D1736590

Gift of
III
TRIAD
GROUP OF COMPANIES
Adnan M. Khashoggi Chairman

THE CAMBRIDGE HISTORY OF IRAN

IN EIGHT VOLUMES

Volume 4

THE CAMBRIDGE HISTORY OF IRAN

Volume 4

THE PERIOD FROM THE ARAB INVASION TO THE SALJUQS

edited by
R. N. FRYE
Professor of Iranian, Harvard University

CAMBRIDGE UNIVERSITY PRESS

Published by the Syndics of the Cambridge University Press
Bentley House, 200 Euston Road, London, N.W.1
American Branch: 32 East 57th Street, New York, N.Y.10022

Library of Congress Catalogue Card Number: 67–12845

ISBN: 0 521 20093 8

First published 1975

Printed in Great Britain
at the University Printing House, Cambridge
(Brooke Crutchley, University Printer)

BOARD OF EDITORS

CONTENTS

PLATES

Between pages 352 and 353

MAPS

PREFACE

The period of Iran's history from the Arab conquests to the Saljuq expansion is very difficult to separate from the general history of the Islamic oecumene. Since the overwhelming majority of the sources are in Arabic, and more concerned with general Islamic affairs than with Iran, the story of the transition of Iran from a Zoroastrian land to an Islamic one is not easy to reconstruct. Under Islam, for the first time since the Achaemenids, all Iranians, including those of Central Asia and on the frontiers of India, became united under one rule. The Persian language was spread in the East, beyond the borders of the Sāsānian Empire, by the conquering armies of Islam, and Persian became the *lingua franca* of the eastern caliphate. The New Persian language written in the Arabic script, and with numerous Arabic words in it, became a marvellous instrument of poetry and literature, similar to the English language, which developed from a simple Anglo-Saxon tongue to one enriched by Latin and French usages after the Norman conquest. Although Firdausī with his *Shāh-nāma* commonly has been proclaimed the founder of New Persian literature, in another sense he was the preserver of the old Persian style of the Sāsānians, not only in epic content, but also in the simplicity of his language without Arabic words. He not only feared the loss of old traditions in Iran, in the face of massive conversions to Islam by his time, but he also sought to preserve the very language which was threatened by permanent change from the use of Arabic, as the language of Islam *par excellence*. Even poetry in Persian had been adapted to Arabic models, and the synonymity of the words "Arab" and "Islam" questioned the very identity of Iranians. This threat was not only evaded by the Iranians, but they gave a new direction to Islam.

Islam was rescued from a narrow bedouin outlook and bedouin mores primarily by the Iranians, who showed that Islam, both as a religion and, primarily, as a culture, need not be bound solely to the Arabic language and Arab norms of behaviour. Instead Islam was to become a universal religion and culture open to all people. This, I believe, was a fundamental contribution of the Iranians to Islam. By Iranians, I mean Soghdians, Bactrians, and other Iranians, ancestors of the present Kurds, Baluchis and Afghans, as well as the Persians, who were joined together under the roof of Islam. Although almost all

Iranians had become Muslims by the time of the creation of the Saljuq Empire, nonetheless they preserved their old Iranian heritage, such that even today the chief holiday in Iran is ancient *naurūz*, "new year's day". This continuity is unequalled elsewhere in the Near East, where in Egypt for example, two great changes erased the memory of the pharoahs from the minds of the inhabitants: first Christianity and then Islam. In Iran Christianity had little influence and Islam was adapted to Iranian customs. So Iran, in a sense, provided the history, albeit an epic, of pre-Islamic times for Islam. After all, the Arabs conquered the entire Sāsānian Empire, where they found full-scale, imperial models for the management of the new caliphate, whereas only provinces of the Byzantine Empire were overrun by the Arabs.

One of the main themes of this book is the process of conversion, how people changed from one religion to another. This process differed considerably from place to place and many monographs should be written before a general picture can be presented. Nonetheless, throughout various chapters in this volume the conversion process is mentioned. The first conversions took place in the cities and towns where Arab garrisons were settled, more in the east on the frontiers of the *dār al-ḥarb*, "the abode of war", than in western Iran. In the east the Sāsānian name for the Arabs became a synonym of "Muslim", such that even today we have Tajiks in Soviet Central Asia who are Iranians, but who carry the ancient designation for "Arab", because they were converted to the religion of the Arab conquerors and were identified with them. It was not until the end of the eighth and especially the ninth century of our era that Muslim missionaries made extensive conversion in the countryside. By the ninth century, except in areas of Fārs province and pockets of non-Muslims elsewhere, the Islamic religion became everywhere predominant even in the countryside. This process must be kept in mind when reading the present volume.

It must be strongly emphasized that this volume is only the history of Iran under Islam, and is not intended to repeat the *Cambridge History of Islam*; yet, as mentioned, it has proved very difficult to separate the two. Some readers will undoubtedly point out that much which occurred in Damascus under the Umayyads, for example, had repercussions in Khurāsān. This is true, but the emphasis of our volume is upon local conditions, even though the sources in this regard are very sparse.

Nonetheless, it is hoped that the reader will find here the information he may want in regard to this period. If omissions have been made, the editor can only take refuge in the Islamic remark that what is presented is in part and not all. Indeed, it would have been impossible to cover the many details of the history of the period, as well as all aspects of culture and civilization. Perhaps one should remember that history can hardly be what Leopold von Ranke decreed, a report of what really happened, nor even what people thought had happened, but rather history is what people believe should have happened. For history at the least is a people's attempt to justify their past for posterity, even if the record be at times rough or even sordid. In the case of Iran after the Arab conquests the record is brilliant as well as fascinating. It was in this period that the foundations were laid for the flourishing of Persian poetry and the arts, so characteristic of Iran after the Mongol conquest. It is hoped that the present book will provide the reader with a record of these formative centuries of Islam in Iran.

Most of the time of an editor is spent on trying to standardize names and to be consistent, an almost impossible task. On the whole, the rules adopted for Volumes 1 and 5 of the *Cambridge History of Iran* have been followed in Volume 4. Naturally, certain transcriptions were changed, since the sources for Volume 4 are overwhelmingly in Arabic rather than in the Persian language. Certain practices, such as italics for the first occurrence of a foreign name and roman type for later appearances, may startle but surely not confuse the reader. Certain names have been spelled in their common English forms while others have been transcribed in their Arabic or Persian forms. In these instances the indulgence of the reader is sought with a passing reference to Emerson's dictum that "a foolish consistency is the hobgoblin of little minds".

It remains to thank deeply all persons who worked upon this volume to make it ready for the final printing. Without the unfailing help of Hubert Darke, the Editorial Secretary of the entire series, this volume would not have appeared. Likewise Peter Burbidge of the Cambridge University Press gave encouragement and help unstinting. Richard Hollick, and others at the Press, patiently had to endure an editor's failings and certainly their help made this book possible. The hospitality of King's College and of Peter Avery made my frequent visits to Cambridge a great pleasure. My peregrinations between Shīrāz and Cambridge, Massachusetts, at times cast a shadow over the progress of the book, and in the end I hope that, in spite of shortcomings, it will prove of use to many readers.

Cambridge, Massachusetts, March 1974 RICHARD N. FRYE

CHAPTER I

THE ARAB CONQUEST OF IRAN AND ITS AFTERMATH

I. IRANIANS AND ARABS IN PRE-ISLAMIC TIMES

The Muslim Arabs' disastrous defeat of the Sāsānian Empire opened a new chapter in the long history of Iran. In distant Ḥijāz in the city of Mecca, Muḥammad b. 'Abd-Allāh had given to an idolatrous and strife-ridden people a new religion, which inculcated monotheism, its message coming to Muḥammad as Revelation, conveyed to his Community later in the Qur'ān, and bade the Arabs to submit as people accountable to God and fearful of his wrath. Some of them were so inspired by this new teaching that they undertook the conquest of the world about them, to achieve at the same time in this holy war the reward of a share in the world to come, Paradise.

Muḥammad's death in 11/632 was followed in his successor Abū Bakr's time by a crisis of apostasy, the *Ridda*, which put both the religion and the government of Medina in jeopardy. The faith and the polity which Muḥammad had promulgated there were shaken, but nonetheless the new Islamic vigour was enough to achieve dominion over all the Arabian Peninsula. Once the apostasy had been suppressed, closer unity followed with greater zeal to sacrifice all in a larger struggle. The end of the Ridda wars left the Arabs poised for Holy War for the sake of Islam, ready to challenge even Byzantium and Iran.

From as early as before the advent of Alexander the Great Arabs had been known to Iran. In the Sāsānian period, from A.D. 226 to 651, their jurisdiction reached as far as the western outskirts of Ctesiphon. According to Ṭabarī, Sh̲āpūr I (A.D. 241–72) had settled some of the tribe of Bakr b. Wa'il in Kirmān.[1] Arab merchants, as well as Arab pirates, frequented the shores of the Persian Gulf. Arab-occupied areas in proximity to so imposing a structure as the Sāsānian state could not escape being under Iran's influence, if not its full dominion. For example, from ancient times Baḥrain and Qaṭīf had been Iranian protectorates. Sh̲āpūr II (A.D. 309–79) had subdued the whole of the

[1] Ṭabarī, in T. Noeldeke, *Geschichte der Perser und Araber* (Leiden, 1879), p. 57.

western side of the gulf, and it seems that from the time of Ardashīr I (A.D. 226–41) the Azd tribes had chosen to settle in 'Umān under Iranian rule. In Baḥrain the Tamīm, 'Abd al-Qais and a section of the Bakr b. Wā'il tribes were, in Hajar in the centre of Baḥrain, under direct Iranian influence. From Shāpūr II's time the Lakhmid kings of al-Ḥīra appointed there their own nominee as *amīr*, but in later Sāsānian times this amīr was generally under the supervision of a high-ranking Iranian revenue official.[1]

Those Arabs under Sāsānian jurisdiction acted under that government's protection especially in the matter of conducting overland trade with Byzantium and Egypt, through Mesopotamia (Iraq) and Syria; and with India, through the Yemen and Baḥrain. The emergence of the Sāsānian navy owed a great deal to the co-operation which existed with the Arabs. Khusrau I (A.D. 531–79) intervened in Yemenī affairs on the pretext of aiding the Arabs against Byzantium, with the result that Iranian forces replaced Ethiopian there. Among the secretaries at the Sāsānian court was one for Arab affairs. He also acted as interpreter and his salary and maintenance were supplied in kind by the Ḥīra Arabs.

Thus from ancient times Iran had had contacts varying in degree of closeness and amity with the Arabs. Before the Sāsānian era, Arab tribes had settled in the Tigris–Euphrates region, though at the beginning of the era Ardashīr I had wrested from them the district known as Maisān, in southern Iraq on the Persian Gulf.

In Ḥīra on the right or west bank of the Euphrates resided the House of Mundhir of the Lakhmid Arabs, who were generally accounted the tributaries of the Sāsānians, as their rivals, the Ghassānids, in the desert of north Syria, were the clients and vassals of Byzantium. The Lakhmids frequently aided the Iranians in their contests with Byzantium. Notwithstanding, in some respects their influence could become a source of annoyance to the Sāsānian state, as for example when 'Amr b. 'Adī, the king of Ḥīra, arose on one occasion in defence of Manichaeism, while in the end Ḥīra became the refuge of Christians. Kavādh I (488–531) arranged with Ḥārith b. 'Amr b. al-Maqsūr al-Kindī, who had ousted Mundhir III from the throne of Ḥīra, that a portion of the revenue from Ḥīra should be his, provided he prevented the tribes of Bakr and Taghlib raiding over Iran's frontiers.

In the time of Khusrau I, otherwise known as Anūshīrvān (531–79),

[1] G. Rothstein, *Die Lakhmiden in al-Ḥīra* (Berlin, 1899), p. 131.

the Bakr tribes joined the Lakhmids and fought against the Ghassānids under the banner of Mundhir III. Khusrau II Aparvīz (591–628), according to Arab tradition, found refuge with Nu'mān Abū Qābūs, Nu'mān III, King of Ḥīra, when fleeing from Bahrām Chūbīn, but when restored to his throne, he ill repaid this assistance by seizing Nu'mān, having him thrown beneath an elephant's feet, and divesting his family of Ḥīra. The state was given to Iyās of the tribe of Ṭayy, a Persian inspector being appointed to oversee what had in effect become an appanage of Iran. This was the end of Lakhmid power. The reason for this imprudence on Khusrau II's part is not clear. Nu'mān's refusal to confer on the Shāhanshāh his horse when the latter was a fugitive, or to give one of his daughters in marriage to a relative of the shah's, do not appear sufficient cause for Khusrau's subsequent treatment of Nu'mān, who had, however, embraced Christianity. It is possible that his leanings towards Nestorianism, whose adherents had promoted a conspiracy against the shah, might have motivated Khusrau against him, especially since the shah had every reason to fear the influence of the Christians in his own court. The name of the Persian inspector is given in the sources as Nakhvēraghān, probably a form of his title.

No doubt the collapse of the puppet kingdom of Ḥīra was welcomed by the Iranian nobles and *mobads*, the former out of contempt for it and the latter out of religious prejudice against it; but the later calamitous events between Arabs and Iranians revealed how lacking in foresight the elimination of this "puppet" Lakhmid house had been. The first warning was the battle known as Dhūqār, from the name of the place, near the present-day Kūfa, where it occurred. The tribes of Bakr b. Wā'il, of the vicinity of Ḥīra, were dissatisfied with the new ruler of Ḥīra, Iyās of Ṭayy. They began raiding across the Iranian border. Near Dhūqār they fell in with two parties of Iranian horse, each comprising a thousand troopers. The tribesmen were equipped with arms the despairing Nu'mān had entrusted for safe-keeping to the chief of the Shaibānids, one of the Bakr b. Wā'il tribes, when leaving to answer the summons of Khusrau II. Thus armed, they were able to defeat utterly the Iranians, who were led by Hāmarz and Khanābarīn, both of whom were slain, their squadrons being decimated. The date of this episode, and indeed its exact nature, are uncertain. In some traditions it is suggested that the battle took place in the year of the prophet Muḥammad's birth; in others that it coincided with his opening of his mission, or a short time after the battle of Badr, 2–3/623–5. Recent research, however, reasonably places it between the years A.D. 604 and 611, a supposition based on the date of the ending of Nu'mān's reign, A.D. 602, and the fact that Iyās's rule lasted only until 611. The episode came to be sung in Arabic legend and verse as one of the *ayyām*: the Arabs' Heroic Days.

The Bakr tribesmen took heart from their success on this day; their raids on the Iranian frontiers increased. The removal of the Lakhmid government meant that there was no longer any restraining force, no paramount local influence to command the tribesmen's respect and have the power to rebuke them if they overstepped the bounds of what, however tenuously, had been accepted as neighbourly convention. It is not possible dogmatically to assert that the presence of the Lakhmid power would have prevented the Muslim attack on Iran and the fall of the already tottering Sāsānian state; but the absence of this screen, however flimsy it may have been, contributed to the boldness of the Muslim Arab warriors – as did the memory of Dhūqār – at the beginning of their inroads into Iran, especially as these began at a time when after Kavādh II, Shērōē (Shīrūya) (A.D. 628–9), there was a period of total insecurity and decline. Thus, amid conflicting claimants for the throne and a rapid succession of incumbents, chance was not given for a planned and continued campaign to counter these mounting inroads.

After a succession of weak monarchs and brief reigns, following the patricide Kavādh, in the year of the death of Muḥammad, the prophet of the Arabs, in Medina, Yazdgard b. Shahriyār, Yazdgard III (A.D. 632–51), was crowned in the temple of Nāhīd at Iṣṭakhr in Fārs. His accession coincided with the emergence of the Arabs into a field of activity the result of which was the conquest of the whole of the ancient dominion of the Sāsānians, in a period of less than a quarter of a century.

II. FROM ḤĪRA TO MADĀ'IN

The first major encounter between the Arabs and Iran occurred during the reign of the first caliph, Abū Bakr (11–13/632–4). In his time the area from Yamāma, the Najd and eastern Arabia as far as the Persian Gulf and Gulf of 'Umān, up to the borders of Ḥīra, was in the hands of the Bakr b. Wā'il tribe, itself divided into numerous sub-tribes. In this area the celebrated Islamic warrior, Khālid b. al-Walīd was still occupied in suppressing the remaining vestiges of the Ridda. The sub-tribes of the Bakr b. Wā'il supplied the raiders against the borders of Sāsānian

Iran where Iranian, Nabatean and Arab peoples were mingled and living as neighbours. The fortifications on the Ḥīra frontier were mainly intended to counter these raids.

The principal Bakr b. Wā'il tribes, at this time in the Euphrates district and apt to raid Iranian soil, consisted of Shaibānids, 'Ijl, Qais and Taim al-Lāt. The Shaibānids and 'Ijlids, from the vicinity of Ḥīra, near the site of present-day Najaf, as far as Ubulla, conducted raids deep across the Iranian frontier. The chief of the Shaibānids was Muthannā b. Hāritha. His raiding grounds were in the neighbourhood of Ḥīra. The 'Ijlids were led by Suwaid b. Quṭba, or one who might have been his father, Quṭba b. Qatāda; they raided in the region of Ubulla and even as far as the area of Baṣra. Both these Bakrī chiefs plundered the frontier cultivators and if pursuit of them were attempted, fled into the desert.

The stronger and bolder of the two was Muthannā, who pitched his tents in a place known as Khaffān, on the edge of the desert not far from Ḥīra, whence he mounted highway robbery and plundering expeditions. In the first stages of the caliphate of Abū Bakr, the Shaibānids and the rest of the Bakr b. Wā'il tribes neither had any contact with Medina nor had they received the Islamic message. As the power of Medina, especially following Khālid b. al-Walīd's success in suppressing the Ridda, spread as far as Yamāma, the various groups of the Bakr b. Wā'il were faced with the choice of either accepting Islam and so uniting with their Muslim Arab brethren, or of submitting to the ancient enemies, the Sāsānians, whose decline had by this time become manifest. For generations they had regarded the desert areas adjoining the scene of their activities as their natural refuge. Their custom was to seek asylum from the Persians in flight towards the desert and among their fellow-Arabs. Consequently it was with the latter that they now chose to ally themselves, in order to ensure a greater measure of immunity in their inroads on Iranian territory, freed from the threat of attack from behind. Thus Muthannā b. Hāritha betook himself to Medina, submitting to Islam and the caliph. Furthermore, he sought the caliph's recognition of him as rightful leader of his people, whom he would bring with him to Islam, to organize them for a campaign into the Sawād of Iraq to spread Islam, ostensibly among the Arabs and Christian Nabataeans residing there.

Abū Bakr issued a decree to this effect. Muthannā returned to Khaffān and summoned his followers to the Faith. His choice of alignment with the Muslims resulted in his gaining the allegiance of practically all the Arabs engaged in raids on the populous and cultivated Iranian frontier regions. The caliph, however, could not place all his confidence in the operations of the new convert. Khālid b. al-Walīd, the same whom the Prophet had awarded the title "The Sword of God", and in whom the caliph had implicit confidence, was immediately despatched to take charge of the campaign in 'Irāq, while Muthannā was ordered to accept his command and in all ways assist him.

The Yamāma and Baḥrain areas having been cleansed of the Ridda disaffection, Khālid addressed himself to 'Irāq, his primary purpose at this stage being the chastisement of those Arabs who had sided with the apostates in the Jazīra. In other words, he was still engaged in mopping up the remnants of the Ridda. Concerning the route Khālid took, Wāqidī relates that it was through Faid and Tha'labīya, that is, across the Arabian desert to the district of Ḥīra. According to a number of other sources, he came from Baḥrain, approaching Ḥīra by way of Ubulla. These sources establish the fact that near Ubulla he fell in with Suwaid b. Quṭba, who joined him. Khālid began his campaign in the Euphrates area, but his operations were little more than skirmishes with Christian Arab tribes, and the completion of suppression of the apostasy.

At that time Abū Bakr was preoccupied in Syria and Palestine. It seems unlikely that thoughts of attacking Iran had yet arisen. Saif b. 'Umar's narrative, that Abū Bakr, following Muthannā's insistence, commissioned Khālid to invade Iran according to a concerted and carefully arranged plan of campaign, would appear to be a romantic historical fiction, of the kind the 'Irāqī Arabs in 'Abbāsid times (A.D. 750–1258) concocted for their own greater glorification.

In any event, and certainly in accordance with Abū Bakr's orders, Khālid reached the Mesopotamian area from Yamāma and Baḥrain, and his operations there are only imperfectly known and subject to dispute, but were chiefly against the Christian Arabs. It is probable that in the course of engagements with the Arabs of this region he met parties of the Iranian frontier forces. That is proved by the encounter known as the battle of Dhāt al-Salāsil in the region between Baḥrain and Baṣra called the Ḥafīr, at a place called Kāẓima.

The Iranian frontier official in this district was called Hurmuzd. He was reputed irascible by temperament, of a tyrannous disposition, particularly in relation to his Arab subjects; so much so that the Arabs of the area made his pride and ill-temper the stuff of proverbs. This Hurmuzd was killed by Khālid in the battle which, apparently because of the resemblance of the ranks of the armoured Iranian cavalrymen to an iron chain, came to be called Dhāt al-Salāsil. The Iranian force he had commanded was routed.

Not long after, another engagement occurred between the two sides, in a place near the present-day Kūt al-'Amāra and called Madhār. On this occasion there is evidence that skirmishing was beginning to develop into more regular warfare; the element of surprise was lacking and preliminary preparations had been made. Two Iranian commanders, of a force comprising fugitives from the army of Hurmuzd, named Qubād and Anūshajān (it is likely that they were princes of the Sāsānid house) made a stand against Khālid, while another leader, Qārin by name, came to their aid from Madā'in. He, as well as Anūshajān and Qubād, was put to the sword with a large number of the Iranian troops, many of whom were drowned in the canal called Thany. Besides considerable booty numerous captives fell into the enemy's hands, Magian and Christian.

A further battle took place in the district of Kaskar at a place named Walaja half way between Ubulla and Ḥīra. The Iranian commander on this occasion is called in Arab sources Andarzghar (his title: *andarz-gar*?), and his force included, in addition to Persian cavalry units, a number of Christian Arabs from the Bakrī 'Ijlids. According to the sources Khālid killed an Iranian veteran named Hazār Savār. Andarz-ghar fled, to perish of thirst in the desert. The triumphant Muslims captured a number of Christians besides Iranians and Khālid invested Ḥīra.

Near Anbār a fourth engagement occurred on the banks of the Euphrates at a village called Ullais. The Iranian commander, whose name was Jābān, was again accompanied by Christian members of the Bakr b. Wā'il tribes. Near the battleground was a channel known as the River of Blood, perhaps connected with the legend that the Arab commander, driven to wrath by the casual air of the Iranians, caused a number of captives to be put to death so that blood flowed as a river, a legend which is, incidentally, associated with several other commanders in the history of the Arab conquests.

The *marzbān* of Ḥīra, called Āzādbih, lost his son in an encounter with Khālid. He fled before the conqueror, who proceeded to lay siege to the fortress and town. The Christian population after tasting the bitterness of the siege sought a compromise, which they gained on condition of paying tribute and agreeing to act as spies among the Iranians on behalf of the Muslims, an arrangement which Khālid also exacted from the inhabitants of Ullais.

The taking of Ḥīra and the pillage of the Arab-inhabited areas on the banks of the Euphrates had only just been completed when Abū Bakr's orders reached Khālid, to decamp with his army for Syria. From Ḥīra, or perhaps to be more precise from 'Ain al-Tamr, he took the desert road to Syria and arrayed himself before the gates of Damascus. This departure of Khālid from what might be described as the "Iranian front" demonstrates that Abū Bakr had as yet no ready plan for the conquest of Iran; rather the Muslims' main preoccupations in those days were still associated with the aftermath of events of the last days of the Prophet's life, and were centred on the "Syrian Problem".

Nevertheless the fall of Ḥīra put the Iranians on their mettle and the youthful Yazdgard began to take the business of the Arabs more seriously. After several years of patience, it began to seem that he too, as Shapūr II had done, was on the point of punishing the refractory Arabs on his borders. When Muthannā felt himself threatened by the Iranian forces, he had recourse to Medina in search of reinforcements, but his arrival coincided with Abū Bakr's death (13/634). 'Umar b. al-Khaṭṭāb succeeded as caliph. Khālid was still engaged in Syria and against Byzantium, while, moreover, 'Umar was dissatisfied with him. Though he was unable, in spite of the new caliph's urging, to muster sufficient men to fight the Iranians, Abū 'Ubaida Thaqafī had no alternative but to go to Mesopotamia, where the caliph placed Muthannā under his command.

Abū 'Ubaida encountered the Persian force, commanded by Bahman Jādūya, at a place near the present site of Kūfa on the banks of the Euphrates, the Arabs being on the west bank in a spot called Mirwaḥa and the Iranians on the opposite bank. As the two places were linked by a bridge, the battle which followed is known as the "battle of the bridge" (A.H. 13 or 14). With great intrepidity Abū 'Ubaida succeeded in crossing this bridge and taking the battle on to the eastern bank of the river, but the sight of the Iranians' elephants and their noise and ferocity terrified the Arabs' horses. Abū 'Ubaida ordered an attack on the elephants and himself wounded a white elephant which in its anger tore him down with its trunk and trampled him under foot. An Arab of the Thaqīf tribe who had witnessed the awful slaying of his Thaqafī leader went and cut the bridge in order to force the Arabs to continue the contest, but they panicked and fled. According to the tales of this battle, Muthannā made a stand against the enemy while the Arabs as best they could with the help of local folk fixed a new bridge and crossed in safety. About four thousand of them perished in this engagement and Muthannā himself received a wound from which he later died. The wonder is that the Iranians, though their victory was not gained without appreciable losses on their side, made no attempt to pursue the fleeing enemy.

Those Arabs who had accompanied Abū 'Ubaida from the Ḥijāz now returned there. A year elapsed during which there was neither thought in Medina of renewing the Persian war nor serious activity on the frontier on the part of Muthannā. Then, apparently after Damascus had been secured for the Muslims, the caliph once more permitted operations against Iran. Volunteers, however, were not at first forthcoming until the Bajīla tribes, who since some time before the advent of Islam had been scattered among the Arab tribes, principally in the hope of booty came forward for the task with Jarīr b. 'Abd-Allāh Bajalī. A number of former apostates, whom, in spite of their repentance, Abū Bakr hitherto had not allowed participation in the *jihād*, or Wars for the Faith, also came. They were joined by groups of the Mesopotamian Arabs under Muthannā. Thus hostilities recommenced a year after the disaster of the battle of the bridge.

The Iranians meanwhile had taken no advantage of their victory to chastise the Arabs but were now under the command of Mihrān b. Mihrbandād and facing the enemy in a place called Nakhīla near present-day Kūfa, through which ran a canal from the Euphrates known as Buwaib. Mihrān crossed the bridge over this stream and made a surprise attack on the Arab camp.

A severe conflict ensued and the Arabs, though Muthannā's brother, Mas'ūd b. Ḥāritha, was slain, did not break. Mihrān was killed and the leaderless Iranian army fled in confusion. Muthannā was able to seize the bridgehead and thus slay or capture many of the retreating Iranians. In this encounter, which occurred in October, A.D. 635, the Arabs, besides gaining considerable booty in cattle and baggage, were able to some extent to make amends for the battle of the bridge. Perhaps more important was the fact that news of this victory drew the caliph's attention to Mesopotamia; the second battle of the Yarmūk in August, A.D. 636 completed the conquest of Syria and the Caliph 'Umar lost no time in ordering part of his Syrian army to the Persian front. He now sought to augment the force on the Euphrates and recruits were called from all the Arab tribes, while ʿUmar himself set out from Medina intending personally to command the expedition. His chief men counselled him against this and he appointed the Prophet's relative and one of the Prophet's companions, Saʿd b. Abī Waqqāṣ, the commander. Muthannā died soon after his success in the battle of Buwaib, from the wound received in the battle of the bridge.

Incensed by the defeat at Buwaib and possibly apprehensive on account of news of the Arab successes against Byzantium, the Iranians also turned their attention to the Euphrates situation, and now hastened to defend that frontier against the Arabs. This defence was entrusted to Rustam b. Farrukhzād, the commander of armies in Āzarbāījān. For a while the two armies confronted each other on the western side of the Euphrates at Qādisīya. The authorities differ regarding the numbers of each force. The Arabs have been enumerated at from six to thirty-eight thousand; the Iranians from twenty to thirty, and by some, from sixty to over a hundred thousand men. It is unlikely that Arab manpower problems and the necessity for garrisoning the Syrian frontier would permit the Muslim army reaching such proportions, while internal troubles in Iran and the extensive frontiers which the Sāsānian rulers had always to watch would equally make the larger numbers given for the Persian army considerably more than actually could have been present. An Armenian historian, Sebeos, has given the Iranian force as eighty thousand and the Arabs as nine or ten thousand with the addition of six thousand men who came to their aid from Syria, but arrived only towards the end of the battle. Though these figures are not free from exaggeration, there can be no doubt that the numbers of the Persians were appreciably greater.

Qādisīya was a small town situated fifteen miles from the site of Kūfa and on the edge of the desert of Ṭaff. It was a frontier post, with a fort, some cultivation and palm groves. Near it at a distance of some four to six miles, was the last stage of the desert, at a spot known as ʿUdhaib, with a spring. Saʿd b. Abī Waqqāṣ had his camp at ʿUdhaib. Rustam had his outside Qādisīya. For a time neither side showed any haste to open hostilities, especially Rustam, for he saw in the desert of Ṭaff an ever-present refuge for the Arabs, to which they could take flight and whence they could again attack. In his view temporizing with them and reaching some reasonable basis for negotiations were the best policies.

He began discussions in order to find out what their ultimate aim in undertaking this expedition and in raiding the frontiers of Iran might be, but the exchange of messengers, some of whom in all probability Rustam even sent to Ctesiphon, bore no fruit. After four months' negotiation and procrastination, and against his private wishes, Rustam opened the battle.

The Iranian lines were drawn up on a canal called 'Aqīq. The Muslims were on the walls of a fort near 'Udhaib, known as Qudais. The battle lasted only three or four days and, in accordance with old Arab custom, each of these days of fighting was to bear its special name, generally, it would seem, after the name of a particular place. Throughout the battle Sa'd b. Abī Waqqāṣ, said to be suffering from either boils or sciatica, neither mounted his horse nor entered the field. He watched the battle from a vantage point. In spite of all the Arabs' efforts, as might have been anticipated the outcome seemed about to be in favour of the Iranians – until the arrival of the Syrian reinforcements. Though they were numerically insignificant, they turned the day to the Arabs' advantage. It goes without saying that victory was not cheaply gained; the Arabs lost about a third of their number, while Iranian losses were also heavy. On the final day Rustam was killed and his army dispersed in flight. Amongst the quantities of spoils which fell into Arab hands was the banner which these victors termed the banner of Kābiyān.

The precise date of the battle of Qādisīya varies in the sources from A.H. 14 to 16, but it would appear to have taken place some months after the second battle on the Yarmūk in Syria, in the middle of the year A.H. 16, a dating confirmed by Ilyās of Niṣībīn, who states that the battle was fought in Jumādā I 16/June 637. The battle's importance for the Arabs was such that it became subject to grandiose treatment in poetry and legend, a reason for treating traditions relating to it with caution.

In any event, after the victory at Qādisīya the fertile lands of the Sawād of 'Irāq lay open to the Arabs. Here too, as in Syria, almost without any obstruction they took over a population of Aramaean cultivators ready to accept the Arabs as liberators. Two months later, in accordance with the caliph's orders, Sa'd marched towards Madā'in or Ctesiphon, the celebrated Sāsānian capital. The Muslims reached the banks of the Tigris without encountering any opposition worth mentioning, and arrayed themselves before the walls of Ctesiphon. This city, which as its name Madā'in implies was a group of cities embracing

Ctesiphon and Seleucia, had been from the time of the Parthians heir to the ancient rôle of Babylon; in fact it comprised seven cities adjoining one another on either bank of the Tigris. The whole complex was surrounded by lofty walls, in which gates had been symmetrically arranged. On the west bank of the Tigris were the cities of Bih-Ardashīr (Bahurasīr), Seleucia, Darzījān, Sābāṭ and Mā Hauza, while Ctesiphon, Asbānbur, Rūmīya, which was also called Vēh-Antiokh-Khusrau ("better than Antioch Chosroes built"), were situated on the east bank.

The shah resided in the White Palace of Ctesiphon, and the Aivān-i Madā'in, the Arch of Chosroes, where receptions took place and banquets were held, was in Asbānbur. After Qadīsīya, Sa'd's first action was to lay siege to the western parts of these cities. Some indication of the extended length of the siege is given by the inclusion in the narratives of the fact that the Arabs twice consumed fresh dates and twice celebrated the Feast of the Sacrifice. Meanwhile within the walls famine broke out and the population fell into sore straits so that in the end the people of Sābāṭ began to sue for peace. They submitted by paying the *jizya*. The people abandoned the section known as Bih-Ardashīr, and when the Arabs entered it, they beheld the White Palace of Ctesiphon and raised their call to the witness of the greatness of Allah. It was spring and the river in full spate. The Persians had destroyed the bridges. The Arabs nevertheless found a crossing and quietly but suddenly made their way across. When the sentries on the gates saw them, they cried, "Devils have come".

Before their arrival Yazdgard with a retinue of several thousand people and all his treasure had left Ctesiphon. After a short and dispiriting engagement, Khurrazād, the brother of Farrukhzād, to whom the shah had entrusted the city, abandoned it and fled towards the Zagros mountains, to Ḥulwān, whither Yazdgard had also gone. Ctesiphon's gates were opened to the Arabs, and the booty, which according to the account given by Balādhurī consisted of carpets, dresses, arms, jewels and so forth, astonished the Bedouin soldiers. It is said that by this time Sa'd b. Abī Waqqāṣ's army had reached sixty thousand men in size, each one of whose share of the spoils amounted to twelve thousand *dirhams*. While acceptance of these figures calls for caution, it still remains clear that an Arab warrior's share of the booty which fell to him on this occasion was great.

On entering the palace of Chosroes, Sa'd had performed eight *rak'ats* prayer for his victory and, because of its appropriateness in recalling the fate of those who reject God, recited the Qur'anic verse (44, 25–7) which begins, "How many gardens and springs have they left". He made a mosque in the citadel and the four-hundred-year-old capital of the Sāsānians became for a time the camping ground of this Muslim general. Then as is well known the caliph sent one of the Prophet's own Persian *mawālī* or clients, Salmān Fārsī, whose Iranian name is recorded as Māhbeh or Rūzbeh and who is said originally to have been an adherent of Christianity before his travels took him into the orbit of Muḥammad at Medina, to be governor at Ctesiphon. Accounts, legends rather, relating to his subsequent life after he had been sent as governor to the ruined capital on the Tigris speak of his gaining his living basket-weaving, thus providing an example of asceticism and humility, an example that has not been lost on the Ṣūfīs or the Shī'īs, especially the Nuṣairīs. He has been claimed as one of the chief pillars and earliest exponents of Ṣūfism, and also as the Grand Master of Guilds (*aṣnāf*). His tomb beside the Arch of Ctesiphon is still a memorial to the fall of Madā'in, and is a shrine guarded by devotees of the ascetic life.

III. THE VICTORY OF VICTORIES

The conquest of Iraq was only the beginning of a larger task, for so long as Media, Khurāsān, Sīstān and Transoxiana remained unsubdued, Iraq could not be securely in the possession of its new masters. They would constantly have to fear the preparation of a fresh army by either the fleeing Yazdgard or some claimant to his throne, with the inevitable attempt to retrieve Iraq. Thus pursuit of Yazdgard and the conquest of central and eastern Iran were undertakings the Arabs could not avoid.

Beyond the Zagros mountains, which mark the dividing line between the Semitic world of Mesopotamia and Aryan Media, in Jalūlā, near the site of present-day Khānaqīn, and probably where Qizil Ribāṭ now is, Sa'd's advance party fell in with the remnant of the Persian army commanded by Mihrān Rāzī. The day went to the Arabs who once more acquired considerable booty. Yazdgard received news of this episode in Ḥulwān, not far from Jalūlā; he elected further flight.

In spite of the victory which had been gained, 'Umar did not evince any great eagerness to embark on extended conquests, and on his command, Sa'd did not remain either in Madā'in or Anbār, where for a while he had established his headquarters. The cities further to the west, on the banks of the Euphrates, were avoided by the desert Arabs because of the discomforts of fever and insects, while the caliph himself writing to Sa'd said that the Arab was like the camel and needed the desert and green pasture, city life not being in harmony with his nature. To make a place suitable for his army Sa'd chose a spot near Ḥīra which, since it was on the right bank of the Euphrates, fulfilled the expressed desire of the caliph, that no natural obstacle, river or mountain, should come between the Arabs of Iraq and their brethren in the Prophet's city of Medina. Thus fourteen months after the conquest of Madā'in the garrison city of Kūfa came into being; Baṣra had already been founded, to be the garrison for the Muslims in Lower Mesopotamia. At first it was the caliph's wish that between Baṣra and Fārs there should be a barrier, just as the Zagros provided a wall between Kūfa and Media. The Arabs were to stand in their two garrisons on what he intended to be their frontier against the Iranian world.

This was neither acceptable to the Iranians who had lost their capital, nor to the Arab warriors, aroused by the hope of further booty and imbued with hope of admission to Paradise, hopes not to be realized by a status quo. Furthermore, since Yazdgard had not yet given up all idea of recovering the position, it was unlikely that the status quo would be tenable, especially when the presence of Hurmuzān, who probably belonged to one of the seven great families of Iran and was related to the shah, among the tribes of K͟hūzistān posed a threat to Baṣra.

Hurmuzān, the ruler of K͟hūzistān, had retired to his realm with its capital at Ahvāz following the battle of Qādisīya. From Ahvāz he occupied himself in raiding the Maisān district, which was held by the Baṣra Arabs. It seems that Yazdgard encouraged him in these exploits. Hurmuzān became a thorn in the flesh of the Arabs and it was not until the Baṣra and Kūfa garrisons united that he was driven back from Maisān. Since he was compelled to seek an armistice, inevitably his defeat resulted in loss of territory. Later, in the course of pursuing a quarrel with an Arab tribe resident near his province, Hurmuzān again opened hostilities against the neighbouring Arabs, only once more to be reduced to asking for peace. He was forced to accept disagreeable terms. When under Yazdgard's urging the men of Fārs united with those of Khūzistān to oppose the Arabs, Hurmuzān's fortunes took a turn for the better. The caliph sent Nu'mān b. Muqarrin to lead the defence against him.

Battle was joined in Arbūq and, though he put up a stout struggle, Hurmuzān was in the end forced to flee. Nu'mān entered Rāmhurmuz while Hurmuzān was at Shustar, whither Nu'mān decided to follow him. There Hurmuzān was surrounded. Abū Mūsā Ash'arī, the Commander-in-Chief at Baṣra, was assigned the task of besieging him, reinforced by a party of men sent on the caliph's orders from Kūfa. The siege of Shustar was protracted, but in the end an Iranian's treachery – his name was Siyā – enabled the Arabs to enter the city. According to some accounts, even after the city's capture, Hurmuzān continued to hold out in the citadel, of which the siege was also long. Those in the fortress with Hurmuzān killed their dependents and threw their possessions into the river rather than let them fall into the Arabs' hands.[1] Ultimately the Arabs' persistence won. Hurmuzān had to surrender, in 21/641–2, on condition that he was sent to the caliph. The siege of Shustar had lasted eighteen months, or, as some accounts have it, two years.

Hurmuzān was sent to Medina in the garb and with the trappings of royalty, to be amazed by the simplicity and austerity which were characteristic of 'Umar, the caliph of Islam. Though after lengthy discussions Hurmuzān maintained his refusal to become Muslim, by some stratagem he was also able to preserve his life. Later he became a Muslim and gained the caliph's confidence, even to the extent of receiving a share of the spoils of the war against Iran. After 'Umar's assassination at the hands of an Iranian Christian named Fīrūz, who was known as Abū Lu'lu', Hurmuzān was seized on suspicion of being in collusion with him and, rightly or wrongly, put to death by 'Ubaid-Allāh, 'Umar's son.

After the capture of Shustar it was the turn of Shūsh and Jundīshāpur, so that city by city Khūzistān fell to the Baṣra Arabs. Meanwhile Fārs became increasingly subject to the raids of the amīr of Baḥrain. Though he was not always successful, Fārs was insecure, never knowing when to expect Muslim raids. Thus, contrary to the wish of 'Umar, Fārs and Khūzistān were the victims of inroads from the Muslim Arabs of Baṣra, and the garrison at Kūfa began crossing the Zagros into Media, which was later to be known as 'Irāq-i 'Ajam, Iranian Iraq.

[1] Ḥasan b. Muḥ. al-Qummī, *Tārīkh-i Qum* (Tehrān, 1313/1934), p. 300.

Yazdgard, who saw his throne lost, decided after Jalūlā once more to equip an army and make an attempt to rid Iraq of the Arabs, or at least prevent their invasion of western Iran. He issued his summons from Ray, requiring his generals and their divisions to be ready to face the Arabs. Nihāvand was considered suitable for this last stand, being situated to the south of the route which makes a circuit round the heights of Alvand and the district of Ḥulwān to join the central regions of Iran.

Yazdgard's decree assembled here the Iranian troops scattered about the country, from both the province of Fārs and the central mountainous region known to the Arabs as the al-Jibāl. The gathering of such a force at Nihāvand excited the anxiety of the Kūfans, and Sa'd b. Abī Waqqaṣ's replacement as governor there, 'Ammār b. Yāsir, approached the caliph for assistance against so formidable a host. The caliph was at once alarmed and for a time contemplated himself moving to Iraq. Instead he appointed Nu'mān b. 'Amr b. Muqarrin, the official responsible for collecting the *kharāj* from the Kaskar district of lower Iraq, to command the army of Kūfa and sent him there with instructions that contingents from the armies of Syria, 'Umān and Baṣra should join him at Kūfa. Nu'mān sallied forth from Kūfa with this composite army towards Nihāvand in the province of Media (Arabic: Māh). The Iranian base there was called Vāykhurd, the Arabs' Isbidhān, and from these two bases the two armies watched each other for several days without engaging. Then the Arabs spread a rumour that the caliph had died and they intended to withdraw, a ruse by which they drew the Iranians from behind their defences onto the wide plain, the type of field preferred by the Bedouin for battle. Here the Arabs gave battle, apparently having received further reinforcements which had given them fresh heart. The engagement lasted three days, from Tuesday to Friday. Nu'mān was killed, but the battle was continued and the Iranian forces were defeated and fled from their last stand. The people of Nihāvand were besieged but finally submitted. Once more the Muslims gained great booty.

With this victory of Nihāvand, which the Arabs called the "Victory of Victories", the Iranians' last concerted stand against the Muslims was smashed. In spite of minor struggles continued by local chiefs, and in spite of the occasional clarion calls which Yazdgard made in attempts to gather an army again, the collapse of Sāsānian power was now final. Thus the four-century-old power which had defied Rome and Byzantium and kept at bay the threats of the Hephthalites, now succumbed to the Arabs with their religion, Islam.

Concerning the real cause of this collapse, undoubtedly one of the most important events in world history, there has been much debate. Certainly one of the causes was the marked difference between classes then prevalent in Iran, and the lack of co-operation between them. Another was the differences of religion which existed, for, together with a tendency towards fatalism and belief in the power of destiny, ideas which prepared the Iranian people to accept defeat, there were also numerous heterodoxies and Christian groups as well, whose followers were sufficiently numerous to impair any concerted effort for the defence of the fire temples and the Sāsānid family. Also, the cupidity and corruption of the mobads and their interference in politics had raised hatred against them. Another factor was the weakness of a government that in the course of four years put no less than eight rulers one after the other on the throne, while the treasury was exhausted and had become solely devoted to the adornments of vain pomp. Further, the aimless wars of Khusrau II also played their part in weakening the government and its finances.

Thus, in a last analysis it can be seen that the chief cause of the downfall of the Sāsānians was the material and spiritual bankruptcy of the ruling class, which especially became apparent after the bad government of Khusrau Parvīz, and which must account for the crumbling of so great a power before the attacks of a hungry people newly arrived on the scene – newly arrived, but inspired by the sense of walking in the way of a Lord whose message had been brought to them by their Prophet, and filled with ardour for adventure.

Not that religion was by any means the sole inspiration of the Arabs at the outset; it cannot be denied that poverty and hunger were powerful goads to action and avarice. The Prophet had promised that the treasures of the Chosroes and Caesars were destined for the Arabs. That promise was now being redeemed in a fashion which must have lent significance to the religious injunction that it was an able-bodied Muslim's duty to spread the Faith. To be killed so doing was meritorious to the extent of being the highest form of martyrdom (*shahāda*) with a place assured in Paradise. The caliph also encouraged the Muslim community to jihād, especially as, since the suppression of the Ridda, the numbers of Muslims in Arabia and on its perimeters day by day increased. It was necessary to send them out to fresh lands, both for the sake of their stomachs and in order to restrain civil strife within the community.

The Arab way of waging war moreover differed from that current among the Byzantines and Iranians, so that, for example in the case of Iran, it had been more viable to combat the Byzantines with Arab mercenaries from Ḥīra than to use the heavily armoured cavalry of the Persians. Unfortunately, however, the principality of Ḥīra had fallen some time before the events which have just been described. This barrier removed, the heavily accoutred Iranian knights had been left exposed to the lightly armed Arabs, all of whose weapons could be borne on one camel with its rider, and whose lightning tactics of attack and withdrawal ultimately paralysed the ponderous panoply of the empire. The victory of Nihāvand spelt not only the final dissolution of Sāsānian power but the end of ancient Iran. It left the rest of the Iranian lands open to the Muslim Arabs.

IV. THE PURSUIT OF YAZDGARD

The victory of Nihāvand in 21 or 22/641–642 marks the beginning of a new era of Iranian history. No further obstacle remained in the path of Arab conquest, for though for a time the fleeing ruler, frontier guardians (the semi-independent marzbāns and *pādhghospāns*) and likewise independent local governors, hindered very rapid Arab expansion, nevertheless in the course of fifteen years after Nihāvand, with the exceptions of the Makrān and Kabul, most of the Sāsānian realm on the Iranian plateau fell to the Muslims. Following the victory there was no co-ordinated resistance. The caliph, moreover, sought to forestall any attempt on Yazdgard's part to raise further organized resistance by nominating groups of Arabs from Kūfa and Baṣra to undertake the gradual subjection of the Iranian region; it was as if an organized infiltration movement into the heart of the distracted and shattered empire was now mounted, at first under the direction of Medina, though later under that of Kūfa and Baṣra, the headquarters of the majority of the Muslim armies engaged in Iran. Certainly the conquest of Iran, contrary to the account of Saif b. ʿUmar, did not by any means reach its completion in the time of the caliphate of ʿUmar b. al-Khaṭṭāb; it in fact continued into Umayyad times, the Umayyad caliphate having begun in 41/661. It was not conducted on a single front, hence the use of the term organized infiltration; for example, the conquest of the west-central region, the Jibāl-Māh area comprising ancient Media, and southeastern Āzarbāījān, followed the capture of Madā'in and was undertaken by Sa'd b. Abī Waqqāṣ. After the episode at Jalūlā, this general entrusted an army to Jarīr b. 'Abd-Allāh Bajalī and sent him to take Ḥulwān. Jarīr took Ḥulwān, then a fertile spot with mineral springs, gardens and orchards, peacefully in 19/640. The way was then open for the conquest of Kirmānshāh, which was apparently the Sāsānian provincial capital for the province of Māh. It too submitted peacefully. Meanwhile Abū Mūsā Ash'arī the governor of Baṣra took Dīnavar and Māsabadhān. Thus the districts of Māh fell half to the Muslims of Kūfa, half to those of Baṣra, so that later the caliph awarded the province of Māh, to be called by the Arabs al-Jibāl or Māhain, the old region of Media, to both the Baṣrans and the Kūfans. The upper portion became Māh al-Kūfa, its centre Dīnavar; the lower portion, Māh al-Baṣra, had as its capital Nihāvand.

Hamadān, the ancient Ecbatana, was taken after Nihāvand, according to one account by Mughaira b. Shu'ba, the governor of Kūfa, or by Jarīr b. 'Abd-Allāh, the commander of his army. Another narrative names Nu'aim b. Muqarrin, whose brother Nu'mān was slain at Nihāvand, as the conqueror of Hamadān, and states that he overcame the brother of Rustam, and several other Iranian generals. It was this same Nu'aim b. Muqarrin who took Ray, whose governor at that time is named as Siyāvakhsh the son of Mihrān the son of Bahrām Chūbīn, for the province of Ray was in fact the fief of the Mihrān family.

Yazdgard III after Jalūlā had come to Ray from Ḥulwān; it was thence that he issued his last summons to his forces, to assemble against the Arabs, the summons which led to Nihāvand. After that battle, Yazdgard resorted to Iṣfahān, leaving Ray in the hands of the local marzbān – the Mihrānid, so that when the Arabs threatened it, Siyāvakhsh organized its defence, gaining assistance from the people of Damāvand. His efforts were in vain. One of the notables of Ray, possibly a certain Farrukhān, joined the Muslims and the Arabs were able to seize the province. Nu'aim punished Siyāvakhsh's strong stand by totally destroying the ancient city of Ray, ordering Farrukhān to construct a new city in place of it. When Ray had fallen, the governor of Damāvand, who had the religious title of Maṣmughān, independently came to terms with the Arabs on payment of jizya fixed at two hundred thousand *dīnārs* a year, an arrangement which for practically a century kept the Maṣmughān immune from Muslim attacks. The conquest of Ray is dated differently in different sources, ranging from 18/639 to 24/645. What seems likely is that portions of the province of Ray fell to the conquerors piecemeal at various dates.

Qazvīn also, which comprised several strong points against the inroads of the Dailamites from the mountains to the north, fell after the battle of Nihāvand. It is reported that Barrā' b. 'Āzib laid siege to it and the city surrendered in 24/644–45, the entire population accepting Islam, presumably in order to gain exemption from payment of the jizya. Henceforth Qazvīn became an Arab garrison against the Dailamite raids which from time to time reached as far as Qum. The reign of the caliph 'Uthmān, 23–35/644–56, saw the taking of the province of Gurgān, one of the Caspian littoral areas, and an important Sāsānian frontier region, by the governor of Kūfa, Sa'īd b. 'Āṣ (30/650); but the real conquest of this region was not effected until Umayyad times, when Yazīd b. Muhallab took it from a Turkish overlord named Ṣūl in 98/716–17.

Similarly during the caliphate of 'Uthmān, Sa'īd b. al-'Āṣ attacked the region of Ṭabaristān, but in those days the Arabs failed to make headway in this area; even as when, in the time of the Umayyad Mu'āwiya (41–60/661–80), Masqala b. Hubaira entered Ṭabaristān with ten, according to some twenty, thousand men and lost most of his forces in the mountains of that inhospitable region. It was only later, during the reign of Sulaimān b. 'Abd al-Malik (96–9/715–17), that Yazīd b. Muhallab again brought Arab arms into Ṭabaristān, and even this great commander was unable to complete a conquest which eluded the Umayyad caliphate.

The conquest of Āzarbāījān likewise began after Nihāvand and was undertaken by the same warriors for the Faith. Among them was Ḥudhaifa b. al-Yamān, who raided Ardabīl, the centre of the province and seat of the governor. After a stiff resistance this city submitted and accepted the imposition of the jizya. According to some accounts, Bukair b. 'Abd-Allāh Laithī also campaigned in Āzarbāījān and defeated and captured there Isfandyādh, the brother of Rustam Farrukhzād. The real conqueror of Āzarbāījān, however, was 'Ataba b. Farqad al-Sulamī, who approached it after the conquest of Mosul by way of Shahrazūr and Urmīya (modern Rezā'īya) and extended the Arab conquest in the northwest. The region of Mūghān, with a part of the lower Aras district, submitted in 22/642 to Sarāqa b. Bukair and later both Walīd b. 'Uqba and Sa'īd b. al-'Āṣ raided in that area.

Mughaira b. Shu'ba, who held Kūfa on behalf of 'Umar, embarked thence on the conquest of Khūzistān but was forestalled by Abū Mūsā Ash'arī from Baṣra. In spite of the stout efforts of Hurmuzān all over the province, only the city of Shustar, which was the site of great hydraulic works as well as being of strategic importance, could hold out against the attackers. Ash'arī later despatched an army northwards towards al-Jibāl, which took Ṣaimara, Sīravān and Mihrajānqadaq and penetrated as far as the neighbourhood of Qum. Likewise Abū Mūsā despatched Aḥnaf b. Qais to capture the city of Kāshān, which did not fall without fighting. Apparently acting on the orders of 'Umar, he sent 'Abd-Allāh b. Budail to Iṣfahān, whose marzbān was an aged man of the rank of pādhghōspān. It is said that since the people were not willing to defend the city against the Arab attack, this pādhghōspān left it with a few companions, but when the Arabs pursued him, he returned and surrendered the city on payment of the kharāj and jizya. Thus did 'Abd-Allāh b. Budail conquer Iṣfahān in the latter part of 'Umar's caliphate (23/644). He remained there until the early days of 'Uthmān's caliphate. Narratives, however, emanating from the people of Kūfa differ: they make Iṣfahān's fall earlier, in 19/640 or 21/642, and its conqueror another 'Abd-Allāh, 'Abd-Allāh b. 'Atabān.

Because many Iranian cities revolted after being taken, the Arabs were repeatedly forced to retake cities they had conquered earlier, a fact which no doubt explains the frequent confusion in the sources over the names of the conquerors and dates of the seizure of cities and localities. Fārs, the cradle of the Sāsānians and seat of several important Zoroastrian fire temples, being situated strategically on military routes, inevitably became exposed to Arab attacks. Thus as early as 19/640 'Alā' b. Ḥadhramī, the *'āmil* of Baḥrain, attacked it, apparently against the caliph's wishes, from the sea and penetrated as far as Iṣṭakhr. He had not reckoned with the forces of Shahrag, the marzbān of Fārs, however, and it was only with very great difficulty and aided by reinforcements sent on the caliph's orders from Baṣra that he was able to fall back on the coast of the Persian Gulf and effect his withdrawal. Some four years later, in 23/644, his successor, 'Uthmān b. Abi 'l-'Āṣ, again attacked from Baḥrain and in a battle near Rāshahr (Bushire) on the coast, which Balādhurī states to have been of no less magnitude or significance than Qādisīya, overcame and killed the marzbān Shahrag. He was joined by the men of Baṣra, and the governor of Iṣṭakhr made peace with this joint Baṣra-Baḥrain Arab host. Shīrāz, Naubandajān in

Shūlistān, Dārābjird and Fasā were also taken. During Caliph ʿUthmān's reign, in 28/648 ʿAbd-Allāh b. ʿĀmir, the amīr of Baṣra, seized Iṣṭakhr from Māhak its governor, and a year later took Gūr (Fīrūzābād).

During the caliphate of ʿUmar and in the early years of ʿUthmān, Iraq, Jibāl and Fārs came under the domination of the new conquerors in such a complete way that the revolutions of the latter part of ʿUthmān's time, and even the sanguinary civil wars in ʿAlī's brief caliphate, afforded various claimants for the Sāsānian throne no opportunity to rally any support or popular sympathy for a general rebellion or an attempt to restore Iranian independence. Nevertheless, sporadic local revolts did occur, especially after ʿUmar's murder in Medina at the hands of an Iranian. The Iranians in an unconcerted manner, and in different regions, frequently seized the opportunity to break truces or terms of surrender which they had made with the Arabs, who were forced once more to renew their attacks and reimpose themselves on refractory areas. This was particularly the case as long as Yazdgard III remained alive. He was perpetually in a state of flight from province to province, and his quest for the means with which to repel the Arabs, in Ray, Iṣfahān, Iṣṭakhr, Kirmān, Sīstān, Khurāsān, forever remained fruitless; nonetheless his presence was from time to time a source of hope. Even after his death, which occurred in 31/651–2, apparently at the instigation of Māhōē Sūrī the marzbān of Marv, at the hands of a miller, the people of some provinces to whom submission to the Arabs and acceptance of their new faith were not agreeable, used every available opportunity to contend with their conquerors. They repeatedly found an excuse to break their treaties of surrender returning to their former religious practices and ancient customs.

Thus after the murder of ʿUmar b. al-Khaṭṭāb the people of the district of Shāpūr rose and Kāzarūn was engulfed in rebellion. Similarly after ʿUthmān's murder in 35/656 and after the murder of the caliph ʿAlī five years later, and almost every time the governors of Kūfa and Baṣra were changed, the Iranians had occasion to revolt. In the early months of the caliphate of ʿUthmān, when Saʿd b. Abī Waqqāṣ was for the second time made governor of Kūfa, the people of Hamadān and Ray staged an insurrection against the Arabs. Saʿd sent ʿAlā b. Wahab to reduce Hamadān, and the population of Ray were once again induced to pay the kharāj and jizya; but the peace which, with the aid of the internal differences between the notables of Ray, was imposed in 25/646 upon the refractory populace was not lasting. Rebellion was endemic and the Arabs were repeatedly compelled to mount armies to suppress them, until finally during the time of 'Uthmān and under the governorship, at Kūfa, of Abū Mūsā Ash'arī, the city was reduced and peace imposed by Qurẓat b. Ka'b Anṣārī. During the period when Walīd b. 'Uqba was governor of Kūfa, again in 25/646, in place of Sa'd b. Abī Waqqāṣ, the people of Āzarbāījān took the opportunity to mount an insurrection. Walīd responded with a fresh invasion taking his army as far as Mūghān, Ṭīlsān (Ṭālishān) and even raiding into Armenia. In Fārs, apparently at the instigation of Yazdgard or at least on account of his brief presence, the people rose against the Arabs. The people of Īdhaj and the tribes of that mountainous district wore out the patience and resources of Abū Mūsā Ash'arī. His successor, 'Abd-Allāh b. 'Āmir, the youthful twenty-five-year-old cousin of the caliph, confronted the rebels, who had killed the Arab general 'Ubaid-Allāh b. Ma'mar near Iṣṭakhr. 'Abd-Allāh b. 'Āmir brought an army into Fārs and after a bloody encounter managed to regain Iṣṭakhr, only to learn of a second outbreak there while he was marching on Dārābjird and Fīrūzābād. Bypassing Fīrūzābād, where it appears Yazdgard was at the time, he returned to Iṣṭakhr, which withstood a long siege and put up a courageous resistance. He pounded the walls with stones from catapults, and the narratives have it that the conduits ran with the blood of the slaughtered. It is said that the remnants of Sāsānian chivalry were decimated in this protracted struggle, in 28–9/648–9, and the hyperbolical estimates of the slain reach figures of between forty and a hundred thousand. The next year Fīrūzābād submitted on payment of kharāj fixed at thirty-three million dirhams a year.

With the Arabs dominant in Fārs, Yazdgard went to Kirmān, but the Arabs of Baṣra and Baḥrain did not leave him any security, even in that remote province. 'Abd-Allāh b. 'Āmir, at this time governor of Baṣra, sent Mujāshi' b. Mas'ūd Sulamī on the heels of the fleeing Yazdgard, but his army perished from snow and the intense cold while Mujāshi', though himself escaping destruction, failed to catch up with the fleeing monarch. The latter's misplaced haughtiness and imperious manner excited the hatred of the marzbān of Kirmān, whence Yazdgard the ill-fated pursued his tragic destiny into Khurāsān (30/650). Mujāshi' meanwhile collected another army to replace the one lost in the Kirmān region, and seized Sīrjān and Jīruft. He also succeeded in repelling an attack launched on him in Kirmān by Iranians from

Hurmuz. It is significant that before his invasion of Kirmān a number of the inhabitants fled in order to preserve their ancestral Zoroastrian religion, seeking refuge in Sīstān, Khurāsān or in the mountains. Some years earlier the Arabs had campaigned in Sīstān and thither 'Abd-Allāh b. 'Āmir now went in pursuit of Yazdgard.

Sīstān comprised the ancient province of Drangiana, whose governor was at this time independent. On retreating from Kirmān, Yazdgard had first gone to Sīstān, where the governor had given him support, which he withdrew on being ordered by Yazdgard to render taxes which had fallen into arrears.[1] It is not known precisely whether in those days the governor of Sīstān was a Sāsānid prince or a local ruler, but in any event he was unable to keep Sīstān free from Arab penetration. In 30/650–1 'Abd-Allāh b. 'Āmir, who was at Kirmān, sent Rabī' b. Ziyād Ḥārithī to Sīstān. Rabī' crossed the desert between Kirmān and that province and reached Zāliq, a fortress within five farsangs of the Sīstān frontier, whose *dihqān* surrendered it to him. Likewise he received the submission of the fortress of Karkūya, mention of whose fire temple in the Song of the Fire of Karkūy has come down to us in the anonymously written *Tārīkh-i Sīstān*. Falling back on Zāliq, Rabī' projected the seizure of Zarang which, though formerly it had submitted to the Arabs, had once more to be subdued. Between Zāliq and Zarang, Rabī' subdued various districts.

The marzbān of Zarang, Aparvīz, however, strongly contested his advance, but in the end was forced to submit to the Muslims. According to the sources, when Aparvīz appeared before Rabī' to discuss terms, he found the Arab general sitting on the corpse of a dead soldier, his head reclining against another, while his entourage had been instructed also to provide themselves with such macabre seats and bolsters. The sight terrified Aparvīz into submission, to spare his people such barbarous cruelty, and peace was concluded on payment of heavy dues. Thus Rabī' with considerable difficulty succeeded in gaining Zarang, the centre of Sīstān, where he chose to remain for several years. Not that Zarang was a safe or quiet place for the Arabs; only two years elapsed before the people of Zarang rose and expelled Rabī''s lieutenant and garrison there. 'Abd-Allāh b. 'Āmir sent 'Abd al-Raḥmān b. Samura to Sīstān to secure it a second time, and he added to the Arab gains the cities of Bust and Zābul. Meanwhile 'Abd-Allāh sent Aḥnaf b. Qais from Ṭabasain, which had been conquered in 'Umar's time by

[1] Balādhurī, p. 315.

'Abd-Allāh b. Budail Khuzā'ī, with a portion of the Baṣra army, to complete the conquest of Kūhistān.

Aḥnaf campaigned for a time in this area, which lies between Nīshāpūr, Herāt, Sīstān, Kirmān and 'Irāq-i 'Ajam. Then 'Abd-Allāh ordered him to set out for Tukhāristān, where either by war or peaceful means he possessed himself of Marv ar-Rūd, Jūzjānān, Ṭāliqān and Fāryāb, reaching as far as the borders of Khwārazm. Ibn 'Āmir himself with his other generals made expeditions in Khurāsān and captured the towns of Jām, Bākharz, Juvain and Baihaq. After taking Khwāf, Isfarā'in and Arghiyān, he marched on Nīshāpūr. The siege lasted several months but in the end, aided and guided by a person from among the local petty rulers of the district, 'Abd-Allāh b. 'Āmir was able to take this important city. Next it was the turn of Abīvard, Nisā and Sarakhs to fall to the Arabs. The *kanārang* or governor of Ṭūs peacefully submitted to the Baṣran Arabs on the condition that he remain governor of the district.

Yazdgard's last refuge was Marv, whose governor was the Māhōē Sūrī already mentioned, who seems to have belonged to the great Sūrēn family. The entrance of the uninvited guest pleased him no more than it had the kanārang, especially as, according to the sources, Yazdgard was accompanied by a retinue of some four thousand non-combatants, secretaries, cooks, ladies, infants and the aged. The monarch also required of him taxes fallen into arrears. The governor incited some Hephthalites under their ruler Nīzak against him, and when the unfortunate monarch learned of the plot, fleeing the city he fell the victim of a nameless assassin in a mill in 31/651.

Māhōē's compact with the Nīzak did not save his realm from the Arabs, for a short while afterwards, when 'Abd-Allāh b. 'Āmir had taken Herāt, Bādghīs and Būshanj, Māhōē sent an emissary to him to discuss surrender terms. According to one account these were payment of two million two hundred thousand dirhams, while others have it that the demand was for one million dirhams in cash and two hundred thousand measures of corn and barley. The treaty included provisions that the Iranians should receive the Muslims in their houses and apportion the payment of the jizya among themselves, the Muslims' task being limited to the receipt of the stipulated returns. According to some authorities, peace was concluded only on condition of payment in slaves, kind and cattle, this being only later converted into and assessed in money. To Māhōē was left the tax collection and during

'Alī's caliphate he went to Kūfa, when the caliph wrote to Māhōē's *dihqāns*, instructing them to render to him their jizya. This was followed by insurrection in Khurāsān, apparently because of discontent with the administration of Māhōē.[1]

Meanwhile Aḥnaf b. Qais conquered Tukhāristān and thus, within a short time after the death of Yazdgard III, nearly all Khurāsān was in the Arabs' hands.

V. THE ARABS IN IRAN

As has been shown, in spite of the victories, the lands conquered did not at once settle into anything like continuous submission: they continued to be the scene of frequent military campaigns. The provinces of Khurāsān and Sīstān, far from the Arabs' headquarters at Kūfa and Baṣra, were especially troublesome for the Arabs. For example, within a year after Yazdgard's death an Iranian local notable named Qārin raised an insurrection in Kūhistān, collecting supporters in Ṭabasain, Herāt and Bādghīs to the extent that it is reported he mounted a body of forty thousand insurgents against the Arabs in Khurāsān. They were able to surprise him, however, so that Qārin and many of his people perished, while many were made captive (32/652–3). This type of regional revolt was a feature of the latter days of the caliphate of 'Uthmān and of the whole of the reign of 'Alī, days when the Arabs themselves were distracted by civil war.

'Uthmān was slain in a general uprising in Medina in 35/655–6 and the people of Iṣṭakhr chose the moment to rise, to be suppressed in a welter of blood by 'Abd-Allāh b. 'Abbās on the orders of his cousin, 'Alī b. Abī Ṭālib, the fourth caliph. Not long afterwards the caliph ordered Ziyād b. Abīhi to put down revolts in Fārs and Kirmān, in 39/659, the Arab civil authorities having been driven out of these areas. The population of Nīshāpūr, also in the time of 'Alī, broke their treaty and refused payment of the jizya and kharāj, so that the caliph had to send an army to bring them back into submission.

After 'Alī's murder, Mu'āwiya, who became caliph in Syria in 41/661, restored 'Abd-Allāh b. 'Āmir to the governorship of Baṣra, a post he had had to relinquish during 'Alī's brief reign. 'Abd-Allāh sent 'Abd al-Raḥman b. Samura to govern Sīstān, and Qais b. Haitham to Khurāsān. When Ziyād b. Abīhi succeeded in the governorship of Baṣra, he followed the Sāsānian practice of dividing Khurāsān into four

[1] *Ibid.*, pp. 408–9, and al-Iṣfahānī, p. 243.

quarters, a governor being appointed to each, so that the Arab position in this area was greatly strengthened.

After Zīyād his son, 'Ubaid-Allāh b. Zīyād, and later Sa'īdb. 'Uthmān, a son of the third caliph who went to Khurāsān on the instructions of Mu'āwiya, began raids on the other side of the Oxus, mainly in quest of plunder. Many are the tales of Sa'īd's military adventures in Transoxiana. He was subsequently dismissed from Khurāsān and brought a number of prisoners from Transoxiana, whom in fact he had retained as hostages, to Medina, where they murdered him. Khurāsān, in spite of efforts at administrative consolidation, and Transoxiana remained, for all the Arabs' efforts and sojourning there, the scenes of military upheavals, and ripe for unrest and dissatisfaction.

In the western and southern regions the populace had less opportunity for raising the head of revolt. After the victory of Nihāvand in the Jibāl, at Ahvāz and Shīrāz, the Arabs had established garrisons. In these regions, at first the local governors and marzubāns had supported with their levies the main Sāsānian armies and also had put up some resistance against the invaders, but in the end each of them had separately negotiated his surrender. By submitting to payment of the jizya and contracting treaties with the Arabs, they had managed to save some of the privileges and inheritance of their families. These negotiated surrenders implied in the beginning little change in the way of life, but the gradual penetration among the people of the Arab tribes and the imposition of the jizya had the effect of making the presence of the Arabs accepted and tolerated, while in response to the burden of the tax more and more, who had at first remained in their former religion, turned to Islam. The real Arab, so to speak, dispersal into Iran began after the initial Islamic victories. Indeed in Sāsānian times, before Islam, there had been Arab tribes in southern and western Persia; but after the conquest, the flood of these desert dwellers onto Iranian soil was suddenly loosed, in particular from the vicinities of Kūfa and Baṣra. In the first century after the Hijra, places like Hamadān, Iṣfahān and Fārs soon began to attract immigrants, to be followed by Qum, Kāshān, Ray and Qazvīn and even Āzarbāījān. Later Arab tribes found settlement in Qūmis, Khurāsān and Sīstān on account of the attractiveness of the climate, or wherever they found the environment most congenial to them. In the midst of these settlers came people bent on jihād on the frontiers, adventurers among whom were those who because of affiliation with the Shī'a or the Khārijites could not or did not wish to remain in Syria and Iraq. Many of these, such as the Sā'ib family who settled in Qum, were subject to persecution in Iraq from the Umayyad officials, so that by removing themselves to distant areas they found freedom from oppression.

In spite of having been defeated, the Iranians did not accept the penetration of these different kinds of immigrants with enthusiasm; on their entrance to Madā'in they referred to the Arabs as devils; in Sīstān they were regarded as adherents of Ahriman. In many places their entrance was contested and when the Arabs assembled in Qum for their prayers, the people came and shouted insults at them, sometimes throwing stones and refuse into their dwellings. The flood was not, however, to be stemmed; gradually the Arabs acquired property and land in these new realms, and, particularly with the notables of different districts, they were able to establish relations which were not slow to move from the formal to the friendly. Marriages between the local residents and the new arrivals cemented fresh ties; the offspring from them brought into being a new class of people whose increasing numbers meant increasing strength. The Arabs' pride in their tribal lineages and Arab patronage served to give this new class cohesion and to augment its influence and status.

In these migrations, the geographical characteristics of Khurāsān were more congenial to the immigrants than those of many other areas. With their camels the Arabs were able to move easily about the deserts of Khurāsān. Accordingly Khurāsān and Qūmis were especially attractive, so that the sources tell us that in 52/672–3 as many as fifty thousand warriors, with their dependants, went to Khurāsān, half of them being Baṣra Arabs, half Kūfans. If the number of soldiers amounted to fifty thousand, the number of non-combatants with them – women, children and others – must be reckoned to have been at least three times this figure. Thus the number of Arabs involved in this large migration must have been of the order of two hundred thousand. In addition to this vast movement of people, in the year 64/683–4 another group of tribes went to Khurāsān. Of these immigrants, some would stay in cities, in their own Arab and tribal subdivision in special quarters, but a large number outside the cities continued to follow their former Bedouin way of life, as in the Arabian Peninsula.

The larger portion of these Arabs were from Baṣra. In Sīstān and eastern Khurāsān, the Bakr and Tamīm tribes predominated. In western Khurāsān and round Qūmis, the Qais were mainly to be found. The

Azd tribe reached Khurāsān a little later, to form another significant group in that region. The ancient, deep-seated rivalry and hostility that existed between the Qaḥṭānī and the ʻAdnānī Arabs reappeared among the immigrants, to be an important factor in bringing about the means by which the Umayyads were eventually unseated through rebellion begun in Khurāsān.

VI. MAGIANS AND MUSLIMS

In the wars between the Iranians and the Arabs, especially during the conquest of the Tigris–Euphrates basin and Iraq, those who fought valiantly against the Muslims either fell in battle or were taken as captives to become part of the victors' booty in the form of slaves. After a fifth of their number, as was the arrangement for all forms of the spoils of war, had gone to the caliph, the remainder were divided among the Muslim warriors. The numbers of these male and female captives, in particular before the time of Nihāvand, were excessive. The conquerors used them for hard labour, the men in farming and building and the women for domestic service. The battle of Jalūlā and the expeditions into Khūzistān were particularly productive of captive slaves. It was one of them, Abū Lu'lu' Fīrūz already mentioned, at first the slave of Mughaira b. Shuʻba, who finally put an end to the life of ʻUmar, the victorious caliph. The condition of these slaves, especially in Iraq and the Ḥijāz, was not at all pleasant, although the majority of them by becoming Muslim gained their freedom. It was a qualified freedom, for they became mawālī (clients) of the Arabs, freed slaves but still dependants who, as second-class citizens, could be exposed to ill-treatment and the contumely of the Arab Muslims.

Iran's submission to Islam, moreover, was only a very gradual process; the speed with which the new faith was spread varied according to region and to the different classes of society concerned. Acceptance of Islam changed the domestic and social life of the people: in the conquered territories it meant, aside from accepting new teachings in religion, taking new manners, customs and laws, and assuming a new way of life. Since Islam legislates for every detail of life, this change of faith meant that any habits and ideas not in conformity with it were abandoned. The conversion to Islam on the part of the whole population, such as is related about Qazvīn, was extremely rare. Although some groups, such as the Zuṭṭ, the Siyābija and a group of Dailamite horsemen, went over as whole bodies to Islam, and even as mawālī fought side by side with the Arabs in the wars in Iran, in several areas, notably Fārs, Jibāl, Gīlān and Dailam itself, the people avoided Arab overlordship and their faith. In other areas taken, too, a section of the population refused to follow the new ways; by accepting the jizya and kharāj they elected to continue in their old religion. After all of Iran had fallen to the Muslim conquerors, the privileges and immunities which those who accepted Islam had over those who remained as *dhimmīs*, became a force more potent than the efforts the conquerors at first made to propagate their new faith. Particularly significant is the fact that the artisan class and the craftsmen of the cities, unlike the cultivators in the countryside and members of the great families, were not deeply attached to the old religious organizations and the rules and taboos promulgated by the Zoroastrian clergy.

The explanation for this lay in the fact that these classes through the nature of their daily tasks could not help perpetually colliding with the taboos and injunctions of the Zoroastrian religion, which forbade the pollution of fire, earth and water, so that in the eyes of the Zoroastrian priesthood the artisans and craftsmen were ritually unclean and neglective, perhaps even of doubtful devotion. Not unnaturally, the new religion seemed to these classes more palatable and less rigorous. It must be admitted also that, while Islam abolished the class society of Sāsānian Iran, in some respects it conformed to what were also ancient Iranian ideas, such as the belief in one God, Allah, and the devil, Iblīs, the angels, the Day of Judgement, the Bridge of Sirāṭ, Heaven and Hell; and even the five diurnal prayers were similar to ancient Iranian cult practices. Thus among the Iranian masses, who witnessed the self-confidence, the enthusiasm and the faith of the new-comers, and were aware of the corruption and weaknesses of the Sāsānian religious organization, gradually hesitation in accepting Islam disappeared.

When the Sāsānian government fell, people who in accordance with the precepts of the Qur'ān were recognized as "People of the Book", that is to say the Jews and Christians, could continue in their former faith as dhimmīs, members of a recognized confessional, on payment of the jizya. Moreover Islam for them spelt liberation from forced labour and military service, which in Iran formerly they had been bound to perform. They enjoyed more liberty in the performance of their religions than had been accorded them under the régime of the Zoroastrian clergy. In return for the jizya Islam took them under its protection. In any event the amount of this tax was in practice generally little in excess of what the Muslims themselves paid in the form of *ṣadaqa* or *zakāt*, while women, infants, the indigent, the disabled and monks were exempt from it. Needless to say the dhimmīs were required to show respect for Islam and the Qur'ān, and not to seek marriage or association with Muslim women, nor to proselytize among Muslims, nor aid those at war against Islam. In addition it was binding upon them that they should not wear the same garb as Muslims and that their buildings should not exceed Muslim edifices in height. The sound of the instruments by which they were permitted to summon their co-religionists to prayer and the sound of their devotions were not to reach Muslim ears. They were not openly to consume wine or show signs of their religion, and their dead were to be interred secretly and separately. They were not to construct new places of worship, nor to carry weapons and ride horses. In accordance with the Qur'ān, payment of the jizya was furthermore to be accompanied by signs of humility and recognition of personal inferiority. On payment of the tax a seal, generally of lead, was affixed to the payee's person as a receipt and as a sign of the status of dhimma.

Islamic rule, especially in the early days of the conquest, sat more lightly upon Christians and Jews than had the rule of the Zoroastrian state. At first the term dhimma applied exclusively to the Jews and Christians as those specifically mentioned in the Qur'ān. Later Zoroastrians, also known as Magians, although the caliph ʿUmar sought to impose very rigorous measures against them, on the precedent that the Prophet was said to have accepted the jizya from Magians in Baḥrain, were counted in the ranks of "People of the Book".

Muslim treatment of the Zoroastrians varied in accordance with the policies of the caliphs and attitudes of different governors. In the early days of the conquest both sides from time to time broke their agreements and ignored the convention which was supposed to exist between them, but after the time of ʿUthmān the dhimmīs in Iraq and Iran lived fairly comfortably. With the exception of the Umayyad governor Ḥajjāj, who went so far as to exact the jizya from monks because he was of the opinion that people became monks to avoid the tax, the Umayyad *ʿummāl*, especially in Iraq, adopted after the example of their caliphs a markedly lenient policy towards the dhimmīs. Khālid b. ʿAbd-Allāh Qasrī displayed positive affection for Christians, his mother having been one, and was moderate in his dealings with the

Magians. It is said that the reason for his dismissal as governor was that he placed a Magian in charge over Muslims.[1]

Nevertheless Muslim treatment of Magians in the Umayyad period, particularly in Fārs and Khurāsān, gradually became increasingly contemptuous and intolerable. It was for this reason that a group of them left the land of their ancestors in order to preserve their ancient religion, emerging from the fortress of Sanjān, which is situated near Khwāf in the vicinity of Nīshāpūr, and departing to Kūhistān and the island of Hurmuz, ultimately to go to Gujerāt by way of the Persian Gulf, there to found a colony in India. The story of the migration of this group, which seems to have been at the end of the first century after the Hijra, about A.D. 718–19, was later made into a Persian odyssey, the *Qiṣṣa-yi Sanjān* ("The Story of Sanjān") by a Zoroastrian poet named Kai-Qubād Nūsārī and is extant.[2] Sixty years after this first group had found safety in Gujerāt, they were joined by another group, and their descendants still preserve their faith and are known as Parsis. Magians also stayed in Iran and by dint of paying the jizya were able to maintain their rites, but in the course of the centuries their sufferings have been considerable.

The adherents of other old Iranian religions, such as Manichaeism and even Mazdakism, found in the time of the Arab invasion more scope than they had enjoyed under the Sāsānians for the practice of what had to the latter been heterodoxies, to be suppressed. The followers of Mānī during Umayyad times in Iraq and Khurāsān maintained a secret existence on a limited scale. Among others, Ibn al-Nadīm is a source for the fact that Manichaeism existed in Iraq and Khurāsān in the reign of Walīd b. ʿAbd al-Malik (86–96/705–15). According to him, for some time prior to this period there had been a difference of opinion among the Manichees about the successor of Mānī; the sect of them known as the Dīnāvariyya, who lived beyond Balkh, were in opposition to the Manichaean chief who resided in Babylon.[3] Among the secretaries of Ḥajjāj one was a Manichee, who built a hospice and oratory in Madā'in for one Zād Hurmuzd, who claimed to be the chief of the Manichees and was moreover recognized by the Dīnāvariyya. The opposing faction came to be called the Mihriyya, after one Mihr, the Manichaean leader in the time of Walīd b. ʿAbd al-Malik. The

[1] Ibn Khāllikān, *Wafayāt al-aʿyān*, ed. Muḥ. ʿAbd al-Ḥamīd, vol. II (Cairo, 1948), p. 8.

[2] Cf. J. J. Modi, *The Kisseh-i-Sanjān* (Bombay, 1917), pp. 8–10.

[3] Ibn al-Nadīm, *Fihrist*, ed. G. Fluegel (Leipzig, 1872), p. 334.

existence of various sects of Manichaeans indicates the degree of freedom with which they were able openly to proclaim themselves, while it would appear that heterodox Muslims in this time were charged with being Manichees.

Followers of Mazdak also, at various intervals, found increased scope for action. The Zoroastrians themselves strove harder than the Muslims against these heresies, as is shown by the manner in which they rejected Bihāfarīd b. Mahfurūdīn, who was in reality the apostle of reform in Zoroastrianism since he apparently wished to remove from it those aspects which struck the Muslims most forcibly and cleanse it of accretions and superfluities. It was the Zoroastrian priests themselves who supported Abū Muslim and the newly arisen 'Abbāsid régime, because both offered them help against heretics.

Bihāfarīd appeared in the last days of the Umayyad caliphate, in about 129/747, at Khwāf in the vicinity of Nīshāpūr, and produced a book in Persian. His appearance indicates a tendency towards sectarianism among the Magians, but he tried to effect a rapprochement between the teachings of Magianism and those of Islam. Although, and to some extent at the promptings of the Magian priests, Abū Muslim destroyed Bihāfarīd, his followers, the *Bihāfarīdiyya*, continued until the fourth century of the Muslim era, the tenth century A.D., to expect his return. However, this piece of collusion on Abū Muslim's part with the Magian authorities against the Bihāfarīdiyya must be accounted part of his policy of taking advantage of a variety of anti-Arab forces in mounting his campaign against the Umayyads.

VII. THE MAWĀLĪ BETWEEN THE SHĪ'A AND THE KHĀRIJITES

With the death of 'Uthmān the centre of the caliphate moved from Medina to Kūfa in Iraq, a city which had been built near to the ancient Ḥīra and half of whose inhabitants were non-Arabs. 'Alī b. Abī Ṭālib, the new caliph, had a considerable following in Iraq both from among the Yemenī Arabs and from among non-Arab Muslim elements, those who were known as mawālī. Under the Umayyads the Arabs and the mawālīs of Iraq continued to show respect for 'Alī's descendants. In any event the internal division which manifested itself during 'Alī's brief reign ended in the separation of the two sects the Shī'a and the Khārijites from the mass of Muslims. Later both acquired a following among the Muslims of Iran. Iranians thus entered the lists of the internal political differences of the Arabs. Generally in order to show their hatred for the Umayyad régime the Iranians supported the Shī'a, which had the best organized platform against the Umayyads, besides being in accord with the Iranians' own sentiments. From these beginnings of internal conflict among the Arabs themselves, and among Muslims in general, the Kūfan Arabs, who were generally Yemenī in origin, showed a marked predilection for 'Alī; they were followed in expressing affection for him by the mawālī of Kūfa.

Most of the mawālī in this instance were humble craftsmen whom the Arabs had received into their city in order to have jobs performed which the Arabs regarded as shameful. The Arabs saw their function as war; any other they regarded as beneath them, the mawālī being held in contempt for the very skills which made their presence desirable and useful. The caliph 'Alī, unlike 'Uthmān, was sympathetic towards the mawālī and treated them with respect, to the extent of arousing complaints on this score from his compatriots. To the anger of the latter, he accorded the mawālī equality in all respects with the Arabs, a factor which also accounted for the mawālī's attachment to him. Some Kūfan Arabs regarded 'Alī as the exponent and support of the ascendancy of Iraq, while subsequently they took the imāmate of his descendants, Ḥasan, Ḥusain and Muḥammad b. al-Ḥanafiyya as the symbol of the greatness and predominance of their city. In the same way Ḥusain b. 'Alī's marriage and connection with the family of Yazdgard or Hurmuzān became one of the principal reasons for Iranians' increased regard for 'Alī's progeny. Perhaps in their imāmate the Iranians envisaged the restoration of Iran's past greatness.

At the bottom of the Shī'ī reverence for the *imām* – the Prophet's successor – and the conception that the leadership of the community was a divine and extraordinary office, lay the Iranians' belief that the *farr-i īzadī*, the Divine Power or Aura, should be an essential attribute of the exercise of sovereignty. This is not to say that the bases of Shī'ī beliefs are in any way derived from Iranian religious tenets; but the attraction these beliefs held for Iranians was in large measure due to the manner in which they were in harmony with and, as it were, echoed older cult conceptions. Nor is it without significance that some of the extremer forms of Shī'ism, such as the Kaisāniyya, Khashabiyya, Khaṭṭābiyya and Rāvandiyya, received their greatest support among the Iranian mawālī.

In contrast the Khārijites may be said to have been a "puritan" party in Islam, entertaining extreme democratic views verging on the anarchistic; if they really had any specific aim it was the creation of an Islamic community in which no one, not even the caliph, should deviate from the dictates of the Qur'ān. This extremist sect believed that to commit any major sin meant, even for the caliph, expulsion from the Faith, to be condemned as an unbeliever.

It happened that since the Khārijites in the issue of the election of the caliph were opposed to the view supported by the Umayyads, they gained the support of the mawālī. With their conceptions of equity and egalitarian tendencies, the mawālī looked with favour upon this sect. They frequently joined them in risings against the Umayyads, so that throughout the period of the Umayyad caliphate not only were the distant regions of Iran the scene of Khārijite rebellions against the caliphate, but also mawālī fought side by side with Arabs in these insurrections. Whatever difference there may have been between different parties of them, the Khārijites were united in the belief that an oppressive caliph must be opposed.[1] It was this same point which brought the mawālī, who were generally labouring under the burden of the kharāj and the oppressive manner of its collection, into the ranks of the Khārijites, both from the towns and the rural districts. For example during the time of 'Alī some of the mawālī of Ahvāz, discontented by the amount of kharāj required of them, joined in the fray. In the case of the rising of Abū Miryam of the Banī Sa'd Tamīm in 38/658, when Kūfa was threatened, most of his army consisted of mawālī. In the interregnum which followed the death of Yazīd b. Mu'āwiya (64/683), both Fārs and Ahvāz were the scene of Khārijite risings, as well as the vicinity of Ray. The conformity between mawālī aims and some of the claims of the Khārijites accounted for such joining of forces as was apparent in the rising of 'Ubaid-Allāh b. al-Māḥūz, one of the Azraqite leaders, when an appreciable number of mawālī were involved, while there were many also among the supporters of Qaṭarī b. Fujā'a, another Azraqite chief who managed for a time to hold Fārs and Kirmān. The emergence of differences between the mawālī and the Arabs, however, did not escape the camps of the Khārijites. While the Arabs took the part of Qaṭarī, the mawālī put up against him 'Abd Rabbihi, causing a division which did as much to destroy the Azraqites as did the arms of the Umayyad commander Yazīd b. Muhallab.

[1] Baghdādī, *al-Farq bain al-firaq* (Cairo, 1948), p. 45.

The mawālī habit of seeking refuge from Arab oppression in the encampments of the Khārijites and joining in their fighting continued until the end of Umayyad times. Similarly in the Shī'ī struggles against the Umayyads, the mawālī played a part. Although in the rising of Hujar b. 'Adī (51/671) and that of Ḥusain b. 'Alī at Ṭaff (61/680) the complexion was completely Arab, with the insurrection of Mukhtār the mawālī were with the Shī'īs; in Mukhtār's army, as is well attested, were twenty thousand of the Ḥamrā', the Kūfan mawālī, all of Iranian origin.[1]

Mukhtār's pretext for rising against the Umayyads was to exact revenge from the slayers of Ḥusain b. 'Alī. At the time, however, even the Shī'īs were doubtful of his sincerity; it was said that he used support of the cause of Ḥusain as a means of attracting to himself the people of Kūfa, in particular the non-Arab element, for the forwarding of his own designs. Nevertheless Mukhtār presented himself to the Shī'īs as the representative and minister of Muḥammad b. al-Ḥanafiyya, who was in the Ḥijāz, and by sending messages to him, persuaded him to express secret agreement with his plans, so that he could win the adherance of the Kūfan Shī'īs and in their name gain the ascendancy over that city.

Mukhtār exhibited a special skill in gaining the support of the mawālī, and their numbers in his forces became so great that the movement might be accounted a movement against the Arabs of Iraq. The Kūfan Arabs were disconcerted by his special regard for the mawālī elements; the complaint gained ground that in his camp not a word of Arabic could be heard.[2] With the support of this non-Arab element, Mukhtār was in fact able to rule Kūfa for eighteen months, taking kharāj from the Sawād, Jazīra and the Jibāl. His own bodyguard was chosen from among the Ḥamrā', and its command was also entrusted to one of them. Moreover, hitherto the mawālī's arms had been limited to a baton and they had participated in battle only on foot and had no share in the spoils of war. Mukhtār mounted them and provided them with weapons. Not only were they to share booty with the Arabs, but he promised that the property of the Arab nobles should fall to them also. Mukhtār's general, Ibrāhīm b. al-Ashtar, who said that these mawālī were the descendants of the knights and marzbāns of Fārs, considered them more suitable for doing battle against the

[1] Dīnawarī, p. 288.

[2] Ṭabarī, vol. II, pp. 647, 724; Dīnawarī, pp. 294–5.

Syrians than any other group. The Arabs of Kūfa, who also as Shī'is to some extent supported Mukhtār, grew angry over this complete confidence in the client class; it would seem that his movement developed into an anti-Arab movement, not solely one against the Umayyads.

Therefore, gradually support was withdrawn from Mukhtār. The Arabs joined Muṣ'ab b. Zubair who was in Baṣra on behalf of his brother, the famous claimant of the caliphate, 'Abd-Allāh b. Zubair. Thus Muṣ'ab b. Zubair, who in effect represented the Arab faction, overcame Mukhtār, who had become little more than the leader of the clients. After taking Kūfa, he left the Arabs free to exact their revenge from the mawālī; it is reported that after defeating Mukhtār, Muṣ'ab visited such excessive cruelty upon the mawālī that he gained the soubriquet *jazzār*, "butcher". More than seven thousand of the Kūfan mawālī are said to have perished.

However, in spite of this heavy death-roll, the important result achieved by Mukhtār's insurrection was the emergence of the mawālī in Iraq as a fighting force to be reckoned with. For example, when a few years later the tyranny of Yūsuf b. 'Umar Thaqafī, who continued the repressive policy of Ḥajjāj in Iraq, compelled Zaid b. 'Ali, Ḥusain b. 'Alī's grandson, to come out against the Umayyads and proclaim himself, again his principal support consisted of mawālī. His venture failed on account of his own vacillations and the lack of unity among his confederates. When he rose, in 122/739, only two hundred and eighteen people of all those who had sworn loyalty to him were mustered. As might be expected, Zaid suffered defeat and was murdered.

Likewise when a short time afterwards, in the year 125/742–3, his son, Yaḥyā b. Zaid, rebelled in Khurāsān and was defeated in Jūzjānān by the governor of Khurāsān, Naṣr b. Sayyār, he too was put to death. The death of this father and son, however, though apparently marking an Umayyad victory, in fact to some degree redounded to the advantage of the 'Abbāsid cause. The deaths of Zaid and Yaḥyā removed rivals who might have been able to prepare those unseen forces awaiting the 'Abbāsid call. After the death of these two, practically all the Shī'ī partisans in their various groupings came over to the secret propaganda of the 'Abbāsids. The latter's programme even came to include the appeal of taking revenge for Zaid and Yaḥyā's forfeited lives.

Zaid wanted to gain the caliphate with, as far as possible, the support of the majority of Muslim sects. To this end he even accepted Khārijites among his sworn adherents. Contrary to the inclination of most Shīʿīs he was unwilling to inculpate Abū Bakr and ʿUmar and, while acknowledging their inferiority to ʿAlī, he insisted upon recognizing the validity of their caliphates. As a result most of the Shīʿīs abandoned him and this was an important factor in his defeat. ʿAbd-Allāh b. Muʿāwiya, the grandson of Jaʿfar b. Abī Ṭālib, had the same experience, to be left, like Zaid, without the support of the Shīʿīs. The Zaidīs, who were a group consisting of many different elements, joined ʿAbd-Allāh b. Muʿāwiya, but his insurrection at Kūfa in the month of Muḥarram 127/October 744, in spite of a demonstration of great courage on the part of the Zaidīs in his defence, met with defeat. Following his flight from Kūfa he was able for a short while to gain power in Iṣfahān, Iṣṭakhr, Ahvāz and Kirmān, and a party of Khārijites joined him, but he was defeated by ʿĀmir b. Ḍubāra and finally went to Khurāsān to Abū Muslim. The latter, who had just placed the ʿAbbāsid propaganda on the road to victory, took him and put him to death in 129/746–7.

The time had passed when the ʿAbbāsid cause could tolerate any kind of vacillation or difference of opinion of the kind which in the past had vitiated all the Shīʿī movements. In any event, at the end of Umayyad times not only were the mawālī, as in the days of Mukhtār and ʿAbd al-Malik (65–86/685–705), co-operating with both major movements, Khārijite and Shīʿī, against the Umayyads, but it would also seem that they were becoming affected by the tenets of these movements. This was especially true with the Zaidī rising and that of ʿAbd-Allāh b. Muʿāwiya; while the Khārijites in order to raise contention against the hated Umayyads sank their differences sufficiently to collaborate with some of the Shīʿī moderate factions. The Umayyad government had learnt to regard the mawālī, as it did the Khārijites and the Shīʿa, not as subjects, but as disturbers of the peace and its unrelenting opponents.

VIII. THE MAWĀLĪ AND ARAB RULE

When the Islamic invasion of Iran began, Yazdgard III was ruling as possessor of the divine glory, blessed and confirmed by God; he saw himself as above and as the guardian of the rest of the people. The ruler and guardian of Muslim affairs, who was called the Prince of Believers, and imām, was simply one among the rest of the Muslims, who, at least in theory, see themselves as brothers and equals. But he was a member of the Quraish, who acted as the deputy of the Prophet in overseeing the execution of the laws of Islam and in guiding the community. It was only on account of his being the deputy of the Prophet of God that obedience to him was required, and opposition to him tantamount to denial of the Prophet. The early caliphs sat in the simplest garb among their people and took with them the simplest of fare. When Hurmuzān the governor of Khūzistān was captured and taken to Medina, he was amazed at the simplicity of the caliph, who lacked both chamberlains and guards.

The Umayyads, having regard to the extraordinary way in which the realms of Islam had expanded and to the variety of elements which now composed the Muslim community, became aware that religion alone was not sufficient as a base for a great empire; some kind of national feeling was also required. They placed the caliphate on a new kind of footing, changing it into a government – an Arab government – which depended upon the protection of the Arab tribes. Naturally in this government new aims and institutions appeared, while the pristine simplicity and strong complexion of theocracy characteristic of the times of the first four caliphs disappeared. In opposition to these new aims and government structures parties arose such as the Shīʿa and the Khārijites, totally ready to disown the bases of this new government. For example, the sects of the Shīʿa, with the exception of the Zaidīs, refused to recognize an elective caliphate, and maintained that the right to be caliph rested exclusively in ʿAlī and his descendants. On the other hand the Khārijites denied the necessity for the imām's being of the Quraish, and in some instances, the necessity for there being an imām at all.

Nevertheless Muʿāwiya made the caliphate like kingship, hereditary in his own family, and gradually by the introduction of various ceremonies and types of etiquette, transformed it into something much more resembling an Arab monarchy, its *raison d'être* the defence of the Arab tribes. Accordingly, as long as the unity of the tribes survived, so did their government. It was only when ancient tribal factions re-appeared, the Qaisīs and Kalbīs, the Muḍarīs and Yemenīs, that their government began to decline. Until then the Umayyads were able to rely upon these tribes to withstand the serious threats being posed against them by the Shīʿīs and Khārijites. The Arab tribes whose chiefs Muʿāwiya had attracted, accepted and lent strength to this new policy.

The Arab conquerors, who in the time of 'Umar had seized from the Iranians the fertile Sawād, were gradually emerging as an élite ruling group which in its heart had no desire to be considered on the same level with mawālī – the Iranians and Nabataeans of Iraq, whose lands had been conquered and whom, though they did accept Islam, the conquerors still regarded as only freed captives and bondsmen. Some of these mawālī were in fact the descendants of captives who during the conquest had fallen into the Arabs' hands and then, on becoming Muslim, gained their freedom. Others were people whose cities had surrendered to the Muslims without resistance, and who had accepted Islam and attached themselves voluntarily to the Arabs for their protection, thus willingly taking on the status of clients of the Arabs. The Arabs looked upon both sorts of mawālī as aliens and, regardless of what class they had belonged to, treated them with scorn and contempt. They led them into battle on foot. They deprived them of a share of the booty. They would not walk on the same side of the street with them, nor sit at the same repast. In nearly every place separate encampments and mosques were constructed for their use. Marriage between them and the Arabs was considered a social crime. The Umayyad caliphs and their governors generally regarded the mawālī with suspicion and aversion. Mu'āwiya, alarmed at the large number of them he found in Iraq, went so far as to contemplate putting many of them to death and exiling others. He did at least send some of them to the Syrian coast and Antioch, apparently as a foresighted move to obviate troubles to come.[1]

Although the conduct of Ziyād and his son, 'Ubaid-Allāh – governors of Iraq – towards the mawālī was not unmixed with mildness, the prevalence of the Arab power there continued to be regarded by these people with disfavour. Thus it was that unceasingly among them men appeared who, in spite of those who supported the Umayyad caliphate, united with the Umayyads' enemies. When 'Abd-Allāh b. Zubair revolted they joined him, but when they found him not to be favourable to non-Arab elements they deserted him. What principally caused the rivalry and enmity which gradually came into existence between the Arabs and the mawālī was that for the governors of Iraq hostility against non-Arabs became obligatory as a form of regular observance, a harsh manifestation of the Arabs' right of patronage. Thus Mukhtār Thaqafī became the victim of the Arabs' wrath and hatred when, in

[1] Ibn 'Abd al-Rabbihi, *al-'Iqd al-farīd*, vol. II (Cairo, 1302/1885), p. 91.

pursuance of his own plans, he deemed it expedient to support the mawālī, giving them their share in the common distribution of booty, a gesture which brought him down in defeat.

The governorship of Ḥajjāj was particularly characterized by profound suspicion of the mawālī, who were, not unnaturally, always in league with his opponents. To prevent this, Ḥajjāj encouraged and compelled them to participate in wars against the Khārijites or in the jihād on the frontiers of Sind, Kabul and Transoxiana; such expeditions were in his eyes the best medicine for the trouble-makers who according to him were prevalent in Iraq. They, on the other hand, did not show much enthusiasm for these distant wars. They preferred remaining in Iraq and since there they were subject to Ḥajjāj's strict surveillance and oppression, they were seldom missing in any movement aimed at his discomfiture. For example, in the rising of Ibn Ash'ath, the mawālī played a considerable rôle. Ḥajjāj b. Yūsuf made this 'Abd al-Raḥmān b. Muḥammad b. Ash'ath, who was a relative of his, the 'āmil of Sīstān, sending him thither with an army composed of Arab and mawālī elements to reduce the king of Kabul. Since Ash'ath saw no likelihood at that time of success in those regions, he wrote and told Ḥajjāj of his intention to return. Ḥajjāj wrote back angrily and did not spare his reproaches, to which the Arab responded by rebelling against Ḥajjāj. On his return to Iraq, Ash'ath was joined by more mawālī; besides the Khārijites, always ready to fight the Umayyad régime, Shī'īs attached themselves to him, as did Murji'īs, whose normal avoidance of taking sides gave the Umayyads an advantage. In these three different sectarian groups were mawālī and, since Ḥajjāj had no alternative before such a concourse but to seek help from Syria, in effect Ibn Ash'ath's motley rising developed into a rising of Iraq against Syria. Ibn Ash'ath's defeat fell heavily upon the mawālī elements, Ḥajjāj's ruthless pursuit of whom and the punishments he meted out to them calling forth protests from the caliph 'Abd al-Malik, who wrote and rebuked him.

So outstanding was the persistence of the mawālī in the Ibn Ash'ath insurrection that the courage of one of their leaders, named Fīrūz, gave Ḥajjāj special cause for concern. It is said that he offered ten thousand dirhams reward to anybody who brought Fīrūz's head. Fīrūz retorted by offering a hundred thousand in return for Ḥajjāj's head.[1] After the defeat of the rebellion, Fīrūz escaped to Khurāsān, where he was captured by Ibn Muhallab. He was sent to Ḥajjāj, and tortured to death.

[1] Ibn Qutaiba, *Kitāb al-ma'ārif* (Cairo, 1960), p. 337.

Apart from Ḥajjāj other Umayyad governors, civil and military, in both Iraq and Khurāsān treated the mawālī with the same harshness and contempt as other Arabs displayed towards them. This treatment by the authorities continued in spite of the fact that the oppression which had been a feature of the reign of 'Abd al-Malik was somewhat relaxed under Sulaimān his son, under 'Umar II b. 'Abd al-'Azīz and even Hishām b. 'Abd al-Malik. In Khurāsān and Iraq the Arabs' attitude towards the mawālī was not based on any assumption of equality or justice. Probably the sources exaggerate, but nonetheless there is plenty of evidence of Arab contempt for the non-Arab Muslim, not least in the scorn poured on them over their genealogies, so that there is every reason to consider this assumption of superiority on the Arabs' part a main cause of the mawālī's dissatisfaction against them. This was aggravated by the fact that the Umayyad governors exerted their oppression in lands which had belonged to the ancestors of the mawālī. In this respect the case of Khurāsān differs from that of western Iraq.

For Mu'āwiya the conquered territories were the means for sweetening potential foes and attracting the allegiance of friends. When Sa'īd b. 'Uthmān complained of Yazīd being made the caliph's heir, he was given Khurāsān as a douceur. Sa'īd fully appreciated the succulent sop brought to him and in a couplet which he composed remarked that if his father, the caliph 'Uthmān, had been alive, he would not have awarded him with more than Mu'āwiya had.[1] The Umayyads saw the granting of governorships in the eastern provinces as a means of rewarding services, and provided that gifts and tribute regularly reached the caliph, these governors were, contrary to the practice under the first caliphs, subject to no supervision. 'Abd al-Malik b. Marwān, inviting the Iraqi chiefs to aid him in his war with Muṣ'ab b. Zubair, promised them governorships, while they in most instances entered into a contract with him for them. For example, forty of them, each one separately, at one time requested of him the governorship of Iṣfahān; 'Abd al-Malik asked in astonishment, "Goodness, what is this Iṣfahān?".

One of the Arabs of the desert appointed by Ḥajjāj to collect the kharāj at Iṣfahān summoned a number of people who had failed to render the tax at the appointed time and cut their heads off, to intimidate others into prompt payment.[2] Influential governors from time to time

[1] (Pseudo) Ibn Qutaiba, *al-Imāma wa'l-siyāsa*, vol. I (Cairo, 1957), p. 192.
[2] Mas'ūdī, vol. v, pp. 390–3.

deposited the taxes to their own account, sending nothing to Damascus. Maslama b. 'Abd al-Malik, who was later governor of Iraq and Khurāsān on behalf of his brother Yazīd, sent nothing out of the kharāj of his governorship to the caliph.[1] Sulaimān b. 'Abd al-Malik, who preceded his brother Yazīd in the caliphate, appointed Yazīd b. Muhallab to Khurāsān, but Sulaimān's successor, 'Umar b. 'Abd al-'Azīz, was forced to imprison Yazīd to extract the dues of the *Bait al-māl*, the Muslim community's treasury, from him.[2]

In those distant provinces the caliphs' officials lent themselves to every form of oppression of subjects, especially as in many cases their office had been acquired by the offering of presents and payment of bribes. The caliph Hishām (105–25/724–43) gave Junaid b. 'Abd al-Raḥman al-Murrī Khurāsān in return for a costly and much appreciated jewelled necklace he had given the caliph's wife, and a similar one presented to Hishām himself.[3] Walīd b. Yazīd (125–6/743–4) granted Khurāsān with Naṣr b. Sayyār and all its revenue, in return for a sum of money, to Yūsuf b. 'Umar, the governor of Iraq; however, before either Khurāsān or Naṣr b. Sayyār could fall into the hands of this cruel purchaser, Walīd was killed and the evil passed.

Enough has been said to illustrate the harsh treatment of the mawālī in the matter of taxation by Umayyad governors who tended to make no distinction between Muslim converts and the dhimmīs. Conduct in such marked contrast to the manner in which the Arabs under the first four caliphs acted caused increasing dissatisfaction. Indeed, during the century that had elapsed since the conquest of the Jibāl and Khurāsān, the Umayyads had changed the Islamic theocracy into something that could only be described as an Arab government, and the enthusiasm and idealism of Islam had been so much weakened that a rising of a group of discontented people in Khurāsān under the title of protecting the Faith and the Family of the Prophet was sufficient to overthrow the Arab government.

IX. JIZYA AND KHARĀJ

The dihqāns, or landed aristocracy, of Sāsānian times remained under the new Islamic dispensation as the government's representatives in rural areas. Their main task was collection of the kharāj from the

[1] Ibn al-Athīr, *al-Kāmil fi'l-ta'rīkh*, vol. IV (Cairo, 1957), p. 181.
[2] *Ibid.*, p. 157.
[3] *Ibid.*, p. 206; Ṭabarī, vol. III, p. 1527.

cultivators and its transference to the central treasury of the Muslim community. The kharāj on land was of course levied from the agrarian classes, and it was the duty of the dihqān to apportion what was due among the peasants who had to pay it. Thus, as in Sāsānian times, under the Muslim government the cultivator continued bound to work the land and render taxes to the government.

In Iraq at first the principal aim of the Muslims was to gain booty and at the same time make the Christian Arab tribes of the Sawād Muslim. The chief purpose was then not to overthrow the Iranian régime. At the time of Ḥīra's fall, when a party of Arabs came out of the city for negotiations, Khālid made three proposals to them – acceptance of Islam; payment of the poll-tax, the jizya; or war. The people of Ḥīra elected to pay the jizya. According to the sources, out of the total population about six thousand were capable of paying the poll-tax. On this basis the sum required was estimated as sixty thousand dirhams. Its collection was entrusted to persons selected by the citizens themselves. Khālid left the "People of the Book" free to continue the practice of their religion. In their turn these promised to forbear from any hostile act and from giving aid to the Iranians. In sundry other cities of Iraq similar arrangements were made between the Muslims and the local population. If, however, an invested town could only be taken by war, its people were put to the sword or made slaves.

Once an administrative centre, Kūfa, had been established in Iraq, the next problem was the division of lands and administration of the tax régime, the kharāj. The conquering Arabs expected to divide the land among themselves, exploiting the peasantry of Iraq for their own benefit, as had been the custom under the Sāsānians. The caliph, 'Umar b. al-Khaṭṭāb, however, abandoned these ideas in the interests of prudence and out of military and religious considerations. For the Faith had to be defended, if not spread. If its warriors were to settle on the lands distributed amongst them in the Sawād, the conquests would be halted, and manpower for Muslim garrisons on the frontiers, against the risings or invasions of enemies, would be short. Distribution of fiefs among the conquerors, moreover, would prevent the regular receipt by the central treasury of fluid assets. Accordingly, 'Umar took counsel with the notables among the Prophet's former companions at Medina and left the Sawād lands as before, in the hands of the dihqāns, and those formerly in control of them, the condition being that they paid kharāj as before on their lands, and jizya on their own heads. The dihqāns had been responsible for tax collection under the Sāsānians; the caliph instituted the same procedure. Surveyors were sent to Iraq to make a cadastral survey. At first the kharāj was restricted to grain-producing lands or to those producing dates, grapes, olives and alfalfa. Since other products implied exemption from the tax, the cultivators tried to sow crops not subject to the kharāj. In consequence, part of the Sawād escaped taxation, until in 22/643–4 the governor of Kūfa, Mughaira b. Shu'ba, drew the caliph's attention to the fact and fresh regulations were promulgated. Thereafter, not only were other crops subject to tax, but also lands not under cultivation were assessed. Though these lands remained under the control of the dihqāns, since they were made mortmain or *waqf*, in trust on behalf of the Muslim community by what was a species of entail, the dihqāns had no way by which to get them exempted from the kharāj. Such exemption could not be gained by selling the lands to Muslims, nor by the dihqāns' turning Muslim.

Besides the lands left under the dihqāns' control, there were estates which had belonged to the former imperial house or to soldiers slain or missing in the wars. These also were left to their former cultivators, but became in effect the *khāliṣa* or, so to speak "crown lands" pertaining to the caliphs, who held them as *ṣawāfī*, i.e. the part of the booty which went directly to the imām as distinct from what was divided among the soldiers. They sometimes distributed them as they wished in the form of iqṭā' fiefs.

From the dhimmīs, besides kharāj, which only applied to those holding land, was also taken the jizya, a capitation tax not limited to land ownership but applicable in accordance with their capacity, and so long as they remained non-Muslim, to artisans and craftsmen and all the inhabitants of the cities. This *gazīt* or jizya, capitation tax, had also been levied in Sāsānian times on the masses, but the nobles, clergy, dihqāns and *dabīrān* (the scribes or civil servants) had been exempt from it. Thus it was a tax which had come to denote a low position in the orders of society. In Islam this levy was in accordance with the direction of the Qur'ān and becoming Muslim meant, in theory at least, its cessation. Kharāj, on the other hand, being a land tax was not affected by acceptance of Islam. Thus though the Muslims took over the Sāsānian tax system in Iraq as it stood, from the beginning they recognized a difference between jizya and kharāj.

The collection of revenue and disbursements out of it depended on the creation of a *dīvān*, a treasury office, and this began in Iraq in the time of Mughaira b. Shu'ba under the direction of an Iranian named Pīrī or Pīrūz(?). After him, his son, Zādān Farrukh was for a time in charge of it. After a short while, the second caliph, 'Umar, expanded this dīvān of Iraq, creating an establishment in which the entire income and expenditure of the Islamic realms were registered along with all those who were entitled to stipends or a share of the booty. Reforms had to be carried out in the operations of the dīvān in the time of Mu'āwiya, when Ziyād b. Abīhi was governor in Iraq. Another problem that arose was the gradual Islamization of the dhimmīs and likewise the unavoidable changes and transferences which occurred in lands and their ownership, with steps taken by recent converts among the mawālī to leave their lands and escape the kharāj by going to the cities – all these matters were a source of concern to the caliphs and their revenue officers.

Ḥajjāj b. Yūsuf, the harsh governor of Iraq, returned to their villages by force those mawālī who fled their lands, and in addition he used to extract from them the jizya, illegally, of course, since according to Islamic law they were exempt from this on conversion. The cultivation and industry of Iraq at this time were principally in mawālī hands. The dīvān, with its significance as the central and most sensitive organ of government, was also in mawālī hands. Up to the time of 'Abd al-Malik, the accounts were still written entirely in Persian notation. Ḥajjāj, who was not happy about the mawālī predominance and prevalence of the Persian language in the dīvān, took measures to have its language changed to Arabic, thereby making the supervision of the affairs of non-Arabs by Arabs more extended. The person who accomplished this for Ḥajjāj was himself an Iranian, one of the clients of the Banī Tamīm named Ṣāliḥ b. 'Abd al-Raḥmān, a Sīstānī. He worked in the dīvān with Zādān Farrukh b. Pīrūz. When the latter was killed in the course of the insurrection of Ibn Ash'ath, Ḥajjāj ordered Ṣāliḥ to effect the change into Arabic, in spite of the fact that Zādān's son, Mardānshāh, endeavoured to obstruct the innovation.

At the same time, following differences with Byzantium, 'Abd al-Malik the caliph established a mint in Damascus to produce coins with Arabic inscriptions, and Ḥajjāj also struck new coinage to replace the old. Until this time the currency of Iraq and Iran had been of the ancient pattern. In spite of the change from Persian to Arabic notation in the dīvān and the new coinage, contrary to what Mardānshāh had foreseen, the Persian vernacular did not disappear, while the governors who succeeded Ḥajjāj, though themselves Arabs, were forced increasingly to take advantage of the presence of mawālī in the dīvān.

In Khurāsān, however, another kind of difficulty arose in connection with the kharāj. The local aristocracy and marzbāns of this region gave up hope of a restoration of the Sāsānians after the fall of Ctesiphon and the final Arab victory, and most of them peacefully submitted to the Arabs. This submission, however, was accompanied by acceptance of an arrangement whereby they were to pay a fixed sum annually to the Arab conquerors. It was by making this kind of peace, whereby a fixed sum should be paid and should not be subject to any arbitrary changes, that the cities of Ṭabasain, Kūhistān, Nīshāpūr, Nasā, Abīvard, Ṭūs, Herāt and Marv fell to the Arabs, each making its treaty separately. Unlike Iraq, where the Muslims had the lands and their extent and taxable value registered in the dīvān and where their officials could interfere directly in the affairs of revenue collection, in Khurāsān this was left to the local *kadkhudās* or overseers, who accomplished it in collaboration with the local religious officials. The revenue collection was carried out according to former practices or in whatever way suited the men responsible for doing it. Of what accrued, only the amount stipulated in the treaties made at the time of the conquest was paid to the Arabs. A portion of what the officials collected was under the heading of jizya and the rest from the land, while the sum which the people of a city paid as a whole to the Arabs was fixed and was more or less based on an estimate of the total of both these components. As elsewhere, becoming Muslim, if one were one of the People of the Book, entailed a diminution of the tax obligation, at least in so far as the jizya was concerned. Although several of the governors in Khurāsān strongly urged that these converts to Islam, in accordance with Qur'ānic precept, be exempt from the poll-tax, those responsible for revenue collection often failed to carry out these injunctions. If they seemed to implement them, they generally found some pretext for manipulating the taxes under one heading or another in such a way that the loss of the jizya was made up and the global sum rendered remained the same as before. Since the tax gatherers were, as has been shown, working in conjunction with officials of the former religions, when they saw one of their own faith turning to Islam or accepting it, not only did they not excuse him taxes, from which in theory he thus became exempt, but, since his conversion was to their disadvantage, they were venal enough to find means to increase the burden of his tax over that paid by those who had retained their former religious allegiance. Bahrām Sīs, who in the last days of the Umayyads was in charge of collecting kharāj from the Zoroastrians of Khurāsān, used this device as did others. Thus at that time nearly thirty thousand new converts still paid the jizya, while eighty thousand dhimmīs were in effect exempted from taxation. The last Umayyad governor in Khurāsān, Naṣr b. Sayyār, tried to correct this situation in favour of the Muslims and with some regard for the teaching of the Qur'ān, and he even proposed to have land taxes reassessed and allocated anew. His attempted reforms, however, began too late to silence the numerous discontented whose patience had been exhausted by years of the injustice of Arab intendants and their Iranian tax gatherers. Moreover his reforms seriously vexed the dhimmīs, upon whom the tax burden fell heaviest. Finally, internal differences among the Arabs gave this last but worthy Umayyad governor no opportunity to continue his ameliorative efforts; it was in the midst of his various difficulties that the secret 'Abbāsid propaganda burst into the open and began to bear fruit.

X. THE 'ABBĀSID PROPAGANDA

There was little possibility of open Shī'ī propaganda making any headway in Iraq because of Umayyad power, but also there were a number of different Shī'ī sects at work, in opposition to each other. From this time began the Shī'ī interest in having recourse to *kitmān* and *taqiyya*, valid dissimulation, to prevent discord and obviate personal persecution, in readiness for the time when the right torn from the House of Muḥammad, the caliphate, might be restored and with the advent of the true imām. To this end, secret underground propaganda began. According to the sources, the secret propaganda was initiated by Muḥammad b. al-Ḥanafiyya, 'Alī b. Abī Ṭālib's son (not by Fāṭima, the Prophet's daughter, but by a wife from the Banū Hanīfa), although it seems more likely that the foundations for it were laid right from the time when Imām Ḥasan came to terms with the Umayyads. After the murder of Ḥusain in the battle of Ṭaff, the majority of the Shī'a gathered round Muḥammad b. al-Ḥanafiyya. His fabled physical strength gave them hope of progress in realizing their cause.

With the rising of 'Abd-Allāh b. Zubair, however, who in a sense was his rival and opponent, this opportunity was not granted, and

Muḥammad himself, despite the high expectations the Shīʿīs entertained of him, refrained from any sort of violence, giving Mukhtār, whose proclamations and incitement to action were in Ibn al-Ḥanafiyya's name, only the most ambiguous verbal support.

His son, ʿAbd-Allāh b. Muḥammad, known as Abū Hāshim, continued his father's secret propaganda but in the presence of the Umayyad officials' suspicion and close observation of Shīʿī movements, found no opportunity to stage a rising. Nevertheless his father's followers, who in his father and him saw the Mahdī of the House of Muḥammad, the Promised Deliverer of Islam, continued secretly to be in communication with him. Among them the Kaisāniyya – after the episode of Mukhtār, who had claimed to be about to realize their plans – secretly retained contact with the son of their imām. They believed him still to be alive but in a state of occultation.

In this way the Shīʿī cause found response among both the Arabs and the non-Arabs of Iraq, for the latter were disaffected by the oppression of non-Arabs on the part of the Umayyad governors; and the former by the Umayyads' having transferred the caliphate from Kūfa to Damascus. Since Mukhtār's policy, however, had gradually lost him the support of the Kūfan Arabs because of their dislike of the mawālī, little by little the real supporters of Shīʿism became almost exclusively the mawālī. This meant that in the course of time Shīʿism became to some extent penetrated by the ideas and practices which had belonged to these people's traditions.

The hope for the advent of the *imām*, a secretly nurtured millennial anticipation, and the need for practising kitmān gradually developed Shīʿism into an underground faction or party. This going into concealment of itself became a cause for the emergence of different movements, in conflict with each other, under various Shīʿī leaders; but in this state of affairs Muḥammad b. al-Ḥanafiyya and his son, Abū Hāshim, had the advantage of long experience in the conducting of secret propaganda. They were able to gain the greatest degree of influence and prestige among the Shīʿīs, while Abū Hāshim, after his father's death in about 81/701 (an episode which seems, as clearly indicated, to have been kept hidden from some of his followers), organized the Shīʿī mission on regular lines.

On the death of Abū Hāshim, which occurred in Syria after a meeting with Hishām b. ʿAbd al-Malik, the Umayyad caliph, in 98/716–17, several different groups of Shīʿīs appeared, each claiming that Abū

Hāshim had assigned the task of leadership to their particular imām. For example, the Bayāniyya, followers of Bayān b. Sam'ān Tamīmī, claimed that Abū Hāshim had conferred the imāmate after himself on Bayān. Likewise a group of the followers of 'Abd-Allāh b. Mu'āwiya – the Ḥārithiyya – chose him and designated him the heir of Abū Hāshim.[1] The Rāvandiyya pretended that when he was dying Abū Hāshim had transferred the leadership of the Shī'īs to one of the house of his paternal uncles – Muḥammad b. 'Alī, the grandson of 'Abd-Allāh b. 'Abbās.

This Muḥammad b. 'Alī, whose ancestry went back to 'Abbās, the Prophet's uncle, hence the name "'Abbāsid" for his descendants, continued the secret propaganda with great caution after Abū Hāshim's death. Two years afterwards he sent agents to Kūfa and Khurāsān. At this time, since the affairs of other propagandists had fallen on evil days because of their carelessness, those of the Rāvandiyya, who exercised the utmost caution and secrecy, prospered. It was thus that the secret propaganda, whose aim was the restoration of the usurped caliphate to the Prophet's family, became in its direction and control transferred from the descendants of 'Alī to those of 'Abbās.

Both out of fear of being discovered, in which event it is probable the 'Abbāsid Imām's life would have been endangered, and also because the majority of the Shī'īs still persisted in their loyalty to 'Alī's family, the 'Abbāsid Imām instructed his missionaries not to mention in their propaganda the name of any specific imām. They were to proclaim a general propaganda, referring ambiguously to the one from the Family of the Prophet whose imāmate would be acceptable to all. The basis of the propaganda was the necessity to rise against the Umayyads and absolute secrecy and obedience to the propagandist or cell-organizer with whom the neophyte was in contact. Besides Kūfa, the chief centre for Shī'ī propaganda in Iraq, the 'Abbāsid Imām paid special attention to Khurāsān. This was because in his eyes the people of Kūfa were still in their hearts supporters of the 'Alids; those of Baṣra, of the 'Uthmāniyya; those of the Jazīra, of the Khārijites; and those of Syria, of the Marwānids. The Khurāsānīs on the other hand were recognized by him as people whose minds were as yet free from any ulterior designs and might incline to his propaganda very rapidly. Khurāsān seemed ripe, and was moreover far from the formidable watchfulness of the

[1] Baghdādī, *op. cit.* p. 135; al-Naubakhtī, *Firaq al-shī'a*, ed. H. Ritter (Istanbul, 1931), pp. 30, 69.

Umayyad officials in Iraq. From the outset he sent people to its various centres.

The chief centre of the propaganda was Humaima in Syria, where the ʻAbbāsid Imām or leader himself resided, and which was situated on the pilgrimage route, so that his missionaries could resort to him for instructions, or to give him gifts, in the guise of pilgrims or merchants. In Khurāsān the Umayyad officials watched these comings and goings with the utmost rigour; their suspicious movements made the missionaries repeatedly the object of pursuit in Iraq, Syria and particularly Khurāsān. Nevertheless Khurāsān was for a number of years the scene of the dissemination of this propaganda.

The essence of the propaganda was exploitation of stories of the Umayyad's abandoning Islam, and exciting the people into support for the Prophet's family by raising hope of the advent of the promised Mahdī, who would come to inaugurate justice in a world woefully filled with oppression – Umayyad oppression. It was this very expectation of the advent of the promised Mahdī or Deliverer that caused a group of Arabs and mawālī in Khurāsān to gather about a person of the Banī Tamīm Arabs, named Ḥārith b. Suraij. He had appeared in Tukhāristān claiming the caliphate; he also displayed the Black Standard as a sign of the good tidings of the Mahdī's appearance. Naṣr b. Sayyār was able in the end to defeat him in the vicinity of Marv, and he was put to death, in 128/745.

The persistence of feuds between the Arabs, the Qaḥṭānī and ʻAdnānī, in Khurāsān gave the ʻAbbāsid Imām, who closely observed developments in that region, a particularly valuable opportunity to add to his other adherents by attracting discontented and restless Arab elements. Finally, when he had found a sufficient numbei of good and faithful leaders, he selected from them some special chiefs or *nuqabā*, twelve in number, of whom four were mawālī and the rest Arabs. These nuqabā for an extended period secretly spread the propaganda in Khurāsān, assiduously preaching against the Umayyads in spite of the unremitting policing and suspicion of their governors. Similarly in Iraq Maisara ʻAbdī and his comrades also carried on the work. Not long afterwards Maisara was able to attract the allegiance to the movement of Bukair b. Māhān, who contributed to it all the wealth he had accumulated in trade with India. After Maisara's death in 105/723–4 leadership of the secret propaganda was transferred to Bukair. He despatched a number of agents to Khurāsān, of whom all except one were seized and executed by the governor, Asad b. 'Abd-Allāh (107/725–6). A few years later another group went to Khurāsān with 'Ammār b. Yazīd who later called himself Khidāsh (118/736). Khidāsh to some extent succeeded in spreading the propaganda, but when he was charged in Marv with being of the Khurramiyya sect Asad b. 'Abd-Allāh arrested him and had him put to death under torture. The 'Abbāsid Imām had no alternative but to send Bukair to Khurāsān (120/738), to demonstrate to the Shī'ī leaders his dissatisfaction with Khidāsh and his views.

On his return to Kūfa, Bukair became the object of the governor of Kūfa's suspicion and in 124/741 he was cast into prison. There he became acquainted with 'Īsā b. Ma'qil 'Ijlī and, since he had Shī'ī leanings, was able to gain his adherence; and, more important, at the same time he gained the allegiance of a young maulā named Abū Muslim, apparently of Iranian origin, although he was attached to the 'Ijlī family. Bukair, who was later released, went to Khurāsān once more, in 126/743–4. This time he went to inform the Shī'ī nuqabā of the death of Muḥammad b. 'Alī and administer to them the oath to his son, Ibrāhim b. Muḥammad. After Bukair's death in 127/744, which occurred on his return from this journey, according to his will the continuation of his work was to go to one of the mawālī of Kūfa, Abū Salama, who later in the caliphate of Ṣaffāḥ was known as the vizier of the House of Muḥammad. Besides Bukair and Abū Salama, who were responsible for the direction and dissemination of the 'Abbāsid propaganda in Iraq, many others were also active in Khurāsān. Of this group, Sulaimān b. Kathīr acquired special influence; he became the object of the utmost respect from the Shī'īs of Khurāsān, and the repository of great confidence from the 'Abbāsid Imām.

XI. ABŪ MUSLIM AND THE MEN OF THE BLACK RAIMENT

In the end the 'Abbāsid propaganda in Khurāsān was declared openly by Abū Muslim, who seems to have joined Muḥammad b. 'Alī towards the end of the latter's life, and to have been sent by his successor, the Imām Ibrāhīm, to Khurāsān in 128/745 with fresh instructions and a special commission. The arrival of this young missionary, who lacked either an Arab pedigree or an outstanding past, was not received with enthusiasm by the Shī'ī leaders, Sulaimān b. Kathīr for example, in Khurāsān, and it was only through the Imām's renewed instructions and endorsement of his credentials, when he met the leaders at the season of the Pilgrimage, that Abū Muslim gained the acceptance and recognition he required to carry out his dangerous mission. This was to lay the preliminaries for publishing a propaganda the foundations of which had been prepared for twenty years in secret, and which the conflicts among the Umayyads and the Arabs in Khurāsān gave encouragement to think might now be revealed. Ibrāhīm had instructed Abū Muslim to take advantage of the conflict among the Khurāsānī Arabs, keeping the tribe of Nizārīs as enemies, while so far as possible attracting the Yemenīs and being wary of the Rabī'a. He was also to put to death everyone who aroused his suspicion; and, if it were necessary, nobody who spoke the Arabic tongue need be left alive in Khurāsān. However he was to take, and heed, the counsel of Sulaimān b. Kathīr.

Regarding Abū Muslim, it seems that from the period of his own lifetime he has been somewhat of a mystery; his name and origins have been the occasion of contention among different sects, and from very early times different accounts have described him as an Arab, Turk, Kurd or Persian. Some have associated him with the 'Abbāsids through the dubious line of Salīṭ b. 'Abd-Allāh. Some have gone so far as to make him a descendant of 'Alī, while other legends have made him Iranian as the descendant of Buzurgmihr. His official name, which appears on a coin, was 'Abd al-Raḥmān b. Muslim, though some have averred that this was the name given him by the Imām Ibrāhīm, his original name being something else, Ibrāhīm b. 'Uthmān, while an Iranian name has also been applied to him, Bihzādān the son of Vindād-Hurmuzd.[1] It is most likely that he was one of the mawālī and in all probability an Iranian.

For a time he continued the propaganda in Khurāsān in secret until the imām ordered the publication of it. Abū Muslim made the propaganda public in the house of Sulaimān b. Kathīr, in the village of Safīdhanj near Marv in Ramaḍān 129/May–June 747. Abū Muslim with Sulaimān b. Kathīr and other associates donned black clothes, either as a sign of mourning for those of the Prophet's family who had been slain, or to signify the raising of the Prophet's banner, which was black, against the Umayyads. In the course of one night the residents of sixty neighbouring villages came and joined him, all donning black and referring to their wooden clubs as infidel-fellers, their asses as Marwān, a satirical reference to the title of Marwān – *ḥimār* – the ass.

[1] Ibn al-Athīr, *op. cit.*, vol. IV, p. 295.

Most of them – people described by one western historian as "black devils"[1] – were peasant cultivators, artisans and other classes of the mawālī, whom the Arabs sarcastically called the saddler's whelps, in allusion to Abū Muslim's reputed former occupation as a saddle-maker.

Naṣr b. Sayyār, the Umayyad governor, sent a party to suppress them, but his army was defeated; Abū Muslim's affairs took a turn for the better. Safīdhanj no longer provided sufficient room for his followers and he moved to the larger village of Mākhwān, where he prepared for a new encounter with Naṣr b. Sayyār, while one by one the cities of Khurāsān began to fall to him. The governor, meanwhile, was preoccupied with the difficulties arising from the Arabs' internecine conflicts, those between the Yemenīs and Nizārīs, to which there seemed to be no end. The episode of Ḥārith b. Suraij had just been settled when Naṣr was confronted with the opposition of an Arab named Judai' b. 'Alī al-Kirmānī, a chief of the Banī Azd, whose contentiousness in fact once more represented a renewal of war between the Nizārīs and the Yemenīs. Before Abū Muslim could attract and unite Kirmānī to himself, Naṣr succeeded in killing Kirmānī, but his son, 'Alī b. Judai', joined Abū Muslim. Thus the latter was able to prevent Naṣr b. Sayyār from uniting the Arabs of Khurāsān against him, while the governor, on account of Umayyad difficulties in those provinces, could not hope for help from Syria and Iraq. It can be said that confronted by the combination of Abū Muslim and Kirmānī's son, Naṣr b. Sayyār fell into a trap, so that he lost the seat of his government, Marv, and was forced into flight.

After consolidating his position in the northeast, Abū Muslim sent Qaḥṭaba b. Shabīb Ṭā'ī after Naṣr, who had fled to Nīshāpūr where others of Abū Muslim's opponents had gathered round him. Moreover, his son, Tamīm b. Naṣr, had taken up a position in Ṭūs, where he was ready for battle against Abū Muslim. After a bloody engagement, Qaḥṭaba was able to wrest Ṭūs from him, on his way to Nīshāpūr. Tamīm was slain and the Men in Black gained great booty. When Qaḥṭaba invested Nīshāpūr, Naṣr with his companions escaped to Qūmis.

In Gurgān Qaḥṭaba met an army which the governor of Iraq had sent against Abū Muslim. It was here that, in order to encourage the Iranians, he delivered a khuṭba in terms calculated to demean the Arabs

[1] J. Wellhausen, *Das arabische Reich und sein Sturz* (Berlin, 1902), p. 332.

and exalt the ancient Iranians.[1] After defeating this Arab force, Qaḥṭaba sent his son, Ḥasan b. Qaḥṭaba, in pursuit of Naṣr b. Sayyār at Qūmis. However, Naṣr, who at this time was in charge of all Arabs in Iran, now suffered the same fate as had Yazdgard a century earlier; he could not remain in Qūmis, but went to Ray, where a number of freshly recruited Arabs were to meet him on the instructions of the caliph, Marwān. At Ray Ḥasan b. Qaḥṭaba was again deprived of the chance to engage him, for Naṣr took to flight. He had fallen ill in Ray and he died at Sāva, in Rabī' I 131/October 748 aged eighty-five. His companions fled to Hamadān.

When Qaḥṭaba himself arrived in Ray, he again despatched his son after the fugitives. Ḥasan surrounded them in Nihāvand, while his father administered a severe defeat to Umayyad forces in Iṣfahān. After this, he went to Nihāvand; the city which a century before had marked their "victory of victories" once again became the site of a "victory of victories", but, though also won by an Arab general, its significance for Arabs was of a different sort (131/748). Nihāvand, as if to reproduce in reverse what a hundred years earlier had happened to the Iranians, was followed by Ḥulwān, where the retreating force was defeated by the Khurāsānīs under one of Abū Muslim's generals, Khāzim b. Khuzaima.

The final and most important engagement took place near Mosul in northern Iraq, so that it was not far from Marwān's capital, Ḥarrān, that the Umayyads were ultimately defeated. 'Abd al-Malik b. Yazīd Khurāsānī, nicknamed Abū 'Aun, on the orders of Abū Muslim, had been deputed to this area, and he defeated 'Abd-Allāh, Marwān's son, close to Shahrazūr, in Dhu'l-Ḥijja 131/July 749. A few months later he confronted Marwān himself, on the banks of the Greater Zāb. In the meantime Qaḥṭaba without any opposition had passed Jalūlā and crossed the Euphrates and, having triumphed in an engagement with Ibn Hubaira, disappeared in mysterious circumstances, but his army reached Kūfa under his son, Ḥasan, thus to gain the Shī'ī centre in Iraq.

A few days before this, the Imām Ibrāhīm had become the object of Marwān's profoundest suspicion and been arrested and put to death. Thus it was his brother, Abu'l-'Abbās 'Abd-Allāh, later known as al-Saffāḥ, whom the Khurāsānīs proclaimed caliph in Kūfa, in Rabī' I 132/October 749. So, in spite of the fight unto the death put up by Ibn Hubaira, Iraq witnessed the establishment of a new régime,

[1] Ibn al-Athīr, *op. cit.*, vol. IV, pp. 313–14.

founded with the help of the Iranian mawālī. The new caliph sent his uncle, ʿAbd Allāh b. ʿAlī, to Abū ʿAun's assistance in the Jazīra, so that Marwān's final defeat might be accomplished. It was. Marwān became a fugitive to Egypt where, at Būṣīr, he was murdered in Dhu'l-Ḥijja 132/July 750.

Iraq and Syria were now in the hands of the Khurāsānīs, to be followed by Egypt and Arabia. The Umayyad government had been overthrown by the Iranians and given way to that of the ʿAbbāsids. Nevertheless the new government very soon disappointed its supporters; Arab and mawālī hopes were dashed. For a few years Abū Muslim managed to maintain his power in Khurāsān, but very soon he fell a victim to the suspicion and morbidity of the second ʿAbbāsid caliph, Manṣūr, to be treacherously put to death. Nonetheless the new régime, fruit as it was of a long secret propaganda and intrigue, did not lose its anti-Arab complexion until nearly a century later, while its new capital, Baghdad of the Thousand and One Nights, near the ruins of the ancient Madā'in, perfected an amalgamation of the culture and institutions of Iran with the religion of the Arabs.

CHAPTER 2

THE ʿABBĀSID CALIPHATE IN IRAN

On 3 Rabīʿ I 132/20 October 749 Abu'l-ʿAbbās ʿAbd-Allāh b. Muḥammad b. ʿAlī b. ʿAbd-Allāh b. al-ʿAbbās, after receiving the oath of allegiance as caliph, spoke in the mosque of Kūfa until, weakened by fever, he sat down in the pulpit while his uncle finished the speech for him. The speech served as an inaugural address for this first ʿAbbāsid caliph and clearly outlined both the discontents which had encouraged the revolution against the Umayyads, and the claims of the ʿAbbāsids to restrict the caliphate of the Islamic community to the members of their own family. Even if the authenticity of the speech is difficult to establish, it faithfully reflects the tone of ʿAbbāsid rule during the following two hundred years:

Praise be to God . . . who has given us ties of relation and kinship with the Messenger of God, and has brought us forth from his fathers . . . and has placed us in respect to Islam and its people in an exalted position . . . He has informed them of our excellence and made it obligatory for them to render us our right and to love us . . . The erring Sabā'iyya have claimed that someone other than us has a greater right than we to leadership, administration and the caliphate . . . How so and why so, oh people? It is through us that God has guided men after their erring and enlightened them after their ignorance . . . God tolerated [the Umayyad usurpers] for a while, until they angered Him; and when they angered Him, He avenged Himself on them at our hands and returned our right to us . . . Oh people of Kūfa, you are the object of our love and affection. You have been constant in that love, your mistreatment by the oppressors has not turned you from it until you reached our time and God brought you our turn in power (*daula*), and so you have become the happiest of people through us and the most honoured by us. We have increased your [yearly] stipends by one hundred *dirhams*. Hold yourselves ready, for I am the pitiless bloodshedder (*al-saffāḥ*) and the destroying avenger.

At this point, Abu'l-ʿAbbās, overcome by his fever, sat down. His uncle continued in the same vein, declaring that the ʿAbbāsids had revolted partly because the Umayyads had mistreated "the sons of our uncle" (the ʿAlids), and had taken exclusive possession "of the revenue rights (*fai'*) of the community which are yours and of your charitable taxes (*ṣadaqāt*) and of your plunder (*maghānim*)". He asserted that, in contrast, the ʿAbbāsids would rule according to the Qurʾān and the example of Muḥammad. He said that "God has given us as our party (*shīʿa*) the people of Khurāsān . . . and has caused a caliph to appear amongst you from the descendants of Hāshim and [shown favour to] you through him and given you ascendancy over the Syrians and transferred the government to you . . . So take what God has given you with gratitude; remain obedient to us; and do not mistake your position – for this is your affair . . . Know," he concluded, "that this authority is ours and will not leave us till we hand it over to Jesus son of Mary."[1]

The ʿAbbāsids, therefore, claimed that recognition of their right to the caliphate was obligatory, and that they received their authority by divine mandate and not by the agreement of men. In this speech, while no genealogical proof of the ʿAbbāsids' right is offered, Abuʾl-ʿAbbās is presented as a descendant of Hāshim – an ancestor of the ʿAlids, the Jaʿfarids and the ʿAbbāsids – and as the common avenger of the entire family of Muḥammad. Only the extremist Shīʿī beliefs of the Sabāʾiyya (or Sabaʾiyya), who revered ʿAlī as divine, are specifically rejected. Up to this moment, ʿAbbāsid propaganda had been carried out and the oath of allegiance taken in the name of *al-riḍā min āl Muḥammad*, "the one of Muḥammad's family who would be agreed upon" – a designation which left room for both ʿAbbāsids and ʿAlids. Abuʾl-ʿAbbās made it clear that the Kūfans, who had especially hated Umayyad rule, were to be materially rewarded and restored to the place of honour which they had held when ʿAlī brought the caliphate to their city. Hence, by implication, the non-Syrian provinces, formerly held in check by the Syrian troops which were the military basis of the Umayyad empire, would be free from this domination. However, not all these provinces would contribute equally to the military basis of the new caliphate, for the "party" which supported the new empire by force of arms was the army of Khurāsān. Many Muslims felt that continued Umayyad government would bring the destruction of Islam, and Abuʾl-ʿAbbās promised them that the ʿAbbāsids would answer the growing desire to see a truly Islamic government, conducted according to the Qurʾān and the *sunna*. The financial rights of the Muslims would be restored to the community as a whole after they had been usurped by the Umayyads.

[1] Ṭabarī, vol. III, pp. 29–33. At least two other dates are given for this speech.

When Abu'l-'Abbās accepted the oath of allegiance or *bai'a*, the success of the 'Abbāsids was far from assured. Marwān II was in Syria preparing for a decisive battle, and his chief lieutenant, Ibn Hubaira, was encamped with an Umayyad army at Wāsiṭ. Even the loyalty of the chief partisan of the 'Abbāsids at Kūfa, Abū Salama al-Khallāl, was doubtful because he had forced Abu'l-'Abbās and his relatives to remain in hiding several weeks after the contingents of the Khurāsānian army had arrived in that city; and it was rumoured that he favoured transferring the caliphate to the 'Alids. The military threat from the Umayyads, however, was soon over; the victory of the 'Abbāsids on the Upper Zāb (11 Jumādā II 132/25 January 750) was complete and the army of Ibn Hubaira surrendered after a long resistance had finally been made hopeless by the desertion of the southern Arabs, who had for years disliked Marwān's rule.

This chapter gives an account of all the principal political events in Iran under the 'Abbāsids, and then discusses the long-term significance of these events for the history of that country; but it should never be forgotten that the 'Abbāsids intended to create and for a time nearly succeeded in creating a universal Islamic empire. When Zaidī 'Alid pretenders rebelled in the Yemen and in Māzandarān they posed essentially similar political threats to the 'Abbāsids. Consequently, the actions of the central government, and the reactions of the Iranian Muslims under 'Abbāsid rule, were always more subject to Islamic considerations than to any specific feeling about Iranians as a group.

The success of the 'Abbāsid revolution has often been viewed as a success by Iranians over Arabs; but a very great number of the soldiers and propagandists who won and maintained 'Abbāsid rule were Arabs, and there is little sign that the Iranian supporters of the dynasty in the early period were anti-Arab. In the Umayyad period the 'Abbāsid family had fostered an extensive and complex network of secret adherents, and the victory of the 'Abbāsids probably encouraged many later Islamic revolutionary movements to imitate their example. The first members of this network in southern Iraq were *mawālī* – non-Arab converts to Islam – and southern Arabs, especially the Banū Musliyya; and the 'Abbāsid movement was sustained right through to its victory by the efforts of both Arabs and Iranians. A document of the late 120s/740s shows that at that time the secret organization in Khurāsān was led by twelve *naqībs*, most of whom were Arab. The original 'Abbāsid army was quite naturally in large proportion and perhaps in

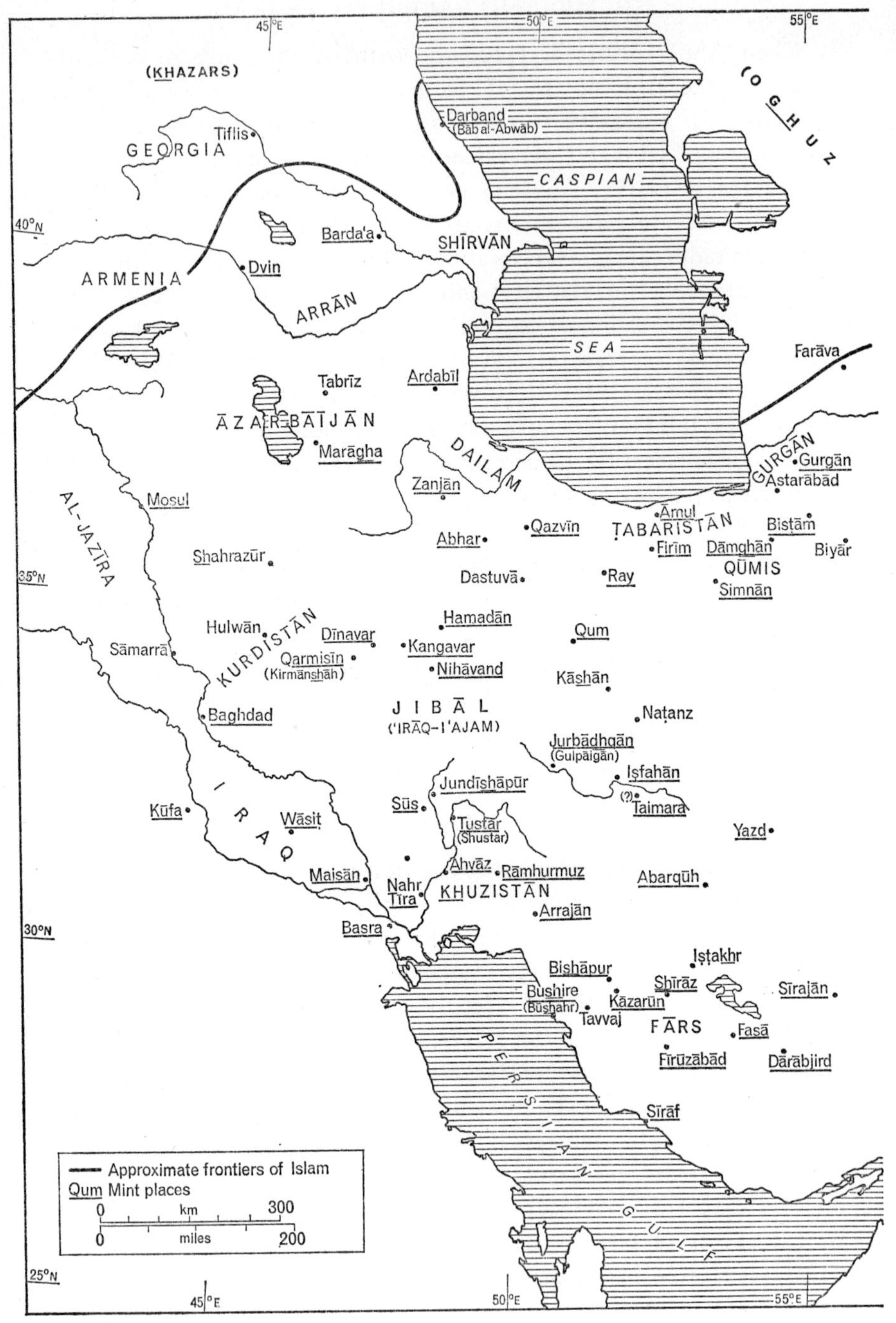

Map. 1. Iran under the 'Abbāsids

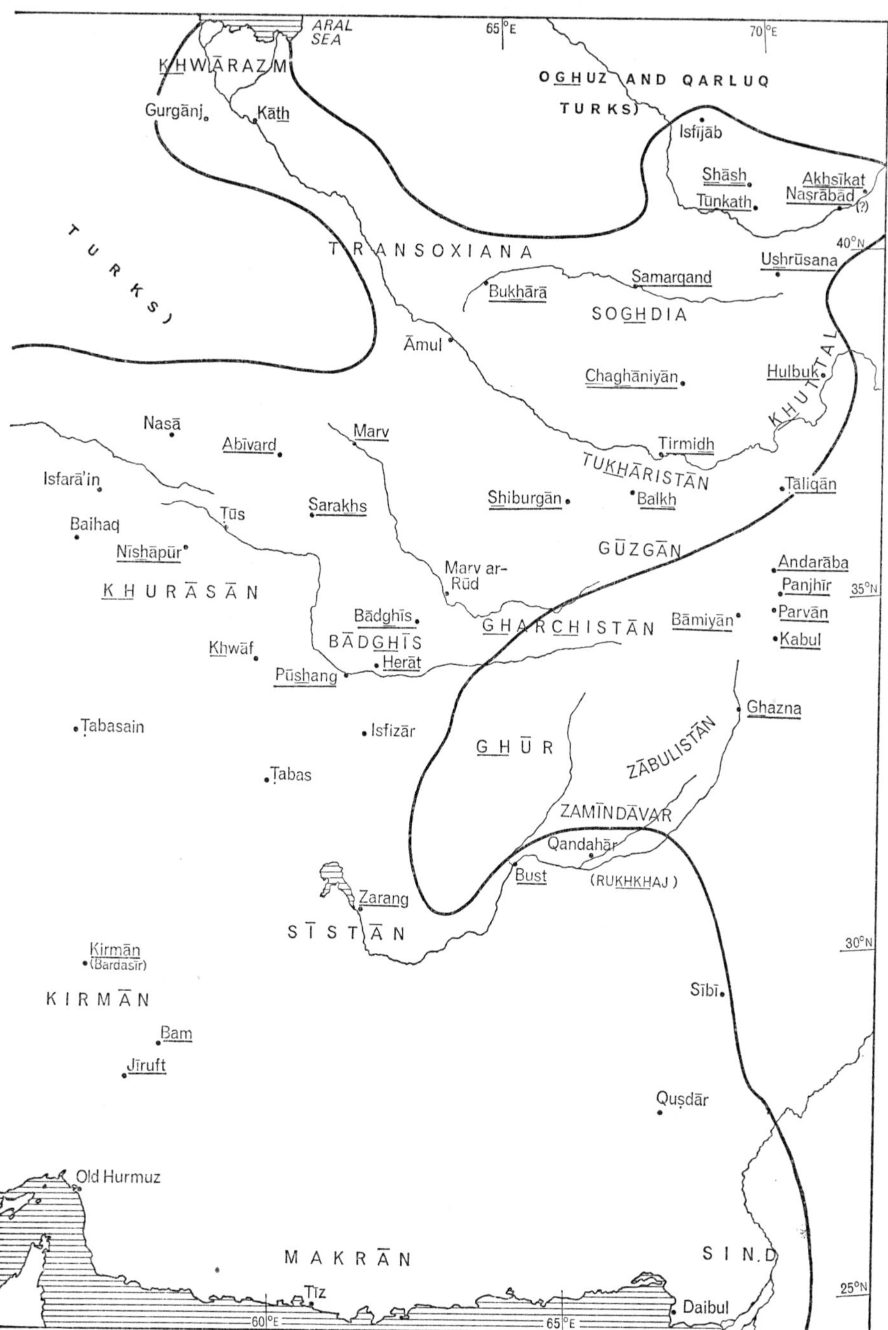
ARAL SEA
65°E
70°E
KHWĀRAZM
Gurgānj
Kāth
OGHUZ AND QARLUQ TURKS
Isfījāb
Shāsh
Akhsīkat
Naṣrābād (?)
Tūnkath
TURKS
TRANSOXIANA
40°N
Ushrūsana
Samarqand
Bukhārā
SOGHDIA
Āmul
Chaghāniyān
Hulbuk
KHUTTAL
Nasā
Abīvard
Marv
Tirmidh
Isfarā'in
TUKHĀRISTĀN
Ṭāliqān
Shiburgān
Balkh
Baihaq
Ṭūs
Sarakhs
Nīshāpūr
GŪZGĀN
Andarāba
Marv ar-Rūd
Panjhīr
35°N
KHURĀSĀN
Parvān
Bādghīs
Bāmiyān
GHARCHISTĀN
Kabul
Khwāf
BĀDGHĪS
Herāt
Pūshang
Ghazna
Ṭabasain
Isfizār
GHŪR
ZĀBULISTĀN
Ṭabas
ZAMĪNDĀVAR
Qandahār
Bust
(RUKHKHAJ)
Zarang
SĪSTĀN
30°N
Kirmān
(Bardasīr)
KIRMĀN
Sībī
Bam
Jīruft
Quṣdār
Old Hurmuz
MAKRĀN
SIND
25°N
Tīz
Daibul
60°E
65°E

majority Arab, for the standing army of the Muslims in Khurāsān was overwhelmingly Arab, and the help of this army was essential to the success of any military effort. Abū Muslim, the Iranian architect of the 'Abbāsid uprising in Khurāsān, recognized the importance of Arab adherents and found among the Arabs as well as among the Iranians many eager to support a complete change of government. A large number of Arab tribesmen in Khurāsān had struck roots in that province and become interested in agriculture and trade, and were unwilling to engage in the continual campaigning which the Umayyad governors had demanded of them. Therefore, they had been dropped from the muster lists, and, to their annoyance, the Umayyad government made them – like the non-Arab population of Khurāsān – pay their land taxes through the largely non-Muslim Iranian large holders called the *dihqāns*. They had lost not only the advantage of being Arabs, but they were even partly governed by non-Arabs; and only a change of dynasty, not merely of governors, seemed likely to improve their lot. When in Ramaḍān 130/May 748 (or, according to other historians, 1 Shawwāl 129/15 June 747) Abū Muslim began recruiting an army openly, he registered soldiers not according to their tribes, as the Umayyads had done, but according to their place of residence. This reform not only diminished the spirit of tribal solidarity which had caused nearly continual war in preceding years but also suited the new situation of the more settled and Iranized Arabs of the Marv region, as well as the situation of the Iranian Muslim population who shared many of their interests. Meanwhile, the fight between the southern Arabs regularly listed on the muster lists and the Umayyad governor Naṣr b. Sayyār, who was also the leader of the northern Arab regulars, was dragging on inconclusively; and Abū Muslim, with great skill, also persuaded many of these southern Arabs to join his army.

If, however, many of the soldiers in the first 'Abbāsid army were of Arab ancestry, the army was seen not as Arab or Iranian but as Khurāsānian. The soldiers of this army spoke *lugha ahl Khurāsān*, the speech of the people of Khurāsān, and do not seem to have greatly cared which of their fellow soldiers were of Arab ancestry, and which of Iranian – for Iranians were unquestionably present in the army. The 'Abbāsid government claimed that it was truly Islamic, and therefore expected the passive obedience of all Muslims; but it reserved a privileged position for the soldiers of this Khurāsānian army who were called "sons of the daula" (*abnā' al-daula*) and whose children inherited this distinction. Even Jāḥiẓ (d. 255/868–9) who wrote when the descendants of this first Khurāsānian army ceased to be important militarily, called the 'Abbāsids "Khurāsānian and non-Arab (*a'jamī*)".[1] Nevertheless, the early 'Abbāsid basis of power was not so much the entire province of Khurāsān, parts of which rebelled repeatedly against the first 'Abbāsid caliphs, as a specific Khurāsānian army stationed in Iraq.

The destruction of the Umayyads did not bring peace to the Islamic empire, and the first two 'Abbāsid caliphs found themselves embarrassingly dependent on Abū Muslim to keep order in their new dominions. The 'Abbāsid revolution had been conducted on behalf of an imām whose name remained hidden until its final stages, and it therefore raised hopes even among non-Muslim peoples, who were affected by the expectation of a universal saviour which had become widespread at the end of the Umayyad period. Forces which had despaired of a change of régimes during the seventy years of Umayyad rule were encouraged by the revolution to come into the open. In the first years of the new caliphate Abū Muslim rendered great services to his 'Abbāsid masters by defeating their external and internal enemies. He received the governorship of Khurāsān, where he had many devoted followers, and of the Jibāl. His lieutenant defeated the Chinese in central Asia in July 751, after which Chinese influence in this area greatly decreased; and a pro-'Alid uprising which started among the Arabs in Bukhārā was suppressed in 133/750–1. In 132 Abū Muslim sent Muḥammad b. al-Ash'ath to govern Fārs and to hunt down the representatives of the philo-'Alid Abū Salama al-Khallāl, who had himself been killed in the same year. The caliph, constrained to get Abū Muslim's approval for Abū Salama's execution even though it took place in Iraq, tried to exert his authority over Fārs by sending his uncle, 'Īsā b. 'Alī, to claim control of that province. But Ibn al-Ash'ath would not let him perform the duties of a governor, and it became increasingly urgent for the caliph to find a way of dealing with Abū Muslim, his over-powerful subject. The caliph, however, was able to control the governorships of Ahvāz and Āzarbāījān. In 135/752–3 Abu'l-'Abbās secretly encouraged two lieutenants of Abū Muslim to revolt in Khurāsān, but they were defeated.

When Abu'l-'Abbās died in the night on 13 Dhu'l-Ḥijja 136/8 or 9 June 754 he was succeeded, as he had arranged, by his brother Abū

[1] *al-Bayān*, vol. III (Cairo, 1947), p. 206, cited in Zarrīnkūb, p. 487.

Ja'far who took the throne title of al-Manṣūr. While the continued life of the new dynasty seemed uncertain in the reign of Abu'l-'Abbās, the long reign of his forceful brother saw the power of the 'Abbāsids consolidated throughout the empire. On his accession al-Manṣūr was faced with the revolt of his uncle who as governor of Syria commanded a large army, and Abū Muslim was sent against him in the hope that one of the two would be eliminated. After his victory (7 Jumādā II 137/26 or 27 November 754) Abū Muslim disregarded al-Manṣūr's order that he stay in the provinces he had occupied, and openly said that "He makes me governor of Syria and Egypt; but Khurāsān belongs to me!" Finally, to prevent Abū Muslim's return, al-Manṣūr gave the governorship of Khurāsān to Abū Dā'ūd whom Abū Muslim had left there as his representative; and Abū Muslim, finding that his way back was blocked, and still hopeful that al-Manṣūr intended no harm, went to the caliph who killed him in Sha'bān 137/February 755.

Abū Muslim's importance as the living link between the emerging central government and the province from which it drew its military manpower and its most fervent adherents was now made apparent by the long series of revolts in Khurāsān which followed his execution. The first of these was the revolt of Sunbādh in 138/755. Sunbādh was not a Muslim and the participation of non-Muslims in most of these revolts indicates how much the non-Arab peoples of Iran and Transoxiana had felt somehow identified with the state under Abū Muslim. Sunbādh was killed seventy days after he revolted but his movement had attracted enormous numbers to its standard, including many farmers from the Jibāl, and helped to form a clandestine religious group called the Bū-Muslimiyya which continued to foster anti-'Abbāsid feeling for many years. In 140/758 dissension which broke out in the 'Abbāsid army in Khurāsān resulted in the death of Abū Dā'ūd, the governor, and the death of the sub-governors of Bukhārā and Kūhistān at the hands of the new governor Abū Ja'far 'Abd al-Jabbār. When the Khurāsānians complained to al-Manṣūr about the harshness of his appointee, the caliph decided that "'Abd al-Jabbār is destroying our party (shī'a)" and sent an army which defeated and killed him.[1]

The revolts of Ustādhsīs and al-Muqanna' like that of Sunbādh had extensive local support. Ustādhsīs, who attracted followers principally from the regions of Herāt, Bādghīs and Sīstān, defeated the garrison

[1] Ṭabarī, vol. III, p. 134.

at Marv ar-Rūd. Finally al-Manṣūr sent a large army which defeated Ustādhsīs in 151/768. The rising of al-Muqannaʿ had a more specifically religious colouring. After starting the rebellion in Khurāsān, he moved to the region of Kish and Nasaf in Transoxiana where supporters of Abū Muslim were numerous and where there had been an earlier and unsuccessful rebellion against the ʿAbbāsids led by Isḥāq the Turk, so called because he had been a *dāʿī* or propagandist sent by Abū Muslim to the Turks. Al-Muqannaʿ was defeated in 162 or 163/778 or 779 after a campaign of two years.

Al-Manṣūr's armies were active in other parts of Iran as well. In 142/759 al-Manṣūr began the conquest of Ṭabaristān which had preserved its independence under its ancient rulers. Armies were also sent to Armenia to decrease the threat of attacks by the Khazars who had raided southward several times, sacking the Caspian port city of Darband (Arabic: *Bāb al-abwāb*) in 145/762. The Khārijites, though defeated by the early ʿAbbāsids in northern Iraq and the Jazīra, continued to be a source of rebellion in Sīstān.

When al-Manṣūr died on 6 Dhu'l-Ḥijja 158/7 October 775, he left the ʿAbbāsid dynasty firmly established and without serious contenders. He had cleverly anticipated and removed many of the traditional sources of disruption to the stability of the state and to smooth transfer of rule from one member of the ʿAbbāsid family to another. As the ʿAbbāsid revolution had used the slogans of the Shīʿa yet rejected their essential goal, some of these contenders were, quite naturally, ʿAlids. Al-Manṣūr purposely provoked a revolt by the most prominent ʿAlid, Muḥammad al-Nafs al-Zakiyya, whose consequent defeat and death in the Ḥijāz on 25 Ramaḍān 145/6 December 762 for a time discouraged the ʿAlids from openly opposing the ʿAbbāsids. Al-Manṣūr had also discouraged the pretensions of the southern Iraqis to control the caliphate by moving his capital from the neighbourhood of Kūfa to a new city, Baghdad, especially constructed so that he would be surrounded by his army which, however, would not be concentrated in one spot but garrisoned on several sides of the city. Baghdad was also near the most convenient pass leading from Iraq to the Iranian plateau and Khurāsān, and the city gate facing this route was appropriately called "Bāb al-Daula". Al-Manṣūr's handling of his own family showed the same firmness as the rest of his administration. Like Abu'l-ʿAbbās he appointed many of his governors from his own family, the only group virtually certain not to feel that the ʿAbbāsid revolution had betrayed them. But he controlled his family as carefully as he controlled the other servants of the state, and in 147/764, after intimidating his relatives by killing his uncle, 'Abd-Allāh b. 'Alī, he changed the line of succession established by Abu'l-'Abbās to make his son al-Mahdī heir apparent.

Under al-Mahdī there was a change in caliphal policy towards religion and administration, a change which al-Manṣūr seems to have intended. This change reflected an inevitable shift from the fervour of a revolution, in which extravagant and ultimately unfulfillable hopes are raised, to a post-revolutionary situation in which an astute government seeks a moderate fulfilment of some of these hopes in order to survive. Al-Mahdī's throne title evoked the atmosphere of the 'Abbāsid revolution at which time the "divinely guided one" or *mahdī* was expected by many Muslims and even by some non-Muslims. Al-Manṣūr seems to have chosen this throne title in an effort to derive whatever support he could for his heir from the devotion to the dynasty formerly shown by the Hā<u>sh</u>imiyya, the network of 'Abbāsid partisans who had plotted against the Umayyads. *Ḥadī<u>th</u>s* in later sources, while contrived to fit the actual course of events, probably reflect the eschatological framework in which the earliest 'Abbāsids had sought support for their rule; one ḥadī<u>th</u> quotes Muḥammad as saying "By God, were no more than one day left to the world, God would cause the downfall of the Umayyads so that al-Saffāḥ (the bloodshedder), al-Manṣūr (he who is rendered victorious) and al-Mahdī would come."[1] (While Abu'l-'Abbās called himself al-Saffāḥ in his inaugural speech, until al-Mas'ūdī who wrote in the early 4th/10th century this title was used by Arabic authors for his uncle 'Abd-Allāh b. 'Alī who killed so many Umayyads.)

Yet by the end of al-Manṣūr's reign the original ideas of the Hā<u>sh</u>imiyya were no longer an important prop to 'Abbāsid rule; and extreme forms of these ideas were a positive embarrassment to the ruling dynasty. When a few hundred members of the Rāvandiyya came from <u>Kh</u>urāsān to worship al-Manṣūr as the living God, he was forced to attack and disperse them. The execution of Abū Muslim, the consequent rebelliousness of <u>Kh</u>urāsān and the continued affection of the Kūfans for the 'Alids had dampened the enthusiasm of the Hā<u>sh</u>imiyya itself. Under al-Mahdī the 'Abbāsids no longer emphasized that – as in

[1] 'Abd al-Raḥmān al-Irbilī, *<u>Kh</u>ulāṣat al-<u>dh</u>ahab al-masbūk* (a *mu<u>kh</u>taṣar* of Ibn al-Jauzī's *Siyar al-mulūk*) (Beirut?, 1885), p. 39.

fact had been the case – their ancestor Muḥammad b. 'Alī had received by testament both the imāmate and the secret organization of the 'Alid Abū Hāshim 'Abd-Allāh, who gave his name to the Hāshimiyya. Instead, "Hāshimiyya" was understood to refer to the supporters of Banū Hāshim, the clan of the Quraish which included Muḥammad and the head of which, after the death of 'Abd al-Muṭṭalib, was, in fact, their ancestor al-'Abbās. On this basis the 'Abbāsids claimed that the imāmate had belonged in their family without interruption from the time of Muḥammad's death. A specific genealogical argument was advanced to support their claim and to disprove the claim of certain descendants of 'Alī. Descent through their ancestor al-'Abbās, they said, was more important than descent through the female line of al-Fāṭima, the eldest daughter of Muḥammad and the wife of 'Alī, or than descent from 'Alī's father, Abū Ṭālib, an uncle of Muḥammad who never openly professed Islam; for al-'Abbās was a paternal uncle of Muḥammad and had become a Muslim. This position allowed the 'Abbāsids to seek the approval of the Sunnīs and those Shī'īs who felt that the 'Alid claim had died with some previous imām. Al-Mahdī furthered this policy of reconciliation by releasing political prisoners, choosing a Shī'ī vizier, and distributing gifts and pensions from the very full treasury left by al-Manṣūr; and if al-Mahdī persecuted Manichaeans, by doing so he probably increased his popularity with the majority of his subjects.

Under al-Mahdī there were some signs of the future weakness of the 'Abbāsids. Like al-Manṣūr, al-Mahdī wanted to change the line of succession established by his predecessor. He encouraged the 'Abbāsid party in Khurāsān to demand that his sons Mūsā and Hārūn be made first and second in line of succession respectively; and to placate the former heir apparent, 'Īsā b. Mūsā, and his son, he distributed enormous sums of money and estates to both of them. He was the first caliph to have the bai'a or oath of allegiance taken to more than one son, a practice which eventually increased the number of pretenders to the caliphate. Al-Mahdī also anticipated the practices of future 'Abbāsid caliphs by his retreat into an exalted isolation which made him increasingly dependent for any suggestions of policy on his chamberlain al-Rabī' b. Yūnus, his wife al-Khaizurān and other immediate associates.

At the accession of Mūsā al-Hādī (22 Muḥarram 169/4 August 785) the army mutinied and demanded additional pay as a gift; they burnt the gate of al-Rabī' b. Yūnus and only returned to obedience after receiving two years pay. This mutiny may have been the result not only of al-Mahdī's clemency and generosity but also of his neglect to keep the army dispersed in detachments which would therefore find it difficult to make common cause with each other. This first entry of the central army into politics without the leadership of a pretender to the caliphate established a precedent which continued to trouble the ʻAbbāsids until their loss of power. Al-Hādī's short reign did not allow him to develop any major policies except a reaction against the attempt to reconcile the ʻAlids, whose support in any case, does not seem to have been won by al-Mahdī; and towards the end of his reign even al-Mahdī seems to have become more hostile to the Shīʻīs, at least to the Zaidīs. Al-Hādī's harsh treatment of the ʻAlids provoked the rebellion, during the pilgrimage of 169/786, of al-Ḥusain b. ʻAlī, a descendant of al-Ḥasan b. ʻAlī, who was easily defeated at Fakhkh in the Ḥijāz. Al-Ḥusain's head was sent to Khurāsān to intimidate the Shīʻīs there who had disliked the anti-ʻAlid policy of the governor in the last years of al-Mahdī's caliphate. The battle at Fakhkh, though of small military importance, seems to have taught the ʻAlids the lesson of the ʻAbbāsid revolution: that efforts to establish a new caliphate should seek support in border provinces which were less accessible to the principal army of the caliphate and in which standing armies accustomed to continual warfare might feel very little loyalty to a remote caliph. From the battlefield at Fakhkh the founder of the Idrīsid dynasty fled to Morocco and Yaḥyā b. ʻAbd-Allāh fled to Dailam where he was the first of many ʻAlids to receive the support of the warlike people of the southern Caspian coast.

Al-Hādī determined to make his son Jaʻfar the heir apparent, but his brother Hārūn, supported according to some accounts by Yaḥyā the Barmakid, refused to withdraw from the succession. Al-Hādī may have been killed by his mother al-Khaizurān, who resented her exclusion from politics and wanted her favourite son Hārūn to remain the first heir. When, therefore, Hārūn al-Rashīd succeeded to the caliphate on 15 Rabīʻ I 170/4 September 786, he felt deeply indebted to his mother and to her allies the Barmakids.

This remarkable Khurāsānian family was descended from the hereditary high priest of a Buddhist temple near Balkh. They had a long history of successful service to the ʻAbbāsids in the course of which they developed a network of contacts and introduced important innovations into ʻAbbāsid administrative practice. Khālid b. Barmak was an adherent of the ʻAbbāsid cause at the end of the Umayyad period, and an important officer in the first 'Abbāsid army. According to al-Jahshiyārī, at Abū Muslim's direction Khālid arranged the land tax (*kharāj*) in Khurāsān at the time of the 'Abbāsid revolution, and he did so with a spirit of fairness which made the Khurāsānians deeply grateful to him.[1] Abu'l-'Abbās put him in charge of the two important ministries of the army (*jund*) and land tax at which time he is supposed to have introduced the system of keeping records in *daftars* or codices instead of separate sheets.[2] Under al-Manṣūr he was demoted to the governorship of Fārs, which he held for two years, and subsequently he became governor of Ray, Ṭabaristān and Damāvand. Under al-Mahdī he was again governor of Fārs where he redistributed the kharāj and dropped a widely disliked and burdensome tax on orchards.

The first five 'Abbāsids continued the centralization and elaboration of administration which had begun under the Umayyads. Al-Manṣūr separated judgeships from governorships, making their personnel and functions discrete, and is said to have been the first caliph personally to appoint judges in the important cities. To obtain better intelligence he required the *barīd* or postal service to report on provincial administration and prices more frequently and in greater detail than any earlier caliph; and even his son and heir al-Mahdī, when he was governor of western Iran, was under its surveillance. To control the increasing number of dīvāns or ministries in the central government, al-Mahdī in 162 created a separate *zimām*, literally, "a halter", to audit each existing dīvān; and in 168/784 he created the *dīwān zimām al-azimma*, a ministry to supervise these auditing bodies. While the central administration continued to be refined by the Barmakids under al-Rashīd, this caliph nevertheless in some respects halted the trend to centralization by allowing provincial governors more freedom than they had hitherto enjoyed. Under al-Rashīd the Aghlabids were permitted to hold a governorship in North Africa hereditarily as a *muqāta'a*, an arrangement which gave the governor financial and military control of his province in exchange for a fixed yearly tribute and acknowledgement of the caliph's position in the Friday prayer and on the coins issued in such a province. This arrangement was to be frequently imitated in Iran. The caliph, however, continued to take a direct hand in the choice of governors in the key provinces, often with unfortunate results. Al-Rashīd disregarded the protests of the Khurāsānians against the unauthorized increase in taxes under the governors 'Abd al-Jabbār b. 'Abd al-Raḥmān and

[1] Jahshiyārī, p. 87. [2] *Ibid.*, p. 89.

al-Musayyib b. Zuhair. When, however, al-Faḍl b. Sulaimān al-Ṭūsī and the Barmakid al-Faḍl b. Yaḥyā, in an attempt to still this discontent, forwarded less money to al-Rashīd during their brief governorships because they burnt the books of arrears and invested taxes in local public works, they were dismissed.

With al-Rashīd's accession, Yaḥyā b. Khālid became vizier, a title which originally had as much religious as administrative meaning. *Wazīr* in the Qur'ān designated the position which Aaron held as the helper of Moses, and it was in the spirit of the Qur'anic verse that the head of the 'Abbāsid *da'wa* in al-Kūfa, Abū Salama, even before the bai'a to Abu'l-'Abbās, was called *wazīr āl Muḥammad*, or vizier of the family of Muḥammad. Before al-Rashīd, the vizier had never been more than the first secretary in the administration; and it was not because Yaḥyā was appointed vizier but rather because both he and his sons and uncles were favoured with appointments to so many specific tasks in the government that their influence under al-Rashīd became great. In 176/792 al-Rashīd made al-Faḍl b. Yaḥyā governor of the Jibāl, Ṭabaristān, Damāvand and Armenia, and in 178/794 he was made governor of Khurāsān where his administration was praised for its excellence. He was succeeded in this position in 180/796 by his brother Ja'far b. Yaḥyā who also supervised the barīd, or post-intelligence system, and the mints – this last an amazing privilege since the mints had always been under the supervision of the caliph alone.

One night in Ṣafar 187/January 803, Ja'far b. Yaḥyā was killed and the other principal Barmakids arrested. The sudden and dramatic fall of the Barmakids, usually represented as a puzzling and totally unexpected event, is associated by some sources with earlier events in Iran. According to al-Ṭabarī, 'Alī b. 'Īsā b. Māhān, the repressive governor of Khurāsān who replaced Ja'far, made al-Rashīd suspicious of the love which the Khurāsānians felt for the Barmakid family; and consequently al-Rashīd imprisoned Mūsā b. Yaḥyā in 186/802, then released him.[1] The affection of the Khurāsānians was certainly not the only reason that the Barmakids had been disgraced, and the arrest of Mūsā b. Yaḥyā was not the only previous sign that al-Rashīd was concerned by their increasing domination of the government. Whatever the causes of their fall, its result was to make clear that even the most powerful bureaucrat was only the servant of the caliph, and no vizier would be allowed full control of the government. V. V. Barthold

[1] Ṭabarī, vol. III, p. 675.

believed that the rôle of the Barmakids in the central government symbolized the co-operation of the Iranian "squirearchy" or class of dihqāns with the ruling family, and that the downfall of the Barmakids signalled the end of such co-operation.[1] The evidence for this very plausible theory is, however, ambiguous. The Barmakids probably favoured some Zoroastrian officials like the Banū Sahl and opposed anti-Iranian officials like Muḥammad b. Laith in their own self-interest and not because they were consciously advancing Iranian interests to the detriment of Arab interests. The two parties at court, the Barmakid party which included al-Khaizurān who died only a year before the Barmakids were disgraced, and their enemies led by al-Rashīd's wife Zubaida, cannot easily be identified as the pro-Iranian and pro-Arab parties since Zubaida's party included Iranians like 'Alī b. 'Īsā b. Māhān. The Barmakids may nonetheless have represented a specifically Khurāsānian interest at court and al-Rashīd's disregard of their support for the protests of the Khurāsānians against the extremely bad administration of 'Alī b. 'Īsā b. Māhān may have been part of an effort to decrease the dependence of the 'Abbāsids on Khurāsān.

Al-Rashīd had started towards Khurāsān in 189/804 because of a rumour that 'Alī intended to revolt; but the governor met al-Rashīd at Ray and, by his lavish gifts, persuaded the caliph not to interfere in his province. The rebellion of Khurāsānians in 191/807 finally brought home to al-Rashīd how far the misgovernment of 'Alī (and, possibly, the downfall of the Barmakids as well) had estranged the people of that province from the 'Abbāsids. The rebellion of 191 was not anti-Arab; for its leader, Rāfi' b. al-Laith, was a descendant of Naṣr b. Sayyār, the last Umayyad governor of Khurāsān. The cause of the rebels was popular not only in Khurāsān, but also in Transoxiana where the kings of al-Shāsh and the Turks supported it. Al-Rashīd made Harthama b. A'yan governor and had 'Alī b. 'Īsā arrested. In 192/808 the caliph, now thoroughly alarmed at the continuing disorder in all the eastern provinces, started travelling eastward during his final illness. Al-Rashīd's progress through western and central Iran was probably an occasion of administrative reform in that area for we know that he reformed the system of taxes in Qazvīn in 189/805 and took some districts away from Hamadān and Abhar-rūd in order to make Qazvīn a separate *kūra* or province, just as he had made Qum a separate kūra.[2]

[1] Article "Barmakids", *E.I.*[1].

[2] Ḥamd Allāh Mustaufī, *Tārīkh-i guzīda*, ed. 'A. Navā'ī (Tehrān, 1339/1961), pp. 777 and 789.

Al-Rashīd died in Ṭūs on 13 Jumādā II 193/24 March 809 leaving the caliphate and most of its western provinces to his younger son al-Amīn while he left the heir apparency and all the provinces from the western borders of Hamadān eastward to his older son al-Ma'mūn, and he made a third son, al-Mu'tamin, third in line of succession as well as governor of the Jazīra and the cities bordering the Byzantine empire. By dividing the empire in this manner al-Rashīd had unintentionally made sure that his dangerous policy of alienating the Khurāsānians from the government in Baghdad would be fully realized. The Khurāsānians accepted al-Ma'mūn as one of their own and, because his mother was an Iranian, called him "son of our sister". The rebellion of Rāfi', which had begun because the distant government in Baghdad would not respond to protests against misrule in Khurāsān, had now lost its point and in 195/810 he surrendered himself to al-Ma'mūn who pardoned him. The poets at al-Amīn's court soon began to represent al-Ma'mūn and his vizier al-Faḍl b. Sahl, a Zoroastrian until 190/806, as opponents of Arabs and, by extension, of Islam itself. One poet said of al-Ma'mūn, "A power continuing that of Chosroes and his religion has gathered and the Muslims are humbled."

In 194/810 al-Amīn removed his brother al-Mu'tamin from the governorship of his provinces and ordered that in the *khuṭba*, or Friday sermon, prayers be said for his son Mūsā as well as for his brothers; on hearing this, al-Ma'mūn stopped the post from Khurāsān to Baghdad. Finally, al-Amīn asked for direct control of al-Ma'mūn's provinces; and when al-Ma'mūn refused, al-Amīn announced in 195/811 that his son was heir apparent to the caliphate, and ordered 'Alī b. 'Īsā b. Māhān to march on Khurāsān. In the face of his brother's hostility, al-Ma'mūn had courted the religious classes in Khurāsān and decreased the kharāj or land tax of that province by one quarter. His inaugural speech, delivered before the Khurāsānians, was surprisingly unautocratic and conciliatory for an 'Abbāsid: "Oh people, I have taken it upon myself before God that, if he gives me charge of your affairs, I will obey him in dealing with you. I will not purposely shed blood except in lawful punishments and obligations imposed by God, nor will I take anyone's wealth . . . if the law forbids me."[1]

Al-Amīn tried to gain the affection of the Khurāsānians by matching his brother's gesture and decreasing the kharāj of Khurāsān by one quarter. But al-Amīn who commanded the central armies of the

[1] Ya'qūbī, p. 167.

caliphate, including the army which had been with al-Rashīd at Ṭūs, foolishly sent the hated 'Alī b. 'Īsā b. Māhān against al-Ma'mūn's brilliant Khurāsānian general, Ṭāhir, who defeated both 'Alī and another army led by 'Abd al-Raḥmān b. Jabala. The third army sent by al-Amīn returned without fighting Ṭāhir, and finally the abnā' al-daula revolted in Baghdad itself and gave the bai'a to al-Ma'mūn, so that Ṭāhir was able to take the city without much difficulty.

This second Khurāsānian conquest of Iraq was accomplished by an army much more clearly Iranian than the army of Abū Muslim. When al-Ma'mūn decided to remain in the East and made al-Ḥasan, a brother of al-Faḍl b. Sahl, governor of Baghdad, the Iraqis felt even more keenly that they were occupied by an alien army. After the Arab general Harthama b. A'yan defeated Shī'ī rebellions in southern Iraq and the Ḥijāz, he travelled to Khurāsān to inform the caliph how deeply al-Ḥasan's rule was disliked in the central provinces; but al-Faḍl persuaded the caliph to imprison Harthama immediately on his arrival. In 201/815 when news of this event came to Baghdad, the troops descended from the old Khurāsānian army, who were now as much or more Iraqi than Khurāsānian, joined the populace and drove al-Ḥasan out of the city, though eventually a peace was arranged and al-Ḥasan returned to Baghdad.

In 201/816 al-Ma'mūn proclaimed 'Alī b. Mūsā heir to the caliphate. 'Alī was the descendant of al-Ḥusain b. 'Alī whom the twelver Shī'īs regarded as the imām; and al-Ma'mūn, who was a philo-'Alid, chose him at least in part out of personal conviction. But when al-Ma'mūn chose for him a throne title which evoked the intellectual climate of the 'Abbāsid revolution, al-riḍā min āl Muḥammad, he seems to have hoped that Muslims would rally to a member of the Banū Hāshim who had no rôle in the quarrel between Iraq and Khurāsān (and within the 'Abbāsid family) which had so deeply divided the empire. Quite the opposite happened – the proclamation revived the quarrel, and the 'Abbāsid princes gladly supported the people and army of Baghdad in their new revolt. Even the Shī'ī Kūfans who presumably favoured the nomination of 'Alī al-Riḍā, put their regional loyalties above their traditional sympathy for the 'Alids, and consequently would not support the hated al-Ḥasan b. Sahl who represented the continued predominance of Khurāsān over Iraq. Al-Faḍl b. Sahl hid the seriousness of the rebellion from al-Ma'mūn until 'Alī al-Riḍā convinced the caliph in 202/817 to start for Iraq. Al-Faḍl b. Sahl and 'Alī al-Riḍā conveniently died on the way; and the rebellion of the Iraqis collapsed on his arrival.

Ṭāhir had been fighting a rebel Arab chieftain in northern Syria, though without enthusiasm because of his dispute with al-Ḥasan b. Sahl, who had refused to supply or support him properly. Ṭāhir was now made governor of "all the West" (*maghrib*), and in 204/820 head of police in Baghdad; but he feared that al-Ma'mūn would hold him responsible for al-Amīn's death, and longed to return to Khurāsān. In 205/821 he was made governor of the Jibāl and of Khurāsān, where he replaced Ghassān b. 'Abbād, a cousin of al-Faḍl b. Sahl. Al-Ma'mūn, whose troops had threatened to mutiny after al-Faḍl b. Sahl was arrested, may have appointed Ṭāhir to keep the affection of his Khurāsānian troops when he removed the remaining members of the Banū Sahl from the government. His son, 'Abd-Allāh b. Ṭāhir, was now given his father's former command, and was later made governor of the Jazīra and Egypt which he reduced to order with his Khurāsānian troops.

Al-Ma'mūn understood that the 'Abbāsids needed a new and wide basis of support to avoid excessive dependence on the increasingly independent Khurāsānians, and to win back the loyalty of the central provinces of the empire. For this reason, and from personal conviction, he attempted to enforce Mu'tazilism as the official form of Islam. He had already tried without success to use the philo-'Alid sentiments among some of the remnants of the original 'Abbāsid party and among his Shī'ī subjects. He therefore turned to the Mu'tazilites, who may have been associates of the earliest 'Abbāsid propaganda and who made the superiority of Abū Bakr over 'Alī a point of basic doctrine. Judges and witness-notaries (*shuhūd*) were required to testify to the central doctrine of the Mu'tazilites, the createdness of the Qur'ān. Ultimately, al-Ma'mūn's campaigns against the Byzantines won him far more respect among the religiously minded than his much resented interference in theology, just as the popular reputation of al-Mahdī and al-Rashīd for piety had been largely based on their pilgrimages and personal campaigns against the Eastern Romans.

In 218/833 al-Ma'mūn started the last significant effort by an 'Abbāsid to conquer the Byzantine empire in its entirety. During this campaign, on 18 Rajab 218/9 August 833, al-Ma'mūn died and was succeeded by his brother al-Mu'taṣim. With al-Ma'mūn's death, the personal tie of the 'Abbāsids with the Khurāsānians was broken and the end of this special relationship brought a fundamental and lasting change in the character of the 'Abbāsid state. Al-Mu'taṣim, whose mother was Turkish, made Turkish slaves bought as boys and raised as professional soldiers the core of the caliphal army. Most of the Turks were from Farghāna and Ushrūsana; and two thousand Turks were sent to the caliph each year as tribute by 'Abd-Allāh b. Ṭāhir. Other elements still existed in the army, including the *maghāriba* (nomadic Arabs from Egypt), Khazars, the old Khurāsānian detachments, and detachments from other parts of Iran.[1] The Turks, however, dominated the army of the central government from this time until the appearance of the Dailamites.

Under al-Ma'mūn appeared the most serious movement of local opposition in Western Iran since the 'Abbāsid Revolution. The rebellion of Bābak, a Mazdakite, which had begun at Badhdh between Arrān and Āzarbāījān in 200 or 201/816, continued an older tradition of Mazdakite or "Khurramī" resistance to 'Abbāsid government in that part of Iran. Bābak received encouragement from Ḥātim b. Harthama b. A'yan, the governor of Āzarbāījān, who revolted when he heard that al-Ma'mūn had imprisoned and killed his father. By 218/833, after defeating four caliphal armies, Bābak controlled most of Āzarbāījān and some of the Jibāl where his followers, who were especially numerous at Masābadān and Mihrajānqadaq, now gathered in a military encampment in Hamadān province. The Bābakīs in the Jibāl were mostly farmers and no match for the troops of Isḥāq b. Ibrāhīm, the governor of the Jibāl; after their defeat, many of them fled to the Byzantines. To defeat Bābak himself in the mountains of Āzarbāījān was more difficult, however, and al-Mu'taṣim chose for this task the Afshīn, the Iranian king of Ushrūsana, who had been converted by al-Ma'mūn and entered the caliph's service with an army of his countrymen. The mountains made supply extremely difficult; therefore, after an unsuccessful campaign, a series of fortresses were constructed from Zanjān to Ardabīl and Bābak was finally besieged in Badhdh which was taken on 20 Ramaḍān 222/26 August 837.

The movement of Bābak left followers in most parts of Iran, and several Iranian nobles were his adherents; but the violent rebellion of Māzyār, a king of Ṭabaristān who had become a Muslim at the hands of al-Ma'mūn, would have taken place even without Bābak's encouragement. Māzyār was governor of Ṭabaristān, Rūyān and Damāvand and, according to some sources, was encouraged by al-Mu'taṣim to take the

[1] Mas'ūdī, vol. VII, p. 118.

governorship of Khurāsān from the Ṭāhirids whom that caliph feared. In any case, in 224/839 Māzyār refused to pay kharāj to the Ṭāhirids. His revolt soon developed into a social revolution; for when he found that the Islamicized land-owners of the Caspian were hostile to him, he came more and more to rely on the peasants and to voice their discontents. He ordered the peasants to attack their *katkhudās* (village headman and usually the largest holder in the village) and to plunder their goods. The caliph, if he had seen any advantage in encouraging Māzyār, now recognized the danger of this rebellion to Islam, and consequently co-operated with ʿAbd-Allāh b. Ṭāhir in putting down the revolt. Māzyār was defeated and killed in the same year. The rebel Mankjūr al-Farghānī, son of the Afshīn's maternal uncle and the Afshīn's representative as governor of Āzarbāījān, was accused of Bābakī sympathies as Māzyār had been. Al-Muʿtaṣim had the same accusation brought against the Afshīn in 226/841 in which year he was tried and killed; but the real reason for his execution was probably al-Muʿtaṣim's desire to rid his army of these powerful Iranian noblemen whose troops were usually more loyal to their commanders than to the caliph, and who, though they had been especially useful in fighting Bābak, were now not urgently needed. Māzyār and Mankjūr may, in fact, have rebelled because they correctly gauged their future under al-Muʿtaṣim's philo-Turkish government.

When al-Muʿtaṣim died on 18 Rabīʿ I 227/5 January 842, he left his heir a prisoner of the Turkish soldiers. Al-Muʿtaṣim had moved the capital to Sāmarrā in 221/836 partly to avoid the frequent street fights between the Baghdādīs and the Turks, but even more to separate the Turks from outside influences so that they should maintain the manner of life which was thought to make them excellent soldiers; they were, in fact, forbidden to marry non-Turkish wives. The new caliph, al-Wāthiq, gave the Turks an excellent pretext for dominating the affairs of the caliphate by not appointing a successor, and it was the Turks who chose al-Mutawakkil to succeed on 23 Dhu'l-Ḥijja 232/11 August 847.

The principal events of al-Mutawakkil's reign were related to his attempts to free himself from his dependency on the Turks. He sought popular support by reversing the pro-Muʿtazilite policy which had pleased only a minority and had led to public protest under al-Wāthiq. His standing as a champion of the Sunnī majority was increased by his oppressive policy to non-Muslims and to the Shīʿīs who were particularly horrified when he ordered the tomb of al-Ḥusain to be destroyed. Al-Mutawakkil seems to have tried to gain more control over the administration by giving the governorship of the empire to his sons on the understanding that they would inherit portions of the government just as al-Amīn and al-Ma'mūn had. According to this arrangement, Ahvāz and the Jibāl were included in the share of the first heir, al-Muntaṣir, while Khurāsān, Āzarbāījān and Fārs went to al-Muʿtazz, the second heir. As al-Muntaṣir, the elder, was only thirteen at the time, a secretary was assigned to administer his provinces. It is likely that al-Mutawakkil tried in this way to avoid assigning provinces to his Turkish generals and to assert more direct control over these areas, since the secretaries were really answerable to the caliph, not to his sons. Five years later, the treasuries and mints in all regions were assigned to his sons. Nothing, however, released him from the control of the Turks. In 242 he contemplated moving the capital to Damascus where non-Arab influence was negligible and the population strongly anti-Shīʿī, but the Turks forced him to return to Sāmarrā. He tried to sow dissension among the Turkish leaders by taking the estates of one general, Waṣīf, and giving them to another, al-Fatḥ b. Khāqān; but Waṣīf and a third general, Bughā, turned this dissension against the caliph and killed him along with al-Fatḥ on the night of 4 Shawwāl 247/11 December 861. With this event whatever awe or respect had surrounded the caliph's person in the eyes of his Turkish troops disappeared. The alarming frequency with which the Turkish generals now changed caliphs made the next decade a period of confusion in which the degradation of the ʿAbbāsid caliphate seemed irreversible.

Al-Muntaṣir, the successor of al-Mutawakkil, had participated in the plot because his father intended to replace him in the succession by his brother al-Muʿtazz. Al-Muntaṣir died either of illness or poison on 3 Rabīʿ II 248/6 June 862, and the Turks made al-Mustaʿīn, a grandson of al-Mutawakkil, caliph. The old Khurāsānian guard disliked this choice and fought the Turks for three days but were defeated. The Turkish generals fought with each other to control the caliph until the caliph moved to Baghdad with Waṣīf and Bughā. The Sāmarrā troops then chose al-Muʿtazz as caliph on 4 Muḥarram 252/25 January 866. Muḥammad b. ʿAbd-Allāh, who held the office of chief of police in Baghdad as many Ṭāhirids had done before him, armed some of the populace and some passing Khurāsānian pilgrims to defend the city, but soon realized that a defence was hopeless; he surrendered to the

Sāmarran troops. Al-Mu'tazz tried to favour the *maghāriba* and *farāghina* as counterweights to the Turks, but delays in pay finally brought the army together against him and he was killed with Waṣīf and Bughā on 27 Rajab 255/11 July 869. The troops made Muḥammad b. al-Wāthiq caliph with the title al-Muhtadī, but Mūsā b. Bughā who was fighting in Khurāsān would not recognize him; and when the Turks in Sāmarrā saw that Muḥammad intended to favour the farāghina and maghāriba to lessen their power, they deposed him on 18 Rajab 256/21 June 870 and killed him four days later.

After Mūsā b. Bughā chose al-Mu'tamid, he agreed to a policy of co-operation with the caliphate which ended the confusion of the Sāmarrā period. The 'Abbāsids had partly won their struggle with the Turks; for the caliph was still powerful enough to encourage factionalism within the army and, increasingly, between the new generation of Turks and the older Turks, so that the resulting anarchy kept the troops irregularly paid and caused the deaths of almost all the leading Turkish generals except Mūsā. The Turks, even if they did not respect the caliph's person, needed a caliph to make the government stable; and they never seriously thought of transferring rule to one of themselves or even to a non-'Abbāsid.

The confusion of the Sāmarrā period allowed the development of independent dynasties, not only because the army of the central government was occupied with affairs in the capital, but also because many governorships were assigned to Turks who stayed in Iraq and only sent representatives to their provinces. Rebellions continued to break out in Āzarbāījān, and one of the most serious of these, led by Muḥammad b. al-Ba'īth, was only defeated in 235/849 after three caliphal armies had been sent there. The Caspian provinces, subjected to bad government by the Ṭāhirids and the more direct representatives of the caliph, rebelled under a Zaidī pretender in 250/864 and were never again fully recovered by the 'Abbāsids. Most dangerous of all were the rebellions of the Ṣaffārids of Sīstān and the Zanj, the black slaves of southern Iraq. At its high point, the Zanj rebellion extended into Ahvāz where they held Ābādān and Wāsiṭ. Mūsā b. Bughā began fighting the Zanj in Dhu'l-Qa'da 259/August 873; but his lack of success and the news that the province of Fārs, of which he was governor, had been occupied by a rebel caused him to withdraw from the campaign. He also resigned his governorship of the East "because of the many who had forcibly seized it [i.e., the eastern provinces of the empire], and because he had no support against them". Al-Muwaffaq, the caliph's brother, trusted by Mūsā and increasingly the actual administrator of the empire, took over these tasks; and with the help of the Turks, he prevented the Ṣaffārid conquest of Baghdad and patiently drove back the Zanj until their complete defeat in Ṣafar 270/August 883.

When al-Muwaffaq died, his son al-Mu'taḍid assumed his father's rôle as actual administrator of the empire, and therefore succeeded his uncle as caliph, on 20 Rajab 279/18 October 892. The reigns of al-Mu'taḍid and his son al-Muktafī (acceded 22 Rabī' II 289/5 April 902) saw important victories in Iraq, where the Khārijites were defeated in the Jazīra, and the recovery of large parts of Iran. Abū Dulaf, al-Amīn's governor of Hamadān, had been followed in that position by his son and grandsons, who had become increasingly independent of caliphal rule. In 281/894 Ḥārith b. 'Abd al-'Azīz b. Abī Dulaf gained control of Iṣfahān and Nihāvand but was defeated in the same year by the forces of the caliph, who now resumed direct control of all the Dulafid territories.

Both of these caliphs sought to preserve the recovered strength of the 'Abbāsids by making the bureaucracy more elaborate and hierarchical than it had been before, so that it could be the effective voice of the caliph in the day-to-day affairs of the government. As a result when al-Muktafī died on 12 Dhu'l-Qa'da 295/13 August 908 without having officially chosen a successor before death, it was a cabal of officials, not generals, which chose his thirteen-year-old son al-Muqtadir as caliph. Under the strong government of the preceding caliphs the army had become accustomed to regarding the vizier as the spokesman of the caliph and, therefore, as their superior. With the accession of the youngest caliph since the 'Abbāsid revolution, the bureaucrats now had almost unrestrained control of affairs. Two factions of clerks, the Jarrāḥids and Furātids took turns in office and the caliph allowed each incoming faction to fine and often torture the outgoing faction in order to enrich the treasury of the state.

A government budget of 306/918 provides an insight into the 'Abbāsid administration of Iran in this period, especially when it is compared with a budget prepared under Hārūn al-Rashīd. Each item in either of these tax budgets might represent several tax districts together, but almost certainly would not represent a fraction of a tax district, since it is not likely that the government would divide out subdistricts after taxes had been reported by a full district. If the budgets are examined with this principle in mind, they give some idea of the change in tax districts between the time of al-Rashīd and al-Muqtadir. The provinces of Khurāsān, Sīstān, Gurgān, Qūmis, Ṭabaristān and Gīlān were no longer under direct ʿAbbāsid control. Āzarbāījān, Ahvāz, Fārs and Kirmān – insofar as they were controlled by the ʿAbbāsids – continued to be tax districts; but the government had separated out the tax districts of Qazvīn, Qum and Sāva, from the districts of Ray, Iṣfahān and Hamadān, and had separated the joint tax district of Nihāvand and Dīnavar into two districts.

At the centre of the government these districts were supervised by the various *dīvāns* (loosely, "ministries") and *majlises* or "committees" under the vizier. Although lists of these dīvāns differ, there was a gradual increase in their number throughout the ʿAbbāsid period and, under al-Muqtadir, there were over twenty dīvāns in Baghdad. Communication of the government's orders to the provinces and classification of letters from provincial officials was the task of the chancery, *dīwān al-rasāʾil*, which was aided in this task by the dīvān of the post (*al-barīd*) which also served as an intelligence service. The dīvān most actively concerned with provincial administration was the *dīwān al-kharāj* which supervised the land tax. This dīvān dealt with the provinces through separate dīvāns in Baghdad for each major tax district or group of districts. One of al-Muʿtaḍid's reforms was to bring these dīvāns together as *dīwān al-dār* or dīvān of the palace. Later the dīvān of the East (*al-mashriq*), the dīvān of the West (*al-maghrib*) and the dīvān of the Sawād, a vast region of southern Iraq, were separated from the dīvān of the palace, which survived as an accountancy or records office for the dīvāns which actually administered the land tax. The *dīwān al-ḍiyāʿ* or dīvān of caliphal estates supervised the vast properties directly owned by the central government. Linked to each of the financial dīvāns was a *dīwān al-zimām* as mentioned above.

The two officials appointed by the central government to run the provincial administration were the *ʿāmil liʾl-ḥarb* or *amīr*, the military governor, and the *ʿāmil liʾl-kharāj*, or financial governor. Probably most military governors were professional soldiers, and they acted as local garrison commanders. Their appointments covered several tax districts, and presumably either their deputies or the heads of the local police were in charge of keeping order in safer provinces. The financial governor may sometimes have been subordinate to the military governor, but was not ordinarily so. He not only paid local taxes but also paid the salaries of local officials and other government expenses out of local revenues, which made him a source of patronage used even by the central government. Ibn Abī Baghl, financial governor of Iṣfahān from 299/911–12 to 310/922–3 became so annoyed by the size of the packet of recommendations one man brought from Baghdad that he cried: "Every day one of you comes to us demanding a situation. If the treasuries of the whole world were at my disposal, they would by this time be exhausted."[1]

Under these officials were clerks, *jahbadhs* or experts in money matters, the *muḥtasib* or market inspector, mintmasters, toll officials and officials in charge of irrigation. Judges were somewhat outside this system, for they were responsible to the chief judge or *qāḍi 'l-quḍāt* in Baghdad. The first Chief Judge was appointed by Hārūn al-Rashīd, but only later were provincial judges subordinated to him. In the confusion of later 'Abbāsid times one or more headmen (singular *ra'īs*) appeared in Iranian towns because the towns needed spokesmen to deal with the rapidly changing governors and soldiers of fortune who held authority over them. These headmen owed their position more to local support than to the favour of the central government, and it is not surprising to hear that the headman of Qazvīn was held hostage by the 'Abbāsids to assure the co-operation of his fellow townsmen. As the history of the Dulafids shows, there was little that distinguished such popular local headmen from some of the "independent" dynasties which appeared in the 3rd/9th centuries except the official maintenance of a professional army.

At first, the excesses of the clerks in Baghdad seemed not to threaten the recovery of the post-Sāmarrā period. The often brilliant if corrupt viziers of this period skilfully used and played off the new semi-independent rulers against each other. The 'Abbāsids, helped by the Sunnī Sāmānids who had replaced the Ṭāhirids as the great power in eastern Iran, continued to regain control over parts of central and western Iran. The Sāmānids were important enough in the empire that the vizier in 296/908 considered their support a significant help if he should replace al-Muqtadir with another caliph. However, the sometimes conflicting ambitions of these two neighbouring powers prevented the Sāmānids from becoming as closely associated with the 'Abbāsids as the Ṭāhirids had been. The ruler of Khurāsān was angry

[1] Tanūkhī, *Nishwār al-muḥāḍara* (London, 1921), p. 183.

when the 'Abbāsid government gave refuge to one of their rebellious generals and his four thousand troops,[1] and sometimes the Sāmānids and 'Abbāsids would actually quarrel over control of certain provinces in central Iran.

Under al-Muqtadir, the regular army was led by Mu'nis, who had risen under al-Muwaffaq and retained some of the loyalty which that 'Abbāsid had inspired among his officers. Mu'nis recovered Fārs in 297/910 from the Ṣaffārids who were weakened both by a quarrel with the governor of Fārs and by the pressure of Sāmānid attacks on Sīstān, their home province. Tribal groups were also used in the caliphal army; and in this period the partly Arab tribal leaders called the Ḥamdānids, who were closer to Mu'nis and to the Jarrāḥid clerks than to the Furātids, became more prominent. They not only defended the Syrian and northern Iraqi borders of the caliphate but they also received assignments in Iran as governors of Qum and the Dīnavar road to K͟hurāsān. More dangerous allies were the Sājids, a family from Us͟hrūsana who, as governors of Āzarbāījān, had created an army in that province loyal to themselves; and finally one of the Sājid rulers, Yūsuf b. Abi 'l-Sāj, took Ray on his own initiative. Mu'nis, after several unsuccessful campaigns, defeated him in Āzarbāījān in 306/918 but gave this ever-rebellious province to Sabuk, one of Yūsuf's retainers, who, like his former master, usually did not forward the taxes to the central government.

All these gains by the 'Abbāsids in Iran were short lived, not only because governors had their own armies, but also because they had so little to fear from the central government. Al-Muqtadir, forgetting that he owed his throne to Mu'nis, who had suppressed a palace revolution in 296/909 and even defeated a dangerous Fāṭimid invasion of Egypt, plotted to kill his general in 315/927. Finally on 27 S͟hawwāl 320/31 October 932 the caliph decided on a direct contest of strength with Mu'nis; he rode against Mu'nis wearing the cloak and carrying the Rod of the Prophet, preceded by descendants of the first Muslims holding copies of the Qur'ān – in short, with all the symbols of caliphal authority. The caliph was killed. Al-Muhtadī had also tried unsuccessfully to evoke pious support in his struggle against the Turks; but the effect of al-Muqtadir's death was much greater. The ineffectiveness of both religious reverence and an extensive administration in the face of any determined opposition by the army was made unmistakably clear to

[1] Miskawaih, *Tajārib al-umam*, vol. 1, p. 16.

Muslims in all parts of the empire. As Muskūya (Miskawaih) (d. 421/1030) wrote, "it emboldened the enemies to achieve what they had never hoped for – to take possession of the capital. Since that time the caliphate has been weakened and the caliph's authority shattered."[1]

The confusion at the centre of the government made it impossible for the 'Abbāsids to maintain their control of Western Iran. When Sabuk died in 310/922 the Sājid Yūsuf was released and sent to govern Āzarbāijān, Ray and the intervening provinces. In 311/924 he captured Ray, which had been lost by the Sāmānids to rebellious governors. Ray was the gateway to central Iran; and the dizzying rapidity with which it changed hands in the next twenty years reflected the anarchy of a period in which there was no stable successor to 'Abbāsid rule in that area. It was occupied by the Sāmānids in 313 or 314, then by an independent commander who was a former Sāmānid governor from 314 to 316, then by the Zaidī ruler of Ṭabaristān, then by the soldier of fortune Asfār b. Shīrūya, who declared his loyalty to the Sāmānids only to be killed by his lieutenant, Mardāvīj. Mardāvīj defeated the caliphal governor of the Jibāl in 319/931 and direct 'Abbāsid rule in central Iran ceased. Shortly after this, 'Alī b. Būya, an officer in the army of Mardāvīj, revolted against that ruler and fled southward to Fārs where he defeated the semi-independent caliphal governor in Jumādā II 322/June 934, and occupied Shīrāz. After this event there was virtually no official on the Iranian plateau responsible to the caliph in Baghdad. 'Alī b. Būya sent his brother Aḥmad to Arrajān where in 326/938 he defeated the governor of Khūzistān and thereafter took Baghdad itself in Jumādā I 334/December 945. Asfār, Mardāvīj and 'Alī b. Būya were from Dailam, a geographical term used in this period for Gurgān, Ṭabaristān, Dailam proper and Gīlān. Henceforth Dailam was to be a major source of military manpower for western Iran and southern Iraq.

When Mu'nis was treacherously killed in 321/933 by al-Qāhir, who had become caliph after al-Muqtadir, the swollen and inefficient army which had just barely been able to hold onto the core of the caliphate could no longer defend the central government. The field was open for a new military leader to establish himself in Baghdad, and the caliph, who was in any case bankrupt, decided to make the best of the situation by choosing this leader himself. Therefore al-Rāḍī, who followed al-Qāhir as caliph on 6 Jumādā I 322/29 April 934, agreed to accept the

[1] *Ibid.*, p. 237.

offer of the semi-independent military governor of Wāsiṭ, Ibn Rā'iq, to defray all the expenses of the government including those of the army and the court. In exchange the caliph made him *amīr al-umarā'*, or supreme commander, and put him in charge of the principal ministries, giving him in effect "the management of the empire". Ibn Rā'iq's name was to be mentioned with that of the caliph in the khuṭba in all lands. Ibn Rā'iq arrived in Baghdad in Dhu'l-Qa'da 324/September 936; and in 325/936 he killed the remaining household troops of al-Rāḍī and thereby deprived the caliph of all actual military power.

Rival governors now fought to be the caliph's keeper or to set up their own candidates for the caliphate. The other supreme commanders, the Turks Bajkam and Tuzun, the Dailamite Kūrankīj and the Ḥamdānid Nāṣir al-Daula were all, like Ibn Rā'iq, professional soldiers. The only civilians to assume control of Baghdad in the decade of the supreme commanders were the clerk Ibn Muqla and the tax-farmer Abū 'Abd-Allāh Aḥmad al-Barīdī; and though both assumed the more traditional civilian titles of vizier, they had to assume the style of military commanders in order to survive; the subordination of the bureaucracy to the army was complete. None of these supreme commanders or viziers, however, gained sufficient strength to keep his office for any length of time, partly because Sunnī circles in the populace, government and army favoured Sunnī contenders, while Shī'īs favoured Shī'īs like the Ḥamdānids; and partly because there was enmity between the Turkish cavalry and the large new contingents of Dailamite footsoldiers.

It was only when the Barīdīs introduced the Būyids, who had a strong military base on the Iranian plateau, that a stable dynasty of supreme commanders arose. The Barīdīs had had the tax farm of Khūzistān since the reign of al-Qāhir, and had become independent in that province in 324/936; but when Ibn Rā'iq briefly occupied Khūzistān, Abū 'Abd-Allāh al-Barīdī took refuge in Fārs with 'Alī b. Būya who supported him. The Barīdīs not only recovered their province, they also occupied Baghdad more than once and were only driven from there by the Ḥamdānid ruler of Mosul in 330/942. The Ḥamdānid ruler, after struggling for a year with the factions of the capital while trying to keep his army of Arabs and Kurds together, left in disgust. But the position of al-Muttaqī, who had succeeded al-Rāḍī as caliph on 20 Rabī' I 329/23 December 940, under the Ḥamdānids foreshadowed the position of the

'Abbāsids for the next hundred years. A ruler who was a Shī'ī had occupied Baghdad at the head of an army united largely on principles of tribal loyalty. Unlike the rule of the earlier supreme commanders, Ḥamdānid rule could not be seen simply as a more severe form of that subjugation to the army which the 'Abbāsids had suffered before al-Muwaffaq. When the Shī'ī Būyids who led armies largely composed of Dailamites occupied Baghdad, the event was therefore not entirely novel in character. But it was appropriately seen by contemporary and later Muslim writers as marking an era in the history of the Muslim caliphate; for the Būyids, firmly in possession of Fārs, came with much greater military power than the Ḥamdānids possessed, and they came to stay. Less than a month after occupying Baghdad Aḥmad b. Būya deposed al-Mustakfī, who had been caliph since 20 Ṣafar 333/12 October 944.

With Aḥmad b. Būya's conquest of Baghdad, Iraq was again loosely tied politically with western Iran where his two brothers had large kingdoms of their own. This conquest therefore revived the long political association of Iraq and Iran, and ended the 'Abbāsid attempt to make Iraq the centre of an empire whose heartlands included Egypt and Syria as much as it included the Iranian plateau. When the first 'Abbāsids had moved the capital from Syria to Iraq, they had made the Islamic empire less of a *ghāzī* state, centred on former Byzantine territory near the new Byzantine borders, and more of a Mesopotamian (or Iraqi) state. To be a Mesopotamian state meant to be constantly compared with a Sāsānian imperial tradition. By force of such comparisons, the 'Abbāsids and their servants sometimes imitated that tradition self-consciously, if not accurately; for many of the "ancient Persian" ceremonials of the 'Abbāsid court, like the Persian etymologies for administrative terms like barīd, were based on historical fictions satisfying to contemporary taste. Those who wished to denigrate the 'Abbāsids were no less eager to create fictitious resemblances to a period when men had lived in ignorance of Islam. Yet the 'Abbāsid empire, for all its real or imagined family likeness to earlier Iranian empires, remained a Mesopotamian empire, not an empire which, though it had a capital in Mesopotamia, retained a special tie with the peoples of the Iranian plateau. The 'Abbāsids in the 4th/10th century lost control of Egypt, Syria and western Iran almost simultaneously; and the temporary loss of Fārs in an earlier period to the Ṣaffārids was no worse a blow than was the temporary loss of Egypt and part of

Syria to the Ṭūlūnids. With the breakdown of the ʿAbbāsid state, an older division reappears, in which Mesopotamia is often the natural extension of the power of the rulers of western Iran or of northern Iraq and Anatolia.

If the ʿAbbāsids had no special tie with the peoples of the Iranian plateau as a whole, they did at first have a special tie with a specific Khurāsānian army and, more loosely, with Khurāsān in general. As Abu'l-ʿAbbās said in his inaugural speech, the people of Khurāsān were especially designated by God to be partisans of the ʿAbbāsids; and when al-Manṣūr found that the Khurāsānians disliked the governor he sent, he decided that this governor was "destroying our party (*shīʿa*)". Nevertheless, whether from overconfidence or from fear of dependency, the ʿAbbāsids loosened this special tie by a series of acts which the Khurāsānians could not easily forgive. Al-Manṣūr killed Abū Muslim, perhaps politically the most justifiable of all these acts. Al-Rashīd disgraced the Barmakids. But by far the worst damage was done by al-Rashīd's division of the empire between al-Amīn and al-Ma'mūn; and with al-Ma'mūn's victory, the ʿAbbāsids found themselves dependent on the Khurāsānians in an altogether more dangerous way. The army of al-Ma'mūn was as loyal to its Iranian patrons as it was to the caliphs; al-Ma'mūn, as we have seen, not only was dependent on the Ṭāhirids but even had trouble with the army when he disposed of al-Faḍl b. Sahl. The civil war and the consequent dependency on Khurāsān also meant that the caliphate had lost all prestige in the eyes of the Arabs. Yet Muslim Iraqis were still passively obedient, because the attacks of the Khārijite and Shīʿī Bedouin offered an alternative much less desirable than ʿAbbāsid government; and by the end of the 3rd/9th century some Iraqi Muslim theologians had made it a definite religious duty *not* to revolt. Nevertheless, this obedience covered a loss of loyalty, and sometimes even a covert hostility.

Al-Muʿtaṣim's Turkish slave army, therefore, was not a personal whim but a pressing necessity. The Khurāsānian tie did not disappear immediately, and the Ṭāhirids, who were parvenus in the eyes of the nobility of eastern Iran, rightly prized the prestige that ʿAbbāsid recognition gave them. The Ṭāhirids continued to be chiefs of police in Baghdad; and it was so automatically assumed that Khurāsānians were their supporters that Muḥammad b. ʿAbd-Allāh b. Ṭāhir armed the Khurāsānian pilgrims to defend al-Mustaʿīn. Al-Ma'mūn's use of the Afshīn was one way of avoiding dependency on the Ṭāhirids; for the people of Farghāna felt themselves to be separate from the Khurāsānians, and the Afshīn disliked the Ṭāhirids. But the most successful alternative to the Khurāsānians was the Turks; and if the Turks for a while chose and deposed caliphs as they wished, the ultimate revival of the 'Abbāsid empire at the end of the 3rd/9th century was militarily a Turkish accomplishment.

To safeguard and pay for this accomplishment al-Muwaffaq, al-Mu'taḍid and al-Muktafī made the administration more elaborate than it had ever been before. More money was needed to maintain slave soldiers and mercenaries than to pay levies of free men, yet more territory was being lost from direct financial control as provincial governors arranged to hold their provinces by way of *muqāṭa'a* for a fixed tribute, which they often withheld in any case. The central government was therefore obliged to get as much revenue as it could from the sources which remained to it. By creating smaller tax districts and more dīvāns the government was able to have a closer and more effective oversight of the collection of revenue; at the same time new auditing dīvāns like the dīwān al-dār allowed a vigorous caliph to have a closer and more effective oversight of the operations of his officials. Not only did the 'Abbāsids create a more refined bureaucracy, they also made greater use of tax-farming and of assignments of revenue rights called *iqṭā'*. These measures were successful as long as there was a strong caliph who kept the bureaucracy under his surveillance; but as soon as al-Muqtadir came to the throne, the bureaucrats destroyed the financial apparatus created in the previous reigns to ensure the maintenance of the army. As al-Muqtadir grew up he proved to be negligent and spendthrift in the same style as the caliphs of the Sāmarrā period; and when he foolishly provoked the army by his opposition to Mu'nis, it was only a matter of a few years before the 'Abbāsids resigned themselves to the necessity of another dynasty's tutelage. The failure of the 'Abbāsids to create anything more lasting and stable than a household administration is a failure which they share with all early Islamic dynasties.

In a sense, the 'Abbāsids were less successful ideologically during their first empire, when they ruled a larger territory and were much more formidable to their enemies, than they were in the revived empire of the 3rd/9th century. There had been an internal contradiction in the ideology of the 'Abbāsid state from the beginning: the empire was to be based on the unity of all Muslims, not an extension of power by a relatively homogeneous group like the Syrian Arabs. Yet the empire was at first essentially an extension of the power of the Khurāsānian army, however much the ʻAbbāsids tried to represent the Khurāsānians as playing only the rôle of military guardians for the Islamic state. From the beginning circumstances forced the ʻAbbāsids to make choices which caused parts of the Islamic community to feel excluded from participation in their rule. They had to choose between the religious groups which had brought them to power: the Hāshimiyya, the Shīʻīs and the anti-Umayyad Sunnīs. They chose the Sunnīs but were never completely successful in convincing the Sunnīs that their interest and that of the ʻAbbāsids was the same. Then, thanks to al-Rashīd's treatment of the Barmakids and the question of succession, the ʻAbbāsids and their subjects had to choose between Iraq and Khurāsān. This choice proved the undoing of the original ʻAbbāsid empire, and only when the new Turkish army agreed to co-operate with the caliphs could a second ʻAbbāsid empire be formed.

The second ʻAbbāsid empire was militarily limited, but ideologically successful, because the ʻAbbāsids, despite their failure to dictate an official form of orthodoxy under al-Ma'mūn, al-Muʻtaṣim, and al-Wāthiq, seem to have convinced most members of the religious class throughout the empire that in principle many Islamic institutions could function properly only if the reigning ʻAbbāsid caliph recognized them. In the vast majority of cases, the ʻAbbāsids had disguised their loss of power by giving the new independent rulers deeds delegating the caliph's authority to them by official appointment. The independent rulers wanted these deeds of appointment for, as Bīrūnī wrote in the 5th/11th century, "the common people in the large cities have become accustomed to the ʻAbbāsid claim, and have been inclined to their rule, and obey them out of a sense of religion, and consider them possessed with the right to command".[1] Most Muslims believed that their community could not be divided against itself, and, though they were often disloyal to individual caliphs, they were nonetheless upholders of the principle of the caliphate. This principle, they felt, not only satisfied established theological requirements, but was to their advantage in that it gave them the same right to "citizenship" in any kingdom within the empire, and the same right to demand (though not always to receive) the protection of the sacred law of Islam, the sharīʻa. Almost everywhere, if no rival caliph was recognized, the ʻAbbāsid caliph's name

[1] Bīrūnī, *al-Jamāhir fī maʻrifat al-jawāhir* (Hyderabad, 1355/1936), p. 23.

continued after 334/946 to be inscribed on coins and mentioned in the Friday prayer. In the long run, the greatest contribution of the ‘Abbāsids to Islamic society was their fostering of Islamic institutions, and they were repaid by the continuing reverence in which their caliphate was held as guarantor of these institutions long after their non-ideological instruments of power had been lost.

CHAPTER 3

THE ṬĀHIRIDS AND ṢAFFĀRIDS

During the 3rd/9th century, four generations of the Ṭāhirid family succeeded each other hereditarily as governors for the ʿAbbāsid caliphs (205–59/821–73). The line is thus often considered as the first dynasty in the east to make itself autonomous of the caliphs in Iraq; their rôle in the dissolution of the political unity of the Islamic caliphate would, according to this view, correspond to the rôles of the Aghlabid governors of Ifrīqiya or Tunisia in the far west and of the Ṭūlūnids in Egypt and Syria. There are, as we shall see below, cogent objections to this view, both from the standpoints of constitutional theory and of the Ṭāhirids' actual behaviour; in many ways, it is a misleading and superficial analysis of affairs. Yet it is probably true that the continuity in power of the Ṭāhirids did favour the beginnings of a resurgence of Persian national feeling and culture, although Spuler is perhaps being unduly dogmatic when he remarks, concerning the succession of the first Ṭāhirids in the governorship of Iran, "In theory, nothing essential had changed, but in practice, the first independent Muslim dynasty had been established on Iranian soil; the political rebirth of the Persian nation began."[1]

Previously, Khurāsān had been economically and socially backward compared with the rest of Persia. It had endured a succession of governors sent out from Iraq, normally Arabs who had little concern for the enduring prosperity of the province; the turnover amongst governors was often rapid, providing a temptation to exploit one's charge and line one's pocket whilst opportunity permitted. The Ṭāhirids were culturally highly Arabicized, but they were nevertheless Persians. The firm and generally just rule which they gave to the eastern Iranian world favoured a material and cultural progress, whereas earlier, the indigenous, older Iranian culture had been weakened by the dynamic impact of Islamic religion and Arab political dominance. The practical effects of these trends inaugurated by the Ṭāhirids were seen somewhat later, in the governmental policies and

[1] Spuler, p. 60.

cultural climate of succeeding dynasties – the Ṣaffārids and Sāmānids in eastern Persia, the various Dailamite and Kurdish dynasties in the west – whose links with the ʿAbbāsid caliphate were perceptibly looser and whose respect for the constitutional theory that all political power was a delegation from the caliphs was much weaker.

The founders of the Ṭāhirid family fortunes were typical of the Persians who had lent their support, first to the anti-Umayyad *daʿwa* of Abū Muslim, and then to the new régime of the ʿAbbāsids which in 132/749 emerged from that upheaval. From the accession in that year of the Caliph al-Saffāḥ to the death of al-Maʾmūn over eighty years later, the Khurāsānī troops formed the backbone of the ʿAbbāsid army and the mainstay of the dynasty, fully meriting their designation of *abnāʾ al-daula* "sons of the dynasty". Their services contributed much to the victory of al-Maʾmūn, who commanded the human and material resources of Persia, over his brother al-Amīn, whose main support came from the Arabs of Iraq. Only with the accession in 218/833 of al-Muʿtaṣim did the Persian element in the caliphal armies take second place to newer groups, most prominent amongst which were Turks from the Central Asian and South Russian steppes.

Ruzaiq, ancestor of the first Ṭāhirid governor of Khurāsān, Ṭāhir b. al-Ḥusain, was a *maulā* or client of Ṭalḥa b. ʿAbd-Allāh al-Khuzāʿī, known as "the incomparable Ṭalḥa" (*Ṭalḥa al-Ṭalaḥāt*), who had been governor of Sīstān towards the end of the 1st/7th century. Ṭāhir's grandfather Muṣʿab b. Ruzaiq played a part in the ʿAbbāsid revolution in Khurāsān, acting as secretary to the ʿAbbāsid *dāʿī* or propagandist Sulaimān b. Kathīr al-Khuzāʿī. As a reward for their services, these early Ṭāhirids acquired governorships in eastern Khurāsān. Muṣʿab was governor of Pūshang and apparently also of Herāt. He was certainly governing Pūshang for the Caliph al-Mahdī in 160/776–7, for in that year he was expelled from the town by the Khārijite rebel Yūsuf b. Ibrāhīm al-Barm al-Thaqafī. These were years of considerable social, political and religious upheaval in Khurāsān, but the Ṭāhirids flourished in an unspectacular way, and their continued grip on Pūshang foreshadowed the wider rôle they were later to play in Khurāsān: both al-Ḥusain and Ṭāhir, son and grandson of Muṣʿab, succeeded at Pūshang. The sources agree that the Ṭāhirids were ethnically Persian and that they acquired the *nisba* or gentilic of al-Khuzāʿī through clientship to the Arab tribe of Khuzāʿa. Ṭāhir b. al-Ḥusain's normal tongue was Persian, and Ibn Ṭaifūr records his dying words in that language. When the Ṭāhirids were at the zenith of their power, attempts were made by their partisans to inflate their modest origins. Mas'ūdī states that they claimed descent from the hero Rustam, and the Arab poet Di'bil b. 'Alī, himself of genuine Khuzā'ī stock, satirizes the Ṭāhirids' attempts to connect themselves on the one hand with Quraish (because Khuzā'a had once in pre-Islamic times controlled Mecca) and on the other with the Persian Emperors.[1]

In 194/809–10 Ṭāhir joined the general Harthama b. A'yan in operations against Rāfi' b. al-Laith, a grandson of the last Umayyad governor of Khurāsān Naṣr b. Sayyār. Rāfi' had in 190/806 raised up a serious and protracted rebellion against caliphal authority, attracting support from the Iranian populations of Transoxiana and Khwārazm as well as from the Turks of the surrounding steppes. By 194/810 the fragile peace between the two 'Abbāsid brothers al-Amīn and al-Ma'mūn, the chief legatees of their father Hārūn al-Rashīd's power, was already crumbling. In the complex succession arrangements made by Hārūn in 182/798 and confirmed at Mecca in 186/802, it had been laid down that al-Ma'mūn, governor of all the Persian lands east of Hamadān, should follow al-Amīn in the caliphate, with a third brother, al-Qāsim al-Mu'tamin, governor of al-Jazīra and the fortresses along the Byzantine frontier, as next in line. Urged on by his vizier al-Faḍl b. al-Rabī' and by 'Alī b. 'Īsā b. Māhān, former governor of Khurāsān, al-Amīn in 194/810 declared the succession rights of al-Ma'mūn and al-Qāsim to be null and void, and he proclaimed his infant son Mūsā as heir, with the honorific *al-Nāṭiq bi'l-Ḥaqq*. Al-Ma'mūn retaliated by dropping his brother's name from the *khuṭba* or Friday sermon in his territories and from the coins minted by him there, and by cutting the *barīd* network of communications between Khurāsān and Iraq.

In 195/810–11 Ṭāhir became commander of the army posted by al-Ma'mūn at Ray to confront al-Amīn's forces at Hamadān. In the subsequent battle, 'Alī b. 'Īsā b. Māhān was defeated and killed; and one of the explanations given for Ṭāhir's nickname of *Dhu'l-Yamīnain* "the man with two right hands" or "the ambidexter" is that in this battle he cut a man in two with his left hand. The historians praise Ṭāhir's skilful generalship in deploying his troops, whom he urged to "attack with the fury of the Khārijites" (*iḥmilū ḥamlat^{an} khārijiyyat^{an}*), and also his use of spies.[2] Al-Ma'mūn's subsequent victory is generally

[1] Mas'ūdī, *Kitāb al-tanbīh*, ed. M. J. de Goeje (Leiden, 1894), p. 348; tr. Carra de Vaux (Paris, 1897), p. 446.

[2] Ibn al-Athīr, vol. VI, pp. 168, 177.

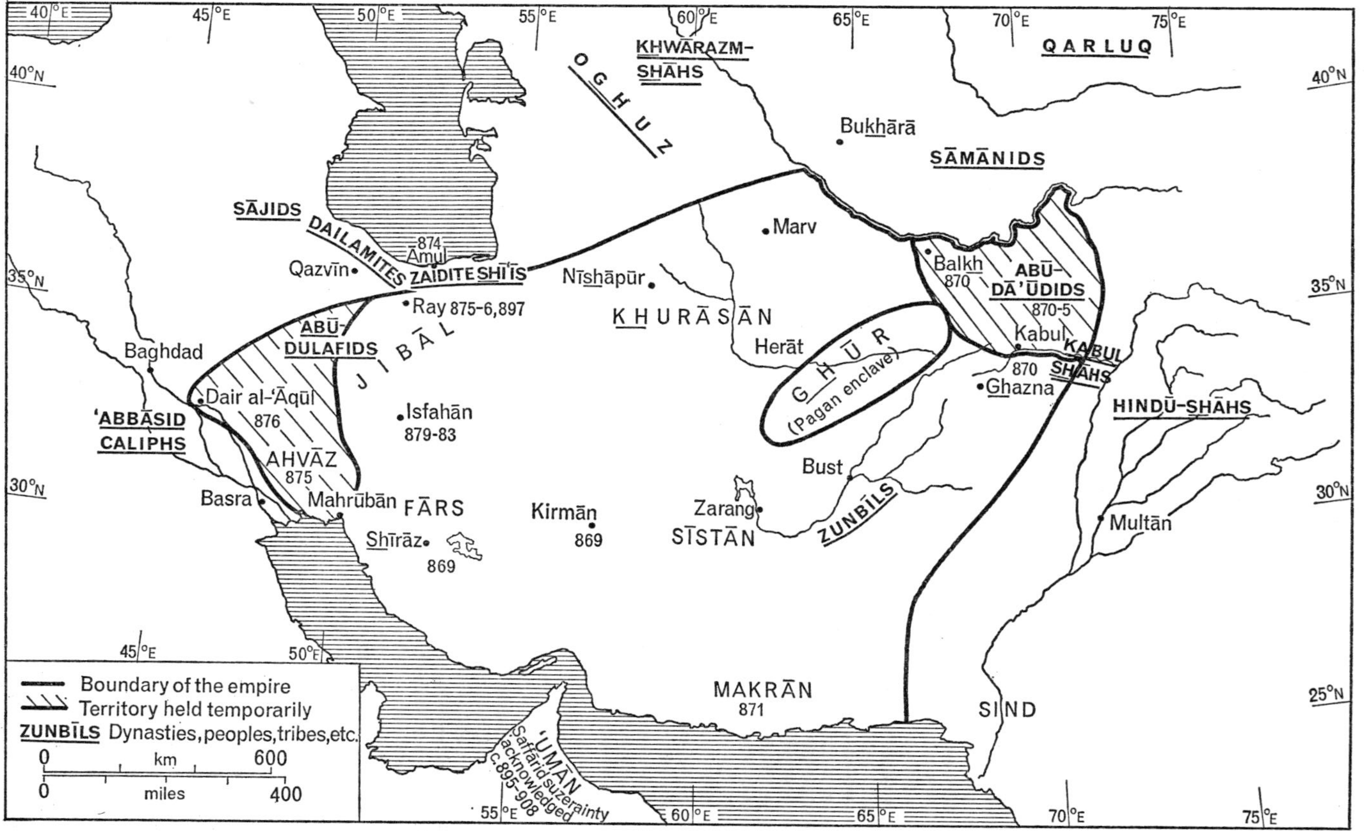

Map 2. The Ṣaffārid empire

regarded as a triumph of the Persian east over Arab Iraq. His cause was certainly helped by local memories of ʿAlī b. ʿĪsā b. Māhān's tyrannical rule in Khurāsān, and by Ṭāhir's denunciations at Ray of the opposing army as being a rabble of predatory Bedouins and mountain brigands; al-Ma'mūn's maternal descent from Marājil al-Bādghīsiyya, one of Hārūn's Persian concubines, and his known Persian sympathies, must also have helped. Ṭāhir pressed on after his victory at Ray and overran the whole of Jibāl, inflicting further blows on al-Amīn's armies and advancing through Ahvāz to the capital itself. When Baghdad at last fell to Harthama and Ṭāhir, Ṭāhir's Persian soldiers slew the captive al-Amīn (198/813); certain sources say that al-Ma'mūn later came to hold Ṭāhir responsible for his brother's murder.

The new caliph al-Ma'mūn remained for several years in his eastern headquarters of Marv. Although Ṭāhir was one of the architects of his triumph, he ordered Ṭāhir to relinquish control of western Persia, Iraq and the Arabian peninsula to al-Ḥasan, brother of his principal adviser, the Persian al-Faḍl b. Sahl, called Dhu'l-Riyāsatain ("the man charged with the two functions, *al-tadbīr wa'l-ḥarb*", i.e. civil and military power). Instead, he was appointed governor of al-Jazīra and Syria, with the specific charge of combating a local Arab chief, Naṣr b. Shabath al-ʿUqailī, who had raised a revolt of pro-Amīnid elements. In the event, he made no real headway, and Naṣr b. Shabath continued to cause trouble for over ten years, until his centre of power at Kaisūm, north of Aleppo, was captured.

Ṭāhir's base during these years was at Raqqa on the Euphrates, but he also acquired further offices in Iraq, becoming *ṣāḥib al-shurṭa*, the officer responsible for public order and police services, in Baghdad, and taking over responsibility for collection of the revenues of the Sawād of Iraq, the fertile and prosperous agricultural region of central Iraq. Whilst the Ṭāhirids have come to be primarily known for their rule in Khurāsān, these administrative charges in Baghdad were hardly of less importance for the maintenance of the family's power; indeed, various Ṭāhirids held on to them till the early years of the 10th century, long after Khurāsān had been relinquished to the Ṣaffārids. They were undoubtedly very lucrative. According to Yaʿqūbī, the *kharāj* or land-tax of Khurāsān under the Ṭāhirids amounted to forty million dirhams, but as well as this, their interests in Iraq brought them an extra thirteen million dirhams, plus other revenue in kind.[1] Within the city of

[1] Yaʿqūbī, *Kitāb al-buldān*, p. 308; tr., p. 138.

Baghdad, the Ṭāhirids were rich property-holders. The Ḥarīm of Ṭāhir b. al-Ḥusain, one of the most opulent buildings in the western side of Baghdad, was the residence of the Ṭāhirid governors of Baghdad, and later, of the caliphs themselves; as early as 'Abd-Allāh b. Ṭāhir's time, it acquired quasi-regal status, with consequent rights of sanctuary (hence the name *ḥarīm* "inviolable place, sanctuary"). By means of these offices, the Ṭāhirids were able to exert influence at the centre of the caliphate, and since their seat was in Baghdad, they were less affected by the violence of the Turkish guards who dominated and often terrorized the caliphs in Sāmarrā. Thus Ṭāhirid pressure in Baghdad compelled the Caliph al-Mu'tamid to take a firm line, if only temporarily, against Ya'qūb b. al-Laiṯẖ when in 259/873 he captured Nīsẖāpūr from Muḥammad b. Ṭāhir.

Ṭāhir became governor of all the caliphal lands east of Iraq in 205/821. He is said deliberately to have sought investiture of these in order to remove himself from court, fearing that al-Ma'mūn had turned against him. The governorship was actually secured by a piece of unpleasant intrigue, in which the intercession of al-Ma'mūn's vizier Aḥmad b. Abī Kẖālid was employed against the incumbent governor of Kẖurāsān, Gẖassān b. 'Abbād, protégé and kinsman of the previous vizier al-Ḥasan b. Sahl. Soon after his arrival in the east, Ṭāhir began leaving al-Ma'mūn's name out of the kẖuṭba, and certain coins minted by him in 206/821–2 also omit the caliph's name; both these actions were virtually declarations of independence from Baghdad. However, at this point he died in Marv (207/822).

It is obviously difficult to gauge Ṭāhir's motives, since we do not know how events might have turned out. There are certain contradictions and differences of chronology in the historians' accounts, and it is possible that Ṭāhir was poisoned on the orders of Aḥmad b. Abī Kẖālid, concerned to vindicate his own fidelity to the caliph now that the man whom he had personally recommended for office had proved rebellious. It is possible that the significance of Ṭāhir's action has been exaggerated. Despite it, the caliphs did not hesitate to appoint Ṭāhir's sons and other members of the family to the governorship of Kẖurāsān, and their power in Baghdad and Iraq continued undiminished. None of these subsequent Ṭāhirids emulated Ṭāhir; all of them behaved circumspectly and entirely correctly towards the caliphs.

When Ṭahir died, his son Ṭalḥa assumed command of the army in Kẖurāsān, although he was powerless to prevent the troops from plundering his father's treasury. Al-Ma'mūn eventually confirmed Ṭalḥa in the governorship of Khurāsān; certain sources say that the caliph at first appointed another son, 'Abd-Allāh b. Ṭāhir, but 'Abd-Allāh's preoccupation in al-Jazīra with Naṣr b. Shabath's rebellion led him to make Ṭalḥa his deputy in the east. Whatever the exact circumstances of Ṭalḥa's succession to power, the significant point is that al-Ma'mūn, apparently on the advice of Aḥmad b. Abī Khālid, maintained a son of Ṭāhir's in Khurāsān. Either Ṭāhir's gesture of rebelliousness was not regarded over-seriously, or else the caliph and his advisers realized that it was wisest in the circumstances to entrust Persia to the indigenous family of the Ṭāhirids. Certainly, caliphal authority was beset by difficulties at this time. The Arab west was not yet fully reconciled to al-Ma'mūn, with Naṣr b. Shabath still at large and with disturbances in Egypt. In the east, Sīstān was still in the throes of the protracted rebellion of the Khārijite Ḥamza b. Ādharak or 'Abd-Allāh, and most serious of all these revolutionary movements, the Neo-Mazdakite Khurramiyya sectaries, under their leader Bābak, controlled Arrān and Āzarbāījān and were threatening Jibāl. On the intellectual plane, the caliph was trying to secure greater religious harmony by making concessions to the Shī'a (seen in the adoption of the Eighth Shī'ī Imām, 'Alī al-Riḍā, as his heir in 201/816), and by encouraging the views of the Mu'tazilite sect on such topics as the createdness of the Qur'ān; these policies had only succeeded in rousing conservative, orthodox forces to the defence of the Sunna, and had aggravated rather than composed religious dissensions within the caliphate. Thus by retaining the Ṭāhirids in Khurāsān, the caliphs took the line of least resistance and ensured a degree of continuity and stability in the east.

Ṭalḥa b. Ṭāhir governed Khurāsān till his death in 213/828. After Ṭāhir's death had been reported to Baghdad, al-Ma'mūn had sent out Aḥmad b. Abī Khālid with military powers, in order to install a caliphal presence in the east. The vizier led an expedition across the Oxus into Ushrūsana, the region lying just to the south of the middle Syr Darya, where the local ruler, the Afshīn Kāwūs, had stopped paying tribute (the successor in Ushrūsana to this Kāwūs was the famous Khaidhar or Ḥaidar, vanquisher in al-Mu'taṣim's reign of the Khurramī Bābak). Aḥmad b. Abī Khālid is also said to have given support to the Sāmānids in Transoxiana, and to have aided Aḥmad b. Asad in Farghāna, a region which was, like Ushrūsana, only partially Islamized (207/822–3). In the next year, the energetic vizier was in Kirmān suppressing a revolt by a dissident member of the Ṭāhirid family, al-Ḥasan b. al-Ḥusain b. Muṣʿab. Aḥmad b. Abī Khālid seems to have been satisfied with Ṭalḥa's *bona fides*, especially as the latter had judiciously given the vizier a munificent offering of three million dirhams in coinage and two million dirhams' worth of presents.[1] During Ṭalḥa's governorship, the main threat to ʿAbbāsid and Ṭāhirid authority in the east came from the Khārijite movement centred on Sīstān and led by Ḥamza b. Ādharak or ʿAbd-Allāh. The movement had a social and political aspect as well as a religious one, for the Khārijites utilized rural discontent against the ʿAbbāsid officials and tax-collectors. The Ṭāhirids could not therefore remain oblivious to the wider implications of Ḥamza's revolt – its dissolving effect on the whole fabric of caliphal authority and Sunnī orthodoxy in Sīstān and the adjacent provinces of the east. Nīshāpūr, Baihaq, Herāt and other towns of Khurāsān proper were at times affected by Khārijite depredations, and Gardīzī records that Ṭalḥa was much occupied with warfare against the Ḥamziyya. Ḥamza did not, however, die till 213/828, the year of Ṭalḥa's own death.

Ṭalḥa is a somewhat shadowy figure in the sources, but there is an abundance of references to Ṭāhir's other son ʿAbd-Allāh, perhaps the greatest of the Ṭāhirids and certainly the one who has left the deepest impression on the history and culture of his time. According to Shābushtī, ʿAbd-Allāh had long been a favourite of al-Ma'mūn's, and the caliph had "treated him like one of his own sons and brought him up (*tabannāhu wa-rabbāhu*)".[2] Much of ʿAbd-Allāh's early career was spent in the west, dealing with the unrest in the Arab lands consequent on the civil war between al-Amīn and al-Ma'mūn. He followed his father Ṭāhir at Raqqa in the operations against Naṣr b. Shabath, and in 209/824–5 or the following year, finally induced the latter to surrender. In 210/825–6 he was also in Egypt, putting down a long-standing uprising led by ʿAbd-Allāh b. al-Sarī, a revolt which had been aggravated by a group of freebooters from Muslim Spain, seizing control of Alexandria. In 214/829 he was at Dīnavar with a commission to attack Bābak, but was then transferred by al-Ma'mūn to Khurāsān in order to combat Khārijite raids there. (The final defeat and capture of the Khurramī leader was to be the work of the Afshīn Ḥaidar, who in 222/837, after lengthy and hard-fought campaigns in Āzarbāījān and Mūghān, captured Bābak's fortress of Badhdh; the Armenian prince

[1] Ṭabarī, vol. III, p. 1066; Ibn al-Athīr, vol. VI, p. 271; Rothstein, p. 162.
[2] Rothstein, p. 162. Jūzjānī, vol. I, p. 192; tr. p. 113.

Sahl b. Sunbādh delivered up Bābak to the Afshīn, and he was executed at Sāmarrā in 223/838.) When in 213/828 the death of Ṭalḥa b. Ṭāhir supervened, his brother ʻAlī was on the spot in Khurāsān, and acted as deputy governor until ʻAbd-Allāh, the official governor, arrived in 215/830 at Nīshāpūr, where he made his capital.

During his fifteen years' rule in central and eastern Iran (215–30/830–45), ʻAbd-Allāh was undisputed master in his own house, without, however, behaving disrespectfully towards the ʻAbbāsids. Both Ṭāhir and ʻAbd-Allāh had been high in al-Ma'mūn's favour. According to Gardīzī, the new Caliph al-Muʻtaṣim (218–27/833–42) hated ʻAbd-Allāh, ostensibly because of a slight he had experienced at court from ʻAbd-Allāh during his brother al-Ma'mūn's lifetime. Al-Muʻtaṣim is alleged to have tried to poison ʻAbd-Allāh, and later in the reign, the Afshīn Ḥaidar was encouraged in his own ambitions for Khurāsān by talk from the caliph indicating that he wanted the Ṭāhirids removed from Khurāsān. This may be so, but on the other hand, al-Muʻtaṣim seems to have had a high regard for ʻAbd-Allāh and his capabilities. At his accession, he confirmed ʻAbd-Allāh in his governorship, and ʻAbd-Allāh retained the long-established interests of his family in Iraq. At his death he held, besides Khurāsān, the provinces of Ray, Ṭabaristān and Kirmān, and was administrator of the Sawād of Iraq and military commander in Baghdad (*wāli al-ḥarb wa'l-shurṭa*), the total revenue from his territories being 48 million dirhams.[1] ʻAbd-Allāh followed a policy of circumspection and non-provocation in his dealings with the caliphs, and would never leave his territories and visit the caliphal court at Sāmarrā. When at one point ʻAbd-Allāh announced his intention to go westwards and perform the Pilgrimage, his secretary Ismāʻīl protested, "O Amīr, you are too sensible to undertake such a senseless business!"; the Ṭāhirid agreed, and said that he had only wished to test him.

ʻAbd-Allāh's governorship was punctuated by spells of military activity. In Transoxiana, Ṭāhirid efforts were devoted to strengthening the position of their Sāmānid vassals, in the hope of achieving the final Islamization of the province and of warding off attacks from the pagan Turks. Sheltered in this way, the early Sāmānids were able to lay the foundations of their later powerful amīrate in Transoxiana and Khurāsān. Thus at one point, ʻAbd-Allāh sent his son Ṭāhir into the Oghuz steppes, probably with Sāmānid help, and Ṭāhir penetrated to places where no Muslim force had ever been. Ṭāhirid concern over

[1] Ṭabarī, vol. III, pp. 1338–9; Ibn al-Athīr, vol. VII, p. 9.

Transoxiana is also in part explicable by the fact that the 'Abbāsid caliphs themselves still had important direct interests there. The commercial links of Transoxiana and Baghdad were kept up, despite the great distance involved; Tha'ālibī mentions the export of Khwārazmian melons to Baghdad during the caliphates of al-Ma'mūn and al-Wāthiq.[1] The caliphs also possessed private estates there. Al-Mu'taṣim was persuaded, albeit grudgingly, to contribute two million dirhams towards the digging of an irrigation canal in the province of Shāsh, and later in the century, al-Mu'tamid made over revenues from property at Ishtīkhān and Iskijkath in Soghdia to Muḥammad b. Ṭāhir b. 'Abd-Allāh.[2] But the prime economic factor here was, of course, the traffic from the Central Asian steppes in Turkish slaves, for which demand (and consequently prices) rose sharply in the course of the 3rd/9th century. The Ṭāhirids, and later the Sāmānids, controlled this traffic; it contributed both to the economic prosperity of Transoxiana and Khurāsān and to the great personal wealth of the Ṭāhirids. These slaves formed a proportion of the tribute forwarded to Iraq by the Ṭāhirids, and they went to swell the ranks of the caliphs' military guards (*ghilmān, mamālīk*); thus on his accession in 232/847 al-Mutawakkil received a gift of 200 slaves of both sexes from the Ṭāhirids.[3] Slaves were also brought from the far eastern fringes of the Iranian world; amongst the tribute sent by the Shāh of Kābul during 'Abd-Allāh b. Ṭāhir's governorship were 2,000 Oghuz slaves valued at 600,000 *dirhams*. It was in the middle years of the century that one of the Ṭāhirids' tributaries, the Abū Dā'ūdid or Banījūrid Amīr Dā'ūd b. Abī Dā'ūd 'Abbās, undertook an obscure but doubtless profitable expedition into eastern Afghanistan and Zābulistān; and it is recorded that in 250/864 Muḥammad b. Ṭāhir sent to the caliph two elephants captured at Kābul, idols, and aromatic substances (? musk from Tibet). These eastern fringes were also the scene in 219/834 of an 'Alid rising led by a descendant of al-Ḥusain, Muḥammad b. al-Qāsim, who appeared at Ṭāliqān in Jūzjān, but was finally captured by 'Abd-Allāh b. Ṭāhir's troops.

Yet the gravest threat to the Ṭāhirid position in Persia came from the Caspian provinces. This was a region whose sub-tropical climate and vegetation made it notoriously unhealthy for outsiders; consequently,

[1] *Laṭā'if al-ma'ārif*, ed. I. al-Abyārī and Ḥ. K. al-Ṣairafī (Cairo, 1960), p. 226; tr. C. E. Bosworth, *The Book of Curious and Entertaining Information* (Edinburgh, 1968), p. 142.

[2] Ṭabarī, vol. III, p. 1326.

[3] Mas'ūdī, vol. VII, p. 281.

it was for long inaccessible to Muslim armies. Islam came here late, and older Iranian practices lingered. When Islam did secure a foothold, some sections of the local population emphasized their continued differentiation by adopting heterodox forms of the new faith, in particular, Zaidī Shī'ism. Ṭabaristān came under 'Abd-Allāh b. Ṭāhir's jurisdiction, but in 224/839 the local ruler, the Ispahbad Māzyār b. Qārin b. Vindādhhurmuz (himself only a recent convert to Islam), refused to pay tribute to the caliphate through the intermediacy of the Ṭāhirids, insisting on direct access to the caliphs. Māzyār thus aimed at reducing Ṭāhirid influence over Ṭabaristān, so that he could pursue unimpeded a policy of aggression which he had already embarked upon in the mountainous hinterland of the province. He had disposed of a rival from the neighbouring Bāvandid dynasty, and was in correspondence with the Afshīn Ḥaidar. At this time, the Afshīn's prestige was high, as the victor over Bābak and as a participant in al-Mu'taṣim's Amorium campaign of 223/838 against the Byzantines. He regarded the Ṭāhirids with envy and coveted the lucrative governorship of Khurāsān for himself, pretensions encouraged, according to Ṭabarī, by al-Mu'taṣim's dislike of the Ṭāhirids. On hearing of Māzyār's defiance, 'Abd-Allāh b. Ṭāhir sent his uncle al-Ḥasan b. al-Ḥusain b. Muṣ'ab to Gurgān and sent forces through the Alburz Mountains to invade Ṭabaristān from the south. By taking advantage of opposition in the mountains to Māzyār's expansionism (Māzyār's power being based on the coastal lowlands and such towns there as Āmul, Sārī and Chālūs), and by suborning other members of Māzyār's family into betraying him, in the end he captured Māzyār and sent him to Iraq. The Afshīn Ḥaidar was now slipping from caliphal favour; he was adversely affected by the revolt of one of his kinsmen in Āzarbāījān, and was suspected of diverting plunder captured from the Khurramiyya to his home province of Ushrūsana and away from the caliph in Iraq. Finally, he was accused of sympathy for the older religions of Transoxiana (Manichaeism or Buddhism?), of apostasy from Islam and of a desire to see the Arabs and Turks abased and the ancient glories of Persia restored. In a celebrated trial, he was condemned, and in 226/841 died in prison. Māzyār confessed at Sāmarrā to involvement with the Afshīn and his plans, and was executed, his body being gibbeted with Bābak's (225/840).

'Abd-Allāh b. Ṭāhir died at Nīshāpūr in 230/end of 844. Ya'qūbī's epitaph on him is that "he had ruled Khurāsān as no-one had ever done before, so that all the lands were subject to him, and his orders were universally acknowledged".[1] According to Ṣūlī and Shābushtī, who cite Aḥmad b. Abī Du'ād, chief qāḍī under al-Mu'taṣim and al-Wāthiq, the caliph at first appointed to Khurāsān a Ṭāhirid from a collateral branch, Isḥāq b. Ibrāhīm b. Muṣ'ab; presumably al-Wāthiq was reluctant to encourage direct hereditary succession of the line of Ṭāhir b. al-Ḥusain. Nevertheless, he then cancelled Isḥāq's nomination and confirmed 'Abd-Allāh's son Ṭāhir, an appointment subsequently confirmed by al-Mutawakkil, al-Muntaṣir and al-Musta'īn. Ṭāhir b. 'Abd-Allāh's just rule and personal virtues are praised by the historians in the same glowing terms as those employed about his father, and Ya'qūbī again says that "he governed Khurāsān in an upright manner (*waliyahā mustaqīm al-amr*)".[2] The historians have, however, little specific to say about events in Khurāsān during his governorship (230–48/845–62); yet we know that political and social disturbances, of the kind exemplified in the rebellions of Bābak and Ḥamza al-Khārijī, continued in outlying parts of Iran. In 231/845–6 the caliphal general Waṣīf had to march into Jibāl and Fārs to suppress unrest amongst the local Kurds, and a year later, a Ṭāhirid, Muḥammad b. Ibrāhīm b. al-Ḥusain b. Muṣ'ab, was appointed governor of Fārs. In Āzarbāījān, there was a rebellion at Marand to the north of Lake Urmīya by a former official, Muḥammad b. al-Ba'īth, which had to be suppressed by al-Mutawakkil's general Bughā the Younger (234–5/848–50). It was also during Ṭāhir's governorship that direct Ṭāhirid control over Sīstān, an administrative dependency of Khurāsān, was lost, for in 239/854 the *'ayyār* leader Ṣāliḥ b. al-Naḍr of Bust assumed power in the capital Zarang, driving out the Ṭāhirid governor and paving the way for the Ṣaffārids' eventual triumph there.

Other members of the Ṭāhirid family continued to hold official posts in Iraq and the central lands of the caliphate. However, the basic stability obtaining in Khurāsān under 'Abd-Allāh and his son Ṭāhir was lacking in the west, and these Ṭāhirids of the west shared in some of the vicissitudes and tribulations of the 'Abbāsids. In 236/850–1 there occurred a sordid sequence of intrigues amongst these Ṭāhirids. Muḥammad b. Ibrāhīm b. al-Ḥusain b. Muṣ'ab, governor of Fārs, opposed the appointment of his nephew Muḥammad b. Isḥāq b. Ibrāhīm to the governorship of Baghdad, an office to which Muḥam-

[1] Ya'qūbī, *Ta'rīkh*, vol. II, p. 586.
[2] Ya'qūbī, *Kitāb al-buldān*, p. 307; tr. p. 138.

mad b. Isḥāq further added responsibility for Baḥrain, the Yamāma, the road across Arabia to Mecca and Medina, and Fārs itself. Muḥammad b. Isḥāq therefore ordered the deposition of his uncle from Fārs and his replacement by al-Ḥusain b. Ismā'īl b. Ibrāhīm, who murdered Muḥammad b. Ibrāhīm and succeeded to his governorship. The outcome of these internecine quarrels was that in 237/851 Muḥammad b. 'Abd-Allāh b. Ṭāhir came from K͟hurāsān to take over the *s͟hurṭa* and governorship of Baghdad and also the governorships of the Sawād and of Fārs, exercising these functions in the west till his death in 253/867. According to S͟hābus͟htī, he further acted as *ḥājib* or chamberlain to the caliphs, and in 251/865 organized the unsuccessful defence of Baghdad for al-Musta'īn against the Turks supporting al-Mu'tazz.[1]

Ya'qūbī says that Ṭāhir's death in 248/862 was greeted by the caliph with relief, "for there was no-one more feared by al-Musta'īn's entourage than the governor of K͟hurāsān". The caliph invited Muḥammad b. 'Abd-Allāh b. Ṭāhir to transfer from Baghdad to K͟hurāsān, but he refused. So al-Musta'īn had to follow Ṭāhir's own *waṣiyya* or testamentary disposition and appoint his young son Muḥammad b. Ṭāhir to K͟hurāsān, Muḥammad b. 'Abd-Allāh being at the same time confirmed as governor of Iraq and the Holy Cities, ṣāḥib al-s͟hurṭa of Baghdad and controller of the finances of the Sawād.

Perhaps because of his final failure in K͟hurāsān and his loss of the province to the Ṣaffārids, Muḥammad b. Ṭāhir is viewed in the sources as a markedly inferior figure compared with his predecessors, and as a weak and neglectful voluptuary. He was unfortunate in that, soon after his assumption of power, the Caspian provinces broke out in a general revolt so serious and lasting in its effects that outside control could never be fully re-imposed there. This Zaidī S͟hī'ī revolutionary movement in Ṭabaristān is, in fact, an early manifestation of the rise of hitherto submerged northern Iranian elements, above all of the Dailamites which was to characterize the 4th/10th and early 5th/11th centuries.

The middle decades of the 3rd/9th century also witnessed widespread activity by various 'Alid claimants, who seized their opportunity as the 'Abbāsid caliphate became paralysed at the centre with uprisings and military coups. In 250/864 there occurred the revolt of Yaḥyā b. 'Umar in the region of Kūfa in Iraq, which was suppressed by Muḥammad b. 'Abd-Allāh b. Ṭāhir's forces. A much more serious threat was posed by the movement of al-Ḥasan b. Zaid in Ṭabaristān. Maladministration

[1] Ya'qūbī, *Ta'rīk͟h*, vol. II, pp. 596, 602, 608–9; Ṭabarī, vol. III, p. 1410.

by members of the Ṭāhirid family and their officials contributed much to popular exasperation there, leading in the end to revolt. ʻIrāq ʻAjamī or western Persia, including the Caspian provinces, came under Muḥammad b. ʻAbd-Allāh, who had appointed his brother Sulaimān as his deputy in Ṭabaristān and Gurgān. Sulaimān's officials, and especially one Muḥammad b. Aus al-Balkhī, behaved oppressively. Particularly resented were the actions of a Christian official of the Ṭāhirids on some caliphal estates at Chālūs and Kalār, on the borders of Ṭabaristān and Dailam, which had been granted to a certain Muḥammad b. ʻAbd-Allāh. This agent had confiscated *mawāt* "dead" lands (i.e. uncultivated ones) formerly used by the local people as common pasture. There followed a rising of the people of Ṭabaristān and Rūyān, headed by two "sons of Rustam", and aided by the Dailamites of the mountains to the west. The ʻAlid al-Ḥasan b. Zaid, called *al-Dāʻī al-Kabīr* "the great summoner to the true faith", then came from Ray. He was generally recognized as amīr of Ṭabaristān; Sulaimān b. ʻAbd-Allāh and the Ṭāhirid tax-collectors were expelled to Gurgān, and for a time, the insurgents even held Ray. Sulaimān's ignominious defeat did not prevent his nomination to the governorship of Baghdad and the Sawād in 255/869, two years after his brother Muḥammad had died in these offices; it did, however, bring down on his head the satires of the poet Ibn al-Rūmī.

Al-Ḥasan b. Zaid was checked in Ṭabaristān, but withdrew westwards into Dailam, where he energetically spread the Shīʻī form of Islam in regions hitherto pagan, and achieved the reputation of a wise and just ruler. In 251/865 there was a further ʻAlid rising against the Ṭāhirid officials in Qazvīn and Zanjān led by al-Ḥusain b. Aḥmad al-Kaukabī, aided by the Justānid ruler of Dailam. Two years later, al-Kaukabī was driven back into Dailam by Mūsā b. Bughā, but al-Ḥasan b. Zaid maintained his position in the Caspian region, and in 259/873 crossed the Alburz Mountains and occupied the province of Qūmis. He continued to rule in Ṭabaristān till his death in 270/884, and his equitable rule there was praised by impartial historians.

The history of Muḥammad b. Ṭāhir's governorship in Khurāsān now merges into that of the first Ṣaffārid, Yaʻqūb b. al-Laith, who gradually extended his power from Sīstān, expelling the Ṭāhirid governors from the towns of eastern Khurāsān, and finally in 259/873 occupying Nīshāpūr and deposing Muḥammad b. Ṭāhir; these events will be treated in more detail below.

Muḥammad b. Ṭāhir's failure marks the end of fifty years' Ṭāhirid control over Khurāsān, although his brother al-Ḥusain held out in Marv for some time longer, and various military commanders hostile to the Ṣaffārids campaigned under the banners of legitimacy and restoration of the Ṭāhirids. Muḥammad b. Ṭāhir was later re-appointed by the caliph al-Mu'tamid to Khurāsān, but never dared to show himself there. He became governor of Baghdad in 270/883–4, and did not die until 297/910 or possibly the next year. His uncle 'Ubaid-Allāh b. 'Abd-Allāh b. Ṭāhir held the governorship and shurṭa of Baghdad on various occasions under al-Mu'tazz and al-Mu'tamid, including after the death of Muḥammad b. Ṭāhir. During the reign of al-Mu'taḍid he fell into a certain amount of hardship, in which he was helped financially by the caliph, and died in 300/913. 'Ubaid-Allāh seems to have been on bad terms with his brother Sulaimān and nephew Muḥammad, and this hostility presumably explains why 'Ubaid-Allāh acted as representative in Iraq for the Ṣaffārids Ya'qūb and 'Amr b. al-Laith during those periods when they were able to exert influence there. The Ṭāhirid family by no means disappeared in the 4th/10th century, even though it no longer exercised any political power. Tha'ālibī mentions one Abu'l-Ṭayyib al-Ṭāhirī, who in the second half of the century lived on revenues from former Ṭāhirid estates granted to him by the Sāmānids, but never ceased to hate the Sāmānids as supplanters of his own family.

The Ṭāhirids thus had fifty years of unbroken rule in Khurāsān, but it is dubious whether one should speak of them as a separate dynasty there. The governorship of Khurāsān was only one of several offices, albeit the most important one, which they held simultaneously, and certain of these offices they continued to hold after the loss of Khurāsān to the Ṣaffārids. The coins of the Ṭāhirids are little different from those of other 'Abbāsid governors. With the exceptions noted above in the case of Ṭāhir b. al-Ḥusain, the caliph's name is always acknowledged, and indeed, coins were minted in many places definitely under Ṭāhirid control which do not mention the Ṭāhirids at all. The evidence seems to show that the Ṭāhirids were retained in Khurāsān because the caliphate in Iraq was increasingly unstable and its direct authority over outlying provinces was shrinking; the Ṭāhirids gave firm government to a large part of Persia, respected the constitutional rights of the caliphate and gave as little trouble as could be expected.

Culturally, the Ṭāhirids shared to the full in the Arab-Islamic civilization of their time. They acted as patrons to many of the great figures of contemporary Arabic literature and music, such as 'Alī b. Jahm, Isḥāq al-Mauṣilī and Ibn al-Rūmī. The poet and author Abu'l-'Amaithal al-A'rābī served both Ṭāhir b. al-Ḥusain and then 'Abd-Allāh, becoming tutor to the latter's son. Almost all the major figures in the Ṭāhirid family achieved some fame as scholars or poets themselves, from Ṭāhir b. al-Ḥusain onwards. Ṭāhir's epistle to al-Ma'mūn on the capture of Baghdad and his moralising charge to his son 'Abd-Allāh on his taking over the governorship at Raqqa became especially famed; al-Ma'mūn ordered copies of the latter to be sent to all his other governors.[1] According to the *Kitāb al-aghānī*, both 'Abd-Allāh and his son 'Ubaid-Allāh composed numerous melodies to which poetry could be sung, but did not like their names to be connected with the unstatesman-like business of composing, so they let them be attributed to their slavegirls. Moreover, 'Abd-Allāh, together with Ibrāhīm b. al-Mahdī, held contests in singing at his court. The *Fihrist* of Ibn al-Nadīm even has a special section devoted to the Ṭāhirids as scholars and littérateurs. 'Abd-Allāh's nephew Manṣūr b. Ṭalḥa, governor in northern Khurāsān and Khwārazm, wrote books on philosophy, music, astronomy and mathematics, and was known as "the wisdom of the Ṭāhirids". 'Ubaid-Allāh b. 'Abd-Allāh is described in the *Kitāb al-aghānī* as "pre-eminent in literature and all its varied aspects, in the transmission and reciting of poetry, in grammar, and in knowledge of the ancient philosophers and authorities on music, geometry, etc., to an extent which is too wide for adequate description and too lengthy to be enumerated". 'Ubaid-Allāh further wrote a history of the poets and a treatise on government, and his epistles to Ibn al-Mu'tazz and his *dīvān* of poetry were collected together.

The Ṭāhirids' attitude towards Persian culture is more difficult to evaluate. 'Aufī and Daulatshāh, both writing several centuries later, allege that they were hostile to Persian lore and literature. Daulatshāh says that 'Abd-Allāh b. Ṭāhir once ordered a copy of the Persian romance of *Vāmiq-u 'Adhrā'* to be destroyed, and all other Persian and Zoroastrian books in his territories to be burnt. This is almost certainly untrue. It is unlikely that the Persian literature appearing in eastern Iran under the first Ṣaffārids did not have precursors in the Ṭāhirid period, and indeed, al-Ma'mūn is said to have been greeted by an ode in Persian when he first entered Marv.

Because of their opulent and aristocratic way of life and their concern

[1] Text of the epistle in Ibn Ṭaifūr, pp. 26–34; Ṭabarī, vol. III, pp. 1046–61.

for the maintenance of the orthodox status quo, the Ṭāhirids are treated with warm approval by later historical sources, and anecdotes illustrating their benevolent and just rule abound in *adab* literature and works of the "Mirrors for princes" genre. Their rule in Khurāsān is rightly characterized by Barthold as one of enlightened absolutism, in which they endeavoured to provide stable rule after the period of social-political and religious upheavals in Persia consequent on the 'Abbāsid revolution. According to the great Saljuq vizier Niẓām al-Mulk, 'Abd-Allāh b. Ṭāhir was always careful to choose honest and pious men as his *'āmils* or tax-collectors; his tomb at Nīshāpūr became a pilgrimage-place, still frequented in the author's own time over two centuries later.[1] He was especially concerned for the restoration of agriculture and the preservation of the peasants from undue exploitation. On hearing of the frequent disputes over water rights and the upkeep of *qanāts* or subterranean irrigation channels, 'Abd-Allāh commissioned scholars from Khurāsān and Iraq to compose an authoritative book on the law and practice regarding water rights; this *Kitāb al-qunīy* was still used in Khurāsān in Ghaznavid times. Ṭāhirid activities for the pacification of the Persian countryside were in large measure directed against such sectarian movements as the Khārijites in Sīstān and the Shī'is in the Caspian provinces, so that the family came to be regarded as the upholders *par excellence* of the Sunna and moral authority of the caliphs. There are nevertheless certain references in the sources imputing Shī'ī sympathies to some of the Ṭāhirids. Thus Sulaimān b. 'Abd-Allāh b. Ṭāhir is alleged to have campaigned in Ṭabaristān against al-Ḥasan b. Zaid's partisans in a lukewarm fashion only, because of his family's 'Alid sympathies. Although this was a period when Shī'ism had not yet crystallized into a dogmatically rigid movement, and it was still possible for good Sunnīs to have an emotional sympathy for the house of 'Alī, these imputations do not seem to have had any firm basis; pro-Shī'ī poets like Di'bil b. 'Alī satirized the Ṭāhirids, and Ṭāhir b. al-Ḥusain rejoiced when al-Ma'mūn and his entourage reached Baghdad in 204/819 and consented, at Ṭāhir's own request, to restore the 'Abbāsid official colour of black (it had been green in the period of attempted rapprochement with the Shī'īs, when the Imām 'Alī al-Riḍā had been proclaimed heir to the caliphate).

The first Ṣaffārids have a significance in the history of the caliphate

[1] Niẓām al-Mulk, p. 63.

disproportionate to the duration of their power, for the period of their florescence hardly extended beyond fifty years. The Ṣaffārids persisted long after this, showing great tenacity, but were rarely a force outside their native Sīstān. The main significance of the early Ṣaffārids is that by establishing a vast but transient military empire in the Islamic east, an empire which stretched from Bāmiyān and Kābul in the east to Ahvāz and Iṣfahān in the west, they made the first great breach in the territorial integrity of the ʿAbbāsid caliphate. The Ṭāhirids arose from the military and official entourage of the caliphs; as governors, they were congenial to the ʿAbbāsids and to the orthodox religious institution. Yaʿqūb b. al-Laith, on the other hand, achieved power in Sīstān with no advantages of birth or official connections. In the parts of eastern and southern Persia which he took over, there was no smooth transfer of power, but rather, the imposition of a régime of military occupation; accordingly, this régime only endured whilst the Ṣaffārid amīrs had the vigour to hold their territories against rivals. When the caliphs confirmed the conquests of Yaʿqūb and ʿAmr – the act of confirmation being regarded from the point of view of constitutional theory as the bestowal of a governorship – this was done only grudgingly. Hence when rivals appeared who could be urged against the Ṣaffārids, such as Rāfiʿ b. Harthama al-Sayyārī or Ismāʿīl b. Aḥmad the Sāmānid, the grants to the Ṣaffārids were promptly withdrawn. It was, in fact, the Sāmānids of Transoxiana who in the end overthrew ʿAmr b. al-Laith, wrested Khurāsān from the Ṣaffārids and eventually extended their own suzerainty over ʿAmr's weaker successors.

It has not in the past been easy to form a balanced picture of the early Ṣaffārids and their achievements. The standard historical sources on the eastern Iranian world, Arabic and then from the 5th/11th century onwards, Persian also, are generally hostile to them. Most of these historians reflect the socially hierarchical and aristocratic atmosphere of the ʿAbbāsid caliphate and the empires of the Sāmānids, Ghaznavids and Saljuqs. They regard with contempt the plebeian origins of the Ṣaffārids, treat them as rebels against the legitimate authority of the caliphs, and on the whole view them as little better than brigands. The early Ṣaffārids seem personally to have had no strong religious feelings, though there is evidence that they were not unaware of the need to conciliate the orthodox religious classes. The historians nevertheless frequently accuse them of heterodoxy, above all, of Khārijite sympathies, for Khārijism persisted in Sīstān much longer than in most of the eastern Islamic world. That they held positive Khārijite beliefs is unlikely, although it is undeniable that Ya'qūb incorporated Khārijite troops into his armies, taking advantage of their fighting qualities. Niẓām al-Mulk, obsessed as he was by the threat to the fabric of the Saljuq empire from the extremist Shī'ī Assassins, even makes Ya'qūb a convert to Ismā'īlism. Only in a writer with Shī'ī sympathies like Mas'ūdī do we find a sympathetic appraisal of Ya'qūb's undoubted qualities as a military leader.

Fortunately, we have in recent decades acquired a vigorous corrective to the hostility of the orthodox Sunnī sources in the *Tārīkh-i Sīstān*, the essential part of which was compiled by an anonymous local author in the middle years of the 5th/11th century. He shows an intense local patriotism and regards the achievements of Ya'qūb and 'Amr with pride, for these leaders had made the peripheral and rather unimportant province of Sīstān for a while the centre of a vast empire, overthrowing the Ṭāhirids and humiliating the 'Abbāsid caliphs. The *Tārīkh-i Sīstān* deals with the Ṣaffārids during the first two centuries of their existence in such detail that it might well be regarded as a special history of that dynasty.

Caliphal control over Sīstān had become tenuous even before the rise of the Ṣaffārid brothers. When the Umayyad Viceroy al-Ḥajjāj b. Yūsuf and his generals cleared the Khārijite sectaries of the Azāriqa from Persia, many of these last fled eastwards into Kirmān, Sīstān and the adjacent regions. During the course of the 2nd/8th century, the savagery of the Azāriqa (who were one of the most extreme of the Khārijite sub-sects) moderated somewhat, although it by no means wholly died down. In the eastern Islamic world, it was only in Sīstān, Kūhistān and Bādghīs (the region around Herāt) that Khārijism retained its vitality, probably because it utilized the social and religious discontent endemic in the Persian countryside during the 2nd/8th and 3rd/9th centuries, the discontent which may also be traced in such outbreaks as those of al-Muqanna', Ustādhsīs and Bābak al-Khurramī. Certainly, the strength of Khārijism in Sīstān lay in rural areas; the large towns, such as the capital Zarang and Bust, were garrisoned by the troops of the caliphal governors and held fast to the official connection. The governors were perpetually harassed by peasant jacqueries and Khārijite outbreaks, movements of local protest against the exactions of the caliphal tax-collectors. These culminated in the great rebellion beginning in 179/795–6 or just after, led by Ḥamza b. Ādharak or 'Abd-Allāh. For thirty years, Ḥamza successfully defied the caliphs and their governors, claimed the title "Commander of the Faithful" for himself, and did not die till 213/828. After this, the khuṭba in Zarang was maintained for the 'Abbāsids, but no revenue was forwarded to Iraq. The Ṭāhirids appointed deputies to govern Sīstān and at times sent troops (one of the commanders employed there was Ilyās b. Asad of the Sāmānid family), but their inability to collect revenue was chronic; the Khārijites remained active in the countryside and the governor's writ rarely extended far beyond the walls of Zarang.

In this period of waning caliphal authority, the orthodox, legitimist elements in Sīstān were thrown back on their own resources. Hence there arose in the towns, above all in Zarang and Bust, bands of vigilantes to combat the Khārijites. These are sometimes called in the sources *muṭṭawwi'a* "volunteer fighters for the faith", but more often by the rather opprobrious term of *'ayyārūn* "ruffians, marauders", for the 'ayyārs were often as much a scourge to the orthodox and law-abiding as to the Khārijites.

Ya'qūb b. al-Laith first rose to prominence through joining one of these 'ayyār bands. He had been born in one of the villages of Sīstān and had worked at the humble trade of coppersmith (Arabic *ṣaffār*, whence the dynasty's name). He and his three brothers, 'Amr, Ṭāhir and 'Alī, had military ambitions. Ya'qūb joined the 'ayyār band of Ṣāliḥ b. al-Naḍr or al-Naṣr, who in 238/852 was recognized by the people of Bust as their Amīr. Ṣāliḥ aimed at taking over the whole of Sīstān, and in 239/854 drove out the Ṭāhirid governor, Ibrāhīm b. al-Ḥuḍain, from Zarang; with Ibrāhīm's expulsion, all direct caliphal control over Sīstān virtually ceased. The ancient rivalry of Bust and Zarang weakened Ṣāliḥ's position in the latter town, and in 244/858 he was replaced there as amīr by another 'ayyār leader, Dirham b. Naṣr. The part of Ya'qūb in these events is unclear, but he was obviously growing in power and reputation, for in 247/861 Ya'qūb himself overthrew Dirham and emerged as amīr of Sīstān.

Ya'qūb's first years as amīr were devoted to strengthening his position within the province. The dispossessed Ṣāliḥ retreated into al-Rukhkhaj or Arachosia, the region around Qandahār in south-eastern Afghanistan, and obtained help from the local ruler there, the Zunbīl. Not till the beginning of 251/865 was Ṣāliḥ captured and killed, the Zunbīl also being slain; two years later, a cousin of the Zunbīl, who had been made governor of al-Rukhkhaj for the Ṣaffārids, rebelled unsuccessfully against Ya'qūb. The pacification of the Sīstān countryside was obviously essential. At the time of Ya'qūb's accession, the leader of the Khārijite bands was 'Ammār b. Yāsir, but Ya'qūb managed in 251/865 to defeat and kill him at Nīshak in Sīstān, after which "The Khawārij all became broken in spirit and fled to the hills of Isfizār (modern Sabzavār, between Zarang and Herāt) and the lowlands of Hindqānān."[1] Ya'qūb's expedition against Herāt in 257/870–1 and his operations in Bādghīs were also the occasion for an attack on the Khārijites of that region. The town of Karūkh, to the north-east of Herāt, was one of their strongholds; over a century later, the geographer Muqaddasī describes them as still numerous there.[2] Karūkh had been for thirty years the headquarters of 'Abd al-Raḥmān or 'Abd al-Raḥīm, who claimed the title of "Caliph of the Khārijites" and the honorific of *al-Mutawakkil 'ala 'llāh*. He mustered 10,000 men, but was defeated and submitted to Ya'qūb. According to Ṭabarī, Ya'qūb killed 'Abd al-Raḥmān, but the more circumstantial account of the *Tārīkh-i Sīstān* says that he submitted and was made governor over Isfizār and the Kurds who nomadized in the surrounding steppes; only after this was he killed by a discontented group of Khārijites who then raised Ibrāhīm b. Akhḍar to be their leader.[3] Ya'qūb settled the whole affair in a manner which he had successfully adopted previously, by incorporating the Khārijite warriors into his own forces. In 248/862 one of Ya'qūb's commanders had won over 1,000 of the Sīstān Khārijites in this way: "Then Ya'qūb gave robes of honour to the Khārijite leaders and said, 'Those among you who are *sarhangs* I will promote to amīrs, those of you who are ordinary cavalry troopers I will promote to *sarhangs*, and those who are infantrymen will become cavalrymen. Moreover, whenever in future I see special ability in anyone, I shall give him particular promotion and honour.'" Similarly, Ibrāhim b. Akhḍar's followers were now incorporated into the Ṣaffārid army and assigned regular salaries from Ya'qūb's dīvān; they formed a special section known as the *jaish al-shurāt*.

One of the most important aspects of early Ṣaffārid policy, of significance for the spread of Islam in Afghanistan and on the borders of India long after their empire had collapsed, was that of expansion into eastern Afghanistan. The early Arab governors of Sīstān had at

[1] *Tārīkh-i Sīstān*, pp. 205–8.
[2] The name of the geographer probably should be read Maqdisī.
[3] Ṭabarī, vol. III, p. 1882; Gardīzī, p. 12.

times penetrated as far as Ghazna and Kabul, but these had been little more than slave and plunder raids. There was fierce resistance from the local rulers of these regions, above all from the line of Zunbīls who ruled in Zamīndāvar and Zābulistān and who were probably epigoni of the southern Hephthalite or Chionite kingdom of Zābul; on more than one occasion, these Zunbīls inflicted sharp defeats on the Muslims. The Zunbīls were linked with the Kabul-Shāhs of the Turk-Shāhī dynasty; the whole Kabul river valley was at this time culturally and religiously an outpost of the Indian world, as of course it had been in earlier centuries during the heyday of the Buddhist Gandhara civilization.

When he had finally disposed of Ṣāliḥ b. al-Naḍr, Ya'qūb had captured several members of the family of the Zunbīl, Ṣāliḥ's ally. In 255/869 the Zunbīl's son escaped from captivity in Bust and speedily raised an army in al-Rukhkhaj, an indication of his dynasty's popularity and deep roots there. He was forced to flee to the Kabul-Shāh, but Ya'qūb was unable to pursue him northwards because of the onset of winter. The Arabic sources refer to the Zunbīl – whether to the man whom Ya'qūb killed in 251/865 or to his son is unclear – not under this title or designation, but under what was apparently his personal name of Fīrūz b. Kabk (?). A raid on Zābulistān from Balkh in the north by Dā'ūd b. al-'Abbās, of the Abū Dā'ūdids of Khuttal, is mentioned in the middle years of the century, and Mas'ūdī speaks with wonder of the impregnability of Fīrūz b. Kabk's fortresses in Zābulistān. Ya'qūb made a further raid into eastern Afghanistan in 256/870, aiming at Kabul, where the Zunbīl's son had fled for refuge. He marched through Panjwāy and Tigīnābād in Zamīndāvar; captured Ghazna and destroyed its citadel; and levied a tribute of 10,000 dirhams per annum on the local ruler of Gardīz, Abū Manṣūr Aflaḥ. He turned northwards to Bāmiyān and then Balkh, where he destroyed the palace of Dā'ūd b. al-'Abbās, who had fled before him. These conquests in the Hindu Kush region gave Ya'qūb control of the Panjhīr river valley and the silver mines of the Andarāba district; the first Ṣaffārid coins extant were minted by Ya'qūb at Panjhīr between 259/873 and 261/875, but after this, possession of Panjhīr reverted to the Abū Dā'ūdids or Banījūrids. Kabul was also taken, and according to Gardīzī here "Fīrūz" (sc. the Zunbīl's son) was captured.

Ya'qūb's activities on these remote frontiers of the Islamic world were widely publicised in the heartlands of the caliphate because of the Ṣaffārids' care to send presents from their plunder to the 'Abbāsids.

Fifty gold and silver idols from Kabul were sent by Ya'qūb to al-Mu'tamid, who forwarded them to Mecca. 'Amr b. al-Laith led an expedition as far as Sakāwand in the Lōgar valley between Ghazna and Kabul, described as a pilgrimage-centre of the Hindus. In 283/896 a sensation was caused in Baghdad when there arrived presents of idols captured from Zamīndāvar and the Indian borders, including a copper idol in a woman's shape with four arms and two girdles of silver set with jewels, with smaller, bejewelled idols before it, the whole being mounted on a trolley suitable for pulling by camels. The next few decades in the history of this region are very dark, but it is symptomatic of the imperfect Muslim control there that in 286/899 or at the beginning of 287/900, during the absence of 'Amr b. al-Laith in Gurgān, two Indian princes attacked Ghazna and temporarily expelled the Ṣaffārid governor. Yet though the power of the local rulers in eastern Afghanistan was not yet entirely broken, Islam did achieve a break-through, and despite our lack of information about the period before the rise of the Ghaznavids, it is probable that the Islamization of the region proceeded apace.

Campaigns against the Khārijites and the infidels of eastern Afghanistan gave the Ṣaffārids prestige in the eyes of the orthodox, but Ya'qūb's ambitions were also fixed on the much richer settled lands of Persia. Here he was bound to clash with representatives of the established order: with the caliphal governors in southern Persia, where some semblance of direct control was still maintained, and with the Ṭāhirids in Khurāsān.

The historian Ya'qūbī says that Ya'qūb invaded the adjacent province of Kirmān soon after he became amīr of Sīstān, and was recognized as governor there by the governor of Khurāsān Muḥammad b. Ṭāhir at the Caliph al-Musta'īn's request (thus placing the event before the beginning of 252/866). This invasion may perhaps have been part of Ya'qūb's general operations against the Khārijites, who were also strong in Kirmān, and especially in the town of Bam. The report may, on the other hand, refer to the undoubted invasion of Kirmān which Ya'qūb undertook in 255/869, i.e. at the end of al-Mu'tazz's caliphate. According to the account in Ṭabarī, Kirmān was a dependency of the Ṭāhirids, but the caliphal governor in Fārs, 'Alī b. al-Ḥusain, sought to add it to his own territories, adducing the feebleness of the Ṭāhirids. Al-Mu'tazz craftily sent investiture patents to both 'Alī and Ya'qūb, hoping to involve these two powerful figures with each other. Ya'qūb defeated ʿAlī's general Ṭauq b. al-Mughallis and soon occupied Kirmān. ʿAlī organized resistance in his capital of Shīrāz, summoning help from the Kurds of Fārs and the mountaineers (Kūfīchīs) of the Jabal Bāriz region of Kirmān, but was defeated and captured by Yaʿqūb. The caliph, whose plan to neutralize the two leaders had misfired, was conciliated by rich presents from the captured plunder.

Caliphal *ʿummāl* or tax-collectors reappeared in Fārs when Yaʿqūb left for Sīstān, but Kirmān remained as a base for a future revanche. Yaʿqūb was in Makrān and Fārs in 257/871 and in Fārs again the next year. After 255/869, Fārs had fallen into the hands of the adventurer Muḥammad b. Wāṣil al-Ḥanẓalī, who had seized power from the caliphal governor. Fārs and Ahvāz were among the territories granted by the caliph al-Muʿtamid to his brother al-Muwaffaq in 257/871, and for a time, ʿAbbāsid authority was restored. But in 261/875 Muḥammad b. Wāṣil was again independent in Fārs, having killed the governor appointed by the Turkish general Mūsā b. Bughā al-Kabīr. So when in 261/875 Yaʿqūb resolved on a large-scale invasion of Fārs, he had a certain specious claim to be ridding the caliph of a rebel. He speedily captured Muḥammad b. Wāṣil's treasury at Iṣṭakhr and defeated him at al-Baiḍāʾ. Yaʿqūb's victories had now brought him to Rāmhurmuz and the borders of Ahvāz (262/875). The rich province of Fārs, upon which the ʿAbbāsids depended for a good proportion of their revenue, was securely in his hands. Further advance westwards would bring him into Iraq, and there was an obvious fear that Yaʿqūb might join forces with the Zanj rebels, the black slaves who had since 255/869 been tying down large ʿAbbāsid armies in lower Iraq and Ahvāz (in fact, Yaʿqūb seems to have rejected offers of an alliance from the Zanj leader ʿAlī b. Muḥammad). Thoroughly alarmed, al-Muʿtamid endeavoured to placate Yaʿqūb by the grant of Khurāsān, Ṭabaristān, Gurgān, Ray and Fārs, in addition to his existing provinces of Sīstān, Kirmān, Makrān and Sind. He was also to have the office of ṣāḥib al-shurṭa in Baghdad in place of the Ṭāhirids, and his name was to appear in the khuṭba in Mecca and Medina; these concessions were publicly proclaimed to the merchants of Baghdad and the pilgrims of Khurāsān by al-Muwaffaq. Yaʿqūb nevertheless continued his advance and occupied Wāsiṭ. Al-Muwaffaq now made a supreme effort, and halted and defeated Yaʿqūb at Dair al-ʿĀqūl on the Tigris, only fifty miles from Baghdad itself (262/876). This was Yaʿqūb's first major defeat, and it saved the capital from what had appeared to be certain capture.

Even so, Fārs remained firmly in Ṣaffārid hands, and between 263/876–7 and 264/877–8 Ahvāz was recovered. Muḥammad b. Wāṣil re-appeared in Fārs as the caliphal nominee for governor, but achieved no lasting success. Just before Ya'qūb's death at Jundishāpūr in 265/879, al-Mu'tamid recognized the strength of the Ṣaffārid hold on Fārs and sent Ya'qūb a diploma for its governorship. Henceforth, Fārs remained fairly continuously under the control of the Ṣaffārid amīrs or their military commanders down to the time of the fifth amīr, Muḥammad b. 'Alī b. al-Laith (298/910–11); a greater number of coins are extant from the Fārs mints of the Ṣaffārids than from the Sīstān or Khurāsān ones.

In 253/867 Ya'qūb marched to Herāt, drove out the Ṭāhirid governor there, Ḥusain b. 'Abd-Allāh b. Ṭāhir, and then defeated at Pūshang the Commander-in-Chief of the Ṭāhirids' army in Khurāsān, Ibrāhīm b. Ilyās Sāmānī. It was after this that operations were undertaken against the Khārijites of Bādghīs. Ya'qūb's attack on Herāt was a deliberate provocation of the Ṭāhirids, but Muḥammad b. Ṭāhir judged it prudent to bow to the obvious strength of the Ṣaffārids, and he invested Ya'qūb with the governorship under the Ṭāhirids of "Sīstān, Kabul, Kirmān and Fārs". With this legitimation of his authority, Ya'qūb had for the first time the khuṭba in Zarang made for himself. In 257/871 al-Muwaffaq sent Ya'qūb a diploma for Balkh and Tukhāristān. According to Gardīzī, this had been seized in the previous year during the course of the Kabul campaign; the Banījūrid Dā'ūd b. al-'Abbās was expelled to Transoxiana, and severe financial levies imposed on Balkh. However, Dā'ūd's successor Muḥammad was in 258/872 minting coins at Andarāba in Badakhshān, and Ṣaffārid dominion over Tukhāristān was obviously only short-lived.

It was increasingly apparent that Ṭāhirid power in Khurāsān was crumbling. On the western fringes, Ṭāhirid authority was threatened by the Zaidī Shī'ī movement in Ṭabaristān under al-Ḥasan b. Zaid. After his successes in Herāt, Fārs and eastern Afghanistan, Ya'qūb felt strong enough directly to provoke a war with the Ṭāhirid amīr. A pretext was found in the latter's sheltering at Nīshāpūr a fugitive from Ya'qūb's wrath, 'Abd-Allāh al-Sijzī or 'Abd-Allāh b. Muḥammad b. Ṣāliḥ. On hearing news of Ya'qūb's approach, he fled immediately to Dāmghān and the Caspian region, leaving Muḥammad b. Ṭāhir to his fate. In 259/873 Ya'qūb entered the capital of Khurāsān without striking a blow, and ended the fifty years' dominion there of the Ṭāhirids.

Muḥammad b. Ṭāhir scorned to flee, and he and several members of his family and entourage (amounting to seventy people, according to Gardīzī) were taken by Ya'qūb into honourable confinement. The *Tārīkh-i Sīstān* says that Muḥammad b. Ṭāhir later died in captivity in Zarang, but the reports in Ṭabarī, Gardīzī and other sources (including a later part of the *Tārīkh-i Sīstān* itself) about his later life, contain the real truth. According to these reports, Muḥammad b. Ṭāhir was taken along with Ya'qūb during the Fārs and Ahvāz expedition of 261/875, and managed to escape to Baghdad after the Ṣaffārid defeat at Dair al-'Āqūl. Al-Mu'tamid re-appointed him governor of Khurāsān after Ya'qūb's retreat from Iraq, but he never deemed it safe or prudent to leave Baghdad and take up the office. In Nīshāpūr, the local notables showed concern about the legitimacy of Ya'qūb's setting-aside of the Ṭāhirids. Ya'qūb is said to have assembled them before him and then to have shown them a naked Yemenī sword, the true symbol of his authority and a more potent one than a mere investiture document. Ya'qūb's prowess as a conqueror now made many of the 'ayyār leaders of Khurāsān rally to his side. The Ṭāhirid treasuries at Nīshāpūr produced a rich haul of money, clothing and weapons; from these, Ya'qūb fitted out 2,000 of his *ghulāms* with shields, swords and gold and silver maces.[1] After this, Ṭāhirid rule in Khurāsān was only upheld sporadically by Muḥammad's brother Ḥusain b. Ṭāhir, on one or two occasions in Nīshāpūr itself, more continuously in Marv; after 267/880–1, however, Ḥusain fades out of Khurāsānian affairs.

'Abd-Allāh al-Sijzī had meanwhile allied with the 'Alid ruler of Ṭabaristān, al-Ḥasan b. Zaid. Ya'qūb pursued him to the Caspian coastlands, and defeated both his opponents at Sārī, after which al-Ḥasan fled into the mountainous interior of Dailam (260/874). Ya'qūb now made harsh financial exactions in the towns of Sārī and Āmul. But the impenetrable jungle of the coastlands and the damp and febrile climate there, defeated the Ṣaffārid just as it had defeated earlier invaders. With his troops decimated by disease, Ya'qūb returned to Nīshāpūr in 261/874–5. 'Abd-Allāh was, according to the *Tārīkh-i Sīstān*, handed over to Ya'qūb by the "Marzbān of Ṭabaristān" (? one of the Bāvandids or Bāduspānids) and killed; according to Ṭabarī and other sources, he fled to Ray, but at Ya'qūb's demand was handed over by the local governor al-Ṣalānī or al-Ṣalābī, the appointee of Mūsā b. Bughā, and killed. Al-Ṣalānī died in 262/875–6, and for a while,

[1] *Tārīkh-i Sīstān*, pp. 222, 224–5.

Ṣaffārid authority was established in Ray, in accordance with the caliphal grant to Ya'qūb in that year; from 262/875–6 dates the sole known Ṣaffārid coin minted at Ray.

The overthrow of the Ṭāhirids in Khurāsān could hardly be ignored by the 'Abbāsids, for as virtually hereditary holders of the shurṭa and governorship of Baghdad, the Ṭāhirid family was very influential there. Ya'qūb had written to al-Mu'tamid announcing the imprisonment of Muḥammad b. Ṭāhir, and sending as a placatory measure the head of the Khārijite 'Abd al-Raḥmān (see above). In 261/874 the caliph assembled the pilgrims of Khurāsān and denounced Ya'qūb's annexation of Khurāsān as unlawful, although the advance of Ya'qūb to the borders of Iraq soon forced al-Mu'tamid to make an undignified volte-face. Whilst Ya'qūb was occupied by his campaigns in Ṭabaristān and southern Persia, a new factor had appeared in the politics of Khurāsān in the person of Aḥmad b. 'Abd-Allāh Khujistānī (from Khujistān, a district of Bādghīs). Khujistānī was a former soldier of the Ṭāhirids who rallied to Ya'qūb when the latter occupied Nīshāpūr. But when Ya'qūb returned to Sīstān after the Ṭabaristān expedition, Khujistānī saw a chance to further his own ambitions. He expelled from Nīshāpūr Ya'qūb's governor Uzair b. al-Sarī and made the khuṭba for the Ṭāhirids (beginning of 262/end of 875). He then marched to attack Herāt, where Ya'qūb had left his brother 'Amr as governor, but in his absence, Nīshāpūr was seized by the ghulām Abū Ṭalḥa Manṣūr b. Sharkab, who, however, kept the khuṭba for Muḥammad b. Ṭāhir (after Ya'qūb's reverse at Dair al-'Āqūl, Muḥammad had once more become titular governor of Khurāsān). Khujistānī reconquered Nīshāpūr, apparently in 265/878–9, defeating Abū Ṭalḥa and his ally, the 'Alid al-Ḥasan b. Zaid.

At this point, 'Amr b. al-Laith succeeded his brother Ya'qūb as amīr. It seems that another brother, 'Alī, was at first the favoured candidate of both Ya'qūb and the army, but 'Amr's craft and ruthlessness secured him the throne. 'Alī was never reconciled to his supersession; 'Amr placed him in captivity, but soon afterwards, he was in treacherous communication with 'Amr's enemy Khujistānī and eventually defected to another opponent, Rāfi' b. Harthama. 'Amr himself is said to have started life as a mule-hirer or stonemason; he had been associated with Ya'qūb in many of his campaigns and in 261/875 had been made governor of Herāt. 'Amr expressed his obedience to the caliph, and was given robes of honour and an investiture patent for Khurāsān,

Fārs, Iṣfahān, Sīstān, Kirmān and Sind (and according to the *Tārīkh-i Sīstān*, for Gurgān and Ṭabaristān as well), in return for tribute of one million dirhams. This legitimation proved a considerable help in the struggle against Khujistānī in Khurāsān, for the *ghāzīs* and religious classes in Khurāsān now gave their support to ʿAmr. He was able to appoint as his representative for the shurṭa of Baghdad ʿUbaid-Allāh b. ʿAbd-Allāh b. Ṭāhir (who was, as we have seen above, on bad terms with other members of his family), and as his representative in Mecca, Muḥammad b. Abi ʾl-Sāj (266/879).

The re-establishment of Ṣaffārid control in Khurāsān was to be a lengthy process. During his last years, Yaʿqūb had been pre-occupied with events in southern Persia and Iraq, and various rivals had appeared in the east. Herāt had fallen into the hands of Abū Ṭalḥa's brother Yaʿmar and then into those of Khujistānī. The latter had himself been campaigning in the Caspian provinces against al-Ḥasan b. Zaid, and now he decisively repelled ʿAmr from Nīshāpūr. ʿAmr had to take refuge in Herāt, whilst Khujistānī went on to invade Sīstān, unsuccessfully besieging Zarang (266–7/880). In Khujistānī's absence, a pro-Ṣaffārid rising took place in Nīshāpūr, led by the ʿayyārs, but Khujistānī returned from Sīstān and restored his authority. ʿAmr acquired, as his ally against Khujistānī, Abū Ṭalḥa, who was at that time in Tukhāristān; but Abū Ṭalḥa could not achieve any significant success. ʿAmr's influence with the caliph secured for a while the imprisonment in Baghdad of Muḥammad b. Ṭāhir, on the plea that the latter had been urging Khujistānī against him. ʿAmr's prestige was high even in distant Mecca. During the Pilgrimage rites of 267/881, ʿAmr's representative was involved in a dispute over precedence with the lieutenant of Aḥmad b. Ṭūlūn, governor of Egypt; in the end, the Ṣaffārid interest prevailed, and ʿAmr's banner was hung from the right-hand side of the Prophet's *minbar* or pulpit.

Until now, Khujistānī had been the nominal vassal of the Ṭāhirids, but during 267/880–1 he ceased mentioning them in the khuṭba at Nīshāpūr, and made it for the caliph and himself only. He also assumed another of the prerogatives of independent sovereignty and minted his own dirhams and *dīnārs*; dirhams of his from Nīshāpūr and Herāt are extant for the years 267/880–1 and 268/881–2. Khujistānī occupied Tukhāristān and Herāt in the first of these two years, but towards the end of 268/882 was killed by one of his own ghulāms. Abū Ṭalḥa took over Nīshāpūr, and for a while, he and ʿAmr were recognized as masters of all Khurāsān, their names appearing jointly on a Nīshāpūr coin of 269/882–3. Ṣaffārid coins were also minted at Iṣfahān in this year. Iṣfahān had been governed by the Abū Dulaf family, and when in 265/879 the town was granted to 'Amr, he retained the Abū Dulafid Aḥmad b. 'Abd al-'Azīz there as his governor; the names of both Aḥmad and his suzerain appear on this dirham of 269/882–3.

One impediment to the establishment of Ṣaffārid authority in Khurāsān had gone with Khujistānī's death, but a further threat arose from Rāfi' b. Harthama, a former partisan of the Ṭāhirids who had become Khujistānī's Commander-in-Chief. Khujistānī's leaderless army acknowledged Rāfi' at Herāt as its leader. Rāfi' restored the Ṭāhirid khuṭba in both Herāt and Nīshāpūr, and raided towards Sīstān as far as Farah. Abū Ṭalḥa was at this point the independent ruler of Marv, and a complex, three-cornered struggle between 'Amr, Abū Ṭalḥa and Rāfi' now followed. During these struggles, Abū Ṭalḥa fled to Sāmānid Transoxiana; he obtained help from Amīr Naṣr's brother Ismā'īl b. Aḥmad, and in 271/885 recaptured Marv. At the end of this year, Abū Ṭalḥa and 'Amr were reconciled, and 'Amr appointed him deputy governor of Khurāsān for his own son Muḥammad b. 'Amr. 'Amr and Muḥammad then left for Fārs in 272/885.

Seizing the opportunity of 'Amr's difficulties in Khurāsān, al-Muwaffaq had in 271/885 assembled the Khurāsānian pilgrims and ordered the public cursing of 'Amr. Muḥammad b. Ṭāhir was re-invested with Khurāsān, and he forthwith made Rāfi' b. Harthama his deputy there. Rāfi''s power grew rapidly. With the help of Sāmānid troops and the commander 'Alī b. Ḥusain Marvarrūdhī, he drove Abū Ṭalḥa from Marv and the latter's deputy from Herāt (272/885–6). In this same year he also raided Khwārazm and returned to Nīshāpūr with rich booty. In 275/888–9 he attacked Gurgān and Ṭabaristān and defeated at Chālūs the 'Alid Muḥammad b. Zaid; and in the following year he went to Qazvīn and then Ray, where he remained till al-Muwaffaq's death in 278/891. It was whilst Rāfi' was in Ṭabaristān that he was joined by 'Alī b. al-Laith, who had fled from Kirmān, where his brother had been holding him captive.

Al-Muwaffaq's enforced concentration on the Zanj revolt in Lower Iraq had meant that 'Amr's grip on Fārs had remained generally firm, leaving him fairly free to deal with the more dangerous situation in Khurāsān. Two campaigns in Fārs by 'Amr are recorded from the early years of his reign, in 266/879–80 and in 268/881. The latter one was to suppress the revolt of the governor there, Muḥammad b. al-Laith (his own son Muḥammad b. 'Amr b. al-Laith?); Muḥammad was captured and his headquarters at Iṣṭakhr plundered. 'Amr used the prestige of his victory to exact 300,000 dirhams' tribute from the Abū Dulafid governor of Iṣfahān, Aḥmad b. 'Abd al-'Azīz, and this money, together with rich presents, was sent to al-Muwaffaq. He also sent a successful expedition to Rāmhurmuz against a Kurdish chief of Fārs, Muḥammad b. 'Ubaid-Allāh b. Āzādmard, a former adherent of Ya'qūb b. al-Laith's, who was suspected of aiding the Zanj rebels. Al-Muwaffaq now gave 'Amr a fresh diploma for his territories, and 'Amr in return sent four million dirhams' tribute to Baghdad (270/883).

But in this year, the Zanj were finally mastered. Also, Rāfi' b. Harthama's star was in the ascendant in Khurāsān, with corresponding difficulties for the Ṣaffārids. As noted above, al-Muwaffaq accordingly dismissed 'Amr from his governorships, and took steps to wrest Fārs from him. In 271/884–5 Aḥmad b. 'Abd al-'Azīz was invested with Fārs and Kirmān. Al-Muwaffaq's vizier, Dhu'l-Wizāratain Ṣā'id b. Makhlad, was sent from Wāsiṭ into Fārs, and a general onslaught was made on the Ṣaffārid position there. Initial reverses forced 'Amr and his son Muḥammad to hurry to Fārs at the beginning of 272/summer 885. The caliphal general Tark b. al-'Abbās was defeated, but in 273/886 Aḥmad b. 'Abd al-'Azīz inflicted a severe defeat on 'Amr; 'Amr withdrew to Sīrjān on the borders of Kirmān, and Fārs passed into the control of al-Mu'taḍid, al-Muwaffaq's son and the future caliph. 'Amr invaded Fārs once more, and in 274/887 al-Muwaffaq came personally with an army. 'Amr was again pushed back into Kirmān; in the course of these operations, 'Amr's ally Abū Ṭalḥa, who had come from Khurāsān, changed sides, and 'Amr's son Muḥammad died. However, al-Muwaffaq did not dare to pursue 'Amr across the desert separating Kirmān from Sīstān.

Threats to the position of the caliphate in Syria and al-Jazīra, where both the Ṭūlūnid Khumārawaih and the Byzantines were active, inclined al-Muwaffaq towards peace. In 275/888–9 'Amr's governorships in Khurāsān, Fārs and Kirmān were restored in return for ten million dirhams' tribute; his name was inscribed on the banners, lances and shields; and his agent 'Ubaid-Allāh b. 'Abd-Allāh b. Ṭāhir was reappointed to the shurṭa in Baghdad. 'Amr's officials came back to take over the administration of Fārs. Yet in the next year, al-Muwaffaq rescinded these grants, and Aḥmad b. 'Abd al-'Azīz was once more commanded to invade Fārs. ʻAmr retaliated by omitting al-Muwaffaq's name from the khuṭba; he defeated Aḥmad and advanced into Ahvāz. Negotiations were opened up with the vizier Ismāʻīl b. Bulbul, and peace was made; the series of coins minted by ʻAmr in Fārs during these years shows that he remained fairly continuously in possession of Fārs down to al-Muʻtaḍid's accession in 279/892.

The last decade of the ninth century saw ʻAmr at the zenith of his power. Rāfiʻ b. Harthama remained a major threat in Khurāsān. In 273/886 Rāfiʻ was in Transoxiana aiding Ismāʻīl b. Aḥmad against the Sāmānid amīr Naṣr, and in 276/889 he established himself at Ray. When al-Muʻtaḍid came to the throne, he endeavoured to remove the threat to Jibāl implicit in Rāfiʻ's commanding position at Ray. He invested ʻAmr with Khurāsān, and the standard sent from Baghdad was publicly exhibited at Nīshāpūr for three days as a visible sign of caliphal favour. Al-Muʻtaḍid demanded of Rāfiʻ that he should evacuate Ray, and commissioned Aḥmad b. ʻAbd al-ʻAzīz to expel him. Rāfiʻ fled to Gurgān, but returned to Ray and decided to make peace with Aḥmad and concentrate on the reconquest of Khurāsān. He conciliated Muḥammad b. Zaid, and was promised a contingent of Dailamī warriors. In Ṭabaristān and Gurgān, he had the khuṭba made for the ʻAlids. This public renunciation of allegiance to the ʻAbbāsids gave ʻAmr a moral advantage in that he could rally the support of the orthodox and the religious classes in Khurāsān against Rāfiʻ. It was at this time (283/896) that ʻAmr sent to Baghdad four million dirhams and the munificent array of presents captured by him in eastern Afghanistan. Rafiʻ invaded Khurāsān, among his commanders being Muʻaddal and Laith, the two sons of ʻAmr's brother ʻAlī. At one point, whilst ʻAmr was at Sarakhs, Rāfiʻ occupied Nīshāpūr, making the khuṭba there for the ʻAlids and adopting the white colours of the ʻAlids instead of the ʻAbbāsid black. He also accused al-Muʻtaḍid of having hastened the end of his feeble-minded uncle, al-Muʻtamid, in order to secure power for himself. Unfortunately for Rāfiʻ, the help promised by Muḥammad b. Zaid never materialized. He was expelled from Nīshāpūr, defeated at Baihaq and Ṭūs and finally killed in Khwārazm (283/896). ʻAmr sent the rebel's head to Baghdad, and with Khurāsān cleared of all opposition, his prestige had never stood higher; in 284/897 the caliph invested him with Ray, in addition to his existing territories. It may be noted that it was probably during these latter years of ʻAmr's reign that Ṣaffārid authority was recognized on the other shore of the Persian Gulf in ʿUmān. This is unmentioned in the literary sources, but a coin from here, dated 295/907–8 and bearing the name of ʿAmr's successor Ṭāhir, is extant; it seems likely to have been ʿAmr rather than the weaker Ṭāhir who established his suzerainty there.

ʿAmr's downfall was now brought about by pride. He aspired to follow his Ṭāhirid predecessor in extending his overlordship beyond the Oxus. At Nīshāpūr he received the homage of one Muḥammad b. ʿAmr al-Khwārazmī, and sent him back to Khwārazm with military support as a Ṣaffārid protégé. This was a provocation of the Sāmānids of Transoxiana, who claimed to exercise suzerainty over the Afrīghid Khwārazm-Shāhs. It was obviously to the astute al-Muʿtaḍid's advantage to widen the breach between the Ṣaffārids and Sāmānids. According to the account of the *Tārīkh-i Sīstān*, ʿAmr's interference in Khwārazmian affairs led to fighting with Ismāʿīl b. Aḥmad, in which the Ṣaffārids were worsted; in his anger, ʿAmr wrote to the caliph seeking the grant of Transoxiana and promising to subdue the ʿAlids of the Caspian region. This seems, however, to be an inversion of the true order of events. In 285/898 al-Muʿtaḍid sent ʿAmr rich gifts and a diploma for Transoxiana and Balkh, and a decree deposing Ismāʿīl was read out in Baghdad to the Khurāsānian pilgrims. ʿAmr marched northwards to take possession of his newly-granted territories, not only from the Sāmānids but also from the petty rulers of Tukhāristān and Jūzjān, the Abū Dāʾūdids and Farīghūnids. There was considerable fighting south of the Oxus, in which first ʿAmr's general Muḥammad b. Bishr was killed and then in 287/900 ʿAmr himself was defeated near Balkh. ʿAmr was captured and eventually sent to al-Muʿtaḍid, who had him killed in 289/902. According to the *Tārīkh-i Sīstān*, Ismāʿīl was at first willing to ransom ʿAmr, but ʿAmr's successors in the Ṣaffārid amīrate, his grandsons Ṭāhir and Yaʿqūb b. Muḥammad b. ʿAmr, would not do so. The caliph was overjoyed at Ismāʿīl's victory, even though it was technically an act of opposition to his previous proclamation deposing Ismāʿīl, and he now invested the Sāmānid amīr with all ʿAmr's eastern possessions.

With ʿAmr's capture, the dynamic of the Ṣaffārid empire, which had dominated the eastern Islamic world for forty years, slackened, and its territories shrank. The Sāmānids took over Khurāsān, and were to hold it for a century until the coming of the Ghaznavids. Fārs was vulnerable to caliphal attacks, and al-Muʿtaḍid was in 289/902 succeeded by his equally-energetic son al-Muktafī. Even so, Fārs and Kirmān were generally retained by the Ṣaffārids or their nominal servant Sebük-eri (Subkarī), and coins of Ṣaffārid type were minted there, down to the definitive assertion of ʿAbbāsid authority in Fārs in 298/911. Also, the heartland of Sīstān itself was defended for a decade until the Sāmānids appeared there.

ʿAmr's successor, Ṭāhir, had been governor of Marv during his grandfather's lifetime, the names of ʿAmr and himself appearing on coins minted there. He was raised to the amīrate in Sīstān by the Ṣaffārid generals, and ruled in close conjunction with his brother Yaʿqūb, but there was also a faction in favour of Laith b. ʿAlī b. Laith, partly because his father ʿAlī had, in fact, been Yaʿqūb b. al-Laith's intended successor. Compared with his predecessors, Ṭāhir emerges from the sources as a weak and frivolous ruler, addicted to hunting and luxurious living. During his reign (287–96/900–909) much of the thirty-six million dirhams which he took over from ʿAmr's treasury at Zarang was expended on palaces and gardens. Whilst this money lasted, taxes went uncollected, income decreased and by 293/906 the treasury was completely empty. Also, the capital Zarang was at this time rent by social-religious factional strife, the two sides corresponding roughly to the adherents of the Ḥanafī and Shāfiʿī law-schools respectively; this division persisted down to the Ghaznavid occupation a century later. The real powers behind Ṭāhir's throne were his uncle Laith b. ʿAlī, the slave commander Sebük-eri (who had been captured during a Ṣaffārid raid into Zābulistān and was one of ʿAmr's freedmen) and the latter's co-adjutor ʿAbd-Allāh b. Muḥammad, of the old Nīshāpūr family of Mīkālīs.

In 288/901 Ṭāhir drove out the caliphal officials from Fārs and established his authority there, but a threatened invasion of Sīstān by Ismāʿīl b. Aḥmad, whose grant from al-Muʿtaḍid of ʿAmr's former eastern territories included Sīstān, forced him to return thither. However, Laith b. ʿAlī held Fārs against the caliphal general Badr until Ṭāhir could return; al-Muktafī was thus in 290/903 obliged to send Ṭāhir a diploma for the governorship of Fārs. Ṭāhir and Yaʿqūb spent much of their time in festivities at Zarang and Bust; Fārs remained in the hands of Sebük-eri, who by 292/905 was showing signs of independence, and cut off all revenue from Fārs and Kirmān to Ṭāhir.

Ṭāhir's financial position was now perilous, and he became completely dependent on Laith b. ʿAlī, who in 295/908 sent him revenue which he had collected from his governorship of Makrān and from

Kirmān. Out of this, Ṭāhir could send tribute to the new Caliph al-Muqtadir, and was confirmed by the latter in his possessions. Laith, however, soon decided to end the feeble and neglectful rule of Ṭāhir. He marched to Zarang, and besieged Ṭāhir in the inner city or *shahristān*. Laith's superior financial resources told in the struggle; most of Ṭāhir's commanders deserted him, the city fell to Laith, and Ṭāhir and Ya'qūb fled westwards (296/909). They thought first of seeking aid from Sebük-eri in Fārs, but were doubtful of his good faith as a servant of the Ṣaffārids, believing him to be inclining to a pro-caliphal policy. This suspicion was justified; Sebük-eri bought over the remaining commanders of Ṭāhir and Ya'qūb, and when the two brothers came into his hands, he sent them captive to Baghdad. Sebük-eri's seizure of Fārs had been without caliphal authorization, but now he was formally invested as governor of the province.

The new amīr Laith (296–8/909–10) had first of all to send his brother Mu'addal to suppress unrest in Zābulistān (297/909), and then he resolved to invade Fārs to punish Sebük-eri for his treachery. He invaded Kirmān with 7,000 cavalry, defeated Sebük-eri and pushed on to Iṣṭakhr and Shīrāz. Sebük-eri appealed to the caliph for help, and the slave general Mu'nis was sent. Mu'nis soon concluded a separate peace with Laith, but Sebük-eri fought on and defeated Laith in Fārs. Laith was captured and sent to Baghdad, dying at Raqqa in 317/929, but Mu'addal escaped to Kirmān (298/910). Sebük-eri's good relations with the caliph did not last long. He could only collect ten of the sixteen million dirhams stipulated as tribute from Fārs, so a punitive expedition was sent against him. Defeated at Shīrāz, he dared not go to Sīstān, but fled across the Great Desert to Herāt and Marv; he was captured by the Sāmānid Aḥmad b. Ismā'īl and sent to Baghdad as a prisoner, where in 305/917–18 he died. Laith b. 'Alī was the last Ṣaffārid to have controlled Fārs; it was now placed under the caliphal slave general Qunbuj al-Afshīnī.

In Sīstān, Laith's brother Muḥammad (298/910–11) became amīr at the beginning of 298/summer 910, but he was only recognized in Sīstān, Zamīndāvar, Zābulistān and Kabul; no coins of his or of his brother Mu'addal seem to be extant. At this point, al-Muqtadir invested Aḥmad b. Ismā'īl with Sīstān and instructed him to end the rule of the Ṣaffārids for good. Muḥammad lacked military experience. He released from captivity Mu'addal, who forthwith treacherously seized Zarang for himself. Muḥammad had to retire to Bust, where he acquired a bad reputation for the exactions he made in his frantic need for money. Accordingly, when amīr Aḥmad came from Farah to Bust, he met little opposition there. Soon afterwards, Muʿaddal surrendered Zarang to the Sāmānid general Sīmjūr al-Dawātī. Both Muḥammad and Muʿaddal were carried off as captives; Ṣaffārid rule was for the moment uprooted from its native province, and a Sāmānid governor appointed there (298/911).

The Ṣaffārid empire in its heyday under Yaʿqūb and ʿAmr was essentially a military creation based on force of arms alone; in an anecdote told by Niẓām al-Mulk, Yaʿqūb boasts to the caliph's envoy that he has achieved his high position not through birth, like the ʿAbbāsids, but through his own boldness and valour (*ʿayyārī wa s̲h̲īr-mardī*).[1] The Ṣaffārids' unashamed proclamation of the superiority of force over the moral considerations which were supposed to underpin the temporal rule delegated by God to man, probably accounts for much of the hostility to them in the standard Muslim sources. On several occasions the amīrs showed their contempt for the constitutional doctrine, generally observed by provincial governors, that all secular power derived from the caliph, and lesser rulers only had *de jure* authority in so far as they obtained investiture from the caliph and forwarded suitable tribute to him. Yaʿqūb and ʿAmr were prepared to fall in with this when it suited their purposes. Thus ʿAmr was aware of the value of caliphal approbation in so strongly orthodox a province as K̲h̲urāsān, and he made much of his campaigns against the ʿAlids of the Caspian region and against the pagans of eastern Afghanistan, forwarding to Baghdad rich presents from the plunder gained there. Yet ʿAmr always knew that the sword was mightier than the diploma, and he expressed this view volubly when in 285/898 he received from al-Muʿtaḍid's envoy the investiture diploma for Transoxiana: "What am I to do with this? This province can only be wrested from Ismāʿīl with the aid of 100,000 drawn swords."[2] It is also said that ʿAmr was the first provincial ruler to place his own name in the k̲h̲uṭba, until then only read in the name of the caliph, but the narrative of the *Tārīk̲h̲-i Sīstān* and other sources such as Nars̲h̲ak̲h̲ī show that Yaʿqūb placed his own name in the k̲h̲uṭba of his territories from *c.* 253/867 onwards.

It is, indeed, abundantly clear that the caliphs and the Ṣaffārids never trusted each other for one moment. The investiture diplomas were

[1] *Niẓām al-Mulk*, p. 23.
[2] Gardīzī, p. 18; Ibn K̲h̲allikān, tr. vol. IV, pp. 326–7.

swiftly cancelled when Ṣaffārid fortunes flagged, when there still seemed chances of restoring the Ṭāhirids to Khurāsān and when the rising power of the orthodox and obedient Sāmānids could be used against the Ṣaffārids. In the *Tārīkh-i Sīstān*, Ya'qūb emphatically lays bare his hatred and mistrust of the 'Abbāsids: "He used often to say that the 'Abbāsids had based their rule on wrong-doing and trickery – 'Haven't you seen what they did to Abū Salama, Abū Muslim, the Barmakī family and Faḍl b. Sahl, despite everything which these men had done on the dynasty's behalf? Let no one ever trust them!'"[1]

Given the military nature of the Ṣaffārid empire, the army was necessarily of prime importance. Ya'qūb and 'Amr were themselves skilled commanders, inured to hardship and following a simple way of life, thereby setting an example to their troops and avoiding the encumbering of their army with unnecessary impedimenta. Ya'qūb's food is described as rough-and-ready, and consisted of the staples of Sīstān diet such as barley bread, leeks, onions and fish. The nucleus of the army consisted of local Sagzī troops and 'ayyārs, both cavalry and infantry; the infantry of Sīstān had been renowned since Sāsānid times, and over a century later, the Ghaznavids employed Sagzī infantry. But the Ṣaffārid army was also influenced by the trends in military organization prevalent in the Islamic world of the 3rd/9th century, in which professional armies of slaves (*ghilmān, mamālīk*) drawn from a multitude of different nationalities were increasingly employed. Ya'qūb and 'Amr similarly welcomed into the ranks of their troops capable soldiers of any race; in addition to the Sagzīs and Khurāsānīs, there were not only the ubiquitous Turks, but also Arabs, Indians and peoples from the Indo-Afghan borderlands. Peasant levies (*ḥasharhā-yi rūstā'ī*) were also pressed into service in times of need, but were often of dubious fighting quality; when Muḥammad b. 'Alī b. Laith was attempting to defend Sīstān against the incoming Sāmānids in 298/911, his *ḥashar* broke at the first charge.

According to Mas'ūdī, who in his *Murūj al-dhahab* quotes from a much longer account of the Ṣaffārids which he inserted in his lost *Akhbār al-zamān*, Ya'qūb exerted an unparalleled discipline over his troops, requiring them to be ready for battle or for moving at a moment's notice, and to refrain from looting till expressly permitted to do so. When a recruit to the Ṣaffārid army presented himself, Ya'qūb personally tested his skill. Then the recruit had to surrender all his

[1] *Tārīkh-i Sīstān*, pp. 267–8.

possessions and equipment; these were converted into cash and credited to him in the dīvān. If he was later found unsuitable and was discharged, this sum was given back to him; but if he stayed in the Ṣaffārids' service, he was fitted out with clothing, weapons and a mount from the army's own stocks, there being a central pool of mounts which was the property of the amīr himself. There are several specific examples in the sources of the amīrs' care to attract good men into their forces. Ya'qūb's winning-over of bodies of the Khārijites of Sīstān and Bādghīs has been noted, as has the interesting fact that one of these bodies preserved its separate identity within the Ṣaffārid army as the *jaish al-shurāt*. After Ya'qūb had ended the rule of the Ṭāhirids in Nīshāpūr and had campaigned energetically against the 'Alids of the Caspian provinces, his reputation caused several of the former commanders of the Ṭāhirids and the 'ayyār leaders of Khurāsān to rally to his side; amongst these were Abū Ṭalḥa Manṣūr b. Sharkab and Aḥmad b. 'Abd-Allāh Khujistānī, both of whom were later prominent in Khurāsānian affairs.

Like other contemporary rulers, the Ṣaffārid amīrs had a body of palace ghulāms, probably in large part Turkish, who were used as an élite force and for ceremonial occasions. When Nīshāpūr was captured, Ya'qūb fitted out 2,000 of these with weapons found in the Ṭāhirid treasury; he then held court like a king, with two lines of ghulāms drawn up before him.[1] The evident similarity in weapons, equipment and functions, of these slave guards to the Ghaznavids' palace ghulāms, is striking, and illustrative of the continuity of military techniques in the eastern Islamic world. Both Ya'qūb and 'Amr were keenly interested in the acquisition and training of these ghulāms. According to Mas'ūdī, watching the progress of his young slaves' education was the sole diversion of Ya'qūb, who had no interests outside his military career. 'Amr is said to have trained young slaves, and then to have attached them to his chief commanders as spies, again a striking anticipation of the Ghaznavid use of such spies or *mushrifs*. As to numbers, 'Amr is alleged to have possessed 10,000 palace ghulāms at his death, but this seems exaggerated.

In order to maintain the morale and discipline of the army, Ya'qūb and 'Amr were careful to see that it was paid promptly and in full. Pay was normally issued in an allotment (*razqa, bīstgānī*) every three months, whilst extra payments might be made after some conspicuous success; thus in 275/888, after his second occupation of Fārs and his peace

[1] *Ibid.*, p. 222.

settlement with the caliph ʿAmr distributed two million dirhams to his army. These payments were made after a general inspection (*ʿarḍ*) of the troops, their equipment and mounts; according to the historian of Khurāsān Sallāmī, the *ʿāriḍ* or head of the Department for Military Affairs inspected everyone, from the amīr himself downwards. Ibn Khallikān, who cites Sallāmī, links these inspections with the practice of the Sāsānid Emperors, and here too we see a continuity with the Iranian past. In addition to normal pay allocations, Ṭāhir b. Muḥammad b. ʿAmr in 289/902 distributed grants of land or *iqṭāʿs* to his troops in Fārs. Whilst this system of supporting troops on the revenues from lands and estates was at this time hardly known in Khurāsān and the east, it was certainly widespread in Iraq and western Persia, and the Ṣaffārids were in this instance merely adapting an established local practice to their own needs.

We know little of the internal administration of the Ṣaffārid empire. In the case of provinces like Khurāsān, Fārs and especially Ahvāz, the amīrs' authority was often broken by the occupations of enemies or rivals. Here, the Ṣaffārid central government was represented principally by tax-collectors (ʿummāl). The expense of maintaining a large, professional army in the field was almost certainly heavy. It is improbable that these tax officials behaved in a tender fashion, although it was apparently newly-conquered or hostile territories which were mulcted most severely. During the course of his campaign of 261/874 against al-Ḥasan b. Zaid, Yaʿqūb's officials exacted a year's kharāj from the people of Āmul and Sārī in Ṭabaristān, and refugees from the Caspian coastlands carried their complaints as far as the caliph in Iraq. But if an amīr were in desperate straits, the heartlands of the empire might suffer equally. Muḥammad b. ʿAlī b. al-Laith so oppressed the people of Bust in 298/910 that they welcomed the appearance of the well-behaved and disciplined Sāmānid army; when he had occupied Bust, the Sāmānid amīr restored to their former owners the goods and property confiscated by Muḥammad. Clearly, the government's demands for money often pressed hard on the *raʿiyya* or subjects. The amīr Ṭāhir refused to collect revenue on the explicit ground that he did not want to incur the odium of oppression and tyranny; nor did he use corvée labour for the building of his new palaces. The general trend towards harsh rule is probably not negated by the emphasis in the *Tārīkh-i Sīstān* on Yaʿqūb's piety and justice, his refusal to exact taxes from the very poor, his hearing of *maẓālim* or complaints of official misconduct, and his care to see that the *amīr-i āb* (the official in charge of the division of irrigation waters, a vital factor in the agricultural prosperity of the eastern provinces) functioned equitably; and the same reserve applies to ʿAmr's charitable works in the shape of new mosques, *ribāṭs*, bridges, stones marking the tracks through the deserts, etc.

Because of the paucity of information, it is difficult to estimate how advanced in organization was the Ṣaffārid administration, and how much it owed to the ʿAbbāsid caliphate for its institutions and techniques, for the caliphal administration was the model for that of its successor-states. Yaʿqūb set about establishing his own dīvān and appointing his own officials as soon as Sīstān was under his control in 247/861, and the head of his chancery seems to have been the poet and littérateur Muḥammad b. Vaṣīf. Not till ʿAmr's reign do we hear of a vizier as the amīr's chief executive, but the office is frequently mentioned from the opening years of the 4th/10th century onwards. ʿAmr's administrative skill and good government are specifically mentioned, and Gardīzī (using information from Sallāmī) describes how he had four treasuries. One was in effect an armoury, and contained a store of weapons. The other three were financial hoards and were entirely at the amīr's personal disposal. The first comprised revenue from the land tax and other imposts, and was used for the army's salaries. The second comprised revenue from the amīr's personal properties and estates (the *māl-i k̲h̲āṣṣ*), which was used for court expenses, food, etc. The third comprised revenue from occasional and extraordinary levies, and confiscations of the wealth of soldiers who had gone over to the enemy; from all this, special rewards and payments were given to outstandingly brave warriors and to spies and envoys. The same author goes on to say that ʿAmr was careful always to make confiscations at suitable times and with plausible pretexts. Out of all this income, tribute was sent only intermittently to the caliphate, though when money was sent, the sum involved might be as high as ten or twenty million dirhams. The good financial management of the first two Ṣaffārids is seen in the well-filled treasuries which each of them left behind. Yaʿqūb left at his death fifty million dirhams and another four million (or alternatively, 800,000) dīnārs, and ʿAmr left thirty-six million dirhams plus a great number of dīnārs, jewels, clothing, weapons, etc.; his improvident successor Ṭāhir got through all this in about six years.[1]

Whatever unfavourable reputation the Ṣaffārids may have left behind

[1] Masʿūdi, vol. VIII, p. 46; Gardīzī, p. 15.

in the provinces outside their homeland, there is much to show that they were genuinely popular inside Sīstān, that they expressed something of the local, particularist spirit there, and that they had in some measure the interests of Sīstān in their minds. In the early years of Ya'qūb's career, when he was an 'ayyār commander in Ṣāliḥ b. al-Naḍr's service, he is said to have restrained Ṣāliḥ's predominantly Bustī troops from plundering Zarang, since impoverishment of the capital could only benefit the rival town of Bust. More explicit are the attempts of a member of the ruling family, Muḥammad b. Khalaf b. al-Laith, to sooth the factional strife between the two groups of the Samakiyya and Ṣadaqiyya. His theme is that the unity and cohesion of Sīstān will suffer from dissensions: "He said, 'Let there be no more strife (*ta'aṣṣub*), for we are already in deep trouble. You have all seen the present state of affairs and the divisions which have arisen since the deaths of Ya'qūb and 'Amr; you must not let any more divisive factional strife arise. Instead, let there be concord amongst you, so that even if all the [outlying] provinces [of the empire] are lost, this province at least will remain in your hands and be inviolate from the grasp of outsiders and unworthy ones.'"[1] Moreover, during their period of rule in Khurāsān, the Ṣaffārids made some endeavour to enlist the support and sympathy of the *'ulamā* and scholars there. Ya'qūb had caused some destruction in Nīshāpūr when he had captured it, but 'Amr added to the Friday mosque and built the *dār al-imāra* or governor's palace there. The Ṣaffārids employed as a secretary the poet Ibrāhīm al-Mughaithī, and it is mentioned that 'Amr rewarded the jurist and traditionist Muḥammad al-Būshanjī with 20,000 dīnārs.

Of undeniable importance is the Ṣaffārid stimulus to the renaissance of New Persian literature and culture in the later part of the 3rd/9th century. In this movement, the plebeian milieu of the Ṣaffārids played a part as well as the feudal, aristocratic Sāmānid court. According to the *Tārīkh-i Sīstān*, Ya'qūb had poets attached to him who, after the conquest of Herāt and Pūshang from their Ṭāhirid governor, eulogised him in Arabic verses. Ya'qūb could not understand these, and asked the secretary of his chancery, Muḥammad b. Vaṣīf, "Why must something be recited that I can't understand?" So Muḥammad b. Vaṣīf composed some verses in Persian. That the appearance of vernacular literature in Sīstān at this time was something new is implied by the local history itself when the author contrasts Ya'qūb's encouragement

[1] *Tārīkh-i Sīstān*, pp. 198–9.

of New Persian literature with the purely Arabic eulogies and verses of the Khārijites of Sīstān. Muḥammad b. Vaṣīf made himself court poet and commentator on events affecting the Ṣaffārids; thus he celebrates 'Amr's pacification of Khurāsān after Rāfi''s death, and mourns the capture of Ṭāhir and Ya'qūb b. Muḥammad b. 'Amr. In this fashion, the Ṣaffārids were some of the catalytic agents in the birth of a specifically Irano-Islamic culture and feeling.

Over succeeding centuries, the Ṣaffārids continued to be the rallying-point for local feeling and desires for independence. The exact genealogy of the later generations of the dynasty is unclear, but the charisma of the Ṣaffārid name, if not the blood connections, plainly persisted. For the 150 years or so after the Sāmānid conquest, undoubted descendants of Ya'qūb and 'Amr and their kinsmen headed resistance to alien control, and it is with these amīrs of the period before the Ghaznavid conquest of 393/1003 (sometimes distinguished as the "second Ṣaffārid dynasty") that we shall finally be concerned.

In 298/911 Sāmānid rule had been imposed on Sīstān, and Manṣūr b. Isḥāq, the amīr Aḥmad b. Ismā'īl's cousin, was made governor there in 299/912. Manṣūr soon made himself unpopular by his excessive fiscal demands, well above the million dirhams regarded as the normal *'amal* or tax-yield of the province. A rebellion against Sāmānid rule was sparked off by one Muḥammad b. Hurmuz, called Maulā Ṣandalī, who, according to Gardīzī, was formerly a Khārijite and then a soldier in the Sāmānid army, but had been dismissed as too old for further service. For a successful popular rising, it was necessary to have a Ṣaffārid at least as a figure-head, and this was found in the person of the ten-year-old boy Abū Ḥafṣ 'Amr b. Ya'qūb b. Muḥammad b. 'Amr b. al-Laith, apparently the only survivor then in Sīstān of the direct lines of Ya'qūb and 'Amr (others were captive in Baghdad at this time). Muḥammad b. Hurmuz raised the 'ayyārs of Sīstān, killed the Sāmānid garrison in Zaranj and seized Manṣūr b. Isḥāq (299/912). Muḥammad b. Hurmuz now made the khuṭba for himself, and not for 'Amr b. Ya'qūb, and his aim was clearly his own personal aggrandisement. However, the pro-Ṣaffārid forces rallied, defeated him and set up 'Amr b. Ya'qūb as amīr. Eventually, a Sāmānid army under Ḥusain b. 'Alī Marvarrūdhī was sent to deal with the rebellion. 'Amr's brief amīrate was ended; he was sent into exile at Samarqand, and the 'ayyār leaders were massacred. A second Sāmānid occupation of Sīstān followed, this time with the Turkish slave general Sīmjūr al-Dawātī as governor (301/913).

In 301/914 a period of chaos and weakness began for the Sāmānid state when the amīr Aḥmad b. Ismā'īl was murdered by his ghulāms. The regency of the kingdom was undertaken for the child Naṣr II b. Aḥmad by the vizier Jaihānī, but the Sāmānid grip on the peripheries of the empire was inevitably relaxed. In Sīstān, it was the occasion for the 'Abbāsids briefly to re-assert their authority; as events turned out, this was for the last time. The governor of Fārs Badr b. 'Abd-Allāh al-Ḥammāmī appointed Faḍl b. Ḥamīd as his deputy in Sīstān. Faḍl and Khālid b. Muḥammad, governor of Kirmān, took over Sīstān, Sīmjūr having fled; by sending expeditions to Bust, al-Rukhkhaj and Zābulistān, they drove out the Sāmānid officials and established caliphal authority as far east as Ghazna. Yet it proved difficult for the 'Abbāsids to hold this distant outpost of the caliphate. The situation in Sīstān continued to be unstable, and very soon, the province was in the hands of 'ayyār bands once more. An adventurer, Kathīr b. Aḥmad emerged as amīr by popular acclamation from 304/917 to 306/919, followed by Aḥmad b. Qudām. Bust seems to have been generally held by a group of the Sāmānids' Turkish ghulāms, originally left there as a garrison; and in 317/929, after the failure of an attempt to raise Naṣr b. Aḥmad's brother Yaḥyā to the throne in Bukhārā, the general Qara-Tegin Isfījābī settled there.

In the midst of these confused happenings, the 'ayyārs of Zaranj broke out in revolt and raised to the throne a member of the Ṣaffārid family, Abū Ja'far Aḥmad b. Muḥammad b. Khalaf, whose grandfather had been a close associate of Ya'qūb and 'Amr's, and who was related also to the founders of the dynasty through his mother Bānū. Amīr Aḥmad (311–52/923–63) soon won over Bust and al-Rukhkhaj to his allegiance, and began to restore Sīstān to prosperity and effectiveness in the politics of the eastern world. The local historian of Sīstān says: "Then they all made a general oath of allegiance to Amīr Abū Ja'far, and his rule was universally recognized. The army, comprising the slaves (*mawālī*), the 'ayyār leaders (*sarhangān*) and the free Sagzī troops, all became united, and all the disorder was ended."[1]

In Aḥmad's early years, a vigorous policy was pursued. In 317/929, a year in which the 'Abbāsids were distracted by the temporary deposition and restoration of al-Muqtadir, and in which the Sāmānid state also was shaken by the *putsch* in Bukhārā mentioned above, Aḥmad's troops marched into Kirmān and collected a million dirhams' taxation;

[1] *Ibid.*, pp. 207, 229, 243, 310–12, 325.

possibly this was connected with an event recorded for the preceding year in which a rebel (*khārijī*) is said to have marched from Sīstān towards Fārs, but to have been killed by his own troops before reaching there. In 320/932 a rising of Qara-Tegin and the Turks of Bust was suppressed. The 'Abbāsids, although increasingly enfeebled and approaching the nadir of their fortunes, were still not disposed to give up Sīstān for lost. In 318/930 al-Muqtadir appointed his son Hārūn governor of Fārs, Kirmān, Makrān and Sīstān, and in the following year Muḥammad b. Yāqūt was invested with Sīstān; but there is no record, historical or numismatic, that these investitures had any practical consequences. In 321/933 the Ṣaffārid Abū Ḥafṣ 'Amr b. Yaq'ūb, who had briefly reigned as amīr from 299/911 to 301/913, returned to Sīstān from Baghdad; possibly the caliph hoped thereby to introduce an element of discord into Sīstān politics. Two other Ṣaffārids, the grandsons of 'Amr b. al-Laith, Ṭāhir and Ya'qūb, had been released from captivity in Baghdad in 310/922–3 and were living there in an honoured state.

Amīr Aḥmad's prestige spread beyond the confines of Sīstān. The *Tārīkh-i Sīstān* lists rich presents sent to him by Naṣr b. Aḥmad, and gives the text *in extenso* of a lengthy ode by the Sāmānid court poet Rūdakī praising Aḥmad as "that foremost one amongst the nobles and the pride of Iran, That just king and sun of the age ... from the glowing orb of the stock of Sāsān"; the poem earned for Rūdakī a present from Aḥmad of 10,000 dīnārs. The last years of Aḥmad's reign saw a certain weakening in the state. The Commander-in-Chief Abu'l-Fatḥ was for a while the dominating influence, but at some time after 341/952–3, he raised a revolt at Jarwardkān and Baskar in favour of a son of the former amīr Ṭāhir b. Muḥammad b. 'Amr. There was some support for this claimant on account of his direct descent from 'Amr b. al-Laith, but Aḥmad suppressed the revolt with the aid of the Turks of Bust.

Aḥmad was murdered by his own ghulāms in 352/963 and succeeded by his son Abū Aḥmad Khalaf, the last and most celebrated of the Ṣaffārids of the 4th/10th century. Khalaf had to set aside another member of the family before he could consolidate his power, and at the beginning of his reign was dependent on Ṭāhir b. Muḥammad (or Ṭāhir b. [Abī] 'Alī) Tamīmī. Ṭāhir had been a general in the Sāmānid army, and had fought against the Dailamite rebel Mākān b. Kākī; in amīr Aḥmad's reign he had been a popular governor in Bust, and then at the Sāmānid amīr's request was made governor of Farah by Khalaf. Ṭāhir's mother was a grand-daughter of the Ṣaffārid 'Alī b. al-Laith, and Khalaf now formally associated Ṭāhir in his rule, their names being proclaimed jointly in the khuṭba. In 353/964 Khalaf left Sīstān to fulfil a vow by making the Pilgrimage to the Holy Places, leaving Ṭāhir as regent. Under Ṭāhir's enlightened rule, the country flourished; apart from the perennial strife of factions in Zarang, the country was at peace, and the kharāj was collected "dirham for dirham", i.e. strictly according to the assessment and not with the usual *dāng* or so demanded in excess. In 357/968 or shortly afterwards, the authority of the great Būyid ruler 'Aḍud al-Daula, who had just conquered Kirmān from the Ilyāsids, was recognized in the khuṭba of Sīstān. Also in 357/968 Ṭāhir led an expedition against the Turks who had again seized control of Bust; Gardīzī implies that these Turks were the former ghulāms of Qara-Tegin. Yet soon afterwards, Bust fell once more into the hands of a Turkish chief called in the *Tārīkh-i Sīstān* Yüz-temür. This man may be the Baituz known from early Ghaznavid sources to have been ruling in Bust when Sebük-Tegin conquered it in 367/977–8 and also known as the minter of an extant copper coin at Bust in 359/970; the famous rhetorician and author Abu'l-Fatḥ Bustī had been secretary to Baituz before passing into Sebük-Tegin's service.

It was perhaps natural that Ṭāhir should be unwilling to relinquish power when in 358/969 Khalaf returned from the west. Khalaf took the precaution of going first to the Sāmānid court and obtaining military aid from Manṣūr b. Nūḥ, but was unable to prevail against Ṭāhir's well-entrenched position in Sīstān; it was not till Ṭāhir's death in 359/970 that Khalaf managed to occupy Zaranj and carry out a purge of Ṭāhir's former supporters. The struggle against Khalaf was now taken up by Ṭāhir's son Ḥusain, of whom a coin is extant. Ḥusain retired to Bukhārā; Khalaf cut off the tribute and presents which he customarily sent to Bukhārā, hence Ḥusain returned with a powerful Sāmānid army, including the general Abu'l-Ḥasan Sīmjūrī. A long siege of Khalaf within the citadel of Zarang followed, but he could not be dislodged (372/982–3). A peace was then arranged by the Sāmānids, but fighting again flared up, this time with Ḥusain shut inside the citadel of Zarang. Ḥusain vainly sought help from Sebük-Tegin in Ghazna, and had to surrender in 373/983–4; peace was made, but Ḥusain died soon afterwards.

Khalaf was now undisputed master of Sīstān. He secured an investiture patent from the caliph and assumed the honorific of *walī al-daula*. Like his father, Khalaf was a great patron of the *'ulamā'* and scholars. One of his eulogists was the great poet and author of *maqāmāt*, Badī' al-Zamān al-Hamadānī. He combined extreme avariciousness and duplicity with ostentatious piety, and is said to have commissioned a grand Qur'ān commentary, which finally ran to 100 volumes; it comprehended all previous commentaries, set forth all the variant readings, explored all grammatical questions and set forth all the sound traditions. Externally, Khalaf felt strong enough in 376/986–7 to send an army to Bust and Zābulistān whilst Sebük-Tegin was absent fighting the Hindūshāhī Rājā Jaipāl, but he had to evacuate Bust on the Ghaznavid's return. An expedition under his son 'Amr was sent in 381–2/991–2 to the Būyid province of Kirmān, taking advantage of dissensions amongst the Būyids after Sharaf al-Daula's death, but the Ṣaffārid troops were eventually driven back. Nevertheless, Khalaf continued to covet Kirmān; in 384/994 his army again invaded the province, but was repelled by the Būyid general Abū Ja'far b. Ustādh-Hurmuz.

After the failure of his attempt to recover Bust, Khalaf's relations with Sebük-Tegin had been good, and he had sent troops to help Sebük-Tegin against Abū 'Alī Sīmjūrī. However, the extension of Ghaznavid authority over Khurāsān was plainly inimical to Ṣaffārid interests, and Khalaf tried to induce the Qarakhānid Ilig Khān Naṣr, who was threatening the last Sāmānids in Bukhārā, to attack the Ghaznavids (386/996). After Sebük-Tegin's death in the next year, his sons Maḥmūd and Ismā'īl were for several months locked in a struggle over the succession, and Khalaf seized the opportunity of wresting Pūshang and Kūhistān from Sebük-Tegin's brother Bughrachuq, the latter being killed by Khalaf's son Ṭāhir (388/998). But once Maḥmūd was firmly in control at Ghazna, Khalaf could only sue for peace, paying a tribute of 100,000 dīnārs or dirhams (both terms are given in the sources), and placing Maḥmūd's name in the khuṭba (390/1000).[1] Khalaf had only one surviving son, Ṭāhir, having put to death 'Amr after the failure of the Kirmān venture. The events of the last years of Khalaf's reign are somewhat confused. Some sources say that Khalaf renounced the throne in favour of Ṭāhir, and then snatched it back again; others, that Ṭāhir rebelled against his father, marched into Kirmān, but was defeated there and had to return to Sīstān. With 'ayyār help he secured Zarang, but was treacherously captured and

[1] 'Utbī, vol. I, pp. 209, 350–65; Gardīzī, p. 63; *Tārīkh-i Sīstān*, pp. 345–6.

killed by Khalaf (392/1002). A severe revulsion of feeling against Khalaf resulted. A group of the military leaders of Sīstān invited Maḥmūd of Ghazna, and after a siege in the fortress of Ṭāq, Khalaf surrendered and abdicated (393/1003). He chose exile with the Farīghūnids of Gūzgān, but after plotting once more with the Qarakhānids during their invasion of Khurāsān in 397/1006–7, was removed to Gardīz for the last two years of his life. Such is the narrative of the historical sources, although the existence of a coin bearing the names both of Ṭāhir and Maḥmūd points to the possibility that Ṭāhir had already acknowledged the overlordship of the Ghaznavids before his death.

Sīstān now became a province of the Ghaznavid empire, under the governorship of Maḥmūd's brother Naṣr, but the province was never reconciled to the yoke of the Ghaznavids and their rapacious tax-collectors. Revolts were frequent; the activities of the 'ayyārs, now more than ever linked with the cause of local patriotism, increased; and it was not long before scions of the Ṣaffārid dynasty re-appeared in their ancestral homeland.

CHAPTER 4

THE SĀMĀNIDS

The original home of the Sāmānids is uncertain, for some Arabic and Persian books claim that the name was derived from a village near Samarqand, while others assert it was a village near Balkh or Tirmidh.[1] The latter is a shade more probable since the earliest appearance of the Sāmānid family in the sources seems to be in Khurāsān rather than in Transoxiana. In some sources the Sāmānids claimed to be descended from the noble Sāsānian family of Bahrām Chūbīn, whereas one author claimed that they were of Turkish origin and belonged to the Oghuz tribe, which is most unlikely, but conceivably may be a later attempt to link them to a Hephthalite or Turkish origin.[2] All traditions relating to the origin of the dynasty, however, have it that Sāmān accepted Islam from Asad b. ʻAbd-Allāh al-Qasrī (or Qushairī), governor of Khurāsān 105–9/723–7, for subsequently Sāmān named his son Asad after the governor. We hear no more of Asad until the time of al-Ma'mūn, when his governor of Khurāsān, Ghassān b. ʻAbbād, rewarded the four sons of Asad for their support of al-Ma'mūn against a rebel Rāfiʻ b. Laith. This was about the year 204/819, and the four sons of Asad were appointed over the following cities: Nūḥ – Samarqand, Aḥmad – Farghāna, Yaḥyā – Shāsh and Ilyās – Herāt. This assignment of rule to the sons of Asad marked the beginning of Sāmānid power in Transoxiana, for the line of Ilyās in Herāt did not fare as well as did his brothers in the north. Ilyās died in 242/856 and his son Ibrāhīm took his place in Herāt. Afterwards Ibrāhīm was called by Muḥammad b. Ṭāhir, governor of Khurāsān, to become his army commander, but he unsuccessfully fought against the Khārijites in Sīstān. When Yaʻqūb b. Laith besieged Herāt, the Ṭāhirid governor sent Ilyās against Yaʻqūb. At a battle near Fūshanj (or Pūshang) in 253/867 Ilyās was defeated by Yaʻqūb and fled to Nīshāpūr, where he later surrendered to Yaʻqūb and was taken as a captive by him to Sīstān.

In Transoxiana, at the death of Nūḥ (227/841–2), the governor of Khurāsān appointed both of Nūḥ's brothers, Yaḥyā and Aḥmad, over

[1] Yāqūt, *Muʻjam al-buldān*, p. 13.

[2] Muḥammad Lārī, Persian ms. Univ. of Istanbul F 725, fol. 234a.

the city of Samarqand, but Aḥmad (d. 250/864–5) survived his brother (d. 241/855) and transmitted power to one son Naṣr in Samarqand, and to another son, Ya'qūb in Shāsh, who ruled there a long time. We do not know exactly what happened between Yaḥyā and Aḥmad, and why the line of Aḥmad replaced that of his brother Yaḥyā. Perhaps Yaḥyā surrendered power to his more energetic brother Aḥmad, who ruled most of Transoxiana, other than the oasis of Bukhārā and Khwārazm, while Yaḥyā remained only a figurehead ruler in Samarqand. It is significant that no coins of Yaḥyā have been found whereas copper coins (*fals*) of Aḥmad begin in 244/858–9 in Samarqand. (The right of the Sāmānids to strike silver coins, *dirhams*, did not exist before Naṣr b. Aḥmad, *c.* 273/886.) With the breakdown of the authority of the Ṭāhirid governors of Khurāsān and the victories of Ya'qūb b. Laith, Naṣr b. Aḥmad found himself the virtually independent ruler of Transoxiana with his capital in Samarqand. He consolidated his power by sending his brother Ismā'īl to Bukhārā which was in a chaotic state in the vacuum left by the fall of the Ṭāhirids. Khwārazmian troops had raided and pillaged the town so Ismā'īl was welcomed by the people who supported him from the outset as the restorer of order. It was not long before disagreement over the allocation of tax money caused strife between Ismā'īl and his brother Naṣr. The story of the conflict between the two, and the victory of Ismā'īl, is related by Narshakhī, as well as by other sources. Although Ismā'īl was the victor in the fratricidal struggle, he did not move to Samarqand but made Bukhārā the new centre of the Sāmānid state.

The Sāmānid state had received recognition in the year 261/875 when the caliph al-Mu'tamid sent the investiture for all of Transoxiana to Naṣr b. Aḥmad, in opposition to the claims of Ya'qūb b. Laith the Ṣaffārid. Even after the victory of Ismā'īl, in the eyes of the caliph Naṣr was still the legal ruler of Transoxiana rather than his brother Ismā'īl, and this legality Ismā'īl recognized until the death of Naṣr in Jumādā I 279/August 892.

Meanwhile, Ya'qūb b. Laith had also died and was followed by his brother 'Amr, who considered himself the heir of the Ṭāhirids, hence *de jure* ruler of Transoxiana, as well as Khurāsān and other parts of Iran. 'Amr persuaded the caliph to send him the investiture for Transoxiana, and this was done possibly with the hope that the Ṣaffārids and Sāmānids would destroy each other. Ismā'īl was victorious, and if the stories about 'Amr's defeat are to be believed, he was captured by

Ismā'īl's troops near Balkh without a skirmish. In any case 'Amr was captured and sent as a prisoner to Baghdad where the caliph ordered his execution. The date of the victory of Ismā'īl over 'Amr is uncertain, but probably it was in the spring of 287/900.

The victory over 'Amr brought recognition to Ismā'īl from the caliph as ruler over all of Khurāsān. This formal recognition, in the form of documents, presents, and a robe of honour, meant only a recognition of the actual situation, since the power of the caliphate had long since ceased to extend to the east. Ismā'īl was the real founder of the Sāmānid state, and is highly regarded in all sources for his good qualities as a ruler, indeed almost an idealized ruler.

Ismā'īl enlarged the Sāmānid domain in all directions. In 280/893 he raided to the north and captured the city of Ṭarāz where a Nestorian church was reputedly turned into a mosque and much booty was taken. This expedition is reported differently by various sources, but they all agree in the success of Ismā'īl. This campaign and another by Ismā'īl in 291/903, although it did not result in a great extension of the Sāmānid frontiers to the north and east, at least made that frontier safe from raids of Turkish infidels, and enabled Muslim missionaries to propagate Islam into the steppes. We may surmise, if we study the extant coinage, that Ismā'īl ended the independent existence of a number of small vassal states in Central Asia, placing them directly under Sāmānid rule. Probably in 280/893 he ended the local dynasty of Ushrūsana in the upper Zarafshān valley, famous as the homeland of the ill-fated Afshīn Ḥaidar b. Kāūs.[1] It is not known when the various parts of Transoxiana submitted to the Sāmānids, but some of them remained under the control of their local rulers, for example in Khwārazm where the country became a part of the Sāmānid state after Ismā'īl's defeat of 'Amr b. Laith, but the local Khwārazmian dynasty continued to flourish until 385/995 in the south of the country, while a governor of the Sāmānids ruled in the north with his capital at Gurgānj. In 385/995 the northern ruler defeated the southern and annexed his domains, but throughout the existence of the Sāmānid state both parts of Khwārazm remained true vassals of the Sāmānids. So Ismā'īl's domains were composed both of provinces of the central government and of vassal princes.

Since after the defeat of 'Amr b. Laith, Ismā'īl had received from the caliph investiture over Ṭabaristān as well as Khurāsān, Ray and Iṣfahān,

[1] In the local language this place was called Ustrūshana.

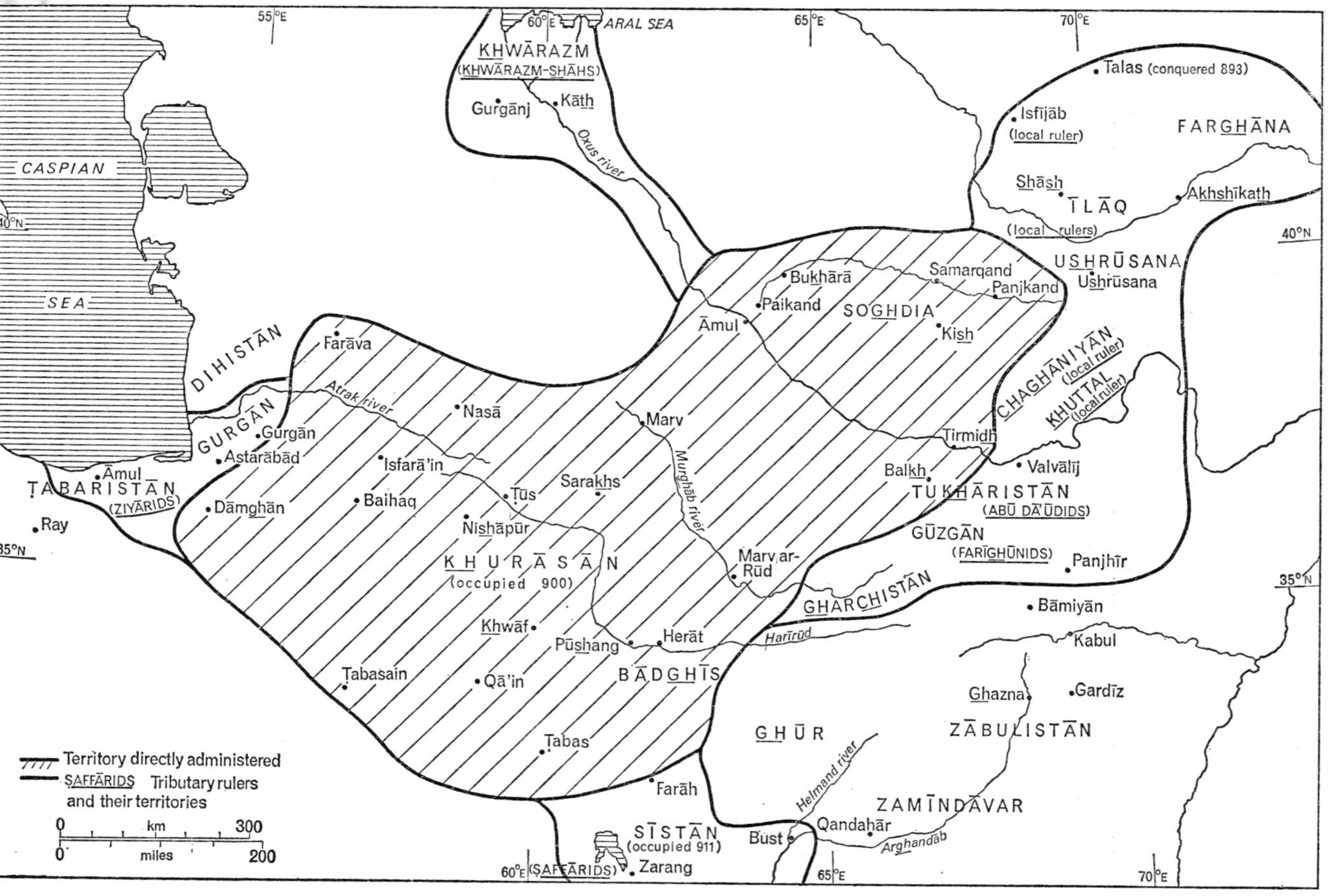

Map 3. The Sāmānid kingdom

he decided to annex these realms to his own. In 287/900 he sent an army against Muḥammad b. Zaid, the *de facto* ruler of Ṭabaristān and Gurgān, despite the attempts of the envoy of Muḥammad to restrain him. Ismāʿīl was successful and defeated and killed the ruler of Ṭabaristān. The general of Ismāʿīl revolted, however, and in the following year Ismāʿīl himself led an army into Ṭabaristān. The rebellious general, Muḥammad b. Hārūn, fled to Dailam and Ismāʿīl re-established Sāmānid rule over Gurgān and Ṭabaristān. Ray and all of Khurāsān submitted to Ismāʿīl but Sīstān and Iṣfahān remained independent. Thus the heart of Ismāʿīl's domains remained Transoxiana with his capital at Bukhārā.

Ismāʿīl has come down in history not so much as a capable general or as a strong ruler, although he was both, but rather as the epitome of the just and equitable ruler. Many stories in this vein about Ismāʿīl are to be found in both Arabic and Persian sources. For example, on one occasion he found that the weights used in the city of Ray to weigh the precious metals for the taxes were too heavy. He ordered them corrected and deducted the amount of excess which already had been collected from the city taxes.[1] Stone weights have been found with Ismāʿīl's name on them, so we may suspect that the ruler systematized the weights and measures in his domains although it is not mentioned in the sources. Ismāʿīl introduced other reforms in his kingdom, and even at Qazvīn, his westernmost outpost, he confiscated the possessions of some of the landowners with the approbation of the common folk.[2] Because of his campaigns, especially to the north against nomadic Turks, the heart of the kingdom, Transoxiana, was so safe from enemy attacks that the walls and other defences of Bukhārā and Samarqand were neglected. As long as Ismāʿīl lived there was no need of defensive walls but later, at the end of the dynasty, the earlier, but now dilapidated, walls were sorely missed.

Ismāʿīl was loyal to the caliph but there is no evidence that he, or any of the Sāmānid rulers, paid tribute or taxes to Baghdad. Gifts were sent, for this was normal procedure, reports on their activities were also sent, and coins were minted in the names both of the caliph and the ruling Sāmānid, while both names were also mentioned in the daily prayers, at least until the rise of the Būyids. Nonetheless relations between the Sāmānids and the caliphs continued to be correct though formal to

[1] Mīrkhwānd, p. 124.

[2] Abu'l-Qāsim al-Rāfiʿī, *Kitāb al-tadwīn fī dhikr ahl al-ʿilm bi Qazwīn*, Arabic ms. Istanbul, Koğuşlar 1007, fol. 147a.

the end of the dynasty. All of the Sāmānid rulers are called *amīr* in the sources, which in that age meant something like viceroy of the caliph, who himself was amīr of all the Muslims. Like the 'Abbāsid caliphs, the Sāmānids took throne names, for example *amīr-i ḥamīd* for Nūḥ b. Naṣr; some also had posthumous names, for example Ismā'īl was called *amīr-i māḍī*, "the late amir", after his death, and Aḥmad b. Ismā'īl was called *amīr-i shahīd*, "the martyred amir", as was noted by Muqaddasī (p. 337).

Ismā'īl became sick and after a long interval died in the month of Ṣafar 295/November 907, the exact day reported differently in various sources. He was succeeded by his son Aḥmad. At the outset of his reign Aḥmad set out to conquer Sīstān which had remained under a Ṣaffārid ruler. By 298/911 most of the province had submitted to Sāmānid rule. The province of Ṭabaristān, however, broke away from the Sāmānids with the revolt of a Zaidī Shī'ī leader called Nāṣir al-Kabīr. Before Aḥmad could take measures to reconquer Ṭabaristān and Gurgān, which had also revolted, he was assassinated by some of his slaves who cut off his head when he was sleeping in his tent near Bukhārā. Some sources say that the slaves killed Amīr Aḥmad because he relied too heavily on learned men for advice, and he had introduced the use of Arabic instead of Persian in orders and decrees, contrary to his father. He died in Jumādā II 301/January 914 and his son succeeded him at the age of eight.

Naṣr b. Aḥmad, surnamed Sa'īd "the fortunate", was just that in having Abū 'Abd-Allāh al-Jaihānī as his prime minister. Jaihānī was not only a capable administrator but also a famous geographer and learned man. The accession to the throne of a boy of eight, however, led to a series of revolts, the most dangerous of which was that of the uncle of his late father, Isḥāq b. Aḥmad, a younger brother of Ismā'īl in Samarqand. Isḥāq struck his own coins and his sons aided him; one of them Manṣūr seized Nīshāpūr and several cities in Khurāsān. After several battles Isḥāq was defeated and captured while his son died in Nīshāpūr. Later Naṣr's own brothers revolted against him, and with difficulty he suppressed those revolts too. In spite of these interior troubles, Naṣr was able to reconquer some of the western provinces which had left their allegiance to the Sāmānids at the death of Amīr Aḥmad. Ray was reoccupied but Ṭabaristān proved much more difficult. Much of the province returned to Sāmānid rule but then a local leader called Mākān b. Kākī not only took over Ṭabaristān but also raided Khurāsān where he was defeated by a general of the Sāmānids in 940. Naṣr died after a rule of twenty-nine years in 331/943. Several sources tell us that the leading officers of Naṣr's army were opposed to Naṣr's support of Ismā'ilī missionaries in his realm and plotted to assassinate the amīr. But Nūḥ, son of Naṣr, heard of the plot and at a banquet to organize the revolt Nūḥ seized and decapitated the chief of the malcontents, promising, however, to put an end to the Ismā'īlīs. He persuaded his father to abdicate and shortly afterwards Naṣr died.

In spite of the revolts and internal troubles, the reign of Naṣr b. Aḥmad might be called the high point or golden age of Sāmānid rule. More than the ruler, his two prime ministers were responsible for the flowering of literature and culture. We have already mentioned Jaihānī who was prime minister from 302/914 to 310/922 and from 327/938 to 331/941. The other was Abu'l-Faḍl al-Bal'amī who held office from 310/922 to 327/938. Jaihānī wrote a geography which has not survived but parts of which were incorporated in other works. This geography contained detailed information about lands and peoples to the east and north of Transoxiana, which the prime minister had obtained from envoys, merchants and others. His interest in geography led him to invite geographers to the court at Bukhārā, but the most famous one of the age, Abū Zaid al-Balkhī, refused to leave his native city of Balkh in spite of the attractions of the amīr's court. But Jaihānī's interests were not limited to geography, since we know from the *Fihrist* of Ibn al-Nadīm that he wrote other books which have not survived. Scientists, astronomers, men of letters and others did come to the capital Bukhārā, such that its fame as a centre of learning spread throughout the Islamic world. Bal'amī, who extended his patronage to many savants and men of literature, was also a man of learning and culture. He replaced Jaihānī, who had been suspected of harbouring Shī'ī beliefs or even Manichaean dualist tendencies and was removed from office. Bal'amī continued the policies of Jaihānī and showed himself an even more skilful administrator when he put down an uprising in the city of Bukhārā led by brothers of Naṣr, by inciting the rebels against one another.

Anthologies of literary figures, such as the *Yatīmat al-dahr* of Abū Manṣūr al-Tha'ālibī, the *Lubāb al-albāb* of Muḥammad 'Aufī and others give us the names and works of poets and authors of this age, and the list is impressive. Not only religious scholars, writing in Arabic, but poets writing in both Arabic and Persian, historians and scientists adorned the court of Naṣr b. Aḥmad. To begin with geographers, not only was Jaihānī famous in this area but Abū Dulaf went on an embassy to China for Naṣr and wrote a report of his travels. Ibn Amājūr al-Turkī was an astronomer active for a time in Naṣr's domain. Theologians were so many they cannot be discussed here. Although al-Fārābī (d. 339/950) was born in Transoxiana, most of his life was spent in Baghdad and elsewhere. Perhaps the most significant group of literary men at Naṣr's court were the Persian poets, principally Rūdakī who died probably in 329/940. The rise of the New Persian language and literature is discussed in another chapter. Suffice it to say that during the reign of Naṣr both Arabic and Persian books were produced in his capital, as well as elsewhere in the kingdom, and a library was assembled at Bukhārā which won the praise of scholars including Ibn Sīnā, who used it later in the Sāmānid era.

The organization of the Sāmānid state was modelled after the caliph's court in Baghdad with its central and provincial divisions. We have mentioned that the ruler appointed local governors, or local dynasts functioned as governors although they were actually vassals of the Sāmānid amīr. The primary duty of both governors and local potentates was to collect taxes and provide troops if needed. The chief governorship in the Sāmānid domains was the huge province of Khurāsān, south of the Oxus River, which was at first entrusted to a relative of the ruler or later to one of his trusted slaves. The governor of this province was usually the *sipāh-salār* (Arabic: *ṣāḥib al-juyūsh*) or commander of the principal army. Slaves, just as in Baghdad, could rise to high positions of authority, and the palace school for court slaves is described in detail by Niẓām al-Mulk in his *Siyāsat-nāma*. The system of training remained a model for succeeding dynasties. Just as at Baghdad, so in Bukhārā Turkish slaves eventually succeeded in usurping authority and the ruler became almost a puppet in their hands.

The division of political functions between the court (*dargāh*) and the chancery (*dīvān*) mirrored similar conditions at Baghdad. The office of prime minister or vizier (*vazīr*), was especially important, for a powerful minister could appoint and dismiss other officials and could even hold command of the army. Theoretically the vizier was the head of the dīvān, the bureaucracy, and thus was the counterpart in the bureaucratic institution of the head of the court, the chamberlain (*ḥājib*). Actually, the vizier became the right-hand man of the amīr, and thus in effect the second in command in the Sāmānid state. The *ḥājib*, or *ḥājib al-ḥujjāb* as he is also called in the sources, was the equivalent of a modern minister of court, although under the early Sāmānids the *vakīl*, or head of the amīr's household seems to have been more influential than the ḥājib. As the Turkish palace guard became more powerful, the office of ḥājib, which included authority over the guard, also increased, primarily at the expense of the vakīl. Thus the constant factor in the government of the Sāmānid state was the bureaucracy, presided over by the vizier, whereas the court could be the scene of conflict for power between the domestic organization managed by the vakīl and the executive branch of the dargāh run by the ḥājib.

The executive branch was composed not only of the palace guard, but also the army. The problem of control of the army was later complicated, however, by the overwhelming importance of the governor of Khurāsān as commander of the army of Khurāsān, and also by the growth of the Turkish slave system at the Sāmānid court. After the reign of Ismā'īl, the Sāmānids turned their prime attention from Central Asia to western Iran, and the Turkish slave system came to dominate the court. Until the middle of the 4th/10th century, however, the limelight was held by the dīvān under the two remarkable viziers of Amīr Naṣr whom we have mentioned above. Under them the dīvān, as described by Narshakhī, received the form which was so admired by Niẓām al-Mulk and later authors. The historian (p. 24) tells us that there were ten ministries in the capital city, that of the prime minister (*vazīr*), the treasurer (*mustaufī*), correspondence (*'amīd al-mulk*), captain of the guard (*ṣāhib shuraṭ*), postmaster (*ṣāhib barīd*), inspector, fiscal as well as general (*mushrif*), the private domains of the ruler, chief of police (*muḥtasib*), religious endowments (*auqāf*), and of justice (*qaḍā*). This central bureaucracy was matched by a similar organization in the provincial capitals, but on a smaller scale. Some provinces, however, were not under the central government but maintained a quasi-autonomous existence under local princes and with varied relationships to Bukhārā. Although the bureaucracy would flourish, or at least exhibit power and influence, under a good vizier, it could and did continue to function, even poorly, under a weak vizier. This instrument of administration, forged under the Sāmānids, continued to exist after the fall of the dynasty. It is not easy, however, to follow the fortunes of the bureaucracy throughout the 4th/10th and 5th/11th centuries. For one matter, we are not certain when Persian replaced Arabic as the official language of the bureaucracy. A remark by Ḥamd-Allāh Qazvīnī, an historian of the 8th/14th century (p. 381), that Amīr Aḥmad b. Ismāʿīl changed proclamations and decrees from Persian to Arabic, indicates that before Aḥmad Persian had been the language of the bureaucracy. In any case, the measure was not popular and had to be rescinded. The language question, however, is more important than a mere bureaucratic change, for it is a keynote of the nature of the Sāmānid bureaucracy, which was to have much influence later.

We must digress briefly to discuss the question of the use of Persian at the court of the Sāmānids. It is generally believed that in the chancellery of the Sāmānids, till the end of the dynasty, Arabic alone was used and all attempts to introduce Persian failed. I believe the situation was different. Since we know that Persian was used as the language of bureaucracy under the Ghaznavids, and the vizier of Sulṭān Maḥmud, Maimandi, failed in his attempt to change usage from Persian to Arabic, one must assume that Persian had been used previously. Furthermore, under the Būyids there was a *kātib al-rasāʾil al-fārisīya* "secretary for Persian correspondence", and the name of one of them, Shīrzād b. Surkhāb, is known. It has been presumed that this bureau was concerned with Zoroastrians and only used Pahlavī, but there is no reason why the scribes could not have written Persian in Arabic characters in the Būyid courts. Rūdakī, the poet of Transoxiana, I believe presupposes some previous development of New Persian in Arabic script. Furthermore, Khwārazmī in his book *Mafātīḥ al-ʿulūm* (pp. 59, 117), although he does not say so, implies the existence of New Persian writing. I suggest that much of the bureaucracy of the court of Bukhārā was conducted in written Persian, while Persian was the "official" spoken language and Arabic was also used for more formal, for religious and for caliphal matters. In effect the Sāmānid bureaucracy was bilingual.

Unfortunately, we do not have enough evidence to reconstruct the central and provincial administration and bureaucracy of the Sāmānid state in detail, but from later books, such as the *Siyāsat-nāma* of Niẓām al-Mulk, it is clear that the Sāmānid state organization provided a model for the Saljuqs and later states. The model itself was not a direct inheritance from the Sāsānian state apparatus but an interesting mixture of Sāsānian, local Central Asian and Arab-Islamic features, for Transoxiana, the domain of the Sāmānids, had not been a part of the Sāsānian

Empire. A brief look into its origins may help to explain some of its general features.

From the beginning of the 2nd/8th century until the second half of the 3rd/9th century Transoxiana had been transformed from an area of many local dynasts, almost what one might call city states, using Soghdian and other Iranian tongues as their "state" languages, into an important part of the ʿAbbāsid Caliphate. If we take Samarqand in the year 725, the "official spoken" language of the city was still Soghdian, witness the Soghdian letters found in 1934 in Mt Mug east of Panjikant. The "official written" language was Arabic, since the Arabs ruled the city. The "religious" language was also Arabic for Muslims, and Avestan with Pahlavī for Zoroastrians. At home Soghdian dialects were spoken. A hundred years later Persian had replaced Soghdian as the "official spoken" language, whereas Arabic remained as the "official written" language though soon (probably under Naṣr b. Aḥmad or Ismāʿīl b. Aḥmad) to be changed to Persian. The "religious" language was now almost exclusively Arabic since most of the population had become Muslim. At home Soghdian dialects were still spoken as well as more and more Persian. As noted above, we do not know where the first writing of Persian in the Arabic alphabet occurred, but the Sāmānid bureaucracy from the time of Ismāʿīl was based on both Arabic and the new Persian form of writing. The Sāmānids were the first to "Persianize" the bureaucracy as copied from Baghdad, which in turn had borrowed from Ctesiphon, the capital of the defunct Sāsānians.

It is probable that the Sāsānian bureaucracy had been strongly under the influence of the Zoroastrian clergy in pre-Islamic Iran. References to *mobads* in the Middle Persian and Arabic literatures, as well as the enormous number of Sāsānian seals with the names of priests on them, indicate the importance of the Sāsānian clergy. The class of scribes, however, did exist and was separate from the clergy, which is why it survived to serve new Arab Muslim masters, whereas the priests, of course, had to retire from any positions of influence in the government after the coming of Islam. The scribes, on the other hand, were of vital importance for the bedouin conquerors, for only the scribes could keep the accounts and help the Arabs rule their new conquests in the east. Consequently, after the Arab expansion the role of the scribes in Iran increased in importance compared to Sāsānian times, where they had performed little more than the bookkeeping for the secular chiefs and for religious officials such as judges and lawyers.

In pre-Islamic Central Asia, on the other hand, the rigid, almost caste system of Sāsānian Iran had not held sway and the scribes, the "priests" (Manichaean, Christian and Buddhist as well as Zoroastrian) and the men of letters were more equal in influence, for the society there was much more a mercantile, trading one rather than a hierarchical caste society as in Iran. The development of an egalitarian Islamic society therefore was more propitious in Transoxiana than in Iran, which is why the well-known "Iranian Renaissance" began in Central Asia rather than in Iran itself. The name "renaissance", however, can be misleading if it signifies a re-birth of the past, for it was rather an Islamic–Iranian Renaissance which flourished under the Sāmānids, and the Islamic part of it was both more important and more characteristic than the Iranian side. The Sāmānids liberated Islam from its narrow Arab bedouin background and mores and made of it an international culture and society. They showed that Islam also was not bound to the Arabic language, and in so doing they earned a significant niche in world history.

The government structure of the Sāmānids reflected this, too, for the three intellectual classes of Islamic society are clearly discernible in the sources on the Sāmānids, the scribes (Pers. *dabīr*, Ar. *kātib*), the literati (Pers. *farhangī*, Ar. *adīb*) and the religious scholar (Pers. *dānishmand*, Ar. *'ālim*), more known in the Arabic plurals, *kuttāb*, *udabā'* and *'ulamā'*. In Bukhārā, the Sāmānid capital, the scribes were the more important of the three in the earlier years of the dynasty and the 'ulamā' at the end of the dynasty. All were eclipsed, however, at the end by the Turkish military institution which will be discussed below.

Society under the Sāmānids thus was far from being a mere reflection of the state government divided between the court and the bureaucracy. Indeed the religious leaders were frequently loath to accept any employment by the government, even a judgeship, which was in the domain of religion. Like the learned men, poets and story-tellers, although frequently supported by the amīr or one of his entourage, at times showed their independence of and opposition to the Sāmānid government. Likewise, merchants, landowners (usually the *dihqāns*, a continuation of pre-Islamic society), and bazaar craftsmen could exert pressure on the state by virtue of their influence and co-operation to secure mutual goals. During the first half of the 4th/10th century economic conditions were good in the Sāmānid domains. The *ghāzīs* were busy on the Central Asian frontiers against the pagan Turks, while the

ʿ*ayyārūn* or *fityān*, who were active in many parts of Iran during this period, were comparatively quiet in Transoxiana. With the conversion of Central Asian Turks to Islam and internal developments in the Sāmānid state, the situation changed in the last part of the 4th/10th century, which will be discussed below. Before turning to the Turks, however, the provincial organization of the Sāmānid state should be examined.

Transoxiana at the time of the Arab conquests was an area of small oasis states which might be divided into three linguistic and cultural areas: Khwārazm on the lower Oxus River and around the Aral Sea, where Khwārazmian was the official written and spoken language, with a local, native era dating from the first century A.D.[1] Greater Soghdiana included not only Samarqand and Bukhārā, but areas of Soghdian influence or colonization to the east such as Farghāna and Shāsh. The Soghdian language, and a culture based on trading as far as China and on the land holdings of the local aristocracy of dihqāns, held sway over this widely extended area. Finally in Bactria, which included Chaghāniyān, most of present Tajikistan and northern Afghanistan the Kushan–Bactrian language in a modified Greek alphabet was in use in the 1st/7th and 2nd/8th centuries. In Bactria, the centre of Iranian Buddhism, that religion still claimed many adherents. Finally, to the south in the Hindukush mountains, in the Kabul valley, Ghazna and in Zamīndāvar, a resurgence of Hinduism had reasserted Indian influence. Although by the time of Ismāʿīl b. Aḥmad most of Soghdiana was Muslim and Khwārazm much the same, large parts of Bactria, and almost all of the Hindukush and southern Afghanistan regions had not been Islamicized. In all these areas, however, no matter what the religious changes, ancient customs and practices of rule continued to exist. In the many valleys of the mountainous areas, the only political reality was expressed in the form of a vassal–lord relationship. Thus the Arabs in their conquests in Central Asia had been obliged to make separate agreements with each town or oasis, which probably considered the new masters in the old vassal–lord relationship which had existed previously in this part of the world. The Sāmānids were heirs of this tradition.

When the four sons of Asad were given governorships under the Ṭāhirids, they not only fitted into the Central Asian pattern of various local dynasts, but the relationship between them was one of family

[1] Cf. V. A. Livshits, "The Khwarezmian Calendar and the Eras of Ancient Chorasmia", *Acta Antiqua Acad. Sci. Hungaricae*, vol. XVI (Budapest, 1968), pp. 433–46.

solidarity, a characteristic of that "feudal" society. We do not know whether the system of rule in pre-Islamic Soghdian society was based on a strong family tradition where the eldest member of the family would succeed to the paramount rule, but if we remember that later among the Būyids the system of the senior amīrate was a political reality, and among the Qarakhānid Turks, after the fall of the Sāmānid dynasty, such a system of succession was practised, one may ask if this system was not an old Iranian rather than a Central Asian custom. We do not have enough information to answer this question, but it seems to have existed in Central Asia at an early date.

In any case, in their dealings among members of their own family and with petty dynasts in the east, the Sāmānids expanded their state on the basis of vassal relationships. We have already mentioned Khwārazm which submitted to Ismā'īl. In Chaghāniyān the local dynasty also accepted Sāmānid rule early, probably submitting to Ismā'īl, and in many sources the ruling family is called by the Arabic name of Muḥtāj (Āl Muḥtāj). One of their members, Abū 'Alī Chaghānī, became governor of Khurāsān about 318/930 and was removed in 334/945, but he revolted and occupied Bukhārā for a short time in 336/947, then was defeated, pardoned and reinstated as governor of Khurāsān, dying in 344/955. Farther to the east, in the present Vakhsh valley, was the principality of Khuttalān which also submitted to Sāmānid overlordship. To the south of the Oxus River the family of the Farīghūnids ruled in Jūzjān, the present-day area of Maimana in Afghanistan, and they were loyal vassals of the Sāmānids to the end of their rule. There were, of course, minor vassals whose existence can be implied only from brief notes in the sources, such as the rulers of Gharchistān, Bust and Ghazna. All in all, Sāmānid rule weighed lightly on their vassals and the benefits of centralized rule were more than any disadvantages. Some local princely families, however, lost their patrimonies, such as the family of the ancient rulers of Bukhārā and other towns in the Bukhārān oasis. On the whole, however, the Sāmānids tried to tie the local rulers to Bukhārā in a vassal relationship, rather than extirpating the local dynasty. Peace was even made with the Ṣaffārids in Sīstān who became vassals of the Sāmānids for a time.

The rise of Turkish slaves to great power in the Sāmānid state should be examined, for they changed the balance of power to their own advantage. Turks were not newcomers in the Near East, for the Arabs had much difficulty fighting them in eastern Khurāsān and in Transoxiana in the time of the Umayyad caliphate. One of the reasons for the efforts of the early Sāmānids to expand their boundaries to the north and east was much more to obtain slaves than to spread Islam. The missionaries who followed the Sāmānid armies, however, did convert many pagans in the course of time. Even before Ismā'īl the Sāmānids had participated in Ṭāhirid raids and conquests in Transoxiana. Under the governorship of Ṭalḥa b. Ṭāhir his general Aḥmad b. Khālid raided Farghāna and Ushrūsana, which had revolted against the rule of Aḥmad b. Asad the governor in Shāsh.[1] In 207/822 Bunjikath, the capital of Ushrūsana, was burned, and under Ismā'īl Ushrūsana was incorporated into the Sāmānid kingdom and the last ruler, called *afshīn*, Sayyār b. 'Abd-Allāh, was killed. His last coin, of copper, is dated 279/892. General order was restored and some conversions made. According to Sam'ānī (*s.v.* Sāmānī) in 225/839–40 Nūḥ b. Asad conquered Isfījāb and built a wall around it to protect the city from the nomadic Turks. It is difficult to gather all of the notices about the expeditions of Ismā'īl against the Turks, but the year 280/893 is memorable for the conquest of Ṭarāz/Talas, where converts to Islam were made.[2] On these expeditions the ghāzīs or warriors for the faith were an important factor in Sāmānid successes. All this time the slave trade in the Sāmānid domains was an important source of revenue for both merchants and the government, which taxed even the transit slave trade to Baghdad and elsewhere. Turkish slaves were highly valued for their martial qualities and the Sāmānid amīrs maintained schools for slaves who prepared for military or for administrative service. It is probable that the amīrs used Turkish slaves in their government because they were more reliable than the local dihqāns and furthermore the slaves were well trained for their positions from childhood. Their numbers grew as did their influence. One Arab geographer says that in the year 375/985 slaves were selling in Transoxiana for twenty or thirty dirhams a head, for the Sāmānids had made so many prisoners, and they monopolized the slave trade so the prices dropped because of the glut on the market.[3] So the number of Turks inside Sāmānid territory was considerable.

The training of slaves at the Sāmānid court is described in detail by Niẓām al-Mulk, and their training prepared them well for positions of

[1] Ṭabarī, vol. III, pp. 1065–6.
[2] Ṭabarī, vol. III, pp. 2138 and 2249; Mas'ūdī, *Murūj*, vol. VIII, p. 144.
[3] Muqaddasī, p. 340.

leadership in the state. These Turkish officials and generals then imported slaves themselves and thus the Turks became more and more important in the army and in the administration. The ultimate Turkification of most of Transoxiana was thus begun in earnest under the Sāmānids, but it was not so much this which brought about the fall of the Sāmānids as the loss of confidence in the dynasty by the population, which in the end abandoned the Sāmānids to their fate.

From the time of Naṣr b. Aḥmad to the end of the dynasty most of the energies of the Sāmānids were devoted to their western frontiers, for the rise of Shīʿī dynasties in western Iran posed a threat to the Sunnī Sāmānids. The rise of the Būyids, and especially their conquest of Baghdad in 333/945, heightened the threat in the west. The amīr in Bukhārā was Nūḥ b. Naṣr, who succeeded his father in 331/943. The new ruler was faced with a revolt in Khwārazm which was suppressed, and then with difficulties from Abū ʿAlī Chaghānī, mentioned above. Abū ʿAlī refused to abdicate his post of governor of Khurāsān in favour of Ibrāhīm b. Sīmjūr, a Turk in the amīr's service. Instead he joined an uncle of Nūḥ, Ibrāhīm b. Aḥmad, and raised the standard of revolt. In 336/947 for a short time Ibrāhīm was recognized as ruler in Bukhārā and Nūḥ had to flee to Samarqand. The populace of Bukhārā, however, did not support the new amīr, so Nūḥ returned and took revenge on his uncle and two brothers by blinding them. Even though Nūḥ succeeded in sacking Abū ʿAlī's capital in Chaghāniyān, he was obliged to make peace in 948 and reinstated Abū ʿAlī in the rule of Chaghāniyān. In 341/952, after the death of the interim governor of Khurāsān, Manṣūr b. Qara-Tegin (Ibrāhīm b. Sīmjūr having died earlier in 337/948), Abū ʿAlī was reappointed governor of Khurāsān and began a war against the Būyids. This struggle was instigated by the Ziyārids of Ṭabaristān who were enemies of the Būyids and allies of the Sāmānids. Abū ʿAlī, though successful in the field, made a compromise with the Būyids in Ray which displeased Vushmgīr the Ziyārid who complained in Bukhārā that Abū ʿAlī was making common cause with the enemy. As a result Abū ʿAlī was again deposed from his governorship. Abū ʿAlī thereupon joined the Būyids and received, through their agency, a diploma from the ʿAbbāsid caliph Muṭīʿ for rule over Khurāsān.

With the death of Nūḥ in 343/954 Abū ʿAlī had seemed to be in a good position to establish his independent rule over Khurāsān, but he too died and Sāmānid rule was re-established. The new governor Bakr b. Malik al-Farghānī had been appointed by Nūḥ, but this Turkish officer, who had carved out a fief for himself at a place called Naṣrābād in the Farghāna valley (a symptom of developments in the Sāmānid state), was killed by the Turkish guard of the amīr less than two years after assuming office.[1] He was succeeded for a time by Muḥammad b. Ibrāhīm Sīmjūrī, while the vizier was Abū Ja'far 'Utbī, from the same prominent family which had produced an earlier vizier. It was clear, however, that the Turkish military establishment in Bukhārā had taken control of the government, for 'Abd al-Malik, son and successor of Nūḥ, was incapable of acting without their agreement. The leader of the Turks was Alp-Tegin and he had himself appointed governor of Khurāsān, at the same time securing the appointment as vizier of Muḥammad b. Abū 'Alī Muḥammad Bal'amī, son of the Bal'amī who had been vizier under Amīr Naṣr. Unfortunately, the son was not as capable as his father and affairs continued to devolve into the hands of the Turks. The death of the Amīr 'Abd al-Malik at the end of 350/961 did not change the picture.

The problem of succession, however, split the Turkish party, for Alp-Tegin supported the son of 'Abd al-Malik whereas another and larger group, headed by a childhood companion of the amīr's brother Manṣūr called Fā'iq, was successful in raising Manṣūr to the throne. Alp-Tegin, seeing his chances dim, left Nīshāpūr the capital of Khurāsān for Ghazna where he established himself independently of the Sāmānids and laid the foundations for the future Ghaznavid empire.

Abū Ṣāliḥ Manṣūr b. Nūḥ ruled for fifteen years in the same tradition as his predecessors, a patron of the arts and literature, but his government was now not only weak but chronically in debt. His governor of Khurāsān, Abu'l-Ḥasan Muḥammad Sīmjūrī, who remained in power from 351/962 to the death of Manṣūr, fought against the Būyids. It was easy to find a pretext for hostilities since Vushmgīr, the Ziyārid prince, had been driven from Ṭabaristān and Gurgān by the Būyids the same year in which Sīmjūrī was appointed governor of Khurāsān. The death of Vushmgīr in the following year put an end to hostilities, but the Būyid ruler 'Aḍud al-Daula agreed to pay tribute to the Sāmānids who were hard pressed to raise money for their troops. The tribute unfortunately did not continue long.

One feature of the last part of Sāmānid rule in both Transoxiana and Khurāsān was the decline of the dihqān class. Not only the rise of the

[1] E. A. Davidovich, "Vladeteli Nasrabada", *Kratkie Soobshcheniya Instituta Materialnoi Kultury*, vol. LXI (Moscow, 1956), pp. 107–13.

Turks through the slave system of the court, but also the decline of the countryside caused the impoverishment of the dihqāns. Compared to the Ṭāhirids, the Sāmānids were a very centralized dynasty, and the growth of the bureaucracy paralleled a growth of cities. Bukhārā, Samarqand, but especially Nīshāpūr, and other cities of Khurāsān increased greatly in size and complexity. For example, the oasis of Bukhārā, which had been dotted with flourishing towns and surrounded by a wall which kept out the desert sands as well as nomads, under the later Sāmānids became a metropolis – Bukhārā, with villages which were almost suburbs, rather than a succession of towns. The wall was neglected, as was agriculture in general, as the sands encroached on the settled areas. Archaeology confirms the sources which indicate that the dihqāns and peasants flocked to the cities in the second half of the 4th/10th century. The dihqān class lost its power and influence, and the city proletariat was swollen in size. The government bought land, or confiscated it in lieu of taxes thus diminishing the taxable land, while land values declined, not helped by the growth of *waqf* or religious endowment lands, attached to a mosque, hospital, school or the like. Revenue from the land dropped considerably, which is one reason why the government was always in search of new revenue. So the old, traditional families gave way to new landowners, including merchants and army officers. The peasantry was more oppressed than previously and they too fled to the cities. Contemporary writers complain of the lack of sanitation and crowded conditions in the cities, while many people suffered from the privileges which others had. For example, *sayyids*, descendants of the Prophet Muḥammad, were exempted from paying taxes by the Sāmānid government as were officers of the guard and others. All of this did not help the revenues of the state.

We have mentioned religion only briefly. The Sāmānid amīrs were devout Muslims, and except for the interlude when Naṣr b. Aḥmad flirted with the Ismāʿīlīs, they remained Sunnīs of the Ḥanafī persuasion. Shāfiʿīs existed but not in great numbers, while Shīʿīs, in general after Naṣr b. Aḥmad, kept themselves underground. The Sāmānid amīrs promoted missionary activities, and patronized the translation of religious works from Arabic into Persian. It was under Manṣūr b. Nūḥ that the *Ṭafsīr* or commentary on the Qur'ān by Ṭabarī was translated from Arabic into Persian by a group of scholars. Other books were put into Persian at the orders of the Sāmānid amīrs to help defend orthodoxy against heresy. Abu'l-Qāsim Samarqandī (d. 342/953) was one of the religious writers active under the Sāmānids and he translated into Persian his own Arabic treatises on orthodoxy. Until the end of the dynasty the ʿulamā were pro-Sāmānid but at the end they too abandoned the dynasty.

The literati who flourished at the courts of the early Sāmānids, such as Rūdakī, continued to enjoy favour later. Not only were religious works translated from Arabic into Persian by order of the Sāmānid amīrs, but secular works too were not neglected. The vizier Abū ʿAlī Muḥammad Balʿamī started his work on the translation of Ṭabarī's great history into Persian in 352/963 and finished it a few years later. Likewise books on medicine and drugs were written in Persian under the Sāmānids, and the court library at Bukhārā was famous. It provided an education for the young Ibn Sīnā who lived in Bukhārā at the end of the Sāmānid dynasty. Another savant Muḥammad b. Yūsuf al-Khwārazmī, who died *c.* 387/997, served in the Sāmānid bureaucracy and composed a small encyclopaedia in which he wrote about the bureaucracy among many other subjects. In short, scholars were welcomed at the court of Bukhārā as well as in the provincial courts of the Sāmānid state which copied Bukhārā. The poets and story-tellers were even more welcome, and the most famous was Daqīqī.

Abū Manṣūr Muḥammad b. Aḥmad Daqīqī was invited to the Sāmānid court by Nūḥ II, the son of amīr Manṣūr who commissioned the poet to write the epic history of pre-Islamic Iran in verse. He did not finish his work, for in 367/977 he was murdered, according to some traditions by his own slave. Daqīqī was only one of a number of poets or story-tellers in the 4th/10th century who were seeking to preserve the heritage of ancient Iran before it was forgotten and absorbed by the new Islamic culture which was changing not only the old Persian language by a massive influx of Arabic words and expressions, but also was substituting new ideas and ideals for the ancient Iranian mores, preserved in the lays of minstrels and story-tellers. Firdausī, who began his work under the Sāmānids but finished it under the Ghaznavids, was not, as he often has been described, the founder of New Persian literature. Rather, he was the saviour of Middle Persian literature. True, he wrote in the Arabic alphabet, but who could read Persian in the cumbersome Pahlavī alphabet in Firdausī's day? It was the Sāmānid court which initiated interest in preserving the pre-Islamic Iranian past and Firdausī was the result of that interest.

Perhaps the main theme of the *Shāh-nāma* is the conflict between

Iran and Tūrān, whose people in Firdausī's day were considered to have been the ancestors of the Turks. Before the great epic poem was finished, however, the Turks had been converted to Islam and had become part of Islamic society. We have already mentioned some of the Sāmānid expeditions against the pagan Turks, but the rôle of dervishes and missionaries who went into the steppes was greater than the military in converting the Turks. Brief notices in the sources merely indicate the activity of such missionaries as Abu'l-Ḥasan al-Kalamātī from Nīshāpūr who, during the reign of Amīr 'Abd al-Malik, was active among the Turks (presumably the Qarakhānids).[1] The raids of the pagan Turks into the Sāmānid domains until at least the end of Ismā'īl's rule, brought volunteers for the faith or ghāzīs from all over the eastern Islamic world to fight in Transoxiana against the infidels. With the conversion of the Turks, however, the services of the fighters for Islam were no longer needed in Central Asia, but still in Anatolia and the Caucasus regions. In the history of the Būyids by Ibn Miskawaih under the year 353/964, it is stated that 5,000 such warriors for the faith came from Khurāsān into Būyid territory and in 355/966 a host of 20,000 of them came from Khurāsān and asked permission to pass through the Būyid lands to go west and fight against the Byzantines. Among these freebooter warriors were undoubtedly many Turks, forerunners of the great movement of Turks to Anatolia in later centuries. In effect the barrier of *ribāṭs* or forts built by the Ṭāhirids and early Sāmānids against the infidel Turks in Central Asia, and manned by warriors for the faith, in the second half of the 4th/10th century lost their purpose and were for the most part abandoned. The population still was predominantly Iranian but Turks had begun to settle on the land and mix with the local people. Since long before the Sāmānids, all nomads had been Turkish, and their close relations with the settled folk helped to speed the process of assimilation.

The end of the dynasty was longer delayed than many expected because the loyalty of the people to the house of Sāmān, in spite of incompetent rulers, persisted for a time. A year before he died in the summer of 366/976, Amīr Manṣūr gave the post of vizier to Abū 'Abd-Allāh Aḥmad b. Muḥammad Jaihānī, grandson of the famous Jaihānī mentioned above, but the new vizier could accomplish little more than his immediate predecessors. In the west the powerful Būyid ruler 'Aḍud al-Daula was able to wrest Kirmān from nominal Sāmānid overlordship

[1] Sam'ānī, *s.v.* "al-Kalamātī".

and to prevail most of the time in Ṭabaristān and Gurgān against the Ziyārid ruler Qābūs b. Vushmgīr, the ally of the Sāmānids. The Sāmānids tried to recover lost lands in the west, but they were not able to prevail against the Būyids.

Nūḥ II b. Manṣūr was a youth when he ascended the throne, and he was assisted by his mother and a new vizier Abu'l-Ḥusain 'Abd-Allāh b. Aḥmad 'Utbī, of the same family as a previous vizier. Khurāsān was governed, one might say almost ruled, separately from Bukhārā, by Abu'l-Ḥasan Sīmjūrī, and the new vizier could only flatter the Sīmjūrid and secretly undermine his position until in 982 he was able to replace Abu'l-Ḥasan by a Turkish general called Tāsh who had been a slave of 'Utbī's father and was devoted to the vizier. Abu'l-Ḥasan fled to his appanage in Kūhistān south of Ṭūs and Herāt. The army of Khurāsān, now the only real standing army of the Sāmānids, was assembled and led against the Būyids later in the same year 372/982, but after initial successes it was decisively defeated by the Būyids and only 'Aḍud al-Daula's death kept the Būyids from invading Khurāsān. Before 'Utbī could reorganize the army, he was assassinated by agents of Abu'l-Ḥasan Sīmjūrī and Fā'iq who had been chamberlain. The governor of Khurāsān, Tāsh, was called to Bukhārā by the amīr to restore order in the city following an uprising which had taken place at the news of the death of the vizier 'Utbī. This he did and prepared to fight Abu'l-Ḥasan and his son Abū 'Alī allied with Fā'iq. Tāsh foresaw future trouble for himself, however, and made peace with his opponents. He persuaded the amīr to assign Balkh to Fā'iq to rule and Herāt to Abū 'Alī, while Abu'l-Ḥasan returned to Kūhistān and Tāsh to Nīshāpūr. The last proved a mistake, for the new vizier Muḥammad b. 'Uzair had been an enemy of 'Utbī and hence of Tāsh, and he lost no time in persuading the amīr to remove Tāsh from the governorship of Khurāsān and reinstating Abu'l-Ḥasan Sīmjūrī in his place. Tāsh at once sought help from the Būyids but even with this help he was defeated by the Sīmjūrīs and Fā'iq at the end of 377/987, and fled to Gurgān where he died the following year.

Abu'l-Ḥasan Sīmjūrī also died shortly afterwards, and his son succeeded him as governor of Khurāsān with more power than any governor before him. Fā'iq quarrelled with Abū 'Alī and in the resulting hostilities the former was defeated in 380/990. Fā'iq in retreat tried to take Bukhārā but was defeated again, this time by Bektuzun a Turkish general serving the amīr Nūḥ. Fā'iq returned to Balkh which he was able to hold against Sāmānid vassals instigated to attack him by Bukhārā. A new menace, however, appeared in Transoxiana with the advance of the Qarakhānid Turks deep into Sāmānid territory.

The Qarakhānid dynasty had been consolidating its power in Kāshghar and Balāsāghūn, north of Isfījāb for several decades prior to their advance into Sāmānid territory. In 370/980 they had taken Isfījāb and possibly earlier than that, in 366/976, they had captured the silver mines of the Sāmānids on the upper Zarafshān valley. More peacefully, however, the Qarakhānids simply inherited the small principalities which had broken away from Sāmānid rule and already were ruled by autonomous Turkish "governors" of the Sāmānids.

The Qarakhānid ruler Bughrā Khān moved at the end of 991 into Sāmānid territory and the first army sent against him by Amīr Nūḥ b. Manṣūr was completely defeated. Nūḥ then turned to Fā'iq, pardoned him and made him governor of Samarqand with a commission to fight the invaders. The course of events is unclear but after some fighting Fā'iq surrendered to Bughrā Khān who advanced on Bukhārā causing Nūḥ to flee. The Qarakhānid ruler entered the Sāmānid capital in the late spring of 382/992. Some sources, such as the *Kitāb al-yamīnī* of 'Utbī claim that Fā'iq invited the khān to invade the Sāmānid domains. Mīrkhwānd, and other later historians suggest that Abū 'Alī wanted to divide the Sāmānid state between himself and Bughrā Khān, so he invited the Qarakhānids to invade Sāmānid territory. These uncertain stories of invitations lead one to suspect that many people in the Sāmānid state were not unhappy to see the advance of a new power. In any case, Fā'iq was re-appointed to Balkh by Bughrā Khān and left the capital.

Nūḥ wrote to Abū 'Alī in Nīshāpūr requesting his help in regaining his throne, but the latter at first refused and then reconsidered. His help was not necessary for Bughrā Khān fell sick in Bukhārā and left the city, dying on the road after leaving Samarqand for the north. Later in the summer Nūḥ returned to Bukhārā, easily defeating the representatives of the Qarakhānids in the city.

The turncoat Fā'iq tried to capture Bukhārā but was defeated, and this time he fled to his former enemy Abū 'Alī whom he joined. The two rebels decided to put an end to Sāmānid rule, but amīr Nūḥ looked to Ghazna for aid, to Sebük-Tegin who had succeeded Alp-Tegin as ruler in Ghazna. Nūḥ also secured the aid of the Khwārazmians and other vassals as well as Sebük-Tegin and in a battle in Khurāsān in

Rajab 384/August 994 the rebels were completely defeated. Both Abū ʿAlī and Fāʾiq fled to Gurgān where they gathered new forces. Nūḥ rewarded Sebük-Tegin and his son Maḥmūd with titles and gave the governorship of Khurāsān to Maḥmūd in place of Abū ʿAlī.

The following year the two rebels returned and forced Maḥmūd to evacuate Nīshāpūr. Sebük-Tegin joined his son and they again defeated Abū ʿAlī and Fāʾiq in a battle near Ṭūs. The two fled northward and Fāʾiq eventually reached Qarakhānid territory after Nūḥ refused to pardon him. Abū ʿAlī, however, was pardoned and sent to Khwārazm where he was imprisoned by the Khwārazmshāh. The Shāh and Abū ʿAlī were both captured by the amīr of Gurgānj in northern Khwārazm and Abū ʿAlī was sent to Bukhārā where the amīr Nūḥ after a time sent him to Sebük-Tegin in 386/996 and he was later executed in Ghazna.

Although Fāʾiq intrigued with Naṣr Khān the successor of Bughrā Khān to attack Nūḥ and Sebük-Tegin, the Qarakhānid instead made peace. In this peace Fāʾiq was pardoned by Nūḥ and even made governor of Samarqand. The situation was stabilized, but the Sāmānid domains had shrunk considerably, now restricted to the Zarafshān valley with Khwārazm only paying lip service as a vassal state. Khurāsān and all lands south of the Oxus River gave no allegiance to the Sāmānids, the Ghaznavids having replaced them in most regions. In 387/997 both Nūḥ and Sebük-Tegin died, leaving very different successors.

Nūḥ's son Abu'l-Ḥārith Manṣūr II was too young to control his strong associates, and when a rebel called on Naṣr Khān for help the Qarakhānid came but arrested the rebel and sent Fāʾiq, who was received by the khān with great friendship, to Bukhārā with a small force. Manṣūr II, not trusting Fāʾiq, fled but was induced to return to Bukhārā, even though power remained in Fāʾiq's hands. Affairs in Khurāsān, after the death of Sebük-Tegin, again invited intervention on the part of the Sāmānids. A Turkish general Bektuzun, mentioned previously, was sent by Manṣūr II to Nīshāpūr as governor of Khurāsān. Fāʾiq, who was the real power in Bukhārā, feared the growing power of Bektuzun and persuaded Abu'l-Qāsim Sīmjūrī, the new ruler of Kūhistān, to attack Bektuzun. A conflict took place in the spring of 388/998, and Bektuzun was victorious. He made peace with Abu'l-Qāsim, however, and returned to Bukhārā, and although he and Fāʾiq did not become friends, they joined forces against a new threat, Maḥmūd of Ghazna, who had succeeded in gaining supreme power in his kingdom after the suppression of his brother Ismā'īl and others. Maḥmūd wanted back the governorship of all Khurāsān, and both Fā'iq and Bektuzun feared that the amīr Manṣūr II might betray them in favour of Maḥmūd, so in Ṣafar 389/February 999 they deposed and then blinded Manṣūr, replacing him with his younger brother Abu'l-Fawāris 'Abd al-Malik.

Maḥmūd saw an opportunity to assert his claims as the avenger of the deposed amīr, so he set out for Nīshāpūr, but he realized that his enemies, Bektuzun and Fā'iq, together with the Sīmjūrīd Abu'l-Qāsim, were possibly too strong for him, so he made peace with them in the early spring of 389/999, retaining Balkh and Herāt under his rule. The allies did not trust Maḥmūd and attacked the rearguard of his army without, however, defeating Maḥmūd. War was renewed and this time near Marv he decisively defeated the allies. Maḥmūd now secured all of the lands south of the Oxus River. Even the rulers of Chaghāniyān and others north of the river submitted to him, and he appointed his brother Naṣr governor of Khurāsān. Power had definitely passed from the Sāmānids to the Ghaznavids south of the Oxus.

The Sāmānid amīr 'Abd al-Malik, together with Fā'iq and later Bektuzun, in Bukhārā attempted to rally support for a campaign against Maḥmūd, but Fā'iq died just as the Qarakhānid ruler Naṣr decided to put an end to the Sāmānid state. The Sāmānid amīr tried to rouse the people of his domains against the invaders but he failed. The people of Bukhārā would not listen to the Sāmānids, especially when their religious leaders assured them that the Qarakhānids were good Muslims like themselves and there was no need to fight for the discredited Sāmānids against them. The Qarakhānids entered the capital without resistance and Bektuzun surrendered, while 'Abd al-Malik was taken prisoner. The Muslim Turks accomplished what the pagan Turks could not have done; the Qarakhānids brought an end to the Sāmānid dynasty and Iranian rule. Thereafter Turks ruled in Central Asia.

There was a romantic postlude to the story of the Sāmānids. A younger brother of Manṣūr b. Nūḥ and of 'Abd al-Malik called Ismā'īl escaped from the Qarakhānid prison and fled to Khwārazm where he gathered support for the Sāmānid cause. He took the name Muntaṣir, "victorious", and he was successful at first in driving the Qarakhānids from Bukhārā and then from Samarqand. But then the main Qarakhānid army was mobilized and at its approach Muntaṣir had to abandon all of his conquests and flee to Khurāsān. At first again he was successful and drove Naṣr, brother of Maḥmūd, from Nīshāpūr, but again with the approach of Maḥmūd's army he had to abandon everything. In 394/1003 Muntaṣir returned to Transoxiana and sought help from a new source, the Oghuz Turkish tribes which had infiltrated the Zarafshān River valley. The latent power of the Turkish nomads, so evident later under the Saljuqs, was revealed when they defeated the Qarakhānids in several battles including the chief ruler Naṣr. Muntaṣir, however, feared that he could not rely upon the nomadic Turks, so he left them and went to Khurāsān.

Attempts to reconcile Maḥmūd of Ghazna and to enlist his sympathy for the house of Sāmān failed, so Muntaṣir returned to the Zarafshān valley where he did secure aid from various supporters, including the Oghuz. In Rajab 394/May 1004 he defeated the Qarakhānids, but in a succeeding battle the Oghuz deserted him and his army disintegrated. Again Muntaṣir fled to Khurāsān and again at the end of the same year he tried his luck with a few followers to cross the Oxus River and rally adherents to his cause. This time the Qarakhānids were prepared and Muntaṣir barely escaped with his life. He took refuge with an Arab tribe near Marv but he was killed by their chief in 395/1005. Thus ended the last attempt of the Sāmānids to regain power.

The descendants of the Sāmānid family continued to live in the oasis of Bukhārā and they were highly regarded by the populace and were well treated by the government in later times. The memory of the Sāmānids, not only as the last Iranian dynasty in Central Asia, but that dynasty which unified the area under one rule and which saved the legacy of ancient Iran from extinction, lasted long in Central Asia, and a kind of "mystique" similar to that which surrounded the Sāsānians with their founder Ardashīr, also grew up regarding the Sāmānids and their founder Ismā'īl. Indeed, in many ways the Sāmānids were compared with the Sāsānids. The union of diverse elements in Transoxiana by the Sāmānids into one state seemed to many almost miraculous, as though the unity of Iran and its culture had been accomplished in Central Asia and not in Iran. Furthermore, this unity was based upon Islam, and the Sāmānids had shown how ancient Iranian culture could be compatible with Islam. This was the great contribution of the Sāmānids to the world of Islam, and of course, to Iran.

GENEALOGICAL TABLE OF THE SĀMĀNIDS

Naṣr b. Aḥmad	c. 261/875–279/892
Ismā'īl b. Aḥmad	279/892–295/907
Aḥmad b. Ismā'īl	295/907–301/914
Naṣr II b. Aḥmad	301/914–331/943
Nūḥ b. Naṣr	331/943–343/954
'Abd al-Malik	343/954–350/961
Manṣūr	350/961–366/976
Nūḥ II	366/976–387/997
Abu'l-Ḥāri<u>th</u> Manṣūr II	387/997–389/999
'Abd al-Malik II	389/999
Ismā'īl Muntaṣir	390/1000–395/1005

CHAPTER 5

THE EARLY GHAZNAVIDS

The establishment of the Ghaznavid sultanate in the eastern Iranian world represents the first major breakthrough of Turkish power there against the indigenous dynasties. The peaceful penetration of Turks into the originally Iranian lands of Central Asia, *sc.* into Transoxiana, Farghāna and Khwārazm, and across the Dihistān Steppe (the modern Qara Qum Desert) towards the Caspian coastlands, had, however, begun several centuries before. The Iranian rulers of Soghdia who opposed the Arab invaders of the 1st/7th and early 2nd/8th centuries received assistance from the Western Turks, before the steppe empire of these Türgesh itself disintegrated. In addition to this, the Soghdian princes hired Turks from the steppes as mercenary soldiers and as frontier guards, thus anticipating the 'Abbāsid caliphs' employment of Turkish slaves in their armies. In what was, before the rise of the Sāmānids, a politically fragmented region, with the independent political unit often little more than the city-state or petty principality, there was frequent internecine warfare and consequent employment for these warriors.

The Sāmānid amīrate in Transoxiana and Khurāsān meant that there was a strong barrier in the northeast against mass incursions from the steppes into the civilized zone. The Iranian world was now protected by a vigorous power, whose central government in Bukhārā had an advanced bureaucracy, utilizing techniques evolved in the 'Abbāsid caliphate, and a well-disciplined professional army. Again, this army followed the 'Abbāsid pattern in that it had a core of Turkish slave guards (*ghilmān*, *mamālīk*) personally attached to the amīr. Hence during the heyday of the Sāmānids – up to the middle of the 4th/10th century – the frontiers of Transoxiana were held firm against pressure from the Turks outside. Such frontier regions as Isfījāb, Shāsh and Farghāna were protected by chains of *ribāṭs* or fortified points garrisoned by *ghāzīs* or fighters for the faith. The amīrs personally undertook punitive campaigns into the steppes when need arose, such as the great expedition to Talas in 280/893 of Ismā'īl b. Aḥmad, when the capital of the

Qarluq Turks was sacked and an immense booty of slaves and beasts taken. Similarly, the Afrīghid Khwārazm-Shāhs in the 4th/10th century led an expedition each autumn into the steppes, the so-called *Faghbūriyya* or "King's expedition".

During this period of Sāmānid florescence, large numbers of individual Turks were brought through Transoxiana into the Islamic world; the greater part of them found employment as military guards in the service of the caliphs and of provincial Arab and Persian governors. During the course of the 3rd/9th century the military basis of the ʿAbbāsid caliphate was completely transformed. Instead of relying on their Khurāsānian guards, or on the remnants of an even earlier system, that of the militia of Arab warriors, the caliphs came to depend almost wholly on slave troops. These included such varied races as Arabs, Berbers, black Sudanese, Balkan Slavs, Greeks, Armenians and Iranians, but Turks from Central Asia were the most prominent of all. Much of the economic prosperity of the Sāmānid state was built on the slave trade across its territories, for the demand for Turkish slaves was insatiable; the Sāmānid government controlled the export of slaves across the Oxus, exacting tolls and requiring licences for the transit of slave boys. The Turks were prized above all other races for their bravery, hardihood and equestrian skill, and provincial governors and ambitious military commanders emulated the caliphs in recruiting for themselves bodyguards of these *ghulāms*. It was the existence of these professional troops which enabled such governors as Aḥmad b. Ṭūlūn and then Muḥammad b. Ṭughj to throw off direct caliphal control in Egypt.

Thus during the 3rd/9th and 4th/10th centuries there was a gradual penetration from within of the eastern and central parts of the Islamic world by these Turkish soldiers. In Persia itself, the two major powers of the Būyids and the Sāmānids supplemented the indigenous Dailamī and eastern Iranian elements of their forces with Turkish cavalrymen, and even the minor Dailamī and Kurdish dynasties of the Caspian coastlands and northwestern Persia added Turks to their local and tribal followings. Numerically, these Turks in the Iranian world did not add up to a great influx – not until Saljuq, Mongol and Tīmūrid times did mass immigrations occur which changed the ethnic complexion of certain regions – but they formed an élite class as military leaders and governors, and in western Persia at least, as owners of extensive landed estates or *iqṭāʿs*. Once the hand of central government relaxed, these Turkish commanders had the means for power immediately at hand:

personal entourages of slave guards, and territorial possessions to provide financial backing.

These considerations clearly play a large rôle in the decline and fall of the Sāmānid empire in the second half of the 4th/10th century, and in the rise from its ruins of two major dynasties, the Qarakhānids to the north of the Oxus and the Ghaznavids to the south of that river. Signs of weakness already appeared in the amīrate of Nūḥ b. Naṣr (331–43/943–54). Power was usurped by over-mighty subjects such as Abū 'Alī Chaghānī, who came from a prominent Iranian family of the upper Oxus valley, and by the Sīmjūrīs, a family of Turkish ghulām origin who held Kūhistān virtually as their own private domain. The expense of dealing with rebellion and unrest in Khurāsān placed the amīrs in serious financial trouble, driving them to impose fresh taxation and thereby increase their unpopularity with the influential landowning and military classes. Uncertainties over the succession allowed the Turkish military leaders and prominent bureaucrats, such as the Bal'amīs and 'Utbīs, to act as king-makers. With centrifugal forces in the ascendant, outlying dependencies of the Sāmānid empire began to fall away from the control of Bukhārā. Thus in Sīstān, a collateral branch of the Ṣaffārid dynasty reappeared and flourished under Aḥmad b. Muḥammad b. Khalaf b. Laith (311–52/923–63) and his son Khalaf (352–93/963–1003) (see Chapter 3). In Kirmān, the Sāmānid commander Muḥammad b. Ilyās founded a short-lived dynasty (320–57/932–68) which ruled in virtual independence until the province was conquered by the Būyid 'Aḍud al-Daula. In Bust and al-Rukhkhaj, in southeastern Afghanistan, the ghulām general and governor of Balkh, Qara-Tegin Isfījābī, held power in the years after 317/929. Forty years later, a further group of Turkish ghulāms under one Baituz was ruling in Bust, and it is possible, though unproven, that there was some continuity here with the earlier régime of Qara-Tegin. Baituz's links with his suzerains in Bukhārā had become so far relaxed that on the sole coin of his which is extant, a copper *fals* of 359/970, the name of the Sāmānid amīr is not mentioned.[1]

The Ghaznavids arose indirectly from this atmosphere within the Sāmānid empire of disintegration, palace revolutions and succession *putschs*. The Turkish Commander-in-Chief of the Sāmānid forces, the *ḥājib* Alp-Tegin, in 350/961 allied with the vizier Abū 'Alī Muḥammad Bal'amī to place their own candidate for the amīrate on the throne. The

[1] J.-C. Gardin, *Lashkari Bazar II, Les trouvailles . . .* (Paris, 1963), pp. 170–1.

coup failed, and Alp-Tegin was obliged to withdraw to Ghazna in eastern Afghanistan, on the far periphery of the Sāmānid empire, wresting the town from its local ruling dynasty of the Lawīks (351/962). Ghazna was not, however, relinquished by the Lawīks without a struggle. They were connected by marriage to the Hindūshāhī dynasty ruling in Kabul (see below), and clearly enjoyed much local support. During the next fifteen years, they returned on various occasions, and at one juncture, Abū Isḥāq Ibrāhīm, Alp-Tegin's son and successor in Ghazna, only regained the town with military help sent out from Bukhārā. Because of this need in the early years for Sāmānid support, the various Turkish governors in Ghazna continued down to Sebük-Tegin's death in 387/997 generally to acknowledge the amīrs on their coins.

One of Alp-Tegin's most trusted supporters was the ghulām Sebük-Tegin (probably to be interpreted as Turkish "beloved prince"). According to a testament of aphorisms on the exercise of kingly power, allegedly left to his son Maḥmūd (the *Pand-nāma*), Sebük-Tegin came from the region of Barskhān on the shores of the Isiq-Göl, in what is now the Kirghiz S.S.R. It is accordingly probable that he came from one of the component tribes of the Turkish Qarluq group. Obsequious genealogists later fabricated a genealogy connecting Sebük-Tegin with the last Sāsānid Emperor, Yazdgard III, it being supposed that Yazdgard's family had fled into the Central Asian steppes and there intermarried with the local Turks, although they were unable to get round the fact of his pagan birth. Captured in the course of intertribal warfare, he was sold as a slave at Nakhshab, and eventually bought by Alp-Tegin. The story of his rise to eminence in Alp-Tegin's service is detailed in the *Siyāsat-nāma* of Niẓām al-Mulk, although this account should be treated with some caution. Sebük-Tegin accompanied Alp-Tegin to Ghazna, passing into the service of the latter's son Abū Isḥāq Ibrāhīm, and quietly building up a following among the Turks in Ghazna. He was prominent during the governorship of Bilge-Tegin, in whose time the town of Gardīz was first attacked (364/974). In 366/977 the Turks of Ghazna deposed the drunken and incompetent governor Böri, and installed Sebük-Tegin as their governor and leader, thereby giving the stamp of formal approval to the substance of power which he had previously enjoyed.

Sebük-Tegin now began a twenty years' reign in Ghazna, ostensibly as governor on behalf of the Sāmānids; the amīrs' names were placed on his coins before his own, and on his tomb the title of *al-Ḥājib al-Ajall* "Most exalted commander" still proclaims his subordinate status. In fact, the foundations of an independent Ghaznavid power, which was to be erected into a mighty empire by Sebük-Tegin's son Maḥmūd, were firmly laid in his time. The economic stability of the Turkish soldiery in Ghazna was helped by reforms in the system of land grants or iqṭā's on which they had settled in the surrounding countryside. The Turks' power radiated out from Ghazna over the region of Zābulistān in eastern Afghanistan. Zābulistān was basically Iranian in population, and it played a notable part in Iranian epic lore, especially in that aspect of it concerned with the hero Rustam-i Zāl; in the 5th/11th century, the popular traditions of Zābulistān were worked up by Asadī Ṭūsī into his epic of the *Garshāsp-nāma*. Before the coming of Alp-Tegin, it is probable that this region was only imperfectly Islamized; certainly, paganism persisted in the inaccessible region of Ghūr in central Afghanistan well into the 5th/11th century. Sebük-Tegin endeavoured to conciliate local feeling by marrying the daughter of one of the nobles of Zābulistān; it was from this union that Maḥmūd (sometimes referred to in the sources as Maḥmūd-i Zāwulī) was born.

The group of Turks in Ghazna was a small one, set down in an hostile environment, and a dynamic policy of expansion may have seemed to Sebük-Tegin the best way to ensure its survival. Soon after his assumption of power, Sebük-Tegin moved against the rival group of Turkish ghulāms in Bust and overthrew Baituz, at the same time adding Quṣdār (*sc.* northeastern Baluchistan) to his possessions. As a result of the Bust expedition, Sebük-Tegin acquired the services of one of the greatest literary men of the age, Abu'l-Fatḥ Bustī, formerly secretary to Baituz; the composition of his new master's *fatḥ-nāmas*, proclamations of victory, and the organization of a Ghaznavid chancery, were now undertaken by Abu'l-Fatḥ.

Most significant, however, for the future history of the Ghaznavids were the beginnings of expansion towards the plains of India. The *dār al-kufr*, land of unbelief, began not far to the east of Ghazna. The Kabul river valley is geographically an extension of the river system of the northern Indian plain; it was often part of the Indian cultural and religious world too, and Buddhism and Hinduism both left their mark there in pre-Islamic times. In the 4th/10th century, the lower Kabul valley, as far west as Lāmghān and Kabul itself, was the centre of the powerful Hindūshāhī dynasty of Waihind (near the modern Attock, at

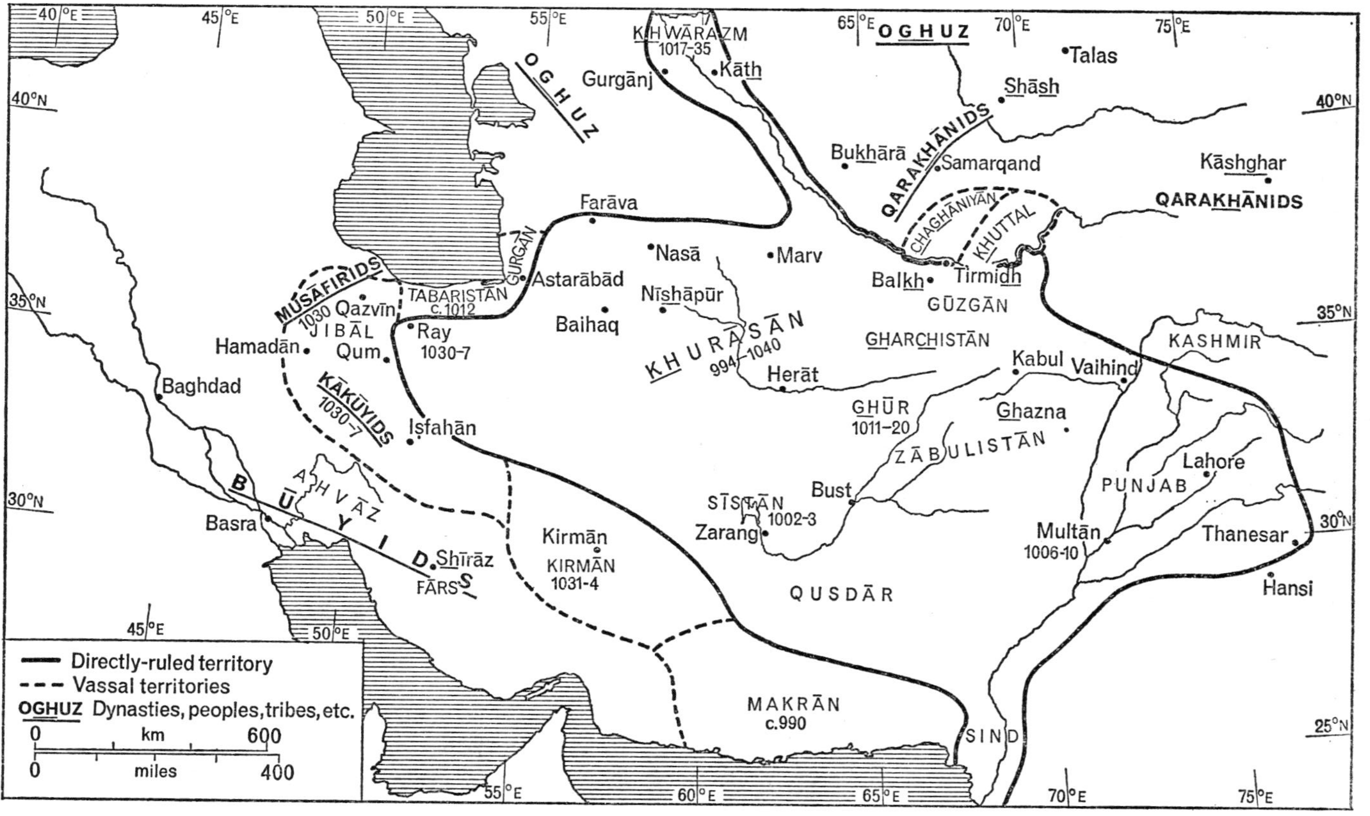

Map 4. The early Ghaznavid empire

the confluence of the Indus and Kabul rivers), and these rulers barred the way for Muslim expansion into northern India. For Sebük-Tegin and his followers, the situation resembled that familiar from Transoxiana. Here too there were frontier fortresses like Ghazna and Gardīz facing a pagan land, but with the difference that the plains of India promised an infinitely richer plunder than the bare Central Asian steppes had ever yielded. It is likely that Sebük-Tegin's first clashes with the Hindūshāhīs were, at least in part, defensive measures; we have noted above that the Hindūshāhīs were related to the dispossessed Lawīks of Ghazna, and on more than one occasion, they supplied help from Kabul to the Lawīks. At some time around 367/986–7 there was sharp fighting in the Kabul–Lāmghān region, in which the Hindūshāhī Rājā was finally defeated, enabling Sebük-Tegin to advance down the Kabul river towards Peshawar and implant the first seeds of Islam there.

Sebük-Tegin's successful maintenance of himself in power at Ghazna and his victories against the Indians now made him a force in the internal politics of the Sāmānid empire, at this time moving towards its final collapse. Internal conflicts so weakened the amīrs' authority that in 382/992 Nūḥ b. Manṣūr was unable to halt an invasion of Transoxiana by the Qarakhānid chief Bughra Khān Hārūn, who for a time actually occupied the capital Bukhārā. An alliance against the crown of two great men in the state, Abū 'Alī Sīmjūrī and the Turkish general Fā'iq Khāṣṣa, drove Amīr Nūḥ to call in Sebük-Tegin in the hope of redressing the balance (384/994). Sebük-Tegin and Maḥmūd now appeared in Khurāsān and routed the rebels; both consequently received a grant of honorific titles from the grateful amīr, and Maḥmūd was invested with command of the army of Khurāsān. By 385/995 rebel opposition had been temporarily crushed, and Khurāsān was in Maḥmūd's hands; once Maḥmūd was secure on the throne of Ghazna three years later, Khurāsān was to be an integral part of the Ghaznavid empire for the next forty years. However, the shrinking Sāmānid dominions continued to be disordered: the Qarakhānids took over the whole of the Syr Darya basin, and the authority of the amīrs was confined to a small part of Transoxiana.

In the midst of this, Sebük-Tegin died (387/997), and Maḥmūd was obliged to leave Khurāsān and allow the Turkish general Bektuzun to occupy Nīshāpūr. Sebük-Tegin had appointed as his successor in Ghazna a younger son, Ismā'īl (possibly because Ismā'īl's mother was a daughter of Alp-Tegin), and the claims of the more experienced and capable Maḥmūd were ignored. Maḥmūd proposed a division of power within the Ghaznavid territories, but Ismā'īl refused this; recourse to arms followed, and after a few months' reign in Ghazna, Ismā'īl was deposed (388/998). The Sāmānid Amīr Abu'l-Ḥārith Manṣūr b. Nūḥ now confirmed Maḥmūd in possession of Ghazna, Bust and the eastern Khurāsānian towns of Balkh, Tirmidh and Herāt, but Maḥmud was left to recover western Khurāsān from Bektuzun. The deposition of the amīr by Bektuzun and Fā'iq enabled Maḥmūd to pose as his avenger, and after further negotiations and renewed fighting, Maḥmūd was in 389/999 at last victorious over all his enemies. Khurāsān was now firmly within his possession, and with the advance of the Qarakhānid Ilig Naṣr to Bukhārā in the same year, the Sāmānid dynasty virtually ended. Maḥmūd established friendly relations with the Ilig, and both sides agreed that the former Sāmānid dominions should be partitioned, with the Oxus as boundary between these two Turkish powers. This cordiality proved to be only transient; very soon, the Qarakhānids were trying to extend their authority into Khurāsān, whilst Maḥmūd later tried to secure a foothold north of the Oxus. Significant for the future orientation of Ghaznavid policy was Maḥmūd's eagerness to secure legitimization of his power from the 'Abbāsid caliph al-Qādir, who at this point sent him the honorific by which he became best known, that of *Yamīn al-Daula* "Right hand of the state". The Ghaznavids were always careful to buttress their authority by caliphal approval and by an ostentatious espousal of the cause of Sunnī orthodoxy (see below).

Maḥmūd's thirty-two years' reign (388–421/998–1030) was one of ceaseless campaigning and warfare over a vast stretch of southern Asia; at his death, the empire stretched from the borders of Āzarbāījān and Kurdistān in the west to the upper Ganges valley of India in the east, and from Khwārazm in Central Asia to the Indian Ocean shores. Not since the early days of the 'Abbāsid caliphate had such a vast assemblage of territories been ruled by one man. This was an entirely personal creation and consequently ephemeral, for Maḥmūd's son Mas'ūd was inferior to his father in skill and judgement and was unable to hold the empire together. Yet the might of Maḥmūd's empire at its zenith immensely impressed succeeding generations of Muslims, and especially excited the admiration of those who held fast to Sunnī orthodoxy and revered the 'Abbāsid caliphs as imāms of the community of the faithful. It was fortunate for Maḥmūd that his campaigns on both flanks of the empire could so often be represented in a favourable religious light. In the east, Maḥmūd achieved his reputation as the great *ghāzī* sultan and hammer of the infidel Hindus. That his motives here were, as is explained below, as much influenced by material as spiritual considerations did not affect the approbation of contemporaries, who knew only that such houses of abomination as the great idol-temple of Somnāth were being cleansed, just as Muḥammad the Prophet had purified the Ka'ba of its 365 idols. In the west, Maḥmūd's main opponents were the Būyids and lesser Dailamī powers like the Kākūyids of Iṣfahān and Hamadān and the Musāfirids of Dailam, and since these were Shī'ī in faith, it was possible to publicize Maḥmūd's campaign of 420/1029 in western Persia as a crusade for the re-establishment of Sunnī orthodoxy.

Finally, Maḥmūd's achievement should be considered within the context of the contemporary Islamic world in general. His victories for orthodoxy came at a moment when the fortunes of that cause were at a low ebb in the more westerly lands of Islam. The extremist Shī'ī Fāṭimids had founded a rival caliphate which stretched from North Africa to Syria, and their capital of Cairo had come to eclipse Baghdad in its splendour and its economic and cultural vitality. To the threat of Fāṭimid expansionism across the Syrian Desert towards Iraq was added danger from without the Islamic world. Under the energetic Macedonian imperial dynasty (867–1057), the Byzantines began to recover ground lost to the Arabs three centuries before. Cyprus, Crete and much of northern Syria were reoccupied, and Greek armies almost reached Damascus and Jerusalem, inflicting a severe blow to Muslim self-confidence. Coming as they did at this time, Maḥmūd's Indian exploits gave a fillip to Muslim spirits; and Maḥmūd was always careful to forward detailed fatḥ-nāmas to the 'Abbāsids in Baghdad, so that his achievements might be publicized. In all of these activities, Maḥmūd acted as a fully independent sovereign, save only for his formal acknowledgement of the caliph's spiritual overlordship, signalled by the appearance on his coins from 389/999 onwards of the title *Walī Amīr al-Mu'minīn* "Friend of the Commander of the Faithful". Recognition of the sovereignty of the Sāmānids, still kept up by Ismā'īl during his brief reign, was now abandoned.

By acquiring Khurāsān, Maḥmūd became master of a rich and flourishing province. Khurāsān had rich agricultural oases, irrigated by means of a skilful utilization of a modest water supply. Its towns were centres for local industry and crafts, with its textiles and other specialties exported far outside the province; it also benefited by its straddling of the long-distance trade route between Iraq and Central Asia. It was also at this time the intellectual and cultural heart of the eastern Islamic world, not only for the traditional Arabic theological, linguistic and legal sciences, but also for the cultivation of New Persian language and literature, a process which culminated in the achievement of Maḥmūd's contemporary and would-be protégé, Firdausī of Ṭūs. In short, the wealth of Khurāsān, as much as that of India, provided the material basis for much of Maḥmūd's imperial achievement.

The sultan was, accordingly, concerned to guard Khurāsān against threats from the Qarakhānids, for despite Maḥmūd's marriage to a daughter of the Ilig Naṣr (390/1000), the khans did not for long relinquish their designs upon the province. Whilst Maḥmūd was away at Multān in India in 396/1006, a two-pronged invasion of Khurāsān was launched. One Qarakhānid army occupied Balkh (where a market belonging to the Ghaznavid sultan, the Bāzār-i 'Āshiqān or "Lovers' Market", was burnt down), and the other occupied Nīshāpūr; at this last place, a large part of the *dihqāns* or landowners had already become disillusioned with the rapacity of the sultan's tax-collectors, and actually welcomed the invaders. With characteristic verve, Maḥmūd raced back across Afghanistan, and hurled the Qarakhānids back across the Oxus. The Ilig Naṣr attempted a revanche in the following year, in alliance with his second cousin Yūsuf Qadïr Khān of Khotan. But a great victory by Maḥmūd near Balkh in 398/1008, in which a charge of the armour-plated war elephants of the Ghaznavids had a demoralizing effect on the invaders, ended the campaign; the Qarakhānid commanders had protested that "it is impossible to put up resistance against those elephants, weapons, equipment and warriors". The Qarakhānid dominions were never ruled as a unitary state, but formed something like a loosely-linked confederation. Internal quarrels and warfare broke out within the dynasty at an early date, and over the next years, the Ghaznavid borders were not again threatened by the khans.

Once he had consolidated his power in Khurāsān, Maḥmūd gradually brought under his own control those regions which had lain on the periphery of the Sāmānid empire and had been loosely tributary to Bukhārā, *sc.* Sīstān, Gharchistān, Jūzjān, Chaghāniyān, Khuttal and Khwārazm.

North of the upper Harī Rūd lay Gharchistān ("land of the mountains"), ruled by a line of local princes who bore the Iranian title of *Shīr* (< Old Persian khshāthriya "ruler"). The Shīr Abū Naṣr Muḥammad acknowledged Maḥmūd's suzerainty right away in 389/999, but some years later, the sultan used the pretext of truculent behaviour on the part of the Shīr's son Muḥammad b. Muḥammad to invade the province and incorporate it in his empire (403/1012). That the family of Shīrs nevertheless survived seems possible, for they are mentioned once more in the Ghūrid period.

Under its dynasty of the Farīghūnids, Jūzjān, the region to the north of Herāt, had been an important vassal-state of the Sāmānids, providing military aid to the amīrs against their rebellious generals. The Farīghūnids had also been patrons of the arts; it was for one of the amīrs that the pioneer geographical treatise in New Persian, the *Ḥudūd al-ʿālam*, was written towards 372/982, and the late Professor V. Minorsky suggested that the author of an Arabic encyclopaedia of the sciences called the *Jawāmiʿ al-ʿulūm*, one Shaʿyā b. Farīghūn, might be a scion of this princely family.[1] The ruler Abū Naṣr Aḥmad fought for Maḥmūd against the Qarakhānids in Khurāsān and also in India, and retained his territories until his death in 401/1010–11, when Gūzgān was placed under the governorship of the sultan's son Muḥammad, who had married a daughter of Abū Naṣr Muḥammad.

It may also be noted at this point that Maḥmūd endeavoured to extend some control over Ghūr, until this time a pagan enclave in the mountains of central Afghanistan. Two expeditions were sent in 401/1011 and 411/1020 and with difficulty procured the submission of certain local chiefs, including Muḥammad b. Sūrī of Āhangarān on the upper Harī Rūd. Teachers were left to inculcate the rudiments of the Islamic faith, but Ghūr was never properly subdued by the Ghaznavids, and the spread of Islam there was to be a slow process.

Another region of Afghanistan, that of Kāfiristān (modern Nūristān), which lies across the Hindu Kush and to the north of the Kabul River, did not become Muslim till the end of the 19th century, when the Afghan Amīr ʿAbd al-Raḥmān Khān led a force into Kāfiristān and replaced the indigenous paganism by Islam. A raid by Maḥmūd is recorded in 411/1020 on the Nūr and Qīrāt valleys, apparently lying in the eastern part of Kāfiristān, but no permanent conquest was attempted.

Because of its distance from Bukhārā, Sīstān had slipped from direct Sāmānid control after the first decades of the 4th/10th century, and a

[1] "Ibn Farīghūn and the Ḥudūd al-ʿĀlam" in *A locust's leg: Studies in honour of S. H. Taqizadeh* (London, 1962), pp. 189–96.

line connected with the Ṣaffārids Ya'qūb and 'Amr b. al-Laith had reappeared there. When Sebük-Tegin annexed Bust, his territories became contiguous with those of the Ṣaffārid Khalaf b. Aḥmad. In 376/986–7 Khalaf tried to take advantage of Sebük-Tegin's involvement with the Hindūshāhī Rājā Jaipāl, and seized Bust for a time; later, he tried to set the Qarakhānids against Sebük-Tegin. Whilst Maḥmūd was disputing with his brother Ismā'īl over the succession, Khalaf's forces seized the district of Pūshang, to the north of Sīstān, and in 390/999 Maḥmūd retaliated by an invasion of Sīstān. On numismatic evidence, Ghaznavid authority was first recognized there in 392/1002, although the literary sources state that it was not until the next year that Maḥmūd finally took over Sīstān, after Khalaf had put to death his own son Ṭāhir and provoked a civil war there. Khalaf was now deposed and the province placed under Maḥmūd's brother Abu'l-Muẓaffar Naṣr. Yet the Sagzīs' attachment to their own local line and their hatred of the alien Turkish yoke remained constant, and Sīstān was never quiet under the Ghaznavids; once the Saljuqs appeared on the fringes of Sīstān during the sultanate of Maudūd b. Mas'ūd, the Sagzīs joined with the Türkmens to expel the Ghaznavid officials.

Quṣdār had apparently been allowed by Sebük-Tegin to retain its local rulers, for in 402/1011 we hear of an expedition by Maḥmūd to restore the ruler to obedience and the customary payment of tribute; this ruler (who is nowhere named) had tried to establish relations with the hostile Qarakhānids. Makrān, the coastal strip of which Baluchistan is the interior, also had its own line of rulers who had in the 4th/10th century acknowledged the Būyids of Kirmān as suzerains, but who had latterly transferred their allegiance to Sebük-Tegin and Maḥmūd. When the ruler Ma'dān died in 416/1025–6, there was a dispute over the succession between his sons 'Īsā and Abu'l-Mu'askar, in which Maḥmūd in the end negotiated a settlement. Just before Maḥmūd's death in 420/1029, 'Īsā tried to assert his independence of Ghazna; it was left to Maḥmūd's son Mas'ūd to bring 'Īsā to heel and replace him by Abu'l-Mu'askar.

The mountain principalities of Chaghāniyān and Khuttal, on the right bank of the upper Oxus, were of strategic importance to the Ghaznavids: they served as bridgeheads into the Qarakhānid dominions, and were the Ghaznavids' first line of defence against predatory peoples like the Kumījīs of the Buttamān Mountains (see below), and beyond them, Turkish peoples of Central Asia. In Sāmānid times, these principalities had been ruled by local dynasties, tributary to Buk͟hārā and descended from indigenous Iranian or Arab families such as the Āl-i Muḥtāj in C͟hag͟hāniyān and the Abū Dā'ūdids or Banījūrids in K͟huttal. It seems, in the absence of specific information to the contrary, that local lines survived in G͟haznavid times as the sultans' vassals; in Maḥmūd's reign, the Muḥtājid Fak͟hr al-Daula Aḥmad was amīr of C͟hag͟hāniyān, and in Mas'ūd's reign, the then amīr was the sultan's son-in-law.

The acquisition of K͟hwārazm was one of the most important events of Maḥmūd's middle years. The province itself was rich agriculturally, with a complex system of irrigation canals for utilizing the waters of the lower Oxus. It derived further prosperity from its position as the Islamic terminus for caravans arriving from the Og͟huz steppes and Siberia, and the geographer Muqaddasī enumerates an impressive list of the products for which K͟hwārazm was the distributing centre. But its strategic value was probably the consideration uppermost in the sultan's mind. Possession of K͟hwārazm enabled him to turn the flank of the Qarak͟hānids in Transoxiana and, above all, to put pressure on one of his most implacable enemies, 'Alī-Tegin of Buk͟hārā and Samarqand (see below). Since 385/995 K͟hwārazm had been ruled from the great commercial centre of Gurgānj by the Ma'mūnid family of amīrs, who had in that year overthrown the ancient family of the Afrīg͟hid K͟hwārazm-S͟hāhs of Kāt͟h. Though nominally dependent on the Sāmānids, the geographical isolation of K͟hwārazm, surrounded as it was by steppeland, had enabled the S͟hāhs to live in almost untrammelled independence. The Amīr 'Alī b. Ma'mūn (387–99/997–1009) was to some extent dependent on the Qarak͟hānids, but in 406/1015–16 the grounds of G͟haznavid intervention were laid when Maḥmūd's sister Ḥurra-yi Kaljī married 'Alī's brother Ma'mūn b. Ma'mūn. The very detailed account of the conquest of K͟hwārazm given by the G͟haznavid offical Baihaqī (quoting al-Bīrūnī's lost *History of K͟hwārazm*), shows how the sultan deliberately provoked the K͟hwārazmians, and by a series of Machiavellian diplomatic moves, secured a pretext for sending G͟haznavid troops into the country. His demands for recognition in the *k͟huṭba* or Friday sermon in K͟hwārazm (in effect, recognition of G͟haznavid suzerainty there) provoked a patriotic reaction amongst the K͟hwārazmians, in which Ma'mūn was assassinated. Maḥmūd could now enter the province, ostensibly to avenge his brother-in-law. After fierce fighting, the G͟haznavid cause prevailed; the Ma'mūnid dynasty was extinguished, a reign of terror unleashed, and the whole land incorporated into the Ghaznavid empire. One of Sebük-Tegin's former ghulāms, the ḥājib Altun-Tash, was installed as governor with the traditional title of Khwārazm-Shāh, and he and his sons ruled there for the next twenty-four years.

The possession of Khwārazm gave Maḥmūd the preponderance over the Qarakhānids, who were by now racked by internal warfare. Not till the latter years of Mas'ūd's sultanate, when the incursions of the Saljuqs were creating general chaos in northern Afghanistan, did a Qarakhānid prince, Böri-Tegin, seriously harry Ghaznavid territory. In the years after his repulse of the Ilig Naṣr's invasion of Khurāsān, Maḥmūd exploited the internal rivalries of the Qarakhānids by allying first with Aḥmad Toghan Khān (d. 408/1017–18) of Semirechye and, till the last years of his life, of Kāshghar also, and then with Yūsuf Qadïr Khān of Khotan and Kāshghar. This last alliance was specifically aimed at the ruler of Bukhārā and Samarqand, 'Alī b. Hārūn Bughra Khān, called 'Alī-Tegin. 'Alī-Tegin had captured Bukhārā in 411/1020, and down to his death fourteen years later, was the most skilful and persistent opponent of Ghaznavid ambitions in Central Asia. In 416/1025 Maḥmūd invaded Transoxiana with the aim of overthrowing 'Alī-Tegin. The sultan met with Yūsuf Qadïr Khān at Samarqand; according to the Ghaznavid historian Gardīzī's account, presents were exchanged on a munificent scale by the two sovereigns, and complex negotiations for a marriage alliance begun. The sultan and the khan joined forces, firstly to scatter 'Alī-Tegin's allies the Saljuq Turks, and then to drive 'Alī-Tegin himself into the steppes. However, Maḥmūd now withdrew from Transoxiana in order to prepare for the Somnāth expedition. 'Alī-Tegin re-emerged and took back his former possessions. Hence Barthold was probably right in surmising that Maḥmūd preferred to leave 'Alī-Tegin in Transoxiana as a counterpoise to the power of Yūsuf Qadïr Khān.[1]

West of Khurāsān stretched the territories of various Dailamī powers, above all, of the Būyids. With the Ziyārids of Gurgān and Ṭabaristān (who were actually orthodox Sunnīs in faith), Maḥmūd had friendly relations, and after the death in 402/1011–12 of Qābūs b. Vushmgīr, this dynasty was virtually tributary to the Ghaznavids. At first, Maḥmūd supported the claims to the succession of Dārā b. Qābūs, who had been a refugee in Ghazna during his father's lifetime; but he

[1] *Turkestan*, pp. 279–86.

soon came to recognize Manūchihr b. Qābūs as amīr, after the latter had been raised to the throne by local interests. The new Ziyārid amīr became Maḥmūd's son-in-law, and on various occasions, sent troop contingents to the Ghaznavid army. In this way, the sultan maintained a friendly power at the western approaches of Khurāsān, and thereby deterred the Būyids from making moves in that direction.

Although it no longer had the cohesion and might which it had had in the days of 'Aḍud al-Daula, the Būyid empire was still territorially impressive, embracing as it did most of Iraq and western and central Persia. But structurally it was weak, in that by the early 5th/11th century, it lacked a single, generally acknowledged head, and this want of a united front weakened Būyid abilities to resist first the Ghaznavids and then the Saljuqs. It would not have been difficult for the sultan to find a plausible pretext for meddling in Būyid affairs: first, the Būyids were Shī'īs, and as long as they held Baghdad, the 'Abbāsid caliph could not be considered a free agent; and secondly, the inability of the later Būyids to keep internal order meant that pilgrims travelling from the east to the Holy Places were constantly harried and financially mulcted whilst crossing the Būyid lands. According to Ibn al-Jauzī, Maḥmūd was specifically reproached in 412/1021 for his lack of interest in the tribulations of these pilgrims, and was unfavourably compared with the Kurdish ruler of Hamadān, Nihāvand and Dīnavar, Badr b. Ḥasanūya, who always gave subsidies and aid to the pilgrim caravans passing through his lands.

In fact, Maḥmūd showed considerable restraint in making no major move against the Būyids till the last year of his reign. It is true that when in 407/1016–17 the Būyid governor in Kirmān, Qawām al-Daula Abu'l-Fawāris, had rebelled against his brother Sulṭān al-Daula Abū Shujā' of Fārs, Maḥmūd had supplied him with military help. But the Ghaznavid troops had been unable immediately to restore Qawām al-Daula to his former position, and when towards the end of Maḥmūd's reign, a fresh succession dispute broke out in Kirmān, he made no attempt to intervene. It is somewhat surprising that Maḥmūd refrained so long from attacking Jibāl, with its capital of Ray, a rich manufacturing centre and strategically the key to northern Persia; for since the death of the Būyid Fakhr al-Daula 'Alī in 387/997 and the succession of his infant son Majd al-Daula Rustam, *de facto* power there had been in the hands of a woman, the Queen-Mother Sayyida. It is recorded in Baihaqī that towards the end of his life, Maḥmūd was asked by his vizier Maimandī why he had not before intervened in Jibāl. The sultan replied that if a man had been ruling in Ray, he would have had to keep an army permanently stationed at Nīshāpūr, whereas, with a woman in Ray, there was no real Būyid threat to Khurāsān.[1]

Sayyida's death in 419/1028 left Majd al-Daula with sole power in Ray, but the last years of his exclusion from real authority had sapped his powers to govern effectively; he was unable to keep his Dailamī troops in order, and foolishly appealed to Maḥmūd for help. It is probable that Maḥmūd was already meditating intervention, and when his army reached Ray, he deposed Majd al-Daula and sacked the city in a frightful manner. The sultan felt bound to justify this act of naked aggression, and in his fatḥ-nāma to the caliph spoke of cleansing Jibāl of the "infidel Bāṭiniyya and evil-doing innovators", who had flourished under Majd al-Daula's lax rule; certainly, those suspected of extremist Shī'ī and Mu'tazilī beliefs were mercilessly hunted down, and many allegedly heretical books burnt. The seizure of Ray opened up the possibility of a drive towards Āzarbāījān and the west. Mas'ūd was given charge of operations here. The Musāfirid ruler of Dailam, Ibrāhīm b. Marzubān, was temporarily dispossessed of his capital Ṭārum and brought to obedience; and then at the beginning of 421/1030 Mas'ūd turned southwards against the Kākūyids of Iṣfahān and Hamadān. The news of his father's death in Ghazna compelled him, however, to leave the Kākūyid 'Alā' al-Daula Muḥammad b. Dushmanziyār, called Ibn Kākūya, as his vassal in Iṣfahān. As it happened, Mas'ūd was never able permanently to subdue the resilient Ibn Kākūya, and Ghaznavid rule in Ray only lasted for some seven years. Yet the Ghaznavids had seriously impaired the Dailamī ascendancy in northern Persia, so that the advance of the Saljuqs through northern Persia a few years later was made correspondingly easier.

So far we have been concerned only with Ghaznavid expansion into Central Asia and the Iranian world. Yet simultaneously, a great military effort was being mounted against India. Each winter, armies of the regular troops, swollen by the ghāzīs and volunteers who flocked thither from all parts of the eastern Islamic world, would descend to the plains of India in search of Hindu temples to sack and slaves to round up. The numerous Indian campaigns of Maḥmūd have been well described by Muḥammad Nāẓim, with a skilful elucidation of the geographical and topographical problems involved in the source

[1] Baihaqī, p. 263; tr. pp. 252–3.

material. The first great obstacle to Ghaznavid penetration of India was the continued existence of the Hindūshāhī kingdom of Waihind, with whose Rājā, Jaipāl, Sebük-Tegin had already clashed. In 392/1001 Maḥmūd defeated and captured Jaipāl near Peshawar, so humiliating him that he committed suicide. His son Anandpāl organized a grand coalition of the Indian rulers of northwestern India, but this too was broken by the sultan at Waihind and Nagarkot (399/1009). The next Hindūshāhīs, Trilochanpāl and his son Bhimpāl, carried on the fight against Maḥmūd in alliance with such rulers as Ganda, Rājā of Kālinjar, but were gradually driven eastwards across the Punjab, and with the death of Bhimpāl in 417/1026, the once-mighty Hindūshāhī dynasty came to an end.

Maḥmūd was not, of course, the first Muslim leader to bring Islam to India. The new faith had been implanted in Sind by the Arab general Muḥammad b. al-Qāsim al-Thaqafī in Umayyad times (90–2/709–11), and had spread up the Indus as far as Multān. During the course of the 4th/10th century, the Muslim communities of Sind had been won over by Ismā'īlī *dā'īs* or missionaries to the cause of extremist Shī'ism. The early Ghaznavids vigorously uprooted all traces of Ismā'īlism in their own dominions, and when in 403/1012–13 the Fāṭimid caliph in Cairo, al-Ḥākim, sent a diplomatic mission to Maḥmūd, the sultan had the luckless envoy executed. Thus Maḥmūd had, in his own eyes, ample reason for taking over the important town of Multān and restoring orthodoxy there. In two campaigns of 396/1006 and 401/1010, the local ruler Abu'l-Fatḥ Dā'ūd was humbled and finally deposed, and the Ismā'īlīs in the city massacred. Nevertheless, Ismā'īlism lasted there for two more centuries; and only thirty years after Maḥmūd's efforts there, in Maudūd b. Mas'ūd's sultanate, a rising of the Multān Ismā'īlīs occurred.

However, the majority of Maḥmūd's Indian campaigns were directed at the Hindu Rājput rulers. Two attempts were made to penetrate into Kashmir (in 406/1015 and 412/1021), but he was held up on both occasions by the fortress of Lohkot, and the mountain barriers proved too much for the invaders; not until the 8th/14th century did a Muslim dynasty, the line of Shāh Mīrzā Swātī, come to rule in Kashmir. The main Ghaznavid effort was directed across the Punjab towards the Ganges–Jumna Dōāb. Here lay Indian towns richly endowed with temples, such as the temple of Chakraswāmī at Thānesar (raided in 405/1014) and the temple at Mathura, reputed birthplace of the hero

Krishna (raided in 409/1018). With these preparatory successes, Maḥmūd was ready to confront the two chief rulers of northern India, the Pratihāra Rājā of Kanauj, Rājyapal, and the Chandel Rājā of Kālinjar, Ganda. Ganda was the most tenacious of Maḥmūd's opponents. In 410/1019 he organized a league of Indian princes against Maḥmūd, but during the expedition of 413/1022 Ganda was besieged in his fortress of Kālinjar and eventually forced to surrender. Yet the climax of the sultan's Indian campaigns was undoubtedly the Somnāth expedition of 416–17/1025–6. For this, Maḥmūd led his troops across the inhospitable Thar Desert to Anhalwāra, and then into the Kāthiāwār peninsula to Somnāth itself. At Somnāth was a famous temple containing a *linga* of the Moon-God Mahādeva, which was served by 1,000 Brāhmans and 350 singers and dancers, and endowed with the income from 10,000 villages. After fierce fighting, the shrine was captured and despoiled to the amount of twenty million *dīnārs*, and finally burnt down. The return journey was arduous and dangerous, and whilst travelling up the Indus valley, the Ghaznavid army was harassed by the local Jāts; Maḥmūd returned in 418/1026 to lead a punitive expedition against these marauders. The news of the Somnāth victory spread rapidly throughout the Islamic world, and contributed much to the image of Maḥmūd as the hero of Sunnī Islam; the 'Abbāsid Caliph sent from Baghdad fresh honorific titles for the sultan and his family.

Ghaznavid military activity in India was, as is clear from the preceding paragraph, essentially composed of plunder raids. From the temple treasures came the bullion which enabled the sultans to maintain a good standard of gold and silver coinage, and the extra currency in circulation stimulated trade all over eastern Islam, reversing for a while the normal drain of specie into the Indian subcontinent. This treasure was also used to finance and to adorn the splendid buildings which Maḥmūd began to erect, such as the '*Arūs al-falak* "Bride of Heaven" mosque and madrasa in Ghazna (built from the proceeds of the expedition of 410/1019 against Trilochanpāl of Kanauj and Ganda of Kālinjar), and the vast complex of palace buildings laid out in early Ghaznavid times on the lower Helmand river at Lashkarī Bāzār near Bust. The slaves imported from India were likewise a great economic asset. According to the historian 'Utbī, 53,000 captives were brought back from the Kanauj expedition of 409/1018, and slave merchants converged on Ghazna from all parts of the eastern Islamic world. Some of these slaves were incorporated into the Ghaznavid armies, where the Rājputs' fighting qualities had good scope, and they were often considered more reliable than the Turks. It was the Ghaznavids who reintroduced into the Islamic world the use of elephants as beasts of war, and numbers of elephants were often stipulated in the peace treaties with Indian princes; they were regarded as royal beasts, and when captured in battle, fell within the sultan's fifth of the booty.

Since financial considerations seem to have been uppermost in the sultan's mind, it is difficult to see Maḥmūd as a Muslim fanatic, eager to implant the faith in India by the sword. Islam made little progress in India during the Ghaznavid period; the succeeding periods of the Ghūrids and the Slave Kings were more important for this. His main aim was to make the Indian princes his tributaries and to use them as milch-cows; the temples were despoiled primarily because of their great wealth. The sultan knew well that if he had tried to impose Islam on the princes as a condition of peace, they would have apostasized as soon as his troops left. It seems that conversion to Islam was not even required of Indian troops recruited into the Ghaznavid forces; the excesses of pagan Indian soldiers at Zarang in Sīstān in 393/1003 are denounced in the local history of that province, the *Tārīkh-i Sīstān* (pp. 355–7). Not till the end of Maḥmūd's reign was there any attempt to set up a Ghaznavid civil administration in the Punjab, and this foundered early in the next reign because of jealousies between the civil and military heads. For the remainder of Ghaznavid rule in India, power was exercised from military garrison points like Lahore and Multān; since ghāzīs and other unruly elements gathered at these places, they were frequently centres for unrest and even rebellion.

Maḥmūd's empire was thus an impressive achievement. For the study of mediaeval Islamic political organization, it has a special interest, for the Ghaznavids are a classic instance of barbarians coming into an older, higher culture, absorbing themselves in it and then adapting it to their own aims. The empire was, indeed, the culmination of trends towards autocracy visible in the earlier 'Abbāsid caliphate and its successor-states. Dynasties like the Būyids and Sāmānids had tried to centralize administration in their territories and to make the amīr a despotic figure, but their attempts had foundered; in the case of the Būyids, because of family rivalries and the impediment of a turbulent Dailamī tribal backing, in the case of the Sāmānids, because of the entrenched power of the Iranian military and landowning classes and of the merchants, all hostile to any extension of kingly power. The Ghaznavids, on the other hand, did not rise to eminence on the crest of a tribal migration or movement of peoples, and had few local, established interests to contend with. Hence they could make themselves far more despotic than their successors in Persia, the Saljuq sultans. Whereas the great Saljuq vizier Niẓām al-Mulk (whose views derived from his family background of service in Ghaznavid Khurāsān) later complained that the Saljuqs did not make full use of the machinery of despotism available to them, the Ghaznavid official Baihaqī denounces Mas'ūd b. Maḥmūd's over-reliance on this machinery, his arbitrary behaviour, and his use of spies and informers, which created an atmosphere in the state of suspicion and mistrust. Leaving their pagan steppe origins behind completely, the Ghaznavids enthusiastically adopted the Perso-Islamic governmental traditions which they found current in their newly acquired territories. This process of adoption was facilitated by a continuity of administrative personnel with the previous régimes. When Maḥmūd took over Khurāsān, most of the Sāmānid officials remained in office and merely transferred their allegiance to the new master. Thus Maḥmūd's first vizier, Abu'l-'Abbās al-Faḍl Isfarā'inī, had formerly been a secretary in Fā'iq's employ. Certain officials, like the qāḍī Shīrāzī, who was civil governor of northern India in the early part of Mas'ūd's reign, had a background of service with the Būyids. Trained men like these were welcomed in the Ghaznavid administration, particularly as the expansion of the empire under Maḥmūd enlarged its sphere of operations and the volume of work with which it had to cope.

In structure, the Ghaznavid administration clearly stems from that of the Sāmānids in Bukhārā, as known to us from Narshakhī and Khwārazmī, which in turn was based on the bureaucracy of 'Abbāsid Baghdad. There were five great departments of state: the *dīvān-i vizārat,* that of the vizier, concerned with finance and general administration; the *dīvān-i risālat,* that of the Chief Secretary, concerned with official and diplomatic correspondence; the *dīvān-i 'arḍ*, that of the *'āriḍ* or Secretary for War, concerned with the mustering, organizing and equipping of the army; the *dīvān-i ishrāf*, that of the chief *mushrif*, concerned with the internal communications and espionage system; and the *dīvān-i vikālat,* that of the *vakīl-i khāṣṣ* or Comptroller of the Royal Household, concerned with the running of the royal palace and the administration of crown properties. All these departments were the preserve of Persian secretaries, who continued in them the traditions and techniques of their craft. Although the sultans listened to advice from their officials, they did not necessarily take it, for their power was theoretically uncircumscribed by any other human being. The position of the vizier was an unenviable one, for any independence of thought or action was resented by his master; most of the viziers of Maḥmūd and Mas'ūd suffered falls from favour and even imprisonment or death. Moreover, there was always an over-riding need for more money, and the vizier suffered unless he could tap fresh sources of taxation. However, in Aḥmad b. Ḥasan Maimandī, called *Shams al-Kufāt* "Sun of the Capable Ones', the sultans had a vizier of outstanding intellectual calibre, with a contemporary fame for his Arabic scholarship and his executive skill comparable with that of the great Būyid viziers.

The ethos of the Ghaznavid "power-state" involved a sharp division between the ruling class and the ruled, the division elaborated by Niẓām al-Mulk in his treatise on statecraft, the *Siyāsat-nāma*, and the division crystallized in later Ottoman Turkish terminology as that of '*Askerīs* and *Re'āyā*. At the top were the sultan and his servants, both military and civilian. Beneath them were the masses of population, including merchants, artisans and peasants, whose duties were to obey the sovereign power and to pay their taxes faithfully; in return, the ruler protected them from outside invaders and internal bandits, and left them freedom to pursue their ordinary vocations. The sultan's control over the provinces was based largely on fear, the expectation of swift punishment for wrongdoing or rebelliousness. Information on what was happening in outlying regions was continuously brought to the court by the agents of the *barīd* or postal and intelligence service, an ancient Near Eastern institution which the Ghaznavids developed to a high degree. Provincial governors and officials were often tempted to appropriate monies or to rebel against the distant central government, and the existence of this communications system was one of the few means of control over peripheral regions which the sultan possessed.

On the ideological and religious plane, the sultan's authority was maintained by a rigid adherence to Sunnī orthodoxy, seen in the sultans' favour to the Ḥanafī law-school and to a conservative, literalist sect like that of the Khurāsānian Karrāmiyya, which was favoured by Sebük-Tegin and, in the early part of his reign, by Maḥmūd. Dissenters, above all adherents of the extremist Shī'a like the Ismā'īlīs, were persecuted as subverters of the *status quo*, and the sultans' zeal is frequently praised in contemporary literature and poetry. Thus Farrukhī, in an elegy on Maḥmūd's death, says that the heretics can now sleep safely:

> "Alas and alack, the Qarmaṭiyān [*sc.* the Ismā'īlīs] can now rejoice!
> They will be secure against death by stoning or the gallows."[1]

A corollary of this zeal was the maintenance of close relations with the 'Abbāsid caliphs, whose support Maḥmūd had sought at the outset after his victory in Khurāsān of 389/999. The sultans clearly felt the need for legitimation of their power by the caliphs, and they also sought caliphal approval for such acts of dubious political morality as the expeditions against Multān and Ray. Both Maḥmūd and Mas'ūd were careful to forward presents to Baghdad from the captured plunder, and in return they received investiture patents (*manāshīr*, sing. *manshūr*) for their possessions and honorific titles (*alqāb*). They refused any contact with the 'Abbāsids' enemies, the Fāṭimids of Egypt; Maḥmūd had a Fāṭimid envoy executed, and Mas'ūd in 422/1031 revived an old charge of contacts with the Fāṭimids as an excuse for condemning to death the former minister Ḥasanak.

The culture of the early Ghaznavids was strongly Perso-Islamic, and much influenced by the Iranian civilization of the lands which they had taken over, above all by that of Khurāsān. The Sāmānids had been great patrons of both Arabic and Persian learning, and their court had nurtured such authors as Rūdakī, Bal'amī and Daqīqī, who had paved the way for the crowning achievement in the early Ghaznavid period of Firdausī of Ṭūs, author of the *Shāh-nāma* or "Book of kings". Maḥmūd and Mas'ūd both had traditional Islamic educations, and they were determined that their court too should be adorned by the greatest talents of the age. They attracted poets from neighbouring territories, so that amongst their poets, Farrukhī Sīstānī came to Ghazna from the service of the Muḥtājid amīr of Chaghāniyān, whilst Manūchihrī Dāmghānī came from the Ziyārid court in Gurgān and Ṭabaristān. According to the later literary biographer Daulatshāh, there were 400 poets in regular attendance at Maḥmūd's court, presided over by the laureate or *amīr al-shu'arā'*, 'Unṣurī, who was himself continuously engaged in eulogizing his master and other court figures. 'Unṣurī may have composed a metrical version of Maḥmūd's exploits, the *Tāj al-futūḥ* or "Crown of conquests". Certainly, the *dīvāns* or collections

[1] *Dīvān*, ed. 'Alī 'Abd al-Rasūlī (Tehrān, 1311/1932), p. 93.

of verse which have survived from a few of these poets show freshness and attractiveness of expression. Maḥmūd also brought to Ghazna the great scholar, scientist and historian Abū Raiḥān al-Bīrūnī (362–c. 442/973–c. 1050) from his native Khwārazm when that province was conquered by the sultan's army. Al-Bīrūnī was therefore able to accompany the Ghaznavid raids into India. He learnt Sanskrit, and his contacts in India and his boundless intellectual curiosity about other faiths and customs enabled him to produce his *magnum opus* on India, the *Taḥqīq mā li'l-Hind*, the first Islamic work dispassionately to examine the beliefs and practices of the Hindus.

The actual court was organized on traditional Persian lines. The sultans were great builders, and constructed for themselves palaces and gardens in all the major towns of the empire. Mas'ūd personally designed and supervised the building of a fine new palace at Ghazna which took four years to complete, cost seven million dirhams and was erected by corvée labour. The surviving ruins at Lashkarī Bāzār, extensively investigated in recent years by the French Archaeological Delegation in Afghanistan, give some idea of the monumental scale and opulence of these palaces. Their upkeep was doubtless a heavy charge on the populations of the towns in which they were situated. The sultans in their court sessions surrounded themselves with their slave guards, sat on a golden throne and engaged in prolonged drinking bouts with their *nadīms* or boon-companions. They had their harem, with the inevitable eunuchs in attendance. Because of the hierarchical nature of court society, strict protocol was observed and the sultan was withdrawn from direct contact with the people. Some links with the masses were nevertheless kept up through the Islamic institution of sessions in which people could lay complaints of oppression or wrongdoing (*maẓālim*) before the ruler. A picture accordingly emerges of the sultans as typical Perso-Islamic rulers, in an environment very similar to other courts of the eastern Islamic world. In fact, a certain qualification should be made: we must always remember that the sultans were racially Turks, and only one or two generations removed from the Central Asian steppes; moreover, their power rested largely on their Turkish soldiery. The early sultans were still Turkish-speaking, and it was always necessary for the sultans to stay attuned to the needs and aspirations of their fellow-nationals. The exclusively Arabic and Persian nature of the sources for the period leaves us only to guess at the extent and influence of this Turkish element in early Ghaznavid life and culture, but this must have been significant; the Persian court poet Manūchihrī was familiar with Turkish poetry, this being presumably of a popular nature.

Since military expansion was the characteristic feature of the empire of the early Ghaznavids, the army was naturally of supreme importance in the state. Much of the work of the civilian bureaucracy, in its search for fresh revenue sources, was directed at supporting this heavy superstructure. The Ghaznavid army was a highly professional one, answerable only to the sultan, and looking to him for successful leadership and a resultant flow of plunder. Being a standing army, it was kept perpetually on a war footing; hence it had to keep occupied as continuously as possible. Regarding numbers, the contemporary historian Gardīzī mentions that Maḥmūd in 414/1023 reviewed outside Ghazna 54,000 cavalry and 1,300 elephants, and that this excluded soldiers in the provinces and on garrison duty. Armies of around 15,000 men were employed in Khurāsān against the Türkmens in Mas'ūd's reign, and 40,000 cavalry and infantry were reviewed on the field of Shābahār outside Ghazna in 429/1038.[1] Following the trend begun in the 'Abbāsid caliphate, the army was built round a body of slave ghulāms, numbering approximately 4,000; these were principally Turks, but also included some Indians and Tājīks. Their commander, the *sālār-i ghulāmān*, ranked next in importance to the commander-in-chief of the army in general, the *ḥājib-i buzurg*. Within this body of slaves was a core of élite troops, the sultan's personal guard (the *ghulāmān-i khāṣṣ*), who were prominent on ceremonial occasions (the appearance of these palace ghulāms, with their rich uniforms and bejewelled weapons, is now known to us from the murals found in the palace of Lashkarī Bāzār, giving remarkable confirmation of the descriptions in the literary sources). Although Turks imported from Central Asia predominated in the army, and Turkish generals held the highest commands, many other nationalities could be found in the army, including Indians, Dailamīs, Arabs, Kurds and Afghans. This racial diversity was regarded by contemporaries as a source of strength, and is praised by both Kai Kā'ūs and Niẓām al-Mulk; it was believed that it discouraged undue dependence on any one group, and that the various races would vie with one another in feats of daring. One obvious advantage of these troops brought in from outside was that they lacked local ties or vested interests, and could be guaranteed not to shrink from such tasks as

[1] Gardīzī, p. 80.

extracting money from the subject peoples of the empire. Maḥmūd's reputation as a war-leader inevitably attracted hosts of ghāzīs and volunteers, especially from Khurāsān and Transoxiana, who supplemented the regular troops. These volunteers were not registered in the dīvān-i ʿarḍ as entitled to regular stipends, but shared in the captured plunder. Most of the troops in the army were cavalrymen, but there was also a corps of infantrymen, used for instance in siege warfare, and often transported to the scene of battle on swift camels.

The sultans made extensive use of war elephants, drawn as tribute from India, and jealously guarded as royal beasts; there was a body of Indian keepers (*pīlbānān*), whose head held the rank of ḥājib or general. Commanders used elephants to secure a vantage-point in battle; armour was placed over their heads, and they were then used to charge the enemy; and they were further employed to drag heavy equipment such as armouries and siege machinery. Although Maḥmūd had a deserved reputation as a dashing commander, a Ghaznavid army fully equipped for the march had a heavy baggage train, with many impedimenta (it must be remembered that the court and administration, though based on Ghazna, usually accompanied the sultan on his marches). The Ghaznavid armies' comparative lack of mobility placed them at a disadvantage against the highly mobile Türkmen invaders of Khurāsān during Masʿūd's reign.

Expenditure on these forces was bound to be enormous, and in any case, the adoption of professional armies has in all phases of human history brought about a sharp rise in state expenditure. Such campaigns as the Indian ones and the Ray one of 420/1029 brought in rich plunder, but this was erratic, whereas taxation levied on the rich Iranian provinces yielded a high, regular income. Hence the Ghaznavids were able to pay their troops largely in cash, whereas the Būyids and later the Saljuqs had to resort to a system of land-grants or iqṭāʿs (this does not necessarily imply that the iqṭāʿ was unknown in the eastern Islamic lands of the early Ghaznavids, but the institution was not yet highly developed there). There are numerous indications in the sources that Ghaznavid administration in the provinces, in its incessant quest for more money, was often oppressive and brutal. The tax-collectors or *ʿāmils* were often concerned to line their own pockets, but they were also driven on by pressure from the sultan, who acted ruthlessly towards ʿāmils who failed to bring in their stipulated quotas. Maḥmūd's vizier Isfarā'inī was removed from office and jailed because he refused to make up tax-deficits from his own pocket. Khurāsān suffered badly from this oppression, and distress there was aggravated by earthquakes and a disastrous famine in 401/1011 followed by plague, when people were at times reduced to cannibalism. In Mas'ūd's time, the governor Abu'l-Faḍl Sūrī similarly drained Khurāsān of its wealth. It is not surprising that the dihqāns and notables of Khurāsān had in 396/1006 encouraged the Qarakhānids to invade, and that in Mas'ūd's sultanate, they were indifferent to the coming of the Saljuqs. The unpopularity of Ghaznavid rule can be further demonstrated from other parts of the empire. In Ray and Jibāl, the Ghaznavid invaders had at first enjoyed a certain popularity, because they promised deliverance from the tyranny and arbitrary rule of the Dailamī soldiery. But disillusionment soon set in, and it is recorded of the Ghaznavid military governor there that "Tash-Farrāsh had filled the land with injustice and oppression, until the people prayed for deliverance from them and their rule; the land became ruined and the population dispersed"; finally, complaints became so loud that Mas'ūd had to send out a new governor and restore more equitable rule. Here, then, is one reason why Ghaznavid rule did not take firm root in the western provinces of the empire and why these lands fell to the Saljuqs comparatively easily: the sultans had done nothing to make the people there feel any attachment to the Ghaznavid cause.

Maḥmūd died in 421/1030, and his son Muḥammad, who had been governor of Gūzgān, succeeded in Ghazna according to his father's will. The situation presents parallels with Sebük-Tegin's choice of Ismā'īl in preference to Maḥmūd, for Mas'ūd had been governor of Herāt and was by far the most experienced and capable of Maḥmūd's sons; but he had latterly been on bad terms with his father, and so was passed over. As events fell out, Mas'ūd's reputation as a war leader, and his recent exploits in Jibāl and the west, gained him the support of the Ghaznavid army, and this was the all-important factor; in a military state like that of the Ghaznavids, a sultan without the full confidence of the army was inconceivable. As Mas'ūd came eastwards from Ray to Ghazna, his uncle Yūsuf b. Sebük-Tegin and the other great commanders all rallied to him, and Muḥammad's first reign ended after only a few months (he was briefly raised to the throne again in 432/1041 by the rebels who murdered Mas'ūd).

The new sultan Mas'ūd was a brave soldier, but in many ways he lacked his father's strength of character. His advisers complained of his capriciousness and deviousness, his refusal to consider unpalatable advice and his dependence on a crowd of sycophants, led by the 'āriḍ Abū Sahl Zauzanī, whom Baihaqī regards as a maleficent influence in the state. Indeed, in his early years on the throne, Mas'ūd conducted a vendetta against all those connected with his father's régime whom he considered had turned Maḥmūd against him. Not a few of these *Maḥmūdiyān* (to use Baihaqī's term) were hounded to disgrace or death: the former vizier Ḥasanak was executed on a trumped-up charge of contacts with the Fāṭimids; Mas'ūd's uncle Yūsuf b. Sebük-Tegin was arrested and jailed; and the assassination of the Khwārazm-Shāh Altun-Tash was attempted (see below). Conversely, the former vizier Maimandī, who had incurred Maḥmūd's displeasure and had latterly been imprisoned, was now released and restored to office for the two years preceding his death in 424/1033. His successor in the vizierate, Aḥmad b. 'Abd al-Ṣamad, soon incurred Mas'ūd's hostility because of his independence and criticism of the sultan's unwise policies.

Mas'ūd was determined that his father's achievement in India should be safeguarded; the death of Maḥmūd should not mean that the Indian princes could sit back and breathe again. Mas'ūd had to give up the idea of going to India in 422/1031, because of the danger on the Oxus from the Qarakhānid 'Alī-Tegin and the Saljuqs, but in 424/1033 he led an expedition which captured Sarsūtī or Sarsāwa, a fortress which his father had been unable to take. In the winter of 429/1037–8, he insisted on personally leading an expedition to the allegedly impregnable "Virgin fortress" of Hānsī near Delhi, in fulfilment of a vow he had made, even though the situation in Khurāsān and the west was at that time highly menacing. We can, indeed, detect a constant tension in Mas'ūd's reign between the claims of India, where the Ghaznavids had gained so much glory, and those of Khurāsān, where the mounting intensity of the Saljuq incursions threatened the loss of all the western lands. The dilemma was made worse for Mas'ūd by the instability of affairs in the Punjab. In 422/1031 he had sent out one Aḥmad Ïnal-Tegin, formerly treasurer to Maḥmūd, as Commander-in-Chief of the Indian garrisons. Because of earlier ill-treatment at Mas'ūd's hands, he seized the opportunity to rebel, rallying the turbulent Turkish ghāzī elements of the garrison towns. Mas'ūd had to send a force under the Indian commander Tilak before Aḥmad Ïnal-Tegin's revolt could be quelled (425/1034).

The succession disputes in the tributary state of Makrān have been already noted. At the beginning of his reign, Mas'ūd deputed his uncle Yūsuf b. Sebük-Tegin to march southwards from Bust with an army, reduce the rebellious governor of Quṣdār, who was two years behind with his tribute, and then go on to Makrān. One of the disputants over the succession, Abu'l-Mu'askar, had appealed to Mas'ūd for help; Yūsuf's army was now able to help him successfully achieve the throne (422/1031). However, there was a deeper motive behind Mas'ūd's despatch of his uncle to Baluchistan. When Maḥmūd died, Yūsuf had in the first place supported Muḥammad, and Mas'ūd, with his intensely suspicious nature, could never forgive him nor trust him thereafter. He deliberately sent Yūsuf away from the centre of power until his own position in Ghazna was secure; then, when Yūsuf returned, he was arrested, dying in prison shortly afterwards. The success of his troops in Makrān encouraged the sultan to intervene in the Būyid province of Kirmān, which bordered on his own dependent territories of Sīstān and Makrān. Being already master of Ray and Jibāl, the acquisition of Kirmān would have rounded off Ghaznavid territory in central Iran. Mas'ūd proclaimed to the new caliph al-Qā'im's envoy that this project was all part of a grand design, one involving a general onslaught on the Būyids; 'Umān would be attacked from Makrān, and ultimately, Ghaznavid armies would sweep westwards, liberate the 'Abbāsids from Būyid tutelage and attack the infidel Byzantines and heretical Fāṭimids. Naturally, the eruption of the Saljuqs into Khurāsān made these plans unfulfilled dreams. Nor was the Kirmān venture successful. The army which had been victorious in Makrān did in 424/1033 occupy Kirmān. But the Ghaznavids' financial exactions there made the Kirmānīs long once more for Būyid rule. 'Imād al-Dīn Abū Kālījār sent from Fārs an army under his vizier Bahrām b. Māfinna, and in 425/1034 the Ghaznavid garrison was ignominiously ejected and had to retreat to Nīshāpūr.

As Mas'ūd's reign progressed, everything else became overshadowed by events in Khurāsān and along the Oxus frontier. The two great disasters which befell Ghaznavid power here were the penetration of Khurāsān by the Oghuz Türkmens and the loss of Khwārazm. The early history of the Oghuz and their gradual migration southwards and westwards from the Central Asian steppes are detailed in *The Cambridge History of Iran*, vol. v. Following the classical pattern of barbarian infiltration into the civilized lands, we find bands of Oghuz, under the direction of the Saljuq family, serving as frontier auxiliaries in Khwārazm and Transoxiana. One group aided Ismā'īl al-Muntaṣir, the last fugitive Sāmānid, before he was finally killed in 395/1005. After this, Oghuz under Arslān Isrā'īl b. Saljuq are found pasturing their flocks on the fringes of Khwārazm and then in the service of the Qarakhānid 'Alī-Tegin, who towards 416/1025 allotted them pastures in the Bukhārā district. They were joined by other Türkmens under Arslān Isrā'īl's brothers Toghrïl and Chaghrï, who had been previously in the service of another Qarakhānid prince. It seems that the military support of the Oghuz was an appreciable factor in 'Alī-Tegin's maintenance of his power in Transoxiana; the high favour which Arslān Isrā'īl enjoyed is shown by 'Alī-Tegin's marriage with one of his daughters.

When in 416/1025 'Alī-Tegin was temporarily driven out of his possessions by the combined operations of Maḥmūd of Ghazna and Yūsuf Qadïr Khān, Arslān Isrā'īl was captured by Maḥmūd and imprisoned in India till he died. His Türkmen followers, numbering 4,000 tents, then sought permission from Maḥmūd to settle on the northern edge of Khurāsān in the districts of Sarakhs, Abīvard and Farāva, where they promised to act as frontier guards. The decision to admit these lawless elements, who as pastoral nomads could not be expected to have any regard for agriculture and settled life, was later recognized by the sultan to have been a mistake. In 418/1027 Maḥmūd had to send a punitive expedition against them, the people of Nasā and Abīvard having complained about their spoliations. But his general Arslān Jādhib failed to master them, and in the next year, the sultan himself came and inflicted a crushing defeat on the Türkmens, scattering them broadcast. Some fled westwards into the Balkhān Mountains on the eastern shore of the Caspian. Others fled into the interior of Persia, where they successively sought employment as mercenaries: first with the Būyid Qawām al-Daula of Kirmān, then with the Kākūyid ruler of Iṣfahān, 'Alā' al-Daula, and finally with the Rawwādid amīr of Tabrīz, Vahsūdān b. Mamlān, who aimed to use them against his rivals the Shaddādids of Arrān and against the Christian Armenian and Georgian princes. It is these Türkmens who are called in the sources the "'Irāqī" ones, because they had entered 'Irāq 'Ajamī, i.e. western Persia. They do not seem to have had any outstanding leaders, and deprived of Arslān Isrā'īl's leadership, they split into undisciplined bands. Eventually, they joined up with other Oghuz who, if the accounts of an expedition under Chaghrï Beg as far as Āzarbāījān and Armenia at some time between 407/1016–17 and 412/1021 are to be credited, had entered northern Persia a few years previously.

Thus despite the momentary stability established in Khurāsān by the time of Maḥmūd's death, the position facing Mas'ūd was far from reassuring. At all stages of human history before the spread of firearms, people of the sown have been at a disadvantage against invaders from the desert or steppe. These last rarely possess anything more than their herds, so have little to lose; their incursions occur over a wide front, and even if repelled, mean the trampling of crops and disruption of the agricultural cycle. So it was with the Oghuz in Khurāsān; and furthermore, Mas'ūd for several years persistently underestimated the danger, unable to conceive that half-starved nomads could seriously damage the imposing edifice of Ghaznavid power in Khurāsān. The war there was left to subordinate commanders, whilst the sultan concerned himself with other projects, such as the campaigns in India or the expedition to Gurgān and Ṭabaristān, or else remained in his palaces, engrossed in pleasure and wine-drinking.

In the succession struggle with his brother Muḥammad, Mas'ūd had himself recruited some of the "'Irāqī" Türkmens under their chiefs Yaghmur, Qïzïl, Bogha and Göktash, and these were used as auxiliary troops, e.g. for Yūsuf b. Sebük-Tegin's Makrān expedition of 422/1031. But they were never a reliable force, and it proved impossible to hold them in check, so that their depredations spread all over northern Persia. Finally, in 424/1033 Mas'ūd sent to Ray his general Tash-Farrāsh, who there seized fifty of the Türkmens' leaders, including Yaghmur, and put them to death. The remaining Türkmens inevitably became implacable enemies of the Ghaznavids.

Meanwhile, the Saljuq family under Toghrïl, Chaghrï, Mūsā Yabghu and Ibrāhīm Ïnal, had remained in Transoxiana, and in 423/1032 were once more allied to 'Alī-Tegin. Their story now becomes intertwined with events in the neighbouring province of Khwārazm. The Khwārazm-Shāh Altun-Tash had always given unswerving loyalty to the Ghaznavids, and it had been his advice which had made many of the army leaders support Mas'ūd in preference to Muḥammad. Yet Mas'ūd's chronically suspicious nature fell on all who might possibly figure as his rivals. In Khwārazm, Altun-Tash disposed of a large army, and he had recruited large numbers of Qïpchaq and other Türkmens as auxiliary troops. These were obviously necessary for the defence of a province so exposed to external attack as was Khwārazm, but the sultan fiercely resented Altun-Tash's military strength. Accordingly, he endeavoured early in his reign to procure the Shāh's assassination, but the plot misfired. The sultan feared that Altun-Tash would now be driven into the arms of the Ghaznavids' old enemy 'Alī-Tegin, but he nevertheless remained loyal and died fighting against 'Alī-Tegin at the battle of Dabūsiya in 423/1032. Warfare with the Qarakhānid khan had flared up because Mas'ūd, when preparing for a struggle with his brother after his father's death, had rashly promised to cede Khuttal to 'Alī-Tegin in return for military aid. The help had not been needed, but 'Alī-Tegin continued to claim his side of the bargain. The full effects of Mas'ūd's earlier attempt to kill Altun-Tash were now seen. The latter's son Hārūn followed his father as effective ruler in Khwārazm, though without the traditional title of Khwārazm-Shāh. A breach opened up rapidly, and Khwārazm now fell away from Ghaznavid control. In 425/1034 Hārūn allied with 'Alī-Tegin for a joint attack on the Ghaznavid territories along the Oxus, and this was only halted when Mas'ūd managed to have Hārūn murdered by his own ghulāms. 'Alī-Tegin also died at this juncture, but the struggle against the Ghaznavids was continued from Khwārazm by Hārūn's brother Ismā'īl Khāndān and from Transoxiana by 'Alī-Tegin's sons. On the upper Oxus, the Kumījī tribesmen of the Buttamān Mountains were stirred up; they were further used by a Qarakhānid prince, Böri-Tegin, to harry Khuttal and Vakhsh in 429/1038. Thus Khwārazm was now totally lost, and one of the bastions against the flooding of the Türkmens into the Ghaznavid territories removed.

When 'Alī-Tegin died, the Saljuqs and their followers moved into Khwārazm at Hārūn's invitation, but there, enmity flared up between them and the head of a rival group of Oghuz, the Yabghu or traditional head of the tribe, Shāh Malik of Jand and Yengi-kent (two towns near the mouth of the Syr Darya). As the Ghaznavids' ally, Shāh Malik eventually reconquered the whole of Khwārazm; but by that time (432/1041), Sulṭān Mas'ūd was dead and the power of the triumphant Saljuqs dominant in eastern Iran. In 426/1035 Shāh Malik routed the Saljuqs and drove them southwards towards Khurāsān. Ten thousand Türkmens, under Toghrïl, Chaghrï, Mūsā Yabghu and Ibrāhīm Ïnal, reached Khurāsān in a desperate condition, and asked the governor Abu'l-Faḍl Sūrī for asylum. Calling themselves "the slaves Yabghu, Toghrïl and Chaghrï, clients of the Commander of the Faithful", they asked for the grant of Nasā and Farāva, promising to act as frontier guards against further incursions from the steppes. It seems that the Saljuqs' intentions were at this time peaceable, and the sultan's civilian advisers suggested a pacific reply, at least until the Saljuqs openly showed their bad faith. But Mas'ūd and his generals were bent on destroying the Türkmens as quickly as possible. He sent an army against them under Begtoghdï, but was astounded to hear that the Saljuqs had defeated this army on the road to Nasā (426/1035). He was forced to yield Nasā, Farāva and Dihistān to them, nominally as governors on his behalf, and in a fruitless attempt to attach them to the Ghaznavid cause, marriage alliances were offered to the Saljuq leaders. Naturally, the latter were merely emboldened by their success, and in 428/1037 asked for the grant of Sarakhs, Abīvard and Marv, together with their revenues.

Only now did the sultan really awaken to the gravity of the situation, for it was impossible for him to give up so important a town as Marv without a fight. The warfare in Khurāsān had already put a severe strain on both military and economic resources. The raiders drove their flocks of sheep and their horses unconcernedly over the rich agricultural oases of Khurāsān, preventing the sowing and harvesting of crops, and intercepting the caravan traffic upon which the province's commercial prosperity depended. One historian says of the distressed state of the Nīshāpūr region, just before it was occupied by the Saljuqs in 429/1038, "That region became ruinous, like the dishevelled tresses of the fair ones or the eyes of the loved ones, and became devastated by the pasturing of [the Türkmens'] flocks."[1] Hence the Khurāsānian towns, though secure from direct onslaught behind their walls and ditches (which the nomads were ill-equipped to assault) were gradually starved out through being cut off from their agricultural hinterlands. Such towns as Nīshāpūr, Marv and Herāt in the end surrendered peacefully to the Saljuqs from economic rather than political motives.

Shortages of food and fodder, and the financial drain of keeping armies continuously in the field, plagued Mas'ūd and his generals. It was these needs which in 426/1035 impelled him to lead an expedition to Gurgān and Ṭabaristān on the Caspian coast, where the local ruler Abū Kālījār was behind with his tribute. At first sight, the military advantages in Khurāsān seemed to be on the side of the Ghaznavids, with their professional troops and generals, their superior weapons and equipment, and their numbers at least equal to those of the Saljuqs, but this was not in practice the case. The Türkmens were poorly armed,

[1] Mīrkhwānd, *Rauḍat al-ṣafā*, vol. IV (Tehrān, 1270–4/1853–6), p. 102.

but were highly mobile; they could leave their baggage and families long distances away, and being accustomed to the rigours of steppe life, could operate with minimal food supplies. As one of Mas'ūd's courtiers said, "The steppe is father and mother to them, just as towns are to us."[1] The Ghaznavid armies were skilfully commanded by such generals as Sü-Bashï, but they suffered terribly from the shortages of food and water in the desert fringes of northern Khurāsān; also, they were burdened by heavy equipment and had to operate from fixed bases.

The early disillusionment of the people of Khurāsān with Ghaznavid rule has already been mentioned, and the lack of a will to resist begins to play a significant part in the Ghaznavid–Saljuq struggle for the province. The notables and landowners there had to endure the burnings and tramplings across their lands of the opposing forces. The sultan seemed impotent, based as he was on distant Ghazna, to master the invaders; was it not preferable to end it all and come to terms with the Saljuq leaders, in the hope that they might then be able to restrain their lawless followers? Consequently, Marv was occupied by Chaghrï as early as 428/1037, and Nīshāpūr opened its gates to Ibrāhīm Ïnal in the next year, being occupied by the Saljuqs for several months before Mas'ūd reappeared with an army. Here in Nīshāpūr, the administrative capital of Khurāsān, Toghrïl had during this occupation mounted Mas'ūd's own throne and behaved as ruler of Khurāsān. Saljuq raiders were now penetrating up the Oxus valley to Balkh and Tukhāristān, and as far south as Sīstān; it was feared that Ghazna itself would be threatened, although the mountain barriers of the Hindu Kush and Pamirs in fact prevented the Saljuqs from reaching eastern Afghanistan. Law and order were everywhere breaking down, and local governors and officials were making the best terms they could with the incomers. Ray and Jibāl were by now, of course, irretrievably lost, for the Türkmens had long been making communication with these western outposts of Ghaznavid power difficult. With the aid of the "'Irāqī" Türkmens whom he had hired as mercenaries, the Kākūyid 'Alā' al-Daula had been emboldened to throw off Ghaznavid control in Iṣfahān. Then, at the beginning of 429/1038, the Ghaznavid garrison in Ray was expelled by the Türkmens and the governor Tash-Farrāsh killed; 'Alā' al-Daula managed to secure control of the town, continuing to acknowledge on his coins the overlordship of Mas'ūd, until

[1] Baihaqī, p. 537; tr. p. 476.

the Saljuqs wrested Ray from him and for a time made it their capital in Persia.

The climax of the struggle for Khurāsān came in 431/1040. The sultan had before this spent a winter unsuccessfully campaigning in Chaghāniyān against the Qarakhānid invader Böri-Tegin (430/1038–9); he had, however, defeated the Saljuqs near Sarakhs (430/1039) and recaptured Herāt and Nīshāpūr. He now decided on a final effort to engage the Saljuqs in the steppes around Marv, and took with him a large army, including a force of elephants. But they found food and water virtually non-existent in the steppes, to such a point that the Ghaznavid cavalrymen were reduced to fighting on camels instead of horses. When Mas'ūd's army engaged some 16,000 Türkmens at the ribāṭ of Dandānqān on the road from Sarakhs to Marv, they were in a dispirited and internally divided condition, so that when the Saljuqs attacked, their "sword-blade fell only on cuirasses already cracked, and on helmets already split". In this crucial battle, the sultan's troops were routed, and a *sauve-qui-peut* back to Afghanistan and Ghazna followed. Khurāsān had to be abandoned to the Saljuqs, and on the battlefield, Toghrïl was proclaimed amīr of Khurāsān.

The towns of Khurāsān all capitulated to Toghrïl and Chaghrï. Mas'ūd tried fruitlessly to get help from the Qarakhānid Sulaimān Arslān Khān of Kāshghar. He became plunged in melancholy; conducted a purge of those of his subordinates whom he considered had failed him; he even considered ceding northern Afghanistan to Böri-Tegin, in the hope that the latter would become embroiled with the Saljuqs. Finally, he decided to give up the struggle and abandon Ghazna for India, even though his advisers assured him – truly, as events showed – that eastern Afghanistan was perfectly defensible against the Saljuqs. He gathered together all his treasure and set off for India, but when his column reached the ribāṭ of Marīkala near Taxila in the Punjab, the army mutinied and plundered his treasury and baggage. The rebels raised to the throne once more Muḥammad b. Maḥmūd, just released from imprisonment, and Mas'ūd himself was killed (432/1041), giving him in the eyes of future generations the designation of *amīr-i shahīd* "the Martyr-King". Mas'ūd's son Maudūd came from Balkh, setting himself up as his father's avenger, and a few months later, according to some authorities, he overthrew and killed Muḥammad in a battle at Nangrahār in the Kabul River valley.

One may consider the early Ghaznavid period as ending at this point. The empire survived with reduced territories, essentially those of eastern Afghanistan, Baluchistan and the Punjab, for another 130 years. In the middle decades of the 5th/11th century, peace was made with the Saljuqs, and the frontier between the two empires stabilized; Sulṭān Ibrāhīm b. Mas'ūd restored some of the glory of his father's and grandfather's age and treated with the Saljuq sultans on equal terms. If we are to evaluate the historical significance of the early Ghaznavid empire, we may note the following points. First, the Ghaznavids exemplify the phenomenon of barbarians coming into the higher civilization of the Islamic world and being absorbed by it. The court culture under Maḥmūd and Mas'ūd, with its fine flowering of Persian poetry and the commanding figure of the polymath Bīrūnī, shows how far this process went, as does the moulding of the administration of the empire within the Perso-Islamic tradition. The sultans also took over one of the historic tasks of the Iranian rulers of the east, the maintenance of a bastion there against further invaders from the steppes. Secondly, the Ghaznavid empire had an essentially military bias. It was built around a highly professional, multi-national army, with a nucleus of slave guards personally attached to the sultan; and because of the connection with India, the sultans were able to keep this standing army generally occupied in the exploitation of the riches of the subcontinent. The constituting of the Ghaznavid army, a fighting instrument so much admired by later political theorists like Niẓām al-Mulk, thus marks the culmination of the general infiltration of the eastern Islamic world by Turkish mercenaries. On these fringes, the Turks managed to overthrow the indigenous Iranian powers and build up a mighty empire of their own, setting the pattern for Turkish political domination over much of the Islamic world for centuries to come. Thirdly, the Ghaznavids have a place in history as the introducers on a large scale of Muslim rule into northern India, and the establishers, through the intermediacy of such scholars as Bīrūnī, of the first direct connection with the culture of the Indian world. In terms of permanent settlement and conversions to Islam, the Ghaznavid period in India was not as important as succeeding ages, but the sultans did by their raids accustom the Turkish and Afghan peoples of Inner Asia to utilize the plains of India as an outlet for barbarian energies; and in the course of these incursions, Islam was made one of the major faiths of the subcontinent. Fourthly, the personalities of Maḥmūd and Mas'ūd were built up in popular minds into great Muslim heroes, and almost into folk-heroes. Maḥmūd is prominent in later literature, in both the *adab* collections of anecdotes and in the poetic romances, in various guises: as the great despot, as the lover of his favourite Ayāz, and above all, as the scourge of the infidels in India. Mas'ūd also, has to a lesser extent a place in the popular mind as a warrior in India and as the "Martyr-Sultan".

CHAPTER 6

THE MINOR DYNASTIES OF NORTHERN IRAN

I. THE CASPIAN PROVINCES

Among the former provinces of the Sāsānian empire, the coastal regions along the southern shore of the Caspian Sea resisted the penetration of the Arabs and Islam most tenaciously. Protected by the lofty Alburz mountain range they escaped the main thrust of the Arab conquering armies as they advanced eastward into Khurāsān. Early Arab invasions were only partially successful. In the year 30/650–1, under the caliph 'Uthmān, Sa'īd b. al-'Āṣ entered Gurgān, the province touching the southeastern coast of the Caspian Sea, and imposed a tribute on its ruler. From there he marched westward to conquer parts of Ṭabaristān. These conquests were lost again during the struggle between 'Alī and Mu'āwiya for the caliphate, and the tribute for Gurgān was frequently withheld. Mu'āwiya soon after gaining sole possession of the caliphate in 41/661 sent Maṣqala b. Hubaira to subjugate Ṭabaristān, but he and his army were annihilated in Rūyān to the west of Ṭabaristān. In the years 61–4/680–3 an attempt to conquer Ṭabaristān resulted in a defeat of the Kūfan general Muḥammad b. al-Ash'ath al-Kindī. Gurgān was not brought under Muslim rule until 98/716–17, when Yazīd b. al-Muhallab defeated the Chöl (Ar. Ṣūl) Turks of the Dihistān steppes north of the Atrak river, who had taken the country from its *marzbān* Fīrūz b. Qūl, and built the town of Gurgān (near modern Gunbad-i Qābūs) which became the capital of the Muslim province. Yazīd's further attempt to conquer Ṭabaristān ended in failure, and he was forced to leave the country after concluding a truce.

Ṭabaristān, the most developed and populous of the Caspian provinces, at this time was ruled by a dynasty of Ispahbads known after their ancestor Dābūya as Dābūyids with their capital in Sārī. They bore the titles Gīlgīlān, Padashwārgarshāh (Patashwārgar being the old name of the mountains of Ṭabaristān; later distorted as Farshwādgarshāh), Ispahbad of Khurāsān, said to have been conferred upon them by the last Sāsānian king Yazdgard III, and claimed descent from the Sāsānian Pērōz through his son Jāmāsp. The early history of the dynasty is, however, shrouded in obscurity. The first mention of an Ispahbad ruling Ṭabaristān in a reliable report concerns the year 79/698. Coins minted in the names of the Dābūyid Ispahbads are known only from 711. They are dated in a post-Sāsānian era beginning in 651. Statements in the later sources that their ancestors before the rise of Islam ruled in Gīlān may be merely an attempt to explain their title Gīlgīlān. The fact that Ṭabaristān in early Islamic times harboured beside the Ispahbads other dynasties of Pa<u>dhgh</u>ōspāns and Ustandārs has been interpreted as reflecting an attempt to reconstitute the higher Sāsānian administrative hierarchy there, perhaps at the time when Pērōz, the son of Yazdgard III, hoped to restore the Persian empire.[1] The use of these titles in Ṭabaristān as names and designations appears, however, only much later. Their adoption among the rulers seems rather to attest the survival of Persian national sentiments, which also encouraged the preservation of the title Ispahbad long after the overthrow of the Dābūyids by the Muslim conquest. The region of Mount Damāvand in the same period was ruled by a dynasty bearing the title Maṣmu<u>gh</u>ān ("Great one of the Magians") indicating a religious function. Another dynasty of Maṣmu<u>gh</u>āns is mentioned in the area of Miyāndūrūd in eastern Ṭabaristān.

Al-Ḥajjāj b. Yūsuf during his governorship of ʿIrāq and the east renewed the Muslim efforts to subdue Ṭabaristān. In 78/697 a group of <u>Kh</u>ārijites under their leader Qaṭarī seeking refuge in Ṭabaristān were hospitably received by the Ispahbad. When Qaṭarī, however, demanded his conversion to Islam on <u>Kh</u>ārijite terms he joined forces with the army sent by al-Ḥajjāj, and Qaṭarī was killed, according to a legendary report by the Ispahbad himself in single combat. Under the pressure of new Arab attacks the Ispahbad agreed to pay tribute but succeeded in keeping the Muslims out of the country. When the ʿAbbāsid revolutionary army reached Ray in 131/748 the Ispahbad <u>Kh</u>ūr<u>sh</u>īd readily followed the invitation of Abū Muslim to transfer his allegiance and pay the tribute to the new power. The Maṣmu<u>gh</u>ān of Damāvand rejected a similar demand and repelled the ʿAbbāsid troops sent against him.

After the execution of Abū Muslim by the caliph al-Manṣūr the Ispahbad <u>Kh</u>ūr<u>sh</u>īd supported the Zoroastrian Sunbā<u>dh</u> who rose in

[1] Marquart, "Ērānšahr", pp. 133ff.

revolt in 137/754–5 claiming revenge for Abū Muslim and offered him shelter in Ṭabaristān after his defeat by the caliph's troops. Sunbādh was killed, however, by a relative of the Ispahbad to whom he refused to show respect. Al-Manṣūr attempted to overthrow Khūrshīd by appointing and crowning a cousin of his as Ispahbad. As this expedient failed to shake the position of Khūrshīd, a settlement was reached under which Khūrshīd promised to pay a heavy tribute. But in 141/759 al-Manṣūr ordered war against the Ispahbad. Within two years Ṭabaristān was conquered by the concerted action of the generals Abu'l-Khasīb, Khāzim b. Khuzaima, Abū 'Aun b. 'Abd-Allāh, Rauḥ b. Ḥātim, and 'Umar b. al-'Alā'. The last-named also took Rūyān and, even further west, Kalār and Chālūs which became the Muslim border towns towards the country of Dailamān. The Ispahbad fled to Dailamān and gathered an army of Dailamites and Gīlites threatening a counter-attack. But when his wives and children were captured by the Muslims he despaired and poisoned himself in 144/761. Damāvand too was conquered by the Muslims, probably a few years later.

Ṭabaristān henceforth was ruled by Muslim governors residing in Āmul. Their first task was to secure the Muslim domination over the newly subdued territories. Though the nobility was generally left unharmed, some prominent Zoroastrian leaders were killed during the first years of the occupation. The third governor, Abu'l-'Abbās al-Ṭūsī, *c.* 146/763 settled garrisons (*masāliḥ*) ranging in strength between two hundred and one thousand Arab and Persian, chiefly Khurāsānian, loyalists (*abnā'*) to the 'Abbāsid cause in more than forty towns and strategic spots from Tamīsha in the east to Chālūs and Kalār in the west. The mountains of Ṭabaristān, however, continued to elude the control of the conquerors. They were ruled by members of two families claiming, like the Dābūyids, illustrious descent in the Sāsānian past. The eastern mountain range, later known as the Sharvīn mountains, was the domain of Sharvīn of the house of Bāvand. His ancestor Bāv was said to be a grandson of Kā'ūs, son of the Sāsānian king Kavādh, and to have come to Ṭabaristān at the time of the flight of Yazdgard III before the Arab conquerors. Bāv is, on the other hand, the name of a *magus*, and it has been suggested that the family was descended from a prominent Zoroastrian priest of Ray at the turn of the sixth century.[1] The seat of the Bāvandids was in Firīm on mount Shahriyārkūh. The central mountain range was

[1] Marquart, "Ērānšahr", p. 128.

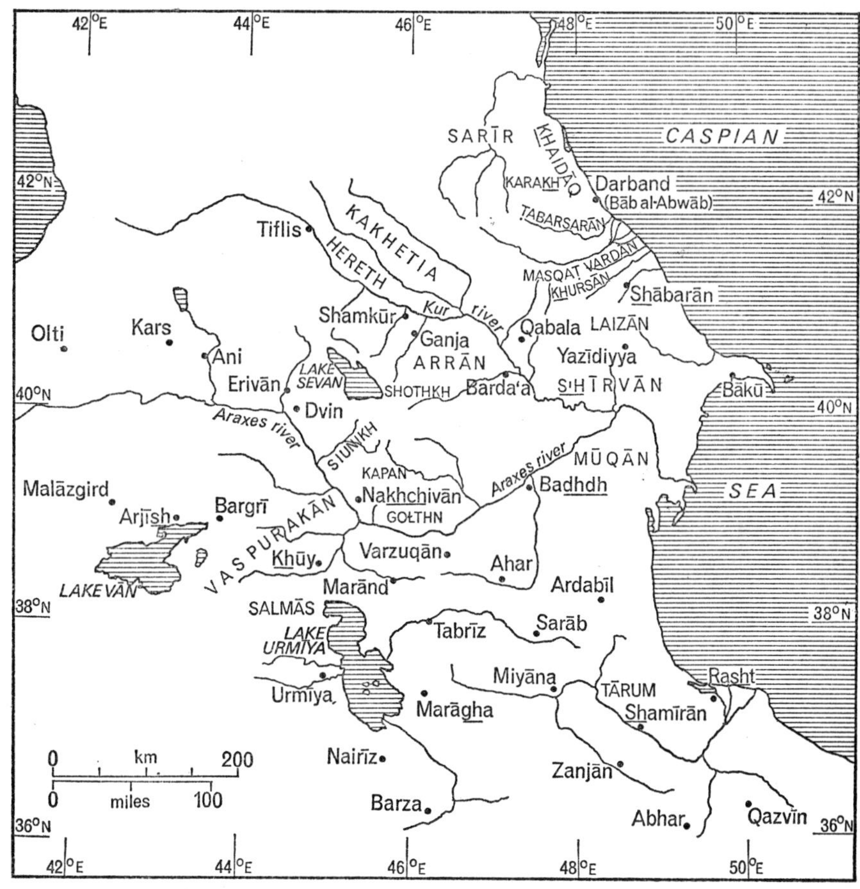

Map 5. Āzarbāījān

ruled by Vindā<u>dh</u>hurmuzd of the house of Qārinvand who resided near Damāvand and in Lafūr. A younger brother of Vindā<u>dh</u>hurmuzd, Vindāspagān, held sway over the western mountains and resided in Muzn at the border of Dailamān. The Qārinvand allegedly were descended from Sō<u>kh</u>rā, the minister of Kavā<u>dh</u>, whose son Kāren was granted parts of Ṭabaristān by Anū<u>sh</u>irvān. Perhaps more reliable is a different account stating that they had been installed in their domains by the Dābūyids a century before. Vindā<u>dh</u>hurmuzd and his successors considered themselves as heirs of the Dābūyids and assumed their titles Gīlgīlān and Ispahbads of <u>Kh</u>urāsān. The Bāvandids in this period were addressed as kings of Tukhāristān and probably also claimed the title of Ispahbad.

Khālid b. Barmak during his governorship in Ṭabaristān (*c.* 151–5/768–72) tried to expand the Muslim influence in the highlands by establishing friendly relations with Vindādhhurmuzd and building towns there. They were destroyed after Khālid's departure by the Bāvandid Sharvīn. In 164/781, at a time of unrest in Khurāsān, the caliph al-Mahdī sent messengers to the ruling princes of the east, among them "the king of Ṭabaristān the Ispahbad" (Vindādhhurmuzd) and "the king of Tukhāristān Sharvīn", and received pledges of their loyalty.[1] Yet two years later Vindādhhurmuzd in alliance with Sharvīn and the Maṣmughān of Miyāndūrūd led a dangerous anti-Muslim rebellion. The local chronicles report, no doubt exaggerating, that all Muslims throughout Ṭabaristān were massacred on a single day. The massacres presumably were confined to the highlands and those parts of the lowlands which the rebels were able to overcome. They defeated the first Muslim armies sent against them and killed some of their leaders. The rising was serious enough for the caliph to send in 167/783–4 his son Mūsā with "a huge army and equipment such as no one previously had been equipped, to Gurgān to direct the war against Vindādhhurmuz and Sharvīn, the two lords of Ṭabaristān".[2] In the following year al-Mahdī sent another army of 40,000 men under Sa'īd al-Ḥarashī to the rebel province. Eventually Vindādhhurmuzd was defeated and wounded and gave himself up to Mūsā in Gurgān on a promise of pardon. Mūsā after his succession to the caliphate in 169/785 took him to Baghdad, but soon permitted him to return to his domains.

Relations with the Muslim governors then remained amiable for some time. Jarīr b. Yazīd, governor from 170/786 to 172/788, sold Vindādhhurmuzd extensive holdings of domanial land outside Sārī. In the later years of the reign of Hārūn al-Rashīd, however, new troubles occurred. The two kings of the mountains in alliance strictly controlled the access to their territories and would not permit any Muslim to be buried there. The men of the Bāvandid Sharvīn murdered a nephew of the governor Khalīfa b. Sa'īd whom the latter had appointed his deputy. In 189/805 Vindāspagān, the brother of Vindādhhurmuzd, killed a Muslim tax collector sent to survey his villages. The caliph, who came to Ray in order to settle matters with a governor of Khurāsān of doubtful loyalty, sent to the two princes of Ṭabaristān bidding them

[1] Ya'qūbī, vol. II, p. 479.

[2] Ṭabarī, vol. III, pp. 518ff.

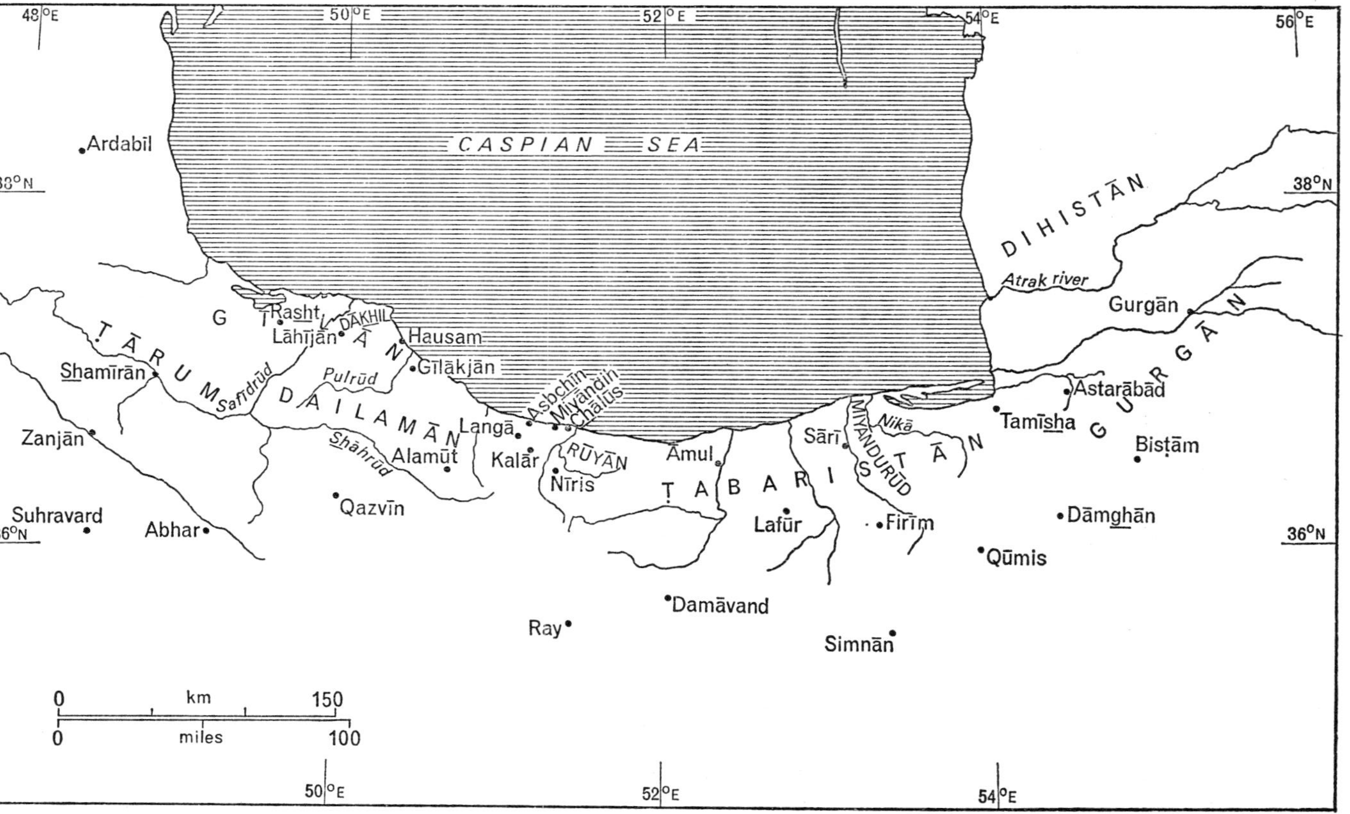

Map 6. The Caspian provinces

to appear before him. Both kings hastened to assure Hārūn of their submission promising payment of the land tax, and Vindādhhurmuzd presented himself to the caliph who confirmed him as Ispahbad. On his request Hārūn replaced the governor of Ṭabaristān, but gave the new governor instructions to restrict the authority of the princes to the highlands. As hostages for their loyalty he took Qārin, the son of Vindādhhurmuzd, and Shahriyār, the son of Sharvīn, to Baghdad. They were returned to their fathers four years later when Hārūn passed through Ray on his way to Khurāsān.

The grandson of Vindādhhurmuzd, Māzyār b. Qārin, was deprived of his kingdom by the Bāvandid Shahriyār b. Sharvīn and his own uncle Vinda-Umīd b. Vindāspagān. He came to the court of the caliph al-Ma'mūn and accepted Islam receiving the Muslim name Abu'l-Ḥasan Muḥammad and gained the caliph's confidence. In 207/822–3 he returned with the governor Mūsā b. Ḥafṣ, a grandson of 'Umar b. al-'Alā', to Ṭabaristān where al-Ma'mūn had granted him the rule of two towns. He first killed his uncle and in 210/825–6 conquered, in concert with Mūsā, the territories of the Bāvandid Shāpūr, successor of his father Shahriyār, and put him to death. Having become the sole ruler of the highlands he adopted the traditional titles of the Ispahbads of Ṭabaristān, built mosques in Firīm and other towns, and carried out successful raids among the Dailamites of whom he settled some 10,000 in the border area of Muzn. His influence also expanded in the lowlands at the expense of the governor Mūsā and, after the latter's death in 211/826–7, of his son Muḥammad. His régime soon ran into the opposition of a section of the native aristocracy and from the descendants of the abnā' who saw their privileged position as the ruling element threatened. As their attempts to discredit Māzyār with al-Ma'mūn failed, an insurrection broke out against Māzyār in Āmul into which the governor Muḥammad b. Mūsā was drawn. Māzyār took the city after a siege of eight months, executed some of the leaders and imprisoned others, among them Muḥammad. Al-Ma'mūn granted Māzyār the government of all of Ṭabaristān, and al-Mu'taṣim, who succeeded to the caliphate in 218/833, at first confirmed him. Māzyār soon became involved, however, in a quarrel with 'Abd-Allāh b. Ṭāhir who as viceroy of the east claimed overlordship over Ṭabaristān. Māzyār refused to transmit the revenues of Ṭabaristān to the Ṭāhirid, instead surrendering them to a representative of the caliph, and rejected 'Abd-Allāh's intercession for the release of Muḥammad b. Mūsā. 'Abd-

Allāh in turn denigrated Māzyār with the caliph and encouraged the internal opposition to him. As the descendants of the abnā' accused him of apostasy and worked for his overthrow, his measures against them became more and more repressive. He took hostages to prevent their leaving the country and abolished their tax privileges as no longer justified since they were no more obliged to fight the infidel Dailamites and mountaineers. Eventually he sent the inhabitants of Āmul and Sārī to prison camps and encouraged the native peasants to revolt against their landlords. The caliph ordered 'Abd-Allāh b. Ṭāhir to take action against him. Betrayed by his brother Qūhyār, Māzyār in 224/839 was captured by the Ṭāhirid army and sent to Sāmarrā where he was scourged to death in the following year.

The sources, invariably hostile to Māzyār and pro-Ṭāhirid, repeat accusations against him that he reverted to Zoroastrianism and conspired with the Khurramī Bābak against Islam. These charges seem to be without any sound basis in fact, though it is evident that Māzyār in his struggle with the descendants of the abnā' came increasingly to rely on native, often Zoroastrian, supporters. Nor is there clear evidence that Māzyār intended to revolt against the caliph. If he was encouraged in his resistance to 'Abd-Allāh b. Ṭāhir by the latter's rival al-Afshīn, he became a victim of the power struggle of these two men. Yet this accusation itself appears from some sources as a trumped-up charge of the Ṭāhirid to prove the treason of his rival.

Ṭabaristān now came under Ṭāhirid rule for over two decades. Qūhyār, who had been promised by the victors possession of the kingdom of Vindādhhurmuzd, was killed by his brother's Dailamite slave guard, and it has been generally assumed that the Qārinvand dynasty came to an end at this time. This assumption is probably wrong. In events of the year 250/864 an Ispahbad of Lafūr, Bādūspān b. Gurdzād, is mentioned. He and his descendants through three generations are occasionally referred to until 318/930 as rulers of Lafūr, Vinda-Umīdkūh and Vindādhhurmuzkūh. One of them is designated in a contemporary source as a Qārinid ("Ibn Qārin"). After 318/930 the dynasty apparently declined to insignificance and is not mentioned for over a century. But towards the end of the 5th/11th century Ibn Isfandiyār again mentions amīrs of Lafūr and expressly calls them Qārinvand. It is thus evident that Badūspān b. Gurdzād also must be a Qārinid, though his exact relationship to Māzyār is unknown.

The Bāvandid Qārin b. Shahriyār, who also had aided the Ṭāhirid conquest, in reward for his services was restored to the rule of the Sharvīn mountains. In 227/842 he accepted Islam. The Islamization of the native population of Ṭabaristān was proceeding rapidly now. The majority adopted Sunnī Islam loyal to the 'Abbāsid régime, especially of the Ḥanafī and Shāfi'ī schools. But oppositional Shī'ism soon also spread. Imāmism found adherents especially in Āmul and east of Ṭabaristān in Astarābād and Gurgān. In Rūyān and Kalār Zaidī Shī'ism was propagated by followers of the 'Alid al-Qāsim b. Ibrāhīm al-Rassī (d. 246/860). One of the chief transmitters of the teaching of al-Qāsim was Ja'far b. Muḥammad al-Nairūsī, a native of Nairūs in Rūyān. From Rūyān with its close connections with the Dailamites – Rūyān had indeed formerly belonged to Dailamān – Zaidism began to spread westward to the Dailamites and Gīlites living outside the territory of Islam.

II. 'ALID RULE IN ṬABARISTĀN

It was in Rūyān, Kalār and Chālūs that the growing dissatisfaction with some Ṭāhirid officials erupted in open revolt in 250/864. The local leaders concluded an alliance with the Dailamites and invited a Ḥasanid from Ray, al-Ḥasan b. Zaid, to become their chief. Al-Ḥasan, who adopted the regnal name *al-Dā'ī ila'l-ḥaqq*, became the founder of the Caspian Zaidī reign. In the following year he was forced by a counter-offensive of the Ṭāhirid Sulaimān b. 'Abd-Allāh to seek refuge in the country of Dailamān, but before the end of the year he was safely in possession of all of Ṭabaristān. From 253/867 on he usually also held sway over Gurgān. Other 'Alids with his support temporarily gained control over Ray (250–1/864–5, 253/867, 256/870, 258/872), Zanjān, Qazvīn (251–4/865–8) and Qūmis (259–66/873–9). On two occasions al-Ḥasan was again compelled to flee to Dailamān. In 255/869 the 'Abbāsid general Mufliḥ and in 260/874 Ya'qūb al-Ṣaffār invaded Ṭabaristān and Rūyān, but both withdrew in short order.

When al-Ḥasan died in Āmul in 270/884, his brother Muḥammad, whom he had named his successor, was in Gurgān. In Ṭabaristān al-Ḥasan's brother-in-law, the 'Alid Abu'l-Ḥusain Aḥmad b. Muḥammad, usurped the rule for ten months until he was overthrown by Muḥammad. The latter, who assumed the same regnal name as his brother, gained popularity with the Shī'is everywhere by restoring the shrines of 'Alī and al-Ḥusain destroyed by the caliph al-Mutawakkil and by sending liberal gifts to the 'Alids outside his domains. In

277–9/891–3 Rāfi' b. Harthama, then in control of Khurāsān, conquered Ṭabaristān and penetrated deep into the regions of Dailamān and Gīlān where the 'Alid had sought shelter. When the caliph al-Mu'taḍid in 279/892 granted the governorship of Khurāsān to his rival, the Ṣaffārid 'Amr, Rāfi' made peace with Muḥammad b. Zaid restoring Ṭabaristān to him and pledging allegiance to him. In 283/896 he occupied Nīshāpūr for a short time and introduced the 'Alid's name in the *khuṭba* there, but 'Amr soon expelled him. In 287/900 Muḥammad set out to conquer Khurāsān. He was defeated and killed by the Sāmānid army under Muḥammad b. Hārūn al-Sarakhsī at Gurgān. His son and heir-apparent Zaid was carried off to Bukhārā, and al-Sarakhsī took possession of Ṭabaristān.

The reign of the two 'Alids was supported most steadfastly in Rūyān and Kalār. In Ṭabaristān and Gurgān initial enthusiasm for the new régime soon gave way either to fickle support or to latent opposition. The reliance of the régime on rough and undisciplined Dailamite soldiers gave cause to complaints in the towns. The official espousal of Shī'ī doctrine and Mu'tazilī theology provoked resistance among the Sunnī *'ulamā'*, which the rulers did not hesitate to counter with stern measures of repression. The Qārinid Bādūspān loyally supported al-Ḥasan b. Zaid, but his son Shahriyār later opposed Muḥammad. The Bāvandid Qārin and his grandson and successor Rustam were traditionally hostile and missed no chance of fomenting trouble and allying themselves with the foreign enemies of the régime. Rustam eventually in 282/895 was imprisoned and tortured to death by Rāfi' b. Harthama, who at that time supported Muḥammad b. Zaid, and the Bāvandid reign lapsed temporarily.

The Dailamites proved to be the most valuable if not always reliable allies of the two 'Alid rulers. They saved their reign several times by giving them shelter and aiding them to regain their lost kingdom. The Dailamite territories in this period extended from the Chālūs river westward along the coast to about the Gavārūd and in the highlands as far as the valley of the Safīdrūd in its middle course. Along the southern slopes of the Alburz the Dailamites occupied the basin of the Shāhrūd, separated from the plains of Qazvīn by a chain of hills. The lowlands around the delta of the Safīdrūd were occupied by the Gīlites. The Dailamites and the Gīlites spoke dialects which were different enough from the language of the majority of Persians to be incomprehensible to them. They were divided into tribes, and political authority was exercised by tribal chiefs on a hereditary basis. A dynasty of "kings of the Dailamites" known as the Justānids was recognized, though it is not clear how far their authority extended outside their own tribe. Their seat was in Rūdbār, in a side valley of the Shāhrūd basin, where in 246/860–1 one of them is said to have built the fortress of Alamūt. The Justānids, whose origins are unknown, are first mentioned in the sources *c.* 176/792 when one of them gave shelter to the ʿAlid refugee Yaḥyā b. ʿAbd-Allāh. Hārūn al-Rashīd during his visit to Ray in 189/805 received Marzubān b. Justān, lord of the Dailamites, and sent him off with gifts. At the time of al-Ḥasan b. Zaid's arrival in Kalār, the Justānid Vahsūdān b. Marzubān at first pledged allegiance to him, but soon withdrew his support and died in 251/865. His successor Khūrshīd was hostile, but the ʿAlid was able to neutralize his influence among the Dailamites, and he was soon replaced by Justān b. Vahsūdān who rendered important services to both al-Ḥasan and Muḥammad. The Gīlites, according to a single source which may not be entirely reliable, recognized kings of their own who belonged to a royal clan Shāhānshāhvand and resided in the Dākhil region north of Lāhījān. The kingship was not strictly hereditary and was transferred within the royal clan and even to another, related clan. The first king of the Gīlites mentioned, Tīrdādh, father of Harūsindān, must have been contemporary with the ʿAlid brothers, though the Gīlites generally remained aloof from support of their cause.

While Ṭabaristān came under the rule of the Sāmānid Ismāʿīl who restored Sunnism and granted generous compensation to many victims of the Zaidī régime, the Zaidī cause was furthered among the Dailamites by an ʿAlid who had belonged to the entourage of the two Dāʿī's. The Ḥusainid al-Ḥasan b. ʿAlī al-Uṭrūsh after the defeat of Muḥammad b. Zaid fled to Ray from where he soon followed an invitation of Justān b. Marzubān who promised him support in avenging the Dāʿī and recovering Ṭabaristān. Two campaigns which they undertook jointly in 289/902 and 290/903 ended in failure. Al-Uṭrūsh later left Justān in order to summon the Dailamites north of the Alburz and the Gīlites to Islam, taking his abode in turn in Gīlākjān, in the valley of the Pulīrūd among the Dailamites, and in Hausam (modern Rūdisar) among the Gīlites. Al-Uṭrūsh converted most of the Dailamites "of the interior" and the Gīlites east of the Safīdrūd who accepted him as their imām with the regnal name al-Nāṣir li'l-ḥaqq. The Zaidī legal and ritual doctrine which he taught them diverged to some extent from the doctrine of al-Qāsim b. Ibrāhīm to which the Zaidīs converted earlier in Rūyān and Dailamān adhered. These divergencies later provoked fanatical antagonism between the Nāṣiriyya, the followers of the school of al-Uṭrūsh, and the Qāsimiyya, the supporters of the doctrine of al-Qāsim. The conflict had wider implications, since a grandson of al-Qāsim, Yaḥyā al-Hādī ila'l-ḥaqq in 284/897 succeeded in founding a Zaidite state in the Yemen. He and his successors there espoused and developed the doctrine of al-Qāsim. The Caspian Qāsimiyya thus was tempted to look for guidance and leadership to the Zaidite imāms of the Yemen. In fact a substantial contingent of Ṭabarīs, probably mostly from Rūyān, rendered al-Hādī effective military aid.

The Gīlites west of the Safīdrūd, the larger part of Gīlān, probably about the same time were converted to Sunnī Islam by a Ḥanbalī scholar from Āmul, Abū Ja'far al-Thūmī. Ustādh Abū Ja'far, as he later remained known, was buried in Rasht. His shrine, located in the quarter of Ustādsarā, became a place of pilgrimage and remained the main sanctuary of Rasht until the early twentieth century, though an inscription of the year 1009/1600–1 identified him as a nephew of the Prophet and milk-brother of al-Ḥusain b. 'Alī.[1] This region of Gīlān produced a number of distinguished Ḥanbalī scholars during the following centuries.

Al-Uṭrūsh's claim to allegiance among the Dailamites clashed with the interests of Justān b. Vahsūdān who resented his loss of authority and tried to prevent al-Uṭrūsh from raising taxes. In the ensuing conflict the 'Alid gained the upper hand, and Justān was compelled to swear allegiance to him. In 301/914 al-Uṭrūsh set out on a campaign to Ṭabaristān. This time the Sāmānid army under Abu'l-'Abbās Ṣu'lūk suffered a crushing defeat at Būrdidah on the river Būrrūd west of Chālūs, and al-Uṭrūsh occupied Āmul. In the following year a Sāmānid counter-attack forced him once more to withdraw to Chālūs, but after forty days he expelled the enemy and brought all of Ṭabaristān and temporarily Gurgān under his sway. The Bāvandid Sharvīn b. Rustam and the Qārinid Shahriyār b. Bādūspān who at first opposed him were forced to submit. The contemporary Sunnī historian Ṭabarī, himself a native of Āmul, pays tribute to this 'Alid ruler stating that "the people had not seen anything like the justice of al-Uṭrūsh, his good conduct, and his fulfilment of the right".[2] Al-Uṭrūsh died in 304/917. The

[1] The grave of Abū Ja'far is now located in the courtyard of the town hall of Rasht.
[2] Ṭabarī, vol. III, p. 2292.

Nāṣirī Dailamites and Gīlites for centuries later made the pilgrimage to his shrine in Āmul and kept an affection for his descendants each of whom was given the honorary surname al-Nāṣir.

The Zaidite supporters of al-Uṭrūsh, other than the Dailamites and Gīlites, were opposed to the succession of any of his sons, whom they considered dissolute and ill-suited for the rule, and favoured the Ḥasanid al-Ḥasan b. al-Qāsim, commander-in-chief of his army. Already during al-Uṭrūsh's lifetime rivalry between his sons and al-Ḥasan had led to quarrels during which al-Uṭrūsh himself was deposed for a brief time by al-Ḥasan. Al-Uṭrūsh nevertheless consented to appoint him his successor. After al-Uṭrūsh's death his son Abu'l-Ḥusain Aḥmad invited al-Ḥasan from Gīlān and surrendered the reign to him. Aḥmad was reproached for this by his brother Abu'l-Qāsim Ja'far who left Āmul with the intention of gaining his father's throne by force. Al-Ḥasan, who adopted the regnal name al-Dā'ī ila'l-ḥaqq, forced the Bāvandid Sharvīn and the Qārinid Shahriyār to pay more tribute and he conquered Gurgān. The people of Ṭabaristān liked him, especially since he kept the Dailamite soldiers under strict control. In 306/919 Abu'l-Ḥusain Aḥmad deserted the Dā'ī and joined his brother Ja'far in Gīlān. Ja'far defeated the Dā'ī and assumed the rule in Āmul. Consequently the two brothers occupied Gurgān. The Dā'ī, who had sought refuge with the Qārinid Muḥammad b. Shahriyār, was seized by the latter and sent to the Justānid 'Alī b. Vahsūdān, at this time 'Abbāsid governor of Ray. 'Alī sent him to Alamūt for detention by his brother Khusrau Fīrūz. The latter released him soon when 'Alī was killed by the Sallārid Muḥammad b. Musāfir. Seven months after his flight the Dā'ī returned to Ṭabaristān with an army he had gathered in Gīlān and defeated Aḥmad near Astarābād. Then he came to terms with him, while Ja'far fled to Ray and Gīlān. Aḥmad usually governed Gurgān for the Dā'ī. In 309/921 the Dā'ī's general Līlī b. "al-Nu'mān" (his father's real name was Shahdūst), king of the Gīlites in succession to Tīrdādh, conquered Dāmghān, Nīshāpūr and Marv, but was ultimately defeated and killed by the Sāmānid army. As the defeated army returned to Gurgān, a group of Gīlite and Dailamite leaders conspired to kill the Dā'ī. The latter was informed, came hurriedly to Gurgān and treacherously killed seven of them, among them Harūsindān b. Tīrdādh, whom the Gīlites had recognized as their king after Līlī. This incident resulted in the disaffection of part of the Gīlite and Dailamite army and eventually in the death of the Dā'ī at the hands of Mardāvīj b. Ziyār, the nephew of Harūsindān through his sister.

In 311/923 Aḥmad again made common cause with his brother Ja'far against the Dā'ī. As the latter fled to the highlands, the brothers entered Āmul, and Aḥmad took over the rule until his death two months later. Ja'far succeeded him and warded off an attack of the Dā'ī who eventually retired to Gīlān. When Ja'far died in 312/925 the Dailamite leaders in Āmul put a son of Aḥmad, Abū 'Alī Muḥammad, on the throne. The constant quarrels among the 'Alids had indeed greatly strengthened the hands of the Dailamite and Gīlite chiefs, who more and more were able to use the 'Alids as pawns in their own power struggle. Two Dailamite leaders soon emerged as the main rivals in this struggle: Mākān b. Kākī and Asfār b. Shīrūya. Mākān and his cousin al-Ḥasan b. al-Fairūzān conspired in favour of a young son of Ja'far, Ismā'īl, who was a half brother of al-Ḥasan through his mother. They seized Abū 'Alī and put Ismā'īl on the throne. Abū 'Alī succeeded, however, in killing the brother of Mākān, who was supposed to kill him, and gained the support of Asfār. Mākān was defeated and fled to the highlands, while Abū 'Alī returned to reign. Within months he was killed in an accident and was succeeded by his brother Abū Ja'far Muḥammad. As his reign was weakened by the revolt of Asfār, Mākān in 314/926 descended from the highlands and expelled him from Āmul. The Dā'ī, who had not responded to earlier overtures of Mākān, now joined him from Gīlān and was once more restored to the rule of Ṭabaristān, while Abū Ja'far found refuge in the highlands. In 316/928 the Dā'ī and Mākān set out on an ambitious campaign and conquered Ray and the province of Jibāl as far as Qum. Asfār, who governed Gurgān under Sāmānid suzerainty, used the occasion of their absence to invade Ṭabaristān. The Dā'ī, without Mākān, returned and met Asfār at the gate of Āmul. As his army was routed, the Dā'ī was mortally wounded by Mardāvīj b. Ziyār, who had entered the Sāmānid service even before Asfār and thus avenged the murder of his uncle Harūsindān. Asfār then defeated Mākān at Ray, and the latter fled to Dailamān.

Zaidī sentiment was still strong among the Dailamites and Gīlites, and Asfār's Dailamite governor in Āmul restored Abū Ja'far al-Nāṣir as the Imām. On the protest of Naṣr b. Aḥmad, Asfār's Sāmānid overlord, Asfār arrested Abū Ja'far and sent him together with some other 'Alids to Bukhārā. In 318/930 Mākān once more conquered

Ṭabaristān, Gurgān and Nīshāpūr. His cousin al-Ḥasan b. al-Fairūzān, whom he left in charge of Ṭabaristān, revolted and again raised his half-brother Ismā'īl as the imām, but the mother of Abū Ja'far, Ismā'īl's cousin, contrived to have the latter poisoned. Abū Ja'far, released from prison in Bukhārā during a rebellion against Naṣr b. Aḥmad, at this time gained the support of Mardāvīj b. Ziyār who had revolted against Asfār and had taken possession of Ray. In 319/931 Mardāvīj sent him with an army to conquer Ṭabaristān from Mākān, but he was defeated. Later Vushmgīr, the brother and successor of Mardāvīj, established him in Āmul as his governor. After the conquest of Ray by the Būyid Rukn al-Daula (331/943) Abū Ja'far came to live there without any political authority until his death. The 'Alids were no longer able to recover their dominion in Ṭabaristān. The descendants of al-Uṭrūsh remained influential in Āmul where they were centred on the shrine of their illustrious ancestor and owned much property. Repeatedly descendants of al-Uṭrūsh are mentioned as governors of the town under both Būyid and Ziyārid rule.

III. ZIYĀRID DOMINATION IN ṬABARISTĀN AND GURGĀN

The Ziyārids, descendants of Ziyār b. Vardānshāh, belonged to the Gīlite royal clan living in the Dākhil region. Vardānshāh is said to have enjoyed great authority among the Gīlites. Like other Persian dynasties of the time, they later claimed pre-Islamic royal ancestry alleging that they were descended from Arghush Farhādān, king of Gīlān in the time of Kai-Khusrau. Mardāvīj b. Ziyār in 318/930 was sent by Asfār together with the latter's brother Shīrzād to conquer the fortress of Shamīrān in Ṭārum from the Sallārid Muḥammad b. Musāfir. During the siege he was persuaded to revolt against Asfār by letters from Mākān and the Sallārid who both promised him aid. With the help of the sons of the Sallārid he took Shīrzād by surprise and killed him together with twenty-nine chiefs of the Varūdāvand, the tribe of Asfār. As he approached Asfār in Qazvīn, the army of the latter went over to him. Asfār fled, and Mardāvīj inherited his territories, Ray, Qazvīn, Zanjān, Abhar, Qum and Karaj. In 319/931 he captured and killed Asfār and in rapid succession conquered Hamadān, Dīnavar and Iṣfahān from the governors of the caliph. Then he turned against Mākān with whom he had at first concluded a treaty after having received his support against Asfār. After an initial defeat, Mardāvīj in 320/932 took

Ṭabaristān and Gurgān. Mākān, whose attempts to recover his territories failed, entered the service of the Sāmānids. In 321/933 Mardāvīj, threatened by an offensive of the Sāmānid Naṣr b. Aḥmad, agreed to a peace treaty under which he surrendered Gurgān and paid tribute for the possession of Ray to the latter. His attention was now drawn toward the south of his domains where the Būyid 'Alī, whom he had appointed governor of al-Karaj, had renounced his allegiance and successfully carried out independent conquests. By the end of 322/934 the Ziyārid army had occupied Ahvāz, and 'Alī, now in Shīrāz, again acknowledged his overlordship. Mardāvīj now was hatching ambitious plans for a campaign to conquer Baghdad and overthrow the caliphate. Then he intended to be crowned in Ctesiphon and to restore the Persian empire. Before he could realize these plans he was murdered in Iṣfahān in 323/935 by his Turkish troops whom he had gravely insulted.

The Ziyārid cause was further weakened by the defection of the Turks, some of whom joined 'Alī b. Būya in Shīrāz while others entered the service of the caliph. 'Alī's brother al-Ḥasan, the later Rukn al-Daula, thus was able to occupy Iṣfahān. The majority of the Dailamites and Gīlites in the Ziyārid army, however, returned to Ray and pledged allegiance to Vushmgīr, the brother of Mardāvīj. Vushmgīr still in 323/935 repulsed Mākān and a Sāmānid army from Ṭabaristān and conquered Gurgān. Then he acknowledged Sāmānid overlordship in order to strengthen his rear in resisting the Būyid advance. Evidently with the same motivation he turned over Gurgān to Mākān in 325/936. In 328/939–40 Mākān was attacked in the main city of Gurgān by the Sāmānid general Abū 'Alī b. Muḥtāj and expelled after a lengthy siege despite the aid which Vushmgīr sent him. Ibn Muḥtāj then marched against Vushmgīr in Ray and defeated him in a battle which cost Mākān his life. Vushmgīr fled to Ṭabaristān where he was faced with a revolt of al-Ḥasan b. al-Fairūzān, governor of Sārī, who accused him of being responsible for the death of his cousin Mākān. Defeated by Vushmgīr, al-Ḥasan joined Ibn Muḥtāj and induced him to undertake a new campaign to Ṭabaristān. Vushmgīr was forced to reacknowledge Sāmānid suzerainty, but as Ibn Muḥtāj left for Khurāsān he regained Ray, only to be expelled from there in 331/943 by the Būyid al-Ḥasan, this time for good. He returned to Ṭabaristān and was defeated there by al-Ḥasan b. al-Fairūzān who previously had occupied Gurgān. While Vushmgīr fled to the Bāvandid Ispahbad Shahriyār and then found refuge at the court of the Sāmānid Nūḥ b. Naṣr, al-Ḥasan b. al-Fairūzān entered into friendly relations with the Būyid giving him his daughter in marriage, though he prudently acknowledged Sāmānid suzerainty once more when Ibn Muḥtāj re-occupied Ray in 333/945. Vushmgīr at this time regained Gurgān with Sāmānid support but was unable to hold it. In 335/947 he again conquered Gurgān and Ṭabaristān with the help of a large Sāmānid army and expelled al-Ḥasan b. al-Fairūzān. In the following year Rukn al-Daula took Ṭabaristān and Gurgān from him. Al-Ḥasan b. al-Fairūzān again made common cause with the Būyid. Vushmgīr could, however, continue to count on the support of the Sāmānids in their feud with the Būyids. In the next years Gurgān and Ṭabaristān changed hands several times until a general peace was concluded between Rukn al-Daula and the Sāmānids in 344/955 under which the former engaged himself not to molest the Ziyārid in Ṭabaristān. Numismatic evidence shows that this peace did not last long. In 347/958 Vushmgīr succeeded in briefly occupying Rukn al-Daula's capital Ray. Two years later Rukn al-Daula in turn occupied Gurgān for a short time, and in 351/962 (and perhaps in 355/966) Vushmgīr temporarily lost both Ṭabaristān and Gurgān to the Būyids.

Vushmgīr was killed by a boar on a hunt in 357/967, just after a Sāmānid army had arrived in Gurgān for a joint campaign against Rukn al-Daula. Bīsutūn, the eldest son of Vushmgīr, came from Ṭabaristān, where he had been governor, to Gurgān, now the Ziyārid capital, to claim the succession. The Sāmānid commander, however, favoured his brother Qābūs, whose mother was a daughter of the Bāvandid Ispahbad Sharvīn. Bīsutūn returned to Ṭabaristān and asked Rukn al-Daula for support acknowledging the Būyid suzerainty. When the Sāmānid army left Gurgān returning to Khurāsān, Qābūs found the support of al-Ḥasan b. al-Fairūzān, who now was ruling Simnān, but Bīsutūn conquered Gurgān and Simnān forcing Qābūs to submit. Bīsutūn confirmed his alliance with the Būyids by marrying a daughter of 'Aḍud al-Daula, the son of Rukn al-Daula, and in 360/971 was granted the title Ẓahīr al-Daula by al-Muṭī', the puppet caliph of the Būyids.

When Bīsutūn died in 366/977 his father-in-law and governor of Ṭabaristān, the Gīlite Dubāj b. Bānī, hastened to Gurgān in order to secure the succession with Sāmānid support for Bīsutūn's minor son, in whose name he intended to rule. Bīsutūn's brother Qābūs gained the support of the army and of the Būyid ʿAḍud al-Daula. He expelled Dubāj from Gurgān and captured his nephew in the fortress of Simnān. In 368/978–9 the caliph al-Ṭāʾiʿ granted him the title Shams al-Maʿālī. A year later Qābūs offended ʿAḍud al-Daula by offering refuge to Fakhr al-Daula, brother of ʿAḍud al-Daula, who had incurred the latter's wrath. Qābūs lost Ṭabaristān in 369/980 to ʿAḍud al-Daula, and in 371/981 Muʾayyad al-Daula, brother of ʿAḍud al-Daula, expelled him from Gurgān. He and Fakhr al-Daula fled to Nīshāpūr. As a Sāmānid army which was sent to restore Gurgān to Qābūs was defeated, the Ziyārid provinces came under direct Būyid rule for seventeen years, while Qābūs lived in exile in Khurāsān. Fakhr al-Daula after the death of Muʾayyad al-Daula in 373/984 was recalled by the latter's vizier, al-Ṣāḥib b. ʿAbbād, and put on the throne in Ray, but he did not permit Qābūs to return to his domains. Only after the death of Fakhr al-Daula and the succession of his minor son Majd al-Daula in 387/997 was Qābūs able to recover them. Supporters of his gained control of Rūyān and Ṭabaristān and then proceeded to conquer Gurgān. In 388/998 Qābūs returned there. After the failure of some Būyid attempts to dislodge him, his reign remained generally uncontested. Though he established friendly relations with the Ghaznavid Maḥmūd, he ruled now without recognizing any overlord other than the caliph. Qābūs was broadly cultured and one of the famous stylists in Arabic epistolography of his time, and he composed poetry in both Arabic and Persian. His court attracted many poets and famous scholars like al-Bīrūnī and Avicenna. His religious sentiments were Sunnī, and he severely curbed Shīʿī and Muʿtazilī activity in his domains. His sanguinary vindictiveness, which cost many of his high officials and army chiefs their lives on the slightest offence or mere suspicion, finally caused his downfall. Some chiefs of the army conspired against him and, though failing to capture him in his castle outside Gurgān, gained control of the capital. They invited his son Manūchihr, governor of Ṭabaristān, to take over the rule. Manūchihr, in fear of losing the throne, joined them and pursued Qābūs to Bisṭām where he had sought shelter. Qābūs agreed to resign in favour of his son and retired to a castle where he would spend the rest of his life in devotion. The conspirators, however, were still afraid of him and contrived to have him freeze to death in 403/1012. His mausoleum near Gurgān, in the shape of a cylindrical brick tower, has remained a landmark.

Manūchihr then was confirmed in his rule and granted the title Falak al-Ma'ālī. He also recognized the overlordship of the Ghaznavid Maḥmūd and promised to pay a tribute to him, perhaps in order to forestall Maḥmūd's support for possible pretensions of his brother Dārā, who previously had joined the court of the Ghaznavid, to the throne. On Manūchihr's request Maḥmūd gave him one of his daughters in marriage. Their relationship, however, did not always remain undisturbed. In 419/1028 Maḥmūd, on his way to conquer Ray from the Būyid Majd al-Daula, invaded the territory of Manūchihr. The latter fled before him and then succeeded in buying his withdrawal for a high sum.

When Manūchihr died soon afterwards, his son Anūshīrvān Sharaf al-Ma'ālī was confirmed by Maḥmūd as his successor in return for a commitment to pay tribute. Anūshīrvān, who was still young, in 423/1032 was practically excluded from the rule by Abū Kālījār, a maternal relative of his and chief of the Ziyārid army. The Ghaznavid Mas'ūd, Maḥmūd's successor, confirmed Abū Kālījār as the ruler of Gurgān and Ṭabaristān upon his commitment to continue paying the tribute and a year later married a daughter of his. The tribute was not regularly paid, however, and in 426/1035 Mas'ūd invaded Gurgān and Ṭabaristān as far as Rūyān. Abū Kālījār fled before the Ghaznavid army, but after its withdrawal regained control and reached a settlement with Mas'ūd promising renewed payment of the tribute. Anūshīrvān later, after 431/1040, succeeded in arresting Abū Kālījār and resumed the rule himself. This unstable situation, however, encouraged the Saljuq Toghrïl Beg to conquer Gurgān in 433/1041–2. Toghrïl installed as his deputy there Mardāvīj b. Bishūī, a former Ghaznavid commander, who soon came to terms with Anūshīrvān under which the suzerainty of Toghrïl was proclaimed throughout Gurgān and Ṭabaristān. The Ziyārid dynasty survived under Saljuq overlordship, until the last quarter of the century.

IV. THE BĀVANDID ISPAHBADS AND THE USTANDĀRS OF RŪYĀN IN THE 4TH/10TH CENTURY

The history of the Bāvandid Ispahbads of Shahriyārkūh in the 4th/10th century can only fragmentarily be pieced together from occasional references in literary sources and some numismatic evidence. Sharvīn b. Rustam, the Bāvandid ruling at the time of the 'Alids al-Uṭrūsh and al-Ḥasan b. al-Qāsim, is last mentioned in events of the year 318/930.

His son Shahriyār is first referred to as the ruler of Shahriyārkūh in 331/943, when the Ziyārid Vushmgīr, his brother-in-law, sought refuge with him. In 336/947–8 Shahriyār personally made his submission to the Būyid Rukn al-Daula when the latter conquered Ṭabaristān. Later he was expelled from Shahriyārkūh by his brother Rustam, perhaps with Būyid support. For in 357/968 Shahriyār is mentioned in Gurgān in the presence of the commander of the Sāmānid army intending to conquer Ṭabaristān. Rustam's rule in Firīm is attested by coins in his name dating from 353/964 to 369/979, on which he regularly acknowledged Būyid overlordship. Inscriptions on these coins also indicate his support of Imāmī Shī'ism. Coins minted in Firīm in 371/981 and 374/984–5 name "al-Marzubān b. Sharvīn" as the ruler recognizing the suzerainty of the Būyid Fakhr al-Daula.[1] This al-Marzubān is probably to be identified as the son of Rustam and the author of the *Marzubān-nāma*, a collection of tales about the pre-Islamic Persian kings originally written in the dialect of Ṭabaristān. Al-Marzubān thus was probably a brother of the famous Sayyida, wife of Fakhr al-Daula, who after her husband's death came to rule in the name of her minor son Majd al-Daula.[2] In 375/985–6, however, an "Ispahbad Sharvān b. Rustam", who is not mentioned in the literary sources, held sway over Firīm according to a coin on which the Būyid suzerainty is not recognized.[3] He may be either a brother of al-Marzubān or of Shahriyār b. Dārā b. Rustam, who according to the numismatic evidence ruled Firīm in 376/986–7 and recognized the overlordship of the Būyid Fakhr al-Daula. Shahriyār evidently was overthrown some time later by his uncle al-Marzubān and allied himself with the Ziyārid Qābūs in his exile in Nīshāpūr. For in 388/998 he conquered Shahriyārkūh which according to al-'Utbī, on whose account all later sources depend, was held then by "Rustam b. al-Marzubān, maternal uncle of Majd al-Daula", and proclaimed the suzerainty of Qābūs. His rival expelled him with Būyid support, but Shahriyār, aided by Qābūs, regained his domains. Soon he claimed independence from the Ziyārid and was attacked and seized by his rival, who had broken with Majd al-Daula and now acknowledged the overlordship of Qābūs. It has been pointed

[1] Unpublished coins in the collection of Mr St. Album and in the Iran Bāstān Museum in Tehrān.

[2] According to Hilāl al-Ṣābi', vol. III, p. 449 and Yāqūt, vol. III, p. 211, the Sayyida was the daughter of Rustam b. Sharvīn. It is to be noted, however, that according to the *Qābūs-nāma* of the Ziyārid Kay-Kā'ūs, whose mother was a Bāvandid princess, the Sayyida was a niece of al-Marzubān, son of Rustam (*Qābūs-nāma*, p. 83).

[3] Coin in the collection of Mr St. Album.

out that al-'Utbī seems to have inverted the name of the rival and meant al-Marzubān b. Rustam, the uncle of Shahriyār b. Dārā.[1] Al-Marzubān is indeed known to have been Ispahbad of Shahriyārkūh when he was visited by the scholar al-Bīrūnī sometime between 384/994 and 393/1004, most likely about 389/999. It is unknown how long he continued to rule. Shahriyār b. Dārā died *c.* 390/1000 in Ray, perhaps poisoned by the vizier Abu'l-'Abbās al-Ḍabbī.

The literary sources do not mention the names of any Ispahbads during the following decades. An Ispahbad of Firīm is mentioned anonymously, however, as aiding Majd al-Daula and his mother against a rebel in 407/1016–17. An Ispahbad of Ṭabaristān in 418/1027 was captured in a war with the Kākūyid 'Alā' al-Daula, in whose prison he died in 419/1028. Almost certainly the first one, and perhaps also the second one, is to be identified with the Bāvandid Ispahbad Abū Ja'far Muḥammad b. Vandarīn, who according to an inscription in 407/1016–17 ordered the building of a mausoleum, known as Mīl-i Rādkān in the upper valley of the Nīkā river southwest of Astarābād and was evidently still alive at the time of its completion in 411/1020. These data, however fragmentary, tend to invalidate the general assumption of modern scholars that the reign of the dynasty lapsed in this period until its new rise in the early Saljuq age.

Rūyān in the 4th/10th century came under the rule of a dynasty bearing the title Ustandār. The revival of this pre-Islamic title denoting a district governor is further evidence for the continued strength of Persian national sentiments in the Caspian region. An Ustandār ruling Rūyān is mentioned in the sources for the first time in events of the year 336/947–8. There are coins minted in Āmul in the years 337/948–9 and 343/954–5 in the name of Ustandārs and scattered references in literary sources mention them, variously as vassals of Būyids, Ziyārids or 'Alids, until around the beginning of the 5th/11th century. These notices do not give any indication as to the origin of this dynasty, nor do they suffice to trace their family relationships. The Ustandārs of the Saljuq and later ages claimed to be descended from Bādūspān, brother of Dābūya, the ancestor of the Dābūyids. Bādūspān allegedly founded the rule of the Ustandārs in Rūyān, which continued without interruption among his descendants. Auliyā' Allāh Āmulī (8th/14th century) in

[1] Cf. P. Casanova, "Les Ispehbeds de Firîm", in *A Volume of Oriental Studies presented to Edward G. Browne*, ed. by T. W. Arnold and R. A. Nicholson, pp. 123ff. F. Justi, *Iranisches Namenbuch*, pp. 197 and 445, proposed to identify Rustam b. al-Marzubān with Dushmanziyār, the father of the founder of the Kākūyid dynasty.

his history of Rūyān furnishes a full pedigree of the Ustandār of his time to this Bādūspān and further back to Adam. Ẓahīr al-Dīn Mar'ashī (9th/15th century) adds information about individual rulers and the length of their reign, on which modern accounts and chronologies of a Bādūspānid dynasty in Rūyān in the early centuries of Islam are based. This information is entirely fictitious.[1] It is doubtful if the Ustandārs of the Saljuq and later times are related to those of the 4th/10th century.

V. THE 'ALIDS IN GĪLĀN AND DAILAMĀN

As the régime of the 'Alids in Ṭabaristān collapsed beyond repair, the solidly Zaidī regions of Dailamān and eastern Gīlān afforded their aspirations a new, if territorially more limited, stage. Hausam, the town at the eastern edge of the area inhabited by the Gīlites, where al-Nāṣir al-Uṭrūsh had been active, became a centre of learning of the Nāṣiriyya and the seat of a series of 'Alid rulers. The founder of the 'Alid régime in the town was Abu'l-Faḍl Ja'far b. Muḥammad, a grandson of al-Uṭrūsh's brother al-Ḥusain al-Shā'ir, who in 320/932 established himself there, adopting the regnal name al-Thā'ir fi'llāh, and reigned for three decades. In the years from 337/948 to 341/953 he thrice occupied Āmul. The first time he was allied with the Ustandār of Rūyān, the second time with Vushmgīr, and finally with Rukn al-Daula, but each time he was dislodged within months. He died in 350/961 and was buried in Miyāndih, 30 km east of Hausam, where his tomb is still standing. Two of his sons, Abu'l-Ḥusain Mahdī al-Qā'im bi'llāh and Abu'l-Qāsim Ḥusain al-Thā'ir fi'llāh, succeeded him in turn. The latter soon was captured by Langar, a son of Vushmgīr, who since the last years of Abu'l-Faḍl al-Thā'ir had been trying to wrest eastern Gīlān from the 'Alids. The Ziyārids were indeed permanently interested in maintaining their influence in their home country. The Būyids of Ray, too, tried to assert their authority in the region, which contained their own original home Liyāhij (later Lāhijān). Rukn al-Daula succeeded in luring Siyāhgīl b. Harūsindān, the king of the Gīlites, to Ray despite the offers which Vushmgīr, his cousin, made in the hope of enticing him to join the Ziyārid camp. After the death of Siyāhgīl Langar had begun to claim the kingship among the eastern Gīlites. He partially blinded al-Ḥusain al-Thā'ir and sent him to his father Vushmgīr, who kept him in prison. Al-Ḥusain was avenged by Abū Muḥammad

[1] Cf. S. M. Stern, "The Coins of Āmul", *NC*, 7th ser., vol. VII (1967), pp. 231, 233.

al-Ḥasan al-Nāṣir, a son of Abū Ja'far Muḥammad who before his death had come to reside in Ray under the protection of Rukn al-Daula. Abū Muḥammad, probably supported or at least favoured by Rukn al-Daula, gained control of Hausam and in 353/964 killed Langar in a battle. Shortly afterwards he was expelled from Hausam by another son of Abu'l-Faḍl al-Thā'ir, Abū Muḥammad al-Ḥasan, known as Amīrkā.

Amīrkā's exactions clashed with the interests of the Justānid Mānādhar, king of the Dailamites, who wrote to Abū 'Abd-Allāh Muḥammad, a son of the Dā'ī al-Ḥasan b. al-Qāsim, inviting him to claim the Zaidī leadership among the Dailamites and Gīlites. Abū 'Abd-Allāh, at this time syndic of the 'Alids in Baghdād, had acquired high erudition in theology and the law and unquestionably fulfilled the requirements for the Zaidī Imāmate in this respect. He is indeed the first 'Alid after al-Uṭrūsh who later was universally recognized as a full Imām by the Zaidīs. In 353/964 he joined Mānādhar in Rūdbār and, after an initial setback, took Hausam from Amīrkā and ruled with the regnal name al-Mahdī li-dīn Allāh. Enjoying wide support among the Dailamite Qāsimiyya as well as the mostly Gīlite Nāṣiriyya, he made great efforts to alleviate the sharp antagonism between the two schools, maintaining that both doctrines were equally valid.

Amīrkā, who had found shelter in a castle near Hausam, continued to harass al-Mahdī until he was captured by him. Faithful to the traditional Zaidī aspirations al-Mahdī then set out to conquer Ṭabaristān. In 355/966 he defeated the Ustandār Naṣr b. Muḥammad al-Kūhī, who was then a vassal of Vushmgīr. A revolt of Amīrkā forced him to return to Hausam. Amīrkā again escaped to his castle and renewed his raids against al-Mahdī. In 358/969 he seized al-Mahdī and kept him imprisoned for a few months, but then was forced by al-Mahdī's supporters and an army sent by Mānādhar to release him. A year later al-Mahdī died and was buried in Hausam.

Amīrkā regained control of Hausam. He was attacked, however, by Abū Muḥammad al-Nāṣir, who had earlier escaped to Ray and had twice come to support al-Mahdī, his maternal uncle, but each time had left him in protest against his leniency toward Amīrkā. He captured and slew Amīrkā and took possession of Hausam. A coin minted there indicates that he acknowledged the suzerainty of the Būyid Rukn al-Daula. The Ziyārid Bīsutūn then released the half-blind Ḥusain al-Thā'ir and supplied him with money in order to battle Abū Muḥammad, but he was defeated and killed by the latter. His son Abu'l-Ḥasan

'Alī undertook to avenge him and succeeded in expelling Abū Muḥammad from Hausam, according to numismatic evidence in 364/974–5. Abu'l-Ḥasan presumably was also supported by Bīsutūn, for he acknowledged the Ziyārid suzerainty. He was still ruling in 369/980 while his rival Abū Muḥammad had lost all power.

After this date information concerning the history of Hausam becomes sparse in the sources. The town evidently remained the object of competition between the Nāṣirid and Thā'irid pretenders to the Zaidī leadership. In 380/990 a contender representing another branch of the 'Alid house appeared in Gīlān: Abu'l-Ḥusain Aḥmad b. al-Ḥusain al-Mu'ayyad bi'llāh of the Buṭḥānī family. Al-Mu'ayyad and his elder brother, Abū Ṭālib Yaḥyā al-Nāṭiq bi'l-ḥaqq, both have gained universal recognition among the later Zaidīs as Imāms for their outstanding rank in religious scholarship. A number of their legal and theological works have been preserved by the Zaidīs in the Yemen. Born in Āmul, they studied in Baghdad and elsewhere and then belonged to the circle of the vizier al-Ṣāḥib b. 'Abbād and the famous Mu'tazilī chief judge 'Abd al-Jabbār in Ray. Al-Nāṭiq later taught for several years in Gurgān and dedicated one of his works to al-Ḥasan al-Muṣ'abī, vizier of the Ziyārid Manūchihr. Though both brothers were also learned in the legal doctrine of al-Nāṣir al-Uṭrūsh, they adhered to, and developed, the doctrine of al-Qāsim and al-Hādī. The cause of the Qāsimiyya school, prevailing in Rūyān and the neighbouring regions of Dailamān, had been furthered before al-Mu'ayyad by the activity of a grandson of al-Hādī, Yaḥyā b. Muḥammad al-Hādī, coming from the Yemen. Though he was evidently not very successful in his political ambitions, he became an important transmitter of the doctrine of his grandfather in the Caspian regions. His stay probably lasted several decades, and he or another 'Alid pretender of this time was buried in Aspchīn, *c.* 30 km west of the Chālūs river.

When al-Mu'ayyad arrived in Gīlān, Hausam was governed by a Dailamite, Shīrzīl, evidently under the suzerainty of the Būyid Fakhr al-Daula, who was disconcerted by the activity of al-Mu'ayyad. The 'Alid occupied Hausam with Zaidī support for a year, but then was expelled and later induced by al-Ṣāḥib b. 'Abbād to return to Ray. When he rose a second time in Gīlān, probably after the death of Fakhr al-Daula (387/997), a Thā'irid, Abū Zaid, was in control in Hausam. Al-Mu'ayyad expelled him and held sway over the town for over two years, but eventually Abū Zaid gained the upper hand since the Nāṣirī

Gīlites gradually turned away from al-Mu'ayyad. He once more returned to Ray. Abū Zaid in turn was driven out of Hausam and killed by a Nāṣirid, Abu'l-Faḍl. The family of al-Thā'ir now offered full support to al-Mu'ayyad in order to avenge the death of Abū Zaid. This time al-Mu'ayyad established himself in Langā, not far west of Aspchīn, among the Qāsimī Dailamites, while Hausam was taken by the Thā'irid Kiyā Abu'l-Faḍl who nominally recognized the Imāmate of al-Mu'ayyad. About the year 400/1009–10 al-Mu'ayyad set out, supported by Kiyā Abu'l-Faḍl and the Ustandār of Rūyān, to conquer Āmul, which was governed by a Nāṣirid for the Ziyārid Qābūs. Al-Mu'ayyad was defeated at Āmul, and his situation was further weakened by the defection of the Ustandār. Later Manūchihr, the successor of Qābūs, who was markedly more sympathetic to Shī'ism than his father, concluded a peace treaty with al-Mu'ayyad and paid him and Kiyā Abu'l-Faḍl a subsidy.

Langā after the death of al-Mu'ayyad in 411/1020 and his burial there remained the seat of the 'Alids claiming the Imāmate among the Qāsimī Dailamites. Al-Mu'ayyad's brother al-Nāṭiq (d. 424/1033?) evidently was active there, though no details are known. In 417/1026 the Ḥusainid Aḥmad b. Abī Hāshim, known as Mānakdīm, claimed the Imāmate in Langā with the regnal name al-Mustaẓhir bi'llāh, but did not stay long. Probably soon after the death of al-Nāṭiq, 'Alī b. Ja'far al-Mahdī li-dīn Allāh of the Ḥuqainī branch of the 'Alid house gained recognition as the Imām there. He also had belonged to the circle of Qāḍī 'Abd al-Jabbār and adhered to the Qāsimī legal school. His reign may have lasted several decades, well into the Saljuq age. He was buried in Langā. Hausam in Nāṣirī Gīlān during the same period no doubt continued to be disputed between Thā'irids and Nāṣirids, though no reports are available until the year 432/1040–1 when the scholars of Hausam set up a descendant of al-Uṭrūsh, al-Ḥusain al-Nāṣir, and after instructing him in the essential religious sciences paid allegiance to him as the Imām. He ruled for forty years in Hausam, where his tomb is still known. The expansion of Saljuq authority into Ṭabaristān and the regions south of the Alburz range did not appreciably hamper the Zaidī activity in Dailamān and Gīlān, but later in the century the spread of Nizārī Ismā'īlism put the Zaidī communities in Rūyān and Dailamān under increasing pressure.

VI. THE JUSTĀNIDS AND THE SALLĀRIDS OF ṬĀRUM IN THE 4TH/10TH CENTURY

The authority of the Justānid kings of the Dailamites, already disputed by the claim of the ʿAlids to allegiance among the Zaidī Dailamites, was further weakened in the early 4th/10th century by family discord and by the rise of the rival Sallārid dynasty of Ṭārum. Justān b. Vahsūdān after a rule of over forty years was murdered by his brother ʿAlī, probably in the last decade of the 3rd century (903–912). ʿAlī then entered ʿAbbāsid service and was governor of Iṣfahān in the years 300–4/912–16. The traditional seat of the Justānids, Rūdbār of Alamūt, fell to another brother, K͟husrau Fīrūz, who presumably had co-operated to some extent with ʿAlī. The murder of Justān was avenged by his son-in-law Muḥammad b. Musāfir, founder of the Sallārid dynasty, who killed ʿAlī in 307/919, shortly after the latter had been appointed ʿAbbāsid governor of Ray. Anti-ʿAbbāsid sentiments may have been mixed in the motivation of Ibn Musāfir with the desire to avenge his father-in-law. Ibn Musāfir also killed K͟husrau Fīrūz in battle, but could not prevent the succession of the latter's son Mahdī, known as Siyāhc͟has͟hm, in Alamūt. Siyāhc͟has͟hm in 316/928 was lured by Asfār, who coveted possession of Alamūt, to accept the governorship of Qazvīn and was consequently killed by him. A son of Siyāhc͟has͟hm is mentioned much later as a leader in the army of the Būyid Muʿizz al-Daula, killed in 347/968 in a campaign against the Ḥamdānids in Mosul. There are no reports about the fate of Alamūt after the death of Asfār in 319/931. In events of the year 336/947 a Mānād͟har b. Justān is first mentioned who later is known as king of the Dailamites ruling in Rūdbār. The identity of this Mānād͟har has been disputed, and it has been held that he belongs either to the Sallārid or to an unknown dynasty. A somewhat obscure passage in a report of the year 379/989 preserved by Yāqūt has been interpreted to mean that the Justānids in this period lost possession of the highlands of Dailamān, including Rūdbār, to the Sallārids and transferred their seat to Lāhījān in the lowlands. There is no solid evidence to support this view. Mānād͟har presumably was either a son or, more likely, a great-grandson of Justān b. Vahsūdān. Under the year 328/940 a chronicle notes the death of a Justān[1] who could well be the father of Mānād͟har. Justān may have been supported by Muḥammad b. Musāfir, presumably his uncle, to gain possession of Alamūt after the

[1] al-Hamadānī, p. 117.

overthrow of Asfār. The Justānids thus did not lose Rūdbār for any prolonged period, though their position was eclipsed by the rise and spectacular success of the Sallārids, and they lost the allegiance of many of the Dailamites to this rival dynasty.

Mānādhar, as has been seen, later supported the ʿAlid al-Mahdī. He died probably between 358/969 and 361/972 and was succeeded by his son Khusrau Shāh, who is named on coins minted in Rūdbār in 361/971–2 and 363/973–4. Relations with the Būyids were close in this period. Mānādhar sent Dailamite troops to aid ʿAḍud al-Daula and gave him a daughter in marriage. ʿAḍud al-Daula in turn sent his physician Jibrīl b. Bukhtyishūʿ to treat Khusrau Shāh. A brother of Khusrau Shāh, Fūlādh, was a prominent army leader under Ṣamṣām al-Daula and later stayed at the court of Fakhr al-Daula in Ray, where he died after 384/994. Khusrau Shāh was probably still alive and ruling in Rūdbār some time between 392/1002 and 396/1006. In the 5th/11th century mention of Justānids occurs only rarely in the available sources. A son of Fūlādh in 407/1016–17 revolted against the Būyid Majd al-Daula, who had refused his demand for possession of Qavzīn, and eventually had to be granted the governorship of Iṣfahān. In 420/1029 Maḥmūd of Ghazna after conquering Ray sent al-Marzubān b. al-Ḥasan b. Kharāmīl, a "descendant of the kings of Dailam", who had sought refuge with him, against the Sallārid Ibrāhīm b. al-Marzubān b. Ismāʿīl. It is unknown who ruled Rūdbār in this period. In 434/1042–3 the Saljuq Toghrīl Beg after his conquest of Ray and Qazvīn received the submission of "the king of Dailam", no doubt a Justānid of Rūdbār. The dynasty evidently disintegrated later in the century.

The Sallārid dynasty is named after its founder Sal(l)ār (also Sālār, from *sardār* prince, leader), whose name was later regularly adopted as a title by his descendants. Sallār used the Muslim name Muḥammad, and his father's name Asvār was arabicized as Musāfir. After the latter name modern scholars also have called the dynasty Musāfirid. In early sources it is referred to as Langarid after an ancestor named Langar.[1] The Langarids at an unknown date, probably in the later 3rd/9th century, took possession of the mountain stronghold of Shamīrān and from it gained control over Ṭārum, the region along the middle course

[1] In Yāqūt, vol. III, p. 149, the name appears as Kankar, and this form was accepted by A. Kasravī and V. Minorsky who called the dynasty Kangarī. In all other sources, however, the first letter of the name is *lām*. The Ziyārid Vushmgīr named two of his sons Salār and Langar. This choice of names may indicate that their mother was a Sallārid princess, most likely a daughter of Muḥammad b. Musāfir.

of the Safīdrūd (Qizil Uzen) before its confluence with the Shāhrūd. Marriage ties with the Justānid family apparently existed even before the marriage of Muḥammad b. Musāfir with Kharāsūya, daughter of Justān b. Vahsūdān, which involved him in the Justānid family feud. Muḥammad built up Shamīrān with spectacular splendour luring expert workmen with the promise of high recompense and then retaining them as forced labourers. His harsh tyranny made him hated even in his family. In 330/942 his sons Vahsūdān and al-Marzubān with the connivance of their mother seized him and shut him up in a castle. While al-Marzubān shortly afterwards conquered Āzarbāījān, as will be related in the context of the history of that province, Vahsūdān remained in Shamīrān and held sway over Ṭārum. A coin minted in his name in 341/952–3 shows that he supported Ismā'īlism. His brother al-Marzubān according to Miskawaih also adhered to the Ismā'īlī movement, though he did not indicate it on coins in his name. Ismā'īlī Shī'ism had indeed gained prominent followers among the Dailamites, chiefly through the activity of the Ismā'īlī missionary Abū Ḥātim al-Rāzī (d. 322/933–4). Asfār b. Shīrūya, the Justānid Siyāhchashm, and the Ziyārid Mardāvīj are all reported to have been converted to Ismā'īlism, though their support of the movement was at most ephemeral. As the coin of Vahsūdān confirms, the Ismā'īlī doctrine spread among the Dailamites in this period did not entail recognition of the Fāṭimid caliphs as Imāms.

Vushmgīr in 355/966 was expelled from Ṭārum by the Būyid Rukn al-Daula, but soon recovered his dominion. He is last mentioned in 356/967. Shamīrān later came into the possession of his son Nūḥ, who died before 379/989–90. In that year the Būyid Fakhr al-Daula married his widow in order to gain possession of the fortress and then divorced her. Her minor son, Justān, was brought to the Būyid court in Ray, where also some other Sallārids were present in this period. After the death of Fakhr al-Daula in 387/997 a great-grandson of Vahsūdān, Ibrāhīm b. al-Marzubān b. Ismā'īl, gained possession of Ṭārum, Zanjān, Abhar and Suhravard. For some time he also held sway over Qazvīn. When Maḥmūd of Ghazna took Ray in 420/1029, he sent the Justānid al-Marzubān to conquer the territories of Ibrāhīm, but he was unsuccessful. Ibrāhīm expelled the Ghaznavid garrison of Qazvīn and defeated Maḥmūd's son Mas'ūd. The latter then succeeded in bribing some men of Ibrāhīm's army and captured him. Ibrāhīm's son could not be induced by Mas'ūd to surrender the fortress of Sarjahān, but was forced to agree to paying tribute. Nothing is known about the later fate of Ibrāhīm. In 434/1043–4 the Sallār of Ṭārum acceded to the demand of the Saljuq Toghrïl Beg, who had conquered Qazvīn, that he recognize Saljuq overlordship and pay tribute. This Sallār most likely was Ibrāhīm's son Justān, who in any case was lord of Shamīrān three years later when Nāṣir-i Khusrau visited the region. The dynasty survived under Saljuq suzerainty for some decades.

VII. ĀZARBĀĪJĀN AND EASTERN TRANSCAUCASIA

Āzarbāījān and the Persian provinces in eastern Transcaucasia as far as Darband, unlike the South Caspian provinces, offered only little resistance to the initial Arab conquest which took place early, partially still under the caliphate of ʻUmar. The Sāsānian marzbān of Āzarbāījān, who at this time submitted to the conquerors agreeing to pay tribute, is not mentioned afterwards. In al-Bāb (or Bāb al-abwāb), as the Arabs called Darband, the commander of the Persian garrison made common cause with them against other enemies, chiefly the Armenians and the Khazars. The latter indeed thwarted the further northward advance of the Arabs and during the following decades repeatedly invaded Arrān, Armenia and Āzarbāījān. When Salmān al-Bāhilī under the caliph ʻUthmān invaded eastern Transcaucasia from Armenia, the local princes from Shakkī in the west to Sharvān in the east and Masqaṭ in the north submitted to him and agreed to pay tribute.

The population of Āzarbāījān at the time of the conquest was predominantly Iranian, speaking numerous dialects. Groups of Kurds had already penetrated into some parts of the province. To the north the provinces of Arrān, between the Kur and Araxes rivers, Sharvān (later Shīrvān), the region north of the Kur, and Darband were located in the territory of the ancient kingdom of Albania (Ar. Arrān). The Albanians, a non-Indo-European people, had been converted to Armenian Christianity and were partially Armenicized in the areas south of the Kur, where Armenians in large groups had settled and intermarried with them. Their language survived, however, and was still spoken in Bardaʻa, the capital of Arrān, in the 4th/10th century. The Albanians since the end of the 6th century had been ruled by the Mihranid dynasty which survived under Muslim suzerainty until 821–2. North of the Kur Iranian immigrants had settled in substantial numbers. Local names like Laizān, Sharvān, Bailaqān suggest that they came from Dailamān and other areas south of the Caspian Sea. Various invaders from the north had also left settlements in the area, most important for this time the Khazars who had occupied the town of Qabala to the west of Sharvān. The variety of the population as well as the mountainous fragmentation of the region favoured the survival of numerous petty principalities, some of which had been established by the Sāsānians with the aim of strengthening the border defence. These local dynasties became tributaries of the Arab conquerors and generally survived intact at least until the late Umayyad age, though little is known about their history. Later some of them disappeared, while in other principalities the rule was taken over by members of the new nobility of the conquerors.

Because of the exposed border location of Āzarbāījān and Transcaucasia, the Arab conquerors were compelled to station strong forces there. Already in the time of ʿUthmān a large number of Kūfan warriors were settled in Āzarbāījān. Consequently tribal Arabs from Kūfa, Baṣra and Syria migrated to Āzarbāījān and gained extensive holdings of land cultivated by the native peasants. About the year 141/758–9 the Muhallabid Yazīd b. Ḥātim, appointed governor of Āzarbāījān by the caliph al-Manṣūr, settled Yemenī tribal groups from Baṣra in various parts of the province. Al-Rawwād b. al-Muthannā al-Azdī, the ancestor of the Rawwādid dynasty, settled between al-Badhdh and Tabrīz, gaining power in the latter. In other towns, too, Arab chieftains came to build their castles and dominated the inhabitants: in Marand Abu'l-Baʿīth Ḥalbas of the tribe of Rabīʿa, in Urmīya Ṣadaqa b. ʿAlī, a client of Azd, in Miyāna ʿAbd-Allāh b. Jaʿfar of Hamdān, in Barza the clan of al-Aud, in Nairīz Murr b. ʿAmr al-Mauṣilī of Ṭayy, and in Sarāb descendants of al-Ashʿath b. Qais of Kinda, one of the early conquerors. These powerful Arab lords and their families caused considerable trouble to the governors of the province in the 2nd/8th and 3rd/9th centuries. The situation was hardly improved by the frequent appointment of governors belonging to these local families. In the north Bardaʿa and later al-Bāb held strong Arab garrisons and served as bases for the wars with the Khazars. Bardaʿa received new fortifications under the caliph ʿAbd al-Malik, and those of al-Bāb were greatly strengthened in 113/731 by Maslama, the son of ʿAbd al-Malik, who settled 24,000 Syrian soldiers there. Arrān was normally governed by the governors of Armenia. Frequently the provinces of Āzarbāījān and Armenia were held jointly by a single governor.

Although according to one report most of the population of Āzarbāījān had accepted Islam and "were reciting the Qur'ān" by the time of the caliphate of 'Alī, this can refer only to limited localities, perhaps in particular Ardabīl.[1] The strength of the Khurramī movement in Āzarbāījān, which under the leadership of Bābak from his stronghold al-Badhdh near the Araxes resisted all attacks of the caliphal armies for over twenty years (201–22/816–37), sufficiently proves the persistence of anti-Islamic and anti-Arab sentiments among part of the population. Islam in Āzarbāījān was predominantly Sunnī in the early centuries, though Khārijism was rampant at times. Serious fighting between Mu'tazilīs and Sunnīs in Barda'a is reported in the time of the caliph al-Ma'mūn. Among the Sunnīs, conservative Ḥanbalism was espoused by the scholars of *ḥadīth*, while Ḥanafism and Shāfi'ism were represented as minority schools.

VIII. THE SĀJIDS, SALLĀRIDS AND RAWWĀDIDS

The revolt of Bābak had only temporarily reduced the power of the Arab chieftains in Āzarbāījān. It was evidently in part with the aim of reducing their turbulent independence and partly in order to check the ascendancy of the Bagratid kings of Armenia that the caliph al-Mu'tamid in 276/889–90 or, more likely, in 279/892 appointed one of his foremost commanders, Muḥammad b. Abi'l-Sāj, governor of Āzarbāījān and Armenia. The Sājid family came from Ushrūsana in Central Asia and was probably of Soghdian origin.[2] Muḥammad's father Abu'l-Sāj Dēvdād b. Dēvdasht distinguished himself in the 'Abbāsid army under al-Afshīn in the final war against Bābak and later served the caliphs in various provinces. After his death in 266/879 his two sons, Muḥammad and Yūsuf, followed his career. The first task of Muḥammad in Āzarbāījān was to subdue the rebel 'Abd-Allāh b. al-Ḥasan al-Hamdānī, presumably a chief of the Hamdān in the province, who had occupied Marāgha. In 280/893 Muḥammad induced him to surrender on a promise of safety, but then confiscated his property and executed him. He took Marāgha as his capital, though later he usually resided in Barda'a. Then he turned his attention to Armenia, where the Bagratid Smbat I had acceded to the throne in 890. Muḥammad had sent him in the name of the caliph a crown and presents,

[1] Al-Balādhurī, p. 329.
[2] V. Minorsky, *Studies in Caucasian History*, p. 111, n. 1.

thus affirming his overlordship. When Smbat in 892 sent envoys to the Byzantine emperor, Muḥammad threatened to attack him, but was pacified by a diplomatic letter of the king. The Bagratid then occupied Dvin (Ar. Dabīl), and in 895 invaded Georgia and Albania. Countering this expansion in the north Muḥammad in the same year occupied Nakhchivān and Dvin, but then suffered a defeat and concluded a peace with Smbat.

Muḥammad soon felt strong enough to revolt against the caliphal government, presumably withholding the revenue of his provinces. Perhaps it was at this time that he assumed the surname al-Afshīn, the traditional title of the kings of Ushrūsana, which appears on a coin in his name minted in Barda'a in 285/898. In the same year he submitted again to the caliphal authority, evidently in preparation for a new campaign against Smbat, and was confirmed in the governorship of Āzarbāījān and Armenia. Penetrating to the heartland of the Bagratid kingdom he took Kars and carried off the wife of Smbat and part of the royal treasury. Dvin was firmly brought under his rule at this time. In 899 he agreed to exchange the queen for Smbat's son Ashot. Shortly afterwards he invaded Vaspurakan and forced its ruler, the Ardzrunid Sargis Ashot, to become his vassal and surrender his brother as a hostage. Then he occupied Tiflis, which was already in Muslim hands, and, breaking his truce with Smbat, again invaded the Bagratid heartland but failed to capture the king. After these spectacular successes his loyalty to the caliphal government once more became suspect, for in 287/900 a plot was uncovered by which he hoped to gain possession of Ḍiyār Muḍar. In the same year he re-invaded Vaspurakan in revenge for the absconding of the brother of Sargis Ashot. As the latter fled before him, he left an occupation force and returned to Barda'a in order to prepare for a new campaign against Smbat. His plans were cut short when he succumbed to an epidemic in 288/901.

After Muḥammad's death the army put his son Dēvdād on the throne, but after five months he was overthrown by his uncle Yūsuf b. Abi'l-Sāj, who transferred the capital to Ardabīl and razed the walls of Marāgha. King Smbat tried to extricate himself from the Sājid overlordship by offering his direct vassalage to the caliph al-Muktafī. When he refused a summons of Yūsuf to present himself to him, the Sājid invaded his country. In 290/903 a settlement was reached, and Smbat received a crown from Yūsuf thus acknowledging his suzerainty. Yūsuf's relations with the caliph, which had never been formalized, became increasingly strained. In 295/908 an army was sent against him from Baghdad. Only after the accession of the caliph al-Muqtadir was a settlement negotiated in Baghdad, evidently with the support of the new vizier Ibn al-Furāt, whom Yūsuf henceforth considered his protector naming him regularly on his coinage, and in 296/909 the Sājid was formally invested with the government of Āzarbāījān and Armenia.

King Smbat in the time of the insubordination of Yūsuf had been encouraged by the caliph to arm against the Sājid. Yūsuf never forgave him this act of disloyalty and immediately after settling his relations with Baghdad set out to enforce his authority in Armenia. He had found an ally in Gagik, the prince of Vaspurakan, who was involved in a dispute with Smbat about the possession of Nakhchivān and offered to become a vassal of Yūsuf. The latter crowned him king and refused the overtures of Smbat putting his envoy, the Catholicos Hovhannes, in fetters. In 296/909 he took Nakhchivān and, aided by Gagik, occupied the country of Siunikh. Pursuing Smbat across the country, he spent the winter in Dvin and in 297/910 defeated the royal army under two sons of Smbat, Ashot Erkath and Musheł, north of Erivan. Musheł was captured and poisoned by the Sājid. As the merciless war dragged on, Smbat was besieged by Yūsuf in an impregnable fortress and finally surrendered voluntarily in order to stop the bloodshed. Yūsuf at first permitted him to leave, but then seized him again and imprisoned him for a year. During the siege of Erenjak, probably in 301/914, Yūsuf had him tortured and killed before the ramparts of the fortress in the hope of inducing the garrison to surrender and then sent his body to be hung in Dvin. The war caused extensive devastation and was accompanied by a wave of religious repression. The geographer Ibn Ḥauqal remarks upon the unprecedented harshness which Yūsuf introduced into the Muslim treatment of the Armenians and states that the people of Baghdad refused to buy Armenian slaves knowing that they were *ahl al-dhimma*.[1] Yūsuf at first also pursued a hostile policy against Ashot II, the son of Smbat, who endeavoured to restore his father's kingdom. After the Ardzrunid Gagik refused to co-operate further with him, Yūsuf set up the Sparapet Ashot as a rival king crowning him in Dvin. As the son of Smbat, however, gained general support in Armenia and Yūsuf's attention turned elsewhere, Yūsuf finally recognized him, probably *c.* 304/917, and conferred a crown upon him.

[1] Ibn Ḥauqal, p. 343.

After the dismissal of Ibn al-Furāt, his protector in Baghdad, Yūsuf had begun to withhold some of his annual tribute to the caliphal government. In 303/915–16 he imprisoned an envoy of the caliph, though later he released him and sent him back with presents and money. After the restoration of Ibn al-Furāt to the vizierate in 304/917 Yūsuf conquered Zanjān, Abhar, Qazvīn and Ray from a Sāmānid governor and claimed in a letter to Baghdad that the previous vizier had invested him with the governorship of that province, evidently in the hope that Ibn al-Furāt would back him up. The caliph al-Muqtadir was thoroughly incensed, however, and an army was sent against the Sājid, who defeated it. When the ʿAbbāsid commander-in-chief Mu'nis approached with another army, Yūsuf withdrew to Ardabīl. Despite the intercession of Ibn al-Furāt for him the caliph still refused to confirm him in the governorship of his provinces. Mu'nis was routed by Yūsuf in a first battle near Ardabīl, but a year later in 307/919 he defeated the Sājid there. Yūsuf was carried to Baghdad where al-Muqtadir put him into prison for three years. In Āzarbāījān his *g͟hulām* Subuk gained control and, after defeating an army sent against him, was recognized by the caliph as governor.

In 310/922 Yūsuf was released and invested with the governorship of Ray, Qazvīn, Abhar, Zanjān and Āzarbāījān. He proceeded to Āzarbāījān where Subuk, who had always remained faithful to him, had died. In 311/924 he defeated and killed the previous governor of Ray, who had rebelled against the caliph, and took over the city. As he left and occupied Hamadān, his deputy soon was expelled by the people of Ray. Yūsuf returned there briefly in 313/925 and went on to Āzarbāījān. In 314/926 he was called by the caliphal government to ʿIrāq to take charge of the war against the Qarmaṭīs of Baḥrain who were ravaging the country. A year later he was defeated near Kūfa by these fierce opponents, even though his army greatly outnumbered them. Yūsuf was captured and a few months later, in 315/928, killed. Some of his Turkish troops entered the caliphal service in Baghdad, where they formed the Sājiyya regiment.[1]

After Yūsuf's death his nephew Abu'l-Musāfir al-Fatḥ, son of Muḥammad al-Afs͟hīn, was invested by the caliph with the government of Āzarbāījān. One and a half years later, in 317/929, he was poisoned in Ardabīl by one of his slaves. Though the Sājid dynasty ended with

[1] The mention of Sājiyya troops under Mu'nis in 311/924 by Miskawaih, vol. 1, p. 116, seems to be erroneous.

him, Āzarbāijān did not revert to the rule of governors sent by the caliphal government. After al-Fatḥ's murder Waṣīf al-Sharvānī gained sway over Āzarbāijān. He was succeeded, probably still in the same year, by Mufliḥ al-Yūsufī, who according to numismatic evidence remained in power at least until 323/935. In 325/937 the Ḥamdānid al-Ḥasan of Mosul sent Naẓīf, an officer of the Sājiyya regiment who had sought refuge with him, to conquer Āzarbāijān, but he had evidently not much success. By 326/938 Daisam b. Ibrāhīm al-Kurdī had taken over the reins. Daisam's father, whose patronymic b. Shādhlūya points to Iranian, most likely Kurdish, origin, was a companion of the Khārijite leader Hārūn al-Wāziqī in Mosul. After the capture of Hārūn by the caliph al-Mu'taḍid in 283/896 Ibrāhīm fled to Āzarbāijān where he married the daughter of a Kurdish chieftain who bore him his son Daisam. Daisam, like his father a Khārijite, was employed by the Sājid Yūsuf and rose in his service to prominence.

Daisam at first relied chiefly on Kurdish troops. The Dailamite expansion, however, soon engulfed Āzarbāijān too. In 326/937 Lashkarī b. Mardī, a Gīlite formerly serving Mākān and the Ziyārids Mardāvīj and Vushmgīr, with an army composed of Gīlites and some Dailamites invaded Āzarbāijān and expelled Daisam, who recovered his dominion, however, with the aid of Vushmgīr. As Daisam's Kurdish warriors became unruly and laid their hands on some of his domains, he began to employ Dailamites, among them Sālūk (Ar. Ṣu'lūk), a son of the Sallārid Muḥammad b. Musāfir, in order to counterbalance their strength and arrested some Kurdish chiefs. Daisam's vizier Abu'l-Qāsim Ja'far b. 'Alī, who had been finance administrator under the Sājid Yūsuf and was also active as an Ismā'īlī missionary, fled in 330/941–2 because of intrigues against him to Ṭārum, where Muḥammad b. Musāfir was overthrown by his sons Vahsūdān and al-Marzubān. He encouraged al-Marzubān to conquer Āzarbāijān and by secret correspondence he gained the allegiance of many chiefs of Daisam's army, especially the Dailamites, to al-Marzubān. When the latter invaded Āzarbāijān in 330/941–2 and gave battle to Daisam, the Dailamites went over to him. Daisam was forced to flee and found refuge with the Ardzrunid king Gagik of Vaspurakan, with whom he had previously had friendly relations.

Al-Marzubān, himself an Ismā'īlī initiate, appointed Ja'far b. 'Alī as his vizier and allowed him to teach Ismā'īlism openly. Soon, however, he gave him reason to fear for his position. Ja'far requested permission to go to Tabrīz, where he invited Daisam to join him and with the aid of the inhabitants killed the Dailamite chiefs. As Daisam arrived in Tabrīz, all the Kurds, whom al-Marzubān had offended, gathered around him. Al-Marzubān with his Dailamite army defeated them and besieged Tabrīz. He made overtures to Ja'far, who once more went over to him and on his own wish was permitted to live freely in his house without official position. Before al-Marzubān occupied Tabrīz, Daisam and his supporters escaped to Ardabīl. Al-Marzubān, aided by his brother Vahsūdān, besieged him there and after bribing his new vizier succeeded in forcing him to surrender in 331/942–3. Daisam was treated well by the Sallārid and on his own request put in charge of al-Marzubān's castle in Ṭārum. The prominent people of Ardabīl, on the other hand, were punished for their support of Daisam by the imposition of a heavy tribute and the demolition of the town wall, which they had to carry out with their own hands. Ja'far later returned to the vizierate, before 344/955 when Ibn Ḥauqal was visiting Āzarbāījān. His missionary activity was evidently successful, for Ibn Ḥauqal notes the presence of many Ismā'īlīs in the province.[1]

Al-Marzubān now held sway over all of Āzarbāījān and eastern Transcaucasia. By 333/945 he also took possession of Dvin according to numismatic evidence.[2] In the spring of that year the Russians (Rūs) came by boat on the Kur river and occupied Barda'a after defeating an army under al-Marzubān's governor consisting mainly of local volunteers. At first the inhabitants were treated well by them, but as the mob openly aided the Muslim armies against the invaders many of them were massacred and others were compelled to surrender all their property. Muslim volunteers from everywhere flocked to join al-Marzubān in fighting the infidel intruders. Despite the great numerical superiority of his army al-Marzubān was several times beaten. Finally after the ferocious enemy had been weakened by an epidemic caused by their overindulgence in fresh fruit he laid a successful ambush in which 700 men and their chief were slain. The rest withdrew into the citadel of Barda'a. As al-Marzubān besieged them he learned that al-Ḥusain b. Sa'īd had been sent by his uncle, the Ḥamdānid al-Ḥasan Nāṣir al-Daula of Mosul, to conquer Āzarbāījān and had reached Salmās, where

[1] Ibn Ḥauqal, p. 349.

[2] Cf. Paul Lemaire, "Muhammadan Coins in the Convent of the Flagellation", *NC*, 5th series, vol. XVIII (1938), p. 299. The coin bears besides the name of al-Marzubān that of Muḥammad b. Musāfir al-Malik indicating that al-Marzubān still recognized his father, despite his confinement, as the Sallārid king.

he was joined by the Hadhbānī Kurds under Ja'far b. Shakūya. Al-Ḥusain in 331/942, when al-Marzubān and Daisam were still at war over the control of Āzarbāījān and Nāṣir al-Daula was in charge of the government in Baghdad, had been invested by the caliph al-Muttaqī with the governorship of Armenia and Āzarbāījān. Al-Marzubān marched against the Ḥamdānid, leaving only a small troop to face the Russians, and defeated him in winter 334/945–6. Al-Ḥusain shortly afterwards was recalled by his uncle for a campaign to Baghdad. About the same time the Russians departed carrying off much booty and captives.

In 337/948–9 al-Marzubān, enraged by an insult his envoy had suffered from the Būyid Mu'izz al-Daula, decided to wrest Ray from the hands of Rukn al-Daula. The latter succeeded by diplomatic overtures to delay al-Marzubān's campaign until the arrival of auxiliary armies from his brothers and with their support thoroughly defeated him near Qazvīn. The Sallārid was captured. The Dailamite chiefs of his army who escaped gathered around Muḥammad b. Musāfir and brought him to Ardabīl, while Vahsūdān, who apparently had been left by al-Marzubān as his deputy, withdrew to Ṭārum. Muḥammad soon offended the Dailamites again and was forced to flee to Vahsūdān, who imprisoned him in a castle where he died before 341/953. Rukn al-Daula in the meantime had provided Muḥammad b. 'Abd al-Razzāq, the former governor of Ṭūs who had deserted the Sāmānids, with an army to conquer Āzarbāījān. In this situation Vahsūdān sent Daisam there, presumably to aid the sons of al-Marzubān during the latter's absence, since he knew the country well and would gain the support of the Kurds. As Ibn 'Abd al-Razzāq invaded Āzarbāījān, Daisam withdrew to Arrān. In 338/949–50 Ibn 'Abd al-Razzāq after a setback left for Ray, and Daisam gained control over Āzarbāījān and Armenia.

In 341/952–3 al-Marzubān, having escaped from his prison, sent an army against Daisam, who had usurped the rule in Āzarbāījān. Daisam was defeated near Ardabīl, as the Dailamite chiefs of his army deserted him, and fled to Armenia where the Christian princes aided him. A year later he was expelled from there, too, and sought refuge in Baghdad with Mu'izz al-Daula, who gave him a royal reception. In 343/954–5 Rukn al-Daula made peace with al-Marzubān and married his daughter. Daisam lost hope in Būyid aid to regain his kingdom and joined the Ḥamdānids. After receiving aid from Saif al-Daula of Aleppo, he occupied Salmās in 344/955–6 acknowledging the suzerainty of the

Ḥamdānid. He was expelled by al-Marzubān and at first found shelter with the Ardzrunid Derenik, son of Gagik. Under pressure from al-Marzubān, Derenik later arrested and surrendered him to the Sallārid, who blinded and imprisoned him. He was killed after the death of al-Marzubān by supporters of the latter.

After the capture of Daisam, al-Marzubān's reign remained undisturbed until his death in 346/957. A list of his tributaries in the year 344/955–6 quoted by Ibn Ḥauqal shows that his suzerainty was recognized by most of the petty princes in the Caucasus area and Armenia. Before his death al-Marzubān named his brother Vahsūdān as his successor. The commanders of the fortresses refused, however, to surrender them to him obeying the previous instructions of al-Marzubān which had provided for the successive rule of al-Marzubān's sons Justān, Ibrāhīm and Nāṣir. Unable to impose his authority Vahsūdān returned to Ṭārum. Justān gained control in Āzarbāījān while Ibrāhīm ruled in Dvin as his deputy. Vahsūdān's efforts to sow discord among his nephews soon bore fruit, especially as Justān devoted more and more time to his harem. In 349/960 a grandson of the caliph al-Muktafī, Isḥāq b. 'Īsā, revolted in Gīlān adopting the caliphal name al-Mustajīr bi'llāh and found support among the Sunnīs of western Gīlān. The former vizier of Justān, who had escaped from prison, invited him to come to Mūqān where he gathered supporters for his cause. Justān and Ibrāhīm defeated them, and the 'Abbāsid was captured and died in prison.

Shortly afterwards Vahsūdān succeeded in luring Justān and Nāṣir together with their mother to Ṭārum, where he imprisoned them. Then he sent his son Ismā'īl to take over the rule in Āzarbāījān. When Ibrāhīm in Armenia gathered an army to oppose Ismā'īl and free his brothers, Vahsūdān executed them and their mother. Ibrāhīm was driven out of Āzarbāījān by the supporters of Ismā'īl, but retained control of Armenia. Just as he again had assembled a strong army, Ismā'īl died, between 351/962 and 354/965 according to numismatic evidence. Ibrāhīm now occupied Ardabīl and devastated the domains of Vahsūdān, while the latter fled to Dailamān. In 355/966 Ibrāhīm was defeated by an army of Vahsūdān, who had returned to Ṭārum. Deserted by his army Ibrāhīm sought refuge in Ray with Rukn al-Daula, while Vahsūdān put his son Nūḥ in charge of the government of Āzarbāījān. Rukn al-Daula treated his brother-in-law most generously and sent his vizier Ibn al-'Amīd with an army to reinstate him in his domains. Ibn al-'Amīd conquered Āzarbāījān and ordered its administration. Then he wrote to Rukn al-Daula proposing to dispossess the Sallārid since he would be unable to keep the country under control and would squander its wealth, but Rukn al-Daula refused to betray the good faith of Ibrāhīm and recalled the vizier.

After Ibn al-'Amīd's departure Vahsūdān in 356/967 again sent an army which burnt Ardabīl. Ibrāhīm concluded a peace with his uncle, ceding to him a part of Āzarbāījān, presumably the region of Miyāna. In the following years he endeavoured, with only partial success, to reimpose his suzerainty on the Muslim principalities of Transcaucasia which had become progressively more independent. During the last years before his death in 373/983 his régime seems to have disintegrated and he was imprisoned. After him Āzarbāījān fell into the hands of the Rawwādids except for a small part (Miyāna ?) which was held by a grandson of Vahsūdān, al-Marzubān b. Ismā'īl. A year later the latter was attacked and seized by the Rawwādid Abu'l-Haijā'. His son Ibrāhīm fled to Ṭārum, where he later was able to restore the Sallārid reign. A son of Ibrāhīm b. al-Marzubān b. Muḥammad, Abu'l-Haijā', is mentioned in an Armenian source as ruling in Dvin in 982–3 when he was incited by King Musheł of Kars to invade the territory of the Bagratid king Smbat II. Probably soon afterwards he attacked Abū Dulaf al-Shaibānī, the first known member of a dynasty ruling in Gołthn and Nakhchivān until after 458/1066, but was defeated and lost his domains to Abū Dulaf. Abu'l-Haijā' later wandered with his family seeking help all over Georgia and Armenia and even visited the Byzantine emperor Basil II. In 989–90 Smbat II provided him with an Armenian army to reconquer Dvin, but then withdrew his support. Abu'l-Haijā' eventually was strangled by his servants.

The Rawwādids who succeeded the Sallārids in the rule of Āzarbāījān were descendants of the Azdī Arab family of al-Rawwād b. al-Muthannā which in the 2nd/8th and 3rd/9th centuries had dominated the town of Tabrīz. With the rapid rise in strength of the Kurdish element in Āzarbāījān in the 4th/10th century, they came to associate closely with it, especially with part of the Hadhbānī tribe, and were themselves generally considered as Kurds. During the captivity of the Sallārid al-Marzubān (337–41/949–53) Muḥammad b. al-Ḥusain al-Rawwādī is reported to have seized some parts of Āzarbāījān, probably Ahar and Varzuqān, northeast of Tabrīz, for which his son and successor Abu'l-Haijā' Ḥusain in 344/955–6 paid tribute to al-Marzubān. A year later

Abu'l-Haijā' occupied Tabrīz. After building a wall around the town he took it in 350/961 as his capital. Tabrīz remained the seat of the Rawwādids even when they later held sway over all of Āzarbāījān.

The history of Āzarbāījān from about 370/980 until 420/1029 is obscured by a lack of source material. There are no reports about the circumstances of Abu'l-Haijā''s rise to independence after the Sallārid Ibrāhīm b. al-Marzubān. Obviously he profited from the decline of the latter's power, and perhaps it was he who imprisoned the Sallārid for some time. After establishing his authority in Āzarbāījān he ravaged in 377/987 the domains of Abū Dulaf al-Shaibānī and took Dvin from him. The Bagratid king Smbat II on his demand paid the arrears of the Armenian tribute. In 378/988–9 he attacked Vaspurakan, but during the campaign he died.

Abu'l-Haijā' was succeeded by his son Mamlān (Muḥammad), who was unable to forestall the re-occupation of Dvin by Abū Dulaf. He faced the opposition of his brother al-Marzubān, whom he captured in 386/996. When the Curopalate Davith of Taikh conquered Malāzgird (Manazkert) between 992 and 994 and expelled the Muslim inhabitants arousing widespread indignation in the Muslim world, Mamlān acted as a defender of the Muslim cause. He penetrated Armenia as far as Valāshgird. Meeting the joint armies of Davith, the Bagratid Gagik I, and the Georgian king Bagrat II, he withdrew without giving battle. In 388/998 he led another army, this time joined by volunteers from 'Irāq and Khurāsān, as far as the village of Tsumb, northeast of Lake Vān, where he was met by the joint Armenian and Georgian armies. The encounter ended against expectation in a severe rout of the Muslim army despite its numerical superiority.

According to the only extant literary source Mamlān died in 393/1001 and was succeeded by his son Abū Naṣr Ḥusain. Mamlān's name, however, appears on coins at least until the year 405/1014. Thus either the date given for his death is mistaken or Abū Naṣr, about whose reign nothing is known, continued to mint coinage in his father's name. According to the same source Abū Naṣr died in 416/1025 and was succeeded by another son of Mamlān, Abū Manṣūr Vahsūdān. Under Vahsūdān the first waves of migration of Oghuz (Ghuzz) Turks reached Āzarbāījān, which gradually were to change completely the composition of its population. Late Armenian sources date the arrival of the Turks even earlier and describe it as one of the causes for the migration of the Ardzrunids and their people from Vaspurakan to Sebastaia (Sīvās) and the cession of the former province to Byzantium in 1021. Such an early date for the coming of the Turks cannot be reconciled with the accounts of the Muslim sources.[1] The early Oghuz immigrants in Āzarbāījān all belonged to the so-called ʿIrāqī Türkmens, who were expelled from Khurāsān by the Ghaznavids while their leader, Arslan Isrāʾīl b. Saljuq, was cast into prison where he died *c.* 427/1034. The first group of Oghuz consisting of about 2,000 tents arrived in 420/1029 and was well received by Vahsūdān and effectively employed against his enemies. The Armenians were strongly impressed by their first encounter with these mounted archers. Their presence did not halt for the moment the eastward pressure of Byzantium. Having previously taken Arjish from the Muslims, the Byzantines in 425/1034 expelled Abu'l-Haijā' b. Rabīb al-Daula, nephew of Vahsūdān and chief of the Hadhbānī Kurds, from the fortress of Bergri northeast of Lake Vān. As Abu'l-Haijā' was at odds with his uncle, the caliph intervened to reconcile them for the sake of recovering the stronghold. Their joint efforts led only to a short re-occupation before the fortress was definitely lost.

A second wave of Oghuz, much stronger than the first, arrived in 429/1037–8 under their leaders Būqā, Göktāsh, Manṣūr and Dānā. Though Vahsūdān established marriage ties with one of their leaders, they soon began to pillage the country. They sacked Marāgha in 429/1039, burnt its mosque, and massacred many of the inhabitants. One group, which had settled in Urmīya, after a successful raid into Armenia was attacked on their return by the Hadhbānīs because of previous friction between them. They killed many of the Kurds and pillaged the countryside. The Hadhbānī leader Abu'l-Haijā' b. Rabīb al-Daula, who held sway over Urmīya, and Vahsūdān united forces to expel the troublemakers. Many of the Oghuz were slain, while large groups left for Ray and Hamadān. Others, however, stayed. In 432/1040–1 Vahsūdān seized thirty of their leaders at a dinner to which he had invited them and then killed many of their men. As a result the Oghuz of Urmīya chose to leave for Mosul. In the next year another large contingent of Oghuz came from Ray fleeing before the Saljuq Ibrāhīm Īnāl. They were defeated and driven out by Vahsūdān. Again in 435/1044 some 5,000 Türkmens returned to Āzarbāījān from Mesopotamia through Diyārbakr and Armenia and occupied the town of Khūy (Arm. Her). The remnants of the ʿIrāqī Türkmens were now firmly

[1] Cf. C. Cahen, "La première pénétration turque en Asie-Mineure", *Byzantion*, vol. XVIII (1948), p. 9.

established in Āzarbāījān. Soon afterwards Qutlumush, the son of Arslān b. Saljuq, joined them to take over their leadership.

Tabrīz was struck in 434/1042 by a severe earthquake which destroyed large parts of the town and its wall; 40,000 or 50,000 inhabitants were said to have died. The palace collapsed, but the ruler, who was in a garden, was unhurt. He made every effort to rebuild the capital in short order. Vahsūdān during most of his reign was the patron of the poet Qaṭrān, who eulogized him in numerous odes.

In 446/1054 Toghrïl Beg came to Āzarbāījān and Arrān to receive the submission of the local rulers. In Tabrīz Vahsūdān submitted to him, introduced his name in the Friday prayer, and surrendered his son to him as a hostage. The Rawwādids thus became Saljuq vassals. Vahsūdān's son Abū Naṣr Mamlān, who succeeded him in 451/1059, once more revolted against the Turkish domination. Toghrïl in 452/1060 vainly invested Tabrīz. Mamlān travelled in person to Baghdad to complain to the caliph al-Qā'im about the depredations of the Oghuz in Āzarbāījān, while many notables sent letters of complaint. The caliph wrote Toghrïl requesting him to prevent the Türkmens from devastating the country, but to no avail. In 454/1062 Toghrïl returned to Āzarbāījān and forced the Rawwādid again to submission imposing a heavy tribute on him.

IX. THE SHADDĀDIDS OF ARRĀN

The Banū Shaddād were chiefs of a Kurdish clan, probably of the Hadhbānī tribe, which roamed the pasture grounds of Armenia. Muḥammad b. Shaddād b. Qurtaq about the year 340/951–2, in the time of the detention of the Sallārid al-Marzubān, gained control of Dvin, probably invited by the Muslims of the town as a protector. Ibrāhīm b. al-Marzubān, who tried to preserve his father's interests, incited a Christian vassal to attack Muḥammad, but the latter defeated him. Ibrāhīm then sent an army of Dailamites and Kurds which expelled the Shaddādid. Soon he was recalled, however, by the people of Dvin, who were dissatisfied with the Dailamite garrison, and foiled an attempt of the Bagratid king Ashot III of Ani to conquer the town. In 343/954–5 he was driven out by a Dailamite army sent by al-Marzubān, who had regained the rule in Āzarbāījān. Muḥammad and his clan found shelter in Vaspurakan. He vainly sought Byzantine support to recover Dvin and died in 344/955–6.

The eldest of Muḥammad's three sons, al-Lashkarī Abu'l-Ḥasan 'Alī, became chief of the clan and entered the service of the Armenian Grigor, ruler of Pharisos, and received from him Shothkh and Berd-Shamiram as fiefs. The youngest brother, al-Faḍl (Faḍlūn), at first served Najā al-Saifī, governor of Diyārbakr for the Ḥamdānid Saif al-Daula. When Najā was killed in 354/965, he returned to his brothers, but as he did not want to serve the Christians he soon left with the intention of joining the Sallārid Ibrāhīm in Āzarbāijān. As he reached Ganja, Ibrāhīm's governor of the town, 'Alī al-Tāzī, invited him to stay and guard it against hostile neighbours. He soon had occasion to prove his usefulness in warding off an attack of the Siyāvurdiyya (Sevordi), Armenicized Hungarians living west of Shamkūr. When he again made up his mind to leave for Āzarbāijān the notables of Ganja persuaded him to stay and invite his brother al-Lashkarī to come to Ganja. Al-Lashkarī at first refused to join al-Faḍl, but the latter induced him by a ruse to come and then was able to persuade him to stay. The people of Ganja co-operated with them arresting the governor and opening the gates for them. Al-Lashkarī in 360/971 took possession of Ganja and killed the governor. The Sallārid Ibrāhīm in 361/971–2 laid siege to Ganja but failed to take it and withdrew after concluding a peace which must have practically recognized the independence of the Shaddādid. Al-Lashkarī took possession of the region, expelling the Dailamites, and gradually expanded his territories as far as Shamkūr to the northwest and Barda'a to the east. He died in 368/978–9.

Although al-Lashkarī had favoured al-Faḍl for the succession, the second son of Muḥammad, al-Marzubān, gained the throne with the support of the army and the subjects. Al-Marzubān proved deficient in his political judgment and lost *c.* 372/982–3 Barda'a to the Sharvān-Shāh Muḥammad b. Aḥmad. Some retainers stirred up discord between al-Faḍl and him. In 375/985 al-Faḍl murdered him seizing his son Shīrvān and ascended the throne.

Al-Faḍl during his long reign greatly expanded the Shaddādid territory despite some setbacks. In 383/993 he occupied Barda'a and Bailaqān. Probably connected with these acquisitions is the report of an Armenian source that he invited Gagiḳ, son of Hamam, the lord of Tandzikh, killed him and seized his country. When the ruler of Pharisos, Grigor, died in 1003–4, al-Faḍl put his son Philip, whom he had previously invited, in fetters and occupied Shashvash and Shothkh of Grigor's domains. At an unknown date he seized the country of the Siyāvurdiyya west of Shamkūr. Probably in 413/1022 he brought Dvin under his rule, imposing a heavy tribute on the Armenians, and appointed his son Abu'l-Asvār governor. In 418/1027 he ordered a bridge to be built over the Araxes (probably at Khudāfarīn), perhaps with the intention of expanding his domains into Āzarbāījān.

Not always successful were his wars with the Bagratids of Tashir, who adopted the pretentious title "kings of Ałvankh" (Albania), and the Georgian kings. Al-Faḍl fought Gurgen of Tashir and after his death *c.* 989 attacked his son Davith Anhołin, but suffered a defeat. Around the same time he invaded Kakhetia and Hereth, but king Bagrat III of Georgia in alliance with king Gagik of Ani invested Shamkūr forcing him to sue for peace. When in 417/1026 the king of Georgia, probably Giorgi, again besieged Shamkūr, al-Faḍl met and defeated him. In 421/1030 al-Faḍl successfully raided Georgia. On his way back he was set upon by an allied army of the Georgian war-lord Liparit, the king of Kakhetia Kuirike III, and the king of Tashir Davith Anhołin and lost 10,000 men and all his booty. In the same year his son 'Askarūya revolted in Bailaqān. Al-Faḍl, who after his defeat fell mortally ill, sent another son Mūsā against him. Mūsā with the aid of a group of Russians who had raided Sharvān took the town and slew 'Askarūya. Al-Faḍl died in 422/1031.

Al-Faḍl's son and successor Abu'l-Faḍl Mūsā ruled only three years until 425/1034, when he was murdered by his son al-Lashkarī 'Alī, who ascended the throne. At first al-Lashkarī's reign was stable and successful. The poet Qaṭrān, who spent some time at his court in Ganja and left not later than 432/1041, in some of his eulogies for him mentions a major victory which he won over the joint army of the kings of Georgia and Armenia. His relations with the Rawwādid Vahsūdān initially were poor. Vahsūdān's employment of the Oghuz Türkmens posed a serious threat, but al-Lashkarī succeeded in bringing some of them to Arrān. Consequently their relations improved, and Vahsūdān even paid a visit to the court of the Shaddādid, probably some time between 427/1036 and 432/1041. Al-Lashkarī also entertained friendly relations with the Muslim ruler of Tiflis, Ja'far b. 'Alī, whom he aided in his resistance against Georgian attacks. After Ja'far's death (1046) al-Lashkarī married his widow Shāh-Khusruvān. During the last years of his reign he came under serious pressure from the Türkmens and the Byzantine expansion. In 437/1045–6 the Oghuz under Qutlumush began a siege of Ganja which lasted one and a half years and was raised only when the Byzantine army under the eunuch Nicephore joined by the Georgian king Bagrat IV approached. Al-Lashkarī was forced to make concessions to his saviour recognizing the Byzantine suzerainty and surrendering his son Ardashīr as a hostage. His situation remained precarious, and he moved his residence from castle to castle until he died in 441/1049 or 50.

Al-Lashkarī was succeeded by his minor son Anūshirvān in whose name the chamberlain Abū Manṣūr reigned. Abū Manṣūr agreed with the army chiefs to surrender several border fortresses to the rulers of Kakhetia, Georgia, to the Dido mountain tribe and to Byzantium in the hope of relieving their pressure on Arrān. This decision still in 441/1049–50 provoked a revolt of the people of Shamkūr, who took the citadel of the town and proclaimed Abu'l-Asvār Shāvur, son of al-Faḍl b. Muḥammad, ruler. Abu'l-Asvār since 413/1022 had ruled Dvin practically independently. Though he was married to a sister of the Armenian king Davith Anhołin of Tashir, he proved a troublesome neighbour to the Armenians and earned the reputation of an exemplary *ghāzī* among the Muslims. He granted asylum to the Armenian nobleman Abirat with his large retinue and then killed him. Around 1039 he invaded the territory of his brother-in-law king Davith pillaging and burning. As he threatened to attack Davith himself, the latter appealed to the kings of Ani, Kapan and Georgia for help. Aided by their troops he inflicted a defeat on the Shaddādid and drove him out of his domains. In 1043 the Byzantine emperor Constantine Monomach, intending to annex Ani and to overthrow its youthful king Gagik II, invited Abu'l-Asvār by letter to attack the territory of Ani and promised him in a golden bull recognition of any conquests he would make. Abu'l-Asvār occupied a number of fortresses and places in Gagik's territory. After the Byzantine conquest of Ani in 1045 the emperor in breach of his promises demanded from him the surrender of the lands formerly belonging to Ani. Upon Abu'l-Asvār's refusal a strong Byzantine army with Armenian and Georgian contingents attacked Dvin. Abu'l-Asvār flooded the country and put his archers in an ambush. The attackers were repulsed with heavy losses. In the next year another Byzantine army took some of the fortresses belonging to Ani. Most serious was the campaign under Nicephore *c.* 1048–9. Abu'l-Asvār withdrew to Dvin, while the enemy laid the countryside waste. He was forced to recognize the Byzantine suzerainty before Nicephore went on to Ganja.

After gaining control of Shamkūr Abu'l-Asvār occupied Ganja and the rest of Arrān. Anūshīrvān and the chamberlain Abū Manṣūr were arrested. Abu'l-Asvār succeeded in restoring to the Shaddādid régime some of its earlier strength. In 445/1053 he took a border fortress from the Georgians and placed a garrison in it. He entrusted his son Abu'l-Naṣr Iskandar with the government of Dvin. When Toghrïl Beg after receiving the submission of the Rawwādid Vahsūdān in Tabrīz came to Ganja in 446/1054, Abu'l-Asvār submitted to him. He later participated in the Saljuq conquest of Armenia. The Shaddādid dynasty survived as Saljuq vassals ruling Ani until the end of the 6th/12th century.

X. THE YAZĪDIDS OF SHARVĀN AND THE HĀSHIMIDS OF BĀB AL-ABWĀB

In the limitrophe provinces of Sharvān and al-Bāb two dynasties, the Yazīdids and the Hāshimids, were able to establish their hereditary rule around the middle of the 3rd/9th century. Until the late Sallārid period they remained generally under the overlordship of the governors and rulers of Āzarbāījān and Arrān, but these interfered only occasionally in their affairs. Much of their efforts was devoted to raiding the non-Muslim petty principalities in the region and repelling their attacks. The two families were also engaged in a long, intermittent feud with each other. The Yazīdids, who had a historical claim to al-Bāb, time and again interfered in the affairs of this neighbour province and usually gained the upper hand. The Hāshimids, whose hold over al-Bāb was also permanently threatened by the power of the chiefs (*ru'asā'*) of the town, were repeatedly expelled and restored within a short time.

The Yazīdids were descendants of Yazīd b. Mazyad, a chief of the Arab tribe of Shaibān and prominent commander under Hārūn al-Rashīd. Yazīd was twice appointed governor of Āzarbāījān and Armenia (171–2/787–9 and 183–5/799–801) and distinguished himself in fighting the Khazars. After him his three sons and his grandson Muḥammad b. Khālid were repeatedly sent as governors to Āzarbāījān, Armenia and Arrān. Muḥammad b. Khālid in 245/859–60 restored the town of Ganja and was granted it together with some estates as a hereditary fief. His brother al-Haitham probably under him became governor of Sharvān. As the disturbances following the murder of the caliph al-Mutawakkil in 247/861 weakened the central government, he was able to retain his dominion and bequeath it to his son. A third brother, Yazīd, in the same period established himself in Laizān, a small region in northern Sharvān. Al-Haitham and Yazīd adopted the traditional titles Sharvān-Shāh and Laizān-Shāh. The dynasty soon became Persianized and claimed descent from Bahrām Gūr.

The Banū Hāshim were descendants of a client of the Arab tribe of Sulaim of unknown origin. The Sulaim were powerful in al-Bāb, and the Hāshimids were one of the families of prominence among them. Al-Najm b. Hāshim is mentioned as the lord of al-Bāb representing the local interests about the year 180/796. When the inhabitants of the town attacked their tax collector, al-Najm was killed by the governor of Armenia. His son Ḥayyūn revolted and asked the Khazars for help, who came with a strong army and penetrated as far as the Kur river causing much damage to the Muslims before they withdrew. Despite this traitorous activity, the Hāshimid family did not lose its influence in al-Bāb. In 255/869 the inhabitants and the ghāzīs of the town raised a great-grandson of Ḥayyūn, Hāshim b. Surāqa b. Salis, as their amīr, and from that date the family reigned on a hereditary basis. Hāshim led two successful raids into the Avar country known as al-Sarīr in 263/876–7 and 265/878–9. After his death in 271/884–5 he was succeeded by his son ʻAmr, who died after a year and was succeeded by his brother Muḥammad. Muḥammad in 273/886–7 carried out a successful raid on Shandān, northwest of al-Bāb, and in 288/901 beat off a Khazar attack. Less fortunate were his relations with al-Sarīr. In 292/905 Muḥammad in a battle was captured together with ten chiefs of al-Bāb by the lord of al-Sarīr, who later released them with generous presents. In 297/909–10 (according to another version in 300/912–13) Muḥammad led another campaign against Shandān jointly with the Sharvān-Shāh ʻAlī, great-grandson of al-Haitham b. Khālid, who had succeeded to the rule after his grandfather Muḥammad and his father al-Haitham. The Muslims suffered a crushing defeat by the army of Shandān, al-Sarīr and the Khazars. The two rulers and 10,000 men were captured. Those falling into the captivity of the Sarīrians as well as the two rulers were freed after a few months, while most of the others were sold into slavery. It was perhaps during the captivity of Muḥammad, between 296/909 and 299/912, that the Sājid Yūsuf came to al-Bāb and rebuilt the walls of the town. Muḥammad died in 303/916 and was succeeded by his brother ʻAbd al-Malik.

In Sharvān ʻAlī b. al-Haitham, not long after his release from captivity, probably in 301/913 faced a raid of the Russians on Bākū. When they withdrew to some islands off the coast, the Sharvānians attacked them in boats, but were badly mauled, and several thousand Muslims were killed. These setbacks encouraged Abū Ṭāhir Yazīd of the Laizān branch of the family, who had succeeded to the rule of that region after the reigns of his grandfather Yazīd b. Khālid and of his father Muḥammad, to overthrow 'Alī in 305/917–18. He killed 'Alī and his son al-'Abbās and took over the rule of Sharvān. In 306/918–19 he built the town of al-Yazīdiyya near Shamākhī as his new capital and gave Laizān as a fief to his son Muḥammad, who later seems to have become his co-regent. The regions of Khursān, Vardān and Ṭabarsarān were annexed to Sharvān under Yazīd.

This northward expansion may have been encouraged by the family quarrel which weakened the Hāshimid power in al-Bāb in this period. 'Abd al-Malik b. Hāshim two months after his accession was overthrown and expelled by his nephew Abu'l-Najm b. Muḥammad with popular support. 'Abd al-Malik fled to Shandān and then to Yūsuf b. Abi'l-Sāj, who formally invested him with the government of al-Bāb and provided him with an army of 6,000 men, which aided him to recover the town in spite of the support of the inhabitants for Abu'l-Najm. A few months later he marched to Shābarān in the hope of capturing his nephew there. Abu'l-Najm eluded his search and was able to reoccupy al-Bāb. 'Abd al-Malik retook the town after a siege, this time aided by the lord of Khaidāq with a Khazar army. He killed his nephew and continued to rule unopposed. A battle with Muḥammad, the son of the Sharvān-Shāh, in 318/930 at Shābarān remained inconclusive and evidently did not reverse the northward expansion of Sharvān. Two successful raids to the region of Shandān were carried out in 326/938. A year later 'Abd al-Malik died leaving a son Aḥmad of four years.

The succession of a minor brought on a new period of troubles in al-Bāb. Aḥmad was expelled after five months by the chiefs of the town, who turned over the rule to al-Haitham b. Muḥammad, grandson of the Sharvān-Shāh Yazīd and governor of Ṭabarsarān. In 329/941 they expelled him and restored Aḥmad, only to overthrow him again after six months. They recalled al-Haitham, but after six months deposed him and invited his grandfather, the Sharvān-Shāh Yazīd, to take over the town. Yazīd sent his son Aḥmad as his deputy, but he in turn was expelled after a few days in favour of the Hāshimid Aḥmad. Yazīd now led a punitive campaign to al-Bāb carrying off much booty and imposing a tribute. Shortly afterwards the Dailamites of the

Sallārid al-Marzubān invaded Sharvān, and Yazīd was forced to seek the support of the people of al-Bāb restoring all the booty and the tribute to them. He drove off the Dailamites, but then concluded a peace with al-Marzubān which evidently entailed recognition of the Sallārid overlordship and payment of tribute.

After the death of Yazīd in 337/948 his son and successor Muḥammad imprisoned his brother Aḥmad, and in his place sent his own son Aḥmad to rule Laizān and confirmed his other son al-Haitham in the rule of Ṭabarsarān. He died in 345/956 and was succeeded by his son Aḥmad. Aḥmad's brother al-Haitham soon became afraid of him and sought refuge among the Lakz (Lazgi). In 357/968 he joined the Sallārid Ibrāhīm b. al-Marzubān and in the next year participated in a campaign intended to reaffirm the Sallārid authority over Sharvān and al-Bāb. The Sallārid army pillaged Sharvān and the countryside of al-Bāb. The Sharvān-Shāh Aḥmad sued for peace and paid tribute.

The demands of the Sallārid were resisted by the Hāshimid Aḥmad, who after having been deposed once more in 342/953–4 for six months in favour of the king of the Lakz Khashram Aḥmad b. Munabbih, had gained firm control of al-Bāb. Al-Haitham now joined the Hāshimid, who vainly tried to persuade the Sharvān-Shāh to grant some territory to his brother. The Hāshimid gathered an army composed largely of Avars from al-Sarīr and sacked and burnt Shābarān carrying off much booty. As the soldiers of al-Sarīr on their return entered al-Bāb one day before the amīr, the inhabitants attacked them, massacred a large number and seized their booty. The Avars took revenge in 360/971, when they defeated the people of al-Bāb near the town and killed 1,000 Muslims.

Maimūn b. Aḥmad, who succeeded his father in 366/976, was soon confined in the government building by the chiefs of al-Bāb, who took over the reins of the rule. Maimūn secretly sought help from the Russians. In 377/987–8 a band of them arrived in eighteen boats and freed Maimūn, but then many of them were massacred by the people of al-Bāb and the rest departed, while Maimūn fortified himself in the citadel of the town with a guard of Russians. In 379/989–90 a popular preacher from Gīlān, Muḥammad al-Tūzī, found an eager audience in al-Bāb and gained complete control over the town. Maimūn was at first swayed by his preaching, but later resisted his demands. He was besieged in the citadel by the people supporting the preacher and was forced to leave for Ṭabarsarān (380/990–1). The preacher invited the

Sharvān-Shāh Muḥammad b. Aḥmad to take over the rule of al-Bāb. Muḥammad, who had succeeded his father in 370/981, pursued a policy of expansion taking possession of the town of Qabala from its ruler ʻAbd al-Barr b. ʻAnbasa (371/981) and of Bardaʻa (*c.* 372/982). He now came readily to al-Bāb, but shortly after his arrival was wounded by a slave of Maimūn who struck him with a battle-axe. While he returned to Sharvān, Maimūn reoccupied al-Bāb. The Hāshimid in 381/991 was once more expelled by the people, who recalled the Sharvān-Shāh. The latter soon departed again, leaving a garrison in the citadel. Maimūn reconquered al-Bāb in 382/998–9 and in the following year also took the citadel. In 385/995 the people of the region of al-Karakh, located in a strategic position on the route from al-Bāb to central Dāghistān, were converted to Islam by him. Maimūn died in 387/997. His brother Muḥammad, who succeeded him, was murdered after ten months by a ghulām of Maimūn. Four months later (388/998) Maimūn's son al-Lashkarī acceded to the rule. The feud with Sharvān flared up again with new vigour.

In Sharvān Muḥammad b. Aḥmad had been succeeded by his brother Yazīd. In consequence to the earlier conquest of Qabala, the Sharvānian army in 382/992 met the army of Shakkī near the town and suffered severe losses. In 389/999 Yazīd took the castle of Gurzūl from ʻAbd al-Barr, the former lord of Qabala. Then he fought the Hāshimid al-Lashkarī in a dispute over an estate. Al-Lashkarī won an initial victory and seized the estate, but later the Sharvān-Shāh routed him at Shābarān and captured his brother Abū Naṣr. When al-Lashkarī died in 392/1002, the people of al-Bāb requested him to release Abū Naṣr. Yazīd, intent on restoring the Sharvānian authority over al-Bāb, proposed that Abū Naṣr should marry his daughter and demanded the surrender of the citadel of al-Bāb to himself. When the people of al-Bāb refused this demand, he killed Abū Naṣr and fought his brother al-Manṣūr, to whom the people of al-Bāb swore allegiance in 393/1003. The war between Sharvān and al-Bāb dragged on with changing fortune until the people of al-Bāb revolted and expelled al-Manṣūr in 410/1019–20 and surrendered the town to the Sharvān-Shāh, who put a garrison into the citadel. Al-Manṣūr recovered town and citadel in 412/1021–2 with the support of the lord of al-Sarīr and fought an inconclusive battle with the Sharvānians at Shābarān. In 414/1023–4 he was again driven out by the people, who surrendered the town to the Sharvān-Shāh, but he reconquered it in 415/1024. The feud was temporarily interrupted when the Sharvān-Shāh in 416/1025 during his absence from his capital al-Yazīdiyya was faced with a rebellion of his son Anūshīrvān there. Anūshīrvān soon lost most of his supporters and fled as his father approached the capital. He was captured and starved to death in prison. Yazīd died in 418/1027 and was succeeded by another son, Manūchihr.

Manūchihr in 420/1029 reopened the war with al-Bāb over the possession of an estate in Masqaṭ. He was defeated, and in 421/1030 the army of al-Bāb raided his domains causing extensive destruction. Later in the same year the Russians landed in Sharvān and inflicted a defeat on Manūchihr near Bākū killing many Sharvānians before they moved on to Arrān. In 422/1031 they again landed at Bākū but were driven out by Manūchihr. They united with the Alans and in 423/1032 took al-Yazīdiyya by force pillaging and slaying. On their way back they were attacked and badly mauled by an army of ghāzīs under the amīr Manṣūr of al-Bāb and lost all their booty and many men. A year later they tried to take revenge on al-Bāb, but were beaten off at al-Karakh.

Both the Hāshimid Manṣūr and the Sharvān-Shāh Manūchihr died in 425/1034, the latter murdered by his brother Abū Manṣūr with the aid of Manūchihr's wife, a daughter of the Shāddadid al-Faḍl. While Abū Manṣūr ascended the throne in Sharvān and married the widow of his brother, al-Manṣūr was succeeded in al-Bāb by his son ʿAbd al-Malik, who was promptly overthrown and expelled by the people, who surrendered the town in 426/1035 to the new Sharvān-Shāh. The latter garrisoned the citadel and put his vizier in charge of al-Bāb. But ʿAbd al-Malik after two months reconquered his domains and killed the vizier. He was able to conclude a peace with the Sharvān-Shāh and in 427/1035 married his sister Shamkūya. The new alliance was viewed askance by the powerful chiefs of al-Bāb. When they murdered the vizier of ʿAbd al-Malik, the latter left secretly for Sharvān. Two of them followed the amīr to persuade him to return. They were detained as hostages by the Sharvān-Shāh while ʿAbd al-Malik returned to al-Bāb and fortified himself in the citadel. In 429/1038 an attack of the people of Shandān on the town was repelled. In 430/1038–9 one of the chiefs, ʿAlī b. al-Ḥasan b. ʿAnaq, revolted and besieged the amīr in the citadel but failed. The people of Khaidāq took the citadel in 432/1040–1 and briefly held the amīr and his wife captive. In the same year the chief ʿAlī b. al-Ḥasan carried out a raid on Shandān. In 433/1041–2 ʿAbd al-Malik again fled in fear of the chiefs, who captured his wife and sent her to her brother the Sharvān-Shāh. ʿAbd al-Malik soon retook al-Bāb, while the chiefs fled, and his wife returned from Sharvān. ʿAbd al-Malik died in 434/1043 leaving a son, Manṣūr, of four years.

Manṣūr was proclaimed amīr, and the chief ʿAbd al-Salām b. al-Muẓaffar b. Aghlab acted as his regent during his minority. After ʿAbd al-Salām's death in 443/1051–2 Manṣūr became the effective ruler. But already in 446/1054 the chiefs revolted, and his reign remained troubled by their opposition until he was eventually murdered by them in 457/1065. In Sharvān Abū Manṣūr b. Yazīd was succeeded in 435/1043–4 by his brother Qubād. In 437/1045–6 Qubād built a wall around the capital al-Yazīdiyya for fear of the Oghuz Türkmens, who at this time were laying siege to Ganja. Qubād was succeeded in 441/1049 by his nephew Bukhtanaṣṣar ʿAlī b. Aḥmad, who was promptly overthrown by his uncle Sallār b. Yazīd. ʿAlī fled but was captured and killed near Bailaqān. Sallār actively pursued the fight against the infidels during his reign. In 445/1053–4 he took the castle of Mālūgh in Shakkī by force and garrisoned it. Next to it he built a town with a congregational mosque.

It is unknown if the rulers of Sharvān and al-Bāb were among the princes who formally submitted to Toghrïl Beg at the time of his campaign to Āzarbāījān and Arrān in 446/1054. Their recognition of the Saljuq suzerainty in any case cannot have been delayed much longer. A decade later the region came under massive Turkish occupation.

CHAPTER 7

IRAN UNDER THE BŪYIDS

During the first decades of the 4th/10th century Iran was divided into three important spheres of power. The east (Transoxiana and Khurāsān) was subject to the Sāmānids, who also exerted a varying degree of authority over the provinces of Sīstān and Kirmān beyond the desert area of Dasht-i-Kavīr and Dasht-i-Lūṭ. The Iranian highlands by the Caspian Sea were controlled by the Zaidite rulers of Ṭabaristān and by various local potentates. In the south they were ruled by ʿAbbāsid governors directly dependent on Baghdad, whose constant ambition however was to establish themselves as independent dynastic rulers. The Sājids of Qazvīn had already succeeded in doing this by the end of the 3rd/9th century in Āzarbāījān in the northwest. The Zaidite rulers of Ṭabaristān and the other smaller princes joined the Sājids, though often involuntarily, to form a barrier effective enough to halt the westward progress of the Sāmānids. Iran's fate for the next hundred years was to be decided in the region on the south shore of the Caspian Sea, an area barely two hundred miles long and sixty miles wide. Within a few years an entirely new power was to emerge in this vacuum, the Būyids, who were able to wrest central and southern Iran from the ʿAbbāsids while the attention of the latter was being diverted by conflicts in Mesopotamia. Thus for the first time in Islamic history this area was released from the centralized control of Baghdad and united under the rule of an Iranian dynasty. In other words, the formation of native states, which had already been in progress for some time in eastern Iran, now began to take place in western Iran. The Būyids achieved even more than this; from the Iranian plateau they descended on Iraq and brought the caliphate itself under their domination. The Būyid period therefore also marks the opening of a new era in the history of the ʿAbbāsid caliphate. The weakening of the central power of the caliphate, it is true, had already begun after the turn of the century; nevertheless it was the Būyids who were to stabilize the situation in Baghdad after a period of considerable confusion. The occupation of Baghdad by the Shīʿī Būyids might well have dealt a mortal blow to the caliphate if they had not decided, for reasons of political expediency, to countenance its continued existence, thereby assuring themselves of the possibility of using it as a political tool both at home and abroad. This gave their rule a more legitimate appearance in the eyes of the majority of their subjects, who were Sunnī, and also increased the respect in which the Būyids were held by foreign powers. Their most dangerous opponents remained the Sāmānids in the east, who in contrast were pursuing a deliberately orthodox Sunnī policy which gave them an excellent pretext for continuing their expansion westwards. The struggles which took place along the frontier between them were to affect Būyid policy for decades to come. It was from this direction too, that in the 11th century the Ghaznavids and then the Saljuqs delivered the counter-blows which first reduced and then annihilated the Būyid state.

The form of government established by the Būyids may be described with reservations as a military dictatorship. The Būyids were Dailamites and were largely dependent on soldiers drawn from their own people. The Dailamites, whose home was in the mountainous area north of Qazvīn, had a long tradition of military prowess dating back to pre-Christian times and including campaigns against Georgia as allies of the Sāsānians. Like the Turks, they already had been playing an important rôle as mercenaries in the period which preceded the emergence of the Būyids, and they had been active in Iran, Mesopotamia and even further westward. This was a factor of some importance in the rapid success of the Būyids, for it was easy to persuade the Dailamites to follow the victorious leadership of one of their own number. Their fighting methods, their strategy and their accoutrement were much the same as they had always been. Being a peasant race possessing cattle but not horses, they were infantry men. Each man was equipped with a shield, a sword and three spears, and, as Islamic sources tell us, they were able to form an impenetrable wall with their large shields when advancing in close formation. They specialized in hurling lances to which were attached burning rags soaked in crude oil. Islamic sources emphasize their hardiness, and their bravery was proverbial. On many occasions the Būyids were able to win victories although their forces were far outnumbered by their opponents. Because the Dailamites could only be employed as infantry, the Būyids were also obliged to make use of the Turks, whose mounted archers provided a tactically essential complement. In addition they also enrolled Kurdish mercenaries in Iran and Arabs in Mesopotamia. The combination of Dailamites and Turks as the backbone of the Būyid army soon led to serious problems. The question of the direct payment of the army out of the state treasury was at least partly solved by the introduction of a form of feudalism. Since the Būyids depended for their initial successes largely on the assistance of their own people the Dailamites, there soon grew up a sort of military aristocracy largely hereditary in character. As a result there was constant friction between them and the Turks, which in turn affected the outcome of many internal Būyid squabbles. Later the Būyids of Iran tended to rely on Dailamites while those in Iraq depended on Turkish support. In addition to this, the feudal system had grave disadvantages, and the supremacy of the military was detrimental to the civilian population. Dailamite oppression became proverbial, as a reliable witness reports.[1]

The roots of this military dictatorship lie partly in the conditions under which the Būyids set up their rule and partly in the situation prevalent in many parts of Iran before they appeared on the scene. The central government was so ineffectual that the mercenaries in Shīrāz and Iṣfahān were left to themselves; consequently they could only be paid and maintained by a leader who possessed a combination of initiative, outstanding military proficiency, conviction and organizing ability. The lack of administrative experience could easily be supplemented by the co-operation of professional civil servants. As we shall see, 'Imād al-Daula, the founder of the Būyid empire, possessed all these essential qualities. In Iran he found the mood of the mercenaries ideally favourable for a take-over of power. The words attributed to the Iṣfahān mercenaries after the death of Mardāvīj are particularly revealing in this respect: "If we remain without a leader, we are lost."[2] In this mood both Turks and Dailamites embraced the Būyid's leadership; the fact that he outstripped numerous rivals is indicative of his qualities.

It lies in the nature of a military dictatorship based on a military aristocracy that attempts to ensure a strictly hereditary line of succession are fraught with difficulty. The Būyid empire was no exception, and it only succeeded in establishing a regular pattern of succession when it was already too late. The army was repeatedly to decide the matter either by an official election or simply by force of arms. Women had always held an important place in Dailamite society and they were to

[1] Tanūkhī, part I, p. 157. [2] Ibn al-Athīr, vol. VIII, p. 105.

wield great political influence and were even to achieve personal rule. An example is Sayyida at the end of the 4th/10th century in Ray. The unique structure of the Būyid empire gave rise to a further problem. It was from the start divided into three spheres of influence, Shīrāz, Ray and Baghdad. In consequence, questions of the unity of the empire and its government occupy a position of the greatest importance in the history of this period. From this point of view Būyid history may be divided into three sections: first, its foundation and rise; secondly, its apogee and the establishment of unity under Rukn al-Daula and 'Aḍud al-Daula; and thirdly, the struggle for the succession of 'Aḍud al-Daula which led in due course to the decline and final collapse of the empire.

I. FOUNDATION OF THE EMPIRE BY 'IMĀD AL-DAULA

In the mountain fastnesses of their homeland the Dailamites had already succeeded in repelling more than a dozen Muslim attacks before the beginning of the 3rd/9th century, when they began to receive Islamic influences. Pretenders to the succession of 'Alī, who were of the Zaidite persuasion, sought refuge amongst the Dailamites and began to proselytize them in the second half of the 3rd/9th century. But the real wave of conversion did not come until the turn of the century, when the Zaidite Imām Ḥasan al-Uṭrūsh spent a considerable length of time in the region. The Zaidite Imāms were supported by the Dailamite family of Banū Justān in their struggle for supremacy in Ṭabaristān, but at the beginning of the 4th/10th century various Dailamite and Gīlān military leaders began to supplant them. It was during this turbulent and uncertain period that 'Alī b. Būya ('Imād al-Daula), the founder of the Būyid empire, began his career.

Our knowledge of 'Imād al-Daula's youth is at best fragmentary. If we accept that he died at the age of 57, he must have been born *c.* A.D. 891–2. It appears that, true to Dailamite tradition, he early embarked on a military career. He himself records that he was in his youth employed at the court of the Sāmānid prince Naṣr b. Aḥmad (301/913–331/943) apparently in the prince's closest entourage. The next step in his advancement occurred when he entered the service of Mākān b. Kākī, either at the suggestion of Naṣr or of his own free will. Mākān was a member of a princely Gīlān family. He had espoused the cause of the 'Alid ruler of Ṭabaristān and in 924 had become governor of Gurgān. After the death of the former ruler he had made successful overture to the Sāmānids and had been appointed governor of the disputed territory of Ray. It is conceivable that 'Imād al-Daula joined Mākān at this date (928). He must certainly have occupied a high position in Mākān's army, for he was able to invite his two younger brothers, Ḥasan (the future Rukn al-Daula) and Aḥmad (later known as Mu'izz al-Daula), to join him and to procure for them commissions in the army and in his own retinue. Ḥasan was then about 30 years old, Aḥmad a boy of just 13. Two years later, Mākān took a politically fatal step when he decided to attack the Sāmānids in Khurāsān; he managed to occupy Nīshāpūr for a time, but was then defeated by Mardāvīj, another Gīlān prince, and forced to abandon Ṭabaristān. 'Imād al-Daula was quick to join the victor's side along with his brothers, and he entered the service of Mardāvīj just when the latter was preparing to subjugate the territory south of the Alburz range as far as Qazvīn, with every intention of proceeding to the conquest of other provinces further south. Mardāvīj soon recognized the capabilities of the Būyid, shortly afterwards entrusting him with the administration of the important town of Karaj, which had been the seat of the Dulafid princes. The itineraries of various geographers would seem to indicate that Karaj was in the neighbourhood of present-day Bahrāmābād, sixty miles southeast of Hamadān. It was situated at an important centre of communications, being at the junction of the north–south route from Ray to Ahvāz and the south-east route from Hamadān to Iṣfahān. After the overthrow of the Dulafids at the end of the 3rd/9th century, a vacuum had occurred here which the 'Abbāsid governors of Iṣfahān and Shīrāz had not been able to dispel. The appointment of 'Imād al-Daula as governor of Karaj may well have taken place in Ṭabaristān, since on his journey to his post he passed through Ray, where Vushmgīr, one of Mardāvīj's brothers, resided, as did the vizier al-'Amīd, whose son was later to play an important part in connection with Rukn al-Daula. Meanwhile Mardāvīj decided to terminate 'Imād al-Daula's appointment, probably because he wanted to administer Karaj himself. However, while in Ray 'Imād al-Daula won the favour of the vizier and from him discovered the prince's plan. In order to forestall his dismissal he speedily left Ray and took over control of Karaj.

The political situation at Karaj was confused. There seems to have been a small garrison of Dailamite soldiers, but these had been left to their own devices and were bored with inactivity. The surrounding mountains were in the hands of the Khurramites, adherents of a religious and political sect combining Shī'ī and Zoroastrian elements. 'Imād al-Daula set about their subjugation systematically and seized a series of fortresses, which enhanced his reputation, and provided him with valuable spoils. Soon the entire region was in his hands. The riches he acquired from the Khurramites enabled him to hire more mercenaries, thereby building up his position. His qualities as a born leader were proved by the failure of Mardāvīj's attempts to stir up the soldiers in Karaj against him. Soon 'Imād al-Daula was in a position to contemplate an extension of his power. But at the same time he was obliged to prepare his army for the likelihood of an impending attack by Mardāvīj, who was bound sooner or later to try to put down his rebellious viceroy. 'Imād al-Daula now made the capture of nearby Iṣfahān his ambition, and there met with an unexpectedly brilliant success. The opposing army, though far outnumbering his own, came over with astonishing alacrity to his side when he appeared before the walls of the city. This in turn enhanced his wealth and his popularity with the mercenaries. He failed, however, to come to terms with the governor of Iṣfahān and, unable to establish the legality of his position, he abandoned the city in the face of Mardāvīj and, abandoning Karaj too, marched on the important town of Arrajān, between Khūzistān and Fārs, which was ruled by the same governor as Iṣfahān. Here the same pattern of victory and spoils was repeated.

His march on Arrajān was probably in the nature of a foray, but he was doubtless already entertaining the prospect of setting up a kingdom in southern Iran. He therefore only spent the winter in Arrajān, and in spring 321/933 set off on a new campaign. In Fārs he ran into an ally in the person of Zaid b. 'Alī al-Naubandagānī, who possessed large estates in the mountains north of Kāzarūn and was on bad terms with the authorities in Baghdad. Judging by his name he may have been a descendant of 'Alī, who hoped that the Būyid would provide military support for the advancement of his religious and political ambitions. Meanwhile Yāqūt, the governor of Iṣfahān and Fārs, had replaced Mardāvīj as 'Imad al-Daula's most immediate antagonist. A series of skirmishes culminated in a decisive battle from which the Būyid emerged victorious. By treating them well, he also won the vanquished over to his side. The way was now open to Shīrāz. In 322/May or June 934 he entered the capital city of Fārs, which was to remain in the uninterrupted possession of the Būyids until 1062.

After the capture of Shīrāz 'Imād al-Daula strove to gain recognition by the caliph in order to forestall the claims of Mardāvīj. This time he was successful, though he had no intention of paying the requisite tribute. He accepted the insignia of his office as viceroy from the caliph's emissary, but then delayed the emissary with promises for two years, until the latter finally died in Shīrāz without having achieved his mission of obtaining the tribute. This episode, insignificant in itself, prefigured the attitude which was to condition the subsequent policy of the Būyids towards the 'Abbāsid caliphate. 'Imād al-Daula and his successors were by tradition Shī'ī and of the Zaidite persuasion. It should be recalled that the Dailamites had been converted to Islam by Zaidite missionaries. Later the Būyids were to bend towards Twelver Shī'ism, and even the Ismā'īlīs were later accepted for brief periods at their court. Their Shī'ī beliefs may have been varied in complexion, but they certainly had no religious reason for seeking the caliph's approval, let alone for setting themselves up as protectors of the caliphate after their capture of Baghdad. But whatever the arguments put forward to explain the moderation of the Būyids' policy towards the caliph and whatever they themselves asserted at the time, there can be no doubt that 'Imād al-Daula's decision to acknowledge at least formally the caliph's supremacy was to have a very considerable influence on future developments. His once valuable ally in Naubandagān meanwhile disappeared from the scene, as did a later Zaidite pretender who had accompanied Mu'izz al-Daula to Baghdad but who then returned to Ṭabaristān to further his own cause.

Mardāvīj was still 'Imād al-Daula's bitterest opponent. In order to sever any possible Būyid links with Iraq, and doubtless also to preclude the westward expansion of the Būyid Empire, Mardāvīj now embarked on a campaign against Khūzistān. He then came to an agreement with the caliph, thus forcing 'Imād al-Daula to recognize Mardāvīj's formal superiority. But this state of affairs came to an abrupt end with the murder of Mardāvīj in January 935. 'Imād al-Daula then began to press his claims to Khūzistān with the caliph, probably building on his position as second only to Mardāvīj. He occupied 'Askar Mukram and then came to terms with the caliph, who confirmed him in the possession of Fārs and gave Khūzistān to Yāqūt, the former governor of Fārs.

The assassination of Mardāvīj in Iṣfahān, followed by the dispersal of his Turkish mercenaries, led to the collapse of Ziyārid rule in central Iran. Two of his Turkish officers, Tuzun and Bajkam, went to Baghdad, both reaching high position. A large number of the Turkish mercenaries joined ʿImād al-Daula in Shīrāz, whereupon the latter felt that the opportunity had come to incorporate in his growing empire Iṣfahān, scene of his earliest triumphs. The command of this campaign he entrusted to his younger brother Ḥasan (Rukn al-Daula), who had distinguished himself in the battles in Fārs and had then been sent as a hostage to the court of Mardāvīj at the time of his brother's truce with him, but had escaped at the time of Mardāvīj's assassination by bribing his keepers. Rukn al-Daula won an easy victory at Iṣfahān, particularly because Vushmgīr, Mardāvīj's brother, was involved in engagements with the Sāmānids, who were again attacking Ray. Owing to internal discords, however, his triumph over the Ziyārids proved short-lived. Vushmgīr took Iṣfahān three years later and Rukn al-Daula was forced to retreat to Fārs. He set up camp before the gates of Iṣṭakhr and there awaited the moment for renewed action.

Soon after the capture of Iṣfahān ʿImād al-Daula sent his youngest brother Aḥmad (Muʿizz al-Daula) to Kirmān, a province which since 862 had been in the hands of the Ṣaffārids. Shortly before the Būyids established themselves in Shīrāz, Abū ʿAlī b. Ilyās of Khurāsān had driven the Ṣaffārids out of Kirmān (from now on they were confined to Sīstān) and had forced them to recognize Sāmānid supremacy in 928. During ʿImād al-Daula's campaigns in Fārs he had made a vain attempt to take Shīrāz in a surprise attack. After the assassination of Mardāvīj ʿImād al-Daula seized the opportunity of expanding his realms towards the southeast. Rukn al-Daula was already in Iṣfahān; Muʿizz al-Daula however was still waiting for a kingdom. He had distinguished himself during the battle which had decided the struggle for Fārs by his intrepid heroism, and now Kirmān fell swiftly before him until he met resistance from the Qufṣ (Kūfichīs) and Balūchīs. He was then recalled by ʿImād al-Daula and sent to Iṣṭakhr, there to await further calls to duty. Nevertheless his campaign in Kirmān resulted in the permanent recognition of Būyid authority by the Banū Ilyās. The province was not to be annexed directly for several decades.

ʿImād al-Daula had already obtained a foothold in Khūzistān, the valuable province linking Fārs and Iraq by occupying the strategically vital town of Arrajān. The Barīdīs, the virtual rulers of the province, now turned to the Būyids for help against their overlord the caliph in Baghdad, and ʿImād al-Daula saw in this a golden opportunity for renewing his old plans of conquering their territory. He despatched the waiting Mu'izz al-Daula to Ahvāz, and the latter soon ousted the Barīdīs and undertook repeated campaigns against Baghdad, where the 'Abbāsids were involved in their own internal disputes. In 945 he entered the city, and the caliph bestowed the honorary title Mu'izz al-Daula on him and the titles 'Imād al-Daula and Rukn al-Daula on his brothers in Iran. He also became the de facto successor to the senior amīrate (*amīr al-umarā'*). In Mesopotamia he found himself confronted by the Barīdīs, who had retreated to Baṣra and Wāsiṭ, second, by a small but impregnable amīrate in the marsh between the two cities, and, most seriously, by the Ḥamdānids in Mosul who, after a vain attempt to expel the Būyids from Baghdad in 946, retired to northern Mesopotamia, where their opposition was to be overcome thirty years later by 'Aḍud al-Daula. In 947 Mu'izz al-Daula subdued the Barīdīs. The small marshland amīrate alone remained, defying the Būyids for almost a century.

Meanwhile, in central Iran, Rukn al-Daula was favoured by fortune as was his brother in Iraq. Clever politics of alliance enabled him to play off the Ziyārids against the Sāmānids and especially their governors in K͟hurāsān, the Banū Muḥtāj. Unlike Mu'izz al-Daula, Rukn al-Daula did not receive support from S͟hīrāz, and his progress was in consequence more erratic. About 940 he recaptured Iṣfahān and then defeated Vus͟hmgīr and occupied Ray with the help of Ibn Muḥtāj, the governor of K͟hurāsān. However, he suffered a severe setback in the very year in which Mu'izz al-Daula took Baghdad, for in the course of one ambitious campaign Ibn Muḥtāj seized the whole of central Iran. Rukn al-Daula was not able to return to Ray until 335/946–7 when the Būyids had made sure of Iraq. He then achieved the annexation of Ṭabaristān and Gurgān. His defeat of the Musāfirids of Āzarbāijān at Qazvīn settled this disputed frontier though spasmodic struggles against the Ziyārids and the Sāmānids continued for many years.

By the spring of 948 the boundaries of the Būyid Empire in Iran and Mesopotamia were clearly defined, apart from some small and unimportant areas later added to it. Little over a dozen years had sufficed to establish in the greater part of Iran a power which was to exert a decisive influence on the 'Abbāsid caliphate for more than a century. Yet it was neither centrally organized nor provided with a strict order of succession. This lack of centralization it shared with other powers of the period. Thus the Ḥamdānid state in northern Mesopotamia was divided between Mosul and Aleppo, neither centre taking pride of place. The Būyid state had more in common with the Ḥamdānids than they had with their eastern neighbours the Sāmānids. In both the Būyid and the Ḥamdānid state there were always at least two rival rulers whose interests did not coincide, the only bond between them being that of blood. The relations between the joint rulers of the Būyid empire were more complicated than in the case of the Ḥamdānids, whose rule depended on the Aleppo–Mosul axis. From the very beginning Būyid leadership centred on ʿImād al-Daula, the eldest of the three brothers. Rukn al-Daula seems to have had free rein in Iṣfahān and Ray. His coins bear witness to absolute authority in his own territory, his name alone appearing beside that of the caliph. This was true also of coins of his elder brother minted in Fārs, proving that the two regions enjoyed equal and independent importance. The youngest of the three, Muʿizz al-Daula, who was only twenty when he occupied Kirmān, acted under the orders of ʿImād al-Daula, and when he did not fulfil the latter's requirements he was recalled to Fārs and only later placed in command of the Khūzistān campaign. His dependence on his brother entitled him to support from Shīrāz but limited his personal authority in the territories he conquered to that of a governor or representative (*nāʾib*) of ʿImād al-Daula. His coins therefore bear three names – those of the caliph and ʿImād al-Daula as well as his own. In the list of dignitaries which al-Ṣūlī gives for the caliphate of Muttaqī (940–4) in his work *Akhbār al-Rāḍī waʾl-Muttaqī billāh* ʿImād al-Daula appears as governor of Fārs and Khūzistān (he had not yet conquered Iraq) whereas Muʿizz al-Daula, being only his brother's representative in Khūzistān, is not even mentioned. Rukn al-Daula on the other hand, as would be expected, appeared in the list as the independent governor of Iṣfahān (al-Jibāl).[1]

Was Muʿizz al-Daula entirely subordinate to his eldest brother? When they met in Arrajān in 948 ʿImād al-Daula is said by Miskawaih to have declared: "Muʿizz al-Daula and Rukn al-Daula are my brothers by blood, my sons by upbringing and my creatures with regard to their power." He certainly regarded himself as senior amīr, although Muʿizz al-Daula, as ruler of Baghdad, de facto held the title, yet he never claimed to be supreme ruler of the whole Būyid empire. Such a connection of the senior amīrate arose only after his death. It is hardly likely that Muʿizz al-Daula had no freedom of action; for instance, the

[1] Ṣūlī, p. 284.

deposition of al-Muktafī and the installation of al-Muṭī' in 946 was undoubtedly his decision, though it was in accordance with his brother's policy towards the caliphate. The problem of the succession, meanwhile, was to remain in abeyance until the approaching death of the childless 'Imād al-Daula dictated a provisional solution. He named his nephew 'Aḍud al-Daula as his successor to the throne of Shīrāz. By this decision the flaw inherent in the question of succession in the Būyid empire was perpetuated; a time would come when none of the Būyid rulers had sufficient moral and military authority to assume responsibility for the whole empire in time of need.

'Imād al-Daula died in Shīrāz in December 949 at the age of fifty-seven and was buried in a tomb which was to become the mausoleum of the Būyid dynasty (*Turbat Banī Būya*). He left no other monument of artistic interest, for he was essentially a man of action, a brilliant commander in the field who also knew how to win the favours of the great and turn their influence to his own advantage. His economic policy was in character, as well as being typical of his time. In the first place, he evaded the traditional payment of 800,000 *dīnārs* annual tribute to the caliph; in the second place, he filled his treasury with enforced gifts (*muṣādara*) from his wealthier subjects; thirdly, and most characteristically, he confiscated land, giving it in fief to his officers in lieu of payment. The result of this policy was to lighten the financial burden of the state but at the cost of a fatal and long-lasting impoverishment of the country. Soldiers make bad landlords, and by the end of his reign his officers were almost as discontented as the dispossessed peasantry. The date at which this form of payment began is uncertain, though it must have been earlier than the conquest of Iraq, since Mu'izz al-Daula would not have introduced it there without a precedent in Iran. In the early period of 'Imād al-Daula's rule in Fārs the traditional method of payment seems to have been the rule, and this would account for the almost legendary reports related by Miskawaih and later chroniclers of how, after the capture of Shīrāz, he discovered the hidden treasure amassed by his predecessor Yāqūt and used it to pay his army, his own treasury being at the time empty. Such accounts may well contain an element of truth. If so, they must have been regarded as further proof of 'Imād al-Daula's "good fortune"; the meteoric rise of a humble officer of Dailamite origin was bound to make a deep impression on his contemporaries regardless of the means whereby it was achieved. We will have to come back later to the legend that the Būyids were of royal stock. In Ibn al-Athīr this legend is combined with another, according to which the father of the three brothers was told by an astrologer that his sons could expect a great future; they were three branches from each of which further shoots would spring. The legend seems to have arisen *c.* 936–7, at a time when 'Imād al-Daula could still have been hoping to produce an heir and Rukn al-Daula had already taken Iṣfahān. Mu'izz al-Daula was then awaiting further orders in Iṣṭakhr after his misfortune in Kirmān, and he does not in fact appear by name in the legend.

The chroniclers all pass favourable judgement on 'Imād al-Daula. Indeed the fearless and outspoken Ibn al-Athīr declares that he was mild (*ḥalīm*) and clever (*'āqil*) and imputes political skill to him both as a ruler and as an overlord. To a great extent we may concur with his opinion, though it is questionable whether the Būyids could have retained control for more than a century over the territory they conquered had not rulers like Rukn al-Daula and 'Aḍud al-Daula appeared after him to consolidate the Būyid empire internally and externally. 'Imād al-Daula was himself too concerned with founding the empire to be able to mould its future development with long-sighted policies. His despatch of Rukn al-Daula to Iṣfahān was intended to provide the latter with territory of his own rather than to achieve a deliberate rounding-off of the Būyid frontiers, and the failure to regulate the latter's official relationship to the senior amīrate was to have evil consequences later when Rukn al-Daula's son, Fakhr al-Daula, made the first moves that were ultimately to lead to the disintegration of the empire. Similarly his despatch of Mu'izz al-Daula to Kirmān and Khūzistān was primarily designed to protect the eastern and western flanks of his own central province, Fārs. This, rather than his youth, was the reason why Mu'izz al-Daula was given only titular sovereignty in the west. His subsequent conquest of Iraq was carried out without his brother's instructions and was not supported by him, although it was tolerated. The Būyids were in fact never really at home in Baghdad. Mu'izz al-Daula almost returned to Ahvāz "because of its better climate" and his immediate successors never took up permanent residence in Baghdad. 'Imād al-Daula's lack of interest in Baghdad and in the position of senior amīr is for its part borne out by the fact that he never visited it, to be confirmed in office by the caliph, let alone made it his own capital. The most westerly point he ever reached was 'Askar Mukram, north of Ahvāz, which he occupied for a short time in the spring of 935 after the death of Mardāvīj. 'Imād al-Daula may therefore accurately be said to have founded the Būyid Empire, but not to have moulded it into shape.

II. THE BŪYIDS AT THE HEIGHT OF THEIR POWER

Rukn al-Daula and 'Aḍud al-Daula

'Imād al-Daula died just under two years after the conference of Arrajān where questions concerning the future position of Iraq with regard to the other parts of the Būyid empire had been discussed. Some months before, he had resolved the question of his succession by summoning Fanā-Khusrau ('Aḍud al-Daula), the eldest son of Rukn al-Daula, to Shīrāz and nominating him as his successor. Fanā-Khusrau was barely thirteen years old, but was the only Būyid prince of the second generation to have grown up to that age. This decision shows that 'Imād al-Daula had every intention of preserving the two or even threefold division of the empire. He does not appear to have contemplated the alternative solutions of adding Fārs to the territories of Rukn al-Daula or of nominating Mu'izz al-Daula, his viceroy and representative in the west, to the overlordship of Fārs, Khūzistān and Iraq. He does not seem to have attached any great importance to the question of who was to inherit the title of senior amīr, though he must have realized that during the minority of his adoptive heir the latter's father would enjoy the title. Rukn al-Daula was indeed quick to seize the senior amīrate, particularly as his son's position in Shīrāz was at first by no means certain. At the news of his brother's death he promptly went to Shīrāz and spent no less than nine months there, despite the fact that his own province was still being threatened by the Sāmānids. His efforts had the practical result of restoring the unity of the empire. Fanā-Khusrau discovered that he was not the ruler of an independent province but that he occupied in Fārs a position towards Rukn al-Daula similar to that which Mu'izz al-Daula had occupied towards 'Imād al-Daula; in other words, he was his father's viceroy and representative, as is borne out by the existence of coins bearing his name *and* that of his father. No opposition was offered in Baghdad to this reorganization of the empire. Mu'izz al-Daula had sent troops to Shīrāz to ensure 'Aḍud al-Daula's accession, and he accepted his brother's new position without demur, carrying out the *khuṭba* in his name and altering the design of his coinage accordingly. The only change, as far as Iraq and

Khūzistān were concerned, was that Rukn al-Daula was now in 'Imād al-Daula's place. Nevertheless the changeover at Shīrāz was not entirely without friction. Shortly after his accession, the new ruler of Shīrāz was honoured by the caliph with the title "'Aḍud al-Daula". The earliest evidence we have for it occurs on a coin now in the Berlin Numismatic Collection, which bears the date 340/951–2. As he was the Būyid representative in Baghdad, Mu'izz al-Daula would have had the last say in the negotiations with the caliph, who alone could bestow such titles. The question of a suitable title was thus the last opportunity for raising a protest, and sure enough, it soon became evident that the changes in the east did not meet with complete approbation in Baghdad. From the *Rusūm dār al-khilāfa* "The Etiquette of the Court of the Caliph" by Hilāl al-Ṣābi' we learn that it was initially intended that the title "Tāj al-Daula" should be conferred on Fanā-Khusrau, but Mu'izz al-Daula not agreeing with this, the title "'Aḍud al-Daula" was chosen instead. The original choice seemed to Mu'izz al-Daula to anticipate Fanā-Khusrau's claim to the senior amīrate, and he therefore opposed it. Certainly "Tāj" (crown) differed from all the earlier titles borne by the Būyids, which had all been based on the epithets "pillar" ('Imād, Rukn) or "strength" (Mu'izz). Mu'izz al-Daula considered that, in the event of Rukn al-Daula's death, the leadership of the Būyid Empire should pass to him by virtue of that very principle of seniority which Rukn al-Daula had just asserted in his own favour. In fact his own death during Rukn al-Daula's lifetime exempted him from pursuing any such claim. The disagreement over the title did however result in laying the foundations of an increasing estrangement between Baghdad and Ray/Shīrāz, which was to become open after Mu'izz al-Daula's death, and which finally led to the exclusion of the Baghdad branch from the succession. Provisionally, however, the seeds of this controversy were to some extent concealed by the lavish gifts which Rukn al-Daula sent from Shīrāz to Baghdad and which may well have had a direct connection with the vexed question of the title. In the eyes of Miskawaih, who was on the side of his patron 'Aḍud al-Daula, and who was out to justify the latter's claims to suzerainty, there was no doubt whatsoever that Rukn al-Daula had been officially declared senior amīr by the caliph himself.[1] It was to be of decisive importance for the future that through Rukn al-Daula's assumption of the senior amīrate the centre of the empire shifted from Fārs to Northern Iran.

[1] Miskawaih, vol. II, p. 120.

Whereas the Būyid hold on Fārs had long been assured and Būyid rule in Iraq was well on the way towards consolidation, Rukn al-Daula's hold on his own province was still far from secure. Now, as senior amīr and eldest Būyid, he was able to turn his moral claims to support from the rest of the empire into official obligations, and in consequence he was repeatedly assisted in the struggles of the next few decades by military support from Mu'izz al-Daula, who was thereby compelled to forgo pressing tasks of his own, for in Mesopotamia the Ḥamdānids of Mosul were still a source of constant danger to Būyid supremacy. Strangely enough we do not hear of any support from 'Aḍud al-Daula until later, when he fought a diversionary campaign into Khurāsān during the Sāmānid onslaught of 356/966–7. This was his first sign of military activity. Fārs was an oasis of peace; it was not attacked, nor did it start any offensive, and its young ruler could grow accustomed to the tasks of government undisturbed and emerge as the great monarch who was later to play such an important part in the history of Iran.

Rukn al-Daula meanwhile was being constantly assailed from within and without. During his absence in Shīrāz for the enthronement of 'Aḍud al-Daula, the Sāmānid governor of Khurāsān overran Jibāl; it was providential for Rukn al-Daula that the governor's sudden death halted this advance. In 342/955–6 he was forced to sign a humiliating treaty with the Sāmānids, followed by a second the same year. These conflicts also resulted in Khurāsān's virtual independence from the Sāmānids, which was to last twelve years and allow Rukn al-Daula to advance to the Caspian Sea, annex the henceforth tributary states of Ṭabaristān and Gurgān, and receive the recognition of Bīsutūn b. Vushmgīr. In 361/971–2 he was in a position to sign a more favourable treaty with the Sāmānids, though his pride still had to suffer the humiliation of paying tribute.

The end of Rukn al-Daula's chequered career was overshadowed by the insubordination of 'Aḍud al-Daula concerning claims to Iraq. The Mesopotamian Būyids were facing problems similar to those of Rukn al-Daula in northern Iran, although their rule was less urgently threatened than was the case in Ray and Iṣfahān. In Mesopotamia the Ḥamdānids provided this threat, and political changes on its frontiers could easily have had a disastrous effect. Such changes were lurking on the horizon when, in 967, Mu'izz al-Daula died in the midst of a campaign against the Shāhīnids in the Mesopotamian marshlands. Just before this he had taken 'Umān, which could command the Persian

Gulf, with the help of troops from Fārs. This success was however of little consequence for his larger Mesopotamian policies. It was at this time that Saif al-Daula died in Aleppo, and with him the chief bastion against Constantinople disappeared. This was followed by Byzantine advances in Syria. The Būyids were forced to act. The Islamic world would be threatened by dire perils if they failed to take action. But Mu'izz al-Daula's son and successor, 'Izz al-Daula Bakhtiyār, contented himself with half-measures; an army of the faithful was assembled to wage the Holy War but never marched – its presence merely aggravated the state of tension. It should be noted that these events coincided with the invasion of Egypt by the Fāṭimids from North Africa.

Mu'izz al-Daula in Baghdad was too concerned with home problems to pay much attention to the changes taking place in northern Syria. The traditional antagonism between the Turkish and Dailamite elements in his army was even more bitter in Baghdad than in the rest of the empire. For more than a century the majority of the caliph's mercenaries had consisted of Turks, but with the Būyid conquest Dailamites began to usurp their privileges. The Turks, however, resisted them. Indeed Mu'izz al-Daula's chief commander, Sebük-Tegin, was himself a Turk. A further reason for the antagonism was religion. The Dailamī were Shī'ī, the Turks Sunnī. Mu'izz al-Daula at first alienated the Turks, but then succeeded in working out a policy of compromise, his concern for the continuation of which is clearly discernible in the political testament which he left his son and successor 'Izz al-Daula and which is recorded by Miskawaih. He specifically recommended that Sebük-Tegin be retained in office and insisted that Turkish claims should receive fair consideration. Two other urgent problems were also dealt with in this testament. One concerned Būyid policy towards the Ḥamdānids, the other advocated the recognition of Rukn al-Daula's supremacy. The young prince was also enjoined to respect and honour his elder cousin, 'Aḍud al-Daula.

At first 'Izz al-Daula followed his father's advice. He continued the campaign against the Shāhīnids in the marshlands, which had come to a halt with his father's death, but victory eluded him. He ignored what was happening on the Byzantine frontier, declaring this to be a matter for the caliph. Indeed when in 971 the Byzantine army penetrated deep into northern Mesopotamia, he did not even return to Baghdad. The volunteer force assembled to defend the faith now became the nucleus of a personal army in the hands of Sebük-Tegin, who felt himself slighted by ʿIzz al-Daula and increasingly driven to oppose him. In 973 ʿIzz al-Daula, against the advice left by his father, undertook an expedition against Mosul in order to avert an impending financial crisis. The result was a complete fiasco – the Ḥamdānids marched on Baghdad and it appears that Sebük-Tegin was in secret collusion with them, hoping thereby to overthrow the Būyids in Iraq. ʿIzz al-Daula now resolved to confiscate the Turkish fiefs in order to overcome his financial straits, and with this end in view advanced on Khūzistān, where most of these fiefs were situated, at the same time declaring Sebük-Tegin dismissed. The latter rallied the forces loyal to himself while ʿIzz al-Daula moved to Wāsiṭ and there entrenched himself. He scornfully rejected Sebük-Tegin's offer to relinquish Baghdad while retaining southern Iraq, whereupon the rebellious Turk marched on Wāsiṭ and laid siege to it. ʿIzz al-Daula's fate might well have been sealed had not reinforcements come to his aid from the eastern territories of the empire.

The campaign to relieve Wāsiṭ was entrusted to ʿAḍud al-Daula. For nearly twenty years he had ruled in peace. He had helped Muʿizz al-Daula capture ʿUmān and then promptly had marched on Kirmān, which had once again become the scene of internal conflicts between the Banū Ilyās. The province was now for the first time directly annexed by the Būyids and Abu'l-Fawāris (Sharaf al-Daula), the seven-year-old son of ʿAḍud al-Daula, was nominally appointed viceroy. These new conquests to the south and east had made Fārs doubly secure, and ʿAḍud al-Daula could now concentrate his undivided attention on the west. His father's decision to entrust him with the relief of ʿIzz al-Daula could scarcely have been more propitious. Since his cousin's accession, he had been viewing the situation in Iraq with growing concern, for as future senior amīr he had more than a casual interest in preserving and strengthening Būyid rule there. He was certainly already contemplating the removal of the Baghdad line because of its proven inability to govern, and this brought him into conflict with his father, who wished to uphold the Iraq branch of the family at all costs. ʿIzz al-Daula had faithfully carried out his father's policy in this respect and had unquestioningly recognized Rukn al-Daula's senior amīrate, but his attitude towards ʿAḍud al-Daula was more complex. The roots of his ambivalent attitude lay in the problem of the rights of succession to the title, discussed above. ʿAḍud al-Daula had granted asylum to a brother of ʿIzz al-Daula who had instigated a rebellion in Baṣra and had been driven to flight. 'Izz al-Daula responded by obstructing the activities of 'Aḍud al-Daula's agents who were in Baghdad to purchase various requirements for his army and court. 'Aḍud al-Daula thereupon seized the opportunity afforded by Mu'izz al-Daula's death of occupying 'Umān and incorporating it in Fārs. These relatively trifling signs of enmity suddenly assumed a new complexion when 'Izz al-Daula ran into serious difficulties and found himself entirely dependent on help from the east. 'Aḍud al-Daula did indeed comply with his father's order to march on Wāsiṭ but he protracted his journey in the hope that his cousin would in the meantime be overpowered, thus leaving the way open for him. But 'Izz al-Daula held out, and 'Aḍud al-Daula found himself reluctantly obliged to reinstate him in Baghdad. There an army mutiny gave 'Aḍud al-Daula the opportunity for which he had been longing. He deposed his hated and despised cousin and assumed power himself. But this action brought him the strong disapproval of his father, who, invoking a pledge given to Mu'izz al-Daula, categorically forbade the exclusion of the Baghdad line. An offer by his son to pay him tribute for the possession of Iraq was promptly rejected. After numerous exchanges between Baghdad and Ray 'Aḍud al-Daula was constrained to return to Shīrāz empty-handed. The sole achievements of his intervention in Iraq were the overthrow of Sebük-Tegin's uprising (the latter had died during the siege of Wāsiṭ) and the provisional retention of his supremacy in Iraq by naming 'Izz al-Daula as his viceroy and leaving one of his own most trusted officers in Baghdad as commander-in-chief of the army. 'Izz al-Daula, however, was so certain of support in Ray that he immediately reverted to the status quo after 'Aḍud al-Daula's departure. He was equally confident that the other powers in Mesopotamia were behind him. Indeed both the Ḥamdānids and the Shāhīnids in the marshlands realized that they fared better when there was a weak Būyid in Baghdad. 'Aḍud al-Daula had demonstrated by his admittedly few but successful undertakings that he was a ruler who had to be taken seriously.

On his return to Shīrāz, 'Aḍud al-Daula must have realized that his intervention in Baghdad had been over-hasty. His prime aim, no doubt, had been to consolidate Būyid rule in Iraq, but at the same time he had not been able to persuade his father to alter the structure of the empire. Now, after this fiasco, he was actually in danger of losing his claim to the succession to the empire as a whole. As the eldest son, and as ruler of the important province of Fārs, he had hitherto been in a position to assume that one day he would succeed his father as senior amīr, even though this actually had never been formulated in so many words. But now his relationship to his father had become decidedly clouded, and there was a very real threat that the latter might decide the question of the succession in a new and completely unforseen way. It was at this juncture that Abu'l-Fatḥ b. al-'Amīd, Rukn al-Daula's vizier, came to his assistance by acting as mediator and arranging a meeting between the two princes in Iṣfahān in January 976. At this encounter Rukn al-Daula appeared in a conciliatory mood and named his son as his successor on the throne, on two conditions: his rule over Ray and Hamadān would have to be indirect, since Ray would go to his second son, Fakhr al-Daula, and Hamadān would be inherited by his third son, Mu'ayyad al-Daula. Both however would have to recognize 'Aḍud al-Daula as senior amīr. In other words the latter would exert direct rule only over Fārs; no mention was made in this settlement of Iraq, nor did 'Izz al-Daula take part in the meeting. It appears that it was tacitly assumed that no regulations would succeed in altering the relationship of Iraq to the eastern provinces of the empire, and that in any case 'Izz al-Daula would duly recognize 'Aḍud al-Daula's supremacy as he had Rukn al-Daula's. 'Izz al-Daula had already been acquainted with this possibility by his father's will, and Rukn al-Daula was justified in hoping that loyalty would be preserved in Baghdad and that no steps would be taken there to alter its traditional dependence on Ray, or rather on Shīrāz. On this point he was however to be proved mistaken. He died shortly after the meeting and settlement, in September 976, and the disintegration of the empire promptly began. 'Izz al-Daula refused obedience to the new senior amīr, expressing this outwardly by the new titles conferred on himself by the caliph, proceedings described by Hilāl al-Ṣābi'. Moreover the caliph also gave him one of his daughters in marriage and thereby declared his assent to 'Izz al-Daula's policy towards the eastern provinces.

It is scarcely probable that Rukn al-Daula's settlement was the result of his own free and unimpeded decision, stemming as it did from a mistaken estimate of future developments. When, on his accession in 949, he had drawn up his first settlement, the situation in Baghdad had been a very different one, but in the meantime 'Izz al-Daula had given ample proof of his incapacity, and the Baghdad viziers were no longer men like Muhallabī, completely and unconditionally loyal to their master. Either Rukn al-Daula was inadequately informed about the changes in Mesopotamian internal and foreign policy, or it was the obstinacy of old age which led him to uphold on principle the settlement drawn up for Iraq in 949. Certainly these were all factors in play at the time, but none was as decisive as the political duplicity of the vizier Abu'l-Fatḥ b. al-'Amīd, who had succeeded his father in that position some years previously. In 974 he had been sent to accompany 'Aḍud al-Daula to Iraq to quell the revolt against the Būyids, and it was there that he began to play his double game; on the one hand he went to Ray as 'Aḍud al-Daula's emissary with the mission of persuading the senior amīr to agree to the deposition of 'Izz al-Daula, on the other he cultivated close ties with 'Izz al-Daula and with the caliph, and was even toying with the idea of moving permanently to Baghdad and of becoming vizier there. In Ray he succeeded in bringing about the reconciliation between his master and 'Aḍud al-Daula. It was undoubtedly due to his exertions that Iraq retained its formal independence in the new order of accession in accordance with the wishes of the Baghdad Būyid and the traditional policy of Rukn al-Daula. The prompt deposition and murder of the vizier following Rukn al-Daula's death was the foreseeable and virtually inevitable consequence. A new imperial policy was now under way, and it needed new men to carry it out.

With the death of his father, the way to Baghdad was open, and 'Aḍud al-Daula, now senior amīr, began his preparations for the campaign while 'Izz al-Daula assembled his confederates in readiness for the coming attack. In the spring of 977 'Izz al-Daula was defeated in a decisive encounter in Khūzistān and withdrew to Wāsiṭ, where he was able to form a new army. But the trial of strength was not in the end to be resumed, for after long drawn-out negotiations 'Aḍud al-Daula granted him freedom of passage to Syria, the one condition being that he was not to make any alliances with the Ḥamdānids. When, in spite of this condition, he allied himself with Abū Taghlib, his fate was sealed. They were defeated at Sāmarrā in the spring of 978, and 'Izz al-Daula, taken prisoner, was put to death with his cousin's consent. 'Aḍud al-Daula then proceeded to conquer the whole of northern Mesopotamia, leaving only the Ḥamdānids of Aleppo as an independent though tributary power. Abū Taghlib for his part was killed while attempting to re-establish himself in Syria. Some of the sons of 'Izz al-Daula went over to the Fāṭimids and the rest were captured and imprisoned in a fortress in Fārs. Next, 'Aḍud al-Daula cleared Mesopotamia of Bedouin and Kurdish marauding bands, not sparing lives and using the harshest form of coercion. This task completed, he turned to deal with the former allies of 'Izz al-Daula; his campaign in the marshlands was a failure, but he was more successful against the Kurds ruled by Ḥasanwaih. With psychological shrewdness but appalling cruelty he executed some of the sons of Ḥasanwaih, who had died just before, while at the same time investing others with robes of honour and naming one, called Badr, as Ḥasanwaih's successor. Every flicker of resistance in Kurdish territory was meanwhile ruthlessly extinguished. During this period he entrusted his undertakings in the east to his brother Mu'ayyad al-Daula. There Fakhr al-Daula, to whom Ray had been given in the settlement of 976, had joined the side of 'Izz al-Daula, hoping thereby to carve out an independent territory for himself in northern Iran. After the defeat of 'Izz al-Daula, he had allied himself to the Ziyārid prince Qābūs, and had counted on Sāmānid support, but his hopes were disappointed. At Mu'ayyad al-Daula's approach, he and Qābūs withdrew to Khurāsān, but Sāmānid support was not forthcoming. Only after 'Aḍud al-Daula's death were the princes able to return to their domains.

By the summer of 980 the fighting was virtually over: 'Aḍud al-Daula returned to Baghdad from Hamadān, the ruler of an empire far greater in size than all the previous subdivisions of the Būyid empire put together, and stretching from 'Umān to the Caspian Sea and from Kirmān to the north Syrian border. The old home of the empire, Fārs, was under 'Aḍud al-Daula's direct control, as were Iraq and the newly conquered province of Jazīra. The rest was governed by Būyid princes or by other tributary rulers; Iṣfahān, Hamadān, Ray, Ṭabaristān and Gurgān by Mu'ayyad al-Daula, the senior amīr's brother, Kirmān by his eldest son Sharaf al-Daula, 'Umān and Khūzistān by his second son Marzubān (Ṣamṣām al-Daula), and the Kurdish territory by Badr b. Ḥasanwaih. A Būyid viceroy resided at Mosul. Of the former Ḥamdānid state only the area around Aleppo remained as a buffer between the Būyid Empire and Byzantium, but Aleppo had to recognize Būyid overlordship. In the east, the Ṣaffārids of Sīstān too were now 'Aḍud al-Daula's vassals, while Makrān, the coastal strip on the Indian Ocean, was annexed to the empire from Kirmān. At the centre of the empire the Shāhīnids of the marshlands still maintained their position as vassals. 'Aḍud al-Daula's attempt to remove them entirely was in fact his only failure. Iraq had ceased to be an independent province.

Although ʿAḍud al-Daula did not return to Shīrāz again, it continued to be regarded as the actual capital of the empire, and it was from Fārs that were drawn the civil servants who replaced most of ʿIzz al-Daula's civil service in Baghdad. These latter, together with the ʿAlid aristocracy, were banished to Fārs. The supreme judge in Baghdad was also dismissed and exiled, and his successor now resided in Shīrāz and was represented in Baghdad by four deputy judges, a decision which infringed the traditional rights of the caliph severely and which also provides an eloquent illustration of the shift of balance from Baghdad to Shīrāz. No doubt ʿAḍud al-Daula had every intention of himself returning to Shīrāz in due course, as his successors were later to do. The restoration and enlargement of the imperial palace in Baghdad need not suggest that he regarded that city as his principal residence. The main offices of state continued to be located in Shīrāz, and communications with that city were maintained and facilitated by a specially organized postal service, to whose quick and effective functioning the senior amīr attached particular importance.

The reasons for ʿAḍud al-Daula's prolonged sojourn in Baghdad were both political and psychological. His new acquisitions had to be consolidated, and they were threatened by the Sāmānids in the east, by a new menace in the form of the Fāṭimids in the west, and by the non-Islamic power of Byzantium in the north. Against Islamic opponents the ʿAbbāsid caliphate was still a valuable weapon in the hands of whoever controlled it. In the face of the Fāṭimid threat to the caliphate, the presence of a moderate Shīʿī power in Baghdad which at least tolerated it, must have appeared relatively tolerable to the markedly Sunnī Sāmānids and, after initial reluctance, they had accepted the situation and recognized the caliph appointed by the Būyids. To the relief of the Sunnīs in Khurāsān and Transoxiana the restriction was lifted, whereby the khuṭba in Friday religious services was said in the name of a deposed or deceased caliph to avoid the name of a caliph appointed by the Būyids, and a more realistic attitude took its place. It is true that ʿAḍud al-Daula was unable to prevent the Sāmānids from granting asylum to Fakhr al-Daula and his ally, the Ziyārid Qābūs, but Bukhārā temporarily lacked the military strength to be able to undertake an aggressive policy against the Būyids. The caliphate was even more necessary to ʿAḍud al-Daula for the consolidation of his internal position than as a means whereby to influence Sāmānid attitudes. The majority of his subjects were Sunnī and regarded the caliph as their sole rightful ruler despite his political impotence; knowing this, ʿAḍud al-Daula had himself formally declared senior amīr by the caliph himself in a solemn ceremony held in the autumn of 977, shortly after his entry into Baghdad. We shall return in due course to the significance of this action and to ʿAḍud al-Daula's conception of the state, which was one which aimed at the coexistence of the caliphate and the senior amīrate and ultimately at a merging of the two.

The city of Baghdad, seat of the caliph, also provided an impressive centre from which to conduct the foreign policies to which ʿAḍud al-Daula now began to devote his energies. From Baghdad he initiated diplomatic contacts with Cairo and Constantinople, and a series of ambassadorial exchanges took place with both capitals. The subjects discussed in his negotiations with Cairo were their policies towards the Qarmatīs, the "Holy War" against their mutual enemy the Byzantine Empire, and the question of the ʿAlid descent of the Fāṭimids. The Qarmatīs had declared their hostility towards the Fāṭimids before 969 at latest, and quite apart from this they had supported ʿAḍud al-Daula in his war against ʿIzz al-Daula. On the subject of the ʿAlid origin of the Fāṭimids the senior amīr at first made some concessions but later withdrew his recognition because it was interfering with his policy towards the caliphate and was also liable to create unrest amongst his S͟hīʿī subjects. His policy towards Constantinople was much assisted by his possession of a valuable hostage, the anti-emperor Bardas Skleros who, having failed in his pretensions to the throne, had sought refuge in Islamic territory and was now being held in confinement at the Baghdad court. Constantinople wanted his return at all costs, and thus ʿAḍud al-Daula was able to arrange a favourable truce. His dealings with the Fāṭimids and with Constantinople clearly reveal his reluctance to embark on further exploits in the north and west. If he did cherish further ambitions, these were thwarted by the decline of his health. Symptoms of a serious disease – the sources speak of epilepsy – had first manifested themselves during his campaign to subjugate the east. This may well explain the depressions which clouded the last years of his life, when he was at the height of his power. He died in March 983 at the age of fifty-three; his imperial rule had lasted not quite six years.

ʿAḍud al-Daula's greatest achievement was that he continued systematically to further his father's attempts to unify the empire. His success was considerable. Although he did not succeed in building foundations both lasting and stable, the period of his rule must, with that of his father's, be regarded as the golden age of the Būyid empire, not only politically but culturally as well. The seeds sown in Rukn al-Daula's reign were to grow and be brought to fruition by 'Aḍud al-Daula. The period dominated by these two rulers does in fact differ in many respects from that preceding which had seen the founding of the Būyid empire, for 'Imād al-Daula had aimed solely at securing his own rule and that of his brothers, whereas his successors went further and sought to provide the empire with an ideological basis.

In Iran forces were stirring which were in favour of a restoration of the Iranian monarchy. The Ziyārid Mardāvīj, 'Imād al-Daula's most redoubtable opponent, had already attempted to exploit such traditions, and it was a policy towards which the Sāmānids also tended. Unlike 'Imād al-Daula, Mardāvīj had had a precise conception of the ideological basis of his own power. He used to celebrate the Iranian New Year with great pomp, and he introduced Iranian court ceremonial in his own palace. At audiences he would sit on a golden throne, wearing a crown of Khusrau. If we are to give credence to Miskawaih's report, his ambition was to conquer Iraq, with the ancient royal city of Ctesiphon/al-Madā'in, recreate the former Persian Empire and assume the title of Shāhanshāh. We are not told what part the caliph was supposed to play in this empire, but the 'Abbāsids would certainly not have derived much comfort from Mardāvīj's aspirations.

At first the Būyids were unusually reluctant to put forward any royal claims. Miskawaih deplores the lack of a royal genealogy in the case of Rukn al-Daula, saying that "in the eyes of the Dailamites he did not possess the authority of an independent ruler". It was under the influence of Ibn al-'Amīd, his vizier, whose father had been vizier under Mardāvīj, that Rukn al-Daula began to acquire a deeper understanding of the significance and requirements of his position, though perhaps the time he spent as a hostage at the court of Mardāvīj may first have aroused his awareness. Now the ideal of a restored Persian monarchy became accepted amongst the Būyids too. Our first record is a commemorative silver medal minted in Ray in 351/962, possibly to celebrate the conquest of Ṭabaristān which occurred that year. On it the senior amīr is depicted as a Persian Emperor wearing a crown; the inscription is in Pahlavī and reads: "May the glory of the King of Kings increase".[1] Indispensable for the support of this claim was the compilation of a genealogy tracing the Būyids back to the Sāsānids, though whether any

[1] Miles, "Portrait", p. 283.

attempt was made in this connection under Rukn al-Daula is uncertain. The frequent choice of Iranian names in the second Būyid generation is however quite striking. The founder of the family bore beside the Iranian name 'Būya' the pseudo-Arab name (or *kunya*) Abū Shujā'. Of the grandfather's names only Fanā-Khusrau is recorded. This suggests that the father was the first to be converted to Islam, and would account for his choice of purely Islamic names for his sons. He behaved in a manner typical of a new convert by calling them 'Alī ('Imād al-Daula), Ḥasan (Rukn al-Daula) and Aḥmad (Mu'izz al-Daula). Rukn al-Daula however returned to Iranian tradition by naming his eldest son ('Aḍud al-Daula) Fanā-Khusrau, and another son Khusrau Fīrūz. The name Fanā-Khusrau is identical with that of the grandfather, who also appears in the fictitious Būyid genealogy which goes back to Bahrām Gūr and was probably only drawn up in its entirety at the court of 'Aḍud al-Daula. We first encounter the complete genealogy in al-Ṣābi''s *Kitāb al-tājī*, a history of the Būyid dynasty composed in Baghdad in 980 at the command of 'Aḍud al-Daula. Although its fictitious character was recognized even by contemporaries, it was to be taken over by numerous authors. Moreover, the fact that it was fictitious led to countless different versions; indeed De Slane refers to no less than seventeen in his translation of Ibn Khallikān's biographical work.[1] A late chronicle, that of Ibn Shiḥna (late 14th century) traces the genealogy as far back as Ardashīr b. Bābak. The likelihood that the provisionally complete version was drawn up at the court of 'Aḍud al-Daula is borne out by the threefold appearance in it of the name Shīrdil, which was the name of 'Aḍud al-Daula's eldest son, who was born *c.* 960 and later became known as Sharaf al-Daula. This detail provides us with the earliest date acceptable for the completion of the genealogy. Shīrdil was certainly regarded as the successor to the crown, a fact which also explains his hostility towards Ṣamṣām al-Daula, who took over the government in Baghdad after 'Aḍud al-Daula's death.

The Būyid claim to kingship runs parallel with that to descent from the Sāsānids. In this respect too, 'Aḍud al-Daula deliberately followed his father's policy both by arranging "suitable" marriages and by assuming fitting titles. Probably as early as his march on Iraq he had already married a daughter of the Dailamite king Manādhar, who may have been descended from the Banū Justān line which had ruled Dailam in the 9th century. As we have already seen, he demanded the title Tāj

[1] Ibn Khallikān, vol. 1, p. 157, note 1.

al-Daula from the caliph immediately after his accession in Shīrāz. When this attempt was thwarted by Mu'izz al-Daula, he continued his policy with greater circumspection but no less determination. On a coin dated 350/961–2 and minted in Shīrāz, he called himself "the just amīr", although names and epithets were till then rarely to be found on coins. In fact the epithet "just" harks back to one which had been the traditional prerogative of Persian kings, and the "mirrors of princes" are full of anecdotes illustrating the "justice" of these monarchs of a former age. It is surely no coincidence that this type of literature, with its typical retrospective emphasis on former Persian kings, now became popular again. Three years after the minting of the coin just referred to, the celebrated Mutanabbī visited the court at Shīrāz and in a *qaṣīda* addressed the amīr as "King of Kings". Although this may partly be explained by his use of poetic hyperbole and by his recourse to flattery in the hope of reward, it nevertheless does reflect the amīr's conception of his own ambitions and position. But a few years were to elapse before he took up arms in order to wage a series of campaigns which were to lead him to Baghdad itself. After his conquest of Kirmān, he commanded the minting of a coin which bore an exact resemblance both in design and inscription to the commemorative medal struck by his father in 351/962. After the capture of 'Umān he went one stage further. The title "Shāhanshāh" now made its first appearance in an inscription. Finally, a coin (not a medal) was minted in 'Umān in 365/975–6 bearing the title "*al-malik al-'ādil*". After his assumption of the senior amīrate in Baghdad nothing prevented him from including this title on coins minted in Ray and Iraq as well. When his series of conquests came to an end in 980, he was in a position to crown his achievements with the official assumption of the title "Shāhanshāh", which was henceforth placed on coins.

This act was preceded at the end of 977 by his solemn investiture in the palace of the caliph, a remarkable ceremony of which al-Ṣābi' gives a detailed description and background. It places the caliph's attitude in a new light. 'Aḍud al-Daula's exaggerated idea of his own importance had led him to insist on two conditions for his reception at the court of the caliph: he demanded the privilege of riding into the audience chamber on horseback, and the erection of a curtain to prevent any of his followers from witnessing the moment when he kissed the ground at the caliph's feet, for fear lest this might lessen the esteem which he had so painstakingly built up for himself in Fārs. The caliph however agreed to neither request. On the contrary, he ordered the erection of a barrier at the entrance of the audience chamber, thereby forcing the senior amīr to dismount and enter it on foot – only to discover the complete absence of the curtain as well. Nevertheless ʻAḍud al-Daula observed all the prescribed ceremonial and prostrated himself before the caliph, giving one of his followers, who asked if then the caliph were God before whom alone one kneels, the quick-witted and appropriate reply: "Not God, but God's shadow on earth." The investiture then took its customary course. After the greeting and a brief dialogue, the caliph pronounced the words of investiture: "It has pleased me to transfer to you the affairs and government of the subjects both in the East and in the West of the earth, excepting my own private possessions, my wealth and my palace. Rule them, begging God to grant you success." At the request of the senior amīr this formula was repeated before witnesses drawn from both parties. ʻAḍud al-Daula then received the robes of honour, the diadem, and two banners, whereupon the deed of nomination was read out. This brought the investiture itself to its traditional close. But the senior amīr had requested a special favour to complete the ceremony. When the diadem was placed upon his head, the court officials entrusted with the investiture itself allowed one of his two locks of hair, adorned with a jewel, to hang loose. At the conclusion of the ceremony, according to the agreed plan, the caliph with his own hand fastened the lock of hair beneath the diadem. This was intended to give the impression that he had actually been crowned by the caliph himself, and in order to ensure that all would go well, he had taken two of his most high-ranking officials with him into the chamber where the robes of honour were put on, apparently to make quite sure that the lock of hair was not fastened beneath the diadem. Presumably this detail was a Persian coronation ceremony unknown at the caliph's court, and the latter had agreed to it unaware of the full significance of what he would be called upon to do. But for ʻAḍud al-Daula this small detail had very great importance indeed; before the eyes of his companions and therefore in a sense of his subjects too, he had been crowned king by the caliph himself. The title which he had demanded as early as 950, shortly after his accession in Shīrāz – Tāj al-Daula ("The Crown of the Empire") – only becomes fully comprehensible in the light of this ceremony. It too was now granted to him, albeit in the altered version "Tāj al-Milla", to avoid the repetition of "Daula".

'Aḍud al-Daula's coronation ceremony provides the clue to his conception of the monarchy. It is true that the concept of monarchy had been in essence superseded by Islam, but in practice this was not quite the case, particularly in Iran. There dates were still reckoned by the era of Yazdgard, the feast of Naurūz was still being celebrated, and numerous fire temples were still serving the Zoroastrian cult, and although countless Persians had already embraced Islam, the concept of an Iranian monarchy still had a meaning. It provided the Būyids with a welcome instrument when they came to consolidate their rule both at home and abroad, it increased the respect in which they were held by the Dailamite leaders who had frequently flouted their authority in the past, and it coincided with the "Persian Renaissance" which in northern Iran was just beginning to make itself felt in the domain of literature. Even the Sāmānids, though strict Sunnīs, displayed considerable reverence for the Iranian royal past, especially when it came to genealogies. But 'Aḍud al-Daula went one step further by obtaining the approval of the caliph, albeit by somewhat devious means, and by claiming descent from the great kings of the past. He was a devout Muslim, and was undoubtedly convinced that the coexistence of caliphate and monarchy would provide a solution for the political and religious problems of the period. Even before his first campaign he must have sensed that he had a vocation; this is something which appears again and again in his surviving official correspondence. It may serve as proof that the ideals which he personified were more than the mere expression of cynical political calculation. In this he was quite unlike Mardāvīj the "unbeliever", who was the victim of his own megalomania and met a miserable death at the hands of discontented Turkish slaves. Of course the caliph was unlikely to be much impressed by his imperial vocation and the new order it entailed. The senior amīr himself came to realize this only too bitterly, in other words, the investiture meant little to the caliph but to 'Aḍud al-Daula its significance was profound and all-important. It led him to reward the caliph with the restitution of all his former rights and privileges, with ostentatious gifts and with the renovation of his palace, although he had no intention of thereby suggesting that he regarded himself as in any way subservient. His idea was a division of power between the caliphate and the monarchy, equivalent to the mediaeval European theories of church and empire. His dismissal of the chief judge might therefore appear as an incomprehensible negation of his ideas; more probably it was a lapse, understandable when one considers how unprecedented his ideas were in Islamic history. Moreover the judge in question had shown that he was likely to be far from sympathetic to the new order contemplated by 'Aḍud al-Daula. This new conception of the division of power presupposed a mutual exchange of tokens of respect. Thus when 'Aḍud al-Daula returned to Baghdad from his eastern campaign in 980 he allowed himself to be conducted into the city by the caliph, an event unprecedented in the history of the senior amīrate. Once again the caliph seems to have failed to appreciate the significance of the ceremony in which he was taking part. It did however lead the senior amīr to conceive a plan which, especially in the eyes of his contemporaries, must have seemed even more unprecedented. He now aspired to unite the two powers in the person of the son to be born of a marriage between his own daughter and the caliph. The marriage took place in the latter half of 980, but the caliph did not consummate it. Similar marriages had often occurred previously, and on this occasion too the caliph declined to see anything more in it than a polite formality to which he ought to consent but which he could always interpret as condescension on his part towards the senior amīr. Thus in the khuṭba held on the occasion of this marriage, the amīr was reminded that the Būyid dynasty was being done a signal honour by being thus permitted to ally itself with the Hāshimid house in wedlock. The caliph's cunning thus came to his rescue; from this point on, relations between him and 'Aḍud al-Daula began to grow decidedly cooler. All that remained of the latter's idea of the division of power were the ceremonials he had introduced.

The attempt, initiated by Rukn al-Daula and continued by 'Aḍud al-Daula, to revive the Persian monarchy by reconciling it with the Islamic form of government was ultimately bound to fail. 'Aḍud al-Daula is not remembered as a Persian monarch. His name was to go down in history rather as a clever, energetic and strong ruler. The title "Shāhanshāh" was not to become generally accepted (although the Saljuqs also at first assumed it); instead the wielder of political power was to bear the title "Sulṭān". It is significant that this title was originally borne by the caliphs; its assumption by the real holder of political authority reveals the extent to which the caliphs had by now delegated theirs. In practice this process had begun long before the advent of the Būyids, from the moment when independent states had arisen in the east and west. The prime concern of the Būyids and above all of 'Aḍud al-Daula was to regulate an area in which the caliph had exerted direct influence until their rise to power. Indeed ʿAḍud al-Daula may even be said to have striven to enhance the authority of the caliphate after a phase during which it had been divested of power. It was an enterprise which presupposed the co-operation of the caliph and the complete supremacy of Būyid power. The first was never really forthcoming, and the duration of the second was too short to provide even a temporary answer to a problem which was at bottom insoluble. ʿAḍud al-Daula's proposal to bring both parties together in a personal union was a daring one, but it overlooked certain essential and theoretically influential doctrines concerning the caliphate, since the Sunnī authorities still regarded the office as elective, not hereditary.

In many areas ʿAḍud al-Daula's achievements were great. Nevertheless we ought not to forget those of his father, Rukn al-Daula. Ibn al-Athīr praises the latter as a just ruler, while the verdict of Miskawaih is rather less favourable, since he is apparently at pains to emphasize the achievements of his own patron, the vizier Abu'l-Faḍl b. al-ʿAmīd, who had served Rukn al-Daula in that capacity from 329/940 to 360/970. At home Rukn al-Daula was faced with two major problems: how to pay the army and how to ward off the incursions of the semi-nomadic Kurds, which were constantly disrupting communications and agriculture not only in their own mountainous area but all over Jibāl. He could not with any confidence embark on a full-scale campaign against them since the Ḥasanwaihids, a Kurdish dynasty, had exploited the confused situation in western Iran in the middle of the 10th century and had built up considerable strength of their own in the area around Hamadān. Rukn al-Daula was compelled to pursue a lenient policy in this direction because he was more concerned with the situation along his eastern frontier. Moreover the Kurds commanded the important route between the Iran plateau and Mesopotamia through which armies from Baghdad would have to pass in order to come to Rukn al-Daula's assistance. Only when the situation on the eastern frontier had been to some extent regulated could he proceed to firmer measures against the Kurds. In 970 he entrusted his vizier with a campaign against Hamadān, but the latter's death brought it to a halt and a compromise solution had to be found. Meanwhile the Ḥasanwaihids continued to increase their power; they were still to have an important rôle to play.

Miskawaih criticized Rukn al-Daula's Kurdish policy and also his liberality towards his troops, though we should not forget that he was more dependent on their loyalty than were the other Būyids. In this respect matters improved once he had consolidated his power, an improvement which the historian naturally ascribes to his own patron Ibn al-ʿAmīd. His complaint that Rukn al-Daula did not concern himself sufficiently with the improvement of the country's economy does not seem to be entirely justified. Information provided by the *Tārīkh-i Qum* indicates that his initially severe taxation policy gradually became more lenient. We know of an inquiry sent by Rukn al-Daula to Baghdad, in which he requested a description of that city and details of the number of the baths it contained (presumably so as to gauge the size of its population?). It seems likely that he wanted to know about the splendours of Baghdad, which he never visited, in order to reflect something of them in Ray or Iṣfahān. He favoured Qum because its inhabitants were Shīʿī, but it was Iṣfahān that he selected as his provisional capital. As late as *c.* 344/955–6, long after the capture of Ray, the senior amīr's harem and treasury were still located in Iṣfahān, and later, when Ray was threatened, the harem was sent back there. The city contained a palace which had originally belonged to the Dulafids of Karaj and had been used by Mardāvīj and then possibly by the Būyids. The extension of the city attributed to Rukn al-Daula was probably begun in 935, shortly after its capture, as was the construction of its new wall, 21,000 paces in circumference, vestiges of which were visible until a few years ago. He had already made the city his residence, and his eldest son Fanā-Khusrau (ʿAḍud al-Daula) was born there the following year. From 938 to 940 he was however forced to abandon the city to the Ziyārids once again. From 940 onwards he was too much involved in endless wars against the Sāmānids to be able to devote much attention to the city. When the court moved to Ray, the young Mu'ayyad al-Daula continued to reside at Iṣfahān as a viceroy, a position he was to hold until his father's death. He had received the *laqab* in 355/965 at the age of fifteen. He too continued to rebuild and beautify the city; indeed most of its extension may probably be attributed to him. He enlarged the palace (*Dār al-imāra*) and it was there that Rukn al-Daula and ʿAḍud al-Daula resided during their celebrated conference to regulate the succession to the empire in the spring of 976. The extent to which Rukn al-Daula was concerned with the economic welfare of his subjects is revealed by the measures he undertook to improve Shīrāz when he spent nine months there in 949 to induct ʿAḍud al-Daula into his new office. He laid out the canal called Ruknābād after him, which was still to be seen in Ibn Baṭṭūta's day; it was fed by a spring located near Sa'dī's grave. One of his earliest viziers, Abū 'Abd-Allāh a-Qummī (d. 328/939–40), was responsible for the restoration of the bridge at Īdhaj in Khūzistān, which was particularly well-known in the Middle Ages. The work was carried out by masons from Iṣfahān at a cost, it is said, of 350,000 dinars.[1]

'Aḍud al-Daula's achievements in all these fields were however very much greater. Its geographical position preserved the province of Fārs intact during all the strife and confusion of the period, and its ruler was able to devote almost twenty years of peace to the improvement of it and above all its capital, since he was more or less spared the expense of military undertakings. Shīrāz, which had superseded the old royal city of Iṣṭakhr after the Islamic conquest, now began to flourish. Rukn al-Daula's canal had marked the beginning of this process, for 'Imād al-Daula does not seem to have made any improvements but simply to have lived in the governor's palace in which, according to legend, he had found the treasure amassed by Ya'qūb and the Ṣaffārids. It was probably in this palace that the enthronement of 'Aḍud al-Daula took place, but the building was soon to prove too humble for a man of his ambition. The geographer Muqaddasī gives an enthusiastic account of the magnificent edifice which now replaced it.[2] It was two storeys high and contained no less than 360 rooms together with a library. At great expense 'Aḍud al-Daula also built a citadel, but he did not see fit to fortify the city itself. This was not to be undertaken until the last years of the Būyid period, when Shīrāz was threatened by the Saljuqs. Soon the city was so prosperous that its confines began to prove too narrow. The amīr thereupon founded a new quarter, calling it Fanā-Khusrau-Gird. It was situated on a canal, half a farsang to the east or southeast of the old city. The ceremonial entry of the amīr to mark its completion, on 27 March 965, was commemorated by an annual celebration. The author of the *Nuzhat al-qulūb*, a late source, states that it was originally intended as a camp for the amīr's troops and was situated to the west, not to the east of the city. Perhaps he was confusing two separate places both founded by 'Aḍud al-Daula, since this camp may well have been on the site of the later Daulatābād, to the west of Shīrāz.

The citadel in Shīrāz and a reservoir in the castle at Iṣṭakhr appear to have been 'Aḍud al-Daula's only military constructions, though we might also include the city wall of Medina, built to discourage the

[1] Schwarz, vol. IV, p. 339 (Yāqūt). [2] *Ibid.*, vol. II, pp. 45–51.

Qarmatīs, before whose appearance there had been no reason to fortify the city; for this wall the sources give the date 360/970–1. All the other buildings erected by him were designed for peaceful uses, either trade, agriculture, religion, or his own glory. First and foremost we should mention the dam situated twenty miles northeast of Shīrāz, which halted the waters of the river Kūr, which had previously flowed into a salt lake some thirty miles away, and diverted them for agricultural use. After Shīrāz the town most favoured by ʻAḍud al-Daula was Fīrūzābād, which may have been the centre of royal estates. Here he often resided, and he reconstructed it entirely, replacing its old name Gūr by its present one because, so Muqaddasī tells us, "Gūr" also means "grave" and was felt to be a bad omen.

The most important port on the Persian Gulf at this time was Sīrāf, west of Lār, though its prosperity was brought to an end by a disastrous earthquake in 977, after which Baṣra seems to have taken its place. It is said to have been rebuilt in the late Būyid period; if so, the Būyid responsible must have ruled Fārs but not Baṣra, and the most likely would therefore be the energetic Abū Kālījār who ruled Fārs from 1027 to 1044, but exerted only indirect influence on Baṣra itself. Long before the conquest of Iraq, ʻAḍud al-Daula had taken at least the coastal areas of the ʻUmān peninsula, which were of paramount importance for shipping. At the same time he also attached great importance to the land links between Shīrāz and Mesopotamia, and in particular the town of Kāzarūn, where he built a settlement for traders which, according to Muqaddasī, brought in an annual revenue of 10,000 *dirhams*.

An approximate picture of the structure of Fārs in the early Būyid period may be reconstructed: Iṣṭakhr and Fasā were military bases on its northern and eastern flanks, Shīrāz performed the functions of administrative capital and principal residence of the ruler, Fīrūzābād served as his alternative residence, while Kāzarūn's importance was primarily that of a commercial centre. In the west, Arrajān occupied a special position. Rukn al-Daula had insisted on keeping it in his personal possession and the revenue from it must have been considerable, since Muqaddasī attributes the following words to ʻAḍud al-Daula: "I want Mesopotamia for the sake of its name, but I want Arrajān for its revenue." Moreover Arrajān may be considered as a kind of central residence of the senior amīr at least until Rukn al-Daula's death, a fact borne out by the peculiar structure of the Būyid empire, by surviving reports of the city, and by its geographical position. Rukn al-Daula, it is true, seldom visited it, but his vizier, the celebrated Ibn al-ʿAmīd, went there frequently, and it was the scene, for instance, of his encounter with Mutanabbī, who was on his way to Shīrāz. Finally, its geographical position in the very centre of the empire was in its favour. If a circle about five hundred miles in diameter were drawn with Arrajān as its centre, it would embrace Baghdad in the west, the Caspian coast in the north, and Kirmān in the east. ʿAḍud al-Daula did not however give the city much concern. Before becoming senior amīr he had no influence there, and his interests subsequently centred mainly on Baghdad.

What has so far been said concerning ʿAḍud al-Daula's building activity and his efforts to develop cities, trade and communications, referred only to the province of Fārs and to the period between 950 and 968. Localities named Tājābād, if connected with him at all, point to the period after 977, for it was only then that the senior amīr received the title Tāj al-Milla; they may therefore be said to provide some evidence that even when he was in Baghdad, he had the welfare of his home province of Fārs at heart. It is hardly surprising that his building activities extended to the areas he acquired after 968. There is however not so much evidence for Kirmān, a report by Muqaddasī being all we have. According to this report, he erected a minaret in Sīrjān (the ruins of which lie five miles to the east of Saʿīdābād), the summit of which was decorated with ornamental woodwork, probably in the form of a balustrade and canopy for the muezzin. He also built a palace there which appears to have been intended for his viceroy, who was his son Abu'l-Fawāris Shīrdil (Sharaf al-Daula). Sīrjān was more accessible from Shīrāz than the older provincial capital of Bardasīr (present-day Kirmān city), which until then had been the residence of the Banū Ilyās, who had accepted Būyid overlordship. In the later Būyid period the viceroys were to return to Bardasīr, and Sīrjān then diminished in importance.

The constructions undertaken by ʿAḍud al-Daula in Iraq (excluding Baghdad) and Khūzistān were concerned primarily with the development of trade and communications. Khūzistān was important as a link between Fārs and Iraq, and Marzubān, who was regarded as the heir to the throne, had been appointed as its governor. Since ʿAḍud al-Daula was particularly eager to establish quick postal services between Baghdad and Shīrāz, he concentrated on improving the roads, though he did not neglect the waterways. An obstacle to communications by ship was the fact that it was necessary to navigate the dangerous route through the Persian Gulf in order to get from the Euphrates and Tigris to the Kārūn in Khūzistān. The senior amīr therefore constructed a canal linking the Shaṭṭ al-ʿArab with the Kārūn, which considerably lessened both distance and dangers. On the land route the bridge over the Hinduwān at Ahvāz was restored. At Ahvāz he also ordered the erection of a magnificently decorated mosque, as Muqaddasī reports. The fact that after 968 he turned his attention to religious edifices may well be connected with his new conception of his task as representative of a restored Persian monarchy. The deliberate fostering of Islam was a component part of his new conception, for only thereby could the monarchy be established on a legitimate basis. As has already been indicated, his Iraq campaign seemed in his eyes to be justified by the strong sense he had of his own religious mission. His erection of religious edifices was likewise intended to justify his occupation of the new territories in the eyes of the caliphate. In Baghdad however he did not build any mosques. According to his theories of the division of power, this was the sole prerogative and responsibility of the caliph himself. It is known that during the Būyid period the caliphs, despite their financial difficulties, were able to build mosques. ʿAḍud al-Daula meanwhile built himself a magnificent imperial palace (*Dār al-mamlaka*) in Baghdad, and drew up grandiose plans for the reconstruction of the city itself, providing house-owners – a strangely modern note – with loans for this purpose. Nevertheless his plans were never to come to full fruition in the few years of his rule in Baghdad, and the city remained in a state of partial decay, covering an area no larger than that of Baṣra.

Two trends may be observed in ʿAḍud al-Daula's activities as a builder. Dams, bridges and bazaars served a practical purpose and were designed to bring in revenue, while his other undertakings, mosques included, served an ideological purpose. Indeed even his most practical constructions had an ideological undertone, and by appearing worthy of past rulers, seemed to bear out his claim to Sāsānian descent and to prove his ability to restore the grandeur of the Persian monarchy. This may savour of personal ambition, and indeed all contemporary observers concur in their verdict that, while undoubtedly a great ruler, ʿAḍud al-Daula was also inordinately vain.

The efforts of Rukn al-Daula and ʿAḍud al-Daula to restore the

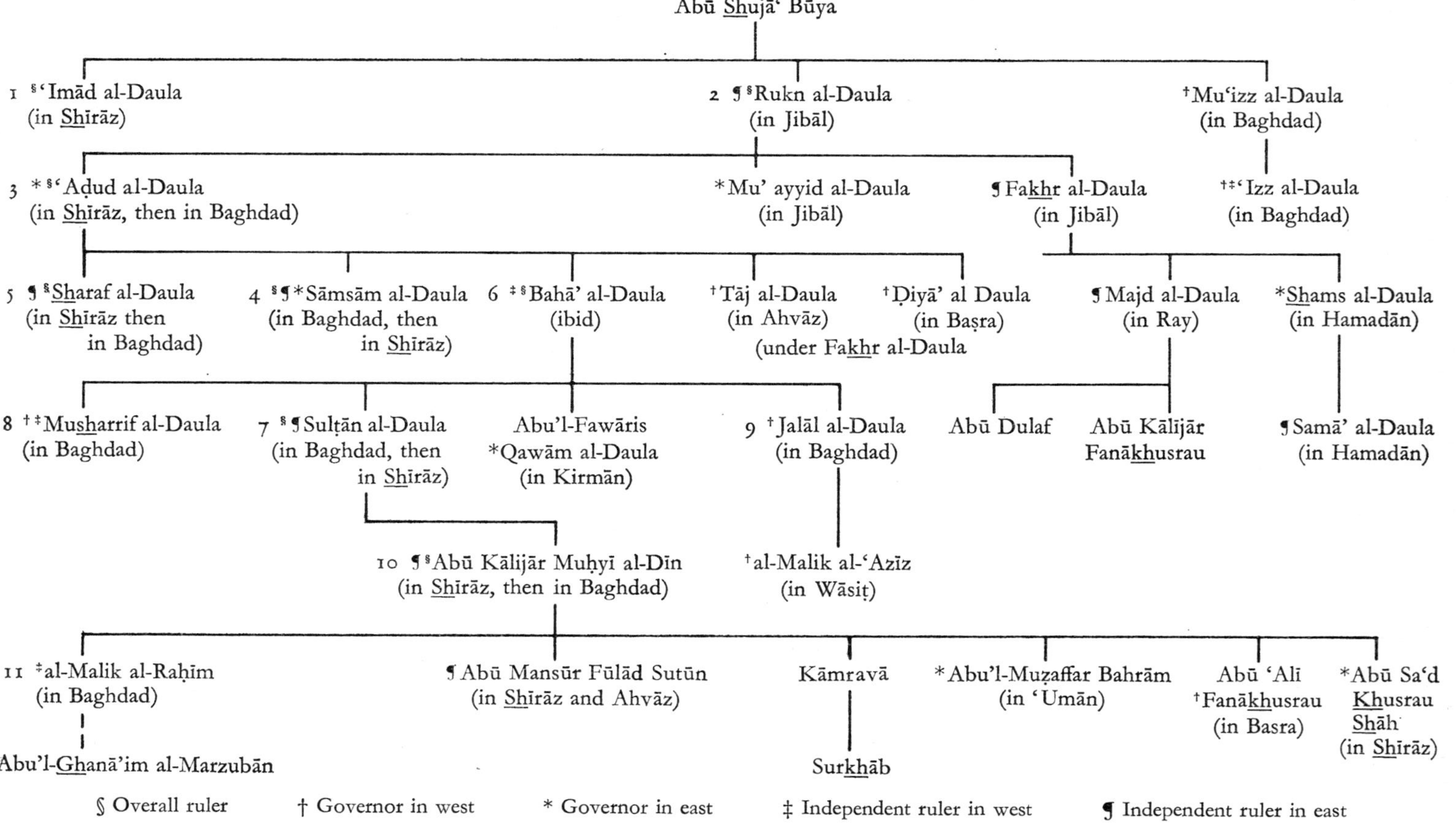
Abū Shujā‘ Būya
1 §‘Imād al-Daula (in Shīrāz)
2 ¶§Rukn al-Daula (in Jibāl)
†Mu‘izz al-Daula (in Baghdad)
3 *§‘Aḍud al-Daula (in Shīrāz, then in Baghdad)
*Mu’ ayyid al-Daula (in Jibāl)
¶Fakhr al-Daula (in Jibāl)
†‡‘Izz al-Daula (in Baghdad)
5 ¶§Sharaf al-Daula (in Shīrāz then in Baghdad)
4 §¶*Sāmsām al-Daula (in Baghdad, then in Shīrāz)
6 ‡§Bahā’ al-Daula (ibid)
†Tāj al-Daula (in Ahvāz)
†Ḍiyā’ al Daula (in Baṣra)
(under Fakhr al-Daula
¶Majd al-Daula (in Ray)
*Shams al-Daula (in Hamadān)
8 †‡Musharrif al-Daula (in Baghdad)
7 §¶Sulṭān al-Daula (in Baghdad, then in Shīrāz)
Abu’l-Fawāris *Qawām al-Daula (in Kirmān)
9 †Jalāl al-Daula (in Baghdad)
Abū Dulaf
Abū Kālījār Fanākhusrau
¶Samā’ al-Daula (in Hamadān)
10 ¶§Abū Kālījār Muḥyī al-Dīn (in Shīrāz, then in Baghdad)
†al-Malik al-‘Azīz (in Wāsiṭ)
11 ‡al-Malik al-Raḥīm (in Baghdad)
Abu’l-Ghanā’im al-Marzubān
¶Abū Mansūr Fūlād Sutūn (in Shīrāz and Ahvāz)
Kāmravā
Surkhāb
*Abu’l-Muẓaffar Bahrām (in ‘Umān)
Abū ‘Alī †Fanākhusrau (in Basra)
*Abū Sa‘d Khusrau Shāh (in Shīrāz)
§ Overall ruler
† Governor in west
* Governor in east
‡ Independent ruler in west
¶ Independent ruler in east

monarchy, and ʿAḍud al-Daula's achievements in both the political and the administrative fields were accompanied by marked emphasis on cultural affairs. Although the Sāmānids had provided a precedent of which the Būyids may have been aware, there can be no doubt that the great flowering of culture which coincided with the apogee of the Būyid empire bore at its outset the imprint of the Arabic–Islamic tradition. At the same time Bukhārā in the northeast was to become the focal point for a synthesis of Islamic and Persian culture, but such a synthesis did not even suggest itself as a remote possibility during the early Būyid period, a fact which may in turn be attributed to various factors, the most decisive being that central and southern Iran had been more strongly subjected to Arab influences than the northeast.

It is open to question whether ʿImād al-Daula and Rukn al-Daula were able to read and write, and their knowledge of Arabic was doubtless limited to the strictly necessary. Yet ʿAḍud al-Daula was to make a name for himself in Arabic literature as a poet and indeed as a stylist of versatility. The vizier Abu'l-Faḍl b. al-ʿAmīd must be given most of the credit for this remarkable achievement. His father had served the Ziyārid Mardāvīj in like capacity and ʿImād al-Daula first became acquainted with him just after he had been nominated as governor of Karaj. Rukn al-Daula rewarded the father's services by appointing the son, Abu'l-Faḍl, as his vizier in 328/939–40. He was to retain this position for thirty years, until his death. Miskawaih provided a somewhat uncritical but nonetheless fitting epitaph on his cultural achievements in his chronicle *Tajārib al-umam*, where he calls him the finest stylist (*kātib*) of his age. Ibn al-ʿAmīd excelled in every subject; indeed he was famous as a designer of siege-machines and in this capacity took part in several military campaigns. In 970 he was entrusted with the direction of the war against the Kurdish leader Ḥasanwaih, dying in the same year before he could bring it to a decisive conclusion. Innumerable poets frequented the court of this enlightened and cultured vizier, singing his praises and hoping for reward. In his anthology *Yatīmat al-dahr*, Thaʿālibī enumerates eleven poets in Ibn al-ʿAmīd's circle, amongst whom is the great Mutanabbī himself, who had deserted the court of Kāfūr for the empire of the Būyids.[1] Another figure at the vizier's court was the philologist Abū Bishr al-Fārisī, who will be referred to later in connection with ʿAḍud al-Daula. It was certainly thanks to the vizier's influence and patronage that scholars

[1] Thaʿālibī, vol. II, pp. 4–8.

and poets were assigned positions of responsibility exceeding their qualifications by Rukn al-Daula. His influence on ʿAḍud al-Daula was to be of paramount importance, as the latter himself conceded by his habit of calling him by the titles *ustād* ("teacher") and *ra'īs* ("master"). It may be possible that Ibn al-ʿAmīd acted officially or unofficially as the young ruler's vizier or adviser in Shīrāz. Only later do the chroniclers mention that he had viziers of his own.

Although ʿAḍud al-Daula was himself the author of occasional verse, he does not appear to have attached much importance to the presence of eulogists at his court at least during the earlier part of his career. Thaʿālibī mentions a great many in connection with the viziers, but none in his section on ʿAḍud al-Daula. The ruler was, however, a great patron of literary men as well as scholars. The full range of his patronage was perhaps even more in evidence in Baghdad than in Shīrāz. Here he founded the famous hospital which was called after him and which was to remain the most exemplary of its kind until the Mongol period. To it were called the most eminent and the most successful doctors of the day, so that it soon became an academy of medicine in which research, teaching and treatment were combined. Meanwhile he also sought out the company of the city's foremost theologians, writers and scientists, and his palace became the meeting-place of learned society.

The Būyids had originally belonged to the Zaidiyya, which was a moderate Shīʿī movement. It seems likely that they only decided to embrace Islam definitely when they first began to appear on the political scene, or perhaps just before. In the *Kitāb al-tājī* this decision is admittedly dated as far back as the period around 865. The information provided by this work must however be accepted with some caution, for implicit in it is ʿAḍud al-Daula's attempt to enhance the glory of his dynasty. It seemed preferable to him to claim that his immediate ancestors were Zaidites than admit that they were pagans. His attitude to the caliphate too is more easily explained if we accept that he had a Zaidite rather than a Twelver Shīa background. At first, however, religious commitment was no great concern of the Būyids and their attitude towards religious and confessional problems was one of indifference, in which practical considerations alone seem to have played a part. The Būyid army was made up of Dailamites and Gīlites (together with Turks and Kurds), and the former, if Muslim at all, were Zaidites, while the latter were Sunnī. Fārs too was, as we have already said, predominantly Sunnī. Thus opposition to the Būyids could easily take the form of religious loyalty to the ʿAbbāsid caliphate. This seems to have been the only reason why ʿImād al-Daula appointed Christians to some positions of responsibility in his administration, a practice which was to be continued by later Būyids. At the height of his power ʿAḍud al-Daula appointed a Christian to the position of vizier. One may say that in the early Būyid period the religious attitude of the imperial government was one of impartiality. Indeed Rukn al-Daula is reported to have compelled the Shīʿīs of Qum to use and pay for the upkeep of the Friday mosque. The official khuṭba for the caliph was naturally enough detested by the Shīʿīs, and they had refused to participate in Friday services; but because the Būyids continued to recognize the caliphate despite the fact that they were Shīʿī, no alteration was made in the khuṭba. This was however Rukn al-Daula's only concession to the caliphate (though his coins bore the caliph's name). In all other respects he gave the Shīʿīs a free hand, thus allowing Qum to develop into the centre of Shīʿī theology. The senior amīr intervened strongly when in 345/956–7 the houses of Shīʿī merchants from Qum were looted during riots between Sunnīs and Shīʿīs in Iṣfahān; the fines he imposed were intended to restore the peace rather than to mark the fact that he intended to protect the Shīʿīs in particular. In Fārs ʿAḍud al-Daula pursued a similar policy of impartiality and religious moderation. When a civil disturbance broke out in Shīrāz between its Muslim and Zoroastrian inhabitants and the latter's homes were wrecked, he ordered those responsible to be severely punished.

By the end of his life, ʿAḍud al-Daula is said to have been the victim of acute melancholia. He must have realized that even his most brilliant successes could never conceal his underlying failure in both the religious and political fields. His ultimate idea of the division of power within the empire had not come to fruition, any more than had his more immediate hopes of a personal union with the caliphate. Both presupposed the caliph's total renunciation of secular power, and for this the time was not yet ripe. The future was to confirm what was in fact already evident now, namely that the ʿAbbāsids were only likely to lend their authority to a temporal ruler whose policies were definitely pro-Sunnī. ʿAḍud al-Daula, for his part, had begun his career by maintaining what amounted to a neutral attitude in religious matters, though by the end of it, he had found himself forced into attempting to regain the confidence of the Shīʿīs. When, after barely six years of rule over the whole empire he died in Baghdad, his successors found themselves faced with a great many serious problems. It was scarcely to be expected that these problems would be solved by the representatives of a dynasty which would not come out openly on the side of the Sunna, but which also lacked the strength and conviction necessary to bring victory to the Shī'ī cause.

III. THE STRUGGLE FOR 'AḌUD AL-DAULA'S SUCCESSION

After 'Aḍud al-Daula's death the empire was once again faced with what had always been a Būyid defect, the lack of any settled order of succession. The late senior amīr's enemies were relatively harmless, perhaps, but they were still there, and new forces were taking shape in Mesopotamia and the Kurdish highlands. The amīr's eldest son, Shīrdil (born *c.* 960), had been sent to Kirmān in 968; after 977 he spent some time in Baghdad, but had again been sent back to his province. His second son, Marzubān (Ṣamṣām al-Daula), born *c.* 963, had come to the fore after the conquest of Iraq, and his father seems to have preferred him to Shīrdil, although he never quite made the final decision of nominating him as his successor. This uncertainty reigned in Baghdad when 'Aḍud al-Daula died. At first Marzubān, who was in the city already, was proclaimed successor to the throne and invested by the caliph. To make quite certain that his designs would succeed, he had kept his father's death secret for a certain time, and had only then arranged for himself to be officially inducted into the office of senior amīr with the title "Ṣamṣām al-Daula". But Shīrdil (Sharaf al-Daula), as the eldest son, naturally also raised claims to the succession. From Kirmān he invaded Fārs, thereby forestalling his brother. Almost at once, the new senior amīr thus found his possessions confined to Mesopotamia, while even there he was compelled to make concessions. A Kurd named Bādh captured the province of Diyārbakr and forced the senior amīr to confirm him in its possession; the latter had to content himself with keeping Bādh out of Mosul.

Shortly after 'Aḍud al-Daula his brother and one of his most loyal supporters, Mu'ayyad al-Daula, also died. Like his brother, he had found it impossible to decide who should be the successor to his considerable possessions. He had remained deaf to the suggestions which his vizier, the celebrated Ṣāḥib b. 'Abbād, began to make beginning from 976. This vizier had succeeded Abu'l-Fatḥ b. al-'Amīd, who had been put to death on account of his opposition to the imperial policy of 'Aḍud al-Daula. Now, after his own master's death, he decided on an unprecedented step. Bearing in mind the fact that the Būyid state was still a military one, and that the military aristocracy had an essential part to play in it in consequence, he summoned a gathering of the army, to which he then suggested the nomination of Fakhr al-Daula, who was in exile in Nīshāpūr. The army assented to the vizier's proposal, and thereupon Fakhr al-Daula hastened to Gurgān, where the gathering had taken place, and was there proclaimed amīr. In dealing with Fakhr al-Daula, the vizier now revealed similar skill and psychological perception. Until now, he had wholeheartedly supported the policies of 'Aḍud al-Daula; indeed his office as Mu'ayyad al-Daula's vizier presupposed such an attitude. In 980 he had met 'Aḍud al-Daula, who had given him his personal instructions concerning the future conduct of eastern policy. His espousal now of the cause of Fakhr al-Daula did not signify a complete break with the attitude he had held until then, for he was in fact to remain a staunch upholder of imperial policy. It is said that, aware of his value as a statesman, he offered Fakhr al-Daula his resignation, knowing full well that the latter would then agree to his continued appointment on his own terms, namely the continuation of 'Aḍud al-Daula's policy. The first tangible result of this was Fakhr al-Daula's refusal to hand Gurgān back to Qābūs b. Vushmgīr, the former vassal of Rukn al-Daula, who had been his companion in exile. He then took the opportunity afforded by Sāmānid quarrels over the province of Khurāsān, and began to show his active interest in the east by giving military support to Abu'l-'Abbās Tāsh, who had been deposed by the Sāmānids from the governorship of Nīshāpūr. Abu'l-'Abbās Tāsh was however forced to take refuge in Gurgān, and Fakhr al-Daula therefore entrusted the government of that province to him before moving to Ray.

In Fārs and Iraq meanwhile 'Aḍud al-Daula's sons had not yet abandoned their struggle for their father's succession. Three spheres of influence had emerged there since his death. Ṣamṣām al-Daula held Iraq, apart from its southern portion and the northern province of Diyārbakr, which he had lost to the Kurdish warrior Bādh. Khūzistān and Baṣra were in the possession of 'Aḍud al-Daula's youngest sons, Tāj al-Daula and Ḍiyā' al-Daula. They had established themselves there when Sharaf al-Daula invaded Fārs from Kirmān. Meanwhile the latter was fighting on two fronts, against Fakhr al-Daula who had now regained the central section of his father's former territory, and against the two rival states in the west. Along his northern frontier he contented himself with giving military support to the Sāmānids in their war against Fakhr al-Daula. The two princes in Baṣra and Khūzistān, caught as they were between his rivals Ṣamṣām al-Daula and Sharaf al-Daula, proceeded to acknowledge Fakhr al-Daula as senior amīr. He for his part had reinforced his claim to the title by already assuming that of "king", a step which none of his rivals had yet dared to take. Since he now had two genuine vassals of his own, in Baṣra and Khūzistān, he proceeded to assume the title of "Shāhanshāh", which amounted to an open and unmistakable declaration that he regarded himself as the sole successor to 'Aḍud al-Daula. Coming after the rejection of the Ziyārids's claim to Gurgān, this was Ṣāḥib b. 'Abbād's second success in his attempt to further 'Aḍud al-Daula's policy uninterrupted.

Despite the successes of Fakhr al-Daula, Sharaf al-Daula was provisionally to prove the strongest claimant to the senior amīrate. After successfully recapturing 'Umān, which had seceded to Ṣamṣām al-Daula, he was free and ready to intervene in the west. Early in 986 he occupied Khūzistān and Baṣra, whose two princes took refuge in Ray. Even Ṣamṣām al-Daula was too weak to counter this new threat with any energy or determination. In a peace treaty signed in May/June 986, he was compelled to recognize Sharaf al-Daula as senior amīr. This now reduced the claimants to the senior amīrate to two. Sharaf al-Daula declined to enter Baghdad before he had destroyed his rival in Ray. But his plans in that direction were suddenly frustrated by events in Baghdad itself. There an insurrection took place against Ṣamṣām al-Daula, which then led to armed conflict between the Turks and the Dailamites. In order to save Iraq from the Kurds and other powers which might exploit this confused situation, Sharaf al-Daula marched on Baghdad in 987, deposed its ruler, and sent him as a prisoner to a fortress in Fārs. By July of that same year he was solemnly invested as senior amīr by the caliph. His struggle with Fakhr al-Daula was now ready to begin. His first move was planned to be the defeat of Badr b. Ḥasanwaih, who was a loyal ally of Fakhr al-Daula. But not only did this campaign fail to produce the desired victory, death suddenly put an unforeseen end to all of Sharaf al-Daula's plans. He died in Baghdad on 7 September 988 at the early age of twenty-eight.

Sharaf al-Daula left two sons, both of whom were too young to be considered as his heirs. The senior amīrate therefore devolved upon 'Aḍud al-Daula's third son, the seventeen-year-old Bahā' al-Daula. He was however unable to take possession of his entire inheritance immediately, because Ṣamṣām al-Daula, who had been partially blinded shortly before Sharaf al-Daula's death, managed to escape from captivity and take Fārs, Kirmān and Khūzistān.

Fakhr al-Daula in Ray now judged that the opportune moment for action had come. His vizier Ṣāḥib b. 'Abbād advocated immediate hostilities to the south and west, and for this the changes of ruler in Shīrāz and Baghdad seemed to provide a favourable opportunity. Accompanied by his vizier, he therefore marched into Khūzistān, with the aim of cutting Baghdad off from Shīrāz. But climate and terrain were against him, and he was obliged to withdraw. This invasion from the north had the result of making the rulers of Shīrāz and Baghdad forget their enmity and draw up a peaceful alliance whereby Ṣamṣām al-Daula confirmed his brother in the possession of Khūzistān and Iraq and himself kept Arrajān, which had already acquired particular importance under Rukn al-Daula, as well as Fārs and Kirmān. Both submitted to the caliph as supreme arbiter, and professed to regard each other as equals. The supplementary title of Ḍiyā' al-Milla which Bahā' al-Daula had assumed on his enthronement, could now no longer be taken as a claim to the senior amīrate. Instead both Būyids made use of the title "king" on their coinage and thereby too acknowledged their equality of rank. This turn of events met with the complete approval of the caliph al-Ṭā'i', who even in 'Izz al-Daula's day had advocated the independence of Iraq. But after his fall and the succession to the caliphate of al-Qādir, Bahā' al-Daula assumed the title of "Shāhanshāh" which had been borne by 'Aḍud al-Daula, and thereby implied that he still aspired to the leadership of the whole united empire and not just an independent Iraq. His prime concern was the removal or at least subjection of his equal and rival, Ṣamṣām al-Daula, who for his part was involved in wars against the Ṣaffārids, who had taken Kirmān almost without a fight after Sharaf al-Daula's death. But Bahā' al-Daula's attack on him met with no success – indeed he now lost Khūzistān, assigned to him in the treaty signed three years before. Nevertheless Ṣamṣām al-Daula also found himself meeting with increasing difficulties, and finally decided that he would recognize the senior amīrate of Fakhr al-Daula on behalf of his entire possessions, namely Kirmān, Fārs, Khūzistān and 'Umān. This step produced a situation virtually identical with that which had prevailed during the reign of Rukn al-Daula. The only differences were that Khūzistān now belonged to the east and, more important, that the Būyid rulers of

Baghdad and Ray both laid claim to the same privileges, bore the title of "Shāhanshāh" and had no intention of yielding to each other's superiority. The empire had fallen into two distinct and independent halves.

Fakhr al-Daula was now the ruler of the whole of Būyid Iran, and could turn his attention either towards Iraq, where Bahā' al-Daula was meeting with increasing difficulties, or towards the Sāmānids, whose rule was growing steadily weaker. His attention was in fact to be occupied almost exclusively by the problem of Khurāsān. Once again he tried to wrest the province, this time from the Ghaznavid Sebük-Tegin, the governor recently appointed by the Sāmānid ruler Nūḥ, but once again, as in 984, his attempt failed despite the large forces which he threw into the campaign. This was probably his biggest mistake. Perhaps some of the blame for it may be attached to the vizier Ṣāḥib b. 'Abbād, but when the latter now died, it was obvious that the Būyid empire had lost one of its most able administrators and that the ideal of imperial unity had lost one of its most fervent and loyal advocates. Whatever his mistakes and omissions – and his failure to realize that the future would be settled in Iraq rather than Khurāsān was the most serious – without him Fakhr al-Daula was lost. Two years later he too was dead without having done anything more to affect the course of the empire's history.

While Fakhr al-Daula's attention was engrossed with the war in Khurāsān, Bahā' al-Daula's strength had begun to revive and Ṣamṣām al-Daula's to wane. Soon Bahā' al-Daula, with the assistance of his new ally the Kurd Badr b. Ḥasanwaih, was able to contemplate an invasion of Fārs. But scarcely had this invasion begun in December 998 than Ṣamṣām al-Daula was himself assassinated while fleeing from Shīrāz by one of 'Izz al-Daula's sons who had escaped from captivity and had organized an armed rising against him. This event gave Bahā' al-Daula the opportunity of taking Shīrāz himself, and before long the opposition of 'Izz al-Daula's sons had been completely broken. Nor did Bahā' al-Daula now have any serious opponent left in Ray where, since Fakhr al-Daula's death and during the minority of his two young sons, the regency had been assumed by their Kurdish mother, the "Sayyida". The elder son, Majd al-Daula, was still in Ray, but the younger, Shams al-Daula, had been appointed governor of Hamadān and Kirmānshāh. Both had recognized Bahā' al-Daula as senior amīr by 400/1009–10 at the latest, and this in turn invalidated their earlier assumption of the title " Shāhanshāh ". Nevertheless Bahā' al-Daula had to content himself with the title of "king" in Ray – a concession which was of theoretical rather than practical significance. Meanwhile the Būyids were no longer proving strong enough to hold the Khurāsān frontier by force of arms and were being forced to accept the loss of valuable territory in the north and west. Both Ṭabaristān and Gurgān now passed into the hands of the Ziyārids for good, and Qābūs b. Vushmgīr reinforced his position towards the Būyids by entering into an alliance with Maḥmūd of Ghazna which made him virtually the latter's vassal. In the west, Zanjān and various other towns fell to the Musāfirids of Āzarbāījān. In the south Būyid freedom of movement was equally hampered, this time by the Kākūyids. Shortly after 398/1007 the Sayyida had entrusted the government of Iṣfahān to the Kurdish prince Ja'far 'Alā' al-Daula b. Kākūya, who was a cousin of Majd al-Daula on his mother's side. This prince had soon succeeded in establishing his de facto independence, and later went on to attempt an extension of his influence to Hamadān and Ray.

Bahā' al-Daula ceased all activity in the north, although the confused situation there and the growing power of the Ghaznavids were making the reinforcement of Būyid strength in Ray more essential than ever. He had entered Shīrāz in 999–1000 and he never left Fārs again. It would seem that he regarded his task complete once he had returned to the capital city of his father and had successfully subjugated his opponents in the east. Perhaps his presence in Iraq would have been even more essential than in the north. There the conquests of 'Aḍud al-Daula had for the most part been lost again. In Diyārbakr, Bādh had laid the foundations for the future rule of the Marwānids; Raḥba and Raqqa had passed into the Fāṭimid sphere of influence, while in Mosul the 'Uqailids had established themselves firmly. They, like the Marwānids, gave only nominal recognition to Būyid authority, though this was at least more than Mu'izz al-Daula had ever obtained from the Ḥamdānids. But whereas the influence of the Ḥamdānids had extended no further than Takrīt on the Tigris, the Bedouin 'Uqailids advanced much further, almost reaching Baghdad in the south and actually including Anbār and Kūfa in the southwest. It was only their internal dissensions that prevented them from providing an even greater threat to the Būyids. The confusion which followed 'Aḍud al-Daula's death had presented an admirable opportunity for the Bedouins to further their attempts to obtain a permanent foothold in the fertile regions, and this was the principal reason for the relative speed of the 'Uqailid advances just described. Bahā' al-Daula, who had spent almost ten years of his reign in struggles with his rival in Fārs, was quite unable to offer any resistance to this wave of Bedouin expansion. By the end of his reign his direct influence in Iraq was confined to Baghdad and Wāsiṭ and the areas immediately surrounding these two cities.

Despite the general confusion which marked the period after 'Aḍud al-Daula's death, and despite the waning of Būyid power which it betokened, the cultural achievements of the Būyid Empire continued. The Būyid princes still found both opportunity and inclination to indulge their scientific and literary tastes. They reverted moreover to the conscious awareness of their Iranian heritage, and western Iran now embarked on the same process which had previously reached such remarkable proportions in the east, namely the deliberate transformation of its Arabic–Islamic culture into a culture specifically Iranian. An important factor in this development was Iran's abandonment of its traditional religion in favour of Islam, which ceased in consequence to be associated with foreign domination and became instead the expression of the religious faith of the nation as a whole. As a result, Arab influence could no longer be regarded as the sole vehicle for the spread of Islam within the confines of Persia, and the Persian language began to permeate court life and to acquire the status of a literary medium. Until the year 1000 however the process of Iranization did not make such rapid progress in Ray and Iṣfahān, where court life was entirely dominated by Arabic–Islamic culture. This was largely due to the cultural and literary activities of the politically even more influential vizier Ṣāḥib b. 'Abbād. Tha'ālibī enumerates no less than twenty-three poets in attendance at the latter's court and singing their patron's praises in Arabic poetry; moreover he kept up a correspondence with all the leading literary figures of his time. A late source ascribes the restoration of the ramparts of Qazvīn to him, as well as the erection of a palace in that city in a quarter thenceforth called Ṣāḥibābād. More often he resided in Iṣfahān, since he was himself a native of nearby Ṭāliqān, and it was in Iṣfahān that he chose to be buried. His death was immediately followed by the confiscation of his property by the impoverished Fakhr al-Daula, who was soon to encounter the opposition of his wife Sayyida who, after his death, took over complete personal control of the government of Ray to the exclusion of her own sons, the elder of whom, namely Majd al-Daula, had been enjoying the most careful education with a view to his future succession. His tutor had been the distinguished scholar and grammarian Aḥmad b. Fāris of Hamadān, whose most illustrious pupil in his native city was Badī' al-Zamān Hamadānī, the literary precursor of Ḥarīrī, the author of the famous *Maqāmāt*. Ibn Fāris was a Persian, but it is significant that, like the vizier Ṣāḥib b. 'Abbād, he was a fervent defender of Arabic against the attacks of the Shu'ūbiyya movement, which advocated the cultivation of Persian at the expense of Arabic.

IV. THE DECLINE OF THE BŪYID EMPIRE

Bahā' al-Daula, after protracted efforts, had finally succeeded in restoring some semblance of unity to the empire. He had, however, also witnessed the beginning of the decline of Būyid power in the north and had had to accept a considerable reduction of his influence in Iraq. He died in Fārs in December 1012, in Arrajān, that city which from the start of the Būyid period had been a favourite seat of the senior amīrs. His reign may with good reason be said to fall into two almost equal halves, the first of which extended from his accession in 989 until the turn of the century and was taken up with the struggles for 'Aḍud al-Daula's succession, and the second being the period of his undisputed senior amīrate which was spent entirely in Fārs and was marked by the absence of any personal intervention in Iraq or in the north. Shortly before his death he had named his son Abū Shūjā', who was born in 993 and lived in Baghdad, as his successor. According to the custom which by now was hallowed by tradition, Abū Shūjā' was given a double title: Sulṭān al-Daula wa 'Izz al-Milla. The new senior amīr promptly left for Shīrāz in order to assume the reins of government and to put the affairs of the empire in order. He allowed his two eldest brothers to participate in this by appointing them to governorships: Abū Ṭāhir Jalāl al-Daula (born 993–4), who had been brought up with him in Baghdad, was made responsible for Baṣra, while Abu'l-Fawāris Qawām al-Daula (born in April 1000) was entrusted with Kirmān.

Like his father, Sulṭān al-Daula regarded Shīrāz as his official residence. He did not even deem it necessary to go to Baghdad to take part in his own solemn investiture; instead the caliph had to send the requisite documents and insignia to Shīrāz. Three years elapsed before he returned to Mesopotamia, and even then he only went as far as

Ahvāz, where he received the governor of Baghdad in audience. In 408/1017–18 he visited Iraq again and revised his relationship with the 'Uqailids. The opportunity which was offered by his absence from Shīrāz was promptly seized by Qawām al-Daula, who now invaded Fārs from Kirmān and occupied the province. In this step he was supported by the Ghaznavids, who had annexed the neighbouring province of Sīstān and were now for the first time playing an active part in Būyid politics. Qawām al-Daula's attack was repulsed. Nevertheless it gave the signal for prolonged contentions between Bahā' al-Daula's sons. After these had continued for several decades, the painstakingly constructed unity of the empire was destroyed. Once Qawām al-Daula had been driven out of Fārs, the senior amīr considered the situation there to be stable enough to allow him to return to Baghdad and concentrate his attention on that sector of the empire, one which had been neglected by his father. This undertaking opened with an outstanding success; he actually succeeded in subjugating the marshlands, that area which had hitherto repeatedly defied all attempts to conquer it. But he soon met with a problem which had always been particularly acute in Iraq, the traditional rivalry between the Dailamites and the Turks. The former had always felt more at home in Iran, and Būyid rule in Iraq had therefore tended to depend largely on the Turks. The latter now demanded that Abū 'Alī (Musharrif al-Daula), Sulṭān al-Daula's youngest brother (born in 1003), be made amīr. Prolonged negotiations resulted in Sulṭān al-Daula's return to Shīrāz and his recognition of his brother in Baghdad as a vassal with the title of "King of Iraq". When he tried to reverse the situation by force of arms and was defeated, he found himself obliged to resign his authority over Iraq. Musharrif al-Daula now assumed the title of "Shāhanshāh" and declared himself to be Sulṭān al-Daula's equal. In a final treaty signed in 413/1022–3, the status quo had to be permanently accepted. The three brothers now all held the title of "Shāhanshāh" and there was no longer any "senior amīr" in the traditional sense of the term.

The first to profit from the disintegration of the empire were the Kākūyids of Iṣfahān. After the death of Badr b. Ḥasanwaih, part of the Kurdish territory had been occupied by Shams al-Daula, the ruler of Hamadān, while the remainder had been overrun by the 'Annāzids of Ḥulwān. Later Shams al-Daula turned to the Kākūyids for assistance in suppressing a rebellion in Hamadān. When he died and was succeeded by his son Samā' al-Daula, the Kākūyids seized Hamadān (414/1023–4) and proceeded to expel the ʻAnnāzids from Ḥulwān. Musharrif al-Daula now intervened. Though the Kākūyids were compelled to withdraw, they managed to hold on to Hamadān and cement their treaty with Musharrif al-Daula by a matrimonial alliance. The centre of their power Iṣfahān now entered a second golden age, comparable to that which it had enjoyed under Rukn al-Daula.

Musharrif al-Daula's position in Baghdad had always been precarious owing to the fact that it depended on the good will of the soldiery who had brought him to power. When he died in May 1025, shortly after his rival, Sulṭān al-Daula, who expired in Shīrāz in December 1024, the choice of his successor was once again in their hands. Not until June 1027 did they finally decide for his brother Jalāl al-Daula, rather than Sulṭān al-Daula's eldest son Abū Kālījār, who had meanwhile become involved in a bitter struggle with Qawām al-Daula of Kirmān. But once Abū Kālījār was rid of Qawām al-Daula – poisoned, as the sources relate – he decided to renew his claims to the throne in Baghdad, and occupied Baṣra. Jalāl al-Daula's authority was by now restricted to the area around Baghdad and Wāsiṭ, and he was caught up in chronic disputes with his own troops with the caliph playing the part of a mediator until they culminated in a mutiny organized by the Turkish general Bārstoghan in 428/1036–7. Abū Kālījār seized this opportunity and marched on Baghdad. Though he failed to occupy it, he succeeded in winning recognition as senior amīr, and had coins minted bearing the title "Shāhanshāh". The ʻUqailids and another Arab tribe, the Asadids, preferred however to see a weak ruler on the throne in Baghdad, with the result that they brought about the reinstation of Jalāl al-Daula. The status quo was thereupon ratified by treaties between the two rival princes, who henceforth ruled over entirely independent states and bore identical titles until the death of Jalāl al-Daula in 1044.

Abū Kālījār might well have become the ruler of the entire empire had his position at home been more secure. But he was faced with problems similar to those of Jalāl al-Daula in Baghdad. His army, which he had begun by handling rather clumsily, was constantly threatening mutiny, and Ibn al-Athīr tells us that he was thoroughly disliked by the inhabitants of Shīrāz.[1] In consequence he preferred to reside at Ahvāz even after he had freed himself from the malign influence of his powerful and cunning tutor, the eunuch Ṣandal. The

[1] Ibn al-Athīr, vol. IX, p. 127.

signing of the peace treaty between himself and Jalāl al-Daula did however allow him to redirect some of his attention to Iran proper, where the influence of the Ghaznavids had been very much on the increase since Maḥmūd had become their leader. He had occupied himself for almost thirty years with campaigns in India, ostensibly to spread the faith but really in search of plunder. In 1029, however, shortly before his death, he crowned his successes with the conquest of Ray, whose ruler, Majd al-Daula, had ironically requested his assistance against his own mutinous troops.

The annexation of Ray by the Ghaznavids produced a new situation in northern Iran. The Ziyārids of Gurgān lost their independence and were obliged to pay tribute, while Maḥmūd's son and successor, Mas'ūd, who had been appointed governor of Ray, had been quick to lay hands on Iṣfahān and Hamadān as well, forcing the Kākūyid 'Alā' al-Daula to turn to Abū Kālījār for help, though in vain, the latter being already engaged in warfare in southern Iraq. After Maḥmūd's death in April 1030, 'Alā' al-Daula made a futile attempt to regain his throne. He was only to be allowed to return to it when some years later he agreed to become a vassal of the Ghaznavids. But Ghaznavid power in Khurāsān and Ray had already passed its zenith, as was proved by their failure to capture Kirmān. A new force had arisen in the area in the form of the Saljuqs, whose base had already shifted during Maḥmūd's reign from Transoxiana to Khurāsān thanks to the collusion of the Turkish Oghuz nomadic tribes in that region. The rise of the Oghuz Turks was astonishingly swift. Only twelve years after their first appearance in the province they inflicted a defeat on the Ghaznavids in 426/1035. In May 1040 another decisive battle was fought at Dandānqān, south-west of Marv, from which the Saljuqs emerged as the victors. At this point the Ghaznavids disappear from the political scene in Iran; from now on their place was to be taken by the Saljuqs.

V. THE FINAL UNIFICATION AND COLLAPSE OF THE BŪYID EMPIRE

The death of Jalāl al-Daula in March 1044 brought Abū Kālījār unchecked rule over both Baghdad and the eastern provinces, a goal for which he had been fighting for many years. He encountered virtually no opposition. There were no longer any serious claimants to the senior amīrate belonging to Jalāl al-Daula's generation, and Fanā-

Khusrau, a son of the Majd al-Daula who had been expelled by the Ghaznavids, was engrossed in waging a losing war to preserve some vestiges of his father's former domains from the ravages of the Oghuz tribes and the Saljuqs. Thus Abū Kālījār's position was all in all by no means unfavourable. Although his ambitions in Iraq had met with no success during Jalāl al-Daula's reign, he had at least taken firm control of Baṣra by appointing his own son as its governor, and he had employed the time during which his rival's power and prestige were waning in consolidating his own authority in Iran. An attack by the Ghaznavids in Kirmān in 422/1031 had been repulsed, and they had been driven out of Khurāsān as well by the decisive victory of the Saljuqs at Dandānqān. The Saljuqs for their part were still busy strengthening their hold on northern Iran, and although Toghrïl Beg had actually appeared in Ray in 434/1042–3 in order to restore order after the province had been devastated by the Oghuz, the situation in Hamadān and Iṣfahān was still far from clear. In Iṣfahān, the Kākūyid 'Alā' al-Daula had died in 1041 and two of his sons were fighting for the succession. The Saljuqs were however not yet strong enough to wrest it from them. Abū Kālījār therefore exploited the unsettled situation and declared his own shortlived nominal authority over it, only to find that both rival claimants preferred to recognize Saljuq authority over both Iṣfahān and Hamadān rather than his own. The situation in Fārs was sufficiently stable meanwhile to allow him to visit Baghdad, there to assume the senior amīrate and receive the supplementary title "Muḥyī al-Dīn" ("Reviver of Religion") together with formal recognition of various Mesopotamian rulers, who all agreed in preferring as senior amīr a Būyid whom they knew to a Saljuq who might well prove to be less tractable. Such success prompted the Kākūyids to return their allegiance to him, but their action quickly led to violent reprisals on the part of Toghrïl Beg, and in due course Abū Kālījār found himself obliged to follow the wiser policy of negotiating a treaty of peace with his Saljuq opponent, which was duly cemented with the customary matrimonial alliances.

The peace which ensued was however to be broken in that province which had for some time been playing a critical part in the political development of the empire, namely Kirmān. Its Būyid governor placed himself under the command of Qāvurt, who was a nephew of Toghrïl Beg and was to become the founder of the Kirmān Saljuq dynasty. Qāvurt seems to have been acting on his own initiative in this, and

Abū Kālījār regarded himself as entitled to take measures against the treacherous governor for his infringement of the peace treaty. It was to be his last campaign. The governor sent emissaries to meet him laden with gifts as a token of his renewed allegiance. Amongst these gifts was a beautiful girl from his harem who was entrusted with a secret task which she duly carried out. In October 1048 Abū Kālījār expired unexpectedly at the age of thirty-eight after partaking of a dish of roast venison liver.

It was Abū Kālījār's intelligence and perseverance that made it possible for him to unite the traditional territories of the Būyids with Iraq. Virtually nothing is known of his cultural and administrative achievements, or of his religious attitudes. The Isma'īlī missionary al-Mu'ayyad fi'l-Dīn, who was in the service of the Fāṭimids and spent some time at Abū Kālījār's court, claimed that he actually converted the senior amīr. But it is more likely that, true to Būyid tradition, he let his attitude to religious questions depend on political considerations. The supplementary title bestowed on him by the caliph is evidence enough of his ability to change course. Much of the administrative duties of the empire fell on the shoulders of his vizier Bahrām b. Māfinnā, a man of exemplary character and considerable learning, who founded a library of some 7,000 volumes in Fīrūzābād, a city which had been flourishing ever since 'Aḍud al-Daula's rebuilding of it. The senior amīr seems for his part to have resided for preference in S͟hīrāz, which he had fortified during the tense period of his confrontation with Tog͟hrïl Beg, but which otherwise still owed most of its splendour to the reign of 'Aḍud al-Daula.

The secession of the governor of Kirmān was the prelude to the disorder which broke out after Abū Kālījār's death and which finally precipitated the collapse of the Būyid Empire. Its immediate causes were once again the shortcomings which had always plagued the dynasty: the unreliability of the soldiery and the dissensions amongst the monarch's sons. Abū Naṣr K͟husrau Fīrūz ascended the throne in Baghdad with the title "al-Malik al-Raḥīm", but nothing is known of his previous career. Kirmān had already been lost and 'Umān followed in 442/1050–1, but more serious than this was the renewed division of the empire into two opposing halves, Iraq and Fārs. The latter had fallen to Abū Manṣūr Fūlād Sutūn, who, instead of concentrating on the more important task of warding off would-be foreign invaders, engaged in a protracted struggle with his rival in Baghdad not so much to gain supremacy over the whole empire as to maintain his authority in Fārs and extend it to Khūzistān as well. In fact this situation amounted to the resumption of the struggle which had been brought to a provisional end by the treaty between Jalāl al-Daula and Abū Kālījār ten years before. At first it seemed that Baghdad would gain the upper hand on this occasion; but having taken Shīrāz al-Malik al-Raḥīm was forced to return to Iraq because of ill-feeling between the Turks and the Dailamī and also because of the worsening situation there. Nevertheless the senior amīr inflicted a defeat on Abū Manṣūr and his allies in 443/1051–2 and thereby succeeded in re-uniting Fārs and Iraq. But Abū Manṣūr turned in his plight to Toghrïl Beg for help, and on retaking Shīrāz in 445/1053–4 he actually recognized him as his overlord in the khuṭba, mentioning the senior amīr in second place – proof enough of the Būyid dilemma during this period and Toghrïl Beg's circumspection in dealing with the Būyids and the caliph; official recognition was his prime objective. By receiving seceders from the Būyid camp with all due honour he astutely enhanced his standing. Soon Khūzistān had fallen to him, laid waste by Turkish pillaging, and the 'Uqailids decided to pay him tribute.

This turn of events isolated al-Malik al-Raḥīm in Iraq; the outlook was bleak indeed. But before acting Toghrïl Beg paused to review his position. His relations with the caliph were strained. The latter held him responsible for the plundering and looting carried out by the Oghuz, though he had in fact had the greatest difficulty in restraining them. Moreover the caliph was by no means eager to be freed from the Shī'ī Būyids by the Sunnī Toghrïl Beg as has hitherto generally been supposed; indeed the caliphate was now, at least in Baghdad itself, enjoying power unprecedented in recent history, and this power was increasing in proportion to the Būyids' decline. To exchange the weak senior amīr for the mighty Toghrïl Beg was hardly a course that recommended itself. At this point a brilliant idea occurred to Toghrïl Beg. He appeared in Baghdad in the guise of a pilgrim bound for Mecca, giving out that on his return he would take up arms against the Fāṭimids. The caliph could not but approve of such pious intentions; moreover Toghrïl Beg's arrival in Baghdad on Friday 17 December 1055 meant that the khuṭba had to be carried out in his name followed by that of al-Malik al-Raḥīm. Magnanimously Toghrïl Beg now consented to regard the Būyid in Baghdad as his vassal, and the caliph wisely recommended the Būyid to his protection. This state of affairs lasted barely one week. Perhaps Toghrïl Beg had foreseen what would happen; the citizens of the town became restive, accusing the Saljuq soldiers of committing acts of looting and calling on the senior amīr to have them expelled from the city. Summoned to the Saljuq camp for negotiations, the senior amīr was himself accused of being responsible for reprisals against the Saljuq troops and, despite the caliph's protestations, was arrested. Būyid rule in Baghdad had come to an end.

The Saljuqs, however, had not yet overcome all opposition in Iraq. An insurrection against them was now organized by Basāsīrī, a slave who had been a favourite of the former senior amīr. For five years the struggle raged with neither side able to gain the upper hand. After countless vicissitudes Basāsīrī turned for financial and military support to the Fāṭimids and was appointed Fāṭimid viceroy in Iraq. The majority of the Arab rulers in Mesopotamia were in league with him, and at the end of 1058 he actually succeeded in taking Baghdad itself, where the khuṭba was performed in the name of the Fāṭimids while the 'Abbāsid caliph was removed from the city and interned at Ḥadītha on the Euphrates. But Toghrïl Beg was ultimately to prove the stronger. As he marched on Baghdad, Basāsīrī's brief moment of triumph came to an end. The insurrection collapsed, and almost exactly one year after his capture of the city he fled from it, only to be killed in a skirmish nearby.

The Būyids in Shīrāz were able to hold out longer than their counterparts in Baghdad. After almost one century of tranquillity, the heart of the Būyid empire had once again experienced the horrors of war during the reign of al-Malik al-Raḥīm, and these were followed by the even starker horrors of Saljuq depredation. Iṣfahān and the surrounding country had already suffered severely when Toghrïl Beg beleaguered the city in 442/1050–1. A similar fate was averted from Shīrāz by Abū Sa'd, al-Malik al-Raḥīm's viceroy in Fārs in 444/1052–3. But in the end the Saljuqs, with their fighting mobility, were to prove superior to the mercenaries of the Būyids, and the rich and unspoilt province of Fārs was not to escape their lust for plunder, especially since the rest of the country had already been laid waste by the Oghuz tribes. In 442/1050–1 Alp-Arslan, the future Saljuq ruler, undertook a foray into the province without the knowledge or consent of Toghrïl Beg. A surprise attack on Fasā inflicted serious losses on its defenders, and, laden with booty, he withdrew without reaching Shīrāz, which had been strongly fortified by Abū Kālījār. But the internal strength of Shīrāz was being weakened by the dissensions amongst Abū Kālījār's sons which had increased in intensity especially after the deposition of al-Malik al-Raḥīm. Abū Manṣūr had removed his brother, Abū Sa'd, but had himself been killed in 454/1062 during a revolt led by the Kurd Faḍlūya, who was to become the founder of the Faḍlūyid dynasty which ruled in Shabānkāra (Dārābjird) until the beginning of the 14th century. In the summer of 1062 Shīrāz was finally taken by the Saljuq governor of Kirmān.

The fate of Abū Kālījār's other sons is lost in the darkness and confusion of the ensuing period. Al-Malik al-Raḥīm for his part died in captivity in the citadel of Ray in 450/1058–9. The Kākūyids alone succeeded at least in part in navigating the perils of this period of Saljuq invasion. On the fall of Iṣfahān after a year-long siege, the Kākūyid Farāmurz b. 'Alā' al-Daula was granted the fiefs of Yazd and Abarqūh by the Saljuqs, and he and his successors raised Yazd to a state of relative prosperity until their dynasty died out and was replaced by atabegs in the mid-6th/12th century. 'Aḍud al-Daula's greater example in Shīrāz thus survived in Yazd, as the Kākūyids embellished it, building mosques, canals and ramparts. One of the last of the atabegs who followed them significantly bore the title 'Alā' al-Daula – that title which had once been borne by the founder of the Kākūyid dynasty.

CHAPTER 8

TRIBES, CITIES AND SOCIAL ORGANIZATION

The problem confronting the writer of this chapter may be summarized in the question: by what process did pre-Islamic Iran turn into the Iran of Islam? Although it is only the social implications of the question which need to be considered here, they are by no means simple. In Iran, as in all the countries of the Near and Middle East, the spoken and written language changed several times over the years, with the practical consequence for modern learning that few scholars are able to study the history of the country continuously from one linguistic period to the others; there are few experts who have a good knowledge of both pre-Islamic and Islamic Iran. Moreover, for pre-Islamic Iran the direct documentary evidence available is unfortunately too meagre to answer all the questions which an Islamicist might in retrospect wish to ask, and even the Arabic documentation which followed the Islamic conquest is, for the first two or three centuries, sadly deficient. The history of the Sāsānian period is often presented with Islamic bias, for the purpose of leading to conclusions which authors of the Islamic period wished to demonstrate, reflecting the conflicts and problems of their times. The same is true of the accounts which they give of the period of the conquests. For these reasons, there are too few substantial studies of the crucial problems of Iranian history during the first centuries after the intervention of Islam for it to be possible to present a synthesis of them. The chapter which follows will therefore consist mainly of somewhat disconnected notes, for the most part of a hypothetical and provisional nature. It is to be hoped that they may nevertheless provide some stimulus for further research and be of help in outlining a programme.

From an ethnical point of view, if the actual penetration by the Arabs themselves be disregarded for a moment, their conquest does not appear to have resulted in any major disturbance of the distribution of the Iranian peoples. Iran therefore has always been populated predominantly by Persians in the strict sense, whose regional differences may for the present be ignored, though they should not be underestimated; it was, incidentally, in Fārs that they preserved their greatest immunity from foreign infiltration. Side by side with them, however, there existed other peoples who, while often deriving from a stock distantly connected with their own, had nonetheless a distinct identity. Sheltered behind the mountains separating the Iranian plateau from the Caspian Sea, or actually among these mountains, were the Dailamites and the Gīlites; in the ranges of the west and the northwest were the Kurds and various groups, such as the Lurs, which the authors of the time associated with them; in the south were the Qufṣ and perhaps the Balūchīs. In the extreme northwest the Armenians straddled both Iran and Asia Minor, and Iranian culture had made inroads among the Caucasian peoples and the Georgians, the limits of which are difficult to determine. In Central Asia and in Afghanistan of today there persisted elements, probably rather heterogeneous, of the confederation known as the Hephthalites, which had an Indo-European core but had been infiltrated by various Turkish elements. The populations which were later to dominate Afghanistan still remained at that time in their mountains, outside the Persian world in its strict sense. The Iranian Soghdians, who had played so important a rôle in the history of Central Asia, had perhaps been partially dispersed without having disappeared. The Khwārazmians, insulated by the desert in their oases, formed a nucleus of social and cultural autonomy. On the fringes of the Iranian world, in Farghāna and other valleys of Central Asia, there were Turks superimposed upon ancient native populations, for the most part Iranian; these Turks were distinct from the Turkish elements in the 'Abbāsid army who, having been uprooted from their places of origin, might find themselves garrisoned or campaigning in Iran.

It was in the midst of this complex of peoples that the Arab intervention occurred. There never was any mass colonization of Iran by the Arabs, who did not care foı the climatic conditions, except in the centre and in the south – the Arabian camel cannot endure cold winters – and their great waves of migration halted at the foot of the Zagros. Nonetheless, in addition to the garrison towns occupied by detachments formed, in the first century, of Arabs, there had been Arab penetration in four regions: on the south coast by sea, originating especially from 'Umān; by Bedouins on the central plateau and in Sīstān; thirdly, in Khurāsān and in Central Asia by mixed groups, half military and half tribal, from Iraq and primarily from Baṣra; and finally in the northwest and on the Armenian–Caucasian frontier by smaller groups of the same kind, coming from Kūfa or from Upper Mesopotamia. It was certainly in Khurāsān that colonization was at its most intensive and most complex, which to some extent accounted for the part played by Muslims of this region in the 'Abbāsid movement. Nevertheless before long a large proportion of the Arabs yielded to their environment and, as a result of mixed marriages, were using a language with Iranian words; conversely, Islamic influence was particularly strong in the zones where Arab penetration was most concentrated. There is thus no need to exaggerate the "national" opposition between the two elements, native and Arab, nor is it necessary to regard the Arabs as constituting a unified whole; they brought with them, especially to Khurāsān, their traditional political and tribal quarrels, which resulted, apparently, in the alliance of certain Arab groups with native groups in opposition to other similar alliances. These features have been dealt with in the chapter on the 'Abbāsids and need not be repeated here.

It would clearly be helpful to know whether the adoption of Islam, which is at one and the same time both a religion and a social law, resulted in important modifications in the life of those peoples converted to it. Polygamy had been practised in pre-Islamic Iran as under Islam, and the shortage of women resulting from it fostered the recruitment of bachelor societies (see below) and propaganda by heterodox sects whom their opponents accused of advocating the communal ownership of women. In other matters it is known that Muslim law, and more specifically Ḥanafite law, which developed over a wide area in Iran, generally authorized pre-Islamic practices, particularly in the field of commerce, or, if it did not authorize them, allowed them to continue. The fact remains that conversion to Islam proceeded at varying rates of progress and did not really gather momentum and become universal until the 4th/10th century, under the "national" Muslim dynasties. The material reasons which are often adduced to explain this process of conversion can only be accepted by taking an over-simplified view of the prevailing conditions. It is, however, impossible to discuss them here and there is only space to record the consequences.

The questions which have just been raised are bound up with that of the *mawālī* (singular *maulā*). This term is known to have been used to denote men of similar status to the "clients" of the Late Roman Empire. In ancient Arab times they could be individuals who, having for one reason or another been excluded from their tribe, put themselves under the protection either of another tribe or of its leaders. Thus it could come about that, in order to safeguard their economic and social position with the Arab conquerors, native inhabitants at all levels placed themselves under the protection either of a group or of a leading personality belonging to the victorious nation. The term could also include liberated prisoners of war who remained attached in some way to their masters. Mawālī of various types existed everywhere within the range of the Arab conquest and were thus drawn from all ethnic sources; they were, however, particularly numerous and influential in Iran. Indeed, in the former Byzantine countries, prominent citizens had been able to flee to Constantinople and from there to redeem their captive compatriots, while the Iranians, on the other hand, whose country was entirely occupied, had little chance of flight nor had they a state at their disposal to ransom their people. Moreover, the part in Muslim history rapidly assumed by Iraq, the seat of the Sāsānian capital, where for a long time there had been a large infiltration of Iranians, gave to the Iranian mawālī who lived there an importance proportionate with that of Iraq; the very size of Iran even allowed them to increase in numbers in Iraq. It is also possible that the communal ties within the Mazdaean church, weakened as it was by schisms, may have been less strong than those of the Jewish or Christian communities, which were more successful in restraining their adherents from yielding to the temptations of Islam. For it must be emphasized that the state of being maulā was conditional on conversion to Islam, that is to say, on integration to a certain degree in the dominant society, albeit on a lower level at first. To represent the mawālī as fulfilling the function of intermediaries between the two societies and cultures may be valid, if what is meant is that they introduced their Arab masters to certain traditions of their ancestral society, but not that they were able actually to serve as interpreters on behalf of the indigenous population with the Arabs, or *vice versa*.

It was under the ʿAbbāsids, who preferred to man their administration and their army with people from Khurāsān, who had been conquered by the Arabs, rather than with their Arab compatriots who were infected with a dangerous egalitarianism, that the mawālī were to attain their most exalted offices and fortunes; hence there arose between them and the Arabs that emulation or rivalry which is described particularly under the literary form of the Shuʿūbiyya; its other aspects, social as well as ethnic, have been ably demonstrated by H. A. R. Gibb.[1] By degrees, with the disappearance of all social differences between themselves and the Arabs, the status of maulā lost its validity and, in the course of the 3rd/9th century, the name, like the state, fell into disuse. In the same way the Arabs became less clearly distinguishable from the native inhabitants in proportion as the latter were converted to Islam, a process which was accelerated in the 4th/10th century, under the Būyids.

In the light of modern "national" movements, there has been a tendency to regard the Arabs and the Iranians as two hostile groups, the latter at first being in subjection and ultimately reasserting themselves with their national dynasties of the 4th/10th century. It is certainly necessary to avoid the opposite extreme of denying that any line of demarcation was apparent or that a great historical and cultural tradition was transmitted from generation to generation in the Iranian consciousness and was, to some extent, communicated to the Arab-Islamic civilization. However, despite the revolts, which were often religious in form, by certain groups in certain regions, there was never a widespread national movement, and the simple fact of the partially national states re-emerging under a Muslim form is a sufficient indication of the limits of the opposition. It has also been alleged that, in their conversion to Islam, the Iranians had at any rate chosen the Shī'a – or opposition – sect; but, whatever may be said at the present day, when Iran is officially and generally Shī'a, mediaeval Iran was never dedicated specifically to Shī'ism, and the Sunnīs were certainly in a majority there, even under the Būyids. The only exception was the Caspian provinces which were isolated and traditionally prone to heresy. The first important centre of the Shī'a was at Qum, a place colonized by the Arabs. There is no need to dwell on these facts in the present chapter, but it was necessary for them to be reviewed from the author's standpoint.

On another matter also there are misunderstandings which have to be cleared. The Arab invasion is sometimes represented as *ipso facto* a penetration by nomads and thus, *ipso facto* negative in its results and harmful to agriculture. Such a view may perhaps be partially true of the later invasions of the Turks and, even more, of the Mongols, but it was not so with the Arabs. In the first place, the town garrisons, even

[1] H. A. R. Gibb, "The Social Significance of the shu'ūbiyya" in *Studia Orientalia Janni Pedersen dicata* (Copenhagen, 1953), pp. 105–14.

when they still retained a strong sense of tribal allegiance, did not hold to the Bedouin way of life, whatever may have been the Bedouin habits of their ancestors. On the other hand, even though certain Arabs, in the most dispossessed regions of the centre and east, were pure Bedouins and frequently insufferable to the inhabitants of the agricultural fringes, economic relations between the nomads and the farmers as a whole, with the resulting exchange of products, were rather a factor of mutual enrichment than of disorder. The nomad economy thus made a positive contribution to regions which without it would have remained empty, because cultivation was not practicable. In this respect the Middle Ages showed an advance on antiquity, for pre-Islamic Iran lacked a sufficient proportion of nomad economy. It is, however, important to distinguish between the semi-nomadism or change of pasture of those who reared sheep in the mountains, as the Kurds had done for many centuries, and the great nomadic movements of Arab camel-drivers on Arab camels, and by certain Turks with the Turkish camel (which was acclimatized to cold winters and suffered in excessive summer heat). The Arab occupation and, even more the subsequent Turkish conquest, were to impose both types of nomadism on the country, but as a whole the Arab occupation made very little change in the semi-nomadism of the mountain regions.

Certain Iranian authors of the Islamic era have produced a summary classification of social divisions, based on a particular aspect of actual social conditions quite independent of the Muslim theoretical system, which paid no heed to them. It might perhaps be possible to discover in this classification, which enumerates soldiers, religious leaders and merchants, but in general makes no mention of peasants, a reflection of the ancient Iranian outlook. It remains, however, too rudimentary and schematic to provide the basis for a description of the true state of affairs under Islam. By and large, and despite overlapping in both directions, it will be simplest to draw a social dividing line between the city and the open country.

There is no doubt that mediaeval Iran continued to be mainly an agricultural country, although it is very difficult, there as in other Muslim and non-Muslim countries, to examine closely the life of the rural inhabitants; in the literature, which is exclusively urban, they are scarcely mentioned, apart from their tax returns. From pre-Islamic times Iran had known flora and fauna (including the silk-worm) which the general Arab–Muslim domination must have distributed over other countries not previously familiar with them; the interest brought to agricultural projects, and especially to irrigation which was essential to them, is demonstrated by the publication, for example, of specialized treatises on the *qanāt*, the subterranean irrigation canals of ancient Iran.[1] It would be useful to know whether the change in sovereignty or subsequent developments provoked notable transformations in the economic and social management of the land. In general, the agreements concluded at the time of the Arab conquest stipulated, in Iran as elsewhere, the right of indigenous owners to retain their property. However, the Muslim state inherited the domains of the Sāsānian state, including private estates which were left without heirs, and distributed them as *qaṭā'i'* (plural of *qaṭī'a*), conferring on the beneficiaries rights which were in effect almost equal to those of true owners. Gradually also, on the legal borderline, quasi-proprietary rights were acquired by prominent persons over lands which, while theoretically remaining the property of their former owners, came under their "protection" by the device of recommendation, *iljā'* or *talji'a*.[2] The large or average-sized property belonging to a native owner by no means disappeared, but it was duplicated by Arab-owned estates from which for practical purposes it was indistinguishable. The owners, whether belonging to one people or the other, often resided in the city, though this characteristic was perhaps not so invariable in many parts of Iran as in the Arab Mediterranean countries, and there were also prominent persons who lived in the country, close to their estates, the development of which they might or might not undertake themselves. These were the *dihqāns,* literally village chiefs, a name which in fact covered a whole gamut of people, from simple cultivators of the soil, who were scarcely better off than their neighbours and subordinates, to true lords of the manor and founders of dynasties. Small properties were often poor, and restricted in scope by debts and mortgages, but at the same time reinforced by the solidarity of the village community, both from the point of view of fiscal responsibility, and because they consisted of developing parcels of land which passed in rotation from one group to another. The great estates, *ḍiyā'*, were for their part cultivated by tenants, *muzāri'(ūn)*, whose methods varied according to the likely yield

[1] Cf. *Istikhrāj-i āb-hā-yi pinhānī* [Extraction of hidden waters] by Abū Bakr Muḥ. b. al-Ḥasan al-Karajī, trans. from Arabic by Ḥusain Khadīvjam (Tehrān, 1345/1967).

[2] Cf. *EI*, 2nd ed. s.v. *ildjā'*, and C. Cahen in *Mélanges Massignon*, vol. 1 (Paris, 1956).

and the local working conditions (particularly as regards irrigation), as has been the case throughout the whole of the Near and Middle East since ancient times.

The word qaṭā'i' has been mentioned, and it is important to clear up numerous misunderstandings concerning its usage in the Muslim world as a whole and also Iran, although it is impossible to give statistics showing the proportions between the various ways of appropriating or exploiting land. It is necessary to repeat here statements which have already been made with regard to the Muslim world in general and which can be found in volume 5 of the present history. By reason of the common Arabic root *q.ṭ.'* of the words qaṭī'a and *iqṭā'* (the latter being the better known), and also because of a regrettable looseness in thought and in translation, the two have often been confused and both indiscriminately have been rendered by the European "fief". Qaṭī'a quite clearly is in no sense a fief; it amounts almost to ownership, carrying with it practically all the rights and indeed also the obligations, as, for example, taxation, and the legal restrictions, that is to say submission to the public administration, which alone had jurisdiction over the lawsuits of the holders. There were of course some estates in inaccessible regions or among semi-autonomous peoples, the masters of which were almost true manorial lords, but such instances were outside the law and were in any case not termed qaṭī'a, nor did they come within the system.[1]

It was precisely because the qaṭī'a was effectively definitive or hereditary in character that the time was bound to come when the state had nothing more to distribute. However, the army still had to be paid and could not be kept waiting. Generally speaking, the land-tax paid by the properties under native ownership was sufficient for this purpose, but the instalments, and especially the actual payment of them, could not always be timed to coincide with the accounts requiring settlement. It was therefore often found more convenient to grant officers the right to intercept at the source revenues to the amount of their pay, and villages or districts known to yield the required totals would be allocated to them with that object. Such was the iqṭā', which is obviously something quite different from the qaṭī'a. The practice appears to have spread over Iraq before actually reaching Iran, and then to have extended over western and southern Iran under the Būyids before affecting eastern Iran; it became progressively more general especially

[1] Cf. *EI*, 2nd ed. s.v. *īghār*.

under the Saljuq Turks in the 5th/11th century. It is sufficient to emphasize that, even though it involved the local administration, it was most often of a temporary nature owing to constant changes in land distribution.

The cultivable lands which had not become state property, whether or not distributed as qaṭā'i', remained theoretically the private estates of their original owners before the Arab conquest. Such was the general rule in the countries conquered by the Arabs, who were discouraged from acquiring land belonging to native inhabitants even by purchase. By and large this policy appears to have been pursued in the Semitic countries of the Near East and in Egypt, that is to say in the parts of the empire which were relatively central and under control. It is more difficult to know what conditions were like in Iran, on which there is less documentary evidence, because so far hardly any research has been devoted to the matter, except in Khurāsān on account of its part in the 'Abbāsid revolt. There is a tendency to believe that private lands were acquired by the Arabs, especially in frontier zones such as the South Caspian provinces. On the other hand it appears that certain peoples who were rapidly converted to Islam may have succeeded in having their lands more or less assimilated with those of the Muslims. It is necessary to understand the financial implications of the matter. The properties which the Arabs possessed in Arabia and the qaṭā'i' which the caliphate had subsequently conceded to them in the conquered countries were subject to a tithe (*'ushr*) on their revenue, while estates belonging to native owners continued to pay the land tax, *kharāj*, which they had been paying under the pre-Islamic system and which, despite the great disparity which existed between lands, was clearly more onerous than the tithe. It had been hoped that, where the holders were converted to Islam, their lands would be transferred to the tithe system, but, for fiscal reasons which are not difficult to understand, the government of the caliphate declared the existing system to be final. The two categories thus remained in opposition, though the contrast was often less marked than might appear, because the holders of estates subject to the tithe did not cultivate the land themselves and the farmers who were the actual cultivators paid them the same amount in rents as they would have had to contribute in kharāj if they had been the owners. There remained also large estates which theoretically were subject to the incidence of the kharāj, but whose owners often found a means of becoming subscribers to a prearranged scale of charges (*muqāṭaʿa*, *īghār*), which simplified the administrative work while allowing them to retain a substantial profit from the rents paid by their tenants. Moreover it appears that in many regions, including particularly almost the whole of Central Asia, at least under the Umayyads, there continued the local land systems which had prevailed before the Arab conquest to the extent that even Arab Muslims were on the same footing as everyone else, without special privileges, the sole personality recognized by the state for taxation purposes being the local dignitary, who was responsible for tribute to be raised from his own land by his own methods. In Iran, as in the rest of the East, fiscal responsibility – and sometimes even farming – was the collective responsibility of a community, which restricted the opportunities for discrimination between individuals.

The tenants paid their rents in kind, according to an agreed percentage. With regard to the tax paid by landowners to the State, however, there were two opposing doctrines in Sāsānian times which continued under Islam. The primitive system, the payment of a fixed proportion in kind, was only workable at times when the economy was short of money. It had, moreover, the disadvantage that the revenues it produced were uncertain and indefinite, and the Sāsānians had converted it for the most part into a tax calculated at a fixed monetary sum per agricultural unit. The peasants frequently had difficulty in raising the required sum when it was due and were thus at the mercy of speculative merchants. Hence in Iraq, where the dense population of Baghdad had somehow to be fed, there was a return to the tax in kind. In Iran it seems that in general the system of fixed taxation persisted and an attempt was made to arrive at the most equitable assessment by taking into account all features of the land and types of cultivation and by allowing rebates and remissions in the event of natural disasters. It is possible, however, that the continuance of the system may have encouraged the peasants to put themselves under the protection of great landowners, to whom they made payments in kind which the landowners were better able than themselves to convert into money.

Under Muslim law, as is well known, there is no right of primogeniture and the successive divisions resulting from this factor led to a splitting-up of great estates at the very time when other forces were working to develop them. Even a practice such as iljā', which was unofficial and lay outside the right of ownership in the strict sense, was treated as an ordinary item in the inheritance and was thus liable to be divided into shares. The practice of iqṭāʿ also superimposed on the right of property another kind of right and this, being combined with a certain service, was not divisible. Until the 5th/11th century it was insecure, however, since the beneficiary was constantly being changed, and, when he strove to acquire some more stable form of property, it became by the same act divisible, like ordinary inherited property. The force of custom was very strong in these matters.

Islam, however, had brought into focus an institution which, from a certain standpoint, allowed the letter of the ordinary law of succession to be bypassed, that of the *waqf*. This institution, guaranteed by the religious law, consisted of the alienation in mortmain of an estate for the benefit of certain defined categories of persons or of public works, it being understood that the administration of the property belonged, according to the founder's injunction, to his family or to certain individual members of it, with the right to deduct from the revenues a sum sufficient to support them and to cover administrative expenses. The result, which had often in fact been the object of the action, was the preservation intact from generation to generation of a certain part of the ownership of the estate in question. In the first centuries of Islam the form of waqf relating to families was much more general than that associated with the maintenance of institutions for the benefit of the public, assured as a whole by the ordinary budget of the State. The balance was to be reversed in later periods which need not be considered here. It should be more or less possible to trace the development of the practice in Iran along the same lines as in Iraq, Syria and Egypt, with special reference to the eventual extension of the waqf for the benefit of the mawālī. In Egypt, on the other hand, only urban properties could be constituted waqfs until the 6th/12th century, to the exclusion of agricultural estates, which in Iraq, by contrast, were predominantly used for the purpose. An attempt should be made to discover what was its position in Iran, and to what extent the waqf for the benefit of mosques, did or did not succeed to trusts previously enjoyed by Zoroastrian institutions, cultural and otherwise. Such a study can perhaps be no more than a pious wish, in the absence of documentary evidence, but a necessary condition for disentangling the problems is first of all to become aware of them.

As a whole, the peasants were despised, although sometimes a voice would make itself heard in their favour. Even if they were not actually attached to the land, the business of the obligations involved in communal development and of tax debts kept them there for practical purposes when they were not in the neighbourhood of a large city. Peasant risings sometimes broke out locally and some of the revolts, presented in the texts from a religious standpoint, have an undeniably social and rural character. It should be understood that the overlords against whom the revolt was directed could be Iranian or Arab indiscriminately. The whole subject is, however, very difficult to elucidate from the documents available and has been too little studied for it to be possible to make any more precise assertions.

Generally speaking the rule of Islam in the Middle Ages is represented as having been accompanied by a significant process of urbanization, whatever the particular region. In respect of Iran, as elsewhere, such a positive statement, without being false, needs to be qualified. It must be admitted that the process of urbanization, which in places dated back to the distant past, was accelerated and intensified by the Sāsānians. Conversely, it can scarcely be denied that many parts of Iran, even under Islam, still remained intrinsically rural and that even the great lords did not always reside in the towns, but were also to be found in fortresses surveying their domains and their people. Despite the importance attained by such provincial cities as Ray, Iṣfahān, Nīshāpūr, Samarqand and certain others at various times, not one of them ever approached the magnitude of Baghdad or Cairo. The Arabs established or re-established, for military reasons, some cities, which then lost their individual character, but the creation of them was not necessarily a gain, for it sometimes resulted in the decline or destruction of earlier cities, just as Iṣṭakhr was replaced by Shīrāz and, in Iraq, Ctesiphon by Baghdad. In Iran as elsewhere, the city was indisputably the centre where the new society and its culture were developed.

Thus it would be most desirable to know the history at least of some of the Iranian cities. With regard to topography, even where some details may be contributed by textual evidence, it is clear that nothing decisive can be settled except by archaeological investigations. Unfortunately, excavations are often impeded by the existence of a modern city superimposed upon the ancient city-site, and, even where a mediaeval city survives to some extent within the modern city, mediaeval archaeology has certainly attracted less interest than remote antiquity, and the monuments of past eras are examined more from the standpoint of artistic merit than for the enlightenment they provide on human affairs. Under such conditions there is no cause for surprise either in the small number of archaeological researches nor in the poverty of the results so far attained. Ray, Nīshāpūr and recently Sīrāf have been the object of expeditions not yet concluded which have been facilitated by the abandonment of the sites, and some other names could be added, such as Bust and Ghazna in Afghanistan. Tirmidh, Samarqand, Panjikent in Central Asia and some other sites have been partially excavated, but here too the efforts are concentrated more on the pre-Islamic past than on the Middle Ages, though it may happen that excavations undertaken for the purpose of investigating ancient sites are obliged to work down through Muslim levels, which is exactly what has happened at Susa, for example.

In any case history in the strict sense can only be founded on textual evidence, involving other difficulties. The geographers make an effort to describe the countryside, but historians, who are most often attracted by the great political centres, in practice if not by design, disregard many of the facts belonging to local history; some regional or local histories have existed, but they have been less well preserved because less often copied. Moreover the diminution of Arab influence in Iran from the 5th/11th century onwards led sometimes to translation, but at other times to the simple loss of works of the first centuries written in Arabic. There existed an abundant supply of literature on cities, some remains of which have survived. They are of a special type and, however disappointing they may often be from the point of view of our present requirements, nevertheless they can and should be utilized much more than has been done. It is relevant here to consider all the biographical dictionaries, the purpose of which was to list all the prominent personages connected with a city and especially, or exclusively, the "men of learning", whose ancestries must be traced in order to establish the soundness of the teachings for which they were responsible. Apart from what may be learned about such persons, the literary material generally includes a more or less lengthy preface praising and describing the city. In exceptional cases an effort was made to write a true history of the city in all its aspects, as was done, for example, in the 6th/12th century by Ibn Funduq in respect of his home town of Baihaq. The accounts of Qum and of Bukhārā, the former only partly preserved, the latter in its entirety (both of them, however, in a Persian translation) are rather histories of provinces or of dynasties than of cities in the strict sense, but are nonetheless worthy of note.

According to tradition, the Iranian city was divided into three parts, a characteristic which distinguished it somewhat from the cities of surrounding countries. There was the citadel (*kuhandiz*), often the original core, the actual city (*shahristān*, in Arabic *madīna*) and a suburb (*bīrūn*, in Arabic *rabaḍ*). This formation, which as a whole was common to all urban agglomerations of normal growth, allowed in detail for the actual city, like the suburb, to consist in its turn of various more or less distinct units, leading a more or less autonomous existence, sometimes even separated by gates. The main roads, which were few, gave access to complexes of lanes or to blind alleys in which, quite clearly defined, dependants or tradesmen were grouped around the residences of the notables. Apart from the great monuments, which themselves were often built of baked brick rather than stone, the ordinary houses, except for the many-storied tenements of the big cities, were constructed of mud or unbaked brick, of which very few traces remain. In certain regions, however, stone or wood made an appearance; at Sīrāf the dwellings of the rich were partly made of teak imported from the Indian Ocean.[1] The life of the house was organized around an interior courtyard or terraces and there was as little access as possible from the street, but here again there were many variations.

The seat of local government was generally in the citadel, but the central monument of the city, in proportion to its degree of conversion to Islam, was the Great Mosque, which did not preclude the existence of small Muslim chapels or, insofar as there were adherents, of the cult-buildings of Mazdaeans, Buddhists or Nestorians (the latter two only in Central Asia).

There has been some discussion in recent times, based particularly on examples in Iran, of the individual or autonomous character of the cities in relation to the country as a whole. Muslim law, of course, took no official cognisance of any intermediate community; it acknowledged the existence only, on the one hand, of the individual, on the other of the general community of believers, the *umma*. It follows also that the various organs of the administration or the religious life were regarded as functions of the state as a whole and not as operating within the limits of the "city". Side by side with this theory, however, there are the actual facts to be considered. It will be seen that there did exist intermediate communities and that, as regards the various agents of the government, not only did they all reside in cities, but some of them had

[1] Ibn Hauqal, ed. Kramers, pp. 281–2; tr. G. Wiet, pp. 277–8.

functions which they would have had no occasion to exercise except in the city. There are other questions which remain unanswered, relating on one side to the economic interdependence of town and country and on the other to the separation between the two. Naturally the country supported the town, by trade, by the rents of the farmers and by the taxation of the landowners, but the town contributed very little to the open country, where the elementary needs of daily life and even implements were supplied by local labour. The great caravans which traversed the country, bringing to the town-dwellers commodities of necessity or luxury not provided by the neighbourhood, were regarded with envy since they contributed nothing to the countryside. They were forbidden to trade outside the city enclosure-walls where they paid their fiscal dues and had their meetings with retail traders.

Subject to the above qualifications, it remains true that many towns were of a semi-rural character and that the villages in their neighbourhood shared in their life and in their conflicts: there was thus, in a sense, an overflow beyond the boundaries of the city. Conversely the framework of local life was often in itself based more on the different quarters or on a particular community than on the city as a whole. This characteristic, which the mediaeval Iranian city shared with many others but possessed perhaps to a particularly high degree, is difficult to interpret correctly, for it was divided not only into quarters but also according to different social levels. In the principal cities and the frontier towns there might be an army, recruited sometimes entirely of foreigners, at other times from Iranian, but not local, stock (Dailamites, for example, or Kurds). There were also government officials (*kuttāb*), who were of great importance socially and culturally, as everywhere else in the Near East, at least until the Turkish epoch. These two classes, however, for lack of sufficiently strong local ties, played a lesser part than did a third category, the religious leaders (including the *qāḍīs* and other men of the law). These latter personages belonged, as they did elsewhere, to various schools: in Iran there were Ḥanafīs, Shāfi'īs (often linked with the "people of the *hadīth*"), Imamian Shī'īs (and Zaidites in the South Caspian provinces), in some places Karrāmiyya, not to mention the secret propagandists of Ismā'īlism or sects which were more or less survivors from the pre-Islamic past. What is remarkable is that these divisions, which were of much greater importance in the realm of theoretical conviction than as applied to practical life, were nevertheless the cause, apparently at least, of topographical and social schisms and the source of perpetual conflicts, even of actual civil wars. With the increase in the mystical forms of religion, prominent rôles were taken by the Ṣūfīs, but in the classical period all the religious leaders and men of the law were important. There was an overlapping of the dividing-lines between doctrines and often between quarters of the town. Sometimes a cross-division could result from the inhabitants of two quarters sharing one ethnic or geographical origin; another time it might happen that the economic activities of the various quarters were not the same and gave rise to conflicts. It has to be admitted, however, that we know little about them.

This question is also related to another, which has received greater attention without being fully elucidated, that of the *futuwwa*. Here evidently there is a mixture of tradition and vocabulary, on the one hand Arabic, on the other Iranian. Arab tradition contributed the *fatā* (plural *fityān*), meaning a brave, generous, chivalrous individual. But in all the old Sāsānian cities there were groups of young men (Persian *javānmardān*) whose community spirit led them to pool their resources in order to achieve the best possible life together, materially and sometimes morally. They had a religion, but it does not appear that religion was the factor which united them, and in any case they came from different religious groups. Almost all of them followed professions, but it would not seem, at any rate before the Turco-Mongolian period, that their union was based on a common profession: their co-operation was of other kinds. It so happened that some of them were poets and from half way through the Middle Ages onwards, the development of certain groups showed a deep appreciation of spiritual values. At the same time certain groups of Ṣūfīs, now organized into communities, were becoming aware of the example of communal life presented by the fityān/javānmardān. Since clearly these were the circles more than any others which produced the writers, there came into existence a complete literature which hinged on the spiritual aspect of the futuwwa (literally "the youth"), a name which was given to their moral principle of cohesion, regardless of the fact that these fityān also had other activities of apparently quite a different kind. In fact they freely professed the legitimacy of theft, provided that it was executed with chivalry to the detriment of the rich and for the corporate benefit of the restricted community. Historians and other authors, in describing the fityān during periods of diminished authority, called them by contemptuous names (adopted as a matter of pride by those concerned), such as *'ayyār(ān)*, *aubāsh*, *shuṭṭār*, etc. (that is, scoundrels, ragamuffins, outlaws) and alleged that they abandoned themselves to various kinds of disorderly behaviour and imposed their "protection" on merchants and on notables at a price. In the large towns the official police forces and the army garrisons held them more or less in respect; in other places, however, they themselves constituted the police, often even to the extent of imposing their own candidate as the head of the town. They frequently had as their leader a *ra'īs*, whose position and functions it is difficult to describe precisely, because the term, which simply means a chief, can perhaps be applied in different ways: sometimes it signifies a kind of local mayor, to confront or oppose the political authority of the prince. Certainly the movements in question were substantial factions (*'aṣabiyyāt*), broader than the communal groups of futuwwa in the strict sense. But there is no doubt that these latter represented both their kernel and their most conspicuous form, a fact which was to be grasped by those ambitious persons who tried to rally the groups of futuwwa in support of themselves. The Ṣaffārid dynasty in Sīstān owed its origin to them.

It is true that in the Semitic, non-Sāsānian, countries of the Near East, there also existed militias, often called *aḥdāth* – another Arabic word meaning "young people", while the fityān/'ayyārān had an actual organization with initiation rites and special insignia (including the "futuwwa trousers"), as well as the moral complexities of their outlook. These features were not to be found among the aḥdāth; indeed the latter were aggrieved with those of their number whom they suspected of wishing to develop along such lines. It is certain therefore that the futuwwa contained an element which, if not purely Iranian, was at least of Iranian–Iraqi and so of Sāsānian origin, representing the strong influence of an Iranian past. Examination of the subject is further complicated by the fact that certain texts appear to confront the reader with the existence not of urban and relatively democratic fityān/javānmardān, but of troops of young aristocrats, of "cavaliers", so to speak, who may have been unrelated to the 'aṣabiyyāt of the towns. Such questions could perhaps be resolved without much difficulty if anything comparable were known in the time of the Sāsānians.

Since the time of the Achaemenids there had been organizations of a similar kind in many other societies but having a purpose which was essentially religious, and it is difficult to form any idea of the manner in which they continued under the Sāsānians. They may have developed so as to be imitated to some extent by the urban associations which appeared after the evolution of the cities. It is possible that the vocabulary and the attitude of mind of Arabs and Iranians, of aristocratic and lower levels, may have undergone a process of intercontamination and it may even be asked whether the Arabic *'ayyār*, which appears in this sense only in the realm under consideration, and the Middle Persian *ayār/yār* = auxiliary, often applied to members of the above-mentioned ancient brotherhoods, may not have interacted on one another.[1]

One other feature must be emphasized which was characteristic of at least a number of Iranian areas. Perpetually exposed as they were to hostile threats from the northeast and the northwest, the Iranians, especially those living in frontier zones, had preserved a military aristocracy and, even in the cities, the tradition of certain "sporting" disciplines, of which there was no exact equivalent in the Arab world. It is true that in Iran, as in the other Muslim countries, the actual practice of arms in the regular army came eventually to be reserved for special racial groups, among which Turkish slaves were bound to play a larger part. On the Arab side the Bedouin retained their custom of war by razzia (predatory raid) which must have provided them with a military function in certain principalities from the 4th/10th and 5th/11th centuries onwards. The Khurāsānīs who, after furnishing the army for the 'Abbāsid victory, had had a semi-monopoly of service in the regular army for three-quarters of a century, continued to play an important if not exclusive rôle in the provincial armies of the Ṭāhirids, Sāmānids and Ṣaffārids, while the Kurds and Dailamites constituted the essential element of the forces of Iran in the west. The Iranians had learned, from contact with the warrior nomads of Central Asia, certain military techniques which, although not enabling them to arrest the Arab advance in the conditions prevailing after the Sāsānian collapse in the 1st/7th century, must have earned the appreciation of their new masters and contributed to their being given the position which they occupied immediately after the 'Abbāsid revolution. In the cities there was training in archery, and fencing was practised in the *zūrkhānas*. It was by no means fortuitous that the subsequent literature of all Muslim countries gave pride of place in this sphere to the Iranian masters. On the other hand, along the borders of the Byzantine Empire, in Central Asia and, to a lesser degree, on the frontier with India, there were to be found, in a semi-permanent state of mobilization, groups of

[1] G. Widengren, *Der Feudalismus im alten Iran* (Cologne, 1969), p. 39.

combatants, religious volunteers (*ghāzīs*), to which, apart from the Bedouin, the Arab world offered no parallel. Some of them simply dwelt in the cities; others were organized in fortified posts along the frontier zones. Of course in the frontier towns there was often overlapping between the ghāzīs and the fityān/ʿayyārān, but it is clear that, whatever has been said to the contrary, the organizations were by no means identical and that there were, in the cities of the interior, fityān who were not ghāzīs, and in the frontier posts ghāzīs who were not fityān. The conversion of the Turks of Central Asia, the conquests of Northern India and of Asia Minor, inasmuch as they deprived the ghāzīs of their employment, were bound ultimately to deal a fatal blow to this section of the Iranian population, whose traditions were adapted by the Turks and must have been transported by them to new theatres of war. Until that time, however, they played an important part.

As already stated, the groups or movements of the fityān/ʿayyārān were not, despite frequent allegations to the contrary, professional in character, in the sense that they were not disposed according to professions and did not concern themselves with organizing the professions. It remains to be seen how in fact those professions were organized which, on a lower level than the political, administrative and religious aristocracies, provided a living for the majority of the population. Here again the matter is complicated, and it is important to dispel misunderstandings.

The general question of the existence of professional corporations in Muslim cities at the peak period of the Middle Ages has been much debated in recent times and does not perhaps present itself in exactly the same terms in the Iranian and the Arab worlds. What is essential is to proceed from a more exact definition than has yet been formulated and to set the problem in its historical perspective. It may be repeated that Muslim law does not recognize any intermediate collective moral entity between the individual person and the community of Believers as a whole, a fact which of course is not enough to establish that such collective bodies did not exist. But here it is important to make a proper distinction between the different historical realities. There could be collective bodies even in the Muslim world, such, for example, as the futuwwa organizations described above, but, as has been pointed out, they do not appear to have been connected, at any rate in the period under consideration, with the "professional" structure of society. There could be, and certainly was, a systematic professional organization involving groups of certain kinds, but, as in the case, broadly speaking, of the Roman Empire and, very definitely, of the Byzantine Empire, which bordered on the Muslim world, what was implied was a state system without independent responsibility of the persons concerned, or any extension of the activities of professional groups beyond the requirements of their calling. Nothing in such a system corresponds exactly with the professional corporations known to European history, namely associations connected with the practice of a profession which assume responsibility for the organization of it and also for large sectors of the extraprofessional life of its members – in short the framework, on a professional basis, of the social structure. Without any clarification of these necessary distinctions, a European terminology, apparently parallel but representing different conceptions, has been used to assert the existence of a state of affairs which is incapable of proof.

Subject to this qualification, it is quite certain that there existed in the mediaeval cities of Iran and Central Asia a topographical grouping of most of the trades, similar to that which prevailed throughout the rest of the Muslim world and in the majority of cities in all mediaeval societies. Such a grouping obviously implied some degree of familiarity, with interests and reactions partly shared for example when threats or disaffection resulted in the closing of the *sūqs*; attendance at the same mosque served to bring together people in the same trade or profession, before they lived in establishments founded by some or other of their members; this came about only at the end of the Middle Ages. The person responsible for living conditions in the trading community, as in the rest of Islam, was the *muḥtasib* "police inspector", or in a large town the *'arīf* (sometimes *amīn*) representing each separate trade under the direction of the aforementioned muḥtasib. Even if this personage himself belonged to the trade (which, for the latter, was by no means always the case), there was nothing to prevent his being appointed by the government to be a government official, without the benefit of any professional "counsel" at his side. The system under consideration, therefore, though perhaps less severe, was in the same category as that which prevailed in Rome and Byzantium. Members of trades or professions were registered by the administration – it was said that they had a *dīvān*. The government agents, at least in certain cases, exercised close control over the manufacture of products (this fact is known with particular reference to the textiles of Kāzarūn). Various trades were obliged, instead of paying other taxes, to make deliveries in kind, the deduction and collection of which obviously suggest a certain degree of organization, though there is not necessarily anything corporate about it. The origin of the muḥtasib himself is not clear,[1] in that he was evidently continuing in a way the work of those agents in the ancient cities with comparable functions, while at the same time answering certain requirements appropriate to Arab-Muslim cities. Existing knowledge of Iranian affairs is too imperfect for it to be possible to specify exactly how the transition from the ancient system to the new was effected.

It remains true, however, that the professional, communal spirit was more pronounced in Iran than in the Arabic-speaking world. Among the Arabs the name of an individual comprised, when given in full, a genealogy of which the final and essential component indicated his membership of a tribe. The non-Arabs of the Muslim world, with certain exceptions such as Berbers, Kurds, etc., were no longer sufficiently mindful of their ancient tribal affiliations to mention them in this way. On the other hand, they indicated, just as clearly and in the same order, their membership of a profession or trade, especially, of course, when it happened to be a fairly exalted one, a practice not peculiar to Iran, but especially in evidence there. Moreover certain texts, admittedly very rare and rather late in date, refer to the existence, in the parts of Central Asia under Persian influence and in Āzarbāījān, of several crafts in which, exceptionally, there was an organization for mutual assistance between members, *tanāṣur*, operative at least for the collection of judicial compensation where damages were due.[2] It is not impossible that the commercial civilization of the Soghdians may have left some legacies of this kind. The course of development certainly proceeded towards the formation of professional corporations in the Turco-Mongolian period, but there is no authority for dating them to an earlier epoch except where indicated above.

It may be inferred that, within each craft, several young apprentices and slaves worked around a master. In general it was a matter of small workshops, which were not always separate either from the dwelling of the master or from the little shop where he marketed the product which had been manufactured more or less under the eyes of the customers. Sometimes, however, it appears that quite a large number

[1] Cf. Benjamin R. Foster, "Agronomos and muḥtasib", *JEHSO*, vol. XIII (1970), pp. 128–45.

[2] C. Cahen in *The Islamic City*, ed. S. Stern and A. Hourani, p. 59.

of workmen were to be found in the same premises working on the same product, though what it amounted to was a juxtaposition of individual crafts rather than a chain of production; at most it represented a series of independent operations. This method appears to have been applied to the manufacture of textiles, spinning being often the province of women, weaving and subsequent processes handled by men. Where costly fabrics were involved, there was state control, as evidenced in Kāzarūn.[1] There were also state workshops in the capital cities for luxury textiles (*ṭirāz*), weapons, coins, paper etc.

In so far as the biographical dictionaries, in giving the names of personages, normally mention the trade or profession to which they or their parents belonged, they give some indication of the nature and statistical distribution of crafts, at least in certain cities. Certainly it is possible to gain some idea at least of the wide diversity of crafts which existed, of which there is independent evidence, and perhaps the variations of time and place might also be ascertained. It is necessary, however, to realize that professions are indicated for only limited classes, and that occupations which are not sufficiently exalted are passed over in silence; the statistical picture may thus be completely falsified; many important textile merchants will be found, but hardly any weavers.

As in the majority of societies before the arrival of large-scale modern capitalism, instances of limited capitalism, where they existed, were commercial rather than industrial, while again in certain cases, such as the textile industry, it is difficult to follow the exact line of demarcation. Indeed, even in the realm of commerce there was not sufficient independence in relation to other sectors of the economy. To a considerable extent the merchants drew the capital with which they conducted their business not only from the profits of previous transactions, but from the revenues derived from land acquired out of those profits or from the estates of prominent persons who were anxious to obtain interest, by means of various contracts of association and commendam, on the income from their property, or again from state revenues which they administered, either when trading for the treasury or as marginal profit on tax-collection. Whatever may have been the social standing of businessmen, they were not the masters – it was the military who were to achieve that eminence.

Although it is not possible in this chapter to contemplate a study of

[1] Ibn Balkhī, as reported by A. Mez, *Die Renaissanz des Islams*, p. 434.

the "international" trade of Iran, it must nevertheless be remembered that in this sphere important differences existed between the various provinces. Central Asia was the great turntable for relations with China, the Eurasian steppe and the Arab–Persian world of the Near East. Baghdad, on the other side of Iran, and Constantinople, beyond the borders of Islam, were two major centres of redistribution. Iran proper took part in this important commerce by means of the great roads which linked Central Asia on the one hand with Baghdad, on the other with Asia Minor and the Byzantine Black Sea. There existed besides the trade of the Indian Ocean which had its terminus at Baṣra in Iraq, with ports of call in the Persian Gulf which became increasingly important with the establishment of the autonomous Iranian principalities. The route from Khurāsān to Iraq was also the pilgrims' road, marked out by cities which owed to it some part of their significance if not the whole – Samarqand, Marv, Balkh, Nīshāpūr, Ray and Hamadān. On the Gulf the great Iranian port was Sīrāf, until in about 390/1000 an earthquake, and also circumstantial changes, which operated in favour of the Red Sea and to the detriment of the Persian Gulf, ruined it without actually producing a substitute. Meanwhile other cities were attracting the merchants, political capitals or rich provincial centres such as Shīrāz, Iṣfahān, Herāt, later Ghazna, and others.

The merchants belonged to different religions and moved about and did business together. Iran was travelled over by Arabs or Arabicized Semites coming from Syria or Mesopotamia and by Jews of more distant provenance, if the account by Ibn Khurdādbih of the Rahdanites is to be taken literally. There is little doubt however that the Iranians themselves formed the majority of the merchants, both on land and in the Indian Ocean from Malaysia (and sometimes even as far as China) to East Africa. A whole history of Persian expansion needs to be worked out. In the realm of commerce, Sindbad the sailor was a symbol, popularized in Arabic, but the vocabulary of business and of navigation (outside the Mediterranean) was, even in Arabic, deeply imbued with Persian.

An attempt has recently been made to analyse the mobility of the population in certain cities which happened to be Iranian by studying the *nisba* (name denoting origin) of persons listed in some of the biographical dictionaries. The merchants, at any rate itinerant merchants, are obviously conspicuous among the mobile elements of the population, but a second category, which can sometimes obscure the former and is more clearly apparent in the sources, is that of the students sometimes of riper years, who went from town to town to complete their education by sitting at the feet of new masters.[1] I recently noted evidence of the presence of some Andalusians at Qazvīn.

In pre-Islamic times Iranian society had been possessed of reserves of slaves and had retained them and probably added to their number under Islam, a factor which enabled them to undertake military or commercial operations on the frontiers of Muslim territory. It is important, however, not to exaggerate or misunderstand the character of this system of slavery. With the exception of the Turks in the army, the slaves, whatever might be their origin (Slavs, Negroes, etc.) were essentially domestic – including concubines – and were limited almost exclusively to the towns; they were not used at all for work on the land and even in cities provided only a part, alongside the free wage-earners, of artisan craftsmanship. Latifundia or large private estates of the Spartacist type, made notorious by the revolt of the Zanjīs of Lower Iraq, on the borders of Iran, were quite exceptional. Again, however, it must be stressed that no study has been made of slavery in the special conditions prevailing in Iran. There also existed, it has to be admitted, in the towns of Iran and especially the large cities, a lumpenproletariat of men without occupations, ready to come to blows for anything or nothing, hangers-on of the rich and ambitious or merely idle starvelings.

In conclusion, it should be reiterated that the above sketch is based essentially on some general knowledge of the problems confronting the Muslim world, whereas Iran has a specific history of its own. Conversely, however, it is possible to gain the impression that certain authors, even in the Muslim epoch, regarded the history of Iran as a separate reality in itself, isolated from its Muslim environment and from integration, more or less, in the Muslim world. Obviously if research is to be productive, consideration must be given both to the state of affairs in the Muslim world as a whole and to the particular traditions of Iran. Such efforts have been made in the realm of political and cultural history, but very little with regard to social matters and here there is an urgent need still to be satisfied.

[1] R. Bulliet, "A Quantitative Approach to Mediaeval Muslim Biographical Dictionaries", *JESHO*, vol. XIII (1970), p. 195.

CHAPTER 9

THE VISUAL ARTS

At this stage of our knowledge it is impossible to write a coherent *history* of Islamic art in Iran before the appearance of the Saljuqs. There are at least three reasons for this state of affairs. One lies in the nature of the documents which are available. Many early monuments of architecture whose existence can be surmised from texts, inscriptions or simple logic have either disappeared or have been so completely transformed in later times (including improperly recorded contemporary restorations) as to make any reconstruction most uncertain. Clearly dated architectural remains from early Islamic times are few for the immense territory of Iran and therefore stylistic or typological classifications are tenuous and liable to modification after every new discovery. Archaeological investigations have not been so far as useful as might have been expected, for the two most important ones, at Ray and Nīshāpūr, have not yet been published, while the very exciting ongoing excavation of Sīrāf has only appeared in the form of preliminary reports. And if one turns to the other arts, matters are both simpler and more complicated. They are simpler because certain series of works such as northeastern Iranian ceramics or the so-called post-Sāsānian silver are at least typologically identifiable. But matters are still complicated because the exact development of styles within either one of these techniques is still very unclear. Furthermore, because of the limited archaeological exploration of Iran in this early period, the degree to which any one type is valid for the whole of Iran is still almost impossible to determine.

A second reason for our difficulty in presenting the material lies in the weakness of the conceptual framework with which scholarship has tended to approach the problem. The fundamental question is whether in matters of functional needs and of artistic taste the Muslim conquest was a revolutionary event which radically and permanently transformed earlier traditions or whether it was but a peculiar spiritual and cultural overlay without major visually perceptible consequences which merely transformed or channelled into new directions an artistic language which had existed before. Whatever answer is to be eventually given to this question, it is affected by a host of variables each of which needs investigation. Since effective Muslim control over any part of Iran took place only after the establishment of a first Muslim architecture in Iraq and Syria, to what extent is the artistic Islamization of Iran affected by an earlier Islamic art in the Fertile Crescent? Conversely, if one recalls the importance of Persians at the ʿAbbāsid court in Iraq, especially after 184/800, should we not at times consider the art of Iraq in the 3rd/9th and 4th/10th centuries as Persian? Inasmuch as totally different pre-Islamic traditions existed in the western and northeastern parts of the Iranian world, were there different modifications brought by Islam to earlier artistic modes? Is the better knowledge we have of Khurāsān and Transoxiana merely the result of more work carried out in these areas than in Fārs or Jibāl or did Islam really become more important earlier in the northeast than in the west? The answer to these questions does not lie only in the study of the monuments but in the investigation of the political, social and cultural conditions of Islamic Iran from the 1st/7th to the 5th/11th centuries. Such studies as do exist have tended to avoid purely archaeological or visual evidence, while art historians and archaeologists have developed hypotheses which are only too little based on a full examination of literary sources. Yet the complexities involved in interpreting properly the fragmentary evidence we possess from either side are of such magnitude that only a systematic co-ordination between written and visual documents can lead to satisfactory conclusions.

Finally in this period – as in so many other periods of the arts of Iran – the lack of monographic studies on individual monuments or on series of monuments is a third reason for reticence in attempting to synthesize the art of the period. Even though recent Soviet scholarship has at least made most of the monuments from Soviet Central Asia comparatively accessible and even though the late E. Kühnel put together the information available to him about one specific moment in the early Islamic art of Iran, we are still in need of many more studies like the forthcoming publication of the Nīshāpūr ceramics by Charles Wilkinson.

For all these reasons the pages which follow will simply attempt to summarize what is already known but their conclusions should be taken essentially as possible hypotheses to be checked against new evidence. Although it seems possible for this particular period to cover separately the two areas of western and northeastern Iran, I have preferred the more traditional approach of discussing individual techniques separately, first architecture and architectural decoration, then the so-called minor arts whose importance is far greater than their slightly pejorative name suggests. In general I have tended to limit my evidence to such areas as are part of the Iranian world proper and to exclude sites like Susa which are strictly speaking in the then predominantly Arab Fertile Crescent. On the other hand the now primarily Turkish but then Iranian-speaking Central Asia is included. Yet it should be realized that the process of Turkification of Central Asia had begun during the centuries under consideration and that the lower Mesopotamian valley had been a Sāsānian province almost as much as Fārs. For a proper definition of the changes effected by Islam, Mesopotamian evidence is essential and one at least of the factors defining the end of our period is the possible impact of Turks on the art and culture of Iran. The full consideration of these two problems would, however, lead us too far astray and require the study of monuments which are outside the narrow definition of Iran. Their existence illustrates however the danger of seeing Iranian art at this time in a narrow regional setting rather than as part of the newly formed Islamic art.

I. ARCHITECTURE AND ARCHITECTURAL DECORATION

The most and almost the only characteristic early Islamic building is the mosque and it is around the development of the mosque that one should attempt to formulate the history of architecture in early Islamic Iran. Unfortunately the evidence is so incomplete and so controversial that such a history cannot as yet be written. On the basis of what is known the following points can be made.

First of all there is no doubt that, as the Arabs introduced Islam to Iran, they brought with them the hypostyle mosque they had created in Iraq some time between 14/635 and 81/700. Hypostyle mosques are known archaeologically at Sīrāf, Nāyīn, Dāmg͟hān (fig. 1),[1] in the Marv oasis, in Buk͟hārā and Samarqand. They can be assumed to have existed in Yazd, Damāvand, Ardistān, Iṣfahān and in any number of other places on the basis of the kind of transformations introduced into

[1] A. Godard, "Le Tari Khana de Damghan", *Gazette des Beaux-Arts*, sixth series, vol. XII (Dec. 1934). For a related monument at Fahraj near Yazd see K. Pirnia, "Masjid-i Jāmi'-i Fahraj", *Bāstān-shināsī va Hunar-i Īrān*, vol. V (1970). Several other early mosques have recently been discovered but have not yet been published.

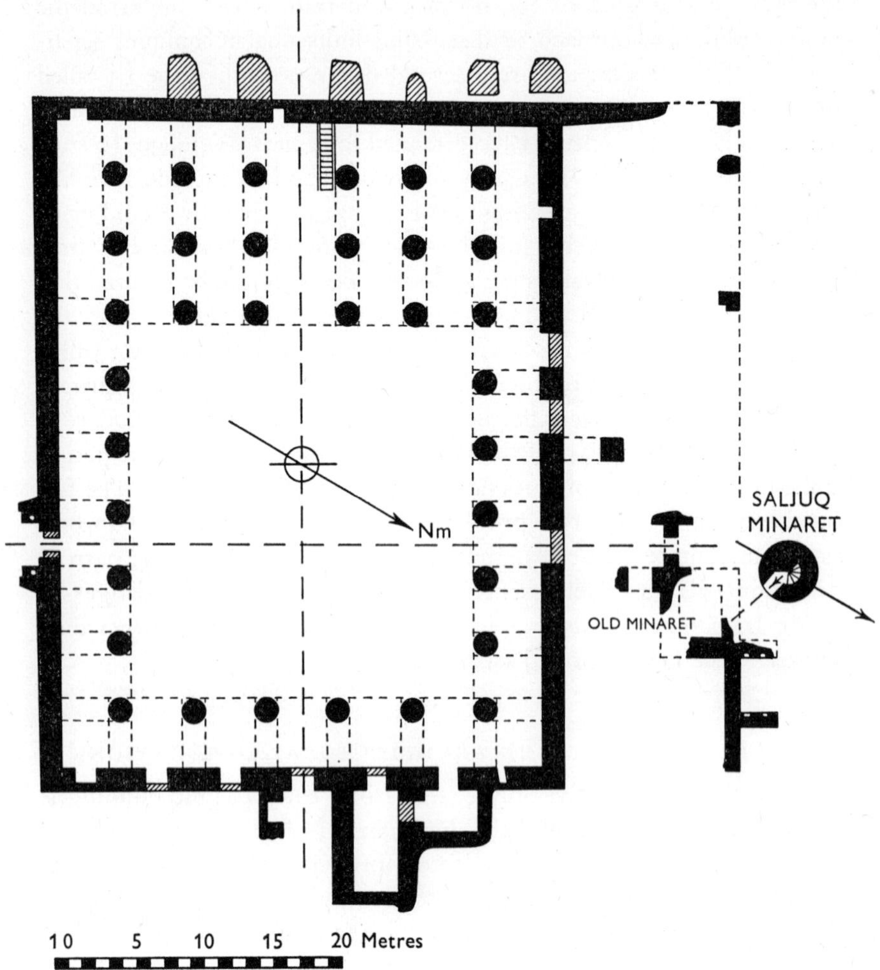

Fig. 1. Plan of Dāmghān mosque.

the main mosques of these cities in the 6th/12th century or later (see bibliography). The existence of hypostyle mosques is also indicated by a number of texts, of which the most celebrated is in Muqaddasī[1] and describes the several stages involved in the construction of the Nīshāpūr mosque. Unfortunately few texts are precise and no clear idea can be formed of the shape given to the twenty-six mosques from early Islamic times listed in a history of Gurgān. Many difficulties occur as

[1] Muqaddasī, *Aḥsan al-taqāsīm*, ed. M. J. de Goeje (Leyden, 1906), p. 316.

one tries to interpret the evidence of the *Tārīkh-i Qum* for a mosque with a large dome or for a mosque with thirteen gates, for, if the latter appears indeed to indicate a large hypostyle building with entrances from many directions, the former may have belonged to another and rarer type to be discussed a bit further on; and the lengthy account by al-Narshakhī of the mosques of Bukhārā, however enlightening it may be on certain details of construction and on various aspects of the life carried on in mosques, tells us almost nothing about the physical type of building involved. If it seems appropriate to suppose that most of these mosques known from literary sources were hypostyle, the reasons lie either in a variety of minor details such as the number of gates and the fires which consumed wooden columns at some stage of the building's history or in the fact that most of them were built by governors appointed from Iraq or Syria, often natives of the Fertile Crescent who can be assumed to have followed the more or less standard models of early Islamic architecture. But it must be admitted that this conclusion is based on an interpretation of early Islamic culture in Iran as derived from the more strongly creative centres outside of Iran rather than on a coherent body of comparable archaeological or literary data.

The same difficulty occurs as one tries to define the architectural characteristics of these hypostyle mosques. They seem to have almost always had one axial nave wider and perhaps higher than the others, thus utilizing principles of organization of space developed, for ideological or formal reasons, in a very specific tradition first known in Syria and avoiding the pure hypostyle of the earliest mosques of Iraq and Egypt. Some of the Iranian mosques were even provided with cupolas, probably in front of the *miḥrāb* as in Mediterranean mosques, although it is not excluded that some other use was given to the dome described by Muqaddasī in Nīshāpūr. The existing archaeological evidence does not make it possible to provide a fully coherent interpretation of texts like Muqaddasī's or like the one in the *Tārīkh-i Qum* which describe the apparently striking domes found in a small number of major mosques.

The walls of most of these mosques were of unbaked brick – hence the collapses so often mentioned in texts as in the *Tārīkh-i Bukhārā* – but baked brick began to make its appearance, especially in eastern Iran. In western Iran the Sāsānian technique of rubble in mortar was used as well. None of the mosques which remain exhibit any sort of sophistication in the use of brick on walls. The main internal support consisted in wooden columns (certainly fairly common in northeastern Iran but probably also known in the west) and in polygonal or circular brick piers (pls. 2, 3). The latter are generally squat and heavy, reflecting the uncertainty about the nature of the single support in an enclosed space which was inherited from Sāsānian architecture. Most of the walls and columns were covered with stucco, at times, as at Nāyīn, decorated (pl. 4). Two types of ceilings and roofs are found. One consisted of a flat roof – often in wood – over heavy arches. A second one, best illustrated in Dāmghān (pl. 1), was made up of long barrel vaults taken from Sāsānian architecture and adapted to the hypostyle's multiplicity of single supports. While the historical importance of this translation of a form developed on heavy walls into a new setting is considerable and has often been recognized, its aesthetic merit is somewhat debatable in spite of the rhapsodic treatment it has received on occasion.

Such seems to be the evidence available for hypostyle buildings, without doubt the most common type in the main cities of early Islamic Iran, especially those with a large influx of Arab inhabitants or utilized as administrative or political centres. Before we can evaluate it properly, however, we must turn to another aspect of mosque architecture in Iran which distinguishes Iran from any other Islamic province during the first centuries of the new faith. Considerable evidence exists for mosque types which are aberrant and considerably at variance from the oecumenical hypostyle. Each of these types poses its own set of problems, most of which have not yet been solved.

The first type is only known archaeologically in the one instance of Yazdikhwāst and consists of the Sāsānian cultic building known as the *chahār ṭāq* transformed into a mosque. It is indeed likely that such transformations occurred elsewhere as well[1] but it should be noted that, on the whole, the evidence of a widespread transformation of pre-Islamic religious buildings into Muslim ones is very scant and in contradiction with the very nature of the early Muslim takeover which was usually not through physical conquest but through treaties which guaranteed the maintenance of former religious buildings. A second aberrant type has recently been isolated quite independently by Dr L.

[1] The evidence for this will be found in a lengthy commentary by R. Ettinghausen on my contribution to vol. 5 of *Cambridge History of Iran* (1968) in *Artibus Asiae*, vol. XXXIX (1969).

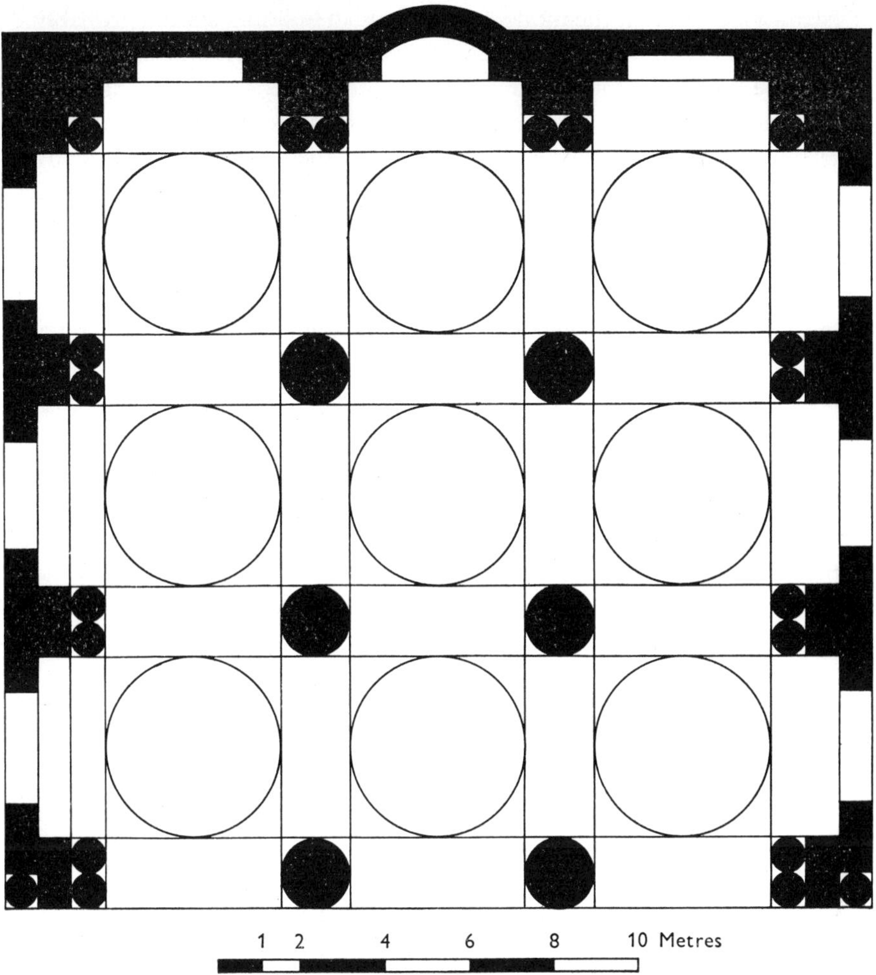

Fig. 2. Plan of Balkh mosque.

Golombek and by Professor Pugachenkova.[1] It consists of a square building divided into nine square bays covered with domes. Its most important example in the Iranian world occurs at Balkh in a mosque (fig. 2) datable in the 3rd/9th century on the basis of its stucco decoration. Two other examples exist as well in northeastern Iran but the interesting point about this type is that, like the hypostyle mosque, it is

[1] L. Golombek, "Abbasid mosque at Balkh", *Oriental Art*, vol. xv (1969); G. A. Pugachenkova, "Les Monuments peu connus de l'Architecture Médiévale de l'Afghanistan", *Afghanistan*, vol. xxi (1968), pp. 18ff.

Islam-wide and that the model for the Iranian building should probably be sought in the west. It is much more difficult to explain the function of these mosques; they were certainly not congregational buildings in the same sense as the large hypostyle buildings and should probably be related to the hitherto little explored type of the private *masjid*. Equally complex is the question of the origin of the form, for, except for a presumably secular *kūshk* in Central Asia, no clear parallel exists for it anywhere.

It may be possible to relate to this type the unique "Digaron" mosque in the small village of Hazāra near Bukhārā, although I would prefer for the time being to consider it differently.[1] On the basis of excavated data the building is not later than the early 5th/11th century. It is essentially a cube, about fifteen metres to the side, with a central cupola held on four large brick piers supporting heavy festooned arches and surrounded by an ambulatory with four corner domes and with barrel vaults in intermediate spaces. The type is connected once again with pre-Islamic religious buildings known in western Iran but not in Central Asia. We shall see later that it is also related to a certain type of early Iranian mausoleum. It should be noted, however, that the presence of this building in a small village makes it very dangerous to give it too much importance and it may altogether be simpler to follow Nilsen's suggestion that a hypostyle model was modified here by some local tradition.

A fourth or third mosque type is equally problematic. But it would be a far more important and far more original type than the previous one if its existence can clearly be demonstrated, for evidence for it occurs both in the western (at Nairīz, fig. 3) and in the northeastern (Bāshān) Iranian worlds and it utilizes a form which will be of considerable importance in later Iranian architecture.[2] The characteristic feature of this type lies in the presence of a huge axial *aivān* which dominates the rest of the building. At Nairīz, whose earliest construction can be dated around 375/985, the construction of the aivān is different from that of the rest of the building and for these reasons it has been suggested that there was a mosque type which consisted originally simply of an aivān and that attendant constructions were generally added at a later time. The evidence still seems to me to be

[1] V. A. Nilsen, *Monumentalnaya Arkhitektura Bukharskogo Oazisa* (Tashkent, 1956).

[2] A. Godard, "Le masjid-e Djuma'a de Niriz", *Āthār-é Īrān*, vol. 1 (1936), and G. A. Pugachenkova, *Iskusstvo Turkmenistana* (Moscow, 1967), p. 112.

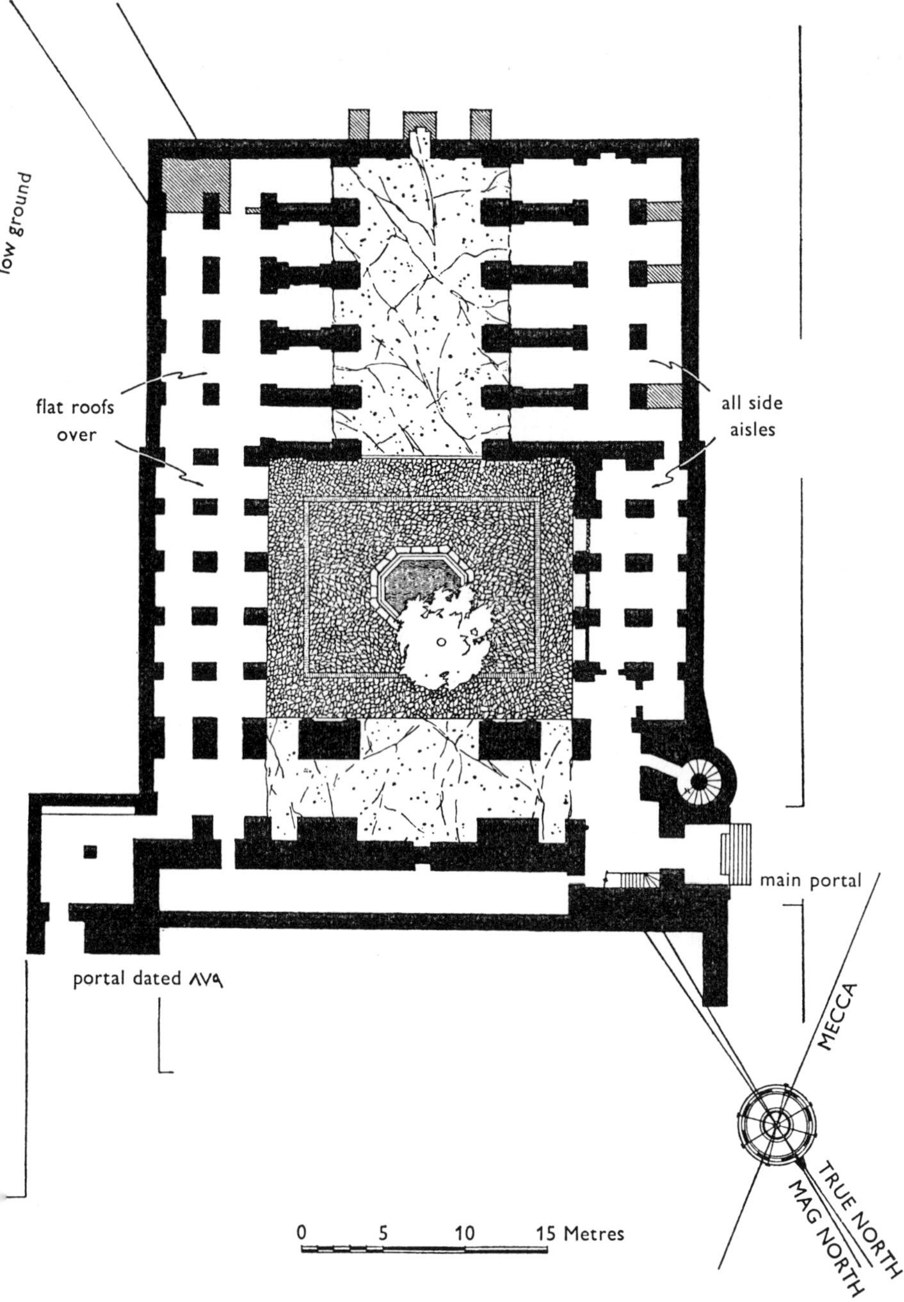

Fig. 3. Plan of Nairīz mosque.

very uncertain and one of the arguments against the hypothesis is that so few instances exist, before or after the Muslim conquest, of the aivān used alone. Furthermore, a good case has been made in the instance of Nairīz for the possibility that the aivān was added later to pre-existing hypostyle building. As to the Bāshān mosque, its archaeological history and its internal characteristics are not available. Thus, while we can obviously not exclude the possibility of this fourth type of aberrant mosque, its actual existence is far from being certain.

Finally no discussion of the early Iranian mosque can avoid mentioning a fifth type which has not remained in a single example but whose existence has been assumed because of a number of peculiarities in later mosques. The type has been discovered and investigated by A. Godard who gave it the name of *mosquée-kiosque*. According to his theory there would have been a type of mosque consisting of a vast space, probably enclosed by a wall and paved, in which the only constructed part was, on the side of the *qibla* and in the centre of the whole composition, a single domed room comparable in form to the Sāsānian chahār ṭāq. The most important and most valid archaeological argument for this hypothesis is that at least twelve 6th/12th-century mosques possess a domed room which is of a different date from and usually earlier than the rest of the building. None of these domes, however, can be dated before the middle of the 5th/11th century, although many of the mosques in which they are found can be proved to have existed since early Islamic times. The historical explanation for the existence of this type lies in the hypothesis of the take-over by early Muslims of the Sāsānian chahār ṭāq as their main religious form. Contrary arguments exist as well. First, as was mentioned before, there is but one instance where it can actually be proved that a chahār ṭāq was adapted to the Muslim cult. Secondly, the main city sanctuaries of pre-Islamic Iran as we know them in Bishāpūr or in Takht-i Sulaimān were far vaster and more complex entities than the simple dome on four supports and some doubt exists as to whether the chahār ṭāq really existed in pre-Islamic times as a totally independent architectural unit. Finally, an alternative explanation has been proposed by Sauvaget for the cupolas of Saljuq times. He suggested that in most instances they were inserted into earlier hypostyle buildings and that they were the *maqṣūras* of princes and governors built on a particularly grand scale by the new feudal rulers of western Iran. While this hypothesis may not solve all the problems posed by the Saljuq buildings, it still seems to me far more likely than the theory of a type of building of which no example remains. But in the context of this volume it may be preferable to conclude that an unsolved problem exists in 6th/12th century architecture for which one *may* have to assume the existence of a *mosquée-kiosque*. It is only through carefully controlled excavations in the major later buildings that the matter will be solved.

Such appear to be the available documents about the Iranian mosque in early Islamic times and a way in which they can be organized according to types of plans. Additional documents do exist. Some are details. Thus, while the Dāmghān mosque shows the existence of the Mediterranean square minaret, the circular minarets which will be the glory of Iranian architecture from the 5th/11th century onward begin to appear in Nāyīn and in Central Asia. None however seems to be clearly datable before the very last decades of the 4th/10th century. Other documents are more difficult to interpret, because they appear for the time being to be in a sort of vacuum. Thus, if it proves to be true that the extraordinary portal found in Iṣfahān is indeed that of the Jurjir mosque known through texts, then we would have here our first example of a work of royal Būyid architecture and the first instance of a complex decorated mosque portal in Iran.[1]

Several preliminary conclusions may be proposed concerning the first Iranian mosque. First it must be repeated that, extensive though it may seem to be, our information is very imperfect not only because of the vastness of the region with which we are concerned but also because small, provincial buildings in minor towns are far better represented than the constructions in the great capitals. While the history of the mosque west of the Zagros is based on Sāmarrā, Baghdad, Damascus, Jerusalem, Cairo, Qairawān and Cordova, in Iran we know next to nothing about the mosques of Ray, Shīrāz, Balkh, Nīshāpūr, Herāt, Marv, Bukhārā and Samarqand. This lopsided view we have of the early Iranian mosque is in remarkable contrast to the situation in Saljuq times and makes it very difficult to use the evidence we do possess either for the history of the mosque in general or for the history of early Islamic architecture in Iran.

Having provided this caveat, we may be justified in emphasizing the variety of the formal types found in early Iranian mosques. While the hypostyle predominates, even when modified by various local traditions, it was certainly not the only available type. The question is why

[1] A. Godard, "The Jurjir Mosque in Isfahan" in *A Survey of Persian Art*, vol. XIV (Oxford, 1967), p. 3100.

did the Iranian world develop a greater variety of forms than the Mediterranean Muslim world. Several reasons can be suggested. One is that many Islamic centres in Iran were far removed from the main creative centres of early Islamic culture. Another one may be that the traditional architecture of Iran at the time of the Muslim conquest was ill-adapted to the needs for a large congregational space, whereas the Mediterranean with its columnar tradition had a versatile unit which could be used for the new culture. It would only be at a later time that certain internal changes in the nature of the faith itself and the development of the monumental four-aivāns plan coincided to create a "classical" Iranian mosque type. Or perhaps already in early Islamic times Iranian Islam did not emphasize the same unitarian tendencies as Arab Islam.

Whatever the reasons there was no clear and typical Iranian mosque form in early Islamic times. Or at least so it seems within the peculiar prism of the information we possess. Yet, even if future excavations show that the mosques of the great Iranian cities tended to be fully in the Islam-wide hypostyle tradition, the facts that this tradition did not seep down to all levels and in all parts of Iran and that thus local traditions were more easily preserved in Iran than elsewhere during the first centuries of Islamic rule will have important consequences in the following period. It is thanks to this conservative tendency that Iran maintained a large number of pre-Islamic architectural forms.

While the early Iranian mosque appears thus as a culturally and historically interesting but artistically secondary architectural development, matters are quite different when we turn to other architectural functions. There on the contrary it is almost from the very beginning that the Islamic architecture of Iran created novelties for which the pre-Islamic past cannot account.

The most important of these new functions of a monumental architecture is the commemorative, mostly funerary, one which is between religious and secular realms. In the 4th/10th century the whole Islamic world began to acquire monuments commemorating the dead, and one of the three most important regions where this development began was the northeastern Iranian world, the other two being Iraq and Egypt. The main reasons for the growth of this new form appear to be two: the importance taken in the 4th/10th century by a whole variety of heterodox movements (especially Shī'ism whose holy cities like Qum in Iran began their spectacular rise at that time) and a new princely patronage of local dynasties, the Būyids of western Iran, the Sāmānids in the East, and various minor princelings in the mountains of the north. It is also likely that the frontier spirit of organized warriors for the faith had something to do with this development, as it probably did in Egypt, but our information is still too scanty on this score. Furthermore the existence on several early Iranian mausoleums of Pahlavī inscriptions next to Arabic ones indicates that, in some fashion yet to be investigated, an attachment to pre-Islamic religious and cultural values or at least practices may have played a part in the appearance of mausoleums. At a certain moment this development takes the form of large sanctuaries in which the holy tomb itself is surrounded by all sorts of service areas and hostels, thus creating the large *mashhads* of later times. Outside of a few uncertainly dated Central Asian monuments and perhaps of a few places at Qum and in Iraq, no such growth of major centres for pilgrimage and for monastic or semi-monastic life can be archaeologically ascertained during the period under consideration. But it is interesting to note that many of the sanctuaries of the 8th/14th and 9th/15th centuries were formed around the more or less apocryphal tombs of holy men from the first four centuries of Islam in Iran.

We are dealing therefore for the most part with single monumental tombs. Almost all of them fall into either one of two groups: the tower-tomb (pl. 5) or the cube covered with a cupola (pls. 6, 7). The first group is mostly characteristic of Khurāsān and of the mountain area south of the Caspian sea, although a monument like that of Abarqūh in southwestern Iran shows that it was not limited to one region alone. Most of the examples from our period consist simply of a tall cylinder covered with a conical roof over a cupola and with a frieze of decorative or epigraphic motifs just under the conical roof. The one exception is the Gunbad-i Qābūs (pl. 5), one of the great masterpieces of Iranian architecture. It is dated 397/1006–7 and was therefore built during the life time of Qābūs; it is possibly for this reason that it was called a *qaṣr* rather than a *qabr* and it clearly belongs to the general category of a secular architecture for conspicuous consumption. Its extraordinary height of nearly sixty-one metres was probably the result of an attempt to protect for ever the body of the prince, as is suggested by a later story. But its most remarkable aspect does not lie so much in its religious or symbolic meanings as in its stunning composition. It is a cylinder of small diameter (less than ten metres) compared to its height. Except for the proportions between height and diameter there is nothing original there, but then the cylinder generates ten angular buttresses which transform the building's surface into a composition of large masses of vertical units. The cylinder becomes a star but is also an abstract composition of pure lines and of a pure relationship between large areas of light and shade. This very contemporary look of the monument is further emphasized by the simplicity of the brick construction, broken only by an inscription and by a small decorative frieze at the very top. In other words an almost perfect balance is achieved between a purpose (princely glory beyond death), a form (cylindrical tower transformed into a star), and a single material (brick).

There is an aesthetic problem posed by this building, which is to know how to fit it into the general style of the time and to this I shall return in conclusion. There is also a historical problem of the tower tombs, which is to explain the origin of the form. It may be connected with the victory towers of later times and thus be simply a princely symbol with possible cosmic connotations. Or it could be connected with Zoroastrian funerary structures which have disappeared. The latter is strongly suggested by a number of peculiarities found in the inscription of the Gunbad-i Qābūs and of other tower mausoleums, such as the use of solar rather than lunar calendars and the occasional use of Pahlavī, but the point cannot really be proved so long as we remain so ignorant of earlier examples of such towers. From the point of view of the art historian, however, the more important point is that the Gunbad-i Qābūs illustrates the transformation of a comparatively common architectural type into a monument with major aesthetic and symbolic purposes.

It is fortunate that two monuments at least have been preserved which illustrate the same modification of a standard type within our second group of mausoleums, the domed cube. The first of these is the celebrated Sāmānid mausoleum of Bukhārā (pls. 6, 8). Datable before 332/943, it is a slightly tapering cube about ten metres to the side, entirely built of baked brick and covered with a large central dome as well as with four small domes in the corners. The main feature of each of its four sides is a monumental recessed arched entrance framed in a rectangular border; in each corner there is a partly engaged circular pier softening the building's corners and emphasizing its upward movement. Inside, its most striking feature is its zone of transition from square to dome. It consists of a squinch-based octagonal zone followed by a sixteen-sided one. The squinches are made of two arches parallel to each other and buttressed by a perpendicular half-arch which abuts against the fake gallery which runs around the upper part of the building.

Two major peculiarities are to be noted about this building. One is its use of brick. Here instead of having each brick so to say disappear into the form of the building as it does in the Gunbad-i Qābūs, each one is also part of an intricate series of designs which cover the whole building like a sheath. The medium of construction has become the medium of decoration. The effect is on the one hand that of a textured, almost tapestry-like surface and on the other of an almost endless development of light and shade contrasts, in total opposition to the massive purity of the Gunbad-i Qābūs.[1] The other peculiarity of the building is that, in spite of the harmony of its proportions, its parts are not architectonically relatable. The corner pillars, the small domes, the gallery, the sixteen-sided zone are not necessary for the building to stand up nor are they related to each other by construction but by a fascinating concern for a three-dimensional ornamental composition. Thus, while the plan of the building is not particularly original and goes back to an old tradition of Mediterranean and Near Eastern origin, the rich surface effect is quite new and gives to the monument the aspect of a rich jewellery box rather than of a sanctuary. It is impossible to be certain about the background for such an effect, but, inasmuch as nothing like it appears anywhere in mosques, it should probably be related to the art of palaces.

Very similar concerns appear in the second masterpiece of this group, the recently discovered ʿArab-atā mausoleum at Tīm (pls. 7, 9), dated 366/976–7. It is distinguished from all other mausoleums of its type by two main features. One is its façade, consisting of a single, large, almost two-dimensional screen set in front of the mausoleum like a sort of loudspeaker broadcasting its holiness. It is for the time being the earliest known dated example of the *pīs͟hṭāq* which will be such an important feature of all later Iranian architecture. It is on the façade that the decoration is concentrated. It includes both brick work and stucco but the more important point is that just a few years after Buk͟hārā's mausoleum with the total ornamentation of the building's surface we see a choice in the utilization of decoration. The reasons for these modifications are impossible to explain at present. One may search for them once again in secular architecture but of far greater significance

[1] *Materialy Khorezmskoi Ekspeditsiya*, vol. II (Moscow, 1963), p. 15, fig. 8.

is the point that we meet here with a development which will dominate much of Iranian architecture over the following centuries. The second novel feature in Tīm's mausoleum is even more important. It occurs in its zone of transition (pl. 9). While the octagonal principle of composition found in Bukhārā is still present, the squinch has become articulated by having the squinch proper shrink in size and by having it framed by a high arch above and by two sections of vaults on the sides. A characteristic tripartite profile is thus given to the squinch and the profile is then reproduced as a flat design on the other four sides of the octagon, thus giving the zone of transition a unified rhythm. A small colonette appears as a leftover from earlier ways. What we find here is the first architectural use of a uniquely Islamic theme, the *muqarnas*. It is still rather clumsy and incompletely thought out, just as it will still be clumsy in a 428/1037 mausoleum in Yazd (pl. 10), so far the earliest known occurrence of the theme in western or south-western Iran.

The problem of the origin of the muqarnas is a complicated one which in many ways escapes the limits of this volume. To keep within the strictly Iranian documentation, an explanation may be derived from the discovery in Nīshāpūr by the Metropolitan Museum of a number of carved stucco niches (pl. 11) similar to the units of a muqarnas. These have been explained as parts of elaborate compositions affixed on the surface of walls.[1] They were found in the secular setting and each one is decorated with its own independent design. But it could be suggested that, following the interest found already in Bukhārā's mausoleum for an impressive zone of transition from square to dome, attempts were made to utilize a primarily ornamental form for structural purposes. In the period with which we are concerned these attempts are still only tentative but in the second half of the 5th/11th century they will be among the most uniquely impressive achievements of Iranian architecture.

The mausoleums of Iran lead to two main conclusions. One is that they illustrate a new purpose whose motivation lies in major cultural and religious changes. The other one is that, far more than the mosque which existed from the very beginning of Islamic Iran, they exhibit not only great variety but also considerable structural and decorative novelties. Almost all of these novelties will remain permanent elements

[1] C. Wilkinson, "The Iranian Expedition", *Bulletin, Metropolitan Museum of Art*, vol. XXXIII (New York, 1938), p. 9, figs. 4–6.

in the further development of Islamic architecture in Iran. Yet one should probably not understand most of them as originating in mausoleums. It is far more likely that the mausoleums, which because of the holiness attached to them, have been preserved, were influenced by and reflect themes and concerns created in secular architecture.

About the latter, unfortunately, we are far less well informed than we would like to be. Textual references to secular buildings abound. Narshakhī's history of Bukhārā, Baihaqī's history of the early Ghaznavids, Ibn Miskawaih's accounts of the Būyids are full of descriptions of all sorts of secular buildings. The most important ones are palaces. These were generally put in gardens with elaborate water systems and the main buildings appeared to have been either single pavilions or groups of residential quarters arranged according to certain patterns, as for instance a palace built "according to the constellation of the Big Dipper with seven stone pillars" (Narshakhī, p. 24). All accounts mention sculpture and painting as the main means of decoration. The difficulty is of course to relate these literary documents, which at least give us the flavour of a rich and luxurious life, to actual monuments.

From the earlier centuries the only available documents come from Central Asia. A large number of single buildings found in Soghdia or in Khwārazm have been interpreted as villas or fortresses belonging to a local aristocracy and some of them may indeed belong to early Islamic times, although there is some uncertainty as to the exact chronology to give to these buildings. In any event they do not seem to exhibit any significant change from earlier buildings. The only major exception is the extraordinary building at Qyrq-qyz near Tirmidh which has variously been interpreted as a palace or as a caravanserai but whose plan (a square with a central cupola and a cruciform arrangement of halls issued from the central cupola) is quite original and without immediately apparent antecedents, or for that matter descendants in the area itself. Its date is also unclear but it has usually been put in the 2nd/8th or 3rd/9th centuries.

Then our information shifts to the early 5th/11th century for the most part and to the comparatively circumscribed world of the Ghaznavids. The excavations at Tirmidh have provided many stucco fragments most of which belong to a later rebuilding as well as parts of palaces, including long pillared halls opening on porticoes surrounding courtyards. These buildings are datable around 421/1030 or before. A palace at Marv with four aivāns around a courtyard also appears to be of the 5th/11th century. A more important palace from the beginning of the century is that of Lashkarī Bāzār in Afghanistan (fig. 4). It was part of an enormous and still largely unexplored complex and its main unit is a large courtyard with four aivāns, but it also includes more original elements such as a cruciform arrangement of interior halls relatable to that of Qyrq-qyz and a pillared aivān similar to what was found in Tirmidh. Finally the still unfinished excavations at Ghazna are bringing much additional material. It is difficult to decide how valid for the whole of Iran and even for the whole of northeastern Iran through four centuries of history are the remarkable group of early 5th/11th-century palaces in Afghanistan and just across the Oxus. Judgement must be reserved until the complete publication of these excavations is available.

It is thus impossible to draw a clear profile about the architecture of the palace in Iran before the middle of the 5th/11th century. Other functions which are even more elusive are the *ribāṭ* and the *madrasa*. Both of these will be known in later times and both are perfectly ascertained through literature, especially in northeastern Iran. But even though a certain number among the fortresses discovered by various Soviet expeditions all over Central Asia could be ribāṭs instead of being private estates, there is nothing certain about this and the architectural type of this characteristically Islamic building is completely unknown. Madrasas, on the other hand, were primarily city buildings. No definite information exists about their form but at least the Metropolitan Museum excavations at Nīshāpūr brought to light the techniques of construction (baked bricks, brick piers, articulated walls) probably used in these buildings, as well as many decorative designs. But no plans of complete buildings are available and even for private houses the only archaeologically clear information we possess comes from Marv, Tirmidh and Ghazna. It should be added, however, that the shops and houses excavated in Sīrāf over the past few years have added considerably to our knowledge of western Iranian houses.

A little more is known about caravanserais, since several large buildings discovered by various Russian expeditions have been so identified. Seen as a group they are quite striking by the variety of their internal arrangement; one of them seems even to have been covered with seventy-seven cupolas. The most spectacular among them is the celebrated Ribāṭ-i Malik (pl. 12) whose date appeared to be secure around 460–2/1068–70 until Nilsen was able to show that the texts

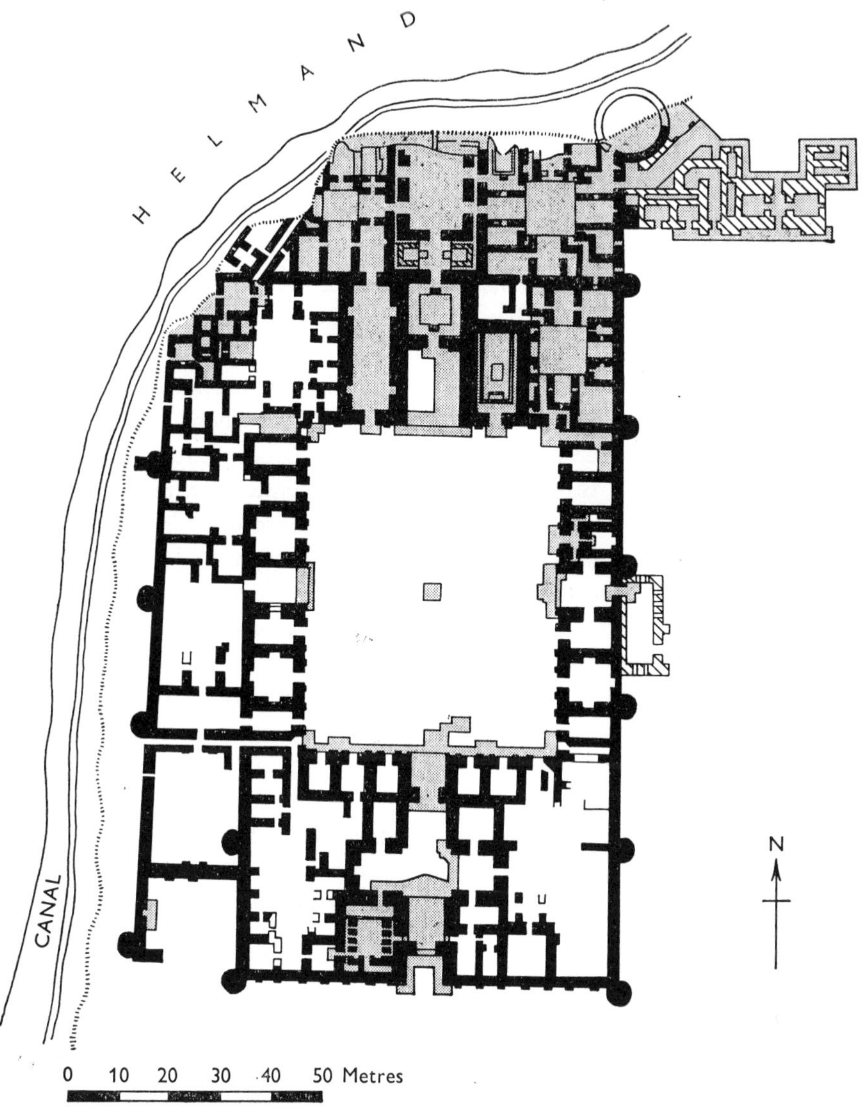

Fig. 4. Plan of La<u>sh</u>karī Bāzār.

and inscriptions used for its identification were not necessarily referring to this building.[1] But regardless of its exact date, the building belongs to our period by its impressive use of baked brick which articulate the outer walls in a manner reminiscent of pre-Islamic Soghdian architecture and by its impressive façade. Of greater interest for the history of cities are the urban caravanserais excavated at Sīrāf and published only in 1972.

This survey of the monuments of architecture known in Iran before the middle of the 5th/11th century is certainly not complete and further studies both of literature and of travel accounts are bound to reveal additional examples. Three main conclusions can be derived from our survey. One is that the northeastern Iranian world appears to have been far more active and far more creative than the western Iranian world. This is due in part to a greater concentration of scientific activity in Afghanistan and in Soviet Central Asia than anywhere else in Iran. But it is also possible to suggest that western Iran which had hardly developed until the Būyid period was mostly under the impact of the imperial ʿAbbāsid art of Iraq and therefore more derivative and less original. But, even though future excavations may modify the picture somewhat, it still seems that Khurāsān and Transoxiana under the Sāmānids and under the first Turkish dynasties was the main centre of Iranian architecture.

Our second conclusion, however, is that, even if we limit ourselves to that area, it is difficult to define a clear architectural style. If anything at all, buildings like the Gunbad-i Qābūs, the mausoleums of Tīm and Bukhārā, the mosques of Nāyīn and Dāmghān, the palaces of Tirmidh and Lashkarī Bāzār illustrate an experimentation with architectural forms and decoration (or lack thereof), especially in the 4th/10th and early 5th/11th centuries. They imply a culture in search of its own ways and of its own formal vocabulary. This vocabulary will be discovered by the culture of Islamic Iran in the following century and precisely in the western Iranian world, i.e. in the hitherto underdeveloped area. The parallel between the various Romanesque provinces and the Gothic, developing in the province least touched by the Romanesque, is striking.

The third conclusion is that this period witnesses in architecture the elaboration of almost all the functions and techniques which will be part and parcel of a classical Iranian architecture: mosques, mausoleums, baked brick, muqarnas, from one to four aivāns around a courtyard,

[1] Nilsen, *op. cit.*, p. 55.

pīshṭāq and so forth. But none of these features appeared as yet as automatic or standard terms in the style of the time. It is also difficult to decide which were clear novelties and which had been adapted from earlier Iranian civilizations. The unit of a single dome on four supports is certainly pre-Islamic; so is the articulation of outer walls through massive piers or even possibly the brick style and the four aivāns plan which has been found in a Buddhist sanctuary of Central Asia and which exists in a simplified format at Kūh-i Khwāja in Sīstān. Yet the combinations of earlier themes made by the early Muslims differentiate their buildings from Sāsānian or Soghdian ones, except possibly in the country villas of Central Asia whose date is uncertain anyway. The main point, it seems to me, is that architectural forms had not yet received by the 5th/11th century standard functional associations and formal characteristics. This transformation of a large number of theses into a precise and classical style will be the main achievement of the following centuries.

Before leaving the subject of architecture a few words should be said about architectural decoration. Throughout our discussion of individual buildings the importance of a wide variety of techniques of architectural decoration was brought up. The most important technique was stucco and it is to it that one must devote most of the discussion. But it was not the only technique used. Aside from the brick so spectacularly used in Bukhārā, and of occasional wooden fragments, numerous examples of representational painting exists as well. The most important ones were found in Nīshāpūr and in Lashkarī Bāzār. Almost all of them are fragments and, except in the instance of the procession at Lashkarī Bāzār and a few grafitti at Nīshāpūr, their exact subject-matter is difficult to interpret. Stylistically they seem to be in the succession of the great Soghdian and Central Asian painting tradition. Painting, however, was not only used for large frescoes with complex iconographies. In Yazd, Sangbast, and Nīshāpūr, among other places, painting was also used simply to cover the walls. Although one can never be totally certain about the exact date of many of the paintings in religious sanctuaries, two decorative themes are present. One is shared with stuccoes and brickwork and consists in inscriptions, usually in the bold strokes of what has been called *coufique fleuri*.[1] The other one (pl. 21) is more original; found in Nīshāpūr it consists in an all-over pattern of scales and leaves in which the main motive ended up with

[1] S. Flury in *A Survey of Persian Art*, vol. IV, p. 1743.

hands and possibly even eyes. The composition is based both on vertical and on diagonal axes and, while it is possible that some of the themes in these panels derive from various textile patterns, if not even at times from the ancient incrustation style, the exact sources of these panels and the meanings which can be attached to them still escape us. With the possible exception of the Nīshāpūr examples and regardless of the qualities of design which exist in some of them, most of these paintings are essentially imitations in a cheaper medium of decorative designs created elsewhere.

The richest medium of architectural decoration was stucco. In almost all instances during the early Islamic period it was applied directly on the surface of the wall to be covered and it is comparatively rarely that one encounters the complicated mixture of media found in later times. From this point of view early Islamic stucco in Iran follows directly in the footsteps of Sāsānian and Central Asian stucco. Where it differs from the latter is primarily in the choice of its subjects. Figural and animal topics have almost entirely disappeared and if one excepts a certain number of friezes emphasizing architectural lines or creating for instance capitals and impost blocks as in Balkh's small mosque, most of the stucco decoration consisted of single panels composed as separate units. Each panel was set, in more or less arbitrary fashion, on the walls, piers or soffits which had to be decorated. Outside of a large number of fragments from Ray which may be late Sāsānian or early Islamic and of single pieces found accidentally, the main groups of stuccoes available for study are found in a 3rd/9th-century mosque at Balkh, in a 3rd/9th-century (or perhaps a little earlier) palace in Afrāsiyāb, in Nīshāpūr, and at Nāyīn. The large groups of stuccoes from Tirmidh, Lashkarī Bāzār and Ghazna are for the most part later than our period. Even though most of them have not yet been fully published, they appear to represent in many ways the culmination of the tendencies developed over the first centuries of Islam.

As in the case of architectural monuments, most of the documents are concentrated in northeastern Iran and I shall therefore limit myself to a few remarks about these, avoiding the question of stylistic chronology which cannot be tackled yet. First, the formal vocabulary of this ornament is comparatively limited: geometric frames and vegetal themes form most of it. The latter have been analysed with some care by Flury and Rempel and included vine leaves usually arranged in rather stilted pairs surrounded by a vaguely circular stem, acanthus leaves, and palmettes or half-palmettes, usually asymmetrically composed. Several different treatments appear for each of these motives, from comparatively natural representations to extreme formalism and stylization (pl. 13). Interlace made of vegetal elements is comparatively rare. But the most important part of this decoration is the geometric order which overwhelmed everything else. Rempel has attempted to show that almost the whole of the geometry was based on a series of exercises on the properties of the circle. Usually a comparatively simple single basic unit is used to generate a variety of shapes and forms which can be both circular and polygonal but all of which can be determined with a compass and a ruler. This principle of generating geometric forms has been called by him the *girih* or knot principle of decoration.[1] Much detailed work is still needed to refine the categories established by Rempel and Flury, but here at least we have working hypotheses with which to begin, and the essential point for this period is that of the powerful impact of geometric considerations over vegetal themes.

The second remaining problem is the historical one of explaining the development of these themes, their use in any one specific instance, and the situation of the Iranian development in relationship to the well dated and well understood art of Sāmarrā. The striking point here is that, even though there are examples of Sāmarrā's bevelled style in Iran, these examples are not very numerous and the most original development in the art of architectural decoration in early Islamic times does not seem to have affected Iran to any great extent. As in much of architecture, we are witnessing an internal refinement of native themes whereby a small number of designs are selected from a fairly rich vocabulary and transformed into a complex exercise in geometry. One may wonder whether there is more to these designs than the pure pleasure of ornamentating surfaces and whether one should attribute some symbolic sense to these developments. But with this question we are moving into the realm of speculation.

II. THE ART OF THE OBJECT

It can be surmised that there was a fairly developed art of painting in Iran before the middle of the 5th/11th century. Some mention was made already of a few remaining fragments of frescoes, mostly with rather

[1] L. I. Rempel, *Arkhitekturnyi Ornament Uzbekistana* (Tashkent, 1961), p. 183, and N. B. Baklanov, "Gerikh", *Sovetskaya Arkheologiya*, vol. XI (1946).

unclear subject. A celebrated text also recalls that a Sāmānid prince had a poetical version of the book of *Kalīla wa Dimna* illustrated by a Chinese or by a Chinese influenced painter.[1] Nothing has remained of this art of the miniature and even later examples hardly ever show traces of a possible earlier art of book painting. The same point can be made about monumental sculpture which may have existed as well. Even though excavations and further studies in texts may modify our conclusion, it seems that most of the sculpture and painting from these first centuries was sponsored by princes and belonged to a rarified royal art. More curious is the point that we know very little about early book calligraphy in Iran and nothing can be compared to the beautiful books known, even though in small numbers, from Iraq and Egypt.

The arts other than architecture are therefore represented almost exclusively by the so-called industrial arts. In the present state of our knowledge only one technique can be described with any degree of completeness, while in two other techniques we can hazard a few hypotheses. The better known technique is ceramics and a few points can be made about metalwork and textiles. It is still almost impossible to cut across various techniques and to put together some statement about the style of the time in the industrial or decorative arts.

It has long been recognized that one of the most uniquely early Islamic developments in the arts was the appearance of an art of luxury ceramics. It was probably a phenomenon of the second half of the 2nd/8th century and its first main centres were in Iraq and in Egypt. Outside of social and cultural forces, to some of which I shall return, the main impetus for this new art of pottery can be found in the desire to imitate metalwork, especially gold, and to copy Chinese ceramics. The second impulse is easily proved by the large number of objects which attempt to recreate the splash or mottled wares of China and many fragments found in Iran show that such objects were used, if not necessarily manufactured, in Iran itself. The first impulse led to the first major invention of mediaeval Near Eastern ceramicists, lustre. Lustre techniques were a carefully guarded secret and, while several Iranian series attempted in various ways to imitate lustre, there is no indication that any lustre pieces were actually made in Iran before the 5th/11th century.

The most important and most original Iranian ceramic seems to have begun in the 3rd/9th century and its production was concentrated in

[1] T. W. Arnold, *Painting in Islam* (New York, 1965), p. 26.

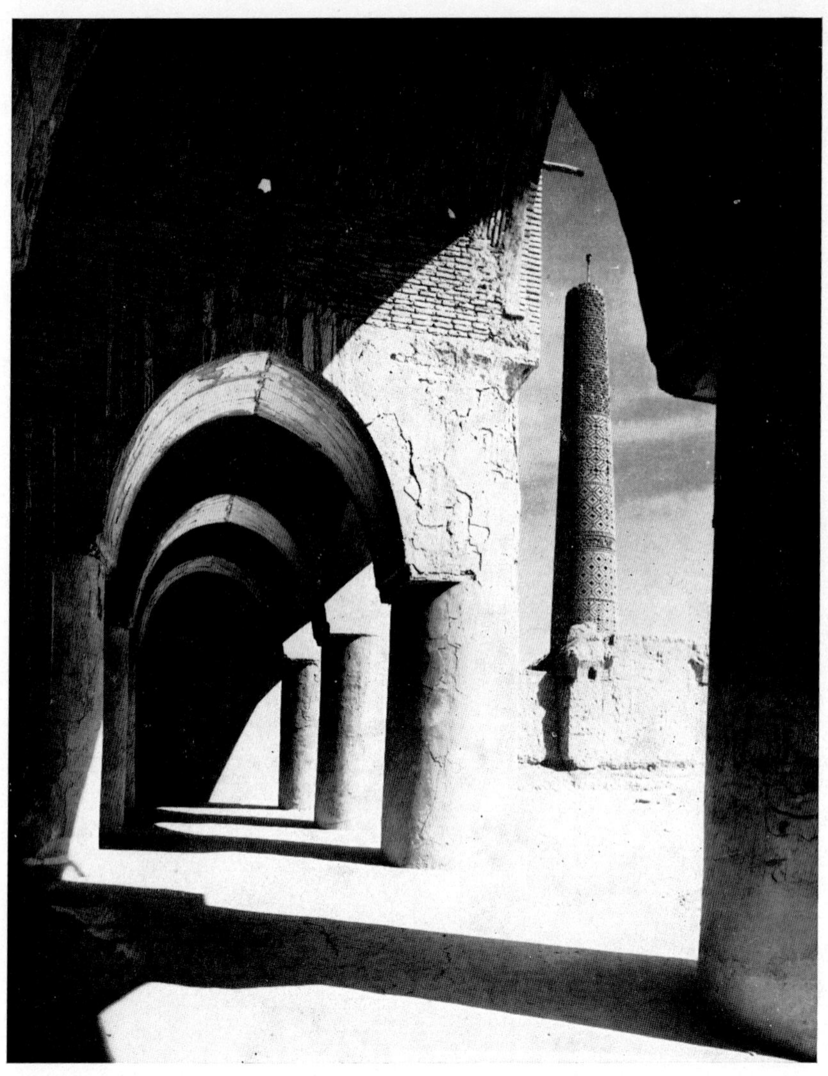

1 Dāmg͟hān mosque.

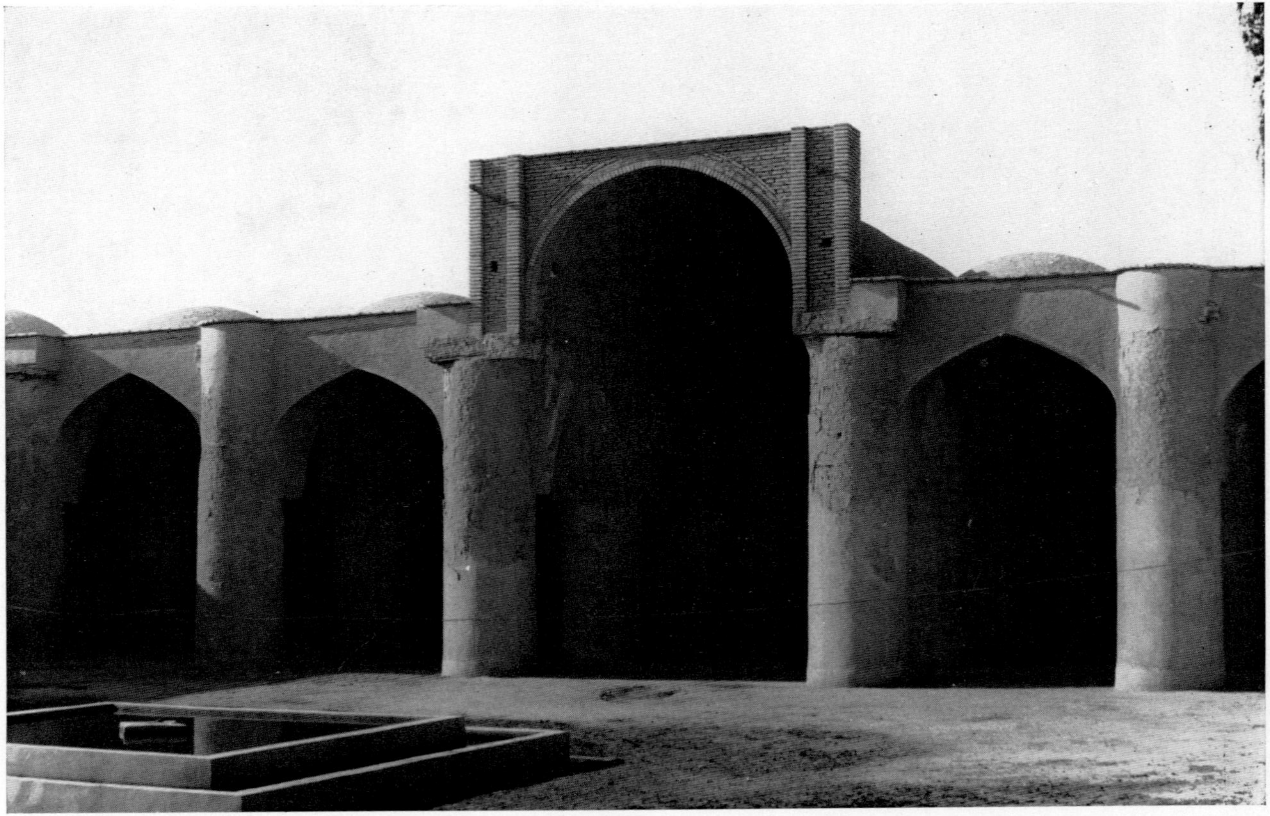

2 General view of Dāmghān mosque.

3 General view of Nāyīn mosque.

4 Stucco decoration: Nāyīn mosque.

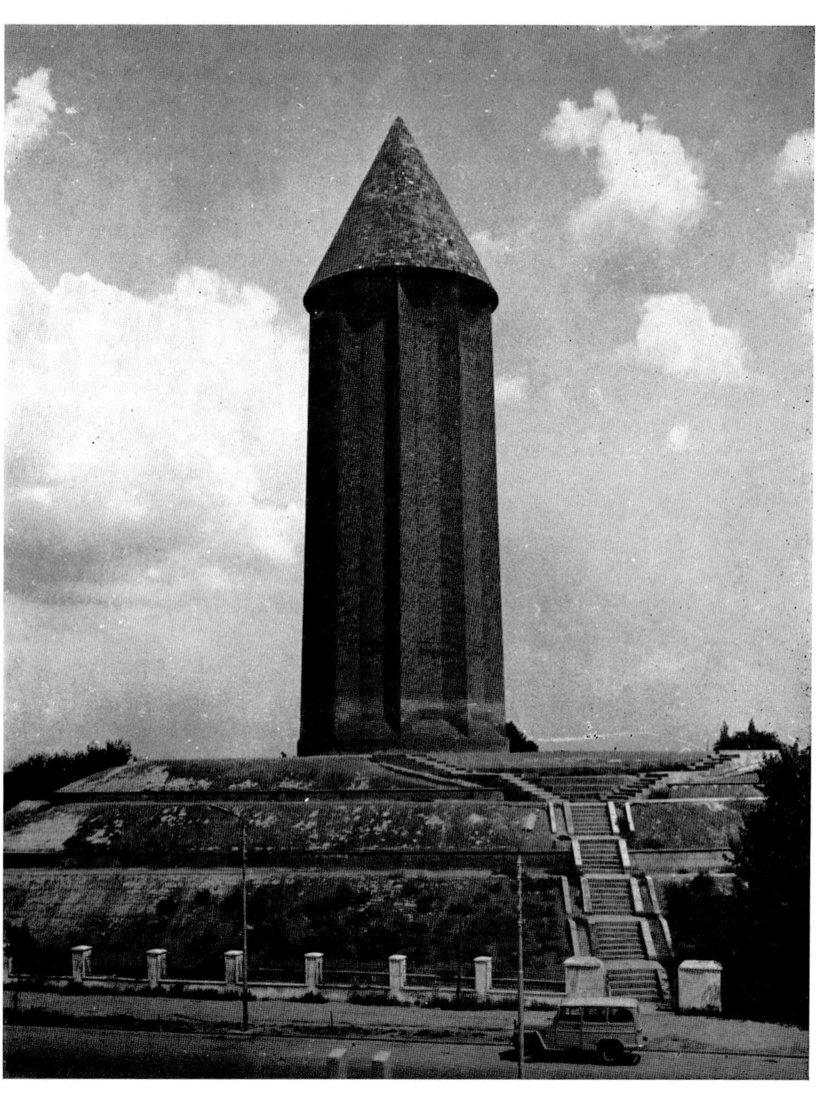

5 Gunbad-i Qābūs.

6 Bukhārā, Sāmānid mausoleum, exterior.

7 Tīm, ʿArab-atā, exterior.

8 Bukhārā, Sāmānid mausoleum, interior.

9 Tīm, ‘Arab-atā, interior.

10 Yazd, Davāzdah Imām squinch.

11 Nī<u>sh</u>āpūr, stucco niche.

12 General view of Ribāṭ-i Malik.

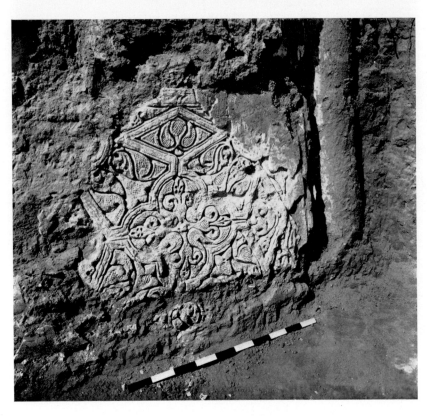

13 Stucco panel from Nīshāpūr.

14 Nīshāpūr plate with inscription.

15 Nī<u>sh</u>āpūr plate, floriated Kufic.

16 Nīshāpūr bowl (see also plate 22).

17 Nīshāpūr plate with figures.

18 Gold ewer.

19 Bronze aquamanile.

20 Būyid silk, compound tabby weave.

21 Painted stucco panel from Nīs͟hāpūr.

22 Nīs͟hâpūr bowl.

23 Western Iranian ceramic.

24 St Josse silk.

the northeastern provinces. Two main centres, Nīshāpūr and Afrāsiyāb-Samarqand, have been identified so far and, while some types were limited to one centre only, others were common to several. For the purposes of this account we shall consider them all together. Although a number of variations do exist, the most common and most significant pottery was a red or buff ware covered with a thick slip which was painted and then covered with transparent or coloured glazes. The main achievement of northeastern Iranian ceramicists was that they discovered ways of keeping a fair number of different colours stable in firing and thus were able to provide their objects with colouristic effects which will remain the hallmark of all Iranian ceramics. Most of the objects were plates and bowls with one single face to be decorated. Jugs and ewers are not unknown but most of them were still at this time unglazed.

The main originality of this eastern Iranian pottery does not lie so much in its technique, even though the latter was a novelty in the arts of the time, but in the nature of its decoration. I shall first discuss the most important themes used in the decoration, then comment on larger stylistic problems raised by this ceramic, and then conclude by bringing up a number of other ceramic types than the main slip-painted ones.

The first and automatically most original subject-matter was writing. A large number of objects (pl. 14) contain simply a single inscription around the plate's border. Most of these inscriptions are legible and consist either of standardized good wishes to an anonymous owner or of proverbs and aphorisms. The flavour of the latter can be given by the following examples: "He who is content with his own opinion runs into danger"; "Patience in learning is first bitter to the taste but its end is sweeter than honey"; "Generosity is one of the qualities of good men." The peculiarities of these inscriptions are that they are all in Arabic and that they tend to express the slightly moralizing morality of a middle class. There are no instances of princely topics among them. The epigraphical style of the writing varies considerably from a strikingly sober and severe Kūfic of long hastae and angular letters all the way to varieties of plaited and flowery Kūfic (pl. 15) or to a transformation of letters into purely decorative forms. Although it is possible to suggest at times a *post quem* date for some of the designs, the exact chronology of this writing and hence of the objects on which it is found still demands further investigation. In all probability several different styles coexisted.

A second major subject consists in animals. The most common ones are birds. They are rarely identifiable from an ornithological point of view and, although here again many variations occur, the idea of a bird – perhaps even abstract shapes suggested by birds – seems to predominate over any sort of representation. The second most common animal is a kind of goat with long horns but the most intriguing beasts are more or less mythical felines illustrating a rather strange bestiary of monsters. For almost all of the animal types it is possible to find prototypes in pre-Islamic art, but their treatment on Islamic ceramics is quite different. Not only do we meet with many variations from one object to the other but the tendency is to emphasize an outline, at times only remotely connected with the original subject, and then to fill the outline with colours, either a single one spread all over the design, or a variety of colours making a design of their own.

A third decorative theme consisted of vegetal elements. These are mostly either rather traditional rinceaux or compositions centred around a single leaf, usually a palmette or an acanthus, arranged so as to fit the surface of the object (pls. 16, 22). Finally, if one excepts a number of rather peculiar designs which for the time being escape definition, northeastern Iranian ceramics provide examples of figural representations. The subjects are riders, dancers, standing or seated personages holding flowers and pitchers, as well as a number of unidentified activities (pl. 17). The greatest originality of these representations lies in their style. A sketchy line outlines the main subjects with very little consideration for bodily proportions and at times with distortions which could be considered as folk caricatures or as wilful modifications of visual impressions. In the latter instance, however, the reasons, formal or iconographic, for the distortions are still impossible to determine. It is also curious to note that almost all the iconographic meanings which can be defined are related to princely art or to the partly religious and partly secular themes of pre-Islamic Central Asian art. Yet the imprecision of the treatment of the figures and especially the lack of clarity of significant details makes it rather doubtful that these were concrete representations of specific personages or even activities. But here we are entering into the problem of the kind of perception of visual forms which existed at the time and which in turn led to the creation of certain forms. For the solution of this problem we do not have as yet the necessary contemporary or theoretical elements. In any event the problem cannot be considered in Iran alone and all one can conclude is that the images on northeastern Iranian ceramics derived from some other source or sources, most of which are still unknown.

Such are the main subjects found on the pottery of eastern Iran. They all share a number of features. First, all of them could be used in two ways, either as a unique and principal subject of decoration or as a detail, at times simply a fill, on objects with other topics. There is in other words an ambiguity in the use and therefore in the likely contemporary significance of most ceramic decorative designs. Second, one of the main concerns of northeastern ceramicists was that of organizing the circular surface of the object, a concern they shared with their Egyptian and Iraqi counterparts. More than the latter, Iranian artisans developed very many different compositions, from simple contrasts between a single central subject and its background or from the effectively sober single inscription on a white background all the way to an immense sophistication of combinations of central axes with clockwise and counterclockwise movements (pl. 23) or to what seem to be an arbitrary filling of the surface with a large number of separate motifs. We are therefore hardly dealing with a single style, but rather with a variety of separate ways of decorating objects, for which some day we may be able to provide more specific regional or social reasons.

The most intriguing question posed by these designs is that of their origins. It seems that, even though animals and human images can be related to various pre-Islamic traditions, a fairly large percentage of the motifs were new inventions, or returns to older traditions with which continuous contact had been broken. Since so few of them exhibit clear princely themes and since Arabic proverbs with a moralizing quality predominate in the inscriptions, we can suggest that this pottery illustrates the taste of an Arab or Arabicized bourgeoisie from northeastern Iran. This was a new social level in Iran and we find it during the centuries under consideration searching for a visual form to express itself. It is for this reason perhaps that its designs illustrate less a style than a mode, i.e. an attitude toward forms whereby experimentation was possible in the process of finding a classical moment. But the classical moment did not occur in the art of ceramics until the following period.

I have emphasized so far the most original and most important group of northeastern Iranian pottery. It was, of course, not the only one, even if one excepts the large number of types which were primarily utilitarian and with little aesthetic intent. One group deserves mention.

It is a sgraffiato pottery in which designs were incised on the slip and then the object was covered with a variety of glazes. A fairly large number of variants exist within this general technical category. Some of the variants are based on the quality of the design itself which can be either very rough and popular as in the so-called Āmul group, or highly organized and planned as in a group of western Iranian ceramics.[1] Or there are variants in the ways in which glazes were used, monochrome ones or polychrome splash types. It is from this group that it has been possible to identify the one group of Persian ceramics (pl. 23) which may be specifically Būyid and western Iranian. Aside from taking too much space, discussion of additional types would be of lesser importance in the context of this essay since their significance is for the time being primarily archaeological and their relationship to the development of a visual taste in Islamic Iran still unclear.

Let us turn, finally, to the other techniques of the industrial arts which characterize the period under consideration. Outside of glass, of which a number of fragments were found in official or clandestine excavations, but whose study is still very incomplete, two techniques may be discussed in greater detail. One is metalwork and the other one textiles.

There is a fairly large number of objects in metal which are commonly assigned to the period between the fall of the Sāsānian dynasty and the middle of the 5th/11th century. The place of discovery of most of this material is generally unknown except for a few finds in Russia and for objects said to have been found in the mountains of northern Iran, the so-called Dailamite region where Islam penetrated only slowly and whence came many of the rulers of western and central Iran from the late 1st/7th century onwards. Partly for this reason much of this metalwork has been considered to be Būyid, or at least not Sāsānian or northeastern Iranian. A further and partial justification for this conclusion is that such objects as are signed or as have the name of an owner – a gold ewer in the Freer Gallery (pl. 18), a silver treasure now in Tehrān, a couple of silver plates in the Hermitage – all can be assigned either to the Būyids themselves or to some small Dailamite dynasty. Needless to say none of the objects was discovered in archaeologically controlled circumstances, doubt has been raised about the date or even the authenticity of some of the pieces, and uncertainty rules over the

[1] E. Kühnel in *Zeitschrift der deutschen morgenländischen Gesell.*, vol. CVI (1956), and A. Lane, *Early Islamic Pottery* (London, 1947), pl. 30 as opposed to plate 32A.

degree to which and the ways in which pieces without specific epigraphical information can be associated with the others. For the main problem of all these objects in metal is to find the means by which to organize them into meaningful groups. Among the possibilities are such categories as techniques, shapes, decorative vocabulary, composition of designs, places of origin, and so forth. Since it is impossible in the context of this essay to investigate each one of these categories, we shall limit ourselves to a rapid mention of the major groups involved according to the metal in which they were made.

One of the most important gold objects is the small ewer in the Freer Gallery (pl. 18) done in repoussé. Its shape with a thick body and a short but wide neck is typical of many objects in metal and ceramics. The design consists of various kinds of borders (among which one may note both geometric and floral themes) compartmentalizing the surface of the object into medallions with a variety of animals. The latter as well as the vegetal features have an archaistic character to them and almost all of them derive from pre-Islamic models. A gold cup in the British Museum may be somewhat later than our period but is interesting in that it contains an inscription with a poem celebrating the drinking of wine and certainly belongs typologically to works of an earlier time. Archaistic themes of Sāsānian origin for the most part also occur on a group of golden medallions from the Būyid period. Some gold jewellery from this period has also remained. While richer in quantity and in quality than anything known from earlier or later periods, these few gold objects are still only a pale shadow of the expressive treasures which adorned for several centuries the various courts of Iranian princes.

Silver objects pose the most complicated problems. Several hoards, mostly in the British Museum and in Tehrān, contain whole sets of drinking vessels, trays, belt plaques, and the like in silver, at times with additional decoration in niello. Most of them have a decoration of animal and floral designs and some have inscriptions mentioning craftsmen or owners, most of whom have never been identified. Seen as a group these objects from Islamic Iran do exhibit certain formal transformations (fewer plates, more ewers, often elongated) which will tend to identify later Islamic metalwork. At the same time, large numbers of plates and ewers continued the traditions of Sāsānian Iran. The latter form what has been known for decades as a "post-Sāsānian" group of silverwork whose main characteristic can be defined in the following manner. While maintaining the shapes, the techniques, and the subjects of pre-Islamic Iran, they show misunderstandings of traditional Sāsānian royal themes, emphases on a life of pleasure rather than on religious or cultic motifs, and a tendency to mix elements from different sources. At the same time they also exhibit a greater interest in ornamental patterns than in iconographically meaningful units. It is even possible that certain new subjects were introduced, such as the story of Bahrām Gūr and Āzāda, but we are still only at the beginning of any sort of understanding of the iconography of these objects. Since many of them differ from certainly Būyid works, it can be concluded that they were northeastern or northern Iranian rather than western Iranian in origin, but here again our information is still too scanty. Nor can we provide an appropriate date for most of them except insofar as some of them are likely to be later than the 5th/11th century.

In spite of our uncertainties about them, gold and silver objects form distinctive groups. The same cannot be said about bronze. There outside of a number of objects (mostly ewers) assumed to be early and Iranian because of their closeness to Sāsānian models, it is difficult to distinguish early Islamic works from later ones and Iranian ones from works made in other parts of the Muslim world, especially Egypt and Iraq. This seems to be particularly true of a large group of zoomorphic objects found all over the world's museums (pl. 19) and of large ewers, of which the most celebrated one is the so-called Marwān ewer in Cairo. Matters are a little bit clearer when we deal with a group of large bronze plates imitating Sāsānian types, for which the latest place of origin has been put in northwestern Iran. It is perhaps more important to note that our period clearly exhibits the beginning of the transformation of bronze manufacture into a major vehicle of artistic creativity and thus leads quite naturally into the great revolution in the art of the bronze object which was to take place in the 6th/12th century. But large numbers of examples remain for which a date somewhere between the 4th/10th and the 6th/12th centuries appears to be the most likely and no clear stylistic, iconographic or functional distinction seems possible for the moment.

Finally a word must be said about textiles. There is little doubt that this was the single most important industrial art of the mediaeval Muslim world and considerable textual information exists about it, although less so for Iran than for the Mediterranean world and especially Egypt. The problem is to relate what is known from literary sources to actually remaining fragments. So far it has only been possible to attribute one hitherto unrelated group of silks to Zandana, a town from the area of Bukhārā.[1] The actual examples are unfortunately datable just before the Muslim conquest but at least a beginning has been made in the complex task facing textile scholarship. Otherwise, if one excepts a number of inscribed *ṭirāz* fragments, what we have left is one unique monument and one group. The monument is the celebrated St Josse textile in the Louvre (pl. 24) with an inscription identifying its owner as one Bukhtakīn who died in 350/961. Its procession of Bactrian camels, its highly stylized affronted elephants, and its inscriptions make it a most appropriate parallel to the ceramic styles of northeastern Iran with which it was contemporary. The group of textiles is that of the so-called Būyid textiles, whose authenticity had been doubted by some but seems to me to have been in recent years proved for the majority if not all of the known fragments. The best examples, some of which are dated, contain a remarkably varied and subtle vocabulary of animal forms (generally two affronted mythical animals set in medallions, pl. 20) and highly original inscriptions, on occasion even whole fragments from contemporary poems. The proper analysis of the iconographic and stylistic characteristics of these textiles has only begun but it is clear that they have played an important part not only in the development of early mediaeval Iranian art but also in its spread beyond the frontiers of Iran proper.

III. CONCLUSIONS

Long though it may be if one considers the lack of major masterpieces from the period between the beginning of Islam in Iran and the middle of the 5th/11th century, our survey is not complete and every scholar will be able to add examples of this or that technique and to illustrate some other aspect of the art of these centuries in Iran. This very fact leads to the first of our conclusions which is that there was no uniform artistic style in Iran during that time. In every technique there was a multiplicity of tendencies which are almost impossible to explain as a group and the better a technique is known, as is the art of pottery in northeastern Iran, the more difficult it is to explain it as a formal entity. Almost every discovery brings to light a hitherto unknown aspect of

[1] D. G. Shepherd and W. B. Henning, "Zandanījī Identified?" in *Aus der Welt der islamischen Kunst* (Festschrift Ernst Kühnel, Berlin, 1959), pp. 15–40.

early Islamic art in Iran. There is hardly ever any possibility to relate the artistic production of any one region or even city of Iran at any one time with contemporary developments elsewhere. It seems to me that, even if we take into consideration the inadequacies of the information in our possession, this state of affairs is not an accident but reflects a peculiarity of the Iranian world which differentiates it considerably from Iraq, Egypt or Spain during the same formative centuries. The peculiarity can be explained if one considers one essential feature of the culture of Iran at that time. It is that the Islamization of Iran was a slow process which affected in totally different ways the dozen or so separate geographical units of Iran and within each region different cities. There remained in Iran far longer than in other Muslim provinces strongholds of non-Islamic traditions whose power and importance varied no doubt from century to century but which were present until the massive arrival of Turks. With the possible exception of some Central Asian traditions which moved farther east into the Ṭārim basin, *all* the pre-Islamic ways, habits, tastes and cultural traits were maintained within the newly created Muslim empire. In the formerly Christian world, on the other hand, the presence of an independent Byzantium and later of a strong Christian west led to the weakening of the Christian traditions under Muslim rule. Things were different in Iran and the development of an Islamic Iranian art must not be seen as a sort of linear growth in time but as consisting of almost as many different times as there were areas or even cities. Even though documents are lacking in most cases other than those of the ceramics of Nīs̲h̲āpūr and of Afrāsiyāb-Samarqand and possibly of mausoleums, there must have occurred a fascinating mutual interaction between various centres, urban or regional, which should form the subject of further archaeological and textual investigations.

Within this plurality of styles and of artistic tendencies one might have expected some sort of crystallization around two dynasties, the Sāmānids and the Būyids. Even though much can be said about an Iranian art under the Sāmānids (I shall return to this point in a moment), this crystallization did not occur in the sense that no "classicism", i.e. no coherent, standardized, and largely exclusive body of forms can be associated with either dynasty. For the Būyids the answer may lie in the fact that, regardless of their importance as the first major builders and patrons in western Iran since the middle Sāsānian period, their political and cultural connections were still too closely tied to the admittedly decadent but still impressive 'Abbāsid culture of Iraq. The instance of the Sāmānids is more puzzling. One may, of course, point out that only one certainly Sāmānid dynastic monument in any technique has remained, the mausoleum of Bukhārā, and that we simply do not have the necessary information. Still this answer is not totally adequate, for so much else has remained from northeastern Iran, in which one might have been able to discover some reflection of a main Sāmānid style. Its absence must somehow be explained. Three factors seem to me to be involved. One is that, even though a certain political stability did reign in northeastern Iran under the Sāmānids, it was still a period of cultural contrasts between various tendencies, local Soghdian, emigré western Iranian, Turkish, Arab Muslim and so forth. It is only later that a sufficient degree of cultural stabilization took place to allow for some sort of artistic unity. But even later, as under the Tīmūrids or the Ghūrids and the Khwārazm-Shāhs, it was largely imposed from above and short-lived. One may wonder whether the geographical and historical fate of northeastern Iran and of Central Asia has not been over the ages to be a great gatherer of influences from all over Asia, at times creative in the invention of certain details but rarely able to form a truly classical style.

Our first conclusion is then that like contemporary Carolingian and Ottonian times in the West, early Islamic centuries in Iran did not create a definable artistic entity – or period style – comparable to what happened later during the so-called Saljuq period.

Yet the artistic creativity of the times was immense and a second conclusion to draw is that this creativity was concentrated in northeastern Iran. Here of course we are the victims in part of our far better knowledge of that area than of any other part of Iran, but it is still striking that almost every major series of early Islamic Iranian monuments is best illustrated through examples from the northeast. Two reasons can be suggested for that. One is that the very complexity of the cultural profile of northeastern Iran most easily led to creativity, inasmuch as the immediately pre-Islamic art of the region was a particularly rich one, possibly richer than the weakened Sāsānian world of the 1st/7th century. The other reason is, paradoxically enough, that northeastern Iran was also the most Islamic of the regions of Iran. Bukhārā, Samarqand, Marv, Nīshāpūr, Herāt, Balkh were major Islamic centres of learning and of propaganda. At the frontier the missionary spirit of Islam exercised itself through any number of institutions which were less often needed elsewhere. It is thus in the combination of a militant Islam with a rich body of earlier traditions that we can see one of the main motivations of creativity in the arts of northeastern Iran.

Finally it is necessary in conclusion to provide some sort of evaluation of the respective importance of the old and of the new in early Islamic art. Are we simply dealing with a continuation of older traditions? Or was Islam a revolutionary phenomenon in Iranian art? The answer is probably negative to both questions. Old themes certainly were continued, such as much of the architectural vocabulary, a number of complete architectural forms like the domed unit, certain kinds of secular constructions, many techniques of decoration, many themes of painting, and several groups of metalwork. In some of these instances it is almost impossible to separate pre-Islamic from Islamic monuments. At the same time, all ceramic techniques, most ceramic designs, hypostyle mosques, baked brick architecture, the utilization of brick for decoration, epigraphical decoration, middle-class patronage for luxury objects, a number of shapes in metalwork and especially in bronze, appear to be mostly new creations. Some of these, such as an art of ceramics, small mosques, bourgeois patronage and epigraphy, are even importations from the earlier centres of Islamic art in the Fertile Crescent. Some day one might be able to draw up a sort of balance sheet of old and new forms and suggest the ways in which little by little the latter replaced the former. Yet it seems that such a balance sheet would not really reflect what happened in the arts for it would substitute a sort of formal accounting for what was clearly a dynamic process, as can be seen in the rapidity with which epigraphy changed on ceramics, and bricks were transformed into decoration. The hypothesis I would like to propose is that all over the Iranian world there took place a conscious process of selection of forms and meanings from the older world to suit the needs of the new. Thus, on the one hand, there occurred an initial impoverishment of decorative themes in the more common techniques of stucco and ceramics, because so many pre-Islamic ones were no longer suited to the new needs of an Islamic culture. On the other hand, as in the case of gold and silver, there were conscious continuations of archaistic themes because princes consciously sought to relate to the earlier, especially Sāsānian, dynasties. Or else ancient themes changed meanings. The floral designs on Soghdian clothes became the background fills of certain groups of Nīshāpūr pottery and formerly religious motifs acquired a secular meaning as in the nude females on silver objects. In a few cases, perhaps very ancient traditional motifs were maintained, as in the instance of birds and of certain other animals.

Much work on individual motifs is needed until one can properly refine and explain the ways in which the process of change and selection took place. But already now one can see emerging a number of elements – baked brick, epigraphy, the muqarnas, brilliant cupolas, ceramics – which were to be the main forms of the classical moments of Iranian art in the Middle Ages. We are dealing therefore with a period of transition and the peculiarity of Iran in the Muslim world is that the transition period lasted longer than anywhere else. It is probably for this reason, above others, that the Islamic art of Iran succeeded over the centuries in maintaining its originality and its uniqueness. At the same time, however original some of its works may have been, the essential process is not Iranian alone but only one aspect of the complex ways in which Islamic art was formed all over the world it had taken over.

CHAPTER 10

NUMISMATICS

When the Arabs entered Iran and in 21/642 defeated the Sāsānian army at Nihāvand they brought with them no coinage of their own. In the first years after the conquest of Byzantine and Sāsānian lands the invaders made use of the existing currency – the Byzantine gold *solidus* or *denarius aureus* and the copper *follis* in Palestine and Syria, the Sāsānian silver *drahm* in the east. Within a very few years, certainly by 31/651–2, the Arab governors in Iran began to imitate the *drahm*, henceforth to be known as the *dirham*, at first anonymously, later with their names rendered in Pahlavī characters, but always with the addition, in the outer margin of the obverse, of a pious legend in Kūfic characters. The prototypes were the drahms of Yazdgard III, Khusrau II and Hormizd IV; by far the commonest "portrait" is that of Khusrau II whose immense output of coinage during the long years of his reign (591–628) had flooded the land and whose image was familiar to everyone in both Iran and Iraq. An example of Khusrau II's drahm is illustrated in pl. 25(1): on the obverse is the bust of the emperor, with bearded head, right, surmounted by a winged head-dress; at the right in front of the face, his name in Pahlavī; in the margin a Pahlavī legend AFD, of uncertain significance. On the reverse is a fire-altar, flanked by attendants; at the left in Pahlavī, the regnal date 26; at the right in Pahlavī, the mint signature NIH, for Nihāvand.

A typical specimen of the Arab–Sāsānian adaptation is shown in pl. 25(2), a dirham of the governor ʿUbaid-Allāh b. Ziyād, struck at Dārābjird in 52/683. It will be observed that the "portrait" is nearly identical with that on the prototype, but that in place of Khusrau's name is a two-line transliteration into Pahlavī of the name of the governor and of his father. The other distinguishing feature is the legend *b'ismi'llāh*, "in the name of Allāh", written in Kūfic, in the lower right-hand quarter. The reverse is likewise similar to that of the prototype, mint signature DA at the right, date at the left. The date, 52, is given in the Yazdgard era. The use of three different eras, Yazdgard, post-Yazdgard and Hijra, on these Arab–Sāsānian coins has contributed to the many problems inherent in the study of this difficult but exceedingly interesting transitional coinage.

Dirhams of the type described above were issued in the names of two caliphs, Mu'āwiya and 'Abd al-Malik b. Marwān, and of at least thirty-seven governors at thirty or more different mints in the provinces of 'Irāq, Khūzistān, Fārs, Jibāl, Āzarbāījān, Arrān, Kirmān, Sīstān and Khurāsān. For the most part these mints were located in cities where Sāsānian mints existed at the time of the conquest, and without any doubt the die-engravers and other craftsmen were Persians trained in the production of the Sāsānian drahm. In fact the letters of the early Kūfic legends in the margins appear to have been composed with Pahlavī punches.

During the latter half of the eighth and the beginning of the ninth decades of the Hijra (last five years of the seventh Christian century and first years of the eighth) a number of innovations were introduced and several radical iconographical changes were experimented with. On coins of the great general and viceroy al-Ḥajjāj b. Yūsuf his name sometimes appears in Kūfic, and an ingenious arrangement of the *shahāda*, or declaration of faith, is introduced into the obverse margin (pl. 25(3), Bishāpūr, 76 A.H.). A remarkable dirham (pl. 25(4)), undated but probably of the year 75/695, depicts on the obverse a figure, *not* the Sāsānian ruler surely, as his head-gear and breast ornamentation are atypical, and on the reverse a *miḥrāb* and the Prophet's *'anaza* or short spear, accompanied by the words in Kūfic, *Amīr al-mu'minīn*, "Commander of the Believers", and *Khalīfat-Allāh*, "Caliph of Allah".[1] The substitution of the prayer-niche and spear for the fire-altar without doubt reflects an attempt to create a purely Islamic iconography representative of the spiritual and temporal leadership of the caliph. Equally remarkable is another dirham (pl. 25(5)), actually dated 75 in a Kūfic inscription on either side of the conventional bust of Khusrau II, with on the reverse the figure of the standing sword-girt caliph, a figure borrowed from the type of Byzantine inspiration introduced by 'Abd al-Malik b. Marwān in Syria and Palestine.[2]

[1] See G. C. Miles, "Miḥrāb and 'Anazah: A study in early Islamic Iconography" in *Archaeologica Orientalia in Memoriam Ernst Herzfeld* (Locust Valley, N.Y., 1952), pp. 156–71. Cf. also Miles, "Some Arab-Sasanian and Related Coins", *ANSMN*, vol. VII (1957), pp. 192–3, nos. 7, 8. See also, with regard to the head-gear, the observations of Richard Ettinghausen, *From Byzantium to Sasanian Iran and the Islamic World* (Leiden, 1972), p. 33.

[2] Cf. G. C. Miles, "The Earliest Arab Gold Coinage", in *ANSMN*, vol. VIII (1967), p. 216, pl. XLVI, 9. The specimen illustrated there, and reproduced here, is now in the

While the sweeping coinage reform of ʿAbd al-Malik which took place between the years 77 and 79/696–9 (with some delays in parts of Iran) by and large resulted in the abolition of figural representations in most regions of the Islamic empire, Sāsānian and quasi-Sāsānian types persisted for several generations in outlying areas. For example, in the mountainous region of Ṭabaristān ʿAbbāsid governors issued dirhams of Sāsānian type (but of reduced module) into the fourth quarter of the second century of the Hijra (A.D. 794). A typical specimen is illustrated in pl. 25(6): a coin of Yaḥyā b. Mikhnāq struck in 165/781. Exceptional is an attempt to "dehumanize" the effigy of the Ispahbad by a governor named Sulaimān (pl. 25(7)): the face is converted into a lozenge enclosing the word *bakh*, "bravo!" From another remote region, Khwārazm, come some very rare thin silver coins with an unusual type of head on the obverse and a horseman on the reverse (pl. 26(1)): behind the rider is the name al-Faḍl, probably al-Faḍl b. Yaḥyā, *c.* 179/795.[1] Finally, datable to the years of al-Mahdī's, Hārūn al-Rashīd's and al-Amīn's rules (158–98/775–813), there are the extraordinary base silver coins of the so-called Bukhār-Khudāhs issued in the Bukhārā area. A specimen of one bilingual variety, with Soghdian (or "Bukhārān") and Kūfic legends, is illustrated in pl. 26(2). The prototype is the coinage of Bahrām V.

Excavations in recent years have disclosed the fact that during the transitional years following the Arab conquest there were local issues of copper coinage, perhaps much more plentiful than the meagre holdings of such coins in the great public collections would suggest. Of crude fabric and usually in a miserable state of preservation these municipal coins seldom find their way into the hands of dealers, but they are actually of extraordinary interest. Modified Sāsānian images are the predominant models, but there are also some Byzantine prototypes and a number of quite original Arab iconographical types, of which the coin illustrated in pl. 26(3) from the Iṣṭakhr excavations is an example. The bust on the obverse is obviously of Sāsānian inspiration but the head-dress is not that of Khusrau II, and behind the head in Kūfic is the name al-Walīd, undoubtedly the Umayyad caliph al-Walīd I

Museum of the American Numismatic Society. The only other known specimen was in the Zubow Collection, Moscow (cf. Walker, *B.M. Cat.* I, p. 25).

[1] Cf. G. C. Miles, *Rare Islamic Coins*, *ANSNNM*, no. 118 (New York, 1950), p. 10, no. 35; and R. N. Frye, *Notes on the Early Coinage of Transoxiana*, *ANSNNM*, no. 113 (New York, 1949), pp. 19ff.; Frye, "Additional Notes on the Early Coinage of Transoxiana", *ANSMN*, vol. IV (1950), pp. 105–8.

(86–96/705–15). The reverse is entirely Muslim of post-reform type, the simple shahāda.

'Abd al-Malik's monetary reform, as mentioned above, began with gold coins in the year 77 and two years later mints in Iran and 'Irāq (and at the capital Damascus in Syria) started issuing the purely epigraphical dirham which was to become the most popular coin in the Near and Middle East and was destined to exert an influence not only on the Byzantine coinage but probably even on the currency of western Europe. A typical example of this chaste and splendidly engraved coin appears in pl. 26(4): mint of Sābūr (Bishāpūr), year 96/714–15. As the Umayyad dirham is to serve as the basic model for several centuries to come, it is well to describe it in some detail. In admirably legible Kūfic characters the obverse area carries the shahāda, "There is no god except Allāh alone, there is no partner with him". Around the area is a circular legend reading, "In the name of Allāh: this dirham was struck in Sābūr in the year six and ninety." The reverse area bears the 112th sura of the Qur'ān: "Allāh is one, Allāh is eternal, He begetteth not and is not begotten, nor is there like unto him anyone." The circular legend reads: "Muḥammad is the messenger of Allāh, he was sent with guidance and the religion of truth to make it prevail over every other religion, averse though the idolaters may be" (Qur'ān, ix. 33). Seventy Umayyad dirham mints have been recorded. Of them sixty-six were located in 'Irāq and Iran; the others were Damascus, Ifrīqiya (Qairawān), al-Andalus (Cordoba) and an uncertain mint. It is interesting to note that the number of post-reform dirham mints is more than double that of the identified mints at which dirhams of Arab–Sāsānian type were issued. Only two (Arrajān and Marv ar-Rūd) or perhaps three (Zanjān?) of the latter were discontinued. The extraordinary uniformity of style of these post-reform dirhams from Spain to eastern Khurāsān and Afghanistan has occasioned some speculation with regard to the possibility that most of the dies, if not the coins themselves, were manufactured in one or two centrally located workshops.[1] The fact of the proliferation of mints after the year 79 would indeed lend weight to this view; at this early stage of the Arab occupation of 'Irāq and Iran where would the Arabs have found the die-engravers and other skilled technicians to man all these newly established mints?

[1] Cf. John Walker, *A Catalogue of the Muḥammadan Coins in the British Museum*, II: *A Catalogue of the Arab-Byzantine and Post-reform Umaiyad Coins* (London, 1956) [hereinafter cited as *B.M. Cat.* II], pp. lxiii–lxiv, to which add P. Balog's observations in *RN* (1958), pp. 230–1.

Our records of mint activity and production of course are not complete, nor will they ever be. However, on the basis of the published corpus, supplemented by the present writer's notes, some observations can be made.[1] Not all the Iranian post-reform mints began activity at the same time: the earliest (79 A.H.) were four in 'Irāq (Abarqubādh, al-Baṣra, al-Kūfa and Maisān); two, or perhaps three, in Khūzistān (Surraq, Sūq al-Ahwāz and Fīl[?]); two in Fārs (Birāmqubādh and Fasā); three in Jibāl (Jay, Shaqq al-Taimara and Māh al-Baṣra, the old Nihāvand); and one in Khurāsān (Marv).[2] The only other mint active in the opening year was the capital, Dimishq, outside our area. Some of these silver mints in the 'Irāq–Iran region ceased production after only a few years: no reliably reported issue of Abarqubādh is known after the year 96, of Maisān after 97, of Surraq after 99, of Fīl after the opening year, of Birāmqubādh after 95, of Shaqq al-Taimara after 82. By the year 131/749 only eight of the seventy Umayyad dirham mints were still producing: al-Andalus (for Spain), Ifrīqiya (for North Africa), Dimishq (for Syria), al-Baṣra and Wāsiṭ (for southern 'Irāq, plus al-Sāmīya, which opened only in the year 131), al-Jazīra (for northern 'Irāq), and al-Bāb (for the Caucasus area). It is remarkable that toward the end of the Umayyad period silver was not being issued at the great cities of Khuzistān, Fārs, Jibāl and Khurāsān (such as Sūq al-Ahwāz, Iṣṭakhr, Sābūr, Jay, Hamadān, al-Ray, Balkh and Marv), but of special interest in this connection is the fact that the production of dirhams is resumed at these and other mints by the partisans of the 'Abbāsid movement, a phase of the numismatic history of Iran which we will touch on briefly below.

To judge by the number of recorded specimens and the immense number seen in collections and in the hands of dealers, by far the most productive of the Umayyad silver mints was Wāsiṭ, the important garrison and administrative city midway between Kūfa and Baṣra founded by al-Ḥajjāj b. Yūsuf in the year 84/703. The earliest issue is dated in that year and specimens are known for every subsequent year down to 132/750, with the very curious and unexplained exception of the years 100 and 102. If indeed the dies for most of the Umayyad dirham mints were centrally produced, Wāsiṭ would appear to be the most probable locality.

[1] Summary in Walker, *B.M. Cat.* II, pp. lx–lxi.

[2] Birāmqubādh is probably to be read as Bizāmqubādh, from Middle Persian *weh az Amīd (kard) Kawād*, "better than Amīd has Qubādh (made this)". This was Arrajān; cf. Yāqūt (ed.).

The ʿAbbāsid and Khārijite movements are well reflected in the coinage. In the years 127–32/745–50 there appear at the mints of Rāmhurmuz in Khūzistān, Iṣṭakhr and Sābūr in Fārs, Jay, Taimara, Māhī (perhaps the two Māhs, Nihāvand and Dīnavar), Hamadān and Ray in Jibāl, and Balkh and Marv in Khurāsān a number of dirhams and a few copper coins with the pro-ʿAbbāsid slogan, "Say, for this I ask no wage of you, save love of my kin" (Qur'ān xlii. 22). At Ray some of the coins bear the name of the revolutionary ʿAbd-Allāh b. Muʿāwiya, and on one issue the name of Abū Muslim himself; elsewhere the coins are anonymous but there can be no doubt that they were all issued on the authority of Abū Muslim. A specimen of this interesting coinage, a dirham of Rāmhurmuz, 128, is illustrated in pl. 26(5). It will be noticed that the reverse is identical with the regular Umayyad coinage but that the obverse differs in that an inner marginal legend with the ʿAbbāsid propaganda is added. Another class of revolutionary coins of this period (al-Kūfa, 128, and Tanbūk, 133, is to be attributed to the Khārijites; they bear the war-cry, "*lā ḥukma illā li'llāhi*", "Arbitration belongs to Allāh alone".[1]

With the enthronement of Abu'l-ʿAbbās al-Saffāḥ on 13 Rabīʿ I, 132/30 October 749 there commences the long series of ʿAbbāsid coins struck at numerous mints in Iran. Gold does not make its appearance in Iran proper until about the year 220/835, but we know of dirhams and *fulūs* (plural of *fals* from Byzantine *follis*) from the mid-130's/750's onward. During the first decade of the dynasty the mints of Baṣra and Kūfa seem to have been the principal sources of silver coinage for the east, but as early as 134 dirhams begin to appear at Persian mints. These dirhams differ little in general appearance from the Umayyad prototype, but there are certain changes in the legends. Except for an attenuation of the letters in the area legend and the date in the margin, the obverse of a dirham of Jundīshāpūr, dated 136/753–4 (pl. 26(6)), very much resembles an Umayyad issue; on the reverse, however, Qur'ān cxii is abandoned and the simple statement, "Muḥammad is the messenger of Allāh" takes its place. The "Prophetic Mission" in the reverse margin remains as before. As time goes on supplementary

[1] An incomplete list of these ʿAbbāsid partisan and Khārijite issues appears in the writer's *Numismatic History of Rayy*, *ANSNS*, vol. II (New York, 1938) [hereinafter cited as *NHR*], pp. 16–17. Supplementary material will be found in D. Sourdel, *Inventaire des Monnaies Musulmanes anciennes du Musée de Caboul* (Damascus, 1953), pp. 5–9; in Miles, *Persepolis Region*, pp. 51–2 and 66–7; in Miles, "Al-Mahdi al-Ḥaqq, Amīr al-Mu'minīn", *RN* (1965), pp. 333–4; and in Ibrahim Artuk, *Denizbacı Definesi* (Ankara, 1966), pp. 36–8.

legends are added, but in style and basic scheme the dirham of the ʿAbbāsids and of the semi-independent dynasts owing allegiance to the caliphs is constant. On a dirham of al-Muḥammadiyya (Ray), 172/788–9 (pl. 26(7)) (*NHR* No. 72D) it will be noted that the reverse carries a six-line inscription; above and beneath, the words *jārib* (?) and *faḍl*, doubtless referring to the excellence of the coinage; and "*Muḥammad rasūl Allāh, al-k͟halīfat al-Ras͟hīd*, among those things ordered by Muḥammad, son of the Commander of the Believers". Al-Ras͟hīd of course is Hārūn al-Ras͟hīd, and Muḥammad is the later caliph al-Amīn.

A dirham of Samarqand dated 203/818–19 (pl. 26(8)) has even more elaborate legends. At the bottom of the obverse area is the word, *al-mas͟hriq*, "The East", and in the outer margin an additional Qur'ānic passage (xxx. 3–4): "Allāh's is the command, before and after; and on that day the Believers shall rejoice in the help of Allāh." The reverse, in seven lines, reads: "To God: *Muḥammad rasūl Allāh*; *al-Ma'mūn, k͟halīfat Allāh*; among those things ordered by the amīr al-Riḍā, heir apparent of the Muslims, ʿAli b. Mūsā b. ʿAlī b. Abī-Ṭālib; *D͟hu'l-ri'āsatain*". Al-Riḍā, the Eighth Imām, had been designated heir apparent by al-Ma'mūn in Muḥarram 201/August 816.[1] *D͟hu'l-ri'āsatain* on the last line, "he of the two authorities" (i.e., the pen and the sword) refers to al-Faḍl b. Sahl, the noted favourite of al-Ma'mūn.

Mention was made above of the fact that the production of gold coinage in Iran begins only toward the end of the first quarter of the 3rd/9th century. As early as 199/814–15 dīnārs were struck in the capital, Baghdad, with the legend al-ʿIrāq, but the earliest issue from a mint in Iran that has come to the writer's attention is a dīnār of Marv dated 220.[2] In the succeeding years a number of other mints began to issue gold. In the list below, wherein the mints in ʿIrāq are included for the sake of completeness, are given the dates of the first gold issues down to the end of the 3rd/9th century known to the writer:[3]

Marv 220
al-Muḥammadiyya 225

[1] For a discussion of these remarkable issues see *NHR*, pp. 103ff.

[2] M. Jungfleisch, "La trouvaille du Cimetière de Sainte-Barbe à Babylone d'Egypte (Juillet, 1948)", *RN* (1949), p. 166.

[3] This list revises and supersedes that in *NHR*, pp. 119–20. Sources are given only for issues unknown to the writer in 1938, as follows:
Sāmarrā: Miles, *Rare Islamic Coins* (New York, 1950), p. 36, no. 140.
Dabīl: ANS, unpublished.
Armīniya: ʿAbd al-Raḥmān Fahmy, *Fajr al-Sikkat al-ʿArabīyah* (Cairo, 1965), p. 607.
Samarqand: Kāmil Muhandis in *Les Annales Archéologiques de Syrie*, 13 (1963), p. 175.

Surra-man-ra'ā (Sāmarrā) 226
al-Baṣra 237
Dabīl 241
Armīniya 243
Samarqand 244
al-Mutawakkiliyya 247
al-Shāsh 248
Wāsiṭ 254
al-Ahwāz 255
Ḥulwān 258
al-Kūfa 266
Qazvīn 268
Hamadān 270
Āzarbāījān 272
Māh al-Baṣra (Nihāvand) 273
Jannābā 275 (Ṣaffārid)
Qum 282
Iṣfahān 293
al-Karaj 293

A typical specimen of an 'Abbāsid dīnār is illustrated in pl. 22(9) (Iṣfahān, 293/905–6). The obverse has the double marginal legend, the inner with the mint-date formula, the outer with Qur'ān, xxx. 3–4; the reverse bears the caliph's name, al-Muktafī bi'llāh.

The humble 'Abbāsid copper or bronze fals, although not particularly appealing to the eye, especially in its usually miserable worn or corroded condition, is frequently of considerable historical interest. Most cities of any importance during the 2nd/8th century struck fulūs, often with the names of governors or *'āmils*, or prefects, whose names sometimes are not recorded in the preserved chronicles. Scientifically excavated sites have provided us with a number of such issues; much interesting unpublished material can be expected from future excavations. At Ray no less than nineteen names of individuals appear on the copper coinage between 138 and 195/755–811.[1] The excavations at Iṣṭakhr and Naqsh-i Rustam have turned up a number of local issues,

al-Shāsh: J. Allan, in *NC* (1919), p. 192.
Wāsiṭ: Ulla S. Linder Welin, "Wāsiṭ", p. 158.
al-Ahwāz: Fahmy, *op. cit.*, p. 633.
Ḥulwān: *ibid.*, p. 636.
Nihāvand: V. G. Tizengauzen, *Moneti vostochnago Khalifata* (St Petersburg, 1873), no. 2077.
Qum: Unpublished, Robert W. Morris collection.
Iṣfahān: Miles, *Rare Islamic Coins*, p. 43, nos. 165–6.
al-Karaj: E. von Zambaur, *Münzprägungen*, p. 204.

[1] Cf. *NHR*, nos. 41–4, 47, 58, 60, 64, 70, 78, 81, 85, 96.

for example: Arrajān, Ardashīr-Khurra, Iṣṭakhr, Birāmqubādh, Tawwaj, Jay, Sābūr, Shīrāz, Fārs, Fasā and Kūrat al-Mahdiyya min Fārs (i.e. Jūr, otherwise known as Fīrūzābād).[1] A specimen from the last-named mint, dated 161/777–8 is shown in pl. 26(10).

Not long after the beginning of the 3rd/9th century the emergence of semi-independent principalities in Iran is reflected in the coinage. The earliest of these so-called "minor dynasties" (not so minor actually, considering the extent of their dominions and their independence from the 'Abbāsid caliphate in all but name) whose coinage has been recognized by numismatists is the Ṭāhirid. The first of the line, the famous general Ṭāhir b. al-Ḥusain, was known as *Dhu'l-Yamīnain*, and this title occurs on coins from the year 206/821 onward. Ṭāhirid mints include Herāt, Samarqand, Bukhārā, Nīshāpūr, Zarang, Bust and al-Muḥammadiyya (Ray). A dirham of Ṭālḥa b. Ṭāhir struck at al-Muḥammadiyya in 210/825–6 (pl. 26(11)) in every way resembles an 'Abbāsid dirham, but it will be noticed that Ṭalḥa's name appears beneath the reverse area, while the caliph's name is not mentioned. Another early dynasty, originating in Sīstān, was the Ṣaffārid. A dirham of al-Laith b. 'Alī issued at the mint of Fārs (Shīrāz) in 297/909–10 is illustrated in pl. 26(12). The flan is larger than the usual 'Abbāsid dirham and there are several distinguishing features: the name of the Ṣaffārid beneath the obverse area, the caliph's name, al-Muqtadir, beneath the reverse, and in the outer margins of both obverse and reverse several isolated "good luck" words, such as frequently appear on Persian glazed pottery, *al-naṣr*, *al-ẓafar*, *al-yumn* and *al-sa'āda*. Ṣaffārid coins are known from seventeen mints: Bust, Zarang and Sijistān in Sīstān; Balkh, Panjhīr, Rīkanz, Marv, Nīshāpūr and Herāt in Khurāsān; Arrajān, Jannābā, Shīrāz (Fārs) and Fasā in Fārs; Iṣfahān and al-Muḥammadiyya in Jibāl; al-Ahwāz in Khūzistān; and 'Umān in Arabia.

As an example of the coinage of one of the lesser dynasties in western Iran a dīnār of the Turkish Sājid Yūsuf b. Dīvdād struck at Armīniya (i.e. Dabīl) in 303/915–16 is illustrated in pl. 27(1). The obverse is in no way distinguishable from an 'Abbāsid dīnār of the period, but the reverse, in addition to the caliph's name, carries that of the dynast. The Sājids issued coins in both gold and silver at Āzarbāījān (Ardabīl or Maragha ?), Arrān (Barda'a), Ardabīl, Armīniya, Barda'a, Marāgha and briefly, al-Muḥammadiyya. Other minor dynasties or families of rulers in western and northern Iran producing coins during the 3rd and 4th/

[1] Miles, *Persepolis Region*, pp. 52ff.

9th and 10th centuries were: the family of Abū Dulaf in Kurdistān and Jibāl (Karaj, Māh al-Baṣra and Māh al-Kūfa, Hamadān and Iṣfahān); several 'Alid princes and pretenders in Qazvīn and Ṭabaristān; the Banījūrids (or Abū-Dā'ūdids) of Tukhāristān, governors of the Sāmānids, coins of whom are known from Andarāba, Balkh, Bāmiyān, Panjhīr and Tirmidh (pl. 27(2)), a dirham of Aḥmad b. Muḥammad b. Yaḥyā struck at Balkh in 297/909–10 (note the very early instance of the use of cursive naskhī script in the engraving of the governor's name beneath the obverse area); the Ṣa'lūkid governors of Ray;[1] the Ziyārids of Ṭābaristān and Gurgān, vassals of the Būyids, descendants of the kings of Gīlān and the Ispahbads of Rūyān (pl. 27(3), a dirham of Bīsutūn b. Vushmgīr, recognizing the Būyid Rukn al-Daula as overlord, struck at Gurgān in 358/968–9; Ziyārid coins are known also from the mints of Astarābād, Āmul, Sārīya and Hausam);[2] the Bāvandids, also of Ṭabaristān (pl. 27(4), a dirham of Rustam b. Sharvīn, acknowledging the Būyid 'Aḍud al-Daula, and bearing on the obverse the Shī'ī motto "*'Alī walī Allāh*", struck at Firīm in 367/977–8 (the only other identified Bāvandid mint is Sārīya);[3] the Sallārids or Musāfirids of Āzarbāījān, Arrān and Ṭārim, with mints at Āzarbāījān, Ardabīl, Armīniya, Barda'a, Marāgha and an unidentified locality Jalālābād (pl. 27(5), a beautiful dirham of the year 343/954–5 issued in the name of Vahsūdān b. Muḥammad with the honorific "Sword of the Family of Muḥammad" and the names of the Ismā'īlī imāms);[4] the Ja'farids of Tiflīs; the Justānids of Dailam (dirhams of the 360's/970's struck at Rūdbār); the Ḥasanwaihids of Kurdistān, with mints at Dīnavar (?), al-Rūr, Sābūr-Khwāst and Hamadān; and the Kākūyids, vassals of the Būyids and later of the Saljuqs, with mints at Asadābād, Iṣfahān, Burūjird, Jurbādhaqān, Sābūr-Khwāst, al-'Askar al-Manṣūr, Qirmīsīn, al-Qaṣr, al-Karaj, Māh al-Kūfa, al-Muḥammadiyya, Hamadān and Yazd. A splendid dirham of Muḥammad b. Dushmanzār, struck in 410/1019–20 at Iṣfahān, is illustrated in pl. 27(6): the obverse carries the name of the caliph and that of the Kākūyid prince, the reverse that of the Būyid overlord Majd al-Daula with the title Shāhanshāh.

[1] *NHR*, pp. 135–40, 144–6.

[2] Cf. G. C. Miles, "Coinage of the Ziyārid Dynasty of Ṭabāristān and Gurgān", *ANSMN*, vol. XVIII (1972), pp. 119–37.

[3] Cf. G. C. Miles, "The Coinage of the Bāwandids of Ṭabāristān", in C. E. Bosworth, ed., *Iran and Islam, In Memory of the Late Vladimir Minorsky* (Edinburgh, 1971), pp. 443–58.

[4] Cf. S. M. Stern, "The early Ismā'īlī Missionaries in North-West Persia and in Khurāsān and Transoxiana", *BSOAS*, vol. XXIII (1960), pp. 72–4. The present writer now knows of four more specimens of this remarkable coin.

We come now to the great dynasties which ruled over vast territories of Iran in the 3rd and 4th/9th and 10th centuries. The first of these was the Iranian Sāmānid house whose dominion at the height of its power extended from the frontiers of India to the central Iranian plateau. The output, particularly of silver, was immense. Sāmānid dirhams predominate in the great silver hoards of the 10th–11th centuries unearthed in Russia, Poland and Scandinavia; for example in a recently published Polish hoard buried probably about 912, more than 68 per cent of the coins were Sāmānid.[1] The earliest Sāmānid coins were of copper and were issued by Aḥmad b. Asad in Samarqand in 244/858–9.[2] There is some overlapping of ʿAbbāsid and Sāmānid issues in the 250's and 260's but the regular production of dirhams begins about 279/892 and of gold about the same time under Ismāʿīl b. Aḥmad. The great series ends a little over a century later with the death of Ismāʿīl b. Nūḥ. A typical dirham of Naṣr II b. Aḥmad, Samarqand, 306/918–19, is shown in pl. 27(7), and a dīnār of Nūḥ I b. Naṣr, Āmul, 343/954–5, in pl. 27(8).

Most Sāmānid dīnārs and dirhams are of conventional types but there are some extraordinary over-sized dirhams (up to 48 mm in diameter) struck in the Hindu Kush area doubtless for local circulation (pl. 28(1), Kūrat Badakhshān, with the names of Nūḥ b. Manṣūr, al-Ḥārith and the caliph al-Ṭāʾiʿ).[3]

The largest number of Sāmānid mints were in Khurāsān and neighbouring areas in the east, but sporadic issues are known also from cities in western Iran. The following list of forty-seven mints is doubtless incomplete: in Farghāna, east of the Jaxartes, Akhsīkat, Ūzkand, Tūnkath Ilāq, al-Shāsh (Tashkent), Farghāna (Andijān ?), Qubbā, Marghinān and Naṣrābād; in Soghdia, between the Oxus and the Jaxartes, Bukhārā, Sughd, Samarqand and Ṭaghāma; in Mā-warā-al-Nahr (Transoxiana), Ushrūsana, Andījārāgh, Badakhshān, Binkath, Tirmidh, al-Khuttal, Rāsht, Zāmīn and al-Ṣaghāniyān; in Sīstān, Farvān and Farah; in Khurāsān, Andarāba, Bāmiyān, Balkh, Panjhīr, Ṭāliqān, Gharchistān, Marv, al-Maʿdan, Nīshāpūr and Herāt; in Qūmis, al-Biyār; in Gurgān, Astarābād and Gurgān; in Ṭabaristān, Āmul and Firīm; in Fārs, Shīrāz (also named Fārs); in Jibāl, Sāva, Qazvīn, Qum, al-Karaj, Māh al-Baṣra, al-Muḥammadiyya and Hamadān.

Almost as prolific as the Sāmānid coinage was the Būyid. The earliest

[1] Cf. M. Czapkiewicz *et al.*, *Skarb monet Arabskich z Klukowicz powiat Siemiatycze* (Wrocław, Warszawa, Kraków, 1964).

[2] A. Markov, *Inventarnii Katalog musulmanskikh Monet* (St Petersburg, 1896), p. 113.

[3] Cf. *ANS Annual Report* (1969), p. 14.

issues are those of 'Imād al-Daula, founder of the dynasty, whose first coins were struck in al-Ahwāz in 320/932; the latest, more than a century later, those of al-Malik al-Raḥīm Khusrau Fīrūz, last of the Fārs and Khuzistān branch of the family, deposed by the Great Saljuq Toghrïl Beg in 447/1055. The Būyid coinage is particularly informative to the political historian, as the amplitude of titles, names and mints throws valuable light on the relationships to each other of the princes of the several branches of the house and of numerous vassals acknowledging their overlordship, and on the extent of their dominions. Recorded mints range from Bisṭām in the east to Baghdad and 'Umān. A list of fifty mints, again probably incomplete, follows: in Qūmis, Bisṭām, Dāmghān and Simnān; in Gurgān, Astarābād and Gurgān; in Ṭabaristān, Āmul, Sārīya and Firīm; in Gīlān, al-Hausam; in Jibāl, Iṣfahān, Ḥulwān, al-Dīnawar, Sābūr-Khwāst, Sāva, Sanjābād, Qirmīsīn, Qazvīn, Qum, Māh al-Kūfa, al-Muḥammadiyya, Nāyīn and Hamadān; in Armīniya, the capital (Ardabīl); in Kirmān, Bardasīr, Bam, Jīruft and al-Sīrajān; in Fārs, Arrajān, Ardashīr-Khurra, Jannābā, Dārābjird, Sābūr, Sīrāf, Shīrāz, Fārs, Fasā, Kāzarūn and Kard Fanā Khusrau; in Khūzistān, al-Abadān min al-Ahwāz, al-Ahwāz, Aidaj, Tustar min al-Ahwāz, Jundīshāpūr, Rāmhurmuz, Sūq al-Ahwāz, 'Askar Mukram, 'Askar min al-Ahwāz and al-Kurdiyya (?); in 'Irāq, Madīnat al-Salām (Baghdad); in Arabia, 'Umān.

The vast majority of Būyid coins, both dīnārs and dirhams, are of conventional type. A typical dirham of rather wide flan is one of Arrajān, 346/957–8 (pl. 28(2)), with the name of Rukn al-Daula Abū 'Alī Būya on the obverse and the names of the caliph al-Muṭī' and 'Aḍud al-Daula Abū Shujā' on the reverse. Exceptional are a few quite extraordinary figural coins. A unique silver piece actually called a dīnār has on one side more or less customary legends in Kūfic, with the name of Rukn al-Daula, the mint al-Muḥammadiyya and the date 351/962; the other side has a remarkable neo-Sāsānian "portrait" accompanied by Pahlavī inscriptions (pl. 28(3)).[1] A comparable "portrait" in the Sāsānian style appears on a gold medallion of Fanā-Khusrau 'Aḍud al-Daula struck at Fārs (Shīrāz) in 359/969–70.[2] There are furthermore

[1] The coin, probably a presentation piece, is the property of M. R. Gurnet of Momignies, Belgium. See G. C. Miles, "A Portrait of the Buyid Prince Rukn al-Dawlah", *ANSMN*, vol. XI (1964), pp. 283–93.

[2] See Mehdi Bahrami in *Archaeologica Orientalia in Memoriam Ernst Herzfeld* (Locust Valley, N.Y., 1952), p. 18, pl. 1, fig. 2a, b. Some suspicion has been expressed about the authenticity of this piece (e.g. Ernst Kühnel, "Die Kunst Persiens unter den Buyiden",

several splendid gold "pièces de cérémonie" issued at Baghdad in 363 and 365/973–976 in the name of ʿIzz al-Daula. One of these, with representations of a seated king and of a musician playing a lute, has been illustrated a number of times. Two others are reproduced here for the first time. One (pl. 28(4)) shows on both sides a lion attacking a stag; the obverse bears the *s̲h̲ahāda* and the mint-date formula in the circular legend, the reverse the name of ʿIzz al-Daula. Another (pl. 29(1)) portrays an eagle seizing a duck on one side, and on the other an eagle devouring a gazelle.

The coinages of two other important dynasties ruling on the eastern frontiers of Iran before the arrival of the Saljuqs remain to be dealt with: the Qarak̲h̲ānids and the G̲h̲aznavids. (The coinage of the second dynasty of the K̲h̲wārazm-S̲h̲āhs, ending with the conquest by Maḥmūd of G̲h̲azna, appears to have been very limited.) The Qarak̲h̲ānid (or Ilig-K̲h̲ānid) coinage, a most interesting and complex branch of Iranian numismatics, deserves much more scholarly attention than it has so far received. The earliest recorded coins are those of Hārūn Bug̲h̲rā K̲h̲ān II, who died in 382/992. Issues in billon, copper and silver are known of some twenty rulers down to the end of the dynasty at the beginning of the 7th/13th century. Recorded mints are: in the Jaxartes region, Banākat̲h̲, Ṭarāz and Kās̲h̲g̲h̲ar; in Farg̲h̲āna, Ak̲h̲sīkat, Ūzkand, Ūs̲h̲, Īlāq, Tūnkat̲h̲ Īlāq, K̲h̲ujanda, al-S̲h̲ās̲h̲, Farg̲h̲āna, Kand, Marg̲h̲inān, Haftdih and Yārkand; in Sog̲h̲dia, Is̲h̲tik̲h̲ān, Buk̲h̲ārā, Sug̲h̲d, Samarqand, Karmīniya, Kis̲h̲ and al-Kus̲h̲ānī; in Transoxiana, Us̲h̲rūsana, Il-Ūrdū, K̲h̲arlug̲h̲ Ūrdū, Dabūsiya, al-Ṣag̲h̲āniyān and Qara Ūrdū; in K̲h̲urāsān, Nīs̲h̲āpūr and Herāt. The types are varied and imaginative, the epigraphy often very fine and quite remarkable, and the titulature rich and complicated. Two specimens are illustrated in the plates: a copper coin (pl. 29(2)) of Naṣr b. ʿAlī Ilig-K̲h̲ān (d. 403/1012–13) exhibiting early examples of plaited Kūfic in the name *Naṣr* on the obverse and in *Muḥammad* on the reverse;[1] and a silver dirham of Yūsuf Qadïr K̲h̲ān, struck at Ūzkand in 423/1032 (pl. 29(3)). Note the fine engraving, the neat epigraphy, the mint-date formula arranged to form a square on the obverse, and the reverse legend reading

ZDMG (1956), p. 85), but particularly in the light of the undoubted genuineness of the Rukn al-Daula "portrait" coin, the present writer accepts the ʿAḍud al-Daula medallion as authentic.

[1] For earlier examples of plaited Kūfic on coins see the remarkable paper of Lisa Volov (Golombek), "Plaited Kufic on Samanid Epigraphic Pottery", *Ars Orientalis*, vol. VI (1966), p. 120.

Plate 25

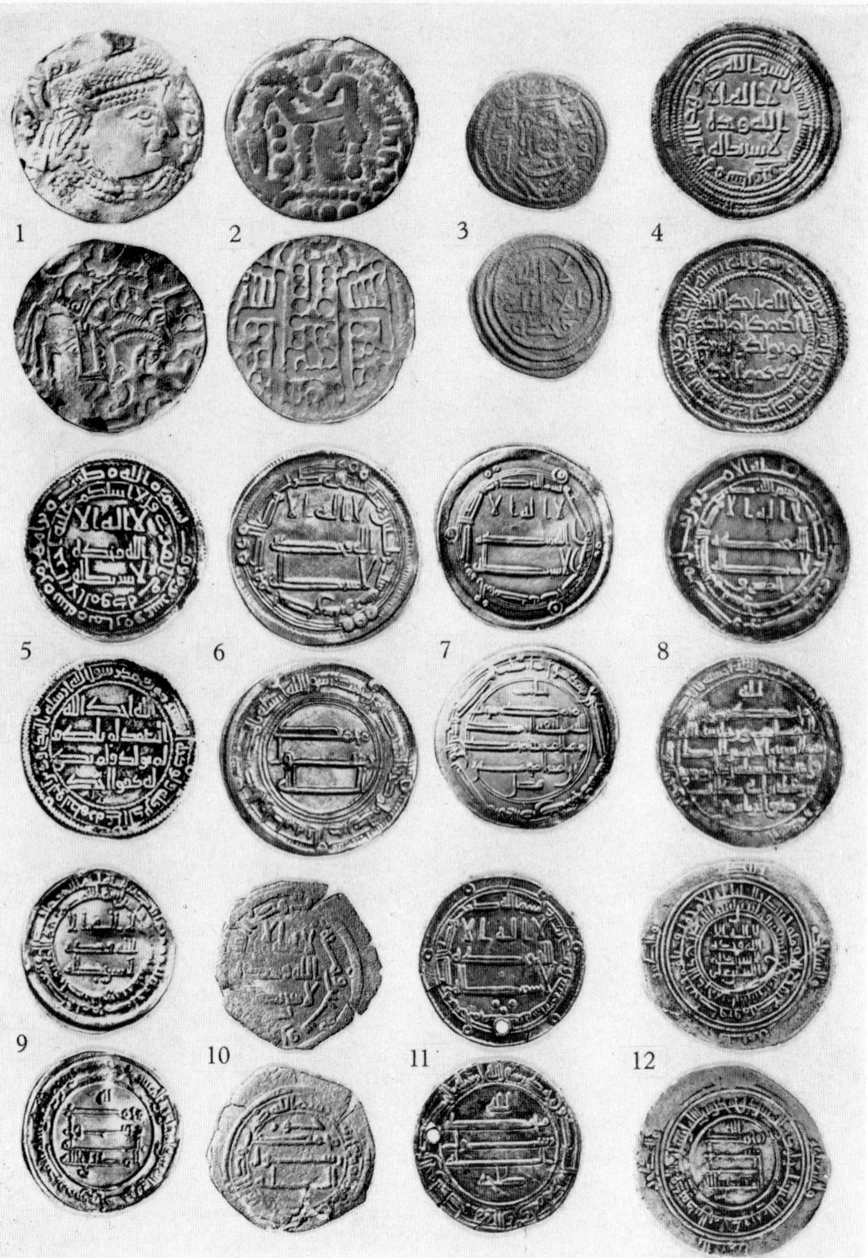

Plate 26

Plate 27

Plate 28

Plate 29

al-Qādir bi'llāh, Nāṣir al-Ḥaqq, Malik al-Mashriq (King of the East), Qadïr Khān.

Finally we come to the great dynasty of the Ghaznavids, whose origins and much of whose history lie beyond the borders of Iran but whose invasion of Khurāsān and Jibāl and defeat of the last Sāmānids bring them into the purview of this chapter. The Ghaznavid coinage is immensely varied and complex, differing widely in type and fabric in various parts of the empire. The earliest coins are those of Alp-Tegin, the Turkish slave in the service of the Sāmānid court in the middle of the 4th/10th century. Thereafter Sebük-Tegin, his great son Maḥmūd and the latter's son Mas'ūd issued dīnārs and dirhams in huge quantities at numerous mints, many of them within Iran proper. While the rise of the Saljuqs puts an end to Ghaznavid domination and mintage in the area with which we are concerned, coins continue to be struck in the East by the successive Ghaznavid princes down to the end of the dynasty in 582/1186. Mints in Iran include: in Soghdia, Karmīniya; in Transoxiana (Badakhshān), Valvālīj; in Sīstān, Sijistān, Ghazna and Farvān; in Khurāsān, Andarāba, Bāmiyān, Balkh, Jūzjān, Nīshāpūr and Herāt; in Fārs; Fasā; in Jibāl, Iṣfahān and al-Ray. Two Ghaznavid issues of Nīshāpūr are illustrated in pl. 29(4), a dirham dated 386/996, with the name of the Sāmānid Nūḥ b. Manṣūr in naskhī characters on the obverse and that of al-Walī Saif al-Daula Maḥmūd, accompanied by a sword diagonally, on the reverse; and (5), a dīnār dated 387/997, with Maḥmūd's name and a sword upright on the obverse, and the Sāmānid overlord's name on the reverse, here with the title *al-Malik al-Manṣūr*.

In this brief survey of the multifarious coinages of Iran from the Arab conquest to the early 5th/11th century no attempt has been made to deal with the important economic aspects of the currency. The emphasis here rather has been on the contributions these coinages offer to the political and cultural historian and to the student of art and epigraphy.

CHAPTER II

THE EXACT SCIENCES

I. INTRODUCTION

The aim of this chapter is to describe scientific activity in Iran during the four centuries beginning about 30/650. In so doing it is convenient to begin with a synoptic introduction, and then to devote a special section to each of the branches of the exact sciences in which significant Iranian work was done. The closing section is a short appreciation of the accomplishments of al-Bīrūnī, a man whose life adorns the period.

As it happens, there is more information about science in Sāsānian Iran than there is about the same subject during the first hundred years of Arab dominance. Although no scientific documents in Middle Persian have survived, it has been established that Greek and Sanskrit works were translated into Pahlavī at the Sāsānian court, and some of these documents exist in the languages from which the translations were made. It is also known that the S̲h̲āhans̲h̲āhs sponsored various versions of the *Zīj-i S̲h̲āh* (or *Zīk-i S̲h̲ahiryār*), sets of astronomical tables for the computation of planetary positions, the prediction of eclipses, and such. Further, by piecing together scraps of information from various early Islamic sources, it is possible to obtain a fair idea of the contents and techniques of the various revisions of the *Zīj-i S̲h̲āh*, including the one made during the reign of Yazdgard III, the last Sāsānian monarch.

During the Umayyad dynasty which followed there is not a single name which has come down, either of a scientific book written, or an astronomer carrying out observations. Yet some work must have been going on at this time, as is witnessed by the considerable number of translators available just afterward to put existing technical books into Arabic from Pahlavī.

The situation changed radically with the rise of the ʿAbbāsids. During the century beginning with 132/750 the exact sciences were cultivated at and near the capital city Baghdad more intensively than anywhere in the world previously. Moreover, in terms of the numbers of scientists at work, the peak of activity then attained was never equalled at any time thereafter during the Middle Ages.

During the final two centuries of our period (235/850–442/1050), reflecting the political decentralization which attended the weakening of the ʿAbbāsid empire, small foci of culture formed at the courts of the various new and competing dynasties, Būyid, Sāmānid and Ghaznavid. As it happened, the break-up in the Baghdad concentration of scientists coincided with a change in the character and quality of the work turned out by the scholars.

Early ʿAbbāsid scientists tended to be astronomer-astrologers whose techniques and theories were inherited from Indian and Sāsānian forebears and whose rôle as innovators was small. Their sole major contribution was in the form of numerous and meticulous astronomical observations. Their computational mathematics was generally unimpressive. In trigonometry their basic function, the sine, was taken over from the Indians. The remaining standard functions, the tangent, secant, and so on, first appear in ʿAbbāsid contexts, but they may have been invented elsewhere. The same statement can be made of the algebra of the quadratic, discussed below.

Beginning with the work of al-Battānī, however, there was a pronounced rise in the level of astronomical theory. He adopted the Ptolemaic planetary models, greatly superior to those of India and Iran, which became permanently displaced in the practice of the abler astronomers. The 4th/10th century also saw the proof of theorems which were decisive in creating trigonometry as a branch of mathematics in its own right, dealing with the solution of triangles, plane or spherical, and without necessary reference to spherical astronomy. Thus, although during the last two hundred years of the period there was a falling off in the number of active scientists, hence a decrease in quantity, the quality and originality of their work was distinctly higher than that of their immediate predecessors.

II. ARITHMETIC

In ʿAbbāsid Iran three distinct and independent systems of calculation subsisted simultaneously: (1) the apparently indigenous *ḥisāb al-kuttāb* (arithmetic of the scribes), (2) *al-ḥisāb al-hindī* (Indian arithmetic), and (3) *ḥisāb al-jummal*, taken over from the Greeks. The leading characteristics of each of these disciplines are described below.

Present knowledge of the scribal arithmetic is due largely to study of a textbook for the use of government employees written by Abu'l-

Wafā' al-Buzjānī (b. 328/940, d. 388/998), a thinker of great originality and power. This system had no special numeral symbols, all numbers being written out in words. The elementary operations as performed upon integers in this arithmetic are of no great interest, but the handling of fractions is distinctive. Considerations of elegance dictated that common fractions appearing in the results of a computation were not to be displayed as such. The well-educated bureaucrat was expected to express an answer, exactly or approximately, as a simple combination of sums and products of "canonical fractions", unit fractions of the form $1/n$, $n \leqslant 10$ (except that the special fraction $2/3$ was also allowed). For instance, he might put

$$\frac{3}{17} \approx \frac{1}{6} + \frac{1}{6}\frac{1}{10},$$

a rather poor approximation. The origins of this cumbersome and strongly convention-ridden system are unknown. The use of unit fractions is immediately reminiscent of the ancient Egyptian arithmetic, but such connection has been contested. Whatever its beginnings, it maintained itself for many centuries alongside the much more efficient imported varieties of arithmetic.

As to the decimal place-value system, its date of transmission from India is unknown. There is a clear reference to the Indian arithmetic by the Syrian monk Sebokht in 42/662, but no examples of its use in Mesopotamia or the Iranian plateau can be exhibited until much later. Of course, the precise form the numeral symbols take is unimportant in itself, whether the "western Arabic" forms common in North Africa, from which the current "Hindu-Arabic numerals" come, or the "eastern Arabic" forms still used in the Middle East – both are demonstrably descendants of Indian numerals. What is essential is the capability of representing any number by the use of a set of numerals including not more than ten different symbols, in which the contribution of any particular symbol to the value of the number is determined not only by the symbol itself, but also by its *place in the set*, hence place-value. E.g. in the set 4609·13 (or ٤٦٠٩٫١٣), the contribution of the symbol 6 (or ٦) to the value of the number displayed is six *hundred* because it occupies the hundreds place, the third to the left of the decimal point.

The earliest known textbook for decimal arithmetic is that written by Muḥammad b. Mūsā al-Khwārazmī (*fl.* 205/820), and it is not extant in the Arabic original but only in Latin translation. In the course of the next two centuries at least ten additional expositions of Indian arithmetic were written. Some of these are extant, and several have been studied in recent years. All give explanations and examples of the elementary operations and usually also of the extraction of square roots. With the single exception of the Damascene arithmetician al-Uqlīdisī (*fl.* 339/950), the authors of these books did not use decimal fractions and the latter were not generally introduced for many centuries.

The third arithmetic system, *jummal* reckoning, was universally employed in astronomy, the only subject in which really serious computation was carried on. In these calculations, letters of the Arabic alphabet (whence *abjad* numbers) were used as numeral symbols. For integers there was a non-place-value decimal notation; for fractions a place-value sexagesimal system – i.e. the base was sixty rather than ten. Sexagesimal arithmetic was by then, of course, quite ancient, having appeared in Mesopotamia some time during the second millennium B.C. For the easier operations, addition and subtraction, numbers were kept in the jummal form. Multiplication and division are more difficult. When the quantities involved were both fractional, the jummal representation was purely sexagesimal, and sometimes products and quotients were calculated directly as sexagesimals. Descriptions of sexagesimal multiplication tables, essential for such computations, exist in the literature, but no actual example is available from this period. Much more commonly these operations were carried out as follows: both numbers involved in the operation were converted into decimal integers, each being the number of the smallest denomination of sexagesimal fractions present, contained in the entire quantity. E.g. $251°17'55''$ would be expressed as 904,675 *seconds* ($= 251 \times 3600 + 17 \times 60 + 55$). The operation was then carried out as a decimal multiplication or division, and the result converted back into sexagesimals. It was essential to attach the proper denomination to the answer, e.g. *seconds* times *minutes* gives *thirds*, and so on.

Computational mathematics did not reach the degree of sophistication it achieved later, in Mongol and Tīmūrid times, but numerical tables of functions were considerably more extensive and precise than those produced by the Greeks and the Indians. In Bīrūnī's astronomical handbook, the *al-Qānūn al-Mas'ūdī* (completed *c.* 427/1036), by way of illustration, the table of sines is carried to four sexagesimal places (hence to a precision better than one in ten million) for each quarter of a degree. Columns of first and second differences are also given for ease in interpolation. In contrast, the analogous table of chords in Ptolemy's *Almagest* is only to three places, and in steps of half of a degree.

Among the more complicated arithmetic processes, the operation of root extraction received considerable attention in ʿAbbāsid times. An extant arithmetic textbook by al-Nasawī (*fl.* 390/1000) contains a method for extracting the cube root which is identical with that of a much earlier Chinese work. This method, to which the name Ruffini-Horner was attached in Europe, may have come to the Near East via India. Both Abu'l-Wafā' and Bīrūnī wrote on the extraction of roots of higher order than the cube, but the treatises themselves have not survived.

III. ALGEBRA

Expressions of the form

$$(1) \qquad ax^2+bx+c = 0, \qquad a \neq 0,$$

where a, b and c are given constants and x is a variable, are known as quadratic equations. A solution of a quadratic is a number which, when it replaces x in the expression above, gives zero for the left-hand side, equalling the zero on the right-hand side. The equation is then said to be satisfied. For example, the numbers 3 and -13 are both roots of the quadratic

$$(2) \qquad x^2+10x-39 = 0.$$

It is now known that every quadratic has two roots, although one or more of the roots may be negative (as above), or irrational (not expressible as a terminating or non-repeating decimal), or complex (containing $\sqrt{-1}$), even when the coefficients a, b and c are all integers.

ʿAbbāsid mathematicians were the first known to mount a systematic attack upon the quadratic, and, subject to limitations in their concept of what constituted a number, they arrived at complete solutions. The best known and perhaps earliest exposition of this doctrine is al-Khwārazmī's *Kitāb al-jabr w'al-muqābala*, whence the modern term *algebra*. Recently published is a similar treatise by one ʿAbd al-Ḥamīd b. Turk, of uncertain date but certainly ʿAbbāsid. For these and the other Muslim algebraists, the notion of a negative number did not exist. In seeking to solve quadratics it was therefore not possible for them to regard all such as typified by the single expression (1), with a, b and c

either positive or negative, and having a single expression which would give all possible solutions in terms of these general coefficients. The equation (2) had the form

$$x^2+10x = 39, \tag{3}$$

and the method of solving it would differ from that worked out for such an equation as

$$x^2+21 = 10x.$$

It must also be borne in mind that the "algebraic" symbols which to some people nowadays are synonymous with the subject itself had no part in al-Khwārazmī's algebra. Equation (3) would be displayed in some such form as "a square and ten roots equal thirty-nine". Modern symbols used here are for convenience only; the Arabic texts contain nothing but words. Should b or c be zero, the effect would be to suppress one of the terms, and hence give rise to a separate case and another method of solution.

Under these circumstances, there are five distinct cases of the quadratic:

$$ax^2 = c,$$

$$ax^2 = bx,$$

$$ax^2+bx = c,$$

$$ax^2+c = bx,$$

and

$$ax^2 = bx+c,$$

where the coefficients are all positive. Such cases as $ax^2+bx+c = 0$ could not exist, since they admit only of solutions in the then non-existent negative or complex numbers. But for each of the five cases listed, al-Khwārazmī gives a verbal rule for calculating the solution in terms of the given coefficients. The rule is accompanied by a numerical example, and in general closely resembles the technique called "completing the square" still in use. This aspect of Islamic algebra, consisting of prescribed sequences of arithmetic operations performed upon sets of given numbers, resembles the content of Old Babylonian algebraic cuneiform texts, to which in some distant way it is undoubtedly related.

Al-Khwārazmī's treatise also has, however, a section giving "proofs" that the rules are valid. In its strongly geometrical character this part of the book is reminiscent of Greek mathematics and has probably drawn ultimately on the algebraic parts of Euclid's Elements, or related works. The procedure involves interpreting the given data geometrically: x^2 is a square whose side is the measure of the unknown: bx is a rectangle with sides of length b and x, and c is a rectangle whose area is c square units. Proof consists of (1) exhibiting a line x constructed by applying geometrically the rule for solving the equation, and (2) showing that the two-dimensional figure which results satisfies geometrically, i.e. in terms of areas, the given equation.

There were also sporadic attempts to solve cubics, polynomial equations of the next degree beyond the quadratic. For instance, Bīrūnī showed that the length of a side of an inscribed regular polygon of nine sides could be calculated in terms of a solution of the cubic

$$x^3 = 1 + 3x.$$

However, the systematic reduction of all types of the cubic was not effected until the end of the 5th/11th century.

IV. TRIGONOMETRY

The branch of mathematics known as trigonometry arose in direct response to the astronomer's need for a means of calculating angular distances on the celestial sphere in terms of other, directly observable, arcs on it. Already by the time of Ptolemy a discipline had been developed which, in principle, provided all that was required. It consisted of two things: a theorem, and a numerical table. The theorem, that of Menelaos, applies to any spherical complete quadrilateral, the configuration formed by any four great circle arcs on a sphere. Menelaos' Theorem establishes a compound proportion involving the chords of three pairs of segments into which any three sides of the quadrilateral are divided by the fourth. The table is a set of chord lengths of a standard circle, tabulated as a function of the arcs the chords subtend. The Menelaos Theorem and the table of chords suffice to solve all the spherical problems in the *Almagest*, but frequently at great cost in ingenuity and computation. The complete quadrilateral, with its four sides and six vertices, is a complicated figure. For each application, a suitable quadrilateral must be found or constructed, so located that five arcs in the compound proportion are known and the sixth is the required unknown. A simpler figure was called for. Furthermore, to ease the burden of calculation, it was desirable to replace the single table of chords by a repertoire of special tabulated functions, carried to more places and at smaller intervals than the *Almagest* table, to increase the ease and precision of interpolation.

The first step to displace the chord function was taken in India, well before the rise of Islam. There it was realized that a table giving for each value of the argument half the chord of twice the given arc was handier than the chord itself. This realization marked the invention of the sine, the fundamental periodic function of modern science. From India the sine travelled to Baghdad, probably via the late Sāsānians. At the hands of the ʿAbbāsid astronomers the new function received marked improvements.

All the trigonometric functions are definable in terms of variable arcs, chords, and tangents to a fixed circle. It turns out that the choice of unity for the radius of this circle simplifies algebraic reductions and saves computation, and this is universal modern practise. For the versions of the sine function which came from India, however, this radius, R, had various values, none of them unity. Most applications of the tables based on these sines involved a division or multiplication by R, which would have been obviated with $R = 1$. The ʿAbbāsid astronomers accomplished almost the same thing by (following the lead of the *Almagest*) putting $R = 60$, the base of the sexagesimal system, and calculating the tabular entries in pure sexagesimals. Multiplication or division of a sexagesimal by 60 is a mere matter of moving the "sexagesimal point" (or its equivalent) one place to the right or left, just as multiplication of a decimally represented number by ten is performed by moving the decimal point one place. At least two 4th/10th-century mathematicians, Abu'l-Wafā' and Bīrūnī, perceived the advantage of putting $R = 1$, and the sine table of the latter (referred to above in the section on arithmetic) is in every respect the modern function.

The operation of division is more tedious than that of multiplication, and the extraction of a square root more troublesome than both. If the calculator solving trigonometric problems has at his disposal only a single function, the sine (or the chord), he is on occasion forced into extracting roots. But if he can count upon tables of the tangent and the secant functions as well, together with their cofunctions, he can confine his arithmetic operations largely to addition, subtraction, and multiplication. The cotangent function may be thought of as a measure of the shadow cast by a vertical gnomon of height R upon a horizontal plane, the sun's angle of elevation being the independent variable. Primitive shadow tables, with the time of day as argument rather than an angle, can be exhibited from several parts of the ancient world. In India the gnomon length $R = 12$ became standard, and sometime before the ninth century the transition in argument from hours to degrees was made, for in the astronomical handbook of al-Khwārazmī a table of $12 \cot \theta$ appears, carried to two sexagesimal places for $\theta = 1°, 2°, 3°, \ldots, 90°$. In the choice of R he was imitated by most of his contemporaries and successors for several centuries. However, another Baghdad astronomer, Ḥabash al-Marwazī (*fl.* 215/830) gives in his astronomical handbook a table in sexagesimals of $60 \tan \theta$ for $\theta = \frac{1}{2}°, 1°, 1\frac{1}{2}°, \ldots, 89°$, carried to three places, thus approaching very close indeed to the modern tangent function.

Although much less common, the secant and cosecant functions were also defined and tabulated in 'Abbāsid times, usually with $R = 12$. In Arabic the cosecant was called *quṭr al-ẓill*, "hypotenuse of the shadow", which is what it is. Thus the tally of computational aids to trigonometry was completed, and we turn to a consideration of advances in the geometrical side of the subject.

The trend was to discard the complete quadrilateral in favour of a much simpler figure, the triangle. A transitional theorem in the process was the "rule of four quantities", which asserts that in any two spherical right triangles which have a pair of acute angles equal, the relation

$$\sin a / \sin a' = \sin c / \sin c'$$

subsists between the sides a and a' opposite the equal angles, and the two hypotenuses c and c'. Just who first proved this theorem is unknown, but various proofs are given by mathematicians of the tenth and eleventh centuries, including one based on the Menelaos theorem.

The rule of four quantities in turn was employed to prove the sine theorem, a landmark in the evolution of trigonometry, involving as it does the sides and angles of any spherical triangle. It is

$$\frac{\sin a}{\sin A} = \frac{\sin b}{\sin B} = \frac{\sin c}{\sin C}$$

where a capital letter denotes an angle, and the same letter, small, refers to the opposite side. Priority for the discovery of the sine theorem was disputed among three contemporaries, Abu'l-Wafā', Abū Maḥmūd al-Khujandī and Abū Naṣr Manṣūr, all three of Khurāsānian origin.

V. THEORETICAL ASTRONOMY – PLANETARY THEORY

From the very beginnings of science the objects in the solar system have stimulated fruitful curiosity, causing men to invent abstract models to enable them to predict the positions and motions of the sun and the planets. The earth, like its sister planets, rotates about the sun in an orbit which is almost a circle. If the earth is thought of as stationary, then it is the sun which rotates about us, carrying with it its satellite planets. For an inferior planet, one whose orbit is smaller than the earth's (or the sun's), its resultant motion with respect to the earth is easy to visualize. It is the motion of a point on a wheel rotating independently at the same time that the wheel's centre rotates upon the rim of a larger wheel. To adopt ancient terminology, the larger wheel (or orbit) is the *deferent*, the smaller the *epicycle*. The case of a superior planet is somewhat more involved, since its orbit is larger than the sun's. But the two orbits can be interchanged without affecting the position of the planet, to retain the deferent as the larger with centre in the vicinity of the earth, and the epicycle as the smaller, outer wheel carrying the planet. Under all circumstances, then, the planet moves with respect to the earth in a series of loops, generally forward, but periodically becoming retrograde. The simple epicyclic model, with all loops congruent, is insufficiently precise for anything but a good approximation. With an actual planet, the size and character of the retrogradations vary, depending upon the region of the sky in which they take place.

Having set up the problem, it is useful to note three ways by which, in various places and times, it was solved:

(*a*) Purely numerical techniques may be used, with no appeal at any stage to a geometric model. This highly sophisticated approach was developed by Babylonian astronomers in the Seleucid period; it then disappeared until the clay tablets on which it was recorded were excavated and deciphered in recent times. Its eschewal of geometry gives it a singularly modern aspect.

(*b*) The simple deferent-epicycle model may be accepted, and the necessary variation in the retrogradations introduced by means of computational schemes which have no immediate geometric motivation or rationale. Unlike (*a*) above, these procedures involve trigonometric, rather than algebraic, transformations because of the implicit presence of the epicycle. They were characteristic of Indian and Sāsānian astronomy.

(*c*) The deferent-epicycle configuration may be modified geometrically, by making the earth eccentric with respect to the deferent and by introducing a periodic variation in the speed of the epicycle centre, in order to improve the correspondence between the model and the facts. This is the method of Ptolemy, and his solution is about as good a job as can be hoped for without abandonment of circular orbits. As with (*a*) and (*b*) the ultimate result is numerical, a set of true longitudes corresponding to given instants. But here computation is postponed until the end, and the figure determines the direction the computation shall take.

We are now in a position to say something about 'Abbāsid astronomy, and it is a reasonably valid generalization to assert that prior to *c.* 336/850 planetary theory was predominantly of type (*b*), and that subsequently it was displaced by the superior type (*c*). It is difficult to be more specific than this and to introduce details about developments in theoretical astronomy during the century ending with the above date. The reason is that extant treatises from this time are few in number, and these few are frequently corrupted with later additions. They are themselves almost our only sources for studying Sāsānian astronomy, there being no astronomical documents in Middle Persian, and there is usually no way of distinguishing between 'Abbāsid doctrine, and Sāsānian technique taken over by the 'Abbāsids. The situation is further complicated by whatever Indian astronomy was brought directly to the court of al-Manṣūr by the legendary ambassador Kanka. This probably comprised the "Great Sindhind", a work closely related to the *Brāhmasphuṭasiddhānta* of Brahmagupta (*fl.* A.D. 630). And it is necessary to introduce additional technical terms.

Any type (*b*) procedure, Indian, Sāsānian or 'Abbāsid, has the following common elements:

(1) There must exist a way of determining the "equation of the anomaly", say e_1, the modification in the planet's position due to its place on the epicycle.

(2) There must exist a way of determining the "equation of the centre", say e_2, the modification in the planet's position due to its situation relative to a point in the sky fixed for each planet, its apogee.

(3) There must exist a rule causing e_1 to affect e_2, and e_2 to affect e_1, since the two equations are not independent of each other.

Usually both e_1 and e_2 were defined by means of numerical tables. In the Indian sources, the earlier versions of the *Zīj-i Shāh*, and the

Sindhind, e_1 tables are computed by use of the epicycle configuration, while the e_2 functions are of the more crude "sinusoidal" form $k \sin t$, where k depends upon the planet, and t is the argument. In the latest version of the *Zīj-i S̲h̲āh* e_1 also seems to be sinusoidal. In the early 'Abbāsid materials this "method of sines" is widespread, as is also the "method of declinations", which substitutes $k\delta(t)$ for the sine function (where $\delta(t)$ is the declination of a point on the ecliptic having longitude t). But whether this is an 'Abbāsid innovation or a Sāsānian carry-over there is no present way of telling.

An Indian method of accomplishing (3), the blending of the equations, is to obtain a preliminary value for e_1, modify the argument by half of e_1, and use the new argument to get a preliminary value for e_2. Obtain a final value for e_2 by using an argument modified by halves of *both* e_1 and e_2. Now obtain a final value for e_1 by modifying the argument with all of the final e_2. This four-step procedure is present in al-K̲h̲wārazmī's astronomical tables, probably via the *Sindhind*. There also exists an 'Abbāsid three-step procedure involving no "halving of the equation", but where it originated is uncertain.

Undoubtedly 'Abbāsid are instances where Ptolemaic parameters were inserted into non-Ptolemaic techniques such as the method of declinations. The general picture is one of earnest practitioners carrying through formal operations with very little understanding of the reasons behind the rules.

From the time of al-Battānī on the situation is easy to describe. He and the better class of astronomers who followed him took over the Ptolemaic planetary theory completely and competently. They used their own observations to improve parameters; in subjects of special interest, as with lunar visibility theory, they developed their own theory, but no fundamental overhaul of the system was attempted.

VI. OBSERVATIONAL ASTRONOMY

In complete contrast to the impossibility of giving a clear and straightforward account of early 'Abbāsid astronomical theory, the materials on astronomical observations, although incomplete, are ample and precise. We proceed to cite some of them in a roughly chronological order.

The earliest reported activity supplied a link with the Sāsānian past. About 184/800, one Aḥmad Nihāvandī was making observations of the sun at Jundīshāpūr, the garrison town and centre of medical studies established in Khūzistān by Shāpūr I. This is the only mention of the place in connection with astronomy, and subsequent reports for a long time thereafter are centred upon Baghdad.

At the latter place, for instance, are the earliest recorded activities of Ḥabash al-Ḥāsib al-Marwazī. Beginning in 204/819 and extending well over forty years is a series of observations of solar and lunar eclipses, planetary positions and conjunctions, lengths of the seasons, and lunar crescent visibility. He, like other astronomers, accompanied the court in its displacements. In 217/832 he was making observations of Regulus from Damascus, and from Sāmarrā he verified that his computations for the new moon of Ramaḍān 245/860 yielded an accurate prediction for the beginning of the month. But by 250/864 he was back in Baghdad observing a conjunction of Jupiter with Regulus.

The career of Ḥabash is paralleled by those of several other astronomers, notably by the brothers Muḥammad and Aḥmad, sons of a reformed highwayman, Mūsā b. Shākir, once the scourge of the roads of Khurāsān and later an intimate of the caliph al-Ma'mūn. The brothers commenced their operations in Baghdad in 225/840, moved to Sāmarrā, but returned to Baghdad, where their last recorded observation is dated in 257/870.

Numerous observations, of planets and of eclipses, are recorded for Muḥammad b. 'Īsā al-Māhānī during the decade beginning in 240/854, all at Baghdad.

Judging from the notices which have survived, the most assiduous of all the Baghdad observers was the group composed of 'Abd-Allāh b. Amājūr, apparently a Turk, together with his son, and a freedman of the son. For the solar eclipse of 28 Jumādā II 316/18 August 928 Ibn Amājūr describes measuring the magnitude of the eclipsed disc by observing its reflection in water – an expedient customary in those times, adopted to avoid injury to the eyes. Commencing in 272/885 and including at least one planetary conjunction observed at Shīrāz, reports of well over twenty observations by the Amājūrs have been transmitted.

By this time the dispersal of scientific activity eastward along the Iranian plateau was well underway. In the city of Balkh (in modern Afghanistan) Sulaimān b. 'Iṣmat al-Samarqandī made numerous observations of meridian solar altitudes over a period of years beginning in 257/871. His main instrument was a four-metre mural quadrant having an alidade mounted on it.

At Shīrāz ʻAbd al-Raḥmān al-Ṣūfī made a series of observations to determine the length of the seasons, commencing with the winter solstice of 359/969. He used a large meridian ring, the scale of which was graduated in intervals of five minutes of arc, and he was assisted by several other well-known savants. The instrument was called the "ʻAḍudī Ring" in honour of al-Ṣūfī's patron, ʻAḍud al-Daula, of the Būyid dynasty.

Ray, near modern Tehrān, was the scene of two separate campaigns. Beginning in the summer of 348/959, and using a mural quadrant, Abū'l-Faḍl al-Hirawī and Abū Jaʻfar al-Khāzin observed a series of meridian transits of the sun in order to determine the latitude of Ray and the obliquity of the ecliptic. The same type of investigation was undertaken in 384/994, but with much more elaborate equipment. In that year Abū Maḥmūd al-Khujandī put into operation a mural sextant far larger than any instrument of the sort previously known. It was part of a trend toward larger and larger instruments designed to increase the precision of observations, a trend continued at the Marāgha (657/1259) observatory and culminating eventually in the gigantic installation at Samarqand (833/1430). Al-Khujandī's "Fakhrī Sextant", so named in honour of the local Būyid ruler Fakhr al-Daula, was graduated to seconds of arc. According to Bīrūnī, however, the results of the observations were untrustworthy because the aperture at the centre of the arc settled slightly after the structure had been completed.

The period closes with the activities of Abū Raiḥān al-Bīrūnī. The earliest of his observations which has come down to us is that of a meridian solar altitude at the summer solstice of 384/994, taken at a village near Khwārazm. Three years later being in Khwārazm, he made arrangements with Abu'l-Wafā', then at Baghdad, that the two of them would make simultaneous observations of a lunar eclipse, in order to determine the longitudinal difference between the two localities. While in political exile in Gurgān in 393/1003 he observed two lunar eclipses, but the following year found him back in his native region, where in the city of Gurgānj he observed another eclipse. Still in Gurgānj in 406/1016, he carried out and recorded numerous observations of the sun. In another two years he had involuntarily entered Ghaznavid service, and all his remaining recorded observations, the last in 412/1021, were made at Ghazna or its vicinity.

The individuals and localities cited above are by no means exhaustive, but they give a fair idea of the scope and character of ʻAbbāsid observational astronomy. The repercussions of these widespread operations on theory were in the nature of routine improvements. Ptolemy's inaccurate value for the rate of precession was corrected, and similar long-term changes were discovered. Mean motion parameters for the sun, moon and planets were recomputed many times. Certain other parameters were sharpened. There was no essential reason why observations of the precision and significance of those made by Tycho Brahe could not have been made during 'Abbāsid times. But there is no evidence, then or in the succeeding five centuries, that such observations were made.

VII. MATHEMATICAL GEOGRAPHY

In his Geography, Ptolemy assembled and digested the totality of quantitative topographical information available to him for the known world. His example was followed by the geographers of the 'Abbāsid empire. There is a well-founded tradition that the caliph al-Ma'mūn called together a commission of experts, their legendary number being seventy, to collate and display in a series of maps the material at their disposal. Their work as such has not come down to us. There does exist, however, a single manuscript copy of a very extensive geographical treatise by al-Khwārazmī, the algebraist and astronomer and a member of the commission, which is based upon the results achieved by Ma'mūn's group. Al-Khwārazmī's geography gives the latitude and longitude of 545 cities alone, plus the locations of mountains, seas, islands and other topographical features. Although it is in great measure derivative from the Ptolemaic geography, much additional material has been added, and certain errors and misconceptions of Ptolemy have been corrected, while others have been retained. Understandably, there is a complete reorganization of localities in Syria, Mesopotamia and Iran. For a few cities, alternative longitudes are given, one Ptolemaic and one independent.

The apparent position of a celestial body is affected not only by the time at which it is observed, but also by the observer's location on the terrestrial sphere. For this reason, most sets of mediaeval astronomical tables contain a list of cities, with their geographical co-ordinates, in order to enable a user to make necessary reductions between positions computed for his station, and the locality for which the tables have been calculated. Thus the *zīj* of Kūshyār b. Labbān (*fl.* 380/990) gives the co-ordinates of ninety cities.

If the co-ordinates of a proposed observatory site were unknown, it was necessary that they be determined. The latitude can easily be calculated in terms of simple and straightforward observations, but longitude determinations are much more difficult. In establishing a base of operations at Ghazna, Bīrūnī was confronted with this problem. He solved it in characteristically exhaustive fashion, describing his efforts in a book (the *Taḥdīd*) which illuminates the whole field of mediaeval astronomical geography. It had been known since antiquity that the longitudinal difference between two places is measured by the time difference between them. It was also understood that one way of finding this difference would be for an observer at each of the two stations to observe an event visible to both – a lunar eclipse being about the only suitable possibility. The method was discussed (and attempted) by Bīrūnī, but the difficulty of fixing the beginning, middle and end of any eclipse led him to prefer another technique. This was to assume that a reasonably accurate estimate of the great circle distance between two points on the earth's surface can be deduced from a knowledge of the caravan routes between them, and the general character of the terrain. The resulting distance was converted from *farsakhs* (or miles) into degrees of arc by application of the accurate conversion factor worked out by geodetic surveys carried through in the time of al-Ma'mūn. Finally, by application of a theorem of Ptolemy on inscribed quadrilaterals, it was possible to compute the longitudinal difference between the two localities in terms of the great circle arc and the known latitudinal difference. By successive applications of this technique, Bīrūnī ran two traverses from Baghdad to Ghazna, one to the north via Ray, Gurgānj, and Balkh, the other to the south through Shīrāz and Zarang. By choosing a value intermediate between the two results he fixed upon the difference in longitude between Ghazna and Baghdad as 24° 20′, a result which is in error by only eighteen minutes of arc, and which, considering the crudity of his data, is creditable indeed.

These and other determinations he incorporated into the geographical tables of his astronomical handbook, the *al-Qānūn al-Mas'udī*. The latter gives the co-ordinates of six hundred cities, more than any other mediaeval source. For India and China alone he reports the co-ordinates of ninety cities given in no source antedating him.

VIII. AL-BĪRŪNĪ

It is fitting that the closing portion of the chapter be a biographical sketch of an individual whose name has already figured in earlier sections. Abū al-Raiḥān Muḥammad b. Aḥmad al-Bīrūnī was born at or near Khwārazm in Turkestān (the modern Khiva) in 362/973. Already in his early twenties he commenced making astronomical observations, but civil war forced him to flee his homeland, and somewhere about 385/995 he arrived at Ray, in very straitened circumstances. After some two years he was welcomed at the court of the Ziyārid dynast Qābūs b. Vushmgīr at Gurgān. Here he completed and dedicated to Qābūs his first major work, the "Chronology of Ancient Nations". This book has as its prime object the description of all known calendars and chronologies accessible to the author, with the regnal years of rulers from early antiquity, the feast days and fasts of many religions, and rules for transforming dates from one calendar to another. But, typically of Bīrūnī, it contains all manner of additional items related in some way to the main topics. By 400/1010 he was able to return to Khwārazm, in high favour at the court of its ruler Abu'l-'Abbās al-Ma'mūn. Eight years later, however, the latter was assassinated, and this event was used as a pretext by Sulṭān Maḥmūd of Ghazna to absorb the entire region into his expanding empire. Bīrūnī, together with other notables, was carried to Ghazna, and this city was the base of his activities for the rest of his long life.

Bīrūnī is said to have accompanied Maḥmūd's army on one or more of its annual campaigns into India, and from this stems his interest in Hindu culture and in the Sanskrit language. His studies culminated in the fascinating "India", for many centuries the only full description of Indian folklore, religions, philosophy, mythology and superstitions existing outside the subcontinent, and still valuable.

Other major works written at Ghazna include the book on mathematical geography described above. An extensive treatise on shadows gives Bīrūnī's notions concerning the nature and propagation of light, reports of optical experiments carried out by him, the history of the trigonometric tangent function, and the use of shadows to determine the Muslim times of prayer. *Al-Qānūn al-Mas'ūdī* resembles the *Almagest* in that it contains not only the numerical tables and accompanying rules for the solution of all standard mediaeval astronomical problems, but it also expounds the theoretical and observational bases from which the rules and tables have been derived. The *Kitāb al-tafhīm* is an exhaustive compendium of astrological lore. Another treatise reports Bīrūnī's very precise determinations of the specific gravities of common substances and describes the instrument he invented for measuring them. When he had passed the age of eighty he was hard at work with a collaborator composing a pharmacology which contains articles on more than seven hundred drugs.

The subjects cited above, diverse as they are, convey a completely inadequate idea of the scope and magnitude of Bīrūnī's attainments and labours. The titles of 148 works written by him are known, of which at least thirty-two comprised sixty folios or more, and of the latter some are very large indeed. Many are the results of extended and sophisticated numerical computations, and all exhibit stupendous erudition, originality and trenchant humour. In addition to his native Khwārazmian tongue he knew and used Arabic, Persian, Sanskrit, Syriac and Greek. In the breadth of his interests he was typical of the scientists of his own time, but intellectual power, critical faculty and tolerance such as his are shared only by the greatest minds, ancient or modern.

CHAPTER 12

LIFE SCIENCES, ALCHEMY AND MEDICINE

I. INTRODUCTION

The Islamic conquest of Persia enabled the Persians to become members of a truly international society and to participate in a world-wide civilization in whose creation they themselves played a basic rôle. A homogeneous civilization which spread from the heart of Asia to Europe, possessing a common religion and a common religious and also scientific language, facilitated the exchange of ideas and prepared the ground for one of the golden ages in the history of science, in which the Persians had a major share. Islamic science came into being in the 2nd/8th century as a result of the vast effort of translation which made the scientific and philosophical traditions of antiquity available in Arabic. This early phase of activity reached its peak in the 4th/10th and 5th/11th centuries just before the Saljuq domination. During this period, which is among the most outstanding in the history of science, Persia was the main theatre of scientific activity, and although there were certainly many Arab and other non-Persian scholars and scientists, most of the figures who contributed to the remarkable philosophical and scientific activity of the age were Persians.

In a sense the scientific activity of this period continued what had been begun during the late Sāsānian period, but on a much greater scale and with a more universal scope. During the late Sāsānian period, there was some notable activity in astronomy, as seen in the *Zīj-i Sh̲ahriyār*, and also in medicine and pharmacology in which the activity of Burzūya, his journey to India and his causing the translation of Sanskrit texts into Pahlavī are reflected in later pages of history. Moreover, Jundīsh̲āpūr had become a major medical centre after the destruction of Edessa by the Byzantines in A.D. 489, and it was the most important medical centre of the ancient world at the time of the Islamic conquests. In botany and pharmacology, there was already a great deal of exchange between Sāsānian Persia and China, as well as some knowledge of Greek sources. Even in the occult sciences, alchemy and metallurgy, it seems that some contacts existed in Iran with Chinese and Alexandrian sources. There are many treatises of the occult sciences of Hermetic origin attributed to Zoroaster and originally translated from Greek into Pahlavī, along with other translations in more openly disseminated sciences such as logic.

This interest in science during the late Sāsānian period is reported in Arabic sources to have been associated more with the Syriac language than with Pahlavī. Although there were certain translations of scientific texts into Pahlavī, the Pahlavī language remained mostly the philosophico-religious language of Sāsānian Persia, as seen in such works as the *Bundahishn* and *Dēnkart*, while most of the teaching and discourse on the sciences in Jundīshāpūr were carried out in Syriac, a sister language of Arabic. This fact itself facilitated the transition to the Islamic period, for soon Arabic, another Semitic language, was to replace Syriac as the scientific language of the region. The Sāsānian experience certainly made it easier for the Persians to make the transition and to learn to master Arabic, a language which enabled the Persians to reach a world-wide audience for the first time. Besides being their religious language, Arabic became for the Persians a scientific language of great precision and wealth which they themselves helped to make the most important scientific language of the world for seven or eight centuries.

It is well known that the Arabic prose connected with the religious sciences such as Qur'anic commentary and *ḥadīth* differs in style from the prose of scientific and philosophical works. Persian scholars like Ibn al-Muqaffa' had a major rôle in developing this scientific prose, and the whole class of clerks and civil administrators which was so responsible for the cultivation of the sciences in the early Islamic centuries consisted mostly of Persians, who entered the civil service in large numbers. Although perhaps it is an exaggeration to say that the Persians created philosophical and scientific Arabic prose, it is certainly justifiable to state that they had a major rôle in its development. They were instrumental in creating a vehicle for the expression of exact thought which enabled them to reach an international audience which had never been available to them before. Besides the spiritual transformations brought about by the Qur'anic revelation, the availability of the Arabic language, and a world-wide civilization which facilitated intellectual communication and the exchange of ideas must be considered as the major factors which enabled the Persians to achieve so much in the domain of abstract thought. If the Achaemenian period is the golden age of Persia politically and the Sāsānian period in administration, city planning and architecture, the first centuries of the Islamic period are without doubt the golden age of Iranian history in the domain of the sciences, particularly medicine and mathematics. To this period belong those Persian scientists who stand among the foremost stars in the firmament of the history of science to this day.

II. THE TRANSLATORS

The transition from the Sāsānian to the Islamic era in the sciences is marked by the period of translation from Graeco-Syriac, Pahlavī and Sanskrit sources into Arabic. In this very important process the majority of translators were Christian and Ḥarranian, but the Persians also had a major rôle, especially in making available works of Pahlavī in the Arabic language, which the Persians, like other Muslims, adopted rapidly as the scientific and philosophical language of discourse. To mention the names of some of the translators of a Persian background, such as Jirjīs b. Bukhtyishū', Yuḥannā b. Māsūya (usually pronounced Māsawaih), Ibn al-Muqaffa', 'Umar b. Farkhān al-Ṭabarī, Muḥammad al-Fazārī, Naubakht al-Ahwāzī and 'Alī b. Ziyād al-Tamīmī, is sufficient to demonstrate the important rôle the Persians had in the process of translation and transmission itself. Moreover, certain Persian families acted as patrons and supporters of the new scientific movement, of which the Barmakids and the Naubakht family are well known examples.

As a result of this concerted effort, encouraged by the caliphate itself, and made necessary by the inner dynamics of the newly born Islamic society, the Persians found themselves in possession of a wealth of sources in the different sciences which could act as raw material for the birth of the Islamic sciences. The availability of these sources, the new cultural climate and the presence of the new scientific language, which the translations themselves had helped forge into a most exact instrument for the expression of abstract thought, all helped to make possible the ever increasing activity in the sciences which reached its crescendo in the 4th/10th and 5th/11th centuries with such figures as Ibn Sīnā and Bīrūnī. As far as the medical and biological sciences are concerned the presence of Jundīshāpūr as a living centre where medicine of the Hippocratic and Galenic traditions had been preserved, along with those of the Persian and Indian, made the transition from the world of ancient science to Islamic science more continuous and coherent. It was upon this existing background that suddenly such giants as Ṭabarī and Rāzī burst upon the scene in the 3rd/9th and 4th/10th centuries.

III. THE LIFE SCIENCES

It has been customary for historians of science in the West to apply categories of modern Western science to Islamic or Indian or Chinese science and then be startled to discover that this or that category does not apply. Such is precisely the case of the life sciences, especially biology. We have often been told that the Muslims did not develop a biology such as that which we find in the specifically biological works of Aristotle but were only interested in "applied biology" such as pharmacology and agriculture. This statement is true only if we seek an "Islamic biology" following the modern conception of what biology is. If we do so, then we do not find a great deal of "Islamic biology", nor for that matter is there much "Chinese biology". But in Islam, as in China, there is a vast amount of material dealing with biology and the life sciences in general in other forms such as in medical treatises, in works on pharmacology, zoology and botany, in texts of natural history, in literary and philological works and even in writings on philosophy and psychology in the traditional sense (*'ilm al-nafs*).

From the Islamic point of view the whole universe is alive and the life sciences really deal with all things. The major distinction is not so much between live and dead matter as it is between different stages, manifestations and degrees of life, which are none other than qualities of universal existence itself on different planes of reality. To speak of life sciences in the matrix of Islamic science is almost to speak of the science of things in general. Even if we seek to limit ourselves to plants and animals, the question of what "life sciences" means is not the same as in the context of modern science. For in Islam the question of "life" is transformed into that of "the moving power" or *anima*; therefore, with Aristotle the Muslim philosophers and scientists focused their attention on psychology as the key to the understanding of life phenomena. For them it was the vegetable soul (*al-nafs al-nabātiyya*) or the animal soul (*al-nafs al-ḥayawāniyya*) which is responsible for all the features we identify with life in plants and animals. Outside the study of these general principles, the understanding of animal and vegetable life was sought in zoology and botany respectively. In these fields there was no longer any question of problems of a general biological nature; the problem was to provide a descriptive account of the features of different living forms and their function and use.

Among the Muslim philosophers who developed the theory of the faculties of the vegetable and animal souls, many of the most important were Persian. Al-Fārābī devoted some attention to it; the Ik͟hwān al-Ṣafā' (Brethren of Purity) spoke extensively of it and Ibn Sīnā gave it its most ample treatment in the sixth book of the physics of his monumental encyclopaedia, *Kitāb al-s͟hifā'*. His view of the faculties of the vegetable and animal souls can be summarized as follows:

vegetable soul (*al-nafs al-nabātiyya*)	faculty of feeding (*g͟had͟hā'iyya*) faculty of growth (*nāmiyya*) faculty of reproduction (*muwallida*)
animal soul (*al-nafs al-ḥayawāniyya*)	faculty of motion (*muḥarrika*) faculty of comprehension (*mudrika*)

The faculty of motion consists in turn of the powers of desire and bodily movement while desire is polarized into the two contradictory but complementary powers of lust and anger, one of which causes attraction and the other repulsion. In this "faculty psychology" and belief in the effusion of the vegetable and animal souls by the "universal or world soul" can be found the basis of the "theory of life" as expounded by the early Muslim thinkers. The appearance of life is not seen as a miracle amidst a sea of dead matter. Rather, beginning with prime matter itself, each stage of terrestial existence is made possible by the effusion of a new form from the Tenth Intellect, which is the "giver of forms" (*wāhib al-ṣuwar*); and each new stage of life, from the mineral to the plant and from the plant to the animal, is due to the appearance of a new "soul" which is none other than a particular faculty of the universal soul which animates the whole cosmos. The life sciences form an intermediary link in a universal chain that stretches from the minerals to the angels.

In fact the key concept which these early Muslim and Persian philosophers and scientists adopted as the framework for their study of the life sciences was the chain of being (*marātib al-wujūd*). The three kingdoms were for them connected, the lowest animal being a grade above the highest plant and the lowest plant a single stage above the highest mineral. The qualities and perfections of the different creatures reflected their ontological status in the "great chain of being". This idea caused much speculation concerning the relation between different living beings both spatially and temporally, and such diverse thinkers as the Mu'tazilī Naẓẓām, Jābir b. Ḥayyān, Bīrūnī and the Ikhwān al-Ṣafā' wrote on the stages of creation and the appearance of different creatures on earth in such a manner that some have misinterpreted them as forerunners of Darwinian evolution. In reality they had in mind gradation rather than evolution and their actual scientific theory was much more akin to that of such natural historians as Cuvier than to the 19th-century evolutionism which cut off the hand of the Creator from creation after the original act.

Sometimes to the central concept of the chain of being was added the correspondence and analogy between the different realms of nature and also between the realms of nature and the archetypal world whose most intelligible symbolism is seen in the world of mathematics. Hence there developed an elaborate science of correspondence between different beings, often linked together by the mathematical symbols connected with each. This "Pythagorean biology" attracted much attention in certain circles of early Shī'ī thought, where it is often combined with Hermetic and alchemical modes of thinking. The biological sections of the Jābirean corpus provide an example of this type of approach, as do the *Rasā'il* or "Epistles" of the Ikhwān al-Ṣafā', where mathematical symbolism is closely allied to the morphological and anatomical study of plants and animals.

Yet another major characteristic of the life sciences of this period, which derives directly from Qur'anic inspiration, is the emphasis upon the view that the goal of the study of nature and especially living things is to observe the "signs of God" (*āyāt*) and to derive moral and spiritual benefits from them. Inasmuch as God has shown His "signs" upon the horizon, as the Qur'anic verse "We shall show them Our portents upon the horizons and within themselves until it will be manifest unto them that it is the Truth" (xli. 53, Pickthall translation) testifies, it is the duty of the Muslim to seek to study these signs so that in this way he might gain a greater understanding of Unity (*tauḥīd*). There was thus a strong religious and spiritual consideration which coloured all studies of the life sciences. The study of nature and especially of living things became combined with a sense of wonder and awe, which we see in so many popular works of natural history, and which has caused so many of these works to be called '*Ajā'ib al-makhlūqāt*, or "The Wonders of Creation".

This Islamic tendency was fortified by an Indian–Persian tradition of natural history which the Muslims inherited and which differed from the biological tradition of Aristotle and Theophrastus. This Indian–Persian tradition combined moral and religious questions with biological and especially zoological ones. The "Tales of Bidpai", rendered from Sanskrit into Pahlavī and then from Pahlavī into masterly Arabic by Ibn al-Muqaffa' under the title of *Kalīla wa Dimna*, is an excellent example of this kind of study. In this work the habits of animals are studied with the view of learning moral and religious lessons from them and not simply for their own sake. Likewise the chapter on the dispute between man and the animals of the *Rasā'il* of the Ikhwān al-Ṣafā', which became so popular throughout the Muslim world, starts from a study of zoology and leads to a most profound exposition of the spiritual relationship between man and the world of living things. In fact this point of view dominates the whole of the *Rasā'il* and many other works on natural history of the period. Along with the principles stated above it is one of the general characteristics of the approach to the study of life sciences observed in the works composed from the 3rd/9th to the 5th/11th centuries.

IV. NATURAL HISTORY, ZOOLOGY AND BOTANY

The works dealing with the life sciences appear under many different categories. Philosophical works usually have chapters devoted to this theme in those sections which deal with natural philosophy (*ṭabī'iyyāt*). Medical works such as the *Qānūn* usually begin with general discussions on the meaning of life and death and the functioning of living beings. General geographical descriptions and works on natural history abound with pages concerned with plants and animals. And even literary and religious works from Qur'anic commentaries to philological studies like the works of Abū Ḥanīfa al-Dīnawarī and al-Jāḥiẓ, and popular tales such as the *Sindbād-nāma* and the "Arabian Nights" contain many valuable pages about the knowledge possessed at that time concerning different branches of the life sciences.

The works specifically devoted to natural history from the beginning of the Islamic era to the 5th/11th century are not as numerous as what one observes during the 7th/13th and 8th/14th centuries when most of the compilations and major zoological treatises such as the *'Ajā'ib al-makhlūqāt*, *Nuzhat al-qulūb*, *Ḥayāt al-ḥayawān* and *Nukhbat al-dahr* were written. But in this earlier period there are major figures in this domain, leading to al-Mas'ūdī who has been entitled the "Pliny of the Arabs". There are also some works dealing with the whole domain of natural history in a manner that is reminiscent of the treatises of the later period. Already in the second Islamic century one can see interest in natural history in the circle associated with the sixth Shī'ī Imām, Ja'far al-Ṣādiq, who is in fact himself considered to be the author of several works on natural history. The Jābirean corpus also, which is so closely associated with the Imām's school, abounds in works dealing with the general field of natural history.

During the 3rd/9th century, while most works in the natural sciences dealt with a specific subject such as zoology or botany, there appeared a strange work entitled *Sirr al-asrār*, "Secretum Secretorum" in its well-known Latin translation, and attributed to Aristotle. Actually this work is probably of Syriac origin, and reflects the late Sāsānian and also Hellenistic "science of the property of objects" (*khawāṣṣ al-ashyā'*, *physikai dynameis* of the Alexandrian school), which combines a physiognomic, magical and occult interest in the properties of natural objects with the more usual type of natural history. This type of "science" is closely connected with Hermeticism and had its centre in both Syria and Persia and especially in Marv just before the rise of Islam. It entered into many works of natural history in Arabic, and through the translation of these works into Latin and even Catalan and other European languages, exercised an appreciable influence upon the "magical school" of natural history in the West. There must have developed a whole school in the late Sāsānian period in Persia and the surrounding regions devoted to this study of the occult properties of objects, of which little trace remains beyond the few works such as the "Secretum Secretorum" that suddenly appears in the 3rd/9th century and exerts so much influence upon a particular school of Muslim natural historians.

There are other figures in the domain of natural history in this early period such as Ibn Qutaiba whose *'Uyūn al-akhbār* contains a wealth of knowledge on the subject. But the outstanding natural historian of this age is Abu'l-Ḥasan al-Mas'ūdī (d. 345/957), who has been compared so often to Pliny. Combining first-hand knowledge of geography attained through extensive travels in Western and Central Asia, India and the Indian Ocean with a philosophical and theological training, he wrote works on natural history that contain elements of history, geography, geology, botany and zoology. His two major works, *Murūj al-dhahab* and *al-Tanbīh wa'l-ishrāf*, which summarize his views, are perhaps the most outstanding works on natural history in the 4th/10th century.

Actually as a historian al-Mas'ūdī was following the tradition of the universal histories of Ṭabarī and al-Ya'qūbī, and as a geographer, the well-known works of al-Khwārazmī, Ibn Khurdādbih, the philosopher al-Kindī, al-Balkhī and al-Iṣṭakhrī. But the distinguishing feature of his works was to emphasize the aspect of natural history. Of course both the Muslim universal histories and many of the geographies contain pages devoted to natural history, but in them there is not the same concentration upon natural phenomena, the acute observation of flora and fauna, and of minerals and geological formations that one finds in al-Mas'ūdī. It is because of these features that the works of al-Mas'ūdī are usually classified with those on science and natural history rather than with those on pure history.

Zoology

The early Muslim treatises on zoology are all in Arabic and are closely associated with philological considerations, as is seen in the works of al-Aṣma'ī and al-Jāḥiẓ. But already in the *Kitāb al-ḥayawān* of al-Jāḥiẓ there are many elements of earlier Persian animal lore. The *Kalīla wa Dimna*, made popular in Arabic through Ibn al-Muqaffa', had made known the Indian and Persian animal lore, which combined scientific and moral interests so closely. This moral concern with animals, which at the same time reveals intimate knowledge of their behaviour, is reflected in much of the literature of the day, even in the "Arabian Nights", many of whose pages reveal specifically Persian elements. It remained, however, for a 7th/13th-century author, al-'Aufī, to write the *Jawāmi' al-ḥikāyāt* ("Collected Stories") which is the most famous Persian literary work dealing with animals.

The early centuries saw a few specifically zoological works such as the *Ṭabāyi' al-ḥayawān* ("Nature of Animals") of the 5th/11th-century author Abū Sa'īd b. Bukhtyishū', and several treatises on different birds and domestic animals. The most important zoological discussions of the period appear in medical and philosophical works where studies are made of the anatomy and physiology of animals. Sections of Ibn Sīnā's

Qānūn dealing with the general nature of animals and their constitution and especially the eighth book of the physics of his *al-Shifā'* illustrate this type of writing. The latter work is probably the most important theoretical work on zoology of the period, continuing the tradition of Aristotle and Galen.

Altogether, however, the interest of Persians like other Muslims in zoology was more practical than theoretical. It either involved moral and spiritual lessons as we see in the *Rasā'il* of the Brethren of Purity and the *Kalīla wa Dimna*, or medical properties of animal parts and extractions as we see in the pharmacological treatises, or their agricultural use as is seen in treatises on agriculture. Even works dealing with a single animal are often concerned with its specific use as in hunting, as we see in some of the well-known works on falconry of later centuries. An important example of this kind, as far as the Persian language is concerned, is the *Bāz-nāma* of Abu'l-Ḥasan 'Alī b. Aḥmad Nasawī, a student of Ibn Sīnā and an acquaintance of Bīrūnī. Nasawī, who is also known for his mathematical works, composed the *Bāz-nāma*, which deals with birds used for hunting, in Persian, basing himself on earlier works of different nations especially the Persians. The treatise indicates the strong interest of Persians in this subject going back to the Sāsānian period, and is itself a fine example of treatises on hunting birds, of which many more are to be found during later centuries.

Treatises on zoology, even when studied philosophically, are concerned more with animals within the total scheme of things, in view of their rôle in the great chain of being and the necessity of their existence to complete the total plan of the Universe. The study of zoology, like botany, was never completely anthropomorphic as one might think. Rather, it was always teleological and aimed at a purpose, whether that be material or spiritual. For in Islamic science there has never been "science for science's sake". Science in Islamic civilization has always been studied with a certain end in view, whether that end be intellectual or material. All the sciences cultivated in Persia at this time and especially zoology and botany conform to this general principle.

Botany and Pharmacology

In botany, as in zoology, one must search in many fields to gather information. Knowledge from the many domains in which the study of plants was carried out must be brought together so as to reveal the contours of this science as it developed among Muslims. Botany was studied from the point of view of natural history and geography, agriculture, philology and literature and most important of all pharmacology, not to speak of theoretical botany which was connected with general studies in natural philosophy (*ṭabī'iyyāt*) as we find in the *Shifā'* and the *Rasā'il* of the Ikhwān al-Ṣafā'. Most of the study of plants was connected with their properties and application to different fields, especially medicine. That is why medical texts, in both Arabic and Persian, are among the most important sources for our knowledge of botany and pharmacology. The field of medicine is inseparable from the study of the plant sciences. In fact the Muslims concentrated so much on vegetable rather than mineral and animal drugs that pharmacology became almost completely an applied botany, and so it is treated here along with botany rather than with medicine where it naturally belongs.

Interest in philology and search for the root of plant names was responsible for many early works in botany which combined philological and scientific interests, in the same way that al-Aṣma'ī and al-Jāḥiẓ pursued the field of zoology with a literary and philological motive. The Persians already possessed much agricultural and botanical knowledge before the rise of Islam, and many plant names in Arabic are to this day of Persian origin. There were also plants whose nomenclature was of Babylonian, Greek and Nabataean origin. This led to the need for extensive research on the origin of plant names and ultimately to a study of their morphology and properties which reached its peak in the Maghrib and Spain with al-Ghāfiqī and Ibn al-Baiṭār.

Of the early writers of Persian origin or background who devoted themselves to this type of philological study one can mention Hishām b. Ibrāhīm al-Kirmānī, author of *Kitāb al-nabāt*; Abū Ḥātim al-Sijistānī, author of *Kitāb al-zar'* and many zoological treatises; Abū Ḥanīfa al-Dīnawarī, author of the most famous early Muslim work on botany of a lexicographical character, also entitled *Kitāb al-nabāt*, which is a precious document for early Muslim knowledge of botany and in which is collected oral and written Arabic traditions of botany as well as much material of Persian origin in Arabic; Ibn Duraid who composed the well-known *Kitāb al-jamhara* containing many plant names; Ibn Khālūya of the court of Saif al-Daula, who wrote the *Kitāb al-shajar* and several other works devoted to plants; and Majd al-Dīn Fīrūzābādī whose *al-Qāmūs al-muḥīṭ* is an authoritative dictionary containing a wealth of information on plants. Many other of the grammarians and philologists of Baṣra and Kūfa could also be included since in one way or another they were in contact with the sphere of Persian culture.

In the domain of agriculture the basis of early Muslim works in this field is as much Persian as Byzantine, and at the same time it is to a certain extent Roman and Nabataean. While, however, the "Geoponica" literature, especially the work of Cassianus Bassus, and the "Nabataean Agriculture" of Ibn Waḥshiyya are known by name, the works of Persian origin have remained mostly anonymous as in so many other cases. Their existence can only be traced through their influence on early works in Arabic and also through the testimony of the actual practice of agriculture in such provinces as Khurāsān, which was certainly the continuation of Sāsānian practices. There has survived the manuscript of a work on agriculture, the *Barz-nāma*, dealing with Persian agriculture and indicative of the type of agricultural knowledge prevalent at that time.

Among geographers and travellers interest in the flora and fauna of different regions was always strong and in most works of this kind there are sections devoted to plants. The first Muslim geographer to have written on plants was Ibn Wādiḥ al-Ya'qūbī followed soon by Ibn Rusta. After that most of the standard authors on geography such as Ibn Ḥauqal and Ibn Khurdādbih, as well as travellers like Bīrūnī in his "India" and Nāṣir-i Khusrau in his "Travels" did not fail to mention something of the plants of each region they described. As a result, the works of geography serve as a valuable source for our knowledge of botany, and most Muslim geographers, especially the later ones like al-Idrīsī, must be also considered as botanists.

It is especially in the field of pharmacology that Muslim scientists excelled, to the extent that recently an authority could write, "In pharmacology and pharmacognosy, the medieval Islamic peoples far surpassed the Greeks and Latins."[1] The Persians were already well-versed in pharmacology in the Sāsānian period, as witnessed by the large number of Persian names for drugs, especially in compounds. They continued this tradition into the Islamic period when the level of knowledge of pharmacology far surpassed what was known by Theophrastus and Dioscorides. This tradition in fact reached its peak much later in the Ṣafavid period, which has been called the "golden age of pharmacology".

[1] M. Levey, p. 3.

The Muslims divided drugs into simples (*mufradāt*) and compounds (*murakkabāt*). Drugs were also called *'aqāqīr*, and the treatises dealing with them were of several types: books on poisons, lists of *materia medica*, synoptic treatises and *Aqrābādhīn*, from the Greek γραφίδιον, meaning a list or registry of drugs or prescriptions. Most Muslim medical treatises, such as the *Qānūn* of Ibn Sīnā, contain elaborate sections devoted to this subject, and there are independent works known by this name such as those of Ibn al-Tilmīdh and Samarqandī that have been famous throughout Islamic history.

The earliest *Aqrābādhīn* is, however, that of Yuḥannā b. Māsūya (Māsawaih), which was later translated into Latin by Pietro d'Abano and which gained for the author the title *pharmacopoerum evangelista*. Of greater fame is that of Sābūr b. Sahl of Jundīshāpūr. The philosopher al-Kindī was also interested in plants and wrote an *Aqrābādhīn* as well as other treatises on drugs and perfumes. The philosopher-physician Rāzī also composed a well-known *Aqrābādhīn* which was later rendered into Hebrew and Latin, while Ibn Sīnā has left a most complete formulary of drugs in the *Qānūn* that is still in use in certain regions of the East. His contemporary philosopher and historian Ibn Muskūya (Ibn Miskawaih) also left behind a *Kitāb al-mufradāt*.

As far as the Persian language is concerned the work on drugs by Abū Manṣūr Muwaffaq b. 'Alī al-Hirawī entitled *Kitāb al-abniya 'an ḥaqā'iq al-adwiya* ("Book of the Foundations of the True Properties of the Remedies"), written between 357/968 and 366/977, is particularly important because it is among the first extant prose works of the Persian language. The author mentions 585 remedies, drawing from Greek, Syriac, Persian and Indian as well as Arabic sources. There is also a general theory of drugs developed which is of scientific interest. But the greatest interest that attaches to this work is from the point of view of the Persian language itself, for Hirawī presages the many future authors like Jurjānī who were to write extensive medical treatises in Persian from the 6th/12th century onward.

Also of particular significance in the field of pharmacology during this period is the *Kitāb al-ṣaidala* ("Book of Drugs") of Bīrūnī, which has not been edited as yet. Like other works of the author, this treatise is a masterpiece of its own, and it was later translated into Persian by Abū Bakr b. 'Alī b. 'Uthmān Aṣfār al-Kāshānī. Bīrūnī, while employing Babylonian, Greek, Syriac, Indian and Arabic sources, draws especially from earlier Persian works many of which are now lost. Besides its intrinsic value as perhaps the most authoritative work of its kind of the period, the *Kitāb al-ṣaidala* is also an important source for our knowledge of the earlier tradition of Persian pharmacology.

Besides the *Aqrābādhīn*, another type of work on pharmacology which is of much interest is that dealing with poisons. This particular subject, like several other branches of pharmacology, drew heavily from Indian sources. The books on drugs were in fact often called *Kunnāsh* ("Pandects"), which is derived from Sanskrit. But in poisons more than elsewhere the elaborate Indian writings show their clear influence. Like the Indians, the Muslims were fascinated by the different ways in which poison could be administered, and men in power as well as physicians were interested in gaining knowledge of different forms of poisons as stories such as the "Arabian Nights" amply demonstrate. Among the important works on this subject is the *Kitāb al-sumūm* ("Book of Poisons") of Jābir b. Ḥayyān. Equally well known is that of Ibn Waḥshiyya. In both cases the close rapport between this branch of pharmacology and the occult property of things can be seen through the names of the two authors, who are among the most famous in Islam to have written on the hidden and occult nature of substances.

V. GEOLOGY AND MINERALOGY

Although geology and mineralogy are not a part of the life sciences, they form an integral part of natural history and, in the context of Islamic science, cannot be separated from the study of zoology and botany. In geology, Muslim authors usually based their theoretical discussions on the works of the Greek natural historians and geographers, but made many original observations not found in earlier sources. There are descriptions in al-Mas'ūdī which indicate direct observation. Of even greater interest is Bīrūnī's description of the sedimentary basin of the Indian sub-continent, found in his "India", and Ibn Sīnā's theories of rock formation and mountain structure as well as his close study of the nature of sedimentary deposits and analysis of meteorites. Many geological phenomena such as diastrophism, tectonic movements and mineral genesis are described by the early Muslim geologists in a manner that is confirmed by current theories and observations.

An important description repeated in the writings of many authors of this period is that of fossils, which the Brethren of Purity and Bīrūnī describe correctly as remains of animals of earlier ages. Unlike the mediaeval West where up to the 18th century fossils remained essentially a mystery, Muslim authors regarded the presence of fossils even on mountain tops as only confirming their theory of cycles separated by cataclysms, a theory somewhat reminiscent of those of Cuvier and other 18th-century Occidental naturalists. There was also a keen awareness of the greater complexity of life forms in later geological ages, but never a theory of evolution in the Darwinian sense, for this would be absurd from the point of view of any metaphysics, the Islamic included.

In mineralogy, the theoretical aspect was closely tied to alchemy, which will be treated later, and even those like Ibn Sīnā who did not believe in alchemical transformations accepted the alchemical sulphur–mercury theory of the structure of minerals and metals. The standard works on mineralogy, however, dealt more with the properties of minerals than with their constitution. The earliest texts of this kind include the *Manāfiʿ al-aḥjār* of ʿUṭārid b. Muḥammad al-Ḥāsib, cited often by Rāzī and other later authorities, and the *K͟hawāṣṣ al-aḥjār* and the *al-Aḥjār*, attributed to Hermes and Aristotle respectively. The *al-Aḥjār* or "Lapidary" of Aristotle, which became well known in the mediaeval period, belongs definitely to the late Sāsānian Persian–Syriac tradition and differs from the "Mineralogy" of Theophrastus. It is certainly an Oriental compilation and contains many Iranian names for stones. Later works of this kind, that is those concerned primarily with the description of stones and their properties, include the *Nuzhat al-nufūs wa'l-afkār fī k͟hawāṣṣ al-mawālīd al-t͟halāt͟ha*, *al-Jauharatain al-ʿaqīqatain* of Abū Muḥammad al-Hamad͟hānī and *al-Aghrāḍ al-ṭibbiyya* of Jurjānī. It is this same tradition which led to the later well-known works on precious stones such as the *Jawāhir-nāma* attributed to Naṣīr al-Dīn Ṭūsī and the *ʿArāʾis al-jawāhir* of Abu'l-Qāsim Kās͟hānī.

The most important Muslim lapidary of the pre-Saljuq period is without doubt the *Kitāb al-jawāhir fī maʿrifat al-jawāhir* of Bīrūnī. This masterpiece of descriptive mineralogy brings together a great deal of information on different stones, combining matters of mineralogical and philological interest. Moreover, the work makes use of such earlier sources as the books of al-Kindī and Naṣr b. Yaʿqūb al-Dīnawarī on precious stones that have been lost.

A book contemporary with the above-mentioned works and representing the summit of mineralogy in its analytical rather than descriptive aspect is the "De Mineralibus" of Ibn Sīnā, long considered as a treatise of Aristotle in the West. This well-known work was originally the fifth section of the physics of the *Shifā'*, which deals with the mineral kingdom within the larger context of Ibn Sīnā's natural philosophy. In its Latin translation, however, it became an independent book that completed in Western eyes Aristotle's treatment of the three kingdoms. In describing the constitution of metals and minerals and their place in the natural order this work is as important as the *Jawāhir* of Bīrūnī, which seeks mostly to describe the qualities and properties of minerals rather than their constitution and place in the hierarchy of existence.

VI. ALCHEMY

The tradition of Islamic alchemy, in Persia as in other parts of the Islamic world, is closely related to the Alexandrian school while at the same time certain links with China can be discerned in many domains, especially in the relation between magic squares and alchemical doctrines. Islamic alchemy, like the alchemy which preceded it in Alexandria and China and the school that followed it in the West, is not a crude chemistry. It is rather a science of the soul based on the symbolism of metals and at the same time on the correlation between the microcosm and the macrocosm, or the operations of nature and those which occur within the soul of man. Its perspective belongs to the period when spirit and matter had not as yet become wholly separated and the sacred was still intimately connected with the symbolic significance of natural phenomena. Alchemy was a way to ennoble matter. It was both a science and a technique, concerned at once with psychology, cosmology and art. It bestowed a spiritual significance upon the work of the artisan and served as a means to achieve spiritual perfection within the cosmic order itself by making use of cosmic and natural forces. The link between Ṣūfism and the craft guilds must be sought in many instances through alchemy, which provided both a symbolic language for Ṣūfīs and an operational method for the artisan. From this tradition through the gradual loss of the "symbolist vision" there grew the science of chemistry which is concerned solely with the material aspect of things. Some of the Muslim alchemists undoubtedly did perform actual experiments with metals and minerals and in fact developed much of the apparatus used for centuries and even now in chemistry laboratories, but their vision was hardly ever limited to the material aspect of substances alone. The colours, forms and material transformations continued to convey a symbolic significance for them. That is why alchemy is a field that is at once concerned with Ṣūfism, cosmology, a traditional and sacred psychology and art as well as chemistry, pharmacology and medicine. It was moreover, the way in which the spirit of Islam was able to penetrate the material environment in which it breathed and to leave upon it its imprint.

The origin of Islamic alchemy is associated with Alexandria and the names of Morianus and K͟hālid b. Yazīd. But there were also definite Persian and Mesopotamian influences present, not to speak of certain Chinese factors, which appear fully in the works of Jābir b. Ḥayyān. Alchemy definitely was widely spread in Sāsānian Persia, and the rôle of the school of Jundīs͟hāpūr in the transmission of this art cannot be in any way neglected. In fact E. J. Holmyard, one of the foremost scholars of the history of alchemy, states that the "fundamental ideas [of alchemy] arose in the ancient Persian Empire, which includes Mesopotamia, Asia Minor, Syria and Egypt".[1] Although there is little knowledge of Sāsānian alchemy, traces of this tradition can be seen in the works of certain later Muslim alchemists, especially Rāzī, whose frequent reference to *nus͟hādur* many scholars such as Ruska have seen as proof of Sāsānian alchemical influence in his works. The coming of Islam brought the different centres of alchemical knowledge and practice together and fused the several different schools of the ancient world, especially the Alexandrian, with the Chinese and Persian and also perhaps Indian into a synthesis which is seen in the Jābirean corpus.

Mystery still shrouds the identity and personality of the founder of Islamic alchemy, Jābir b. Ḥayyān. Some have even doubted his existence, while others like Kraus have cast doubt upon the authenticity of the works attributed to him. But when all the evidence is examined, it is hardly possible to doubt that such a person existed, that he was an alchemist and that he also belonged to the circle of the sixth S͟hī'ī Imām, Ja'far al-Ṣādiq. It is also clear that some of the works in the Jābirean corpus are later accretions of Ismā'īlī inspiration. There is a link between Jābirean alchemy and Ismā'īlism in such works as the *Kitāb al-mājid* ("The Book of the Glorious"), and also many links with the general tradition of Ṣūfism in such questions as the symbolism of letters.

Jābir is entitled in traditional sources as al-'Azdī, al-Kūfī, al-Ṭūsī, al-Ṣūfī. There is a debate as to whether he was an Arab from Kūfa who

[1] E. J. Holmyard, "Alchemical Equipment" in *A History of Technology*, ed. E. Singer *et al.*, vol. II (Oxford, 1957), p. 731.

lived in Khurāsān, or a Persian from Khurāsān who later went to Kūfa, or whether he was, as some have suggested, of Syrian origin and later lived in Persia and Iraq. What remains certain is that he and his family lived much of their life in Ṭūs in Khurāsān, that he spent a good part of his life, which stretches over the 2nd/8th century, in Kūfa and at the court of Hārūn al-Rashīd in Baghdad, that he was a Ṣūfī, and that he was also in the circle of Imām Ja'far. Recently some have claimed to have discovered his tomb in western Persia. He was both the founder of Islamic alchemy and the prototype of the Muslim alchemist in later centuries.

The works of Jābir deal not only with alchemy but also with cosmology, psychology, natural philosophy and even the science of language. In alchemy they contain a whole philosophy of nature dominated by the idea of the "balance" which symbolizes the harmony of various tendencies of the world soul. There is also a great deal of chemistry and the descriptions of such processes as the preparation of nitric acid and compounds of copper. The alchemical descriptions are dominated by the sulphur–mercury theory of the structure of metals which became known to the West in the writings of the Latin Geber. There is also a great deal of emphasis upon the elixir (*al-iksīr*), a term which Jābir uses for the first time in its specifically alchemical sense. For Jābir *iksīr* and *kīmiyā'* (from which comes the term alchemy) mean nearly the same thing. Both signify the agent causing transmutation rather than transmutation itself.

Two fundamental alchemical texts that appeared soon after Jābir are the *Sirr al-khalīqa*, probably of Syriac origin, written during the reign of al-Ma'mūn and at the end of which appears the famous "Emerald Table", and the "Turba Philosophorum" by the Egyptian alchemist, 'Uthmān b. Suwaid. These works bridge the gap between Jābir and Muḥammad b. Zakariyyā' al-Rāzī, the Latin Rhazes, who was his real successor in alchemy. Rāzī held a different view about religion and nature from Jābir and in fact opposed the fundamental Shī'ī doctrine of hermeneutic interpretation or *ta'wīl*, through which the Shī'ī and Ṣūfīs seek to penetrate into the inner meaning of both revelation and natural phenomena. And in so doing Rāzī converted alchemy into a science of material substances or chemistry. Yet, his alchemical writings follow the titles of the works of Jābir and he was profoundly influenced by him, except that he had no interest in the Jābirean balance. He still moved in the atmosphere of Jābirean alchemy; "A study of Razi's writings, however, conveys the impression that he was much more interested in practical chemistry than in theoretical alchemy."[1]

The best-known works of Rāzī on alchemy include his *Sirr al-asrār* ("Secret of Secrets") and the *Asrār* ("Secrets") which has until recently been mistaken for the *Sirr al-asrār*. The *Asrār*, edited by Ruska as *Sirr al-asrār*, contains descriptions of alchemical apparatus and reveals clearly Rāzī's concern with laboratory work and experimentation. Rāzī described many substances, animal, vegetable and mineral alike, and in fact he is the first to have classified substances into these categories. He also described many chemical processes, such as calcination. The writings of Rāzī must be considered as the first documents of chemistry, although still shrouded in the language of alchemy.

The tradition of alchemy continued in Persia after Rāzī as we see in the writings of Qāḍī 'Abd al-Jabbār, a Mu'tazilī who wrote the *Risāla fi'l-kīmiyā'* ("Treatise of Alchemy"), and Abu'l-Ḥākim Muḥammad al-Kāthī, author of the *'Ain al-ṣan'a wa 'aun al-ṣinā'a* ("Origin of the Art"). In later centuries, most of the authors continued to rely on the writings of the early masters, especially Jābir and Rāzī, who in fact brought Islamic alchemy to its peak early in its career. Alchemy continued to survive both as an operational science connected with the crafts and a mystical science of the soul attached to Ṣūfism, in which form it has continued to produce works of note from the alchemical treatise of Mīr Findiriskī in the Ṣafavid period to the alchemical poems of the Qājār Ṣūfī poet, Muẓaffar 'Alī Shāh.

VII. MEDICINE

The major link between Islamic and Greek medicine must be sought in late Sāsānian medicine, especially in the School of Jundīshāpūr rather than in that of Alexandria. At the time of the rise of Islam Jundīshāpūr was at its prime. It was the most important medical centre of its time, combining the Greek, Indian and Iranian medical traditions in a cosmopolitan atmosphere which prepared the ground for Islamic medicine. The combining of different schools of medicine foreshadowed the synthesis that was to be achieved in later Islamic medicine, and the practices and institutions then established influenced much that is seen several centuries later in Baghdad and other centres of Islamic civilization. "To a very large extent the credit for the whole hospital system must be given to Persia. The hospitals of the Mohammadan period

[1] E. J. Holmyard, *Alchemy*, p. 86.

were built very largely upon the ideals and traditions of the Sāsānian hospital of Jundīshāpūr."[1] The well-known hospitals of 'Aḍud al-Daula in Shīrāz and Baghdad, as well as the later hospitals of Damascus and Cairo, were based upon the Jundīshāpūr model. The first products of Islamic medicine were also from this important medical centre.

Although one of the Companions of the Prophet, Ḥārith b. Kalada, studied at Jundīshāpūr, the earliest medical figures in Islamic history were Christians and Jews, the most outstanding among them being Ḥunain b. Isḥāq, to whom we owe the best translations of the Hippocratic and Galenic corpus and also major independent treatises on medicine. The physicians of the caliphs continued to be Christians and Jews until the time of the caliph al-Mu'taḍid who had a Persian Muslim physician, Aḥmad b. al-Ṭayyib al-Sarakhsī. Among the Christians also there were some of Persian origin or at least of immediate Persian background, among whom the most important are the Bukhtyishū' and Māsūya (Māsawaih) families. The members of the Bukhtyishū' family were directors of the Jundīshāpūr hospital and produced many outstanding physicians. One of them, Jirjīs, was called to Baghdad by the 'Abbāsid caliph al-Manṣūr, to cure his dyspepsia. Due to his success he became court physician of the caliphs, and after him the whole school was transferred to Baghdad marking the real beginnings of Islamic medicine. As for the Māsūya family, the father was a person of definite genius who gained knowledge of medicine through experience in the hospital of Jundīshāpūr without formal training. He later came to Baghdad at the time of Hārūn al-Rashīd to seek fame and fortune. All his three sons became physicians. Among them Yuḥannā b. Māsūya (the Latin "Mesue Senior") is best known. In fact he was the outstanding physician in Baghdad during the first half of the 3rd/9th century, was the first in Islamic civilization to perform dissection of animals and wrote the first Arabic treatise on ophthalmology. Also of importance among the early physicians of the Persian world at this time are Sābūr b. Sahl of Jundīshāpūr and Yaḥyā b. Serapion.

From the 3rd/9th century onward Muslims themselves began to cultivate interest in medicine and henceforward became the main figures in the history of medicine. The greatest of these figures, who ushered in the golden age of Islamic medicine and who are discussed separately by E. G. Browne in his *Arabian Medicine*, are four Persian

[1] C. Elgood, p. 173.

physicians: ʿAlī b. Rabban al-Ṭabarī, Muḥammad b. Zakariyyāʾ al-Rāzī, ʿAlī b. al-ʿAbbās al-Majūsī and Ibn Sīnā. These four figures dominated the scene during the two centuries stretching from the 3rd/9th to the 5th/11th, overshadowing other figures of significance such as Abu'l Ḥasan Aḥmad b. Muḥammad al-Ṭabarī, the author of *al-Muʿālajāt al-buqrāṭiyya*; Abū Bakr Rabīʿ al-Akhwīnī al-Bukhārī, the student of Rāzī who is the author of the oldest known Persian medical text, entitled *Hidāyat al-mutaʿallimīn fi'l-ṭibb*; Abū Manṣūr b. al-Ḥasan al-Qamarī, the teacher of Ibn Sīnā in medicine; and Abū Sahl ʿĪsā b. Yaḥyā al-Jurjānī, whose *Kitāb al-miʾa fi'l-ṣināʿat al-ṭibbiyya* served as a model for Ibn Sīnā's "Canon".

ʿAlī b. Rabban al-Ṭabarī, who was a convert from Zoroastrianism to Islam, is the author of the first major work on Islamic medicine, entitled *Firdaus al-ḥikma* ("The Paradise of Wisdom"). The work combines the Hippocratic and Galenic traditions of medicine and is also of particular interest for its last section, devoted to Indian medicine. The value of the book lies especially in its treatment of pathological and pharmacological questions.

Ṭabarī was the teacher of the real founder of clinical medicine in Islam, Rāzī. This great scientific figure of the 4th/10th century devoted the earlier part of his life to the study of alchemy, music and philosophy and became attracted to medicine only in the later period of his life. Yet his mastery in this domain became so great that soon he became the head of the hospital in Ray and later the chief director of the hospital in Baghdad. Long experience with different patients helped make Rāzī an outstanding authority in observation and prognosis. In fact he is probably the greatest clinical physician of Islam. His magnum opus, the *al-Ḥāwī* (translated into Latin as "Continens"), is the most precious existing document on clinical medicine in Islam and bears testimony to the author's mastery in observation. Rāzī wrote altogether fifty-six works on medicine and related subjects of which, after the *al-Ḥāwī* the most important in the history of medicine are the *Kitāb al-manṣūrī*, also rendered into Latin, and his small masterly treatise on smallpox and measles, *Kitāb al-jadarī wa'l-ḥasba*, published along with several other of his shorter works in Latin as "Opera Parva Abubetri" and translated later into several European languages.

Rāzī was the first to describe smallpox, and the first to write an independent treatise on pediatrics. He is usually credited with the isolation of alcohol and its use in medicine as an antiseptic, and also the use of mercury as a purgative. The "Album Rhasis" of the Latin Middle Ages is named after him. Altogether Rāzī had a profound influence in both East and West and is, after Ibn Sīnā, the most influential of all Muslim physicians.

Between Rāzī and Ibn Sīnā the outstanding medical figure was 'Alī b. 'Abbās al-Majūsī al-Ahwāzī, of whom little is known save that he was the physician of 'Aḍud al-Daula and came from Ahvāz or possibly Bihbahān. His masterpiece, *Kāmil al-ṣinā'a* or *Kitāb al-malikī*, known in the West as "Liber regius", is the outstanding work after *al-Ḥāwī* and became a standard medical text until the appearance of Ibn Sīnā's "Canon". Ahwāzī studied medicine with Abū Māhir Mūsā b. Sayyār al-Qummī and was well acquainted with both the Greek and earlier Muslim authorities. He knew Rāzī well and criticized *al-Ḥāwī* for its disorderliness. His own *Kitāb al-malikī* is known for its organization and order. It is divided into two main sections devoted to theoretical and practical medicine respectively, and each section is in turn subdivided into ten chapters. Of particular significance is the chapter on surgery, which is the most original part of the work. The last chapter is devoted to pharmacology and is also of much interest.

After Ahwāzī there were many physicians of note, especially Abū Sahl 'Īsā b. Yaḥyā al-Masīḥī al-Jurjānī, who was a contemporary of Ibn Sīnā and perished during the flight with Ibn Sīnā to Khurāsān. But his name, like that of all other physicians of the latter half of the 4th/10th century was overshadowed by the towering figure of Ibn Sīnā, who is the most influential medical figure of the mediaeval period in both East and West. Ibn Sīnā was already a well-known physician at the age of eighteen and did not cease to practice until his death. He combined the acute observational powers of the earlier physicians with a philosophical mind that sought to create a philosophy of medicine and of living things in general, as we find in the first book of his "Canon". He was in a sense Hippocrates and Galen combined in a single figure. His observations led to the discovery of specific illnesses and their correct description, as in the case of meningitis, described correctly for the first time by him. His knowledge of the human psyche led to a remarkable development of psychosomatic medicine in his hands. But perhaps most important of all, his philosophical mind succeeded in creating a philosophy of medicine which is still of much value.

Ibn Sīnā wrote one great medical masterpiece, the *Qānūn* or "Canon", which has remained the best-known medical work in the East, is still studied and consulted by *ḥakīms* today, and was known almost to the same extent in its Latin translation in the West. This monument of Islamic medicine is the synthesis of all that came before and the basis of all that followed. Ibn Sīnā also wrote shorter medical treatises such as the *Urjūza* or "Poem of Medicine" and the treatise on the pulse, *Dānish-i rag* or *Nabḍiyya*, in Persian, which is particularly important for its being one of Ibn Sīnā's definitely authentic Persian works. His concern in medicine ranged from pharmacology to psychology, and he established a school which is among the major medical systems of the world and is still of value in many fields of medicine.

After Ibn Sīnā, Islamic medicine acquired a more local character. One can discern for example an Andalusian and Moroccan school, an Egyptian school or a Persian one. The latter begins to use the Persian language more frequently. The *Dhakhīra-yi Khwārazmshāhī* of Jurjānī, a vast medical encyclopaedia in Persian, is based on the *Qānūn*, as are the many works produced in Ṣafavid Persia and Moghul India. Thus, in medicine as in the life sciences, the first few Islamic centuries produced many prominent figures, most of them connected in one way or another with the Persian climate, who determined the nature and future course of the Islamic sciences.

CHAPTER 13(*a*)

PHILOSOPHY AND COSMOLOGY

To discuss philosophy and cosmology in Persia from the rise of Islam to the Saljuq period is almost synonymous with studying the first phase in the development of Islamic philosophy and cosmology itself. During the first four centuries of Islam the most important intellectual centres wherein such branches of the intellectual sciences (*al-'ulūm al-'aqliyya*) as philosophy were cultivated were either Baghdad, Kūfa and Baṣra, on the border between Arab and Persian worlds, or the cities of Persia itself, especially those of Khurāsān. During this period only a few centres outside of these areas, such as those of Fāṭimid Egypt, were of any significance for the development of Islamic philosophy, and even there Persian elements were far from being absent. Therefore, in order not to repeat and summarize in a few pages the genesis and early history of Islamic philosophy in general, we shall seek to concentrate more on the distinctly Persian elements and also on lesser known schools of Islamic philosophy associated with the Persian world. Such important figures as the Arab al-Kindī we shall therefore have to leave aside, although he is in a sense the founder of Islamic philosophy, and the later stages of its development would not be comprehensible without him. Likewise Fārābī, although from Khurāsān, we shall discuss only in passing, for he also has been treated amply in many studies. Of the well-known Peripatetics of the early period, only Ibn Sīnā will be treated more fully, because in addition to the fact that he has played a central rôle in Islamic philosophy in general, the whole later intellectual life of Islamic Persia would be inconceivable without him.

The Persians played a central rôle in the elaboration of Islamic philosophy from the very beginning, and Persia was destined to become the main home and theatre of activity of this aspect of Islamic culture throughout history. During the period of the assimilation of the early sciences by Islam most of the translators were Christians of Mesopotamian or Syrian background, but the Persians also played an important rôle. More and more today the importance of later Sāsānian philosophical works, in origin either Pahlavī or ultimately Greek rendered into Pahlavī, is evident, and such works must be considered an important component in the formation of Islamic philosophy. Moreover, the Persian translators and the whole class of secretaries (*kātibs* or *dabīrs*) who cultivated philosophy were important in creating the new style of philosophical prose in Arabic. The rôle of Ibn al-Muqaffaʿ was particularly central in this connection, and he as well as other members of his school did much to form a new technical vocabulary and style which helped to make Arabic the major world language of philosophical discourse for many centuries. The Persians played an important rôle in the development of Arabic philosophical vocabulary not only at its genesis but also throughout its later history, and they are the authors of most Islamic philosophical works even in the Arabic language. Throughout Islamic history they have used Arabic as a vehicle for their thoughts and only after the 4th/10th century did they begin to develop Persian as a language for traditional philosophical discourse.

The early history of Islamic philosophy and theology (*Kalām*) during the 3rd/9th century is connected with the cities of Baghdad, Baṣra and Kūfa, in all three of which the Arab and Persian elements were mixed, such that it is often difficult to separate them. It can in fact be said that the Islamic sciences were founded by the co-operation of these two major elements of Islamic civilization, the Arabs being more devoted to kalām and the Persians to the intellectual sciences including philosophy, although as mentioned earlier there were Arabs like al-Kindī who played a major rôle in the cultivation of philosophy, and Persians who were outstanding among the Muʿtazilī and later As͟hʿarī theologians. It is only later, in the 4th/10th century, when the centre of philosophical activity shifts from Baghdad to K͟hurāsān, that the Persian element becomes more distinct.

Usually in discussing the early period of Islamic philosophy attention is focused on the Peripatetic (*mas͟hs͟hāʾī*) school that dominated the scene. In actuality the situation was much more complex than most studies would indicate. There were many tendencies and schools, of which the Peripatetic is but one branch, albeit an outstanding one. There was the Hermetic school associated at the beginning with the city of Ḥarrān and later with Jābir b. Ḥayyān and his school, which left an important effect upon certain branches of S͟hīʿī theology, both Imāmī and Ismāʿīlī. There was the Neopythagorean element which manifested itself in the works of different authors such as the Ik͟hwān al-Ṣafāʾ without developing into a completely distinct school of its own. There was the Ismāʿīlī school of philosophy, which developed parallel with the Peripatetic but which is hardly ever considered in the general works on Islamic philosophy. In all of these schools and tendencies as well as in Ṣūfism, Kalām and many of the lesser-known fields, the Persians played a notable rôle, so that in any comprehensive study of philosophy in Islamic Persia all of these schools must be taken into account.

The first person mentioned in traditional sources as having devoted himself to philosophy in the Islamic period is Abu'l-'Abbās Īrānshahrī, who flourished in the 3rd/9th century and came from the vicinity of Nīshāpūr. Nothing is known of his life and works save for a few quotations found in the writings of such later authors as Bīrūnī, who cites his name many times in the *al-Qānūn al-Mas'ūdī*, *Taḥqīq mā li'l-Hind* and *al-Āthār al-bāqiya*, and Nāṣir-i Khusrau, who refers to him several times in his *Zād al-musāfirīn*.[1] From these sources we learn that he was well versed in astronomy and philosophy. According to Nāṣir-i Khusrau he was the teacher of Muḥammad b. Zakariyyā' Rāzī. Nāṣir-i Khusrau calls both of them "followers of the school of *hylé*" (*aṣḥāb-i hayūlā*) but respects Īrānshahrī's synthesis of philosophy and religion whereas he attacks Rāzī violently. We also learn from the same source that Īrānshahrī composed two books called *Jalīl* and *Athīr* on philosophy and that he considered space (*makān*) to be eternal and the external manifestation of the power of God. The author of the work on religions called *Bayān al-adyān* adds that Īrānshahrī claimed to be a prophet among the Persians and brought a book in the language of an angel called Being (*hastī*)![2]

This sketchy information may not lead us far in understanding the teachings or the influence of Īrānshahrī. It does show, however, the significance of this forgotten figure as the first person in the Islamic period to have become interested in philosophy, which was soon to find its first systematic expositor in the figure of Kindī. Īrānshahrī's name, moreover, is symbolic in the sense that in addition to referring to the name of a place near Nīshāpūr from which he hailed, it means one from the "land of Iran", which was to become the heartland for the later development of Islamic philosophy.

The written record of Islamic philosophy begins with the "philosopher of the Arabs" Abū Ya'qūb al-Kindī, who wrote extensive treatises in Arabic on philosophy and the sciences during the 3rd/9th

[1] See M. Mīnuvī, "Abu'l-'Abbās Īrānshahrī", *RFLM*, vol. 1, nos. 2–3 (1344/1966), pp. 133–9; M. Mohaghegh, pp. 16–19.

[2] See editions of this work by M. T. Dānishpazhūh in *Farhang-i Irānzamīn*, vol. x (Tehrān, 1341/1963), pp. 283ff. and Hāshim Raḍī (Tehrān, 1342/1964), p. 67.

century, relying most of all on the translations of Syriac scholars as well as of course on Islamic sources. For reasons already mentioned we must pass over this astounding figure in our present study. His famous students, however, who were nearly all Persians, must be mentioned if we are to understand the link between Kindī and the remarkable flowering of intellectual activity during the following century.

Among Kindī's most famous associates are the two Balkhī's, Abū Zaid and Abū Ma'shar. Both are better known in geography and astronomy and astrology than in philosophy but they were also knowledgeable in the latter field. Abū Zaid was highly reputed by his contemporaries as an outstanding philosopher who harmonized religion and philosophy. He was the greatest scholar of his day, of the same stature as Jāḥiẓ and Abū Ḥanīfa Dīnawarī.[1] As for Abū Ma'shar, although celebrated as the foremost authority on astrology in East and West, he was also thoroughly acquainted with both Hermetic and Aristotelian philosophy and it was in fact through the Latin translation of his *al-Mudkhal al-kabīr*, known as "Introductorium in astronomiam Albumasaris Abalachii octo continens libros partiales", that Aristotelian philosophy was introduced to the West for the first time.

Probably Kindī's most important disciple in the domain of philosophy was Aḥmad b. Ṭayyib al-Sarakhsī from Khurāsān, who was born between 218/833 and 222/837 and died in 286/899, according to some sources by suicide. Although well-known in his own lifetime, having been the instructor to the 'Abbāsid prince al-Mu'taḍid, even becoming his boon companion (*nadīm*) when the prince became caliph and being given charge of some state duties by him, he fell from favour late in life and was imprisoned. This fact may have contributed to his becoming rapidly forgotten; even his works, of which there were many, were mostly lost or neglected. Enough has been recounted of them, however, to enable us to reconstruct an image of him. He wrote in nearly every field, following the example of his teacher. His writings embraced religion, philosophy and the sciences and ranged over fields as far apart as music, in which he wrote a major work, and politics, in which his *Ādāb al-mulūk* still survives. In geography and especially literature (*adab*) he had many original ideas while in philosophy he followed closely the teachings of Kindī. His tragic life coincided with the period when the intellectual climate of Baghdad was changing, preparing the

[1] See Yāqūt al-Ḥamawī, *Mu'jam al-udabā'*, vol. I (Leipzig, 1866), p. 125 (Appendix on Aḥmad b. Dā'ūd Abū Ḥanīfa al-Dīnawarī).

way for the spread of philosophy beyond the inhospitable atmosphere of the capital to the cities of Persia and especially Khurāsān, which were soon to become its new home. One of Sarakhsī's students, Rāzī, was in fact to carry the transformation to an extreme, by not only shifting the centre of intellectual activity away from Baghdad but also opposing completely the Peripatetic school of thought established by Kindī and followed by Sarakhsī.

With Muḥammad b. Zakariyyā' Rāzī, the Latin Rhazes, we come face to face with a singular personality and a philosopher who holds a unique position in the annals of Islamic philosophy in the sense that he was opposed and criticized on one philosophical ground or another by nearly everyone, from the theologians (*mutakallimūn*) to the Ismā'īlī *dā'īs* or missionaries. Rāzī was born in 250/864 in Ray and died in the same city in 313/925. His career embraced several phases. Early in life he was interested in alchemy and only at a later age, in the middle of life, did he turn to medicine. He spent the first part of his life in Ray and after gaining fame as a scientist and physician went to Baghdad where he became known as the foremost authority on medicine. His knowledge in this field was proverbial even in his own day and it is in fact in the fields of medicine and alchemy that he has left his profoundest mark upon history. This aspect of his activity, however, does not concern us here and belongs to the history of science rather than to philosophy.

Rāzī was also a philosopher of note who, however, never entered the mainstream of Islamic intellectual life, precisely because of the nature of his thought, which stood against the "prophetic philosophy" characteristic of Islam as a whole. His philosophical works were in fact lost sight of for centuries and have been partially recovered only during the past decades, mostly through the efforts of P. Kraus. Rāzī was an independent figure who did not belong to any of the established schools of thought and considered himself as an equal of Plato and Aristotle, who were able to found new philosophical schools by themselves. He was given by nature to controversial questions and wrote against such theologians and philosophers as Abu'l-Qāsim Balkhī, a student of the Mu'tazilī Khayyāṭ, and Shahīd Balkhī, the famous poet and philosopher-theologian, as well as the aforementioned Sarakhsī, against whom he wrote a separate treatise.[1]

His writings in turn caused intense interest on the part of such

[1] See Mohaghegh, pp. 45–7.

outstanding scholars as Bīrūnī, who in fact wrote a catalogue of his works, as well as severe reactions from many quarters. The Ismā'īlī philosophers and theologians reacted against him most violently, and Abū Ḥātim Rāzī, Ḥamīd al-Dīn Kirmānī and Nāṣir-i Khusrau wrote a great deal about him, to the extent that their writings contain many fragments of his treatises which otherwise would have been lost. The Peripatetics such as Fārābī also criticized him as did such scientists and physicians as Ibn al-Haitham and 'Alī b. Riḍwān. The only places where he did exercise some philosophical influence were among a few Shī'ī theologians, who adopted his theory of pleasure, and also among later Ismā'īlīs, inasmuch as his writings on alchemy, in spite of his difference of view on their interpretation, entered into the Jabirean corpus, to which was wed the Hermeticism that had been integrated into the Islamic perspective following the period of translation in the 2nd/8th century.

Over two hundred works by Rāzī dealing with nearly every branch of learning have been mentioned in various traditional sources. As far as those on philosophy and related subjects are concerned, some of the most important titles include *al-Madkhal ila'l-manṭiq* and *Kitāb al-burhān* in logic; *Sam' al-kiyān*, *Fi'l-zamān wa'l-makān* and *Fi'l-lidhdha* in natural philosophy; *al-Nafs al-ṣaghīr*, *al-Nafs al-kabīr*, *al-Shukūk 'alā Abarqalus*, *al-Shukūk 'alā Jālīnūs*, *Maidān al-'aql*, *al-'Ilm al-ilāhī*, *al-Ṣīrat al-falsafiyya* and *al-Ṭibb al-rūḥānī* in philosophy, of which the last three are particularly important for our understanding of Rāzī's thought. Many of these treatises are lost and only segments can be recovered from the works of later authors. Such is the case with the major opus, *al-'Ilm al-ilāhī*, parts of which can be found in Nāṣir-i Khusrau's *Zād al-musāfirīn* and some of the other later philosophical works.

The most characteristic features of Rāzī's philosophy are his "five eternal principles" (*al-qudamā' al-khamsa*) and his theory of the nature and history of the soul, a theory which displays gnostic tendencies and is related to his conception of nature. The five principles, consisting of the Creator, Soul, Matter, Time and Space, are well known and reflect both the influence of Manichaeism and of Plato's *Timaeus* and its later commentaries. Rāzī's belief in a Creator (*bārī'*) was firm but the other four "principles" stood co-eternal with him. Rāzī believed in both a partial or limited space and an absolute one. Likewise, following both Plato and possibly Zurvanite and Manichaean models, he distinguished between limited and absolute time, the latter being conceived as a substance independent of matter and equal to eternity or *dahr*, which was the same as the Greek *aion*.

As for matter, Rāzī expounded an original atomistic theory differing completely from the atomism of the theologians (*mutakallimūn*) as well as from the well-known atomism of Democritus. For Rāzī atoms possess extension and mix in a void to produce the five elements.[1] They thus differ from the *juz' lā yatajazzā'* of the mutakallimūn which is devoid of extension. Whether this atomism came from Buddhist sources as thought by Pines or from late and unknown interpretations of the school of Democritus as believed by H. A. Wolfson, there is no doubt that it represents one of the most interesting forms of atomism in Islamic philosophy.

Rāzī's theory of the soul, in contrast to other aspects of his philosophy, which have a "materialistic" tinge, reflects mystical interpretations of the entanglement of the soul in the prison of the body. According to Rāzī the soul wanted to unite with matter in order to produce forms that would be the source of bodily enjoyment. Matter, however, refused to participate in this union. The Creator then created this world with lasting forms in order to enable this enjoyment to take place. The soul, however, possesses life but not knowledge, through which it could discern its own situation. Therefore, from his own divinity the Creator produced the intellect (*al-'aql*) and sent it into this world in order to awaken the soul from its dream and redeem it from the prison of matter into which it has fallen. And this takes place only through the use of the intellect in philosophy. For Rāzī, therefore, philosophy has a redeeming and salvatory character.

Strangely enough it is just this belief in the presence of the intellect within all men that turned Rāzī against the belief in the necessity of revealed religion and prophets. For Rāzī, since all men possess this intellect and are equal in this respect, there is no need for prophets and they cannot have spiritual superiority over other men. It was this aspect of Rāzī's thought, contained in his two books *Fi'l-nubuwwāt* and *Fī ḥiyal al-mutanabbiyyīn*, that was most violently attacked by all Islamic philosophers and theologians, from Bīrūnī to Abū Ḥātim. In fact later texts of Islamic theology, continuing to the present day, contain chapters devoted expressly to the refutation of the theses of Rāzī and Ibn al-Rāwandī on the denial of the necessity of prophecy.

[1] See S. Pines, Chapter 2.

In ethics Rāzī was much influenced by Socrates, whom he deeply respected. His *al-Ṭibb al-rūḥānī* and *al-Ṣīrat al-falsafiyya* contain the major theses of his ethical theory, of which the most notable feature perhaps is his well-known theory of pleasure, according to which pleasure is nothing more than a return to normal conditions.

Abū Naṣr al-Fārābī, the second major figure of the Peripatetic school after Kindī, has also been treated so often elsewhere that we need only to review rapidly his specific significance for the tradition of Islamic philosophy in Persia. Fārābī, who lived from around 257/870 until 339/950, spent half of his life in Khurāsān and the other half in Baghdad and Aleppo. This fact in itself indicates the importance that Khurāsān was beginning to gain in the field of intellectual activity, to such an extent that a generation after Fārābī it, rather than Baghdad, became the central arena for Islamic philosophy.

Fārābī is becoming recognized, even more than Kindī, as the real founder of Islamic philosophy, and a great deal of attention has been focused upon him of late. His logical works, both in the form of original treatises and commentaries upon the *Organon* of Aristotle, set the foundations for logic among the Muslims. His combining of the political thought of Plato, the ethics of Aristotle and Islamic political theory in several works, of which the *Ārā' ahl al-madīnat al-fāḍila* is the most important, has established him as the founder of Islamic political philosophy. His attempt to harmonize the philosophies of Plato and Aristotle in *al-Jam' bain ra'yai al-ḥakīmain Aflāṭūn al-ilāhī wa Arisṭū* set a tendency that was pursued by most of the later Muslim philosophers, while he discussed the philosophies of Plato and Aristotle separately and in greater depth in other treatises. His *Fuṣūṣ al-ḥikma*, also attributed by some to Ibn Sīnā, has been studied in the Islamic world for a millennium and has been a major source for Islamic philosophical terminology. It has also combined gnosis and philosophy in a remarkable way.

Finally, in the domain of metaphysics Fārābī was the author of major works, of which the *Kitāb al-ḥurūf* is particularly significant for an understanding of his ontology. He also wrote the commentary on Aristotle's *Metaphysics*, entitled *Aghrāḍ mā ba'd al-ṭabī'a*, which, although short, deeply influenced Ibn Sīnā in the latter's understanding of Aristotle. Through the later Peripatetics and especially Ibn Sīnā, Fārābī became a permanent influence upon all later Islamic philosophy and a figure who must be taken into consideration in any study of the many facets of Islamic philosophy as it developed from the 4th/10th century onward.

Abu'l-Ḥasan Muḥammad b. Yūsuf al-'Āmirī is certainly the most important figure between Fārābī and Ibn Sīnā, although he was soon to become over-shadowed by the towering figure of the latter. Born early in the 4th/10th century in Nīshāpūr, he studied most likely with Abū Zaid Balkhī and spent most of his life in his home province. He visited Baghdad in 364/974–5 but did not like the city and therefore soon returned to Nīshāpūr where he died in 381/991. He was held in great respect by his contemporaries and is cited often by Sijistānī, Tauḥīdī, Muskūya and many other later philosophers. In his *Milal wa niḥal* Shahristānī calls him one of the great philosophers of Islam, and the title "Master of Philosophers" (*ṣāḥib al-falāsifa*) was bestowed upon him.

At least twenty-three works by 'Āmirī have been cited.[1] Only recently, however, have some of his works, such as *al-I'lām bi manāqib al-islām* on the defence of Islam and *al-Sa'āda wa'l-is'ād* on ethics, been published. His major history of philosophy, *al-Amad 'ala'l-abad*, remains to be edited as do several other of his works. He also wrote the *Manāhij al-dīn* on Ṣūfism, which influenced Kalābādhī in his *al-Ta'arruf*, commentaries upon Aristotle, *al-Fuṣūl fī ma'ālim al-ilāhiyya* and *Farrukh-nāma-yi yūnān dastūr*, this last in Persian.

'Āmirī must be noted for his political theory, in which he was influenced not only by Greek sources but also by Persian material of the pre-Islamic period, for his strong defence of Islam, unique in its tone and argument among the Peripatetic philosophers, and for certain strictly philosophical and metaphysical views such as the unity of the intellect and the intelligible. Although attacked by Ibn Sīnā and thereby eclipsed by this powerful figure who was to succeed him on the philosophical scene, 'Āmirī continued to be studied and quoted by the later philosophers, and even as late as the Ṣafavid period such a figure as Mullā Ṣadrā quotes him several times in his *Asfār*. Through his works and his students, of whom Ibn Hindū was the most important, 'Āmirī left a greater impact upon Islamic philosophy than has been realized until now, and he is one of the early Islamic philosophers most deserving to be studied more closely.

Although after the first few decades of the 4th/10th century Khurāsān became the main focus and centre of Islamic philosophy, Baghdad

[1] See M. Mīnuvī, "Az khazā'in-i turkiyya", *RFLT*, vol. IV, no. 3 (1336), pp. 60–83.

continued to be an important centre of intellectual life to the very end of the century. During the second half of the 4th/10th century the philosophical scene in Baghdad was dominated by a Persian originating from Sīstān, Abū Sulaimān al-Sijistānī, entitled Manṭiqī. This title, which means "logician", is indicative of his powers in the domain of logic. In fact the Baghdad school of Peripatetic philosophy during the latter part of the 4th/10th century turned more and more toward an interest in logic to the detriment of other aspects of philosophy.

Sijistānī trained many students and was the leading figure in the intellectual circles of Baghdad, which were visited by many important figures such as ʿĀmirī and the authors of the *Rasā'il* of the Brethren of Purity. Perhaps this contact with so many different scholars was one of the reasons that led Sijistānī to compose the very important *Ṣiwān al-ḥikma* on the history of philosophy from the beginning until his own time. This work, complemented by Baihaqī's *Tatimma ṣiwān al-ḥikma*, remains to this day one of the basic sources for our knowledge of early Islamic philosophy.

The record of the philosophical sessions revolving around Sijistānī is to be found in the works of his disciple, Abū Ḥayyān Tauḥīdī, who was a Ṣūfī and also a literary figure of much talent. His *al-Imtāʿ wa'l-mu'ānasa* and *Muqābasāt* mirror the rich and diversified intellectual life of Baghdad of the late 4th/10th century. Although not a noted philosopher himself, Tauḥīdī remains, nevertheless, a key figure for an understanding of the intellectual life of that period.

During the last decades of the 4th/10th century there appeared a collection of fifty-one treatises dealing with nearly all fields of knowledge and known as the *Rasā'il* of the Brethren of Purity (I<u>kh</u>wān al-Ṣafā'). This group of authors, whose identity has never become completely clear, was certainly of <u>Sh</u>īʿī inspiration although perhaps not as specifically Ismāʿīlī as it came to be considered later. The group was also associated with a secret organization and probably had its centre of activity in Baṣra. The *Rasā'il* served as a means of disseminating the teachings of this society to a wider audience. The Ismāʿīlīs made the *Rasā'il* their own during later centuries and two treatises, *Risālat al-jāmiʿa* and *Jāmiʿat al-jāmiʿa*, which were written later and contain the essence of the *Rasā'il*, were taught both esoterically and to a smaller group of Ismāʿīlī adepts.

The *Rasā'il* exercised a wide influence and were read by most of the later Muslim intellectual figures, from <u>Gh</u>azzālī to Ibn ʿArabī to Mullā

Ṣadrā. Because of their simple exposition of the sciences and philosophy and also because of their attempt to harmonize philosophy and religion they attracted much attention almost immediately after their dissemination. The *Rasā'il* expound a Neopythagorean philosophy combined with Peripatetic tenets and of course Islamic teachings. They are related, therefore, to early Peripatetic philosophy as well as to Jābir and early Hermeticism, not to speak of the Sabaeans, from whose teachings they must have also drawn. Here it should be remembered that the Sabaeans of Ḥarrān were the heirs to late Greek Neopythagoreanism and Hermeticism.

The backbone of the philosophy of the *Rasā'il* is a numerical symbolism and mathematical theory which sees numbers and figures in a Pythagorean manner, not only as quantity but also as symbols of metaphysical realities and principles of things. The sciences are integrated into the religious point of view through the symbolic aspect of these sciences. The *Rasā'il* present a synthesis of the knowledge of the day and at the same time one of the best-known efforts made during the 4th/10th century to harmonize religion and philosophy. Considering the comprehensive nature of the *Rasā'il*, their simple style of exposition and the crucial questions discussed by their authors, it is not surprising that Peripatetic philosophers, theologians and Ṣūfīs, men from all shades within the wide spectrum of Islamic intellectual life, came to read and be influenced by them.

One of the notable figures of the 4th/10th century, at once philosopher and historian, is Abū 'Alī Aḥmad b. Muḥammad Ya'qūb Muskūya, known usually by the Arabic form of his name, Miskawaih. It is not certain whether he was a Zoroastrian converted to Islam or belonged to a Muslim family that had been converted generations before.[1] There is also a debate as to whether his real name was Muskūya (Miskawaih) or Ibn Muskūya (Miskawaih). Muskūya was born in 325/936 in Ray. He later went to Baghdad where he frequented the circle of Sijistānī and became a close associate of the vizier al-Muhallabī. During this period he led a life of pleasure and composed mundane poetry. But upon the death of al-Muhallabī he changed his way of life. He returned to Ray to join the circle of Ibn al-'Amīd, whom he served as librarian. There he studied deeply in a rich library in that city and underwent a

[1] These two views are to be found in M. Arkoun, *Contribution à l'étude de l'humanisme arabe au IVe/Xe siècle : Miskawayh philosophe et historien* (Paris, 1970), the most extensive and scholarly work on Muskūya to date; and M. Abdul Haq Ansari, *The Ethical Philosophy of Miskawaih* (Aligarh, 1964).

transformation in his outlook. In 365/976 he returned to Baghdad to serve the Būyid ruler ʿAḍud al-Daula as librarian and ambassador. Only in 372/983 after the death of ʿAḍud al-Daula did he begin to study philosophy. Later he joined the service of the Khwārazm-Shāh as physician and there he met Ibn Sīnā. Finally at the age of ninety-six he died in Iṣfahān in 421/1030, having spent decades in scholarly activity and having lived a life of virtue after turning away from the life of pleasure of his early years.

Muskūya was interested in alchemy and medicine, for both of which he has been remembered in later Islamic history. But his reputation rests most of all on his historical masterpiece *Tajārib al-umam* and his philosophical works such as the *Tartīb al-saʿādāt wa manāzil al-ʿulūm* on the classification of the sciences, *al-Fauz al-aṣghar*, *al-Fauz al-akbar* and *al-Ḥawāmil wa'l-shawāmil* on theological problems and his two most famous ethical treatises, *Tahdhīb al-akhlāq* and *Jāvīdān khirad.*

The most lasting contribution of Muskūya was in the field of ethics. Following the example of ʿĀmirī and some of the other earlier authors, he elaborated a philosophical ethics based upon the teachings of Islam, the philosophy of Plato and that of Aristotle, the latter two seen in the light of late Greek philosophy, especially the works of Galen. The *Tahdhīb al-akhlāq*, which contains this synthesis, reveals also certain novel features originating with Muskūya himself. Muskūya revived the importance of *eros*, which Aristotle had neglected, and applied it in new ways. He also spoke of the love between the spiritual teacher and the disciple in a way that is not found in Greek sources but which is to be seen later in the Christian West. One can also see the influence of certain pre-Islamic Iranian elements in Muskūya, both in the *Tahdhīb* and especially in the *Jāvīdān khirad*, whose very title indicates its relation with the wisdom (*khirad*) of the ancient Persians. The text as well speaks of the wisdom of the Persians of old going back to Hūshang. This work, written in Arabic despite its Persian title, is one of the important sources of the Islamic period containing the ethical aphorisms and sayings which were the principles of the ethical teachings of the ancient Persians. Muskūya has lived in later Islamic history – and especially in Persia – not only because of his *Tahdhīb* but especially as a result of the paraphrase of this work in Nāṣir al-Dīn Ṭūsī's *Akhlāq-i Nāṣirī*, which is without doubt the best-known work of philosophical ethics in the Persian language.

Although Abū Raiḥān al-Bīrūnī (362/973–442/1051) belongs more to the history of Islamic science than to philosophy, it is not possible to pass over him in silence when discussing the latter field. Through his studies of chronology as in *al-Āthār al-bāqiya* and his incomparable study of India in *Taḥqīq ma li'l-Hind* we can learn something of his philosophical outlook as a Muslim scientist who combined a keen sense of observation with a power of critical and rational analysis and who was at the same time open to the verities of revelation and intuition. But it is especially in his questions and answers exchanged with Ibn Sīnā that one can measure Bīrūnī's philosophical importance as a most powerful mind who judges clearly and independently and is at the same time a critic of the prevalent Peripatetic philosophy. Bīrūnī must in fact be considered as one of the chief critics of Aristotelian natural philosophy in the Middle Ages.

Bīrūnī's works are also important in the field of comparative religion, of which he may in a sense be considered the founder. In this domain he was not only an observer of facts but also possessed a metaphysical perspective which enabled him to be an acute observer and student of religions other than his own. Although he did not write independent philosophical treatises, this intellectual figure of first magnitude wrote enough pages of philosophical significance within his other works to qualify him as an important philosophical figure of his period, one who did not, however, identify himself completely with any of the well-established schools of his day.

Few men have left as profound an effect upon their civilization and its subsequent history as Ibn Sīnā has left upon Islamic civilization, especially in its Persian zone. An extraordinary genius gifted at the same time with the power of synthesis and analysis, and possessing unusual physical and mental powers, he was able to achieve a lasting synthesis in the domains of both philosophy and medicine. No intellectual figure in the subsequent history of Islam can be said to have been totally free of his influence, whether that figure be a physician or a logician. Even the theologians and other authorities in the religious sciences adopted some of the basic tenets of his metaphysical doctrines.

Ibn Sīnā, who was born in 370/980 and died in 428/1037, lived during a tumultuous period of Persian history. His birthplace of Bukhārā and the adjacent areas underwent not only a political but also an ethnological transformation with the coming of the Turkish Ghaznavids, who were to replace the Sāmānids. Forced to leave his home at the early age of twenty-one he wandered during the rest of his life from one Būyid capital to another making his livelihood as a physician and occasionally as a statesman and vizier. The longest period of relative peace in a life otherwise punctuated by unrest and uncertainty was the nine years spent at the court of 'Alā' al-Daula in Iṣfahān. But even this short calm was to be broken abruptly by the invasion of that city by Maḥmūd of Ghazna's son, Mas'ūd. Having spent his energies all too freely and excessively, Ibn Sīnā burned out the candle of his life much more rapidly than would be expected for a man of his unusual physical stamina and died at the age of fifty-seven in Hamadān.[1]

The exceptional power of concentration and intellectual insight of Ibn Sīnā were such that they could not be eclipsed even by the hectic life that he was destined to lead. Already well-known as a physician at the age of sixteen and a master of the traditional sciences by eighteen, he entered maturity fully equipped from an intellectual point of view, and as he was to write in his autobiography, which he dictated to his favourite disciple, Abū 'Ubaid al-Juzjānī, he knew as much in breadth at the age of eighteen as he did at the end of his life. Only the depth of his knowledge had increased.

One of Ibn Sīnā's chief characteristics was his insatiable thirst to know and to perfect himself through knowledge. There was no form of science, from logic and mathematics to pure metaphysics, from prosody to Qur'anic commentary, that did not attract his attention. In fact he was to make major contributions to every branch of the "intellectual sciences" save perhaps certain branches of mathematics, in which his chief contribution is limited to musical theory and the philosophy of mathematics. Characteristic of his quest after totality and perfection was his attitude toward Arabic. Criticized by some scholars that his philosophical works such as the *Shifā'* were written in the style of "Persian Arabic" (*'ajamī* in both senses of the word), Ibn Sīnā spent much effort and time while in Iṣfahān to perfect his Arabic style. As a result of this period of study he was able to compose a long work on the Arabic language, which is now lost. But the fruit of this effort is to be seen in the much more refined prose style of his last works, such as the *Ishārāt*.

Ibn Sīnā wrote over two hundred works, many of which still survive, and yet despite his fame all of them have not been studied. Aside from the scientific and medical works of which the best known is the *Qānūn*

[1] Some claim that he died in Iṣfahān. There is an *Imāmzāda* in that city which a few scholars of Iṣfahān claim to be his tomb.

or "Canon", the *summa* of classical Islamic medicine, his philosophical works alone comprise over a hundred treatises. These works range from the monumental *al-Shifā'*, known in Latin through its partial translation as "Sufficientia", to short questions and answers and essays devoted to a single philosophical, theological or metaphysical subject. The *Shifā'*, consisting of four books devoted to logic, natural philosophy, mathematics and metaphysics, contains in reality the sum of his Peripatetic philosophy, into which all the natural and mathematical sciences known at that time have been integrated. Throughout the millennium that has followed its composition it has remained the most advanced text of mashshā'ī philosophy and still today it is studied and taught in the *madrasas* of Persia.

It is in this work and its briefer version, *al-Najāt*, as well as in the numerous treatises which develop individual arguments of these more comprehensive works, that one finds that classical formulation of Islamic Peripatetic philosophy which began with Kindī and reached its maturity with Ibn Sīnā himself. The persistent concern with ontology, to the extent that Ibn Sīnā has been called most of all a "philosopher of being", is to be seen in these works. The whole of his metaphysical exposition rests upon the fundamental distinction between Being (*wujūd*) and essence or quiddity (*māhiyya*) and the tripartite division of Being (*wujūd*) into the Necessary (*wājib*), the possible (*mumkin*) and the impossible (*mumtani'*). Upon this division is based Ibn Sīnā's cosmology which is closely wed to the concept of a hierarchical Universe beginning with God and the series of intelligences (*'uqūl*) and including an angelology, again related to the separate intelligences which act as the source of both knowledge and existence in the sub-lunary world. Likewise, Ibn Sīnā develops a psychology based upon Neoplatonic interpretations of Aristotle's *De Anima* that is again closely related to his ontology and also reveals Islamic, Neoplatonic and Aristotelian influences.

It was characteristic of Ibn Sīnā that once having attained the summit of this rational knowledge, which, since it was based upon correct intuitions, became the most plausible and legitimate form of rational philosophy, he should seek to transcend his very synthesis by reaching for the unlimited horizons of the "theosophy of illumination". During his later life Ibn Sīnā wrote the *Manṭiq al-mashriqiyyīn* in which he announced his "philosophy for the elite" (*khawāṣṣ*). Although the major portion of this telling document seems to have been lost, enough material has remained in the form of the visionary recitals, the masterly *al-Ishārāt wa'l-tanbīhāt* – his last major work – and certain other pieces, to enable us to reconstruct the "oriental philosophy" toward which he turned later in life.

A philosophy, or more strictly speaking a theosophy (*theosophia* in its original Greek sense and not the modern deformation), in which knowledge and experience were wed and which led to an immediate experience of the supra-formal states of being, the "Oriental philosophy" of Ibn Sīnā was of utmost importance in the later intellectual life of Islamic Persia. It marked the first step in the direction which was to be followed with such remarkable results a century and a half later by the "Master of Illumination", Suhravardī.

Ibn Sīnā was also important for the later intellectual life of Persia in another sense. He was the first to have attempted to write Peripatetic philosophy in Persian. His *Dānish-nāma-yi 'alā'ī*, which is more or less a Persian version of the *Najāt*, was beset by great difficulties of language and did not succeed in becoming a popular work in the Persian speaking world, as perhaps the author had hoped. But together with Bīrūnī's Persian *al-Tafhīm* and a few other works of the 4th/10th and 5th/11th centuries it prepared the ground for making Persian a major intellectual language of the Islamic world. Without these early efforts the Persian writings of Suhravardī, Afḍal al-Dīn al-Kāshānī, Naṣīr al-Dīn Ṭūsī and others would have been hardly possible.

Ibn Sīnā also trained a whole group of capable students who carried his teachings into the latter part of the 5th/11th century and kept the torch of Peripatetic philosophy burning, albeit dimly, until its revival by Naṣīr al-Dīn Ṭūsī. Among Ibn Sīnā's foremost students must be mentioned Jūzjānī, who completed several of the master's works and accompanied him throughout his life; Bahmanyār, the author of the *Taḥṣīl*, a major Peripatetic work; Ma'ṣūmī, who was respected as Ibn Sīnā's most learned student; and Ibn Zaila, who commented upon the master's more esoteric treatises. Such men as Khayyām and Lūkarī were second generation students of Ibn Sīnā through the above-named figures. The "Prince of Physicians" and the master of the Peripatetics was thus to leave through his works and his students a permanent hegemony in the intellectual life of Islam.

Parallel with the well-known Peripatetic school, which culminated with Ibn Sīnā, there developed during the early centuries of Islam a most elaborate cosmology and metaphysics connected with Ismā'īlism that has not received the attention it deserves until now. While during this period Twelve-Imām Shī'ism was concerned mostly with the collection of *ḥadīths* and the other religious sciences, as witnessed in the monumental works of Shaikh Muḥammad al-Ṭūsī, Kulainī and Ibn Babūya, Ismā'īlism was elaborating its great metaphysical expositions. Of course there is not just one Ismā'īlī philosophy but at least three schools, usually named the Fāṭimid, the Yemenī and the Alamūt. However the Fāṭimid school contains the basis for all later Ismā'īlī philosophical and theological speculations of both the Yemenī and Alamūt branches. And as far as the Fāṭimid school is concerned, except for Qāḍī Nu'mān all of its important figures were Persian, and together they produced the earliest corpus of philosophical writings in the Persian language, although they of course also wrote much in Arabic.

The earliest Ismā'īlī philosophical work – the term philosophy being used here in its traditional and Islamic context as *Ḥikmat* – is the *Umm al-kitāb*, dating probably to the 3rd/9th century. This work, which is still considered as a sacred text by the Ismā'īlīs of the Pamirs, displays a strong belief in the "five principles" for which the Ismā'īlīs were called *al-mukhammasa* (literally "the fivers") and reveals at the same time Manichaean influences. The author of this famous text with gnostic colour is unknown, but it reveals the earliest stages in the elaboration of Ismā'īlī theosophy and philosophy, which was to find many competent expositors in the 4th/10th century.

The earliest and one of the foremost of these Ismā'īlī philosophers and theologians of the 4th/10th century is Abū Ḥātim al-Rāzī, who hailed from Ray and died around 322/933–34. Known especially for his refutal of Muḥammad b. Zakariyyā' Rāzī in his celebrated *A'lām al-nubuwwa*, he also wrote the monumental *Kitāb al-zīna* on theology, *Kitāb al-jāmi'* on jurisprudence, an esoteric commentary (*ta'wīl*) upon the Qur'ān and the *Iṣlāḥ*, which is the most important early systematic treatise on Ismā'īlī theology and philosophy. These works and the intense missionary activity of Abū Ḥātim were certainly very instrumental in the spread of Ismā'īlism in Persia.

Abū Ḥātim was followed by Abū Ya'qūb al-Sijistānī, who died in 408/1017 and was the author of the *Kashf al-maḥjūb*, the Persian translation of which is among the earliest examples of Persian philosophical prose. The book consists of seven chapters and each chapter of seven headings, revealing the central rôle played by the number seven in all Ismā'īlī theosophy. Although criticized by Nāṣir-i Khusrau for his defence of transmigration, Sijistānī must be considered as one of the important successors of Abū Ḥātim along with such other celebrated Ismā'īlī missionaries (*dā'īs*) as Muḥammad b. Aḥmad al-Na<u>khsh</u>abī (Nasafī), who was his near contemporary.

Another 4th/10th-century Ismā'īlī figure of interest is Abu'l-Hai<u>th</u>am Aḥmad b. Ḥasan al-Jurjānī, known especially for his *Qaṣīda* upon which both Muḥammad b. Sur<u>kh</u> al-Nai<u>sh</u>ābūrī and Nāṣir-i <u>Kh</u>usrau wrote commentaries. In fact he exercised much influence upon Nāṣir-i <u>Kh</u>usrau. The *Qaṣīda* is particularly interesting for its discussion of the relation between astrology and prophetology, seen of course in the light of the cyclic doctrines of the Ismā'īlīs.

A foremost Ismā'īlī philosopher of this age and the author of the *Rāḥat al-'aql*, which many consider as the most authoritative source of Fāṭimid Ismā'īlī doctrines, is Hamīd al-Dīn al-Kirmānī, who lived at the time of the Fāṭimid caliph al-Ḥākim bi'llāh and was entitled *Ḥujjat al-'irāqain* because he journeyed between Iraq and "'Irāq-i 'ajam" in Persia. He composed the *Rāḥat al-'aql* in 411/1020 and died probably shortly thereafter. Altogether he wrote thirty-two works including, besides the above-mentioned masterpiece, the *Tanbīh al-hādī wa'l-mustahdī* on the esoteric meaning of ritual acts and *al-Aqwāl al-<u>dh</u>ahabiyya* in the defence of Abū Ḥātim and criticism of Muḥammad b. Zakariyyā' and especially his *al-Ṭibb al-rūḥānī*. Not without reason Kirmānī has been called "the <u>Sh</u>ai<u>kh</u> of Ismā'īlī philosophers".[1]

The *Rāḥat al-'aql* reveals the depth of Kirmānī's knowledge of Aristotelian and Neoplatonic philosophy, the philosophy of Kindī, some of whose technical terms he employs, and the later Muslim philosophers such as Fārābī, the I<u>kh</u>wān al-Ṣafā and Ibn Sīnā. He presents a synthesis of the general principles of Islam, philosophy and Ismā'īlī doctrines and possesses many ideas similar to those of Ibn Sīnā. The celestial hierarchy issuing from the Divine creative act (*ibdā'*) characterizes his metaphysics and cosmology. The *Rāḥat al-'aql* is a systematic exposition of Ismā'īlī cosmology and metaphysics bringing together in a synthesis various components to be found in one form or another in the writings of the other members of this Fāṭimid school of Ismā'īlism.

A younger contemporary of Kirmānī, Nāṣir-i <u>Kh</u>usrau, is certainly the most influential and enduring figure of Ismā'īlism in Persia. Born in Qubā<u>dh</u>iyān near Bal<u>kh</u> in 394/1004 in a family of government

[1] See the introduction of Muḥammad Kāmil Ḥusain and Muḥammad Muṣṭafā Ḥilmī to *Rāḥat al-'aql* (Cairo, 1371/1952), p. 17.

officials, he became converted to Ismā'īlism in the middle of life, probably from Twelver Shī'ism. He spent six years in Fāṭimid Cairo, having become a high official in the Ismā'īlī hierarchy, and returned to Balkh in 444/1052 to continue his activities as a missionary in Persia. He died sometime between 465/1072 and 470/1077 in Yumgān, where his tomb is still to be found today. His tomb has become over the centuries a centre of pilgrimage as the tomb of a Ṣūfī saint and its Ismā'īlī character has been forgotten.

Seventeen works are said to have been written by Nāṣir-i Khusrau, of which nine are extant. These latter include the *Dīvān*, which is one of the masterpieces of the Persian language, *Raushanā'ī-nāma* (poetry), *Raushanā'ī-nāma* (prose), the famous *Safar-nāma*, *Wajh-i dīn*, *Zād al-musāfirīn*, *Khwān al-ikhwān*, *Gushāyish wa rahāyish* and finally his most famous work, the *Jāmi' al-ḥikmatain*. All of these works were written in Persian and represent one of the most important corpora of Persian philosophical writings.

The *Jāmi' al-ḥikmatain* (which means literally the "sum of two wisdoms") seeks to synthesize Greek philosophy and Ismā'īlī theosophy basing itself on the *Qaṣīda* of Abu'l-Haitham alluded to above. Nāṣir-i Khusrau follows the cardinal Islamic teaching of the universality of revelation and belief in the fact that there were men of other religions before Islam who possessed knowledge of Unity (*tauḥīd*) and its mysteries. Therefore he considers the ancient sages and philosophers as among the *ḥunafā* (that is, men who possessed the doctrine of tauḥīd from primordial times) and seeks to harmonize their teachings with those of Islam and its esoteric teachings as reflected in Ismā'īlism. He thus treads a course similar to that of Fārābī but in the context of Ismā'īlī theology and philosophy.

Nāṣir-i Khusrau, like Abū Ḥātim and Kirmānī, was violently opposed to the theses of Muḥammad b. Zakariyyā' Rāzī and refuted him in many of his works. He was opposed to Rāzī especially on three points: nature, the soul and prophecy.[1] Nāṣir-i Khusrau believed that nature is engendered by the cosmic soul, possesses activity and is in fact the principle of motion and rest, in contrast to the "inert" rôle assigned to it by Muḥammad b. Zakariyyā'. Nāṣir-i Khusrau also opposed the idea of Rāzī that the soul is held captive by matter. Similarly he attacked violently the "egalitarianism" of Rāzī according to which he denied prophecy, for it stands at the antipode of Nāṣir-i Khusrau's hierarchical

[1] See Corbin's Chapter 16 below.

conception of knowledge and the esotericism which in his view is reserved for the élite.

Thanks to his poetry, which is among the best examples of religious poetry in the Persian language, as well as his prose writings, Nāṣir-i Khusrau has enjoyed wide popularity in Persia to this day and has certainly been the best-known Ismā'īlī intellectual figure during the later centuries of Persian history. As a sage whose sayings enlighten the minds of men he is hardly ever thought of as being specifically Ismā'īlī. As a technical philosopher and expositor of Ismā'īlī theosophy he has attracted, outside of the Ismā'īlī community, only the attention of the intellectual élite and the few scholars concerned with the history of Islamic philosophy and theology. This latter aspect of his writings needs to be explored much more extensively and he deserves to be known for what he is, namely one of the important philosophers of Islamic Persia, who belonged to a school of thought the significance of which has not yet become fully recognized.

After Nāṣir-i Khusrau Ismā'īlī philosophy continued to flourish for some time but its development lies outside the period with which this essay is concerned. We need only mention one Persian contemporary of Nāṣir-i Khusrau because of his eminence within the Fāṭimid school of Ismā'īlī philosophers. He is Mu'ayyad Shīrāzī, who entered Cairo in 439/1047 and died in that city in 470/1077. His works remain very popular among Ismā'īlīs to this day. These works include the *Majālis* in eight volumes and 800 discourses, *al-Majālis al-mustanṣariyya* containing the author's observations on the assemblies of al-Mustanṣir bi'llāh, his *Dīvān* and the *Jāmi' al-ḥaqā'iq*, all in Arabic. His only Persian work, the *Asās al-ta'wīl*, is a translation of one of the works of Qāḍī Nu'mān.

The metaphysical basis of the doctrines contained in the writings of the Ismā'īlī philosophers from Abū Ḥātim Rāzī to Mu'ayyad Shīrāzī is the distinction between the Source of all reality as the Absolute, that is Supra-Being or Beyond-Being, and creation, which is not an effusion but rather the result of an act of the giving of being (*ibdā'*) by this Source, who is thus called *Mubdi'*. It is this feature which especially distinguishes Ismā'īlī doctrines from those of the Peripatetics, where God is considered as Pure Being from whom the states of being emanate. For the Ismā'īlīs the *Mubdi'* is the origin of being Who through the act "be!" (*kun*) brings into being (*ibdā'*) the First Intellect, which comprises the highest state of being. From the First Intellect the

Second Intellect is brought into being and so on, each state possessing its own limit (*ḥadd*) which at the same time defines it and determines the state beyond, which the lower state aspires to attain.

In the celestial hierarchy, which is generated in a manner similar to the heavenly intellects of Ibn Sīnā after the first act of ibdā', there are ten Intellects, of which the first two together correspond in their metaphysical significance to the Reality of Muḥammad (*al-ḥaqīqat al-muḥammadiyya*) of Twelve-Imām S͟hī'ism and Ṣūfism. With the Third Intellect, however, an event occurs which determines all the history of the cosmos and man, for the Third Intellect, which is the "spiritual Adam" (*Ādam-i rūḥānī*) and the prototype of man, falls into a state of negligence and stupor. Once it is awakened from this state it discovers that it has been relegated to the rank of the Tenth Intellect. Henceforth it seeks to regain its original state. The creation of the cosmos is only for this purpose, and the fundamental importance of the number seven in the Ismā'īlī scheme is based on the difference in range between the Third and the Tenth Intellect. This "retardation of eternity", if it can be so called, is the prototype of time and of history, both of which are cyclic and based on the number seven.

There are seven cycles in the history of the present humanity, in each of which there are seven prophets each with seven Imāms, or several groups of seven, and the prophets and cycles alternate through periods of manifestation or "speaking" (*nāṭiq*) and occultation or "silence" (*ṣāmit*). There is created around this cyclic idea, which has its prototype in the transhistorical drama of the negligence of the "Spiritual Adam", a remarkable cosmology, prophetology and anthropology which can hardly be set aside in any serious consideration of Islamic intellectual life and which moreover represent a most important fruit of the intellectual and philosophical life of Persia during the early Islamic centuries.

In treating Islamic philosophy during the early centuries we have spoken of figures many of whom, like Kirmānī and Ibn Sīnā, have dealt extensively with cosmology. Therefore, in speaking separately about cosmology we wish only to bring out the different types of cosmology that were developed in Persia during the early Islamic centuries. Cosmology in its traditional context is the application of metaphysical principles to the domain of contingency and is therefore inseparable in any traditional civilization from the principles of the tradition in question. This holds true as much for Islam as any other tradition. The cosmologies developed by Muslims in Persia as elsewhere are incomprehensible without recourse to the principles of Islam, of which they are applications, in the same way that the cosmology of the *Bundahishn* is related to Zoroastrianism. Even if the material for these cosmologies was drawn in some cases from non-Islamic sources, it was integrated into the Islamic view and was Islamized before being accepted.

With this principle in mind we can now turn, albeit briefly, to the different cosmologies developed by the Muslims. The first and most essential is of course the Qur'anic cosmology, based on the text of the Qur'ān and consisting of the *'arsh*, the *kursī* and the angelic hierarchy with all the symbolic imagery that is connected with them in the *Ḥadīth* literature concerning cosmology. The cosmologies based on the Qur'ān and Ḥadīth were followed by many early elaborations, both Sunnī and Shī'ī. As far as Shī'ī sources are concerned the *Uṣūl al-kāfī* of Kulainī contains many pages devoted to cosmology, which were elucidated by later commentators. The Qur'anic commentaries of the early centuries, Arab and Persian alike, also developed the cosmology implicit in the Qur'anic text itself.

Inspired by the idea of Unity and the unicity of all created things as taught by the Qur'ān, many cosmologies developed which applied these principles in different ways to the levels of cosmic existence, with the purpose of bringing out their interrelatedness and hierarchical relationship. On the one hand there was the Hermetico-alchemical cosmology developed by Jābir b. Ḥayyān and based mostly on the cosmic polarization between the active and passive principles.[1] On the other hand based on the same sources as well as others, there developed the Neopythagorean cosmology of the Brethren of Purity, who also drew from Aristotelian elements. Ismā'īlī authors elaborated their own cosmology in which the states of being were correlated with the cycles of prophets and Imams, as seen in the *Rāḥat al-'aql* of Kirmānī.

There were also the Peripatetics, who expounded a cosmology which under the guidance of the Islamic principle of *tauḥīd* integrated both Aristotelian and Neoplatonic elements into its perspective. This cosmology had its genesis with Kindī and like so many other aspects of Peripatetic philosophy reached its apogee with Ibn Sīnā. Likewise, scientific cosmologies were developed by astronomers and physicists during this period, men like Thābit b. Qurra, Bīrūnī and Ibn al-

[1] See P. Kraus, *Jābir b. Ḥayyān*, vol. II (Cairo, 1942), pp. 139ff.

Haiṯham. These, however, were never secularized and in them the cosmos continued to be viewed in the light of metaphysical principles.

Altogether the cosmological doctrines of this period of Islamic history were inseparable from the more comprehensive metaphysical doctrines in whose bosoms they grew. And like them they acquired the colour of the particular school that nurtured them. With the coming of the Saljuqs and the emphasis upon Aṣẖʿarī kalām most of the intellectual and philosophical schools of the 3rd/9th and 4th/10th centuries suffered an eclipse. But paradoxically, enriched by the very attacks of the theologians, these schools were mostly revived in the 7th/13th century in new forms that were destined to exercise a permanent influence upon the history of Islamic Persia continuing to this day.

CHAPTER 13(*b*)

ṢŪFISM

I. THE BEGINNING OF THE ṢŪFĪ TRADITION

The spiritual transformation of a people and their participation in the life of a new spiritual universe brought into being by a fresh revelation from heaven is too profound a reality to be reduced simply to socio-political or economic factors. It involves an aspect of the destiny of that people and is ingrained as an innate possibility within the religion that embraces that nation. The Islamization of Persia presents a perfect example of such a transformation. Beyond all external causes, there existed the possibility within Islam to embrace the Persians, a possibility that had to be and in fact came to be actualized fairly rapidly. And there existed in the destiny of the Persians the necessity for such a transformation, which took place in such depth that it not only altered profoundly the later phases of Persian history, but also made the religion, culture and history of the Persians inseparably intertwined with those of the rest of the Muslim world. This sharing of a common universe of discourse with other Muslims, and particularly the Arabs, is to be seen most of all in the field of Ṣūfism which deals by definition with Divine Unity and the universal order, with the realm where man stands before God not dressed in his particular ethnic or racial garb but shrouded with the light of the spirit which dwells in him and which represents his most universal aspect.

To speak of Ṣūfism in the early period of Islamic history in Persia, therefore, is to speak of the origin of Ṣūfism itself, for nowhere is it more difficult to separate Arab and Persian elements than in the Ṣūfism of these early centuries, which flourished mostly in centres where both ethnic elements were present. In some cases such as the Ṣūfīs of Egypt like Dhu'l-Nūn or Rābi'a, who hailed from Jerusalem, or Uwais al-Qaranī who came from the Yemen, one can make categorical distinctions between Arabs and Persians; but it is not possible to understand the development of Ṣūfism in Persia itself without studying such figures. We are therefore forced to speak of early Ṣūfism itself, emphasizing, however, the schools and individuals of Persian origin or associated with the Persian world. It might also be added that while Ṣūfism is a single tradition which cannot be segmented ethnically, particular types of ethnic genius have of course been able to find their fulfilment in Ṣūfism and to give it the different types of expression it has received in its outward manifestations in each ethnic world. The Persians in this sense have given their own characteristic features to the universal teachings of Ṣūfīs, as can be seen in later Persian Ṣūfī poetry. They also played a very important rôle in expounding the verities of Ṣūfism during the earlier centuries when the sole language of discourse was Arabic, and Persian had not as yet come into play.

To study the history of Ṣūfism in Persia during the first few centuries of Islamic history, we must turn to the study of the origin of Ṣūfism from the first decades of Islamic history. Ṣūfism, in its inner reality, and not necessarily in all the formulations it has adopted throughout its history to expound its perennial truths, is rooted in the Qur'ān and the *Sunna* and *Ḥadīth* of the Prophet of Islam. To become a Ṣūfī is to realize in depth the doctrine of unity (*tauḥīd*) contained in the Holy Book and to live a life based on the model of the life of the Prophet.

Ṣūfism was not the creation of any particular race, whether it be Arab, Persian or Indian, but a Divine "Mystery" contained inwardly within the Qur'anic revelation and instructed by the Prophet to a few of his choice Companions, who in turn transmitted this esoteric knowledge to their worthy students and disciples.

The word *ṣūfī* is generally said to have been used for the first time in the 2nd/8th century by Abū Hāshim al-Ṣūfī, while according to the *Kitāb al-luma'* of Abū Naṣr al-Sarrāj,[1] Ḥasan al-Baṣrī, who died in 110/728, had already used it in the famous sentence "I saw a Ṣūfī circumambulating ... (*ra'aitu ṣūfiyyan fi'l-ṭawāf* ...)". The spiritual élite in the earlier generations were called *ṣaḥābī*, then *ahl al-ṣuffa*, then *tābi'ī*, then *'ābid*, *zāhid*, *nāsik*, etc. Only in the second Islamic century did the term *ṣūfī*, whose origin has been discussed extensively in both traditional and modern sources, come to replace all these appellations and to denote in itself the class of men who devoted themselves fully to the spiritual life in Islam and after receiving initiation trod the spiritual path (*ṭarīqa*). Among the class of the earliest spiritual figures and ascetics (*zuhhād*) most were of course Arabs but there were also some Persians who in fact increased in number as the centre of Ṣūfism

[1] Ed. R. A. Nicholson (Leiden, 1914), p. 22.

became established in Baṣra and later Baghdad and Khurāsān. While Khurāsān is integrally Persian, all the activity that was carried out in Baṣra and Baghdad must also be included in any comprehensive study of Ṣūfism in the Persian world, because Arabic and Persian elements in these two centres were so mixed that it is impossible to separate them in any meaningful way.

The assertion of the truth that Ṣūfism existed from the beginning and only gained a new name in the 2nd/8th century and that it is a continuous tradition with its roots in the Qur'ān and its branches stretching over all the periods and lands of Islam, might be opposed by some who would point to the "development" of Ṣūfism from early asceticism to a mysticism of love and finally to gnosis. This apparent "development" does not however contradict the assertion, which the Ṣūfīs themselves have repeated over the ages, of the continuity of the Ṣūfī tradition and its Qur'anic roots. It is true that there is a gradual movement in the historical unfolding of Ṣūfism from the emphasis upon fear (*makhāfa*) to love (*maḥabba*), then to gnosis or sapiental knowledge (*ma'rifa*). In fact Ṣūfism in a sense recapitulates within its own history the unfolding of the ternary aspects of the Abrahamic Tradition in which Judaism emphasizes fear, Christianity love, and Islam knowledge of God. But in the same way that this emphasis does not mean exclusivity and that one finds in Judaism a place for the love and knowledge of God, in Christianity certain modes of spirituality based upon fear and knowledge, and in Islam a gnosis that is never divorced from love or fear, so does one find in Ṣūfism the presence of love and knowledge from the beginning; only the accent changes as the tradition unfolds.

From the early Mesopotamian ascetics, who emphasize the aspect of Divine Majesty and man's fear and awe before Him, to Rābi'a, Ḥallāj and Aḥmad al-Ghazzālī, who speak especially of love and finally to 'Ain al-Quḍāt al-Hamadānī and Ibn 'Arabī, who emphasize gnosis (*'irfān*), there is, needless to say, a "movement" and change of emphasis. But first of all, because of the gnostic character of Islamic spirituality itself, the element of knowledge is present throughout the tradition of Ṣūfism. Secondly, even among the early Ṣūfīs all the basic elements, including maḥabba and ma'rifa, exist and are discussed by certain figures. And thirdly, although the accent shifts in the historical unfolding of Ṣūfism from fear to love to knowledge, all of these possibilities existed from the beginning in the seed contained in the soil of the revelation and were later manifested according to the laws of the life cycle of the tradition. The manifestation of Ṣūfism in its various phases, or what appears outwardly as its "development", if viewed with discernment is itself proof of the continuity of a living, spiritual tradition rooted in the world of the spirit, in the same way that the ages through which man passes are themselves the best proof of the fact that he is alive and that his life possesses organic continuity.

These different phases of Ṣūfism, which must be viewed as the unfolding of a permanent truth rather than either a progress or a deviation as some have thought, make evident the falsity of the claim made by certain modern scholars to identify the ascetic and "dry" phase of Ṣūfism exclusively with the Arabs and the "warm" type of Ṣūfism in which love plays a major rôle with the Persians. Although, as already mentioned, ethnic temperament does play a rôle in the expression of spirituality, and Ṣūfism has adapted itself for people with completely different types of psychic and mental make-up, this type of identification of Persians or Arabs with one kind of Ṣūfism is simply an error. The element of asceticism (*zuhd*), as well as love and knowledge, is to be found among both Persian and Arab Ṣūfīs as well as among Ṣūfīs of other nations such as the Turks and Indians who embraced Islam later. One finds pure gnostics and esotericists among early Ṣūfīs in both the Persian and the Arab worlds, for example Abū Yazīd al-Bisṭāmī and Dhu'l-Nūn al-Miṣrī. In the same way one finds in both worlds Ṣūfīs who composed exquisite poems using the language of love, as for example 'Aṭṭār and Ibn al-Fāriḍ. Therefore, rather than identifying the main types of expression of Ṣūfism with a particular ethnic group, it is more meaningful to state that the Persians and Arabs have shared in the unfolding of the life cycle of the Ṣūfī tradition in which they have both participated and that Ṣūfism in both parts of the Islamic world has unfolded itself through a cycle which embraces the three stages of makhāfa, maḥabba and ma'rifa.

In the same way that the unity of Ṣūfism is preserved in spite of ethnic divisions by means of its elaborate teaching about the spiritual hierarchy, so is this unity continued by means of the hierarchy of invisible men (*rijāl al-ghaib*) who rule over the human world and play an especially important function in initiation and the connection of the spiritual master with the spiritual world. After the Prophet the first spiritual poles (*quṭb*) were among the Arabs, save for Salmān who was a Persian. As for Shī'ism, the Imāms, who play the same rôle as the quṭb in Ṣūfism, belong of course to the "Household of the Prophet". But in the later history of Ṣūfism the different levels of the spiritual hierarchy (the *abdāl*, *autād*, etc.) were connected to the Arab and Persian world alike and many Persian Ṣūfīs, such as Abu'l-Ḥasan al-Kharraqānī, were considered as the supreme pole (quṭb) of their time. Here again the fundamental unity of Ṣūfism imposed itself upon all ethnic diversities and the "development" of Ṣūfism in Persia has remained throughout history organically bound with the Ṣūfī tradition in its totality.

During the early centuries, even more than the later ones, not only the doctrine and method but also the outward expression and transmission of teaching was contained within a single whole embracing all Muslims. The journeys of the Egyptian Dhu'l-Nūn to the East and his many Persian disciples, one of whom, Yūsuf b. Ḥusain al-Rāzī, preserved and distributed his sayings, or the number of Arab disciples of the Persian Junaid, are far from being exceptional. Rather, they represent the rule during the early centuries when personal encounters between outstanding Ṣūfīs of different lands occurred often, and when Ṣūfīs from the eastern and western lands of Islam usually travelled to the central areas of Iraq and Persia as well as, of course, to the holy cities to make the pilgrimage and to meet the Ṣūfīs of those regions.

II. THE SPREAD OF ṢŪFISM AMONG THE PERSIANS

The first link between the Persians and Ṣūfism is through the same figure who was the first among them to make contact with Islam. Reputedly the first Persian to have embraced Islam, Salmān-i Fārsī or Salmān-i Pāk, is among the foremost of the early Ṣūfīs (counted among the ahl al-ṣuffa) and one of the few to have received the esoteric message of Islam directly from the Prophet. The exemplary life of the Persian in quest of the true Prophet, the seeker of the truth who after a period of slavery finally found his way to Medina, is told in many versions in both Sunnī and Shī'ī sources. Salmān became so attached to the Prophet that he was given the honour by the Prophet himself to be a member of his household (*Salmān min ahl baitinā*). Traditional biographies mention that he was one of the sixteen Companions who were allowed to participate in the rite of fraternization when the Prophet arrived in Medina. After the Prophet, Salmān became a close companion of 'Alī and was for a while the governor of Madā'in where he continued to live in simplicity; and he died there in 35/655 or 36/656. His mausoleum is found to this day in that location, being a centre of pilgrimage for people of all schools.

Salmān was respected later by Sunnīs and Shī'īs alike. The Ṣūfīs in the Sunnī world honour him as one of their greatest early forerunners and Ibn 'Arabī even considers him the prototype of the spiritual pole (quṭb). Shī'īs view him as one of the foremost members of the early Shī'ī community and a main factor in the spread of the teachings of 'Alī, especially in interpreting the meaning of the Qur'ān. Certain extremist sects such as the Nuṣairīs even consider Salmān as being the archangel Gabriel himself who brought the revelation. In the alphabetical symbolism of certain Shī'ī schools *mīm* stands for Muḥammad, *'ain* for 'Alī and *sīn* for Salmān, and it is said that sīn symbolizes initiation and is the necessary link between mīm and 'ain or between prophecy and the imāmate.[1]

Putting aside his important rôle in Twelver and Ismā'īlī Shī'ism as well as in many different sects from the Nuṣairīs to the Musha'sha'a, Salmān remains the primordial link between Persia and Ṣūfism. It is noteworthy that in the earliest Islamic community, besides the Arabs, there were a Persian and a Black African, Salmān and Bilāl, whose very presence symbolized the future spread of Islam among these peoples. Moreover, the esoteric function of Salmān and his important rôle in early Ṣūfism was also a symbol of the later spread of Ṣūfism among the Persians and the important rôle of the Persians in the exposition and orchestration of the teachings of Ṣūfism.

After Salmān, the generation of zuhhād spread the teachings which later gained the name of Ṣūfism. Baṣra soon became the centre for these teachings and through its influence the schools of Baghdad, Khurāsān and Egypt came into being. The Persians were involved in all of these schools, save the Egyptian, and produced many outstanding Ṣūfīs during this early period. But Salmān continued to dominate the horizon and remain in the memory of later generations as the earliest link between the Persians and the tree of prophecy whose branches were to spread so rapidly during the following decades and whose spiritual flowers were to blossom so remarkably in the schools of Baṣra, Baghdad and Khurāsān from the 2nd/8th century onward.

[1] On the different sects based on the relations between *mīm*, *'ain* and *sīn*, see L. Massignon, "Salman Pak et les prémices spirituelles de l'Islam iranien" in *Opera Minora*, vol. 1 (Beirut, 1963), pp. 470–2.

III. THE EARLY GENERATIONS OF ṢŪFĪS AND THE SCHOOL OF BAṢRA

The first manifestations of Ṣūfism, in reality if not as yet in name, are to be found, after the Prophet, ʿAlī and a few other of the closest Companions, in several of the figures who came to be known throughout the early community for their asceticism and piety. Among the earliest of these figures was Abu'l-Dardā', himself one of the Companions, who emphasized the importance of meditation (*tafakkur*) and claimed that reverential fear (*taqwā*) was preferable to forty years of worship (*ʿibāda*) without taqwā. In him are to be seen the characteristics which have always distinguished the Ṣūfīs from the rest of the community.

Another early figure respected by Ṣūfīs and Shīʿīs alike, Abū Dharr al-Ghifārī, was an intimate companion of ʿAlī. While participating in political movements for the sake of social justice and opposing the Umayyads for religious reasons, he lived a strict life of simplicity combined with great asceticism and emphasized the purity resulting from the cleansing of the soul, which lies at the heart of Ṣūfism. His contemporary Ḥudhaifa b. Yamān was also opposed to political injustice and misrule. But he did not support any form of revolt. Like Abū Dharr he also lived a life of simplicity and emphasized the importance of the purity of the heart for the attainment of perfection of faith. A few years his younger, ʿImrān b. Ḥusain al-Khuzāʿī lived in Baṣra and was renowned as the most pious and the greatest of the Companions still living in that city when he died in 52/672. He lived a life devoted completely to religious worship and trained some disciples, of whom the most famous was Ḥasan al-Baṣrī. Finally, belonging to the same group of early saints is the famous Uwais al-Qaranī, the Yemenite, who never met the Prophet but became his disciple from far away. He became among the choicest of the Companions and fought with ʿAlī at Ṣiffīn. Few men in the history of Ṣūfism have left as profound an influence as Uwais, who became the prototype of a particular type of spirituality in Islam.

All these early saints of the first generation were Arabs but their relation with the spiritual life of Persia was profound, especially as far as Abū Dharr and Uwais are concerned. Abū Dharr has remained to this day a Persian national hero. His feats and actions are still celebrated from the pulpit of mosques and his spiritual station is looked upon with respect by the Persian Ṣūfīs. As for Uwais, he has exercised the deepest influence in the development of Ṣūfism in Persia. The type of Ṣūfī who is initiated into the Way and guided by the "invisible master" or al-Khaḍir (Khiḍr in Persian) without the intercession of a living master can be seen throughout Persian history and even today there are many "Uwaisīs", one of whom, the late Muḥammad Ṣādiq 'Anqā', was among the most accomplished spiritual figures of Persia during this century.

The founder of the Baṣra school of Ṣūfism, which is itself the source for all later Ṣūfī schools, is the celebrated Ḥasan al-Baṣrī, who was born in Medina in 21/642, the son of a Persian slave, and who died after a long and fruitful life in Baṣra in 110/728. The story of his conversion, apocryphal though it is, has become famous in the annals of Ṣūfī literature especially as told by 'Aṭṭār in the *Tadhkirat al-auliyā'*.[1] Ḥasan is well-known as a transmitter of prophetic ḥadīth and also as the founder of Kalām in its formal phase of development. In addition he is the patriarch of Ṣūfism, the head of the spiritual chain (*silsila*) of many orders and also one of the founders of craft initiation in Islam. He was also an exegete of the Qur'ān and an outstanding orator.

Although famous and in an exalted social position, Ḥasan lived a life of complete purity and asceticism like his saintly predecessors. He based Ṣūfism upon fear of God (*wara'*) and detachment from the world or asceticism (*zuhd*). His famous letter to the pious Umayyad Caliph 'Umar b. 'Abd al-'Azīz begins with these lines: "Beware of this world with all wariness; for it is like to a snake, smooth to the touch, but its venom is deadly. Turn away from whatsoever delights thee in it, for the little companioning thou wilt have of it; put off from thee its cares, for that thou hast seen its sudden chances, and knowest for sure that thou shalt be parted from it; endure firmly its hardship, for the ease that shalt presently be thine . . ."[2]

Ḥasan's teachings were not limited only to the purgation of the soul of its earthly defilements. He also spoke of gnosis, of the direct vision of God in paradise, and of the significance of the nocturnal ascension (*mi'rāj*) of the Prophet. He analysed the different spiritual states (*aḥvāl*) so much developed in later Ṣūfism, and emphasized the significance of meditation (*fikr*) in the spiritual life.[3] Altogether, many of the

[1] 'Aṭṭār, *Muslim Saints and Mystics*, tr. A. J. Arberry (London, 1966), pp. 20–2.
[2] A. J. Arberry, *Sufism*, p. 33.
[3] On the aḥvāl see Naṣr, *Sufi Essays*, Chapter 5, and C. Rice, *Persian Sufis*, Chapter 5.

fundamental aspects of Ṣūfism were formulated by Ḥasan and he left a profound and enduring influence upon nearly all later schools of Ṣūfism throughout the Islamic world. He has been remembered by posterity not only through his works and orations but chiefly through the training of many disciples and the establishment of a school. Perhaps the most famous member of this circle was the woman saint Rābi'a al-'Adwiya, who was born in Jerusalem but lived and died in Baṣra, and was the first among Ṣūfīs to develop the theme of Divine love and union.

IV. THE SCHOOL OF KHURĀSĀN

From its early home in Baṣra and also to a certain degree in Kūfa Ṣūfism spread to two main centres, Khurāsān and Baghdad, each of which became the home of a school known by the name of that locality. The school of Khurāsān, whose members Junaid called the "people of the heart", was known especially for its emphasis upon poverty and indifference towards the opinion of the public, even to the extent of inviting their blame (*malāma*) and accusation. It is not accidental that the school of the Malāmatiyya, that is the people who invited blame upon themselves, associated with Ḥamdūn al-Qaṣṣār, arose in Khurāsān and had most of its later development there.

The founder of the school of Khurāsān, one of the earliest of Ṣūfīs, is Ibrāhīm b. Adham, who was born in Balkh around 100/718 and died probably in Syria around 165/782, although many other localities in the vicinity of the Muslim–Byzantine borders have also been mentioned as the site of his death. The story of the conversion of Ibrāhīm is one of the most celebrated in the annals of Ṣūfism. It is an echo of the story of the conversion of Shakyamuni Buddha from the life of a prince to that of an illuminated being. The story is not just a fictitious tale of later origin. It is an echo in the bosom of Islam of an archetypal reality which found its supreme manifestation in the life of the Buddha. Ibrāhīm, like Prince Gautama, was from a royal family in Balkh, itself a centre of Buddhism before Islam. He became attracted to Ṣūfism through contact with the school of Imām Ja'far al-Ṣādiq by way of Ṣufyān al-Thaurī with whom he corresponded. As a result he left his princely life for one of severe asceticism and poverty in Syria and adjacent areas where he also encountered some saintly Christian monks including a Father Simeon, his meeting with whom was an occasion for the descent of gnosis into his heart. Ibrāhīm emphasized the importance of silence. As Abū Nu'aim recounts in his *Ḥilyat al-auliyā'*, Ibrāhīm said, concerning the way of serving God: "The beginning of service is meditation and silence, save for the invocation and recollection (*dhikr*) of God."[1] Already the supreme method of realization of Ṣūfism is alluded to by this early saint, whose memory has been kept alive through the centuries not only as recounted by Ibn Baṭṭūṭa when he visited his tomb in the 8th/14th century, but even today by the stories of the lives of saints as they are told in *khānaqāhs* and, on a more popular level, in inns by storytellers. He is also remembered for the transmission of two sacred traditions (*ḥadīth qudsī*).[2]

Of Ibrāhīm's students the most famous is Shaqīq al-Balkhī (d. 194/810) who emphasized the importance of reliance upon God (*tawakkul*) and was the first Ṣūfī to define it as a spiritual state (*ḥāl*). He was also much concerned with giving a more systematic character to the self-discipline which lies at the heart of Ṣūfism and which was developed to such an extent by the Ṣūfīs of the next centuries. Some of the sayings of Shaqīq on spiritual discipline are recorded by his student Ḥātim al-Aṣamm who was himself a leading member of the school of Khurāsān but who also spent some time in Baghdad, returning to Khurāsān to die near Tirmidh in 237/852.

Other important figures of the Khurāsānī school in the early period include 'Abd-Allāh b. Mubārak (d. 181/797) who was known as an authority on ḥadīth, Fuḍail b. 'Iyāḍ (d. 187/803) who is responsible for the transmission of a "sacred tradition", and in the 3rd/9th century such men as Abū Turāb al-Nakhshabī (d. 240/854), Ibn Karrām (d. 255/869) and Yaḥyā b. Mu'ādh al-Rāzī (d. 258/872). After being influenced by the later development of Ṣūfism in Baghdad and elsewhere, the Khurāsān school gave birth to some of the most celebrated Ṣūfīs of later centuries, from Bāyazīd to Abū Sa'īd b. Abi'l-Khair and finally to the great Ṣūfī poets of the Persian language starting with Sanā'ī.

V. THE SCHOOL OF BAGHDAD

Almost contemporary and parallel with the school of Khurāsān there grew the school of Baghdad which was direct heir to Baṣra and Kūfa but whose origins are also related to Khurāsān. The foundation of this school is attributed in traditional sources to Ma'rūf al-Karkhī (d. 200/815), the simple and probably illiterate companion of Imām Riḍā, the

[1] Arberry, *Sufism*, p. 37.

[2] Anawati and Gardet, p. 31.

eighth Shī'ī Imām who died and was buried near Ṭūs in Khurāsān. Karkhī's disciple, Sarī al-Saqaṭī (d. 253/867), who was also a simple man, dealing in second hand goods, was the uncle of the celebrated Junaid. Actually not only the school of Baghdad but the whole of later Ṣūfism has been influenced by the writings of two men of that school, namely Muḥāsibī and Junaid, who, although of somewhat different temperament and possessing different approaches to Ṣūfism, provided, each in his own way, the early intellectual and doctrinal formulations of Ṣūfism.

Al-Ḥārith b. Asad al-Muḥāsibī "whose preserved writings may truly be said to have formed to a large extent the pattern of all subsequent [Ṣūfī] thought"[1] was born in Baṣra in 165/781 but spent most of his life in Baghdad where he died in 243/857. A master of the religious sciences, especially Ḥadīth and Kalām, he wrote the first systematic works on Ṣūfism, which have carried an immense influence. His masterpiece, the *al-Ri'āya li ḥuqūq Allāh* was definitely the model for Ghazzālī's *Iḥyā' 'ulūm al-dīn* as his *al-Waṣāyā* served as source of inspiration for Ghazzālī's much more celebrated *al-Munqidh min al-ḍalāl*. His *Kitāb al-tawahhum* dealing with eschatology left its profound marks on the last section of the *Iḥyā'*. In this same book Ghazzālī speaks about Muḥāsibī in these terms: "He harmonized and combined the science of the Truth (*ḥaqīqa*) and the science of the law (*sharī'a*). He spoke to the people in a manner comfortable to their condition. As a result the doctors of jurisprudence (*fuqahā*) had confidence in him as did the Ṣūfīs."[2]

The characteristic approach of Muḥāsibī to Ṣūfism is the examination or taking account (*muḥāsaba*) of the conscience, from which he in fact took the title by which he has been known throughout history. Muḥāsibī developed the method, still emphasized in many Ṣūfī orders, by which the adept examines methodically the fruits of his action in the light of the rights of God and the effect of these actions upon the soul. This is a way to purify the soul from the negative effects of evil actions and prevent the concordant reaction from defiling the soul. In this way and through serving God alone a transformation takes place within man leading to an actualization of wisdom within him. Muḥāsibī develops this fundamental theme in his chief work *al-Ri'āya*, taking into

[1] Arberry, *Sufism*, p. 46.

[2] Quoted in the Arabic introduction of A. Amīn, *Kitāb al-tawahhum*, ed. A. J. Arberry Cairo, 1937), p. *dāl*.

consideration the relation between human action and the intentions behind them as well as the effect of different vices and evils upon the soul. The work is a masterpiece of Ṣūfī psychology and contains many insights into the relationship between the psyche and physical acts on the one hand and the psyche and the spirit on the other.

In his *Kitāb al-tawahhum*, Muḥāsibī turns to the question of the after-life and man's posthumous becoming until he is blessed with the supreme vision. In this remarkable work the transformation of man's vision from the sensual to the spiritual is described in majestic terms. Finally mention must be made of his treatise on love (*Faṣl fi'l-maḥabba*), preserved only partially, in which he discusses the love of God in unprecedented terms. Because of these, and also his properly speaking theological works, Muḥāsibī must be considered one of the most important intellectual figures of early Islamic history, a man who left an indelible mark on Ṣūfism as well as on Kalām and the Islamic religious sciences in general.

With Abu'l-Qāsim al-Junaid, who was born in Nihāvand, or possibly in Baghdad from parents who had migrated from Nihāvand, around 210/825, we reach the other peak of the school of Baghdad. Junaid studied first law and Ḥadīth and only later was he attracted to Ṣūfism, becoming a disciple of Muḥāsibī. He lived a long life in Baghdad, where he died in 298/910 and where his tomb is to be found to this day. This most famous master of the school of Baghdad trained many disciples and wrote a number of treatises, many in the form of letters, which have preserved his influence throughout Islamic history. Few Ṣūfīs have ever gained the degree of fame and universal acceptance enjoyed by Junaid, the master of the "sober" school of Ṣūfism.

Junaid was the first Ṣūfī to have discussed in depth the meaning of spiritual union. With him the early development of Ṣūfī doctrine reaches its peak. In his exposition of Ṣūfism he was, moreover, more of a pure gnostic than Muḥāsibī and opposed the employment of Kalām in the way that can be seen in the writings of the latter. Junaid was also completely opposed to the rationalist Kalām of the Mu'tazilites, who were all-powerful in Baghdad during his days. He thus formulated the Ṣūfī doctrine of Unity (*tauḥīd*) in sharp contrast to the theological definition of the Mu'tazilites. In a definition that has become famous in the history of Ṣūfism and even among doctors of law and theologians, Junaid defines Unity as follows: "*al-tauḥīd ifrād al-qadīm 'an al-muḥdath*" ("Unification is the separation of the Eternal from that which has originated in time"). The whole doctrine of Junaid may be said to depend upon the two principles of tauḥīd and sobriety (*ṣaḥw*), the first of which is the goal and the second his method of realizing it.

Ṣūfīs distinguish between two schools or spiritual styles in Ṣūfism: that of "drunkenness" (*sukr*) and that of sobriety (*ṣaḥw*). In the early period Junaid may be said to be the chief representative of the second and Bāyazīd of the first. Junaid defines ṣaḥw as follows:

He is himself, after he has not been truly himself. He is present in himself and in God after having been present in God and absent in himself. This is because he has left the intoxication of God's overwhelming *g͟halaba* (victory), and comes to the clarity of sobriety, and contemplation is once more restored to him so that he can put everything in its right place and assess it correctly. Once more he assumes his individual attributes, after *fanā'*. His personal qualities persist in him, and his actions in this world, when he has reached the zenith of spiritual achievement vouchsafed by God, become a pattern for his fellow men.[1]

This doctrine implies that after the sukr caused by annihilation (*fanā'*) there is a "return" to the state of subsistence (*baqā'*) which for Junaid is the same as ṣaḥw and which implies a full realization of tauḥīd. To comprehend fully the process of the realization of tauḥīd, whose end is ṣaḥw, it is essential to understand two cardinal doctrines, to each of which Junaid in fact devoted a separate treatise, namely, covenant (*mīt͟hāq*) and annihilation (*fanā'*). Junaid refers to the famous Qur'anic verse "And (remember) when thy Lord brought forth from the Children of Adam, from their reins, their seed, and made them testify of themselves, (saying): Am I not your Lord? They said: Yea, verily. We testify",[2] of which he gives the esoteric meaning that has been repeated over the ages by Ṣūfīs. He says concerning this verse:

In this verse God tells you that He spoke to them at a time when they did not exist, except so far as they existed in Him. This existence is not the same type of existence as is usually attributed to God's creatures; it is a type of existence which only God knows and only He is aware of. God knows their existence; embracing them he sees them in the beginning when they are non-existent and unaware of their future existence in this world. The existence of these is timeless.[3]

Man possesses a mode of being in the Divine which is infinitely more real than his terrestrial existence. Fanā' and baqā' or ṣaḥw mean first a

[1] *Ibid.*, p. 90.

[2] Qur'ān vii. 172 (Pickthall translation), and S. H. Naṣr, *Ideals and Realities of Islam*, pp. 25–6.

[3] Ali Abdel-Kader, *The Life, Personality and Writings of al-Junayd*, p. 76.

loss of one's terrestrial existence and then a realization of one's self as one is and has always been in God, in that state when man said, "Yea". Through fanā' man must die to himself in order to be born *in divinis* and to become once again what he has always been and *is* in reality. This is the true end of mystical union whereby man returns to his divine mode of existence in the state before he was even endowed with the separative existence of a creaturely kind.

Junaid trained many disciples, both Arab and Persian, who are themselves among the celebrated figures of Ṣūfism. Abū Bakr al-Shiblī, his close companion (d. 334/946), was constantly in a state of divine attraction (*jadhb*) and was finally committed to an asylum. His constant companion Abu'l-Ḥusain al-Nūrī (d. 295/908) composed many beautiful Ṣūfī poems which gained prominence as a new literary style. Abū Sa'īd al-A'rābī (d. 341/952) composed the first "history" of Ṣūfism, entitled *Ṭabaqāt al-nussāk*, while another direct disciple of Junaid, Abū Muḥammad Ja'far al-Khuldī, composed the *Ḥikāyāt al-auliyā'*, so highly esteemed by the scholars of Baghdad during the following century. Both these important hagiographies have been lost but many fragments of them have survived in later works. Moreover, both were very influential in the large systematic studies of Ṣūfism that appeared in the 4th/11th century.

The best-known disciple of Junaid was of course Ḥusain b. Manṣūr al-Ḥallāj, the most striking figure of early Ṣūfism, whose words have echoed throughout the history of Ṣūfism and who has also become well known to the West thanks to the indefatigable efforts of L. Massignon. Born around 244/858 near Baiḍā' in Fārs in southern Persia, he studied in Baghdad and visited Mecca. Then he started a long series of journeys which were to take him throughout Persia, Central Asia and India. Everywhere he spoke openly of esoteric knowledge and union with God and found it his vocation to arouse the religious conscience of men by throwing before everyone the pearls of wisdom which Ṣūfism reserves for the spiritual élite. He finally returned to Baghdad, continuing to scandalize the public through his open divulgence of the divine mysteries until finally, accused of preaching against the principles of Islam, he was condemned to death and crucified in 309/921. His open espousal of death and the manner in which he died in the cause of Ṣūfism left an indelible impression upon the Muslim mind in a manner which Massignon has compared to the "passion" in its Christian setting, although of course the scale of the two is quite different. Later Ṣūfīs from 'Aṭṭār, Suhravardī, Ibn 'Arabī and Rūmī to the saints and sages of the last centuries have all re-echoed the unforgettable utterances of Ḥallāj, especially the "I am the Truth" (*ana'l-ḥaqq*) for which he was particularly condemned. Of course from the Ṣūfī point of view it was not the ego or *nafs* of Ḥallāj making this utterance which would have been blasphemous, but God within him as is in fact the case in all the theophonic locutions or paradoxes (*s̲h̲aṭḥiyyāt*) of the Ṣūfīs.

Ḥallāj is the first great poet of Ṣūfism to leave behind a voluminous amount of poetry. Some of his poems are among the finest mystical verses of the Arabic language and he has often been ranked along with Ibn al-Fāriḍ and Ibn 'Arabī as one of the outstanding Ṣūfī poets of the Arabic language. It is of interest to note that before choosing Persian poetry as their vehicle of expression, Persian Ṣūfīs made outstanding contributions to Arabic Ṣūfī poetry of which Ḥallāj's poems form a significant part. How simply and beautifully has Ḥallāj expressed mystical union in these immortal verses:

I am He Whom I love and He whom I love is I,
We are two spirits indwelling one body
When thou seest me, thou seest Him,
And when thou seest Him, then thou doest see us both.

VI. THE DEVELOPMENT OF ṢŪFISM IN PERSIA AFTER JUNAID

Based upon the early development of Ṣūfism in K̲h̲urāsān and benefiting fully from the teachings of the school of Baghdad, Ṣūfism spread extensively in Persia during the middle and latter parts of the 3rd/9th and throughout the 4th/10th century. Although most of the outstanding figures continued to rise from K̲h̲urāsān, which for this reason was called the "land whose product is saints", men of eminence in Ṣūfism began to appear in other parts of Persia, although during this period at least most of them still had contact with the masters of K̲h̲urāsān. Ḥallāj is an exception in that he went from Fārs to Tustar and then Baghdad; but even he was deeply influenced by Bāyazīd Bisṭāmī who hailed from K̲h̲urāsān.

An outstanding Ṣūfī of the 3rd/9th century and a contemporary of Junaid but not of his school is Ibn Karrām, who was born in Sīstān around 190/806, studied in K̲h̲urāsān and then after making the pilgrimage to Mecca returned to Sīstān. But because of numerous difficulties that he encountered in his homeland and also in K̲h̲urāsān especially in Nī<u>sh</u>āpūr where he was imprisoned for some time, he left Persia for Jerusalem where he preached at the mosque of the Dome of the Rock. After a life spent in strict asceticism he died in that city in 260/873 and beside his tomb was constructed a *madrasa* and the *<u>kh</u>ānaqāh* of the Karrāmiyya school named after him. Ibn Karrām was both a Ṣūfī and a theologian. In his writings he revised the technical vocabulary of both Ṣūfism and kalām. He stood theologically between the traditionalist school which opposed rationalist kalām altogether and the Mu'tazilites who supported fully the rationalist approach. His influence is in fact to be seen most of all in the Māturīdī school. His ideas travelled far and wide and were known as far away as India. He also trained many disciples of whom the most famous is Yaḥyā b. Mu'ā<u>dh</u> Rāzī of Nī<u>sh</u>āpūr who died in 258/871.

A contemporary of Ibn Karrām who dominated the spiritual horizons of Ṣūfism in <u>Kh</u>urāsān at that time is Bāyazīd of Bisṭām, one of the most famous of all Ṣūfīs, who died in Bisṭām near the present-day city of <u>Sh</u>āhrūd in 261/874, where his tomb and even the cell where he made his spiritual retreat (*<u>kh</u>alwa*) stand to this day. Bāyazīd was a pure gnostic of the highest order who lived nearly all of his life in the mountains of Māzandarān and Gurgān. He left little behind in writing save a few supplications (*munājāt*) and theophonic locutions (*<u>sh</u>aṭḥiyyāt*), which were later assembled and commented upon by Rūzbahān Baqlī of <u>Sh</u>īrāz. But these few lines and verses are sufficient to establish him as one of the foremost "esotericists" in Islam, a person who expressed the purest teachings of Ṣūfism in a language that can only be comprehended through the vision provided by gnosis. He was the foremost representative of the so-called "intoxicated" school of Ṣūfism and influenced immensely even some of the students of Junaid, the master of the "sober" school, of whom Ḥallāj must be especially mentioned.

Bāyazīd, or Abū Yazīd as he is also called, has been accused once again of incorporating Vedantic teachings into Ṣūfism. R. C. Zaehner, who is the latest to present this argument, points to several elements such as the resemblance between the term *<u>kh</u>ud'a* used by Bāyazīd and *maya*, the famous saying of Bāyazīd "Glory be to me" (*subḥānī*) and "Homage, homage to me" (*mahyam eva namo namaḥ*) of *Bṛhatsannyāsa Upaniṣad*, the resemblance of his "thou art that" (*anta <u>dh</u>āka*) with the famous Vedantic *tat tvam asi* and the fact that his spiritual teacher was Abū 'Alī al-Sindī who is claimed to be a convert from Hinduism.[1] But

[1] R. C. Zaehner, *Hindu and Muslim Mysticism* (London, 1960), p. 95.

as already shown by Arberry[1] none of these arguments can withstand serious criticism. What we observe in the case of Bāyazīd is not a borrowing from the Vedanta but an expression of purely Islamic gnosis (*'irfān*), which because of its very nature closely resembles pure gnosis in any other tradition, including of course Hinduism, where the purely esoteric and gnostic teachings are found in the Vedantic school.

The locutions of Bāyazīd all echo the state of supreme union which he had reached through years of travelling upon the path and purifying his spirit through catharsis (*tajrīd*) of all limitation and darkness. It is related that someone knocked on the door of Bāyazīd. He asked, "Whom do you want?" The man said, "I want Bāyazīd." Bāyazīd answered, "For thirty years Bāyazīd has been looking for Bāyazīd and has not been able to find him. How can you see him?" Another of his sayings is, "Oh God, thou hast become my mirror and I have become thy mirror."[2] These and many other sayings reveal the exalted degree of esoteric knowledge possessed by him and the supreme realization which he gained by traversing all the stages of the Path and "unpeeling" all the outer shells of his own being until he reached the centre of the heart where resides the "Throne of the Compassionate" (*'arsh al-Raḥmān*).

Besides his importance in expounding the mysteries of tajrīd, fanā' and baqā', Bāyazīd is especially known in the history of Ṣūfism as the first person to have described fully the esoteric meaning of the nocturnal ascension (*mi'rāj*) of the Prophet and to have written his own experience of it. Bāyazīd's account as told by Hujvīrī is as follows:

> I saw that my spirit was borne to the heavens. It looked at nothing and gave no heed, though Paradise and Hell were displayed to it, for it was free of phenomena and veils. Then I became a bird, whose body was of Oneness and whose wings were of Everlastingness, and I continued to fly in the air of the Absolute, until I passed into the sphere of Purification, and gazed upon the field of Eternity and beheld there the tree of Oneness. When I looked I myself was all those. I cried: "O Lord, with my egoism I cannot attain thee, and I cannot escape from my selfhood. What am I to do?" God spake, "O Abū Yazīd, thou must win release from thy thou-ness by following my Beloved [*sc.* Muḥammad]. Smear thine eyes with the dust of his feet and follow him continually."[3]

[1] A. J. Arberry, "Bistamiana", *BSOAS*, vol. xxv, part 1 (1962), pp. 28–37.

[2] Baqlī, *Sharḥ-i shaṭḥiyyāt* ["Commentaire sur les paradoxes des soufis"], ed. H. Corbin (Tehrān–Paris, 1966), pp. 102, 105.

[3] Arberry, *Sufism*, pp. 54–5.

The spiritual mi'rāj, which is an emulation of the example of the Prophet, became the supreme model for Ṣūfīs to follow and its details become more elaborated by later Ṣūfīs and poets such as Sanā'ī and Abu'l-'Alā al-Ma'arrī. It even found a permanent place in the Christian world by becoming incorporated into the structure of the *Divine Comedy* by Dante, where again the spiritual experience is depicted as a journey through the cosmos and the various levels of universal existence.

Another Ṣūfī from Khurāsān whose expositions of Ṣūfism had a definite intellectual and gnostic character was Abū 'Abd-Allāh Muḥammad b. 'Alī al-Tirmidhī, known in the history of Ṣūfism as Ḥakīm Tirmidhī, who was born during the first quarter of the 3rd/9th century and died somewhere around its end probably in Tirmidh, where his tomb is said to be located. The details of his life are obscure and only the general contours can be discerned, mostly from his own writings. It is known that he came from a family of scholars of ḥadīth and that the region of his upbringing was also the centre for the study of ḥadīth in the Islamic world at that time. He was himself well versed in ḥadīth and his writings reveal his profound knowledge of this science. He also knew the Qur'ān by heart and, as accounted by himself, was taught the esoteric science by al-Khaḍir or Khiḍr.

The title Ḥakīm or "theosopher" given to Tirmidhī is due to his embarking upon the type of gnostic and theosophical discussions which were to find their full exposition in Ibn 'Arabī, Jīlī and other later masters of that school. Of course Tirmidhī's writings are not limited to Ṣūfism alone. Of his approximately sixty-five works a large number are devoted to the strictly religious sciences such as Qur'anic commentary, Ḥadīth, Kalām and even jurisprudence or fiqh in which, however, the Ṣūfī perspective is never absent. But in his strictly Ṣūfī works, in which he followed in many ways Ibn Karrām, he began to expound basic metaphysical teachings which had remained latent in the writings of the earlier Ṣūfīs until that time. Perhaps the most influential of these works is the *Khatm al-auliyā'* where he embarks upon the question of the relation between prophecy (*nubuwwa*) and sainthood (*wilāya*) and the very delicate question of the "seal of sanctity". It is enough to read the *Futūḥāt al-makkiyya* of Ibn 'Arabī to realize how great was the influence of Tirmidhī upon later Ṣūfism.

This particular question of the "seal of sanctity" was also a point of contention between the Sunnī and Shī'ī followers of Ibn 'Arabī as we see in the writings of Sayyid Ḥaidar Āmulī. Centuries of discussion upon a most difficult and subtle teaching of Ṣūfism revolved around the themes first exposed by Ḥakīm Tirmidhī, who was also the first Ṣūfī to have some acquaintance with the metaphysical and cosmological teachings of the Greeks. His influence upon the gnosis ('irfān) of the school of Ibn 'Arabī on the one hand and on Bahā' al-Dīn Naqshband and the later masters of the Naqshbandiyya order on the other hand was both profound and permanent.

A contemporary of Ḥakīm Tirmidhī, Aḥmad b. 'Īsā al-Kharrāz, lived in Baghdad where he associated with Sarī Saqaṭī and Bishr al-Ḥāfī but travelled later in life to Egypt where he met Dhu'l-Nūn and where he died in 286/899. Known mostly for his sole existing work, the *Kitāb al-ṣidq* ("The Book of Truthfulness"), which is an early masterpiece of Ṣūfism, Kharrāz was one of the earliest authorities to give a clear definition of fanā' and baqā'. He was also particularly attracted to the esoteric science of letters (*jafr*) and to spiritual concerts (*samā'*). In his *Kitāb al-ṣidq* he treats Ṣūfism from the point of view of the cardinal virtue of truthfulness and applies this virtue to all the other elements of the Path such as patience, repentance and knowledge. His writing is clear and the treatise is one of the most direct and lucid expositions of early Ṣūfism written in a concrete and "operative" style and somewhat removed from the intellectual and more "doctrinal" expositions of Tirmidhī.

In addition to the schools of Baghdad and Khurāsān, there were other centres and figures of significance for the development of Ṣūfism during the 3rd/9th century. One of these figures was Abū Sahl al-Tustarī, who was born in Tustar (the modern Shustar, near Ahvāz), where Ḥallāj was also to study later, in 200/815 and died in Baṣra in 261/874. Tustarī, like so many Ṣūfīs of his day, travelled widely, during which period he studied with Ṣufyān al-Thaurī and met Dhu'l-Nūn. In contrast to some of his Ṣūfī contemporaries like Muḥāsibī who were also theologians, Tustarī was opposed to the teachings of kalām and felt that the study of it would turn the mind away from God. He taught especially the importance of turning the mind to God at every moment of life through repentance (*tauba*) which must constantly be renewed. For him the light of faith dominated over reason and all the other faculties of man.

Tustarī wrote the first Ṣūfī commentary upon the Qur'ān and developed the doctrine of the correspondence of the letters of the Qur'ān with the spiritual light, which influenced so many Ṣūfīs such as Ibn Masarra. Many of his esoteric utterances on Divine Unity also influenced Ḥallāj. But the teachings of Tustarī were transmitted to later centuries mostly through his disciple Ibn Sālim of Baṣra, who founded the famous Sālimiyya School and who edited the master's "Thousand Questions". This school lasted for two centuries and nurtured many important figures of Ṣūfism such as Abū Ṭālib al-Makkī and Ibn Barrajān. It finally died out as a result of attacks, mostly from Ḥanbalī circles, and accusations of anthropomorphism.

In Shīrāz also there appeared in the 3rd/9th century a Ṣūfī of lasting fame and influence. Ibn Khafīf, of royal descent, was born in Shīrāz in 270/883. He travelled to Baghdad where he met Ḥallāj and other members of the school of Baghdad and made the pilgrimage to Mecca six times. He also visited Asia Minor and Egypt and returned to Baghdad, where he died in 371/982. He wrote extensively and is especially known for his support of kalām and his attempt to make use of it for the cause of Ṣūfism. He is also known to posterity as the patron saint of Shīrāz, an honour which he shares with another eminent Ṣūfī of that city, Rūzbahān Baqlī.

VII. ṢŪFISM IN THE 4TH/10TH CENTURY

The tree of Ṣūfism which had by now sunk its roots deeply into the soil of Persia continued to bear remarkable fruit in the 4th/10th century. On the one hand there appeared great masters of the type of the 3rd/9th century, such men as Abu'l-Ḥasan Kharraqānī, who was considered the pole (*quṭb*) of his day and whose special spiritual relation with Bāyazīd is related so beautifully in the *Tadhkirat al-auliyā'* of 'Aṭṭār. On the other hand a new type of Ṣūfī writing appeared in the form of syntheses, compilations and histories. The authors of most of these works, which have been the mainstay of Ṣūfī literature to this day within the khānaqāhs, were Persians, such men as Kalābādhī, Sarrāj, Makkī, Sulamī and Abū Nu'aim.

Abū Bakr al-Kalābādhī who died in Bukhārā in 390/1000, is known for his *al-Ta'arruf li madhhab ahl al-taṣawwuf*, which is a classic of Ṣūfī literature and which became popular almost from the moment it was written. Moreover, the book possesses a commentary in Persian by Abū Ibrāhīm Mustamlī al-Bukhārī, who might have been Kalābādhī's student. The commentary, which has never been fully studied, is one of the richest sources for the study of the history and doctrine of early Ṣūfism.

Abū Naṣr al-Sarrāj from Ṭūs, who died in 378/988, was a student of Ja'far al-Khuldī and through him became attached to the school of Junaid. Sarrāj's *Kitāb al-luma' fi'l-taṣawwuf* is one of the fundamental and authoritative accounts of Ṣūfism and its teaching. Rather than just giving an account of the life of the Ṣūfīs, it expounds in a clear and systematic fashion basic Ṣūfī teachings, especially concerning the spiritual states and stations and the spiritual portrait of the Prophet, who is emulated by all Ṣūfīs. The work is also rich in documentation and reference to the sayings and works of early Ṣūfīs. In its intellectual basis it is akin to the school of Junaid.

Abū Ṭālib al-Makkī was born in Persia but went to Mecca where he studied with another of Junaid's students, Abū Sa'īd al-A'rābī and where he died in 386/996. Drawn especially to the school of Muḥāsibī, Makkī was able to give a very successful synthesis of different aspects of Ṣūfism in conformity with the teachings of the Sharī'a. His *Qūt al-qulūb*, which has always competed with the *Kitāb al-luma'* as an early authoritative statement of Ṣūfism, contains fewer quotations but a greater number of arguments than the latter. It is one of the finest works of Ṣūfism in Arabic from a literary point of view and one whose study requires much effort and attention. It was to exercise much influence over many later Ṣūfīs, particularly Ghazzālī, whose *Iḥyā' 'ulūm al-dīn*, which as already mentioned was influenced also by Muḥāsibī, has even been called an enlargement of the *Qūt al-qulūb*.

The first known systematic history of the lives of saints in Islam in the form of *Ṭabaqāt* literature is the *Ṭabaqāt al-ṣūfiyya* of Abū 'Abd al-Raḥmān al-Sulamī of Nīshāpūr who died in 412/1021. The author wrote many works on Ṣūfism, but it is especially the *Ṭabaqāt* that is important both in itself and also as a source for Anṣārī's better known *Ṭabaqāt al-ṣūfiyya*, which are lectures in the local dialect of Herāt based upon Sulamī's work. Also most of the later biographers of Ṣūfism such as 'Aṭṭār and Jāmī drew from Anṣārī and Sulamī, while some historians who included a study of Ṣūfism in their works, such as Dhahabī in his *Ta'rīkh al-islām*, drew from Sulamī's work. The *Ṭabaqāt* of Sulamī is a precious summary of the teachings of the early Ṣūfīs, especially the school of Junaid.

At the end of the 4th/10th and beginning of the 5th/11th century Ṣūfism spread widely throughout the Islamic world and with it there appeared a larger number of works dealing with its doctrines, practices and history. Abū Nu'aim al-Iṣfahānī, who lived at this time and died in 430/1038, wrote what remains to this day the most monumental encyclopaedia of the history of Ṣūfism, covering ten large volumes in its modern printed edition. This vast reference work, based on many earlier biographies and hagiographies that are now lost, does not contain an intellectual structure and is not a systematic exposition of Ṣūfism in either its theoretical or operative aspects. But it does contain a wealth of information of different "classes" of Ṣūfīs starting with the Companions of the Prophet. The last two volumes give a careful description of the Ṣūfism of the two preceding centuries.

With the coming of the Saljuqs many political and intellectual transformations took place which changed completely the direction of the development of philosophy, the sciences and kalām. Also the development of Shī'ī gnosis, both Ithnā'asharī and Ismā'īlī, which are part of Islamic esotericism and closely akin to Ṣūfism but which we were forced to leave out of our present discussion, altered its pattern with the advent of the Saljuqs. But in Ṣūfism the course charted in the 4th/10th century was continued in nearly the same direction. The syntheses of men like Sarrāj and Makkī were continued in the 5th/11th century by Qushairī in his celebrated *Risāla* and by Hujvīrī in the first Persian prose treatise on Ṣūfism, the *Kashf al-maḥjūb*.

The well-known Ṣūfīs of the Saljuq period who began to employ the Persian language as a vehicle for their teachings, such men as Abū Sa'īd, Anṣārī, and later Sanā'ī and 'Aṭṭār, as well as those who were not poets but outstanding Ṣūfīs who wrote in prose like Ghazzālī, are branches of the same tree, some of whose fruit has been examined here. It was the seed of Ṣūfism planted through the revelation of Islam in the Persian soil that produced over the centuries the majestic tree which from the 5th/11th century onward began to spread its branches over the field of Persian literature itself. From the Ṣūfī tradition, whose Persian members had already produced so many of the literary masterpieces of the earlier period in Arabic, there continued to flow that spiritual presence and grace that began to exercise to an ever more evident degree the profoundest influence upon all the arts in Persia, especially literature. From the wedding of this spiritual force and the latent genius of the Persian language there was born the incomparable Persian Ṣūfī poetry which became not only the most universal part of Persian literature but also was destined to play a crucial rôle for many centuries in the spiritual and religious life of numerous nations of Asia, near and far.

CHAPTER 14

THE RELIGIOUS SCIENCES

I. THE ISLAMIZATION OF IRAN

There is a strange persistence in many Western studies of the religious history of Islamic Iran to be concerned almost solely with small sects and extremist religious movements. Far too little attention has been paid to the contribution of Iran to the mainstream of Islam and its traditional sciences, whether these be Sunnī or Shī'ī. To be sure the religious climate of Iran has been witness throughout Islamic history to the rise of many sects, some of which were on the fringe of the spectrum of Islam and a few even outside of it, especially during the first few centuries of the Islamic period. But such movements as that of Bābak Khurramdīn, for example, are minor rivulets on the margin of a vast river which was a major source feeding the sea of knowledge identified with classical, orthodox Islam. Without a clear understanding of the rôle of Iranian scholars in the cultivation of the basic Islamic sciences, such as Qur'anic commentary (*tafsīr*), tradition (*ḥadīth*), jurisprudence (*fiqh*) and its principles (*uṣūl al-fiqh*) and theology (*kalām*), the meaning of the Islamization of Iran on the one hand and Iran's rôle in the elaboration of Islam and its civilization on the other can never be fully understood.

Those who speak of the military conquest of Iran by the Arab armies as being synonymous with the Islamization of the country can perhaps present in support of their thesis arguments claiming that the newly converted Persians performed public prayers because of what might be termed "public pressure". But they would find it difficult to explain why the Persians produced so many great Islamic scholars. It might be thought that a people, if forced, could submit outwardly to another pattern of life, but not that a people could be forced to contribute creatively and profoundly to this pattern unless it were transformed inwardly by the new way of life. The depth of the Islamization of Persia and the transformation of the very substance of its people's soul by this process is best proved by the intensity of interest and the quality of the knowledge and scholarship of the Persian scholars who played such a basic rôle in the development and even creation of so many of the Islamic sciences.

In the same way that for Persians the domain of knowledge became Islamicized as a result of their conversion to Islam so the environment in which they lived underwent a major transformation. In a sense even the cosmic milieu "participated" in the process of Islamization, a similar occurrence being observed in the establishment of every new religion on earth. The stories told about lakes, mountain passes or ravines being formed in different parts of present-day Iran and Afghanistan on the night of the descent of the Qur'ān or through the supernatural powers of some of the Companions, especially 'Alī, cannot be simply brushed aside as old wives' tales. They symbolize the Islamization of the natural and cosmic environment for the Persians, a process which was the complement to the transformation of the content of their minds and thoughts. The two poles of knowledge and existence both became deeply transformed in the new spiritual universe of Islam and as a result the Persians began to devote themselves wholeheartedly to the cultivation of the Islamic sciences, in which their contribution is hardly less central than in the fields of Ṣūfism and philosophy. Moreover, this transformation was permanent and not in any way related to external forces, so that with the termination of Arab political domination over Iran, the intense activity of Persians in the Islamic religious sciences, far from subsiding, reached its peak in both Sunnī and Shī'ī studies, in the late 3rd/9th and 4th/10th centuries.

A notable feature of the Islamization of Iran that is reflected in the work of the Persian scholars of this time who were concerned with the religious sciences is strong opposition to the *Zanādiqa* and similar heterodox groups. Both Abū Ḥanīfa and Muḥammad al-Ṭūsī, the one Sunnī and the other Shī'ī but both Persian, were more severe with the *Zanādiqa* than the Arab jurists, although the background of the *Zanādiqa* movements derives of course from pre-Islamic Iranian religious currents, especially Manichaeism. Likewise, the Persian jurists were usually more strict at this time than others towards those who indulged in debauchery, excessive luxury and worldly pleasures, although the Persians themselves had had the experience of a more luxurious and mundane life than the Arabs in pre-Islamic times, and certain Persians in fact had been the first to introduce this type of life into the Ḥijāz. The Persian scholars were, moreover, more insistent than many of the Arab jurists of this early period on the necessity of maintaining equality between different races in Islam, and they even came to call themselves the "people of equality" (*ahl al-taswiya*). Finally it must be mentioned that the more violent opposition to the extremists of the Shuʿūbiyya movement, which claimed racial superiority for the Persians over the Arabs, came from the Persians themselves – such men as Zamakhsharī in the introduction to his *al-Mufaṣṣal* and Thaʿālibī in the introduction to his *Sirr al-adab fī majārī kalām al-ʿarab*. These and similar attacks finally put an end to this type of movement in the early Islamic period. All these facts indicate the thorough integration of Persians into the Islamic *umma* from the earliest period and the central rôle their writings were to play in the very foundation of the Islamic sciences, which began to crystallize from the fountainhead of knowledge in Islam, namely the Qur'ān and the Ḥadīth.

II. THE QUR'ANIC SCIENCES

Having been revealed to the Arabs, the Qur'ān, along with the sciences concerned with it, was naturally first studied by them, or more specifically by that group among the Companions and their students who were gifted with the necessary qualifications to undertake such studies. Furthermore, having been written in Arabic, the Qur'ān was naturally more easily understood and more easily psalmodized by the Arabs than by the non-Arab Muslims, who first had to overcome the language barrier. As a result the first Qur'anic scholars were all Arabs, save for Salmān al-Fārsī, who is credited with having made the first translation of the Holy Book and the first commentary upon it in another language. Persian became, therefore, the first language into which the Qur'ān was translated.

As the process of Islamization continued among the Persians, love for the Qur'ān combined with a lack of knowledge of its language became an incentive for them to turn to an avid study of Arabic and the Qur'ān, whose language they sometimes tended to analyse even more carefully than the Arabs, precisely because Arabic was not their mother tongue and they were therefore more conscious of the necessity to understand all its intricacies.

The sciences dealing with the Qur'ān are divided traditionally into those dealing with the recitation of the Book (*qirā'a*) and those dealing with commentary upon it and the meaning of its content (*tafsīr*). The science of qirā'a was taught by the Prophet to the Companions and through them reached the next generation or "followers" (*tābiʿīn*), when Persians first began to learn this science. Some have thought that the science of qirā'a, which was transmitted orally at the beginning, was first compiled and systematized by Abū 'Ubaid Qāsim b. Sallām al-Hirawī in the 3rd/9th century. But in reality there were works composed in this science before him by Ḥamza b. Ḥabīb and before Ḥamza by Abān b. Taghlib, who was a contemporary of Ja'far al-Ṣādiq.

Among the authorities on qirā'a seven are considered to be the most outstanding: 'Āṣim, Nāfi', Ibn Kathīr, Kisā'ī, Abū 'Amr b. al-'Alā', Ḥamza b. Ḥabīb and 'Abd-Allāh b. 'Āmir. Of these four were Persians: 'Āṣim b. Abi'l-Najūd, whom Ibn al-Nadīm lists among the *mawālī*, Nāfi', whom the same source considers as having originated in Iṣfahān, Ibn al-Kathīr and Kisā'ī, whose full name, 'Alī b. Ḥamza b. 'Abd-Allāh b. Bahman b. Fīrūz, reveals his Persian origin.[1] The major contribution of the Persians to this all-important Qur'anic science therefore becomes evident simply by studying the background of the early authorities of this traditional science, whose names have been inseparable from it to the present day.

As for Tafsīr among the early Muslim commentators, there are those whose views are echoed in later works but of whom no independent writing has survived and those who have left behind written commentaries. Of the first group, of nearly twenty men like Ibn 'Abbās, Ibn Mas'ūd and Ubaiy b. Ka'b who are considered the earliest authorities on Tafsīr, only Muqātil, Ṭā'ūs, A'mash and Farrā' were Persians. Muqātil b. Sulaimān was from Ray or Khurāsān and died in 150/767–8. He was so well known that Imām al-Shāfi'ī said of him, "People are Muqātil's dependants in the science of Tafsīr."[2] Ṭā'ūs was also a Persian but resided in the Yemen, while Sulaimān b. Mahrān al-A'mash was originally from Damāvand and also died in 150/767–8.

As for Farrā' b. Yaḥyā b. Ziyād al-Aqṭa', he was one of the most famous grammarians of the early period and was himself a student of Kisā'ī and teacher of the children of al-Ma'mūn. He composed an important commentary and died around 207/822 or 208/823. Ibn Khallikān has given an interesting account of how this commentary, entitled *al-Maʿānī*, was written.[3] One of Farrā''s friends wrote to him complaining that in his association with Ḥasan b. Sahl Dhu'l-Riyāsatain he was often asked questions about the Qur'ān which he could not

[1] Ibn Nadīm, pp. 63–4.
[2] Ibn Khallikān, vol. IV, p. 341.
[3] Ibn Khallikān, vol. III, pp. 226–7.

answer, and therefore he requested Farrā' to send him instructions or to introduce a book on the subject for him to study. Upon receiving the letter Farrā' called in his students and declared his intention to dictate a book on the Qur'ān. A particular day was chosen and a chanter of the Qur'ān (*qāri'*) was brought who began to recite the Qur'ān from the beginning while Farrā' recited his commentary to the students. In this way the whole of the Qur'ān was commentated in a vast work of a thousand folios, which moreover gained immediate acceptance. Unfortunately, it has not survived.

The second group of commentators, whose works have survived, is great in number and their names have been enumerated in most traditional works dealing with the "classes of commentators" (*ṭabaqāt al-mufassirīn*). Among those who were Persian and who lived up to the 5th/11th century there are to be found both Shī'ī and Sunnī authorities on tafsīr. The most famous Persian Shī'ī commentators of this period are:

1. Ḥusain b. Sa'īd al-Ahwāzī, who was a contemporary of the fourth Shī'ī Imām Jawād Zain al-'Ābidīn.

2. 'Alī b. Mahziyār al-Ahwāzī, who lived at the time of the eighth Shī'ī Imām 'Alī al-Riḍā.

3. Muḥammad b. Khālid al-Barqī, also a contemporary of Imām Riḍā.

4. Ḥasan b. Khālid al-Barqī, again a contemporary of Imām Riḍā.

5. 'Alī b. Ibrāhīm al-Qummī, who was still alive in 306/918–19.

6. 'Alī b. Bābūya (Bābawaih) al-Qummī, who died in 323/935.

7. 'Ayyāshī al-Samarqandī, who in addition to his mastery of tafsīr was well-versed in jurisprudence, Ḥadīth, medicine and astronomy. He lived in the 3rd/9th century. By the time Ibn al-Nadīm wrote his *al-Fihrist*, al-'Ayyāshī's books were widely known in Khurāsān. His commentary is well-known and has survived fully.

8. Abu'l-'Abbās al-Isfarā'inī, who lived in the second half of the 3rd/9th century.

9. Abu'l-Qāsim Ḥusain b. 'Alī, known as Ibn al-Marzubān, who was a descendant of the last Sāsānian king. He composed a book entitled *Khaṣā'iṣ al-Qur'ān* and died in 418/1027–8. He was buried in Najaf.

10. Faḍl b. Shādhān al-Naishābūrī.

11. Shaikh Abū Ja'far Muḥammad b. al-Ḥasan al-Ṭūsī, the celebrated Shī'ī scholar known also as Shaikh al-Ṭā'ifa and the author of the well-known commentary *al-Tibyān*, which has been printed many

times. Shaikh al-Ṭūsī left Khurāsān at the age of twenty-three for Baghdad where he studied with Sayyid Murtaḍā and Shaikh al-Mufīd and soon became himself the leader of Shī'ism. Towards the end of his life he left Baghdad for Najaf where he established a university for the Islamic sciences which still survives as a major centre of Shī'ī learning.

As for Persian Sunnī commentators, according to al-Suyūṭī's *Ṭabaqāt al-mufassirīn* the best-known are as follows:

1. Abū Yaḥyā Ja'far b. Muḥammad al-Rāzī al-Za'farānī, whom al-Suyūṭī calls "the imām of commentators". He died in 279/892–3.[1]

2. Muḥammad b. Jarīr al-Ṭabarī, the well-known historian, scholar of Ḥadīth, jurisprudent and commentator, whose commentary, *Jāmi' al-bayān*, is so famous. This work was translated into Persian by Bal'amī at the order of Nūḥ b. Manṣūr, the Sāmānid ruler. Al-Ṭabarī died in 310/922–3.

3. Abu'l-Maḥāmid Maḥmūd b. Aḥmad al-Faraj al-Samarqandī, who was born in 208/823–4 and died in 250/864–5. It is said of him that he was an outstanding authority in all the religious sciences, including Tafsīr, Ḥadīth and jurisprudence.

4. Aḥmad b. Fāris b. Zakariyyā' al-Lughawī, who originated in Qazvīn and was at the beginning Shāfi'ī but later became Mālikī. He wrote a commentary entitled *Jāmi' al-ta'wīl* and another work by the name of *Gharīb i'rāb al-Qur'ān*. He died in 395/1004–5.

5. Abū Isḥāq Aḥmad b. Muḥammad b. Ibrāhīm Tha'labī al-Naishābūrī, whose work entitled *Tafsīr al-Tha'labī* is well known. Al-Suyūṭī called him "Unique in his time in the science of the Qur'ān".[2] Tha'labī died in 427/1035–6.

6. Abū Bakr Aḥmad b. Muḥammad al-Fārsī, preacher and commentator from Nīshāpūr whose sermons were attended by thousands of people.

7. Abū Ḥāmid Aḥmad b. Muḥammad al-Hirawī, the *muftī* of Herāt who was a Shāfi'ī and a teacher of the well-known scholar of ḥadīth, Ḥākim al-Naishābūrī. Abū Ḥāmid died in 355/966 or 358/968–9.

8. Abū 'Abd al-Raḥmān al-Ḥīrī al-Naishābūrī, who was both commentator and chanter of the Qur'ān. Al-Naishābūrī, who was blind, was born in 360/970–1 and died in 430/1038–9.

9. Abū 'Uthmān al-Ṣabūrī al-Naishābūrī, both commentator and scholar of ḥadīth, whose piety and acute intelligence were proverbial. He was born in 373/983–4 and died in 449/1057–8.

[1] al-Suyūṭī, p. 10.

[2] al-Suyūṭī, p. 5.

10. Abu'l-Qāsim Ḥasan b. Muḥammad al-Naishābūrī, commentator and preacher whom al-Suyūṭī has called the most famous commentator of Khurāsān. He was a teacher of Tha'labī and died in 406/1015–16.

11. Abū Sa'īd Ḥusain b. Muḥammad al-Iṣfahānī al-Za'farānī, who was a source for Abū Nu'aim al-Iṣfahānī and died in 369/979–80.

12. Abu'l-Ḥasan 'Abd al-Jabbār b. Aḥmad al-Hamadānī al-Asadābādī, who died in 415/1024–5.

13. Abu'l-Ḥasan 'Alī b. Mūsā b. Yazdād al-Qummī al-Ḥanafī, who was the imām of Ray and died in 350/961–2.

14. Abū Bakr Muḥammad b. Ibrāhīm b. al-Mundhir al-Naishābūrī, who lived in Mecca and about whom al-Suyūṭī writes that he composed a commentary that was incomparable. He died in 318/930–1.

There are still other commentators whom one could mention, mostly from the cities of Khurāsān and also Iṣfahān. The above list, however, suffices to demonstrate the major rôle played by Persian scholars in the cultivation of the Qur'anic sciences, in both Sunnism and Shī'ism.

III. THE SCIENCE OF ḤADĪTH

The rôle of the Persians in the field of Ḥadīth was no less outstanding than their services to the Qur'anic sciences. After the death of the Prophet of Islam a group of the Companions opposed the recording of ḥadīth in order to guard the purity and uniqueness of the Qur'anic text, while another group, headed by 'Alī, favoured recording the ḥadīth, referring to the saying of the Prophet, "May God make happy that servant who, having heard my words, preserves them in his mind and transmits them to the person who has not heard them."[1] The partisans and friends of 'Alī, like Anas b. Mālik, were, therefore, the first to collect the ḥadīth and favour the cultivation of the sciences connected with them. With the Sunnīs the systematic collection of ḥadīth began with 'Umar b. 'Abd al-'Azīz. Considering the great significance of the ḥadīth for the life of the Muslim community as a whole, however, there is no doubt that activity in this field played a major rôle in the religious life of both parts of the community much earlier, that is, from the very beginning of Islamic history.

The Persian contribution to the science of Ḥadīth was extensive in both the Sunnī and Shī'ī worlds. Among the Persian Sunnī scholars of ḥadīth the earliest is most likely Nāfi', the Dailamite slave of 'Abd-

[1] al-Kulainī, vol. 1, p. 403, and Ḥasan b. 'Alī b. Shu'ba, p. 42.

Allāh b. 'Umar, who is one of the well-known transmitters (*ruwāt*). In Sunnism the transmission of a ḥadīth from Shāfi'ī, through Mālik b. Anas, Nāfi', 'Abd-Allāh b. 'Umar and finally the Prophet, is called "the golden chain" (*silsilat al-dhahab*).[1] Nāfi' died in 117/735–6 or 120/738. After him the earliest Persian scholar of ḥadīth was Yaḥyā b. Ma'īn, who died in 233/847–8 and who was a teacher of Bukhārī. His contemporary, Abū Ya'qūb Isḥāq b. Rāhūya (Rāhawaih), who died in Nīshāpūr around 230/844–5, was also a teacher of Bukhārī as well as of Muslim and Tirmidhī.

After this period commences the age of the authors of the six canonical collections of Sunnī ḥadīth (*al-ṣiḥāḥ al-sitta*), all of whom were Persian. The authors of the six collections are as follows:

1. Muḥammad b. Ismā'īl al-Bukhārī, the author of the best known of the *ṣiḥāḥ*, which he composed over a period of sixteen years. Traditional sources quote Bukhārī as saying that he did not record any ḥadīth before performing his ablutions and praying. Bukhārī died near Samarqand in 256/869–70.

2. Muslim b. Ḥajjāj al-Naishābūrī, who died in Nīshāpūr in 261/874–5 and whose *Ṣaḥīḥ* is second in fame only to that of Bukhārī.

3. Abū Dā'ūd Sulaimān b. Ash'ath al-Sijistānī, a Persian but of Arab descent, who died in 275/888–9.

4. Muḥammad b. 'Īsā al-Tirmidhī, author of the well-known *Jāmi' al-Tirmidhī*, who was a student of Bukhārī and died in 279/892–3.

5. Abū 'Abd al-Raḥmān al-Nisā'ī, who was from Khurāsān and died in 303/915–16.

6. Ibn Māja al-Qazwīnī, who died in 273/886–7.

Besides the authors of the six canonical collections there were two other outstanding scholars of ḥadīth of Persian background who are especially worthy of note: 'Abd-Allāh b. 'Abd al-Raḥmān al-Samarqandī, known as Dārimī, the author of the *Sunan* of Dārimī, which some people have substituted for the *Sunan* of Ibn Māja as one of the six canonical collections,[2] and Muḥammad b. Yaḥyā, known as Ibn Manda, who originated in Iṣfahān and died in 301/913–14.

During the 4th/10th century also there were several outstanding Persian scholars of ḥadīth, including:

1. Abū 'Abd-Allāh Ḥākim al-Naishābūrī, known as Ibn al-Bayyi', who composed many works including a history of Nīshāpūr. His fame in Ḥadīth depends mostly upon his well-known *al-Mustadrak 'ala'l-*

[1] Ibn Khallikān, vol. v, p. 4.

[2] Tabrīzī, vol. II, p. 206.

ṣaḥīḥain. He lived during the Sāmānid period and was for some time the judge (*qāḍī*) of Nīshāpūr and Gurgān. He was also sent by the Sāmānids as their ambassador to the Būyids. He died in 405/1014–15. He had Shī'ī tendencies to the extent that Ibn Taimiyya considered him a Shī'ī.[1]

2. Abū Sulaimān al-Bustī, who was a teacher of Ḥākim al-Naishābūrī and who composed many works on ḥadīth. He died in Bust in 388/998.

3. Abū Nu'aim al-Iṣfahānī, the well-known Ṣūfī author of *Ḥilyat al-auliyā'* and *Ta'rīkh al-Iṣfahān*, who died in 430/1038–9 and who was an ancestor of the great Shī'ī scholar of the Ṣafavid period, Majlisī.

This list reveals the extent to which Persians contributed to the sciences dealing with ḥadīth in Sunnism. Their contributions to the Shī'ī branch of the same discipline are no less striking. The first Persian to have recorded the text of a ḥadīth was Salmān al-Fārsī, who recorded and commented upon the ḥadīth of Jāthilīq, the Roman.[2] Parts of this ḥadīth appear in different places in the *Tauḥīd* of Ibn Bābūya (Bābawaih) (known as Shaikh al-Ṣadūq or more commonly in Persian Shaikh-i Ṣadūq).[3] After Salmān, Maitham al-Tammār, who was a Persian residing in Bahrain and a companion of 'Alī and who died in 60/679–80, wrote a book on ḥadīth.

Since in Shī'ism the sayings of the Imāms are included in the ḥadīth collections along with the words of the Prophet, those who collected and recorded these sayings must also be considered. Among these many were Persians, especially in the circle of the fifth and sixth Imāms, when the Imāms had greater freedom to teach the religious sciences. Some of the men whose names have already been mentioned among Qur'anic commentators such as Ḥusain b. Sa'īd al-Ahwāzī, 'Alī b. Mahziyār al-Ahwāzī, Muḥammad b. Khālid al-Barqī and Faḍl b. Shādhān al-Naishābūrī were also among those who recorded the sayings of the Imāms. "Four hundred principles" (*uṣūl arba'a mi'a*) of ḥadīth, which became the basis of later compilations, were systematized and organized by students ot the fifth and sixth Imāms.

After the 3rd/9th century Shī'ī scholars devoted themselves to the compilation of the major Shī'ī canonical collections, which appeared during the 4th/10th century. Here also, as in the case of the six Sunnī canonical works, all the authors of the four major collections were Persians. They are as follows:

1. Muḥammad b. Ya'qūb al-Kulainī (from near Ray), who travelled

[1] Ṣadr, p. 209. [2] Ṣadr, p. 280. [3] al-Ṣadūq, pp. 182, 286, 316.

a great deal to collect ḥadīth and finally settled in Baghdad, where he wrote his masterpiece, the *Uṣūl al-kāfī*, and where he died in 329/940–1. Altogether he assembled 16,099 ḥadīths consisting of sayings of juridical, moral and spiritual significance.

2. Abū Ja'far Muḥammad b. Bābūya (Bābawaih) al-Qummī (Shaikh-i Ṣadūq), who also travelled extensively in search of ḥadīth and who died near Tehrān in 381/991–2. His *Man lā yaḥḍuruhu'l-faqīh* consists of 9,044 sayings.

3. Abū Ja'far Muḥammad b. al-Ḥasan al-Ṭūsī, already mentioned as a Qur'anic commentator, who wrote two major works on ḥadīth: *Tahdhīb al-aḥkām*, consisting of 13,590 sayings, and *al-Istibṣār*, comprising 5,511 ḥadīths.

These four works have remained throughout the history of Shī'ism as the most widely accepted authoritative collections of ḥadīth. The rôle of Persian scholars in compiling these and the similar canonical collections in Sunnī Islam is so great that even if they had not made any other contributions to the Islamic religious sciences their share in these sciences would have remained fundamental.

IV. JURISPRUDENCE AND ITS PRINCIPLES

According to both the Shī'ī and Sunnī interpretations of Islam, the practice of giving opinions on questions of sacred law (*ijtihād*) and therefore the foundation of jurisprudence goes back to the Prophet himself, who is the source of this science, the substance of which derives first and foremost from the Qur'ān and the prophetic *Sunna*. Of course the meaning of ijtihād is not the same in all the Sunnī schools of law or in the Shī'ī, as can be seen in the differences between the rôle played by analytical reasoning (*qiyās*) in the Ḥanafī and Shī'ī schools. But the fact that the roots of this science go back to the very origins of Islam holds true in the case of all orthodox Islamic schools.

As far as Shī'ism is concerned, the first scholars of jurisprudence, who lived from the 1st/7th to the 3rd/9th centuries, were the students of the Imāms and have not always been known specifically as jurisprudents. Some of the better-known of these, a few of whom have already been mentioned in their rôle as Qur'anic commentators and scholars of ḥadīth, include Ḥarīz b. 'Abd-Allāh al-Sijistānī, Ḥasan b. Sa'īd al-Ahwāzī, Ḥusain b. Sa'īd al-Ahwāzī, Muḥammad b. Khālid al-Barqī al-Qummī, his son Aḥmad – who is the author of *Kitāb al-maḥāsin* –

'Alī b. Hāshim al-Qummī, Muḥammad b. Aḥmad al-Ash'arī al-Qummī (who was the teacher of al-Kulainī), 'Īsā b. Mahrān, Aḥmad b. Muḥammad b. 'Īsā al-Qummī, Abū Ja'far al-Qummī – known as Ibn al-Walīd – Abū Sa'īd Sahl b. Ziyād al-Rāzī and Abū Isḥāq Ibrāhīm al-Iṣfahānī. During this period the centre of Shī'ism in Persia was primarily Qum, where there lived mostly Persians of Arab origin, and to a certain extent Ray.

Among the Persian jurists of the 3rd/9th and 4th/10th centuries whose works have survived and whose opinions are still discussed and transmitted are such figures as 'Alī b. Ḥusain al-Bābūya (al-Bābawaih) and his well-known son, Shaikh-i Ṣadūq, and al-'Ayyāshī al-Samarqandī, whose works were so popular in Khurāsān. Perhaps the foremost Shī'ī jurist of this age, however, was Shaikh Abū Ja'far Muḥammad al-Ṭūsī (Shaikh al-Ṭā'ifa), who is one of the pillars of the fiqh of the Ja'farī or Twelve-Imām Shī'ī school.

As for Sunnī fiqh, it can be divided, up to the 5th/11th century, into three periods: that preceding the four Imāms of the established Sunnī schools of law (*madhhabs*), the period of the four Imāms themselves and of their contemporaries and the period following them. The period before the four Imāms, which is the age of the "followers" (*tābi'īn*), is dominated by seven main figures: 'Abd al-Raḥmān b. Ḥārith b. Hishām al-Makhzūmī, Sa'īd b. Musayyib al-Makhzūmī, Qāsim b. Muḥammad b. Abī Bakr, Khārija b. Zaid b. Thābit, 'Ubaid-Allāh b. Abd-Allāh b. 'Utba b. Mas'ūd, 'Urwa b. Zubair and Sulaimān b. Yasār. Of these seven jurists (*al-fuqahā' al-sab'a*), Sulaimān b. Yasār was most likely Persian while according to traditional accounts the mother of Qāsim b. Muḥammad was the daughter of the last Sāsānian king, Yazdgard. The other five were pure Arabs. But there are two other jurists who, although not officially among the seven, were their contemporaries and held in high esteem. They are Ṭā'ūs b. Kīsān, who was a Persian residing in the Yemen and died in 104/722–3 or 106/724–5, and Rābi'at al-Ra'iy, also a Persian, who was the teacher of Mālik b. Anas. Rābi'a is said to have been the first to use qiyās, which was later adopted by Abū Ḥanīfa. He died in 136/753–4. Ḥasan al-Baṣrī and Ibn Sīrīn, who both died in 110/728–9, may be said to belong to the same class, although they were more scholars of ḥadīth and Ṣūfīs than jurists.

As for the period of the four Imāms, one of them, Abū Ḥanīfa, who is often called "the grand Imām" (*al-imām al-a'ẓam*), was Persian. His complete name is Nu'mān b. Thābit b. Nu'mān b. al-Marzubān. He died in 150/767–8. As for Ibn Ḥanbal, although of pure Arab blood, his father lived in Persia and his mother was expecting him when she left Marv for Baghdad. Ibn Ḥanbal died in 241/855–6. During the period of the four Imāms, which lasted from the beginning of the 2nd/8th to the middle of the 3rd/9th centuries, there appeared several outstanding Persian jurists, such as 'Abd-Allāh b. Mubārak al-Marwazī, who died in 181/797–8, Sulaimān al-A'mas͟h al-Damāwandī, who died in 148/765–6, Lait͟h b. Sa'd al-Iṣfahānī, the jurist of Egypt who died in 175/791–2, Ḍaḥḥāk b. Muzāḥim al-Balk͟hī and 'Aṭā' b. Abī Muslim al-K͟hurāsānī, who died in 150/767–8.[1] There were also two Persians, Dā'ūd b. 'Alī al-Ẓāhirī al-Iṣfahānī, who died in 270/883–4, and Ṭabarī, the well-known historian and scholar of ḥadīt͟h mentioned above, who established their own schools of jurisprudence, which had certain followers during the lifetimes of the founders and for some time to come. Some of their disciples are even listed by such men as Ibn al-Nadīm and Abū Isḥāq al-S͟hīrāzī.

Among the Persian students of al-S͟hāfi'ī during the 3rd/9th century can be mentioned Abū Ja'far Muḥammad Naṣr al-Tirmid͟hī (d. 295/907–8), Muḥammad b. Isḥāq Sulamī al-Nais͟hābūrī (d. 312/924–5), Abū 'Abd-Allāh Muḥammad b. Naṣr al-Marwazī (d. 294/906–7), Abū 'Alī Ḥasan b. Qāsim, and especially Qāḍī Abu'l-'Abbās al-Suraijī (d. 306/918–19).[2] Altogether there were many prominent Persian jurists who followed the school of al-S͟hāfi'ī during the 3rd/9th century and even later.

As for the early Persian jurists who followed the Ḥanafī school, one can mention such figures as Abū Muṭī' al-Balk͟hī; Abū Bakr al-Marwazī (d. 211/826–7), who studied with Muḥammad b. al-Ḥasan al-S͟haibānī, the famous student of Abū Ḥanīfa; and Muḥammad b. Muqātil al-Rāzī. In the 3rd/9th century famous Ḥanafīs include Muḥammad b. S͟hujā' al-Balk͟hī, known as Ibn al-T͟haljī (d. 266/879–80), Abū 'Alī Daqqāq al-Rāzī, Abū Bakr al-Jūzjānī, Aḥmad b. Muḥammad al-Rāzī, Abū 'Alī 'Abd-Allāh b. Ja'far al-Rāzī and Abū Sa'īd al-Bard͟ha'ī (d. 317/929–30).

In the 4th/10th century a great many S͟hāfi'ī jurists continued to appear in Persia. Some of the more outstanding among them are Abū Bakr 'Abd-Allāh b. Muḥammad al-Nais͟hābūrī, Qāḍī Abū Ḥāmid al-Marv-ar-Rūdī, Abū Zaid al-Marv-ar-Rūdī, Qāḍī Abu'l-Qāsim al-Dīnawarī, Qāḍī Abū Muḥammad al-Iṣṭak͟hrī, Abū Ḥāmid al-Isfarā'inī (d. 406/1015–16) and Abū Isḥāq al-Isfarā'inī (d. 417/1026–7). There were

[1] Ṭās͟hkubrāzāda, p. 18.

[2] al-S͟hīrāzī, pp. 78–94.

also a large number of jurists who were students of al-Suraijī, such as Abū Sa'īd al-Iṣṭakhrī (d. 328/939–40), Qaffāl al-Shāshī (d. 336/947–8) and Abū Isḥāq al-Marwazī (d. 340/951–2).

During the 4th/10th century there were also several well-known Ḥanafī jurists, including Abū Bakr b. Shāhūya (Shāhwaih; d. 361/971–2), Abu'l-Ḥusain, known as Qāḍī al-Ḥaramain (d. 351/962–3), Abū Bakr Aḥmad b. 'Alī al-Rāzī, known as Ḥaṣṣāṣ (d. 370/980–1), Abū Bakr al-Khwārazmī (d. 403/1012–13), Abū Manṣūr al-Māturīdī, Abu'l-Faḍl Muḥammad al-Marwazī, who was killed in 344/955–6, Abu'l-Qāsim, known as Ḥākim al-Samarqandī (d. 342/953–4), Abū Ja'far al-Hindawānī (d. 362/972–3), Abū Ḥāmid al-Marwazī, known as Ibn al-Ṭabarī, Abū Bakr al-Jurjānī, Abu'l-Laith al-Samarqandī (d. 383/993–4) and Abu'l-Haitham Qāḍī al-Naishābūrī.

The Mālikī school had very few followers in Persia, being confined mostly to the Maghrib of Islam and having some adherents in Medina and occasionally Egypt. In his *Ṭabaqāt al-mufassirīn*, al-Suyūṭī tells the story that Aḥmad b. Fāris b. Zakariyyā' al-Lughawī was first a Shāfi'ī and later became a Mālikī, giving as reason for this change his feeling sorry for Imām Mālik, who did not have a single follower among jurists in Ray.

Likewise, the Ḥanbalī school had very few adherents in Iran and Persian jurists of this madhhab are rare. Abū Isḥāq al-Shīrāzī considers Abū Bakr al-Marwazī (d. 275/888–9) and Abū Dā'ūd al-Sijistānī (d. 275/888–9) as Ḥanbalites.[1] Also Ibn al-Nadīm writes that Isḥāq b. Rāhūya (Rāhawaih) was a Ḥanbalī jurist.

The Ẓāhirite school, founded by Dā'ūd al-Iṣfahānī, as can be expected also had some followers among Persian jurists, including Abū Bakr Muḥammad al-Kāshānī, Abū 'Alī al-Samarqandī, Qāḍī Abu'l-Ḥasan al-Kharazī and Qāḍī Abu'l-Faraj al-Shīrāzī. Abū Isḥāq al-Shīrāzī writes in fact that even after the Ẓāhirite school became extinct in Baghdad it continued to have some followers in Shīrāz, students of Abu'l-Faraj al-Shīrāzī.

In the seventh section of the sixth chapter of *al-Fihrist* Ibn al-Nadīm mentions a few followers of the juridical school of Ṭabarī, including 'Alī b. 'Abd al-'Azīz al-Dūlābī, Abu'l-Ḥasan al-Ḥulwānī al-Ṭabarī and Abū Isḥāq Ibrāhīm al-Ṭabarī, all of whom lived in the 4th/10th century. Altogether there were few followers of this and the other Sunnī schools save the Shāfi'ī and the Ḥanafī, which were very widespread at

[1] al-Shīrāzī, p. 104.

this time, the Shāfi'īs being centred mostly in Fārs, Iṣfahān, Ray and Ṭabaristān, and the Ḥanafīs in Khurāsān and Transoxiana.

V. THEOLOGY

If by kalām we mean rational discussion of religious questions, it can be said that this discipline goes back to the first Islamic century, although the word kalām itself was not used until the 2nd/8th century. At this time in the Sunnī world Mālik b. Anas opposed the scholars of Kalām referring to them as "*mutakallimūn*" and in Shī'ism certain of the companions of Imām Ja'far al-Ṣādiq such as Ḥamrān b. A'yan, Mu'min al-Ṭāq, Qais b. al-Māṣir and Hishām b. al-Ḥakam were also called "*mutakallim*".[1]

The Qur'ān itself provides in many places intellectual evidence and demonstration for its arguments and is the example for all later developments of Islamic religious sciences in which rational arguments are provided for articles and principles of faith. Also, among the Companions, 'Alī was known especially for his intellectual discourses upon questions of metaphysics, cosmology and eschatology, examples of which are found especially in the *Nahj al-balāgha*. Thus many have considered him the founder of Kalām in its specifically Islamic sense as well as the other "intellectual sciences" which deal with the origin and end (*al-mabda' wa'l-ma'ād*) of things. Likewise in the sayings of the other Shī'ī Imāms, particularly Zain al-'Ābidīn al-Sajjād, Ja'far al-Ṣādiq and 'Alī al-Riḍā, there are numerous intellectual proofs and demonstrations, which have given a particularly intellectual character to Shī'ī religious and theological thought throughout its history. That is why whenever Shī'ism has been dominant there has been a more favourable climate for the cultivation of the "intellectual sciences" (*al-'ulūm al-'aqliyya*).

Some have thought that the Persian ethnic element has been the only determining factor in providing a more congenial background for the development of the intellectual sciences and particularly philosophy in Persia. But a closer examination of the situation will reveal that also a most important determining factor making Persia the main homeland of Islamic philosophy was the more favourable attitude of Shī'ism toward the intellectual sciences. It must always be remembered that the Persian Sunnī scholars of ḥadīth such as Bukhārī, Muslim and Tirmidhī

[1] al-Kulainī, p. 171.

display the same attitude towards the intellect (*al-'aql*) as the Arab Sunnī scholars.

S͟hī'ī kalām was discussed generally by the Imāms in the sessions of instruction held with their disciples, but certain among these disciples became known officially as *mutakallims*, such men as 'Alī b. Ismā'īl b. al-Mait͟ham al-Tammār. His grandfather was a Persian from Bahrain known as an orator. 'Alī b. Ismā'īl himself is considered the first formal S͟hī'ī theologian. Another early Persian S͟hī'ī theologian is His͟hām b. Sālim al-Jūzjānī, who is well-known as a transmitter of ḥadīt͟h and who was a disciple of Imām Ja'far al-Ṣādiq. Also well-known as theologians are certain members of the Nauba͟kht family, such men as Abū Sahl Ismā'īl b. 'Alī, his brother Abū Ja'far, his nephew Ḥasan b. Mūsā, who wrote *Firaq al-s͟hī'a*, Faḍl b. Abī Sahl, who was in charge of the *Bait al-ḥikma* and translated several works from Pahlavī into Arabic, Isḥāq b. Abī Sahl, his son Ismā'īl b. Isḥāq and several others.

Other Persian S͟hī'ī theologians of this early period include Faḍl b. S͟hād͟hān, already mentioned above, who was a contemporary of Imām Riḍā and transmitted many of the Imām's sayings, Abu'l-Ḥasan Sūsangirdī, who was a slave of Abū Sahl al-Nauba͟khtī, and Ibn Qibba al-Rāzī, who was a contemporary of al-Ka'bī (3rd/9th century) and who carried out theological debates with him.[1] Also well known during this period is Abū 'Abd-Allāh Muḥammad, known as His͟hām al-Jawālīqī, who was originally from Gurgān but lived in Iṣfahān and who was a contemporary of al-Jubbā'ī, therefore living in the 3rd/9th century.

In the 4th/10th century S͟hī'ī theologians are not as numerous if we confine ourselves to men who were only theologians and do not take into account such figures as Kulainī and Ibn Bābūya, who were first and foremost scholars of ḥadīt͟h but theologians as well. Of the former group, namely those who contributed to religious studies mainly in the field of theology, one can name Abū 'Alī b. Muskūya (Miskawaih), who died in 431/1039–40. He is of course best known as a philosopher and physician, but in terms of his specifically religious works he must be considered a leading S͟hī'ī theologian of his day. One may also mention as an important theologian of the period Abu'l-Qāsim 'Alī b. Aḥmad al-͟Kharrāz al-Rāzī, author of the *Kifāyat al-at͟har*, who was a student of Ibn Bābūya.

As far as Persian scholars of Sunnī kalām are concerned one must begin with Ḥasan al-Baṣrī, who was both Ṣūfī and theologian, as well

[1] Ibn Nadīm, pp. 439, 441.

as his student Wāṣil b. 'Aṭā' al-Ghazzāl (d. 131/748–9), who, as is well known, began the Mu'tazilite school as a movement which broke off from the circle of Ḥasan. After these two early figures the important Persian Sunnī theologians are as follows:

1. Abu'l-Hudhail al-'Allāf, whom some have considered as the founder of systematic Sunnī kalām. Abu'l-Hudhail was well acquainted with philosophical arguments and carried out a well-known debate with Ṣāliḥ b. 'Abd al-Quddūs al-Shakkāk (the Sceptic), which Ibn al-Nadīm has recounted. He had a Zoroastrian (*majūs*) secretary named Mīlās and through him a religious debate was arranged with Zoroastrian scholars in which Abu'l-Hudhail triumphed, and it is said that Mīlās and thousands of Zoroastrians were thus converted to Islam. Abu'l-Hudhail died in 235/849–50 during the rule of al-Mutawakkil.[1]

2. Ibrāhīm b. Sayyār, known as al-Naẓẓām, who was a student of Hishām b. al-Ḥakam. He was known particularly for his keen intelligence and must be considered as one of the basic figures of Mu'tazilite kalām. His views on the nature of bodies and of colour and smell were well known to both theologians and philosophers of the later period. Naẓẓām was originally from Balkh. He was a nephew of Abu'l-Hudhail and died in 221/836–7.

3. Abū 'Alī al-Jubbā'ī, from Khūzistān (b. 235/849–50; d. 303/915–16), was the head of the Mu'tazilite school of Baṣra and the teacher of Abu'l-Ḥasan al-Ash'arī, who rebelled against his teachings and established the Ash'arite school.

4. Abu'l-Qāsim al-Ka'bī al-Balkhī (d. 317/929–30), whose views are repeated so often in books on kalām as well as on philosophy and jurisprudence.

5. 'Amr b. 'Ubaid b. al-Bāb, who had Khārijite tendencies and was a contemporary of the 'Abbāsid caliph al-Manṣūr.

6. Ibn al-Munajjim, who was the chamberlain of the caliphs al-Muwaffaq and al-Muktafī and himself a descendant of the last Sāsānian king, Yazdgard.

7. Ibn Fadrik al-Iṣfahānī, both orator and theologian (d. 406/1015–16).

8. Abū Manṣūr al-Māturīdī al-Samarqandī (d. 333/944–5), who established a new school of kalām with views in many ways intermediate between those of the Mu'tazilites and the Ash'arīs.

The Persians also made major contributions to other branches of the

[1] Amīn, vol. 1, p. 379, and Shahristānī, vol. 1, p. 71.

Islamic sciences such as literature, philosophy, the natural and mathematical sciences, Ṣūfism, etc., which have been treated elsewhere and need not be repeated here. But the universality of the Persian contribution to all facets of Islamic learning must be kept in mind in any study of the relationship between Persia and Islamic civilization.

The extensive efforts of Persian scholars in helping to lay the foundation of so many of the Islamic sciences during the early period continued with the same force into the Saljuq and Tīmūrid periods. So many of the works of this later period which are to this day standard texts in Muslim *madrasas*, both Sunnī and Shī'ī, works of such men as Ghazzālī, Fakhr al-Dīn al-Rāzī, Zamakhsharī, Baiḍāwī, Naṣīr al-Dīn al-Ṭūsī, Taftazānī, Sayyid Sharīf al-Jurjānī and Jalāl al-Dīn al-Dawānī, to cite just a few of the better known names, are connected with the Persian world. Ghazzālī alone would be sufficient to underline the significance of the contribution of Persia to Islamic civilization, in the same way that a figure such as he is also an outstanding example of the result of the downpouring of the grace of the Qur'anic revelation upon the soil of Persia.

The history of Persia cannot be understood without grasping the depth of penetration of and the subsequent transformation brought about by the Islamic revelation in Persia. Likewise, the rôle of Persia in the construction of Islamic civilization can never be understood if one confines this rôle to the production of a few extremist sects that stood at the margin of the Islamic religious panorama. As some of the names cited in the present chapter show, the Persians participated in the creation of the mainstream of the Islamic sciences in a direct and central manner, and all that we identify with classical, orthodox Islam in both its Sunnī and Shī'ī aspects would be unimaginable in its existing historical form without the extensive efforts of Persian scholars, who worked along with Arab scholars in creating that vast world of Islamic learning to which other peoples also became subsequent heirs and contributors. For this reason the rôle of Persia in the elaboration of Islamic civilization and the Islamic sciences has remained central throughout Islamic history.

CHAPTER 15

SECTS AND HERESIES

The religious evolution of Iran during the centuries from the Arab conquest to the rise of the Saljuqs was determined by a number of factors which, so far, have not been adequately isolated and analysed. A religious history of Iran during this period still lacks data and analyses to enable the student of the history of religions to make a religious typology, and to differentiate its internal structure and verify its socio-political connections. In dealing with heterodoxy in Iran, the difficulty of focusing on problems is further compounded by the fact that, in most instances, one cannot rely on contemporary sources, which might be properly characterized as "heterodox", as free expressions of the antithesis to the official religious set-up of Iran following the Arab conquest. The oldest and most exhaustive work on Shī'ī heresiography, Naubakhtī's *Firaq al-shī'a*, only dates from the 4th/10th century.

One is thus faced by interpretations which are biased from the very beginning, due to the strongly felt need of condemning heresy and keeping it at a safe distance so as to leave no doubt as to the "orthodox" soundness of the sources. Alternatively, most of the material employed reflects the centrally oriented and Islamic views of the caliphal empire, within which Iran, as any other province, was a mere ramification of a single, powerful centre which was bound, by the nature of things, to peripheral repetition of its basic modules and patterns.

By concentrating on one area or province one can attain a more realistic, although possibly still universal vision, which is important for a number of interrelations between the various areas or provinces, and above all takes into account whatever each area more or less consciously chose to preserve, in a "national" sense as one might say today, out of the supranational whole of aims and interests which the caliphate's Islamic ideology expressed in different occasions and forms, within the territorial boundaries of the caliphate.

A not merely religious but even more simply historical understanding of the revolts documented in Iran primarily during the 'Abbāsid period, and of their underlying theories, requires some consideration of those factors which allow one to reconstruct the socio-economical, political and hence religious texture of caliphal Persia.

One cannot, of course, aim at a detailed and specific analysis of such factors, which would lie outside the scope of this essay, but only by starting with a few general remarks on the history of Persia during the period in question can one understand two main currents of thought which, though inadequate to describe the complexity of the phenomena in question, are complementary to each other. One can identify the politico-economical dimension of these rebellions and heresies, and at the same time single out a few recurring and typical traits deserving the attention of the student of Iranian religious phenomena.

The first indispensable element of such an enquiry is the need of interpreting the religion of Iran at the time of the conquest; i.e. "religion" and not "church"; for the Mazdaean church of the Sāsānian age does not seem in itself to have provided all the religious and social developments inspired by the ancient Persian religion. Not only does this "unofficial" Iranian religion need at least approximate definition, but the Iranian heresies *par excellence* of pre-Islamic times, such as Manichaeism and Mazdakism, should be considered against its background as well as that of the official state religion. The picture would, however, still appear limited and restricted in its historical implications if its scope were not extended to include the whole phenomenon known as Iranian gnosis, which seems to consist in a synthesis of disparate, not strictly Iranian elements. All of these elements, in our view, can act as a framework for the study of the region's transition to an Islamic ideology (it being still too early to speak of conversion to Islamic monotheism as a well-defined religion).

The second basic factor is the economic and social situation of Iran at the time of the conquest. It seems essential to discern in Persian social texture the opportunities for penetration by an external element, in this instance the Arabs and the ideology they brought along with them. One could establish the external element's rôle in setting up a new internal economic and social structure, which was not necessarily innovating but did provide local unrest and endemic demands with a new form of expression, disguised under the camouflage of a new external contribution, and yet substantially not different, for the time being, from traditional forms. This factor can only be determined through a point-by-point analysis of the Arab conquest's stages. The central government's attitudes and reactions as the conquest proceeded are an important factor in clarifying the problems.

A third necessary element, more strictly connected with religious enquiry, is a definition, however approximate, of the Shī'a, which avoids the classic models proposed by traditional heresiographers and generally accepted by students. Such models, in fact, artificially reduce the Iranian religious outlook to a pattern which ultimately depends on the so-called Shī'ī religious conception, viewed almost as an Iranian discovery, or rather the Iranian response to Arab Islam both in the Islamic formulation of the theory of power and, even more so, in its mass religious manifestation.

These factors might together define the field of enquiry: the meaning of the "Iranian substratum" from the religious point of view; the nature of the social and ethnic elements making up Iran; and the new synthesis formed after the coming of Islam onto the Iranian plateau, or rather the nature of the new religious outlook to which Shī'ī heterodoxy contributed.

The first point, however, is extremely tenuous. Reference is often made to the rapid collapse of the Sāsānian empire before the thrust of the first invading Arab armies. That the traditional forms in which power found expression in Iran underwent some sort of collapse is fairly obvious. Whether this coincided with an actual breakdown of Iran's socio-economic structures is not entirely clear. There *was* the collapse of a dynasty and of a church, the Mazdaean hierarchy being allied with, and sharing in, official power, but the landowning and merchant class which wielded economic power underwent no obvious upheaval. The conquerors introduced a religion, as well as a language which was its most obvious vehicle, but they did not force them upon the country. This is in itself a democratic and egalitarian trait; but being conscious of his own material interests the Islamic missionary did not encourage his new subjects toward a condition of parity, while he allowed them a theoretical freedom of choice by granting them a clearly defined juridical status and thus obtained the desired economic results. Any conflict in extending the sway of Islam to Iran at first was hardly felt at all. The important consideration was that the right of control should stay in Islamic hands; apart from that the traditional structures were left unchanged and were actually used by the conquerors for a long time.

The Iranian world thus preserved its own "Iranian" character; the innovation consisted in ending allegiance to the official aristocratic and reactionary church, oppressive by its own quality of court church and, more generally, by the artificial aspects of its cult.

What the Iranian masses believed, and how they expressed themselves in the religious field, is still not clear. The two great movements known to us, which seem to have enjoyed popular support, were Manichaeism and Mazdakism, both directed primarily against the official church. Naturally enough the Mazdaean church of the Sāsānians stubbornly opposed them. This is not to say that a number of Iranian, which we may call Mazdeo-Sāsānian, elements did not find expression in attempts at creating a new religious alternative. The concept of light and darkness, for instance, were poles of a constant dualism within which the Mazdakite catchwords of social justice also found their ideological place.

Unfortunately, however, popular religious feeling can on the whole only be assumed and derived from the negative formulations aimed at official Mazdaism, and from those historically documented rebellions which are Iranian in their dynamism and in the messianic mythology to which they are related most of the time, though already Islamized. One might add the subsequent need of providing the elements of their own myth with historical sanction. It should be noted, however, that the latter circumstance reflects an atmosphere not so much of "conversion" as of reduced religious pressure; in other words, such a constant feature of Islamic religious outlook as the need to provide every suggested element with historicity before making it operative, was bound to be accepted first as a form of liberation from absolute patterns handed down from above as symbols of religious manifestations, and secondly as a platform for actual adhesion to the Islamic creed. Though lacking direct sources, we do have literary and annalistic references, and it is quite obvious that in Firdausī or Asadī no less than in Ṭabarī or Tha'ālibī ancient myth is historicized to the point of persuading us that by A.D. 1000 this process was already long concluded.

In this sense, it is precisely in the field of religious politics that the convergence of Iranian subjects towards Islam was presumably so widespread as to include Christians and Jews in the Sāsānian empire. In this connection, interpreting the Shu'ūbiyya as an ethnico-religious development (Arab versus non-Arab, Muslim versus non-Muslim) does not seem justified. On the contrary, this was possibly a typically Islamic way of voicing claims and demands, according to a dynamic process which placed on the same political plane positive (autonomous) and negative (not necessarily Arab Bedouin) definitions within a system which was wide enough to tolerate such an organization of dissent without serious danger.

It seems obvious that an atmosphere which was less repressive and at any rate more amenable to stimuli, however disparate these might be, should have allowed the recovery – in a strictly religious sense – of mainly hidden undercurrents of Iranian mentality leading to a gnostic syncretism of Judeo-Christian origin, filtered by Iranian mythological structure.

Regarding the second point, it is obvious that by the conquest of Iran one does not mean in this connection the battles of Qādisīya or Nihāvand, which were merely landmarks attesting, among other things, the ability of Arab caravans to pursue their commercial interests in safety and ensuring control over eastern routes. One should consider the history of a few Iranian provinces of Umayyad times with reference to their adjustment to Islamic power and their occasional attempts at independence. From this point of view the most interesting provinces are Fārs, Khurāsān, Sīstān, the Caspian area and, to a lesser degree, Āzarbāījān, whose vicissitudes are connected with the campaigns against Byzantium. The starting points of the Arab armies on their way towards Iran were Baṣra or Kūfa and the eastern provinces' fate became tied to Iraqi politics, and the unrest of the Mesopotamian cities repeatedly found echo and support in the eastern part of the empire.

After 29/650, when 'Abd-Allāh b. 'Āmir, having pacified Fārs, headed toward Khurāsān with Nīshāpūr as his goal, we find a succession of military waves radiating out from Iraq to reach ever further east towards Transoxiana and Farghāna. Arab garrisons were left in Khurāsān to act as bridgeheads for subsequent campaigns, which were not so much expeditions of actual conquest as plundering forays towards Sīstān and the Oxus provinces. Initially, therefore, the Arabs acted as supervisors and new managers of the caravan routes to China, but by 47/667 the governor of Baṣra, Ziyād b. Abīhi, had already established in Khurāsān without modifying their tribal structure 50,000 families from Kūfa and Baṣra, mainly of the Banū Qais, Tamīm and Banū Azd tribes, with the purpose of consolidating previous conquests and establishing a reservoir of manpower for future campaigns. Marv became the Arabs' general headquarters, and not all of the local Arab colony was engaged in warlike activities. This was the beginning of the process of acculturation and of Arab penetration into the existing Sāsānian structures of Iran, which gave birth in Khurāsān to the Abū Muslim faction and was to constitute, in Iran as a whole, an element of potential alliance against the central power in the history of revolts of the times.

There is no evidence of any reaction to the Arab conquest in the guise of popular rebellion, but we do know of many local uprisings in response to each new Arab campaign, organized and directed by the ancient landowning class, such as the short-lived Nīshāpūr and Balkh rebellion of 32/653 led by Qārin, a certain Sāsānian nobleman.[1]

We are thus faced with a common trait in the history of Arab conquests: on the one hand conservation of the existing administrative order (the *dihqāns* and *marzbāns* being entrusted with the task of tax gathering); on the other hand the speedy participation of the Arabs in local politics led them to an anti-Umayyad rôle. The Damascus government repeatedly tried to exert direct control over Iran and particularly Khurāsān by resorting to administrative pressures, for a centralized form of administration had been introduced by 46–50/667–70. The administrative division introduced by Ziyād b. Abī Sufyān, which subjected the finances of Khurāsān to those of Iraq, should be viewed in this perspective. Furthermore, Damascus regularly quartered in Khurāsān Syrian troops, disliked by the locals who had to bear the ensuing financial burden, as well as by the settled Arabs who had to submit to their control. Umayyad politics thus proved ineffective as far as the Iranian territories were concerned, and only such a governor as Ḥajjāj succeeded in enforcing them. As a matter of fact the acts of the governor of Khurāsān often proved incompatible with the central government's policy, both in taxation (regarding the proportion due to Damascus, as well as the degree in which their administration fell to local authority), and as regards recruiting the local population into the Arab military structure. The latter problem, of course, was connected with the former insofar as the question existed of whether to grant or not the inscription of the *mawālī* on the rolls of the Iraqi *dīvān*.

To all this one should add the conversion problem. At first taxation was kept on a *per-capita* basis to the landowners' benefit, which makes one wonder about the historical authenticity of any alleged Arab policy of conversion in the area. Such a policy materialized only under excep-

[1] Cf. M. A. Shaban, p. 26.

tional circumstances, as under ʿUmar II, or when the Umayyad caliphs extended to Arab landowners the obligation of *k͟harāj*.

In the eastern areas of Iran economic power was shared between the Arab conquerors and local merchants. In the patchwork of anti-Umayyad alliances between the Arab settlers and the local wealthy classes, commercial capital played a special rôle; it was placed at the central authority's service when this promoted new campaigns to safeguard the security of the major caravan routes. Such was, for instance, the rôle of the merchants of K͟hwārazm or Sog͟hdiana, where our sources bear witness to the presence of well-organized foreign colonies among the local traders. On the other hand capital was directed to local parties whenever trade required a policy of peace and good neighbourliness rather than aggression.

This then is the context which provided ample scope for the political and organizational capacities of Abū Muslim, whose name cannot be omitted from any typological analysis of the Iranian, or more particularly K͟hurāsānian, rebellions of the first centuries of the caliphate.

During the first decades of the Arab conquest, the elements to be stressed in terms of a typological survey seem to be essentially four. First, we find the unchanging presence of a landed aristocracy acting as large estate owners, and also a lesser farming aristocracy which held titles to their estates against payment of taxes and generally took the lead in anti-Arab risings. Second, there was a wealthy merchant class which generally supported and promoted local political initiatives. Third, we find an Arab colony of more than military nature settled in K͟hurāsān with clearly defined local interests similar to those of the merchants and lesser farming aristocracy. An important example of this was Mūsā b. ʿAbd-Allāh b. K͟hāzim's revolt which secured local support. Finally a popular layer was free, at least in principle, from any direct influence exerted by the new Islamic ideology, through the setting up of new administrative structures, and hence seems to have maintained many old Iranian traditions.

Another problem is the meaning which should be attributed to the S͟hīʿa during this period. As far as official power is concerned, the active opposition party – whether initially anti-Umayyad or subsequently anti-ʿAbbāsid – seems to exhibit those features which are normally associated with the Zaīdi form of S͟hīʿism. In other words, political S͟hīʿism envisaged a seizure of power, and envisaged it in terms of armed insurrection. The fact that this was later codified through the theory stating that the caliph should not be appointed by universal consent, but on the basis of his military victory over any competitors, is not fundamentally important from the point of view of political practice, inasmuch as it amounts to an *a posteriori* motivation of a political attitude. This theory may even go back to remote ideological roots in a form of *ghulūw* (extremism) which was later denied and contradicted by the Zaidite movement itself. Devotion to the cause which found religious expression in the Kaisānites' extreme beliefs, whose inheritance was most fruitfully exploited by the 'Abbāsids themselves, seems on the other hand to have evolved around a few fundamental, typically Islamic themes, a cultural and religious framework which was to provide substance and nourishment for Twelver-Shī'ī and proto-Ismā'īlī religiosity with its doctrines and beliefs which are often and incorrectly considered as borrowed from the Iranian world.

Such a statement does not, of course, rule out the countless opportunities for the recipient of a religious message to interpret and pass it on according to well-known patterns; but this should not deter one from considering as purely Islamic the concept of *Ahl al-bait* (the prophet's family), and the process of *waq'a* undergone by a given historical figure, which is thus moved to a symbolical level. This process was to be variously acted out by those Shī'īs of Iran who were members of a more or less radical wing of Shī'ism, but its origins are nevertheless to be found in entirely Arab surroundings centring on the figure of Muḥammad b. al-Ḥanafiyya.[1]

If one were to generalize the notion of Shī'a, with some risk of inaccuracy and bias, one might say that every Shī'ī-inspired upheaval of the first two centuries of Arab conquest, whether it be Mukhtār's revolt or the rising of the Rāvandīs, shows Zaidite connotations in its exoteric aspect, as far as its goal and the organization of ways and means to achieve it are concerned. All revolts show also Qur'anic and "proto-Islamic" religious connotations, even those of the Qarmaṭīs or the 'Abbāsid revolution. For the extreme religious element stems from an originally Islamic mould to the extent in which the Qur'anic message itself is viewed as deriving from and re-interpreting the Hellenistic-Christian-Iranian gnostic culture of the age. A more peripheral, less Islamic, possibly Iranian character seems on the other hand attributable to the constant social pressure which found expression in revolts which

[1] Naubakhtī, pp. 48–50.

appear to be linked by a common denominator even when inspired by strictly non-ghulūw-affected principles, as in the case of the Khārijites in Sīstān.

In this connection the vicissitudes of the Shīʻa in Iran must claim a place apart in our analysis of Iranian upheavals and heretical theories. By this we mean not so much the vicissitudes of Zaidite Shīʻism, which as regards its diffusion in the north of Iran was an expression of ʻAbbāsid political will, as those connected with the formation of a proto-Ismāʻīlī platform in Persia and those pertaining to the religious inheritance left by the Iranian revolts which we shall deal with in the wake of what we propose to call the local expression of Shīʻī, particularly Imāmite, religiosity.

The most intense period of such upheavals covers roughly the second century of the Muslim era. As already mentioned, the change of dynasty may be considered a symptom of many social troubles in the caliphal empire. Khurāsān in particular became a disappointment to the ʻAbbāsids, gathering a number of elements of discontent among the local people. This continued to the end of the ʻAbbāsid caliphate, when the continuity of socio-religious protest seemed to give way to a more far-reaching and pervasive organization of dissent, such as the Ismāʻīlī and subsequent military-heretical-mystical movements. An actual chronicle of the Iranian revolts of this period lies outside the scope of this chapter, but we shall try to consider their political and social development by analysing their factual background before proceeding to a religious interpretation.

The first movement which should be mentioned is the Bihāfarīd revolt (129/746–7 to 131/748–9). The sources referring to it are primarily Ibn Nadīm, Thaʻālibī, Bīrūnī and Khwārazmī, as well as the heresiographers, particularly Shahristānī.[1] The area where Bihāfarīd b. Mahfurūdīn, a native of Zūzan, began to operate was Khwāf, one of the districts of Nīshāpūr. The religious motives characterizing this rebel's nature will be mentioned later; what should be stressed here is that there is no mention in the available texts of any armed action undertaken by Bihāfarīd's followers. The ensuing repression was cruel, however, which suggests at least some degree of organization. The founder-leader embarked on propaganda, or rather put forward a few suggestions which might roughly be viewed as an attempt at mediation

[1] Ibn al-Nadīm, p. 344; Thaʻālibī, p. 32; Bīrūnī, vol. II, pp. 210–11; Shahristānī, vol. II, p. 71.

between a Zoroastrian kind of religion – not *the* Zoroastrian religion – and the new creed introduced by the Arabs. He set himself up as a new prophet, and as such had attributed to him a book. The socially significant features of the revolt are three: first, the so-called book of Bihāfarīd was written in Persian; second, one of its operative rules was to maintain the upkeep of "roads and bridges, with the means provided by one-seventh of all property and the fruit of toil"; and third, those who in Nīshāpūr requested Abū Muslim's intervention against Bihāfarīd in the name of common interests were the local *mobad* and *herbad*. Abū Muslim rose to the occasion and asked 'Abd-Allāh b. Sa'īd (or Shu'ba) to capture the rebel. He was caught in the Bādghīs highlands and led in chains to Abū Muslim; the latter had him put to death together with as many of his followers as he managed to capture.

The revolt's context seems to be interpretable as a peasant movement opposed to traditional Zoroastrian–Sāsānian authority. The Persian language was obviously chosen because, unlike the protagonists of Abū Muslim's revolution, the followers of Bihāfarīd were only local people. The traditional Zoroastrian clergy's hostility lends the event a popular dimension and reveals the innovating scope of some ideas suggested by Bihāfarīd, such as the restriction of dowries to an amount not exceeding 400 *dirhams*.[1] Such tenets might have been adopted by the poorer layers of the population, who saw in Bihāfarīd a leader capable of giving these beliefs official sanction, by taking advantage of the possibility of innovations in the government of Khurāsān at the time of transition from one dynasty to another. A peasant context also emerges from the expression of interest in roads and bridges. Such interest would have found quite different expression had the viability of a major trade route been in question, and hence commercial security jeopardized. Again, as subsequently happened more than once, the rebel found refuge in the highlands, and available texts mention few instances of local "collaboration" with the representatives of legal authority.

This movement was important because it led to another, more momentous rising, that of Abū Muslim. In the history of insurrections in Iran, the so-called 'Abbāsid revolution played a primary rôle. Abū Muslim, who was to become a hero of legend and epic, turned into a rallying point for many uprisings which were spurred by his own unavenged death and inspired by his political programme. A popular motif seems to underlie many revolts, but its presence in the 'Abbāsid

[1] Bīrūnī, vol. II, p. 211.

revolt of Khurāsān is not in our view to be taken entirely for granted. Reference has been made above to the rather fluid political situation existing in Khurāsān. One of the reasons for such a situation lay in a coincidence of interests, which had not always materialized in the conquests of the first period of Islam, between local traders, small landowners and craftsmen on the one hand, and Arabs who had settled in Khurāsān without being completely tied to the Arab occupation army. Such interests were obviously contrary to those which were expressed by the central government, whether Umayyad or 'Abbāsid; by guaranteeing the stability of the existing social structure both had found a natural ally in the great landowning aristocracy entrusted by the caliphate with the task of administering and gathering taxes.

By resorting to present-day political terminology one might say that in addition to a conservative party reflecting landowning interests and deeply rooted in local tradition, though at the same time acting as the conquerors' spokesman, there was a "petit-bourgeois" party which had spontaneously grown out of Arabs and Persians alike on the common ground of hostility to the perpetuation of the landowners' privileges, which were apt to prove even more unbearable and at any rate more final as the occupation continued. Being more susceptible to new ideological influences – even if Arab in origin – the petit-bourgeois party carefully safeguarded its own class interests by protecting the local merchant and artisan economy and even by promoting economic development within wider boundaries, while at the same time refusing all integration into an economy whose centralized guidelines were laid down from outside the country. Such then was the context which provided Abū Muslim with scope for his political manoeuvring. This consisted in exploiting bourgeois conservative interests as well as the demagogical potential of the common people cut off from the political arena. He brought pressures to bear on the big landowners, who had to rely on external support and were threatened with dangerous consequences whenever they could not manage to switch allegiances at the right time. The ally of the great landowners was ultimately identified with the source of established power.

A number of clichés are thus laid open to question, for example, what is the point, when dealing with Abū Muslim's revolt, of contrasting local inhabitants and the Arabs, or linking together mawālīs and the occupiers?

After its semi-clandestine preparation, Abū Muslim's rebellion developed along extremely straightforward lines. Once the Iraqi situation appeared ripe and ready for acceptance of the Khurāsānī contingents as liberators, and Syrian discontent rendered an effective counter-offensive unlikely, Abū Muslim raised the black flag of the 'Abbāsids in 129/747 and began military operations, first in the Marv district, then in north-eastern Khurāsān; he appointed himself "*amīr āl Muḥammad*" and set off for Kūfa.

The interesting features of Abū Muslim's revolt are, however, complex and blurred. Abū Muslim's revolt broke out in Khurāsān after a first attempt at fiscal reform by the Umayyad government, following an uprising in Marv (116–17/734–5) which seems to have been aimed against the dihqāns (local lords) who supported the governor (first 'Āsim and later Asad) by the Arabs who had been long settled there and saw their interests threatened both by the newly recruited Syrian units and by the presence of "foreign" communities such as the Hephthalites who, it seems, monopolized a large proportion of local trade. The reform (121/739) was carried out by Naṣr b. Sayyār who appropriately enough was Abū Muslim's main antagonist. One thing that is clearly established is that Naṣr b. Sayyār tried to deprive the dihqāns of control over tax gathering, a development which might be viewed in terms of the local converts' interests, possibly urging them to join in protest, or it may merely represent a new departure in the supervision of power rather than a new way of using power on the governor's part. At any rate things had not changed much by 128/746, and the 'Abbāsid spokesman had ample scope for recruiting a revolutionary army. In such a situation it would be daring to depict the events in alternative terms as a contest between mawālīs and Arab conquerors. The fact that one of Abū Muslim's first revolutionary gestures was the laying down of a new "Khurāsānī" dīvān, which was no longer based on the distinction between Arabs and mawālīs, at least suggests which were the circles considered by Abū Muslim as objective allies in his enterprise.

An analysis of the composition of Abū Muslim's army might shed some new light on the soundness and historical authenticity of an antithesis between the native and foreign, Arab elements, both of which were undergoing a process of mutual integration.

On this point various views have been put forward by European scholars: peasants, Marv mawālīs, Yemenī Arabs, Arab merchant missionaries and so forth are in their turn considered as the prevailing element, although it is clear that the hard core of Abū Muslim's force was made up of the *ahl al-taqaddum*, who are none other than the Arab colonists of Khurāsān. Whatever socially inspired indications generally may be drawn, without venturing to select any hypothesis as to the components of the army which led the ʻAbbāsids to their power, but accepting them all as possible interpretations, we may consider the revolt along two main lines.

First, the local enemies of Abū Muslim were the big landowners representing the Umayyad government's interests and empowered in their name to exploit both the local and the Arabic population, thus safeguarding their own privileges and time-honoured position of power. This circumstance should not be underrated, as it proved to be a recurring factor in a number of revolts which were directly inspired by Abū Muslim and based on his programme. Second, it would be a mistake, in our view, to equate the demagogical element of Abū Muslim's propaganda with anything substantial, inasmuch as the object of his efforts was not so much the peasant (as one might be led to believe by the Māzyār rebellion) even if Abū Muslim was indeed the dihqān's most direct enemy; it was the trading and landowning bourgeois, who aimed at seizing power and considered Abū Muslim's rôle as more representative of an Islamic state in a process of territorial expansion. The dihqāns themselves, with whom according to Balʻamī Abū Muslim had some contacts, tried to climb onto the ʻAbbāsid bandwaggon, particularly after Naṣr b. Sayyār's defeat.[1] In later revolts we can detect the demagogical and pseudo-revolutionary attitude of some members of Iran's landed aristocracy.

A cultural and religious interpretation of the revolt naturally leads one to consider the practical syncretism adopted by Abū Muslim in Khurāsān in his patchwork of alliances. The fanaticism which in the Khurāsān ʻAbbāsid revolution seems to be represented by those Arab merchant-missionaries who had followed in the wake of the conquering troops and emerged among Abū Muslim's followers, supported the growth of a local religious spirit which we emphatically consider as belonging to a certain kind of Zoroastrianism, which was not the religion represented by the Mazdaean clergy. On the demagogical level the result of a policy of tolerance, or rather superimposition of assimilable and conspicuously stressed elements, is obvious: it can, at any rate, serve as a starting point for an understanding of the religious

[1] Balʻamī, vol. IV, p. 357.

theories evolved by the sects inspired by Abū Muslim. Abū Muslim's religious policy, as far as we can reconstruct it, introduced a new connection between the local and Arab "bourgeoisie"; this was the opportunity of welding together local and Islamic beliefs, leading to a religiosity unprecedented even in Islam – a tendency, so to speak, to an extreme Shī'ī development such as the later Ismā'īlī movement. This stemmed from a playing down of internal rivalries and contrasts into a Khurāsānian common denominator, which led, however far-reaching the underlying differences, to a common configuration. This is proved, both by the ever-resurgent revolutionary potential of Khurāsān and by the formation of a Khurāsānian army which even when serving under the central government (as under al-Ma'mun) exhibited a will of its own. The Khurāsānians showed a well-defined ideological configuration exerting a certain weight in giving or withholding support to the ruler of the day.

From a typological point of view, the most significant among the uprisings inspired or justified by Abū Muslim's example was that of the Rāvandīs (141/758–9), which though occurring in Iraq was started, according to our sources, by Khurāsānian soldiers.[1] The life of the caliph al-Manṣūr himself was for a brief moment in jeopardy, as the rebels succeeded in surrounding his palace where no security measures had been taken. Apart from their Khurāsānian origin, the extreme nature of this group's underlying ideas will be dealt with when analysing religious motivations. One factor, however, should be stressed, namely the identification of the enemy as the ruling sovereign, which goes back to the idealized prototype of the leader, as embodied in Muḥammad b. al-Ḥanafiyya, that is, the concept of a sovereign who was such because he was divine and was divine because he ruled as a sovereign.[2] This, of course, goes against the theme, beloved in early Islam, of the true prince recognized as such by his subjects, in whose conceptions he could not help but recognize himself. With regard to the Rāvandīs, who incidentally were butchered without a qualm, this did not prevent the occurrence of a number of Zoroastrian motifs in the popular meaning we have given this term.

Within two months of Abū Muslim's death, Sunbādh the Magian raised the standard of rebellion in the murdered propagandist's name (138/755–6), setting himself up as his avenger and heir. According to

[1] Bal'amī, vol. IV, p. 371, and Ṭabarī, vol. III, pp. 129–33.
[2] Naubakhtī, p. 53.

our sources he had been appointed general under Abū Muslim, had grown rich with him and now claimed Abū Muslim's treasure from the caliph. Nearly all historical sources, from Baladhurī and Ṭabarī to Ibn al-Athīr, mention this revolt, which met with a certain success.[1] According to Sadighi it gave birth to four traditions, which differ somewhat particularly as to its length, and the number of actual followers.[2] Sunbādh is however portrayed by all as a Mazdaean from Nīshāpūr. The route of his propaganda and search for reinforcements is also relatively undisputed: Qūmis, Ray, Ṭabaristān. Niẓām al-Mulk further points out that these places were chosen as being inhabited by Rāfiḍites and Mazdakites.[3] We have thus before us an obvious indication of the prospective recipients of Sunbādh's propaganda, as well as an obvious recourse to Abū Muslim's method of joining Muslim and non-Muslim when faced with the need for common action. For such an orthodox and fanatically anti-Shī'ī author as Niẓām al-Mulk, the meeting ground is provided by heterodoxy; this however did not prevent the movement in question from gaining a foothold even in "Arab" territory, or from taking the daring step of making the destruction of the Ka'ba their pass-word. This union of Muslim and non-Muslim happened, in our view, because common ground was reached through the religious syncretism mentioned above, on the basis of common interest in a decentralization of central power.

The leader's wealth stressed by our sources and the claim to Abū Muslim's treasure do not allow one to bracket this revolt together with other purely "protest" movements. On the other hand Spuler indicates that Sunbādh's followers included mountain dwellers.[4] Though this factor was to become a fundamental one only in later uprisings, it helped to define a new geographical focus, apart from Khurāsān, where rebel forces concentrated and found a hinterland for their operations; this was Qūmis–Ṭabaristān and the Bādghīs mountain area which had already been the scene of Bihāfarīd's activities.

Though the insurrection officially ended with the repression carried out by the 'Abbāsid general Jauhar b. Marrār in 138/756 the movement, or rather certain elements connected with it, survived as in Bihāfarīd's case and were subsequently stimulated and organized by the inheritors

[1] Cf. Ṭabarī, vol. III, pp. 119–20; Ibn al-Athīr, vol. v, pp. 368–9.
[2] G. H. Sadighi, pp. 133–4, 138, 143–4.
[3] Niẓām al-Mulk, p. 182.
[4] B. Spuler, p. 50.

of the rebel's leadership, without any ideological revision of the underlying motivations.

This supports our hypothesis about a common ground based on syncretism in religion and on opposition to the big landowners, and hence of an anti-ʿAbbāsid nature, from 131/749 onwards. Even if the official chroniclers of these heresies leading into open rebellion often discriminate between the Abū Muslimiyya and the Khurramiyya, who emerged as protagonists of the Bābak and Māzyār uprisings, they cannot adequately uphold such a distinction when faced by concrete instances.[1] In Sunbādh's case, too, reference is made to the Khurramiyya, just as Abū Muslim continues to provide a signpost even for those movements which are not officially considered linked with him.

Al-Manṣūr's rule saw another uprising similar to Sunbādh's, which also bore the twin label of Abū Muslimiyya and Khurramiyya. This was the revolt led by Isḥāq the Turk, who is also considered a *dāʿī* (missionary) of Abū Muslim's. The most interesting references to Isḥāq are to be found in Ibn Nadīm's *Fihrist*.[2] One is faced first of all with a number of hypotheses regarding Isḥāq, who is variously portrayed as a dāʿī of Abū Muslim's; as an ʿAlid descendant of Zaid, or more precisely a son of Yaḥyā b. Zaid, killed in Jūzjān in 125/742–3 in Naṣr b. Sayyār's time, or as a Transoxiana Turk settled in Transoxiana after Abū Muslim's death to work as a missionary among the local Turks, whence his *laqab*; or even as an illiterate person of Transoxiana origins, instructed by *jinns*.

Judging by his name, Isḥāq does not sound like a Mazdaean, but rather like a Jew or Arab. The conflicting reports as to Isḥāq's origin again indicate that such uprisings were non-specific, being neither Mazdaean, nor strictly Iranian or anti-Arab. The fact that Isḥāq's rebellion was one of a number of uprisings sparked by the army of the Khurāsān governors Abū Dā'ūd Ibrāhīm b. Khālid and ʿAbd al-Jabbār between 137/754–6 and 140/757–8, does however enable us to classify it. After his death in dubious circumstances in Khurāsān, Abū Dā'ūd was succeeded by ʿAbd al-Jabbār. In spite of the former's repression, rebellion still smouldered and ʿAbd al-Jabbār had a few of its leaders imprisoned, but the caliph, angered by the lingering unrest, sent in an army led by his son Mahdī. At this stage ʿAbd al-Jabbār chose white as his colour and joined forces with the rebels, who since Isḥāq's death

[1] E.g. Naubakhtī, p. 67–8, and Baghdādī, pp. 241, 251.
[2] Ibn al-Nadīm, pp. 344–5.

were led by one Barāz. Defeat was a foregone conclusion and 'Abd al-Jabbār was handed over to Mahdī's general.[1]

It would be pointless to insist on the social aspects of the rebellion's leadership, since the sources themselves acknowledge the community of interests of the ruling governor and the rebels *vis-à-vis* the central power. If there was a new factor, this was the revival of what had been a major plank in Abū Muslim's and his predecessors' autonomous, Khurāsān-oriented policy, namely a special consideration for Transoxiana and an appeal to the Christian and local trading bourgeoisie based on a common interest in keeping local control out of the central government's hands. This was tantamount to freedom of initiative in the commercial and hence also in the military field, on whether or not to expand, found settlements, form alliances with the infidels and the like. The peasant, alongside a merchant bourgeoisie, is the second constantly recurring factor of the uprisings in question; it is precisely in Transoxiana that a well structured and even culturally defined peasant element is suggested, for instance by the *Tārīkh-i Bukhārā*, particularly in connection with the great cotton growing districts and associated marketing areas.[2] In this instance the peasant element, which might elsewhere be viewed as the object of mere demagogical propaganda, could be derived from a more conscious alliance with merchants against the big landowners.

Another conspicuous uprising in al-Manṣūr's time was that of Ustādhsīs (148–51/765–8), which spread through the districts of Herāt, Bādghīs and Sīstān and might indeed be identified as the Bust rising mentioned, without further elucidation, in the *Tārīkh-i Sīstān*.[3] References to this rebellion are to be found in most historians such as Ṭabarī, Bal'amī, Ya'qūbī, Maqdisī, Gardīzī, Ibn al-Athīr and Ibn Khaldūn. Its Persian and Khurāsānian leader took up Bihāfarīd's efforts initially in Bādghīs, exactly in the area where Bihāfarīd and his followers had sought sanctuary. The numbers of Ustādhsīs' followers are stated as being about 300,000 men. The task of putting down the revolt fell to a general, Khāzim b. Khuzaima, who according to most sources managed to slay 70,000 rebels.[4] Ustādhsīs himself was however taken to Baghdad and apparently executed there, while another 30,000 people who had been captured together with him were set free. Some sources

[1] Ṭabarī, vol. III, pp. 128, 135–6.
[2] Narshakhī, pp. 11–12, 14, 16.
[3] *Tārīkh-i Sīstān*, pp. 142–3.
[4] Ṭabarī, vol. III, pp. 355–8.

state that Ustādhsīs' daughter later gave birth to Hārūn al-Rāshīd and al-Hādī.

Such references to this rising as are available suggest a survival in Khurāsān of Abū Muslim's party, which not fortuitously drew into its ranks, among others, Bihāfarīd's successors, though these had been attacked by Abū Muslim himself. What, however, is more specific, is the persistence of unrest even after the heavy repression to which reference has already been made, not merely in an endemic form, but also in active opposition up to 151/768 with inconstant success and especially with a number of converging local religious alliances as reported in the chronicle of Sīstān.[1]

Muqanna''s rebellion seems however to exhibit the whole gamut of motivation under consideration though the length attributed to the revolt varies from seven to thirteen years in the sources. An exhaustive analysis of the sources and the discrepancies in their information concerning such features as the protagonist's name and the length of the uprising is to be found in Sadighi. Such other details as are provided in turn by other sources should also be viewed not as conflicting with, but rather as complementing, the generally accepted data on the history of the rebellion, and as clarifying its interpretation by the official chronicles which mention or ignore them.

Some of these data are purely religious, but most discrepancies or rather nuances deal with the social context of the revolt. The revolt, whatever its actual length, took place during the first years of al-Mahdī's rule and spread initially to Khurāsān, Marv and Balkh, and later to Transoxiana and particularly to the Kish district. On the protagonist's surname of Muqanna', the veiled one, there is unanimous agreement, while the discrepancies on his own and his father's actual names in available references enable one to formulate a number of hypotheses as to his origin and social condition. His own name was 'Aṭā' according to Ibn Khallikān and Jāḥiẓ before him; his father's was unknown (but according to Ibn Khallikān possibly Dādūya); Hāshim b. Ḥakim was his name according to Bīrūnī; Ḥākim was to be read as Hāshim, once his mission had started, according to Ibn al-Athīr; Hāshim b. Ḥākim was his name according to the *Tārīkh-i Bukhārā*, and he was said to have lived in a Marv village, Kāzak or Kāza.[2]

[1] *Tārīkh-i Sīstān*, p. 143.

[2] Cf. Ibn Khallikān, vol. II, pp. 205–6, vol. II, I, p. 436; Bīrūnī, vol. II, p. 211; Ibn al-Athīr, vol. VI, pp. 25–6; Narshakhī, p. 63.

The point of such names as 'Aṭā', Hāshim and Ḥākim and their religious meanings seems obvious enough, but there is no comparable evidence as to his family's social background. His family may have found its way into the Arab administration. His father, who hailed from Balkh, seems to have been an officer in the governor of Khurāsān's army under al-Manṣūr; hence he may have been a native integrated into the new system; at the same time he might have been a Mazdaean, inasmuch as a decidedly Mazdaean origin is attributed to the leaders of the uprisings in question. The name of Dādūya would in fact support such an interpretation.

When dealing with his activity the texts yield more explicit data, depicting him as a laundryman, having also a knowledge of the occult, as a military chief in Khurāsān under Abū Muslim and after the latter's death as the secretary of 'Abd al-Jabbār, the very governor who was later to join Ustādhsīs rebellion.

There would seem to be some likelihood in the hypothesis which views as a topos the ascription of low occupations to anybody who was considered a heretic. This would on the contrary emerge as a positive feature in a Shī'ī environment which we might define, in accordance with our line of interpretation, as belonging to an "Arab" type of extremism, and which, according to the sources, Muqanna' belonged to as a follower of the Rizāmiyya sect, linked with and possibly an offshoot of the Rāvandī.[1] This group supported Muḥammad b. al-Ḥanafiyya's claim to the imāmate and the esoteric transfer of power from the latter to the 'Abbāsids through Abū Muslim, whom however the Rizāmiyya held to have really died. During Ustādhsīs' revolt, though with all likelihood in his capacity as 'Abd al-Jabbār's secretary, Muqanna' performed his first *ẓuhūr*, claiming a prophetic mission for himself. He was jailed in Baghdad and later set free, and in accordance with a time-honoured pattern, he was officially consecrated as rebel chief and leader. But whom did he turn to, and who followed him? Let us first of all analyse his socio-political demands. The most explicit words on this subject are to be found in Bīrūnī: he bade himself and his followers obey the laws and institutions established by Mazdak, which in an orthodox source implies a number of clichés such as sexual licence and so forth, but it also indicates a radically different choice, compared with the Islamic one, as far as the leader's rôle is concerned. The leader is no longer a representative or trustee of God's order on earth, though

[1] Baghdādī, p. 243; Naubakhtī, p. 68.

without partaking of a prophetic mission and bound to follow the model of the prophet's legislative rôle; rather he is a leader entitled to modify the social order, to give religious sanction to such a change, and to apply it within his own social group. The fact that Bīrūnī claims to have dealt with al-Muqanna' in his book on the Qarmaṭīs is, in our view, no coincidence.

The superficially progressive nature of such a promise to apply Mazdak's laws and institutions, which was not unlike the Qarmaṭīs' community programme, is belied first and foremost by the actual main goal of such uprisings, namely the ruler's removal through military organization and activity. It is also more substantially refuted by the planned experiment's failure to proceed beyond the organizing movement which, externally, exerted pressures and constraints undistinguishable from those of the very official power it was supposed to replace. One cannot neglect the fact that our sources mention a village in the Nakhshab area, probably Bazda, which not only rejected the propaganda of the "white-clad ones" but actually launched a night attack against the rebels, killing their leader. Muqanna''s revenge was merciless and not unlike the reprisals organized by 'Abbāsid troops against insurgents.

On his way back from Baghdad, Muqanna' began to spread his word in Transoxiana, and his followers came to be identified as the wearers of white garments. The link actually consisted in officially adopting Mazdak's line in Transoxiana, in order to enlist the support of those who were known to Islamic heresiographers as Mazdakites, and locally as wearers of white garments. Their first occurrence seems to date to the 6th century A.D., and they apparently mixed in Manichaean, Turkish (particularly in Soghdiana) and trading circles throughout the area and as far as China.[1] In Transoxiana, moreover, propaganda was made easier by the fact that since the Arab conquest that territory had witnessed a number of disturbances, which can be understood only by recognizing the opposition of interests between big landowners and central power on the one hand, and Arab immigrant or local small farmers and traders on the other. In 133/750–1 a man called Sharīk had engineered a revolt in Bukhārā, where he met with the opposition of the local *Bukhār-khudāt's* son, Qutaiba, who helped Abū Muslim in putting down the rising but later deserted in his turn from the 'Abbāsid

[1] Cf. A. Yu. Yakubovskii, "Vosstanie Mukanny-Dvizhenie Lyudei v belykh odezhdakh" in *Sovetskoe Vostokovedenie*, vol. v (Moscow, 1948), pp. 35–54.

ranks, perjured Islam and was killed on Abū Muslim's own orders.[1] A brother of his later joined Muqanna''s movement. It should be noted that the leader of the rebellion, Sharīk b. Mahdī, was of Arab origin, and that an attempt was made to extend the rebellion to Samarqand. It thus seems likely that Muqanna' emerged as the leader of a local opposition movement whose extreme fringe was represented by the wearers of white, but whose ranks included, even though in different relations to each other, different segments of the population whose anti-'Abbāsid discontent was often exploited by local Arab leaders. Sharīk's revolt was not the only case in point. Yūsuf al-Barm's Khārijite revolt (160/776–7) in Khurāsān and Bukhārā helped to aggravate a critical situation to Muqanna''s advantage. This rebellion also followed the pattern of the other "Iranian" revolts under consideration. After a few initial victories its leader proclaimed himself a prophet, took over a certain area (Marv-ar-Rūd/Ṭāliqān/Jūzjān), was attacked by Yazīd b. Māzyād acting on the caliph's orders, captured, taken to Baghdad and executed.

The details of Muqanna''s activity are not much different: the village of Subakh near Kish went over to him and the Arab amīr was killed with the help of the local feudal lord. In Bukhārā the local Bukhār-khudāt, called Bunyāt b. Tughshāda, was led to join the revolt by the hope of setting up an independent state. Muqanna' established his headquarters in the mountain area of Sanām, also in the Kish district. Raids were essentially plundering forays, according to our sources, such as the typical raid against the Arab, or at any rate pro-Arab, village of Numijkat or Bumichkat. The movement's poles of resistance also included the town of Narshakh, which did not fall into Arab hands until 159/776, after which the white-clad rebels' stronghold was moved toward Soghdiana and particularly the Zarafshān valley. In Narshakh, the rebels were led by a woman, the widow of one of Abū Muslim's officers, whom the latter had ultimately condemned to death. Such was the only bond of joint anti-'Abbāsid opposition which had led the woman to throw in her lot with Muqanna', without however sharing his religious beliefs. The task of putting down the rebellion fell to a number of governors and generals, ranging from Ḥumaid b. Qaḥṭaba who had a watch kept on the Oxus banks to stop Muqanna' from crossing the river to Jibrā'īl b. Yaḥyā al-Khurāsānī, appointed governor of Samarqand in 159/775–6 to help restore order in Bukhārā, and

[1] Ibn Kathīr, *al-Bidāya wa'l-nihāya* (Cairo, 1932–9), vol. x, p. 56.

Mu'ādh b. Muslim who rose to the governorship of Khurāsān after the Khārijite revolt (161/777–8). The latter managed to draft an army with the aid of the local aristocracy and secured the support of Sa'īd al-Harashī, the governor of Herāt. The latter circumstance enabled him to extend operations over a wide region at the same time, thus cutting a number of the rebels' contacts and supply routes, and it led to the siege of the Sanām stronghold by Sa'īd al-Harashī, followed by its capture and the fabulous death of Muqanna' and his women.

Having thus roughly established the facts, we have yet to characterize Muqanna''s followers as something more than just rebels merely opposed to the 'Abbāsids and the big landowners.

Yakubovskii's hypotheses on the white-clad fraternity can be shared insofar as they assume the presence of a peasant element, or rather of peasant organizations, in this case of fortified villages along the Zarafshān and Kashka Daryā valleys, which occasionally joined the new ideology together with their leaders. This peasant element differs from its counterpart in the previous risings, for here they were not merely willing to co-operate, but also organized to the point of suggesting consciousness of their own interests (cotton growing and marketing), jeopardized by the new authority as represented, though not exclusively, by the fiscal system introduced by the Arab administration. The movement also included the mainly urban merchant class to which reference has already been made, to which one might add the craftsmen, if on the basis of existing data one were not inclined to view the distinction between craftsmen and petit-bourgeois urban traders as irrelevant. The situation had obviously not evolved to the point of allowing one to distinguish strictly artisan interests on the one hand and trading interests on the other. It looks as if the urban reality upon which Muqanna''s enterprise was able to prosper may have been of a merchant-artisan type, that is his propaganda struck echoing chords among those city dwellers who were engaged in productive activities and jealous of their local interests, and hence of their autonomy. There was an exception, however, that craftsmen engaged in military production would stay loyal to official authority. Available texts unfortunately do not mention whether Muqanna''s followers had any particular equipment which would enable them to conduct tactically diversified operations and reprisals in the context of some sort of guerrilla warfare. Another element on whose support Muqanna' relied were the Turks, mainly from Soghdiana as some of his Bukhāran generals' names seem to suggest. As already mentioned, the Turks had already made their appearance under this label during Isḥāq's revolt. What should be stressed here is that the sources mention Turks, not Turkish peasants or soldiers, as though referring to tribes, just as Turkish tribes acted as vehicles of Manichaean and Nestorian missionary propaganda in the eastern areas of Transoxiana, toward China.

Unlike the uprisings mentioned so far, the Khurramiyya or Khurramdīn movement, which also gave birth to the revolts of Bābak al-Khurramī and Māzyār prince of Ṭabaristān, seems to yield more information on its social components and aims.[1] No movement, however, is defined by our sources with greater vagueness. The very term of Khurramdīn can in fact incorporate a number of meanings ranging from ambiguous though plausible identification with a reformed branch of new Mazdakism adjusted to Islamic pattern, to a vague sort of common denominator for a number of small sects mentioned by heresiographers, such as the Kūdakiyya, Kurdshāhiyya or Ludshāhiyya and others.[2] Some Khurramiyya groups, of course, can be included in the wider Abū Muslimiyya pattern on the basis of an ever increasing assimilation by a group which, though not the basic one, enables one to determine, through its definition, a common identifying theme compared with other heterodox doctrines. This is not to mention the problem of placing the Muḥammira, the red-wearers (*surkh-jāmagān*) or the red-standard bearers (*surkh-'alamān*) who are often identified with the Khurramiyya.

To sum up, by Khurramiyya one means the whole wide movement which operated throughout Iran, with a possible focus in Āzarbāījān and Ṭabaristān. The latter province is mentioned by the heresiographers but not by the historians. This movement came to be variously coloured and named according to the time and place of its transformation into actual outward insurrectional manifestations, marked (not unlike the risings already mentioned) by every feature of organized opposition to centralized government and, by and large, to its representative, the local governor. This also enables one to understand the "conversion" mentioned by some historians, of the Khurramiyya to Qarmaṭism, once the latter seemed likely to gain the upper hand in the struggle for the Arab caliphate.

[1] Cf. Sa'īd Nafīsī, pp. 8–15. The *Tabṣirat al-'awām* gives an "ideological" summary of the movement.

[2] Mas'ūdī, vol. VI, p. 187.

Not only did a movement such as the Khurramiyya – like the whole Iranian–Mazdaean heresy whose components we are trying to analyse – objectively aid Ismā'īlī propaganda, but the fact that the struggle against the Sulṭān's power and urban or administrative aristocracy waged by Ismā'īlism during the 5th/11th and 6th/12th centuries exploited the same slogans first used by the Iranian heretical movements prevents one from considering the Ismā'īlī movement as unitarian from the point of view of class, even at its inception.

On the Khurramiyya we have a number of sources and abundant if, as usual, biased data. Apart from the heresiographers the most quoted texts are those of Ibn Nadīm, Ṭabarī particularly as regards Bābak's revolt, and Niẓām al-Mulk who also relates some traditions slightly diverging from Ṭabarī's, particularly on Bābak's capture and death.[1]

The very meaning of Khurramiyya appears uncertain to the authors dealing with it. It is usually related to the meaning of the Persian term *khurram* "joyful", so as to stigmatize the movement as "licentious" and justify its dependence on Mazdakism, which was considered as too tolerant from the point of view of ethics. This dependence, however, was occasionally related to Mazdak's wife, Khurrama, held to have given her name to Mazdak's followers after his death. There is also a geographical explanation of the name (from a village called Khurram), which is the least likely interpretation.

Before isolating the movement's basic themes, we should briefly outline its activity, while at the same time touching on a number of lesser, Khurramiyya-linked risings, which can be viewed and interpreted only within the scope of the insurrectional movement promoted in Iran by the Khurramiyya in their different connotations and facets, from 118/736 onward.

In 118/736 Muslim authors mention 'Ammār or 'Umāra b. Yazīd, a Christian convert supporter of Muḥammad b. 'Alī and later of the 'Abbāsids, who upon being sent to Khurāsān by the great Missionary of Kūfa gathered a certain following and began to propagate the Khurramiyya doctrine, pronouncing cult-worship non-mandatory and preaching the common ownership of women. He changed his name to Khidāsh and was ordered to be killed by the governor of Khurāsān, Asad b. 'Abd-Allāh. The Khurramiyya are mentioned in all the risings which occurred after Abū Muslim's death, particularly in 137/754–5 in the mountain areas of Khurāsān. According to some sources the red-

[1] Ibn al-Nadīm, pp. 342–4; Ṭabarī, vol. III, pp. 1201–33; Niẓām al-Mulk, p. 204.

clad fraternity intervened on Muqanna''s and Yūsuf al-Barm's side in Khurāsān and Transoxiana during al-Mahdī's caliphate. In 162/778–9 the Muḥammira under 'Abd al-Qahhār raised the flag of revolt in Gurgān and were joined by the local Khurramiyya. They proclaimed Abū Muslim's simulated death and, purporting to be led by his son Abu'l-Gharra, they made their way to Ray, while the caliph, al-Mahdī, ordered 'Amr or 'Umar b. 'Alā to scatter them. In the same year the Khurramiyya were in a state of unrest in Iṣfahān, Ya'qūbī claiming that the area was inhabited by Kurds and Persians of humble social extraction.[1] According to Ṭabarī another Muḥammira revolt took place in Gurgān in 180/796–7, their alleged leader being a *zandīq* (Manichaean,) 'Amr b. Muḥammad al-'Umarakī, while Ibn al-Athīr mentions a similar revolt in Khurāsān during the following year.[2] In 192/807–8, simultaneously with Rāfi' b. Laith's revolt in Khurāsān, the Khurramiyya rose in Āzarbāījān, whither Hārūn sent an army of ten thousand horse under 'Abd-Allāh b. Mālik to restore order. In the same year Dīnawarī mentions a Khurramiyya rebellion in the Jibāl, which might coincide with the preceding one.[3] Bābak's insurrection originated about 200/816 and lasted until his death in 223/837–8, a date that does not however mark the end of the movement's military activities. The date attributed to the revolt is no coincidence, occurring as it does at the same time as an alleged deposition of Ma'mūn in Iraq, also the appointment of 'Alī al-Riḍā as heir presumptive and the end of hostilities between the caliph's commander in the field Harthama and his secretary Faḍl b. Sahl because of Harthama's violent death which exasperated the situation in Iraq. One must also mention a famine which occurred in Iran during the following year. The area of operations was the Badhdh district in Āzarbāījān, which could provide Bābak a route of withdrawal to Armenia and the Byzantine territories. The legendary features surrounding the name of Bābak, variously identified as the son of a Nabatean or a descendant of Abū Muslim, as a shepherd and the son of a blind mother, will be dealt with later; suffice it for the time being to touch on the main stages of his military and political career. He made his appearance on the political scene under Jāvīdān, one of the leaders of the rebel movement and a rival of Abū 'Imrān's.[4] He secured the goodwill of Jāvīdān's wife, and after Jāvīdān's death which followed shortly afterwards from wounds inflicted in mysterious cir-

[1] Ya'qūbī, p. 275.

[2] Ṭabarī, vol. III, p. 645; Ibn al-Athīr, vol. VI, p. 109.

[3] Dīnawarī, p. 387.

[4] Cf. Ibn al-Nadīm, p. 343.

cumstances, the deceased's wife staged an investiture in Bābak's favour and married him with the consent of the members of the sect. Bābak's first action was a large-scale foray against a Muslim village, carried out in a bloodthirsty manner which contrasted with the Khurramiyya's customary gentle and mild habits acknowledged by the sources themselves. His watchword seems to have been: Bābak shall seize the earth, kill the tyrants and restore the religion of Mazdak; he who had been humbled shall be honoured and the humble shall become great. He was practically in control of the whole Badhdh area, while the Arabs had withdrawn to Marāgha; for security reasons he had destroyed villages and towns all around his stronghold. This marked the beginning of a succession of campaigns which Ma'mūn launched against Bābak, led by the governor of Armenia and Āzarbāījān, but the balance of power remained undisturbed for about twenty years, in spite of a few critical moments when central power was in jeopardy. In 217/832, owing to internal strife, the governor of Armenia and Āzarbāījān, 'Alī b. Hishām, joined forces with the rebels and was subsequently defeated and captured by his successor Ujaif b. 'Anbasa. In 218/833 the rising overflowed into Fārs and Kūhistān under 'Alī b. Mazdak, who easily gained control of the region's mountain areas.

Bābak's insurrection was defeated only under al-Mu'taṣim, who entrusted one of the Transoxiana princes, Afshīn (220/835), with the direction of operations. Bābak was betrayed by local dihqāns whom he believed to be his allies and fell into enemy hands. He was handed to Afshīn's troops by Sahl b. Sunbādh, an Armenian prince in 222/836–7, and executed in Sāmarrā (223/837) while his brother and assistant 'Abd-Allāh was delivered to the prince of Ṭabaristān, Ibn Sharvīn, who had him put to death in Baghdad. This rebellion was followed almost immediately in Ṭabaristān by Māzyār's conflict with the governor of Khurāsān, 'Abd-Allāh b. Ṭāhir, as well as, in Āzarbāījān, by the insubordination of Afshīn's brother-in-law Mankjūr, who refused to deliver to the caliph a portion of Bābak's booty. 'Abd-Allāh b. Ṭāhir sent his troops against Māzyār, while Afshīn was accused of inciting the latter to resistance and talking his brother-in-law into not yielding up the treasure, in the belief that any troops sent by the caliph were sure to join the rebels.

Māzyār was put to death in Sāmarrā the following year in front of Bābak's gallows, and Afshīn's trial seemed to be an inquisition purporting to prove his guilt through his alleged false conversion to Islam.

Whether or not Afshīn had actually engineered a plot is hard to judge on the basis of historical data; it is however noteworthy that the sources ideologically and religiously equate these three figures – Bābak, Māzyār and Afshīn – as upholders of some vague Iranian restoration and defenders of the "white religion" against the "black religion" of Islam.

Rebellion continued even after the major leaders had disappeared: one Maḥmūd, who agitated in 235/849–50 under al-Mutawakkil in the Nīshāpūr area, seems to have started his active opposition by staging a sort of sit-in in front of Bābak's gallows. Revolts clearly labelled as Khurramiyya went on throughout the 3rd/9th century, particularly in the Āzarbāījān–Ṭabaristān areas, without however attaining the same significance as during the early ʿAbbāsid period. As already mentioned, the context of Khurramiyya activity seems on the whole easier to determine, compared with other movements.

In the case of Bābak's revolt the presence of a peasant element is beyond doubt; Bābak's allies consistently include dihqāns, identifiable as smallholders in contrast with the big landowners who were the targets of the movement. When dealing with Bābak's first armed expedition, it is said that his men, the dihqāns were unused to war, and learnt the technique of attack during first clashes, and thus became brave. Until the decline of Bābak's fortunes the local dihqāns naturally considered themselves as his allies and he had no objection to their support.

A closer scrutiny of the texts shows that Māzyār's revolts and Afshīn's own alleged betrayal can only be understood by assuming that the movement underwent an involution. The texts more or less accurately mention people of base origins (Bābak himself was allegedly the son of an itinerant oil vendor), but both Bābak's alleged alliance with the emperor of Byzantium, and the fact that his inheritance included a booty large enough to become a bone of contention, as well as the possible support on which Afshīn's brother-in-law might have relied in the area, suggest the existence of interests and intrigues on a higher level compared with those of the Khurramiyya risings before Bābak's time and the rebellions which have been analysed above. To sum up, one might venture to suggest the following interpretation: starting from the hypothesis that both Bābak's and Māzyār's goal consisted in attacking the large Arab estates in the provinces west and south of the Caspian Sea,[1] this goal eventually changed as some sort of

[1] Ṭabarī, vol. III, p. 1269 and pp. 1278–9.

army was organized and effective control had to be exercised over a given area with a view of supplanting the ancient landed class with a new one, which, however, was not necessarily more amenable to such egalitarian slogans. No clarifying data on the way the area was administered by Bābak are provided by the sources, apart from a reference to his general, Tarkhān, who was captured and killed "while on his way to the village where he lived in the winter", as though taking it for granted that this kind of person had a rôle in the local agricultural structure, while at the same time being called upon at fixed intervals to take part in military operations.[1]

By this we mean that the ideology of the dihqāns, who were the mainstay of most risings in Bābak's time, aimed at and succeeded in exerting on the central government and the big landowners such pressure as to bring about a changing of the guard within the ruling class, without any actual substitution of classes or any real social innovation. Bābak's own programme, to which reference has already been made, partly confirms this, and a further indication should be seen in the subsequent convergence of the Khurramiyya into the Qarmaṭī movement, which also took shape according to a demagogical-revolutionary pattern operating at least roughly in the forefront of the movement, but amounting to no more than a mere change in traditional authority.

From a social point of view Bābak's Khurramiyya revolt enables one to identify a number of features of Iranian society at the time. Before stressing the elements of religious (Iranian, gnostic, Christian) syncretism, reference should be made to the feminist trend which seems to underlie the Khurramiyya movement. One of Mazdak's wives is said to have organized the movement, giving it her own name. Jāvīdān's wife engineered the transfer of power to Bābak, and her rôle received full recognition. Islamic texts mention, if contradictorily, a communistic status of women, and refer to women's right to a second husband, any issue from this second marriage enjoying the same rights as the children born in the first. A particularly striking rule, furthermore, was laid down by Bābak, stating that a man's place of residence should follow the woman's.[2] It is quite likely that this rule rested on more fundamental patrimonial and agricultural considerations, which on the whole must not have been unfavourable to women.

Another factor consists in two anti-Jewish quotations mentioned in

[1] Sadighi, p. 255.

[2] Bal'amī, vol. IV, p. 543.

the texts. Referring to the Arabs he is being handed to, Bābak tells the dihqān who betrayed him, "You have sold me to these Jews." And when general Afshīn leads his children and wife out of Bābak's stronghold, he comments, "Should I be afraid of these Jews, to keep my wife locked up in a fortress?" In a mainly agricultural and Iranian context, these two incidents seem at any rate peculiar.[1]

Iran's insurrectional landscape would be incomplete without reference to the Khārijite and Zaidite revolts typical of the 'Abbāsid empire of the day, though of course they seem less significant to the purpose of isolating from such movements a possible Iranian common denominator or a possible peculiarity of social background providing fertile soil for any given rising.

Many of the Khārijite slogans and even more of the Zaidite catchwords impregnated with Ma'mūn's triumphant Mu'tazilism and somehow linked to the troubles and internal difficulties of the empire are known to match the official interpretation of such movements, which has been dealt with in every heresiographical text. That is why instead of trying to give as complete as possible a picture of the Zaidite and Khārijite presence in Iran, we shall confine ourselves to a couple of examples: Yaḥyā b. 'Abd-Allāh b. Ḥasan's flight from Iraq to Iran and Ḥamza al-Khārijī's revolt in Sīstān. The former was linked to the foundation of an 'Alid dynasty south of the Caspian Sea, accompanied by Zaidite penetration and slow but constant conversion of the local people to the Zaidite branch of Islam, and the second includes some characteristic features within the development of Khārijite revolts.

Yaḥyā b. 'Abd-Allāh did not reach Iran directly, but spent some time in Yemen, Egypt and Maghrib. Hārūn had a price put on his head. Yaḥyā went to Iraq and then to Ray, and left for Khurāsān where the local governor failed to capture him. He made his way to Transoxiana where a Turkish leader, the *Khāqān*, a secret convert to Islam, gave him his support. Thence he went to Qūmis, to the mountain area of Ṭabaristān, and then to Dailam, where he was welcomed by local lords and began to spread his doctrine with the approval of the local jurisconsults and apparently of al-Shāfi'ī himself. The interesting point is that precisely in Iran Zaidite propaganda enjoyed the orthodox jurists' support. This should not be viewed as a strange coincidence in the history of Iran-mediation between different doctrines growing out of an imperfectly Islamized context; this occurred through law, that is

[1] *Ibid.*, pp. 532, 544.

through a routine of legal administration which was bound to be one of the institutions most likely to exhibit an open and democratic aspect of Islam compared with the old order of things. It indicates one of the ways through which Iran was basically Islamized, and seems to confirm once more the possibility of interpreting the syncretism of certain Irano-Islamic movements of the age as a conscious effort toward the unification of different points of view on the everyday, routine level. This was similar to what orthodox Islam itself was doing in Iran *vis-à-vis* heretical Islam, which was nevertheless recognized and pigeonholed in the classical schemes of *firaq* classification.

Once Faḍl b. Sahl's political activity gave the 'Alids control of the area, the caliph could find no weapon capable of opposing his minister except such juridical opposition as he could muster by obvious arrangement through the Qazvīn, Ray or Hamadān *qāḍīs* led by Abu'l-Ba<u>kh</u>tarī Wahb b. Wahb, setting Justān against Yaḥyā by proclaiming Yaḥyā a slave of Hārūn's. Yet an 'Alid presence, more than any other factor, might have provided Iran with an alternative to the caliph, as the obvious result of the old 'Abbāsid propaganda based on the *ahl al-bait* and particularly on the motto "*Muḥammad yā Manṣūr*", that is the slogan in the name of Nafs al-Zakiyya and revenge for the Zaidī martyrs.

The <u>Kh</u>ārijite revolt (181/797–8 to 213/828–9), which can be practically identified with its leader Ḥamza b. 'Abd-Allāh al-<u>Sh</u>ārī al-<u>Kh</u>ārijī's armed activities, is particularly significant as being precisely the rising to which reference is made both when trying to prove an alleged constant heterodoxy of Sīstān within Islam, and when claiming that <u>Kh</u>ārijite success in the area rested upon some ancient proclivity to certain vague forms of religious strictness which had dovetailed into, and become identified with, the <u>Kh</u>ārijite creed.

Without going into the problem it should be pointed out, as far as this revolt is concerned, based on the account contained in the *Tārī<u>kh</u>-i Sīstān*, that by and large, throughout the heresies considered, Islam appears as the new medium of ancient concepts or needs felt by the local people, who express them in more or less heterodox Islamic terms.[1] This is nothing new in religious history. In Iran's case it becomes more particularly striking, because only by considering such a development in the context of the origin of the movement in question, can one somehow form a picture of the social and religious situation of Iran on the local level, apart from the official catchwords of 'Abbāsid his-

[1] *Tārī<u>kh</u>-i Sīstān*, pp. 156–80.

torians. Any hint at a heritage from the past is therefore a valid step towards a reconstruction of Iranian religiosity which, however undocumented owing to its divergence from the Sāsānian Mazdaean church, and latent at the time of impact with the conquerors' religion, was nevertheless sufficiently vital to warrant the later existence of an Iranian Islam. Such an Iranian Islam, which is all too often confused with Shī'ism, was at any rate strong enough to operate, on the theoretical level, until such time as a new version of the Ismā'īlī message should appear. The *Umm al-kitāb* represents the beginning of this synthesis as well as the link between Ismā'īlism and the Kaisāniyya. Islam in Iran on the operational level created an orthodox Islamic country capable of accepting a heretical superstructure without any shock, almost as the prerogative of a well-established ruling class, such as the Persian administrative class of the following centuries.

The protagonist of the Khārijite revolt was a Sīstānī nobleman, born in a "pagan" family claiming mythical Iranian kings as their ancestors; he after going on the pilgrimage to Mecca returned home ready to start armed operations in the district of Zarang. The rebel's first clash, with Ḥafs b. 'Umar b. Tarka, governor of Zarang, was about to end in a duel between the two leaders but the governor did not accept. Ḥamza addressed his first proclamation to the people and their leaders, bidding them pay no taxes to the Baghdad government, an attitude which was to remain constant throughout the rebellion, while the *khuṭba* continued to be read in the caliph's name.

With a view to securing control of the area, a number of alliances were made between the governor and the local *'ayyārs* or bandits, which led to actual popular risings against the Khārijites and, eventually, to a truce arranged by the governor, Laith b. Faḍl, due to the fact that Laith had to enlist Ḥamza's aid against a man of the people, Ḥarb b. 'Ubaida, supported by Ṭarabī, the outgoing governor. Ḥamza's and Laith's victory secured for Laith, the Khārijites and the local 'ayyārs four years (201–5/816–20–1) of continuous peace, apart from the unrevoked ban on the payment of taxes.

We see here a nobleman leading a revolt against central authority and meeting with the active opposition of a number of officials belonging to the structure upon which caliphal power rested. The latter availed themselves of catchwords as demagogical as his own, or they even concocted so-called popular uprisings which they exploited to their own ends; their goal was mere conservation of the *status quo*, while the

Khārijites claimed an autonomous, and hence more equitable, policy, which found partial expression in non-payment of taxes to the local administration, which on the other hand was not considered in itself hostile. This background which does not much differ from the Muqanna' rebellion, for example, does not include religious syncretism and hence the convergence of native elements. Compared with contemporary revolts, the Khārijite movement in Sīstān was subdued by the central government after Ḥamza's death, though some outbursts of independent vitality were in evidence up to at least Ṣaffārid times. It might be qualified as more aristocratic than previous revolts, thanks to its wholehearted adoption of an imported scheme as a medium of protest.

This latter statement should be justified by a restrictive definition of heresy in Islam. Orthodox Islam always proved capable of including different elements on the religious-theoretical level, and allowed a practical application of them which might by itself either prove or refute their validity, without jeopardizing the whole social and political structure. An example of this was Mu'tazilism under al-Ma'mūn. When faced with the need of making a choice, which could not be avoided without prejudice to its official qualification, heresy always led in practice to rigidity and inability to assimilate historical data. As a result, what was meant as an innovating experiment turned into the medium of reaction and fanaticism, even when in defeat, the faction in question appeared in the victim's rôle.

Khārijism and Ismā'īlism are but two of the many obvious examples which one might quote in this connection.

A strictly religious interpretation of the movements in question should not adopt the single label of extremism-Shī'ism-Iranianism. One should rather look for a unifying background by isolating the constant components and only subsequently relating them to a possible "Iranian-heterodox" religious typology.

We shall therefore try to isolate a few motifs and consider their operation within the specific context of the heresies in question, consciously adopting a method that will restrict the field of enquiry and enable us to determine a few essential points basic to a definition of these religious forms' Iranian or non-Iranian character.

The goals of such an analysis ultimately reflect a search for a lunar kind of Islamic component and a solar type, or Iranian component. This qualification of the field of enquiry immediately leads us to choose a fundamental motif, which is at the same time a constant factor in the movements under review: the colour motif.

In more than one context Islam is defined as "the black religion" in contrast with "the white religion" which should be revived, and which our sources oversimplify into the religion of Zoroaster, often described by heresiographers, on the other hand, as the religion of Mazdak.[1]

Black is the colour of night, and black is the 'Abbāsid standard raised by Abū Muslim when openly proclaiming his *da'wa* in the 'Abbāsid family's name. Black is also the colour of the Mahdī, who in the fullness of time will bring justice upon earth, which in religious psychology is tantamount to accepting a positive view of death as the rebirth of true life (the Mahdī's justice). This is at the same time a deliberate decision to hide and conceal oneself, to disappear while persisting (like the moon) and waiting for an opportunity, which is to be determined by an alien, solar active factor, to come back to a new life and shape.

On the other hand, black is also the colour of mourning, particularly according to the Shī'a, and black were the garments worn by Bābak's followers when, according to Abū Tammān's verses, they seemed to want to conceal their secret from the curious, veiling themselves like the moon while waiting for its new cycle.[2] Black was the sheep that Afshīn strangled every week (for so he was accused), cutting it in two halves so that he could pass between them before eating the meat.

It is no coincidence that black, in Islam, should be complemented by green, the classical colour of Islam which is also a night-colour, a colour of rest and waiting, connected with the female element, with milk and the mother's womb. This is the 'Alid colour, and at the same time the wonderful colour of Chinese silk brought back by Bihāfarīd, and of the veil covering Muqanna''s splendour.[3] It is the colour linked to the concept of "*regressus ad uterum*", as well as to the food (liver) eaten by Bihāfarīd during his "apprenticeship" leading to his birth (*ẓuhūr*).

The most interesting point is precisely the connection between China/East and green in Bihāfarīd's case, which merely seems to focus a mysterious, magical feminine origin, to which one has to appeal before proving worthy of one's new mission. China is also the place where one learns art, and materializes its rôle in green silk, which provided Bihāfarīd with the need to wear a veil while waiting for the moment of appearance. Muqanna''s veil acts partly in a similar, though

[1] Cf. Ṭabarī, vol. III, p. 1311, and Baghdādī, p. 251.

[2] E. G. Browne, vol. I, p. 330.

[3] Bīrūnī, vol. II, p. 211.

less complex, fashion. The sight of the divine essence can only filter through thanks to a passive, feminine reflection, inasmuch as it fulfils the primary task of reception and transmission, by adjusting this function to a cycle of preparation and appearance in accordance with the lunar pattern which we suggest.

In other traditions connected with Muqanna', anyhow, green is replaced by a golden mask, gold implying already a transition to white, that is towards inversion from a lunar, passive, feminine situation to a solar, male, active one.[1]

Gold fulfils in our context a rôle similar to red. Red, which in the heretical movements in question is often represented by metal, is still a genetically feminine colour, but in its active stage, at the time of unfolding, it leads to the opposite principle, represented in Iran by white. The need of focusing the component of creation in its feminine form it also reflected in the blood covering Bābak's naked body as he slept under the tree, and in the wine drunk by Bābak during his investiture at the head of the movement.

The fact that whole movements, such as the Muḥammira or Mubayyiḍa, are identified with a colour is less readily attributable to a general principle. Red, however, appears in various cultures as the colour symbolizing a break with tradition and an urge towards not only a new life, but a new world as promised by the Mahdī, verified and materialized in time. As far as our analysis is concerned, it is red, in connection with gold, which leads to white, the seminal-solar, daytime and masculine colour *par excellence*.

Grey-white is the colour of the Mahdī's horse, the first concrete manifestation of future life, a fire- and death-resistant phoenix-salamander. Such is the mount which Bihāfarīd will ride when, according to his followers, he returns in the fullness of time.

What seems most worthy of analysis is the white dove into which Abū Muslim was turned while waiting for the Mahdī. This is neither the normal symbol of the soul and the spirit, nor an image of the immortal ambrosia or vital sperm which knows neither corruption nor death. White seems to be something more – a symbol showing the way followed by different doctrines such as Islam and the old Iranian religion in integrating and building up a single, globally interpretable religious structure.

The religious contents of the movements in question are hardly ever

[1] Ibn Khallikān, vol. II, pp. 205–6.

reflected in our sources by any theory at all. One is faced instead with a number of facts which should provide the historian with the opportunity of formulating a judgment, and the heresiographer with a method of classification. Hence, as noted at the beginning of this essay, since the historical sources reflect the central authority's "truth", their basic judgment is bound to be negative and biased. The heresiographer's classification is, however, even more schematic and based on standard, officially formulated definitions aimed at placing all heretical movements within a set frame which separates the just from the false and lays down the boundaries of the Islamic community.

This is nothing more than one could expect after assuming the need of safeguarding orthodoxy from a threatening heretical development. What does seem typical of Islamic heresiography is its acting as negative propaganda; the heresiographer's self-appointed task seems to consist in teaching what a good Muslim should not do or believe, rather than pointing out where heretics go wrong and lose all hopes of salvation.

The fact therefore that S̲h̲ahristānī includes the Abū Muslimiyya among Mazdakite-inspired groups while the Muḥammira and Mubayyiḍa fall under the wider definition of g̲h̲ulūw merely helps us to choose the general guidelines, to identify in practice the connections between "white" and "black" religion, while the ideological elements typical of such elements are not clarified.[1] One is left at any rate with the facts and descriptions with which Islamic historiographers always accompanied their subject-matter, and which provide one with the material to be divided up into factors of masculine and feminine derivation, in accordance with the interpretation of the masculine–feminine dichotomy which is generally accepted in most psycho-religious analysis.

In Bihāfarīd's movements his proof of his own prophecy consisted in a version of the *mi'rāj* equivalent to communication with the divine level, which he renounced in order to fulfil his prophetic mission. The typology of the mi'rāj seems to assume a solar context, in which ascent acts as the masculine, dynamic element, and is performed twice by the prophet in question: at the start of his mission and at the end of his life. Descent upon earth, which is also dual, merely serves to prove the assumption's reliability, which is stressed by insistence on the numeral seven. Bihāfarīd spent seven years in China and handed down seven prayers to his followers. Sunbād̲h̲ the Magian also chose the sun as the new *qibla*, and set out to destroy the Ka'ba, while the notion of

[1] S̲h̲ahristānī, vol. II, p. 87.

returning at the end of time turns up again in the legend of Muqanna', whose spirit is supposed to be embodied in a grey man returning to be lord of the earth on the usual grey horse.

Messianic elements also appear as a constant of orthodox Islamic ideology, and it is hard to determine to what extent they dovetail into an Iranian vision of rebirth through the sperm which is to recreate life, and to what extent they are merely one of the many expressions of the Islamic concept of alternating phases of death and life, of *g͟haiba* and ẓuhūr. As a matter of fact, both Abū Muslim and Muqanna', destined as they were by legend to share in the Mahdī's mission, either as a substitute (Muqanna') or in a threefold manifestation (Mahdī, Mazdak and Abū Muslim) of the Mahdī himself, appear to be immersed in a feminine, lunar kind of religious reality. Abū Muslim did not ascend to heaven, and hid instead on the mountains near Ray waiting for the resurrection; or he concealed himself in the Mahdī's copper castle.

To sum up, one should go back to the model handed down by primitive Islam for subsequent elaboration, transplanted into Iran and all too simplistically identified with "Iranian religiosity", that is, to the legend of Muḥammad b. al-Ḥanafiyya with its lunar, feminine principle and situation. He too disappeared, hid in the mountains or rather in a cave where he waited for the day of judgment; he too appeared as a mirror of the Mahdī's, rather than as the Messiah himself; he too, like Abū Muslim, was assimilated to an angelic category of creatures; he too seemed to choose apparent death and negation of his own individuality to return into the earth, indeed into the cosmological egg, thence to come forth at the end of time, when the very concept of individual identification will have lapsed into desuetude.

The extremism with which our movements are accused grew out of Muḥammad b. al-Ḥanafiyya himself, or rather out of his legend, and it should be stressed that the "extreme" element was derived from Semitic Islam and was transplanted to the texture of Iranian religiosity in modified form, in accordance with our hypothetical analysis, as an alternative or a complement to Iranian "solarity". Thematic and symbological identification between the 'Alid and an ancient, Iranian mythical figure did in fact explicitly occur in eastern Iran; but this was, significantly enough, not an identification between Muḥammad and Jams͟hīd, or Farīdūn, or Gars͟hāsp, but between Muḥammad and Zaḥḥāk, the prisoner and at the same time the guardian of the egg. The most glaring expression of Muqanna''s lunar, feminine context is the story of the moon which he caused to rise out of the well in which he had placed a phial of mercury. This miracle should be related to the other miracle of his public appearance in full daylight, arranged so that the dazzling rays reflected by a system of mirrors should give his followers a measure of his own divine nature. We have before us a reflected, passive divinity, just as the moon he caused to rise out of the well did not differ from the light of the sun whose reflection Muqanna' appropriated.

There seems to be no point in insisting on the magical attitudes which accompany the protagonists of the movements in question; suffice it to mention food. Reference has already been made to Bihāfarīd's miraculous food. The marriage between Bābak and Jāvīdān's wife becomes official when she offers him a sprig of basil. Muqanna' gives his wives poison. Bābak's investiture is marked by a banquet, and the sacrificed animal's meat eaten by Afs͟hīn is one of the charges he will have to answer. Bābak's biography, too, is marked by wine; wine was drunk by his father while staying with Bābak's mother; there was wine at the banquet organized to celebrate his appointment, and Jāvīdān had Bābak's mother buy wine on the day when he chose him as his servant. A similar magical rôle is attributed to the father of Bābak singing in a foreign language, or to Bābak's making music, if only by playing the drum during his normal, legendary span of life as an orphan and a shepherd. All such elements stress, in our texts, Islam's dislike for all alien forms viewed as disrupting the fundamental relation which is supposed to be set up between God and his creatures. At any rate, this sketchy review of motifs, or rather constant factors of these movements, which attempts to go beyond the heresiographical stereotypes of g͟hulūw, *tanāsuk͟h* (transmigration) and sexual sin, would seem inadequate if it did not touch upon another theme, that of the one-eyed person, which is also linked to the feminine principle and to colour. Even if the female presence is a constant element in our movements the one-eyed person shows up in contexts characterized by a particularly strong female presence, as in the episodes of Muqanna' and Bābak.

Bābak's mother, the object of a strange passion conceived by his father, the stranger, had only one eye.[1] She acted as the nurse and the guardian of the orphaned child, before giving him up to Jāvīdān, but in Bābak's life the maternal rôle was carried on by Jāvīdān's wife, who loved him, prepared his succession and provided him, so to speak, with

[1] Ibn al-Nadīm, p. 343.

the ointment of investiture, by stating that the late Jāvīdān's spirit had moved into his young servant, Bābak. The woman was the exoteric, eloquent element, in contrast with Bābak who merely accepted and, according to texts, spoke with difficulty and stuttered. Bābak is therefore he who speaks through a woman, and is silent in his quality as a guide.

Muqanna' was one-eyed, and according to some sources, stuttered too. His one-eyedness is the exoteric motive of his chosen mask. We have thus a male figure and a female figure sharing this feature, but the fact that Muqanna' is "the veiled one" *par excellence* enables one to classify him, too, in a feminine category, not only because of his rôle, to which reference has already been made, but also because he willingly wears a mask, thus changing his features, and chooses the mystery of his own person as an irreversible fact, becoming a woman from the point of view of symbology.

Generally speaking, a one-eyed person represents a negative factor: one-eyed and blind people are not allowed to perform sacrifices, for instance. But when the negative datum is projected on to an extremely wide area, it represents the Almighty, or rather the Omnipotence linked to the nature represented by the one-eyed person and identified, like him, with violent manifestations such as a storm, a volcano, a thunderbolt, the most obvious example being provided by Odin.

The one-eyed person is however also the hero who willingly gives up an eye in order to penetrate the inner truth of things, that is to provide himself with a strength which is no longer merely natural, but rather magical. That is the force which one acquires by perceiving the essence of things and not stopping at their outer appearance. This clarifies the case in question, together with the fact that the one-eyed person often turns up in hendiadys with some other figure, disabled or lacking a limb, a typical instance being the case of Horatius Cocles and Mutius Scaevola. In our context two disablements, stuttering and partial blindness, coexist in the same figure.

The fact of stuttering might be linked to the importance of the spoken word as a fundamental factor of prophecy and a necessary requisite of the law-making prophet. If however eloquence is a positive fact in orthodoxy, i.e. exotericism, it becomes negative in the opposite field of esotericism. Here the prophetic rôle, which is mediation between the form of life and its essence, between that which is visible and the invisible, is entrusted to the silent, the non-speaking, the *imām-i ṣāmit* who does not speak, in the tradition of the Shī'a, to 'Alī as opposed to Muḥammad in the mystical, gnostic tradition.

An intimate relation probably exists, therefore, between seeing the invisible, not saying the possible, while waiting for the intrinsic truth of things, and the feminine, lunar rôle of suspension performed by Muqanna' or Bābak.

On a more precisely factual level, one can but hazard a few hypotheses. Having accepted the fact that Muqanna' does not ascend to the divine level by a form of mi'rāj, one must at all events find a link between the spiritual and human levels, there being no rebirth of the protagonist, as there is for instance in Bihāfarīd's case. Hence the person accidentally characterized by this natural element (this being the first possible interpretation of one-eyedness) is changed into someone who has an esoterical, magical vision of reality, which is the second way of interpreting the same phenomenon.

Alternatively, the one-eyed person (the eye that does not see, but which can be unsealed, its power thus becoming unleashed) represents, from the iconographical point of view, the female matrix itself, and the hypotheses mentioned above should be viewed as the effect, not as the motive of this fact. Here one should however proceed mainly on the basis of analogy with other mythological forms and different cultures, where the "deformation of the eye" seems to fulfil this very rôle.

A final hypothesis might connect the whole field of enquiry with an interpretation capable of orienting the geographical characterization of the eastern Iranian area, in which the protagonist operates towards a search for the reasons why the land of the Ariamaspoi, or for that matter of the Amazons, should have been related to Alexander's Iranian campaigns, or towards a search for any interactions and interminglings of local elements of an existing divinity, or a particular cult, having its Islamized epigones in Muqanna' and Bābak, though in a different form.

CHAPTER 16

NĀṢIR-I KHUSRAU AND IRANIAN ISMĀ'ĪLISM

I. PERIODS OF ISMĀ'ĪLISM

In order to appreciate the importance of Nāṣir-i Khusrau in the history of Iranian thought, it is necessary to place him in the setting of Ismā'īlism as a whole, for he was one of its most outstanding personalities. Ismā'īlism existed, indeed, outside the world of Iran and the monuments of Ismā'īlī thought produced by Iranians are not all in the Persian language. In the history of philosophy the works of Nāṣir-i Khusrau present the interesting feature of being written entirely in Persian, and it is important to recall in the first place to what extent the Ismā'īlī religion influenced the spiritual destiny of Iran and what has survived of its literature in Persian. For this purpose a summary description is required of the different periods of Ismā'īlism.

The Ismā'īlī religion, it is well known, is a branch of Shī'ism. It has been designated by several names, sometimes being identified with the Qarmaṭīs, sometimes referred to simply as the party of the "heretics" (*malāḥida*). There are more precise denominations, for example *Sab'iyya* or "Seveners", an allusion to the heptadic pattern which the Ismā'īlī discerns in all the planes of existence. The succession of seven imāms or of heptads of imāms is merely the expression of it in the plane of hierohistory and this is one of the points which distinguish the Ismā'īlī doctrine from Twelver Shī'ism, since the latter recognizes a succession of twelve imāms, but without a recurrence of the cycle. There is the more general designation of *Bāṭiniyya*, literally and strictly "Esoterics", and finally there are the names which the Ismā'īlīs give to themselves, such as *Ahl-i bāṭin* (Esoterics), *Ahl-i ta'wīl* (those who practise the interpretation [Hermeneutics] of symbols), *Ahl-i ta'yīd* (those who are assisted by divine inspiration), etc.

It may be said that Ismā'īlism began its official existence on the death of the imām to whom it owed its proper name: the Imām Ismā'īl, son of the Imām Ja'far al-Ṣādiq, who died shortly before 148/765. It is very difficult to state anything with historical certainty about the character of this young imām, whose death was the cause of so many difficulties and troubles, or exactly what part he played in the group of fervent gnostics included in the entourage of his father, those whose passionate devotion to the person of the Imām Jaʿfar, which even he himself rejected, was to transfer itself to Ismāʿīl. Was there a close association between Ismāʿīl and the disciples of the unfortunate Abu'l-Khaṭṭāb and was he himself disavowed by his own father? In non-Ismāʿīlī tradition he is regarded as a reprobate, while Ismāʿīlī sources confer on him divine status, numbering him among those "absolutes who absolve" from servitude (*arbāb-i iṭlāq*), in disagreement, certainly, with the literal votaries of the legalitarian religion, but as a being whose contemplation was directed on the object of absolute contemplation (*manẓūr muṭlaq*).

Alongside research into positive facts, however, on which the historian requires to be reassured, there is another field of enquiry which is strictly phenomenological; it is concerned with those accounts regarded by history as legends which, on the contrary, constitute the most authentic expression of a religious community's knowledge of itself, the expression of the *spiritual reality* to which it owes its origin and of the spiritual reality that it has, if not knowledge, at least the pre-science of formation and existence. This aspect is demonstrated most particularly in Ismāʿīlism, in which thought is inspired by the ta'wīl, the science of hermeneutics which at the same time both establishes symbols and interprets them. The result is that in the Fāṭimid and post-Fāṭimid texts the picture produced by Ismāʿīlism of its own history does not extend to a past in the sense understood by our own scientific history; what emerges may be conveniently called a hierohistory, that is to say the representation of matters resulting not from empirical statements, but from an *a priori* sacral image which is at one and the same time the organ both of perception and of interpretation of reality. Prophetology and the Ismāʿīlī table of the succession of the prophets have their origin in this hierohistory, which relates the *daʿwat*, the Ismāʿīlī "convocation" to an eternal "convocation" having had its "prologue in Heaven". Needless to say the system comprises the account which the Ismāʿīlī community gives of its own history during the obscure period extending from the death of the Imām Ismāʿīl until the accession of the Fāṭimids. However strict and coherent this account may be, and whatever interest it may have in the eyes of the phenomenologist, it cannot fail to lead the historian astray, since it probably does not recognize the claims of historical criticism. This misdirection is manifested in the wide divergency of opinions voiced by Orientalists concerning the origins of Ismāʿīlism – a divergency which is maintained and aggravated by the depreciations and falsifications of the heresiologists (Baghdādī, Dailamī, Nuwairī) either in ignorance or bad faith.

At this point it is necessary to determine the simplest plan which will make it possible to form a mental picture of the periods of Ismāʿīlī literature, classified as follows: (1) A primitive period of fermentation and incubation, continuing until the accession of the Fāṭimid dynasty in Egypt (297/909). (2) The Fāṭimid period itself, until the death of al-Mustanṣir bi'llāh in 487/1094. (3) The period after the great schism caused, on the death of al-Mustanṣir, by the brutal dethronement of the prince Nizār, legitimate heir to the Imāmate, in favour of the prince al-Mustaʿlī. The Ismāʿīlī religion then split into two branches: (*a*) the Western Ismāʿīlīs of the Fāṭimid tradition (the *Mustaʿliyān*), whose history includes a Yemenite period, after the assassination of the last titular Fāṭimid imām (al-Amīr 524/1130), when the centre of the daʿwat was transferred to the Yemen, and an Indian period when, at the end of the 16th century, the headquarters of the head of the community (the *dāʿī muṭlaq*) was moved to India. (*b*) The other branch, the Eastern Ismāʿīlīs, represented the *Nizārī* tradition of the reformed Ismāʿīlism of Alamūt, the principal centre of which was the fortress of that name in Iran. After the destruction of Alamūt by the Mongols in 654/1256, Ismāʿīlism survived in Persia under the cover of Ṣūfism, with the result that Iranian Ṣūfism frequently assumes the appearance of a crypto-Ismāʿīlism. A tide of emigration also flowed towards India.

In the history of Persian Ismāʿīlism after the fall of Alamūt, W. Ivanow discerned, as late as the 16th–17th centuries, a kind of renaissance; he termed it the period of Anjūdān, an important market-town situated some twenty miles to the east of Sulṭānābād (the Arāk of today), which was at one time the place of residence of the imāms and the centre of this spiritual awakening. Reverting to those who took refuge in India, their descendants are now called the *Khojas* and they recognize as their spiritual leader His Highness Karīm Āghā Khān, the forty-ninth Imām. However, the origins of the Ismāʿīlī community in India date back to a much earlier epoch than that of the Mongol invasions, when a flood of Ismāʿīlī refugees was swept in the direction of India (13th century). Before the advent of the Fāṭimids in Egypt the Ismāʿīlī *dāʿīs* or missionaries had succeeded in creating in Sind a state with its capital at Multān. One result, among others, of habits of mind dating back to such an early origin is that certain sections of the Khojas have the extremely interesting characteristic of showing a state of transition between Islam in its Ismāʻīlī form and Hinduism. Unfortunately the literature in Persian of the Eastern Ismāʻīlīs breaks off completely after the fall of Alamūt and the destruction of the Ismāʻīlī centres in Kūhistān (south Khurāsān). Extreme poverty and terrible persecution made it impossible for major works to be produced and almost all those already in existence had been destroyed. The majority of the works which survived were preserved in Central Asia, in Badakhshān and the neighbouring provinces. It is there that Nāṣir-i Khusrau produced most of his works.

As regards the branch of religion followed by the Mustaʻliyān, the disaster which it had to survive, some 130 years before that of Alamūt, was nothing less than the collapse of the Fāṭimid dynasty (524/1130), at which a mortal blow had indeed been dealt by the death of the Imām al-Mustanṣir. The daʻwat found a ready-prepared refuge in the Yemen; it is today distributed between the Yemen and India (where the Ismāʻīlīs of this branch are called *Bohras*) and is divided into two sections: the Sulaimānīs (not very numerous in India) and the Dā'ūdīs, who recognize only the spiritual authority of their own dāʻī muṭlaq. Of the two great branches of the Ismāʻīlī religion, only the Mustaʻliyān have been able to preserve a significant number of important writings. They are all in Arabic and difficult of access.

Shahristānī (d. 548/1153) referred to Fāṭimid Ismāʻīlism as *daʻwat qadīma*, "the ancient *daʻwat*", and to the Ismāʻīlism of Alamūt as *daʻwat jadīda*, "the modern *daʻwat*", something like reformed Ismāʻīlism. Reform indeed it was, and if the meaning of this reform be considered with the help of texts which have recently become available, and in the light of the fortunes of Ismāʻīlism, its large-scale disasters and its determination to survive, one query cannot fail to arise. When questions are asked about the meaning of Iranian Ismāʻīlism, it also involves the meaning of the Fāṭimid phase which is the more formidable because Sunnī "orthodox" propaganda was so militant against its enemies that it is tempting to reverse the image which it presents of the Fāṭimid dynasty. It is to be feared, however, that such a reversal might also undermine the true grandeur of the Fāṭimid concept. In order to judge both its grandeur and its adversity, there is another point of view to be adopted than that of an "orthodoxy" which is opposed to it. For with the aid of the proto-Ismāʻīlī works, in addition to the great speculative systems of the Fāṭimid period, it is not very difficult to reconstruct the dream of Ismā'īlism and to compare with this dream the grandiose concept of the Fāṭimids: "the unification of Islam under the authority of the Imām, that is to say of the legitimate theocratic sovereign, member of the family of the Prophet". This view presupposes, however, a certain idea of the imām, which is fundamental to the Ismā'īlī theosophy. Would it be true to say that out of political opportunism the Fāṭimids had shown themselves ready to sacrifice the theosophical system for the benefit of the positive religion? By doing so, they would have destroyed the balance between the *ẓāhir* (exoteric) and the *bāṭin* (esoteric), between the *tanzīl* (revelation descending in the letter) and the *ta'wīl* (interpretation leading back to the hidden meaning); they would indeed have sacrificed the essentials – the hidden meaning (*bāṭin*) and the esoteric exegesis (*ta'wīl*). What would then have remained of the Ismā'īlī religion?

In fact, the piety with which Nāṣir-i Khusrau speaks of the Imām al-Mustanṣir and even represents himself as his spokesman on the most technical theosophical questions makes it difficult to imagine that the Fāṭimid Imāms condescended to interest themselves in such matters solely in order to satisfy "the spirit of the age". Such systems belong neither to popular works nor to spontaneous inspiration: their circulation presupposes the existence of minds which have attained an advanced degree of philosophical culture. If the Fāṭimid concept was Ismā'īlī, it could not have encountered dilemmas such as the choice between the alternatives of theosophy or Islam. It was precisely the union of the two on which the concept was founded, and this must surely be the lesson which emerges from such a book of Nāṣir-i Khusrau as the *Jāmi' al-ḥikmatain* ("The Sum of the two Philosophies" hereafter referred to as *Jāmi'*). In reality the problem is a different one: is it possible for an esoteric brotherhood (that is to say one founded upon the bāṭin and the ta'wīl) at a given time to take possession, publicly and officially, of the historical scene (ẓāhir) – a scene which at that time extended from the shores of the Atlantic to the easternmost limits of the Islamic world? Could it do so without ceasing to be itself? When a doctrine contains an eschatology as an integral part and when an incident of visible, physical history comes to be proclaimed as demonstrating this eschatology, then either history must be fulfilled or the doctrine must be abandoned. It is a situation which has recurred more than once in the course of time and one with which religious philosophy is quite familiar. Political victory constitutes the failure of the doctrine; if the latter survives this, it will be thanks to a failure which makes amends for that victory and will have restored the spiritual vision to its freedom. History does not stand still and the works of a Nāṣir-i Khusrau or a Hamīd Kirmānī preserve their philosophical value and maintain their spiritual gesture independently of each political reign and of all the visible royalty of the imāms. In this respect the reformed Iranian Ismā'īlism is found to be of particular interest. The proclamation of the "Great Resurrection" at Alamūt was to invert the problem raised by the political reign of the Fāṭimids: if the latter had been tempted to sacrifice the bāṭin, was not Alamūt sacrificing the ẓāhir? In any case the reign of pure religion in spirit and in truth appears paradoxical in the known conditions of our humanity. It is the survival of Ismā'īlism under the mantle of Ṣūfism which comes nearer perhaps to revealing its true grandeur and the inspiration of its distant origins, rather than in the brilliant setting of the Fāṭimid court.

II. IRANIAN ISMĀ'ĪLISM IN THE PERSIAN LANGUAGE

On the basis of such data an attempt may be made to evaluate Iranian Ismā'īlism in the Persian language and literature. Indeed it is from this Iranian Ismā'īlism that the works of Nāṣir-i Khusrau, written in Persian in the days of the Fāṭimids, draw their significance and the reason for their influence. Badakhshān, which like the Yemen was privileged to remain apart from the highroads of history, succeeded in preserving a small part of the Ismā'īlī literature in Persian, and in the *Jāmi'* an otherwise unknown prince of Badakhshān holds an important place. The prince 'Alī b. Asad, himself an Ismā'īlī, must have been the comforter of Nāṣir taking refuge in Yumgān, the place of his exile and of his tomb, for it was he who prompted the composition of this *Jāmi'*. Moreover Badakhshān in the broad sense, a country of the upper Oxus, not only provided a repository for writings destroyed elsewhere, but was the scene of that fusion of traditions which gave to Ismā'īlī Persian literature its distinctive characteristics. The Ismā'īlīs of Central Asia regarded themselves as Nizārīs, but at the same time the religious literature revered by them incorporated elements of earlier date than the reform. From this fusion there resulted a very complex whole, the stratifications of which reveal how the system developed. These stratifications appear in the following order:

1. The earliest stratum relates to the primitive period; there is very little effective knowledge of its literature. However, the work entitled *Umm al-kitāb*, venerated by the Ismā'īlīs of the Pamir as one of their sacred books, had its origin, whatever may be the date of its publication in Persian, in the spiritual environment of the period, which may be designated as proto-Ismā'īlī; it makes known the ideas professed among Qarmaṭī and Khaṭṭābī adherents at this time.

2. The next stratum is exemplified by the work of Nāṣir-i Khusrau, that is to say his authentic work, with the addition of a certain number of texts which have been falsely attributed to him. Nāṣir's authentic work is as representative of the state of the doctrine in Fāṭimid times as may be that of his great Iranian contemporaries writing in Arabic. In the precise state of existing knowledge, it is not possible to determine when and how the junction between the "orthodox" disciples of Nāṣir-i Khusrau in Badakhshān and the Nizārī Ismā'īlīs of the Alamūt reform was effected.

3. A new stratum is defined by this junction, which was of capital importance for Persian Ismā'īlism. The period which followed may be designated that of the "coalescence of Ismā'īlī ideas with Ṣūfism". That it was a genuine coalition is attested, for example, by the Ismā'īlī ta'wīl which is found in the celebrated mystical poem *Gulshān-i rāz* ("The Rose-Garden of the Mystery") by Maḥmūd Shabistarī, by the Ismā'īlī adoption, as one of their own books, of the great treatise on Ṣūfism, *Zubdat al-ḥaqā'iq* ("Quintessence of Metaphysical Truths"), by 'Azīz Nasafī (d. 661/1262), and by the fact that the Ismā'īlīs regarded the great Ṣūfī poet Farīd al-Dīn 'Aṭṭār (d. *c.* 627/1230) as one of themselves.[1] In addition, Ismā'īlī philosophical writers are to be found throughout the whole of Persian Ṣūfī literature, as well as in the great Shī'ī works of philosophy produced in the Ṣafavid period.

This very summary account may now be illustrated by some facts.

The *Khaṭṭābiyya* were the disciples of Abu'l-Khaṭṭāb, a prominent personality whose ideas, influence and school of adherents would merit a book to themselves. Abu'l-Khaṭṭāb appeared in the 2nd/8th century as the first to conceive and to organize a movement of a specifically bāṭinī type, that is to say esoteric and gnostic. He was a close friend of the fifth and sixth Imāms, Muḥammad Bāqir and Ja'far Ṣādiq, up to the point when the latter disavowed him. The degree of their intimacy may be inferred from a solemn episode when the Imām Ja'far, laying

[1] W. Ivanow, *A Guide to Ismaili Literature*, pp. 104–5, 118.

his hand on the breast of Abu'l-Khaṭṭāb, addressed him in these words: "Remember and do not forget. Thou knowest that which is hidden. Behold, thou art become the casket of my knowledge, the lodging-place of my secret. I have entrusted to you our living and our dead." Such a consecration contained within it the pathetic secret of the disavowal which was to follow. Some of the doctrines attributed to the man thus proclaimed the "casket of the knowledge of the imām" are in close agreement with the fundamental idea of Ismāʿīlism – for example, the distinction between the *Nāṭiq* (prophet *enunciator* of the Law) and the *Ṣāmit* (*silent* imām, possessor of the esoteric meaning); without this distinction the very concepts of bāṭin and ta'wīl would be deprived of their purpose. There are, however, other doctrines also attributed to Abu'l-Khaṭṭāb which correspond more with the views professed by the so-called extremists (*ghulāt*) of the Shīʿī Gnosis and it is traces of these doctrines that seem to reappear in the writings subsequent to the reform of Alamūt, adopting more or less the terminology of Ṣūfism.

In the light of the above facts, it is difficult to reconstruct the tragic events which attended the early fortunes of Ismāʿīlism; the victims were those enthusiastic spirits to whose aspirations the young Imām Ismāʿīl was to lend his support. The act of disavowal by his father, the Imām Jaʿfar, aroused consternation, and seventy devotees of Abu'l-Khaṭṭāb assembled in the mosque at Kūfa were massacred by order of the governor; Abu'l-Khaṭṭāb was captured and crucified in 145/762.[1] The survivors transferred their allegiance to Ismāʿīl and from that time Khaṭṭābism became identified with Ismāʿīlism. But who knows what secret drama was experienced by the Imām Jaʿfar at the martyrdom of followers who had been faithful to him until death, even after the impact of his disavowal? For the Imām is described, during an intimate conversation, as weeping himself and allowing tears of compassion to be shed.

The doctrines of Abu'l-Khaṭṭāb and his school have been preserved in the *Umm al-kitāb* ("The Mother [or Archetype] of the Book") mentioned above. It is stated there that "the Ismaili religion is that founded by the children [disciples] of Abu'l-Khaṭṭāb, who sacrificed their lives for love of Ismāʿīl, the son of Jaʿfar Ṣādiq, and it will remain throughout the Cycle of Cycles". Moreover, the sacred symbol of the sect calls down the divine blessing jointly on Salmān and on Abu'l-Khaṭṭāb as

[1] Or in 138/755 according to Kashshī in B. Lewis, *Origins of Ismailism*, p. 33.

adoptive members of the Family of the Prophet (*ahl-i bait*), just as the solemn formula pronounced by the Imām Jaʿfar transposed to Abu'l-Khaṭṭāb the terms used by the Prophet with regard to Salmān the Persian. It may also be noted that the book is deemed to contain the sayings of the Imām Muḥammad Bāqir in reply to the questions of his disciples and that, with a striking resemblance to certain apocryphal Gospels relating to Jesus, the Imām is here represented in the guise of a five-year-old child. There is no need to dwell further on this ancient Persian work, preserved by the Ismāʿīlīs of the Upper Oxus regions as one of their earliest and most sacred books. It may be remembered, however, that the pentadic plan of spiritual archetypes which is found in Nāṣir-i Khusrau already constituted one of the characteristic themes of the *Umm al-kitāb*, and clear reflections of Manichaeism may be discerned. On the other hand the same work offers lines of thought which recall the books of Henoch, and the Valentinian gnosis. Similarly, for the triad of archangels (*Jadd*, *Fatḥ*, *Khayāl*: Seraphiel, Michael, Gabriel) encountered in Nāṣir-i Khusrau, some unpublished chapters by Abū Yaʿqūb Sijistānī point to the Mazdaean *Xvarnah*.[1]

The work of Nāṣir-i Khusrau, appearing as the second stratum in the literature preserved by the Ismāʿīlīs of Badakhshān, represents indeed the doctrine in the systematic form which it acquired from the Fāṭimid period onwards. It was related to the writings of those great thinkers who although they were for the most part Iranians, composed monumental works in the Arabic language – Abū Ḥātim Rāzī (d. 322/933), Abū Yaʿqūb Sijistānī, Aḥmad b. Ibrahīm Nīshāpūrī (5th/11th century), Hamīd al-Dīn Kirmānī (d. *c.* 408/1017), Mu'ayyad Shīrāzī (d. 470/1077). The great problem is the connection, the "missing link" between the works of the primitive period and this burgeoning of perfectly constituted systems. Only two stages can be determined in the transition period: there is the celebrated encyclopaedia of the "Brotherhood of the pure heart" (*Ikhwān al-ṣafā*), the authorship of which is attributed by Ismāʿīlī tradition to the second, concealed imām (Aḥmad b. ʿAbd-Allāh, first half of the 3rd/9th century) of the *satr* period (dating from those imāms who succeeded the son of the Imām Ismāʿīl until the accession of the Fāṭimids). There is also the *Kitāb al-maḥṣūl* mentioned by Nāṣir-i Khusrau and attributed to the martyr-shaikh Nakhshabī. Other questions remain, such as the following: how did the subsequent fusion come about between the Nizārī and the unreformed Fāṭimid traditions?

[1] Cf. *Jāmiʿ*, pp. 91–112.

How was the reform of Alamūt itself effected? To what extent did this reform of the Ismā'īlīs in Persia cause a "reactivation" of primitive Ismā'īlism, even of Qarmaṭism? There is also the problem of the compatibility of an esoteric brotherhood with an *official* state, even that of the Fāṭimids, where poor Abu'l Khaṭṭāb would have had more difficulty in finding a place for himself than in the Ismā'īlī "commanderies" of Alamūt and Kūhistān.

The reform must have instituted a collection of doctrines "symbolizing with" the state of souls aroused from death, that is to say from the death which is represented by every legalitarian religion (*sharī'a*) and by enslavement to the letter of the positive revelation (*tanzīl*). From the idea of the eternal Imām, as the single and identical Being manifesting itself from Cycle to Cycle in the person of the successive "Imāmic personalities", the concept of the imām is exalted to the metaphysical plane and enters the category of the divine, insofar as it is revealed. No longer is it the announcement of the Revelation which reveals the divine; this annunciation still represents a *deitas abscondita*. That which reveals this *absconditum*, this bāṭin, is the decipherment of the symbol in which it is formulated, whence is derived the predominance of the Silent One (*Ṣāmit*), the imām enunciating "incorporeally" the symbolic meaning, over the Prophet, the Enunciator. Indeed the last imām of a Cycle, the Resurrector, has the prerogative of proclaiming the *Qiyāmat* that is to say the Resurrection which marks the end, the *eschaton*, of the sharī'a. This proclamation establishes the religion in spirit and in truth; it abrogates all the earlier prescriptions of the Law, substituting for them their spiritual significance.

It is necessary to envisage the spirit of the reform of Alamūt as being characteristic of Iranian Ismā'īlism in the Persian language, in order to gain some idea of how, during centuries of persecution, Ṣūfism was able to provide for it a refuge and an alibi. The major part in initiating this reformation is attributable to two persons: to the imām who proclaimed the *Qiyāmat* in 559/1164, Maulānā Ḥasan *'alā dhikri-hi'l-salām*, and to Ḥasan-i Ṣabbāḥ (d. 518/1124), the man who, before his time, had been the founder of Ismā'īlī power at Alamūt. This extraordinary man of destiny (whose memory has been defaced by the evil fictions of the anti-Ismā'īlī historians) is mentioned in the texts as "the Jesus of the Cycle of the Resurrection who revealed the works of his father", as "the great *Ḥujjat* of our Lord, the Imām of the Resurrection (*maulānā qā'im al-qiyāmat*), the Christ (*masīḥ*), who caused the trumpet of the Resurrection to sound".[1] It would be a valuable indication of the continuity of Iranian Ismā'īlism, if it were confirmed that Ḥasan-i Ṣabbāḥ, a Shī'ī by birth, could, at the time of his conversion and of his final adherence to the Ismā'īlī religion, have been influenced by Nāṣir-i Khusrau.

The Event of the "Resurrection of Resurrections" (*qiyāmat-i hama qiyāmāt*) or the "Great Resurrection" was solemnly proclaimed at Alamūt on 17 Ramaḍān 559/8 August 1164, in an impressive setting. The sermon preached on that day by the man who was in fact the leading *Khudāvand*, the first grand master of Alamūt, Maulānā Ḥasan *'alā dhikri-hi'l-salām*, is an anthology piece. "Rise up, for the Day of Resurrection has dawned. The awaited Signal is now made manifest. Behold the dawn of the Resurrection which is the culmination of all Resurrections. Today there is no longer need to seek for proofs and tokens; today Knowledge no longer depends on the Signs [the verses of a Book] nor on speeches, nor on allusions, nor on bending the body in acts of devotion . . ."[2]

On that day, which was spent at Alamūt in mutual congratulation and in exchanging vows and of which an annual commemoration was instituted, no one foresaw what a catastrophe would strike the Ismā'īlī order less than a century later, destroying its commanderies and its fortresses throughout Iran. The last imām of Alamūt, Rukn al-Dīn Khūrshāh, was killed in the flower of his youth by the Mongols in 654/1256, but he had fortunately succeeded in hiding his son and heir, Shams al-Dīn Muḥammad. Henceforward the latter and his successors lived for the most part like Ṣūfī shaikhs; they were to be rediscovered in the 16th century at Anjūdān (on the ancient route from Iṣfahān to Hamadān), during the short renaissance mentioned above.

The leaven of the Ismā'īlī religion as the religion of personal salvation, the "religion of the Resurrection", is subsequently to be found incorporated in everything which in Iran is called *'irfān*, *ḥikmat*, *taṣawwuf*, and long and attentive study is still required to estimate its effects. Perhaps they are apparent in this nostalgia for a manifestation of the divinity which allows the inner eye of the heart to behold it, not through incarnation, but through "docetist" transparition by means of a phantasma of flesh, by the flash of beauty transfiguring a face. The concept of

[1] *Haft bābi bābā saiyid-nā*, anonymous Persian text ed. W. Ivanow in *Two Early Ismaili Treatises* (Bombay, 1933), p. 21.

[2] *Jāmi'*, p. 23, and in *Mercure de France* (February, 1965), p. 298.

the eternal imām, divine *anthrôpos* and *logos*, fosters this expectation of divine anthropomorphosis and an Ismā'īlī treatise on the tradition of Alamūt contains pages of pure Ṣūfism. The following passage may be quoted: "Just as the Creation is the veil of God, just as the creative state is the veil of the Deity, so religion (*sharī'a*) is the veil of the Resurrection (*qiyāmat*)."[1]

Thus it is within the framework of the periods of Ismā'īlism which preceded it and those which followed it that the work of Nāṣir-i Khusrau acquires its major significance – a significance which is revealed as much in its affinities with what came before and afterwards as in the differences. Moreover, the spread of this Iranian Ismā'īlism testifies to the importance of the part played by the Persian language, comparable with that of Arabic. As far away as the high plateaux of Central Asia, as far even as the lands of China, wherever an Ismā'īlī community existed, the Persian language too was sanctified as a liturgical language, a "church language".

III. THE LIFE AND WORK OF NĀṢIR-I KHUSRAU

Abū Mu'īn Nāṣir b. Khusrau was born in 394/1003–4, in Qubādhiyān, a small town in the neighbourhood of Balkh. He belonged to a family of government officials in comfortable circumstances and he had two brothers. One of them, Abū Sa'īd, was to accompany him on the great journey which led him as far as the Egypt of the Fāṭimids. The two brothers seem to have been united by strong affection. Nāṣir refers to it in his *Dīvān* and Abū Sa'īd, for his part, composed a funerary elegy in memory of Nāṣir.[2] One question arises: did Nāṣir, by reason of his family connections, have a right to the title of *sayyid*? The Ismā'īlīs of Badakhshān were convinced that he had, and their letters always contain references, it would appear, to convincing evidence on this point. His ancestors, of Iranian stock, probably left Baghdad to settle in Balkh or in Qubādhiyān, cities which at this period were attached to Khurāsān. With regard to his education and upbringing, some clues are to be gleaned from his works. There appears to be no compelling reason for questioning his own testimony concerning the scientific fervour of his youth which led him to interest himself in all the realms of

[1] *Kalām-i pīr*, Persian text ed. W. Ivanow (Bombay, 1935), p. 113.

[2] *Dīvān* of Nāṣir-i Khusrau, introd. by S. H. Taqīzāda (Tehrān, 1929), p. 254, line 2. For Abū Sa'īd see the introduction to the Persian part of *Jāmi'*, pp. 19–20.

philosophy and science, and indeed, no less significantly, in the various religions. Nor are there any serious grounds for discrediting his recollections of the important positions which he occupied, his reception at the court of the Ghaznavids and his frequent attendance on princes and celebrities. Contrary to some opinion, he seems to have been in complete mastery of his own ideas and of the Persian language in which he expressed them. Likewise his books were by no means designed for a popular circle of readers, for the higher teaching of the da'wat was not *ad usum populi*. Indeed, the fanaticism of his contemporaries caused him both indignation and sadness, because this fanaticism annihilated the "two wisdoms" and not at all because of disappointed ambitions for his own career. He had renounced a career on the day when he tendered his resignation as a financial official at Marv, so as to be free to depart for Egypt, and he was to return from there invested with a wholly spiritual mission and entirely dedicated to the Ismā'īlī cause. Though his indignation might burst forth in vibrant pages, it was the eternal indignation of the sage, provoked less by the blind fanaticism of the masses, than by the false scholars who were their abettors.

The question which dominates his whole spiritual biography, of much greater importance than his position in relation to his corporeal family, is to know at what stage Nāṣir-i Khusrau was converted to Ismā'īlism and was received into the esoteric brotherhood. Although it has been thought that he was a Sunnī by birth, it is not at all impossible that he was a Shī'ī. While his references to Sunnism are noticeably hostile, it is to be observed that he passes over the imāms and the doctrines of duodecimal Shī'ism without comment. In fact, if the case represented by conversion from the Shī'ism of the twelve imāms to Ismā'īlism be analysed, the spiritual event was not such that it had to be accompanied by a "resentment" which could not be contained in silence, an element not invariably absent from religious conversions. In any event, the awakening of the conscience on the spiritual plane represented by the Ismā'īlī gnosis necessarily preserved the neophyte from any aggression complex. To hear the da'wat ("call"), to be converted to the religion of the Resurrection (*qiyāmat*), here was nothing which could be translated in terms of a change in confessional denomination. It implied acceding to an esoteric understanding which in essence included something of the "oecumenical". Moreover, the propagation of this higher knowledge by the "missionaries" of the

Ismāʿīlī daʿwat was quite unlike what the history of the Christian churches has generally caused to be known by the name of "missions". It was not a matter of converting crowds, of publicly proclaiming a message, but of discerning, one by one, those individuals who were suitable to receive in confidence initiation and secret instruction.

Over too long a period a very trite "cliché" has been accepted as adequate to explain the conversion of Nāṣir. It was imagined that until Nāṣir reached the age of forty-two his adherence to Islam was somewhat modified by a life of pleasure. One fine morning, however, as the result of a dream, he decided to change his way of life and undertook the pilgrimage to Mecca. The road to Mecca brought him close to Egypt, where he was converted to the Ismāʿīlī doctrine of the Fāṭimids and he returned to his native country invested with the rank of *ḥujjat*. If this interpretation is accepted as it stands, in conformity with the law of least resistance, no questions are even asked about the inner motives which could have guided Nāṣir to his encounter with the Ismāʿīlī doctrine. It is not even debated whether the event may not have been the goal of a spiritual quest.

Two pieces of decisive evidence are available on this point which it is sufficient to read in the subtle spirit of the ta'wīl: (1) the description of the dream which provided the motive for the departure for Egypt, while giving the official pretext of the pilgrimage to Mecca, and (2) a long *qasīda* in which, with some reference to the ta'wīl, it is possible to read the whole spiritual confession of Nāṣir.

(1) On a certain night Nāṣir saw in a dream a personage who reproached him with taking a delight in drunkenness, to which Nāṣir replied that, for the purpose of forgetting the torments of this world, the sages had not discovered anything better. The vision persisted and established the point that the loss of consciousness and self-possession did not mean the liberation of self or the finding of repose. But how was that state to be attained which fortifies the intelligence and the conscience? The reply came that he who seeks is also he who finds, and without another word the vision indicated with a gesture the direction of the *qibla*. Aroused from that night's sleep, Nāṣir resolved as follows: "It is necessary for me to awake from a sleep which has lasted for forty years."[1]

Herein are to be found archetypical themes, and the whole significance of this dream becomes apparent when the method is discovered

[1] *Safar-nāma*, pp. 2–3 of text and 3–4 of French translation.

of deciphering the symbolic narrative. The questions to be asked are the following: *Who* was the vision? *What* was the order given by it? To know the imām of the time and to recognize him through his disguise (this too can have several different meanings) is the great concern and preoccupation which mobilises all the spiritual energies of a devout Ismāʿīlī. From the depths of the subliminal consciousness the ideal image of the imām emerges with the clarity of the dream and the "Silent One" conveys his order incorporeally by a simple gesture. It may perhaps be said that for an Ismāʿīlī the "quest for the imām" had the same significance as the "quest for the Grail" represented for our mystical knights and minstrels.

Drunkenness and sleep, or the lethargy of drunkenness which is equivalent to unconsciousness and ignorance, these are the archetypical symbols which are always recurring in all these accounts of spiritual metamorphosis. Indeed, the narrator speaks of a sleep which has lasted forty years (that was the age of the author). This drunken sleep with which the sleeper is reproached is simply the conventional and routine practice of purely legalitarian and formalist religion (*sharīʿa*). To awake from this lethargy of unconsciousness is to learn the hidden significance of the exoteric religion and what this meaning implies. In short, it is not simply a matter of *one* night in a cycle of twenty-four hours, but of *the* night of unknowingness, a single night which lasted from the birth of the author into this earthly world. Putting an end to this night a messenger, the Ismāʿīlī *dāʿī*, came to provoke the awakening. It was because Nāṣir was already an Ismāʿīlī that he left for the Fāṭimid kingdom (just as Ḥasan-i Ṣabbāḥ was sent there after his conversion); it was not because he happened to be in Egypt that he became an Ismāʿīlī. Hence a whole train of strange circumstances can be explained from this juncture, such as the suddenness of the departure (6 Jumādā II 437/20 December 1045). Nāṣir must already have been an Ismāʿīlī for seven years by the time the order came. He left immediately for Marv to hand in his resignation as an official in the department of finance. Without waiting for the great caravan of the *ḥajj*, which would have assured his comfort and relative security, he departed accompanied merely by his brother and by a little Indian servant, with a modest turn-out and slender provisions. Nevertheless at each stage the travellers always found the help necessary for reaching the following stage, as though their itinerary had been planned with reference to the "lodges" of brothers ready to welcome and help them.

(2) The impression is confirmed if, with the aid of the ta'wīl, the long qaṣīda be deciphered in which Nāṣir set down the apologia for his life, the date for the composition of which can be fixed at about 456/1064.[1] After a prologue in which Nāṣir recalls his youth and his presentiments of the existence of the imām, five subjects follow in order: 1. The oath of fidelity (Qur'ān 48. 18). 2. The quest for truth. 3. *al-balad al-amīn* (the sacrosanct domain of the imām). 4. Wisdom unveiled. 5. The oath of the secret. Finally, salutations and prayers for the imām.

There seems no doubt that the recipient to whom the qaṣīda was addressed was the high dignitary and prolific author Mu'ayyad fi'l-Dīn Shīrāzī Salmānī, a native of Shīrāz or of Ahvāz, who arrived in Cairo during the same year as Nāṣir (439/1047) and died there thirty years later (470/1077). The receiving of his oath of allegiance refers not to the conversion of Nāṣir, but to his admission into the service of the "missionaries" of the da'wat, after he had been found suitable. Having received the necessary pedagogic instruction, Nāṣir was to be allocated to his own country, as being particularly likely to succeed there.

The evocation of the verse of the Qur'ān (48.18) referring to the oath of fidelity taken to the Prophet under a tree, inspires these reminiscences: "I asked myself these questions: what has now befallen this tree and this hand? Where shall I seek this hand, this site? They said to me, it is no longer there, neither the tree nor this hand, for this hand has been mutilated, the assembly has been dispersed."[2] With this reference to the "quest for the imām" is linked the account of the philosophical quest: "I rose from my place and left on my journey. No regret came over me for my house nor for my garden, nor for the familiar surroundings." The enchanted city at which the seeker arrives, where Mu'ayyad Shīrāzī is the "guardian of the threshold", is not the material city of Cairo, it is al-balad al-amīn (Qur'ān 95. 3), it is the "virtual paradise" which is the da'wat typifying on earth the *dār al-ibdā'*, the celestial pleroma of the archetypes of Light.

The sojourn of Nāṣir-i Khusrau in Cairo was to be prolonged for some six years, at the end of which he must have been thoroughly well qualified to fulfil the task expected of him by the "cause"; his mission required that hermeneutic flexibility of the ta'wīl revealed in all his books as his own personal contribution. He was back at Balkh on

[1] *Dīvān*, pp. 172–7, and English tr. in W. Ivanow, *Nāsiri Khosraw and Ismailism*, pp. 17–35.

[2] *Dīvān*, p. 173, lines 23–4.

26 Jumādā II 444/23 October 1052, and from that time the obscure period of his biography begins. There are still, however, two dates which stand out: the year 453/1061, mentioned in the *Zād al-musāfirīn* ("The Travellers' Viaticum"), as marking the completion of this book, and the year 462/1070, in which the *Jāmiʿ* was undertaken. The *Zād al-musāfirīn*, which was finished at Yumgān in 453/1061, refers to those ignorant fanatics who, on the pretext that he was an infidel (*bad-dīn*), attacked his house and hounded him from his home and country.[1] Is it really possible that such an attack could have been made on a personage who had every appearance of being a pious *ḥājjī* returning from Mecca? Some interval of time must have elapsed to allow for Nāṣir's behaviour to have given rise to suspicions. On the other hand it is known that his spiritual functions brought him to Māzandarān and the region bordering the Caspian Sea. The ties which this region had with Shīʿism, as well as its dense forests, offered the chance of an easy refuge to the secret missionary of Ismāʿīlism. It is therefore probable that this journey took place between the two dates, the year of Nāṣir's return and the year given by the *Zād al-musāfirīn*, and that after his journey to Māzandarān he had returned to Balkh.

On this point the *Jāmiʿ* appears to contribute valuable information. Nāṣir says in his *Dīvān*: "The Turks have chased him out of Khurāsān. The amīr of Khurāsān did not want him, nor the Shāh of Sijistān, nor the amīr of Khuttalān."[2] But the subject of the *Jāmiʿ* is a correspondence with an amīr of Badakhshān, not mentioned elsewhere hitherto, so far as is known, at any rate under his true name. This prince was an Ismāʿīlī whom Nāṣir appears to have known well and he praises him in the very warmest terms. It was not the despatch of the qaṣīda of Abu'l-Haitham which was to be the reason for their relationship; on the contrary, it was the cordiality of the relationship which was to be conducive to such an overture from the Prince ʿAlī b. Asad; hence it seems that an indication is provided as to the reasons guiding Nāṣir in his choice of Yumgān as a "city of refuge"; in other respects the place does not appear to have combined many of the conditions of a charmed abode.

Yumgān is the name of a district, a valley which forms a lateral branching-off from the chain of the Hindu Kush, irrigated by a watercourse which today bears the Turkish name of Kokcha (blue river), a tributary of the upper Oxus. The district begins some miles above the

[1] *Zād al-musāfirīn*, pp. 402, line 12, and 280, line 4, for the date 453/1061.

[2] *Dīvān*, p. 331, line 20.

city of Jarm (4,800 feet) and rises rapidly in a southerly direction until it reaches an altitude of 6,000 feet. In summer the valley is hot, dry and dusty; in winter it is very cold. There is little cultivation and it is sparsely populated. There, on a mound, the tomb of Nāṣir-i Khusrau is to be found – a very modest one, according to the accounts of numerous Ismāʿīlīs who have gone there on pilgrimages. Strangely enough, the local people who regard themselves as sayyids and descendants of Nāṣir-i Khusrau, are today fanatical Sunnīs. They believe that Nāṣir was a Ṣūfī *pīr*, a Sunnī like themselves, having no connection with Ismāʿīlism. They also apply a pious zeal to discourage the pilgrimages that the Ismāʿīlīs of Badakhshān (in the wider sense) are naturally anxious to undertake.

More than once Nāṣir evokes his exile and his nostalgia in terms of touching sadness. However, he gives scarcely any solid facts about his life and his activities. It is not difficult to imagine that his spiritual task as an Ismāʿīlī dignitary must have occupied all his time. He himself wrote: "Each year I used to send into the world a book of daʿwat."[1] Thus he was in communication with the rest of the world, with his brothers of the daʿwat and with Egypt, and this was what mattered. It may also be conjectured that his relations with the prince of Badakhshān, ʿAlī b. Asad, must have brought him some consolation in his exile.

It was the prince of Badakhshān who in 462/1070 commissioned the book to which Nāṣir gave the title of the "Sum of the Two Philosophies" (*Jāmiʿ*). The author must by then have reached the age of sixty-seven years, since he was forty-two years of age when he undertook his great journey in 437/1045. From this time onwards there is nothing more to be said. Even the date of his death is by no means certain and it is necessary to search for traces; according to the pilgrims, there is no date at all on the tomb of Nāṣir. A date somewhere between the years 465/1072 and 470/1077 appears to be the most probable.

IV. NĀṢIR-I KHUSRAU AND RHAZES

There can be no question of expounding here, even summarily, the philosophical system of Nāṣir-i Khusrau, and in fact it would be necessary to make an exposition at the same time of the whole of Ismāʿīlī philosophy as it existed at that period. It is, however, at least possible to specify certain tenets assumed by our philosopher on the

[1] *Dīvān*, p. 298, line 3.

occasion of his polemic against an eminent man who, in his lifetime, had been bitterly opposed to the Ismā'īlī thinkers, namely Abū Bakr Muḥammad b. Zakariyyā' Rāzī, better known in the West since the Middle Ages under the Latin form of his name, Rhazes. To judge from the *Jāmi'*, the criticisms of the work of Rhazes are related to three main subjects: Nature, the fall of the Soul and the mission of the prophets.

From the outset, when the connection between the alchemy of Jābir and the Ismā'īlī gnosis is considered, the fact that the concepts of Jābir seem to be unknown to Rhazes is indicative. To ignore the Jābirean science of the "balance" is indeed to disregard the fundamental principle of the ta'wīl, of which the alchemic work is an outstanding example. There is to be observed in Rhazes a deep-seated inclination to reject all esoteric and symbolic explanations of natural phenomena. Just as in the *Jāmi'* Nāṣir gives a favourable account of the arguments of the Greek philosophers, because the ta'wīl allows him to reconcile them with those of Ismā'īlī philosophy, so conversely he reveals a nervous irritability when he mentions the opinions of Rhazes.

(*a*) *Nature:* A primary contention of Rhazes appears in connection with Aristotle's doctrine defining Nature as a "principle of movement and of rest". This hypothesis is not accepted by Rhazes and Nāṣir-i Khusrau makes the following observation: "Muḥammad b. Zakariyyā' Rāzī does not accept this hypothesis, according to which, he says, it would be necessary for the Natures (*ṭabā'i'* – the four natural elemental qualities) to have come from the Creator into material forms. If they came from the Creator, it must follow that Nature existed in God. But this is completely inadmissible."[1]

At the root of this dissimulation is a radical conflict with regard to the concepts of the Soul and of Nature. According to the Ismā'īlī philosophy of Nāṣir-i Khusrau, Nature is born into Matter by a contemplation which the Soul projects in the latter, just as the Soul proceeds to being by a contemplation of the Intelligence directed upon itself. The Soul is in this sense the child of the Intelligence; in the same way Nature is the child of the Soul, its pupil and its disciple. For this reason she can act and produce actions which will be in imitation of the activity of the Soul and, in consequence, she can be the principle of movement. According to Rhazes, the Soul wished to be united with Nature so as to produce sensate forms, but became instead its pitiful captive. It is this myth of the fall of the Soul, as conceived by Rhazes,

[1] *Jāmi'*, para. 122, p. 126.

which the Ismā'īlī thinker rejects, and a rejection of the physical theory of Rhazes means, *eo ipso*, a rejection of his doctrine of the Soul.

(*b*) *The fall of the Soul:* This myth is a characteristic feature of the philosophy of Rhazes. It is known to us from the record of discussions preserved by the Ismā'īlī dā'ī Abū Ḥātim Rāzī and by Nāṣir-i Khusrau himself. There are, according to Rhazes, five eternal (*qadīm*) principles (the Creator, the Soul, Matter, Time, Space), while the world had its origin in time (*muḥdath*). If the world began to exist, it was because an ardent desire set the soul in motion towards something, which might be the world, for the purpose of interpenetration. It did not then know, however, what misery would thenceforth cling to it. The Creator sends the Intelligence (*'aql*, *nous*) to waken the Soul from its lethargy in the habitation (*haikal*) which is the human being. Hence arise the function and the message of the philosophers, which are the deliverance of souls by means of philosophy, since it is through philosophy that the Soul learns to know the world which is truly its own.

Nāṣir-i Khusrau opposes this myth with a vigorous denial; his reply implies a refusal to admit that the Soul, the second hypostasis of the Pleroma, may have fallen into Matter for the purpose of producing Forms. In order to initiate such Forms there, it had only to project its contemplation into this Matter for the active *physis* to be manifested there. It is not the Soul (the second archangel of the divine Pentarchy, according to the system of Nāṣir) who was seduced by Matter and allowed itself to be subjugated by her. They are the partial or individual souls which have emanated from her, ignorant and unconscious, that are the victims of this fall. To awaken these souls is beyond the power of the philosophers. Indeed, is it not the band of philosophers which has been most often flouted and ignored? There is need of the word of the prophets. Besides, "The Sum of the two Philosophies" reveals a true piety in respect of the *Anima mundi*, which is the term used for *tauḥīd* by the philosophers. Nāṣir thus takes up their defence against Rhazes himself. Since the *Anima mundi* is "the lord of the souls of the philosophers", what would be the sense of their tauḥīd and their piety if this *Anima mundi* had succumbed to Matter and become its captive? Therefore it is not the Soul of the world which has been taken captive by Matter, but the partial souls issued from it and these must be awakened from their lethargy. As to the awakening, Nāṣir defies Rhazes to provoke it. It is with reference to the prophets that the conflict appears in its fundamental importance. For, according to Rhazes, souls not redeemed by philosophy wander *post mortem* about the world; these are the bad souls which seduce certain human beings through their pride, suggesting to them that they should proclaim themselves prophets. For the Ismā'īlī, on the contrary, these bad souls are the agents of Iblis-Satan, harassing the prophets, against whom each of the prophets has had to struggle. For the Ismā'īlī thinker, the mission of the prophets – and essentially that of Islamic philosophy – is a divine mission, while for Rhazes it is a Satanic curse. The conflict breaks out in all its violence.

(*c*) *The mission of the prophets:* On this point the antagonism of Rhazes is certainly that of a man of genius, but one who fiercely ignores all "dimensions", not merely of creed but perhaps even of religion. The extreme interest of the situation lies in the fact that here the rationalist challenge is taken up not by the doctors of the Law, by the "orthodox" theologians of Islam, but by the esoterics (*Bāṭiniyān*), whose entire spiritual effort and *raison d'être* are aimed in fact at rising above the letter of the positive legalitarian religion and so at rising above the *tanzīl* and the *ẓāhir* (the exoteric). They themselves incur the worst suspicions of the "orthodox" authorities and are exposed to the worst outrages of their official counter-propaganda. Nāṣir-i Khusrau himself experienced their severity. Probably the Ismā'īlī – or generally Shī'ī – concept of the mission of the prophet (the *nāṭiq*, the enunciator of the letter) is not the same as that of the Sunnī majority. It is no less indispensable to the whole structure of the esoteric religion and to its vision of the correspondence of the worlds and inter-worlds, as well as to the mystery of initiatory salvation, which, for the devotee, constitutes a spiritual birth (*wilādat rūḥānīya*), an inner event quite different from mere redemption by philosophy. To sum up, what has to be considered here is not a commonplace opposition between philosophical rationalism and religion in the current or confessional sense of the word, but a far more radical opposition between the spirit – esoteric, religious, initiatory – and a will which is hostile to all that this spirit implies.

In his profession of faith Rhazes expresses a basic *egalitarianism*, deeming it unthinkable that God should have selected certain men for the purpose of giving them superiority over the masses, conferring on them the prophetic mission and constituting them, as it were, guides for humanity. Rhazes resents the inequalities of nature and the law as an intolerable injustice and combats it with a ferocity which is the more determined for being turned against himself, since at heart he is perfectly aware of his own eminent superiority. It was this aspect which Abū Ḥātim brought, very delicately, to his attention, in the course of their controversy, by a formidable argument *ad hominem*. Rhazes expresses himself with all the passion of a "grievance", the psychological origins of which elude discovery. The pretensions of the prophets are, for him, responsible for the dogmas of inter-contradictory religions and, consequently, for the wars and massacres unleashed in the name of vain beliefs.

The Ismā'īlī thinker, for his part, is equally far removed, or even more so, for different reasons, from religious and all other fanaticism. Regarding the mortal contradictions denounced by Rhazes, the Ismā'īlī knows very well that they arise and become inflamed only at the level of the letter of the law, of the exoteric. Indeed, the whole of Ismā'īlī teaching consists in training devotees who are capable of proceeding beyond the literal appearances, the exoteric, of the Law. The ta'wīl, the spiritual hermeneutic which provides the means of esoteric initiation, postulates the view of history moving in cycles, according to which Time returns to its origin, towards the conclusion of the Great Resurrection. "If men," writes Nāṣir-i Khusrau, "were to seek this spiritual hermeneutic, the prophetic religions would stand upright, each in the place where it stands."[1] Men would understand that each one constitutes one of the "six days" of the creation of the religious cosmos. One day does not oppose another; it succeeds it.

The greatness of the Ismā'īlī thinker lies perhaps in the conception of an eternal transgressor. In the eyes of the rationalist philosopher, he transgresses reason because he upholds the appearance of religion; never does his ta'wīl wound it in the face. In the eyes of the doctor of Law, he transgresses the latter, because he interprets the dogmas of the faith in an inward and spiritual sense. It is this point which is summed up with full awareness in an admirable passage by Nāṣir-i Khusrau: "If," he writes, "in the event of an absence of moral sense taking control of mankind, it were necessary for the sages and the scholars to keep silent and renounce wisdom, then it would have been necessary for the Sage of Sages, the Seal of the prophets, Muḥammad the Elect, to have withheld from men completely this treasure of Wisdom, this mine of essential truths of all the sciences, which is the Holy Book. The truth is quite otherwise. God gave him this command: Recite to the created world the portions of the Book which have been revealed to

[1] *Jāmi'*, p. 165.

you; institute prayer, for prayer preserves from baseness and from evil actions" (Qur'ān 29. 44). These lines, which might have provoked the wrath of Rhazes, could not but appear very edifying to a doctor of the Law.

However, Nāṣir-i Khusrau continues: "The exoteric (*ẓāhir*) of Prayer consists in adoring God with the postures of the body, in directing the body towards the *qibla* of the body, which is the *Ka'ba*, the Temple of the Most High God situated at Mekka. To understand the esoteric of Prayer (*ta'wīl-e bāṭin*) means adoring God with the thinking soul and turning towards the quest of the gnosis of the Book and the gnosis of positive religion, towards the qibla of the spirit, which is the Temple of God, that Temple in which the divine Gnosis is enclosed, I mean the Imām in Truth, salutations to him."[1]

Here it is the doctor of the Law who will denounce, with indignation, Shī'ī extremism! It is for this reason that such a passage, by showing to best advantage the standpoint of an Iranian Ismā'īlī thinker such as Nāṣir-i Khusrau, confers an exemplary grandeur on his solitude.

[1] *Jāmi'*, p. 308.

CHAPTER 17

ZOROASTRIAN LITERATURE AFTER THE MUSLIM CONQUEST

In the preceding volume a survey was made of that part of extant Mazdaean literature the content of which could have been known in the Sāsānian era, even though the books were probably or even certainly compiled under Islam. Only those works were excluded which showed obvious signs of contact with Islam, and it is these which are now to be considered.

They were in the first place characterized by a tendency to be explanatory as well as polemical. Their prime object was to set forth the Mazdaean doctrine, whose liturgical texts, however ancient and widespread in usage, were not of a kind to re-establish didactically, still less to defend rationally, that doctrine, which was threatened on all sides. It was a fact that Islam made rapid progress in Iran and even recruited there its principal doctors and upholders, while the number of Mazdaean *mōbads* qualified to resist them steadily declined. Still more regrettable was the growing scarcity of priests necessary for the conduct of services and purifications, by whom alone the liturgy could be maintained, as the axis of the truly religious life, together with custom and law. Preoccupation with this state of affairs was to be expressed not only in the form of casuistry, to deal with the practical problems raised by this diminution of the priesthood, but also by concern to provide the instruction which was lacking. Thereafter this instruction and catechizing seemed to become more explicit and were addressed, at any rate in the writings, to adult persons who were threatened by conversion to Islam, by indifference or at the very least by ignorance. Such instruction was indeed the chief concern of the mōbads and explains why they should have written the books and also why they should have been particularly anxious to preserve them when most of the various works of Sāsānian (or post-Sāsānian) Pahlavī literature had disappeared or, as in the case of epic, had been absorbed into Persian literature of an ostensibly Muslim nature. Thus the literature now under consideration is both religious and didactic, and is sometimes apologetic and polemical. If it presents very few "literary" features, it is at least superior to the literature of the preceding period (and it must be stressed that only what has survived to the present day is under review) in that it reveals the workings of a certain line of thought. Though lacking in aesthetic merit, it is not without interest for the history of philosophical and theological speculation, at the very period when Islamic thought was in full spate. The Mazdaism of the 3rd–4th/9th–10th centuries deserves to be better known not only for itself but also for its contribution to our knowledge of the theoretical tenets opposed to it by Islam.

I. ĀTURFARNBAG I FARRUXZĀTĀN

The first author for consideration is a mōbad named Āturfarnbag i Farruxzātān, of whom it is known that he lived under the ʿAbbāsid Caliph Ma'mūn (198/813–218/833) and that he was chief of the Mazdaeans of Fārs. A short work records the disputation to which he was challenged by a Mazdaean convert to Islam who had changed his name from Dādv-Ohrmazd to Wahballāh (usually called Abališ or Abaleh owing to the ambiguities of Pahlavī script). He had also summoned Jews and Christians to take part in the argument. The Caliph Ma'mūn, as is known, favoured such rhetorical jousts, and an account of this one has been preserved in a document which may well have come from Āturfarnbag himself. In his questions the renegade made an attack on the consequences of dualism: the existence of opposites in the world, fire-worship, the pains of Hell imposed by Ohrmazd, the state of the bodies of infidels after their death, the wearing of the *kūstīk*. To each of these questions Āturfarnbag put up a defence and is said to have won the approval of the caliph, which seems very unlikely.

The allusions in the *Dēnkart* to the activities of Āturfarnbag support the belief that he took a major part in the collection of the Avestan texts which had been dispersed at the time of the Muslim conquest and, moreover, that he was the author of an *Advēn nāmak* which was drawn upon by the last editor of the *Dēnkart*. The latter indeed gave the *Dēnkart* its name and took a considerable extract from it for his Book V; it is not impossible that this is the celebrated *Āyīn-nāma* referred to in the *Fihrist* of al-Nadīm and quoted by Ibn Qutaiba. Āturfarnbag is mentioned also in the *Dātistān-i dēnīk*, as an authority on the tariffs of the cult, and in the "Epistles" of Manuščihr. A series of answers given by him, contained in the same manuscript as the *Great Bundahišn* (TD 1), was only published recently. The answers are short and never give a general view of the problems or of the legal principles at play, as is the case with some of the other works we are about to examine. Indeed the greater number are concerned only with very minor points of legal purity and are often repetitious. Some however are interesting as bringing some light on the legislation of marriage and the laws of inheritance, and sometimes apropos of the conversion to Islam of a member of the family. Two answers tell us that next-of-kin marriage was still a living practice; the *xvētōdāt* was even enforced against the will of a sister or daughter, but not without the consent of the husbands. The many cases of defilement owing to contact with an impure person or object seem to show that the laws digested in the *Vidēvdāt* were by way of being forgotten and give sense to the report from the *Dēnkart* that Āturfarnbag had collected the dispersed fragments of the Avesta accessible until that time to an ever-diminishing number of *ērpats* and mōbads.

The most important extracts, however, which also come from the *Advēn nāmak*, constitute Book IV of the *Dēnkart*. The book begins with a sort of philosophical exposition of the "procession" of the *Amešа Spenta* in terms reminiscent of Neoplatonism. From the non-created Unity which is at the beginning proceeds Vahuman, the first-created, whose creation is in a way a counterpart to the assault of Ahriman; there is thus already a duality, in consequence of which the coming into being of the other Primordial Creatures is easily explained. Passing on to Šahrevar, who represents the power of arms and the militant aspect of royalty, the author lists the early Sāsānian rulers who played a part in preserving Mazdaean orthodoxy. It seems probable that their decrees are quoted here *verbatim*, the pompous style of such documents being easily recognizable. Proceeding next to the creatures of the *gētī* the author takes the opportunity of dealing very briefly with a large number of theological questions, on which *Dēnkart III* gives more detailed instruction. It is probable that Book IV is not merely a summary of the material contained in Book III, but represents an attempt to build up the theological and philosophical doctrines by which Mazdaean thought had been sustained for several centuries before and after the coming of Islam into a system based upon two main dogmas, of dualism and of creation by a wise and provident God.

II. MANUŠČĪHR-I GOŠN-YAM

This mōbad, a descendant of Āturfarnbag, was chief of the Mazdaeans of Fārs and Kirmān, lived in the second half of the 3rd/9th century, and is known from two very different written sources. The first is a collection of three letters concerning the liturgical controversy in which he opposed his brother Zātspram, mōbad of Sirkān, the inhabitants of which had made a complaint about their priest. He had in fact taught that the purification rite of *baršnum*, which played such an important part in the life of the Mazdaeans, could in general be replaced by a lesser purification. Manuščīhr addressed himself in the first instance to the inhabitants of Sirkān, and his line of argument is to establish the paramount authority of the Avestan text in this matter, maintaining that it was in no way diminished by the variety of opinions between the Mazdaean divines, who very likely had been called in to justify the legality of the innovation made by Zātspram. There are quotations here and there from the corpus of jurisprudence which, as was already known, had long ago been created by jurists and commentators on the Avestan laws. In the second letter, addressed to Zātspram himself, a similar line of defence was employed, insofar as this difficult text can be understood. Manuščīhr (II, ii, 9–12) was concerned to show how an authorized interpretation could, in a particular instance, be supplemented by another interpretation, more apt but equally well authenticated, such as is the case with the differences between Afarg and Mētyōmāh or of Āturfarnbag, Vindāt and Āturbocēt; this argument might be applied to the use which was made simultaneously of the astronomical tables of the Empire (i.e. Iran), of India and of Ptolemy for the purpose of determining the position of the sun, Saturn (Kēvān) or Mars (Varahrān). The epistle continues on a note of severity: Manuščīhr informs his brother that he has already written to the people of Sirkān and that he is sending a decree, Letter no. III, to all the Mazdaeans of Iran forbidding them to follow the practice of Zātspram.

The interest of these documents, whose main purpose is now of little consequence, lies in their disclosure of the functioning of the Mazdaean hierarchy under conditions in which it no longer enjoyed the support of the state. The sustained deferential tone of the letters is in contrast with the dry and somewhat inquisitorial exposition of the religious policy of the first Sāsānids when dealing with "deviations" (*Dēnkart IV*, English tr. by Zaehner, *Zurvān*, pp. 7–9). The solemn and weighty style of Manuščīhr is not at all abusive and he appears to be using his authority only to put the flock of Zātspram on their guard against their leader.

Manuščīhr's other work is his *Dātistān-i dēnīk*. In this he discusses many questions which might perhaps have been taken for granted: there was actually, at this period, good reason for recapitulating points of doctrine and of practice which the Mazdaeans were in danger of forgetting. There is no decisive evidence whether this work was written before or after the "Epistles", in spite of the striking differences of style between them – the open letters and proclamation being couched in solemn and meandering prose, while the *Dātistān* is much more clear and direct, doubtless because more impersonal. It is a collection of ninety-one answers to questions put by a certain Mihr-Xvaršēt i Ātur-Māhān and by other unnamed Mazdaeans. After beginning with a preface in a ceremonial style which is very close to that of the "Epistles" it proceeds forthwith to a series of fairly closely related problems, as follows.

Questions 1–3 deal with the "just" man, that is to say, the archetype, not only Gayōmart, the first or primordial man, but also Zartušt, the bringer of Revelation, and his last son, Sōšyans, born posthumously, who closes the cycle of creation and introduces the eschatological transfiguration (*fraškart*). This traditional doctrine, which places Zartušt in the middle of the history of the world, may have been revived in opposition to Islamic speculation on the *Insān al-kāmil*, unless of course the reverse was the case and the Iranian theologoumenon served as a model for the Muslim – a dilemma we often meet. In any case, the purpose of the Perfect Man is, according to the main theme of Mazdaism, the perfect cult of the supremely good God and the struggle against evil; the wisdom which presides over the divine government provides for each period a ruler devout in the Faith. This quest after perfection is not to be without its difficulties (questions 4–6), a fact which serves only to emphasize the militant character of the religion. Questions 8–14 examine the effect of the actions accomplished either by a man himself or by others on his account, depending on whether he has or has not ordered them to be carried out after his death – an important matter in view of the prayers and rites which are required during and after the death of a Mazdaean. When the body has been delivered up to dogs and birds of prey for rending, it may be asked whether the soul, which although separated from the body is still close to it, can still suffer (questions 15–17). Here it may be noted that dogs are always mentioned as well as birds of prey, which would suggest a practice different from the present, when the body is exposed to the birds alone, the function of the dog being simply to drive away the demons by glancing at the corpse (*sag-dīd*). Question 18 deals with the vision of Ohrmazd and of Ahriman afforded to the dead, and the answer, based on an Avestan text, recalls an ancient myth hitherto attested only in its Manichaean form. Ohrmazd replies to the demand made on him by Zartušt to hold out his hand by telling him to take the hand of Gayōmart – all this takes place in a pre-eternity in which the passing of time is transcended – in return for which he will see him, Ohrmazd, at the resurrection of the body. Thus it will be the impious who will benefit from the apocatastasis, while the just will see God and will rejoice on arrival at the Ohrmazdian existence. The next questions (19–33) deal with the places of the dead and the whole subject of individual eschatology, before proceeding (34–7) to the resurrection of the body.

All these chapters contribute precise details to the study of Mazdaean anthropology and bear witness to the interest taken by the theologian of this period in the nature of bliss in Paradise, a feature which is in contrast with popular works of the Sāsānian period like the "Book of Artā Vīrāf", the author of which took a special pleasure in describing the pains of Hell. An argument of great importance is developed in Chapter 36: the offensive in the struggle between Ohrmazd and his creatures on one side and Ahriman and his supporters on the other is to be blamed entirely on Ahriman; the ills for which Ohrmazd is responsible are, strictly speaking, punishments or acts of legitimate defence. It may be noted incidentally that there is no trace of any dispute regarding the perpetuity of the pains of Hell; such controversy was not to arise until later.

Question 38 proceeds to an examination of the liturgy and considers the manifold significance of the sacred girdle of the Mazdaeans, the kūstīk, symbolizing at the same time the bondage of man (*bandakīh*) in relation to Ohrmazd and the distinction between the upper and lower parts of the body; the kūstīk has as a celestial archetype the Milky Way and the *Dēn* itself. The symbolism of its composition is dealt with in the next question and also the offences connected with it, such as walking without the kūstīk and talking while eating. Since the wearing of the kūstīk is a Mazdaean characteristic, a discussion is inserted here on the gravity of the sin of aspostasy (question 40) and on the merit of those who strive to prevent it from being committed (question 41). There follow further questions on the *drōn* (question 42) and on sacrifice, *yazišn* (question 47), and a collection of questions on the relative values of theoretical and practical knowledge for priests, some of them knowing the texts by heart while others are experts on ritual, all of which has an appreciable effect on their stipends (questions 43–6, 65). These questions contain a mine of information on the state of the Mazdaean clergy two centuries after the conquest of Iran by the Arabs. Priests are few, badly-educated, and impoverished, and it is asked what crafts they can practise in order to survive (question 45). There is frequent discussion of their stipends (questions 81–8) and also of the morality of economic transactions, such as buying goods cheaply and selling them dear and, particularly, of doing business with non-Mazdaeans and non-Iranians. (In this category are to be reckoned not only the Arab invaders, whose total numbers were not very great, but also the Semitic populations of the former Iranian Empire, Christians and Jews who had long ago settled in the country.) For a survey of the demography of Iran before Islam or in the early years of the conquest such data are of the greatest interest. They provide the back-drop for a study of the relationship between early Islam and its non-Muslim "subjects" which is too often undertaken merely on the basis of information on countries populated by Jews and Christians, such as Egypt and Syria.

A characteristic feature of this relationship was the maintenance of the personal law of the *ahl al-kitāb* and suchlike. To questions 53–61 Manuščihr replies with long dissertations on such essential institutions of Iranian family law as authority over the family (*dūtak-sardārīh*) which, especially if the family possesses property, must never fail and for which provision must be made. Sometimes the state of the family itself may offer a solution, or the head of the family may have decided it for the future, before his death. Public officials may, as a last resort, intervene to designate the person most suitable in the circumstances to be the new *paterfamilias*. A more original institution is that of the *stūrīh*, which is the responsibility given (again in accordance with the customs regulating the devolution of the *sardārīh*) to a person for the administration of property of a certain value, instead of and in place of the *de cujus*, who has no legitimate or adoptive heir. This system of devolution made it possible to ensure the continuity of the family by preserving permanently the property designed to maintain it. The subject cannot be discussed further here, though it should be of considerable interest to sociologists and to legal historians. The *Mātigān-i hazār dātistān* mentions it frequently, but provides no substitute for the almost didactic exposition set forth in the *Dātistān-i dēnīk*. Another practice which the Islamic occupation did not abrogate and which was to be found continuing as customary Mazdaean law was consanguineous marriage, xvētōdāt, treated in question 64. Questions 71–7 are devoted to sexual offences, particularly paederasty, which is so often referred to in any discussion of Mazdaean morals.

Manuščihr replies, in irregular order, to questions on various cult observances, *gētī-xrīt*, *zīndak-ruvān*, *hamāk-Dēn* (questions 79, 80, 82) and repeats such expositions of cosmogony as may be read in the *Bundahišn* or the "Selections" of Zātspram: it is what might be called mythological physics, based entirely on tradition, with the exception of question 90 which is very obscure and discusses, in quasi-philosophical terms, the movement of the heavens.

The book ends with a selection of "sayings of the ancients" which recapitulates the beginning of Book VI of the *Dēnkart*. Both texts are somewhat corrupt and serve as correctives to one another. There is no need to assume that either text has borrowed from the other: the aphorisms are clearly of greater antiquity than the two works themselves and it is probable that they formed a thesaurus to which recourse was made as needed. It has already been noted (Vol. 3) that the author of *Šāyast nē šāyast* made use of it in concluding the second part of his book.

III. THE "RIVĀYAT" OF EMĒT I AŠAVAHIŠTAN

The author of this work was Manuščihr's nephew. He exercised after him the authority of a mōbad over a large part of southern Iran in the first half of the 4th/10th century. It consists of a small collection of his answers to questions put to him by a certain Ātur-Gušasp i Mihr Ataš i Ātur-Gušasp and deals almost entirely with concrete examples arising out of the position of the Mazdaeans in Iran under Islam. Muslim influence is very much more apparent here than in the *Dātistān-i dēnīk* or in the *Dēnkart* and is shown to interfere with the laws which still govern the Mazdaean community, especially family law and, in particular, the institution of stūrīh. The opportunity is taken to explain clearly how it works and to describe the status of woman both in her own family and in that of her husband. According to whether her father has or has not an heir, natural or adopted, apart from herself, she is either free or not free to contract a "plenary" or "authorized" (*pātixšāyihā*) marriage which alone entitles her to dispose of her entire property in favour of her husband or her children. Likewise, if she has been married before, she is merely the *cagar* wife of her second husband. (Her position if she had children by her first husband is not, however, made very clear.) As regards repudiation, it is stated (question 7) that it is valid only when the woman is definitely at fault or alternatively if she agrees (deriving an advantage out of it is not enough). In questions of succession, the conversion to Islam of a male member of the family almost always has the effect of altering the status of the woman; if one of her brothers dies and the other becomes a Muslim and thus, by doing so, incurs under Mazdaean law a civil death, her status changes and remains changed even after the new marriage which she may contract (questions 1, 2). The property acquired by the apostate when he was a Mazdaean cannot be allowed to remain in his possession, since an ancient juridical saying lays down that property which has once belonged to a Mazdaean must not be permitted to slip from Mazdaean hands (question 4). In a diminished and defenceless Mazdaean community, however, matters could not always be so arranged (question 25). Repentance and return by an apostate are likewise provided for, and he will benefit from the same spiritual advantages after death as other Mazdaeans (question 26). The proximity of non-Mazdaeans (*akdēn*) is liable to result in contamination and Mazdaism, as is well known, is very scrupulous in this respect. On no account should the hot baths of Muslims be used (question 19), and it is essential, if a Muslim has been down into a well to clean it, that it should be purified afterwards with the utmost care (question 36). The sin of adultery committed with a non-Mazdaean woman is all the more serious if it results in the birth of a child who will be reared in the Evil Religion (question 42). With regard to contamination and the purification it calls for, difficulties arise not only from the presence of Muslims but also owing to the scarcity or the incompetence of the purifiers, that is of all Mazdaean ērpats. It appears in fact that this is the main preoccupation of the book, to judge from the number of times it is mentioned, an ērpat being required not only for purposes of purification but also for the appointment of Mazdaeans to exercise the functions imposed by family law. Where no ērpat is available, recourse must be had to some reasonably well educated man or at least to a man of good repute (question 6). There must often have been ērpats who abandoned their office in order to take up some more lucrative occupation, such as that of soldier or brigand; in the event of their return, they would be suspended from their sacred office (questions 10 and 11), a factor which tended to reduce their numbers still further. Moreover, if they had failed to discharge a debt or fine, they could not in future be employed except for minor functions (question 9). It is hardly surprising therefore that certain poorly qualified persons should have usurped their office (question 12).

One seemingly quite practical question as to the praise or blame attaching to a man who, after deciding to build a bridge for the use of his fellow-citizens, changes his mind and devotes the money to other purposes, provokes a long and subtle dissertation on the relative merits of undertakings according to the circumstances and the manner in which they are accomplished (question 17).

With the publication of the *Rivāyat* of Ēmēt a few years before that of the *Rivāyat* of Āturfarnbag (see above) one of the surprises in store must have been the small group of questions devoted to the forms of marriage between close relations (xvētōdāt), the existence of which, even in remote antiquity, was vehemently contested in the last century. The answers leave no room for doubt concerning the practice of the custom, its various forms (marriage with sister, daughter or mother), its quasi-solemnization (verbal promise, witnesses) and, especially, as regards belief in the meritorious nature of the act, be it actually performed by a man, or intended and subsequently frustrated, or encouraged among others, with or without the hope of progeny (questions 22, 24, 25, 28, 29, 30). In the light of the historical context, as revealed by the book, it is astonishing that such a custom should have persisted in full vigour within the Mazdaean community, surrounded as it was on all sides by Islam. It may be wondered whether the Muslim authorities were actually ignorant or preferred to appear ignorant of practices which belonged strictly to the personal law of their non-Muslim "subjects". In any case, against this evidently historical background, the discussions aroused by these questions can certainly not be regarded as either idle or academic.

It may be noted in passing that in two passages a distinction is made between "apostates" and persons who are born into the "Evil Religion" (questions 4, 6) but who have, notwithstanding, practised the Mazdaean virtues (questions 26, 28).

Two chapters contain brief replies to a collection of theological questions. The first series (question 39) recalls the principal points of individual eschatology: the fate of the soul after death and before the resurrection of the body, the effect of the confession of sins (*patēt*) or, failing confession, of the ritual of the three nights (*satuš*), the perpetuity of the pains of Hell only until the resurrection, the protection of the souls of the deceased by the Creator, even in Hell, the existence of an intermediate region for "moderate" sinners, the difference between the state of the just and that of the damned – the just man enjoying the society of his kind, while each of the damned believes himself to be alone. The second series (question 40) considers various aspects of the important problem, so often discussed by Mazdaeans and Muslims alike, of the extent to which a man's actions are governed by divine predestination or by his own freewill.

This book, like the works of Manuščihr, clearly contributes some valuable evidence on the practical life of the Mazdaeans at a time when they were on the defensive against Islam. Following the *Rivāyat* of Āturfarnbag in Ms. TD 2 is another series of four questions asked by ērpat Spenddāt – Farruxburzīn, with answers of the head mōbad Frēhsrōš i Vahrāmān in A.D. 1008. The only significant one presents us with the rare occurrence of a conflict between Mazdaeans of Khurāsān and an official (*sūltānīk*) of Baghdad who had enforced an intercalation in the calendar, one Abū Manṣūr (?) who was obviously a Muslim. Following on the colophon of this rivāyat come thirty more questions on points of liturgy. There is no indication of their being by the same author as the previous rivāyat. The theoretical works now to be examined reflect not so much the historical situation as the radical conflict of doctrine in which the Mazdaeans changed over to the attack.

IV. "DĒNKART III"

A survey was made in the previous volume of the parts of the *Dēnkart* whose contents must certainly have been known to the Mazdaeans of the Sāsānian period. Here special attention will be given to Book III, the most important theological work left by the Mazdaeans. The other "doctrinal" books, IV and V, appear to be versions of or extracts from earlier writings of one or of several authors. The author or editor of Book III was a mōbad named Āturpāt i Ēmētān; according to information provided by Mas'ūdī and Ḥamza he may be placed chronologically near the middle of the 4th/10th century and he is known to have exercised spiritual authority over the Mazdaeans in southern Iran. He himself reveals nothing of his identity until the final chapter of Book III, in which he traces the history of the transmission of the Avesta and the part played in it by Āturfarnbag. His own work was rather to collect and epitomize the sum of religious thought expressed in later books, chiefly in the *zand*, in the sayings of the Ancients, and in the *Advēn nāmak* of Āturfarnbag which was probably already a compilation. We know nothing of what was contained in Books I and II of his *Dēnkart*. The content of Book III is made perfectly clear by the clause: "from (or according to) the teachings of the Good Religion" that comes at the end of the titles of almost all the chapters, except those dealing with the outward form of the Dēn. This goes to show that the author's purpose is to systematize the Religion, and to bring out the (metaphysical) principles that give force and life to its structure.

The book opens with twelve short answers to questions put by sundry "heretics" and sixteen other answers to questions put by a disciple. The page containing the first question has been lost in the only surviving manuscript, and the succeeding pages are damaged. The manuscript is, moreover, very imperfect and requires continual correction; even the scribe was aware of this in several instances and chose to repeat a complete chapter which he himself copied badly or copied from an original which was in itself bad. Despite the ingenuity of modern scholars, numerous pages will continue to remain obscure.

Apart from some very long chapters on xvētōdāt (Chapter 80), on gētī (Chapter 123), and on medicine (Chapter 157), no chapter exceeds three or four pages in length. Their order is quite arbitrary: some, like those which contain answers to opinions formulated in the previous chapter, are in the right order, but most frequently the connection between them is weak and depends on words rather than on the sense. There is, however, no doubt regarding the unity of the book: the same subjects are pursued and the same ideas are discussed from points of view which at times scarcely differ from one another.

Moreover, the single preoccupation which governed the compilation of the book becomes apparent from the ideological circumstances in which it was written. It must not be forgotten that, at the time and place of its origin, the development of Muslim thought was in full spate; its purpose therefore was both to consolidate the faith of Mazdaeans who – in direct proportion to their intellectual level – were tempted to desert their ancient religion with its load of myth and ritual, and also to explain it in comprehensible and convincing terms to those most apostolic invaders who must have been holding it up to ridicule. But their own religion was surely subject to criticism, and hence the defence of Mazdaism would imply almost inevitably an ordered attack on the new faith. This offensive is directed seldom at the texts but in full measure at those doctrines universally accepted by the enemy, and to this end, since the appeal to any authority would not be valid here, it is rational philosophy which predominates, the rational argument which alone can carry conviction.

There is here something quite different from dialectical opportunism; when the Muslim *mutakallim* argues with Greek philosophers or with Muslim *falāsifa*, he concentrates on seeking out internal contradictions in tenets of his opponents so as to discredit them completely. These are rational arguments which may be used to oppose the processes of reason itself. The Mazdaean line of argument runs an entirely different course: it is founded on the great truths of metaphysics in opposition to the narrow metaphysical system – often deliberately, theoretically narrow – of the Muslim theologians. The omniscience of God, His justice, His providence, His wisdom are the pillars of knowledge and thus the criteria of that truth which is under discussion. Inevitably this starting point will be compared with the Mu'tazilite viewpoint, and it may be thought that, when the latter were accused, in a famous *ḥadīth*, of being the "*majūs* of Islam", it was not simply on account of their theory of human freedom, but rather because both sides, basing their argument on the justice of God, deduced as a consequence what should or should not be properly attributed to God. This line of thought must have appeared as imposing a limit to the omnipotence of God and, in any case, as authorizing an interpretation of the spirit of the revealed texts going far beyond the letter. Indeed, the Mazdaism which is defined and illustrated by the third book of the *Dēnkart*, far from disputing on words, recognizes from the outset a natural (they will say "innate") knowledge of God and regards "innate reason" (*asn-xrat*) and the Good Religion as fundamentally one. It follows that, at least in Book III, the *Dēnkart* says comparatively little about the revelation, as such, about the communication made to mankind by Ohrmazd, through the mediation of the prophet Zarathustra, or the knowledge of such truths as eschatology, which cannot be attained by deduction. In ethics, on the other hand, the Mean (*patmān*) is the norm and source which is that of reason in the realm of knowledge; both attributes are, of themselves, the prerogative of every man. It is these characteristics of accessibility and of universality which give to Mazdaism the superiority emphasized by its theologian throughout the book.

A more detailed survey is desirable, however, of the adversaries either mentioned by name or indirectly implied by the context. Most frequently mentioned are the "doctors" (*kēšdārān* = *'ulamā'*), who are almost invariably Muslims but without being specified as such. In nearly fifty chapters the doctrine set out in the title is followed by a demonstration of the incompatibility of a true conception of God with the doctrines, briefly summarized, of the kēšdārān.

Direct references to Qur'anic doctrine are typical, in relation to the kēšdārān; their prophet represents himself as the Seal of Prophecy; the Creator, after forbidding any cult but His own, commands the angels to worship man. In particular, the eternity of the pains of Hell seems to conflict with the justice of God and, still more, with the wisdom of His providence, the perfection of His original plan. The omnipotence of God is not consistent with the fact that His will is contradicted by the sin of His own creatures and, indeed, how is the all-goodness of God to be reconciled with any kind of responsibility for evil, be it nothing more than mere "permission"? Some of the attacks are aimed more particularly at a Mu'tazilite belief: the non-existence in God of such eternal attributes as the source of action in time.

In at least one instance the kēšdārān are Christians: Chapter 40 deals with the Trinity and with the absurdity of father and son appearing simultaneously in time. With regard to the Jews, it is sometimes difficult to decide whether their faith or practices are the real target since these are common to Jews and Muslims alike. Thus, for instance, the mythological personage Dhahāk (Zohāk), the enemy of Yim, is regarded as the ancestor of Abraham, while in the *Shāh-nāma* he is first and foremost the ancestor of the Arabs. The Manichaeans are not overlooked; their "precepts" are in direct opposition to those proclaimed by Āturpāt i Mahraspandān, and the *zandīk* (a term which in Muslim heresiology was applied specifically if not exclusively to Manichaeans) are rightly held responsible for the doctrine of the two souls, which Saint Augustine both expounded and refuted for posterity.

The author then appears to be fairly well informed on the beliefs of his opponents and cannot be accused of either distortion or misunderstanding; again his attack is not a dialectical exercise but comes to grips with reality.

Without any attempt being made to summarize all the chapters of Book III, the important doctrines set out in them may be considered with the purpose of showing the way in which they cohere and are linked together. The basic dogma is clearly that of "classical" Mazdaism (disregarding the *Gāthās*, which still present a problem of some obscurity), which postulates the existence, in addition to Ohrmazd the Creator, of Ahriman, the principle of Evil. From Good, however, only good can ensue and the principle of Good must necessarily bring everything to a good conclusion for its creatures. Evil is thus ultimately condemned, if not annihilated, a matter on which little explanation is given but which follows from the fact that it is *mēnōg* (transcendant) like the principle of Good and even more exclusively so. Indeed, while the Creator, whose mēnōg state was coveted and assailed by Evil, causes his creatures to pass from the mēnōg state to the state of gētī in which they are armed to struggle with and triumph over Evil, Ahriman, for his part, does not create in the true sense but makes use of gētī beings as his agents. It is they who, at the end of time, will disappear in a burst of dissolution or, in the case of men who have served their time in Hell, will be purified, transfigured and rendered immortal and blessed. Man has thus a militant function in the service of salvation. He is the lord of creation owing to his own free will thanks to which his nature (*cihr*) becomes a wilful nature (*kāmakih*) and he is guided towards his object within the framework of society, according to the four classes of mankind – priests, warriors, husbandmen and craftsmen – topped by the good Iranian king. The part played by the last is thus moral and cosmic as well as political, and royalty, together with the Good Religion itself, is the pillar of the world. The alliance of the two is indissoluble and both enjoy a charisma – royal or religious – bearing the name *xvarrah*. It is possible to foresee what this doctrine, which runs through both the theology and the epic of Iran, was to become in the purely religious and esoteric context of Ismā'īlism and in the Iranian world where, under Islam, people continued to live on their nostalgia for the charisma of royalty. The foundations had already been laid in the theological history of Zoroastrianism, in which Vištaspa was the "lay" champion of the new religion, which conferred legitimacy upon him. On the other hand the Islamic conquest represented a foreign conquest at the same time, so much so that the defeat of Zoroastrianism came to be linked with that of the Iranian Empire in the sacred historiography which became part and parcel of the religious and national mythology.

To return to the question of human free will; it should be noted that this idea is traditionally Mazdaean, since the *Gāthās* so plainly insist on the "choice" of the primordial Good Spirit, but that it has been revived and subjected to philosophical analysis making use of the distinction between voluntary and natural action. There is, further, in the matter of divine responsibility a flat rejection of the view which can be, and which has been, deduced from the Qur'anic texts. Not only is God held to be in no way responsible for the evil committed by his creature, but the problem of the relationship between the free will of man and the causality of God is not even raised. The Mu'tazilites were more explicit: good and bad actions alike both lie outside the influence of God; their solution in support of human responsibility is radical. It is unlikely that the Mazdaeans deliberately adopted it, but the Mu'tazilites could understandably be thought to have followed the same trend of thought.

Although moral dualism was preserved complete by Mazdaism in its later period, the conception of "physical" dualism required some adjustments to comply with new information provided by Hellenistic physics which had long been common knowledge. Clearly the oppositions and contradictions which are apparent in the physical world could not be brought within the twofold scheme of good and evil, a fact which had been realized for some time. The physics of the elements and their opposites allowed for a systematic treatment which withdrew these realities from the moral sphere, even if transcendent. Herein lies the interest of the chapters which deal with the physical world, even though they bring in the assault of Evil, by relating it directly to the creation and to the "evolution" of the gētī as such. Little reference is made to the fact that the mēnōg had passed into the gētī state by reason of the Assault and, so to speak, "as a means of defence". This subject gives rise to some very interesting chapters on the stages of creation of the gētī, starting with the original "production" of matter, which then became subdivided into elements. These elements made up groups determined by their form (*dēsak*) and thence were evolved the autonomous and complex individuals who constitute the world. The elaboration of these ideas is not very advanced or very precise, but they are set out in such a way as to make it clear that this field of study was not overlooked by the Mazdaeans of Iran, a country which at about the same time was providing Islamic culture with some of its greatest philosophers.

From natural science the book proceeds to psychology, ethics and medicine in relation to both body and mind; abundant information is to be found in the most ancient Mazdaean texts on all these studies, and especially with regard to the powers of the mind and to the various spiritual elements of which it is composed. The clarification of these concepts may perhaps make it possible, in spite of the lapse of time, to establish more exactly the meaning of certain words which date from the Avesta, for here, rather more than in natural science, the Iranian – perhaps even Indo-Iranian – heritage predominates. For instance, at the apex of the pyramid of the mental powers is "wisdom unborn" (*asn-xrat*), coupled with "wisdom acquired by hearing" (*gōš-asnūt-xrat*). In the later period of Mazdaism these concepts become "inborn intellect" and "acquired intellect", but, despite this modification, they retain something of their former cosmic dimensions. In all these chapters on psychology, however, there is nothing that can compete with Greek science and the richly developed researches of Neoplatonism, or with Indian speculation, in spite of the fact that the former had already penetrated the Arabic-speaking world of Islam, largely through the agency of Syriac-speaking Christians. Analysis appears here only in rudimentary form and is chiefly concerned with the classification of ancient beliefs in the course of transformation.

The systematic treatment of ethics is conducted along more rigorous lines; here also the ideas are traditional, but the tabulation of virtues and vices is borrowed largely from the peripatetic school. There are grounds for the belief that this borrowing is not of recent date but can be traced back to the lost Nasks of the Avesta, as is suggested by the rich miscellany of ethical learning which makes up Book VI of the *Dēnkart*. There are two factors which tend to confirm the supposition that the knowledge of Greek ethics was fairly widespread in the Iranian world. On the one hand the Sāsānian Empire was to offer hospitality to the Greek philosophers of the School of Athens when it was closed on the orders of Justinian, an invitation which can only be explained if the Iranians had already come into contact with Greek thought. Secondly, the discovery in Afghanistan of rock inscriptions bearing some of the edicts of Priyadarsi-Aśoka, in a Greek translation which is both elegant and scholarly, shows that there existed in the Iranian world a public which was well versed in the technicalities of Greek philosophical thought. At this point there is a link with the principle of the Mean, presented as the distinctive feature of Iranian ethics, which should appeal to the sympathies of all good minds (while at the same time diverting them from Islam and Christianity). Nevertheless, within this Greek setting it is indeed the Iranian virtues which reappear. The synthesis or fusion was successfully achieved and was to leave its mark on the whole rich field of ethics known to mediaeval Muslim Iran.

In this summary an attempt has especially been made to sort out the fundamental doctrines, which can easily be traced throughout all these chapters in spite of their haphazard arrangement. Even in this study of the theoretical texture we can see the link with the doctrines of the past. In reading Book III it must not be forgotten that in Book VIII the author elected to recapitulate, in very great detail, all the Nasks of the Avesta which had survived the shipwreck of Mazdaean culture, and that in Book IX he collected, in a Pahlavī translation, numerous passages from the lost Avesta which illustrated Gāthic teachings by means of myth. There is thus no question of a religion which has given way to philosophy or which would have abandoned the imagery of the revelation of Zarathustra. Even in Book III many references are to be found to doctrines of this type, in addition to rational justifications of the ritual and use of the Avestan vocabulary, only slightly transposed into Pahlavī, which serve as reminders of the vitality and the continuity of this religious tradition. The fact remains that Book III marks a stage of the greatest importance.

V. "ŠKAND-GUMĀNĪK VICĀR"

The author of this last great treatise of the later period of Mazdaism, Martān-Farrux i Ohrmazddātān, gives himself as a man in search of truth and eager to set his faith on a solid foundation while establishing its superiority over the other religions – Judaism, Christianity, Manichaeism and Islam, all of which he refutes in great detail. In this theoretical undertaking he relies on the works of his predecessors, describing himself as their pupil and populariser. There is firstly a certain Āturpāt i Yāvandān (?), of whom nothing is known, not even the exact form of his father's name, but he appears to be connected with Āturfarnbag i Farruxzātān, mentioned in every instance as the author of the *Dēnkart*. He also refers to Rōšn i Āturfarnbagān, author of a

Rōšan nīpīk which is the one mentioned in the *Fihrist* of al-Nadīm (the title occurs quite frequently).

The book is divided into two parts: one of them is theoretical, in the form of replies to various questions put to him by a certain Mihrayyār i Mahmatān, who may have been a Muslim, and expositions of theories of cosmogony and cosmology, all tending to establish the truth of dualism. The other part, which is a polemic, deals with the four religions and also with the *dahriyya*, the sophists and the atheists. Here is a confrontation not only of the established religions but of those currents of irreligious or even anti-religious thought against which all the others must do battle. The arguments directed against any adversary could be utilized by one or other of the opponents whereas it could be turned round against the allies of a moment ago. It is accordingly not easy to determine which side has fathered this or that argument, but at least it may be imagined that the arguments against Judaism and Christianity were polished and tested at the time when Mazdaism found itself at close quarters with them, that is to say in the Sāsānian period, and that this arsenal may have been later reassembled and utilized by the same Iranians after they had become Muslims. It is also possible that in these early times the three established religions may have had to deal with all kinds of "irreligious" persons. In any case it is remarkable that the first compilations of arguments against the other religions – and the first more or less objective expositions of those religions as viewed by their Muslim opponents – should have been almost contemporaneous with a book like the *Škand-gumānīk vicār* and of the same type.

The first chapter – the division into chapters is the work of modern editors – gives an all-round picture of the world of the gods and the world of the gētī with the Dēn, which is like a tree, its trunk being that Mean whence come all the hierarchy of which mankind and human society are composed. The problem which at once arises of the opposites and contradictions lying at the heart of the Good World is the subject of Chapter 2; the solution of it leads directly to the question of the ultimate responsibility for evil and there follows an endeavour, in the face of all objections, to establish that evil never truly results from good, in spite of appearances arising from the interplay within the celestial sphere of the stars of Ohrmazd and the planets of Ahriman (Chapters 3 and 4). Confutation of atheists and of the dahriyya (Chapters 5 and 6) begins with a substantial piece of epistemology on the ways leading to knowledge and especially to the knowledge of God: the starting point being the argument on responsibility and predetermination. The whole dissertation culminates in a demonstration of the belief that, in order to account for the existence of evil, leaving out the Prime Cause, which cannot be otherwise than good, wise and all-powerful over that which originates from it, there must be a principle which is external to God (Chapter 7). Corroboration is provided by an analysis of what takes place in the gētī, the anti-type of the mēnōg, which is engulfed in the struggle but is provided by the Creator with a means of defence. Everything suggests that Evil is a principle and a principle which is unique (Chapter 8). It follows that the struggle against evil is the very purpose of the divine act of creation, having been foreseen before the constitution of the beings of the gētī, who are to be the principal performers: it is thus imposed upon the Creator and on creation (Chapter 9). This chapter quotes a whole chapter of *Dēnkart III*, only the title of which is actually found in the *Dēnkart*. It looks as though that chapter had been literally torn out of the archetype of the extant manuscript – a fact which suggests that there were very few copies of the *Dēnkart* in circulation. The strictly speculative part of the book ends with Chapter 10 which deals with the inner aspects of the history of Mazdaism. Man, by means of the Dēn which is the organ of religious knowledge, succeeds in resisting the enticements of the Antagonist, a process that makes up the religious (e.g. Mazdaean) history of humanity. The opportunity is taken to give a brief summary of the history of Zoroastrianism, which first faithfully follows the traditional legend of Zoroaster's mission, the conversion of Vištaspa and the religious war; then it becomes quasi-historic since it mentions the ordeal to which Āturpāt i Mahraspandān submitted in order to bear witness to the truth of the Religion against the heretics.

Next comes the full array of polemics. Chapters 11 and 12 significantly begin with an attack on Islam, as being a typically monist religion. All the critical arguments of the *Dēnkart* are taken up, recapitulated and directed specifically against numerous texts in the Qur'ān, selected mainly from the first forty *suras*, in addition to attacks aimed at beliefs which are peculiar to the Mu'tazilites; since their premises were often identical with those of the Mazdaeans it was easy to confront them persistently with the existence of evil in order to coerce them into admitting the existence of the Antagonist.

Chapter 12 takes account of the criticisms directed by Islam against

Mazdaism and replies to them by expounding the fundamental optimism of the Good Religion, according to which the existence of evil and its ravages, for which God is in no way responsible, are held in check and strictly limited by the prescience and the power of God who will not tolerate an everlasting mixture of good and evil, and at the end of time will deliver all his creatures. This defence of Mazdaism is manifestly based on the *Dēnkart*.

In his criticism of Judaism (Chapters 13 and 14) the author refers initially to the texts of the first chapters of Genesis and particularly to the account of the fall of man, a theme already touched upon in connection with the Qur'anic texts on the same subject. The Biblical version used, although generally consistent with the Hebrew, shows traces of Targumic and even of Syriac translations. According to the Armenian authors who supply us with information on the controversies between Christians and Mazdaeans under Yazdgard II, the latter were not ignorant, at that period, of the doctrines, nor probably of the Biblical texts, of either the Old or the New Testament. In addition Jewish *midrašim* are also quoted here, for purposes of ridicule; it is not quite certain whether the author had first-hand knowledge of them from the Hebrew or Aramaic texts, but the later *midraš* is known to have been echoed sometimes in the Muslim ḥadīth and traces are to be found even in the "Thousand and One Nights", a collection which contains, as is well known, a fair amount of Iranian tradition.

The review of Christianity (Chapter 15) deals with the principal Christian mysteries: the Incarnation, the redemptive death of Christ and the revelation of the Trinity. The important texts of the New Testament are quoted freely and, what is more interesting, all those which may be adduced in support of a true dualism are exploited accordingly. Christianity is given the name which it continued to bear in Iran of the religion of the "Godfearing" (*tarsākīh*). In Chapter 40 of the *Dēnkart* a direct attack had already been made on the doctrine of the Trinity.

The final chapter (16) is devoted to Manichaeism and provides a very objective and competent exposition of its cosmology, followed by systematic criticism, of which only the beginning has been preserved. It deals with the description of the first "age" of cosmic history, when the two infinites of spirit and matter coexisted in juxtaposition. The Manichaean account of this state is given in terms which are clearly mythical, allowing for the drastic criticism of the Mazdaean author.

Other Mazdaean texts give more pertinent criticism of the dogma, customs and ethics of the Manichaeans. A false dualism, starting from the postulate that evil comes from matter, must have seemed all the more dangerous to a dualism like the Mazdaean, which was not in the least "Platonic". Indeed, Mani had been put to death by order of the Iranian government at the instigation of the clergy led by Kartēr. During the Muslim period the *zandīqs* who were prosecuted and condemned by the authorities were mostly fellow-travellers of Manichaeism, though care must be taken not to interpret the word "Manichaean" more literally in relation to the Muslim controversy than when it appears in the Christian polemics of the Patristic period or mediaeval periods. It was easy to treat as "dualism" the least semblance of deviation from strict Christian or Muslim monotheism and easier still to designate as "Manichaean" any appearance of dualism. However, the eastern world had a first-hand experience of Manichaeism which must have lasted for a long time: the charge of Manichaeism levelled against an alleged heretic was damning. There is hardly any direct information on the history of Iranian Manichaeism after the execution of Mani, but the fact remains that all the documents found in Central Asia, in Soghdian, Old Turkish, Kuchean or Chinese, have been translated from Parthian and Middle Persian, the two dialects of western Iran.

The Zoroastrian scholars living under Islamic rule did not confine themselves to writing in Pahlavī, for the internal use of their own community. They also wrote in Persian, a language and above all a script which was known to non-Mazdaeans as also to the new generations of Mazdaeans who could read Pahlavī only a little or with difficulty. Among the works which have survived are translations or adaptations of Pahlavī books, complete or fragmentary, including some verse which does not, however, show much poetic inspiration. These translations are of interest in that they reveal how religious knowledge has been preserved and handed down; they also dispose of the belief which is an over-simplification, but widely held, that the life of the Mazdaean community completely disappeared from Iran under Islamic rule, as though from the 4th/10th century onward it was to be sought in India alone. Although it is in fact in India that the vast majority of Mazdaean manuscripts known today are to be found, it must be remembered that they did not all arrive there in the 4th/10th century. On the contrary, the ignorance of the Indian communities can be gauged by the numerous epistolary consultations in which they engaged with the Mazdaeans who had remained in Iran – and this was from the 9th/15th century onward – for the purpose of renewing or checking their knowledge on questions of doctrine or ritual. The replies have been preserved and published, very unsystematically, in collections vaguely designated as rivāyāt, which also contain the translations mentioned above and short writings on religious controversy or propaganda. The most important of them will now be considered.

'Ulamā-yi Islām is the title of a kind of dialogue between Muslim and Mazdaean divines, in which the latter reply at length to the questions of the former. On the subject of cosmogony it is striking that the exposition emphasizes the part played by Time, regarded as "uncreated" and prior to Ohrmazd, whom it nevertheless serves notwithstanding the services it renders to Ahriman. This is in fact the Zurvānist doctrine, known to both Christian and Manichaean polemicists of the Sāsānian period and more so to the Muslim heresiologists. This does not mean that all speculations about time should be listed as deriving from the myth of Primordial Time, father of the twins Ohrmazd and Ahriman, which does not incidentally even appear in its achieved form in the *'Ulamā-yi Islām*. The latter, however, provides very good evidence of the astronomical speculations connected with Zurvānism. Another short book which bears the same title (known as *'Ulamā-yi Islām I*) is a miscellany of answers to Muslim objections; in it is to be found a direct appropriation of a well-known Muslim tenet expressed by saying that God is "a thing which is not like other things".

In considering Mazdaean culture in Muslim Iran one should remember that all the important treatises analysed here are contained in manuscripts which were written in Iran, particularly in Fārs and in Kirmān, and were not brought by the Parsees to India until quite late, in the 18th and, still more, the 19th century. At that time the intellectual level of the Zoroastrians of Iran was not very high and their social position was in most cases precarious, while among the Parsees in India some of the large fortunes which resulted from the modernization of the sub-continent made it possible for schools to be opened and for young scholars to be educated. The progress of this community had its effect ultimately on the conditions of their coreligionists in the mother country; meanwhile, however, the patrons of learning and the scholars had stripped what was left of the private libraries of Iran.

CHAPTER 18

ARABIC LITERATURE IN IRAN

I. THE UMAYYAD AGE IN IRAN

Although Arabic literature in Iran can be traced from the 1st/7th century onwards, it is nevertheless true that for the first two centuries or so the sources available are scanty and widely dispersed in later works. But this is a problem affecting all Arabic literature in the early period of Islam. Another obstacle is that at the outset little attention was paid to the Iranian part of the Muslim world, for the centre of the stage was held by the pace-setters in the Ḥijāz at first, then later in Damascus and Baghdad. This was due in large part to the origins of Islam in the Ḥijāz and to the subsequent displacements of its capital and the consequent downgrading of cultural centres elsewhere in Iran to the east or in Africa and Spain to the west.

As for Iran in particular, the rôle of Persians in Arabic literature could hardly be over-emphasized. Arabic literature ceased to be the exclusive property of the Arabs after the 1st/7th century, and it is most unjust and hardly objective to compile histories of Arabic literature that give the impression that somehow all the great authors were Arabs; but this is precisely the case ever since modernist Arab nationalists have taken to composing histories of Arabic literature, not to mention their histories of Islamic civilization.

If the Persians played more than just a passive rôle in Arabic literature, and even in the greater formulation of Islamic traditional culture, this is in great measure because the entire extent, and not merely a part, of the ancient Sāsānian empire, with all of its institutions and cultural traditions, fell to the lot of the Arab conquerors. They conquered the Persians but did not do away with the age-old cultural institutions of that people; on the contrary, the Arabs were in their turn conquered, culturally speaking, by the Persians.

To be sure, there had been contacts between Iran and the Arabs long before the coming of the Arab Muslims. These contacts had taken place mostly in the Tigris–Euphrates region and on the southern coast of Iran across from the Arabian peninsula. As a matter of fact, the Sāsānian rulers, seeing the necessity of having good relations with neighbouring Arab kingdoms and tribes, had established a sort of ministerial post of Arab affairs in their court at Ctesiphon. One of the famous pre-Islamic Arab poets, ʿAdī b. Zaid, who died around the beginning of the 1st/7th century, occupied that post. He was likewise a master of Persian letters, meaning of course the Pahlavī variant of his day. But what is of interest to us is that he was a scribe (*kātib*, pl. *kuttāb*) who had taken over his father's post, just as his father had done from ʿAdī's grandfather, and just as ʿAdī's son would do after him. Such a system of hereditary transmission, almost approaching a caste-like state, was an important Persian institution. It was to play a rôle of considerable influence in the unfolding of Islamic culture when the Persian scribes brought all of their talents to bear within the new tradition.

The Persian contribution to Arabic letters and Islamic civilization in general is already adumbrated in the particular case of Salmān al-Fārisī, the famous and even legendary Persian Companion of the Prophet. Upon the latter's death, the other Companions chose Abū Bakr as his successor in accordance with the consultative customs of the Arabs. Salmān, feeling that they had neglected the more just claims of ʿAlī, burst out with the Persian phrase *kardīd va-nakardīd*, meaning: "You have chosen but have not chosen rightly!" Al-Jāḥiẓ (d. 255/869), the Arab prose stylist, in discussing Salmān's outburst, explains it by saying that Salmān was accustomed to the hierarchic society of Persia and could not readily grasp the Arab ways of election; for in Persia, he goes on to say, in Sāsānian times a scribe could not become a warrior and a craftsman could not become a scribe; everyone had his pre-ordained place through tradition.[1]

Al-Jāḥiẓ, needless to say, is making an equation between Islam and Arab customs, a confusion not limited to him alone. Salmān, on the other hand, had made no such equation but seems to have been judging things through his own discernment as a Muslim without regard to the particular social customs of the Arabs. One might even go further and say that, apart from the question of ʿAlī and Abū Bakr, Salmān incarnated the more universal aspect of Islam and that he was in a sense the prefiguration of the eventual broadening of Islam not only in Iran but elsewhere. This would have its reflections in Arabic literature.

Salmān's devotion to Islam is well illustrated by the fact that he helped in the very conquest of his own country. Once, as the head of an

[1] *al-ʿUt̲h̲māniyya*, p. 186.

Arab army laying siege to a Persian fortress, he called out to the Persians in their own language: "I am only a Persian like you! Can you not see that the Arabs obey me? If you become Muslims, then you benefit from our religion and fall under its obligations; but, if you wish, you may keep your own religion and pay the poll-tax out of subordination!" Finally, he had to take the fortress by storm.[1]

The case of Salmān has a bearing on Arabic literature in Iran just as it has on Islam as a whole. Was the literature, like the religion that inspired it, to be a Persian imitation of Arab tastes and forms in every sense? Was Islam, for that matter, to be a faithful copy of the tribalistic society of the Arabs in regard to its cultural institutions? The answers to those questions came over a period of time. The Arab conquest of Iran up to the confines of Transoxiana was over by 30/651, and such questions were then only academic, but would not remain so for long.

The hierarchic society mentioned by al-Jāḥiẓ was indeed what the Arab nomads found in Iran. Groups of Arab colonists settled in eastern Iran because of the proximity of the Holy War at the frontiers. They were but a minority within the confines of Iran. Soon important centres of Islamic culture came into being at Nīs͟hāpūr, Marv, Herāt, Sarak͟hs and elsewhere in the eastern province, for western Iran was really the centre of Zoroastrianism and would remain so for quite some time.

If Islam was to be implanted firmly on Persian soil, and if the Arabic of the Qur'ān was to prosper, then measures had to be taken to transmit these things from one generation to the next. It is here that we find the origins of Arabic literature in Iran. How was this transmission effected?

The greatest Muslim teachers of early times were, of course, the Companions of the Prophet and then the Followers of the Companions. Their presence in any given place guaranteed the integrity of the Islamic message. Now, because of the ever-present Holy War on its frontiers, K͟hurāsān attracted many of these fervent Muslims. It is with them that Arabic literature, both sacred, which is that of the Qur'ān, and non-sacred, which is the poetry and prose of the Arabs as such, begins its long history in Iran.

All indications permit us to see that K͟hurāsān had more than its share of these early teachers. Qut͟ham b. 'Abbās, a Companion of the Prophet, died in Samarqand; Buraida b. al-Ḥuṣaib, another Companion, died in Marv in the caliphate of Yazīd b. Mu'āwiya. When Qutaiba b. Muslim

[1] Abū Nu'aim al-Iṣfahānī, vol. 1, p. 192.

conquered Samarqand, one of the many people invited to see his spoils was a venerable old man, al-Ḥuḍain b. al-Mundhir, who had been standard-bearer to 'Alī. The famous Ḍaḥḥāk b. Muzāḥim al-Khurāsānī, a teacher of children and an early religious scholar, was a Follower who died at Balkh (*c.* 105/723). The list could go on; the important thing to keep in mind, however, is that Khurāsān became a stronghold of Islamic studies and therefore of Arabic literature.

It was through the efforts of such religious figures that Qur'anic studies were begun and transmitted in Iran. They, and many others besides, taught in one of the three places of instruction that we know existed everywhere in Umayyad times. The first place, meant for children, was the Qur'anic elementary school, or the *kuttāb* (which must not be confused with the plural of *kātib*, or scribe); the second was the home (*dār*) of a particular religious scholar; and the third was the mosque (*masjid*). The teacher, imitating the Prophet, would sit on the ground with his students, young or old, seated around him in a circle (*ḥalqa*), a mode of instruction that was to endure for centuries, even down to the present day. The religious college (*madrasa*), introduced into Islam in the 5th/11th century in Khurāsān itself, would change nothing of the essentials for it was but a mosque with accommodation for students.

At the elementary school, the children learned Qur'anic Arabic, indispensable for Islamic religious observations, and at times they might learn Arabic poetry, arithmetic and writing, depending on the capabilities of the teachers. These elementary schools for children were not of Islamic origin, but had existed in pre-Islamic times in Arabia; Islam simply continued their use, infinitely expanded their numbers, and gave them an Islamic cast through the Qur'anic instruction available in them. As Dodge well says, the Qur'ān was "the foundation stone of Muslim education".[1] One began in these elementary schools at an early age, learning the Qur'ān and occasionally other disciplines. Not all of the teachers were of a calibre that drew praise. Al-Jāḥiẓ says that in his day it was quite common to say: "More stupid than the teacher of an elementary school!" But he takes exception to this and remarks that some of the great figures of early Islam were teachers of schoolchildren, amongst them being al-Ḥajjāj b. Yūsuf, 'Abd al-Ḥamīd (a Persian who was a great prose stylist in Arabic), and Ḍaḥḥāk b. Muzāḥim.[2] He could also have mentioned the almost legendary

[1] Dodge, p. 2.

[2] al-Jāḥiẓ, *al-Bayān*, vol. 1, pp. 248, 250–1.

Abū Muslim, who was so instrumental in bringing down the Umayyads.

Those who went deeper into Islamic studies, and they were perhaps not many, did so either at the home of a Muslim sage or else at a nearby mosque. The mosque, it will be recalled, was the focal point of Islam, so that just as it was "the centre of town life, the place for political and social meetings as well as for worship, so it was also the place for teaching".[1] It would be well to remember that a mosque is not necessarily a stone structure having a given shape, but a place where one performs the ritual obligations of Islam, and this could be even a tent or a small inconspicuous building, as can be seen even in the present day in the Muslim world. The number of such mosques in Iran after the initial wave of conquest must have been considerable. Islam itself lays great stress on the acquisition of religious knowledge; the Muslim is under obligation to say his prayers and perform other religious duties using Qur'anic Arabic. He might even ignore Arabic literature, in the conventional sense, and prefer his own colloquial speech, but he could not ignore the Arabic of the Qur'ān, which is deemed to be sacred and inviolate because of Islamic teachings on its divine origins as the Word of God. It is not Arabic literature that is sacred, but the Qur'ān, which is not considered "literature". Consequently, elementary education, with its almost unique emphasis on learning the Qur'ān, was bound to be widespread amongst the Muslims, both Arabs and Persians, in Iran in those early days.

We have, then, no problem in envisaging how Arab Muslims transmitted their religion and literary culture to their offspring. But what about the Persian Muslims, who soon formed the vast majority of Muslims in Iran? We do know that Salmān al-Fārisī taught a vast number of Persians in their own language till such time as they learned Qur'anic Arabic for ritual purposes. Persian Muslim children, of course, went to the Qur'anic elementary schools, and from thence to the other places of learning mentioned above, if they went at all, and not everyone could have had a compelling reason to do so. Once these Persians became religious scholars in their own turn, they taught others; but these scholars did not then have those well-defined characteristics that one associates with the *'ulamā'* of later times. On the contrary, the early religious sages seem to have formed a very fluid and indefinable group. Often they were greengrocers and warriors.

[1] Tritton, p. 30.

The process by which the Persian Muslims picked up the Qur'anic disciplines directly from the Arabs could not have taken a very long time. In the very first generation of Islam in Iran there must have been Persian Muslims who taught not only Persians but Arabs as well. Being an Arab, it goes without saying, implied no automatic monopoly over Islam and no instantaneous comprehension of the Qur'ān. Otherwise, why did the Prophet have to explain so many verses of the Qur'ān to his auditors in his own day? As a matter of fact, al-Jāḥiẓ records the case of a certain Persian called Mūsā b. Sayyār al-Uswārī (a descendant, no doubt, of the Sāsānian cavalry, the *asāwira*, that embraced Islam in the very first days of the conquest), who was one of the teachers of his period, when the *quṣṣās* were not merely story-tellers but teachers. This Mūsā would sit in his meeting-place with the Arabs to his right, the Persians to his left, and then read aloud a verse of the Qur'ān, explain it to the Arabs in Arabic, then turn to the Persians and explain it to them in Persian.[1]

While we can see how Islam was responsible for the establishment of Arabic studies in Iran, and therefore the motivating cause for their preservation and transmission – for without Qur'anic Arabic, which must be distinguished from conventional Arabic literature, there could be no Islam amongst the Persians of Iran – we are not on such sure ground when it comes to determining how the non-Muslim Persian scribes of Iran came by their knowledge of Arabic. Since the scribes simply continued in Islam with much the same caste-like arrangements that obtained under the Sāsānians, one wonders if even the Persian Muslim scribes did not have their own system of education in Arabic quite apart from the Qur'anic schools mentioned above. We shall have to return to this question when dealing with early 'Abbāsid days, for it was at that epoch that we see the Persian scribes, Muslims or not, come back into the picture with the same important rank and attributes of power that they had in Sāsānian times.

But during the Umayyad epoch Arabic literature in Iran was not much different from what obtained elsewhere in the Muslim world. The literary genres were not rich in diversity; poetry was of course the chief literary vehicle of expression; letters are to be found, composed by governors or important figures in Iran. All of this is imbedded in later collections referring back to Umayyad days, and is characterized by a certain straightforward simplicity and conciseness of spirit that

[1] al-Jāḥiẓ, *al-Bayān*, vol. 1, p. 368.

reflect, no doubt, the virtues of the early Muslims, Persians or Arabs, who asked few questions.

As was said, poetry was the dominant genre of the times. The usual themes of Arabic poetry, couched in the time-honoured form of the Arabic ode (*qaṣīda*), were cultivated: poems of praise (*ḥamd*), of glorification (*fakhr*) either of the tribe or of one's self, of elegy (*marthiya*), of satire (*hijā'*), and of other sorts. This is not exceptional for its day. It reflects, likewise, the martial spirit of early Islam, its virile and robust nature, its directness and earthy realism. Much of it is connected with the famous Muhallabid dynasty that governed the vast areas of Khurāsān, which was all of the regions in eastern Iran and even beyond. They seem to have set themselves up as munificent patrons of poetry and culture in those lands far from the caliphal seat at Damascus, and were at the same time engaged in both military and commercial adventures in the east. Khurāsān, one will recall, was the main source of tribute for the Umayyad caliphs; but, even so, much of that tribute remained in Khurāsān.

One of their poets was Ka'b al-Ashqarī, an Azdite and companion of al-Muhallab b. Abī Ṣufra, and known for his poems of praise and of satire. The reigning caliph, 'Abd al-Malik (65–86/685–705), when he heard Ka'b recite, was astonished at his talents and asked why his own poets did not praise him after the fashion of Ka'b towards al-Muhallab. His fame was such that al-Farazdaq was moved to say that the poets of his day were four: himself, al-Akhṭal, al-Jarīr, and Ka'b.[1]

Still another Muhallabid poet was al-Mughīra b. Ḥabnā', an Arab known for his satire. Both he and Ka'b were in constant verbal battle with a poet of the day called Ziyād al-A'jam. The last-mentioned poet is of special interest to us because he was a Persian who had mastered Arabic verse forms and was the first of a long line of Persian masters in succeeding ages who would number in their ranks such great poets as Abū Nuwās and Bashshār b. Burd of the 2nd/8th century. Ziyād died early in the reign of Hishām (105–25/724–43), and is known for his elegy composed at the death of al-Mughīra b. al-Muhallab in 82/701. As can be seen, it did not take the Persians very long after the conquest of Khurāsān in 30/651 before they too began reciting Arabic poetry, which implies more than just a passing acquaintance with its forms. Though he mastered the forms, Ziyād seems to have been deficient in pronunciation on one or two points. Ibn Qutaiba (d. 276/889–90), the

[1] Abu'l-Faraj al-Iṣfahānī, vol. XIV, pp. 283–301.

Persian literary critic, feels that Ziyād was at times deficient in his grammatical knowledge.[1] However that might be, Ziyād, like the other poets of his day, had a *rāwī* who not only learned Ziyād's poems but could recite them for him as well.

It is owing to Ziyād's occasional use of Persian words that Ibn Qutaiba voices his criticism; but apart from that, Ziyād's poems are stamped with the Bedouin traits of his Arab contemporaries. This, however, would be a fleeting phenomenon amongst Persians composing Arabic poems.

For truly Persian content in the poetry of the age, one must turn to the Persians Ismā'īl b. Yasār and his son Ibrāhīm in the time of the caliph Hishām (105–25/724–43). Though Ismā'īl came from western Iran and spent most of his life outside his native land, he is nonetheless known for his poems wherein the Persian kings and traditions are glorified. He went even so far as to glorify them to the face of the caliph Hishām, who promptly ordered that Ismā'īl be thrown in a pool of water. Though he is sometimes called a *Shu'ūbī*, or partisan of things Persian, he was in reality a Persian engaged in glorifying his own kings and culture much in the same way as the Arabs did for their particular tribes.

Some of the poetry reflects the religio-political issues of those early times of Islam. Thābit Quṭna, an Arab warrior-poet from Khurāsān, and companion of Yazīd b. al-Muhallab in the days of the caliph Sulaimān (96–9/715–17), was a *murji'ite* who sided neither with the reigning Umayyads nor with the claims of the Shī'īs nor with those of the Khārijites, but preferred to leave all questions on the caliphate to God's judgement.

The issue of the caliphate was but one of the questions then under investigation. The reigning caliphs were Umayyad Arabs. Their abusive fiscal policies toward Muslims who were not Arabs provoked outbursts of protests even from Arabs. Nahār b. Tausi'a al-Yashkurī, an Arab poet in eastern Iran at the time of Qutaiba b. Muslim, had this to say of the tribalistic feelings of his fellow-Arabs: "My father is Islam! Whenever they pride themselves on Tamīm or Qais, I have no other father!"[2] But his was a voice crying in the wilderness when compared with the chorus of Arabs who insisted that Islam and Arabism were one and the same thing. This was a sort of latter-day version of

[1] Ibn Qutaiba, *al-Shi'r*, p. 259.
[2] al-Mubarrad, vol. III, p. 179.

Judaism based on the concept of a "chosen people", but impossible to sustain for long in view of the ever-increasing number of Muslims whose allegiance was to Islam, not to Arabism.

What can one say, however, of the Arabic poetry of Iran in those days? Certainly, the influence of Iran made itself felt in the contents, if not in the forms, of the poems. Iranian place-names, feasts (*naurūz* and *mihragān*), and even Persian words figure in the poems. The ancient poetical forms were used by both the Persians and Arabs, but with a different touch when compared with pre-Islamic poetry. This was in part the result of the conditioning of Islam that affected all Arabic poetry of the 1st/7th century; it was in part due to the psychological change taking place in the previously nomadic Arabs who were now beginning to settle down; and in part it was the influence of the *mawālī*, or non-Arabs, on Arabic literature, an influence which was by no means negligible. "On account of the mawālī," says Nallino, "after the middle of the 1st century, the poetry of the Arabs was transformed little by little into a poetry of different Muslim peoples while remaining Arabic in tongue."[1]

In addition, to turn to the Arabs in Iran, one must bear in mind that the conquerors of Iran soon succumbed not only to the culture of the land but also to its speech. They were, after all, but a small minority in a land the culture of which was still intact, however decadent the Zoroastrian traditions might seem. They passed on to the Persians the new Semitic religion they had brought with the conquest and were in turn the recipients of Persian culture. A famous Arab poet of the day, Ibn Mufarrigh, is a case in point. He had spent some time in Khurāsān and, like many other Arabs there, if not all of them, knew Persian. Shortly before his death in Kirmān (69/689), he composed the earliest Persian verse recorded in Arabic literature, one which contained both Arabic and Persian words.[2]

Nevertheless, the hold of the Arabs over their empire and the identification of Islam with Arabism persisted down to the end of the Umayyads. Naṣr b. Sayyār (d. 131/748), the last Umayyad governor in Khurāsān, incarnated that identification. In a letter addressed to the last Umayyad caliph, Marwān (d. 132/750), he warned the caliph of Abū Muslim's activities and what their eventual results would be to Arabism and Islam, for the two were one and the same thing in his eyes.

[1] Nallino, p. 211.

[2] al-Jāḥiẓ, *al-Bayān*, vol. 1, p. 143.

In the last line of a poem appended to the letter, he said: "Flee from your homes and bid a last farewell to Islam and the Arabs!"[1]

Long before that fateful moment, a group of generally silent, but highly purposeful men, had spent most of the Umayyad period carrying out the burden of administrative duties in Iran. These were the Persian scribes. They were to be found outside Iran likewise, and everywhere their impact in those early times was quiet but decisive. In Arabic letters alone, no other group in the Muslim world had more direct influence in steering the course of Arabic literature away from the narrow straits of early days into the deeper waters of later times. With the Umayyads gone, they came upon the stage conscious of their millennial background in Iran and ready to reaffirm their ancient status and prerogatives.

II. THE EARLY ʿABBĀSID EPOCH

Mention was made of the Persian scribes (*kuttāb*) in Iran when we dealt with the question of how the Persians learned and transmitted Arabic literature, both sacred and profane. The possibility was left open that perhaps they did not learn or transmit their knowledge of Arabic in the usual channels open to the Persian Muslims (elementary Qur'anic school, the home of a sage, and the mosque).

When the Arabs came to Iran, they had none of the administrative institutions called for by the establishment of an empire which they had to direct. They were nomads, and nomads have no bureaucracy. The Persians, however, did have one. The scribal caste there had already an ancient history behind it. In Sāsānian times they kept their own style of records, wore distinctive garments, and formed a caste of their own, examining all neophytes to the profession and accompanying all armies into the field to supervise the course of events.

Pahlavī was the script that the scribes used to keep their records, and the same script was used when the Arabs took over the reins in Iran. The order to Arabicize the financial records went out in the reign of ʿAbd al-Malik, in the year 78/697. The actual implementation of the order throughout Iran seems to have been gradual. Most of the scribes in Naṣr b. Sayyār's time in Khurāsān were Zoroastrians and still used Pahlavī. It was only in 124/742 that the governor of Iraq, Yūsuf b. ʿUmar, sent Naṣr an order to employ only Muslims as scribes and to

[1] Ibn Qutaiba, *al-Imāma*, vol. II, p. 138.

convert the financial records from Pahlavī to Arabic, which he did with the help of one of his secretaries. This means, if literally interpreted, that almost a hundred years elapsed, between the conquest of Khurāsān in 30/651 and the order of Yūsuf, before the secretaries finally adopted Arabic.

In reality there had been scribes in eastern Iran prior to Yūsuf's order who were Muslims and knew Arabic, and these were mainly Persians. It is very likely that the Persian scribes, Muslims or Zoroastrians, taught their skills to their own offspring just as the artisans of the day bequeathed their trade secrets to their sons. The very fact that the scribal families formed a caste-like group, with its own professional status, and tended to perpetuate their function through several generations, shows that they were under no need to pass through the usual centres of Islamic learning to master Arabic. Moreover, they did not even have to be Muslims to stay within the chancery ranks, in spite of the order given by Yūsuf b. 'Umar in 124/742. We know, for example, that the famous scribal family, or dynasty, of the Sahlids, who were from Sarakhs in eastern Iran, were still Zoroastrian scribes when they enter Islamic history with a perfect mastery of both Arabic and Pahlavī letters. Indeed, they had been sponsored by yet another great scribal family, the Barmakids, who likewise came from eastern Iran. It was only in 190/805 that al-Faḍl b. Sahl, the famous vizier of al-Ma'mūn, was converted to Islam at the hands of the caliph; yet al-Faḍl's Arabic eloquence was appreciated long before his conversion to Islam. All of this seems to imply that, from the very first days of the conquest, there had been Zoroastrian scribes in Iran who saw the handwriting on the wall and mastered Arabic letters in addition to their own Pahlavī.

The Persian scribes introduced new themes into Arabic literature. The first great prose stylist in Arabic was the Persian secretary to the last Umayyad caliph, 'Abd al-Ḥamīd (d. 132/750). When asked how he came to his masterful knowledge of Arabic, he replied that it was through studying the eloquence of 'Alī, the fourth caliph. 'Abd al-Ḥamīd is credited with being the first to elongate his epistles. On closer examination, there is more to his distinction than that. His epistolary style breathes the influence of Persian culture within an Islamic context. Some of his epistles, moreover, show Persian influence in their contents, as when he counsels rulers on how to govern, how to conduct themselves in court, which are old Persian themes. And even his epistles on hunting, for example, show a fresh departure from the conventional Arab descriptions hitherto employed, and reveal the subtle influence of his Persian background. But in no epistle does this background break forth with more evidence than in his epistle to the scribes, wherein the ancient dignity of the scribal profession is reaffirmed within an Islamic framework. It is by no accident that this famous epistle was composed in the last days of the Umayyad régime, for the scribes, with their eminent positions of power and diversified culture, were then coming into real prominence, and were ready to influence the patterns and style of Islamic civilization on the bases of the essentially Semitic contents of the Qur'ān. A synthesis had already been worked out between the Arabs and Persians by 'Abd al-Ḥamīd's time. This is shown in his epistle to the scribes wherein he says that the scribe must look into every type of knowledge and either master it or take enough to suffice him; he must know the duties of religion. Addressing the scribe, he says: "Begin with knowledge of the Qur'ān and religious obligations; then proceed to Arabic, for that sharpens your tongue; then master calligraphy, the ornamentation of your writings. Get to know poetry, its rare words and ideas, and know also the battle-days of both the Arabs and Persians, their history and biographies, all of which serves to inspire you."[1]

In short, for the scribes, it was not enough to know the battle-days of the Arabs alone, but also Persian battle-days. But one may be sure that more than just the "battle-days" of the Persians would be brought into Arabic literature by the scribes. Many of them were equally at home in Pahlavī literature and were expert translators into Arabic of much of the literary material available in Pahlavī. Al-Faḍl b. Sahl, already mentioned, got his start in that fashion, though none of his translations has come down to us.

The name of Ibn al-Muqaffa' (d. *c.* 139/757) is the second in importance in the development of Arabic prose. He was a Persian who hailed from the region of S͟hīrāz and was a scribe in the areas of Nīs͟hāpūr and Kirmān in the days before the Umayyads fell. Though there has been some dispute as to whether he was a Muslim or not, his writings radiate an Islamic flavour. He too claimed that the utterances of 'Alī were his main inspiration for his Arabic prose style. Like his predecessor, he introduced into Arabic letters the genre of animal fables which we see in his work *Kalīla wa Dimna*, a translation from Pahlavī that goes back eventually to Indian roots. His other translations are no longer extant.

[1] Kurd 'Alī, p. 225.

Kalīla wa Dimna was an instant success due to its limpid and flowing Arabic, and has remained so down to the present day. His epistles also reveal their Persian background when it is a question of manners, or of friendship, or of the type of conduct between rulers and ruled, and the like.

It is through such scribes as Ibn al-Muqaffaʿ and the great scribal families of early ʿAbbāsid times (the 2nd/8th and 3rd/9th centuries), like the Sahlids and Barmakids, that Arabic prose was widened in subject-matter and given a much more flexible nature. They so mastered Arabic letters that al-Jāḥiẓ was moved to say: "As for myself, I have never seen a more exemplary style than that of the scribes in rhetoric."[1] Many of them, in addition to their own contributions to Islamic culture, were at the same time, by virtue of their commanding positions in society, the patrons of science and learning. The Banū Naubakht were a Persian scribal dynasty whose members were models in such diverse fields as theology, astrology, letters, and translations from Pahlavī into Arabic. The Banū Jarrāḥ, in the 3rd/9th century and later, were another Persian family known for their talents in Arabic letters. These people were in a position to influence both literature and institutions because, as Mez points out, the vizier stood higher in rank than all the generals, yet he was but the chief scribe.[2] Al-Jāḥiẓ remarks that common people prove their ignorance by taking the scribe as the paragon of all desirable traits; and he does not hesitate to give the scribes a tongue-lashing for their attachment to Persian culture. Al-Jāḥiẓ was himself attached to Arab culture, yet neither he nor the Persian scribes could extricate themselves from the Islamic civilization of their day which was primarily a synthesis of Perso-Arab elements, however much other cultures, such as the Greek, Hindu, or even the Chinese, are taken into consideration. The issue of Shuʿūbiyya, fought over in the 2nd/8th and 3rd/9th centuries between the Arabs and Persians, has perhaps been given too much emphasis: the Perso-Arab synthesis just mentioned was too vast an affair to be left to the whims of the belles-lettrists.

Apart from the influence of the Persians on the contents of Arabic letters, both prose and poetry, mention must be made of their decisive contributions in both Arabic grammar and lexicography. When one considers that the greatest name in Arabic grammar belongs to Sībawaih (d. *c.* 180/796), the Persian Muslim whose work entitled *al-Kitāb* has held its unique place down to the present day, and that he is but the

[1] al-Jāḥiẓ, *al-Bayān*, vol. 1, p. 137.

[2] Mez, p. 89.

first of a long line of Persians over the centuries who have left their mark on Arabic grammar, the question arises why a Persian, and not an Arab, was so instrumental in crystallizing Arabic grammar in such magistral fashion.

Ibn Khaldūn is probably quite right when he credits the Persians with the foremost rôle in the development of the philological, grammatical, and other Islamic disciplines, while reserving for the early Arabs a sort of political eminence. The implications here are in accordance with his well-known theories about the interplay of sedentary and nomadic cultures, the former possessed of all the trappings of civilization, the latter having none but characterized nevertheless by a certain virility. The Persians would be the cultivated city-dwellers, with the arts and sciences at their disposal, the early Arabs the virile, nomadic group without the refinements of learning at their disposal.

Moreover, by the end of the 2nd/8th and the beginning of the 3rd/9th centuries, the Quraishite style of speech, with its full panoply of inflection (*i'rāb*), was a stilted archaic tongue. In the 1st/7th century, when the Arab military conquests were taking place, the Quraishite style was "the language of prestige, as well as perhaps some kind of military *koine* used in the military expeditions". But even then, the Arabs who were settling down in the cities had to be careful and could only maintain the proper style by sending their children into the desert (*bādiya*), where the pure nomads still used it, in addition to their own dialects. The caliph 'Abd al-Malik (65–86/686–705), for example, failed to send al-Walīd (86–96/705–15) into the desert, with disastrous results for al-Walīd's speech. "Our love for al-Walīd," lamented 'Abd al-Malik, "redounded against us, for we did not impose the desert upon him."

Al-Jāḥiẓ maintains that it was the intrusion of foreign words into the Quraishite Arabic style that corrupted its inflection.[1] But this is only part of the story. The urbanized Arabs had undergone a psychological change which could not but affect their language. It is not written Arabic that we are speaking of here; this Arabic has remained essentially the same throughout the centuries, apart from vocabulary accretions, for the Qur'ān has exerted an overwhelming influence on it. Nor are we discussing the dialects of Arabic, which even in the pre-Islamic days were distinguished from the Quraishite manner of speech, the prestige style of the day, that was carried over into Islam and served as the unifying speech of the Arabs under the Umayyads.

[1] al-Jāḥiẓ, *al-Ḥayawān*, vol. 1, p. 282.

Quraishite Arabic was characterized by the inflection of words, and by the 3rd/9th century this inflection had disappeared in the great urban areas of the Arabic-speaking world; to use it in imitation of the Bedouin was considered a mannerism and pedantic. Some of the best poets of the 2nd/8th century, such as Abū Nuwās (d. *c.* 198/813), sometimes insert Persians words in their poems to a point where it is difficult to say if we are in the presence of an Arabic or a Persian poem.[1] A grammarian such as Sībawaih, therefore, was writing for both the urbanized Arabs as well as for the non-Arabs on the basis of what he had learned from the pure speech of the desert Arabs, who kept their good style until well into the 4th/10th century. By that time Arabic dialects had arisen everywhere in the Arabic-speaking part of the Muslim world.

It was not only in grammar that the Persians, inheritors of an ancient civilization, made their influence felt. Lexicography in Arabic owes much to the culture of Iran. In that science Haywood affirms that we must "take note not only of Persia, but also of the province of Khurāsān". He sees certain resemblances between the alphabetical order of the dictionary (*Kitāb al-'ain*) composed by al-Khalīl b. Aḥmad (d. 175/791) and that of Sanskrit, and attributes this to Indian influence in the eastern areas of Iran. Al-Khalīl, though an Arab from 'Umān, is said to have produced the first Arabic dictionary while he was in Khurāsān and with the co-operation of a native of that region. Indeed, because of the predominant part played by the Persians and others in Arabic lexicography, not only in early but also in much later times, Haywood concludes that "the lexicography was undoubtedly Arabic; it was not Arab".

It is interesting to observe that the Persians of eastern Iran had maintained from the early days of Islam till the coming of the Saljuqs a very high degree of religious scholarship and fervour. This was applied even to their handling of Arabic. While it is true that the presence of an Arabic-speaking agent here and there in Iran had about as much influence on the dialects of the Persians "as that of the English agents on the languages of modern India", nevertheless, amongst the Persian Muslim scholars, a tradition of pure Arabic speech, with complete inflection (*i'rāb*), was maintained even when it was no longer used in the Arabic-speaking urban centres outside of Iran. As was said, in the 3rd/9th century the inflection and other peculiarities of good Arabic speech were considered a mannerism in the Arabic-speaking world.

[1] Mīnuvī, pp. 62–72.

But the Khurāsānī Persian scholar could not be ridiculed by the ordinary Persian for giving his Arabic the inflection and Umayyad overtones that he used, for the ordinary Persian knew only Persian. It is perhaps because of the Umayyad purity of his style that al-Jāḥiẓ remarked that when a Khurāsānī spoke Arabic, "in spite of his inflecting Arabic and choosing his words, you know by his articulation that he is a Khurāsānī". This tradition continued into the 4th/10th century, when all over the Arabic-speaking world, in the urban centres, the different dialects had arisen. The geographer al-Muqaddasī (d. 390/1000) says that the Khurāsānīs used the purest Arabic he had occasion to hear in his long journeys throughout the Muslim lands of the East and West. But he is clearly not saying that the Khurāsānīs were Arabs. The only Arabs who inflected their speech in the 4th/10th century were the pure nomads in certain regions of Arabia and elsewhere; these came by their good Arabic by birthright and therefore effortlessly. Elsewhere in the Arabic-speaking world the regional dialects had arisen. Al-Muqaddasī is referring to a minority of cultivated and erudite Persian Muslim scholars who, to use his words, "went to great pains" to learn that correct Arabic.[1] These were undoubtedly the religious scholars, or 'ulamā', of Khurāsān, for he says that they were highly honoured in that area and had had a notable past tradition of Islamic studies, whereas in the western part of Iran it was the scribes who were held in esteem. When al-Muqaddasī says that the Khurāsānīs used the purest Arabic he had heard, he meant not only their inflection of Arabic but also, perhaps, their use of it with traditional, or Umayyad, nuances.

It goes without saying that he was quite right in referring to the remarkable tradition of Islamic studies in Khurāsān prior to the 4th/10th century. The great Persian Muslim scholars of that region have left behind the foremost collections of the *ḥadīths* of the Prophet. This genre of literature is second only to the Qur'ān in its significance. The collection made by al-Bukhārī (d. 256/870), sometimes called an "Arab" traditionist, but really the grandson of a Persian named Bardīzbih, is perhaps the most noteworthy. The collection made by yet another Khurāsānī, Muslim b. Ḥajjāj, who died near Nīshāpūr in 261/875, is also of great importance, as is that of al-Tirmidhī, who died in 270/884 in Tirmidh. These are but a few of the leading names in that genre of Arabic literature.

And in still another field, that of the mystical sayings and composi-

[1] al-Muqaddasī, p. 32.

tions of the Ṣūfī masters, the 2nd/8th and 3rd/9th centuries show that Khurāsān was a bastion of Ṣūfism. This likewise is a new genre of literature. We have only brief utterances, chiefly of a compactly suggestive nature, from the early masters, such as Abū Yazīd al-Bisṭāmī (d. 261/874). In addition, a more expository and discursive genre of mystical literature appears for the first time in the Muslim world in the literary works of al-Ḥakīm al-Tirmidhī (d. 285/898), a Khurāsānī who paves the way for the later masters. The eastern Iranian frontiers were still aflame with holy war and no doubt this fact alone accounts for the abundance of Ṣūfīs there. Early Islamic mysticism was "militant, and it was generally after having participated in the holy war on the frontiers that the mystics took up a cloistered life in those hermitages that were soon fortified because they were on the frontiers".[1] Under such circumstances, mystical literature was bound to be more abundant there than, say, in western Iran.

Though the beginnings of the New Persian literature are sometimes traced to the 3rd/9th century, the cultivated Persians of that time used Arabic as their literary medium and Persian for ordinary conversation. The Ṭāhirids of the first half of the 3rd/9th century were Persians whose command of Arabic letters, both prose and poetry, was famous in their day. They used Persian in their court but gave Arabic a certain preference. In that century prose had supplanted poetry in eminence as a literary tool and the founder of the dynasty, Ṭāhir, has left behind a famous epistle to his son 'Abd-Allāh, composed when the latter was appointed governor of Egypt in 206/822 by the caliph al-Ma'mūn. Here, once again, we meet the ancient Sāsānian influences and models of courtly conduct issuing through the Arabic pen of a Persian Muslim, for Ṭāhir counsels his son on the best ways of governing and meting out justice, and uses a magnificent Arabic style in doing so.

Mention must be made, too, of another great Persian, Abū Ḥanīfa al-Dīnawarī (d. *c.* 290/902), who is ranked with the finest prose masters of Arabic literature. His compositions deal with history, botany, astronomy, and other fields; unfortunately, this much-neglected author's works have come down to us in fragmentary form except for his brilliant history dealing with Persia, *al-Akhbār al-ṭiwāl*, or "The Long Narratives". Though it is written from a purely Persian point of view, this in no way implies that he was a Shu'ūbī; rather, he was intent merely upon giving his work a certain perspective. He uses a concise,

[1] Massignon, p. 234.

unornamented but well-chosen Arabic, attesting to his perfect command of the resources of that language.

Another Persian master of Arabic letters in that day is Ibn Qutaiba (d. 276/889–90), also one of the best prose stylists of Arabic, who only recently has begun to receive the attention he deserves. He embodies in his own person and works the Perso-Arab synthesis mentioned previously in the chapter. He even defended the Arabs to a certain extent from the barbed shafts aimed at them by the Persian scribes conscious of their own great past. However, in his anecdotal work, *ʻUyūn al-akhbār*, he draws his material from both Persian and Arab sources. Though he was primarily a religious scholar, and had even been a qāḍī for a while, he nonetheless saw fit to compose a manual of good Arabic usage addressed to the scribes of his day and called *Adab al-kātib*, which has since become one of the indispensable manuals for all students of literary Arabic. In the introduction to his work, apart from excoriating the scribes for their defective Arabic (probably he had the run-of-the-mill secretaries in mind), he lays down much the same rules for the scribe's training (religious, arithmetical, literary) as his great predecessor ʻAbd al-Ḥamīd had already done in the 2nd/8th century in his epistle to the scribes.

By Ibn Qutaiba's time the new class of belles-lettrists, or *udabā'*, had come to the fore with al-Jāḥiẓ as their model, but they had not really displaced the scribe in importance. Rather, the range of the belles-lettrist's subject-matter had been widened and approached that of the highly cultivated scribes. The religious scholar, or *ʻālim*, on the other hand, tended then more and more to concentrate on a given aspect of religious studies. "If you want to be an *ʻālim*," said Ibn Quṭaiba, "then specialize in one type of knowledge; but if you want to be an *adīb*, then take the best part of everything."[1] But, more often than not, the religious scholar could be a belles-lettrist, as the case of Ibn Qutaiba himself so well illustrates. Whether an author is to be considered primarily as a religious scholar or a belles-lettrist or a scribe depends, not on fixed traits and categories, but rather on the degree of his commitment to one of these fields. Some, like the famous ʻAbbāsid vizier ʻAlī b. ʻĪsā (d. 334/946), one of the members of a great family of Persian scribes, seem to be religious scholars, belles-lettrists, and scribes at one and the same time.

Other genres of Arabic literature appear in this early ʻAbbāsid period.

[1] Ibn Qutaiba, *ʻUyūn*, vol. II, p. 129.

These have to do with geography, cosmology, and even astrological and mathematical subjects, not to mention medicine and allied fields. In those fields the Persians were most active. This enlargement of the range of Arabic literature was due in great part to the translations into Arabic from Pahlavī, Greek, Syriac and Sanskrit, which were circulating amongst the cultivated classes and leaving their imprint. We can single out for brief consideration only two of the many Persians whose contributions were of great importance in the development of Islamic sciences in those days. Abū Ma'shar al-Balkhī (d. 272/886), who came from eastern Iran, was a rather famous astrologer and astronomer. He was known to the Latin West as Albumasar and his work on astronomy, *Kitāb al-madkhal al-kabīr*, was translated into Latin. Aḥmad b. Ṭayyib al-Sarakhsī (d. 286/899), a disciple of al-Kindī, likewise came from eastern Iran. Though he was the author of diverse philosophical and scientific works, he is known mainly as an astrologer. He seems, however, to have been the first author of a work on geography bearing the title *Kitāb al-masālik wa'l-mamālik*, a title that was to reappear in other geographical works of later times. These men, and others like them, were not specialists in the present-day sense of the word, but had a world-view that was essentially Islamic in its ontology even though Greek, Hindu, and other influences supplied the technical or even terminological framework.

It was perhaps in the 3rd/9th century that Iran begins to pull away more openly from the tight control of the caliphal seat at Baghdad. The Ṭāhirids reigned in the first half of that century, and though they were attached to Arabic letters, they ruled as masters in their own house with considerable independence. They were eclipsed by the Ṣaffārids in the second half of the century. Ya'qūb, the founder of the dynasty, though nominally attached to the caliphal seat, was really subject to no one. By that time the caliphal authority at Baghdad was in decline. It is of interest to note that Ya'qūb did not care to have poetry recited to him in Arabic and that some accounts place the origins of the New Persian literature in his day, though others would place it even earlier. One has the impression, in any case, that the ethnic genius of the Persians, having absorbed the Islamic message and even contributed to its expression in Arabic, was now moving toward the moment when it would break forth in its own tongue.

III. THE EPOCH OF THE BŪYIDS AND THE SĀMĀNIDS

Iran saw two important dynasties arise on its soil in the 4th/10th century: the Būyids, who ruled in the south and also in Iraq, and the Sāmānids, who ruled in the east from their court at Bukhārā. They were both of Persian origin and tongue.

The Būyids conquered Baghdad in 334/946. They were Shī'ī Muslims but created no difficulties for the reigning caliph of Sunnī Islam; quite the contrary, the caliph was given ample liberties although he did not really rule. This extension of Persian rule into the heart of Sunnī Arab Islam by a Shī'ī dynasty is interesting enough in itself; however, west of Baghdad, in Egypt, we find another Shī'ī dynasty, equally magnificent, coming into being in the 4th/10th century with the Fāṭimids. Like the Fāṭimids, the Būyids were great patrons of the arts and sciences, even though in their beginnings they had been only uncouth Dailamites. The fact that they ruled over Baghdad and had general attachments to Iraq, where Arabic letters prevailed, made them patrons more of Arabic letters than of the New Persian literature then flourishing in the eastern part of Iran. There were, nevertheless, poets in western Iran who wrote in the New Persian tongue in Būyid times. Arabic letters, however, prevailed over Persian in western Iran.

The libraries of the Būyids in Iran, at Shīrāz, Ray and Iṣfahān, were the marvels of their day. Moreover, we still see what was evident in preceding times: the chief scribes, that is to say, the viziers, are Persians whose mastery of Arabic is joined to an astonishing culture that roams over all the fields of learning. A Persian kātib like Ibn al-'Amīd (d. 359/969–70) is a good illustration of this broad culture and technical virtuosity in Arabic. Philosopher, philologian, religious scholar, poet, and prose stylist, his name has been juxtaposed to that of his Persian predecessor, 'Abd al-Ḥamīd, in the field of epistolary compositions. 'Abd al-Ḥamīd is said to have given them a new dress and Ibn al-'Amīd, "the second al-Jāḥiẓ", is said to have brought them to an end. But a distinction must be made. 'Abd al-Ḥamīd's epistolary style is virile and not overly ornamented. Ibn al-'Amīd's style, on the other hand, like that of his successor in the Būyid ministry, the Persian Ibn 'Abbād, called the "Ṣāḥib" (d. 385/995), was charged with figures of speech and cast in the rhymed prose style then coming into fashion. There is here a kind of *terminus ad quem* in Arabic letters which is not flattering to the Būyid ministers just mentioned.

But that, after all, is only in the strictly belles-lettrist domain of Arabic literature. No such defect can be found in the Persian historian and moral philosopher Ibn Muskūya (Miskawaih) (d. 431/1040), who had been a scribe and courtier under Ibn al-'Amīd. His historical work called *Tajārib al-umam* ("The Experiences of Nations") is in straightforward prose and characterized by an objective historical attitude.

Historical literature was becoming a matter of first-rate significance at that time. This was due in part to the great impetus given it by the work of the Persian religious scholar al-Ṭabarī (d. 310/923), from Ṭabaristān, whose *Ta'rīkh al-rusul wa'l-mulūk* ("The Annals of the Messengers and the Kings") is a vast universal history dealing with both the Prophets and Persian kings. In part, too, history in the traditional Islamic world was cultivated by way of pinning down all of the events surrounding the origins and subsequent history of the Community. Other historians, such as Hamza al-Iṣfahānī (d. *c.* 360/971), who was also a philologian, stress Persian history in particular.

An insatiable curiosity characterizes the 4th/10th century both in Iran and elsewhere, a curiosity that is not merely occupied with history. All of the domains of Islamic learning were affected. Though that age is sometimes considered by Western historians as belonging to the "golden age" of Islam, it was not considered as such by its contemporaries. The 3rd/9th century had already laid the foundations for the curiosity about the world and its workings which explodes in all directions in the 4th/10th. The great Baṣran Ṣūfī master and sage, Abū Ṭālib al-Makkī (d. 386/996), taking the pulse of his contemporaries, sees them as being far removed from the state of affairs in the beginning age of Islam. He notes that people no longer pose simple questions as of yore, and even in ordinary greetings one is forced to submit to complete interrogations; new sciences, such as theology, logic, argumentation and the like, have arisen; grammar is pursued with passionate attachment; and even Heaven is petitioned in rhymed prose. All of this he calls "decadence" (*fasād*).[1]

While it is true that a spate of questions were now being posed in all domains, the traditional sages were very much in evidence under the Būyids. The latter encouraged Shī'ī literature, which bursts forth in the 4th/10th and 5th/11th century with a veritable cascade of works. It must be recalled that the "major occultation" (*al-ghaiba al-kubrā*) for the Twelver Shī'īs took place in 329/940, when the Twelfth Imām,

[1] Abū Ṭālib al-Makkī, vol. 1, pp. 164–6.

al-Mahdī, disappeared. The great Shīʿī canonical collections of ḥadīths come into being in this period, such as the *Uṣūl al-kāfī* of al-Kulainī (d. 329/940), certainly the most authoritative collection amongst the Shīʿīs, and the collection of Ibn Bābūya (d. 381/991–2); and theological treatises of maximum importance also come into the open buttressing the Shīʿī doctrines.

One of the most interesting of the Shīʿī authorities under the Būyids is Sayyid Sharīf al-Raḍī (d. 406/1016). The Būyid Bahā' al-Daula took him under his care. As a descendant of the Caliph ʿAlī, al-Raḍī enjoyed great prestige. His poems in Arabic breathe the Shīʿī perfume of devotion to the ʿAlid house and have always been considered as paramount in Arabic literature. But, of course, his renown in both the Shīʿī and Sunnī world has been due to his compilations of the sayings, letters, and sermons of ʿAlī in the work called *Nahj al-balāgha*, the third most fundamental text in the Shīʿī world after the Qur'ān and the ḥadīths of the Prophet.

Another personality of touching appeal in Būyid days is the Persian Shīʿī poet, Mihyār al-Dailamī (d. 428/1037). He began his career as a scribe in one of the chanceries of the ruling dynasty. A Zoroastrian of the same Dailamite origins as the Būyids, he converted to Islam at the hands of Sharīf al-Raḍī. His poems show both his love for Shīʿism and a wonderful skill in Arabic verse forms. Mihyār was proud of his Persian ancestry and of Islam at one and the same time.

It was under the Būyids, also, that numerous scholars in all fields wrote their works. Geographers, mathematicians, astronomers and physicians, have left us considerable material wherewith to judge the Būyids' patronage of the sciences. The great Shīʿī scholar, Abu'l-Faraj al-Iṣfahānī (d. 356/967), a Persian from Iṣfahān who is sometimes called a "pure Arab" because of his genealogical tree on his father's side, compiled his justly famous *Kitāb al-aghānī* ("The Book of Songs") under the Būyids. In it he has preserved a mass of poems, anecdotes and brief accounts of great historical value concerning personalities in Arabic literature from pre-Islamic times till the end of the 3rd/9th century.

But it is perhaps Ibn Sīnā, the great Muslim philosopher from Bukhārā who died in Hamadān in 428/1037, who gives us a striking example of Būyid culture. He even served as a minister of the Būyids for a while. Though he wrote his philosophical and cosmological treatises in Arabic, he nevertheless used Persian for his *Dānish-nāma-yi*

'*Alā'ī*, dedicated to 'Alā' al-Daula, ruler of Iṣfahān. His works, especially the early ones, such as *al-S͟hifā* and *al-Najāt*, are considered by S. H. Naṣr as "the most complete expressions of the philosophy of the Peripatetic school in Islam", but there are also his mystical and visionary narratives, that form the point of departure of what was later to be called the *Is͟hrāqī* school of thinking, or the Illuminationist school.

The fact that Ibn Sīnā produced a work in Persian demonstrates this important point: while poetry is the main instrument in the revival of Persian letters in the 4th/10th and 5th/11th centuries, prose also played its rôle. Indeed, already in the 4th/10th century, there were books in Persian representing practically all of the sciences of the day. This shows to what an extent Arabic letters were then ceding the field to Persian. It is precisely in that century that in the Arabic-speaking countries the diverse regional dialects had arisen and invaded the speech even of the grammarians. Written Arabic had by then crystallized into a definite grammatical structure. It therefore remained above the fray; but the dialects rendered easy communications between one region and another a thing of the past. If such was the case in the Arabic-speaking part of the Muslim world, then the time had indeed come for the rise of Persian letters in Iran.

There was a genre of Arabic literature cultivated in Iran in the 4th/10th and 5th/11th centuries that deserves more attention than it gets. This is the Ṣūfī literature, which of course had roots in the past. A more developed prose style is now in evidence. The *Kitāb al-luma'* of Abū Naṣr al-Sarrāj al-Ṭūsī (d. 378/988), a classic in its field, is an explanatory Ṣūfī treatise containing the sayings of previous masters together with extracts from their compositions. A later Ṣūfī master, Abū 'Abd al-Rahmān al-Sulamī (d. 412/1022), fills his *Ṭabaqāt al-ṣūfiyya* with a mass of statements from great Ṣūfīs prior to his day, especially those in Iran. Though this is not to be considered simply as belles-lettrist literature, the Ṣūfīs have unwittingly produced some of the finest Arabic known, due no doubt to the seriousness of their subject-matter, which admits of no bantering or mere playing with words.

It remained for Abū Nu'aim al-Iṣfahānī (d. 430/1038), a Ṣūfī and a religious scholar, to string together, in his *Ḥilyat al-auliyā'*, a mass of information and sayings emanating from the sages and ascetics of Ṣūfism from the very early days of Islam till his own. His work is remarkable for showing how Ṣūfism, far from being an extraneous element, or even a foreign body, within conventional Islam, actually penetrates its deeper significations and inner domains. Abū Nu'aim was himself an example of this balance between inner and outer Islam; he was one of the greatest authorities on ḥadīths of the Prophet in his day and wrote a history of Iṣfahān (*Dhikr akhbār Iṣfahān*), and at the same time he was a Ṣūfī.

We may turn now to the Sāmānids of eastern Iran. Like the Būyids in the south and west of Iran, the Sāmānids were also great patrons of the arts and sciences. But their patronage was not limited to the sole domain of Arabic letters. They were sponsors also of Persian letters, which had less brilliance at the Būyid court due, as was mentioned, to the influence of the Arabic-speaking caliphal seat at Baghdad which the Būyids controlled. By that time the whole Muslim world was a congeries of distinct cultural entities, so that even the Ḥamdānids of Aleppo or the dynasties in Morocco or eastern Iran drew upon their own resources to produce the cultural brilliance that we see.

Something of the self-sufficiency of the different Islamic cultural areas is seen in the story of Abu'l-Ḥasan al-'Āmirī's visit to Baghdad. This great Persian philosopher, little known in the West, was born in the Nīshāpūr of Sāmānid times and it was in that area that he gained his philosophical training. He belonged to that school of Muslim philosophers who tried to establish a harmony between religion and philosophy. Between the days of al-Fārābī (d. 339/950), the great political philosopher and musical theoretician, not to say mystic (as his work *Fuṣūṣ al-ḥikam*, which must not be confused with Ibn al-'Arabī's work with the same title, shows so well), who likewise came from eastern Iran, and the days of Ibn Sīnā (d. 428/1037), Abu'l-Ḥasan al-'Āmirī (d. 381/992) is probably the most important author in this class of literature. Many of his works survive, though insufficient attention has been paid him. When Abu'l-Ḥasan paid a visit to the Baghdad philosophers, the latter, according to Abū Ḥayyān al-Tauḥīdī (d. 414/1023), did not care for Abu'l-Ḥasan because he had not come from Baghdad! But the aversion was mutual and Abu'l-Ḥasan returned to his native Khurāsān. It was as if both sides were content to live with their own cultural heritage without intrusions from the outside world.

Occasionally, however, Baghdad, because of the symbolic attraction of the Sunnī caliphal power, was given more than just nominal recognition by the Sāmānids. We recall that the geographer al-Muqaddasī (or al-Maqdisī) said that the religious scholars were held in high esteem in Khurāsān and that he considered the Arabic used in Khurāsān (no doubt by these same Persian scholars) as the purest he had heard anywhere in his extensive travels. Nevertheless, the Sāmānid king Nūḥ b. Naṣr (331–43/943–54) and his vizier Bal'amī saw fit to address a letter containing hundreds of questions on Arabic and the Qur'ān to the great Persian grammarian and *qāḍī* of Baghdad, Abū Sa'īd al-Sīrāfī al-Marzubānī (d. 368/978), addressing him as the "Imām" of the grammarians. This could be interpreted as two Persians recognizing the superiority of another Persian in Arabic letters. But it likewise shows that Baghdad had a certain magnetic attraction in spite of its political decline.

While the Būyids laid great stress on Arabic literature, the Sāmānids patronized both Arabic and Persian letters. The fact, however, that the Būyids were closer to the Arabic-speaking world, and indeed ruled in Iraq, does not imply that the Arabic literature produced under them was somehow more "Arabic" than that produced under the Sāmānids. One will recall that the literary Arabic of the 4th/10th century, an extremely flexible tool, was the end-result of a long process of development in which the Persians, especially the great scribes, or secretaries, played more than just a minor rôle.

We have in the *Yatīmat al-dahr* of the Persian scholar Abū Manṣūr al-Tha'ālibī (d. 429/1038) a remarkable collection of the poems and prose compositions produced in Arabic in both Iran and elsewhere. His sources, generally speaking, do not go back earlier than the 4th/10th century. No similar works exist for the 3rd/9th century, or earlier. Hence, for periods earlier than the 4th/10th century we must rely on disparate sources to arrive at some idea of the state of Arabic belles-lettres in Iran, particularly its eastern part. Had it not been for his collection, even the 4th/10th century would have been just as difficult to investigate, as far as belles-lettres are concerned, as previous ages. Ironically, his collection of Arabic works, mostly poems composed by both major and minor figures, throws light on the state of Arabic belles-lettres produced by Persians at the very moment that New Persian literature comes into view.

Our remarks on Sāmānid Arabic literature, or more generally, on the belles-lettres composed in eastern Iran will be confined to what is found in the *Yatīma*. For one thing, we know that, apart from a few exiles from Baghdad, the eastern authors cited by al-Tha'ālibī were all Persians. In this respect they are not ethnically different from the great Persian masters of Arabic farther to the west of Iran under the Būyids, such as Ibn al-ʿAmīd or Ḥamza al-Iṣfahānī or Ibn Muskūya, and a host of others. This is well to remember when one is looking for the "Persian mind" amongst the belles-lettrists of Khurāsān exclusively. For another thing, it is quite clear that the eastern Persian authors were all highly urbanized men and used to the patterns of life that Islamic civilization had long before established. In short, they were not Arab nomads, but rather, they were the products of the Perso-Arab cultural synthesis, under the aegis of Islam, that had been worked out, even in the domain of literary Arabic.

Therefore, the contents of 4th/10th-century Arabic belles-lettres in eastern Iran were bound to differ from what the conquering Bedouins produced there in the 1st/7th century, for at that time only the beginnings of a synthesis could have been made. To look for characteristics of the Persian mentality in the Arabic-using poets of Khurāsān in Sāmānid times by citing, as Browne does, such criteria as references to Iranian feast-days, a presupposition of a knowledge of the Persian language, or the use of "Persian" verse-forms such as the *ghazal* and the Arabic equivalent of the *mathnavī*, is really to overlook the fact that these criteria are at best quite external. References to Persian feast-days are found in Arabic poetry of the 1st/7th century; the use of Persian words in Arabic poems is to be found even amongst the Bedouins with some knowledge of urban ways of life. Al-Jāḥiẓ gives an example of this latter point when he cites the poem of a certain al-ʿUmmānī who praised Harūn al-Rashīd: the rhyming words of the poem are all in Persian.[1] One must not forget, moreover, that the "Persian mind" of the 4th/10th century had been considerably Semiticized through the tincture that Islam invariably gives its adherents, to say nothing of the psychological influence of Arabic, and Islam in that day was irrevocably established in Iran even though Zoroastrianism still flourished in parts of the west. On the other hand, and this is likewise important, from the 1st/7th century onwards, the Persians had Aryanized, or Iranized, their Semitic co-religionists, the Arabs, that is to say the urbanized Arabs, and by the 4th/10th century the latter formed the immense majority of Arabs, while the Bedouin retreated into obscurity.

Consequently, if it is difficult to discern the "Persian mind" in the Khurāsānī belles-lettrists of the day, it is because of the significant transformations that had been going on for some time in the cultural expressions of Islam, and in Arabic. If one wishes to compare the

[1] al-Jāḥiẓ, *al-Bayān*, vol. 1, pp. 141–2.

Khurāsānīs with others, it is therefore not with their contemporaries further to the west of Iran, who were likewise Persians, that they might be compared, but rather with the 1st/7th-century poets. The latter were by and large of a nomadic disposition, with a psychology and cultural ambiance that seem rough, warlike, and close to the savage beauty of the desert and its strangely rigorous world. But by the 4th/10th century much had changed. The pure Bedouin was too rough for the taste of the times. Even the 4th/10th-century Arab poet, al-Mutanabbī, was not a Bedouin, but a poet who combined the smooth civility of the city-dweller (for that is what he was, in spite of his brief stint in the desert), with a touch of the ancient savagery: hence his popularity.

Amongst the belles-lettrists of eastern Iran in the 4th/10th century, no one cries over the camp-fire remains of some beloved's departed tribe, no one wastes away his camel's strength in crossing the desert. In their poems the themes attaching to the finest specimens of ancient Arabic poetry are not to be found; in fact they despised the Bedouins, and could easily say, with Abū Bakr al-Khwārazmī (d. 383/993), the great Arabic prose stylist of Iran: "Loathsome to me are the Bedouins' witticisms; odious to me is the number of Bedouins."[1]

Some of the poets mentioned in the *Yatīma* are Persians who excelled in both Arabic and Persian letters. It was as if they had two tongues to express one and the same Islamic culture. No doubt, this provoked questions of cultural affinity. Abu'l-Fatḥ al-Bustī (d. 383/993), a major poet of the day, is a good example of these two-tongued Persians, while Abū Sa'īd al-Rustamī, a minor poet of the day, seems to incarnate the question of cultural affinity. The latter, who came from a more westerly part of Iran, has this to say of his Arabo-Persian background: "As far as my ancestors are concerned, I belong to the house of Rustam, otherwise my poetry comes from Lu'ay b. Ghālib" (a pre-Islamic Arab poet).[2] But, in truth, he is speaking of the forms of Arabic poetry, not the contents. The ideals of the early nomadic Arabs, or of the Bedouins in general, hardly fascinated him or the other belles-lettrists of his day in Iran, and he seems to sum up the whole question of cultural affinity and scorn of the Bedouins' ideals when he says in a poem:

Openly and secretly I am known as a Persian of Arabic culture:
Would that I knew how people situate me when my name is evoked!
My origins are clear enough, and I am of good stock.

[1] al-Tha'ālibī, vol. I, p. 226.
[2] *Ibid.*, vol. III, p. 272.

I do not scurry about praising kings and exhausting riding-mounts;
Nor do I roam about in the desert![1]

It might be true, as Barbier de Maynard points out, that the poetical extracts in the Khurāsānī section of the *Yatīma* are as "unremarkable in poetic invention as in style", but there is, nevertheless, a considerable variety of themes that one would never find in the Arab Bedouin poetry, for the psychological climate, the temperament, the ideals of our Khurāsānī belles-lettrists are imbued with that curiosity and restless mentality that Abū Ṭālib al-Makkī stigmatized as the signs of the decadence (*fasād*) of his day. There are poems to celebrate a house newly built (*dāriyyāt*); poems that reveal a certain preoccupation with the stellar universe and its influence on human destiny (*nujūmiyyāt*); poems loaded with legalistic casuistry (*fiqhiyyāt*), and so on.

Looking at the prose works of such great eastern authors as Badīʿ al-Zamān al-Hamadānī (d. 398/1007), the inventor of the *maqāmāt* literary genre in Arabic, and Abū Bakr al-Khwārazmī (d. 383/993), both of whom spent much of their time in Nīshāpūr or elsewhere in Khurāsān, one is struck by their incredible literary skill. Al-Hamadānī, for example, was so at home in both Arabic and his own Persian tongue that people would fling Persian verses containing rare words at him and he would translate them on the spot into Arabic with amazing rapidity. Even the genre of maqāmāt literature, the genre al-Hamadānī perfected, probably on the basis of the works by Ibn Duraid (d. 321/933), is couched in an overly embroidered Arabic. Like Abū Bakr al-Khwārazmī, al-Hamadānī seems to have reached the terminal point in Arabic letters.

While the decadence mentioned by al-Makkī had as its happy sequel the tremendous outpouring of energy in the intellectual and cosmological sciences of the day, which we have only touched upon, its reflection in the belles-lettres literature of Iran in the 4th/10th century, especially in the prose works of both western and eastern Persian authors, is not a happy one. There is a sort of exaggerated skill in these Persian masters of Arabic. Their figures of speech, their ornamented rhymed prose, the very rapidity with which they can toss off a composition, even a qaṣīda, on the spur of the moment, all point to a perfection that is almost acrobatic, as if they were all superb jugglers.

In truth, one feels that in Iran the masters just mentioned had finally, after several centuries, reached the point where they had exhausted the belles-lettrist possibilities of Arabic and were now very busily burning

[1] *Ibid.*, vol. III, pp. 278, 282.

up its resources. How much further can one get in perfection than al-Hamadānī? He could compose a book on a certain theme, beginning with the last line and working back, line by line, to the first line, and it would be a marvel of rhetorical artistry.

That could not be the start of a new golden age of Arabic belles-lettres in Iran. Rather, it is the last movements of a literary current begun in the 1st/7th century, a sort of galvanized prestidigitation before the curtain falls. It is surely not by accident that the New Persian letters, with their own fresh, untapped sources, were coming upon the scene precisely at that moment.

True, in the 4th/10th century, Arabic would be the main vehicle for the Persian man of culture. But the rise of Persian letters would soon change that situation. Even though great masters of Arabic would appear in later centuries, by the time of al-Bīrūnī (d. 442/1050), on the eve of the Saljuq reign in the Near East, the cultivated Persians no longer gave Arabic a unique place. This great Muslim scholar, who was a cosmologist, historian, mathematician, and indeed a man of many parts, had a great love for Arabic, which in his eyes was a wonderful tool for scientific expression, while Persian seems to have been relegated by him to the domain of poetry. In his *Kitāb al-ṣaidala* he tells us that his contemporaries in Persia prefer Persian to Arabic; they asked: "What is the point in knowing the nominative and accusative declensions and all of those other things you know regarding defective formations, or rare words, in Arabic?"

As was said, the knowledge of Arabic and its use amongst cultivated Persians would not disappear from Iran with the coming of the Saljuqs in the 5th/11th century and the triumphal manifestation of the ethnic genius of that people in the New Persian literature. But the 4th/10th and 5th/11th centuries did see the swan-song of Arabic belles-lettrist compositions in this sense that, henceforth, that genius had its own Islamicized tongue, Persian, at its immediate disposal. This was not a repudiation of Islam. On the contrary, the Arabic of the Qur'ān would always remain sacred to the Persian Muslims; but ordinary Arabic literature was something else again. Moreover, the distinction between Arabism and Islam had long before been made. Thus, when the Persians took to fostering the growth of their own language, they did not "bid a last farewell to Islam", as Naṣr b. Sayyār would have said, for Islam was firmly implanted in the Persian soul, but they did "bid a last farewell to the Arabs", for by then no single ethnic group had a monopoly on Islam.

CHAPTER 19

THE RISE OF THE NEW PERSIAN LANGUAGE

I. INTRODUCTION

New Persian literature, like that of many other countries, begins with poetry. According to the earliest anthology, the *Lubāb al-albāb* of Muḥammad 'Aufī (618/1221–2), the first Persian poem was a *qaṣīda* composed in 193/809 by a certain 'Abbās or Abu'l-'Abbās of Marv on the occasion of the entry into that city of the future caliph Ma'mūn. This information is very questionable, however, and the few couplets quoted by 'Aufī are certainly apocryphal, for the command of classical rhetoric in them is unlikely to be achieved in a first attempt. In fact the earliest poems which have been preserved date from the middle of the 3rd/9th century. The *Tārīkh-i Sīstān*, a local chronicle compiled in the 5th/11th century, attributes the production of the first poetry in Persian to the Sīstānians. According to this interesting account, the victory of Ya'qūb b. al-Laith the Ṣaffārid over the Khārijite 'Ammār in 251/865 was celebrated after the custom of the time by panegyrics in Arabic. Ya'qūb was an uneducated military leader (condottiere) with no knowledge of Arabic. "Why," he asked, "do you compose verses which I do not understand?" One of his secretaries, Muḥammad b. Vaṣīf, then had the idea of composing in the same strain a qaṣīda in Persian, which is quoted in the *Tārīkh-i Sīstān*, and his example was followed by two of his compatriots. The anthologies make no mention of these Sīstānian poets, but the *Chahār maqāla* of Niẓāmī 'Arūḍī (550–1/1155–7) and the *Lubāb al-albāb* of 'Aufī quote some verses by a poet of the Herāt region, Ḥanẓala of Bādghīs, whose work is certainly earlier in date than 259/873. Both traditions therefore attribute the beginnings of Persian classical poetry to the same period.

In addition to Ḥanẓala, 'Aufī mentions a small number of poets living at the time of the Ṭāhirid and Ṣaffārid dynasties, and many more in the Sāmānid period. The court at Bukhārā remained throughout the century a brilliant centre of Persian and Arabic literature, while the local courts of Khurāsān and Transoxiana also patronized poets. The output was certainly abundant, but only isolated fragments have survived. These however suffice to give an idea of the splendour and variety of this first poetic activity. Henceforth Persian poetry could be considered mature; its subjects and forms were fixed and the same tradition was to inform all the poetry which followed, from the rich output of the first Ghaznavid period onwards. It was also in the 4th/10th century and in the same part of Iran that Persian prose had its origin; the first extant works date from the middle of the century.

Until this time literary activity in Persia had been confined to eastern Iran. It began in such regions as Sīstān, Khurāsān and Transoxiana, and penetrated only gradually into western Iran. Towards the end of the 4th/10th century several poets writing in Persian were to be found at the court of Qābūs b. Vushmgīr, amīr of Gurgān, and in the entourage of the Ṣāḥib Ismāʿīl b. ʿAbbād at Ray. It was not until the following century, however, that Persian literature was to become the main form of expression of the Iranian territories as a whole.

The language known as New Persian, which was usually called at this period by the name of *darī* or *parsī-i darī*, can be classified linguistically as a continuation of Middle Persian, the official, religious and literary language of Sāsānian Iran, itself a continuation of Old Persian, the language of the Achaemenids. Unlike the other languages and dialects, ancient and modern, of the Iranian group such as Avestan, Parthian, Soghdian, Kurdish, Pashto, etc., Old, Middle and New Persian represent one and the same language at three stages of its history. It had its origin in Fārs (the true Persian country from the historical point of view) and is differentiated by dialectical features, still easily recognizable from the dialects prevailing in north-western and eastern Iran.

Phonetically and grammatically, the degree of evolution from Old Persian to Middle Persian is considerable, the differences being comparable with the differences between Latin and French, for example. On the other hand New Persian remains in many respects quite close to Middle Persian. The adoption of the Arabic script, which reflects and marks the break with Middle Persian tradition, is an event of enormous importance to civilization, but it must not hide the fact that the phonetic development from Middle to New Persian is very slight, especially New Persian at its early stage. The relationship existing between Old, Middle and New Persian is well illustrated by the word for "king" – Old Persian *khshāyathiya*, but Middle Persian and New

Persian *s͟hāh*. Phonetic differences between Middle and New Persian are generally not greater than in the example Middle Persian *ārāstag* "decorated" and New Persian *ārāsta*. The grammatical structure has also undergone only minor changes, chiefly in relation to verbal morphology and syntax. It is particularly in its vocabulary that New Persian departs from Middle Persian, in two different ways. First, New Persian contains many words which are originally foreign to Persian proper and are betrayed by their form as belonging to other, northern or eastern Iranian dialects: New Persian owes much to Parthian and to related dialects and it has also borrowed from Sog͟hdian. Secondly, it has admitted a considerable proportion of Arabic words, a proportion which has increased with time in the literary language and which also varies between the different literary forms: rare in epic poetry, considerable from the outset in lyrical poetry and significant even in the earliest prose. It is evident that no one has ever written "pure" Persian, that is completely free from Arabic elements. An Arab author, Abū Ḥātim of Ray (d. 322/934), observes that in order to express many ideas it is necessary for a Persian to have recourse to Arabic words.[1] The mixed character of the New Persian vocabulary, as well as being an important fact of civilization, is a basic feature of the language, so that in this respect Persian may be compared with English, the Arabic element holding the same place and playing the same part in Persian as the Latin element combined with the original Anglo-Saxon in English. On the whole, therefore, New Persian appears to have been from the start a mixed language, based on the Persian dialect but bearing marked traces of other Iranian dialects and infiltrated with Arabic words. It may be thought that this diversity was a factor in making it the common language of the Iranian countries and, over the centuries, the main literary and cultural language of the eastern Muslim world.

The emergence of the New Persian language and literature presents considerable historical problems. How was this new literary language formed? What necessity gave rise to it? How does it happen that, in spite of its original connection with the regions of the south-west, it seems to have appeared first in the east, at the opposite extremity of the plateau? Why did literature develop initially in Transoxiana, an outlying region where, until the Islamic conquest at the beginning of the 2nd/8th century, the common and literary language was Sog͟hdian, a

[1] *Kitāb al-zīna*, ed. al-Hamdānī (Cairo, 1957), p. 71.

fundamentally different Iranian language? Moreover, from its beginning or very nearly so, Persian poetry is in full possession of its techniques, verse-forms, rhetorical devices, genres and subjects. It emerged like Minerva from the head of Jupiter, fully equipped from the shadows of history. How were its literary rules formed? On what sources did the early writers draw and how much did they owe to Iranian tradition and how much to the imitation of Arabic poetry? Such questions are controversial for the documents naturally do not give a direct answer. Nevertheless sufficient indications may be found for the consideration of certain probabilities.

II. THE LANGUAGES SPOKEN IN IRAN DURING THE FIRST CENTURIES UNDER ISLAM

In an account passed down by the *Fihrist*, Ibn al-Muqaffaʿ describes the linguistic situation in Iran at the end of the Sāsānian period. The Iranians, he says in effect, have five languages: *pahlavī*, the language of the Fahla country, that is to say of ancient Media, the Jibāl of the Muslims, *darī*, the language of the capital (Ctesiphon or Madā'in), *pārsī*, language of the *mōbads* and scholars, *suryānī*, spoken in Sawād, and *khūzī*, used in Khūzistān. Of these five languages two are not Iranian in the sense accepted by linguists; suryānī is Aramaic, at that time the common language of the population of Mesopotamia, while khūzī was probably a relic of the ancient Elamite. The official language of the state and of the Zoroastrian religion was evidently pārsī, that is to say literary Middle Persian, the vehicle of literature later known as Pahlavī; for, as the result of a shift of meaning which has caused much confusion, the name Pahlavī, originally meaning Parthian, was used in the Islamic period to indicate the only ancient language then still known, Middle Persian, and continues to be the name usually applied to it today. Ibn al-Muqaffaʿ, however, had no knowledge of such a usage; he gave Middle Persian its proper name of pārsī (in Middle Persian itself *pārsīg*) and used the term pahlavī to describe the dialect of Media, historically close to Parthian. As regards darī, it was the usual spoken language not only in the capital but probably throughout a large part of the empire too.

This description, which is limited to western Iran, makes it possible to reconstruct the situation as follows. The official language, and the only written one, was Middle Persian, a language already fixed in its archaic form before the beginning of the Sāsānian period and reserved for official and literary use. In everyday talk darī was employed, its name being derived from *dar*, the "Porte", that is to say the court or the capital. Originally this language must scarcely have differed from the written language, but while the latter remained almost static, the spoken tongue developed to such an extent that towards the end of the Sāsānian period the differences were finally noticed and the need was felt to give it a proper name. Pārsī (Middle Persian literary) and darī were not, strictly speaking, two languages, nor even two separate dialects, but rather two stylistic levels of the same language, pārsī being the medium of the administration, of religion and of written literature, and darī that of everyday oral communication, that is to say the common vernacular of Iran. Alongside darī there existed of course local dialects, the most important of which was pahlavī, probably upheld by the prestige of an oral literature inherited from the Parthian poetic tradition.

During the first centuries under Islam the sources do not provide a general picture of the languages of Iran, but it is possible to glean some items of information from the geographers and the historians. There were numerous local dialects. K͟hūzī persisted in K͟hūzistān; it was said to be a language which could not be put into Arabic script. Āzarbāījān was the domain of *ād͟harī*, an important Iranian dialect which Mas'ūdī mentions together with darī and pahlavī; other idioms also occurred which may have been "Caucasian". The Ardabīl district was remarkable for its mixture of languages: according to Muqaddasī there were seventy of them in use. Among Caspian dialects *dailamī* was the language of the rough soldiery who spread over western Iran and Iraq; *ṭabarī* was sufficiently vigorous to become the vehicle of a written literature in about the 4th/10th century. At Astarābād, in Gurgān, two distinct idioms were spoken. The Pahlavī of Jibāl gave its name to the *fahlawiyyāt*, which were poems in dialect. There were dialects in the open country of Kirmān; the Kōfc͟h (or Kōc͟h, Arabic Qufṣ) tribes and the Balūc͟hīs had their languages, probably different from one another, as did the inhabitants of Makrān. In the north-east K͟hwārazmian, the mother-tongue of Bīrūnī, flourished. Under the Muslim conquest Sog͟hdian lost its function as an official and cultural language, but it survived as the spoken language of the region of Samarqand. Not long after the conquest the inhabitants of Buk͟hārā were speaking a dialect very much like Sog͟hdian which persisted in the country districts until at least the 4th/10th century. Ushrūsana also had its dialect. In what is now Afghanistan, Gharchistān had its own idiom, as did the land of Ghūr, whose inhabitants in 411/1020 could communicate with Mas'ūd of Ghazna only by means of an interpreter. Many other dialects existed in the Iranian countries and Muqaddasī in his description of Khurāsān stated explicitly that almost everywhere in the country districts "another tongue" was spoken, that is to say a dialect distinct from the common language.

This common language was of course darī and a most important feature of this period was the fact that it spread considerably. It probably lost ground in Iraq (though it remained in use among the townspeople at least until the 4th/10th century), but it gained immense territory in the east. Probably already in the Sāsānian period it had ousted from Khurāsān proper the Parthian which had been the common language there in the 3rd century A.D. Supported by the prestige of the empire darī had perhaps also begun to spread quite widely in Bactria and beyond the Oxus. It was certainly at the time when Transoxiana and the present Afghanistan had been integrated into the caliphate that the Muslim conquerors imposed it in all north-eastern regions. Even the name *tājīk*, which is still used today to designate the Persian-speaking populations of Transoxiana and of the whole of the eastern part of the plateau, is the Soghdian form of the Persian word *tāzī*, which was the Iranian name for Arabs, but could also mean "Muslim", as shown by Tavadia.[1] These "Arabs" were actually for the most part Iranians converted to Islam: their victory was also that of the darī language which, first taking root in the towns, eliminated from there the local dialects and confined them to the country districts with the result that eventually most of them died out. In the 3rd/9th century, perhaps even earlier, it had become the common spoken language of the Iranian lands as a whole.

A spoken language which extends over vast territories without having the support of a written tradition tends to assume a diversity of forms and darī was no exception to this rule. Its local variants in the different regions where it took root were influenced to a greater or lesser degree by the dialects which it replaced. In the Sāsānian period the darī spoken in Khurāsān was certainly not identical with that of Fārs or of Iraq and even today the Persian spoken in Kabul and the colloquial Persian of Tehrān are very different and the users of these

[1] *ZDMG*, vol. CII (1952), p. 384.

two colloquial forms cannot easily understand each other. Even within the frontiers of each Persian-speaking country, despite the tendency towards unification imposed by modern social conditions, there are many local forms of speech. In Iran those of Khurāsān and of Sīstān for instance preserve a markedly individual character, while in Afghanistan and also in Tājīkistān there are numerous Persian dialects. These differences are of ancient date. The geographer Muqaddasī in his description of each region always devotes a few lines to the language of its inhabitants. The forms of speech to which he refers are for the most part only local variants of the common language, but he distinguishes practically as many of them as there are important towns or political districts. The indications given by him, although both summary and subjective, are interesting as evidence of the existence of linguistic discrepancies which were apparent to people living at that time. On the other hand, a close examination of early Persian texts enables us to gain some idea of the dialectology of darī. The output of the 4th/10th and 5th/11th centuries, especially in prose (since prose works are less literary and have been better preserved in their original form than the poetry), reveals various dialectical shades of difference. The early Judaeo-Persian writings provide a quantity of instructive information on the forms of speech in south-western Iran and supplement what can be deduced from texts in Arabic script, which were composed mostly in eastern regions. Taking them as a whole, it is possible to detect among the local forms of the common language of about a thousand years ago two main groups, belonging to the east and to the west respectively, each group containing sundry variants. The darī used in the south-west, both in its vocabulary and in various grammatical features, remained closer to Middle Persian, while the darī of Khurāsān was encumbered with more elements coming from non-Persian Iranian dialects, particularly Parthian. It was the darī of Khurāsān which penetrated into what is now Afghanistan and into Transoxiana; in this latter region it acquired a number of Soghdian words.

Alongside both the early dialects and darī, which had spread everywhere with a greater or lesser degree of local variation, Arabic had also taken root in Iran. It was of course the everyday language of the Arab immigrants: certain towns such as Dīnavar, Zanjān, Nihāvand, Kāshān, Qum and Nīshāpūr had a considerable Arab population and Arab tribes had also settled in Khurāsān. However, these Arab elements were more or less rapidly assimilated: in the middle of the 2nd/8th century the majority of the Arabs in the army of Abū Muslim spoke darī. Arabic gained little ground among the Iranian population except as a cultural language and in this respect the Iranian countries differed fundamentally from almost all other parts of the empire of the caliphs. While in the Fertile Crescent and in Africa Arabic was gradually taking the place of Aramaic, Egyptian and the Berber languages as the language of daily communication, the same function was being performed in the east by darī at the expense of the other Iranian languages. It was darī, not Arabic, which was the language of the eastern conquests. Paradoxically Arab domination and the extension of Islam had the effect of largely unifying the spoken language of the Iranian countries, a factor which was decisive in the formation of literary New Persian.

III. LITERARY LANGUAGES IN USE UNTIL THE 3RD/9TH CENTURY

During the first two centuries of Islam, the medium for written expression and literature in Iran was provided by two languages of unequal importance, one of them declining and the other in the ascendant – Middle Persian (called Pahlavī) and Arabic. It is well known that at first the conquerors were necessarily dependent on the former Iranian civil service and that its officials continued to keep the financial registers in Middle Persian until 78/697–8 (or 82/701–2) in the west and until 124/741–2 in Khurāsān, the years in which Arabic replaced Middle Persian as the administrative language. Although it is fairly safe to assume that during the same period Middle Persian continued to be the medium by which the intellectual activity of the cultivated Iranian was expressed, its use became increasingly restricted with the progress of Islamic influence and the vigorous development of Arab culture. Abandoned by the new Muslim converts, it persisted only among the Zoroastrians, particularly – perhaps even exclusively – among the priests, who were the trustees of the ancient culture. The major part of Pahlavī literature which has survived dates from the 3rd/9th century, a period of relatively intense productivity, but this activity was limited to subjects connected with the Mazdaean religion, which the priests wanted to defend against the triumphant extension of Islam. It was the work of clerics and remained geographically confined to Fārs.

Indeed from the 2nd/8th century onwards, the principal cultural language of Iran was Arabic and it had been openly adopted as such by the Islamicized Iranian aristocracy. Although in certain remote provinces it was still ignored by such local princes as Vindādhhurmuzd, king of Ṭabaristān, who was able to converse with the caliph Hārūn al-Rashīd only by means of an interpreter, it was understood and used by many Iranian nobles and by the intelligentsia. It was not merely the administrative language, essential for anyone who held a position of any authority, but also the medium of science and of literature. That Arabic should have fared thus in Iran was due not simply to its being the language of the Qur'ān, the Word of God, and of the exegesis and of the cult recently adopted by the mass of the population, but also resulted from its having become the repository of most of the treasures of the Iranian tradition. The ancient books of history, wisdom and science, the romances, stories and fables had all been translated into Arabic and they were known to educated Iranians much more from these translations than from the original works in Middle Persian. Even some Arabic poetry was, as it seems, permeated with the influence of Sāsānian poetry. In the 3rd/9th century, with the exception of those works which were strictly Mazdaean, there was probably nothing of importance to be found in Middle Persian texts which was not available, more conveniently, in Arabic. Arabic literature was therefore not foreign to the Iranians: they contributed to it themselves as translators and as original writers and it is known that many of the greatest "Arabic" writers and scholars were Iranians. In the Golden Age of 'Abbāsid civilization Arabic literature no longer belonged to the Arabs alone, but was the common property of the peoples of the caliphate, among whom Iranians played a leading part. It offered them riches obtained from various sources, Arab, Iranian, Greek and Syriac, and all alike rediscovered and reanimated their own traditions, renewing them with those of their neighbours. This does not mean that the peoples were blended and lost their separate identities; far from it. The controversy of the Shu'ūbiyya provides a striking demonstration of the extent to which the Iranians were aware of their own ethnic affiliations, when they came up against the Arabs. This "national" consciousness did not, however, manifest itself in the sphere of language; linguistic nationalism is a modern invention and did not exist in those days, as is best proved by the fact that the arguments of the Shu'ūbites were all conducted in Arabic. The Arabic language was the instrument which the most ardent Iranian partisans used quite naturally and to the same degree as their opponents in discussing their ideas.

Linguistic usage in Iran in about the 3rd/9th century may be summed up as follows: there were two languages in use all over Iran at the same time on different levels. One of them, darī, was used, but only in speech, by the bulk of the population; the other, Arabic, was the medium of religion and the administration, of science and of literature, being written and spoken only by educated people. This situation was to continue in some degree even after the emergence of Persian literature: in the 4th/10th century Persian and Arabic poetry flourished side by side at the courts of Khurāsān and for a long time afterwards Arabic remained the chief instrument of science and of philosophy. There was nothing exceptional about such a state of affairs in the Middle Ages – similar conditions prevailed in the countries of western Europe, where Latin, the educated language, was superimposed on the common speech, which was only gradually promoted to nobler usage.

Side by side with the highly cultivated literature in Arabic, however, there also existed an oral literature in the common parlances, repository of the Sāsānian tradition. It is now known that pre-Islamic Iran possessed some brilliant poetry, although the extant traces of it remained unrecognized for a long time. The reason why only minute fragments have survived is, as M. Boyce has pointed out, because this poetry was oral. It was composed by professional minstrels, poet-musicians who sang at the royal and seigneurial courts and also at gatherings of all kinds and at all levels of society. Parthia was a particularly active centre of this kind of poetic production. The beautiful poems in Parthian devoted to the Manichaean religion, of which numerous fragments have been found by archaeologists, must surely have been based on an elaborate tradition. Moreover the Parthian minstrels (*gōsān*) remained famous for a very long time. From miscellaneous indirect evidence it may be inferred that "the gōsān played a considerable part in the life of the Parthians and their neighbours, down to late in the Sāsānian epoch: entertainer of king and commoner, privileged at court and popular with the people; present at the graveside and at the feast; eulogist, satirist, story-teller, musician; recorder of past achievements, and commentator of his own times".[1] There was also, however, poetry in Persian (Middle Persian or darī) as is testified by some pieces preserved in Pahlavī literature and by fragments

[1] Boyce, "The Parthian *gōsān*", pp. 17–18.

transcribed into Arabic script, particularly the hymn of the fire-altar of Karkūy, quoted in the *Tārīkh-i Sīstān*, if it really dates from the pre-Islamic period. The surest piece of evidence, and the most interesting, is a short passage discovered recently by Shafīʿī Kadkanī in a work of Ibn Khurdādbih (d. 230/844) which runs as follows:

Qaiṣar māh mānadh u Khāqān xurshēdh
ān i man xudhāy abr mānadh kāmghārān
ka xᵛāhadh māh pōshadh ka xᵛāhadh xurshēdh

The Qaiṣar is like unto the moon and the Khāqān to the sun.
My lord is like unto the cloud all-powerful:
At will he veils the moon and at will the sun.

This fragment is attributed to Bārbad, a famous minstrel of the time of Khusrau II Parvīz.[1] In any case the content makes it clear that it belongs to the Sāsānian period.

After the Arab conquest this poetry inevitably declined, giving way in the princely courts to Arabic poetry. There is nothing, however, to indicate that it disappeared; on the contrary, everything suggests that it persisted in lower levels of society. Since it had been so much appreciated by all classes in pre-Islamic times, it is hard to imagine that it did not survive afterwards among the masses for whom Arabic remained a foreign language. It continued to exist among the people and probably also in the courts of local lords, the *dihqāns*, who were deeply attached to tradition. In fact several short pieces handed down from various sources afford proof of its existence. One of them, *āb-ast-u nabīdh-ast*..., has been attributed to the Arab poet Yazīd b. Mufarrigh, who is said to have composed it extempore at Baṣra during the years 60–4/679–84. Another poem, *az Khuttalān āmadīh*..., is a satirical piece addressed by the inhabitants of Balkh to a defeated amīr in 108/726–7 or 119/737–8; a third, *Samarqand-i kandmand*..., which seems to be a lament on the ruin of Samarqand, is attributed to about the year 200/815–16, and another, *āhū-i kūhī*..., also appears to be of very early date. These pieces, whose versification apparently belongs to the same type as pre-Islamic poetry, are in darī. The places mentioned (Khūzistān, Bactriana, Transoxiana) suggest that this popular or semi-popular poetry in darī was cultivated practically everywhere in the land of Iran.

[1] "Kuhantarīn namūna-yi shiʿr-i fārsī".

IV. THE EMERGENCE OF THE NEW PERSIAN LITERARY LANGUAGE

The emergence of Persian literature involved the elevation of a widely distributed oral language, darī, to the rank of a language of general culture. This process took at least two centuries, from the 3rd/9th to the 5th/11th, in the course of which literary Persian was progressively extended from popular poetry to poetry of an elevated style and thence to science and administration; its territory was likewise enlarged from Eastern Iran to the regions of the West. At the same time it must itself have undergone a relative unification and stabilization. The darī in everyday use was, as has been seen, subject to variations in numerous local dialects. The literary language was originally based on the colloquial forms of speech of the East, in particular those of Transoxiana, where poetry was first cultivated, as is shown by its vocabulary, which contains many local words unknown in other parts of Iran. The earliest extant Persian dictionary, the *Lug͟hat-i furs* of Asadī, was compiled towards the middle of the 5th/11th century precisely with the object of explaining these words to readers belonging to Western Iran. The author gives a brief explanation of his aim, stating in the introduction that he has encountered poets of merit "with little knowledge of Persian words". This assertion, which at first sight seems surprising, is corroborated by Nāṣir-i K͟husrau, a poet and writer from Bactriana, who relates in his celebrated *Safar-nāma* that in 437/1045 he met in Tabrīz Qaṭrān, "a good poet, but one who did not know Persian very well", and that he was obliged to explain to him the *dīvāns* of Daqīqī and of Munjīk – meaning that Qaṭrān, although expert himself in manipulating the language of literature, was not familiar with the local expressions which occurred in the work of the earliest poets of K͟hurāsān and of Transoxiana. This interesting observation, together with the dictionary of Asadī, bears witness to the local idiosyncrasies of Eastern origin which were originally contained in the literary language. These were later discarded, while the language was probably enriched with elements drawn from other dialects, not to mention innumerable loans from Arabic, and so became the cultivated language of the whole of Iran.

It is of course not known at what period darī first came to be written. In the Middle Ages, as we know, script, much more than language, was connected with religion. At a very early date the Jews were writing darī in Hebrew characters; the inscriptions of Tang-i Azao in Afghanistan of A.D. 752–3 and a fragment of a private letter found at Dandan-Uiliq near Khotan in Chinese Turkestan, also attributed to the 2nd/8th century, appear to be the earliest records of New Persian in any script. The Christians used the Syriac script, as is proved by a fragment of a Persian translation of the Psalms found at Turfan, undated but also very early. From the same oasis come several fragments in New Persian and in Manichaean script, copied in the first half of the 4th/10th century or earlier by the communities of Central Asia. It is also likely that the Iranian Muslims, when they were not sufficiently well educated to use the Arabic language, had long before the introduction of literature written down their own language in Arabic script to serve their practical needs, private correspondence or business accounts. Such practices no doubt involved many fluctuations in spelling, traces of which can still be found in the Persian words and names quoted by Arab authors.

The only detailed account of the origin of literary poetry is that given in the *Tārīkh-i Sīstān*. Being a local chronicle this book naturally aimed at exalting the glories and merits of its own province and is thus limited to a small area. It cannot be expected to supply information which is valid for the whole of Iran. Although the verses quoted seem more authentic because of the clumsy style and the metrical irregularities, we cannot be sure that Muḥammad b. Vaṣīf was the very first poet to compose a poem (a *qaṣīda*) in Persian on the Arabic model. It is likely that similar attempts were made elsewhere at about the same time or a little before: Ḥanẓala of Bādghīs seems to be of earlier date and, for various reasons which will be considered later, it may be inferred that these early efforts were themselves the result of a long preparation.

The account given in the *Tārīkh-i Sīstān*, however, reveals certain aspects of the conditions of the emergence of Persian poetry of the classical type. The scene was the court of an Iranian king, Ya'qūb b. al-Laith: a panegyric in Arabic was rejected by this prince, who did not understand the language. Muḥammad b. Vaṣīf was thus obliged to seek another means of celebrating his patron in verse and it was then that he ventured to compose a qaṣīda in Persian. Now there was already another kind of poetry in Persian: the popular or semipopular poetry which must have existed in Sīstān as elsewhere, and it may be asked why, failing Arabic, no recourse was made to it. The reason is that, precisely because of its popular nature, it was unsuitable for singing the praises of a great king. Muḥammad b. Vaṣīf, who was a secretary, nurtured on Arabic literature, must have been particularly sensitive to the difference in dignity and suitability between the noble Arabic poetry and this literature which was considered scarcely more than folklore; it was accordingly necessary for him to create a new medium.

It is quite possible that the same circumstances may have arisen elsewhere, perhaps at an earlier date, in the courts of less important potentates. There is nothing surprising in the fact that these experimental pieces have not been preserved for posterity; that of Muḥammad b. Vaṣīf is known only from a book of local interest, the sole manuscript of which was long afterwards discovered by a fortunate chance. It may be conjectured that the new poetry, written in darī but borrowing its verse-forms from Arabic literature, made its first appearance in the obscure courts of local princes. Ḥanẓala of Bādghīs, the first poet commemorated by the anthologies, seems himself to have been known chiefly in his own province. The *Chahār maqāla* indeed relates that it was a couplet of Ḥanẓala which fired the ambition of the adventurer Aḥmad b. ʻAbd-Allāh Khujistānī; he was, however, a compatriot of Ḥanẓala, Khujistān being a district of the province of Bādghīs, in the region of Herāt, and it was actually in his own country, according to the *Chahār maqāla*, that he read the dīvān of the poet. Thus it may be concluded that the latter exercised his talent within his own native territory and that his fame can scarcely have crossed its frontiers. Ḥanẓala in Bādghīs and Muḥammad b. Vaṣīf in Sīstān were therefore local poets and they are the only ones whose names have been preserved, but others like them were probably to be found in Eastern Iran in the 3rd/9th century: such men were the creators of Persian poetry for Iranian patrons who had little knowledge of Arabic but wished to imitate persons of importance and like them to be praised in a noble style.

It may be asked why Persian literature first appeared in the East and why its development was confined to Khurāsān and Transoxiana until about the end of the 4th/10th century. The explanation usually given is that it was obviously due to the distance of these regions from the capital and the existence of Iranian dynasties which were practically independent of the caliph. Princes, especially the Sāmānids, are credited with the desire to promote a "national" literature, but such a desire, if it existed, could not have been the sole or even the principal factor, since it could come into being only as the result of a strong collective movement deeply-rooted in social conditions. The political aspect is less important than the remoteness from the centres of culture of the caliphate. In Fārs and Jibāl the relationship with these centres, particularly with Baghdad, was much closer and the country was certainly much more affected by Arab influence. In the east, on the contrary there existed a whole class of dihqāns who were not only devoted to the memory of ancient Iran but were very little touched by Arab culture. It was probably under their patronage that there was a gradual development of a poetry which was at the same time modelled on the ceremonial Arabic compositions and nurtured by Iranian traditions preserved in popular and semi-popular verse.

Another factor could also have contributed to this development. In the west, at any rate in Fārs, literature in Middle Persian was still flourishing in the 3rd/9th century. The Mazdaeans occupied an important place in society there and retained considerable power. A well-organized class of mōbads preserved the legacy of the past within the rigid conventions of the Sāsānian tradition and when they wrote it was in Middle Persian, a language supported by its old prestige. Thus while Arabic was widely used by the aristocracy, the intelligentsia and the Arabs, who were quite numerous in the towns, Middle Persian was the medium of that ancient culture which was now desperately defended by the mōbads, and between them there was little room for a new literary language based on the vernacular. The situation was quite different in the east, especially in the north-east, where darī did not have to face powerful competition of this kind. The use and knowledge of Arabic were less widespread and there was certainly no Iranian literary language still sufficiently vigorous to prevent the formation of a new medium arising out of the spoken language. Mazdaism had not been so strongly rooted there and although communities survived down to the 3rd/9th and 4th/10th centuries, at this period it was much enfeebled, so that there existed no clerical caste able to maintain the tradition of Middle Persian. The purely Iranian culture was not the privilege of clerics and lived on not in the form of dogmatic writings but to a large extent orally with narratives and poems in darī. As a semi-popular culture, it was opposed to the Arabic-inspired culture of the high aristocracy and in order to take its place beside the latter it needed only to produce works in the noble genres.

To sum up: the use of the Persian language for literature appears to have originated in the following manner:

(1) Persian poetry, that is to say the noble poetry in darī as distinct from the traditional oral poetry, began as court poetry.

(2) It came into being in local courts, where the language was darī and Arabic was either unknown or little known by the princes and their entourage.

(3) This process occurred in the eastern provinces because the country was much less impregnated by Arab culture and also because there darī did not have to compete, as in western Iran, with the ancient Iranian literary language.

(4) This poetry, which was at first exclusively lyrical (panegyric) imitated Arabic models, although it may also have been subject, in both form and content, to the influence of oral Iranian literature, a point which will be considered later.

Darī became the new literary language of Iran because it was the most widely known. The same conditions, however, which saw the emergence of Persian literature also inspired literary composition in other dialects, in places where they were sufficiently vigorous. Such output occurred chiefly in regions around the Caspian, which, being geographically isolated, were late to come under the influence of Islam and the Arab world, and which in any case had always been centres of pronounced individualism, so that it is not surprising that they were also centres of a certain amount of literary activity in the local idiom. The date when this activity began is not known, but it was perhaps inspired by the example of Persian literature. The work of a Māzandarānī poet, Amīr Pāzvārī, has survived and the names are known of two works by Marzubān b. Rustam b. Sharvīn, a prince of Ṭabaristān who lived in the 4th/10th century: the *Marzubān-nāma*, a collection of stories which was adapted into Persian by Varāvīnī in the 7th/13th century, and a book of verse entitled *Nīkī-nāma*. A whole group of writers using the same dialect lived at the court of Qābūs b. Vushmgīr (366–403/976–1012), the famous scholar-prince of Ṭabaristān. Similar ventures occurred also in Jibāl: Bundār (or Pindār) of Ray (d. 401/1010) wrote verse in the dialect of his city and a little later Bābā Ṭāhir used a kind of Persian characterized by traces of dialect. The existence of a dialect poetry in this region is not at all surprising. As late as the 7th/13th century the author of a treatise on versification, Shams-i Qais of Ray, emphasized the fondness of the inhabitants of (Persian) Iraq for their local poetry (*fahlawiyyāt*) and it is quite possible that it was the means by which the tradition of the splendid Parthian poetry (pahlavī in the true and original sense of the term) was continued down the centuries.

These literary experiments in dialect which occurred in about the 4th/10th century were scarcely followed up in later times. Various Persian writers, including some of the most important, made use on occasion of dialect, but only for satirical or humorous verse, that is to say in a colloquial kind of writing which had nothing to do with poetry of the exalted style. In the beginning these dialects could perhaps have competed with Persian, but soon the conflict became too unequal between the idiom limited to its own province and the general language which permeated all the countries of Iran. After the flourishing of Persian poetry under the Sāmānids, once its first masterpieces had established its supremacy, literature in dialect was confined to folklore.

V. THE ORIGIN OF THE FORMS AND THEMES OF PERSIAN POETRY

The appearance of New Persian literature is usually represented as the most obvious sign of an Iranian renaissance after an eclipse of at least two centuries, during which Arab culture reigned alone. According to another interpretation, it was not so much a renaissance as the birth of a culture which was completely new and Islamic and was scarcely connected at all with ancient Iran. Should we say renaissance or new birth, continuation or break with the past? In the light of present knowledge, this way of viewing the problem seems to be an over-simplification. Despite the upheaval of the Arab conquest with its destruction of the Sāsānian political structure, despite the social changes caused by the presence of the invaders and the economic development which took place during the first centuries under the caliphate, despite also the ideological revolution which resulted from the influence of Islam, Iranian culture did not disappear but was modified in its content, so as to give an important place to Islam, and in its form, as a consequence of the adoption of the Arabic language. The Iranians did not sink into barbarism, nor even into silence, for three centuries, but shared in the intensive efforts which produced the new civilization of the Islamic East and were among the most energetic contributors to this burst of activity, infusing into it a large part of their ancient culture. At the same time certain aspects of this culture, more or less Islamicized, survived at the humbler level of oral literature. It was in this soil that literature in darī was brought forth, being unquestionably inspired by Arabic models, but also fertilized by local traditions. It was neither a pure and simple resurgence of the ancient culture nor the expression of an entirely fresh culture of Arab-Islamic origin. The links with ancient Iran had been established partly perhaps by such of the Middle Persian writings as were still being read, but surely much more by what had been handed down to Arabic literature and by what still remained, more or less modified and brought up to date, in the living oral tradition. It is in these two sources, Arabic literature and oral Iranian literature, that the origin of the forms and themes of Persian poetry must be sought.

The question of form is outside the scope of this chapter, and discussion of it here will be confined to a few observations. From the techniques of pre-Islamic Iranian poetry to those of Persian poetry the distance is considerable. In the one there is accentual unrhyming verse, in the other quantitative verse, that is to say verse based on a definite succession of long and short syllables, arranged in poems of fixed form. The chief lyrical verse-form, the qaṣīda, was certainly borrowed from Arabic poetry, and it is extremely probable that the principle of quantitative versification and the use of rhyme were directly inspired by it. It would indeed be very unlikely for Iran to have developed this quantitative poetry independently, since there was no sign of it in the pre-Islamic period and since numerous Arabic examples were at hand. The same argument may be applied to rhyme, although it occurs in two Middle Persian poems; one of them, however, definitely belongs to the Islamic era and there is no certainty that the other is any earlier. It is possible that the traditional poetry was familiar with certain devices of rhyme or assonance (they are to be found in the pieces of folk-lore type mentioned above and in the hymn of the fire-altar of Karkūy), but the use of a single rhyme in a long poem and the appearance of this rhyme at the end of each couplet (*bait*) and not of each line (*miṣrā'*) conform too closely to the rules of Arabic poetry not to have been directly imitated.

The differences between Arabic and Persian versification are, however, great. On the one hand certain classes of poems, such as the *mat͟hnavī* and the *rubā'ī*, are widely used in Persian but not in Arabic, which suggests an Iranian origin and also demonstrates that the founders of Persian poetry did not restrict themselves to imitation, but also worked creatively. On the other hand, a discrepancy which is more subtle and perhaps even more significant, the usual metres of each language, although described by theorists by means of the same concepts and the same technical terms, do not in general tally. If New Persian versification is, like the Arabic, quantitative and is actually an imitation of it, the types of verse are in fact different; although the principle is the same, it is not applied in the same way in each case. Persian metres therefore are an original invention, imposed by the phonetic structure of the language, and all the evidence points to the conclusion that this invention did not occur *ex nihilo* but was largely inspired by the traditional Iranian rhythmic patterns, a view which was indeed held and expressed as early as 1932 by E. Benveniste: "L'originalité des Persans en matière de technique poétique a consisté à assujettir le mètre syllabique iranien à la prosodie quantitative arabe. De cette adaptation, dont l'exemple le plus ancien et le plus achevé est le *mutaqārib* épique, sort la poésie noble de la Perse moderne."[1]

So there are grounds for seeking the origin of the various types of New Persian verse in the versification of pre-Islamic Iran, which unfortunately is too little known for the precise genealogical relationship to be understood: it would be necessary to define exactly the analogies between a given New Persian quantitative metre and a given type of accentual verse in the ancient poetry. There are only a few instances in which it is possible to form an idea of the connection: for example, the metre of the rubā'ī, which has no parallel in Arabic poetry and stands in isolation in the Arabic–Persian metrical system, might well be an adaptation of the type of (non-quantitative) verse represented by the poem *āhū-i kūhī*, which certainly belongs to traditional poetry. It is also possible that several quantitative metres are derived from the same type of accentual verse and that, conversely, several accentual types may have given rise to one and the same metre, for, since the principles are different, it cannot be expected that there will be close conformity in detail. The essential fact remains that the dominant features of the traditional rhythmic patterns must have been taken over as the framework of New Persian versification. These rhythms, in their ancient form, were still alive in oral poetry, probably without alteration, for the language did not undergo any important modification between the 1st/7th and the 3rd/9th centuries. They were certainly well known to the creators of Persian poetry, whose function it was to mould from them new types of verse based on the quantitative principle.

It is a long way from the non-rhyming accentual poem to the qaṣīda and numerous tentative experiments must have preceded the standard-

[1] *Journal Asiatique*, vol. CCXX, no. 2 (avril–juin 1932), p. 293.

ization of the rules of metre, prosody and rhyme. It is still possible to find traces of intermediate forms. Metrical irregularities not infrequently occur in the earliest examples of Persian poetry; they must originally have been more numerous, for the copyists have certainly eliminated a number of them. Some have persisted in popular poetry even to the present day: for example, lines of the quatrains (*dubaitī*) in their first syllables show a wavering between long and short which is alien to the classical metrical system. As regards rhyme, the rules deal with its phonetic form (simple assonance not being allowed), with its position within the poem (rhyming couplets in the mat͟hnavī, a single rhyme appearing at the end of each couplet in the lyrical forms) and the kind of words to be used (the same word may not be rhymed a second time in the same poem). These rules are infringed in several early pieces: the two poems in Middle Persian discovered by Henning and Tavadia, the hymn of the fire-altar of Karkūy contained in the *Tārīk͟h-i Sīstān*, which is perhaps a transcription from Middle Persian, and two poems in New Persian and in quantitative verse (not without irregularities) which are quoted in the *Tuḥfat al-mulūk* of ʿAlī b. Abī Ḥafṣ Iṣfahānī (7th/13th century) and certainly date from an early period. From these various pieces it is possible to form an idea of some of the stages in the progress of poetry from the pre-Islamic type towards classical poetry. Broadly speaking, the evolution must have proceeded as follows:

(1) Unrhymed accentual versification (pre-Islamic poetry).

(2) Accentual versification with rhymes which are irregular in relation to the classical system (poems in Middle Persian found by Henning and Tavadia, hymn of Karkūy).

(3) Irregular quantitative versification with irregular rhymes (New Persian poems of *Tuḥfat al-mulūk*).

(4) Irregular quantitative versification with regular rhymes (early examples of Persian poetry, popular quatrains).

(5) Regular quantitative versification with regular rhymes (classical poetry).

Thus, as regards its forms, Persian poetry is indebted both to Arabic literature and to the Iranian tradition. The same holds good of its content. In lyrical poetry the content appears to be identical with that of contemporary Arab poetry; detailed studies of subject-matter are still lacking, however, and they might perhaps reveal shades of difference, at present overlooked, in the choice of themes and their importance in relation to one another. It is doubtful, nevertheless, whether the list of subjects would be appreciably different, which is hardly surprising, for at the time when Persian poetry first developed in Eastern Iran, Arabic poetry continued to be in vogue. The courts of the Sāmānid amīrs and of their vassals were frequented by numerous Arabic-speaking poets and Tha'ālibī was able to present a brilliant picture of their activity. Towards the end of the 4th/10th century the amīr Qābūs b. Vushmgīr at Gurgān and the vizier 'Ismā'īl b. 'Abbād at Ray, themselves men of letters, were both patrons of Arabic learning and at the same time of Persian learning, which was then making its first appearance in those regions. Poets writing in Persian and in Arabic attended the same courts and had the same patrons – in fact they were themselves often the same person. Bilingual poets were numerous, such as, to mention only a few examples, Shahīd, Mus'abī, Murādī, Āghājī, Khusravī, Abu'l-Fatḥ of Bust, Rābi'a of Quṣdār, Kisā'ī, Bundār of Ray; nor must Muḥammad b. Vaṣīf, the innovator of Sīstān, be forgotten; as M. I. Zand says, "The poet who wrote his works in both Arabic and Pārsī, the poet *dhū-lisānain* . . . who commanded two languages . . . was a characteristic figure of those times." Since lyrical poetry both in Arabic and in Persian was addressed, at least in aristocratic circles, to the same audiences and readers and often shared the same authors, it naturally dealt with the same subjects, in the same way. It is obvious that the Arabic lyric imposed its patterns upon the Persian.

In Persian literature, epic poetry is at the opposite pole to lyric poetry. This genre, unknown in Arabic, is completely Iranian and illustrates in the clearest fashion the continuity between pre-Islamic literature and that of Muslim Iran. The subject-matter, even when transmitted partly by means of historians writing in Arabic, is entirely traditional, a fact which is so evident that it need not be emphasized. Another respect in which Persian poetry is connected with the ancient Iranian culture, by ties which are less apparent though very strong, is through ethical thought, expressed not only in many passages of the "Book of Kings" but also in specific works like those of Abū Shukūr (4th/10th century) and even in many verses of the lyrical poets. A whole body of practical rules and advice based on the conception of *khirad* (moral intelligence, innate ability to perceive good and evil) and on a sense of the transience of the things of this world was for a long time to inspire a considerable part of Persian literature. It was influenced very little by Islam and certainly had Iranian roots which were as ancient as they were deep.

Even some of the more important subjects of lyrical verse are not without parallel in ancient Iranian literature. Descriptions of nature and of the seasons, which are the daily bread of Persian poetry of the 4th/10th and 5th/11th centuries, also furnish the theme of some charming verses among the fragments recovered from Manichaean writings. Iranian festivals such as the *naurūz* and the *mihragān* must certainly have been celebrated in verse under the Sāsānians as they were under their Muslim successors; a specimen of this poetry is perhaps recognizable in the speech of the great mōbad quoted by the *Naurūz-nāma*, which seems indeed to have been transcribed from Middle Persian. The glorification of wine, a completely non-Islamic theme, is too much in accordance with the references to it in Middle Persian prose texts and with what is known of court life in the Sāsānian period not to have been the subject of poetry at that time. Even panegyric has its Iranian antecedents, as is proved by the piece attributed to Bārbad and quoted above (*Qaiṣar māh mānadh* . . .); the image would take its place quite naturally in the panegyric part of a New Persian qaṣīda.

All these themes existed of course in Arabic poetry of the ʿAbbāsid period; they had probably been introduced partly under the influence of the Iranian civilization. On the other hand it may be stated without much risk of error that they also survived in oral poetry in darī and in the dialects. They were thus available on all sides to the founders of Persian poetry, who did not have to invent them, but needed only to find suitable methods for developing and harmonizing them, that is to say to invent a rhetorical system.

It is a surprising fact that this rhetoric makes its appearance, at the middle of the 3rd/9th century, fully formed from the outset. In fact, even though the verses of Muḥammad b. Vaṣīf and of his emulators in Sīstān show signs of the clumsiness and rigidity of style which are to be expected in an art which is still "primitive", the poetry of the earliest authors quoted by the anthologies shows an astonishing mastery. The two couplets by Ḥanẓala of Bādghīs reveal a notable maturity, and Fīrūz Mashriqī, who followed him a little later, provides some good examples of very well constructed verse. In a piece like the following,

> The harp, saddened by the rose, raises her voice in lament.
> With hair dishevelled she rends her face with her nails.

The bottle now prostrates itself in prayer
Now a gulp of blood pours forth from its heart,

the description makes use of images which are truly classical, such as the personification of inanimate objects and subtle metaphors. It may be suspected that such verses have been touched up by the copyists or the anthologists, but not to the extent of being entirely rewritten. The imagery certainly belongs to the original and suggests that the poet already had at his disposal a craft elaborated by his predecessors. Here again it is apparent that the first examples of Persian poetry represent the culmination of preparatory labours which had called for repeated and prolonged efforts by a number of obscure creative writers.

VI. LYRICAL POETRY

Since Persian poetry originated in courts for the glorification of Iranian princes, lyrical poetry was the first genre to appear. Its *raison d'être* was the panegyric and its form the qaṣīda, in imitation of Arabic poetry for which it began as a substitute and which it was soon to rival. Without doubt it was generously cultivated under the patronage of the Sāmānid amīrs at Bukhārā, which was a brilliant literary centre, and also under certain vassal princes, such as Fakhr al-Daula Abu'l-Muẓaffar, amīr of Chaghāniyān (second half of the 4th/10th century), who was the patron of Daqīqī and of Munjīk and whose fame as a benefactor to learning attracted Farrukhī at the start of his career. From all this activity, however, up to the end of the 4th/10th century, there remain only fragments, short pieces or isolated verses quoted in the anthologies and dictionaries which, if they do not impart full knowledge, give an inkling of the talent or stature of the poets of this period. The evidence of later times is as important here as the works themselves, or rather the little that remains of them. Farrukhī, Manūchihrī, Mu'izzī and other later poets recall with respect and admiration some of their predecessors of the 4th/10th century. This period left to posterity the memory of a kind of Golden Age, of munificent kings heaping unheard-of favours upon the panegyrists who had succeeded in pleasing them. Even when allowance is made for legend, the fact remains that this fame is not unfounded: the Sāmānids and certain of their vassals gave powerful support to the upsurge of Persian poetry.

The most impressive figure among these poets is Rūdakī (d. 329/940–1), to whom tradition attributes a considerable output and an important influence on the mind of the king Naṣr I b. Aḥmad. Poets of his own time paid homage to his genius and he was regarded as the father of Persian poetry. In fact, as has been observed, the themes and the forms had already been established before him, but he doubtless gave to them a breadth and a brilliance hitherto unknown. One of his contemporaries from western Iran, Abū Ḥātim of Ray (d. 322/934), who wrote in Arabic but probably knew Persian, stated contemptuously: "What has recently been created in Persian by way of poetry is only talk without meaning, without titles and without usefulness: there is no dīvān among the Persians",[1] a remark which proves that the predecessors of Rūdakī had not yet succeeded in bringing their work to the notice of literary circles and having it recognized as true literature. After him, however, it had become an accomplished fact. The fragments of his poems which have survived make it possible to surmise the reason for his reputation. They reveal a generous disposition and a free and brilliant style, in which nobility is allied to simplicity.

The poets of the Sāmānid epoch mentioned in the anthologies are quite numerous, and the isolated verses or fragments of poems which have been preserved give some idea of the general features of that poetry but not, usually, of the personality of the individual authors. It is possible, however, to discern some characteristics of several of the contemporaries or successors of Rūdakī. Shahīd of Balkh was older than Rūdakī, who composed a funeral elegy on his death. He was a poet who wrote in both Persian and Arabic and also a philosopher, known as such because of a controversy in which he engaged with Abū Zakariyyā' Rāzī (Rhazes) on the nature of pleasure. The appearance of a personality like Shahīd in the early days of Persian poetry suggests that poetry was not simply the work of "entertainers" concerned solely with pleasing their patrons by some happy verbal invention. It could contain more serious thought and some verses by Shahīd, Rūdakī and others reveal an inspiration both philosophical and religious. Such preoccupations played an important part during the reign of Naṣr I b. Aḥmad, under the influence of Ismā'īlism which was active in propaganda and had succeeded in gaining the favour of the sovereign, and they must to some extent have left their mark on the Persian poetry of the day. Further evidence is to be found in the curious qaṣīda of the Ismā'īlī Abu'l-Haitham of Gurgān, a kind of catalogue in verse of philosophical questions designed to stimulate reflection, with commen-

[1] *Kitāb al-zīna, op. cit.*, pp. 122–3.

taries in prose firstly by an anonymous disciple of Abu'l-Haitham and later by Nāṣir-i Khusrau.

Daqīqī (d. between 365/975 and 370/980), well known as a predecessor of Firdausī in the creation of epic poetry, was also one of the most talented lyrical poets of this period. He appears to have made an important contribution to the development of rhetoric and himself declared in verse:

Panegyric was bare when he came to me;
I gave him all his finery.
Now decked in cloak and robe goes he.

He is mentioned with reverence by his successors. Abu'l-'Abbās of Rabinjan (*fl.* 331/943) seems to stand apart from the poets of his time: most of the verses preserved are satirical and recall the humble realities of daily life. Satirical inspiration also has an important place in the work of Munjīk of Tirmidh (about the end of the 4th/10th century), who was equally famous as a panegyrist. Rābi'a of Quṣdār was the first poetess of the Persian language and the author of love-poems of a touching sincerity. Kisā'ī of Marv (b. 341/953, died at an advanced age), after singing the praises of the Sāmānids and of Sulṭān Maḥmūd of Ghazna, turned later to religious poetry of Shī'ī inspiration and was the first to compose poems glorifying the twelve Imāms.

The western regions of Iran had remained devoted exclusively to Arabic literature until about the middle of the 4th/10th century. At this period the literary movement which had originated in Khurāsān spread westward to the courts of Qabūs b. Vushmgīr, the Ziyārid amīr of Gurgān (366–403/976–1012) and of Majd al-Daula, the Būyid prince of Ray, whose vizier, the Ṣāḥib Ismā'īl b. 'Abbād (367–85/977–95), the protector and cultivator of Arab learning, also gave encouragement to Persian poetry. The output from Gurgān and from Ray is known only from fragments but seems, so far as can be judged, to have come particularly under the influence of Arab rhetoric. Manṭiqī of Ray, for example, one of the protégés of the Ṣāḥib who appreciated his work, is found to have indulged in subtle figures of speech, in contrast with the simplicity of the early masters. This taste for artifice is perhaps less a characteristic of the poet himself than of the court of Ray, where refinements of style were highly esteemed. It was before the Ṣāḥib that Badī' al-Zamān al-Hamadānī, the future author of the *Maqāmāt* in Arabic, famous for their florid style, made his first appearance.

At the beginning of the 5th/11th century the centre of Persian literary life was transferred to Ghazna. Poets were naturally attracted by the brilliance of the court of the most powerful prince of the day and by the hope of obtaining greater honours and more ample rewards from him than from amīrs of lesser importance. This concentration of literary men and scientists at Ghazna, however (according to legend the poets alone numbered four hundred), also resulted from the deliberate policy of Maḥmūd, who realized the importance of associating intellectual prestige with political and military power. He gathered around him, whether they liked it or not, a large proportion of the best poets and the greatest minds of his time. This attention paid to what is now called propaganda was rewarded by the legendary popularity which clung to his name in the Persian literary tradition and even in folklore. Maḥmūd created the title and the office of *malik al-shu'arā*, "prince of poets", which implies some organization of poetical activities at court. In fact the output was abundant and brilliant. While the works of the previous century seem to have been lost very early, those of some of the poets belonging to this first Ghaznavid period have remained as models of the style known as *khurāsānī* which lyrical poetry followed until the 7th/13th century.

The most famous poet of the time of Maḥmūd was 'Unsurī of Balkh (d. 431/1039–40), "prince of poets", who retained the favour of the sultan throughout his life and was the leader of a school. His dīvān, of which only quite a small part has been preserved, is of interest mainly because of his skill in panegyric. Farrukhī of Sīstān (d. 429/1037–8) is now considered to have been the best poet of the period. He excelled at describing the seasons and the aristocratic festivals in a style of noble ease infused with gaiety and provides a good example of a poet whose inspiration is in agreement, it would seem spontaneously, with the rhythm of life at court. The fact that more than nine thousand couplets from his dīvān have survived until the present day shows the extent of his popularity over the centuries. Manūchihrī of Dāmghān (d. *c.* 432/1040–1), the panegyrist of the Sulṭān Mas'ūd, son of Maḥmūd, occupies a special position slightly apart from the main stream: a lover of pre-Islamic Arabic poetry, which he imitated in several poems, he was also the author of numerous descriptions of nature, abounding in beautifully observed details relieved by ingenious comparisons and metaphors which have lost none of their charm for the modern reader. He was the first to employ, in addition to the qaṣīda, strophic forms (*musammaṭ*) which gave a new breadth to lyrical poetry. Of the work of other poets of the period there are only fragments or isolated remnants.

The themes of Persian lyrical poetry during this first period were relatively few in number. Constantly repeated and refined they impress the reader with a very special aesthetic vision of the world. Panegyric of the patron was the essential aim of the poem: it praised his fame, his power, his virtues, the happiness of his peoples, his unconquerable bravery in battle, or, if a vizier was the subject, the wisdom of his administration, and in any case certainly his inexhaustible liberality, which the poet expected to see in the form of a handsome reward. These praises were sung in an exaggerated style which very soon became the rule for this kind of poetry. It was, however, the first part of the qaṣīda, on another subject, which gave the poem lasting interest. In early Arabic poetry this first part often recalled the love of the poet for some beauty from whom nomadic life had parted him, the grief of separation and the journey, on a faithful steed, over a perilous desert. This theme is treated repeatedly by Manūchihrī, but it rarely occurs in Persian poetry, where it is purely conventional. Far more often the Persian poet takes his inspiration from life at court. He often sings of festivals, especially the great Iranian feasts, naurūz, the feast of the New Year and the spring, mihragān, the feast of autumn and the wine-harvest, *sada*, the feast of mid-winter celebrated by great fires at night. Descriptions of the seasons, of spring, autumn and winter in the country and in the gardens are usually associated with royal entertainments, at which, in pomp and luxury, the cup is handed round among the guests, to the sound of musical instruments. The glorification of wine is an important subject: sometimes the poet describes the ripening of the grape, the harvests and the miraculous transformation of the juice into a delectable wine; in other passages he invites the guests to intoxicate themselves with this vintage which dispels the cares of the world and turns a man into a superman. These themes are closely related to the aristocratic life of the time; it is sufficient to read the chronicle of Abu'l-Faḍl Baihaqī to see the importance of drinking-parties (*majlis-i sharāb*) in the lives of kings and important personages. Love is naturally not absent from this poetry: the beauty of the loved one and the grief of the lover dying of desire are described in accordance with a convention which became standardized at an early date. Among other subjects treated in the qaṣīdas or in the shorter pieces which may be either extracts from qaṣīdas or were perhaps deliberately composed as "fragments" (*qiṭ'a*), mention should be made of the enigma, in which the subject is not actually named but ingeniously implied by allusions, the funerary lament, moral reflections on the inconstancy and injustice of the world, and more personal themes such as regret for youth (a celebrated qaṣīda by Rūdakī is one of the best examples of this type), complaints by the poet about his own state and the satirising of such rivals and enemies as he could not fail to have at court.

All these subjects are treated in a language which shows marked traces of Arabic influence and reflects the great impact of Arabic models on the development of lyrical poetry in Persian.

VII. NARRATIVE AND DIDACTIC POETRY

Here we shall deal with narrative poetry, with the exception of epic poetry which will be dealt with in the next section. The difference between them depends solely on the subject-matter and its treatment, for the verse-form is the same for each. It is the mat͟hnavī, a poem in rhyming couplets, the length of which is not subject to any rules. Having much greater freedom than the qaṣīda, it lends itself to long descriptions as well as to brief anecdotes and to the exposition of moral, philosophical, mystical and even scientific reflections. Although very rare in Arabic poetry, it was widely used in Iran from the beginnings of Persian literature and occupied a position at least equal to that of lyrical poetry.

Romances and collections of stories and fables existed in the literature of pre-Islamic Iran; the most famous of them was a collection of fables of Indian origin, the *Panchatantra*. A Pahlavī version of it was produced under K͟husrau I Anūs͟hīrvān and it was translated into Arabic by Ibn al-Muqaffa' under the title of *Kalīla wa Dimna* (the names of the two jackals who were the leading characters in one of the stories). Renowned as a manual of wisdom, this same book provided the material for the first known Persian mat͟hnavī. It was rendered into verse by Rūdakī himself at the request of Abu'l-Faḍl Bal'amī, vizier to the Sāmānid Naṣr II b. Aḥmad, but the poem has unfortunately been lost, apart from some fragments. The same fate has overtaken other mat͟hnavīs composed by Rūdakī, notably a *Sindbād-nāma*, another collection of stories also of Indian origin and also transmitted in an Arabic version. The extant fragments show that Rūdakī employed the same metres which were to occur most frequently in mat͟hnavī throughout the whole of

Persian literature – *mutaqārib*, *hazaj*, *khafīf*, *ramal*; this last metre, which was used in *Kalīla* and in the *Sindbād-nāma*, and in many other poems, was also to be the metre of the great mystical poem by Jalāl al-Dīn (Maulavī), known as the "Mathnavī" *par excellence*. On this point it may be noted that the tradition had been well established from the beginning of the 4th/10th century.

The first successor of Rūdakī was Abū Shukūr of Balkh, who also composed several mathnavīs and, in particular, an *Āfarīn-nāma* (written in 333–6/944–8), a poem of moral import in which the ideas were probably illustrated by anecdotes. These works are lost, but from such verses as have been preserved it may be seen that Abu Shukūr was a direct heir to the moralizing literature of pre-Islamic times; many of the sentences which he put into verse are to be found in the Middle Persian books of *andarz*. He had an important influence on Persian didactic poetry, for the Iranians always had a taste for this moral literature and remained constant to the same source of very ancient ideas.

W. B. Henning has discovered a fragment, in Manichaean script, of a rendering in Persian verse of the famous romance of Buddhist origin *Bilauhar-u Būdāsaf* ("Barlaam and Josaphat"), which also dates from the time of Rūdakī. This piece is the single example of its kind belonging to the 4th/10th century, but in the following century 'Unsurī was the author of several verse romances, all of which have disappeared. They included a narrative, *Shādbakht-u 'ain al-ḥayāt*, which was summarized in Arabic by Bīrūnī, *Khingbut-u surkhbut*, "The white and the red idols", a local legend connected with the two great statues of Buddha which can still be seen at Bāmiyān in Afghanistan, *Vāmiq-u 'Adhrā'*, the story of two lovers which seems to have been of Hellenistic origin. Another romance, named *Varqa-u Gulshāh*, the work of a certain 'Ayyūqī, can probably also be attributed to the time of Maḥmūd of Ghazna. This poem tells a love story in an Arab setting; although rather weak in plot and in style, it is interesting as the earliest extant example of a genre destined to have a brilliant future. In the period under consideration it is especially interesting to note the diversity of origin of the narratives put into verse: Iranian, Indian, Arab and Hellenistic sources alike contributed to the making of a literary form which appears to have been very much in fashion.

The *Zarātusht-nāma*, a legendary history of Zoroaster written by a Mazdaean poet, stands somewhat apart from the main tradition. C.

Rempis has shown that this poem, which was for a long time attributed to the 7th/13th century, was actually composed by a certain Kai Kā'ūs, son of Kai Khusrau of Ray, a little before 368/978. It is thus the earliest mathnavī which has survived to the present day. Mention should also be made of one other poem of the same period but of quite a different type, the *Dānish-nāma*, "Book of Science" by Maisarī, written in 367–70/978–81, which is simply a medical treatise in verse. Without having any poetical pretensions, it is significant in providing evidence of a genre, that of scientific exposition in verse, not otherwise known to have existed in Persian at so early a date. The style of Maisarī, which is firm and clear, suggests that he was heir to an already established tradition.

VIII. EPIC POETRY

Persian epic, which is completely unique in type, consists of the recital in verse of the whole of the history, factual or imaginary, of Iran from the creation of the world to the end of the Sāsānian dynasty. It comprises elements of various origins, the most ancient of which are the old Indo-Iranian myths already recalled in the *Avesta*. Then come evocations of the periods before and after the beginning of Zoroastrian Mazdaism, a history of Alexander derived chiefly from the fictional work of the pseudo-Callisthenes and finally the history of the Sāsānians. In addition to tales of royal deeds, there are legends relating to various local heroes, the most important of which are those concerning Rustam, the prince of Sīstān who became the great champion of epic Iran. This mass of material was accumulated gradually over many centuries. Khurāsān appears to have been the principal centre of this activity, but other Iranian regions also contributed to it. Towards the end of the Sāsānian period the essential elements were collected and arranged in chronological order in a book written in Middle Persian entitled *Khwadāy-nāmag*, the "Book of Kings", the last edition of which appeared at the very end of the Sāsānian epoch under Yazdgard III (632–51). This work, which has long since disappeared, was a learned compilation. In addition to it there certainly existed a multitude of fragmentary accounts composed more freely in prose or in verse. Ḥamza al-Iṣfahanī (d. 360/970), in an interesting passage translated by Shaked, says: "As regards the Persians, their dispersed [historical] accounts and reports, and their scattered stories concerning lovers, were turned into verse for their kings, registered in books and permanently deposited in storehouses which were libraries. The number of these books assembled was so large that it cannot be specified. Most of them were lost when their kingdom disappeared, though remnants of them survived, the number of which exceeds ten thousand sheets written in their Persian script. These are poems all composed in a single metre which is similar to *rajaz*. They resemble Arabic verse by the fact that they are composed in regular metres but they differ from it by the fact that they have no rhyme." A single example has survived – the poem entitled *Yādgār ī Zarērān*, the "Memorial of Zarēr", which describes the exploits of an Iranian hero of the time of Zoroaster.

The *Khwadāy-nāmag* was translated or adapted into Arabic several times. The translation which was both the earliest and the best known was the work of Ibn al-Muqaffaʿ (d. *c.* 142/759–60). The names are recorded of eight other adaptations, complete or partial, but all have been lost. The little that is known suggests that they were subject to important variations of contents, implying that their authors had used various other sources apart from the *Khwadāy-nāmag*. With the development of New Persian literature it was inevitable that similar works in Persian should appear. Under the Sāmānids a lively interest in ancient Iran was encouraged by the amīrs themselves and certain of their vassals. Abu'l-Mu'ayyad of Balkh, also known as a poet of the time of Nūḥ II b. Manṣūr (365–87/976–97), was the author of a lengthy *Shāh-nāma*, "Book of Kings", in prose, fragments of which have survived. Of another *Shāh-nāma*, written by a certain Abū ʿAlī also of Balkh, hardly anything is known except the name. There is a little more information regarding a third work, compiled in 346/957 by order of Abū Manṣūr Muḥammad b. ʿAbd al-Razzāq, governor of the city of Ṭūs. The preface, which alone has been preserved, explains that it was put together by a college of four Zoroastrians who apparently used accounts from various sources in addition to the *Khwadāy-nāmag*.

All these works were in prose, but the notion of putting the material into verse was bound to occur before long. Indeed, this immense collection of narratives constituted the national memorial of the Iranian people and was a valuable treasure, rich in information, which it was essential to preserve. Versification could help to perpetuate it. Firdausī himself was well aware of this fact and he stated, with regard to the book of *Kalīla wa Dimna* rendered into verse by Rūdakī: "He bound together by means of metre the words of this prose work . . . For an educated reader this form lends an additional grace; for an ignorant person it is beneficial: a prose narrative (*parākanda*) disperses (*parākanad*) the recollection of it, but when it is bound together by metre (*paivasta*) it satisfies the soul and the mind."[1] Narratives which were historical or regarded as such were therefore a subject of poetry in the same way as the tales and maxims already turned into verse by Rūdakī: the mat͟hnavī was the ideal form for them. Moreover, they had already been treated in poetry in Middle Persian. Many of them certainly remained very popular and continued to be circulated in oral literature: there is no reason why some of them should not have been in verse. The existence of epic poems based on folklore among the Kurds and the Baluc͟hīs of the present day makes this a probable hypothesis. It is known, moreover, that elegies on the death of the hero Siyāvus͟h were sung at Buk͟hārā by popular minstrels.

The first poem of this kind in New Persian mentioned in our sources was composed by a certain Mas'ūdī of Marv, probably near the beginning of the 4th/10th century; the three couplets which remain and several allusions to it indicate that it embraced all the traditional history of the kings of Iran from their origin to the end of the Sāsānian dynasty, but its precise extent is not known. It is said to have been held in great esteem among the Iranians. Several decades later Daqīqī in his turn undertook the composition of a *S͟hāh-nāma* in verse, but the work was cut short by his premature death. About a thousand couplets of it, telling of the preaching of Zoroaster under king Gus͟htāsp, were preserved by Firdausī and incorporated into his own poem. It is known from Bīrūnī that Daqīqī composed more than this. His epic talent has been assessed in varying terms by the experts, some of them finding him dull and dry, compared with his great successor, while others perceive scarcely any differences of style between the passage by Daqīqī and the rest of the *S͟hāh-nāma*. It is certain in any case that the epic style was already well established before Firdausī. The *mutaqārib* metre employed by Daqīqī remained the only one used in epic and the language was clearly differentiated from that of lyrical poetry: it was much less arabicized, and instead was full of archaic Iranian words, which were probably already no longer in daily use at that time. This low proportion of Arabic vocabulary was also a feature of prose works on the same subjects, to judge from the preface to the *S͟hāh-nāma* of Abū Manṣūr. These particular characteristics of the language of epic

[1] *S͟hāh-nāma*, p. 2507.

were most likely the result of the influence of Middle Persian sources and perhaps also of the influence of the oral tradition.

Firdausī (b. between 320/932 and 330/941–2; d. 411/1020–1 or 416/1025–6), dihqān of the neighbourhood of Ṭūs, began his work in about 365/975–6 and finished it probably in 400/1009–10; the whole poem amounts to some fifty thousand couplets. After being supported in his work by members of the aristocracy of his native city, the poet sought the patronage of the Sulṭān Maḥmūd of G͟hazna, when the latter had become the most powerful sovereign of the age. General hearsay and the more reliable but less specific indications furnished by the *S͟hāh-nāma* suggest that this attempt met with no success. For Firdausī, like his contemporaries, the subject he was treating was the real history of ancient Iran and his work was scientific as well as poetical (witness the epithet *ḥakīm*, "doctor", which has remained appended to his name). As a scholar he did not write fiction, but scrupulously followed his sources, chief of which was the prose *S͟hāh-nāma* of Abū Manṣūr, though he also made use of others. One of the merits of Firdausī was that he carefully selected from the mass of material available to him and that he compiled a corpus of the stories which were to remain in the memory of the Iranians and of the other peoples, Turks and Indians, who were at one time nurtured on Persian literature. He incorporated once and for all the "Sīstānian cycle" concerning Rustam and his family into the national tradition; on the other hand he omitted various legends of lesser interest, some of which were treated by his successors and imitators. Nevertheless he owed his fame even more to his art, which consisted in giving life, by means of brilliant narrative, to the great men of the past. "Rustam," he exclaimed, "was hitherto merely a warrior of Sīstān; I have made him Rustam the son of Dastān." "From this verse," writes Bausani, "it may be seen how Firdausī understood his task, which was not to revitalize symbolic 'legends', but to transfigure, by means of poetry, the true facts which, when presented simply as historical material, remained arid."[1]

The *S͟hāh-nāma* has miscellaneous contents. Alongside heroic narrative, which constitutes the central and strictly epic section, it includes romantic descriptions, like the charming story of Bīz͟han and Manīz͟ha, instructive or amusing anecdotes and collections of aphorisms (*andarz* or *pand*) derived directly from moral literature in Middle Persian. The ideology which is found in the work and unifies the poem belongs to

[1] Bausani, "Letteratura", p. 614.

Sāsānian Iran, a time when the major preoccupations were with the legitimacy of kings, the loyalty of vassals towards their sovereign and the eternal struggle of good and evil reflected in the war between Iran and Tūrān. Only the characteristic features of the Mazdaean religion are blurred, to the point of disappearing completely, in favour of a vague monotheism compatible with Islam. The *Shāh-nāma* is a compendium of all kinds of legacies from Iranian antiquity. In the 4th/10th century, these memories were still vivid, especially among the class of the dihqāns to which Firdausī belonged, and for them it was not a matter of simple narrative, of a curious or instructive nature, which was to be found in ancient books, but the very essence of their past and the mainstay of their national consciousness.

It was this feeling which gave Firdausī the inspiration necessary to bring his gigantic poem to a successful conclusion, and his greatness lies in his having used his exceptional poetic gifts in its service. He was aware of the value of his work and believed in the eminent dignity of the art of language. "The soul of the poet," he said, "finds happiness when speech (*sukhan*) is united with intelligence (*khirad*)."[1] As regards the art of speech, he was clearly indebted to his predecessors, all those Persian poets who, for more than a century, had cultivated the language, constructed the system of rhetoric and had brought to perfection the literary instrument by means of which he was able to work the very rich but amorphous material into the brilliant form which gave it eternal life. However great the genius of Firdausī, the *Shāh-nāma* could not have been produced if the Persian language and the Persian art of poetry had not been brought already to maturity. Ancient in content, modern in form, it was the product of a unique moment of equilibrium when the memories of the past still lived on in the Iranian mind (the class of dihqāns was soon to disappear and the ideology to undergo a fundamental transformation) and when the new literary language was already sufficiently well developed to allow the composition of a masterpiece.

IX. PROSE

Of the prose works produced before the end of the first thirty odd years of the 5th/11th century, there are very few, in fact scarcely a dozen, which have not been lost, but the total output was certainly more numerous. We know the titles of some books whose text is missing and

[1] *Shāh-nāma*, p. 523.

manuscripts of unknown works may be discovered (there are precedents). It is a relatively varied literature. The prose *Shāh-nāmas* have already been mentioned, and history in the strict sense of the term is represented by the adaptation made in 352/963–4 by Abū 'Alī Bal'amī, vizier of the Sāmānid amīr Manṣūr b. Nūḥ, at the latter's command, of the Arabic *Annals* of Ṭabarī; it is the earliest large piece of New Persian prose to have been preserved to the present day. It remained the standard work of general history in Iran until the Mongol period. Geography is treated in the interesting *Ḥudūd al-'ālam*, "The Regions of the World", written in 372/982–3 for a prince of Jūzjān. The demands of religious propaganda, revived by the struggle between Sunnism and Ismā'īlī Shī'ism, played an important part in the development of Persian prose. The commentary on the Qur'ān (*tafsīr*) by Ṭabarī was rendered into Persian by a college of learned men convened by order of Manṣūr b. Nūḥ (350–65/961–76). It was the first tafsīr in Persian; two others, anonymous and undated, the so-called Cambridge and Lahore tafsīrs, were also written at a very early period. The commentary on the sacred text is limited to descriptions of the preaching of Muḥammad and the history of earlier prophets; it is patently addressed not to experts, but to a wide public. To combat the progress of heresy, Nūḥ b. Manṣūr (365–87/976–97) ordered the translation of a brief treatise on orthodoxy written by a Ḥanafite doctor, Abu'l-Qāsim Samarqandī (d. 342/953–4), the text of which has been preserved. There was also some Ismā'īlī literature in Persian, from which an anonymous commentary has survived on the philosophical qaṣīda of Abu'l-Haitham mentioned above. Finally the first mystical work in Persian appeared in the 5th/11th century – a commentary on the *Kitāb al-ta'arruf* of Kalābādhī by Abū Ibrāhīm Mustamlī of Bukhārā (d. 434/1042).

All the other extant books are on science or philosophy. The *Hidāyat al-muta'allimīn*, "Guide to Students", by Abū Bakr Akhavainī of Bukhārā, a pupil of the celebrated Abū Zakariyyā' Rāzī (Rhazes) is an interesting medical treatise, the author of which, by his scholarly spirit and his clinical observations, chiefly of mental disorders, shows himself to be worthy of his master. The *Kitāb al-abniya 'an ḥaqā'iq al-adwiya*, "Book of the Foundations of Pharmacology" by Abū Manṣūr Muvaffaq of Herāt, has survived in a manuscript copied in 447/1056 by the poet Asadī of Ṭūs, which is the most ancient Persian manuscript known. Astronomy and astrology are represented by two works, the *Kitāb al-mudkhal ilā 'ilm aḥkām al-nujūm*, "Introduction to Astrology", by

Abū Naṣr of Qum, and the *Kitāb al-tafhīm li-awā'il ṣinā'at al-tanjīm* by Bīrūnī. An Arabic version of both of them also exists and in both cases it is probably the original. The *Kitāb al-mudkhal* was compiled at Qum in 364–5/975–6 and the *Kitāb al-tafhīm* at Ghazna in 419–20/1028–9; the Persian translations must have been made a little later. Finally Avicenna, who resided in Iṣfahān from 412/1021 until his death in 428/1037, wrote two of his works in Persian there for the Kākūyid amīr 'Alā' al-Daula: the encyclopaedia of philosophy and science entitled *Danish-nāma-yi 'Alā'ī*, "Book of Science for 'Alā'", and a medical treatise dealing with the pulse.

As may be observed, prose literature was still purely utilitarian and had no aesthetic pretensions, for at this time literary art was concerned exclusively with poetry. If an author wrote in prose, it was solely for purposes of instruction or of propaganda. Commentaries on the Qur'ān, religious controversy, mysticism, history, geography, mathematics and astronomy, medicine and natural sciences and philosophy, the area staked out by these works covered a large part of what was considered science at that time. Most of them were translations, from Middle Persian chiefly for the *Shāh-nāmas*, from Arabic for all the rest. Arabic remained beyond question the principal language of thought and of science in Iran; it was used quite naturally for their basic works by scholars such as Avicenna and Bīrūnī, both of whom spent the whole of their lives in Iranian countries. The interesting fact is, however, that a need was felt to render into Persian a part of the knowledge accumulated by Arabic-speaking authors. The translators were aware of the reasons for their work and often explained them. It is stated, for example, in the Arabic preface to the Persian adaptation of the *Annals* of Ṭabarī: "I have translated this book in order that all, princes and subjects alike, may have access to it, so as to read it and know it." The introduction to the *Tafsīr-i Ṭabarī* mentioned that the Arabic original had been brought to Bukhārā from Baghdad and that the amīr Manṣūr b. Nūḥ, finding it difficult to read, took steps to have it translated into Persian. The translator of the dogmatic pamphlet of Abu'l-Qāsim Samarqandī wrote: "The amīr of Khurāsān (Nūḥ b. Manṣūr) ordered that this book should be translated into Persian, so that, being already available to experts (*khāṣṣ*), it might also be useful to the masses (*'āmm*), to the end that all might have a good knowledge of religion and keep themselves apart from innovation."[1] Similar statements are to be found

[1] Quoted by Ṣadīqī, p. 118.

in various other works of the 4th/10th and 5th/11th centuries. They show that there existed in Iran a wide public sufficiently interested in intellectual matters to wish to be informed, but not very familiar with the Arabic language; the Sāmānid amīrs were among them and their individual action contributed to the development of Persian prose.

Prose was not able to advance, however, without a considerable effort being made to improve the language. The fact was that neither the darī spoken in daily usage nor the language of poetry provided the whole vocabulary needed for dealing with matters of doctrine or science. This difficulty was fully realized by Bīrūnī who, in a famous passage, spoke with some severity about the Persian language: "If I compare Arabic with Persian," he wrote in the preface to the *Ṣaidana*, "two languages of which I have an intimate knowledge, I confess that I prefer invective in Arabic to praise in Persian. And anyone will acknowledge that my remark is well founded if he examines what happens to a scientific text when translated into Persian; it loses all clarity, its horizon becomes blurred and its practical application disappears. The function of the Persian language is to immortalize historical epics about the kings of bygone ages and to provide stories to tell on night-watches."[1] The polemical tone is rather surprising – Bīrūnī was probably irritated, at a time when the Persian language was in full expansion, by some adulators who extolled it beyond its justifiable claims – but it must be recognized that his judgement was valid for that period. Arabic was then a precision instrument for the expression of scientific thought; Persian had given brilliant proofs of its ability in poetry, but abstract and technical vocabularies still had to be invented. A comparison of the two versions of the *Kitāb al-tafhīm* is sufficient to demonstrate this truth.

The effort of Persian authors and translators is thus all the more noteworthy. When writing about religion, they easily surmounted the difficulty by adopting, as was natural, Arabic terms. In scientific and philosophical treatises they made very interesting attempts to produce technical vocabularies from Iranian stock. This effort is particularly apparent in Ismā'īlī literature, firstly in the anonymous commentary on the qaṣīda of Abu'l-Haiṯẖam and later in the works of Nāṣir-i K̲h̲usrau; it can be observed also in the *Dānis̲h̲-nāma* of Avicenna. These authors did not abstain from using Arabic words, but their work also contains

[1] After Massignon's French translation in *Al-Biruni commemorative volume* (Calcutta, 1951), p. 218.

a number of abstract Iranian words, which are partly neologisms and partly philosophical terms existing in Middle Persian, so that some contact with Pahlavī literature is indicated. The same tendency is revealed in science and may be observed in the Persian version of the *Kitāb al-tafhīm*, the author of which, instead of reproducing Arabic technical terms, often endeavoured to translate them, or, failing anything better, to paraphrase them.

Indeed he was not the only one to do so. A later author, Shahmardān b. Abi'l-Khair, in his *Rauḍat al-munajjimīn*, "Garden of the Astronomers", written in 466/1073–4, criticized his predecessors in the following terms: "The most astonishing thing is that, when they write a book in Persian, they state that they have adopted this language in order that those who do not know Arabic may be able to use the book. Yet they have recourse to words of pure Persian (*darī-yi vīzha-yi muṭlaq*) which are more difficult than Arabic. If they employed the terms currently in use it would be easier to understand them." He adds that for his part he does not avail himself of any but ordinary terms, that is to say Arabic, which can be learned by anyone in five days.[1] This interesting passage confirms that in the 4th–5th/10th–11th centuries there was a definite movement for the creation of a scientific vocabulary which was authentically Persian. At the same time it makes it clear that the movement was unsuccessful: in the second half of the 5th/11th century it was the Arabic vocabulary which prevailed.

[1] Boldyrev, "Iz istorii", p. 85; Lazard, *La langue*, p. 105.

CHAPTER 20 (*a*)

THE "RUBĀ'Ī" IN EARLY PERSIAN LITERATURE

In the western conception of Persian literature the words *rubā'īyāt* and *'Umar Khayyām* have become practically synonymous, and it is only recently that scholarship in this field has brought a growing realization that this picture is incomplete. Before then we can consider to what extent Khayyām contributed to the development of this particular Persian literary form, we must go back a few centuries.

We need not concern ourselves here with the argument whether the classical Persian metres derive from Persian or Arabic sources; the one metre whose purely Persian origin has never been challenged is the *rubā'ī*. The arguments in favour of a Central Asian, Turkic origin for the rubā'ī put forward by Bausani[1] are by no means to be dismissed, in spite of some rather dubious assumptions; but they have no bearing on the question of the metrical pattern, which is quite common in Persian but unknown elsewhere. Tradition indeed claims that it was invented by the early 4th/10th century poet Rūdakī. According to Shams-i Qais,[2] writing in the 7th/13th century, Rūdakī (or some other poet) overheard the excited cry of a small boy (said by the 9th/15th century biographer Daulatshāh to have been the son of Ya'qūb b. Laith) as he was rolling nuts into a ditch:

ghaltān ghaltān hamīravad tā bun-i gav
– –   – – ∪ – ∪ –   – ∪ ∪ –

Rolling along it goes to the edge of the ditch

Inspired by the balanced rhythm of this sentence, the poet went home and proceeded to write quatrains in this and equivalent metres, which in due course came to be known as rubā'ī (four-line poem), *dūbaitī* (two-couplet poem), or *tarāna* (poem of freshness and youth).

Leaving legend aside, it is sufficient to note that from a fairly early

[1] Pp. 533–7.
[2] *al-Mu'jam*, pp. 83–4.

date the term rubā'ī began to be used for a poem having two main characteristics:

(1) two verses (*bait*) or four hemistichs (*miṣrā'*), with the rhyme-scheme either *aaaa* or *aaba*;

(2) the metre known in Arabic terminology as *hazaj muthamman akhrab aw akhram maqbūḍ makfūf majbūb*, or more simply

– – ∪ ∪ – ∪ – ∪ – – ∪ ∪ – – ∪

The second, metrical, requirement however seems to have been a gradual development, since in the earliest stages of known Persian poetry we find what appear to be quatrains in other metres. It must be emphasized at this point that our treasury of early Persian poetry is so scanty that we have to be cautious about basing conclusions on it. Much of it has had to be gathered from non-literary sources – dictionaries, grammars and works on prosody, in which isolated verses are used to illustrate rare words or linguistic subtleties, or histories and biographies, where the purpose is to enliven or emphasize a point in the narrative. The result is that our material consists of unrelated scraps of poetry selected for specialized interests, and not necessarily typical of their author's work. In particular we cannot know whether a four-line fragment is an independent unit or part of a longer poem now lost. The rhyme scheme may be a guide: *aaaa* is almost certainly an independent verse, *abab* almost certainly not, while *aaba* could be either an independent quatrain or the opening verses of a longer poem. The two fragments by Ḥanẓala Bādghīsī (*fl.* 250/864) that are conventionally regarded as the earliest authentic verses by a named poet are both in quatrain form and independent in sense, but have respectively the *aaba* and *abab* rhyme-schemes:

yār-am sipand agarchi bar ātish hamī figand
az bahr-i chashm tā na-rasad mar-varā gazand
ū-rā sipand u ātish nāyad hamī bi-kār
bā rūy-i hamchu ātish u bā khāl-i chūn sipand

My love may burn the wild rue for a charm
To keep her untouched by the evil eye.
Yet what need has she of such magic spells?
Her cheek is fire, the mole thereon wild rue.

*

mihtarī gar bi-kām-i shīr dar ast
shau khaṭar kun zi kām-i shīr bi-jūy
yā buzurgī u 'izz u ni'mat u jāh
yā chu mardān-t marg-i rūyārūy

If lordship lies within the lion's mouth,
Be not afraid, go, seek it even there.
Thus either wealth and glory will be yours,
Or like a man you'll come to grips with death.

*

An almost contemporary poet, Maḥmūd Varrāq (*fl.* 260/873), wrote:

nigārīnā bi-naqd-i jān-t nadham
girānī dar bahā arzān-t nadham
giriftastam bi-jān dāmān-i vaṣlat
diham jān az kaf ū dāmān-t nadham

Beloved, life's too cheap a price for you;
I will not sell so rich a prize for nothing.
I clasp you to me with my very life;
I'll give my life, I will not let you go.

The metrical pattern of this verse, ⏑ – – – ⏑ – – – ⏑ – –, though not that subsequently established for the formal rubā'ī, was nevertheless widely used for quatrains in popular literature, and indeed the term dūbaitī was often used to distinguish this form from the rubā'ī proper. The dūbaitī was never to become popular as a literary form, though in folk-literature it survives to the present day. The only ancient poet to use this form almost exclusively was the dervish poet Bābā Ṭāhir 'Uryān (the Naked) of Hamadān (*fl.* 5th/11th century), whose quatrains are still extant in the dialect form in which they were probably first sung, side by side with later Persianized versions:

mū (man) ki sar dar biyābūnum (biyābānam) s̲h̲av (s̲h̲ab) ū rūj (rūz)
sirís̲h̲k az dīda bārūnum (bāranam) s̲h̲av ū rūj
na tav (tab) dīrum (dāram) na jāyum (jāyam) mīkarū (mikunad) dard
hamī (hamīn) dūnam (dānam) ki nālūnum (nālānam) s̲h̲av ū rūj

I wander through the desert day and night,
My eyes are wet with weeping day and night.
No fever racks me, and I feel no pain;
All that I have is sorrow day and night.

*

bi-īn bī-ās̲h̲yūnī (ās̲h̲yānī) bar kiyān (kīhā) s̲h̲am (s̲h̲avam)
bi-īn bī-k̲h̲ānumūnī (k̲h̲ānumānī) bar kiyān s̲h̲am
hama gar mū birūnan (birānand) vā ta (sū-yi tu) āyam
ta (tu) az dar gar birūnī (birānī) bar kiyān s̲h̲am

Needy and destitute, where shall I turn?
Driven from house and home, where shall I turn?
Rebuffed at every door, I turn to you;
If you reject me too, where shall I turn?

Nevertheless the distinguishing feature that marks out the rubā'ī from all other verse forms is the metre, which is not only virtually unique to the quatrain form, but also enjoys the unusual facility of combining two different patterns within the same poem:

(1) the repeated alternation of two long and two short syllables:

– – ᴗ ᴗ – – ᴗ ᴗ – – ᴗ ᴗ –

(2) the more typical pattern in which the above sequence is combined with a section in which single long and short syllables alternate:

– – ᴗ ᴗ – ᴗ – ᴗ – – ᴗ ᴗ –

When to these are added the variants permissible for all Persian metrical patterns (the substitution of one long syllable for two consecutive short syllables, and of one overlong syllable for a consecutive long and short syllable), the poet is equipped with a metrical form that is unique even in Persian poetry in its simplicity, balance and flexibility. (A short syllable is a consonant plus short vowel; a long syllable is a consonant plus long vowel, or a consonant plus short vowel plus consonant; an overlong syllable is a consonant plus long vowel plus consonant, or a consonant plus short vowel plus two consonants.) Ignoring variations in the last syllable, which may be either long or overlong, the other variations provide in theory sixty-two different hemistichs, flexibility enough without the additional possibility of treating a wide range of syllables as either long or short according to metrical requirements (the *iḍāfa*, the ending *-a* (*h*), *va/u* (and), short syllables followed by an initial *hamza*, to mention only a few examples). Particularly striking is the possibility of "changing gear" in mid-poem, though this is not always exploited when pattern (2) (which itself incorporates such a change) is used. A check of 172 rubā'īyāt attributed to the earliest poets up to Manūchihrī (d. 432/1040) shows that 51 follow pattern (2) throughout, 59 use pattern (1) once, 45 twice, and 15 three times, while only two keep to pattern (1) throughout. Or to put it another way, there are 486 hemistichs in pattern (2), as against 202 in (1). This division into two patterns has nothing to do with the two "trees" beloved of the classical prosodists, which are distinguished by a much less significant difference.

Perhaps the most surprising feature of the rubā'ī metre is the fact that, in spite of its easily assimilated rhythm, it is confined in use almost exclusively to the quatrain form. The qualification "almost" is necessary because, as Mujtabā Mīnuvī has shown,[1] poets have been known

[1] Mujtabā Mīnuvī, *Pānzdah guftār* (Tehrān, 1967), pp. 335–7.

to experiment with it in other forms. However even this indefatigable scholar has only been able to turn up five examples, and one of these, a *qaṣīda* by Farrukhī (d. 428/1037), even though Shams-i Qais classifies it as in the rubā'ī metre,[1] should rather be scanned according to the pattern – ∪ ∪ – – ∪ – ∪ – ∪ ∪ – – (*munsariḥ muthamman maṭwī manḥūr*). Of the other four examples, the best known is a *musammaṭ* by Manūchihrī, while the others include a *qiṭ'a* by 'Ain al-Quḍāt Hamadānī (*c.* 492/1099–525/1131), another by Abū Ṭāhir Khātūnī (*fl.* 500/1106) also quoted by Shams-i Qais, and a qaṣīda by the little-known poet Jamāl al-Dīn Abu'l-Maḥāsin Yūsuf b. Naṣr, quoted in the 7th/13th century *Lubāb al-albāb* of Muḥammad 'Aufī.

The sources of the rubā'ī metrical pattern can probably no longer be traced, but they certainly pre-date the age of Rūdakī. Even the fully-fledged rubā'ī metre was already current in his time, if we may judge from the earliest recorded examples – a possibly spurious verse attributed to Abū Ḥafṣ Sughdī (*fl.* 300/912), and two attributed to Shahīd Balkhī (d. 324/936), a slightly older contemporary of Rūdakī:

būs ū naẓaram jamāl bāshad bā yār
in fatvā man girifta-am az churgar

Beauty is in the kisses of my love;
Such is the *fatvā* of the holy man.
(Abū Ḥafṣ Sughdī)

*

pīsh-i vuzarā rukhna-yi ash'ār-i marā
bī-qadr makun bi-guft guftār-i marā

Present (?) my poems to the men of state;
Do not condemn with words my humble verse.
(Shahīd Balkhī)

*

ai qāmat-i tū bi-ṣūrat-i kāvanjak
hastī tu bi-chashm-i har kasī bulkanjak

Your body's twisted as a cucumber,
You are to every eye an uncouth clown.
(Shahīd Balkhī)

However the same metrical patterns are encountered in even earlier poems; the simpler pattern (1) is already found (with different syllabic lengths) in poems by Muḥammad b. Vaṣīf, Bassām Kurd and Muḥam-

[1] *al-Mu'jam*, p. 92.

mad b. Mukhallad, all of whom were at the court of the Ṣaffārid Ya'qūb b. Laith (253/867–265/878):

ai amīrī ki amīrān-i jahān khāṣṣa va 'āmm
banda vū chākir u maulāt va sagband u ghulām

Prince, before whom the princes of the world
Humble themselves in abject slavery . . .
(Muḥammad b. Vaṣīf)

*

har ki nabūd ūy bi-dil muttaham
bar athar-i da'vat-i tū kard na'am

All those who had no evil in their hearts
With one accord cried "Yes!" to your command . . .
(Bassām Kurd)

*

juz tu na-zād ḥavvā v-ādam na-kisht
shīr-nihādī bi-dil ū bar manisht

Eve never bore, nor Adam sired, a son
Like you, a lion in valour and resolve . . .
(Muḥammad b. Mukhallad)

Pattern (2) appears a little later in a verse by Fīrūz Mashriqī (d. 283/896), in a form one syllable shorter than the rubā'ī metre:

murghīst khadang ai 'ajab dīdī
murghī ki hama shikār-i ū jānā
dāda par-i khwīsh kargasash hadya
ta bachcha-sh-rā barad bi-mihmānā

The arrow flies like a bird, but what a bird!
A bird whose prey is every living soul.
The vulture yields its feathers as a gift
That they may bear their children to the feast.

Abū Salīk Gurgānī, a contemporary of Fīrūz Mashriqī, provides us with two verses in a yet shorter variant, later a favourite for *mathnavī* (rhyming couplet) epics and romances:

dar janb-i 'ulūv-i himmatat charkh
mānanda-i vushm pīsh-i chargh-ast

Before your boundless zeal the very heavens
Tremble as does a quail before a hawk.

*

az farṭ-i 'aṭā-yi ū zanad āz
paivasta zi imtilā zarāghan

So generous is his bounty, greed itself
Belches aloud from utter satisfaction.

So the rubā'ī in its final form contains no elements that were not familiar at least in the century before Rūdakī's lifetime. True, we have more rubā'īyāt attributed to Rūdakī than to any of his predecessors or contemporaries; the dictionaries and other sources have yielded, amongst much other material, thirty-nine rubā'īyāt. But only one of these appears in a work earlier than the beginning of the 10th/16th century, and even that is no earlier than the 7th/13th century prosodical work of Shams-i Qais:[1]

vājib nabuvad bi-kas bar ifḍāl u karam
vājib bāshad har āyina shukr-i ni'am
taqṣīr nakard khwāja dar nā-vājib
man dar vājib chigūna taqṣīr kunam

God's law demands munificence of no man;
What it demands is gratitude for favours.
My lord excels in what is not demanded;
How then can I fail in my obligations?

The problem of the authenticity of Rūdakī's quatrains is indeed even more puzzling than the case of 'Umar Khayyām, of whose poetic gifts some scholars still remain sceptical. In 'Umar's case the earliest recorded rubā'īyāt in his name appear some seventy years after his death; for Rūdakī the gap is more like three centuries, and even then we have only one example, and must wait another three centuries for the remainder.

We should not however be too discouraged by such anomalies. The rubā'ī is one of the most foot-loose of Persian verse-forms, a fact largely explained by its brevity and its uniformity of metre and form. One rubā'ī is much like another; in most cases neither language nor subject-matter are copious enough to enable us to place a particular one in the right century, let alone with the right author. The problem of the "wandering" quatrains is always with us, though it is much more acute when, as in the case of 'Umar Khayyām or Abū Sa'īd b. Abi'l-Khair, the poet has written virtually nothing else.

The suggestion has been made that the rhyme-scheme may help in the problem of dating rubā'īyāt. Bausani appears to regard the *aaba* as the original form, and cites its appearance in Turkic and Chinese literature, as well as in Persian, as evidence of its radiation outwards from a common Central Asian source. Tirtha on the other hand takes the view that quatrains with the *aaaa* rhyme-scheme are likely to be

[1] *al-Mu'jam*, p. 175.

the older.[1] This is not borne out by those attributed to Rūdakī (but we have already noted the dubious authenticity of these); of 37 whose rhyme-scheme can be determined, 12 have four rhymes and 25 three. Scattered verses by other poets up to the middle of the 5th/11th century show 15 *aaaa* and 17 *aaba*. On the other hand the figures for those 5th/11th-century poets whose rubā'īyāt have survived in substantial numbers lean heavily towards the four-rhyme type: Farrukhī (d. 428/1037) – 37 *aaaa*, 1 *aaba*; Qaṭrān (d. 464/1072) – 130 *aaaa*, 21 *aaba*; 'Unṣurī (d. 430/1039) – 59 *aaaa*, 8 *aaba*; Azraqī (d. *c.* 464/1072) – 88 *aaaa*, 20 *aaba*; Abu'l-Faraj Rūnī (d. *c.* 491/1098) – 43 *aaaa*, 5 *aaba*; Mas'ūd Sa'd Salmān (437/1046–515/1121) – 399 *aaaa*, 8 *aaba*; Amīr Mu'izzī (d. 518/1124) – 149 *aaaa*, 28 *aaba*. These figures contrast with an overall ratio for classical Persian poets of 30 per cent *aaaa* to 70 per cent *aaba*. The difference is sufficiently marked to lend colour to the belief that the *aaaa* form was the earlier, but it does not really help us, since the three-rhyme form certainly existed at a very early stage – Farālāvī (*fl.* 318/930) has one, for instance.

The shape of the rubā'ī has remained unchanged throughout its long career in Persian literature. The first two hemistichs set the scene; the third stands poised on the brink, and the fourth emphasizes the point. It is as characteristic in its genre as the Greek epigram or the Japanese *haiku*, with both of which it has been compared. In contrast to the more substantial *qaṣīda* and *ghazal*, it was usually a vehicle for improvization, and contemporary accounts suggest that, as still today, many well-known rubā'īyāt originated as impromptu thoughts thrown out at random during informal literary or religious gatherings. This would also explain the simple, almost earthy language of most of them, which contrasts noticeably with the highly chiselled and polished style of the more formal verse-forms, even as early as the 5th/11th century. Nor was it long enough for the sustained ecstasy of mystical inspiration; even mystics like Abū Sa'īd b. Abi'l-Khair and Khwāja 'Abd-Allāh Anṣārī, whose poetic output was confined almost exclusively to the rubā'ī, used it rather to emphasize and illustrate points already elaborated in prose sermons and prayers.

It has been suggested that long stanzaic poems were sometimes composed in rubā'ī form, but the evidence is very slim. Mīnuvī quotes four examples,[2] but two of these (from the 8th/14th-century *Mi'yār-i Jamālī* of Shams Fakhrī Iṣfahānī, and the 9th/15th-century prosodist

[1] Bausani, pp. 534–6; Tirtha, p. 134.
[2] Mīnuvī, *op. cit.* p. 335.

Mu'īn al-Dīn 'Abbāsa) are acknowledged prosodist's *tours de force* – a fact that in itself proves the rarity of the device.[1] The other two examples (three quatrains in the 7th/13th-century *Tārīkh-i Ṭabaristān* and a series of 123 attributed to Afḍal al-Dīn Kāshī (7th/13th century) seem rather to be collections of independent quatrains grouped according to subject-matter, a practice not uncommon among anthologists before the introduction during the 9th/15th century of the alphabetical arrangement under rhyming letters. In any case the stanzaic poem is comparatively rare in Persian literature. The musammaṭ by Manūchihrī mentioned above is one of the earliest examples, and we must look to the 6th/12th and 7th/13th centuries for its formal development.

The subject-matter of the rubā'ī, in contrast to its form, is virtually unrestricted; it has been used for the complaints of the lover, the celebration of wine, the eulogizing of the patron, the satirizing of enemies, the thoughts of the philosopher, and the expression of mystical ecstasy. Rūdakī is usually the plaintive lover:

bī-rū-yi tu khwurshīd jahān-sūz mabād
ham bī tu chirāgh 'ālam-afrūz mabād
bā vaṣl-i tu kas chu man bad-āmūz mabād
rūzī ki turā na-bīnam ān rūz mabād

Your face brings ardour to the burning sun,
Your eyes increase the brilliance of the moon.
In your embrace I rest immune from evil;
Far be the day that you are far from me!

*

dil sīr na-gardadat zi bīdādgarī
chashm āb na-gardadat chu dar man nigarī
īn ṭurfa ki dūst-tar zi jānat dāram
bā ānki zi ṣad hazār dushman batarī

Your cruel heart is never satisfied,
You shed no tears at my predicament.
How strange that I should love you more than life,
Though you are harsher than a thousand foes!

Sometimes he gives us more straightforward and as yet unconventionalized descriptions of beauty:

ai az gul-i surkh rang barbūda va bū
rang az pay-i rukh rabūda bū az pay-i mū
gul-rang shavad chu rūy shū'ī hama jū
mushkīn gardad chu mū fishānī hama kū

[1] Shams Fakhrī Iṣfahānī, pp. iv–v.

You have stolen colour and fragrance from the rose,
Red for your cheeks and perfume for your tresses.
The stream becomes rose-coloured when you bathe,
The lane musk-scented when you comb your hair.

An occasional note of pessimism about life and destiny reminds us of 'Umar Khayyām nearly two centuries later:

hān tishna-jagar majūy zīn bāgh thamar
bīdistān ast īn riyāḍ-i bi-du dar
bīhūda mamān ki bāghbānat bi-qafāst
chūn khāk nishasta gīr u chūn bād guzar

Ho, thirsty one, there's no refreshment here;
This double-gated garden's but a desert.
Waste no more time, the gardener's close behind you;
Pause like the dust, and pass on like the wind.

One of the most widely quoted of Rūdakī's rubā'īyāt is the following:

chūn kār-i dilam zi zulf-i ū mānd girih
bar har rag-i jān ṣad ārzū mānd girih
ummīd zi girya būd afsūs afsūs
k-ān ham shab-i vaṣl dar gulū mānd girih

My heart is stifled by her curling locks,
My longings stifled in my quivering veins;
I hoped my sobs would move her, but alas!
That night they too were stifled in my throat.

It is tempting to place a Ṣūfī interpretation on these verses, which display some of the characteristics of later Ṣūfī poetry; but it would be an anachronism to do so. All the evidence suggests that Persian mystical poetry is a phenomenon of the 5th/11th century onwards. The resemblance arises presumably from the fact that the mystical poets embedded their experiences in conventional lyric poetry; and indeed had this lyric tradition not been already established by earlier poets like Rūdakī, Farrukhī, 'Unṣurī and Manūchihrī, it could hardly have served as a vehicle for mystical ideas.

The next century provides us with few complete rubā'īyāt. That prolific writer Abū Shukūr of Balkh (*fl.* 340/951) has left us only one, characteristic however in its balance and ingenuity:

ai gashta man az gham-i farāvān-i tu past
shud qāmat-i man zi dard-i hijrān-tu shast
ai shusta man az farīb u dastān-i tu dast
khwud hīch kasī bi-sīrat u sān-i tu hast

Humbled by constant grieving over you,
My body bowed by pain of separation,
I wash my hands of all your tricks and falsehoods.
Who in the world would be so cruel as you?

Daqīqī (329/941–367/978), better known for his epic verse later expanded by Firdausī into the *Shāh-nāma*, also composed an ingenious rubā'ī in the same vein:

chashm-i tu ki fitna dar jahān khīzad az ū
la'l-i tu ki āb-i khiḍr mīrīzad az ū
kardand tan-i marā chunān khwār ki bād
mīyāyad u gard u khāk mībīzad az ū

Your eyes, from which stems all the world's dissension,
Your ruby lips, whence streams the water of life,
These have so wasted my poor body, that
The wind sweeps through it in a cloud of dust.

The rubā'ī was generally felt to be too short for panegyric sentiments, which required the more lavish scope of the qaṣīda. However an unknown Ṣāni' or Ṣāyigh of Balkh in about 354/965 is recorded in the *Tārīkh-i Sīstān* as having addressed the following to a Ṣaffārid prince:[1]

khān-i gham-i tu past shuda vīrān bād
khān-i ṭarabat hamīsha ābādān bād
hamvāra sar-i kār-i tu bā nīkān bād
tu mīr-i shahīd u dushmanat mākān bād

May the house of sorrow never rise for you!
May the house of pleasure prosper where you are!
May your dealings always be with righteous men!
Thrive like our late Amīr, your foes like his!

The opening of the 5th/11th century coincided with the rise of three poets who may be claimed as the founders of the Persian poetical tradition, if only because they are the first to have left a substantial corpus of unchallenged work. All of them were court poets to Sulṭān Maḥmūd of Ghazna and his son Mas'ūd. Certainly the distinction of Farrukhī, 'Unṣurī and Manūchihrī is first and foremost in the fields of the qaṣīda and the ghazal, but their rubā'īyāt show something of the quality of their more formal compositions, and provide opportunities for the display of verbal dexterity and rhetorical skill. Farrukhī, for

[1] P. 324.

instance, uses the *su'āl u javāb* (question and answer) device in the following quatrain:

guftam rukh-i tū bahār-i khandān-i man ast
guft ān-i tu nīz bāgh u bustān-i man ast
guftam lab-i shakkarīn-i tu ān-i man ast
guft az tu darīgh nīst gar jān-i man ast

I said, "Your cheek is like the smiling spring";
She said, "Yours is a scented flower-garden."
I said, "Your sugar-lip belongs to me."
She said, "My life is yours, without restraint."

'Unsuri provides the following example of *jam' va taqsīm* (combination and division):

si chīz bi-burd az si chīz-i tu mithāl
az rukh gul u az lab mul u az rūy jamāl
si chīz bi-burd az si chīzam hama sāl
az dil gham u az rukh nam u az dīda khiyāl

Three things have modelled themselves on three of yours –
Rose on cheek, grape on lip, beauty on face.
Three things each year are taken from three of mine –
Grief from heart, tears from cheek, fancy from eye.

Characteristic of Manūchihrī is:

dar bandam az ān du zulf-i band andar band
nālānam az ān 'aqīq-i qand andar qand
ai va'da-yi fardā-yi tu pīch andar pīch
ākhir gham-i hijrān-i tu chand andar chand

I am a prisoner of those tangled locks,
Tormented by those sugared ruby lips.
Tomorrow's tryst with you convulses me,
Still more the pain of parting at the end.

However the 5th/11th-century name that springs most readily to mind in connection with the rubā'ī is Abū Sa'īd b. Abi'l-Khair (357/967–440/1048). True, there is a fairly clear statement in the biography written by his great-great-grandson Muḥammad b. Munavvar between 553/1158 and 599/1203 that Abū Sa'īd wrote virtually no poetry himself.[1] The passage describes how Abū Sa'īd wrote a verse on the back of a letter sent to him by a dervish of Nīshāpūr, and continues: "The

[1] *Asrār al-tauḥīd*, p. 218.

Shaikh al-Islām, grandfather of the present writer, related that some are of the opinion that the verses recited by the Shaikh [Abū Sa'īd] were composed by him, whereas this is not so. He was so immersed in God that he had not the leisure to compose poetry, except for this one verse."

This statement has been taken in its overt sense by such European scholars as Zhukovskii, Bertel's, Fritz Meier and Rypka; but Sa'īd Nafīsī, in his edition of the verses of Abū Sa'īd, contradicts this and adduces a variety of evidence in support.[1] We do not need to enter into this argument, since there is general agreement that, even if the rubā'īyāt are not by Abū Sa'īd himself, they were learnt by him from his teachers, and have certainly been attached to his name from a very early date. Nafīsī notes that of the 726 complete rubā'īyāt in his edition, 172 are also attributed to other poets, notably 'Umar Khayyām (55), Bābā Afḍal (40), Rūmī (30), Auḥad al-Dīn Kirmānī (35) and Bākharzī (23). This still leaves well over five hundred for whom no other author has ever been suggested. This is not conclusive evidence of Abū Sa'īd's authorship, but it at least leaves it open. What can certainly be stated without qualification is that the rubā'īyāt attributed to Abū Sa'īd constitute the first major corpus of Ṣūfī quatrains, and indeed one of the earliest collections of Persian Ṣūfī verse in any form. There is also no question that Abū Sa'īd was widely recognized during his lifetime as a Ṣūfī teacher of great authority, and a representative of the eastern, "intoxicated" school of Ṣūfī thought of which Bāyazīd Bisṭāmī was the first and greatest figure.

mā kushta-i 'ishq-īm u jahān maslakh-i mā-st
mā bī-khwar u khwāb-īm u jahān maṭbakh-i mā-st
mā-rā nabuvad havā-yi firdaus az ānk
ṣad martaba bālātar az ān dūzakh-i mā-st

For love's sake we are butchered by the world,
The greedy world robs us of food and sleep.
We have no need of Paradise, because
Our Hell exceeds it by a hundred-fold.

*

bāz ā bāz ā har ānchi hastī bāz ā
gar kāfir u gabr u but-parastī bāz ā
īn dargah-i mā dargah-i nūmīdī nīst
ṣad bār agar tauba shikastī bāz ā

[1] Rypka, p. 234; Nafīsī, pp. 35 ff.

Come back, come back! Whoever you are, come back!
Infidel, guebre, idolater, come back!
Here in these courts of ours is no despair,
Sin and repent unceasing, but come back!

*

gar murda buvam bar āmada sālī bīst
chi pindārī ki gūram az 'ishq tuhīst
gar dast bi-khāk bar nihī k-īnjā kī-st
āvāz āyad ki ḥāl-i ma'shūqam chīst

Though I lie twenty years beneath the soil,
Never suppose that love will leave my grave.
Touch but the earth and ask, "Who lies beneath?"
Then hear the answer, "How fares my beloved?"

*

avval ki marā 'ishq-i nigāram birabūd
hamsāya-i man zi nāla-i man naghunūd
v-aknūn kam shud nāla chu dardam bifuzūd
ātish chu hama girift kam gardad dūd

When first my loved one stole my heart away,
My neighbours knew no rest from my lament.
Now my lament is less, my pain is more;
When all is burnt away, no smoke remains.

*

'ishq āmad u shud chu khūnam andar rag u pūst
tā kard marā tuhī va pur kard zi dūst
ajzā-yi vujūdam hamagī dūst girift
nāmī-st zi man bar man u bāqī hama ū-st

Love flowed like blood through every vein of mine,
Drove out all else and filled me with the Friend.
My Friend embraces every limb of me,
Only my name remains, the rest is He.

One of the most famous of Abū Sa'īd's verses has been the subject of several commentaries:

ḥaurā bi-naẓāra-i nigāram ṣaf zad
riḍvān bi-'ajab bi-mānd u kaf bar kaf zad
ān khāl-i siyah bar ān rukhān miṭraf zad
abdāl zi bīm chang dar maṣḥaf zad

The houris stood in ranks to see my love,
Heaven became amazed and clapped its hands.
Seeing her cheeks veiled by the dusky mole,
The saints from fear grasped at the Holy Book.

The next author whose name is particularly associated with the rubā'ī is Khwāja 'Abd-Allāh Anṣārī (396/1006–481/1088) of Herāt, though in fact his quatrains have never been separately collected, but remain scattered throughout his theological and mystical writings, notably his *Munājāt*, *Rasā'il* and other works in rhymed prose interspersed with verse. It may also be that some of the numerous rubā'īyāt quoted in Maibudī's *Kashf al-asrār*, written in 520/1126, can be attributed to Anṣārī, since this work is avowedly an expanded version of the latter's now lost *Tafsīr al-Qur'ān*. In any case these are obviously of early date, and come therefore within the period under consideration. Once again we find rubā'īyāt, together (less frequently) with other scraps of verse, used to illustrate or emphasize points in the discourse rather than as an art-form in their own right.

'aib ast 'aẓīm bar kashīdan khwud-rā
v-az jumla-i khalq bar guzīdan khwud-rā
az mardumak-i dīda bi-bāyad āmūkht
dīdan hama kas-rā va na-dīdan khwud-rā

It's a sad fault to raise yourself aloft,
To set yourself above the common herd.
Learn this much from the pupil of the eye:
See all the world, but never see yourself.

*

ān kas ki tu-rā shinākht jān-rā chi kunad
farzand u 'ayāl u khānumān-rā chi kunad
dīvāna kunī har du jahānash bakhshī
dīvāna-i tū har du jahān-rā chi kunad

He who has known you, what is life to him?
What shall he do with children, wife and home?
Treat him as mad, the universe is his;
Why should your madman want the universe?

*

paivasta dilam dam-i havā-yi tu zanad
jān dar tan-i man nafas barāyi tu zanad
gar bar sar-i khāk-i man giyāhī rūyad
az har bargī bū-yi vafā-yi tu zanad

My heart is yearning for you ceaselessly,
My soul within me breathes of nothing else.
The flowers that blossom from my funeral earth
Give off the scent of my undying love.

*

andar rah-i dīn du ka'ba āmad ḥāṣil
yak ka'ba-i ṣūrat-ast u yak ka'ba-i dil
tā bi-tvānī ziyārat-i dilhā kun
k-afzūn zi hazār ka'ba bāshad yak dil

Two shrines we find upon the road of faith,
The Ka'ba and the temple of the heart.
Make all your pilgrimages to the heart,
One heart is worth a thousand of the other.

*

nai az tu ḥayāt-i jāvidān mī-khwāham
nai 'aish u tana''um-i jahān mī-khwāham
nai kām-i dil u rāḥat-i jān mi-khwāham
chīzī ki riḍā-yi tu-st ān mī-khwāham

I do not seek eternal life from Thee,
I do not want the pleasures of this world.
I do not look for ease and peace of mind;
All that I ask is that which pleases Thee.

The decline of the Ghaznavids and the rise of the Saljuqs were marked by the appearance of a new generation of panegyric poets, of whom Qaṭrān, Azraqī and Rūnī, and somewhat later Mas'ūd Sa'd Salmān and Amīr Mu'izzī were the most distinguished figures. The Tabrīzī poet Qaṭrān (d. 465/1072) lived mainly at the courts of local rulers in Āzarbāījān and the Caucasus, to whom his panegyric *qaṣā'id* are addressed, as also many of his rubā'īyāt, of which 151 are recorded in his dīvān.

dāranda-i dād u dīn malik mamlān-ast
chūn shīr bi-rūz-i kīn malik mamlān-ast
bā dānish u dīn qarīn malik mamlān-ast
tā ḥashr bi-āfarīn malik mamlān-ast

Mamlān dispenses sanctity and justice,
Mamlān is like a lion in his fury,
Mamlān is paramount in faith and learning,
Mamlān is praised throughout eternity.

Other verses of his are savagely satirical:

ānī ki vafā na-bāyad az mihr-i tu just
dar va'da mukhālif-ī u dar paimān sust
bī-sharmī u bīdādgarī pīsha-i tu-st
dast az tu bi-ṣābūn-i rayī bāyad shust

No one can hope for lasting love from you,
You break your promise, you forget your oath.
Shamelessness and injustice are your craft,
Ray soap one needs to wash one's hands of you.

For an example of impromptu ingenuity, we need look no further than the quatrain composed by the Herātī poet Azraqī (d. 526/1132) to console the young Ṭug͟hānsh͟āh for an unsuccessful throw at dice:[1]

gar s͟hāh du s͟his͟h k͟hwāst du yak zak͟hm uftād
tā ẓan na-barī ki ka'batain dād na-dād
ān zak͟hm ki kard rāy-i s͟hāhans͟hah yād
dar k͟hidmat-i s͟hāh rūy bar k͟hāk nihād

The king sought sixes, but the dice gave ones;
Yet this was no injustice on their part.
The dice, knowing full well the royal wish,
In homage bowed their faces to the ground.

Amīr Mu'izzī (440/1048–518/1124), court poet to Malik-S͟hāh and Sanjar, followed in the footsteps of Farruk͟hī, 'Unṣurī and Manūc͟hihrī.

s͟hāhā at͟har-i ṣabūḥ kārī 'ajab-ast
nāzad bi-ṣabūḥ har ki s͟hādī-ṭalab-ast
bāda bi-hama vaqt ṭarab-rā sabab-ast
līkan bi-ṣabūḥ kīmiyā-yi ṭarab-ast

O King, the morning drink's a splendid thing,
All who seek pleasure love the morning drink.
At every hour wine is a source of mirth,
At dawn it is the elixir itself.

The function of the poet as royal entertainer is also illustrated in the poetry of Mas'ūd Sa'd Salmān (438/1046–515/1121), who served the G͟haznavid court in India after the expulsion of that dynasty from Iran. In his case there is often a note of wry wit, reflecting his own troubled fortunes, which included several periods of imprisonment:

gar ṣabr kunam 'umr hamī bād s͟havad
v-ar nāla kunam 'adū hamī s͟hād s͟havad
s͟hādī-yi 'adū na-jūyam u ṣabr kunam
s͟hāyad ki falak dar īn miyān rād s͟havad

[1] *C͟hahār maqāla*, pp. 86–8.

In sufferance will my life pass like the wind,
But grumbling too will make my enemies glad.
I will not please my foes, I will be patient;
Perhaps too Heaven will soon be generous.

A contemporary at the same court was another poet of Persian origin, Abu'l-Faraj Rūnī; for him the qaṣīda and ghazal were primarily panegyric vehicles, and it is only in his rubā'īyāt that we sometimes find a note of tenderness:

az dard-i firāqat ai bi-lab shakkar-i nāb
nai rūz marā qirār u nai dar shab khwāb
chashm u dil-i man zi hijrat ai durr-i khwushāb
ṣaḥrā-yi pur ātish ast u daryā-yi pur āb

Through hopeless yearning for my sweet-lipped love
Days know no rest, and nights are robbed of sleep.
My eyes and heart, seeking that peerless pearl,
Burn like the desert, billow like the sea.

By the end of the 5th/11th century the development of the rubā'ī was complete. Perhaps it attained its highest peak in the hands of the poet (or poets) who wrote under the name of 'Umar Khayyām (439/1048–525/1131); from his time onwards poets did little more than embroider on a well-established tradition. For this reason, if for no other, it is virtually impossible to establish with any degree of certainty which of the many rubā'īyāt attributed to Khayyām are in fact his. Until the end of the nineteenth century this does not seem to have worried anybody. Manuscript, lithographed and printed editions contained hundreds, even more than a thousand, quatrains. By the turn of the century however scholars were becoming aware of two curious circumstances: first, early sources for Khayyām's verses were almost non-existent, and secondly, a number of those commonly attributed to him are to be found in the collected works of other poets.

So far as sources are concerned, there are none contemporary with Khayyām, and the only one dating from the 6th/12th century is the *Sindbād-nāma* of Ẓahīrī Samarqandī, written in 555/1160, which contains five anonymous quatrains attributed to Khayyām in later sources:

chūn nīst maqām-i mā dar īn dahr muqīm
pas bī mai u ma'shūq khaṭā'ī-st 'aẓīm
tā kai zi qadīm u muḥdath ummīdam u bīm
chūn man raftam jahān chi muḥdath chi qadīm

I am not here forever in this world;
How sinful then to forfeit wine and love!
The world may be eternal or created;
Once I am gone, it matters not a scrap.

*

ma-shnau sukhan az zamāna-sāz-āmadagān
mai khwāh muravvaq bi-ṭarāz-amadagān
raftand yakān yakān farāz-āmadagān
kas mī-na-dihad nishān zi bāz-āmadagān

Ignore the fools who temporize with Fate;
Your darling friends will pour you sparkling wine.
So many postured here awhile and went,
And never has a man of them returned.

*

bar gīr piyāla ū sabū ai dil-jūy
tā bi-khrāmīm gird-i bāgh ū lab-i jūy
bas shakhs-i 'azīz-rā ki charkh-i bad-khūy
ṣad bār piyāla kard u ṣad bār sabūy

Lift up the cup and bowl, my darling love,
Walk proudly through the garden by the stream;
For many a slender beauty Heaven has made
Into a hundred cups, a hundred bowls.

*

az jumla-i raftagān-i īn rāh-i darāz
bāz āmada kīst tā bi-mā gūyad rāz
pas bar sar-i īn du-rāha-i āz u niyāz
tā hīch namānī ki namī-ā'ī bāz

Of all the travellers on this endless road
No one returns to tell us where it leads.
There's little in this world but greed and need;
Leave nothing here, for you will not return.

*

īn charkh-i falak ki mā dar ān ḥairān-īm
fānūs-i khiyāl az ān mithālī dānīm
khwurshīd chirāgh dān u 'ālam fānūs
mā chūn ṣuvar-īm k-andar ān gardānīm

This sphere of Heaven in which we wander lost
Seems to me rather like a shadow-lantern;
The sun's the lamp, the world's the twirling shade,
And we the figures painted round about.

Khayyām's name first appears as the author of rubā'īyāt in 7th/13th-century sources, by which time we are already a century after his own time, more than sufficient for corruptions and interpolations to have taken place. Even so the material is still very scanty. A treatise on the Qur'ān by the Imām Fakhr al-Dīn Rāzī, written at the beginning of the century, provides us with one:

dāranda chu tarkīb-i ṭabāyi' ārāst
az bahr-i chi ū fikandash andar kam u kāst
gar nīk āmad shikastan az bahr-i chi būd
v-ar nīk nayāmad īn ṣuvar 'aib kirā-st

Our elements were merged at His command;
Why then did He disperse them once again?
For if the blend was good, why break it up?
If it was bad, whose was the fault but His?

A Ṣūfī work, the *Mirṣād al-'ibād*, written by Shaikh Najm al-Dīn Dāya in about 619/1222, attacks Khayyām for impiety and quotes against him the above rubā'ī together with the following:

dar dāyira-ī k-āmadan ū raftan-i mā-st
ān-rā na bidāyat na nihāyat paidā-st
kas mī-na-zanad damī dar īn ma'nī rāst
k-īn āmadan az kujā va raftan bi-kujā-st

This circle within which we come and go
Has neither origin nor final end.
Will no one ever tell us truthfully
Whence we have come, and whither do we go?

In 658/1260 'Aṭā Malik Juvainī wrote his history of the Mongol invasions *Tārīkh-i Jahān-gushā*, in the course of which, by way of comment on the massacre of the people of Marv, he quotes the following verse by Khayyām:

ajzā-yi piyāla-ī ki dar ham paivast
bi-shkastan-i ān ravā namī-dārad mast
chandīn sar u pā-yi nāzanīn az sar-i dast
bar mihr-i ki paivast u bi-kīn-i ki shikast

Even a drunkard never would propose
To smash to bits his neatly-fashioned cup.
By whom then were so many comely bodies
Fashioned in love, yet smashed in angry hate?

In this period we must also include a recently discovered anthology, *al-Aqṭāb al-quṭbīya*, even though internal evidence suggests that it is not altogether a reliable source. This was written by 'Abd al-Qādir b. Ḥamza Āharī in 629/1232, and the oldest extant manuscript is dated 666/1268. It contributes the following additional rubā'īyāt to our stock:

dar justan-i jām-i jam jahān paimūdam
rūzī na-nishastam u shabī na-ghnūdam
z-ustād chu rāz-i jām-i jam bi-shnūdam
ān jām-i jahān-namā-yi jam man būdam

I scoured the world in search of Jamshid's bowl,
Not resting days nor sleeping in the night.
And then a teacher told me the plain truth:
That world-revealing bowl is – I myself.

*

mā'īm dar īn gunbad-i dīrīna-asās
jūyanda-i rakhna'ī chu mūr andar ṭās
āgāh na az manzil u ummīd u harās
sar-gashta va chashm-basta chūn gāv-i kharās

Here we are, trapped beneath this ancient vault,
Scurrying like ants in search of some escape;
We're lost, and yet feel neither hope nor fear,
Confused and blindfold, like the miller's ox.

*

mā lu'batakānīm u falak lu'bat-bāz
az rū-yi haqīqatī na az rū-yi majāz
bāzī chu hamī-kunīm bar naṭ'-i vujūd
raftīm bi-ṣandūq-i 'adam yak yak bāz

We are the pawns, and Heaven is the player;
This is plain truth, and not a mode of speech.
We move about the chessboard of the world,
Then drop into the casket of the void.

*

z-āvardan-i man na-būd gardūn-rā sūd
v-az burdan-i man jāh u jalālash nafzūd
v-az hīch kasī nīz du gūsham nashnūd
k-āvardan u burdan-i man az bahr-i chi būd

What gain did Heaven get from making me?
What kudos did it earn from my demise?
Yet I have never heard from anyone
Why I was brought here, and why taken away.

Thus up to a century and a half after Khayyām's death we have at most a dozen quatrains plausibly attributed to him. The following century is a little more generous; sources like the *Mu'nis al-aḥrār* (740/1339), the *Nuzhat al-majālis* (731/1331), the *Tārīkh-i guzīda* (730/1330), two manuscripts in the Majlis Library in Tehrān, and a manuscript of the *Lam'at al-sirāj* written in 695/1296, give us another 55, making a total of 67 up to the end of the 8th/14th century – still a very modest figure. It is only during the 9th/15th century that we find the first major collections of Khayyāmic rubā'īyāt – the Bodleian MS of 865/1460 with 158, the *Ṭarab-khāna* of 867/1462 with 373, and various other manuscripts of comparable date and bulk in Istanbul, Paris and elsewhere. We can scarcely doubt that this steadily rising curve was the result of a growing acceptance of Khayyām as an accredited writer of rubā'īyāt, to whose name almost any quatrain could plausibly be attached.

This would also account for the phenomenon of the "wandering" quatrains, first noted by Zhukovskii in 1897. The Russian scholar drew attention to 82 quatrains included in J. B. Nicolas's edition of Khayyām's rubā'īyāt published in 1867, which he had found in the dīvāns of some forty different poets ranging from Firdausī (321/933–411/1020) to Ṭālib Āmuli (d. 1034/1625). Since Zhukovskii's time the researches of such scholars as Arthur Christensen, E. Denison Ross, Friedrich Rosen[1] and Christian Rempis have at one and the same time added to the number of "wandering" quatrains and whittled away the sum of "authentic" ones. The two extremes are represented by H. H. Schaeder, who in 1934 roundly declared that Khayyām's name "is to be struck out of the history of Persian poetry", and Swami Govinda Tirtha,[2] who in 1941 listed no fewer than 756 "vagrants" out of the total of 2,213 quatrains he had found in Khayyām's name. These 756 were distributed over a list of 143 poets ranging over six centuries and reading like a roll-call of the great and small figures of classical Persian literature.

Clearly, if any sense is to be made out of this confused scene, we must accept, first, that many of the rubā'īyāt are not by Khayyām, and secondly, that even the authentic ones were probably improvised by him in his leisure moments, and did not achieve the dignity of written record until after a century or more of oral transmission. To sift the

[1] "Zur Textfrage der Vierzeiler Omar's des Zeltmachers", in *ZDMG* (1926), pp. 265ff.

[2] H. H. Schaeder, "Der geschichtliche und der mythische Omar Chajjam", in *ZDMG*, Band XIII (88) (Leipzig, 1934), pp. *25*–*28*; Tirtha, p. 182.

true from the false, some criterion of authenticity over and above manuscript evidence needs to be adopted, and something of this kind has been attempted in recent years by Iranian scholars. Muḥammad ʿAlī Furūghī in 1942 used the 66 rubāʿīyāt in the earliest manuscript sources then available to him as "key" quatrains, and rejected any later additions that did not seem to him to be consistent with the outlook characteristic of these. This left him with a total of 178. In 1966 ʿAlī Dashtī, using a rather more cautious approach, accepted only 36 "key" quatrains, but filled out his picture of Khayyām's view of life by reference to his prose writings and to contemporary and near-contemporary biographical records. On this basis he found himself able to add another 65 as probably authentic – out of which total of 101, 79 figure in Furūghī's list. The discrepancy illustrates the difficulty of arriving at any conclusive answer, but at least the Furūghī and Dashtī lists present a more or less consistent picture of their author, which is more than can be said for some of the amorphous collections of the 10th/16th century and later. A few characteristic examples, which would probably be accepted as authentic by most scholars and critics, are given below, and present a clear enough picture of a rationalist, sceptical enquirer, uncomfortably aware of the limitations of the scientific method, seeking vainly for a rational explanation of the contradictions of life and death, creation and destruction, compounding and dissolution, existence and non-existence. His scientific and philosophical writings, his public image, reveal none of these doubts; only in his impromptu verse do we see something of the private fears and misgivings that made it impossible for him to surrender either to the certainties of science or to the spiritual consolations of religion.

īn baḥr-i vujūd āmada bīrūn zi nihuft
kas nīst ki īn gauhar-i taḥqīq bi-suft
har kas sukhanī az sar-i saudā guftand
z-ān rūy ki hast kas namī-dānad guft

The boundless universe was born of night;
No man has ever pierced its secrets yet.
They all have much to say for their own good,
But none can tell us who he is, or why.

*

yak qaṭra-i āb būd u bā daryā shud
yak dharra-i khāk bā zamīn yak-jā shud
āmad-shudan-i tu andar īn ʿālam chīst
āmad magasī padīd u nā-paidā shud

A drop of water fell into the sea,
A speck of dust came floating down to earth.
What signifies your passage through this world?
A tiny gnat appears – and disappears.

*

vaqt-i ṣaḥar ast khīz ai māya-i nāz
narmak narmak bāda dih ū chang navāz
k-īnhā ki bi-jāyand na-pāyand darāz
v-ānhā ki shudand kas namīyāyad bāz

The dawn is here; arise, my lovely one,
Pour slowly, slowly wine, and touch the lute.
For those who still are here will not stay long,
While those departed never will return.

*

har yak chandī yakī bar āyad ki man-am
bā niʿmat u bā sīm u zar āyad ki man-am
chūn kārak-i ū niẓām gīrad rūzī
nāgah ajal az kamīn dar āyad ki man-am

Once in a while a man arises boasting;
He shows his wealth, and cries out, "It is I!"
A day or two his puny matters flourish;
Then Death appears and cries out, "It is I!"

*

har dharra ki bar rūy-i zamīnī būda-st
khwurshīd-rukhī māh-jabīnī būda-st
gard az rukh-i nāzanīn bi-āzarm fishān
k-ān ham rukh-i khūb-i nāzanīnī būda-st

Each particle of dust upon this earth
Was once a moon-like face, the brow of Venus;
Wipe gently from your loved one's cheek the dust,
For this same dust was once a loved one's cheek.

*

faṣl-i gul u ṭarf-i jūybār u lab-i kisht
bā yak du si ahl u luʿbatī ḥūr-sirisht
pish ār qadaḥ ki bāda-nūshān-i ṣabūḥ
āsūda zi masjid-and u fārigh zi kinisht

The rose-clad meadow by the water's edge,
Two or three friends, a charming playmate too;
Bring out the cup, for we who drink at dawn
Care nothing for the mosque or synagogue.

*

ayyām-i zamāna az kasī dārad nang
kū dar gham-i ayyām nishīnad dil-tang
mai nūsh dar ābgīna bā nāla-i chang
z-ān pīsh k-at ābgīna āyad bar sang

He merely earns the odium of Fate
Who sits and grumbles at his wretched lot.
Drink from the crystal cup, and touch the lute,
Before your cup is dashed against the ground.

*

ān-rā ki bi-ṣaḥrā-yi 'ilal tākhta and
bī ū hama kārhā bi-pardākhta and
imrūz bahāna-ī dar andākhta and
fardā hama ān buvad ki dī sākhta and

Though man be driven into black despair,
Life goes on well enough without his aid.
Today is nothing but a make-believe;
Tomorrow all will be as it was planned.

CHAPTER 20 (*b*)

'UMAR KHAYYAM: ASTRONOMER, MATHEMATICIAN AND POET

Ghiyāth al-Dīn Abu'l-Fatḥ 'Umar b. Ibrāhīm al-Khayyāmī (the full name of 'Umar Khayyām as it appears in the Arabic sources) in Persian texts is usually called simply 'Umar-i Khayyām, that is, 'Umar the tent-maker, and it is reasonable to assume that his father or grandfather followed that trade. He was almost certainly born in Nīshāpūr, where he passed the greater part of his life and where his grave is still to be seen. Our earliest authority, the *Tatimma ṣuwān al-ḥikma* (or *Ta'rīkh ḥukamā' al-Islām*), by Ẓahīr al-Dīn Abu'l-Ḥasan Baihaqī, written some time before 549/1154–5, states quite categorically that 'Umar was a Nīshāpūrī by birth, as also were his father and his ancestors.[1] On the other hand, a late work, the *Tārīkh-i alfī* of Aḥmad Tatavī (988/1580) refers to another tradition according to which his family came from a village called Shamshād near Balkh, though he himself was born in the vicinity of Astarābād at the north-east corner of the Caspian. So, too, the 9th/15th-century writer Yār Aḥmad Rashīdī Tabrīzī in his *Ṭarab-khāna* says that 'Umar was born near Astarābād and passed his early life in Balkh.

The dates of his birth and death have only recently been established; thanks to the researches of the Indian scholar Govinda Tirtha and the Soviet scholars Rozenfel'd and Yushkevich, the editors of 'Umar's scientific works, it is possible to name, with almost absolute certainty, the actual date not only of his birth but also of his death. It so happens that Baihaqī, our oldest authority, gives the full details of his horoscope, and on the basis of these data Govinda was able to calculate the exact day of 'Umar's birth. The Institute of Theoretical Astronomy of the Academy of Sciences of the U.S.S.R. checked Govinda's calculations and reached the conclusion that between the years 1015 and 1054 the astronomical conditions of the horoscope were satisfied on one day only, 18 May 1048 – the very date that had been calculated by Govinda.

[1] E. D. Ross and H. A. R. Gibb, "The earliest account of 'Umar Khayyām", *BSOS*, vol. V (1928–30), pp. 467–73.

Now according to Niẓāmī 'Arūḍī Samarqandī, our second oldest authority, in a passage in his *Chahār maqāla* he must have died in 526/1131–2, for Niẓāmī visited his tomb in 530/1135–6, *four* years after his death. From evidence in the *Ṭarab-khāna* Rozenfel'd and Yushkevich were also able to calculate that the precise date of his death was Thursday, 12 Muḥarram 526/4 December 1131. Born then in 439/1048 'Umar lived to the age of 83.

Of 'Umar's early life we know nothing. We must assume that he pursued his studies in Nīshāpūr, but the famous story of the Three Friends, familiar from FitzGerald's preface to the *Rubā'īyāt*, can now be finally dismissed as pure legend. 'Umar, it will be remembered, was said to have been a fellow-student at Nīshāpūr with Niẓām al-Mulk, the vizier of the Saljuq sulṭāns Alp-Arslān and Malik-Shāh, and Ḥasan-i Ṣabbāḥ, the founder of the sect of the Ismā'īlīs or Assassins of Alamūt. If, however, 'Umar was born, as seems reasonably certain, in 439/1048, then Niẓām al-Mulk, who was born in 410/1020,[1] would have been about thirty years of age at the time of his birth, and they cannot possibly have been fellow-students. That 'Umar and Ḥasan-i Ṣabbāḥ should have studied together presents no chronological difficulties, but there is not the slightest evidence that Ḥasan, a native of Ray, received his education in Nīshāpūr.

We first hear of the adult 'Umar in Samarqand; it was here that he composed his treatise on algebra under the patronage of the chief qāḍī Abū Ṭāhir 'Abd al-Raḥmān b. 'Alaq. By Abū Ṭāhir he must have been presented to the Qarakhānid ruler Shams al-Mulk Naṣr b. Ibrāhīm (460/1068–472/1080), who, so Baihaqī informs us, "used to show him the greatest honour, so much so that he would seat the Imām 'Umar beside him on his divan". He was presumably still at Shams al-Mulk's court in Bukhārā in 466/1073–4, when peace was concluded with Sulṭān Malik-Shāh, who had invaded the khan's territory, and it must have been then, at the age of twenty-six, that 'Umar entered Malik-Shāh's service. The reformation of the Persian calendar and the building of an observatory at Iṣfahān, undertakings in which 'Umar played a leading part, are mentioned by the 7th/13th-century Arab historian Ibn al-Athīr under the year 467/1074–5. The new calendar, named Malikī or Jalālī was more accurate than the Gregorian, although five hundred years earlier. The observatory remained in use until the death of Malik-Shāh in 485/1092–3, but after that it was disused.

[2] Baihaqī, *Tārīkh-i Baihaq*, p. 130.

With Sulṭān Malik-Shāh 'Umar was on terms of intimacy, being admitted to the company of his *nadīms* or favourite courtiers, but Sulṭān Sanjar, whom he had treated as a boy for small-pox, conceived a dislike for him, and it is perhaps significant that we have no record of his activities after Sanjar's accession to the sultanate in 511/1118. He seems in fact to have fallen from grace after Malik-Shāh's death; he went on the pilgrimage and, upon his return, retired to Nīshāpūr, where he appears to have lived the life of a recluse. We do not hear of him again until 506/1112–13, when he was in Balkh in the company of Abu'l-Muẓaffar Isfizārī, who had collaborated with him in the computation of the Jalālī era: it was here that Niẓāmī 'Arūḍī heard him make his famous prophecy about his place of burial. In 1113 or 1114, probably in Nīshāpūr, he was visited by Baihaqī and his father and catechized the former, then a boy of eight, on Arabic philology and geometry. Finally, in the winter of 508/1114–15 we find him at Marv, whence he was summoned to make a weather forecast for the sultan, who wished to go hunting; this is, presumably, Sulṭān Muḥammad, the second son and third successor (498/1105–511/1118) of Malik-Shāh; it is less likely to have been his brother Sanjar, although the latter had ruled over Khurāsān (of which Marv was then part) since 489/1096. The story is told by Niẓāmī 'Arūḍī:

In the winter of the year A.H. 508 [A.D. 1114–15] the King sent a messenger to Marv to the Prime Minister Ṣadr al-Din [Abū Ja'far] Muḥammad b. al-Muẓaffar (on whom be God's Mercy) bidding him tell Khwāja Imām 'Umar to select a favourable time for him to go hunting, such that therein should be no snowy or rainy days. For Khwāja Imām 'Umar was in the Minister's company, and used to lodge at his house.

The Minister, therefore, sent a messenger to summon him, and told him what had happened. So he went and looked into the matter for two days, and made a careful choice; and he himself went and superintended the mounting of the King at the auspicious moment. When the King was mounted and had gone but a short distance, the sky became over-cast with clouds, a wind arose . . . and snow and mist supervened. All present fell to laughing and the King desired to turn back; but Khwāja Imām ['Umar] said, "Let the King be of good cheer, for this very hour the clouds will clear away, and during these five days there will not be a drop of moisture." So the King rode on, and the clouds opened, and during those five days there was no moisture, and no one saw a cloud.

'Umar was in his sixty-seventh year when he made his prediction. Over the remaining sixteen years of his life there is drawn an impenetrable veil. His death scene is described by his brother-in-law, the Imām

Muḥammad al-Baghdādī, who told Baihaqī that "he used to use a golden toothpick. He was studying the metaphysics in Avicenna's *Shifā*, and when he came to the chapter on 'The One and the Many', he placed the toothpick between the two pages and said, 'Summon the righteous ones that I may make my testament.' He then made his testament, arose and prayed, neither ate nor drank. When he prayed the last evening prayer he prostrated himself saying as he did so, 'O God, Thou knowest that I have sought to know Thee to the measure of my powers. Forgive my sins, for my knowledge of Thee is my means of approach to Thee', and died."

For an account of his final resting place we turn again to Niẓāmī 'Arūḍī:

In the year A.H. 506 [A.D. 1112–13] Khwāja 'Umar-i-Khayyāmī and Khwāja Imām Muẓaffar-i-Isfizārī had alighted in the city of Balkh, in the Street of the Slave-sellers, in the house of Amīr . . . Abū Sa'd Jarrah, and I had joined that assembly. In the midst of our convivial gathering I heard that Argument of Truth [*Ḥujjat al-Ḥaqq*] 'Umar say, "My grave will be in a spot where the trees will shed their blossoms on me twice a year." This thing seemed to me impossible, though I knew that one such as he would not speak idle words.

When I arrived at Nīshāpūr in the year A.H. 530 [A.D. 1135–6], it being then four years since that great man had veiled his countenance in the dust, and this nether world had been bereaved of him, I went to visit his grave on the eve of a Friday (seeing that he had the claim of a master on me), taking with me one to point out to me his tomb. So he brought me out to the Ḥīra Cemetery; I turned to the left, and found his tomb situated at the foot of a garden-wall, over which pear-trees and peach-trees thrust their heads, and on his grave had fallen so many flower-leaves that his dust was hidden beneath the flowers. Then I remembered that saying which I had heard from him in the city of Balkh, and I fell to weeping, because on the face of the earth, and in all the regions of the habitable globe, I nowhere saw one like unto him. May God (blessed and exalted is He!) have mercy upon him, by His Grace and His Favour!

'Umar Khayyām, says Baihaqī, "was niggardly in both composing and teaching, and wrote nothing but a compendium on physics, a treatise on Existence, and another on Being and Obligation, though he had a wide knowledge of philology, jurisprudence and history". In fact, his surviving scientific works, if one excludes the spurious *Naurūz-nāma*, a treatise on the Persian New Year's Day, occupy only 130 pages in Rozenfel'd's translation. For an assessment of these works the reader is referred to his and Yushkevich's introductory essays and commentary and to Professor E. S. Kennedy's chapter ("The Exact Sciences in Iran under the Saljuqs and Mongols") in Volume 5 of the *Cambridge History of Iran.* It is the *rubā'īyāt* or quatrains which, mirrored in FitzGerald's masterpiece, have won for 'Umar the poet a fame far greater than was vouchsafed to 'Umar the scientist. Though not disdained by the professional poets, these brief poems seem often to have been the work of scholars and scientists who composed them, perhaps, in moments of relaxation to edify or amuse – for their content can be both grave and gay – the inner circle of their disciples. We have *rubā'īs* by Avicenna (d. 428/1037), the greatest of the Persian philosophers, whom 'Umar regarded as his master and whose encyclopaedic work, the *Shifā*, he was reading at the time of his death; by Ghazzālī (d. 505/1111), a contemporary but no friend of 'Umar; and by Naṣīr al-Dīn Ṭūsī (d. 672/1274), an astronomer like 'Umar and the builder of an observatory of which, unlike 'Umar's, the remains can still be traced. Such *vers d'occasion* would at first have been transmitted mainly by word of mouth, but writers of the next generation or two would quote them in their works and gradually, over the centuries, they would be collected together in anthologies, etc. This is at any rate what happened to 'Umar's poems. Not until the middle of the 9th/15th century – three hundred years after his death – do the first attempts appear to have been made to collect together the whole corpus of his poems. Of these collections the best known by far is the Bodleian MS. used by FitzGerald: it was compiled in Shīrāz in 865/1460–1 and contains 158 rubā'īs. Of the manuscripts preserved in the Istanbul libraries one, bearing the same date as the Bodleian MS., has as many as 315, while another, four years older, has only 131 rubā'īs.

From now onwards the rubā'īyāt were copied with greater frequency and increased in number with each copy, the copyists tending to incorporate the work of other poets and sometimes, perhaps, their own as well. In addition to the Bodleian MS. with its mere 158 rubā'īs FitzGerald also consulted the transcript of an undated Calcutta MS., probably 12th/18th century, which contained no less than 516. So, too, Nicolas's edition of the Persian text (Paris, 1867), based on a Tehrān lithograph, comprised a total of 464 rubā'īs. Even these figures pale into insignificance compared with the 604 in the Bankipur MS. and the 770 in the Lucknow lithographed edition of 1894–5. The quantity was however drastically reduced by the researches of such scholars as Zhukovski, Ross and, above all, Christensen. The final verdict of the last-named scholar was that of more than 1,200 rubā'īs known to be ascribed to 'Umar, only 121 could be regarded as reasonably authentic. E. G. Browne as long ago as 1906 declared "that while it is certain that 'Umar Khayyām wrote many quatrains, it is hardly possible, save in a few exceptional cases, to assert positively that he wrote any particular one of those ascribed to him". It was and, despite apparent evidence to the contrary, is still possible to argue that his status as a poet of the first rank was a comparatively late development and that to his contemporaries and to the immediately succeeding generations he was a scientist pure and simple.

The question of 'Umar's feelings about mysticism has been disputed. Some Ṣūfīs have claimed him as their own, others just the opposite. Now while he may well, like Avicenna before him, have had his mystical side, he was after all, like his master, a philosopher, that is, a champion of Greek learning, and as such regarded with equal hostility by the orthodox and the Ṣūfīs – we have seen that he was disliked by Ghazzālī, who was in a sense a representative of both parties. That the Ṣūfīs – or some of them – adapted his poems to their own ideas we know from an often-quoted passage from the "History of the Philosophers" of Qifṭī (568/1172–646/1248): "The later Ṣūfīs have found themselves in agreement with some part of the apparent sense of his verse, and have transferred it to their system, and discussed it in their assemblies and private gatherings, though its inward meanings are to the [Ecclesiastical] Law stinging serpents, and combinations rife with malice." On the other hand the celebrated Ṣūfī mystic Najm al-Dīn Dāya (d. 654/1256) speaks of 'Umar as one of "those poor philosophers, atheists and materialists who . . . err and go astray" and as proof of this assertion quotes two of his rubā'īs, which, he says, demonstrate "the height of confusion and error". Similar sentiments are expressed by a witness whose authority is beyond question: the celebrated Ṣūfī poet and thinker Farīd al-Dīn 'Aṭṭār (*c*. 537/1142–3 to *c*. 617/1220), the author, in addition to his *mathnavīs* or narrative poems, of the *Tadhkirat al-auliyā* ("Memorial of the Saints") containing ninety-seven biographies of ancient mystics. In his *Ilāhī-nāma* or "Book of the Divinity" he tells the story of a clairvoyant who could read the thoughts of the dead. Taken to the tomb of 'Umar Khayyām the seer is asked to practise his art, and speaks as follows:

> This is a man in a state of imperfection.
> At that Threshold towards which he turned his
> face he laid claim to knowledge.

Now that his ignorance had been revealed to him,
his soul is sweating from confusion.
He is left between shame and confusion; his
very studies have made him deficient.[1]

Thus this great expert on Ṣūfism, writing less than a century after 'Umar's death, saw in the astronomer-poet not a fellow-mystic, but a free-thinking scientist, who all his life had exalted Reason over Revelation and who now, in his tomb, awaited with fear and trepidation the final reckoning on Judgment Day.

[1] 'Aṭṭār, *Ilāhī-nāma*, ed. H. Ritter (Istanbul, 1940), p. 272, ll. 12–15; ed. F. Rouhani Tehrān, 1340/1961), p. 215, ll. 5173–6.

BIBLIOGRAPHY

Volume Editor's Note

The bibliographies printed below are selective and not intended to be complete; in general they include those works used by each author in the preparation of his chapter. It has not been possible to check the source references of all authors, especially where rare editions of texts have been used. As a rule books and articles superseded by later publications have not been included.

The abbreviations and short titles used in the bibliographies are listed below.

AA	*Arts asiatiques* (Paris)
AESC	*Annales: économies, sociétés, civilisations* (Paris)
AGNT	*Archiv für die Geschichte der Naturwissenschaften und der Technik* (Leipzig)
AGWG	*Abhandlungen der königlichen Gesellschaft der Wissenschaften zu Göttingen* (Berlin)
AI	*Ars Islamica* (Ann Arbor, Mich.)
AIEO	*Annales de l'Institut d'Études Orientales* (Paris–Algiers)
AIUON	*Annali, Istituto Universitario Orientale di Napoli* (Naples)
AJSLL	*The American Journal of Semitic Languages and Literatures* (Chicago)
ANS	American Numismatic Society
ANSMN	*American Numismatic Society Museum Notes* (New York)
ANSNNM	*American Numismatic Society Numismatic Notes and Monographs* (New York)
ANSNS	*American Numismatic Society Numismatic Studies* (New York)
AO	*Ars Orientalis* (continuation of *Ars Islamica*) (Ann Arbor, Mich.)
BAIPAA	*Bulletin of the American Institute for Persian Art and Archaeology* (New York)
BGA	*Bibliotheca Geographorum Arabicorum*, 8 vols. (Leiden)
BIFAO	*Bulletin de l'Institut Français d'Archéologie Orientale* (Cairo)
BSOAS	*Bulletin of the School of Oriental and African Studies* (London)
EI	*Encyclopedia of Islam* (Leiden)
GMS	"E. J. W. Gibb Memorial" series (Leiden–London)
IA	*Iranica Antiqua* (Leiden)
IC	*Islamic Culture* (Hyderabad)
IQ	*Islamic Quarterly* (London)
Iran	*Iran* (journal of the British Institute of Persian Studies) (London–Tehrān)
Iraq	*Iraq* (journal of the British School of Archaeology in Iraq) (London)

IS	*Islamic Studies* (journal of the Central Institute of Islamic Studies, Karachi) (Karachi)
Der Islam	*Der Islam* (Zeitschrift für Geschichte und Kultur des Islamischen Orients) (Berlin)
JA	*Journal asiatique* (Paris)
JAOS	*Journal of the American Oriental Society* (New York)
JESHO	*Journal of Economic and Social History of the Orient* (Leiden)
JNES	*Journal of Near Eastern Studies* (continuation of *American Journal of Semitic Languages*) (Chicago)
JRAS	*Journal of the Royal Asiatic Society* (London)
JSS	*Journal of Semitic Studies* (Manchester)
MRASB	*Memoirs of the Royal Asiatic Society of Bengal* (Calcutta)
MSOS	*Mitteilungen des Seminars für orientalische Sprachen* (Berlin)
MW	*Muslim World* (Hartford, Conn.)
NC	*Numismatic Chronicle* (London)
NHR	Miles, G. C. *The Numismatic History of Rayy*. New York, 1938 (*ANSNS*, vol. II)
NZ	*Numismatische Zeitschrift* (Vienna)
RENLO	*Revue de l'École Nationale des Langues Orientales* (Paris)
RFLM	*Revue de la Faculté des Lettres de Meched* (Mashhad)
RFLT	*Revue de la Faculté des Lettres et des Sciences Humaines de Téhéran* (Tehrān)
RN	*Revue numismatique* (Paris)
SBWAW	*Sitzungsberichte der Wiener (Österreichischen) Akademie der Wissenschaften* (Vienna)
Syria	*Syria* (revue d'art oriental et d'archéologie) (Paris)
WZKM	*Wiener Zeitschrift für die Kunde des Morgenlandes* (Vienna)
ZDMG	*Zeitschrift der deutschen morgenländischen Gesellschaft* (Wiesbaden)

CHAPTER 1

1. *Primary sources*

Balādhurī. *Futūḥ al-buldān*, ed. M. J. de Goeje. Leiden, 1866.
Dīnawarī. *al-Akhbār al-ṭiwāl*, ed. V. Guirgass. Leiden, 1888.
Ḥamza al-Isfahānī. *Kitāb ta'rīkh sinī mulūk al-arḍ wa'l-anbiyā'*, ed. S. H. Taqizadeh. Berlin, 1921.
Mas'ūdī. *Murūj al-dhahab* (*Les prairies d'or*), 9 vols., ed. and tr. C. A. Barbier de Meynard and A. J. Pavet de Courteille. Paris, 1861–77.
Ṭabarī. *Ta'rīkh al-rusul wa'l mulūk*, 15 vols., ed. M. J. de Goeje *et al.* Leiden, 1879–1901.
Ya'qūbī. *Ta'rīkh*, 2 vols., ed. M. T. Houtsma. Leiden, 1883.

2. *Secondary sources*

Cahen, Claude. *Der Islam*, vol. 1. Frankfurt, 1968.
Spuler, Berthold. *Iran in früh-islamischer Zeit.* Wiesbaden, 1952. (Extensive bibliography.)
Zarrīnkūb, 'Abd al-Ḥusain. *Tārīkh-i Īrān ba'd az Islām*, vol. 1. Tehrān, 1343/1965. (Extensive bibliography.)

CHAPTER 2

Bal'amī, Abu 'Alī Muḥammad. *Tarjuma-yi tārīkh-i Ṭabarī.* Tehrān, 1337/1959.
Dūrī, 'Abd al-'Azīz. *al-'Asr al-'Abbāsī al-awwal.* Baghdad, 1363/1945.
Jahshiyārī, Abū 'Abd-Allāh Muḥammad b. 'Abdūs. *Kitāb al-wuzarā' wa'l-kuttāb.* Cairo, 1357/1938.
Lewis, Bernard, "'Abbāsids", *EI*, 2nd ed.
Mas'ūdī. *Muruj al-dhahab* (*Les prairies d'or*), 9 vols., ed. and tr. C. A. Barbier de Meynard and A. J. Pavet de Courteille. Paris, 1861–77.
Miskawaih. *Tajārib al-umam*, vol. 1. Cairo, 1914–15.
Qummī, Ḥasan b. Muḥammad b. Ḥasan. *Tārīkh-i Qumm*, ed. Jalāl al-Dīn Ṭihrānī. Tehrān, 1313/1934.
al-Ṣābi', Hilāl. *al-Wuzarā'.* Cairo, 1958.
Sourdel, Dominique. *Le Vizirat 'Abbāside*, 2 vols. Damas, 1959–60.
Spuler, Bertold. *Iran in früh-islamischer Zeit.* Wiesbaden, 1952. (Extensive annotated bibliography.)
Ṭabarī. *Ta'rīkh al-rusul wa'l-mulūk*, 15 vols., ed. M. J. de Goeje *et al.* Leiden, 1879–1901.
Ya'qūbī. *Ta'rīkh.* Najaf, 1939.
Zarrīnkūb, 'Abd al-Ḥusain. *Tārikh-i Īrān ba'd az Islām*, vol. 1. Tehrān, 1343/1965.

CHAPTER 3

1. *Primary sources*

'Arīb. *Ṣilat ta'rīkh al-Ṭabarī*, ed. M. J. de Goeje. Leiden, 1897.

'Aufī, in M. Niẓāmu 'd-Dīn, *Introduction to the Jawámi'u 'l-ḥikáyát of Muḥammad 'Awfí*. London, 1929 (GMS, n.s. vol. VIII). Facsimile partial text. Tehrān, 1335/1956.

Gardīzī. *Zain al-akhbār*, ed. M. Nāẓim. Berlin, 1928. Ed. 'Abd al-Ḥayy Ḥabībī. Tehrān, 1347/1968.

Ibn al-Athīr. *al-Kāmil fi 'l-ta'rīkh*, 7 vols., ed. C. J. Tornberg. Leiden, 1851–76.

Ibn Khallikān. *Wafayāt al-a'yān*, 4 vols., tr. M. de Slane. Paris–London, 1843–71.

Ibn Ṭaifūr. *Ta'rīkh Baghdād*. Cairo, 1368/1949.

Iṣfahānī, Abu 'l-Faraj. *Kitāb al-aghānī*. Bulaq, 1285/1868; Beirut, 1956–7.

Maqātil al-ṭālibiyyīn, ed. A. Ṣaqr. Cairo, 1368/1949.

Jūzjānī. *Ṭabaqāt-i Nāṣirī*, ed. 'Abd al-Ḥayy Ḥabībī. Kabul, 1342–3/1963–4. Tr. H. G. Raverty. London, 1881–99.

Kitāb al-'uyūn, ed. M. J. de Goeje and P. de Jong in *Fragmenta historicorum arabicorum*, vol. I. Leiden, 1869.

Malik-Shāh Ḥusain b. Malik Ghiyāth al-Dīn. *Iḥyā' al-mulūk*, ed. M. Sutūda. Tehrān, 1344/1966.

Mas'ūdī. *Murūj al-dhahab* (*Les prairies d'or*), 9 vols., ed. and tr. C. A. Barbier de Meynard and A. J. Pavet de Courteille. Paris, 1861–77.

Miskawaih. *Tajārib al-umam*, with the continuations of Rūdhrāwarī and Hilāl al-Ṣābi', ed. and tr. H. F. Amedroz and D. S. Margoliouth in *The Eclipse of the 'Abbasid Caliphate*, 6 vols. Oxford, 1920–1.

Narshakhī. *Tārīkh-i Bukhārā*, tr. R. N. Frye as *The History of Bukhara*. Cambridge, Mass., 1954.

Niẓām al-Mulk. *Siyar al-mulūk* (*Siyāsat-nāma*), ed. H. Darke, 2nd ed. Tehrān, 1347/1968. Tr. H. Darke as *The Book of Government or Rules for Kings*. London, 1960.

Ṭabarī. *Ta'rīkh al-rusul wa'l-mulūk*, 15 vols., ed. M. J. de Goeje *et al.* Leiden, 1879–1901.

Tārīkh-i Sīstān, ed. Bahār. Tehrān, 1314/1935.

'Utbī. *al-Ta'rīkh al-Yamīnī*, with commentary of Manīnī. Cairo, 1286/1869.

Ya'qūbī. *Kitāb al-buldān*, ed. M. J. de Goeje. Leiden, 1892 (*BGA*, vol. VII). Tr. G. Wiet as *Les pays*. Cairo, 1937.

Ta'rīkh, 2 vols., ed. M. T. Houtsma. Leiden, 1883.

2. *Secondary sources*

Barthold, W. "Zur Geschichte der Ṣaffāriden" in *Orientalistische Studien zu Theodor Nöldeke gewidmet*, vol. I (Giessen, 1906), pp. 171–91.

Turkestan down to the Mongol Invasion. London, 1928.

"'Amr b. al-Laith", "Ṭāhirids". *EI*, 1st ed.

Bosworth, C. E. "Notes on the pre-Ghaznavid history of eastern Afghanistan". *IQ*, vol. IX (1965), pp. 12–24.

Bosworth, C. E. *Sīstān under the Arabs, from the Islamic Conquest to the Rise of the Ṣaffārids (30–250/651–864)*. Rome, 1968.
"The Armies of the Early Ṣaffārids". *JRAS* (1968).
"The Ṭāhirids and Arabic Culture". *JSS*, vol. XIV (1969), pp. 45–79.
"The Ṭāhirids and Persian Literature". *Iran*, vol. VII (1969), pp. 103–6.
"An Early Arabic Mirror for Princes: Ṭāhir Dhu'l-Yamīnain's Epistle to his Son 'Abdallāh (206/821)". *JNES*, vol. XXIX (1970), pp. 25–41.
Browne, E. G. *A Literary History of Persia*, vol. I. London, 1902.
Marquart, J. "Ērānšahr nach der Geographie des Ps. Moses Xorenac'i". *AGWG*, n.f. vol. III (2) (1901), pp. 133ff.
Miles, G. C. *The Numismatic History of Rayy*. New York, 1938 (*ANSNS*, vol. II).
Muir, Sir W. *The Caliphate, its Rise, Decline and Fall*, 4th ed. Edinburgh, 1915.
Nafīsī, S. *Tarīkh-i khāndān-i Ṭāhirī*, vol. I, *Ṭāhir b. Ḥusain*. Tehrān, 1335/1956.
Nāẓim, M. *The Life and Times of Sulṭān Maḥmūd of Ghazna*. Cambridge, 1931.
Nöldeke, T. "Yakúb the Coppersmith and his Dynasty" in *Sketches from Eastern History* (London, 1892), pp. 176–206.
Rabino di Borgomale, H. L. "Les préfets du Califat au Ṭabaristān". *JA*, vol. CCXXXI (1939), pp. 237–74.
Rothstein, G. "Zu aš-Šābuštī's Bericht über die Ṭāhiriden (Ms. Wetzstein II, 1100 fol. 44ᵃ–64ᵃ)" in *Orientalistische Studien zu Theodor Nöldeke gewidmet*, vol. I (Giessen, 1906), pp. 155–70.
Sadighi, G. H. *Les mouvements religieux iraniens au IIe et au IIIe siècle de l'hégire*. Paris, 1938.
Sourdel, D. "Les circonstances de la mort de Ṭāhir Ier au Ḫurāsān en 207/822". *Arabica*, vol. V (Leiden, 1958), pp. 66–9.
Spuler, B. *Iran in früh-islamischer Zeit*. Wiesbaden, 1952.
Stern, S. M. "Ya'qūb the Coppersmith and Persian National Sentiment" in *Iran and Islam, in Memory of the Late Vladimir Minorsky*, ed. C. E. Bosworth (Edinburgh, 1971), pp. 535–55.
Vasmer, R. "Über die Münzen der Ṣaffāriden und ihrer Gegner in Fārs und Ḫurāsān". *NZ*, vol. LXIII (1930), pp. 131–62.
Walker, J. "The Coinage of the Second Saffarid Dynasty in Sistan". *ANSNNM*, no. 72 (New York, 1936).
Wright, E. M. "Bābak of Badhdh and al-Afshīn during the Years 816–41 A.D. Symbols of Iranian Persistence against Islamic Penetration in North Iran". *MW*, vol. XXXVIII (1948), pp. 43–59, 124–31.

CHAPTER 4

1. *Primary sources*

Gardīzī. *Zain al-akhbār*, ed. M. Nāẓim. Berlin, 1928. Ed. 'Abd al-Ḥayy Ḥabībī. Tehrān, 1347/1968.
Khwārazmī, M. b. Yūsuf. *Mafātīḥ al-'ulūm*, ed. G. van Vloten. Leiden, 1885.
Mīrkhwānd. *Rauḍat al-ṣafā*, ed. and tr. M. Defrémery. Paris, 1845.

Miskawaih. *Tajārib al-umam*, with the continuations of Rūdhrāwarī and Hilāl al-Ṣābi', ed. and tr. H. F. Amedroz and D. S. Margoliouth in *The Eclipse of the 'Abbasid Caliphate*, 6 vols. Oxford, 1920–1.

Muqaddasī. *Aḥsan al-taqāsīm*, ed. M. J. de Goeje. Leiden, 1906 (*BGA*, vol. III).

Narshakhī. *Tārīkh-i Bukhārā*, ed. C. Schefer (Paris, 1892), pp. 1–97. Tr. R. N. Frye as *The History of Bukhara*. Cambridge, Mass., 1954.

Qazvīnī, Hamd-Allāh Mustaufī. *Tārīkh-i guzīda*, abridged tr. E. G. Browne and R. A. Nicholson. Leiden, 1913 (GMS, o.s. vol. XIV (2)).

Sam'ānī. *Kitāb al-ansāb*, facsimile. Leiden, 1912 (GMS, o.s. vol. XX). Ed. M. 'Abd al-Mu'īd (Hyderabad, 1962ff.).

Tha'ālibī, 'Abd al-Malik. *Yatīmat al-dahr*, vol. IV. Damascus, 1304/1886.

Yāqūt. *Mu'jam al-buldān*, 6 vols., ed. F. Wüstenfeld. Leipzig, 1866–73.

Further references will be found in the translation of Narshakhī, pp. 163–6.

2. *Secondary sources*

Barthold, W. *Turkestan down to the Mongol Invasion*. London, 1928; new ed., 1968 (GMS, n.s. vol. V).

Frye, R. N. *Bukhara, the Medieval Achievement*. Norman, Okla., 1965.

Gafurov, B. G. (ed.). *Istoriya Tadzhikskogo Naroda*, vol. II. Moscow, 1964.

Spuler, B. *Iran in früh-islamischer Zeit*. Wiesbaden, 1952.

CHAPTER 5

For surveys of the sources, see Barthold, *Turkestan*, "Introduction – Sources", pp. 18–24; Nāẓim, *Sulṭān Maḥmūd*, chapter on "Authorities", pp. 1–17; Bosworth, *The Ghaznavids*, "Note on the Sources", pp. 7–24, and "Bibliography", pp. 308–14; Bosworth, "Early Sources for the History of the First Four Ghaznavid Sultans (977–1041)", *IQ*, vol. VII (1963), pp. 3–22. The relevant items in the bibliographies in Spuler, *Iran in früh-islamischer Zeit*, pp. 532–94, and Rypka *et al.*, *History of Iranian Literature* (Dordrecht, 1968), pp. 751–861, should also be consulted.

1. *Primary sources*

Baihaqī, Abu 'l-Faḍl. *Tārīkh-i Mas'ūdī*, ed. Ghanī and Fayyāḍ. Tehrān, 1324/1945. Tr. A. K. Arends as *Istorya Mas'uda (1030–1041)*, 2nd ed. Moscow, 1969.

Baihaqī, Ẓahīr al-Dīn Abu'l-Ḥasan 'Alī b. Zaid. *Tarīkh-i Baihaq*, ed. A. Bahmanyār. Tehrān, 1317/1938.

Bundārī. *Zubdat al-nuṣra wa-nukhbat al-'uṣra*, ed. M. T. Houtsma in *Recueil de textes relatifs à l'histoire des Seljoucides*, vol. II. Leiden, 1889.

Faḍlī, Saif al-Dīn. *Āthār al-wuzarā'*, ed. Jalāl al-Dīn Urmavī. Tehrān, 1337/1959.

Fakhr-i Mudabbir. *Ādāb al-mulūk wa kifāyat al-mamlūk*. India Office MS. no. 647.

Gardīzī. *Zain al-akhbār*, ed. M. Nāẓim. Berlin, 1928. Ed. 'Abd al-Ḥayy Ḥabībī. Tehrān, 1347/1968.

Hilāl al-Ṣābi'. *Ta'rīkh* in *The Eclipse of the 'Abbasid Caliphate*, vols. III, VI, ed. H. F. Amedroz and D. S. Margoliouth. Oxford, 1920–1.

Ḥusainī, Ṣadr al-Dīn. *Akhbār al-daula al-saljūqiyya*, ed. M. Iqbāl. Lahore, 1933.

Ibn al-Athīr. *al-Kāmil fi 'l-ta'rīkh*, ed. C. J. Tornberg. Leiden, 1851–76.

Ibn al-Jauzī. *al-Muntaẓam*. Hyderabad, 1357–9/1938–41.

Jurbādhqānī. *Tarjuma-yi tārīkh-i Yamīnī*, ed. 'Alī Qavīm. Tehrān, 1334/1957.

Jūzjānī. *Ṭabaqāt-i Nāṣirī*, ed. 'Abd al-Ḥayy Ḥabībī. Kabul, 1342–3/1963–4. Tr. H. G. Raverty. London, 1881–99.

Kai Kā'ūs b. Iskandar. *Qābūs-nāma*, ed. R. Levy. London, 1951 (GMS, n.s. vol. XVIII). Tr. Levy as *A Mirror for Princes*. London, 1951.

Kirmānī, Nāṣir al-Dīn. *Nasā'im al-asḥār*, ed. Jalāl al-Dīn Urmavī. Tehrān, 1337/1959.

Niẓām al-Mulk. *Siyar al-mulūk* (*Siyāsat-nāma*), ed. H. Darke, 2nd ed. Tehrān, 1347/1968. Tr. Darke as *The Book of Government or Rules for Kings*. London, 1960.

Niẓāmī 'Arūḍī Samarqandī. *Chahār maqāla*, ed. M. M. Qazvīnī. London, 1910. Tr. E. G. Browne as *Revised Translation of the Chahar Maqāla*. London, 1921 (GMS, o.s. vol. XI (1, 2)).

Qazvīnī, Ḥamd-Allāh Mustaufī. *Tārīkh-i guzīda*, ed. 'Abd al-Ḥusain Navā'ī. Tehrān, 1339/1960.

Rashīd al-Dīn. *Jāmi' al-tawārīkh*, vol. II, part 4, ed. A. Ateş as *Sultan Mahmud ve Devrinin Tarihi*. Ankara, 1957.

Rāvandī. *Rāḥat al-ṣudūr wa āyat al-surūr*, ed. M. Iqbāl. London, 1921 (GMS, n.s. vol. II).

Shabānkāra'ī. *Majma' al-ansāb fi 'l-tawārīkh*. Istanbul MS. Yeni Cami 909.

Tārīkh-i Sīstān, ed. Bahār. Tehrān, 1314/1935.

'Utbī. *al-Ta'rīkh al-Yamīnī* with commentary of Manīnī. Cairo, 1286/1869.

Ẓahīr al-Dīn Nīshāpūrī. *Saljūq-nāma*, ed. I. Afshār. Tehrān, 1332/1953.

2. *Secondary sources*

Barthold, W. *Turkestan down to the Mongol Invasion*. London, 1928; new ed. 1968 (GMS, n.s. vol. V).

"A History of the Turkman People" in *Four Studies on the History of Central Asia*, vol. III. Leiden, 1962.

Biberstein-Kazimirsky, A. de. *Ménoutchehri, poète persan du onzième siècle de notre ère*. Paris, 1886. (Includes a detailed résumé of Baihaqī's *Tārīkh-i Mas'ūdī*.)

Bombaci, A. "Ghaznavidi" in *Enciclopedia Universale dell'Arte*, vol. VI (Venice–Rome), pp. 6–15.

Bosworth, C. E. "Ghaznevid Military Organisation". *Der Islam*, vol. XXXVI (1960), pp. 37–77.

"The Imperial Policy of the Early Ghaznawids". *IS*, vol. I (3) (1962), pp. 49–82.

"The Titulature of the Early Ghaznavids". *Oriens*, vol. XV (1962), pp. 210–33.

The Ghaznavids, their Empire in Afghanistan and Eastern Iran 994–1040. Edinburgh, 1963; 2nd ed. Beirut, 1974.

Bosworth, C. E. "Mahmud of Ghazna in Contemporary Eyes and in Later Persian literature". *Iran*, vol. IV (1966), pp. 85–92.

"The Development of Persian Culture under the Early Ghaznavids". *Iran*, vol. VI (1968), pp. 33–44.

"The Turks in the Islamic Lands up to the Mid-11th Century". *Philologiae Turcicae Fundamenta*, vol. III (Wiesbaden, 1971).

"Ghazna", *EI*, 2nd ed.

"Dailamīs in Central Iran: the Kākūyids of Jibāl and Yazd". *Iran*, vol. VIII (1970), pp. 73–95.

"Kākwayhids", *EI*, 2nd ed.

Browne, E. G. *A Literary History of Persia*, vol. II. London, 1906.

Cahen, C. "Le Malik-Nâmeh et l'histoire des origines seljukides". *Oriens*, vol. II (Leiden, 1949), pp. 31–65.

Dames, M. L. "Maḥmūd of Ghazna", *EI*, 1st ed.

Elliot, Sir H. M. and Dowson, J. *The History of India as Told by Its Own Historians*, II: *The Muhammadan Period*. London, 1869. (Corrected by S. H. Hodivala in *Studies in Indo-Muslim History*. Bombay, 1939.)

Ganguly, D. C. "Ghaznavid Invasion" in *The History and Culture of the Indian People*, V: *The Struggle for Empire* (Bombay, 1966), pp. 1–23.

Gelpke, R. *Sulṭān Mas'ūd I. von Ġazna. Die drei ersten Jahre seiner Herrschaft (421/1030–424/1033)*. Munich, 1957.

Habib, M. *Sultan Mahmud of Ghaznin*. Delhi, 1951.

Haig, Sir Thomas W. "The Yamīnī Dynasty of Ghaznī and Lahore" in *Cambridge History of India*, vol. III: *Turks and Afghans*. Cambridge, 1928.

Khalīl Allāh Khalīlī. "Ghaznaviyān" in *Tārīkh-i Afghānistān*, vol. III. Kabul, 1336/1957.

Nāzim, M. *The Life and Times of Sulṭān Maḥmud of Ghazna*. Cambridge, 1931.

"The Pand-Nāmah of Subuktigīn". *JRAS* (1933), pp. 605–28.

Pritsak, O. "Der Untergang des Reiches des Oğuzischen Yabğu". *Fuad Köprülü Armağanı* (Istanbul, 1953), pp. 397–410.

Ray, H. C. *The Dynastic History of Northern India (Early Mediaeval Period)*, vol. I. Calcutta, 1931.

Sachau, E. "Zur Geschichte und Chronologie von Khwârazm". *SBWAW*, vol. LXXIII (1873), pp. 471–506; vol. LXXIV (1873), pp. 285–330.

Schlumberger, G. "Le palais ghaznévide de Lashkari Bazar". *Syria*, vol. XXIX (1952), pp. 251–70.

Shafi, I. M. "Fresh Light on the Ghaznavids". *IC*, vol. XII (1938), pp. 189–234.

Sourdel-Thomine, J. "Ghaznavids. Art and Monuments", *EI*, 2nd ed.

Spuler, B. *Iran in früh-islamischer Zeit*. Wiesbaden, 1952.

"Ghaznavids", *EI*, 2nd ed.

Zakhoder, B. N. "Selçuklu Devletinin Kuruluşu Sïrasinda Horasan". *Belleten*, vol. XIX (Ankara, 1955), pp. 491–527.

CHAPTER 6

1. *Primary sources*

A. Arabic and Persian

'Arīb b. Sa'd al-Qurṭubī. *Ṣilat ta'rīkh al-Ṭabarī*, ed. M. J. de Goeje. Leiden, 1897.

Auliyā' Allāh. *Tārīkh-i Rūyān*, ed. 'A. Khalīlī. Tehrān, 1313/1934.

Baihaqī, Abu'l-Faḍl. *Tārīkh-i Mas'ūdī*, ed. Ghanī and Fayyāḍ. Tehrān, 1324/1945.

Balādhurī. *Futūḥ al-buldān*, ed. M. J. de Goeje. Leiden, 1866.

Buṭḥānī, Yaḥyā b. al-Ḥusain. *Kitāb al-ifāda fī ta'rīkh al-a'imma al-sāda*. MS. Berlin, Glaser 37.

Hamadānī, Muḥammad b. 'Abd al-Malik. *Takmilat ta'rīkh al-Ṭabarī*, 2nd ed., ed. A. Y. Kan'ān. Beirut, 1961.

Hilāl al-Ṣābi'. See Miskawaih.

Ḥudūd al-'ālam, tr. V. Minorsky. London, 1937 (GMS, n.s. vol. XI).

Ibn Ḥauqal. *al-Masālik wa'l-mamālik*, ed. J. H. Kramers. Leiden–Leipzig, 1938–9 (*BGA*, vol. II).

Ibn 'Inaba. *'Umdat al-ṭālib fī ansāb āl Abī Ṭālib*, ed. M. Ḥ. Āl al-Ṭāliqānī. Najaf, 1961.

Ibn Isfandiyār. *Tārīkh-i Ṭabaristān*, 2 vols., ed. 'Abbās Iqbāl. Tehrān, 1320/1942.

Ibn Wāṣil. *Ta'rīkh-i Ṣāliḥī* (extract) in B. Dorn (ed.), *Muhammedanische Quellen zur Geschichte der südlichen Küstenländer des kaspischen Meeres*, vol. IV. St Petersburg, 1858.

Ibn Ẓāfir al-Azdī. *Akhbār al-duwal al-munqaṭi'a*. (1) On the Sājid dynasty: in G. W. Freytag (ed.), *Locmani Fabulae*. Bonn, 1823. (2) On the Ziyārid dynasty: MS. Ambrosiana, Milan, G/6.

Kai Kā'ūs b. Iskandar. *Qābūs-nāma*, ed. R. Levy. London, 1951 (GMS, n.s. vol. XVIII). Tr. R. Levy as *A Mirror for Princes*. London, 1951.

Mar'ashī, Ẓahīr al-Dīn. *Tārīkh-i Ṭabaristān u Rūyān u Māzandarān*, ed. M. H. Tasbīḥī. Tehrān, 1966.

Mas'ūdī. *Murūj al-dhahab*, 9 vols., ed. and tr. C. A. Barbier de Meynard and A. J. Pavet de Courteille. Paris, 1861–77.

Miskawaih. *Tajārib al-umam*, with the continuations of Rūdhrāwarī and Hilāl al-Ṣābi', ed. and tr. H. F. Amedroz and D. S. Margoliouth in *The Eclipse of the 'Abbasid Caliphate*, 6 vols. Oxford, 1920–1.

Muḥallī. *Kitāb al-ḥadā'iq al-wardiyya fī manāqib a'immat al-Zaidiyya*, vol. II. MS. Vienna, Hofbibliothek, Glaser 116.

Munajjim-bāshī, Aḥmad b. Luṭf Allāh. *Ṣaḥā'if al-akhbār*. (1) On the Shaddādid dynasty: in V. Minorsky (ed.), *Studies in Caucasian History*. London, 1953. (2) On the Yazīdid and Hāshimid dynasties: in V. Minorsky (ed.), *A History of Sharvān and Darband in the 10th–11th Centuries*. Cambridge, 1958.

Muqaddasī. *Aḥsan al-taqāsīm*, ed. M. J. de Goeje. Leiden, 1906 (*BGA*, vol. III).

Qaṭrān. *Dīvān*, ed. M. Nakhchivānī. Tabrīz, 1333/1954.

Rūdhrāwarī. See Miskawaih.

Ṣābī, Abū Isḥāq Ibrāhīm. *Kitāb al-tājī fī akhbār al-daula al-Dailamiyya.* Fragment. MS. Ṣan'ā', Great Mosque.

Sahmī. *Ta'rīkh Jurjān.* Hyderabad, 1369/1950.

Sibṭ b. al-Jauzī. *Mir'āt al-zamān fī ta'rīkh al-a'yān*, ed. Ali Sevim. Ankara, 1968.

Ṭabarī. *Ta'rīkh al-rusul wa'l-mulūk*, 15 vols., ed. M. J. de Goeje *et al.* Leiden, 1879–1901.

Ya'qūbī. *Ta'rīkh*, 2 vols., ed. M. T. Houtsma. Leiden, 1883.

Yāqūt. *Mu'jam al-buldān*, 6 vols., ed. F. Wüstenfeld. Leipzig, 1866–73.

Yūsuf al-Jīlānī. *Kitāb ilā 'Imrān b. al-Ḥasan b. Nāṣir al-Hamdānī.* MS. Ambrosiana, Milan, B 83.

B. Armenian, Georgian, and Greek

Anonymous Georgian chronicle. *Histoire de la Géorgie*, tr. M. Brosset. St Petersburg, 1849–51.

Hovhannes Catholicos. *Jean VI dit Jean Catholicos, Histoire d'Arménie*, tr. Saint-Martin. Paris, 1841.

Matheos Urhayetsi. *Chronique de Mathieu d'Edesse*, tr. E. Dulaurier. Paris, 1858.

Skylitzes, Ioannes. *Excerpta ex breviario historico*, ed. I. Bekker in Cedrenus, Georgius. *Historiarum Compendium.* Corpus Scriptorum Historiae Byzantinae, vol. xxxv. Bonn, 1839.

Stepanos Asołik. *Des Stephanos von Taron armenische Geschichte*, tr. H. Gelzer and A. Burckhardt. Leipzig, 1907.

Stepanos Orbelian. *Histoire de la Siounie*, tr. M. Brosset. St Petersburg, 1864–6.

Thomas Ardzruni. *Histoire des Ardzrouni*, tr. M. Brosset in *Collection d'historiens arméniens*, vol. I. St Petersburg, 1874.

Vardan Areveltsi. *Universal History*, tr. M. Emin (into Russian). Moscow, 1861.

2. *Secondary sources*

Amedroz, H. F. "On a Dirham of Khusru Shāh of 361 A.H., etc." *JRAS* (1905), pp. 471–84.

Bïkov, A. A. "Daysam ibn Ibrāxīm al-Kurdī i ego monety". *Epigrafika Vostoka*, vol. x (Moscow, 1955).

Bosworth, C. E. "On the Chronology of the Ziyārids in Gurgān and Ṭabaristān". *Der Islam*, vol. XL (1964).

Cahen, C. "La première pénétration turque en Asie-Mineure". *Byzantion*, vol. XVIII (1948).

"Qutlumush et ses fils avant l'Asie-Mineure". *Der Islam*, vol. XXXIX (1964).

Canard, M. *Histoire de la dynastie des H'amdanides de Jazîra et de Syrie*, vol. I. Algiers, 1953.

Casanova, P. "Les Ispehbeds de Firîm" in T. W. Arnold and R. A. Nicholson (eds.), *A Volume of Oriental Studies Presented to Edward G. Browne.* Cambridge, 1922.

Defrémery, M. "Mémoire sur la famille des Sadjides". *JA*, 4th series, vols. IX, X (1847–8).

Dunlop, D. M. *The History of the Jewish Khazars.* Princeton, 1954.

Huart, C. "Les Ziyârides". *Mémoires de l'Institut National de France, Académie des Inscriptions et Belles-Lettres*, vol. XLII (1922).
"Les Mosâfirides de l'Adherbaidjân" in T. W. Arnold and R. A. Nicholson (eds.), *A Volume of Oriental Studies Presented to Edward G. Browne*. Cambridge, 1922.
Kasravī, Aḥmad. *Shahriyārān-i gumnām*. Tehrān, 1335/1957.
Madelung, W. *Der Imam al-Qāsim b. Ibrāhīm und die Glaubenslehre der Zaiditen*. Berlin, 1966.
"Abū Isḥāq al-Ṣābī on the Alids of Ṭabaristān and Gīlān". *JNES*, vol. XXVI, 1967.
"The Alid Rulers of Ṭabaristān, Daylamān and Gīlān". *Atti del III Congresso di Studi Arabi e Islamici*. Naples, 1967.
"Further Notes on al-Ṣābī's *Kitāb al-Tājī*". *IS*, vol. IX (1970).
Marquart, J. "Ērānšahr nach der Geographie des Ps. Moses Xorenac'i". *AGWG*, n.f. vol. III (2) (1901), pp. 133ff.
Miles, G. *The Numismatic History of Rayy*. New York, 1938 (*ANSNS*, vol. II).
"The Coinage of the Bāwandids of Ṭabaristān" in C. E. Bosworth (ed.), *Iran and Islam, in Memory of the Late Vladimir Minorsky*. Edinburgh, 1971.
Minorsky, V. *La Domination des Daylamites*. Paris, 1932.
"Māzandarān", "Māzyār", "Musāfirids", *EI*, 1st ed.; "Daylam", *EI*, 2nd ed.
Studies in Caucasian History. London, 1953.
A History of Sharvān and Darband in the 10th–11th Centuries. Cambridge, 1958.
Mīnuvī, M. In S. Hidāyat and M. Mīnuvī, *Māzyār*. Tehrān, 1320/1942.
Rabino, H. L. *Mázandarán and Astarábád*. London, 1928.
"Les Provinces caspiennes de la Perse. Le Guilan". *Revue du monde musulman*, vol. XXXII (Paris, 1917).
Stern, S. M. "The Early Ismā'īlī Missionaries in North-west Persia and in Khurāsān and Transoxania". *BSOAS*, vol. XXIII (1960), pp. 56–90.
"The Coins of Āmul". *NC*, 7th series, vol. VII (1967).
Sutūda, M. *Az Āstārā tā Astarābād*, vol. I (1). Tehrān, 1349/1970.
Vasmer (Fasmer), R. R. "O monetax Sadžidov" in *Izvestiya obshchestva obsledovaniya i izucheniya Azerbaidzana*, vol. V. Baku, 1927.
"Die Eroberung Ṭabaristāns durch die Araber zur Zeit des Chalifen al-Manṣūr". *Islamica*, vol. III (Leipzig, 1927), pp. 86–150.
"Zur Chronologie der Ǧastāniden und Sallāriden". *Islamica*, vol. III (Leipzig, 1927), pp. 165–86.

CHAPTER 7

1. *Arabic and Persian sources*

Abū Dulaf Mis'ar. *Abū-Dulaf Mis'ar b. Muhalhil's Travels in Iran*. Text with tr. by V. Minorsky. Cairo, 1955. Tr. by P. G. Bulgakov and A. B. Khalidov. Moscow, 1960.
Abū Nu'aim. *Geschichte Isbahans*, 2 vols., ed. Sven Dedering. Leiden, 1931–4.
Hamadānī, Muḥammad b. 'Abd al-Malik. *Takmilat ta'rīkh al-Ṭabarī*, ed. Albert Yūsuf Kan'ān. Beirut, 1961.

Ḥamza b. al-Ḥasan al-Iṣfahānī. *Ta'rīkh sinī mulūk al-arḍ wa'l-auliyā'* (Hamzae Ispahanensis annalium libri x), 2 vols., ed. J. M. Gottwaldt. St Petersburg–Leipzig, 1844–8.

Hilāl al-Ṣābi'. *Rusūm dār al-khilāfa*, ed. Mīkhā'īl 'Awwād. Baghdad, 1383/1964. And see Miskawaih.

Hunarfar, Luṭf-Allāh. *Ganjīna-yi āthār-i tārīkhī-yi Isfahān*. Iṣfahān, 1344/1966.

Ḥudūd al-'ālam, tr. V. Minorsky. London, 1937 (GMS, n.s. vol. XI).

Minorsky, V. "Addenda to the Ḥudūd al-'Ālam". *BSOAS*, vol. XVII (1955), pp. 250–70.

Ibn al-Athīr. *al-Kāmil fi'l-ta'rīkh*, vols. VIII, IX. Cairo, 1303/1885–6.

Ibn al-Balkhī. *Fārs-nāma*, ed. G. le Strange and R. A. Nicholson. London, 1921 (GMS, n.s. vol. I).

Ibn Ḥauqal. *al-Masālik wa'l-mamālik*, ed. J. H. Kramers. Leiden–Leipzig, 1938–9 (*BGA*, vol. II).

Ibn al-Jauzī, Abu'l-Faraj 'Abd al-Raḥmān. *al-Muntaẓam fī ta'rīkh al-mulūk wa'l-umam*, parts 5–10. Hyderabad, 1357–8/1938–9.

Ibn Khallikān. *Wafayāt al-a'yān (Ibn Khallikān's Biographical Dictionary)*, 4 vols., tr. de Slane. Paris–London, 1843–71.

Ibn Taghribirdī, Abu'l-Maḥāsin Jamāl al-Dīn Yūsuf. *al-Nujūm al-ẓāhira fī mulūk Miṣr wa'l-Qāhira*, ed. W. Popper. Berkeley–Leiden, 1909–29.

Ibrāhīm b. Hilāl al-Ṣābi', Abū Isḥāq. *al-Mukhtār min rasā'il Abī Isḥāq al-Ṣābi'* ed. Shakīb Arslān. Beirut, 1966.

Kai Kā'ūs b. Iskandar. *Qābūs-nāma*, ed. R. Levy. London, 1951 (GMS, n.s. vol. XVIII). Tr. R. Levy as *A Mirror for Princes*. London, 1951.

Māfarrukhī, al-Mufaḍḍal b. Sa'd. *Maḥāsin Isfahān*, ed. Jalāl al-Dīn Ṭihrānī. Tehrān, 1933.

Mīrkhwānd. *Rauḍat al-ṣafā*, 10 vols. Tehrān, 1938–9.

Mirchond's Geschichte der Sultane aus dem Geschlechte Bujeh, ed. and tr. F. Wilken. Berlin, 1835.

Miskawaih. *Tajārib al-umam*, with the continuations of Rūdhrāwarī and Hilāl al-Sābi', ed. and tr. H. F. Amedroz and D. S. Margoliouth in *The Eclipse of the 'Abbasid Caliphate*, 6 vols. Oxford, 1920–1.

al-Mu'ayyad fi'l-Dīn, Abū Naṣr. *Sīrat al-Mu'ayyad fi'l-Dīn dā'i al-du'āt. Tarjuma ḥayātihi li-qalamihi*, ed. Muḥammad Kāmil Ḥusain. Cairo, 1949.

Muqaddasī. *Aḥsan al-taqāsīm*, ed. M. J. de Goeje. Leiden, 1906 (*BGA*, vol. III).

Niẓām al-Mulk. *Siyāsat-nāma*, tr. K. E. Schabinger Freiherr von Schowingen. Freiburg–Munich, 1960.

Qazvīnī, Hamd Allāh Mustaufi. *The Geographical Part of the Nuzhat al-qulūb*, tr. G. le Strange. Leiden, 1919.

Qummī, Ḥasan b. Muḥammad b. Ḥasan. *Tārīkh-i Qumm*, ed. Jalāl al-Dīn Ṭihrānī. Tehrān, 1313/1934.

Rūdhrāwarī, Abū Shujā'. See Miskawaih.

Ṣāḥib b. 'Abbād, Abu'l-Qāsim Ismā'īl. *Rasā'il al-Ṣāḥib b. 'Abbād*, ed. 'Abd al-Wahhāb 'Azzām wa Shauqī Ḍaif. Cairo, 1947.

Ṣūlī, Abū Bakr Muḥammad b. Yaḥyā. *Akhbār al-Rāḍī wa'l-Muttaqī bi'llāh*, tr. M. Canard. Algiers, 1950.

Tanūkhī, Abū 'Alī al-Muḥassin. *Nishwār al-muḥāḍara*, parts I, II, VIII, ed. D. S. Margoliouth. Damascus, 1921–30. Tr. Margoliouth as *The Table Talk of a Mesopotamian Judge*, parts I, II, VIII. Oxford, 1921–32.
Tha'ālibī, 'Abd al-Malik. *Yatīmat al-dahr*, 4 vols. Damascus, 1304/1886.
Yāqūt. *Mu'jam al-buldān*, 5 vols. Beirut, 1374/1955.
Irshād al-arīb ilā ma'rifat al-adīb, ed. D. S. Margoliouth. Leiden, 1907–31.
Zarkūb-i Shīrāzī, Abu'l-'Abbās Aḥmad. *Shīrāz-nāma*, ed. Bahman Karīmī. Tehrān, 1350/1931.

2. *General studies and monographs, archives and coins*

Amedroz, H. F. "Three Years of Buwaihid Rule in Baghdād, A.H. 389–93". *JRAS* (1901), pp. 501–36, 749–86.
"The Vizier Abu-Faḍl b. al-'Amīd from the 'Tajārib al-Umam' of Abu 'Ali Miskawaih". *Der Islam*, vol. III (1912), pp. 323–51.
"An Embassy from Baghdad to the Emperor Basil II". *JRAS* (1914), pp. 916ff.
Bahrami, M. "A Gold Medal in the Freer Gallery of Art" in *Archaeologica Orientalia in Memoriam Ernst Herzfeld*. New York, 1952.
Bivar, A. D. H. and S. M. Stern. "The Coinage of 'Umān under Abū Kālījār the Buwayhid". *NC*, 6th series, vol. 18 (1958), pp. 147–56.
Bosworth, C. E. "The Imperial Policy of the Early Ghaznavids". *IS*, vol. I (3) (1962), pp. 49–82.
Bowen, H. "The Last Buwayhids". *JRAS* (1929), pp. 225–45.
Bürgel, J. C. *Die Hofkorrespondenz 'Aḍud ad-Daulas und ihr Verhältnis zu anderen historischen Quellen der frühen Buyiden*. Wiesbaden, 1965.
Busse, H. *Chalif und Grosskönig. Die Buyiden im Iraq (945–1055)*. Beirut, 1969.
Cahen, C. "Quelques Problèmes économiques et fiscaux de l'Iraq buyide d'après un traité de mathématiques". *AIEO*, vol. X (1952), pp. 326–63.
"L'Évolution de l'iqṭā'". *AESC*, vol. VIII (1953), pp. 25–52.
"Une correspondance būyide inédite" in *Studi Orientalistici in onore di Giorgio Levi Della Vida*, vol. I (Rome, 1956), pp. 83–97.
"Note pour l'histoire de la ḥimāya" in *Mélanges L. Massignon* (Damascus, 1956), pp. 287–303.
Canard, M. *Histoire de la dynastie des Ḥ'amdanides de Jazîra et de Syrie*. Algiers, 1953.
Covernton, J. G. "Two Coins Relating to the Buwayhid and 'Okaylid Dynasties of Mesopotamia and Persia". *NC*, 4th series, vol. III (1903), pp. 177–89.
Frye, R. N. "Die Wiedergeburt Persiens um die Jahrtausendwende". *Der Islam*, vol. XXXV (1960), pp. 42–51.
"The Charisma of Kingship in Ancient Iran". *IA*, vol. IV (1964), pp. 36–54.
Hasan, Saeed. *The Early History of the Buwaihids*. Allahabad, 1948.
Houtsma, M. T. "Zur Geschichte der Selǧuqen von Kermān". *ZDMG*, vol. XXXIX (1885), pp. 362–402.
Houtum-Schindler, A. *Eastern Persian Irak*. London, 1897.
Huart, C. "Les Banou-Annāz". *Syria* (1922), pp. 66–79, 265–79.

Kabir, Mafizullah. *The Buwayhid Dynasty of Baghdad (334/946–447/1055).* Calcutta, 1964.

Khan, M. S. "The Eye-Witness Reporters of Miskawaih's Contemporary History". *IC*, vol. XXXVIII (1964), pp. 295–313.

"A Manuscript of an Epitome of al-Ṣābī's Kitāb al-Tāǧī". *Arabica*, vol. XII (Leiden, 1965), pp. 27–44.

Lambton, A. K. S. "An Account of the Tārīkhi Qumm". *BSOAS*, vol. XII (1948), pp. 586–96.

Lane-Poole, Stanley. *Catalogue of Oriental Coins in the British Museum*, vols. I–III (London, 1875–7), vol. IX (London, 1889).

"Fasti Arabici IV". *NC*, 3rd series, vol. VI (1886), pp. 227–32.

Madelung, W. "Fāṭimiden und Baḥrainqarmaṭen". *Der Islam*, vol. XXXIV (1959), pp. 34–88.

Makdisi, G. *Ibn ʿAqīl et la résurgence de l'Islam traditionaliste au XIe siècle (Ve siècle de l'Hégire).* Damascus, 1963.

Markov, A. K. *Inventarnyi katalog musul'manskix monet Imperatorskago Ermitaža.* St Petersburg, 1896.

Miles, George G. *The Numismatic History of Rayy.* New York, 1938.

"A Portrait of the Buyid Prince Rukn al-Dawla". *ANSMN*, vol. XI (1964), pp. 283–93.

Minorsky, V. *La Domination des Dailamites.* Paris, 1932.

Nöldeke, A. *Das Heiligtum al-Ḥusains zu Kerbelā.* Berlin, 1909.

Østrup, Johannes. *Catalogue des monnaies arabes et turques du Cabinet Royal des Médailles du Musée National de Copenhague.* Copenhagen, 1938.

Schwarz, P. *Iran im Mittelalter nach den arabischen Geographen.* Leipzig, 1929–35.

Spuler, B. *Iran in früh-islamischer Zeit.* Wiesbaden, 1952.

Zambaur, E. von. "Nouvelles Contributions à la numismatique orientale. Monnaies inédites ou rares des dynasties Musulmanes de la collection de l'auteur". *NZ*, vol. XLVII (n.f. vol. VII) (1914).

CHAPTER 8

For general information: W. Barthold, *Turkestan down to the Mongol Invasion*, ed. C. E. Bosworth (London, 1968); Ziya Bunyatov, *Azerbaidžan v 7–9 vv.* (Moscow, 1965); C. Cahen, "Histoire economico-sociale et islamologie" in *Correspondance d'Orient*, vol. V (Brussels, 1961); M. A. Shaban, *The ʿAbbāsid Revolution* (Cambridge, 1970); B. Spuler, *Iran in früh-islamischer Zeit* (Wiesbaden, 1952); and with reserve, J. Wellhausen, *Das arabische Reich und sein Sturz* (Berlin, 1902).

On juridical sources: C. Cahen, "Note sur l'utilisation des ouvrages de droit musulman pour l'histoire" in *Atti dell Terzio Congresso di Studi arabi ed islamici* (Naples, 1967).

For geography and cities: Xavier de Planhol, *Les Fondements géographiques de l'histoire de l'Islam* (Paris, 1968) and the review in *JESHO*, vol. XII (1969), pp. 218–20; N. Pigulevskaya, *Les Villes de l'état iranien* (Paris, 1963); A. Hourani and S. Stern (eds.), *The Islamic City* (Oxford, 1970), especially the article of J. Aubin; A. K. S. Lambton, *Islamic Society in Persia* (London, 1954). Still useful are A. Mez, *The Renaissance of Islam* (Patna, 1937); I. M. Lapidus (ed.), *Middle Eastern Cities* (Berkeley, 1969); article by O. Tskitishvili in *JESHO*, vol. XIV (1971), pp. 311–20.

On Sīrāf: see various articles in *Iran.*

On taxation and commerce: C. Cahen, "L'Évolution de l'iqtā'", *AESC*, vol. VIII (1953), pp. 25–52; A. K. S. Lambton, *Islamic Society in Persia* (London, 1954); D. C. Dennett, *Conversion and Poll Tax in Early Islam* (Cambridge, Mass., 1950); F. Løkkegaard, *Islamic Taxation in the Classic Period* (Copenhagen, 1950); A. K. S. Lambton, *Landlord and Peasant in Persia* (Oxford, 1953); C. Cahen, "Reflexions sur le waqf ancien", *Studia Islamica*, vol. XIV (Paris, 1961); C. Cahen, "Mouvements populaires et autonomisme urbain dans l'Asie musulmane du Moyen Age", *Arabica*, vols. V, VI (Leiden, 1958–9); R. B. Serjeant, "Materials for a History of Islamic Textiles", *AI*, vols. IX–XIV (1942–8) (and see under *Textiles*, p. 681); H. J. Cohen, "The Economic Background and the Secular Occupations of Muslim Jurisprudents", *JESHO*, vol. XIII (1970), p. 16; C. Cahen, "Quelques problèmes concernant l'expansion économique musulmane au haut Moyen Age", *Settimane di Studio del Centro Italiano di Studi sull'Alto Medioevo*, vol. XIII (Spoleto, 1965), pp. 391–432; R. W. Bulliet, *The Patricians of Nishapur, A Study in Medieval Islamic Social History* (Cambridge, Mass., 1972); *Sociétés et compagnies de commerce en Orient et dans l'Ocean Indien*, ed. M. Mollat (Paris, 1970); and the translations from Arabic texts made by A. Ben Shemesh under the title *Taxation in Islam* (Leiden, 1965–9).

CHAPTER 9

Items are listed in the order in which subjects are discussed in the text.

General

Grabar, O. *The formation of Islamic Art.* New Haven, Conn., 1973.

Architecture

Godard, A. "Les Anciennes Mosquées de l'Iran". *Āt͟hār-e Īrān*, vol. I (1936) and *L'Art de l'Iran* (Paris, 1962), pp. 321ff.

Pugachenkova, G. A. *Puti Razvitiya Arxitektury Yuznogo Turkmenistana.* Moscow, 1958. *Istoriya Iskusstv Uzbekistana.* Tashkent, 1965.

Nilsen, V. A. *Arxitektura Srednei Azii V–VIII vv.* Tashkent, 1966.

Mosques

Sīrāf: D. Whitehouse. "Excavations at Siraf, Second Interim Report". *Iran*, vol. VII (1969), fig. 2.

Nāyīn: S. Flury and H. Viollet. "Un monument des premiers siècles de l'hégire". *Syria*, vol. II (1921).

Dāmg͟hān: A. Godard. "Le Tari Khana de Damghan". *Gazette des Beaux Arts*, 6th series, vol. XII (Paris, 1934).

Marv: Pugachenkova. *Iskusstvo Turkmenistana*, p. 112.

Samarqand: A. Yakubovskii. "Arxeologicheskoe Izučenie Samarkanda". *Trudy Otdela Vostoka Ermitaža*, vol. II (1940), p. 303.
Yazd: M. Siroux, "La Masjid-e-Djum'a de Yezd". *BIFAO*, vol. XLIV (1947), p. 128, fig. 3.
Damāvand: M. B. Smith. "Material for a Corpus of Early Islamic Architecture". *AI*, vol. II (1935).
Iṣfahān: A. Godard. "Les Anciennes Mosquées de l'Iran", *op. cit.*
E. Galdieri, *Isfahan, masjid-i jum'a*, vols. I, II. Rome, 1972–3.
Gurgān: A. Dietrich. "Die Moscheen von Gurgan zur Omaijedenzeit". *Der Islam*, vol. XL (1964).
Qum: *Tārīkh-i Qumm* (Tehrān, 1935), pp. 36–8, and A. Houtum-Schindler, *Eastern Persian Iraq* (London, 1897), pp. 64–5.
Yazd-i Khwāst: M. Siroux, "La Mosquée Djum'a de Yezd-i Khast". *BIFAO*, vol. XLIV (1947).

Secular buildings

O. Grabar. "The Earliest Commemorative Structures". *AO*, vol. VI (1969).
A. Godard, "Les Anciennes Mosquées de l'Iran", *op. cit.*
Hunarfar, Luṭf-Allah. *Ganjīna-yi āthār-i tārīkhī-yi Isfahān* (Iṣfahān, 1966), p. 51.
E. Diez. "Die Siegestürme in Ghazna als Weltbilder". *Kunst des Orients*, vol. I (Wiesbaden, 1950).
Sāmānid mausoleum in Bukhārā: L. Rempel in *BAIPAA*, vol. IV (1935).
Arab-atā: G. A. Pugachenkova. *Iskusstvo Zodčix Uzbekistana*. Tashkent, 1963.
Qyrq-qyz: B. Veimarn. *Iskusstvo Srednei Azii* (Moscow, 1940), p. 22.
E. Herzfeld. "Damascus I". *AI*, vol. IX (1942), p. 34, figs. 24–5.
Lashkarī Bāzār: D. Schlumberger. "Le Palais ghaznévide". *Syria*, vol. XXIX (1952).
The Samarra bevelled style: R. Ettinghausen in *Archaeologica in Memoriam E. Herzfeld*. New York, 1952.

Ceramics

A. Lane. *Early Islamic Pottery*. London, 1947.
A Survey of Persian Art, vol. IV (Oxford, 1938–9), pp. 1446ff.
C. Wilkinson. *Iranian Ceramics*. New York, 1963.
Nishapur, Pottery of the Early Islamic Period. New York, 1973.

Inscriptions on pottery

O. G. Bolshakov. "Arabskie Nadpisi na Polivnoi Keramike". *Epigrafika Vostoka*, vols. XII–XVIII (1958–67).
L. Volov. "Plaited Kufic on Samanid Epigraphic Pottery". *AO*, vol. VI (1966).

Glass

R. W. Smith. *Glass from the Ancient World* (Corning, N.Y., 1957), pp. 227ff.
M. G. Lukens, "Medieval Islamic Glass". *Bulletin of the Metropolitan Museum of New York* (Feb. 1965).

Silver and gold

I. I. Smirnov. *Vostočnoe Serebro.* St Petersburg, 1909.
D. Barrett. *Islamic Metalwork in the British Museum.* London, 1949.
O. Grabar. *Persian Art before and after the Mongol Invasion* (Ann Arbor, 1959), no. 14.
O. Grabar. *Sasanian Silver.* Ann Arbor, 1967.

Bronze vessels

U. Scerrato. "Oggetti metallici di età islamica in Afghanistan". *AIUON*, vol. XIV (1964), pp. 673–714.
R. Ettinghausen. "The Wade Cup". *AO*, vol. II (1957).

Textiles (for sources)

R. B. Serjeant. "Materials for a History of Islamic Textiles". *AI*, vols. IX–XIV (1942–8). Reprinted in book form as *Islamic Textiles, Material for a History up to the Mongol Conquest.* Beirut, 1972.
G. Wiet. *Soieries persanes.* Cairo, 1948.
F. E. Day in *AI*, vols. XV–XVI (1951), pp. 231–51.
D. G. Shepherd and E. Kühnel. "Buyid Silks" in *A Survey of Persian Art*, vol. XIV (Oxford, 1967).

CHAPTER 10

For the Arab–Sāsānian coinage see John Walker in *A Catalogue of the Muhammadan Coins in the British Museum*, vol. I: *A Catalogue of the Arab–Sassanian Coins* (London, 1941), hereinafter referred to as *B.M. Cat* I.

On the Bukharan coinage *ibid.*, pp. lxxx-xcvii, 162–9 and note 3; Frye, Richard N. (ed.), *Sasanian Remains from Qasr-i Abu Nasr* (Cambridge, Mass., 1973), Miles, George C., "The Coins", pp. 26–36; Gaube, Heinz, *Arabosasanidische Numismatik* (Brunswick, 1973).

On general Islamic coinage in Iran see Brown, Helen W. Mitchell, "Oriental Numismatics", in *A Survey of Numismatic Research, 1966–1971*, vol. II (International Numismatic Commission, New York, 1973), pp. 315–46; Miles, G. C., *The Numismatic History of Rayy*, New York, 1938 (*ANSNS*, vol. II); Miles, George C., *Excavation Coins from the Persepolis Region*, *ANSNNM*, no. 143 (1959), hereinafter referred to as Miles, *Persepolis Region.*

For Islamic mint names in general (excluding India) see Zambaur, E. von, *Die Münzprägungen des Islams* (Wiesbaden, 1968), supplemented recently by Miles, "Additions to Zambaur's Münzprägungen des Islams", *ANSMN*, vol. XVII (1971), pp. 229–33.

On local coinage see Miles, *Persepolis Region*, where the bibliography of earlier literature will be found. A few specimens were described by J. Walker in *Mémoires de la Mission Archéologique en Iran*, vol. XXXVII (Paris, 1960), pp. 49–65.

On Byzantine–Arab coin relationships consult Miles, "Byzantine Miliaresion and Arab Dirhem: Some Notes on Their Relationship" in *ANSMN*, vol. IX (1960), pp. 189–218.

Ṭāhirid coins: E. von Zambaur, "Contributions à la numismatique orientale", *NZ* (1905), pp. 119–42. An important monograph on Ṣaffarid coins is R. Vasmer's "Uber die Münzen der Ṣaffāriden und ihr Gegner in Fārs und Ḫurāsān", *NZ* (1930), pp. 131–62. For a *dirham* hoard containing Ṣaffārid coins, quite possibly the property of a soldier in Ya'qūb b. al-Laiṯ's army, see Miles, "Trésor de dirhems du IXe siècle", *Mémoires de la Mission Archéologique en Iran*, vol. XXXVII (Paris, 1960), pp. 67–145.

Sājid coins: The coinage of the Sājids is discussed in a detailed monograph by R. Vasmer, "O monetax Sadžidov" in *Izvestiya Obsledovaniya i Izučeniya Azerbaidžana*, no. 5 (Baku, 1927), pp. 22–48. Cf. *NHR*, nos. 155C, 156A,B.

'Alid coins: For some very curious 'Alid dirhams of the early 3rd/9th century, see Miles, "Al-Mahdi al-Ḥaqq, Amīr al-Mu'minīn", *RN* (1965), pp. 329–41, where references will be found to a number of other revolutionary issues.

Ja'farids of Tiflis: See E. A. Pakhomov, *Moneti Gruzii* (*Zap. Num. Otd. Imp. Russ. Arxeol. Obščestva*), vol. I (1910), pp. 49–52; D. G. Kapanadze in *Vestnik Gosudarstvennogo Muzeya Gruzii*, vol. XII-B (1944), pp. 183–90 (in Georgian, with Russian summary).

Justānids of Dailam: See R. Vasmer, "Zur Chronologie der Ǧastāniden und Sallāriden", *Islamica*, vol. III (Leipzig, 1927), pp. 165–86, 482–5; W. Madelung, "Abū Isḥāq al-Ṣābī on the Alids of Ṭabaristān and Gīlān", *JNES*, vol. XXVI (1967), pp. 52–7.

Ḥasanwaihids of Kurdistān: Miles, "Trésor de dirhems", *op. cit.* p. 145.

Kākwaihids: See Miles, "The Coinage of the Kākwayhid Dynasty", *Iraq*, vol. V (1938), pp. 89–104; Miles, "Notes on Kākwayhid Coins", *ANSMN*, vol. IX (1960), pp. 231–6; Miles, "A Hoard of Kākwayhid Dirhems", *ANSMN*, vol. XII (1966), pp. 165–93; Miles, "Another Kākwayhid Note", *ANSMN*, vol. XVIII (New York, 1972), pp. 139–48, with additional bibliography.

On Samanid coinage: Hennequin, Giles, "Grandes Monnaies sāmānides et ghaznavides de l'Hindu Kush, étude numismatique et historique", *Annales Islamologiques*, vol. IX (Cairo, 1970), pp. 127–77.

On Sāmānid hoards in eastern Europe: M. Czapkiewicz *et al.*, *Skarb monet Arabskich z Klukowicz powiat Siemiatycze* (Wrocław–Warszaw–Krakow, 1964). For a general introduction to the Viking Age hoards, see N. L. Rasmusson in *Commentationes de nummis saeculorum IX–XI in Suecia repertis, Pars Prima* (Stockholm, 1961), pp. 3–16; Ulla S. Linder Welin, *s.v. Arabiska mynt in Kulturhistorisk Leksikon för nordisk middelader*; Linder Welin, *Atti Congr. Int. di Numismatica, Roma, Settembre 1961*, vol. II (Rome, 1965), p. 499. For a recent investigation of the "silver famine" problem: A. M. Watson, "Back to Gold – and Silver", *The Economic History Review*, vol. xx (London, 1967), pp. 1–34.

Buyid coins: No comprehensive treatment of the complex Buyid coinage exists. J.-C. Lindberg's "Essai sur les monnaies coufiques frappées par les Emirs de la famille des Bouides" in *Mémoires de la Société Royale des Antiquaires du Nord* (Copenhagen, 1840–4), pp. 193–271, was an admirable pioneer work, but an immense amount of material since that date has become available in scattered publications and in unpublished collections. Roy P. Mottahedeh is now engaged in compiling a major corpus and monograph on the subject. Some important data on the coinage drawn from literary sources have been assembled by Claude Cahen in "Quelques Problèmes économiques et fiscaux de l'Irâq Buyide d'après un traité de mathématiques", *AIEO*, vol. x (1952), pp. 338–41. On Būyid "ceremonial" gold pieces see Sir Thomas W. Arnold in *Painting in Islam* (Oxford, 1928; New York, 1965), pl. LIX. Cf. J. Walker in *ANS Centennial Publication* (New York, 1958), p. 694, fig. 2.

Qarakhānids: The only numismatic monographs, both limited in their treatment, are R. Vasmer's "Zur Münzkunde der Qarāḫaniden" in *MSOS* (1930), pp. 83–104, and E. A. Davidovitch's "Numizmatičeskie materiali dlya xronologii i genealogii sredneaziatskix Karaxanidov" in *Numizmatičeskii Sbornik* (Moscow, 1957), pp. 91–119. See also O. Pritsak, "Die Karachaniden", *Der Islam*, vol. XXXI (1953), pp. 17–68, and his article "Kara-Hanlilar" in the Turkish *Islam Ansiklopedisi*, and C. E. Bosworth, "Ilek-Khans", *EI*, 2nd ed.

CHAPTER II

1. *General works*

Battānī, Muḥammad b. Sinān b. Jābir. *al-Zīj al-Ṣābi'*, 3 vols., ed. and Latin tr. C. A. Nallino. Milan, 1899–1907.

Braunmühl, A. von. *Vorlesungen über die Geschichte der Trigonometrie*, 2 vols. Leipzig, 1900.

Haddad, F. I. and Kennedy, E. S. "Place Names of Medieval Islam". *The Geographical Review*, vol. LIV (New York, 1964), pp. 439–40.
Ibn Yūnis, Abu'l-Ḥasan 'Alī b. 'Abd al-Raḥmān b. Aḥmad. *al-Zīj al-kabīr al-Ḥākimī* (*Le Livre de la grand table Hakémite*), ed. and tr. J. J. A. Caussin de Perceval in *Notices et extraits des manuscrits de la Bibliothèque Nationale etc.*, vol. VI (1) (Paris, an XXI de la république), pp. 16–240.
Juschkewitsch, A. P. *Geschichte der Mathematik im Mittelalter*. Leipzig, 1964.
K͟hwārazmī, Muḥammad b. Mūsā. *al-Kitāb al-muk͟htaṣar fī ḥisāb al-jabr wa'l-muqābala*, ed. and tr. F. Rosen as *The Algebra of Mohammed bin Musa*. London, 1831.
Kitāb ṣūrat al-arḍ, ed. H. von Mžik. Leipzig, 1926.
Levey, M. *The Algebra of Abū Kāmil...in a Commentary by Mordecai Finzi*. Madison, Wisc., 1966.
Levey, M. and Petruck, M. *Kūshyār ibn Labbān, Principles of Hindu Reckoning*. Madison, Wisc., 1965.
Luckey, P. "Zur Entstehung der Kugeldreiecksrechnung". *Deutsche Mathematik*, vol. V (Leipzig, 1941), pp. 405–46.
Nallino, S. "Al-Khwārizmī e il suo rifacimento della geografia di Tolomeo". *Raccolto di scritti editi e inediti*, vol. V (Rome, 1944), pp. 458–532.
Neugebauer, O. *The Astronomical Tables of al-Khwārizmī*. Copenhagen, 1962.
Sayili, A. *Abdulhamid ibn Turk'un... (Logical Necessities in Mixed Equations by 'Abd al-Ḥamīd ibn Turk)*. Ankara, 1962.
The Observatory in Islam. Ankara, 1960.

2. *Works of al-Bīrunī*

al-Āt͟hār al-bāqiya, 2 vols., ed. E. Sachau. Leipzig, 1878. Tr. E. Sachau as *The Chronology of Ancient Nations*. London, 1879.
Kitāb al-tafhīm li awā'il ṣinā'at al-tanjīm, tr. R. Wright as *The Book of Instruction in the Elements of the Art of Astrology*. London, 1934.
Boilot, D. J. "L'Œuvre d'al-Beruni, essai bibliographique" in *Mélanges de l'Institut Dominican d'Études Orientales*, vol. II (Cairo, 1955), pp. 161–256.
Kitāb fī taḥqīq mā li'l-Hind..., ed. E. Sachau. London, 1888. Osmania Oriental Publications. Hyderabad–Deccan, 1958. Tr. E. Sachau as *Alberuni's India*, 2 vols. London, 1910.
al-Qānūn al-Mas'ūdī, 3 vols. Hyderabad–Deccan, 1954–6.
Taḥdīd al-amākin, tr. Jamil Ali as *The Determination of the Coordinates of Cities*. Beirut, 1967.

CHAPTER 12

al-Bīrūnī. *Kitāb al-ṣaidala* (edition being prepared by 'A. Zaryāb K͟ho'ī of the University of Tehrān).
Browne, E. G. *Arabian Medicine*. Cambridge, 1921.
Burckhardt, T. *Alchemy – Science of the Cosmos, Science of the Soul*, tr. W. Stoddart. London, 1967.

Campbell, D. E. H. *Arabian Medicine and Its Influence on the Middle Ages*, 2 vols. London, 1926.
Corbin, H. with S. H. Nasr and O. Yahya, *Histoire de la philosophie islamique*, vol. I. Paris, 1964.
Dīnawarī, Abū Ḥanīfa Aḥmad b. Dā'ūd. *Kitāb al-nabāt*, ed. B. Lewin (Uppsala Universitets Årsskrift, 1953: 10). Uppsala–Wiesbaden, 1953.
Elgood, C. *A Medical History of Persia and the Eastern Caliphate*. Cambridge, 1951.
Fonahn, A. *Zur Quellenkunde der persischen Medizin*. Leipzig, 1910.
Holmyard, E. J. *Alchemy*. London, 1957.
Holmyard, E. J. (tr.). *Avicennae de congelatione et conglutinatione Lapidum*. Paris, 1927.
Ibn Qutaiba. *'Uyūn al-akhbār*, tr. L. Kopf as *The Natural History Section from a 9th Century "Book of Useful Knowledge"*. Paris–Leiden, 1959.
Ibn Sīnā. *al-Qānūn*, tr. O. C. Gruner, as *A Treatise of the Canon of Medicine of Avicenna, Incorporating a Translation of the First Book*. London, 1930.
'Īsā Bak, Aḥmad. *Ta'rīkh al-bīmāristānāt fi'l-'ahd al-islāmī*. Damascus, 1939.
Ta'rīkh al-nabāt 'ind al-'arab. Cairo, 1944.
Kindī, Ya'qūb b. Isḥāq. *al-Aqrābādhīn*, ed. and tr. M. Levey as *The Medical Formulary...* Madison, Wisc., 1966.
Kraus, P. *Jābir ibn Ḥayyān*, 2 vols. Cairo, 1942–3.
Leclerc, L. *Histoire de la médecine arabe*, 2 vols. Paris, 1876.
Meyerhof, M. "Das Vorwort zur Drogenkunde des Bêrûnî". *Quellen und Studien zur Geschichte der Naturwissenschaften und Medizin*, vol. III (iii) (1933), pp. 1–52 (151–208).
Mieli, A. *La Science arabe et son rôle dans l'évolution scientifique mondiale*. Leiden, 1938.
Nasr, S. H. *An Introduction to Islamic Cosmological Doctrines*. Cambridge, Mass., 1964.
Islamic Studies. Beirut, 1967.
Science and Civilization in Islam. Cambridge, Mass., 1968.
Three Muslim Sages. Cambridge, Mass., 1964.
O'Leary, De Lacy D. *How Greek Science Passed to the Arabs*. London, 1949.
Ruska, J. "Al-Razi's Buch Geheimnis der Geheimnisse". *Quellen und Studien zur Geschichte der Naturwissenschaften und Medizin*, vol. VI (1937), pp. 1–246.
Salammoniacus, Nušādir und Salmiak. Heidelberg, 1923.
Das Steinbuch des Aristoteles. Heidelberg, 1912.
Ṣafa, Z. *Tārīkh-i 'ulūm-i 'aqlī dar tamaddun-i islāmī*. Tehrān, 1336/1957.
Sarton, G. *An Introduction to the History of Science*, vol. I. Baltimore, 1927.
Sharif, M. M. (ed.). *A History of Muslim Philosophy*, 2 vols. Wiesbaden, 1963–6.
Siggel, A. *Das Buch der Gifte des Ǧābir ibn Ḥayyān*. Wiesbaden, 1958.
Stapleton, E. with R. F. Azo and M. Hidāyat Ḥusain. "Chemistry in 'Iraq and Persia in the Tenth Century A.D.". *MRASB*, vol. VIII (6) (1927), pp. 317–418.
Wiedemann, E. "Aus der Botanik des muslimischen Volkes". *AGNT*, vol. III (1911), pp. 299–306.
"Beitrage zur Mineralogie usw. bei der Araben" in *Festschrift O. Lippmann* (Berlin, 1927), pp. 48–54.

CHAPTER 13(*a*)

Afnan, S. *Avicenna, His Life and Works*. London, 1958.

Corbin, H. *Avicenna and the Visionary Recital*, tr. W. Trask. New York, 1960.

Corbin, H. with S. H. Naṣr and O. Yahya. *Histoire de la philosophie islamique*, vol. I. Paris, 1964.

Fārābī, Abū Naṣr. *Kitāb al-ḥurūf*, ed. M. Mahdi. Beirut, 1969.

Ivanow, V. *A Guide to Ismaili Literature*. London, 1933. Second, enlarged edition under the title *Ismaili Literature*. Tehrān, 1963.

Kraus, P. *Jābir ibn Ḥayyān*, vol. II. Cairo, 1942.

Mohaghegh, M. *Fīlsūf-i Rayy, Muḥammad ibn Zakariyyā' Rāzī*. Tehrān, 1349/1970.

Nāṣir-i Khusrau. *Jāmi' al-ḥikmatain*, ed. H. Corbin and M. Mu'īn. Tehrān–Paris, 1953.

Gushā'ish va rahā'ish, ed. S. Nafīsī. Bombay–Leiden, 1950. Tr. Filippani-Ronconi into Italian as *Il Libro dello Scioglimento e della Liberazione*. Naples, 1959.

Nasr, S. H. *An Introduction to Islamic Cosmological Doctrines*. Cambridge, Mass., 1964.

Islamic Studies. Beirut, 1964.

Science and Civilization in Islam. Cambridge, Mass., 1968.

Three Muslim Sages. Cambridge, Mass., 1964.

Pines, S. *Beiträge zur islamischen Atomenlehre*. Berlin, 1936.

Qazvīnī, M. *Abû Sulaimân Manṭiqî Sidjistânî*. Chalon-sur-Saône, 1933.

Schuon, F. *Dimensions of Islam*, tr. P. Townsend. London, 1970.

Sharif, M. M. (ed.). *A History of Muslim Philosophy*, 2 vols. Wiesbaden, 1963–6.

CHAPTER 13(*b*)

Anawati, G. C. and Gardet, L. *Mystique musulmane*. Paris, 1961.

Arberry, A. J. *The Doctrine of the Sufis*. Cambridge, 1935.

Sufism. London, 1950.

Arberry, A. J. (tr.). *Muslim Saints and Mystics: Episodes from the Tadhkirat al-Auliya' by Farid al-Din Attar*. London, 1966.

Asin Palacios, M. *Obras Escogidas*, 3 vols. Madrid, 1946–8.

Burckhardt, T. *An Introduction to Sufi Doctrine*, tr. D.M.Matheson. Lahore, 1959.

Dermenghem, E. *Vies des saints musulmans*. Algiers, n.d.

Ess, M. von. *Die Gedankwelt des Ḥārith al-Muḥāsibī*. Bonn, 1961.

Ḥallāj, Ḥusain b. Manṣūr. *Akhbār al-Ḥallāj*, ed. and tr. L. Massignon. Paris, 1957.

Kāshānī, 'Izz al-Dīn. *Miṣbāḥ al-hidāya wa miftāḥ al-kifāya*, ed. J. Humā'ī. Tehrān, 1325/1947.

Kharrāz, Abū Sa'īd. *Kitāb al-ṣidq*, ed. and tr. A. J. Arberry as *The Book of Truthfulness*. London, 1937.

Maḥmūd, 'Abd al-Ḥalīm. *al-Mohāsibī*. Paris, 1940.

Maḥmūd, ʻAbd al-Qādir. *al-Falsafat al-ṣūfiyya fi'l-Islām*. Cairo, 1966–8.
Massignon, L. *Essais sur les origines du lexique technique de la mystique musulmane*. Paris, 1954.
La Passion d'al-Hosayn ibn Mansour al-Hallaj, 2 vols. Paris, 1922–3.
Receuil de textes inédits concernant l'histoire de la mystique en pays d'Islam. Paris, 1929.
Molé, M. *Les Mystiques musulmans*. Paris, 1965.
Nasr, S. H. *Islamic Studies*. Beirut, 1966.
Ideals and Realities of Islam. London, 1967.
Sufi Essays. London, 1972.
Three Muslim Sages. Cambridge, Mass., 1964.
Nicholson, R. A. *The Mystics of Islam*. London, 1914.
Rice, C. *The Persian Sufis*. London, 1964.
Schuon, F. *Dimensions of Islam*, tr. P. Townsend. London, 1970.
Understanding Islam, tr. D. M. Matheson. London, 1963.
Smith, M. *An Early Mystic of Baghdad*. London, 1935.
Readings from the Mystics of Islam. London, 1950.
Sulamī, Abū ʻAbd al-Raḥman. *Ṭabaqāt al-ṣūfiyya*, ed. J. Pedersen. Leiden, 1960.

CHAPTER 14

Amīn, Aḥmad. *Ḍuḥa'l-islām*, 3 vols. Cairo, 1956.
Browne, E. G. *A Literary History of Persia*, vol. IV. Cambridge, 1924.
Corbin, H. *En Islam iranien*, 4 vols. Paris, 1971.
Donaldson, D. M. *The Shiʻite Religion: A History of Islam in Persia and Irak*. London, 1933.
Gobineau, A. *Les Réligions et les philosophies dans l'Asie centrale*. Paris, 1923.
Ḥasan b. ʻAli b. S͟huʻba. *Tuḥaf al-ʻuqūl*. Tehrān, 1378/1958.
Ḥusainī, Abū Bakr b. Hidāyat-Allāh. *Ṭabaqāt al-s͟hāfiʻiyya*, printed with al-S͟hīrāzī's *Ṭabaqāt al-fuqahā'*. Baghdad, 1356/1937.
Ibn Juljul. *Ṭabaqāt al-aṭibbā' wa'l-ḥukamā'*. Cairo, 1955.
Ibn K͟hallikān. *Wafayāt al-aʻyān*, 6 vols. Cairo, 1367/1948.
Ibn al-Nadīm. *The Fihrist of al-Nadīm*, 2 vols., tr. B. Dodge. New York–London, 1970.
Kulainī. *Uṣūl al-kāfī*. Tehrān (Āk͟hūndī), n.d.
Nasr, S. H. *Ideals and Realities of Islam*. London, 1966.
An Introduction to Islamic Cosmological Doctrines. Cambridge, Mass., 1964.
"It͟hnā-ʻas͟harī Shīʻism and Iranian Islam" in A. J. Arberry (ed.), *Religion in the Middle East*, vol. II. Cambridge, 1969.
"Persia and the Destiny of Islamic Philosophy" in *Studies in Comparative Religion*, vol. VI (1972), pp. 31–42.
Ṣadr, S. H. *Ta'sīs al-s͟hīʻa*. Baghdad, 1354/1935.
Ṣadūq, S͟haik͟h. *al-Tauḥīd*. Tehrān, 1387/1967.
S͟hahristānī. *al-Milal wa'l-niḥal*. Cairo, 1368/1948.
S͟hīrāzī, Abū Isḥāq. *Ṭabaqāt al-fuqahā'*. Baghdad, 1356/1937.
Sulamī, Abū ʻAbd al-Raḥmān. *Ṭabaqāt al-ṣūfiyya*. Cairo, 1372/1952.

Suyūṭī, Jalāl al-Dīn. *Ṭabaqāt al-mufassirīn*, ed. A. Meursing. Leiden, 1839.
Tabrīzī, M. *Raiḥānat al-adab*, 2nd printing. Tabriz, n.d.
Ṭāshkubrāzāda. *Ṭabaqāt al-fuqahā'*. Mosul, 1961.
Watt, W. M. *Islamic Philosophy and Theology*. Edinburgh, 1962.
Wickens, G. M. "Religion" in A. J. Arberry (ed.), *The Legacy of Persia* (Oxford, 1953), pp. 148–73.
Yādnāma-yi Shaikh al-Ṭā'ifa... Ṭūsī, vol. I. Mashhad, 1348/1970.

CHAPTER 15

1. *Primary sources*

Baghdādī. *Kitāb farq bain al-firaq*. Cairo, 1910.
Balādhurī. *Futūḥ al-buldān*, ed. M. J. de Goeje. Leiden, 1866.
Bal'amī. *Chronique de Tabari*, 4 vols., tr. H. Zotenberg. Paris, 1958.
Barhebraeus, Abu'l-Faraj Gregorius. *Ta'rīkh mukhtaṣar al-duwal*. Beirut, 1890.
Bīrūnī. *al-Āthar al-bāqiya*, 2 vols., ed. E. Sachau. Leipzig, 1878.
Dīnawarī. *al-Akhbār al-ṭiwāl*, ed. V. Guirgass. Leiden, 1888.
Ibn al-Athīr. *al-Kāmil fi'l-ta'rīkh*, 13 vols., ed. C. J. Tornberg. Leiden, 1851–76.
Ibn Khallikān. *Wafayāt al-a'yān*, 4 vols., tr. M. de Slane. Paris–London, 1843–71.
Ibn al-Nadīm. *Fihrist*, 2 vols., ed. G. Fluegel. Leipzig, 1871–2.
Mas'ūdī. *Murūj al-dhahab* (*Les Prairies d'or*), 9 vols., ed. and tr. C. A. Barbier de Meynard and A. J. Pavet de Courteille. Paris, 1861–77.
Narshakhī. *Tārīkh-i Bukhārā*, ed. C. Schefer. Paris, 1883.
Naubakhtī. *Firaq al-Shī'a*. Najaf, 1959.
Niẓām al-Mulk. *Siyāsat-nāma*, ed. C. Schefer. Paris, 1891.
Shahristānī. *al-Milal wa'l-niḥal*, 3 vols. Cairo, 1368/1948–9.
Ṭabarī. *Ta'rīkh al-rusul wa'l-mulūk*, 15 vols., ed. M. J. de Goeje *et al.* Leiden, 1879–1901.
Tārīkh-i Sīstān, ed. M. S. Bahār. Tehrān, 1314/1935.
Tha'ālibī. *Kitāb al-ghurar* in M. T. Houtsma, "Bihafrid". *WZKM*, vol. III (1889), pp. 32ff.
Ya'qūbī. *Kitāb al-buldān*, ed. M. J. de Goeje. Leiden, 1892 (*BGA*, vol. VII).

2. *Secondary sources*

Abdel-Kader, 'Ali. *The Life, Personality and Writings of al-Junaid*. London, 1962 (GMS, n.s. vol. XXII).
Bausani, A. *Persia Religiosa*. Milan, 1959.
Bertels, E. E. *Nasir-i Khosrov i Ismailizm*. Moscow, 1959.
Blochet, E. *Le Messianisme dans l'hétérodoxie musulmane*. Paris, 1903.
Browne, E. G. *A Literary History of Persia*, vol. I. Cambridge, 1928.
Darmesteter, J. *Le Mahdi*. Paris, 1885.
Grignaschi, M. "La riforma tributaria di Ḥosro I e il feudalesimo sassanide". *La Persia ed il Medioeva* (Rome, 1971), pp. 87–147.
Laoust, H. *Les Schismes dans l'Islam*. Paris, 1965.

Madelung, W. *Der Imam al-Qasim b. Ibrahim und die Glaubenslehre der Zayditen.* Berlin, 1965.
Nafīsī, S. *Bābak-i Khurramdīn.* Tehrān, 1341/1963.
Rekaya, M. "Māzyār, prince-gouverneur du Ṭabaristān". *Studia Iranica,* vol. II (Leiden, 1973).
Sadighi, G. H. *Les Mouvements religieux iraniens au II et au III siècle de l'hégire.* Paris, 1938.
Scarcia, G. "Lo scambio di lettere fra Hārūn al-Rašīd e Ḥamza al-Ḫāriǧī secondo il Ta'rīḫ-i Sīstān". *AIUON,* vol. XIV (1964), pp. 623–45.
Shaban, M. A. *The 'Abbāsid Revolution.* Cambridge, 1970.
Składanek, B. "Powstanie Charydzyckie Hamzy al-Hāriǧī w Sistanie". *Przegląd orientalistyczny,* vol. XXXIII (Warsaw, 1960), pp. 25–32.
Spuler, B. *Iran in früh-islamischer Zeit.* Wiesbaden, 1952.

CHAPTER 16

1. *Sources*

The literature of the Ismā'īlīs is listed by W. Ivanow in *Ismaili Literature* (Tehrān, 1963). A list of the works of Nāṣir-i Khusrau according to the chronology of their composition (numbers in parentheses refer to Ivanow's book above):

A. Authentic works of Nāṣir preserved

1. *Dīvān* (750), ed. Naṣr Allāh Taqavī. Tehrān, 1929; reprinted 1951.
2. *Raushanā'ī-nāma* (743), a treatise in verse, edited as above, continuation of *Dīvān.*
3. *Safar-nāma* (746), ed. and tr. C. Schefer. Paris, 1881. Kāviyānī Press, Berlin, 1341/1922.
4. *Wajh-i dīn* (744). Kāviyānī Press, Berlin, 1341/1922.
5. *Zād al-musafirīn* (749). Kāviyānī Press, Berlin, 1341/1922.
6. *Khwān al-ikhwān* (748), ed. Yaḥyā al-Kashshāb. Cairo, 1940.
7. *Raushanā'ī-nāma* (745) in prose, ed. W. Ivanow as *Six Chapters or Shish Faṣl.* Leiden, 1949.
8. *Gushā'ish va rahā'ish* (747), ed. S. Nafīsī. Bombay–Leiden, 1950. Italian tr. Pio Filippani-Ronconi as *Il Libro dello Sciolimento e della Liberazione.* Naples, 1959.
9. *Jāmi' al-ḥikmatain* (751), ed. H. Corbin and M. Mu'īn. Tehrān–Paris, 1953.
10. *Risāla* (752), published as an appendix to the *Dīvān,* pp. 563–83. It is a somewhat haphazard succession of *abstracta* from the *Jāmi'.*

B. Works mentioned by Nāṣir himself of which no manuscript has so far been found

11. *Bustān al-'uqūl* (755), mentioned in *Zād al-musafirīn,* p. 339, line 17, and in *Jāmi',* p. 137, line 12.
12. *Kitāb al-miftāḥ wa'l-miṣbāḥ* (754), mentioned in *Khwān al-ikhwān,* p. 23.
13. *Dalīl al-mutaḥayyirīn* (753), mentioned in *Khwān al-ikhwān.*

14. *Kitāb al-dalā'il* (753)? mentioned in *Khwān al-ikhwān*, perhaps the same as 13?

15. *Kitāb 'ajā'ib al-ṣan'āt* (758), mentioned in the *Jāmi'*.

16. *Kitāb lisān al-'ālim* (757), mentioned in the *Jāmi'*.

17. *Kitāb ikhtiyār al-imām wa ikhtiyār al-īmān* (756), mentioned in the *Jāmi'*.

18. *Gharā'ib al-ḥisāb wa 'ajā'ib al-ḥussāb* (759), mentioned in the *Jāmi'*.

C. There remain eleven titles mentioned by Ivanow, the attribution of which to Nāṣir is either dubious or impossible. Most celebrated is the *Kalām-i pīr* (761), much revered by Ismā'īlīs of Central Asia. The *Gauhar-rīz* (742) is a romanticized biography of Nāṣir. The *Sa'ādat-nāma* (760) was for a long time attributed to Nāṣir, but in fact it belongs to a man of the same name, Nāṣir-i Khusrau of Iṣfahān who died in 753/1352. The rest of the works have nothing to do with our Nāṣir and need not be considered.

2. *Secondary works*

Corbin, H. *Histoire de la philosophie islamique*. Paris, 1964.

Ivanow, W. *The Alleged Founder of Ismailism*. Bombay, 1946.

A Brief Survey of the Evolution of Ismailism. Bombay–Leiden, 1952.

Nasiri Khosraw and Ismailism. Bombay–Leiden, 1948.

Lewis, B. *The Origins of Ismailism*. Cambridge, 1940.

The Assassins. London, 1968.

Stern, S. M. "The Early Ismā'īlī Missionaries in North-west Persia and in Khurāsān and Transoxania". *BSOAS*, vol. XXIII (1960), pp. 56–90.

CHAPTER 17

1. *Zoroastrian texts in Middle Persian*

Āturpāt i Farrux-zātān. *Dēnkart*, book IV (see bibliography, *Cambridge History of Iran*, vol. III).

Gujastak Abalish, ed. and French tr. A. Barthélemy (Paris, 1887); ed. and English tr. H. F. Chacha (Bombay, 1936); Persian tr. Ṣādiq Hidāyat (Tehrān, 1318/1940).

The Pahlavī Rivāyat of Aturfarnbag and Farnbag-Sroš, ed. and tr. B. T. Anklesaria. Bombay, 1969.

Manuščihr i Gōšn-Yam. *Epistles*, ed. B. N. Dhabhar (Bombay, 1912); tr. E. W. West in *Sacred Books of the East*, vol. XVIII (Oxford, 1882).

Dādistān i dēnīk: questions 1–40, ed. T. D. Anklesaria (Bombay, 1911); questions 41–92, ed. P. K. Anklesaria (thesis, London, 1958); English tr. West, *op. cit.*

Emēt i Ašavahistān, ed. B. Anklesaria (Bombay, 1962); French tr. of parts J. de Menasce in *Revue de l'histoire des religions* (Paris, 1962) and *Festschrift für Eilers* (Wiesbaden, 1967).

Dēnkart, book III (see bibliography, *Cambridge History of Iran*, vol. III); French tr. J. de Menasce (Paris, 1973).

Škand Gūmānīk vicār, ed. H. J. Jamasp-Asana and E. W. West (Bombay, 1887); English tr. E. W. West in *Sacred Books of the East*, vol. XXIV (Oxford, 1885); ed. with French tr. and commentary by J. de Menasce (Fribourg-en-Suisse, 1945).

2. *Zoroastrian texts in Persian*

Dārāb Hormazyār's Rivāyat, 2 vols., ed. M. R. Unvala (Bombay, 1922); English tr. of large parts and from other *Rivāyats* B. N. Dhabhar as *The Persian Rivayats of Hormazyār Framarz* (Bombay, 1932).

'Ulamā-yi Islām I is given in Unvala's text, vol. II, pp. 72–80, and in Dhabhar's translation pp. 437–49.

'Ulamā-yi Islām II is given in Unvala's text, vol. II, pp. 80–6, and in Dhabhar's translation pp. 449–57; also in R. C. Zaehner, *Zurvan, A Zoroastrian Dilemma* (Oxford, 1955), pp. 409–18, and in French tr. by E. Blochet in *Revue de l'histoire des religions*, vol. XXXVII (Paris, 1898), pp. 40–9.

CHAPTER 18

Abu'l-Faraj al-Iṣfahānī. *Kitāb al-aghānī*. Cairo, 1345/1927.

Abū Ḥayyān al-Tauḥīdī. *al-Imtā' wa'l-mu'ānasa*. Cairo, 1373/1953.

al-Muqābasāt. Cairo, 1347/1929.

Abū Nu'aim al-Isfahānī. *Ḥilyat al-auliyā'*. Cairo, 1351/1933.

Abū Ṭālib al-Makkī. *Qūt al-qulūb*. Cairo, 1310/1893.

Barbier de Meynard. "Tableau littéraire du Khorassan et de la Transoxiane au IVe siècle de l'hégire", *JA*, 5th series, vol. I (1853), pp. 169–239; vol. III (1854), pp. 291–361.

Blau, J. *The Emergence and Linguistic Background of Judeo-Arabic: A Study of the Origins of Middle Arabic*. Oxford, 1965.

Browne, E. G. *Literary History of Persia*. Cambridge, 1928.

Christensen, A. *L'Iran sous les Sassanides*. Paris, 1936.

Dodge, B. *Muslim Education in Medieval Times*. Washington, D.C., 1962.

Fück, J. W. *'Arabīya*. Berlin, 1950. French tr. Claude Denizeau. Paris, 1955.

Goldziher, I. "Education (Muslim)" in *Hastings Encyclopaedia of Religion and Ethics*, vol. V, New York, 1912.

Haywood, J. A. *Arabic Lexicography: Its History, and Its Place in the General History of Lexicography*. Leiden, 1960.

Ibn 'Abd Rabbih. *al-'Iqd al-farīd*, vol. II. Cairo, 1364/1945.

Ibn Khaldūn. *al-Muqaddima*. Beirut, 1956.

Ibn Qutaiba. *Adab al-kātib*. Cairo, 1377/1958.

al-Imāma wa'l-siyāsa. Cairo, 1377/1958.

al-Shi'r wa'l-shu'arā', ed. M. J. de Goeje. Leiden, 1904.

'Uyūn al-akhbār. Cairo, 1343/1925.

Ibn Sa'd. *al-Ṭabaqāt al-kubrā*, ed. E. Sachau. Leiden, 1904–28.

Jāḥiẓ. *al-Bayān wa'l-tabyīn*. Cairo, 1380/1960.

Dhamm akhlāq al-kuttāb in *Three Essays*, ed. J. Finkel. Cairo, 1344/1926.

Jāḥiẓ *al-Ḥayawān*, 7 vols. Cairo, 1356–63/1938–44.
al-'Uthmāniyya. Cairo, 1374/1955.
Jahshiyārī. *Kitāb al-wuzarā' wa'l-kuttāb*. Cairo, 1357/1938.
Krenkow, F. "Bērūnī and the MS. Sulṭān Fātiḥ No. 3386" in *al-Bīrūnī Commemoration Volume*. Calcutta, 1951.
Kurd 'Ali, M. (ed.). *Rasā'il al-bulaghā'*, 4th ed. Cairo, 1374/1954.
Lazard, G. *La Langue des plus anciens monuments de la prose persane*. Paris, 1963.
Masse, H. *Firdausi et l'épopée nationale*. Paris, 1935.
Massignon, L. *Essai sur les origines du lexique technique de la mystique musulmane*. Paris, 1954.
Mez, A. *The Renaissance of Islam*. Patna, 1937.
Mīnuvī, M. "Yakī az Fārsiyyāt-i Abū Nuwās". *RFLT*, vol. 1 (3) (1333/1954), pp. 62–77.
Mubārak, Zakī. *al-Nathr al-fannī fi'l-qarn al-rābi'*. Cairo, 1352/1934.
al-Mubarrad. *al-Kāmil*. Cairo, 1376/1956.
Muqaddasī. *Aḥsan al-taqāsīm*, ed. M. J. de Goeje. Leiden, 1906 (*BGA*, vol. III).
Nallino, C. A. *La Littérature arabe des origines à l'époque de la dynastie umayyade*, tr. Charles Pellat. Paris, 1950.
Nasr, S. H. *An Introduction to Islamic Cosmological Doctrines*. Cambridge, Mass., 1964.
Ṣafwat, A. Z. *Jamharat rasā'il al-'arab*. Cairo, 1356/1937.
Sadighi, G. H. *Les Mouvements religieux iraniens au IIe et au IIIe siècle de l'hégire*. Paris, 1938.
Sprengling, M. "From Persian to Arabic". *AJSLL*, vol. LVI (1939), pp. 175–224.
Tha'ālibī. *Yatīmat al-dahr*. Cairo, 1353/1934.
Tritton, A. *Materials on Muslim Education in the Middle Ages*. London, 1957.

CHAPTER 19

With exceptions for some important or special studies, this bibliography is limited to the most recent works. There will be found mention of others in the reference works, chiefly Rypka, *History of Iranian Literature* (Dordrecht, 1968).

1. *General works and miscellaneous studies*

Bausani, A. "Letteratura neopersiana" in A. Pagliaro and A. Bausani, *Storia della letteratura persiana*. Milan, 1960.
"Considerazioni sull'origine del ghazal", *La Persia nel medioevo, Problemi attuali di scienza e di cultura*, no. 160 (Rome, 1971), pp. 195–208.
"Note sui prestiti arabi nella più antica poesia neopersiana" in *Studia classica et orientalia Antonino Pagliaro oblata* (Rome, 1969), pp. 173–88.
Bertel's, E. E. *Izbrannye trudy: Istoriya persidsko-tadzikskoi literatury*. Moscow, 1960.
Persidskaya poeziya v Buxare X. vek. Moscow–Leningrad, 1935.

Boldyrev, A. N. "Iz istorii razvitiya persidskogo literaturnogo yazyka". *Voprosy yazykoznaniya*, no. 5 (1955), pp. 78–92.

"Nekotorye voprosy stanovleniya i razvitiya pis'mennyx yazykov v usloviyax feodal'nogo obščestva". *Voprosy yazykoznaniya*, no. 4 (1956), pp. 31–7.

Bosworth, C. E. "The development of Persian culture under the early Ghaznavids". *Iran*, vol. vi (1968), pp. 33–44.

"The Ṭāhirids and Persian literature". *Iran*, vol. vii (1969), pp. 103–6.

"The Ṭāhirids and Arabic culture". *JSS*, vol. xiv (1969).

Boyce, M. "Some remarks on the transmission of the Kayanian heroic cycle" in *Serta cantabrigiensia* (Wiesbaden, 1954), pp. 45–52.

"The Parthian *gōsān* and Iranian minstrel tradition". *JRAS* (1957), pp. 10–45.

Braginskij, I. S. *Iz istorii tadžikskoi narodnoi poezii*. Moscow, 1956.

Daudpota, U. M. *The Influence of Arabic Poetry on the Development of Persian Poetry*. Bombay, 1934.

Fouchecour, C. H. de Salivet de. *La Description de la nature dans la poésie lyrique iranienne du XIe siècle. Inventaire et analyse des thèmes*. Paris, 1969.

Frye, R. N. "Development of Persian literature under the Sāmānids and Qarakhanids" in *Yādnāma-yi Jan Rypka* (Prague, 1967), pp. 69–74.

"The New Persian renaissance in Western Iran" in *Arabic and Islamic Studies in Honor of Hamilton A. R. Gibb* (Leiden, 1965), pp. 225–31.

"Die Wiedergeburt Persiens um die Jahrtausendwende". *Der Islam*, vol. xxxv (1960), pp. 42–51.

"Zoroastrier in der frühislamischen Zeit". *Der Islam*, vol. xl (1965), pp. 198–9.

"The problem of New Persian and Dari". *Indo-Iranica*, vol. xvi (Calcutta, 1963), pp. 30–2.

Henning, W. B. "A Pahlavi Poem". *BSOAS*, vol. xiii (1949–51), pp. 641–8.

"Persian Poetical Manuscripts from the Time of Rūdakī" in *A Locust's Leg. Studies in Honour of S. H. Taqizadeh* (London, 1962), pp. 89–104. (On New Persian in Manichaean script.)

Lazard, G. "Ahu-ye kuhi...Le Chamois d'Abu Hafs de Sogdiane et les origines du robai" in *W. B. Henning Memorial Volume* (London, 1970), pp. 238–44.

"Deux poèmes persans de tradition pehlevie". To appear in *Mélanges J. de Menasce*. Tehrān–Paris. (On poems quoted in the *Tuḥfat al-mulūk*.)

"Dialectologie de la langue persane d'après les textes des Xme et XIme siècles ap. J.-C.". *Revue de la Faculté des Lettres de Tabriz*, vol. xiii (1340/1961), pp. 241–58.

"La dialectologie du judéo-persan". *Studies in Bibliography and Booklore*, vol. viii (Cincinnati, Ohio, 1969), pp. 77–98.

"Les emprunts arabes dans la prose persane du Xe au XIIe siècle: aperçu statistique". *Revue de l'École Nationale des Langues Orientales*, vol. ii (1965), pp. 53–67.

La Langue des plus anciens monuments de la prose persane. Paris, 1963.

"Les Origines de la poésie persane". *Cahiers de civilisation médiévale*, vol. xiv (Poitiers, 1971), pp. 305–17.

Lazard, G. "Pahlavi/pahlavâni dans le Šâhnâme". *Studia Iranica*, vol. I (Paris, 1972), pp. 25–41.

"Pahlavi, pârsi, dari: les langues de l'Iran d'après Ibn al-Muqaffaʿ" in C. E. Bosworth (ed.), *Iran and Islam, in Memory of the Late V. Minorsky* (Edinburgh, 1971), pp. 361–91.

Les Premiers Poètes persans (IXe–Xe siècles). Fragments rassemblés, édités et traduits, 2 vols. Tehrān–Paris, 1964.

Maḥjūb, M. J. *Sabk-i khurāsānī dar shiʿr-i fārsī*. Tehrān, 1345/1966.

Osmanov, M. N. "Iz istorii literatury narodov Xorasana i Maverannaxra VIII–IX vv.". *Sovetskoe Vostokovedenie*, no. 2 (Moscow, 1956), pp. 105–18.

"Svody iranskogo geroičeskogo eposa ('Xuday-name' i 'Šaxname') kak istočniki 'Šaxname' Firdosi". *Učennye zapiski Instituta vostokovedeniya*, vol. XIX (1958), pp. 153–89.

Rempis, C. "Die altesten Dichtungen in Neupersisch". *ZDMG*, vol. CI (1951), pp. 220–40.

Rypka, J. *History of Iranian Literature*. Dordrecht, 1968.

Sadīqī, Gh. "Baʿḍī az kuhantarīn āthār-i nathr-i fārsī tā pāyān-i qarn-i chahārum-i hijrī". *RFLT*, vol. XIII (1345/1966), pp. 56–126.

Ṣafa, Dh. *Tārīkh-i adabiyyāt dar Īrān*, vol. I. Tehran, 1335/1956.

Shabbī. *al-Adab al-fārisī fi'l-ʿaṣr al-ghaznawī*. Tunis, 1965.

Shafīʿī Kadkanī (M. Sirishk). "Kuhantarīn namūna-yi shiʿr-i fārsī: yakī az khusruvānīha-yi Bārbad". *Ārish* (Mashhad, 1342/1963), pp. 18–28.

Shaked, S. "Specimens of Middle Persian verse" in *W. B. Henning Memorial Volume* (London, 1970), pp. 395–405.

Spuler, B. *Iran in früh-islamischer Zeit*. Weisbaden, 1952.

Stern, S. M. "Yaʿqūb the Coppersmith and Persian National Sentiment" in C. E. Bosworth (ed.), *Iran and Islam, in Memory of the Late V. Minorsky* (Edinburgh, 1971), pp. 535–55.

Tavadia, J. C. "A Rhymed Ballad in Pahlavi", *JRAS* (1955), pp. 29–36.

Taqīzāda, S. H. "Shāh-nāma-yi Firdausī" in *Hazāra-yi Firdausī*. Tehrān, 1323/1944.

Zand, M. I. "A Few Notes on Bilingualism in Literature of Transoxiana, Khurasan and Western Iran in the 10th century A.D." in *Yādnāma-yi Jan Rypka* (Prague, 1967), pp. 161–4.

"Antixalifatskie i sotsial'no-obličitel'nye motivy v tadžikskoi poezii X v.". *Trudy Akad. nauk. Tadž. SSR, Institut istorii, arxeologii i etnografii*, vol. XXVII (1954), pp. 185–223.

"Doislamskie prazdnestva v poezii Sredney Azii i Irana X v." *Kratkie Soobsceniya Instituta Narodov Azii*, vol. LXIII (Moscow, 1963), pp. 55–65.

2. *Editions, translations and surveys of the works*

Afshār, I. *Kitābshināsī-yi Firdausī*. Tehrān, 1347/1968 (Intishārāt-i anjuman-i āthār-i millī 59).

Ayyūqī. *Varqa va Gulshāh*, ed. Ṣafā. Tehrān, 1343/1964 (Intishārāt-i dānishgāh-i Tehrān 897).

"Le Roman de Varqe et Golšāh, essai sur les rapports de l'esthétique littéraire et de l'esthétique plastique dans l'Iran pré-mongol, suivi de la traduction du poème", by A. S. Melikian-Chirvani. *AA*, vol. XXII (numéro spécial) (1970).

Akhavainī, Abū Bakr Rabī' b. Aḥmad. *Kitāb hidāyat al-muta'allimīn fi'l-ṭibb*, ed. J. Matīnī. Mashhad, 1344/1965 (Intishārāt-i dānishgāh-i Mashhad 9).

Bal'amī, Abū 'Alī Muḥammad. *Tārīkh-i Bal'amī (Tarjuma-yi tārīkh-i Ṭabarī)*, ed. M. T. Bahār. Tehrān, 1341/1962.

Boldyrev, A. N. "Novopersidskie obrabotki epičeskix predanii v zapadnom Irane". *Kratkie Soobsceniya Instituta Narodov Azii*, vol. LXVII (Moscow, 1965), pp. 127–35.

Dabīrsiyāqī, M. *Daqīqī va ash'ār-i ū*. Tehrān, 1342/1963.

Firdausī. *Shāh-nāma*, Beroukhim ed., 10 vols. Tehrān, 1934–5.

The Epic of the Kings, tr. R. Levy. London, 1967.

Hiravī, Muvaffaq al-Dīn Abū Manṣūr 'Alī. *al-Abniya 'an ḥaqā'iq al-adwiya ba khaṭṭ-i Asadī-yi Ṭūsī* (facsimile). Tehrān, 1344/1965 (Intishārāt-i bunyād-i farhang-i Īrān 2).

al-Abniya 'an ḥaqā'iq al-adwiya, ed. A. Bahmanyār. Tehrān, 1346/1967 (Intishārāt-i dānishgāh-i Tehrān 1163).

Islāmī Nudūshan, M. 'A. *Zindagī va marg-i pahlavānān dar Shāh-nāma*. Tehrān, 1348/1969 (Intishārāt-i anjuman-i āthār-i millī 62).

Lazard, G. "Abu'l-Mu'ayyad Balxi" in *Yādnāma-yi Jan Rypka* (Prague, 1967), pp. 95–101.

"Le poète Manteqi de Rey" in *Mélanges d'iranologie en mémoire de feu Saïd Naficy* (Tehrān, 1972), pp. 56–82.

Maḥjūb, M. J. "Vāmiq-u 'Adhrā-yi 'Unṣurī". *Sukhan*, vol. XVIII (Tehrān, 1347/1968), pp. 43–52, 131–42.

Massé, H. "The Poetess Rābi'a Qozdāri" in *Yādnāma-yi Jan Rypka* (Prague, 1967), pp. 103–6.

Matīnī, J. "Dar bāra-yi dānishnāma-yi Maisarī". *RFLM*, vol. VIII (1351/1972), pp. 593–628.

Mīnuvī, M. *Firdausī va shi'r-i ū*. Tehrān, 1346/1967 (Intishārāt anjuman-i āthār-i millī 56).

Mirzoev, A. M. *Rudaki: žizn i tvorčestvo*. Moscow, 1968.

Mustamlī, Abū Ibrāhīm Ismā'īl b. Muḥammad. *Sharḥ-i kitāb al-ta'arruf li madhhab al-taṣawwuf*, part 1, ed. H. Minūchihr. Tehrān, 1346/1967 (Intishārāt-i bunyād-i farhang-i Īrān 22).

Rajā'ī, A. 'A. "Shāh-nāma barāy-i daryāft-i ṣila surūda nashuda-ast". *RFLM*, vol. IV (1346/1967), pp. 255–93.

Rempis, C. "Qui est l'auteur du Zartusht-Nâmeh?" in *Mélanges d'orientalisme offerts à Henri Massé* (Tehrān, 1342/1963), pp. 377–42 (Intishārāt-i dānishgāh-i Tehrān 843).

Starikov, A. A. *Firdausī va Shāh-nāma*, tr. R. Ādharakhshī. Tehrān, 1346/1967.

Tafsīr-i Qur'ān-i pāk (facsimile). Tehrān, 1344/1965 (Intishārāt-i bunyād-i farhang-i Īrān 1).

Tarjuma-yi Tafsīr-i Ṭabarī, 7 vols., ed. H. Yaghmā'ī. Tehrān, 1339–44/1960–5 (Intishārāt-i dānishgāh-i Tehrān 589, 661, 717, 787, 881, 946, 993).

'Unsurī, *Vāmiq-u Adhrā of 'Unsurī*, ed. M. M. Shafī'. Lahore, 1967 (Panjab University, Shahanshah of Iran's Grant Publications Series, vol. III).

Yūsufī, Gh. "Dānish-nāma-yi Maisarī". *Rahnamā-yi kitāb*, vol. VII (1343/1964), pp. 283ff.

CHAPTER 20

Abū Sa'īd. *Sukhanān-i manzūm-i Abū Sa'īd b. Abi'l-Khair*, ed. Sa'īd Nafīsī. Tehrān, 1334/1955.

Asadī Ṭūsī. *Lughat-i furs*, ed. 'Abbās Iqbāl. Tehrān, 1319/1940.

Anṣārī. *Munājāt-i Khwāja 'Abd-Allāh Anṣārī*. Tehrān, 1336/1957.

Azraqī Hiravī. *Dīvān*, ed. Sa'īd Nafīsī. Tehrān, 1336/1957.

Bābā Ṭāhir. *Dīvān*, ed. Vaḥīd Dastgirdī. Tehrān, 1331/1952.

The Lament of Bābā Ṭāhir, Being the Rubā'īyāt of Bābā Ṭāhir, Hamadānī, ed. Edward Heron-Allen. London, 1902.

Baihaqī, Ẓahīr al-Dīn Abu'l-Ḥasan 'Alī b. Zaid. *Tatimma ṣiwān al-ḥikma*, ed. M. Shafī'. Lahore, 1935.

Tārīkh-i Baihaq, ed. Kalīm-Allāh Ḥusainī. Hyderabad, 1968.

Bausani, Alessandro, "La Quartina" in Antonino Pagliaro and Alessandro Bausani, *Storia della letteratura persiana* (Milan, 1960), pp. 527–78.

Boyle, J. A. "Omar Khayyam: Astronomer, Mathematician and Poet". *Bulletin of the John Rylands Library* (Manchester), vol. LII (1) (1969).

Christensen, Arthur. *Recherches sur les Rubā'iyāt de 'Omar Ḥayyām*. Heidelberg, 1905.

Critical Studies in the Rubá'iyát of 'Umar-i-Khayyám. Copenhagen, 1927.

Dabīr-Siyāqī, Muḥammad. *Ganj-i bāz-yāfta. I. Aḥvāl u ash'ār-i Labībī – Abū Shakūr Balkhī – Daqīqī – Abu Ḥanīfa Iskāfī – Ghaḍāyirī Rāzī – Abu'l-Ṭayyib Muṣ'abī*. Tehrān, 1334/1955.

Dashti, 'Alī. *Damī bā Khayyām*. Tehrān, 1345/1966; 2nd revised ed. 1348/1969. Tr. L. P. Elwell-Sutton as *In Search of Omar Khayyam*. London, 1971.

Farrukhī, Sīstānī. *Dīvān*, ed. 'Alī 'Abd al-Rasūlī. Tehrān, 1311/1932.

Khayyām, 'Umar. *Rubā'īyāt*, ed. Muḥammad 'Alī Furūghī. Tehrān, 1321/1942.

Lazard, Gilbert. *Les Premiers Poètes persans*, 2 vols. Tehrān–Paris, 1964.

Maibudī, Abu'l-Faḍl Rashīd al-Dīn. *Kashf al-arsar va 'uddat al-abrar, ma'rūf bi-Tafsīr-i Khwāja 'Abd-Allāh Anṣārī*, 10 vols., ed. 'Alī Aṣghar Ḥikmat. Tehrān, 1331–9/1950–60 (Intishārāt-i dānishgāh-i Tehrān 158–658).

Manuchihrī. *Dīvān*, ed. Muḥammad Dabīr-Siyāqī. Tehrān, 1326/1947.

Mas'ūd Sa'd Salmān. *Dīvān*, ed. Rashīd Yāsimī. Tehrān, 1318/1939.

Muḥammad b. Munavvar. *Asrār al-tauḥid fī maqāmāt al-Shaikh Abī Sa'īd*, ed. Dhabīḥ-Allāh Ṣafā. Tehrān, 1332/1953.

Mu'izzī. *Dīvān*, ed. 'Abbās Iqbāl. Tehrān, 1318/1939.
Niẓāmī 'Arūḍī Samarqandī. *Chahār maqāla*, ed. Muḥammad Qazvīnī and Muḥammad Mu'īn. Tehrān, 1334/1955. Tr. E. G. Browne, London, 1921 (GMS, o.s. vol. XI (2)).
Qaṭrān Tabrīzī. *Dīvān*, ed. Muḥammad Nakhjavānī. Tabrīz, 1333/1954.
Rashīdī, Yār Aḥmad. *Ṭarab-khāna*, ed. Jalāl Humā'ī. Tehrān, 1342/1963.
Rempis, Christian. *Beitraege zur Ḫayyam-forschung*. Leipzig, 1937.
Ross, E. Denison. Introduction to Edward FitzGerald, *The Rubaiyat of Omar Khayyam*. London, 1900.
Rozenfel'd, B. A. and Yushkevich, A. P. *'Omar Khaiyām. Traktaty*. Moscow, 1961.
Rūnī, Abu'l-Faraj. *Dīvān*, ed. Maḥmūd Mahdavī Dāmghānī. Mashhad, 1348/1969.
Rypka, J. *History of Iranian Literature*. Dordrecht, 1968.
Ṣafā, Dhabīḥ-Allāh. *Ganj-i sukhan*, vol. I. Tehrān, 1339/1960.
Tārīkh-i adabiyyāt dar Īrān, vol. I, 2nd ed. Tehrān, 1335/1956. Vol. II. Tehrān, 1336/1957.
Shams al-Dīn Muḥammad b. Qais al-Rāzī. *al-Mu'jam fī ma'āyīr ash'ār al-'Ajam*, ed. Muḥammad Qazvīnī and Mudarris Raḍavī. Tehrān, 1314/1935, 1336/1957 (Intishārāt-i dānishgāh-i Tehrān 374).
Shams Fakhrī Iṣfahānī. *Vāzha-nāma-yi Fārsī: bakhsh-i chahārum-i mi'yār-i Jamālī*, ed. Ṣādiq Kiyā. Tehrān, 1337/1958 (Intishārāt-i dānishgāh-i Tehrān 468).
Tīrtha, Swāmī Govinda. *The Nectar of Grace. 'Omar Khayyām's Life and Works*. Allahabad, 1941.
Tārīkh-i Sīstān, ed. Bahār. Tehrān, 1314/1935.
Zhukovskii, V. A. "Omar Khaiyam i stranstvuyuščiye četverostišiya" in *al-Muzaffariya*. St Petersburg, 1897.

INDEX

Figures in italics indicate a main entry.

M.E. DS 272 .C34 v.4
The Cambridge history of
Iran
v.4
MAR
M.E. DS 272 .C34 v.4
The Cambridge history of
Iran
DATE
ISSUED TO
MAR 8 1979